# THE UNITED STATES

# THE UNITED

THIRD EDITION

*Prentice-Hall, Inc.*

Englewood Cliffs, New Jersey

# STATES

Richard Hofstadter

William Miller

Daniel Aaron

# PREFACE

THE UNITED STATES, *Third edition*
*by Hofstadter, Miller, and Aaron*
©*1972, 1967, 1957 by Prentice-Hall, Inc.,*
*Englewood Cliffs, New Jersey.*
*Printed in the United States of America.*
*ISBN 0-13-938423-5*
*Library of Congress Catalog Card No. 79-160528*

*10  9  8  7  6  5  4  3  2  1*

*Maps by Hagstrom Company, Inc.*
*and J & R Services*
*Picture consultant: Frances L. Orkin*
*Design by Walter Behnke*

PRENTICE-HALL INTERNATIONAL, INC., *London*
PRENTICE-HALL OF AUSTRALIA, PTY., LTD., *Sydney*
PRENTICE-HALL OF CANADA, LTD., *Toronto*
PRENTICE-HALL OF INDIA PRIVATE LTD., *New Delhi*
PRENTICE-HALL OF JAPAN, INC., *Tokyo*

When the authors said to a rich lady of their acquaintance, one accustomed to the sense of power, that the present age was a watershed in American history, she asked, how then are we to bring the new age about? We replied that the new age had already come about, or in any case that a great divide had been passed. We added that some time would elapse before scholars gave the new age its name. After all, not until Adam Smith, writing in the early capitalist age in Britain, was the name mercantilism used to describe the age, already dead, that preceded it; and not until Karl Marx, writing in exile from his native Prussia about a century later, was the name capitalism given to the age of private power already being superseded in Europe by the power of the state.

Historical watersheds are discoveries of scholars and the subjects of their books. Scholars could be wrong, of course. We do not share the "illusion of finality" which R. G. Collingwood describes in *The Idea of History*. Nor do we offer our book as a work of historical discovery in the grand sense. At the same time, we conceive of it as an interpretation of the course of American life—not a teaching machine. Even for students who may have taken American history more than once in their earlier school years we hope to open up the subject and not close it, as many textbooks do.

To write history without interpretation, were it possible at all, would be to write history without meaning. The mere selection of topics is an act of interpretation, however unconscious it may be. The interpretation in our book will emerge in the telling. The authors subscribe to the pragmatist William James's dictum, "Mind engenders truth upon reality"; and we hope our minds have done this. But we also feel that the range and quality of contemporary incident and quotation here are suggestive enough to impel other minds to engender their own truth, if they will.

Teachers who used *The United States* before often commended the chapter openings, and these, many of them freshly conceived, we have retained. One of the distinctive new features of the third edition is the series of pictorial essays ranging from the early Puritans—"The Chosen People and Their Visitations"—to our own day of "Violent Peace." All the captions in these essays are contemporary statements by spokesmen from different walks of life. By presenting a virtual anthology of contemporary ideas, these captions, we believe, enhance the visual materials.

So many other changes have been made in this edition that we feel we may say of it, as we said of our earlier revision, that it is again largely a new book. Its fresh organization and ideas are reflected in the Table of Contents, where no fewer than nineteen of the thirty-three chapters have new substantive titles—for example, Chapters Seven and Eight, "Federalist Nationalism" and "The Jeffersonian 'Empire for Liberty.'" Again, in Chapter Seventeen, we no longer talk of "The Reconstructed South" after the Civil War but of "The Reclaimed South" dragooned back into the Union (even if largely unreconstructed) as part of the process of encompassing the continent.

Farther on, Chapter Twenty-four no longer bears the dated tag "The Progressive Movement" but is called "Twentieth-Century Optimism," stressing the expansiveness of a new world power rather than the "search for order." This is but one example of our weighing the most recent scholarship and departing somewhat from it.

Much of modern scholarship, of course, we do accept gratefully, not least in the largely new last four chapters on the new world order since World War II and the atomic revolution. A considerable part of modern scholarship deals with two very lively subjects, black history and foreign relations; and we suggest that the main heads and subheads in our Table of Contents be inspected from first to last for our coverage of these areas. Both bear heavily on such increasingly significant subjects as militarism and police power, executive aggrandizement and secrecy, and the challenge these offer to traditional liberties and community life.

Until his death in the fall of 1970, Richard Hofstadter was for many years DeWitt Clinton Professor of American History at Columbia University. Few could feel a deeper sense of loss at his passing in the prime of life than his collaborators, his friends since graduate school days.

William Miller, who has devoted himself largely to the care and feeding of our joint books in the past few years, has been Ford Distinguished Visiting Professor of Behavioral Science at Michigan State University and Visiting Lecturer in American History at Yale. Daniel Aaron is Mary Augusta Jordan Professor of English Language and Literature and Director of American Studies at Smith College. We both wish to thank our friends at Prentice-Hall for their unfailing personal and professional consideration.    W.M.    D.A.

# CONTENTS

vii

# MAPS AND CHARTS

# PART ONE

# Encompassing a continent

Detail of lithograph by Charles Bodmer showing Fort Union on the Missouri River, 1833. (Courtesy, Rare Book Division, New York Public Library, Astor, Lenox and Tilden Foundations)

# THE DISCOVERY OF AMERICA BY EUROPEANS

CHAPTER ONE

A half hour before dawn on Friday, August 3, 1492, the pull of the moon began to draw the waters of the Atlantic Ocean back from their crest on the Rio Tinto at the little port of Palos in Andalusia in Spain. As the tide ran out to sea that morning, it carried from the security of Palos harbor three fated ships, *Niña, Pinta,* and *Santa Maria.* Aboard *Santa Maria* sailed the "captain-general" in command, long-faced, hawk-nosed Christopher Columbus, an aging mariner many thought mad. His destination: "the lands of India," a storied realm of wealth and power somewhere to the east of the Mohammedan world that gravely menaced Christendom. "I should not go by land, the usual way, to the Orient," Columbus the Genoese told his royal backers, King Ferdinand and Queen Isabella of Spain, but by water, westward, "by the route to the Occident, by which no one to this day knows for sure that anyone has gone."

His ships, Columbus said himself, were "well furnished with much provision and many seamen." The season was sounder than he knew for an ocean voyage on the course he proposed to follow. The morning of departure his sails hung limp in the windless air, but by eight o'clock the river tide had floated his small vessels to open water where they caught a strong sea breeze.

By sunset on the first day officers and men lost sight, over the curving rim of the earth, of dear, familiar shores, visible havens from the unknown terrors of the deep that claimed so many of the seagoing clans. But Columbus's mariners, seasoned in ocean navigation, knew, or thought they knew, something of what lay ahead and did not worry yet.

Six days out, 660 miles "South and by West" of Palos, the little fleet reached the Canary Islands, owned and already settled by Spain for nearly a hundred years. These islands cluster just off West Africa's turbulent coast at 28° north latitude, the very parallel, Columbus believed, on which lay Cipangu—Japan—the richest part, according to the information he trusted most, of "the lands of India" he sought.

Columbus and his men rested in the Canaries for a month while their ships underwent needed repairs and supplies were replenished. The captain-general fell in love with the lady ruler of the island of Gomera, Doña Beatriz de Peraza. But Columbus loved his mission more than his mistress, and in the early hours of September 6, his prayers said and his vessels bulging with fresh wood and water, wine, biscuit, and cheese, he weighed anchor at San Sebastián, Doña Beatriz's pleasant port.

For nearly two days Columbus's fleet stood becalmed off the island of Tenerife, its fiery 12,000-foot volcano marking the tallest point in the Canaries. Then, at 3 A.M. Saturday, September 8, as the commander recorded, "the wind come fair" from the northeast, and he set his bold new course: *Oeste: Nada del noroeste, nada del sudoeste*—"West: nothing to the northward, nothing to the southward."

The next day he did something bolder still. What this was he put down in the privacy of his journal, in the third person, as was his practice: "he decided to reckon less than he made," to doctor the log, that is, "so that if the voyage were long the people," as he called the crew, "would not be frightened and dismayed." The people, that Sunday morning

and afternoon, still could see the westernmost of the Canaries, the island of Ferro, and lofty Tenerife breathing smoke. By dusk, each last point of land had faded out. By nightfall, the three small ships bobbed alone on the uncharted sea, their crews, mostly Spanish, restive under a foreign captain they did not fully trust.

Thirty days out, on October 10, having doubled all records for ocean sailing beyond sight of shore, *Santa Maria's* people mutinied. The very uneventfulness of the lengthening voyage had overstrained the nerves of sailors made idle by the easy passage. Only Columbus's promise to turn back if no land were raised in three days quieted the crew. Then, just past 2 A.M. on October 12, the deadline nearing, *Pinta's* lookout called, *"Tierra! Tierra!"*

After three false landfalls on recent days, this cry in the night awakened mixed feelings in the men. But a light on an island in the Bahamas had indeed been sighted six miles off. As soon as daylight made debarkation safe on this engaging gateway to the New World—"all is so green that it is a pleasure to gaze upon it," wrote the captain-general in his journal—the momentous "Landing of Columbus" took place.

"To the first island which I found," Columbus later wrote to his sovereigns, "I gave the name 'San Salvador,' in remembrance of the Divine Majesty, Who had marvellously bestowed all this; the Indians call it 'Guanahaní.'" Soon, "I found very many [other] islands," Columbus added in his letter to Ferdinand and Isabella, "filled with innumerable people, and I have taken possession of them

3

*No fully authenticated portrait
of Columbus painted in his life time exists,
but Columbus scholars agree
that the figure on the far left,
"in rich robes, with light gray hair,
beard and mustache, fair complexion, long
face and aquiline nose," to quote
S. E. Morison, perhaps best
represents the Discoverer as he is described
in written sources. The painting
itself is of "Our Lady of the Fair Winds,"
by Alejo Fernandez (about 1520),
who may have known Columbus.*

4

all for their Highnesses, done by proclamation and with the royal standard unfurled, and no opposition was offered to me."

On his part, on this first contact, Columbus was quick to answer native kindness with aggression: "As soon as I arrived in the Indies, in the first island which I found, I took some of the natives by force, in order that they might learn and might give information of whatever there is in these parts." When he then mended his manners, it was not without ulterior motives of enduring consequence:

*I gave them a thousand handsome good things, which I had brought, in order that they might conceive affection for us and, more than that, might become Christian and be inclined to the love and service of Your Highnesses and of the whole Castilian nation, and strive to collect and give us of the things which they have in abundance and which are necessary to us.*

# I   The New World before Columbus

### Challenge of Indian culture

America has been discovered many times. When we say, "Columbus discovered America," we mean only that his voyage across the Atlantic Ocean in 1492 first opened the New World to permanent occupation by people from Europe, itself a complex and challenging term perhaps most usefully defined by the geographer Derwent Whittlesey as "the habitat of western civilization, a dynamic society not paralleled in any other part of the earth, until Europeans carried their expansive mode of life overseas."

The most recent estimates place the arrival in America of the earliest known discoverers

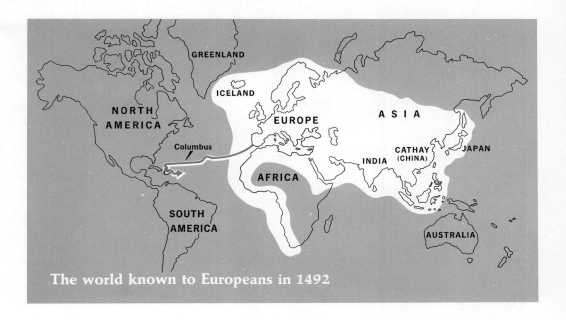

The world known to Europeans in 1492

and settlers—Columbus was the first to call these tawny Mongoloids "Indians"—between 40,000 and 20,000 years ago. These people, or more properly this mixture of peoples, having moved eastward across Asia over thousands of years (while others, somehow differently mixed and grown fatefully fair in complexion, were moving into European lands), apparently crossed from Siberia to Alaska by way of an ancient land bridge, now 300 feet beneath Bering Strait, whose long existence modern science recently established.

With the conspicuous exception of the late-arriving Eskimos, the newcomers gradually spread southward in pursuit of the big game on which they chiefly lived. Some settled permanently on the high plains of what is now the arid Southwest of the United States where, until a sharp climatic change occurred about 8000 B.C., a lush forest afforded ample greenery on which mammoths, wild bison, antelopes, and mountain goats fed. This fare thinned out farther west where a "desert culture" developed. For thousands of years small desert groups, occasionally finding shelter in mountain caves where their traces have been uncovered, eked out the big game with smaller carnivores such as coyotes, gophers, bobcats, and rats, and, more significantly, with

plant food. After 8000 B.C., with the forests of the high plains dying because of the dwindling water supply, the plains Indians also turned to scrub plants for their principal food. Some 2000 years later they were successfully gathering, preserving, and planting seeds, and cultivating regular crops with crude tools of wood and stone.

As early, according to recent findings, as 12,000 B.C., husbandry had also begun in the "valley of Mexico," where the largest numbers of Indians had settled down after the southward trek. The stable society husbandry made possible turned Mexico, and neighboring Guatemala and Honduras, into the "heartland of Middle America." Here and in Peru, during the early centuries of the Christian era in Europe, which we call the Dark Ages, Indian culture flowered.

Widespread if unconnected disasters—earthquakes and epidemics, prolonged droughts and dynastic civil wars—seem to have disrupted many areas of Indian life in the century or two before the catastrophic European invasion. Such misfortunes helped prepare the way for the Europeans' success among the dark worshipers of the sun in heaven, who innocently welcomed white men coming from the direction of the sun's rising as the true

Lee Boltin

*Colossal (8 foot, 3 inch) statue
of Coatlícue (Serpent-Skirt), headless Aztec
goddess of earth and mother of fierce
warrior gods, her face formed by serpents
rising from her neck, her necklace
made of human hearts and hands and pendant
skull, from corpses on which she fed.*

children of the gods. Yet, even in the years of their decline, when they first were encountered by the Spanish *conquistadores* (see p. 16), the Aztecs of Mexico, the Incas of Peru, the Mayas of Guatemala and Yucatán aston-

ished the newcomers with their wealth and artistry; and to this day their accomplishments, and those attributed to predecessor peoples they themselves had mastered, challenge the mind. When Albrecht Dürer, the great German artist, viewed the trophies sent from Mexico by Cortez for the coronation at Aix-la-Chapelle in 1520 of Charles I of Spain as Holy Roman Emperor, he wrote in his diary: "In all the days of my life I have seen nothing which so rejoiced my heart as these things, . . . and I marveled over the subtle genius of these men in strange countries."

For all the stunning beauty of their environment—the sturdy causeways, for example, and the enchanting ponds and lakes and canals of Mexico formed man-made parts of intricate irrigation systems—the Aztecs were a brutal and terrifying people, much given to human sacrifice. The Incas of Peru, inheritors, like the Aztecs, of an earlier advanced culture, at least equalled the Aztecs in building and design. In imperial and social organization and administration, they outdistanced them. At the time of the Spanish invasion, the Inca empire stretched along South America's western coast from 2° north to 37° south latitude and included much of modern Ecuador, Peru, Bolivia, and Chile, all bound together by roads and runners the Romans would have admired. Nor were their rulers lacking in the consciousness of power. When urged by Pizarro's chaplain, on his way to the conquest of Cuzco, the glittering Inca capital, to accept Christ as his Lord, the Pope as his master, and Emperor Charles as his monarch, the reigning Inca sovereign, Atahuallpa, replied: "I will be no man's tributary."

In the "classic age" of their Theocratic Period, which seems to have ended catastrophically about 900 A.D., the Mayas, possessors of the third great Indian culture, were the uncontested masters of the science of the sky. Their gods were many and were associated with the peaceful pursuit of husbandry. Their efficiency in cultivation supplied the wherewithal for the support of priestly learning, and

6

especially the learning that had to do with the weather, the seasons, the round of the year. Mayan priests specialized in astronomy, to which mathematics was the key. Abstract thought itself was the key to mathematics. The Mayas' brilliant achievements along all these lines culminated, before the end of the

*Inca gold female figurine, 9.5 inches,*
*from about 1500, one of the few*
*to escape the Spanish melting pot.*

seventh century A.D., in their extraordinary 365-day calendar, one better than Europeans generally would have for a thousand years. Mayan triumphs in art equalled those in science.

7

Indian Mexico and Peru, at their peak, held a population (possibly 30 million) almost as large as that of western Europe at the time of the Renaissance; and their principal cities, despite much controversy over their precise size, far outnumbered Paris and London at that time. The simple fact that such populations and urban concentrations were adequately fed for centuries testifies to the technological standards and political stability of what we may appropriately call the old New World. Invading Spanish soldiers, fearful of the Devil's retribution, destroyed Mayan cities as they destroyed those of Aztec Mexico and Inca Peru. So also, in the 1560s, intrusive Spanish missionaries, fearful of the Devil's words, burned almost all the Mayan books. Such desecration heightens the challenge to our understanding of Indian culture, while revealing some of the barbarism in Europe's own.

From Mexico and Peru, long before the white man's arrival, aboriginal peoples had spread once more far into the temperate zones, north and south, to join those already living there. The farther they moved from their great heartland, like Europeans from their Mediterranean havens, generally speaking the cruder and harsher their culture seems to have become.

Yet, even as far north as the St. Lawrence River Valley the earliest explorers from overseas marveled at the cities they encountered. One such was Hochelaga, the site of modern Montreal, of which the French explorer Cartier reported to his king in 1535 how impressed he was by "the immense numbers of peoples living there" and "their kindness and peacefulness." Ralph H. Brown, in his *Historical Geography of the United States*, remarks that "it has often been suggested, among other explanations, that originally the name 'Canada' signified a place of large Indian lodges." Brown goes on to describe the "underestimation of the extent to which the Indians had been engaged in agriculture," the frequency of Indian towns farther south, and the "Indian old fields" so commonly encountered and so zealously coveted for their open spaces by the first English settlers in what was to become the eastern United States.

Of the Indians in the rest of the future United States something new is being discovered almost every day as archaeological remains in the great river basins are exposed by the rush to develop hydroelectric power and establish flood control. And most of what is being discovered tends to undermine the myth of Indian savagery by which the first white settlers, on each new advance into fresh territory, comforted themselves and assuaged their guilt.

By their step-by-step resistance to encroachment for almost 300 years these Indians are said by some to have hardened the fighting qualities in the American character. Their more peaceful contributions to white civilization include the canoe and the snowshoe, the tobacco leaf that was to become the first staple of the English mainland colonies, and Indian corn, that remarkable man-made hybrid, which remains to this day the staple of much of the Middle West.

### Foreshadowings in fact and fancy

While America was developing in isolation a still mystifying civilization, other parts of the world were themselves much more restless than our casual inattention to them suggests. Only now are we beginning to gain some knowledge of the internal history—the distant commerce, the wars, beliefs, and communication—of Africa south of the Sahara and west of the Nile, the source of one of the earliest and eventually one of the largest, though involuntary, migrations of people to the New World.

For hundreds of years, moreover, while Europe slumbered, China developed the most advanced civilization on earth and was to bequeath to the West such basic instrumentalities for its own later expansion as the compass, gunpowder, and printing. As early as the thirteenth century, European travelers moving over land had penetrated the recesses of the Orient to carry home accounts of unmatched splendor. Marco Polo's *Travels* became the most famous of such accounts and most enticing to Columbus later on (see p. 11). Such travelers also reported that China bordered an eastern sea and thus might be reached by water. And far in advance of the white man in America, in fact, Chinese and Japanese fishermen, swarming on this water known to us as the north Pacific, almost certainly were blown by the prevailing winds to British Columbia, Oregon, and California, from which they were powerless to find their way home. In the mid-1960s, strong evidence was uncovered of Japanese presence as far south as modern Ecuador as early as 3000 B.C.

The earliest authenticated account of white men in the New World is that of the Norwegians who moved from Iceland to Greenland late in the tenth century A.D. The instigator of this adventure was Erik the Red, who—on being expelled from the Iceland republic for disrupting the peace—sought to lure settlers to Greenland's barren wastes by giving the great island its more attractive name. Boasting only small colonies of Eskimo fishermen in its most distant parts, Greenland was settled by whites from Iceland in 986 and became a colony of Norway in the thirteenth century, when its population had reached about 4000. For reasons still obscure, Greenlanders lost contact with Europe fifty years or more before 1492. When John Davis visited the great island in 1585 and gave his name to the strait that separates it from Baffin Island, he found the white man extinct. Not until the eighteenth century did white settlers return.

Around the year 1000, Erik the Red's son Leif set out from Greenland to explore the American mainland coast. Conjecture says he sailed as far south as Massachusetts, but that remains doubtful. The first lands he sighted probably were Baffin Island, named by him Helluland, land of flat stones, and forested Labrador, which he called Markland, or woodland. The voyagers came ashore at last at the place they called Vinland, "in accordance with the good things they found in it."

Vinland for centuries tried the historians' imagination, until in 1964 its most likely location was fixed. The artifacts left behind by Leif and his company, who remained for ten to twelve months, and by successors who for three years tried to build a permanent colony there, testify (since their discovery in the 1960s) that the place was the small fishing village known today as L'Anse au Meadow, the bay of the meadow, at the northernmost tip of Newfoundland Island. A land of grass, as its Norse etymology indicates (not a land of vines and grapes), "Vinland the good" was named by thankful Greenlanders for its fine grazing fields. What killed their colony was the hostility toward the strange Europeans of the natives they called *Skraelings,* or screechers. Far outnumbering the trespassers, they eventually drove the survivors among them back to Greenland.

By the time Columbus first conceived his "enterprise of the Indies," even this certain discovery and attempted settlement of America by Europeans had been lost to memory— except simply as one more strand in the richly embroidered tales of other worlds by which the medieval imagination was possessed. These tales and morsels of truth which they contained, went back to the Old Testament story of the Garden of Eden and to pagan Homer and the classic Greeks. As part of the mythology and learning of Western culture, they were more important in motivating Columbus and his successors than the hazy discoveries of the more recent past.

Almost 2500 years before Columbus, the poet Homer, in the story of Odysseus, placed the Elysian Fields—the *earthly* paradise—on the river Oceanus, "at the world's end where all existence is a dream of ease." Thereafter, successive Mediterranean civilizations took heart from visions of new Edens across the western ocean.

Four hundred years after Homer, the philosopher Plato wrote of the lost island of Atlantis, once the site, he said, of an ideal commonwealth just beyond the Strait of Gibraltar. For a full millennium and more, few would sail beyond this Strait, "where Hercules his landmarks set as signals," as Dante wrote in the

9

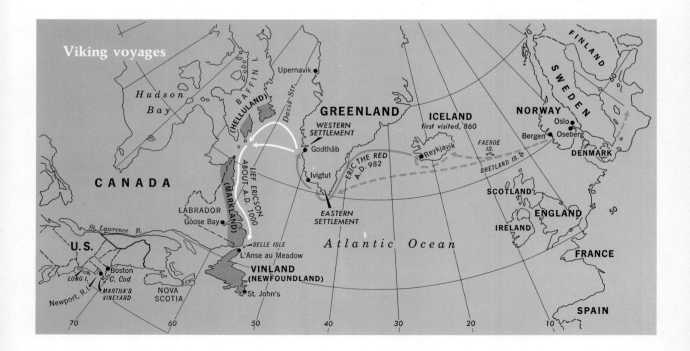

thirteenth century, "that no man farther onward should adventure." As long as men failed to disprove the existence of Atlantis, Plato's pleasing myth or invention grew ever more real to the European mind.

During the Middle Ages, imaginary Atlantic lands multiplied and exercised an enduring spell. One was the Island of the Seven Cities, also known in Columbus's time as Antilia, where each of seven Christian bishops, fleeing the Mohammedan invasion of Spain in the eighth century, was said to have built a gilded town, one more lovely than another. From it comes the name Antilles, given derisively to the Caribbean islands by some of Columbus's own mariners, skeptical that they were in fact in the *Indies,* as their captain claimed.

The peak of medieval misdirection was reached in that popular fourteenth-century phantasmagoria, *The Travels of Sir John Mandeville,* which Columbus and his men knew well. "And man may well prove by experience and subtle compassment of wit," wrote the author of *The Travels of Mandeville,* "that a man might go by ship all about the world above and beneath . . . and turn again to his country. . . . And always he should find men, lands and isles," while circumnavigating the globe.

### The reach of geographic speculation

The morsels of "experience and wit" in *Mandeville* and similar medieval concoctions derived largely from the geographical learning of antiquity which the Arabs preserved and enlarged. This learning Europe began to regain in Columbus's early years, when it was given greater currency than ever before by the spread of printing and by the growing secular interests of scholars and scientists upon which the printers fed.

As early as the fourth century B.C., Aristotle's mathematical proofs had caused most learned Greeks to agree that the earth was more or less a sphere. By then, too, commerce and war with neighboring Mediterranean lands had familiarized even ordinary Greeks with the nearest borders of three continents— Europe, Asia, and Africa. In 327–325 B.C. Alexander the Great's armies crossed northern India almost to Tibet. This exploit pushed Greek knowledge of the inhabited world well over 1500 miles eastward and opened up the more distant vistas of Oriental marvels which thereafter held Europeans enthralled.

The farther their knowledge was extended, the more interested did the Greeks become in the size of the whole sphere and the extent of its watery parts. The principle of symmetry, or balance, the first general principle in the history of geographical science, dominated their thinking. Aristotle himself argued from the occurrence of elephants in both Africa and India, and from the assumed difficulty of carrying them by sea from one place to the other, that the watery surface of the sphere was limited and the ocean passage from the western bulge of Africa to the eastern extremity of Asia was short. This conclusion sailed through the ages on Aristotle's immense authority as a seer and was quoted often and energetically by Columbus.

Since most Greeks agreed that land was heavier than water, and that these elements must nevertheless balance one another by weight, it followed from the belief in a small watery surface that the heavier land surface of the sphere must be smaller still. By such reasoning Aristotle reached a second long-lived geographical conclusion: that the short ocean passage from Africa to Asia was uncluttered by islands. The land mass known to the Greeks in Europe, Africa, and Asia, he said, was ample to balance all the water on the sphere.

For all his authority, Aristotle's reasoning about the occurrence of elephants and the absence of islands did not go unchallenged even in his own time. Some Greeks held that since there was a habitable land mass on the one surface of the sphere known to them, there must be at least its antipode on the opposite side. Indeed, said some, there may be a number of unknown lands, each in balance with one another, and hence a very much larger ocean than Aristotle spoke of with water enough to balance all.

The principle of balance also led certain Greeks to divide the sphere latitudinally into five climatic zones—two frigid zones balancing each other at the poles; a broad torrid zone girdling the center; and between the torrid zone and each frigid zone, two temperate zones in balance in the northern and southern latitudes. These Greeks and most of their followers for almost 2000 years held that the frigid zones were too cold and that the torrid zone was too hot to sustain life even if there were land. But about the familiar north temperate zone they were willing to make bold non-Aristotelian predictions. Eratosthenes, who lived and wrote in Alexandria during the third century B.C., was responsible for one of the most remarkable of these:

*If the extent of the Atlantic Ocean were not an obstacle, we might easily sail from Iberia [Spain] to India, on the same parallel. . . . It is quite possible that within the same temperate zone there may be two or even more inhabited earths.*

A brilliant mathematician, Eratosthenes calculated the circumference of the sphere at 25,000 miles, almost precisely right. A successor of his in Alexandria in the second century B.C., Hipparchus by name, was the first to divide the sphere by parallels of latitude and meridians of longitude and to attempt to locate habitable points on it in terms of degrees. A third Alexandrian, known to us as Ptolemy, who lived in the second century A.D., made what may have been the very first atlas of the world employing the method Hipparchus developed.

Ptolemy's atlas accompanied his work on world geography, which reflected much of the ancient Greek tradition, corrected, as he thought, by all the evidence he could gather from the itineraries of sailors and the reports of travelers. But many of Ptolemy's corrections proved to be erroneous. Most significant for the future was his espousal of the idea of a sphere much smaller than that of Eratosthenes. This led him to calculate each of the sphere's 360 degrees as itself much smaller than it was in reality. Ptolemy also brought West Africa and East Asia far too close to each other.

These errors, embalmed in the geographical writings he absorbed, proved irresistible to Columbus. Indeed, so possessed was he by his notion of finding a short sea route to the Orient that he even improved on Ptolemy. He was encouraged to take this step by a more recent source to whose accuracy on virtually every point modern scholarship has testified, except the one point on which Columbus most relied. This source was Marco Polo.

On his return to his native Venice in 1298, after nearly thirty years in China in the service of the Great Khan, Polo published his famous *Travels* only to be scoffed at by his countrymen ("Marco's millions," they jeered) for the Oriental wonders he reported. Numerous handwritten copies of Polo's work, no two alike, circulated among the learned in Europe before it was printed for the first time in 1477. Thereafter, all aspiring ocean navigators devoured it, Columbus's copy with his marginal markings dating from 1485. Polo reserved his choicest language for the wonders of Japan, which he never visited and of whose extent his knowledge remained vague.

By indefensible manipulations of fanciful Arabic evidence, Columbus compulsively shrank each short Ptolemaic degree by 10 percent. And on the basis of Polo's second- and third-hand information, he stretched Asia no less than 30 degrees nearer West Africa, so that, as S. E. Morison writes, "Japan almost kissed the Azores." Columbus's calculations, in fact, placed Japan almost precisely where he made his Bahamas landfall.

11

## II  Expansion of Europe

### Menace of Mohammedanism

When Columbus first sought the support of the Portuguese king early in the 1480s for his proposed westward voyage to the East, vast historical changes had already assured the Atlantic primacy over the Mediterranean in Europe's future, and Portugal, at land's end, primacy over Europe's other maritime nations in Atlantic navigation. At the heart of these historical changes lay the menace of Mohammedanism, or Islam, to Christianity.

Spain, of which Portugal was long a part, had been the first Christian country to succumb to the Mohammedan invasion of Europe from North Africa in the eighth century. Thereafter, although checked in western Europe by Charles Martel of France in the memorable battle of Tours in 732, Mohammedanism quickly spread to Mediterranean islands, Adriatic and Aegean lands, the entire Middle East, and ever farther south in Africa, ever farther east in Asia. Tolerant of captives willing to join the easy brotherhood of Islam, Mohammedanism gradually absorbed the legends, lore, and learning of the world from Persians, Hindus, Jews, Egyptians, Greeks, and others.

Within the vast expanse of Islam by the end of the tenth century lay most of the great cities known to man: Cairo and Alexandria, Baghdad, Damascus, and Antioch, Tabriz, Samarkand, and Jerusalem. In such cities of the Levant, or the land of the rising sun, were to be found all the luxuries of the yet more distant East, their value in no way diminished by the mysterious remoteness of their origins.

The Christian counteroffensive gained momentum with the start of the Crusades in 1096, and reached a peak three years later when holy Jerusalem was regained. The Crusades solidified the authority of the Roman popes in Christendom and solidified the leadership of the Italian city-states in the Mediterranean trade. Merchants of Pisa, Genoa, and Venice in particular, profiting from carrying pilgrims eastward from Europe to Jerusalem, greatly enlarged their fortunes by carrying westward from the Levant the spices, silks, gems, tapestries, and other exotic wares which Europe's upper classes craved.

By the thirteenth century, however, Christianity's crusading spirit had spent itself. Jerusalem had once again fallen to the Mohammedans, and the onslaught of Islam on Europe from the East had taken on renewed force under Turkish leadership, culminating in the sack of Constantinople in 1453. The Levantine trade was so hard hit by this reversal of fortune that Pisa, Genoa, and Venice, struggling to retain worthwhile shares of the trade that remained, fought suicidal wars among themselves. With prices of oriental goods soaring because of the disruption of the traditional lines of supply, the rest of Europe began to yearn for new routes to the Indies which would somehow circumvent the formidable Turkish strongholds.

### Portugal takes the lead

As early as 1291 two brothers, Ugolino and Vadino Vivaldo of Columbus's native Genoa, embarked on what may have been the first deliberate effort to reach the East by sailing west. They appear to have perished on the voyage. Early in the next century, other Italians, and Spaniards and Frenchmen, beginning to explore the west coast of Africa in search of the way around that continent, came upon and occupied the Canaries, the somewhat more westerly Madeiras, and ultimately the still more westerly Azores. But it remained for the Portuguese, after 1420, to begin the systematic collection of geographic information which dissipated ancient fears of the "green sea of gloom," as the Arabs called the Atlantic, and transformed that waterway into a path of adventure and commerce, not least commerce in enslaved blacks whom the Portuguese first brought to Europe in 1442.

After freeing herself from Spain in 1140, during the next century Portugal had rid herself of the last Mohammedan enclaves. Then, while consolidating their home territory, her rulers prepared to pursue the Mohammedans in Africa. The legend of Prester (that is, Priest) John, which began to spread through beleaguered Europe late in the twelfth century, emboldened the Portuguese. Prester John was said to be a mighty Christian potentate somewhere in the heart of Islam who had withstood Mohammedan expansion and might help the Europeans subdue the infidel. Portugal's quest for Prester John was intensified after 1415, when her forces invaded Africa and took the Islamic port of Ceuta, opposite Gibraltar.

**13**

*Sixteenth-century engraving of the port of Lisbon in Portugal's great period.*

14

In 1420 Prince Henry, third son of King John I and famous in history as Henry the Navigator, set up his great academy on seafaring at Sagres, on Portugal's southernmost tip, "where the two seas, the Mediterranean and the Great Ocean fight together." Here, for forty years, until his death in 1460, he conducted a veritable laboratory in astronomy, cosmography, cartography, ship and sail design, and instruments of navigation. Some of his most valuable information came, as we say of returning astronauts, from "debriefing" returning ocean sailors and ship captains. The tropics, Ptolemy held, were "uninhabitable because of the great heat"; "and we found quite the contrary!" exclaimed one of Prince Henry's men. "The illustrious Ptolemy who wrote so well on many things, was quite mistaken here!" Prince Henry's work was crowned in 1488, many years after he died, and after Prester John had proved to be nothing more than an Abyssinian native chieftain, when Bartholomeu Diaz at last rounded *Cabo Tormentoso* (Cape of Storms), at Africa's southernmost tip, and thereby opened the first all-water route from Europe to the Indies. So impressed was the King of Portugal with the prospects afforded by this feat that he promptly renamed the treacherous neck of land "Cape of Good Hope."

Nine years after Diaz's voyage a flotilla of four Portuguese ships under Vasco da Gama sailed for Calicut from Lisbon and returned in 1499 laden with spices and jewels. Da Gama's voyage marked the end of Levantine supremacy in the Oriental trade, the eclipse of the Italian merchants, and the decline of the Mediterranean. The Portuguese, moreover, soon drove Mohammedan merchants from the Indian Ocean itself, reduced their strongholds at the sources of supply for Oriental goods, and established an Oriental empire of their own that lasted, at least in fragments, to our day.

In 1500, on a voyage to the Orient, a Portuguese captain, Pedro Alvarez Cabral, finding himself blown off his course onto the New World shore, promptly claimed it for his native land. Cabral's discovery became known as Brazil for the bright red wood found there similar to the "brazil" wood imported from the Far East for making red dye. But Portu-

guese interest in the New World languished until, half a century later, other European nations showed sharp interest in her possession there.

### Spain's gamble

Columbus had sailed as a youth in the Portuguese service in caravels similar to his *Niña, Pinta,* and *Santa Maria* of the future. On making his early bids in Lisbon for royal support of his proposal for a short sail westward to reach the East, he was laughed out of court by the King's experts. It was by persisting on this theme that he won the reputation for madness that thereafter clung to him.

When Columbus left Portugal in 1485 to try his luck with Ferdinand and Isabella of Spain, he found them immersed in ridding their own country, after 700 years, of the last Mohammedan bases. Five years later, after failures in England and France as well as Portugal once again, Spain's own royal experts judged his scheme "impossible and vain."

In 1492 Columbus's fortune changed. In January that year the Spanish monarchs at last expelled Islam from its last foothold in Granada and then moved immediately to wipe out all other non-Catholic elements in the Spanish population, including the Jews whose wealth had helped immensely in financing the long wars. The instrument was the Spanish Inquisition; its penalties, expulsion or death. These harsh measures foreshadowed the violent Catholic Counter-Reformation which Spain was to finance in sixteenth-century Europe with the golden hoards Columbus's successors would soon send back from the New World (see p. 16). In 1492, the hope of converting the "princes and people" of the Indies to the holy faith and conscripting their fabled treasure for Spain's depleted treasury at last prompted Ferdinand and Isabella to capitulate to the importunings of Columbus's influential friends. In April, they gave their blessing and backing to the explorer's quest for "the route of the Occident" to the Orient and agreed further, as Columbus noted for himself, "that henceforth I might call myself by a noble title and be Admiral-in-Chief of the Ocean Sea and Viceroy and Perpetual Governor of all the islands and mainlands that I should discover, . . . and that my eldest son should succeed me, and thus from rank to rank for ever."

We know now what Columbus found. After a few months spent exploring in the Caribbean, where the climate constantly reminded the Admiral of "spring in Andalusia," he left some of his men behind in Hispaniola, modern Haiti, and set out for Spain with a few gold nuggets and a few red Indians to prove the success of his venture. None of the Indians survived the voyage.

In September 1493 Columbus set sail once more with 1500 settlers for his islands in the Ocean Sea and for further exploratory work. In 1498 and again in 1502, only four years

before his death, he made two more voyages. His search, on these visits, was for a passage through the tantalizing barrier just beyond which, he remained certain, must lie Japan, his goal. Naturally, Columbus found no passage. Not until Magellan's men circumnavigated the globe in the service of Spain (1519-1522) did the truth become known about how enormously long was the westward passage to the East—as Eratosthenes and other Greeks had foretold. But Columbus, nevertheless, had his compensations. During his third visit in 1500 he wrote from America: "God made me the messenger of the new heaven and the new earth of which He spoke in the Apocalypse by St. John, after having spoken of it by the mouth of Isaiah, and He showed me the spot where to find it."

So little trust did Ferdinand and Isabella place in the Admiral's claims to have reached Japan, that as early as 1493 they had the Pope, himself a Spaniard, divide the newly discovered world between themselves and the Portuguese. The next year, in the Treaty of Tor-

**15**

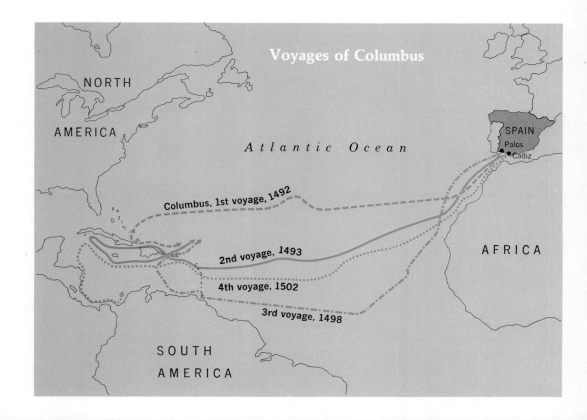

desillas, Spain and Portugal agreed on the specific boundary separating their portions of the sphere. Portugal, in effect, received the Orient and Spain the New World, except for the region that became Brazil. Spain soon encouraged others besides Columbus to occupy her claim, to search out its limits, convert its inhabitants, and uncover its wealth.

One of the first to sail under her colors was a Florentine, Amerigo Vespucci, who in 1497 began a series of voyages on which he explored the American coastline southeast from Mexico all the way to Brazil. Historians now feel that he well earned the fame that attached to his name ever since a German geographer, in 1507, first called the New World "America."

*Spanish ascendancy in the New World*

More useful to Spain than the navigators who followed Columbus under her flag in seeking the passage to India were many of her old *conquistadores.* Freed now from fighting the Mohammedan at home, they boldly crossed the sea to establish Spain's ascendancy over the Indian and the land in America.

Very soon after Columbus's first discoveries, these rough opportunists lorded it over Hispaniola. From this base they extended their grasp to Jamaica in 1509, Cuba in 1511, and Puerto Rico in 1512, thereby completing Spain's occupation of the Greater Antilles. By then rumors of immense wealth on the mainland had begun to exert their charm, and the *conquistadores,* disappointed with their rewards in the islands, left the Lesser Antilles to later adventurers and embarked on the conquest of Central America, Mexico, and Peru.

The first Spanish settlement on the American mainland was made in Panama in 1508 by Alonzo de Ojeda. In 1513 Vasco Nuñez de Balboa worked his way across the Panama isthmus to sight the Pacific, and Ponce de Léon began his quest for the fountain of youth in Florida. But the two greatest exploits were yet to come. The first was the conquest of the Aztecs of Mexico, beginning in 1519, by youthful Hernando Cortez and his mighty horsemen. The second, beginning in 1528, was the yet more cruel conquest of the Incas of Peru by the aging Francisco Pizarro. Here, at last, was the wealth Spain sought, stored up in hoards more magnificent than any European could imagine, and at hand for her superior arms to claim.

From Mexico and Peru, their appetites sharpened by the finds of their superiors, other *conquistadores* set out to discover hoards of their own, but with little success. Tough Hernando de Soto led his men on a fruitless search through the gloomy forests from Florida to the Mississippi River, which he discovered in 1541 only to die of fever on its banks. In the same year Francisco de Coronado, seeking the mythical Seven Cities of Cibola and the gold they held, began his broad explorations of the American Southwest which he disgustedly called the "great American desert," a description which helped retard settlement there for 300 years. On the water, moreover, Spanish ship captains, by 1600, had ranged as far south as Chile and Argentina and as far north and west as the shores of upper California.

Long before other Atlantic nations challenged her in the New World, Spain had established a vast empire in the West Indies and on the Spanish Main. The Spanish regime was in many respects inflexible and harsh. Their obligation to the Pope worked sufficiently on the consciences of Spain's rulers for them to send active missionaries overseas; and these missionaries themselves sometimes proved to be humanitarians. Most notable among them was Bartolomé de Las Casas, who devoted his life to combating the enslavement and extermination of the Indians. But other missionaries soon fell themselves into the ways of the *conquistadores.* Indeed, the priesthood became one of the most exploitive of the Spanish castes and eventually controlled more than half the land of the empire.

The *encomienda,* a system of enforced native labor on large estates, still colors the land

and labor policies of many Latin American countries. This system eventually drew more wealth from the soil than was ever drawn from the mines, but at a high cost in frightful abuses which were ignored by the absentee owners and the authoritarian bureaucrats in the mother country. Above the oppressed natives rose the *mestizos,* Americans of mixed Indian and white ancestry, and the *creoles,* native-born whites. Each of them exploited the caste below, and both, in turn, were harshly discriminated against by the Spanish-born officials in New Spain.

It is true that many Indians, like the fierce Caribs whom Columbus encountered on West Indian islands he visited on his later voyages, as well as mainland Aztecs, Incas, and Mayas, resisted and sometimes withstood enslavement, just as did many fierce tribes of blacks who scared off the slave trade's Iberian minions in Africa. But it is also true that other Africans were first introduced into the New

World by *conquistadores* who, having literally depopulated entire islands (they called them "useless," for their lack of gold) by carrying off the aborigines as short-lived bondsmen, required a continually replenished labor supply.

One of the lasting myths of the Negro's past is that he took docilely to enslavement, a myth fed largely by the contrasting myth of the Indian's brave preference for extinction. But in those tropical regions where they were most numerous, millions of Indians were extinguished (and additional millions and their descendants were repressed) *by* enslavement; and in the same regions many of those blacks who were successfully carried into slavery chilled their captors with the menace of servile revolts.

Spanish New World annals are stained with blood, yet Spain's colonial adventure was remarkably enduring; indeed, her New World empire survived intact twice as long as the British empire in North America. The sway of her cultural institutions perhaps contributed as much to this result as the severity of her material exploitation. In 1544 the first New

**17**

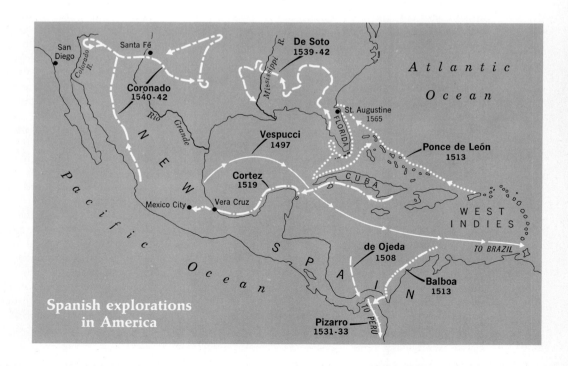

Spanish explorations in America

World printing press was set up in Mexico City. Its initial publication was a *Compendium of Christian Doctrine, "en lengua Mexicana y Castellana."* In 1551, the first New World universities were opened in Mexico City and in Lima, Peru. Shortly thereafter imposing cathedrals were to be found in the important coastal cities, while all over the land hundreds of monasteries plied their business of saving souls.

## III   National rivalry in America

*Religious transformation in Europe*

If the menace of Islam underlay the extension of Portuguese and Spanish power to the most distant habitable regions of the globe, a religious revolution within Christendom fostered the *permanent settlement* of Europeans in the New World, especially in its northern parts.

This religious revolution, which we call the Protestant Reformation, had been fed for generations by the corruption of the Roman church before it broke into the open in 1517. In that year, the deeply troubled German monk and teacher Martin Luther posted his famous 95 theses on the church door in Wittenberg, denouncing in particular the "deception" practiced on "the greater part of the people" by the "indiscriminate" sale of "pardons" for sins. Men, Luther asserted, were not saved by such "good works" (by which he meant largely these and similar contributions to church coffers forcibly exacted by heartless clergymen from easily frightened believers) but by a deep and abiding faith that came directly from God. Christians, he added, should learn about religion not through priestly intermediaries, themselves often ignorant and unprincipled, but directly from the Bible, the word of God, and he translated the Bible into magnificent vernacular German.

Luther aimed at a drastic reformation of the church, not its abolition, but his doctrine pointed toward the radical notion of the priesthood of all believers—"all Christians are truly of the spiritual estate," he argued in 1520. After the Pope excommunicated Luther in 1521, the monk gained the support of many German princes and Scandinavian rulers who had their own quarrels with Rome (see p. 20) and in 1529 "protested" the Pope's efforts to crush the reform movement. Luther, in turn, acknowledged that the state might dominate his church the better to insure, as he said, that "the glorious Teutonic people should cease to be the puppet of the Roman pontiff."

In 1536, almost twenty years after Luther's revolt, John Calvin, harried from his native France to Geneva in Switzerland, presented his ideas to the world in his *Institutes of the Christian Religion,* written in Latin for the learned. Like Luther, Calvin believed that men were saved by the inner light of faith alone, kept steady and bright by daily study and contemplation of the Bible. Confessions, intercessions, mortifications, and reformations in themselves he held mere superstitious acts. But Calvin stressed much more than Luther the idea that if what a man did on earth could not save him, then, if men were actually saved, their eternal reward must be predestined. Calvin was more radical still: the slough of immorality in which men obviously wallowed on every side must mean that only a few choice spirits were preordained by God to participate in the Covenant of Grace—a few choice spirits, that is, and their children; for by the Covenant of Baptism, a kind of inheritance by sacrament, they alone might grow into the "elect," the illuminated countenances, the vessels of Christ.

In Geneva, moreover, Calvin promptly took over the government and afforded his zealous followers elsewhere a model of a purified or "puritan" regime. Although Calvinism was in theory undemocratic, it strengthened the cause of individual freedom by insisting on the privacy of religious experience, by making all "callings" equally honorable, by giving laymen a vital role in church government, and by teaching that the authority of the states was limited by a higher, divine law concerned with the individual soul.

On religious grounds Calvinism was as much a menace to the papacy as Lutheranism. On political grounds it was far more of a menace than Lutheranism to those monarchs who remained, in the Calvinists' estimation, impure and Godless men even though the Pope had given them his blessing. Chief among these monarchs was Charles I, who became King of Spain in 1516 when his grandfather Ferdinand (Isabella had died in 1504) went to his reward. Three years later, Charles's other grandfather, Maximilian, the Hapsburg Archduke of Austria and Holy Roman Emperor, also died, and Charles succeeded him as well, thereby becoming suzerain of all the German princes as Charles V and chief protector of the Roman popes. Charles also became the principal enemy of France, whose territory his Spanish and German holdings virtually hemmed in and many of whose great nobles would soon become "Huguenots," or "confederates" of Calvin.

As early as 1521, Charles swore to Pope Leo X that in undertaking to crush the Lutheran heresy he would not spare his "dominions, friends, body, blood, life, and soul." In 1522 Charles began to impose the Spanish Inquisition on his subjects in non-Spanish lands. In 1534 he approved the creation, by the Spanish monk Ignatius Loyola, of the Society of Jesus, whose task it became to help reclaim Europeans to Catholicism and convert the heathen masses overseas to the old religion. The Jesuits, the members of this Society, zealously pursued their mission; and yet, Protestantism—in the form of Lutheranism, Calvinism, and other rising sects—spread far in Europe. Outside of Germany and France, most irritat-

19

Musée Historique de la Réformation, Geneva

*John Calvin in 1534.*

ing to Charles was the infection of his Dutch subjects in the Spanish Netherlands with the most virulent brand of Calvinism and the infection of England with Anglicanism, a local form of Protestantism declared to be the state religion in 1534 after Henry VIII, in defiance of the Pope, annulled his marriage to Charles's aunt, Catherine of Aragon, and was excommunicated.

In 1556, worn out in the service of the popes, Charles retired to a monastery and left the immense burden of his crusade against the Reformation to his son, who ruled Spain and the other extensive Hapsburg holdings as Philip II. Philip also claimed to be King of England, for in 1554 he had married Queen

Mary, the Catholic daughter of Henry VIII and Catherine. Between them, Philip and Mary restored Catholicism in England, the Queen earning notoriety as "Bloody Mary" for executing some 300 Protestants. When Mary died in 1558, Philip sought to marry her successor, her half-sister Elizabeth, but the new queen rejected both Philip and his faith.

In 1563 Elizabeth strengthened the position of Anglicanism in England by subscribing to the Thirty-nine Articles of religion, which made clearer and more specific the differences between the new Church of England and the old Church of Rome. By taking this step, however, she severed the attachment of the many remaining English Catholics to the throne and also weakened the loyalty of the growing numbers of English Calvinists who wished to go much farther than the Thirty-nine Articles in eliminating the last vestiges of Romanism in English belief and worship.

These religious divisions in her island—which were profound enough to lead eventually to civil war—tempered Elizabeth's policies in many ways. And yet having declared unequivocally for her own brand of Protestantism at home, she soon offered to aid anti-Catholics elsewhere in Europe. Elizabeth especially aided the Dutch, who had revolted against Philip in 1568. In 1570, the Pope excommunicated her and absolved English Catholics of allegiance to the throne.

Spain and England now became more bitter enemies than ever, and the "scepter'd isle" at last turned her attention to mastery of the seas. The principal lures on the seas were the Spanish galleys carrying the wealth of Mexico and Peru to Philip's treasury for the support of his Catholic armies. The Elizabethan "sea dogges" pursued these galleys unremittingly, Francis Drake in *Golden Hind* bringing home the most magnificent catch of all in 1580—£1,500,000 in gold and silver gained in raiding the Spanish Main and Spanish New World islands, as well as Spanish shipping. The blow to Philip was made all the more pointed by Elizabeth's promptly knighting the buccaneering sailor.

The final insult came in 1587, when Elizabeth, impelled by the urging of her council, her Parliament, and most of her people, or-

dered the execution of her Catholic cousin, Mary, Queen of Scots. Twenty years earlier, when Mary had been forced to abdicate by Calvinists led by John Knox in her own country, she found a refuge in England, where she repaid Elizabeth's calculated hospitality—the better to keep an eye on Mary—by conspiring constantly with Philip's English friends to help him grasp the throne. As English relations with Spain worsened, Mary had to be dispatched.

Philip now declared open war on England, sending out in 1588 the Grand Armada with which he hoped to destroy Elizabeth, proceed to victory over the Dutch, and assist the Catholic party in France to crush the Huguenots. The Armada's defeat by Sir Francis Drake and the bold Dutch "water beggars" who sailed down to join the battle, frustrated Philip's plans and initiated his decline. In 1589 the wars between Catholic and Protestant forces in France ended in victory for the Huguenot Henry of Navarre, who as Henry IV became the first Bourbon king. Along with the Protestant English and Calvinist Dutch, Henry was soon to establish his own claims to New World lands in defiance of Catholic Spain's monopoly.

### Economic and political nationalism

Protestantism so rapidly transformed so much of sixteenth-century Europe largely because Catholicism had fallen on evil days. The failure of the late Crusades against Islam had placed the papacy at once in debt and on the defensive. As calls for funds on Catholic rulers grew more frequent and burdensome, their resistance to paying matched in ingenuity and intensity the popes' importunities. One reason why the Reformation began in Germany was that the popes were forced increasingly to seek their funds from the German people on whom, as subjects of the Holy Roman Empire, they had the most direct claim. Methods so crude and corrupt were used to wring money from the Germans that they became profoundly disenchanted with the materialism of their priests and their religion. This widespread popular discontent with Rome made all the more practical the lust of the German princes themselves for the vast lands of the church, and for control of church offices and income. For similar reasons the spark of the German Reformation quickly inflamed much of the rest of Europe.

As sides were drawn, other always volatile elements—ancient feudal family rivalries, dynastic ambitions of rising clans, greed for commercial monopolies—fed the blaze. The very nature of European civilization was altered with extraordinary speed. Powerful new nations emerged out of the searing chaos of contending principalities. New national armies incurred heavy costs not only in establishing the new monarchs but also in protecting and extending their authority. To meet these costs the monarchs sought new national taxes and loans. These, in turn, could be most effectively obtained by abating the old church doctrine against high profits and interest.

One of the most obvious sources of high profits in still largely agricultural communities was improved land use. Such improvement often entailed the dislodging of many small husbandmen and the combination of their fields into extensive estates producing cash crops. Then, as later, the removal of families from the land supplied many new hands for commercial and industrial enterprises, for the growing national armies and navies, and for settlement in colonial outposts overseas. Improved land use and commerce in cash crops, in turn, made available the wherewithal for heavy-interest loans to royalty, and also for investment in colonial enterprises. Naturally these enterprises were usually promoted and manned in newly Protestant countries by those in revolt against Roman Catholic ideas and institutions. In England especially, during the early decades of Elizabeth's reign, a strong new impulse was given to the modernization of society. In keeping with emerging "mercantilist" theories of national competition (see p. 49), the commercialization of agriculture, the development of mining and manufacturing, the improvement of facilities for domestic commerce all were speeded up. The object was to make the Protestant Queen "a prince of power" by promoting English self-sufficiency to the extent that nature and improved technology permitted. At the same time, every national advantage was sought in extending foreign trade.

Much else, of course, in what we may justly call the New World of Europe fostered the development of the New World in America. With the resurgence of interest during the Renaissance in classical society and the imperial grandeur of Rome, the very idea of empire grew more attractive even in Catholic lands. The attack of Protestant thinkers on the mysticism, not to say the superstition, of the old Church strengthened the rising spirit of secularism and science, including the science of discovery. Discovery itself raised profound questions about the origins of strange beasts and people which the Bible inadequately accounted for. Such questions culminated centuries later in the Darwinian theories of evolution and the science of anthropology. The concern with empire, secular thought, and scientific study spread across Europe after the fifteenth century; but it most deeply altered life in the new maritime (as against the old Mediterranean) nations of the north, especially France, the Netherlands, and England.

### The way of the French

As early as 1523, more than half a century before Drake in *Golden Hind,* Jean Fleury, a French corsair, intercepted Spanish galleys carrying the gold and silver of the New World to the treasury of Charles V. The next year, King Francis I of France sent Giovanni Verrazano to North America in search of the northwest passage to the Indies. Verrazano explored the coast from North Carolina to Newfoundland, to which Dutch mapmakers, mocking Spanish claims to the whole New World, soon gave the name "New France." In 1534 Jacques Cartier, on a mission similar to Verrazano's, began the exploration of the Gulf and River of St. Lawrence and thereby strengthened French claims to the sites of future Quebec and Montreal.

Soon after Cartier's expedition, France was ravaged by religious wars, and exploration ceased for almost 75 years. But free-lance French corsairs continued so to harass Spanish shipping from the New World that Spain, in 1565, was forced to set up a base at St. Augustine, Florida, from which to combat the marauders. This was the first European settlement on land that was to become part of the continental United States. Far to the north other Frenchmen on fishing voyages to Newfoundland had begun exchanging precious bits of metal for the rich pelts the native red men would bring to the shore. The trade in fur (soon enlarged by the exchange of brandy and guns as well as scraps of iron) became the staple of New France after exploration and settlement were resumed under the leadership of Samuel de Champlain in 1603.

Champlain was France's greatest explorer. He and his men pushed French claims, and French friendship with the Indians who would support their claims, well past the "inland sea" we know as the Great Lakes. The fur trade, in turn, carried its followers, red and white alike, ever deeper into the North American wilderness in search of beaver and other fur-bearing game. To Quebec and Montreal soon would flow a stream of gifts for the Indians and supplies, instructions, and news from home for the traders. From these growing ports New France would soon send much wealth to the mother country. But the fur trade abhorred settlers who would enclose and cultivate the land and thereby drive off the fur-bearing animals. Thus while the French ultimately could lay claim to an area in North America far more vast than that of the English huddled along the coast, they had far from sufficient numbers to make good their claim when the final showdown with the English came in the middle of the eighteenth century.

### The way of the Dutch

Although the French led the way in attacking Spain on the sea, the Dutch far outdid them in pirating Spanish gold. The Dutch

Macpherson Collection, The National Maritime Museum, Greenwich, England

had other capabilities as well. To their shores they welcomed many Jews exiled from Spain after 1492. Strengthened by these versatile capitalists, the Dutch developed their own manufactures, fisheries, trade centers, and banks. Splendidly situated between booming Scandinavia, which was supplying Europe with much of its timber and naval stores, and booming France and England, which were exporting wines, woolens, and coal, the Dutch became the prosperous middlemen on the northern water routes, as the Italians once had been on the southern paths of commerce.

Once the Portuguese had opened their direct trade with the Orient, moreover, the Dutch worked out an agreement with them to meet their ships at sea in order to pick up and speed the delivery of Oriental wares to the northern countries. They also were licensed to serve as carriers between Lisbon and Brazil. When Portugal fell to Spain once more in 1580, the Dutch were engaged in their own

Havana

Dutch Admiral Piet Hein's capture,
with his few small ships,
of a Spanish treasure fleet off Havana, 1628.
In all the Dutch booty was worth
12 million florins,
for the loss of which the Spanish commander
was executed on his return home.

successful revolt against their Spanish rulers. The Dutch promptly included Portugal among their enemies and soon supplanted her in the Oriental and Brazilian trade. Indeed, having set up the Dutch East India Company in 1602 to consolidate their Oriental interests, the Dutch quickly established a Far Eastern empire of their own that remained intact until 1949.

In 1609 the Dutch East India Company sent Henry Hudson in *Half Moon* to make its own futile search for the elusive northwest passage. Hudson failed; but while anchored in the vicinity of modern Albany on the river named for him, he entertained a band of Mohawks of the great Iroquois nation and made them gifts of "firewater" and firearms. Iroquois friendship helped the Dutch in their contest with the French, which began in 1614 when another Dutch party established Holland's first fur-trading post near Albany. The English inherited Iroquois good will when

they ousted the Dutch from North America in 1664. In April 1610, this time employed by English adventurers, Hudson set forth on his last voyage, on which he discovered Hudson Bay.

On the model of the East India Company, the Dutch, in 1621, also created a West India Company to extend their grip on Portuguese Brazil and break the Spanish Caribbean monopoly. The Dutch gained their first successes in Brazil in 1630 and by 1637 controlled 1200 miles of coastal lands, on which they grew brazilwood, tobacco, and above all, sugar cane. When, in 1640, Portugal rewon her independence from Spain, Brazilian Catholics, shocked by a Portuguese-Dutch agreement recognizing Dutch holdings, revolted against both the Portuguese and the Dutch. By 1654, faced with crises elsewhere, the Dutch completed their withdrawal, taking with them their slaves, their tools, and their invaluable knowledge of sugar production.

By 1630 the Dutch West India Company had also smashed Spanish shipping in the Caribbean and largely taken charge of the carrying trade there themselves. The fury of their attack so weakened the Spanish hold in the region that English, French, and Scandinavian adventurers, as well as the Dutch, swarmed in, each to grasp islands for their own flag.

The attraction of such islands lay initially in their value as bases for smuggling and piracy; but the English settlers on the islands soon tried to make a go of it by growing tobacco for the European market. The Virginia variety, however, had already proved of higher quality (see p. 36). The Dutch watched the islanders' losing struggle with concern, and in order to keep full the holds of their own vessels in the Caribbean trade they began, as early as 1637, to teach the English and the French the intricacies of sugar growing and manufacture. The Dutch also supplied them with capital and equipment and with the enslaved Africans who soon displaced the white workers and laid the foundation for the heavy black concentration in the population of these islands to this day. After 1650 sugar produced by slave labor on large plantations made the islands in the Lesser Antilles the most precious of New World colonies.

In 1626 the Dutch West India Company purchased Manhattan Island from the local braves as a base for its own fur-trade operations and changed its name to New Amsterdam. The Company next extended its claims up the Hudson Valley and outward to Hartford on the Connecticut River, to Camden on the Delaware, and to Long Island. In 1629 it made its first immense grants of land along the Hudson to the patroons who were expected to bring in permanent tenants. In 1638 Scandinavians established New Sweden on Dutch claims in the Delaware vicinity, and the Dutch Company for a few years made no move to dislodge them.

In 1638, flouting mercantilist theory (see p. 49), the Dutch opened New Amsterdam to mariners of all nations. This step alone showed that the Dutch, a nation of a mere 2.5 million souls, had begun to overreach themselves; but long after they surrendered New Amsterdam to the English in 1664 they remained a power to reckon with elsewhere.

### The way of the English

The French and the Dutch exposed the weakness of Spain's hold on America, but it was England that most effectively contested Spanish claims and most successfully colonized the northern hemisphere.

In 1497 Henry VII, the first of the Tudor line, who established the modern national monarchy in England by his victory in the War of the Roses twelve years earlier, sent out John Cabot, a naturalized Venetian, to seek the fabled northwest passage to Asia. Upon Cabot's single visit to Labrador, England's New World claim long rested. Almost a century later, in 1576, the Cathay Company, formed to develop English trade with China, sent Martin Frobisher on the first of three voyages duplicating Cabot's quest, but nothing came of them except reinforcement of English reluctance to chase this will-o'-the-wisp any longer. Drake's voyage in *Golden Hind* in 1577 confirmed the greater value of chasing Spanish galleys.

While Elizabethan sailors were scourging the seas, Elizabethan soldiers dreamed their own dreams of adventure and wealth. In 1578 Humphrey Gilbert, Walter Ralegh's half-brother, obtained from Elizabeth the first charter for a North American settlement. Gilbert was not without ambitions to emulate Drake; nor

*Sir Walter Ralegh at age 44, artist unknown.*

National Gallery of Ireland

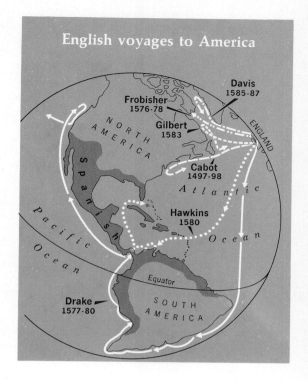

**English voyages to America**

had the lure of the northwest passage altogether died in him. His path-breaking goal was a permanent North American base for his endeavors.

The outcome of Gilbert's first voyage in 1578–1579 remains a mystery. In June 1583 he embarked on his second voyage in command of five ships and 260 men with the aim of establishing a settlement in Newfoundland. Insubordination and foul weather plagued the enterprise from the start, and most of the participants, including Gilbert, perished at sea on the voyage home. Ralegh then took up the mission, only to exhaust his fortune on three profitless expeditions. On the first of these, in 1584, the year he was knighted, his captains made their landfall in the vicinity of Roanoke Island, to which, on their return with enchanting reports, Ralegh gave the name Virginia for the virgin queen, Elizabeth. After an abortive second expedition in 1585, Ralegh made his most serious attempt at colonization in 1587, when he sent 120 persons to Virginia under the leadership of John White. Once he had landed his passengers and selected the site for their settlement, White sailed home for supplies. On his return to Virginia in 1590 he found the settlement deserted. No one, to this day, knows its fate.

The Crown looked upon Ralegh's ventures as a way for him to recoup his fortune, not to improve the fortunes of England. What helped change England's mind about colonies was, if not the promotional work of Richard Hakluyt the younger beginning in 1589, then the conditions Hakluyt described and which he claimed colonization overseas would relieve.

Hakluyt's *Voyages,* numerous publications in which he gathered every scrap of information he could find about foreign lands, revealed much of the outside world to his insular countrymen. Hakluyt argued persuasively for a North American settlement as a source of raw materials for English industry, a market for English goods, and an attraction for the "able men" who "pestered" English pris-

ons. When Hakluyt wrote, the English statute books listed some 400 capital crimes. Many felons in the sixteenth century—given the choice of deportation or death—preferred the perils of the newly discovered world to the mysteries of that "undiscovered country" from which (as Shakespeare reminded them) no travelers returned.

But not all Englishmen who eventually left for the New World acted from such desperate motives. Some dutifully followed the clerical injunction to "marry this land, a pure virgin, to thy kingly son Christ Jesus." For others less concerned with converting the heathen, "a Land more like the Garden of Eden than any part else of all the earth" offered another congenial challenge. Reports of exotic animals and plants, variations in climate, unusual customs, and rare "objects for contemplation" also whetted the appetite for adventure. Prospects of new Inca and Aztec hoards, moreover, continued to sharpen the greed of "right worthy" promoters as well as the avarice of the settlers they sent out.

# For further reading*

The new world of Europe, from which emerged the impulse to seek new worlds overseas, is the subject of R. L. Reynolds, *Europe Emerges: Transition Toward an Industrial World-Wide Society 600-1750* (1961). On this theme see also E. P. Cheyney, *The Dawn of a New Era 1250-1453* (1936), and Derwent Whittlesey, *Environmental Foundations of European History* (1949).

Digging into the earth for archeological survivals is going on as actively as the exploration of space. New findings are often presented in authoritative fashion in such magazines as *Scientific American* and *National Geographic*. An example from the first is W. C. Haag, "The Bering Strait Land Bridge" (January 1962); of special interest in the second is Helge Ingstad, "Viking Ruins Prove Vikings Found the New World" (November 1964), a study elaborated in Ingstad's *Westward to Vinland* (1969). Background for the discovery and settlement of Vinland is best supplied in two books by Gwyn Jones: *The Norse Atlantic Saga* (1964) and *A History of the Vikings* (1968).

G. R. Willey, *An Introduction to American Archaeology* (vol. 1, 1966; vol. 2, 1971), and George Kubler, *The Art and Architecture of Ancient America* (1962), are authoritative. Excellent on the Aztecs and Mayas are M. D. Coe, *Mexico* (1962) and *The Maya* (1966); and on the Incas, John Henning, *The Conquest of the Incas* (1970). Still valuable on pre-Columbian culture are the American classics by W. H. Prescott and Francis Parkman. Most germane here are Prescott's *History of the Conquest of Mexico* (3 vols., 1843), and *History of the Conquest of Peru* (2 vols., 1847), both abbreviated in paperback editions, and Parkman's Introduc-

tion on "Native Tribes" in his *The Jesuits in North America in the Seventeenth Century* (2 vols., 1867). This Introduction is reproduced in the excellent edition of selections from Parkman, *The Parkman Reader* (1955), edited by S. E. Morison. A contemporary classic on the Spanish invasion of the American mainland is Bernal Díaz del Castillo, *The Discovery and Conquest of Mexico*, edited in a satisfactory one-volume edition by I. A. Leonard (1956). Cortez's dispatches from Mexico are available in I. R. Blacker and H. M. Rosen, *Conquest* (1962). Of unusual interest are M. Leon-Portilla, *The Broken Spears, the Aztec Account of the Conquest of Mexico* (1962), and R. C. Padden, *The Hummingbird and the Hawk, Conquest and Sovereignty in the Valley of Mexico 1503-1541* (1967). W. E. Washburn, *The Indian and the White Man* (1964) is an invaluable anthology.

J. E. Gillespie, *A History of Geographical Discovery 1400-1800* (1933), is a good short introduction. Rhys Carpenter, *Beyond The Pillars of Hercules* (1966), is outstanding on classical exploration and geographic thought. A. P. Newton, ed., *Travel and Travellers of the Middle Ages* (1930), and Boies Penrose, *Travel and Discovery in the Renaissance 1420-1620* (1960), are excellent on the background for Columbus's adventure. Sir Henry Yule and Henri Cordier, eds., *The Book of Ser Marco Polo* (2 vols., 1921), is the best edition of the famous travels. M. C. Seymour, ed., *Mandeville's Travels* (1968), is a modern English version of that book. C. E. Nowell, *The Great Discoveries and the First Colonial Empires* (1954), is a short, authoritative survey. The outstanding biography of Columbus is S. E. Morison, *Admiral of the Ocean Sea* (2 vols., 1942). See also C. O. Sauer, *The Early Spanish Main* (1969). The best edition of Columbus's writings and related materials is S. E. Morison, ed., *Journals and Other Documents on the Life and Voyages of Christopher Columbus* (1963). E. P. Hanson, ed., *South from the Spanish Main* (1967), provides revealing material on "South America Seen through the Eyes of its Discoverers." J. B. Brebner, *The Explorers of North America 1492-1806* (1933), is indispensable for the opening of that continent. R. H. Brown, *Historical Geography of the United States* (1948), is excellent on the character and use of the land.

---

* So many scholarly books are now published only in paperbacks, or are published in paperbacks simultaneously with or very shortly after hard-cover editions, that we have given up identifying paperback titles as a practice too rapidly dated. Instead, we recommend to our readers the use of *Paperbound Books in Print*, published quarterly (with monthly supplements) by the R. R. Bowker Company, a comprehensive listing of such books by title, by author, and by subject. Current issues should be available in every college and school library.

On Portugal and her empire, see C. E. Nowell, *A History of Portugal* (1952); Elaine Sanceau, *Henry the Navigator* (1947); and C. R. Boxer, *Race Relations in the Portuguese Colonial Empire 1415-1825* (1963). On the Spanish empire, besides Prescott, see J. H. Parry, *The Spanish Seaborne Empire* (1966); F. A. Kirkpatrick, *The Spanish Conquistadores* (1934); and L. B. Simpson, *The Encomienda in New Spain* (1950). A. P. Newton, *The European Nations in the West Indies 1493-1688* (1933), is invaluable for Spain and her rivals. On the great event of 1588, see Garrett Mattingly, *The Armada* (1959). On France in the New World, in addition to Parkman, see W. B. Munro, *Crusaders of New France* (1920), and G. M. Wrong, *The Rise and Fall of New France* (2 vols., 1928). On the expansion of Holland, see C. R. Boxer, *The Dutch Seaborne Empire: 1600-1800* (1965).

The background for English expansion is presented in numerous works by J. A. Williamson, for example, *Maritime Enterprise 1485-1558* (1913). K. R. Andrews, *Drake's Voyages* (1967), is an authoritative modern interpretation. Extracts from Richard Hakluyt's twelve volumes of *Voyages* are presented in the excellent World's Classics edition by Janet Hampden (1958). *The England of Elizabeth* (1951) and *The Expansion of Elizabethan England* (1955) by A. L. Rowse capture the spirit of the age. Rowse's *The Elizabethans and America* (1959) is excellent on early colonization attempts.

# AN ENGLISH NATION

In July 1603, a few months after James I became King of England, Sir Walter Ralegh was locked up in the Tower of London for treason. His personal fortunes had sunk as low as the fortunes of his colonial enterprises in North America almost twenty years earlier, but he still clung to his old hopes for Virginia which he expressed as late as 1602: "I shall yet live to see it an English nation."

When in 1618 Ralegh at last was executed under his old sentence, Virginia had indeed become an English colony. But the English *nation* Ralegh had in mind was a far grander enterprise than the feeble settlement planted at Jamestown in 1607. This settlement, which tried in every way to emulate the Spanish *conquistadores,* was to be a disastrous failure for a generation. Ralegh's idea had been not to emulate but to evict the Spanish. He would so develop the economy of his territory that the "shipping, victual, munition, and transporting of five or six thousand soldiers may be defrayed." With this force he would march on and conquer New Spain. Ralegh's Virginia was to be nothing less than the New World itself, unshared, unpartitioned, a mighty imperial accession for the English.

Ralegh, as we know, failed in his grand design. New Spain prospered. New France, in turn, continued to occupy most of the northern part of North America until the English took it in 1763. A mere twenty years later, the English themselves were driven out of what was to prove the gateway to the richest region of the Western Hemisphere by the rebellious inhabitants of their own "plantations," assisted by the French who hankered to return. About half a million of these rebels—approximately one-fourth of the white population of the thirteen colonies in 1775—were of non-English extraction, mainly German, Scotch, Dutch, and Irish, but including also Spanish and Portuguese Jews, French Huguenots, and a mixture of Scandinavians, predominantly Swedes. Another half a million Americans were Negroes from Africa or of African descent.

And yet Ralegh's hopes for Virginia were not altogether unfulfilled. Although surrounded by foreign enemies and inhabited by many foreign peoples, the American colonies became an "English nation" in language, law, and tradition. So deeply did the English feel this that they would not enlist to fight their "brothers" in 1775 and 1776, and the Crown had to hire Hessians to try to put the rebellion down. The Americans, in fact, quickly became

more English than the English in those very qualities which helped distinguish the English from their continental rivals other than the Dutch—nonconformism in religion, representative government, economic and social opportunity for the common man. So deeply, on their part, did the rebels feel *this* that when they enlisted in their state militias in 1775 and 1776 to fight the outrages of Parliament, they signed up officially to serve "in His Majesty's Service . . . for the preservation of the Liberties of *America*." One of the principal causes of the rebellion was the Americans' recognition of their own continental destiny which the English, after 1763, had tried to hedge in. As late as the 1890s, Sir Walter's grand vision of the New World with "but one flag and one country" continued to animate American policy.

# I  Impulse to leave England

## The Stuart succession

Much is often made of "the English birthright," of the "Liberties, Franchises, and Immunities," as the first Virginia charter put it in 1606, of English subjects living under the rule of law and not of men. That these are more than mere phrases history attests. Yet we are not to confuse them, or even the aspirations they suggest, with the egalitarian concepts of our own day, however liberal the tradition they inspired, especially in America.

The reign of the Tudors, brought to a close by Elizabeth's death in 1603, remained a despotism with a long roll of martyrs to conscience, to conviction, and to convenience. Many troublesome books were burned publicly, their possessors executed, their authors expelled from the country. Freedom of expression meant no more than the Commons' right to introduce legislation not proposed by the Crown, and it usually was denied. Freedom of assembly and of petition were considered seditious goals. Religious dissidents were persecuted mainly on political grounds, the numerous Catholics (except under "Bloody Mary") as agents of a foreign foe, the growing number of Puritans as enemies of monarchy; but these were grounds enough to kill the bloom of toleration.

By and large, among Englishmen still habituated to doffing the cap, bending the knee, and prostrating themselves in supplication, the Tudors' was a popular despotism satisfying, however imperfectly, the deep yearning for domestic peace. It may fairly be said of Elizabeth in particular—gracious, clever, confident—that she ruled more by "progresses"

than by "prerogative." Elizabeth owned numerous palaces, rallying points of national pride. And she was constantly on the move across the country from one palace to another, her living presence filling such pride to overflowing. Each of her progresses was an act of state, meticulously thought out. No one knew better than the Tudors, as a contemporary of Elizabeth said, that "in pompous ceremonies a secret of government doth much consist." To the people, she said herself, "no music is so sweet as the affability of their prince." Yet even Elizabeth wore out her welcome, especially among Puritans who never tasted the affability of their prince and who hated pompous ceremonies.

*An Elizabethan "progress." Her subjects in provincial cities and towns as well as in London lined the streets for hours awaiting her approach.*

Near the end of Elizabeth's reign, Puritans probably made up a majority of the kingdom. With their friends in the Commons, mainly lawyers and justices of the peace aroused to the defense—really, the revolutionary extension—of their privileges by the Queen's intransigence in religious matters, they certainly commanded an overwhelming majority of Parliament. Elizabeth's secret choice as her successor was James VI of Scotland, son of Mary, Queen of Scots, whom she herself had ordered executed in 1587 (see p. 20). To prepare James, Elizabeth long engaged in secret correspondence with him, tutoring him in English ways. In one letter she observed, "There is risen a sect of perilous consequences, who would have no kings but a presbytery. . . . Suppose you I can tolerate such scandals! " James's early years had been spent in terror of warring Protestant groups; and while well trained in Calvinism as befitted a Scottish king, he soon disavowed equally with Elizabeth that part of the doctrine stated by John Knox himself to Mary: "If . . . princes exceed their bounds, Madam, they may be resisted and even deposed."

Whatever else Elizabeth attempted to teach James about England seems never to have taken hold. James's Calvinism commended him the more readily to many Puritans who, having grown tired of combating a woman's wiles, were eager to have a king. Catholics, on the other hand, despaired. Yet Puritans, as it turned out, had as much to fear from James as Catholics, and England more to fear than both. Still, the Stuarts did have a chance to win English hearts.

James's peaceful accession brought a welcome lull in England's bitter border wars with Scotland which ravaged the northern frontier. When his assumption of the throne was followed in 1604 by his making peace at last with Spain, and when this peace was followed with new commercial treaties, the reign enjoyed an unprecedented expansion of trade which further gilded its prospects. Yet James, sometimes known for his studiousness and

dogmatism as "the wisest fool in Christendom," out of ignorance and intolerance quickly cast these added advantages away.

In the midst of his first progress to the throne, spokesmen for a thousand reform clergymen placed in his hand the Millenary Petition requesting alterations in Church of England doctrine and worship far milder than those which had driven Elizabeth to extremities. In January 1604 James yielded sufficiently to call a conference at Hampton Court to consider the petition and, as was his wont, he argued learnedly with the members before smiting them with the fury of his wrath. "If you aim at a Scottish Presbytery," he cried, "it agreeth as well with monarchy, as God with the Devil." The reformers had expressed no such aim, but grasping his hat to signalize the end of the conference, James shouted: "If this be all your party hath to say, I will make them conform themselves or else harry them out of the land."

Shortly thereafter, hundreds of reform clergymen were evicted from their livings, and thousands more, for conscience' sake, embraced the Puritan position. The radical Separatists, recognizing the bleakness of their plight, began preparations for their exodus to Holland and eventually to a haven in the New World (see p. 39). At the same time, the royalist clergy took to announcing their own divinity and infallibility, a position sustained by the ecclesiastical courts. Royalist judges, in turn, assented to ecclesiastical court encroachments on the jurisdiction of the common-law courts. In self-defense, common-law lawyers were impelled ever more strongly toward nonconformist ranks.

James spent as little time dallying with Catholics as he had with the Protestant reformers. Under Elizabeth, Catholics had been the hunted pariahs of the realm. James's own goal in the Spanish peace was to bring an end to Spanish subversion of the Catholic underground in England. This accomplished, he even restored diplomatic relations with the Pope and gave other signs of toleration. Having thus drawn Catholics out of hiding, he promptly conjured up the old blood-curdling fears among all Protestants, to which, indeed, Catholic leaders had quickly given some substance. As early as February 1604 the royal reaction began, and Catholics found themselves worse off than ever. Certain Catholic leaders now worked out the elaborate Gunpowder Plot in which Guy Fawkes and others planned to blow up both the King and Parliament, initiate a civil war, and call Spain in to restore order. The great explosion was planned for December 1605, but the plot was uncovered in November, when Fawkes and his co-conspirators were arrested and soon tried, convicted, and hanged. Thereafter, with only occasional intermissions, Catholics knew no more peace in England, and like the radical Protestants they turned their eyes to havens abroad.

### Resumption of the American enterprise

During the great surge of economic expansion in the early years of Elizabeth's reign (see p. 21), the joint-stock company, a device borrowed from the Dutch especially for distant trading, had come into general use in England. Joint-stock companies, by selling shares to those rising on the economic scale and accustoming themselves to the long-term risks of far-off ventures, could quickly amass far larger capital funds than most individuals had at their disposal. Anyone with money could subscribe to company stock, participate in the profits, and even gain a voice in management—features that favorably distinguished joint-stock enterprises from the traditional trading guilds with their prohibitive fees and tests, and the hated monopolies by which court favorites ate out the substance of the country.

In the early decades of Elizabeth's reign, joint-stock companies had extended English commerce to Russia, Scandinavia, and the Levant, even to Africa and the Orient. Elizabeth's interminable Spanish war checked economic expansion, but James's peace with Spain in 1604 led to its spectacular revival.

Joint-stock undertakings in America followed directly upon the voyage to the Maine coast in 1605 of Captain George Waymouth in search of a Catholic refuge. In Maine, Waymouth kidnapped five Indians, an act local tribes were to hold against all later white visi-

tors, and when he displayed them in London on his return, having trained them to talk of the wonders of their native land, they caused a sensation. Sir Ferdinando Gorges, one of the organizers of the Virginia Company of Plymouth late in 1605, declared that "this accident" of the red men's arrival "must be acknowledged the means under God of putting on foot and giving life to all our plantations."

A year after Gorges's company, a second Virginia joint-stock enterprise, the Virginia Company of London, was organized, with Sir Thomas Smith, governor of the English East India Company, prominent among its directors. The possibility of finding a short route to China by way of Virginia rivers, an objective

*"The Right Worshipful Sir Thomas Smith of London, Knight." From the original portrait by an unknown artist.*

dear to the East India Company, no doubt contributed to his enthusiasm for the venture.

The release of mercantile energies during the early years of James's reign promoted what may be called the *colonizing* activity of the nation. James himself, and Charles I after him, unwittingly secured the permanence and profitability of colonies, particularly in America, by promoting the *settlement*—the flight, really—of large numbers of Englishmen overseas. The Stuarts accomplished this, as we have seen, not only by religious persecution, but also by denouncing the rule of law as treason just when Parliament, dominated by Puritans, was making its most portentous efforts to curb monarchical absolutism.

James had come to the throne with obligations to many backers. Insecure in his new eminence, he sought, furthermore, to enlist the support of leading courtiers with lavish grants. He also inherited large war debts from Elizabeth. The thirst for funds had forced James in his early years as King, as it had forced Elizabeth in her waning years, to call session after session of Parliament; but the members would yield little while their growing grievances, especially on religious and legal issues, went uncorrected.

The struggle between Crown and Commons deepened when James, and Charles after him, deprived of funds by the House, began to reach out for other sources of revenue by royal proclamation. Among the tastiest of these were the "impositions," or duties, on imported goods, which had grown greatly in value during the economic boom. When the Commons, in 1610, asked that "a law be made to declare that all impositions set upon your people . . . save only by common consent in parliament, . . . shall be void," James, in a rage, closed the session. When a new Parliament in 1614 presented even stronger religious and legal demands in exchange for "supplies" for the King, James not only dissolved it immediately but sent four of its leading members to the Tower. With his new chief minister, George Villiers, whom he made

Duke of Buckingham, James now ruled without restraint. Impositions soared; peerages were sold for huge sums; new monopolies were granted to the rich. At the same time, economies so ruined the navy that Turkish pirates enslaved English seamen in the Channel itself, while the Dutch captured much of London's trade.

When Charles I succeeded James in 1625, Buckingham embarked on military and maritime adventures to regain mercantile support. But these were such costly failures that the Crown itself was brought into ever worse repute and Parliament into outright rebellion. Parliament's refusal to vote money for further adventures like Buckingham's brought Charles at last to the policy of "forced loans," refusal to lend carrying with it the penalty of imprisonment without trial. A compliant clergy attempted to aid Charles by declaring nonpayment of taxes and loans a sin. This reminder of papal corruption completed the mortification of the Puritans who had already become alarmed by the sincere efforts of Charles's new archbishop, William Laud, to reform the Church of England. Unfortunately, Laud's reforms went directly opposite to those the Puritans themselves demanded, bringing in many Roman innovations to attract worshippers who did not in fact have Christ in their hearts. Laud, at the same time, intensified the persecution of nonconformists.

In 1629, Parliament, with Sir John Eliot showing the way, proposed the famous "Three Resolutions" to Charles, demanding that the King declare "as a capital enemy to this kingdom and commonwealth" not only him who lays and him who pays taxes "not being granted by Parliament," but him also who "shall bring in innovation in religion." Charles rejected the Resolutions. When Parliament voted them despite his opposition, Charles dissolved the body, not to recall it until April 1640, when he again needed funds to suppress an uprising of Scotch Presbyterians. This Short Parliament was immediately dissolved when it insisted on reforms first. By then no less than 70,000 Englishmen had migrated to the West Indies and North America.

A settlement with the Scots committed Charles to still further outlays, and in November 1640 he called the fateful Long Parliament, which resisted his demands, raised its own army, touched off the Civil War, and paved the way for the dictatorship of Oliver Cromwell. The Long Parliament held office until the Restoration in 1660. During its turbulent career, Cromwell welded his army of "Roundheads" into an irresistible force. Soon after Parliament ordered the beheading of the King in 1649, Cromwell became Lord Protec-

34

tor of the Commonwealth, as the kingdom came to be called. In the Commonwealth period, the flow of dissenters to America slackened, and only a few royalists were prepared to leave England, joyless and austere though the land now seemed.

## II   Rude beginnings on the Chesapeake

### Survival in Virginia

Sir Ferdinando Gorges's Virginia Company of Plymouth outdid its rivals in getting under way. Its first expedition set sail in August 1606, only to fall prey to Spaniards in the West Indies. In May and June 1607 Gorges dispatched two more ships, one of them carrying Waymouth's pilot, to the region of Waymouth's visit (see p. 32), and there, on the Sagadohoc River, the lower Kennebec today, the Plymouth Company's first and only colony endured one "extreme, unseasonable and frosty" winter and quit. Thereafter, fishermen from all expansionist nations of Europe regularly visited the Maine coast but established no lasting bases.

In December 1606, meanwhile, *Susan Constant, Godspeed,* and *Discovery,* with 160 men, all under the command of Captain Christopher Newport, an experienced West Indian buccaneer had quietly weighed anchor for the London Company, and on April 26, 1607 sighted "the Bay of Chesupiac," or Chesapeake. A few days later, the expedition sailed some 50 miles up the river they named the James and chose a site they named Jamestown, one well situated for defense. Here, although only after the most distressing experiences, not excluding cannibalism, England won her first foothold in America. During the bleak winter of 1608-1609, the "starving time," only the efforts of Captain John Smith had held the colony together. But when Smith, having taken authority upon himself, was injured in 1609 and left Virginia for good,

**Early settlements in Virginia**

Potomac R.
Delaware Bay
Chesapeake Bay
Atlantic Ocean
James R.
York R.
● Williamsburg
Jamestown ●
Roanoke Island

*(Opposite) "A particular of such necessaries . . . for their better support at their first landing in Virginia," published in 1622 to help new colonists avoid "The inconveniencies that have happened to some persons which have transported themselves from England."*

# THE INCONVENIENCIES
## THAT HAVE HAPPENED TO SOME PERSONS WHICH HAVE TRANSPORTED THEMSELVES

from *England* to *Virginia* , vvithout prouisions necessary to sustaine themselues, hath greatly hindred the *Progresse of that noble Plantation : For preuention of the like disorders* heereafter, that no man suffer, either through ignorance or misinformation; it is thought requisite to publish this short declaration : wherein is contained a particular of such necessaries, as either priuate families or single persons shall haue cause to furnish themselues with, for their better support at their first landing in Virginia; whereby also greater numbers may receiue in part, directions how to prouide themselues.

### Apparrell.

*Apparrell for one man, and so after the rate for more.*

| | li. | s. | d. |
|---|---|---|---|
| One Monmouth Cap | oo | oi | 10 |
| Three falling bands | — | oi | o3 |
| Three shirts | — | o7 | c6 |
| One wast-coate | — | o2 | o2 |
| One suite of Canuase | — | o7 | o6 |
| One suite of Frize | — | 10 | oo |
| One suite of Cloth | — | 15 | oo |
| Three paire of Irish stockins | — | o4 | — |
| Foure paire of shooes | — | c8 | c8 |
| One paire of garters | — | oo | 10 |
| One doozen of points | — | oo | o3 |
| One paire of Canuase sheets | — | c8 | — |
| Seuen ells of Canuase, to make a bed and boulster, to be filled in *Virginia* 8.s. / One Rug for a bed 8. s. which with the bed seruing for two men, halfe is | — | c8 | oo |
| Fiue ells coorse Canuase, to make a bed at Sea for two men, to be filled with straw, iiij.s. / One coorse Rug at Sea for two men, will cost vj. s. is for one | — | o5 | oo |
| | o4 | oo | oo |

### Victuall.

*For a whole yeere for one man, and so for more after the rate.*

| | li. | s. | d. |
|---|---|---|---|
| Eight bushels of Meale | o2 | oo | oo |
| Two bushels of pease at 3.s. | — | o6 | oo |
| Two bushels of Oatemeale 4.s. 6.d. | — | o9 | oo |
| One gallon of *Aquauitæ* | — | o2 | o6 |
| One gallon of Oyle | — | o3 | o6 |
| Two gallons of Vineger 1. s. | — | o2 | oo |
| | o3 | o3 | oo |

### Armes.

*For one man, but if halfe of your men haue armour it is sufficient so that all haue Peeces and swords.*

| | li. | s. | d. |
|---|---|---|---|
| One Armour compleat, light | — | 17 | oo |
| One long Peece, fiue foot or fiue and a halfe, neere Musket bore | o1 | o2 | — |
| One sword | — | o5 | — |
| One belt | — | o1 | — |
| One bandaleere | — | o1 | o6 |
| Twenty pound of powder | — | 18 | oo |
| Sixty pound of shot or lead, Pistoll and Goose shot | — | o5 | oo |
| | o3 | o9 | o6 |

### Tooles.

*For a family of 6. persons and so after the rate for more.*

| | li. | s. | d. |
|---|---|---|---|
| Fiue broad howes at 2.s. a piece | — | 10 | — |
| Fiue narrow howes at 16.d. a piece | — | o6 | c8 |
| Two broad Axes at 3.s. 8.d. a piece | — | o7 | c4 |
| Fiue felling Axes at 18.d. a piece | — | o7 | o6 |
| Two steele hand sawes at 16.d. a piece | — | o2 | o8 |
| Two two-hand sawes at 5. s. a piece | — | 10 | — |
| One whip-saw, set and filed with box, file, and wrest | — | 10 | — |
| Two hammers 12.d. a piece | — | o2 | oo |
| Three shouels 18.d. a piece | — | o4 | o6 |
| Two spades at 18.d. a piece | — | o3 | — |
| Two augers 6.d. a piece | — | o1 | oo |
| Sixe chissels 6.d. a piece | — | o3 | oo |
| Two percers stocked 4.d. a piece | — | oo | c8 |
| Three gimlets 2.d. a piece | — | oo | c6 |
| Two hatchets 21.d. a piece | — | o3 | o6 |
| Two froues to cleaue pale 18.d. | — | o3 | oo |
| Two hand bils 20. a piece | — | o3 | o4 |
| One grindlestone 4.s. | — | c4 | oo |
| Nailes of all sorts to the value of | o2 | oo | — |
| Two Pickaxes | — | c3 | — |
| | c6 | c2 | c8 |

### Houshold Implements.

*For a family of 6. persons, and so for more or lesse after the rate.*

| | li. | s. | d. |
|---|---|---|---|
| One Iron Pot | co | c7 | — |
| One kettle | — | o6 | — |
| One large frying-pan | — | o2 | c6 |
| One gridiron | — | o1 | oo |
| Two skillets | — | o5 | — |
| One spit | — | o2 | — |
| Platters, dishes, spoones of wood | — | o4 | — |
| | o1 | o8 | oo |

For Suger, Spice, and fruit, and at Sea for 6 men. — oo | 12 | c6

So the full charge of Apparrell , Victuall, Armes, Tooles, and houshold stuffe, and after this rate for each person, will amount vnto about the summe of ---- 12 | 10 | —
The passage of each man is ---- 06 | 00 | —
The fraight of these prouisions for a man , will bee about halfe a Tun, which is ---- 01 | 10 | —

*So the whole charge will amount to about* ---- 20 | oo | oo

Nets, hookes, lines, and a tent must be added, if the number of people be greater, as also some kine.
*And this is the vsuall proportion that the* Virginia *Company doe bestow vpon their Tenants which they send.*

Whosoeuer transports himselfe or any other at his owne charge vnto *Virginia*, shall for each person so transported before Midsummer 1625. haue to him and his heires for euer fifty Acres of Land vpon a first, and fifty Acres vpon a second diuision.

Imprinted at London by FELIX KYNGSTON. 1622.

the settlement remained, in his words, "a miserie, a ruine, a death, a hell."

The Virginia undertaking had three principal objectives: (1) to find a northwest passage to the wealth of China; (2) to exploit the gold and silver of America; (3) to scout the immediate environs for a suitable "plantation" where later settlers might produce the silks and dyes which England was now constrained to buy from hated France and Spain. All three objectives were promptly frustrated. The James River scarcely penetrated the immense North American barrier to the Pacific. Worse still, Smith's own explorations of the river aroused the suspicions even of the most helpful Indians, who realized that the English had come not to trade metal for corn but to take their land. Soon, as one Virginian observed, the Indian was "as fast killing without as the famine and pestilence within." Little or no gold, in turn, could be found; but that did not deter the "decayed gentlemen" the Virginia Company had mistakenly sent out as settlers from spending so much time seeking precious metals that none remained for providing shelter or food let alone establishing plantations for silks and dyes.

In 1610, although Newport on successive visits had augmented the first settlers with almost 200 newcomers, only sixty persons lived in Jamestown, and Virginia was on the verge of going the way of Sagadohoc. The Virginia Company council in London had gradually learned of Virginia's travail from those who fled home with Newport from time to time and by other means, and it made a great effort to improve their enterprise. Yet by 1624, when James I revoked the colony's charter and made Virginia a royal province, about 6000 persons had set out for Jamestown, of whom about 4000 had perished on the ocean voyage or in the New World. Hundreds of others had the wisdom to flee home; a mere 1200 were left.

By then, however, conditions had begun to improve. The first settlers in Virginia had been mere "servants" of the promoters, men who had signed contracts called "indentures" by which they agreed to work for a certain number of years in exchange for their passage to the New World. Once they reached Virginia these servants became very hard to control. Many ran off to seek gold on their own hook. Those who fulfilled their indentures had little incentive to work. The promoters recognized the shortcomings of this system in 1619 when they gave to each of the "ancient planters" (those who had arrived before 1616) 100 acres of his own. They also instituted the "head right" system, under which each new settler received 50 acres of land for himself and an additional 50 acres for every servant he himself induced to come to America. The government of the colony also was liberalized by the creation of the House of Burgesses, the first legislature of elected representatives in America, which held its first meeting on July 30, 1619.

As important as these formal changes was the discovery, about 1615, that tobacco could be grown successfully in Virginia. This discovery probably saved the whole enterprise, but it also brought a host of new problems that were to plague Virginia and her neighbors for generations.

A market for tobacco had been growing in Europe since the middle of the sixteenth century. In 1618 Virginia shipped 30,000 pounds of tobacco to England, mostly for reexport to the Continent. By 1627 the colony was exporting more than 500,000 pounds a year. By then the first Negro workers had been added to the labor force, but not until the 1660s were they stigmatized and fully segregated as "servants for life," or slaves. By 1710 their number had risen to 12,000 and their lives had come under ever stricter regulation. By then profits from the tobacco trade had created a Virginia aristocracy of great landholders who used their standing in the colony to dominate its politics and their political power to enhance their wealth and escape the heavier burdens of taxation.

Tobacco was a crop that quickly depleted the soil. In their quest for more and more land, the Virginia planters gradually pushed the small farmers from the rich coastal plain, called the tidewater, into the piedmont areas of the backcountry and eventually into the barren mountains. Here the small farmers led a precarious existence, made no easier by the taxes levied on them by the House of Burgesses, where they had few or no representatives. The legislature also failed to protect them from Indian raids to which they were increasingly exposed on the frontiers. One reason for this failure was the value the aristocracy placed on Indian friendship in the conduct of the trade in furs which the Indians supplied.

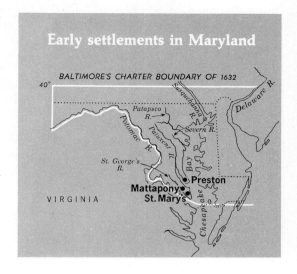

**Early settlements in Maryland**

### The Maryland refuge

Virginia's first neighbor was Maryland, which was created by Charles I in 1632 when he granted to Sir George Calvert, the first Lord Baltimore, that part of the Virginia territory between the Potomac River and the fortieth parallel, north latitude. Two years later Sir George's son Cecilius sent out the first Maryland settlers, the leaders among whom were Catholics like the Calverts. Their instructions were to deal fairly with the Indians, and soon after their arrival at the mouth of the Potomac in March 1634, they purchased from them a healthful and accessible tract which they named St. Mary's.

The Baltimores realized from the start that most English Catholics fleeing persecution at home would seek refuge in Catholic countries in Europe and that in Maryland, as elsewhere in America, most settlers would be Protestants. Thus, although Catholics were offered a place to go to freely if they wished, the proprietors warned them from the outset that "no scandall nor offence" be given to Protestants. When Virginia's loyalty to the Crown in the 1640s led to increasing harassment of Puritans in that colony, Maryland in 1648 invited hundreds of them to come to her. Rightly fearful of Puritan tyranny now, the reigning Lord Baltimore, in 1649, sent over his "Act Concerning Religion," justly famous as his Toleration Act, to protect Catholics from Puritan intolerance. The Maryland assembly, established in

1635, promptly approved this measure. Although the Toleration Act made the denial of the Trinity a capital offense, it nonetheless advanced the cause of conscience by requiring the hostile Christian denominations to suffer one another peacefully.

Despite attempts to negotiate with the Puritan rulers in England after 1649, the Baltimores lost control of their colony. From 1650 to 1657, the Puritan element managed Maryland's affairs. In 1654, the assembly repealed the Toleration Act, and in 1655 a force of 200 men under the proprietor's deputy-governor was routed by a troop of Puritan planters during a brief civil war. But the antiproprietary group exercised authority for only a few years, and by 1657 Baltimore had regained his privileges.

Maryland quickly picked up from Virginia the art of cultivating tobacco and the practice of using Negroes in the fields. Her great landholders also became as adept as those in the first colony in corralling the best land for themselves and relegating the poorer husbandmen to the interior. By 1691 social conflicts, embittered by religious differences, had become so menacing that the Crown took Maryland from the Calvert family and made it a royal province. In 1715, however, Maryland was returned to its old proprietors and it remained in Calvert hands thereafter until the Revolution.

## Bacon's Rebellion and the moving frontier

The commitment of the Chesapeake planters to the one-crop system brought into focus all the grievances that culminated in Bacon's Rebellion in Virginia in 1676.

By 1670 the Virginia frontier had been pushed only 50 miles inland, a shallow and slow penetration which for 30 years had helped keep the general peace with the Indians of the region, who served as buffers between the colony and unfriendly tribes deeper in the interior. Yet the pressure on all the red men steadily mounted. In 1671 and again in 1673 expeditions sent out by the most influential Virginia fur traders and land speculators pierced the Appalachian barrier for the first time. These explorations greatly enlarged the Virginians' vision of empire; they also sent a quiver of dismay through the Indian nations upon whose country they trespassed. Meanwhile, the day-to-day encroachment of tobacco planters on Indian towns and farms close to white settlements, as well as the enslavement of Indian captives, was making the tribesmen wild with fear. Hardened Virginians, in turn, had already learned to shoot first, "it matters not whether they be Friends or Foes Soe they be Indians."

In Maryland in this period, planter and speculator ambitions northward had consequences similar to those of Virginia's westward surge. Distant enemy tribes, disturbed by the white man's land hunger, soon were pushing Maryland's protective Susquehannock Indians, far up at the head of Chesapeake Bay, southward toward the older settlements. Here they met what had become the usual hostile reception not only from the white men but also from the local braves who, like the tribes in Virginia, had grown exceptionally excitable. Food shortages soon drove the Susquehannocks and other Indians to raid frontier plantations in Maryland, with accompanying atrocities. In September 1675, a combined force of Maryland and Virginia militia failed in an attempt to wipe out the Susquehannocks, who then poured across the Potomac in roving bands that became the scourge of the Virginia frontier.

Berkeley's failure to enlist a force sufficiently powerful to check the unprecedented Indian violence of 1675 gave the firebrand Nathaniel Bacon his chance. A young aristocrat with a shady past, Bacon was in his twenties when he arrived in Virginia as recently as 1674 and set himself up on more than 1000 acres of fine land in the interior up the James. Berkeley, forty years his senior, was his cousin by marriage, and within a year of Bacon's arrival had given him a coveted seat on the Governor's Council. Bacon, however, was not won over to the Governor's side. The country, he said in June 1676, wanted dead Indians, not friendly ones; and he demanded that Berkeley grant him a military commission to do the job against the red men that the Governor had mishandled. When Berkeley angrily refused, Bacon set himself up as the leader of the anti-Berkeley party, collected a force of willing volunteers, and led them in successful raids not only against the red men but against Jamestown itself. Bacon's followers actually captured and burned the capital; but when their leader suddenly died in October 1676, his band became a disorderly mob. Berkeley vindictively hanged twenty-three of the rebels before the King, now Charles II, recalled him.

Bacon was not the "Torchbearer of the Revolution," as he has been painted. If his rebellion did in fact hasten the Revolution, which, it must be recalled, did not begin for another hundred years, it could only be because of the impetus it gave to the tightening of English control on colonial expansiveness. When news of the uprising first reached England in September 1676, 1100 soldiers under Colonel Herbert Jeffreys were promptly shipped out to Virginia to restore order. Jeffreys himself was to take over as Lieutenant-Governor. This military force, one of the very first sent to America, with a military man placed in charge of the colony, showed the determination of the Stuarts to bring the far-off freemen to book.

The policy in relation to the Indians, henceforth, was to keep the Americans away from them, the land the settlers already held, it was said in 1677, "being more than they either will or can cultivate to profitt." Beyond that, the hope of peaceful relations was surrendered, the goal of conversion to Christianity abandoned, the policy of swift extermination rejected as too costly in money and men. Indian and white man both knew that the aborigines' hold on the land was sure to be broken. In 1682, when Jeffreys' force was recalled after the Virginia assembly refused to bear the cost of it, the formal policy was adopted that was to be followed along the whole course of the moving frontier: It was acknowledged that the Indians would never yield peacefully; to reduce the hazards of retaliation to the minimum, the system of frontier rangers was initiated. These rangers, armed and mounted at their own expense, rode regular patrols to learn of menacing Indian movements and to warn the settlers to prepare for attacks.

The frontier settlers themselves, meanwhile, as a Virginia statute of 1701 put it, were to designate and equip enough "warlike Christian men" to lead the defense of each warned community. Such soon became the task of the German and Scotch-Irish immigrants in particular, who were shunted to the frontier by great landholders in all the English mainland colonies (see Chapter Three).

## III   Puritan colonies of New England

### Pilgrims in Plymouth

In 1614 Captain John Smith, now in the employ of London merchants still in quest of gold and copper mines in the New World, sailed to the northern reaches of Virginia, brought back fish and furs instead, and a map from which, in 1616, the name New England first was given to the region.

The very next year a number of the most dedicated Puritan Separatists who had fled from persecution in England in 1608 and 1609 to a refuge granted them in the Netherlands, having grown disenchanted with life in a foreign country, decided that their best hope "was to live as a distinct body by themselves" on the virgin land of America.

Three years of the most disheartening haggling passed before the Pilgrims gained the financial backing of London businessmen who had obtained a grant from the Virginia Company for a colony of their own. At last, on September 16, 1620, in the ship *Mayflower*, thirty-five Pilgrims, led by the deacon John Carver and William Bradford, his second in command, set out with a rough company of some sixty-six "strangers"—artisans, indentured servants, and soldiers, including John Alden and Captain Miles Standish, hired as their military leader. On finding themselves off Cape Cod in November 1620, Carver and his colleagues decided to forego Virginia and to seek a suitable site in the region where God had led them. This decision made, they felt the urgency to form "a combination . . . before they came ashore, being the first foundation of their government in this place." Why they did this is well told by Bradford in his *Of Plymouth Plantation*. This "combination," Bradford writes, was

*occasioned partly by the discontented & mutinous speeches that some of the strangers amongst them had let fall from them in the ship—That when they came ashore, they would use their own liberty; And partly that such an act by them done . . . might be as firm as any patent, and in some respects more sure.*

This "combination" was the memorable Mayflower Compact by which the forty-one members of the expedition who signed it on November 11 "solemnly . . . covenant and combine . . . together into a civil Body Politick, for our better Ordering and Preservation." A month later their search for a good site was rewarded by the discovery of the place they called Plymouth, where they "found divers cornfields and little running brooks." That first winter half the colonists died, and only the friendship and tutelage of Squanto and his Indian friends, "a spetiall instrument sent by God for their good," preserved the remainder for another year. In November 1621 the ship *Fortune* arrived with provisions to augment the first crops. Her arrival inspired the first Thanksgiving feast, a celebration that reduced supplies once more.

The Pilgrims by 1626 felt sufficiently well established to buy out the London investors who themselves had made no profit from the venture. This step severed all effective connection with the mother country. In 1636, when new towns had been added to Plymouth and problems of government had grown more complex, the colony adopted the "Great Fundamentals," the first basic system of laws originating in the English colonies. These Fundamentals instituted a system of representative government in place of the arbitrary rule of the Pilgrim founders. Only those with the rank of "freeman" were given the franchise. While evidence of material well-being was required to attain this rank, in Plymouth, as in Massachusetts Bay, aspirants had also to survive strict examination by the divines, who

rejected all those found "insufficient or troublesome."

Until 1691, when it was absorbed into Massachusetts Bay, the Pilgrim community led an austere but independent existence, sustained chiefly by trade in fish and fur. "Let it not be grievous to you," one of their friends wrote from England, that "you have been but the instruments to break the ice for others; the honor shall be your's till the world's end."

### The Bible Commonwealth of Massachusetts

Separatists made up only a small minority of English Puritans, most of whom remained, in their own estimation, the only loyal members both of the Kingdom and the Church of England. But even these Puritans felt by 1629, in the words of the lawyer, John Winthrop, that God was "turning the Cup toward us also, & because we are the last our portion must be, to drink the very dregs that remain." In March 1630, under Winthrop's direction, the Great Migration "to inhabit and continue in New England" began.

The Puritans had been anticipated in New England not only by the Pilgrim Fathers but also by a group of settlers on Cape Ann sent out in 1624 by promoters from Dorchester. In 1628 a number of Puritan merchants and others, organized as the New England Company, obtained the rights of the Dorchester promoters and sent to Salem, the name taken by these settlers, a vanguard of forty Puritans under John Endecott, who became governor there. They strengthened their title to the land by obtaining a patent under "covert and surreptitious" circumstances for territory between the Charles and the Merrimack rivers still claimed by Sir Ferdinando Gorges. In 1629 the New England Company was reorganized as the Massachusetts Bay Company with a new charter from Charles I confirming its land title, which included the Salem settlement.

This company's charter resembled those granted to other trading companies. The col-

*Plymouth Harbor, as drawn by Champlain.*

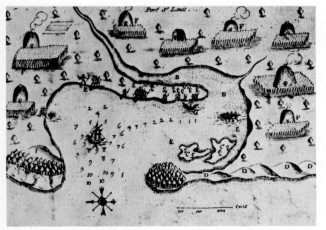

ony was to be administered by a governor, a deputy-governor, and a council of assistants elected by the freemen sitting as its general court or "assemblie." It neglected, however, to specify the company's official residence or to declare that the colony must be administered from England. Winthrop, named governor of the company, and his colleagues hungrily seized upon this oversight to transfer the whole enterprise to Massachusetts, where, as Cotton Mather later explained, "we would have our posterity settled under the pure and full dispensation of the gospel; defended by rulers who should be ourselves." By winter 1630 a thousand picked settlers had been landed in Massachusetts, and radiating from Boston, the Puritan capital, seven other towns were laid out. Within a decade, 25,000 persons had journeyed to the commonwealth. Winthrop and his colleagues, however, struggled manfully to keep control in the godly minority he headed.

At the outset the freemen, who alone had the franchise, constituted less than 1 percent of the adult population. As the colony thrived and disfranchised rich men demanded a voice in the government, certain liberalizing steps were taken, chief among them being the extension of the rank of freemen to all church members. To become a church member, however, a man must still undergo intense scrutiny of his life and character by the Puritan divines, a test some refused to undergo.

By an act of 1635, the General Court adopted the historic measure giving the freemen of the separate towns unprecedented freedom in town government. This act inaugurated the general town meeting at which to this day in many small communities the entire body of voters acts directly on such important matters as schools, roads, water supply, and police. But here, too, there was a catch. Since only Puritan church members could be freemen, this measure in effect extended the power of the oligarchy over localities.

By 1644, the towns won the right to send representatives to a Chamber of Deputies

41

Phelps Stokes Collection, New York Public Library

*A center of power in Massachusetts— meeting house of the Third Church of Boston, 1669, the largest to be built in seventeenth- century New England. Building is shown on right with three gables and tall turret topped by weathervane, from William Burgis, "View of Boston," 1722.*

which became the lower house of the General Court, while the upper house of assistants still retained most power. But even where the machinery of government was liberalized, the strength of the clergy persisted either because of formal prerogatives or moral prestige.

In 1648, the oligarchy having withstood for thirteen years the demand for an explicit legal code, the General Court published the "Book of the General Lawes and Libertyes concern-

42

ing the Inhabitants of the Massachusets." Public laws made by self-governing freemen were now to take precedence over the Mosaic code and other laws of God. Even so, the Court said, "we had opportunity put into our hands . . . to frame our civil Polities, and Laws according to the rules of his most holy word whereby each do help and strengthen other (the Churches the civil Authoritie, and the civil Authoritie the Churches)," and the opportunity was not missed.

The year 1648 saw another momentous event in the running conflict between the "elect" and the others, with the elect again having their way. On learning that year of Oliver Cromwell's admission of Baptists, Quakers, and members of other radical sects into his "New Model" Army, the Massachusetts General Court called a synod, or council, of Puritan clergymen to meet at Cambridge expressly to sever all remaining ties with Presbyterianism at home. This synod promulgated the Cambridge Platform, making the secular government the explicit agent for enforcing the religious and moral decrees of the Puritan—now the Congregational—clergy. The "dictatorship of the visible elect," in Perry Miller's phrase, soon became known as "the New England Way."

The Cambridge Platform's appeal to the power of the state, nevertheless, seemed gradually to diminish the moral force of Puritanism. When the Anglican church was reestablished in England on the restoration of the Stuarts in 1660, and thus enjoyed a revival in America as well, those tired of Puritan engrossment found a welcome escape within the Anglican structure. Aware of this competition, and fearful of an English investigation of their "tyranny" under the New England Way, the Massachusetts General Court and the Congregational General Synod in 1662 agreed to the "Half-Way Covenant." Those who preferred not to run the rigors of seeking membership in the Congregational church might now become freemen without it and participate equally with the elect in civic affairs. They might also have their children baptized into the Covenant of Grace.

Winthrop warned that New England's marked material success (see p. 44) would

make the colonists "fall to embrace this present world and prosecute our carnall intentions." Yet Yankee merchants quickly came to the support of churches which, of course, were built in Massachusetts from the first. They also supported the college that was organized in 1636 to train the "learned clergy" of the future, and gentlemen as well. In 1638, John Harvard, no stranger to wealth as it was judged at the time, bequeathed the new college his library and half his estate, and since then it has borne his name.

In 1642 and again in 1647, noting that "one chief point of that old deluder, Satan, [was] to keep men from a knowledge of the Scriptures . . . by keeping them in an unknown tongue," the General Court adopted legislation to further public education and even "to fit youths for the university." This legislation proved ineffective (see p. 99); but it established the principle of compulsory public education, new to the English-speaking world, and served as an inspiration to other New England settlements and those which Yankees later established on the moving frontier.

## Radicals of Rhode Island

Concessions like the legal code of 1648 and Half-Way Covenant of 1662 had come hard to the leaders of Massachusetts Bay. In earlier times they used harsher means to deal with what Winthrop called "seditious and undermining practices of hereticall false brethren."

Among the first of the "false" was Roger Williams, "a man," to quote Bradford, "having very many precious parts, but very unsettled in judgment," who arrived in Massachusetts in 1631 after having encountered the wrath of Archbishop Laud at home. In Massachusetts he promptly raised embarrassing issues—by asserting, for example, that the Bay Colony had no just claim to Indian lands, and by denying, as the Boston magistrates claimed, that "the powers that be are ordained by God, . . . and they that resist shall receive to themselves damnation." Williams doubted that "Judges are God upon earthe." Threatened with banishment to England, in the winter of 1635 he fled to the region of Narragansett Bay. The following spring, having been joined by some of his sympathizers, he established his own community there, which he called Providence, the foundation of later Rhode Island.

In 1638 the Massachusetts clergy banished another troublemaker, Anne Hutchinson, the sharp-witted wife of a mild Puritan merchant, who had moved from practical discussions of midwifery in Boston to more touchy analyses of sermons she heard on Sundays. Early in 1639 the Hutchinson family left Massachusetts for Rhode Island and there founded a town, later called Portsmouth. On her husband's death in 1642, Mrs. Hutchinson moved with her children to present-day New York State where, the next year, all were massacred by Indians.

The establishment of Providence also drew voluntary exiles from Massachusetts who founded towns nearby. To insure the land titles of these loosely federated settlements, Williams sought a charter from Parliament, which he received in 1644. For many years Rhode Island was the only colony in which all Christian sects enjoyed "liberty in religious concernments," as the charter put it, including the liberty to vote, whether a church member or not. Perhaps such libertarianism lay behind the attitude of the other New England colonies, which regarded Rhode Island as "Rogues' Island"—"nothing else than the latrina of New England."

## Expansion of New England

In the 1630s and 1640s refugees from Massachusetts had also settled in present-day Connecticut, New Hampshire, and Maine. The exodus to Connecticut was led by Thomas Hooker, a determined minister who was dissatisfied both with the quality of the soil and the care of souls in Massachusetts. Under his direction first Hartford and then Wethersfield and Windsor were established in the rich Connecticut River Valley. In 1639 they were joined together under the Fundamental Orders of Connecticut. Similar governments ruled in the New Haven settlement on Long Island Sound, founded by the Reverend John Davenport and Theophilus Eaton in 1638, and in the neighboring towns that soon affiliated themselves with New Haven (1643–1656). In all of them Puritan orthodoxy persisted, and only church members could vote. Connecticut emerged as a separate colony in 1662 when the Crown joined New Haven with the river towns to the north.

Massachusetts asserted its authority over the northern territory between the Merrimack and Kennebec Rivers in 1640 when settlers from the Bay Colony were already moving into future New Hampshire and Maine. New Hampshire was established as a distinct royal colony by Charles II in 1679. Ten years earlier Maine had been formally annexed to Massachusetts in whose jurisdiction it remained until 1820.

The Puritans in Massachusetts, like the Pilgrims in Plymouth, had at first encountered the smallest and least thickly settled Indian tribes of the entire eastern seaboard, who seemed content to be friendly with the new-

Massachusetts, Rhode Island, and Connecticut settlements

44

comers. The rapid expansion of New England settlements and encroachments on Indian lands in the 1630s, however, soon gave the tribes a common grievance, which was deepened by the rivalry of the English with the French to the north and the Dutch to the south for Indian allies in the fur trade. Indian raids on white frontier settlements, in turn, changed the Puritan attitude from one of peaceful attempts to convert the red men to fearful retaliation.

In an effort to strengthen resistance to the common danger, and also to promote common interests, Massachusetts Bay, Plymouth, Connecticut, and New Haven joined together in 1643 to form "The Confederation of the United Colonies of New England," the first of a series of colonial efforts to work together without thinking to consult the mother country. The Confederation boycotted Rhode Island, whose lands the members coveted as strongly as they detested her principles. Although the Confederation had languished by the middle 1660s, its sternest test lay ahead. In June, 1675, a combination of Indian tribes under the Wampanoag, King Philip, attacked settlements around Plymouth. Soon a full-scale war was being waged between the braves and the New England Confederation. This war lasted an entire year; and while the Indians succumbed in the end, the cost of King Philip's War to New England was immense in men and property. The Confederation itself lasted until 1684 when it foundered on Massachusetts's overbearing attitude toward the other members.

### New England's material foundations

With the exception of the Connecticut and Merrimack Valleys, the New England terrain was much more hilly and far less fertile than the Chesapeake region, and the section was destined to be covered with small farms, not large plantations. Farm families settled in compact villages around the church and the green instead of being dispersed over the countryside, as in most of the regions to the south.

The villages, or towns, were themselves set up under the jurisdiction of the central authorities and not by speculators. When a group wished to establish a new town, they obtained permission from the General Court to settle a block of land of approximately 6 square miles adjoining an older one. All freemen were eligible to draw for the town lots and to make use of the undistributed woods and meadows. The richer settlers sometimes got additional lots, but even the most favored never received more than two or three times as much land as the poorest.

This system of establishing new towns carried with it certain disadvantages. The original proprietors, for example, by retaining control over the future distribution of undivided land, could discriminate against latecomers, who in fact soon formed a disgruntled majority along with landless and voteless tenants and laborers. Disputes between the old settlers and the new often ended with the newcomers moving west or north to areas beyond the regime's control, and gradually the New England system of planned expansion broke down. During most of the seventeenth century, however, the New England plan worked effectively, and the culture of the region was carried to new frontiers more or less intact.

About 85 percent of New England settlers in this period engaged in subsistence agriculture and home industry, with little hired help or bound labor. As early as 1644 iron was being smelted commercially in Massachusetts, while rum distilled from West Indian molasses and cider pressed from local fruits had become available for sale locally and overseas. New England craftsmen also made many of the commodities needed in the colony, such as furniture, silverware, pottery, hardware, and tools, articles which the Puritans, who did not have a big export staple such as the southerners had in tobacco, could not easily pay for abroad.

While most New Englanders clung to the soil or serviced the farm families, a more enterprising 15 percent or so, finding the land intractable, had turned to the water. Fishing off the banks of Newfoundland became so important in the Massachusetts economy that the cod was placed on the commonwealth's coat of arms. Enough fish were caught for export to the West Indies and elsewhere, along with foodstuffs, timber, and even captive Indians to be sold as slaves.

Puritan business in black slaves began in 1638 when the Salem ship *Desire* brought home the first Africans from Barbados in the West Indies. Thereafter blacks were landed only spasmodically in New England; yet by 1700 the region's population of 90,000 included about 1000 colored people, most of them slaves. It was the traffic *to* the West Indies, not from it, that soon dominated the New England slave trade. Early in the 1640s, Puritan captains began visiting the main slave marts on West Africa's Guinea coast; here in their efforts to fill up their holds with black cargoes they engaged in shooting wars which quickly earned them Massachusetts indictments for murder, "these acts and outrages being committed where there was noe civill government which might call them to accompt." It was English, Dutch, French, and

Portuguese competition, nevertheless, rather than Massachusetts views of "the haynos and crying sinn of man stealing," that at first drove the Puritans from the Guinea coast, forcing them to seek their black cargoes in Madagascar and other *east* coast islands heavily frequented by pirates. But the Puritans were not to be intimidated for long, and before the end of the century, Massachusetts and Rhode Island merchants in particular had become heavily engaged in the Guinea trade, their main customers being found in the Caribbean islands. Gradually they won larger markets in the mainland tobacco colonies as well, where the English slave traders predominated.

Commerce, like fishing, greatly stimulated shipbuilding; and New England vessels proved at once so seaworthy and so cheap that they soon were being built for foreign as well as domestic merchants and captains.

Once on the sea, Puritan ships, like those of other maritime nations, sought out all kinds of cargoes and sailed to every beckoning port, legal or illicit, to make a trade. When they reached home at last they might land goods from around the world. As early as 1675, Boston was described as, "a magazine both of all American and European commodityes for the furnishing and supplying of seaverall countreys."

## IV   Completion of mainland colonization

### Carolina and Georgia

Between 1640 and 1660, during the English civil war and the Cromwellian Protectorate (see p. 34), emigration to America practically ceased. With the restoration of the Stuarts in the person of Charles II in 1660, new men came into power with claims on the new king and designs on the New World. During the following three-quarters of a century seven new colonies, most of them established by such men, and all growing from proprietary grants, completed the roster of those that first formed the United States.

The first of the Restoration colonies was called Carolina and extended from the southern boundary of Virginia to the borders of Spanish Florida and westward as far as the continent itself. This princely domain was granted by Charles II in 1663 to eight of his friends who had been instrumental in placing him on the throne. Among them were rich men who had made their fortunes in sugar growing in Barbados. Their aim in America was to people their land with Barbadians squeezed off their farms by the growth of the great sugar plantations on the island. The proprietors brought in the first contingent of

Barbadians in 1665; but within two years this experiment failed. Many of the Barbadians returned home, the rest scattered elsewhere.

46 The first permanent Carolina settlement was begun in March 1670, off Port Royal Sound, with the arrival of an expedition of Englishmen augmented by new Barbadians and other West Indians picked up on the way. Fear of the Spanish this far south prompted a northward move a month later to the Ashley River. Twenty-five miles up the river Charles Towne was begun. In 1680, the town was moved to its present site where the Ashley and Cooper rivers meet. By then wars with the local braves had convinced the red men that they had better cooperate with the Charles Towne adventurers by supplying furs, deer hides, and other skins, as well as more captive Indians for the slave trade. This traffic rapidly made Charles Towne a flourishing commercial community whose population grew even more cosmopolitan after 1685, when Louis XIV resumed persecution of the Huguenots and French Protestant refugees poured in.

In the 1690s, as rice became South Carolina's export staple, the plantation system spread. Negro slavery, with many harsh as-

pects more characteristic of the West Indies than the mainland, became common, and here as in Virginia it fed the sense of superiority among the masters. The first "Fundamental Constitutions of Carolina," set forth in 1668, was an extraordinary document that provided for a hereditary nobility sharing power with a governor appointed by the proprietors in England. New World conditions forced a gradual liberalization of the government, yet the aristocratic spirit of the colony persisted, and the large landholders who emerged held firmly to the reins of power in Charleston where most of them lived as absentee landlords.

In 1664 the South Carolina proprietors gave a deputy governor to the distant residents in the northern part of their territory which had been settled by Virginia malcontents since 1653. Bad soil and limited access to the sea contrived to keep these settlers poor, and South Carolina aristocrats looked down upon the region as a haunt of pirates, debtors, runaway slaves, and other discreditable persons. In 1721 South Carolina was proclaimed a royal colony and in 1729, when the proprietors at last yielded their charter to the Crown, King George II declared North Carolina a distinct royal colony as well.

Spain, outraged by the formation of South Carolina on the Florida border, grew more furious when George II, having reclaimed the unsettled southernmost part of the colony in 1729, granted it in 1732 to a group of philanthropists whose spokesman was the reformer James Oglethorpe. The next year, Oglethorpe landed the first hundred settlers of Georgia, as he called his grant, above the mouth of the Savannah River, where they established the town of Savannah.

The Crown regarded Georgia as a military outpost; the proprietors hoped to make it an asylum for Englishmen imprisoned for debt; Oglethorpe himself envisioned a community of small farmers who might also constitute a yeoman militia. At the start, landholdings were limited to 500 acres, rum and brandy were banned, while for strategic as well as

Settlement of the Carolinas and Georgia

humanitarian reasons slavery was prohibited. These regulations did not sit well with newcomers from abroad and South Carolinians who came to Georgia to improve their fortunes. Under their pressure the ban on rum was removed in 1742, and by 1750 slavery was permitted, landholdings grew in size, and rice planting spread. Georgia became a royal colony in 1752, but Spain never conceded her existence, and not until the United States purchased Florida from Spain in 1819 was the incendiary southern border of Georgia defined.

### The Middle colonies

While the expansion of New England encroached on New France in the north and the establishment of the Carolinas encroached on New Spain in the south, England's principal maritime rival, the Dutch, with their colony of New Netherland, split England's growing mainland empire in two. Even before the Dutch had been forced to cede New Netherland to the English in 1664, Charles II had given his brother James, Duke of York, the immense territory between the Connecticut and the Delaware rivers. The Dutch regained New York, as James renamed the place, in 1673, but again yielded it to the English the next year.

Four new English colonies were carved from the Dutch mainland empire—New York, New Jersey, Pennsylvania, and Delaware. Until 1683, New York was ruled as the Dutch had ruled it, with an absolute governor and council, and with the same unfortunate results. In 1683 a new governor, Colonel Thomas Dongan, arrived in New York with instructions to create an elected assembly privileged to meet every three years and to impose provincial taxes. By the time this assembly held its first meeting in 1686, the Duke of York had ascended the throne as James II and had made New York a royal colony. When the assembly's legislative efforts reached him for approval, he rejected them, restored the absolute rule of governor and council, and ordered the assembly dissolved.

New York had to wait a few years yet, and to endure a violent rebellion in the bargain, before it joined the other colonies in enjoying a representative government. Not until well into the eighteenth century, moreover, did New York begin to take advantage of its unparalleled harbor and rich inland soil to develop its economy.

The second colony carved from James's holding was New Jersey, made up of the fertile country between the Hudson and Delaware rivers which James had granted in 1664 to two of his friends, Sir George Carteret and John, Lord Berkeley. New Jersey was made a royal colony in 1702 under the governor of New York, by which time it had long been a haven for persecuted Quakers and other dissenting sects. New Jersey did not have a royal governor of its own until 1738.

The third colony carved from James's domain on land between the Delaware River and Maryland was Pennsylvania. William Penn had received this land in 1681 in payment of a debt owed his father by James II, and he immediately proceeded with his "Holy Experiment" here of a model republican and religious community.

Penn had been infected with Quaker ideas

**47**

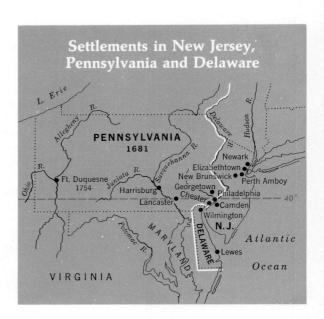

Settlements in New Jersey, Pennsylvania and Delaware

*William Penn in 1696, drawn by Francis Place.*

as a young boy and kept them despite the attempts of an angry father to make him renounce the principles of this despised sect. George Fox (1642–1691), the founder of the Religious Society of Friends, as the Quakers called themselves, preached that man's love for God could best be shown by man's love for man and that salvation was possible for all. Every Quaker regarded himself as a member of the priesthood, since all men possessed the "inner light" that enabled them to "hear" God's voice. The radical egalitarianism of the Quakers—their refusal to swear oaths, to fight wars, to accept class distinctions—seemed a threat to the existing order, and they were savagely persecuted both in Europe and America. Yet they prospered through diligence and frugality.

Penn laid down a plan of government for his colony that was perhaps the most liberal in the world. It called for a governor appointed by the proprietor, and a bicameral

*Penn's first announcement of his good fortune in acquiring his grant in America, 1861: "I thought it not less my Duty [than] my Honest Interest, to give some public notice of it to the World, that those . . . that are inclin'd to Transport Themselves or Families beyond the Seas, may find another country added to their Choice."*

A brief Account of the

## Province of Pennſylvania,

Lately Granted by the

# KING,

Under the GREAT

# Seal of England,

TO

# WILLIAM PENN

AND HIS

# Heirs and Aſſigns.

Since (by the good Providence of *God*, and the Favour of the *King*) a Country in *America* is fallen to my Lot, I thought it not leſs my Duty, then my Honeſt Intereſt, to give ſome publick notice of it to the World, that thoſe of our own or other Nations, that are inclin'd to Tranſport Themſelves or Families beyond the Seas, may find another Country added to their Choice; that if they ſhall happen to like the Place, Conditions, and Government, (ſo far as the preſent Infancy of things will allow us any proſpect) they may, if they pleaſe, fix with me in the Province, hereafter deſcribed.

I. *The* KING'S *Title to this Country before he granted it.*

It is the *Jus Gentium*, or Law of Nations, that what ever Waſte, or unculted Country, is the Diſcovery of any Prince, it is the right of that Prince that was at the Charge of the Diſcovery: Now this *Province* is a Member of that part of *America*, which the King of *Englands* Anceſtors have been at the Charge of Diſcovering, and which they and he have taken great care to preſerve and Improve.

A        II. William

legislature with the members of each house to be elected by the freemen. The upper house would propose legislation; the lower house would ratify or reject it. Since the ownership of a small amount of land or the payment of taxes entitled a man to vote, the franchise was widely held. No church was "established" and freedom of Christian worship prevailed. Even so, the non-Quakers in the colony fought his administration from the start. Moreover, boundary disputes with New York and Maryland, together with charges in 1692 that he favored the cause of the exiled James II (see p. 52), made his position insecure. In 1692, he in fact lost his charter, and his colony was directed for the next two years by the governor of New York.

In 1694, the Crown restored the proprietorship, but Penn remained in England until 1699. In 1701, though disgusted with his enemies in the colony, he liberalized his government even further, the "Charter of Privileges" granted that year reducing proprietary authority to a minimum. One provision of this Charter detached from Pennsylvania the so-called lower counties west of the Delaware, which once belonged to the Swedes but had been granted to Penn in 1682, and gave them their own legislature. This body first met in 1704. The "lower counties," eventually known

as Delaware, remained under the jurisdiction of the governor of Pennsylvania until they became a separate state in 1776.

The immediate success and extraordinary progress of Pennsylvania indicate how much practical wisdom the colonists had accumulated since the days of Jamestown and Plymouth. Penn carefully selected the site for Philadelphia before the first settlers had even arrived, and he laid out his city with foresight. That his province turned out to be fertile and that its beginnings happened to coincide with religious persecutions on the Continent were, of course, accidental. But Penn skillfully took advantage of his opportunities. He advertised his colony widely abroad, attracting colonists of all faiths by guaranteeing toleration for anyone who worshiped God. By 1689, about 12,000 people lived in Pennsylvania, including 250 Negroes. As in New England, a flourishing trade quickly sprang up with the West Indies, where Pennsylvania pork, beef, wheat, and flour were in great demand. Pennsylvania ship captains also engaged in the slave traffic, although Quaker scruples in this early period seemed stronger than Puritan ones in keeping their number small.

William Penn's colony soon became the richest in North America, but the proprietor did not share in its good fortune. After returning to England in 1701 to keep the Crown's grasp off his charter, Penn met financial difficulties and even spent a short time in the debtor's prison. He died in 1718.

## V  Consolidation of the imperial system

*Spirit of mercantilism*

The permanent settlement of the mainland colonies, their economic growth, political maturity, and strategic expansion, all took place within the framework of the emerging mercantilist system. Of course, many colonists went largely untouched by this system. Perhaps as many as nine of every ten mainland families lived on subsistence farms or otherwise personally supplied their basic needs of food, clothing, and shelter. For such items as salt, iron, and ammunition, which they could not make at home, they would barter their surplus crops locally. Thus the vast majority of Americans in all sections shared an independence of the market, of the ups and downs of international trade. From time to time, however, even the most isolated were caught up in the problems of government, war, and rebellion.

Under the mercantilist system, economic activity was organized and controlled—insofar as organization and control could be applied—for the advantage not of the individual but of the rising national state. Spain, Portugal, France, the Netherlands, and England all lived under some sort of mercantilist system from the fifteenth to the nineteenth century. Such a system, indeed, was the means by which each of these states mobilized its economic resources behind its national aims. Since these aims usually were in conflict and often led to war, one of the fundamental goals of the mercantilist system was to preserve and enlarge a nation's gold supply by which armies and navies were supported. The rush to America in the sixteenth and seventeenth centuries was strongly motivated, as we have seen, by the quest for gold hoards and gold mines.

Where there was little or no gold, as in the English mainland colonies, bullion was sought through the regulation of trade. Stated simply, colonies were useful for selling raw materials cheaply to the mother country and buying her manufactures dearly, thereby giving the mother country a favorable edge in the exchange which, by further exchange elsewhere, she could convert into gold. An important corollary of this mode of exchange, lest gold be paid out to foreigners for services, was the requirement that commodities going in either direction be carried in national or colonial ships. Lest gold also be paid to foreigners for goods, another corollary of the mercantilist system was the granting of bounties to colonial settlers to encourage the production of critical commodities. The British, for example, paid Americans bounties for producing hemp for ships' ropes, for refining tar for pitch, for cutting timber for ships' masts.

The mercantilist system worked best in connection with overseas colonies that produced great agricultural staples—such as the tobacco of Virginia and Maryland and the sugar of the West Indian islands. The planters of these staples found a protected market for their products in the mother country. They were also granted extensive credit for the manufactures they bought. British exporters, assured of payment in marketable crops each year, encouraged the colonial planters to live well, indeed beyond their means.

The mercantilist system had fewer attractions to the merchants of the Middle colonies and fewest of all to those of New England who had to roam the world in their ships to get sufficiently ahead in their transactions to earn money for the good life. Earn it they soon did, but in ways that brought little benefit to the mother country.

## Administration of the navigation acts

As early as 1620 the English ordered Virginia tobacco to be exported exclusively to England in English ships even though its principal users were on the Continent. Later "navigation acts" placed additional colonial products under similar mercantilist restrictions. The system was enlarged under Cromwell in the early 1650s, when Dutch carriers took advantage of English internal conflicts to encroach on English overseas trade. After the restoration of the Stuarts in 1660, the Crown was urged to tighten the reins on its New World settlements in order to improve the revenues of the kingdom. Heretofore, only occasional parliamentary committees were charged with the responsibility for administering the navigation acts. Early in the 1660s, Charles II created a "civil list" of Crown employees to give full time to colonial regulation, while Parliament stiffened the navigation code.

One of Parliament's new measures was the Navigation Act of 1660, reenacted by the first regular Restoration Parliament in 1661. This act provided that no goods or commodities could be brought to or sent from any English colony except in ships owned by Englishmen, operated by English masters, and manned by crews at least three-fourths English. These requirements worked no hardship on the colonials, because the term "English" was understood to include them as subjects of the British monarch.

The Act of 1660/1661 also extended the list of "enumerated articles" grown or processed in colonies that could be sold only to England or another colony. Tobacco remained the only such article of major importance to the mainland settlements, but other items were added from time to time. This measure was intended primarily to keep rival nations from obtaining colonial commodities, but the mother country had no intention of harming colonial trade itself. To assure the colonials full benefit of the English market, the act forbade both tobacco growing in England and English importation of foreign tobacco.

In 1663 Parliament passed another Navigation Act giving English merchants a monopoly of colonial trade, and this one affected the colonists more seriously. With a few exceptions, the new act required that all European goods destined for the colonies be shipped by way of English ports on English ships. Import and export duties were charged on landing and reloading such goods, but a system of rebates enabled the colonists to buy foreign goods coming by way of England about as cheaply as Englishmen could buy them at home. The colonial merchants, nonetheless, complained that the required stopover in England sometimes added an extra leg to the return voyage from the Continent. They now began to violate the Act of 1660/1661 by shipping enumerated articles directly to European ports and to violate the Act of 1663 by carrying foreign goods directly home.

To close up loopholes in these early measures, Parliament passed a third Navigation Act, which became effective in 1673. Colonial captains, for example, would pretend that they were carrying enumerated articles simply to another colonial port, but after having cleared that port they would strike out for Europe with their illegal cargoes. To stop this practice, the Act of 1673 assessed duties on colonial products *at the port of clearance,* un-

less the captain would bind himself to take the cargo to England. To collect these new export duties, English officials were sent to America and friction quickly developed between them and the merchants.

After the Restoration in 1660, much of the authority to make recommendations on colonial policy and colonial trade had been granted to the Committee for Trade and Plantations of the Privy Council, more commonly known as the Lords of Trade. As early as 1664, this committee had sent a royal commission to America to bring the colonists up to date on their obligations to the restored Crown and to investigate and arbitrarily correct evasions. The commission succeeded in most of the provinces, but the Bible Commonwealth of Massachusetts proved exceedingly reluctant to surrender her "independency for government" in economic as well as in religious and political matters. Her reluctance stumped the commissioners, who returned home in 1665 with a very negative report.

Following the Navigation Act of 1673, the Lords of Trade made a new effort to bring the Puritans to book. Their instrument this time was Edward Randolph, who arrived in 1676 and for a generation thereafter proved so tireless in searching out infractions that he rose to be "surveyor-general" of His Majesty's customs in all of British America. Hateful to the Puritan merchants, Randolph made Massachusetts so hateful to the Crown that Charles II annulled her charter in 1684. The next year, on succeeding Charles, James II put Massachusetts and other northern colonies into one administrative unit, called the "Territory and Dominion of New England." This "Dominion" included all the New England colonies, together with New York and East and West New Jersey—an unwieldy realm administered from Boston by the dictatorial Sir Edmund Andros, James's governor.

Andros abolished the colonial assemblies and even tried to force the colonists to worship in the Anglican Church. No one could have reconciled Massachusetts to these steps, but Andros made matters worse by his insolence toward Yankee sentiments and his attempt to undermine Yankee land titles. In

1687 Massachusetts sent her leading minister, Increase Mather, to England to try to retrieve the charter and effect Andros's recall. Mather failed to do either while James held the throne. After the "Glorious Revolution" of 1688, Massachusetts at least regained her identity as a distinct colony.

## The Glorious Revolution in England and America

Edward Randolph and Sir Edmund Andros were not the only members of the Stuart "civil list" to incite the Americans. Both Charles II and James II filled colonial offices with indigent court favorites to help them make or recoup their fortunes at the Americans' expense. They also sent royal zealots who boldly overrode not only colonial liberties but those of English merchants engaged in the colonial trade as well. Before long, such merchants so tired of James's administrators and of the King himself that they joined with others in forcing James to flee the throne and escape to France in 1688. Most of these others had been aroused by James's militant Catholicism, first evident in 1685 when on taking the throne he put down a Puritan revolt under the Duke of Monmouth with such zeal that Anglicans too took fright. By placing many Catholics in positions of power, James also flouted the Test Act of 1673, which prohibited all but Anglicans from holding public office in England. Such measures shook even royalist Tories who believed in the divine right of kings. When James fathered a son in June 1688, the dire menace of a new Catholic succession chilled the English soul, and Tories and Whigs together drove James out.

A parliamentary committee itself now boldly invited to England William of Orange, the Dutch Protestant husband of James's daughter Mary. After some months devoted, as one historian has put it, to "decently covering up the unpleasant rents in the fabric of the constitution," the reign of William and Mary, or of William III, began in February 1689. At that time, Parliament also adopted the Bill of Rights, opening with an array of accusations against James II foreshadowing those arrayed against George III by the Americans in July 1776. The famous Bill then proceeded to set forth the rights of Englishmen under the law. No Catholic, furthermore, could henceforth occupy the throne. Dissenters might worship openly as they pleased, but public office remained closed to them as to others not members of the Church of England.

Such was the peaceful Glorious Revolution, which, at least for English constitutional theory during the life of the new rulers, seemed to give the elected representatives of the people superiority over their "elected" king. As elaborated by John Locke (see p. 101), this theory became one of the pillars of the colonists' own argument later that since they did not participate in the election of parliamentary representatives in England, their allegiance must be only to their own local "parliaments" and the king *these* parliaments chose to recognize.

On learning of James's abdication, the Puritans of Massachusetts, even before news of the Glorious Revolution reached America, conducted a bloodless revolution of their own. In April 1689, an armed band of Boston citizens led by young Cotton Mather, son of Increase, marched against Andros, forced him to seek refuge in a fort, and aroused the public to such a high pitch of feeling against him that he capitulated and went to jail. An ad hoc "council" of the General Court ruled Massachusetts until the Commonwealth was brought under a new royal charter in 1691. This charter reflected the failure of Increase Mather's mission. No longer would Massachusetts elect its own governor. Henceforth, he would be appointed by the Crown. His council would be elected by the General Court, subject to the governor's veto. General Court legislation itself was to be subject to review in England. The new charter also ended Plymouth's independent existence. Along with Maine it was incorporated in Massachusetts Bay. Andros's downfall in Massachusetts had prompted

Connecticut and Rhode Island to resume their old regimes, which they were now permitted to continue.

In New York, meanwhile, Andros's deputy, Francis Nicholson, resigned on learning of his superior's plight. In May 1689, Jacob Leisler, a German trader in Manhattan since its Dutch days, took advantage of Nicholson's absence to call upon neighboring counties and towns to set up a representative government for the first time. Backed by dissident elements alarmed by rumors of a French invasion and a Catholic conspiracy, Leisler managed civil affairs vigorously and efficiently for several months. But by disregarding a message he had intercepted from the Crown ordering Nicholson to conduct colonial affairs until new authorities took over, he gave support to the charges of his enemies that he was a revolutionist and a usurper. When in March 1691 Leisler resisted the deputy sent by William III, he was captured and soon tried and sentenced to death along with seven of his men. Leisler and his son-in-law, his closest follower, were hanged in May. The others were pardoned by the Crown, which proceeded to establish royal and representative government in New York.

### The navigation system after 1696

William III brought with him to England his traditional continental rivalry with the Catholic French, which was intensified by Louis XIV's hospitality to the ousted James II. As early as 1689, this rivalry flared up in the War of the League of Augsburg, the opening conflict in the world wars of the eighteenth century over the domination of North America as well as other regions (see Chapter Three). To bolster his position at home, William III undertook to strengthen the Anglican establishment. To bolster his position in the New World he enlarged the number of royal colonies, as we have seen, and in other ways strengthened the position of the royal governors. Starting in 1696, he also revamped the administration and extended the reach of the navigation system.

As the Crown's chief representative in the colonies, the royal governor came to possess broad powers. He could summon and dissolve assemblies, veto their legislation, and appoint minor officials. The upper house, or council, served as his advisory board, with executive, legislative, and judicial functions. Except in Massachusetts, this house was chosen from among leading colonials by the Board of Trade in England. But since the governor's recommendations influenced the Board's choices, his friendship counted for much among wealthy and aspiring Americans. With all his dignity and authority, however, the governor found himself caught between colonial and royal crossfire. As the symbol and spokesman of the Crown, he was expected to follow instructions from England that reflected the rigid policies of British officialdom made thousands of miles from the scene of their application. At the same time he had to respect the needs of his colony and its leaders, among whom he had to live. The job called for remarkable tact, but even the best of governors gradually lost their primacy to the colonial assemblies.

The changes in the navigation system at the end of the seventeenth century did little to improve the governors' prospects of good relations with the Americans. In May 1696, the Lords Commissioners of Trade and Plantations, commonly known as the Board of Trade, supplanted the Lords of Trade (see p. 51). With the Privy Council, the Board administered colonial relations until the Revolution. New navigation acts strengthened the Board's hand.

Under the new legislation, new customs offices were to be set up in each colony, with customs officials given the same powers as those in England, including access to "writs of assistance" by which they could invoke constabulary aid in forcing their way into suspect private premises. Offenders against the new navigation code were henceforth to be tried in admiralty courts. Manned by royal, not provincial, judges, these new courts could try colonial merchants without juries. The admiralty

54

courts became one of the most detested of all English institutions. The navigation code itself was strengthened by the "enumeration" of more commodities to be shipped exclusively to England. Parliament also began to ban the export to England of colonial wheat, flour, and fish which competed with England's own. Starting with the Wool Act of 1699, moreover, colonial craftsmen were forbidden to export and later even to make many manufactured goods in which English merchants thereby gained a monopoly.

And yet the colonies prospered, the richness of America's natural resources contributing heavily to their success. Smuggling and other modes of evasion, moreover, continued to go largely unpunished. American as well as English merchants also benefited from the exclusion of the Dutch and others from the imperial trade and from protection against enemies on the sea. The Americans' growing prosperity and self-reliance, at the same time, encouraged them first to refine the arts of evasion and protest against British regulations, and finally to defy British authority. British demands grew harsher as the costly wars with the French approached their showdown phase, and mounting British pressure on the colonies rekindled the spirit of independence that had marked the early settlements.

## For further reading

The books by A. L. Rowse cited at the end of the readings for Chapter One afford a stirring introduction to the English background of American settlement. S. T. Bindoff, *Tudor England* (1950), and G. M. Trevelyan, *England under the Stuarts* (1904), are scholarly accounts, updated but not outdated by Roger Lockyer, *Tudor and Stuart Britain 1471-1714* (1964), and H. R. Trevor-Roper, *The Crisis of the Seventeenth-Century* (1968). Wallace Notestein, *The English People on the Eve of Colonization* (1954), affords a useful summary but must be supplemented by Carl Bridenbaugh, *Vexed and Troubled Englishmen 1590-1642* (1968).

The first three volumes of C. M. Andrews, *The Colonial Period of American History* (4 vols., 1934-1938), offer the most satisfactory extended account of American settlement. The fourth volume is excellent on Britain's commercial and colonial policy. Three books by T. J. Wertenbaker cover the social history of the early colonial period under the general title, *The Founding of American Civilization*. There are *The Old South* (1942); *The Middle Colonies* (1938); and *The Puritan Oligarchy* (1947). W. F. Craven, *The Southern Colonies in the Seventeenth Century 1607-1689* (1949), is outstanding on Virginia and her neighbors. P. L. Barbour, *The Three Worlds of Captain John Smith* (1964), is the best biography. See also the exceptional collection,

J. M. Smith, ed., *Seventeenth Century America, Essays on Colonial History* (1959). L. B. Wright's modern edition (1947) of Robert Beverley, *The History and Present State of Virginia* (first published in 1705), affords an invaluable early account, especially of Indian relations. W. E. Washburn, *The Governor and the Rebel: A History of Bacon's Rebellion in Virginia* (1957), stresses the importance of these relations. V. W. Crane, *The Southern Frontier 1670-1732* (1929), is excellent on early Carolina history, for which see also Readings for Chapter Three.

William Bradford, *Of Plymouth Plantation 1620-1647* (in the S. E. Morison edition, 1952), is the best work on its subject. George Langdon, *Pilgrim Colony: A History of New Plymouth 1620-1691* (1966), is the outstanding modern account. Of Perry Miller's many works on Massachusetts Bay and its satellites, the following may be noted: *The New England Mind: The Seventeenth Century* (1939); *The New England Mind: From Colony to Province* (1953); and *Orthodoxy in Massachusetts 1630-1650* (1933). Perry Miller and T. H. Johnson, eds., *The Puritans* (1938), is an excellent anthology of Puritan writings, as is E. S. Morgan, ed., *Puritan Political Ideas* (1965). E. S. Morgan, *The Puritan Dilemma: The Story of John Winthrop* (1958), is a somewhat disenchanted biography. See also D. B. Rutman, *Winthrop's Boston: A Portrait of a Puritan Town*

1630-1649 (1965). O. E. Winslow, *Master Roger Williams* (1957), and Emery Battis, *Saints and Sectaries* (1962), on Anne Hutchinson, are good on the religious malcontents.

A. T. Vaughan, *New England Frontier, Puritans and Indians 1620-1675* (1965), is a well-written study of Puritan attitudes and actions. G. L. Haskins, *Law and Authority in Early Massachusetts* (1960), affords an excellent introduction to the American legal tradition. Bernard Bailyn, *The New England Merchants in the Seventeenth Century* (1955), is a useful supplement to the still valuable older study by W. B. Weedon, *Economic and Social History of New England 1620-1789* (2 vols., 1890). Richard Pares, *Yankees and Creoles, the Trade between North America and the West Indies before the American Revolution* (1956), is illuminating for this period and later ones. S. C. Powell, *Puritan Village, The Formation of a New England Town* (1963), is full of insight and evidence.

Two special studies help broaden the picture of early New York: J. R. Reich, *Leisler's Rebellion, A Study of Democracy in New York 1664-1720* (1953), and A. W. Trelease, *Indian Affairs in Colonial New York, the Seventeenth Century* (1960). E. D. Bronner, *William Penn's "Holy Experiment," the Founding of Pennsylvania 1681-1701* (1962), is a sound, straightforward account. F. B. Tolles, *Meeting House and Counting House, The Quaker Merchants of Colonial Philadelphia 1682-1763* (1948), is outstanding on God and Mammon in Pennsylvania.

On British colonial regulation, in addition to C. M. Andrews, cited above, the standard older works are those by G. L. Beer, *The Origins of the British Colonial System 1578-1660* (1908) and *The Old Colonial System* (2 vols., 1912). L. H. Gipson, *The British Empire before the American Revolution* (13 vols., 1936-1967), is a monumental modern account. Special studies of importance include L. A. Harper, *The English Navigation Laws* (1939); M. G. Hall, *Edward Randolph and the American Colonies 1676-1703* (1960), a valuable study of the most persistent British inquisitor, and T. C. Barrow, *Trade and Empire, The British Customs Service in Colonial America 1660-1775* (1967). M. G. Hall, L. H. Leder and M. G. Kammen, eds., *The Glorious Revolution in America, Documents on the Colonial Crisis of 1689* (1964), is an illuminating anthology.

# EXPANSION AND CONFLICT IN NORTH AMERICA

In 1614 Captain John Smith had written of North America:

*As for the goodness and fine substance of the land, we are for the most part yet altogether ignorant of them, but only here and there where we have touched or seen a little, the edges of these large dominions which do stretch themselves into the main, God doth know how many thousand miles.*

By the time Georgia was settled in 1733 as the last of the mainland colonies originating overseas, the English had clinched their hold on 1200 miles of Atlantic seaboard. For all its turbulence and dangers, the Atlantic formed a bridge to the culture and commodities of the Old World. It also provided a path of communication among the settlements of the New World from Labrador to the Caribbean islands and the Spanish Main. In the eighteenth century, the English seaboard merchants became the principal organizers of this New World unity, with even New France and the Caribbean islands dependent for their very food and materials for shelter, as well as for their trade, largely upon Yankee, Yorker, and Quaker coasting vessels, irregular though their sailings were.

Well to the west of this first range of established English settlements, the rivers then known to most colonials began their course to the sea. Beyond the "fall line" of these rivers, where cataracts 200 feet high dramatically signaled a halt to upstream navigation, the Susquehanna Valley in Pennsylvania and the "Great (Shenandoah) Valley" of Virginia tied the "back parts" of the English colonies together. In the eighteenth century, along with English frontiersmen and functionaries, thousands of the non-English immigrants settled in these valleys each year, gradually penetrating farther south and southwest. By the 1750s, issues of Indian relations and runaway slaves and servants, as well as of squatters' rights, church administration, participation in politics, law enforcement, and commercial growth all dictated the need for easier intercourse between this hinterland and the tidewater plantations and cities and harbors of the seaboard. Forward-looking seaboard leaders like the Washingtons and Jeffersons of Virginia, the Norrises, Morrises, and Franklins of Pennsylvania, had begun to press for east-west roads and bridges to link up the natural north-south routes.

To all but a few Americans of the eighteenth century, the country beyond the Appalachians still loomed as a trackless wilderness so densely wooded that the sun seldom penetrated the foliage beneath whose cover lurked wild brave and beast and terrifying creatures of the mind. Yet as we know, this land too was far from empty, and when, after 1768, permanent settlers at long last penetrated the region, "they found weatherbeaten trails," as J. B. Bartlett writes in his fine study of *The Explorers of North America,* "skilful, knowledgeable guides, and Indians who had dealt with the white man for a century."

When the war for this North American wilderness was fought out between Britain and France in the middle of the eighteenth century, the British mainland settlements, a new nation despite their differences, played an American rather than a British role. In a sense, the American Revolution was a late phase of this war which red men, Spaniards, Frenchmen, and Britons had been waging intermittently for more than a hundred years and which, in fact, did not finally flicker out until the end of the Indian wars on the plains following the American Civil War.


## I   The new American population


### Extraordinary growth and spread

Britain's ultimate success against France in North America sprang largely from the astonishing growth of her mainland colonies, the vigor of whose people already gave European rulers cause for wonder and alarm. After 1700, the population of these colonies almost doubled every twenty-five years. In round numbers, the 200,000 settlers in 1688 had grown to about 1,600,000 in 1760. At that time there were but 65,000 Europeans in New France.

The most heavily populated mainland colonies lay in the South, which in 1760 numbered some 700,000 inhabitants. Of these about 300,000 were Negroes, all but a few of them slaves. Approximately 500,000 people,

12,700 of them black, lived in New England at this time, and some 400,000, almost 30,000 of them Negroes, in the Middle colonies, which were growing most rapidly. In all but the lower New England commonwealths, Indians, although unenumerated, continued to make their presence felt.

58

Among the white colonials an extraordinarily high birth rate accounted in large part for the remarkable rise in population—it has been estimated that the average colonial family increased by one child every two years. The large immigration from the British Isles and elsewhere helped swell the total. Less is known of the birth rate among the blacks, boasts of their fertility as evidence of good care distorting the sketchy figures; but their death rate was high, those who survived the terrors of the ocean passage to America often succumbing to grief as well as to disease, violence, malnutrition, and overwork.

During most of the seventeenth century, the English mainland settlers remained hostile to newcomers of other nationalities. In the eighteenth century, the overpowering need for workers and fighters in the rapidly growing settlements induced the English colonials to alter their policies if not their attitudes.

In the early years of the eighteenth century, especially on the southern frontier, slaves and free Negroes sometimes were enlisted in the militia along with whites to fight the Indians and the Spanish; but as the number of slave workers grew, their restiveness and rebelliousness persuaded their masters no longer to arm them. Indeed, in most southern colonies, however exigent the planters became for slave labor, their "great fear and terror" of slave revolts soon induced them to place heavy provincial tariff duties on Negroes to discourage their further importation. The proceeds of such duties, in turn, helped defray the cost of bounties and land grants, and of agents overseas, used to draw white foreigners to America to offset the growing disproportion of blacks and to police them, as well as to fight the Spaniards and Indians. In northern and southern, older and newer colonies alike, the dominant English also compelled white immigrants who came in more conventional ways to serve as "frontier guards."

The American need for workers and fighters in the eighteenth century coincided with social conditions in western Germany and northern Ireland to create a large pool of discontented persons willing if not eager to migrate overseas. The "Palatines," the name Americans carelessly bestowed upon most Germans, even those from principalities other than the Palatinate, and the "Scotch-Irish," as those from the province of Ulster in northern Ireland came to be called, made up by far the largest contingents of white eighteenth-century newcomers.

*The great German influx*

Continuous German immigration began in 1683, when small groups of Mennonites and Quakers, harassed elsewhere for their radical Christianity, established Germantown, near present-day Philadelphia. For thirty-six years until his death in 1720, Francis Daniel Pastorius reigned as Germantown's chief citizen. He is perhaps best remembered for having led in 1688 the first organized religious protest in the English mainland colonies against the practice of keeping slaves, at least by Quakers. During the next three decades other radical German Protestants founded such Pennsylvania towns as Bethlehem, Lititz, and Nazareth. These early immigrants were mainly well-educated people, who paid their own passage, brought property from the Old World, and bought land on their arrival in the New. They built substantial communities where many original buildings still stand.

All the German radical sects were profoundly anti-Erastian, that is, opposed to domination of the church by the state, a position that took its most provocative form in the refusal of their members to bear arms. Their refusal to swear oaths also made them thorns in the flesh to British administrators of the navigation acts and to other political and judicial functionaries.

Along with the sects, intensely Erastian German Lutherans and German Reformed (the established church of those principalities that went Calvinist) were also permitted to settle in Germantown early in the eighteenth century. These denominations, since they were official state religions, numbered by far most of the Protestants in Germany, with Lutherans predominant among them; and they numbered by far most of the German-speaking immigrants to America. As members of the established denominations these immigrants are usually called "church people," but

*George Keith, who*
*after the death of George Fox in 1691*
*aspired to the international leadership*
*of the Society of Friends, issued*
*this "Exhortation & Caution" against*
*enslaving Negroes, "for whom Christ hath*
*shed his precious blood . . .*
*as well as White Men."*

Rare Book Division, New York Public Library, Astor, Lenox and Tilden Foundations

( 1 )

## An Exhortation & Caution
TO

# FRIENDS
Concerning buying or keeping of

## Negroes.

SEing our Lord Jesus Christ hath tasted Death for every Man, and given himself a Ransom for all, to be testified in due time, and that his Gospel of Peace, Liberty and Redemption from Sin, Bondage and all Oppression, is freely to be preached unto all, without Exception, and that *Negroes*, *Blacks* and *Tawnies* are a real part of Mankind, for whom Christ hath shed his precious Blood, and are capable of Salvation, as well as *White Men*; and Christ the Light of the World hath (in measure) enlightened them, and every Man that cometh into the World; and that all such who are sincere *Christians* and true Believers in Christ Jesus, and Followers of him, bear his Image, and are made conformable unto him in Love, Mercy, Goodness and Compassion, who came not to destroy mens Lives, nor to save them, nor to bring any part of Mankind into outward Bondage, Slavery or Misery, nor yet to detain them, or hold them therein, but to ease and deliver the Oppressed and Distressed, and bring into Liberty both inward and outward.

A                                    Therefore

on the whole they were less devoted to their faith than the sectarians, and partly on that account succumbed more rapidly to the frontiers stripping them of much of their Old World culture.

Most of the church people were too poor to pay their way to America and came mainly as "redemptioners," one of the various forms of white servitude. The "indentured servants" who were first shipped to Virginia and Maryland early in the seventeenth century had made contracts with the joint-stock companies or proprietary agents abroad to work in the colonies in exchange for their passage across the Atlantic ocean. Redemptioners of the eighteenth century sold themselves to ship captains or "soul brokers" in European ports. Because of overcrowding and related conditions, on the average a third of the redemptioners, and a much higher proportion of their children, died at sea. On one ship arriving in Philadelphia in 1745, only 40 of 400 passengers had survived; on another in 1752, a mere 19 of 200 lived.

Once landed in America, the redemptioners contracts or "indentures" were sold to the highest bidders. Thereafter, their situation was the same as the earlier white servants. The usual term was from four to seven years, at the expiration of which the servant was to receive "freedom dues," usually 50 acres of land, tools, and clothing, and perhaps a bit of cash to get started on his own. The evidence suggests that these dues often were withheld or, when granted, that the servant sold off his land for a pittance in ready money. On the other hand, runaways were frequent and often went unapprehended.

German immigration reached its high point between 1749 and 1754 when to the dismay of the English colonists who feared they were being engulfed, over 5000 Germans arrived in American ports each year, most of them debarking in Philadelphia. Late in the 1720s the church people had begun to move through recently discovered "gaps" in the Appalachians to the Shenandoah Valley in Virginia and farther south to the Carolina Piedmont, some of them selling their Pennsylvania farms for a profit to break cheaper land on a new frontier (a reverse flow of Maryland, Virginia,

59

and Carolina farmers from slavery north to freer Pennsylvania also developed at this time).

While many of the German church people who stayed on in Pennsylvania strove, to the dismay of their leaders, to take on English ways, others held tenaciously to their frontier homesteads and national traditions. As the open space filled up around them, the village if not the communal example of the sects re-

vived, and the love of the soil, so profound among the Godly, entered others as well. In a nation notorious for using up the land, the Pennsylvania Germans became celebrated throughout the country for their rich gardens and orchards, their stout barns and well-

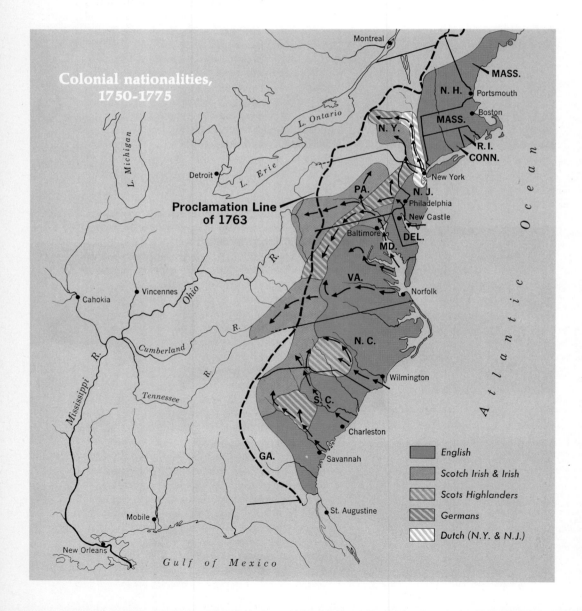

Colonial nationalities, 1750-1775

Proclamation Line of 1763

English
Scotch Irish & Irish
Scots Highlanders
Germans
Dutch (N.Y. & N.J.)

tended livestock, their sturdy self-sufficiency. German artisans developed the famous long rifle, first manufactured in Lancaster and later adopted and improved by frontiersmen everywhere. Equally important innovations were the iron stove and the Conestoga wagon—the stove a vast improvement over the heat-wasting open hearth of the English-style dwelling, the wagon a durable, efficient vehicle for carrying goods and people over rough frontier trails.

### Ulstermen from northern Ireland

Alarmingly numerous though they became, the German immigrants in the English colonies in the eighteenth century were exceeded in numbers by the so-called Scotch-Irish, whose record in America is at once simpler and more profound than that of most other immigrant nationalities. It is simpler in that by and large the Scotch-Irish came (those who came voluntarily) for the single purpose of bettering themselves; more often than others, they arrived not even as families but as individuals who eventually married and bore large numbers of children to improve their chances of success. Their record is more profound in that their readiness to penetrate ever deeper across the Indian frontier formed them and their descendants into the characteristic American type, the model of those who, with eye turned from the sea and the Old World, looked ever westward toward America's continental destiny.

Lowland Scotch Presbyterians, the forebears of the Scotch-Irish, began to cross the North Channel for Ulster at the urging of James I early in the seventeenth century to strengthen Protestantism there, at least by numbers. The men found for this mission naturally were those with least to lose at home. But however they began, the Scots in Ulster prospered sufficiently as farmers and manufacturers to draw thousands of their countrymen in their wake. Scottish well-being in Ireland lasted until the restoration of the Stuarts in England in

1660 brought about the "renewal of episcopal aggression" against Presbyterians. Stricter enforcement of newly discriminatory navigation acts there as in America after the Glorious Revolution of 1688 also deepened economic distress. The final blow came when British absentee landlords, around 1717, demanded practically double the rents the Scotch-Irish had long been paying for the renewal of leases that expired that year and the next. Heretofore emigrating in hundreds, Ulstermen now began leaving in thousands. Many "mere Irish," that is Catholic Irish passers, stole out along with them, and their number surely would have been larger were they not explicitly excluded from America as "papists."

Poverty in Ireland as in England helped fill the prisons as well as the ranks of the poor. In time of war, whatever happened to female offenders, males often were thrust into the army; but when poverty spread during periods of peace, as it did during the twenty-five years following the Peace of Utrecht, 1713 (see p. 77), new expedients were needed to relieve the jails besides the common penalties of "burning in the hand and whipping." The transportation of convicts had a long history in England, and it has been reliably estimated that during the eighteenth century more than 20,000 English felons were shipped to Maryland and Virginia to work in the tobacco fields. A Treasury decision in 1716 to pay merchants liberally for carrying felons overseas, meanwhile, created a powerful special interest behind the perpetuation of the practice. Transportation of convicts, or at least their banishment, had been practiced in Ireland for some time before the Irish Parliament in the 1720s made carrying terms as attractive to Irish as to English merchants. About 10,000 persons appear to have been shipped involuntarily from Ireland to the American mainland "plantations" in the eighteenth century, at least half of them felons, the rest vagabonds and derelicts.

Scotch-Irish paying passengers probably accounted for no more than one in ten of the free Ulster immigrants. The rest, like most of the Germans, obtained their passage by signing indentures similar in virtually all respects to those signed by the "Palatines." Many of the paying passengers debarked in Charleston, South Carolina, where white frontier guards were most in demand and liberal offers of land attracted them. Many of the convicts debarked in the Chesapeake colonies. Most of the servants landed in Philadelphia or in nearby Newcastle, Delaware.

Quickly marked as "bold and indigent strangers" by the Pennsylvania authorities, as the Scotch-Irish spread from the port to the country they incurred all the strictures the German church people endured for clearing land not their own and resisting the proprietors' quitrent collectors with guns. Their "Irish" origins also raised the specter of a "papist" invasion among those who could not or would not distinguish Scots from Celts. The convict taint, moreover, marked even the most law-abiding among the voyagers.

As newcomers continued to arrive by the thousands each year and indentures expired, the Scotch-Irish penetrated beyond the Germans on Philadelphia's northern frontier, becoming especially numerous in this region in the Delaware Valley. They also moved across the Susquehanna to the Cumberland Valley where the mountain passes led naturally southwestward to Maryland, western Virginia, and North Carolina. This course took them along the outer rim of the Germans who had earlier moved in the same direction. Only then did they resume their push westward in Pennsylvania, pressing across the Allegheny River beyond present-day Pittsburgh in the 1760s.

Runaways and hence castaways were more numerous among the Scotch-Irish than among the Germans. Those who triumphed over every frontier trial clung the more tenaciously to the rewards and methods of their success, permitting no cessation in the defense and enlargement of their property. Others, having found constraint unbearable, sometimes refused to constrain their fellowmen. In both characters the Scotch-Irish encountered familiar models among the English gentry with whom they quarreled over religion and politics as well as property. After the Revolution, many Ulstermen mingled with the gentry as soldiers and speculators, but also as distinguished ministers, lawyers, orators, and political leaders. With no lingering loyalties to some Old Country abroad, they fell the more readily into the American grain.

## Blacks among whites

The severity of language in which the fortune of the average eighteenth-century white immigrant to America is described, reflecting the severity of his life, is outdone even in the most abstract and objective accounts of the fate of the black African. Elizabeth Donnan, for example, the compiler of four volumes of *Documents Illustrative of the History of the Slave Trade to America* (1930–1935), says of her subject, "this traffic was not business but crime, and crime of so intolerable a nature that it must be outlawed by civilization." More recently, W. D. Jordan, in *White Over Black* (1968), described the fully developed slave codes of the eighteenth century as the means employed by popularly elected legislatures to "coerce" the "slaveholding gentry . . . as individuals . . . toward maintenance of a private tyranny which was conceived to be in the community interest." Jordan quotes another scholar who said of slaves apprehended in New York in 1708 for murders they may or may not have committed, that they were "put to death with all the torment possible for terror to others."

In *The Atlantic Slave Trade: A Census* (1969), Philip D. Curtin has made a valiant effort to assess the innumerable estimates of the numbers of Africans sold or surrendered into slavery during the 350 years of the slave trade. Curtin puts total slave imports in the New World at between 8 and 10.5 million, with 90 percent or more going to tropical America. He places the total for British North America at 275,000 to 1790, with 70,000 more coming before the formal closing of the slave trade by the United States Constitution in 1808, and some 54,000 smuggled in between 1808 and the Civil War.

The cruelty of slavery began at the very instant of capture (or of kidnaping, a secondary source of supply) and during the marches, often hundreds of miles, from inland wars and defeat to the shore. Here, for those who survived the trek, chained imprisonment, branding, flogging, and even murder on sufficient provocation despite the Negro's value now as property, characteristically preceded the bestial voyage. Despite the careful organization of the trade at its maturity, vessels engaged in it frequently sat idle in ports for weeks before acquiring a full load or finding a favorable wind. Slaves mutinied more often during these periods than on the high seas, some even, on becoming unfettered, throwing themselves into the shark-infested waters in seeking to regain their liberty.

Britain was one of the last of the Western

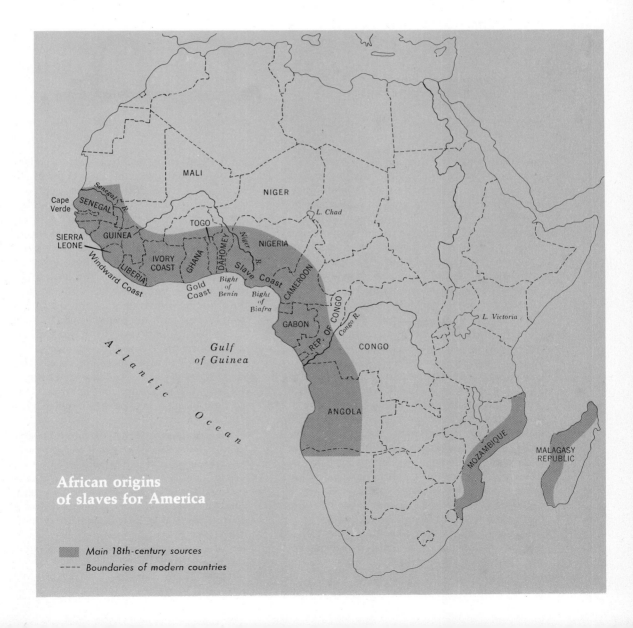

African origins of slaves for America

Main 18th-century sources

- - - Boundaries of modern countries

*From eighteenth-century "Methods of Procuring Slaves": (1) "Manner of yoking slaves" for marching to port. (2) Mouthpiece and necklace, with hooks, so placed as to prevent escape when pursued in woods. (3) Placing dealer's red hot brand on purchased slaves. (4) Slave leg bolts used aboard ship on the middle passage. (5) Stowing blacks on slave ship below decks.*

powers to enter the African slave trade on a commercial basis and only gradually enlarged her interest in it. Britain's mainland colonies, at the same time, only gradually fell prey to the "peculiar institution" as a labor system. In the eighteenth century as in the seventeenth, many of the slaves in these colonies had been "seasoned" in the Caribbean sugar islands before coming to the mainland staple plantations. The majority of eighteenth-century mainland slaves, however, landed straight from Africa, a situation that deepened the planters' fear and terror of their blacks, as yet unbroken to plantation discipline and the constraints of the "quarter."

This circumstance heightened, as we have said, the planters' determination to secure white immigrants whom they could arm in their defense. At the same time, the spread of slavery soon expropriated the white immigrants's opportunities. A Carolina merchant in 1740 made clear what was to become a distressingly persistent southern condition: "Where there are Negroes," he said, "a white man despises to work, saying, *what will you have me a Slave and work like a Negro?*"

If black gang labor turned whites from work in the fields, white legislation soon discouraged blacks from seeking work off the fields. The fully developed slave codes and related ordinances of the early eighteenth century barred slaves and free Negroes alike from many occupations reserved for whites. This became true in northern as well as southern colonies. The latter, moreover, as the slave system matured and its danger grew, closed in on Negro life in numerous other ways, tightening "the bonds on their personal and civil freedom," as Jordan writes, and "loosen[ing] the traditional restraints on the master's freedom to deal with his humanity as he saw fit."

The Negro's response to this trend became apparent in the number of runaways and the groundswell of resistance and revolt. No one phrased the pervasive psychology of the slaveholder in midcentury better than William Byrd of Virginia in a private letter in 1736:

*We have already at least 10,000 men of these descendants of Ham, fit to bear Arms, and these numbers increase every day, as well by birth, as by Importation. And in case there should arise a Man of desperate courage amongst us, exasperated by a desperate fortune, he might with more advantage than Cataline kindle a Servile War. Such a man might be dreadfully mischievous before any opposition could be formed against him, and tinge our Rivers as wide as they are with blood.*

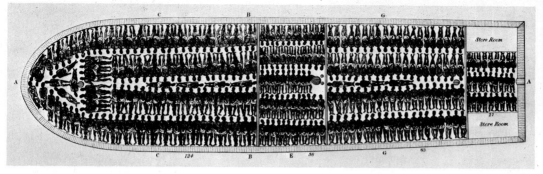

## II Colonial society at its peak

### Tidewater gentry

Throughout the colonial period, most of the population of the Chesapeake region, of tidewater Virginia and Maryland, and of adjacent parts of North Carolina, remained of English extraction. Here, although grain and other food crops continued to be widely grown, the production and export of tobacco gave the strongest impulse to economic expansion, with land speculation offering a hedge against the uncertainties of staple agriculture for distant and fluctuating markets.

Led by a small elite group, the Chesapeake planters kept close ties with the mother country and aped the manners of her aristocracy. The Carters, Lees, Byrds, Randolphs, and Fitzhughs of Virginia, and the Carrols, Dulanys, and Galloways of Maryland lived in Georgian mansions far grander than the seventeenth-century farmhouses of their grandfathers. They filled the well-proportioned rooms with the finest imported furniture, or hired able artisans to carry out the designs of foreign cabinetmakers. Contemporary artists painted the Chesapeake gentry in all their imported finery, yet their middle-class American expressions are not altogether obliterated.

A few Chesapeake planters boasted large libraries with books in several languages which they were capable of reading. Yet cultural interests and institutions languished.

William and Mary College, well endowed by the established Anglican church, opened in Williamsburg, Virginia, soon to become the provincial capital, in 1693; but few students spent more than a year there, that year usually given to indolence and sport. Some planters sent their sons to England for sound classical instruction; but those who profited from such excursions often remained permanently abroad. Observers noted that the Chesapeake gentry were an outdoor people, fonder of fox hunting and horse racing and long weekend house parties than of polite learning.

The Chesapeake planters were forced to take the management of their plantations seriously. But they seemed driven as well to keep up the good life or at least the appearance of it. Land, which represented their greatest wealth, was also their downfall. "Such amazing property," observed Philip Fithian, tutor to the Carters in their heyday, "no matter how deeply it is involved [in debt], blows up the owners to an imagination, which is visible to all." They "live up their suppositions," a Londoner remarked, "without providing against Calamities and accidents."

From the 1730s to the 1750s, when the price of Virginia tobacco soared, the rising profits from their staple also put a premium on the planters' land. In this period, the Chesapeake gentry enjoyed their "golden age," the age of "the gauntlet and the glove," in which the

Courtesy Louise A. Patten; photo Colonial Williamsburg, Virginia

*Robert Carter (1708–1804)*
*of Nomini Hall, Virginia, a James River*
*manor house; painted by Joshua Reynolds.*

myth of southern chivalry and romance took root. Yet few could afford for long the high life of cavaliers, the expenditures for clothes, carriages, and body slaves, mansions, parks, and wine. Eventually, the Virginians' debts for imported indulgences grew so calamitously high that Governor Francis Farquier remarked in 1766 that their "Blood . . . is soured by their private distresses." To those who crashed, the West loomed more beguilingly than ever as a refuge or new springboard to success. It also fed ideas of empire among such Virginians as young George Washington and Thomas Jefferson, whose vision encompassed the entire continent, even the entire hemisphere.

Of all the mainland settlements, tidewater South Carolina, extending inward about 60

miles and southward to the Savannah River, quite distinct from the Chesapeake Country, was closest to the West Indian sugar islands, most distant from England, in character. Eighteenth century South Carolina was the only mainland colony in which blacks outnumbered whites, as in the islands. The whites below the 2000 leading families, moreover, although most earnestly sought for militia service, were the most depressed on the continent, showing the lowest literacy rate and the strongest antagonism to the ruling group.

Under the navigation acts, Carolina rice had been made an enumerated commodity in 1704, requiring that it be sent exclusively to the mother country for reshipment by English merchants to the European continent, which offered the major market. Spoilage from excessive handling and delays in reaching users soon forced the English to reconsider, and in 1729 they allowed rice once more to go directly to European ports. This decision helped greatly to enlarge South Carolina's trade.

By the 1750s, their land hunger as great as that of the Virginians, South Carolina's planters had extended their fields and their forest holdings well into neighboring Georgia, soon virtually their captive colony. By then, too, encouraged by a parliamentary bounty, many of the rice planters had turned to growing indigo, heavily in demand as the source of a dye much wanted in the booming English textile industry. Indigo, together with rice, provided Carolinians with incomes less subject to price fluctuations and other market hazards than tobacco. The Carolina grandees, unlike the Chesapeake gentry, thus were less victimized by debt.

Since the Carolina rivers, unlike those of the Chesapeake region, did not afford seagoing vessels sufficient depth for sailing inland direct to the plantations, the colony's produce usually was brought down to Charleston for shipment abroad. Where the Chesapeake region remained virtually devoid of towns for generations, and its culture rural, Charleston by the 1750s had become the fourth largest colonial city. Its midcentury population of 10,000 was almost equally divided by color, with a sizable proportion of the blacks serving as household and body slaves to planters who maintained homes there. The masters living most of the year distant from the hot and enervating fields left overseers with responsibility for getting out the crops, come what may. This situation aggravated relations between blacks and whites, already tense because of the heavy preponderance of blacks on the plantations. A petition of the South Carolina assembly to the Board of Trade in London as early as 1728 spoke of "such vast numbers of enemies, as are the Spaniards on one side, the Indians on the other and a more dreadful one amongst ourselves, viz., such vast quantities of negroes to grapple with."

There were probably more rich men in South Carolina in the 1760s than in any other colony. At the same time, the concentration of wealth in Charleston seems to have supplied an unusually strong impulse for further accumulation and display. "Their whole lives," said the *South Carolina Gazette* of the colony's leaders on the eve of the Revolution,

*are one continued Race in which everyone is endeavoring to distance all behind him; and to overtake or pass by, all before him; everyone is flying from his inferiors in Pursuit of his Superiors. ... Every Tradesman is a Merchant, every Merchant is a Gentleman, and every Gentleman one of the Noblesse. We are a Country of Gentry. ... We have no such Thing as a common People among us: Between Vanity and Fashion, the Species is utterly destroyd.*

## "Back parts" of the South

On the eve of the American Revolution, about 250,000 persons—runaway slaves and servants, recent immigrants and migrants from the tidewater, and others—had displaced most of the aborigines of the Chesapeake back country and the "back parts" of South Carolina and Georgia.

Although the entire back country at first offered a paradise for hunter and trapper, a mixed subsistence agriculture producing cereals, potatoes, fruits, and meat, as well as flax and hemp, gradually developed in the Chesapeake hinterlands. Soon small market centers emerged along the main routes and at the ferry crossings, and even before midcentury such thriving crossroads communities as Fredericksburg and Hagerstown in Maryland (dominated by the German newcomers), and Martinsburg and Winchester in Virginia, and Charlotte in North Carolina (where the Scotch-Irish prevailed) had been built, each with its grist mills, country stores, bakers, masons, and other artisans. Yet rough conditions continued to breed rough manners.

The back parts of the Carolina country were more isolated and much rougher even than those of the Chesapeake region. It must have been particularly hard on settlers fresh from Ulster or German villages to spend lonely years in a country still ringing with the cries of wolves and panthers. Malaria was endemic here and only added to the difficulty of facing the prospect of unending labor to clear the land. Many settlers soon fell back into the nomadic life from which civilization had worked for centuries to raise mankind, some becoming herdsmen of wild swine and cattle, often stolen from the red men. Itinerant clergymen reported with dismay how the people in this region dwelt together in "Concubinage, swapping their wives as Cattel, and living in a State of Nature, more irregularly and unchastely than the Indians." A few, nevertheless, made fortunes out of meat and skins and tallow, forming a regular back-country gentry living on the most extensive cattle ranges on the entire mainland.

Gradually, tidewater institutions, both legal and political, were imposed on the Maryland and Virginia back country, although not without resistance. Antagonism to Charleston domination in hinterland South Carolina and Georgia was even stronger. Throughout the eighteenth century, the back parts of these colonies complained frequently of the "mixt Multitidue" of "white-collar parasites" from Charleston, the "mercenary tricking Attorneys, Clerks, and other little Officials," who came to prey upon them. "Finding ... they were only amus'd and trifled with," they said at last, "all Confidence of the Poor in the Great is destroy'd and ... will never exist again."

### Pennsylvania grandees and grumblers

During the eighteenth century the Middle colonies formed the most heterogeneous part of British North America. Pennsylvania, the newest, quickly became the largest and most diversified of these colonies. By 1755, Philadelphia, with 28,000 inhabitants, had passed Boston for first place among colonial cities.

Though Quakers no longer were a majority in Philadelphia, Quaker merchants comprised

the city's wealthiest group and dominated the whole settlement. The Quakers' religious beliefs, like the Puritans' inspired the thrift, industry, and reliability essential to business success. The persecution of the Friends for their beliefs both in Europe and America had scattered them over the western world, a circumstance they also turned to commercial advantage. "The intelligence which they received through their correspondence and from itinerant 'public Friends' ... from Nova Scotia to Curaçao and from Hamburg to Lisbon," writes F. B. Tolles, the historian of colonial Quaker life, "was chiefly concerned with prices current and the prosperity of Truth."

The industrious farmers Penn brought to the back country of his colony supplied Philadelphia merchants with excellent grain and other staples for export and a thriving market for imported goods. Philadelphia shipyards

*Philadelphia grandees kept elaborate carriages to carry them from the metropolis to their country estates, like the one shown here belonging to Isaac Norris, reproduced from a drawing of 1717.*

The Historical Society of Pennsylvania

ISAAC NORRIS
hif
Howfe
at
FAIRHILL
MDCCXVII

turned out vessels the equal of any in the world, and their captains were second to none, especially in evading the British Navigation Acts.

Before the end of the seventeenth century, rich Quaker merchants had already begun to turn Anglican in order to escape from having to report their private affairs publicly at the Friends' meetings. Others soon became known as "wet Quakers," a term whose origin is unknown but whose meaning was clear; they had grown too sophisticated to be true believers and had fallen off from their religious observances. Still others, drawn perhaps by their traditional attachment to "Laborious Handicrafts," became involved with Newtonian science and experimentation. Such men frequently became Deists, for whom God was but the "Heavenly Engineer." Far from unknown among the educated planters of Virginia and the intellectuals of New England, Deism flourished in Philadelphia. Its greatest New World apostle was Philadelphia's leading citizen, Ben Franklin.

The liberal government Penn had created for his settlement was, by the early years of the eighteenth century, already on the way to being corrupted by his absentee successors at the expense of the local assembly. After 1740 the struggle quickened between the proprietary party (which stood for centralized authority in the hands of the governor and council) and the popular party (composed of city merchants and property-holding farmers). Liberal suffrage laws and the support of the German element enabled the antiproprietary Quaker party to outmaneuver the Penns' deputies.

For a time, the assembly enjoyed the confidence of all sections of the colony. But in 1754 its failure to protect the frontier from Indian raids the frontiersmen themselves had inspired by land grabbing and violence brought the assembly under attack. The Pennsylvania frontier continued right up to the Revolution to be the scene of bloodshed as the "thirst for large tracts of land . . . prevailed with a singular rage" among the grandees and the hunger for space at the red man's expense remained unappeased among the frontier settlers.

## Progress in New Jersey and New York

Travelers passing through New Jersey in the eighteenth century sometimes stopped long enough to comment on its natural beauty, its prosperity, or the succulence of its oysters. But there was little more to detain the curious, who usually hastened on to New York. Jerseyites often felt the same way about their settlement. In the 1750s about 70,000 people lived in New Jersey, and many of them looked upon it as a "keg tapped at both ends," the colony transporting its surplus hemp, grain, flax, hay, and Indian corn either to New York or Philadelphia for shipment overseas.

Nature endowed New York City with the finest harbor in the Atlantic world, yet its growth was far slower than that of Philadelphia, Boston, or Charleston. Patroon control of the Hudson River Valley and Indian control of the interior were partly responsible for New York's low state. Until 1720, the pirate taint also held back the development of legitimate trade. New York merchants liked pirate goods, which they could buy cheap and sell dear. A pirate rendezvous, however, offered no attraction to legitimate captains and shippers who could easily ply an active trade elsewhere. Early in the 1700s, New York's governor pressed London for vessels swift enough to "destroye these vermin who have hitherto made New York their nest of safety." But a quarter of a century passed before effective action was taken.

At midcentury, New York City boasted 13,000 inhabitants, many of them living in houses built, as a visitor then said, "after the Dutch model with their gravell ends fronting the street." Otherwise, the city had begun to lose many of its Dutch features, and the Dutch language itself was less commonly heard.

Having noticed the decline of Dutch influence in New York City, travelers sailing north by sloop were the more sharply struck by its persistence in the Hudson Valley. The voyage up the Hudson was punctuated by stops at small settlements like Poughkeepsie. Long before Washington Irving exploited the romance and mystery of this region, visitors experienced delicious shudders as they surveyed the solitary river scenery "where nothing presents but huge precipices and inaccessible steeps, where foot of man never was." At the end of this scenic route lay Albany, where the Dutch language remained the predominant one as late as the 1740s.

Exposed to Indian raiders from French Canada until the British dislodged the French in 1763, colonial Albany kept the look of a frontier outpost. Wooded palisades enclosed the town. At its center stood a square stone fortress, but the domestic architecture was comfortable enough.

From the start of the eighteenth century, British governors of New York, emulating the Dutch, rewarded their favorites with land grants ranging from 50,000 to a million acres in the Hudson Valley. Such owners sometimes paid nothing but a token tax on their property and thus had small incentive to sell or lease. German, Scotch-Irish, and other squatters, however, took advantage of the unpatrolled country. Between 1720 and 1756 New York's population grew from 30,000 to 85,000, much of the increase occurring up the Hudson. When, in later years, the patroons tried to collect rents from families that had squatted there for generations, they were forcibly resisted.

### Eighteenth-century New England

Eighteenth-century Boston was regarded by many as the most impressive and the most English city in the colonies. Many roads led to Boston, but the most common way from the Middle colonies, or at least from New York, was to sail out Long Island Sound to New London, Connecticut, or to cross over from Long Island itself by ferry. From New London, most travelers would stop first at Newport, Rhode Island, the fifth largest city in the colonies, and one already renowned among vacationists for its pleasing and healthful climate. Besides the tourist trade, the city thrived on the slave trade.

Newport was the home of one of America's first artists, Robert Feke, whose portraits tell us so much about the values and aspirations of the New England and Pennsylvania aristocracy. In Peter Harrison, the town could claim the most distinguished American architect, who in the 1750s introduced the classical temple form that was eventually adopted everywhere in the colonies. King's Chapel in Boston, completed in 1754, is perhaps Harrison's most famous structure, but other fine examples of his work are Christ Church in Cambridge, Massachusetts, and the Touro Synagogue in Newport itself.

The slave trade, although no worse in Rhode Island than elsewhere, seemed only to confirm for outsiders the outcast tradition of the colony. Dr. Alexander Hamilton, on his visit to Rhode Island in 1744, decided with his usual tolerance that, with its "rural scenes and pretty frank girls," it was the most agreeable place he had struck in his travels; but he had to admit that the people had "as bad a character for chicane and disingenuity as any of our American Colonies."

The city of Boston, if not yet the "hub of the universe," was the heart of Massachusetts, as Massachusetts was the heart of New England. Even prejudiced observers from other sections, who came with preconceived notions about the "canting" Yankees, were amazed by the graciousness of Boston's upper-class life and the comfort of the rest of the people. North of Boston such ports as Salem, Marblehead, and Gloucester, which much later were to supply many of the "proper Bostonians" of the Victorian era, were already enjoying a thriving trade. But the capital of the commonwealth, with over 15,000 people in 1750, the best harbor, and the biggest hinterland markets, stood far ahead of the other towns and was growing faster.

In the seventeenth century Boston's merchants had been quick to take all the advantage they could of England's wars with the Dutch, which diverted the vessels of the two greatest commercial nations from the world's trading routes. Early in the eighteenth century, peace rather than war gave the strongest impetus to Boston's prosperity, especially the Peace of Utrecht of 1713 (see p. 77). In the West Indies, the growing demand for all necessities sent prices and profits soaring. By the terms of the Peace of Utrecht, Britain obtained Newfoundland and Nova Scotia from France, and the vast fisheries of their waters were opened to Yankee enterprise. At the same time, Nantucket whalers began to sail far from their home waters on long voyages to the Arctic Ocean and Brazilian shores. "Farm-

*The elaborate interior of Peter Harrison's King's Chapel, Boston's leading Anglican church, with its double Corinthian columns supporting vaulted ceiling, contrasts sharply with seventeenth-century Congregational meeting houses.*

Wayne Andrews

ing the sea," as the Yankee said, was itself procreative. The demand for more and better ships promoted such land-based businesses as rope- and sailmaking. These drew artisans from nearby and foreign towns, and their growing number fostered new home and business construction and a surge of prosperity in the surrounding countryside as town populations had to be fed.

As in Pennsylvania and the South, so in Massachusetts, wealth enlarged the demands of nature. Calvin, it is true, warned the Saints "resolutely [to] exert themselves to retrench all superfluities and to restrain luxury." He particularly commanded the "elect" to "give an account of thy stewardship." But by the eighteenth century, the richest Puritans, like the richest Quakers, had moved away from the old religion to the more congenial Anglican communion, where there was no requirement to make "a public relation of their experiences." Boston's "codfish aristocracy" and its emulators in other Yankee ports now affected swords, satins, and sturdy English broadcloths as well as comfortable "colonial" homes which replaced the rude structures of pioneer days. The growing secularization so characteristic of colonial society everywhere in the eighteenth century showed itself clearly in the irreverence of life in the cities. When Cotton Mather warned a local reprobate that every time he drank rum he was selling the blood of Christ, this was the response: "Truly, Sir, when we are going to make ourselves drunk, we never think of that."

Self-indulgence gave still another impetus to trade; but Massachusetts had no staple that was wanted where the luxuries she craved originated. Problems involving the imperial navigation system only enlarged the challenge to Yankee ingenuity on the sea. In resolving their problems, Yankee merchants were not constrained by conscience or by consciousness of crime. Like others, they engaged in much illicit traffic, and some did not scruple about practicing sheer piracy. New England's most lucrative legitimate voyages involved the so-called slave-trade triangle, in which Bostonians gained their full share.

Distant commerce always involved a strong element of risk. To reduce the risk, Yankee

71

merchants often installed their brothers, sons, and in-laws as their agents in foreign lands. In Britain itself they turned, when they could find them, to relatives who had resisted the lures of the New World. Family connections failing, they, like the Quakers sought out their coreligionist. As a last recourse, in Dutch or Spanish, French or Portuguese ports, they employed their own countrymen to look after their interests. Characteristically, family businesses were enlarged and family ties multiplied by intermarriage among mercantile families. In this way, wealth was consolidated; yet a strong start could be made with little capital and the established elite itself was pleased to make room for proven competitors, especially when it had daughters to provide for.

North, south, and west of Boston new settlements were springing up everywhere in the first third of the eighteenth century, and to conservatives they displayed a shocking disregard for authority. These "ungospelized" plantations, according to Cotton Mather, were "the very Brothel houses of Satan." But to the outsider, rural New England villages still seemed remarkable for their tidiness and decency.

Living frugally in simple frame houses, tilling an indifferent soil, the New England farmers developed into the tough, uncommunicative (though sometimes garrulous) American stereotype. Travelers thought them too democratic and careless of social distinctions. "They seem to be a good substantial Kind of Farmers," remarked one visitor, "but there is no break in their Society; their Government, Religion, and Manners all tend to support an equality. Whoever brings in your Victuals sits down and chats to you." When they did "chat," moreover, their superior education, compared to that of rustics farther south, soon became evident. One observer from the South seemed surprised that these people, who looked "rather more like clowns, than the riff-raff of our Maryland planters," should discuss matters "that in our parts would be like Greek, Hebrew, or Arabick."

## III   The spirit of provincial politics

### Bonds of social intercourse

When John Adams of Massachusetts, while attending the Continental Congress in Philadelphia in 1774, first saw in the flesh well-horsed, saber-rattling southerners with their flashy body slaves, he suffered the greatest anxiety of his life. He hastened to write home to his wife how he dreaded "the consequences of this dissimilitude of character" between Yankees and planters, and added that, "without the utmost caution on both sides, and the most considerate forbearance with one another, ... they will certainly be fatal."

Long before Adams's unsettling experience it had become apparent to many that a country so diverse geographically and culturally as the American mainland colonies had become was not likely to unify itself. Idiom, custom, and economic interest divided the provinces. The vague definition of boundaries in the colonial charters was the source of many conflicts, which grew especially acrimonious in the middle of the eighteenth century when great land speculators from different colonies staked out overlapping claims. Such disputes eventually turned colony against colony in feuds that later helped drag out the Revolutionary War and postponed the establishment of a permanent federal government once independence had been declared. The movement of speculators and settlers westward also stirred the Indians to stronger resistance, and the colonies again fell out among themselves in trying to meet the recurrent challenges. Other issues involving the exchange of currency, piracy and smuggling, religion and politics, further soured colonial relationships—to such a degree that many saw the stabilizing control of the mother country as the only check on anarchy.

And yet, unifying influences also were at work, especially among colonial leaders who despite their differences shared many interests, beliefs, experiences, and aspirations. Waterways and roads brought the businessmen of New York, Philadelphia, Boston, and Charleston into a vital economic network. Well-to-do families paid visits to distant kin; Quakers and Jews sought out their scattered coreligionists. The colleges at Princeton, New Haven, and Cambridge attracted students from the South and the West Indies as well as from neighboring colonies. Fraternal societies, which were organized in the principal cities as early as the 1730s, welcomed members from afar; Washington, Franklin, and other colonial leaders were Masons even before their revolutionary activities brought them together. Finally, colonists read one another's newspapers, circular letters, sermons, pamphlets, and almanacs. The literate colonial had at his disposal a variety of information on matters outside his immediate sphere of interest—political, cultural, and economic—that linked him with the destiny of his continent. When the time came, colonial spokesmen were able to appeal to a set of widely shared beliefs and experiences, especially among a few thousand leading families, a few hundred in each colony, whose remarkable gains in wealth and power underlay their more subtle claims to primacy.

## The seat of political power

Nowhere was the emergence of a colonial elite more evident than in the structure and tendency of colonial politics. In each of the colonies in the mid-eighteenth century, the governor nominally was at the head of the government. Only in Connecticut and Rhode Island was he elected by the legislature. In Maryland and Pennsylvania he continued to be appointed by the absentee proprietor in England. In all the other colonies, including Georgia after 1752, he was appointed by the king. The governor himself appointed his council, which formed the upper house of the legislature. The lower house, usually called the assembly, represented those qualified electors who bothered to exercise their franchise. Local government differed from colony to colony; but even in Virginia, where the governor, like the king at home, appointed the justices of the peace, the most important local officers, they firmly resisted interference once they had their commissions.

The governor's main strength lay in his right to veto provincial legislation. If he was a man of acumen and ability, he could of course influence the legislators to act in conformity with the king's policy before abrasive vetoes became necessary. But success in managing the elected representatives depended on confidence between governor and legislator, and confidence dwindled by midcentury.

The assembly's main strength lay in its control of appropriations, including those for the governor's salary and for carrying out relevant parliamentary measures. In the eighteenth century, most of the colonial assemblies, like Parliament in England, used their control of the purse to seek control of the entire government. The leading families, in turn, used their wealth and standing to control the assemblies.

Two conditions helped perpetuate oligarchic power. One was the limitation of the franchise in practically all the colonies to those with considerable property, preferably in land. In some colonies, to be sure, such as Massachusetts and Pennsylvania, property qualifications were low enough and land ownership common enough to insure a substantial electorate, more or less representative of the whole adult population. But even in the North, as in New York and Connecticut, for example, many could not meet the property qualifications; in the South, the requirements usually were higher than in the North, and eligible voters relatively fewer. Certain colonies also had religious qualifications for vot-

73

74

ing, but with the exception of the almost universal disfranchisement of Catholics and Jews, these qualifications tended to be questioned less and less frequently where property qualifications could be met. So-called plural voting also was common. In Virginia and elsewhere, those who met the specific property qualification in each of two or more counties could vote two or more times; to make it easier for the gentry to exercise this privilege where they held land, election dates often were staggered. Property qualifications for officeholding, in turn, were usually much higher than for the franchise itself. A member of the South Carolina assembly, for example, had to own at least 500 acres of land, 10 slaves, or other property worth at least £1000.

The second objective condition tending to perpetuate oligarchic control was the underrepresentation of new inland settlements in the assemblies. The assemblies themselves often refused to establish new counties and towns in distant regions and to reapportion seats in the legislature in accordance with changing population density. Inland regions sometimes were happy to be left without the responsibility for paying for county or town government or for representation in the assembly and often did not complain of neglect until crises involving Indians or taxation aroused them.

These objective characteristics of colonial politics may have made it more difficult to overthrow the oligarchs in times of stress; but their rule tended to be sustained by even stronger sanctions arising from the popular recognition of merit based on family and fortune.

Colonial history is well marked with local rebellions against the ruling oligarchs. One of the most persistent issues between them, on the one hand, and businessmen on the make and the general population, on the other, was the supply of money. The primary need for currency among the small farmers who made up by far the majority of the white population everywhere was for taxes, which in their judgment—and usually they were right—were both too high and unfairly apportioned. At the same time, many such farmers along with enterprising business and professional men,

noting the expansive tendency of the entire colonial economy, became increasingly engaged in trade, and also in land speculation to a degree commensurate with their aspirations if not their means. Since money, or at any rate credit in the form of liberal issues of negotiable currency, was the food of trade and the drink of speculation, such men naturally sought a plentiful supply of it, far above the quantity needed to meet mere tax obligations and other current debts.

The normal scarcity of specie in the colonies was aggravated by the mercantilist system which drained gold and silver to the mother country. Thus it became the common practice for those seeking financial assistance to demand more and more paper money. Often enough their demands were heeded. But since paper money had a tendency to be overissued and thus to decline in value, easy-money policies usually were reversed at what appeared to be the most inconvenient times. At such times, taxes, interest, rent, and loans would go unpaid, and creditors trying to collect what was due them might be tarred and feathered and chased from the debtors' vicinity at gun point.

A classic battle over the currency supply occurred in Massachusetts in 1740 and 1741, when many enterprising colonists, after an agitation of nearly twenty years, sought to establish a land bank to lend money in the form of "bills of credit," or paper notes, on the security of land mortgages. The realization that the Indian menace on the frontiers had receded to such an extent that such mortgages on western lands at last had become safe investments gave them new hope at this time.

Unfortunately for the land bank promoters, their opponents among the richest Boston merchants and creditors in the Governor's circle were on the alert. These men had a constitutional loathing for paper money, especially if unsecured by specie or by their own high character. To undermine the land bank they immediately set up a silver bank, with notes to be redeemable only in specie. The advocates of each plan sought government approval; and while the land bank gained much support in the assembly elected in May 1740, Governor Jonathan Belcher and his council backed the silver scheme. Within six months their campaign of abuse had wholly discredited land-bank paper. Early the next year, on their application, Parliament prohibited land banks in Massachusetts. Evenhandedly, the London authorities extended the prohibition to the silver bank as well, a move Boston's leaders could bear with resignation since their principal goal in establishing the silver bank had been the destruction of the land bank, a goal now fully gained. Their success, however, led to such widespread discontent that their friend Belcher was recalled before the year 1741 ended. The destruction of the Massachusetts land bank, John Adams observed a generation later, "raised a greater ferment in the province than the stamp-act did" in 1765.

Conflicts over the money supply, taxation, and debt were not necessarily sectional ones, although they became most acute where the "back parts" felt the weight of tidewater and town leaders. Other political conflicts were specifically sectional in origin. One of the most persistent of them arose over the complaints of new settlers on the moving frontier against the failure of the provincial governments to protect them from the Indians, the French, and the Spanish. The failure of the provincial governments to provide passable roads to markets was a second source of sectional conflict. A third was the failure of such governments to set up courts in the back country and thus save the farmers the heavy cost of several days' travel and neglect of crops to have even minor controversies settled. A fourth was the collection of tithes for the established churches, which had few ministers and few communicants in the wilderness. The failure to extend representation and the suffrage to back-country residents grew into a major issue largely because of the gentry's reluctance to correct the back country's other grievances.

Courtesy Wadsworth Atheneum, Hartford, and Mrs. Norman J. Marsh

*Governor William Shirley of Massachusetts, who succeeded Governor Belcher in 1741 and proved adept enough to hold his position until 1760.*

Yet the colonial rank and file rarely challenged patrician claims to political place and power. Probably a fourth of the white population of the colonies was illiterate; probably a fifth of those who could read and write knew little or no English. Many others used it awkwardly. Most rustics, moreover, illiterate or not, could think of no more unnerving experience than having to address constituents in public meetings or to take effective places in legislative bodies. City artisans, shopkeepers, and laborers no doubt shared the misgivings of their country cousins. By and large, the common run of voters were still proud to be represented by the great men of their neighborhood or of the colony as a whole. Thus they returned to office generation after generation of Byrds, Carters, Harrisons, and Washingtons in Virginia; of Van Rensselaers, Schuylers, and Livingstons in New York; of

Logans, Norrises, Pembertons, and Dickinsons in Pennsylvania. Even in Massachusetts, where the suffrage qualifications were light and educational levels and literacy higher than elsewhere in America, Hutchinsons, Hancocks, Olivers, Bowdoins, and Brattles all were repeatedly returned to rule. A popular political genius like Sam Adams in Massachusetts, the first great rabble-rouser in the colonies, developed a "machine" of his own, known at the outset of the Revolution as the Caucus Club. But even an Adams made little progress against the oligarchs until they wanted his support to meet the British challenge.

## IV  Exclusion of the French

### The ancien régime in Canada

With the elimination of the Dutch from New Netherlands in 1664 and the establishment of Carolina as a buffer against the Spanish in the 1670s, only France remained as a menace to the English colonies on the American mainland.

For a century and more after the establishment of Quebec and Montreal (see p. 22), French explorers had pushed west and south ever more deeply into the continent. One of the early leaders of this movement was the ambitious empire builder Jean Talon, who in 1672 named Louis Joliet to test rumors of the Mississippi flowing westward to the Pacific. Later that year he agreed to permit the Jesuit Father Marquette to accompany Joliet "as chaplain and Christian spokesman." In the spring of 1673, Joliet and Marquette reached the Mississippi and proceeded downstream as far as present-day Arkansas, where they learned from the Indians that the great river "discharged . . . not to the east in Virginia . . . or to the west in California," but emptied into the Gulf of Mexico. Fearful of falling into Spanish hands, they then turned back.

Nine years later the most intrepid of French explorers, Robert Cavelier, Sieur de La Salle, completed the journey all the way down the Mississippi to the Gulf and on April 19, 1682, claimed for the King of France "possession of that river, of all the rivers that enter it and of all the country watered by them." Following La Salle's exploit, France bolstered her claims by building a line of forts from the Great Lakes to New Orleans. The northern anchor of this system was Fort Detroit, completed in 1699. In 1718, the fort was completed at New Orleans, the southernmost citadel of the French North American empire.

France, it is often said, had many advantages over Britain in the contest for North America. Among them were (1) the absolute power of the governor-general of Canada, especially in emergencies, in contrast to the multiplicity of authorities in the British colonies; (2) the professionalism of the permanent military forces in Canada, in contrast to the improvised citizen militias of the British provinces; and (3) the success of French missionaries in converting the natives and of French administrators and fur traders in holding their affections and allegiance, in contrast to the hatred with which the red man viewed the permanent British settlers who were depriving them of their ancient lands.

But on analysis these alleged French advantages appear dubious. The governor-general of Canada in fact shared power with the "intendant" (really the King's independent spy on the governor) and the resident bishop; and since each depended for his authority on rivals for authority at home, New France was always riven by petty jealousies and selfish cliques. The good relations of the French with the Indians, moreover, were preserved at the cost of erecting solid and self-sufficient communities in the New World upon which their professional military forces might depend. For generations the domestic food supply of New France remained poorer even than that of the Indians before the white man came. The vaunted professional soldiers of New France had always to look to the home country and on neighboring New England for sustenance.

Canadian industry was even more backward than its agriculture, which meant that the regime had to rely on ocean-going vessels to bring in munitions, trading goods, and other hardware. But the only navigable entry to French warehouses in Montreal and Quebec was by way of the St. Lawrence, which was either frozen or clogged with ice floes half the year. This inadequate supply line from the sea made it easy in times of crisis for the British navy and British and Yankee privateers to offset nominal French military superiority.

Besides its internal problems, the French regime in Quebec faced other difficulties. Compared, for example, with the lush sugar islands of the West Indies, Canada ranked low in the French scheme of overseas empire. Louis XIV and his successors considered Canada an Arctic waste, little better than a place of exile for aristocratic busybodies and other nuisances. All the more astonishing, then, are the successes these outcasts and a handful of devoted empire builders achieved in the distant reaches of North America.

## Europe's wars and American empire

The series of world wars that ultimately settled the future of North America in favor of the British and the Americans began in Europe in 1689, when William III became king of England with a strong personal motive for warring against Louis XIV of France (see p. 53). Known in Europe as the War of the League of Augsburg and in America as King William's War, this struggle dragged on until 1697.

William's League got none the worst of the fighting on the Continent, but the French had all the best of it in America. At the same time, their success alerted other parties to the emerg-

ing universal conflict to the need to strengthen their New World positions at France's expense. The Iroquois, the most powerful and strategically situated of the Indian nations, and once friendly to the English settlers, had grown estranged from them because of their aggressive occupation of the land. But fearful now of French military aggression, they pledged themselves once more to their old friends. It was on this pledge that English claims to the Ohio and Mississippi Valleys came to rest when the Iroquois had become too weak to defend themselves. Americans in the Carolinas, meanwhile, pushed their own hunting and trading activities to the very shores of the Mississippi below St. Louis. To check them and the French in Louisiana, Spain strengthened her outposts in Texas, New Mexico, and West Florida, and in 1696 established a base at Pensacola, Florida.

The peace of 1697 came to a violent end in 1702. Two years earlier, the Spanish king had died without an heir and Louis XIV had grasped the opportunity to extend Bourbon influence to the Iberian Peninsula by installing his grandson on the throne. William III, backing a candidate of his own, allied himself with other continental powers to expel Louis' protégé. With an eye to the balance of power in the New World, moreover, they agreed among themselves, as one of their treaties said, "especially . . . that the French shall never come into possession of the Spanish Indies nor be permitted . . . to navigate there for the purpose of carrying on trade." When William died in 1702, his successor Queen Anne, persisting in his policies, fought France and Spain for eleven bitter years in the conflict known in Europe as the War of the Spanish Succession, in America as Queen Anne's War.

In this war, the French and their Spanish allies eventually were defeated everywhere and Spain henceforth declined as a world power. The Peace of Utrecht of 1713 confirmed the Bourbons' occupation of the Spanish throne, which remained in their family until 1931. But in the New World, France surrendered the rich island of St. Christopher in the West Indies to her Protestant enemy, confirmed British supremacy over Hudson Bay, and yielded Acadia as well. Above all, the

French recognized the Iroquois as British subjects and the Iroquois empire as a British domain. Britain also won commercial concessions from both France and Spain that boosted her own as well as American trade with the Spanish Main and Spanish Caribbean islands.

For a generation after 1713 internal problems occupied both France and Britain, and they were content to avoid open war. In 1715 Louis XIV died, leaving his bankrupt and starving countrymen to recover as best they could under his five-year-old grandson, Louis XV. Actually, under Louis's Regent, the Duke of Orléans, and for a time under Louis himself, France did well. Her aristocrats reclaimed many of the rights they had surrendered to the absolute "Sun King"; and young nobles like the Baron de Montesquieu joined commoners like Voltaire in learning to admire if not ape British political institutions. French trade and industry also flourished, to such a degree indeed that the political frustrations of the increasingly prosperous but powerless middle class help explain the ferocity of the Revolution which so shocked the world in 1789.

A year before Louis XIV's death, Queen Anne died in England. Her successor was George I, Elector of Hanover, the closest Stuart "cousin" who was not a Catholic. Many British Tories preferred the "pretender," James III, and in 1715 (and again in 1745 when "Bonnie Prince Charlie" had succeeded to James's role) they rebelled against the new royal family. George I and George II, neither of whom learned English, spent little time away from their Hanover estates. The Whigs, however, were committed to the succession. While the "Whig Oligarchy" thus was kept busy quieting rebellion, it was also left free to develop these institutions of parliamentary (aristocratic) supremacy which the French *philosophes* liked so much but which George III and his American colonists both were to challenge fiercely.

In British America this post-Utrecht period of relative peace, and especially the years 1721–1742 during which the great Whig, Robert Walpole, virtually governed the United Kingdom, is usually called the era of "salutary neglect." The same conditions which prompted the mother country to forgo war with her rivals also bade her leave her colonies to their own devices. It was under this regime that colonial life flowered.

Even the period of "salutary neglect" was broken from time to time by violent confrontations. The British took such gluttonous advantage of Spain's commercial concessions of 1713 that the Spanish organized a special Caribbean coast guard, manned by the roughest pirates they could enlist. In 1739 a British officer named Captain Jenkins was haled before Parliament by the "war party" that was growing in opposition to Spanish manhandling of British seamen. In a little box he carried a carefully preserved human ear, which he claimed a Spanish officer had cut from his head as a bloody warning. This dramatic tableau created a sensation, and Britain promptly embarked on "The War of Jenkins' Ear." While disaster followed disaster for the British, no decision was reached until a new general European war broke out in 1745, this time over the Austrian succession.

After the War of the Spanish Succession, the French built a mighty fortress at Louisbourg on Cape Breton Island, just north of Acadia, which commanded the entrance to the Gulf of St. Lawrence. In the War of the Austrian Succession, or King George's War (1745–1748), Massachusetts forces assaulted Louisbourg and, to everyone's surprise, including their own, they managed to capture it. Colonial love for the mother country was hardly warmed by British restoration of Louisbourg to the French in the Peace of Aix-la-Chapelle, which ended this latest struggle. In return, Britain received Madras in India.

### The French and Indian War

The Treaty of Aix-la-Chapelle was more a truce than a permanent settlement. Even before it was signed, both the French and the British had begun preparations for a final showdown. In 1747, with the formation of the Ohio Company of Virginia, Britain had embarked on a shrewd program of encouraging colonial land speculators to stake out huge tracts in the Ohio Valley, "inasmuch as nothing can more effectively tend to defeat the dangerous designs of the French." In 1749, the governor of Canada sent his own representatives to occupy the valley, and soon other Frenchmen followed to work out a system of military defenses. Governor Dinwiddie of Virginia, an investor in the Ohio Company, caught wind of French activity in 1753 and ordered young George Washington to travel west with a protest. When this mission failed, Washington was sent out the next year with a small force and orders to halt the French. This mission ran up against the newly erected French Fort Duquesne at the forks of the Ohio, the site of modern Pittsburgh. Washington proceeded to build his own Fort Necessity at nearby Great Meadows, but in July was forced to capitulate to a French attack upon it. Although the formal declaration of war between the French and the English did not come until 1756, actual fighting had already begun, appropriately enough, in the New World.

The extension of French fort building in the West caused the Privy Council in London to look to its own strength in America. This rested heavily on the Iroquois; but the British now sensed the growing discontent of their native allies in the face of such expansive policies as that which prompted the creation of the Ohio Company itself. In an attempt to restore Iroquois confidence, the Privy Council called for a meeting at Albany, New York, in June 1754, at which delegates from all the northern colonies were to meet with Iroquois and other Indian leaders. At the Albany Congress the Iroquois accepted lavish British gifts but made no promises. Their growing respect and fear of French military strength counseled caution.

It was at the Albany Congress that Benjamin Franklin and others proposed the first general "Plan of Union" to the mainland colonies. The delegates accepted this plan for a general colonial government superimposed on the individual provinces. But when the provincial legislatures themselves and the British as well rejected the far-sighted proposal, the plan died. "The Assemblies," Franklin wrote, "... thought there was too much *prerogative* in it, and in England it was judged to have too much of the *democratic.*"

Neither the French nor the British welcomed a resumption of the world conflict; in fact, the Duke of Newcastle, the First Secretary of State, hoped at first that the war might be localized. Seeking to gain his objective with a great show of strength, in April 1755, he sent General Edward Braddock and 1400 regulars to America to level Fort Duquesne. Braddock was to be assisted by 450 colonials under Washington. Unfortunately for British hopes, Braddock's entire force was ambushed and savagely mauled in July by a force of French

**79**

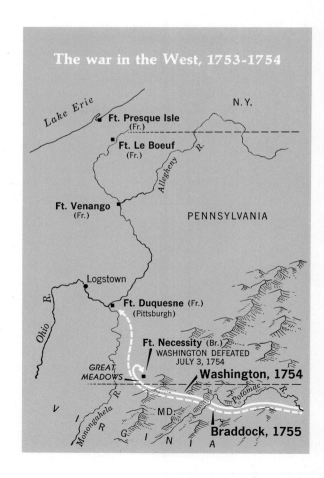

The war in the West, 1753-1754

and Indians on the Monongahela River about eight miles below the fort, and Braddock himself was mortally wounded. Braddock's defeat opened the eyes of the colonials, whose regard for British redcoats declined swiftly thereafter. It also weakened the waning prestige of the British among the Indians.

By 1756 the war that had started in the American wilderness spread over the continent of Europe. To check the ambitions of Frederick the Great of Prussia, France now allied herself with Austria. The better to keep down France, Britain in turn allied herself with Frederick. France and Austria opened the European phase of the war with great land victories; but when William Pitt became chief minister in Britain in 1758, he so heavily subsidized Frederick's armies that they were able to withstand the enemy on land. Britain herself, meanwhile, pursued the war on the sea and in America. For Pitt the central strategic objective was the conquest of Canada and the capture of the American interior. To this end he used British superiority at sea to strike hardest at the two focal points of French power—Louisbourg and Quebec.

In 1758 the British recaptured Louisbourg, the key to the St. Lawrence River and the Atlantic fisheries, and a standing threat to New England. The event was celebrated with

great bonfires in London, Philadelphia, Boston, and New York. In the same year George Washington, now on the staff of Brigadier John Forbes, had the satisfaction at last of taking part in the capture of Fort Duquesne, now known as Pittsburgh. With Frederick turning the tide on the Continent, Clive began to tame the French in India. The climax of the fighting came in September 1759, when the brilliant young James Wolfe, after bringing a large army up the St. Lawrence from Louisbourg, stormed the Heights of Abraham outside Quebec and took the city from a smaller force under General Montcalm. Both Wolfe and Montcalm were killed in the battle, but Wolfe lived long enough to know that he had won Canada for the empire. Since the British were also winning on the sea, in the West Indies, in India, and in the American West, the crisis in the war had passed. "Some time ago," said Pitt in the midst of all these triumphs, "I would have been content to bring France to her knees, now I will not rest till I have laid her on her back." Thus the war dragged on until 1763.

By the Treaty of Paris, concluded in February, 1763, Britain won from France all of Canada and all the great interior east of the Mississippi except for the port of New Orleans. France (to the dismay of Pitt, who had been dismissed by George III) retained fishing rights on the Newfoundland banks and two small islands as fishing bases there. Britain also returned to her the captured West Indies islands, Martinique and Guadeloupe. Spain, in turn, surrendered East and West Florida to the British in exchange for Cuba, which the British had captured from her in 1762. By a separate treaty in 1762 France yielded to Spain, as compensation for her assistance in the war, all French territories west of the Mississippi as well as New Orleans.

Even before the negotiations leading to the Treaty of Paris, British statesmen realized that they could not have both the rich sugar island of Guadeloupe and the vast empty wilderness of Canada—that if they demanded both, the

Campaigns in the North, 1755-1760

Captured by British

Wolfe 1759

C A N A D A

Quebec
Montreal
St. Lawrence R.
L. Champlain
Crown Point
Ft. Ticonderoga
L. Ontario
Ft. Niagara
L. Erie
Boston
Ft. Duquesne
Louisbourg
NOVA SCOTIA
British 1755
Atlantic Ocean

French would continue the fight. Perhaps most influential in the decision to keep Canada and renounce Guadeloupe was the pressure exerted by plantation owners in the British West Indies, who feared the competition they would encounter from Guadeloupe's sugar if that island were brought into the empire. But more general considerations also had their effect. Most important among these was the rise in importance of Britain's mainland colonies, especially the rapidly growing Middle colonies and New England, as markets for British goods. Heretofore, the American empire had been valued mainly as a source of raw materials—tobacco, rice, and indigo in the mainland South, sugar in the West Indies; in 1698, seven-eighths of Britain's American trade had been with these staple-producing regions. By the 1720s one-fourth and by the 1760s more than two-fifths of Britain's American exports were going to areas north of Maryland. Removing France from adjacent Canada, even at the cost of another sugar island, seemed sound policy.

During the argument over the treaty, it was asked whether Canada would not some day revolt and win its independence of Britain. It was also said that if the French were expelled from Canada, the American colonists themselves would no longer feel so dependent on the mother country for protection. Benjamin Franklin, then in London as a colonial agent, wrote a pamphlet on the subject in which he argued for retaining Canada as part of the British American empire. The idea of independence Franklin brushed aside. If the North American colonists had been incapable of uniting against the French and Indians, he asked, was there any likelihood that they would unite against "their own nation" which "they love much more than they love one another?" A union among the colonies, he went on, "is not merely improbable, it is impossible."

But here Franklin added an explanation which, though he did not mean it as a warning, might well have been taken as such: "When I say such a union is impossible, I mean without the most grievous tyranny and oppression."

## For further reading

M. L. Hansen, *The Atlantic Migration 1607–1860* (1940), is the standard account of the movement of Europeans to America before the Civil War. A. E. Smith, *Colonists in Bondage* (1947), is authoritative on white-servant immigration. Much useful material on this subject will also be found in M. W. Jernegan, *Laboring and Dependent Classes in Colonial America 1607–1783* (1931). Dietmar Rothermund, *The Layman's Progress, Religious and Political Experience in Colonial Pennsylvania 1740–1770* (1961), offers a penetrating analysis of the religious sects. Rufus Jones, *The Quakers in the American Colonies* (1911), a standard study, may be supplemented by S. V. James, *A People Among Peoples, Quaker Benevolence in Eighteenth-Century America* (1963).

On the major national groups the following older works remain invaluable: A. B. Faust, *The German Element in the United States* (2 vols., 1909); F. R. Diffenderffer, *The German Immigration into Pennsylvania through the Port of Philadelphia 1700-1775,* bound with his *The Redemptioners* (1900); and H. J. Ford, *The Scotch-Irish in America* (1915). R. J. Dickson, *Ulster Emigration to Colonial America 1718-1775* (1966), is especially valuable for conditions in North Ireland. F. J. Turner, *The Frontier in American History* (1920), is the classic account of the penetration of the interior.

J. H. Franklin, *From Slavery to Freedom, a History of Negro Americans* (1967), the standard work with an up-to-date bibliography, covers the colonial period in detail. Elizabeth Donnan, ed., *Documents Illustrative of the History of the Slave Trade to America* (4 vols., 1930-1935), is the prime source. P. D. Curtin, *The Atlantic Slave Trade, A Census* (1969), supplants all previous work on numbers and scope of this traffic. W. E. B. DuBois, *The Suppression of the African Slave-Trade to the United States of America* (1896), is valuable for many aspects of the "institution." D. B. Davis, *The Problem of Slavery in Western Culture* (1966), and W. D. Jordan, *White Over Black, American Attitudes toward the Negro 1550-1812* (1968), are indispensable modern studies.

J. T. Adams, *Provincial Society 1690-1763* (1927), is a substantial general account. See also the books by T. J. Wertenbaker cited for Chapter Two. Carl Bridenbaugh, *Myths and Realities: Societies of the Colonial South* (1952), is short, iconoclastic, and stimulating. Chesapeake society is well described in D. S. Freeman, *The Young Washington* (2 vols., 1948). On Charleston and its leadership, see M. E. Sirmans, *Colonial South Carolina, a Political History 1663-1763* (1966). V. W. Crane, *The Southern Frontier 1670-1732* (1929), is excellent on life in the interior.

Besides the works on the immigrants cited above, the following are valuable on eighteenth-century Pennsylvania: Carl and Jessica Bridenbaugh, *Rebels and Gentlemen: Philadelphia in the Age of Franklin* (1942); and F. B. Tolles, *Meeting House and Counting House* (1948). Urban life here and elsewhere is authoritatively dealt with by Carl Bridenbaugh in *Cities in the Wilderness . . . 1625-1742* (1938) and *Cities in Revolt . . . 1743-1776* (1955). Bridenbaugh, ed., *Gentleman's Progress* (1948), is the account, by Dr. Alexander Hamilton, of his trip from Maryland to New England in 1744.

New England society is adequately if not impartially covered in J. T. Adams, *Revolutionary New England*

*1691-1776* (1923). Correctives for Adam's anti-Puritan bias will be found in K. B. Murdock, *Increase Mather, the Foremost American Puritan* (1925); and Perry Miller, *The New England Mind: From Colony to Province* (1953). C. K. Shipton, *New England Life in the 18th Century* (1963), affords a vivid panorama. W. B. Weeden, *Economic and Social History of New England 1620-1789* (2 vols., 1890), remains the best survey.

Leonard Labaree, *Royal Government in America, a Study of the British Colonial System before 1783* (1930), is a comprehensive survey. T. C. Barrow, *Trade and Empire* (1967), emphasizes the central role of commerce in colonial–mother-country relations. Sectional works of importance for imperial politics include J. P. Greene, *The Quest for Power, the Lower Houses of the Assembly in the Southern Royal Colonies 1689-1776* (1963), and J. A. Schutz, *William Shirley, King's Governor of Massachusetts* (1961). The colonial franchise and representation have been thoroughly restudied in such works as R. E. Brown, *Middle-Class Democracy and the Revolution in Massachusetts 1691-1780* (1955); and Theodore Thayer, *Pennsylvania Politics and the Growth of Democracy 1740-1776* (1953). Their general conclusions about the liberality of the franchise are challenged in such works as C. S. Grant, *Democracy in the Connecticut Frontier Town of Kent* (1961), and C. S. Sydnor, *Gentlemen Freeholders, Political Practices in Washington's Virginia* (1952). The early chapters of Chilton Williamson, *American Suffrage, from Property to Democracy 1760-1860* (1960), afford a scholarly survey of colonial practice.

Two general works on exploration and settlement give much attention to the international struggle for control of North America: V. B. Holmes, *A History of the Americas From Discovery to Nationhood* (1950); and Bernard DeVoto, *The Course of Empire* (1952). The background is brilliantly set forth in W. L. Dorn, *Competition for Empire 1740-1763* (1940). Max Savelle, *The Origins of American Diplomacy, the International History of Anglo-America 1492-1763* (1967), also is outstanding. The eight volumes of Francis Parkman's classic, *France and England in North America,* first published between 1851 and 1892, have been successfully abridged in one volume, *The Parkman Reader* (1955), edited by S. E. Morison. H. H. Peckham, *The Colonial Wars 1689-1762* (1964), offers a short, scholarly account. See also, G. T. Hunt, *The Wars of the Iroquois* (1940). The most elaborate account of the French and Indian War is to be found in L. H. Gipson, *The British Empire before the American Revolution* (13 vols., 1936-1967).

# The chosen people and their visitations

*Oh yes! oh yes! oh yes!* All you the people of Christ that are here
Oppressed, Imprisoned and scurrilously derided, gather yourselves together, your Wives
and little ones, and answer to your severall Names as you shall be shipped
for his service, in the Westerne World, and more especially for planting the united
Collonies of new England. . . . *know this is the place where the Lord will create
a new Heaven, and a new Earth in, new Churches, and a new Common-wealth together.*
(Edward Johnson, Wonder-Working Providence of Sions Saviour, *1654*)

*. . . the eies of all people are uppon us; soe that if wee shall deal falsely
with our god in this worke we have undertaken and soe cause him to withdrawe his present
help from us, wee shall be made a story and a by-word through the world.*
(John Winthrop, A Modell of Christian Charity, *1630*)

*. . . hence it is the righteous God hath heightened our calamity,
and given commission to the barbarous heathen to rise up against us
. . . heerby speaking aloud to us to search and try our wayes, and turn againe unto
the Lord our God, from whom wee have departed with a great backsliding.*
(Records of . . . Massachusetts Bay, *1675*)

*An Army of Devils is horribly broke in upon the place which is the Center,
after a sort, the First-born of our English Settlements: and the Houses
of Good People there are fill'd with the doleful Shrieks of the Children and Servants,
Tormented by Invisible Hands with Tortures altogether preturnatural.*
(Cotton Mather, The Wonders of the Invisible World, *1693*)

*Religion has both a natural and moral tendency to promote
the Prosperity of a People: if Religion flourishes the country will
flourish; and we shall prosper whithersoever we turn ourselves.*
(John Hancock, Rulers Should be Benefactors, *1722*)

BRATTLE STREET CHURCH, Boston, built in 1699, earliest New England church with
tower and spire at one end. Detail of William Burgis's "View of Boston,"
1722. (Phelps Stokes Collection, New York Public Library)

Detail of the JOSEPH TAPPING GRAVESTONE, King's Chapel, Boston, 1678. (Allan I. Ludwig)

*Suppose thou heardest*
*the Devils roaring, and sawest Hell*
*gaping, and flames of everlasting*
*burnings flashing before thine eyes;*
*it's certain it were better*
*for thee to be cast into those*
*inconceivable torments than to commit*
*the least sin against the Lord:*
*Thou doest not think so now,*
*but thou wilt find it so one day.*
*(Thomas Hooker, A True Sight of Sin, 1659)*

*Mercy they did deserve*
*for their Valour, could we have had*
*Opportunity to have bestowed it.*
*Many were burnt in the Fort, both Men,*
*Women and Children. . . . Great*
*and doleful was the bloody Sight*
*to the View of young Soldiers that*
*never had been in War, to see so many*
*Souls lie gasping on the Ground.*
*(John Underhill, Newes from America, 1638)*

CICATRIX (wound on a tree that in healing took form of a witch) from 17th-century Salem. (Essex Inst., Salem, Mass.)

*Samuel Sewall sensible of the reiterated strokes of God*
*upon himself and family; and being sensible, that as to the Guilt*
*contracted upon the opening of the late Commission of Oyer and Terminer*
*at Salem he is, upon many accounts, more concerned*
*than any that he knows of, Desires to take the Blame and shame*
*of it, Asking pardon of men, And especially desiring prayers that God,*
*who has an Unlimited Authority, would pardon that sin*
*and all other his sins, personal and Relative.*
*(Statement read at the request of Judge Samuel Sewall*
*at the South Meeting House, January 14, 1697)*

MASSACRE OF THE PEQUOTS by New England soldiers, 1637. From John Underhill, *Newes from America . . .*, London, 1638. (Rare Book Division, New York Public Library)

TITLE PAGE OF COTTON MATHER'S *The Wonders of the Invisible World*, Boston, 1693. (Rare Book Division, New York Public Library)

SAMUEL SEWALL, a judge at the Salem witch trials; painting by Nathaniel Emmons, c. 1730. (Massachusetts Historical Society)

Richard Mather *(1596–1669)*: "A man may
have money in his purse, bread in his house
or other supplies, and yet this
needs not, ought not to hinder his dependence
upon the providence and blessing of God,
even for his daily bread."

Increase Mather *(1639–1723)*: "It is sad
that ever this Serpent should creep over into
this Wilderness, where threescore
years ago he never had any footing."

Cotton Mather *(1663–1728)*: "I were
a very degenerate person, if I should not
be touched with an Ambition, to be a
Servant of this now famous Countrey, which
my two Grand-fathers COTTON and MATHER
had so considerable a stroke
in the first planting of;
and for the preservation whereof
my Father, hath been so far Exposed."

RICHARD MATHER, dynastic founder; first woodcut
printed in America, by John Foster, Cambridge, 1670.
(Massachusetts Historical Society)

INCREASE MATHER, Harvard president; first colonial cop-
perplate portrait, by Thomas Emmes, Boston, 1702.
(Metropolitan Museum of Art, Bequest of Charles
Allen Munn, 1924)

COTTON MATHER, seer and scribe; America's first known mez-
zotint engraving, by Peter Pelham, Boston, 1728. (Prints Division, New York Public Library)

"It is a matter of saddest complaint that there should be no more serious piety in the seafaring tribe": Cotton Mather. New England "SEA CAPTAINS CAROUSING AT SURINAM" (Dutch Guiana); painting by John Greenwood, a footloose Boston artist, c. 1758. (City Art Museum of Saint Louis)

TITLE PAGE OF NATHANIEL AMES' *Almanack,* Boston (Rare Book Division, New York Public Library)

*An Astronomical DIARY:*
OR, AN
# ALMANACK
For the Year of our Lord CHRIST
1758.
Being the second Year after BISSEXTILE or LEAP-YEAR
In the 31st Year of the Reign of King GEORGE II.

*Wherein are contained the Lunations, Eclipses of the Luminaries, Aspects, Courts, Spring-Tides, Judgment of the Weather Sun and Moon's Rising & Setting, Time of High-Water, &c*

Calculated for the Meridian of Boston in NEW-ENGLAND, Lat. 42 Deg. 25 Min. *North.*

## By Nathaniel Ames.

THE Starry Parliament, whose twinkling Eyes,
With myftic Characters imboft the Skies,
And fparkle on the Brow of fhady Night ;
Heav'n's high Expanfe with their portent'ous Light
Is fill'd ; and glorious Blazes play
In Knots of Light along the Milky-Way.
Vaft Worlds of Light in feeble Orbits glow :
Their Space immenfe muft needs ordain it fo :
Worlds without Number worthy of their GOD
And of bright Seraphims perhaps th' Abode

BOSTON; NEW-ENGLAND:
Printed by J. DRAPER, for the Bookfellers.

*But* Solomon *tells,* That there is nothing
better under the Sun than for a Man to Eat and Drink,
and Enjoy the good of his Labour:
*So that I believe we ought not to be sordidly
Covetous, and deny ourselves the Comfort of what
we Work for, but Eat and Drink as our Circumstances
will afford, so as not to abuse the Favour
of Heaven to Voluptuousness.*
("A Letter From a Gentleman etc." Boston, 1720)

*O ye unborn inhabitants of America!
Should this page escape its destined conflagration
at the year's end, and these alphabetical
letters remain legible,—when your eyes behold
the sun after he has rolled the seasons round for
two or three centuries more, you will know
that in Anno Domini 1758, we dreamed of your times.*
(Nathaniel Ames, Almanack, 1758)

# THE MATURE COLONIAL MIND

Epithets like "provincial" and "colonial" often suggest narrowness of view, rusticity, isolation from the main stream of thought and action in the world. And it is true of many parts of eighteenth-century America that few colonials were able to find the time for contemplative pursuits.

Yet even in the realm of traditional religious observance important changes had been effected in the New World because of new influences from the Old. By the beginning of the eighteenth century the traditional churches, the Anglican, Presbyterian, and New England Congregationalist, were losing ground in a number of ways. The once hot fires of sectarian commitment seemed to have been banked. Comfortable, often wealthy members of seaboard congregations relaxed the severity of their religious views and chose preachers who made smaller emotional demands upon them, preachers who themselves often were broadened intellectually by new currents of thought. Some of the more advanced divines, like their advanced parishioners, even flirted with the "religion of reason," and this tendency grew stronger as the century wore on.

Traditional churches were also afflicted by a quite different kind of loss. Preachers who had surrendered the old orthodoxies and yet had no stomach for the new modes of thought simply became cold and ineffectual and left their congregations dissatisfied. Many members of such congregations soon turned to the revivalist preachers of the 1730s and 1740s who aroused waves of religious enthusiasm during the Great Awakening (see p. 90). Revivalist passions often split established congregations and denominations into irreconcilable camps, so much so that by the end of the colonial period America embraced an extraordinarily wide range of religious views, running from austere rationalism to obscure pietism.

Although Europeans, and Englishmen in particular, continued to scorn the colonials as bumpkins and barbarians, certain Americans had begun to give a distinctive New World cast to secular as well as religious ideas. By the eighteenth century American prosperity permitted a cultivated minority, at least, to engage in nonutilitarian pursuits and to keep up with the latest intellectual developments on the Continent. This minority created a staunch little world of its own where American savants could talk and speculate and experiment. The Enlightenment became the intellectual hallmark of the eighteenth century; and Americans not only shared in the new universe it opened to the mind but actually broadened its perspectives and its scope. The idea of political independence itself most probably would have gone unthought of had not intellectual independence and maturity preceded it.

## I   The religious mind

### Puritans under stress

The sapping of orthodoxy in religion became particularly striking in New England, where the old divines had been most rigorous and most rudely shaken by the growing wealth and cosmopolitanism of the townspeople. Both the Half-Way Covenant of 1662 and the introduction of Anglicanism in the 1680s (see pp. 42, 52) gave evidence of their decline, which was hastened on also by the revised Massachusetts charter of 1691 that substituted property for religious tests for voting. The excesses of the Salem witchcraft hysteria that followed in 1692 further weakened ministerial authority.

This episode began when two Salem girls accused certain townspeople of bewitching them. Soon a perfect epidemic of witch-hunting infected the community, claiming twenty lives by execution after trials under leading ministers and magistrates. A hundred others were jailed and stood awaiting their fate until the judges, finding some of the most eminent and respected citizens among those charged with being the Devil's emissaries, at last came to their senses. Both Increase and Cotton Mather had inadvertently encouraged the outbreak by publishing books proving the existence of witches—this at a time when William Penn dismissed a case against a woman charged with riding on a broomstick by saying "that there was no law in Pennsylvania against riding on broomsticks." During the trials, the Mathers had cautioned the court not to accept as evidence the reports of persons allegedly afflicted by witchcraft. Since neither the Mathers nor the other ministers actively opposed the trials, however, they were subsequently blamed for the abuses, and their reputations suffered.

90

### Jonathan Edwards: Yankee revivalist

The theological luminary of the next generation was the great revivalist, Jonathan Edwards (1703-1758). A devoted Congregationalist, Edwards was nevertheless strongly attracted to new modes of religious contemplation. In his concern for truths that lay beyond concrete experience, in his rapturous and at the same time astute analysis of religious feeling, evil, and grace, Edwards demonstrated a characteristically American spirit as diverse and contradictory as the country itself: visionary and down-to-earth, deeply radical and solidly conservative, coldly prudent and unexpectedly wild.

Edwards, in 1729, succeeded his grandfather, the eminent Solomon Stoddard, in the Northampton, Massachusetts pastorate where he served for twenty-one years before his congregation dismissed him. Ever since his student days at Yale, Edwards had been a reader of Newton and John Locke; the science and philosophy of the Enlightenment interested him enormously. But his mystical and poetic disposition prevented him from becoming a rationalist like Charles Chauncy of Boston, his chief theological opponent.

Between 1733 and 1735, under the influence of Edwards's teachings, Northampton underwent an intense religious revival. Edwards attacked the widely held doctrine that salvation depended on "moral sincerity" and good works. In place of the humanized Deity, genial and benevolent, who made salvation easy for reputable citizens (the God of his grandfather, Stoddard), he resurrected the jealous God of Calvin. His revival efforts in the mid-1730s won him as many as thirty conversions a week but also further divided his congregation and forced some of the members to abandon it in favor of the more hospitable Anglican communion. Edwards's unswerving devotion to the revived Calvinism eventually led to his dismissal in 1750. By

Courtesy of the New-York Historical Society

*Jonathan Edwards (1703-1758).*

then, in New England and elsewhere in America, revivalism had gained many more converts, thanks to the frequent visits of the electrifying English evangelist George Whitefield, one of the precursors of American Methodism. But revivalism, as preached by Whitefield's cruder imitators, had also gained numerous enemies and sharpened sectarian divisions in Protestantism.

### The Great Awakening

In the early decades of the eighteenth century, religion had fallen even further in esteem outside of New England than in it. In some frontier areas, no provision at all was made for religious observance. Whitefield's tours soon brought widespread changes in religious practices and in other areas of American life.

The Great Awakening was actually part of a worldwide evangelical movement that had put down its roots in Germany and England. Its leading native spirits in the colonies, in addition to Jonathan Edwards, were Theodore Frelinghuysen, a Dutch-Reformed minister living in New Jersey, and William Tennent and his sons, Pennsylvania Presbyterians. The full force of the Great Awakening in America began to be felt during Whitefield's first tour, 1739-1741, when he and some seventeen assistants harangued enormous crowds from Georgia to Massachusetts. Many listeners traveled miles to attend his theatrical performances. Although Whitefield did not mix politics with religion, some of his enthusiastic coworkers offended conservatives by their extravagant behavior and upset the social order by rejecting all forms and creeds.

Enemies of the revival were shocked by ministers grotesquely enacting the sufferings of Christ on the pulpit. Revivalist preachers who passed from place to place censuring the local clergy for their lack of piety found themselves most severely censured. In his *Seasonable Thoughts on the State of Religion in New England* (1743), Charles Chauncy referred to these itinerant preachers as "Men who, though they have *no Learning,* and but *small Capacities,* yet imagine they are able, and without Study too, to speak to the *spiritual Profit* of such as are willing to hear them." Chauncy especially deplored the contention that the sudden awareness of sin with the motions that usually accompanied it—"bitter *Shriekings* and *Screaming; Convulsion-like Tremblings* and *Agitations, Struggling* and *Tumblings*"—signified conversion.

Between archconservatives like Chauncy and uncompromising revival enthusiasts like Tennent, stood a third group—moderates typified by Edwards and Benjamin Colman in Boston. Unwilling to condone the excesses of the Great Awakening, they nevertheless welcomed it, at least in the beginning, as a mighty manifestation of God's spirit moving over the land. Many others, recognizing the isolation and spiritual starvation of frontier life in particular, shared their view. It is easy to harp on the extravagances of the Great Awakening, but it cannot be dismissed as a mere emotional orgy. Its consequences, moreover, appear to have been far-reaching.

RELIGIOUS CONSEQUENCES The Great Awakening split the old denominations into two main groups, one espousing traditional doctrines or forms, the other adopting the "New Divinity," a religion of personal experience as against one of custom or habit. The "New Light" or "New Side" wing, as the revivalists were called, demanded a universal priesthood of believers, a kind of spiritual democracy. The great revival increased membership in the small dissenting sects at the expense of the established denominations. Presbyterians and Baptists, for example, made impressive gains, and in the back country a new group, later to be known as the Methodists, gathered strength. Large numbers of the unchurched were converted. In New England alone, some 40,000 to 50,000 joined new congregations, badly shaking the establishment.

POLITICAL CONSEQUENCES Some historians believe that the weakening of the established Anglican church helped to loosen British authority in the colonies, particularly in Virginia where the Baptists and Methodists led the fight against state-supported churches. Elsewhere, too, it has been argued, the Great Awakening served as a leveling movement, preparing the way for the extension of liberty of conscience to economic and political liberties.

SOCIAL CONSEQUENCES The huge crowds that came to hear Whitefield and the other preachers yearned for social contact. In the vast outdoor meetings that were to become a common feature of subsequent revivals, they found release for social and spiritual emotions long repressed. Despite the excesses accompanying the Great Awakening and the backsliding that followed, morals and manners improved as a result of it.

Although many revivalists mistrusted an educated clergy who (in James Davenport's words) were "leading their People blindfold to Hell," the Great Awakening spawned a number of educational institutions. William Tennent's famous "Log College" at Neshaminy,

Pennsylvania, founded in 1736, fathered similar schools for the preparation of Presbyterian ministers. The Baptists lagged behind the Presbyterians, but they established their own schools—Hopewell Academy, and later the College of Rhode Island (Brown) in 1764. Princeton (Presbyterian), Rutgers (Dutch-Reformed), and Dartmouth (Congregational) all started under the impetus of the revival movement. The new colleges hardly represented the spirit of the Enlightenment, for their main purpose was to prepare ministers in an atmosphere uncontaminated by the doctrines of rival denominations or by secular infidelities. In time, however, the new colleges disavowed narrow sectarian objectives, and some grew into great universities.

The Great Awakening, furthermore, quickened the humanitarian spirit of the eighteenth century. When Jonathan Edwards defined virtue as "love of Being in general," he was suggesting that there was a divine element in everyone that ought to be recognized out of love for God. Orphans, paupers, Indians, and slaves shared in this Being and became the objects of Christian concern.

For the Negro, in particular, the Great Awakening was to have momentous consequences. The revivalists did not try to invalidate slavery as an institution, but in preaching that every man, no matter what his color, was (as Whitefield reminded the planters) "conceived and born in sin," the spiritual equality of the Negro could no longer be denied. That point assured, the antislavery men could now move on to the radical correlative: the sinfulness of enslaving a fellow being endowed with an immortal soul. Well-known Quakers like John Woolman and, later, Anthony Benezet, led the way. Each spoke out eloquently on behalf of the despised blacks and eventually persuaded other Quakers and other sectarians as well to join their quiet crusade.

Woolman (1720–1772), a mild but determined humanitarian, began his opposition to slavery in 1743 and from then until his death never ceased to admonish his coreligionists in New Jersey, Maryland, and Virginia on the sin of human exploitation. Nor did he fail to warn against the spiritual debasement of the white overlords:

*Placing on men the ignominious Title, SLAVE, dressing them in uncomely Garments, keeping them to servile Labour, in which they are often dirty, tends gradually to fix a notion in the Mind, that they are a sort of people below us in Nature, and leads us to consider them as such in all our Conclusions about them.*

Woolman never resorted to harsh abuse, but his journal, as the Quaker poet and abolitionist John Greenleaf Whittier said later, was a lifelong testimony against wrong, and one of the finest expressions of eighteenth-century benevolence.

### Church life

Despite a strong Bible orientation in the seventeenth century and the Great Awakening in the eighteenth, at the time of the Revolution most Americans had no church affiliation. Established churches (those officially supported by the state) existed in some colonies—Anglican in the South, Congregational in New England. But when Quakers, Anglicans, Presbyterians, Dutch-Reformed, Catholics, and Jews lived in the same province, as they did in Pennsylvania, an established church became inadvisable if not impossible. The dissenting spirit of Protestantism did not fade away in America. Rather, it took on a new energy as denominations splintered and new sects sprang up. The very multiplicity of religions, at the same time, promoted a practical tolerance even for most noncommunicants and the acceptance of what finally came to be the American principle of the separation of church and state.

Despite the variety of sects and the ethnic and geographical divisions among the denominations, the following generalizations about colonial religion in the 1750s seems valid:

*First,* colonial religion was overwhelmingly Protestant. Although the colonies provided a refuge for the persecuted of all the Old-World religions, only about 25,000 Catholics and 2000 Jews were living in America on the eve of the Revolution. The Protestant colonists, in a real sense children of the Reformation, differed markedly among themselves in creed and doctrine yet stood united in their opposition to Rome. Catholics were not physically molested in eighteenth-century America, but they were the targets of anti-Catholic propaganda spread by Protestant ministers, educators, editors, and publishers of the popular almanacs. England's wars with Catholic France partly explain this anti-Catholic feeling, but the hostility went far deeper.

*Second,* the doctrine and organization of American churches reflected the social background of the members. The most powerful and influential denominations in the New World were the New England Congregationalists, the Presbyterians, and the Anglicans. These Churches numbered among their adherents many plain folk, in addition to most of the established mercantile and landed middle-class families; but a higher proportion of persons of modest means was found in the Baptist churches, among the Methodists who emerged in the late 1760s, and in various small sects. By their frankly evangelical appeals, they reached elements in the colonial population hitherto neglected by the elite communions. Yet by their frugality, perseverance, and industry—the practical morality characteristic of the sects—the Evangelicals themselves prospered and thereby gained acceptance and respectability. This cycle was repeated again and again throughout American religious history.

*Third,* the churches of the non-English-speaking settlers in the eighteenth century that survived the strains of frontier life had little influence on the main currents of colonial religion yet served as vital social organizations. It took some time for European immigrants to accommodate themselves to American ways, and they often looked to their respective religious leaders for guidance. The German immigrant churches survived best and thus by the middle of the eighteenth century were most strongly confronted with the question that ultimately faced all foreign-language groups: Should English be substituted for their native tongue? Only by insisting on racial and cultural distinctiveness could the religious leaders prevent their compatriots from being absorbed by the aggressive American sects.

*Fourth,* the tendency throughout the eighteenth century was toward greater religious freedom. To the sectarian-minded worshipper of the seventeenth century, tolerance, or "polypiety," was the greatest impiety. But even in orthodox New England the persecution of Quakers and Baptists had ceased by 1700, and a robust minister like John Wise of Ipswich could almost single-handedly foil the attempt of an organized clique of ministers to centralize church government and destroy the autonomy of the independent congregation. In defending the congregational principle and church democracy, Wise introduced arguments that were to be adopted later by the Revolutionary patriots in defense of political democracy. All men are born free, he said; "Democracy is Christ's government in Church and State." In 1763, the possibility that an Anglican bishop might be appointed for New England to dragoon the nascent rebels into the King's communion aroused as much heat as the Stamp Act was to generate two years later. Even southern Anglicans agreed with northern dissenters in opposing the appointment of an American bishop.

### Between faith and reason

As eighteenth century Americans became more humanitarian, secular, and liberal, turning their attention away from God in Heaven toward man on earth, their God also grew more tractable, less demanding, more involved with the happiness of His children. By 1755 John Adams could speak of "the frigid John Calvin," and turn elsewhere for peace of mind.

The new way of looking at the world comes through strongly in the lives of three men on the eve of the Enlightenment:

Samuel Sewall (1652–1730), Boston-born and -bred, bore the stamp of his Puritan forebears, yet easily adopted the secular attitude.

As one of the "Stewards" of his province, a conservative man of affairs and a bulwark of the church, he necessarily spoke in the accents of piety. His wonderful *Diary*, a record of his activities between 1674 and 1677 and from 1685 to 1729, is full of reports of sermons, funerals, weddings, of visits to graveyards ("an awful yet pleasing treat"), and humorlessly amusing accounts of his courtships. But hard as Sewall tried to present himself as a pious and otherworldly man ("The Lord add or take away from this our corporeal weight," he heavily comments on his durable 193 pounds, "so as shall be most advantageous for our spiritual growth"), we are always aware of him as the curious busybody, the humanitarian who opposed the selling of blacks, the chronicler of succulent dinners. His religious sense and training told him that life on earth was transient; every accident, from losing a tooth to breaking a glass, became for him a lesson of mortality. Yet Sewall made much the best of his earthly passage. This side of him emerges in the diary entry: "Six swallows together flying and chippering very rapturously."

If Sewall typified Boston's merchant class in the age of transition, William Byrd II (1674-1744) represented the Virginia planter aristocracy of the same period. Byrd grew up in a society preoccupied with hunting and horseracing, politics, military pursuits, and so-

cial affairs. Yet such gentry were by no means irreligious or freethinking. Byrd himself, educated in London and displaying the manners and sometimes the looseness of Restoration courtiers, had his serious side. His graphic and candid diary shows him to have been a scholar who, besides reading Hebrew every morning, read several pages of the Greek version of Josephus, and perhaps a bit of Bishop Tillotson, the liberal English Anglican churchman. His library of 3600 volumes was equaled in North America only by Cotton Mather's. Like Sewall, Byrd deplored the slave trade, and his religious credo, rational and benevolent, evokes the spirit of the new secularism:

*I believe that God made man ... and inspired him with a reasonable soul to distinguish between good and evil; that the law of nature taught him to follow the good and avoid the evil because the good tends manifestly to his happiness and preservation, but the evil to his misery and destruction.*

Cotton Mather (1663-1728), grandson of Richard Mather, one of the original Massachusetts "Saints," a "very hard student" and inflexible Puritan, reflected the transition from faith to reason in a more interesting way than his contemporaries, Sewall or Byrd. A pious son of a pious father ("I began to pray, when I began to speak," he wrote of himself), he saw in Nature's laws the best antidote to atheism. His religious zeal in no way interfered with his lively interest in medicine, agriculture, and other rational means of human betterment. In fact, his curiosity about every aspect of the natural world, his loving attention to the humblest practical problem—which drew from him the characteristic observation, "The very wheelbarrow is to be with respect looked upon"—sprang directly from his Christian piety. Implicit in Puritanism was the conviction that scriptural truths might be discerned by "right reason," and although God might set aside natural laws when He chose to do so, He created a rational universe

*The library at Westover, the Virginia mansion of William Byrd II.*

94

whose order any rational man might detect. Peter Ramus, a French Protestant scientist much in vogue among New England thinkers, sanctioned this view, and Cotton Mather (without abandoning his faith in God's miraculous ways nor his belief in the threat of the Devil's) saw God's hand in the visible order of the universe.

It may seem a far cry from the kind of rationalism espoused by Puritan thinkers like the Mathers to the rationalism of the later Deists. And yet both believed that the Almighty had given them a thoroughly rational physical universe and the rational faculties with which to understand it. Puritans might use these faculties more for the glory of God, Deists more for their own pleasure.

Deism offered a mechanical universe run by a Heavenly Engineer who had no need to resort to miracles to demonstrate His glory. Deists dismissed the Trinity, the divinity of Christ, and the Biblical account of the creation of man as superstitions. The moral truths of Christianity, they said, were the heart of it, and were better defended by science than by revelation. They emphasized the ethics of Jesus and his way of life on earth, not his ascension. The Deists were not atheists (although they were so labeled by their enemies); but neither were they mystics. As rational men, the truest was for them the clearest, and the most logical. A philosophy of life rather than a religion, Deism reflected the emerging secular view of the world and also promoted it.

## II  The secular mind

### The Enlightenment

After Nicholas Copernicus, a Polish mathematician and astronomer, published his *Concerning the Revolution of Heavenly Bodies* in 1543, the traditional earth-centered universe around which the planets revolved gave way to the solar, or sun-centered system. Copernicus thus cast suspicion on man's kinship with the angels and suggested that all of creation was governed by unchanging natural laws. Subsequently, a growing number of scholars, philosophers, and scientists began to study man and his environment more objectively, to make orderly observations and experiments. Their discoveries in astronomy, physics, anatomy, geology, and chemistry further weakened Biblical dogmas. By the eighteenth century the learned world accepted the idea of the universe as it appeared in the treatises of the great English mathematician Sir Isaac Newton (1642-1727). On his conception rested the major principles of the Enlightenment in philosophy.

According to Newton, neither chance nor miracle governed the physical world. Instead, it appeared to be a perfect mechanical structure functioning under fixed mathematical laws. If that was the character of the universe, it must also be the character of mankind, who was part of it. Thus the Enlightenment philosophers extended Newton's idea of the physical world to the moral world as well. They held bad environment rather than original sin responsible for social evils. By means of science and reason, philosophers could create an ideal environment in which the natural man would flower. The philosophers of the Enlightenment carried their optimism even further. The qualities they valued most highly in the study of physics and political economy—reasonableness, clarity, balance—they made the criteria of art and literary expression.

### Benjamin Franklin

The exemplar of the American Enlightenment and one of the greatest men of his age was the renegade Bostonian and adopted

The Metropolitan Museum of Art, Bequest of Charles Allen Munn, 1924

*Franklin in an engraving after the portrait
painted by Mason Chamberlain in 1762,
when Franklin was 56. At upper right
is the lightning rod he put up
on his Philadelphia house ten years earlier.*

Philadelphian, Benjamin Franklin (1706–1790), a living example of what might be accomplished by reason, measure, and clarity. Franklin, like the other *philosophes,* abhorred mysteries and metaphysics. Incapable of deep religious emotion, he worked out a complacent practical faith for himself and a cool tolerance for the beliefs of others. In his own eyes, he never "sinned"; rather, he "erred." In that distinction we may measure the gulf between the piety of his seventeenth-century forebears and the naturalism of the eighteenth century.

Franklin's worldliness was neither greedy nor materialistic. His close attention to the humblest as well as to the loftier occupations arose from his desire to produce "something for the common benefit of mankind." When he had acquired enough money to support himself (by the conscientious application of the principles he outlined in his celebrated *Autobiography),* he gave up business and devoted his energies to science, politics, diplomacy, and writing. He wanted people, he once confessed, to say after his death that "He lived usefully" rather than that "He died rich."

And so Franklin improved the printing press, tinkered successfully with smoky chimneys, suggested changes in the shape and rigging of ships, plotted cyclonic storms, introduced new plants into the New World, drained swampy land, improved carriage wheels, founded the first American club for mutual improvement, invented the bifocal lens, designed an effective iron stove, recommended a more practical watering trough for horses, showed navigators how to shorten the crossing to Europe by following the Gulf Stream, demonstrated a way of heating public buildings, and constructed a fan for his chair to keep off the flies. This is only a partial list of his accomplishments, which included pioneer work in the science of electricity, studies in American population growth, and an extraordinarily long and successful public career. Franklin took out no patents on his inventions, because "as we enjoy great advantages from the inventions of others, we should be glad of an opportunity to serve others by any invention of ours." His entire life was a fulfillment of one of his deepest beliefs: "Serving God is doing good to men."

Through his writings Franklin expressed the values of thousands of his fellow Americans, the common citizens whose virtues he so uncommonly represented. Their materialistic aspirations he caught in his capitalistic homily, "The Way to Wealth." But his shrewd practicality went beyond concern for the dollar. In his humorous maxims he embodied the folk-wisdom of the American people:

*Fish and visitors stink in three days. Write with the learned, pronounce with the vulgar. Eat to please thyself but dress to please others. Neither a fortress nor a maid will hold out long after they begin to parley. Let thy maid-servant be faithful, strong, and homely. Keep your eyes wide open before marriage, half shut afterwards. Where there's marriage without love there will be love without marriage. The most exquisite folly is made of wisdom spun too fine.*

Even Franklin's scientific papers, which won him worldwide acclaim during and after his lifetime, were couched in terms that could be readily understood. As Franklin's younger contemporary, the chemist Sir Humphry Davy, expressed it in his fine tribute to the American:

*Science appears in his language in a dress wonderfully decorous, the best adapted to display her native loveliness. He has in no instance exhibited that false dignity, by which philosophy is kept aloof from common applications; and he has sought to make her a useful inmate and servant in the common habitations of man, than to preserve her merely as an object of admiration in temples and palaces.*

### Science in the colonies

The brilliance of Franklin's career and his exalted reputation abroad have obscured the attainment of his lesser contemporaries whose investigations he encouraged and assisted. They shared his reliance on Enlightenment thought and like him believed not only that natural philosophy demonstrated the immutable ways of God but also that it could be put to practical use. "Science," Francis Bacon had written, "must be known by its works. It is by the witness of works rather than by logic or even observation that truth is revealed and established. It follows from this that the improvement of man's lot and the improvement of man's mind are one and the same thing." The American scientists who shared the Baconian attitude were not mere utilitarians, but like scientists in Europe they were motivated by disinterested curiosity and a desire for scholarly recognition. Living in a society without wealth, without patronage, and without a learned class, they naturally looked to Europe for sustenance.

Fortunately for the physicians, the teachers, the self-taught botanists, and the amateur mathematicians and astronomers who made up the scientific community in North America, the European savants were keenly interested in the New World. They encouraged the Americans to report their findings on flora and fauna, Indian ethnology, medical lore, earthquakes. By collecting unknown plants, for example, the Americans could help the Swedish scholar Carl Linnaeus to complete his biological classifications. By the middle of the eighteenth century, European scientists had developed a system of communication which kept them informed about one another's findings, and they made the Americans a link in this intellectual chain. Thanks to the efforts of Peter Collinson, a Quaker merchant of London and an influential member of the Royal Society, the reports of the Americans were transmitted to interested Europeans. Through Collinson, isolated Americans also were kept informed of the activities of colleagues in other colonies.

New England from the outset assumed the leadership in scientific investigation. Many of her leaders and professional men had been trained in English universities, and Harvard teachers and graduates had been elected to the Royal Society before 1700. John Winthrop, Jr., of Connecticut, a charter member of the Society, donated a telescope to Harvard in 1672, the one that enabled Thomas Brattle to observe the comet of 1676. Newton used Brattle's observations in his *Principia Mathematica* to illustrate how the orbits of comets are fixed by gravitational force. No less important were the 82 letters the formidable Cotton Mather sent to the Royal Society's *Transactions* between 1712 and 1724. Among them were reports on the hybridization of plants and inoculation against smallpox.

But New England soon lost its preeminence to Philadelphia, which by 1750 had become the center of colonial science. Commercial prosperity was partly responsible for the willingness of Philadelphians to support scientific enterprises (see p. 69). Equally important was the Quaker connection of certain Philadelphians with intellectuals abroad. It was the English merchant, Collinson, again, who put the self-taught naturalist John Bartram in touch with Linnaeus. When Peter Kalm, a pupil of Linnaeus, visited America in 1748, he came straight to Philadelphia to see Bartram. Their discussions, according to Kalm, ranged from silk culture, vineyards, stalactites, and truffles to Indian pottery, hummingbirds, and cures for snake bite. Bartram had a genius for collecting specimens and a knack of communicating his enthusiasm to others. Half mystic, half rationalist, this independent Quaker saw "God in his glory" through the telescope, the first instrument of space exploration.

Bartram received aid and encouragement from another notable Philadelphian, James Logan, the Penns' representative, who made his fortune in land speculation and Indian trade. Logan conducted important experiments on the role of pollen in the fertilization of plants. He also befriended Thomas Godfrey,

the inventor of an improved quadrant, and Cadwallader Colden, a plant collector highly honored in Europe and author of one of the earliest scholarly treatises on the Indians.

In 1743 Franklin and Bartram tried without success to set up a scientific society to correlate the work of experimenters throughout the colonies. Twenty-five years later (1768), their plan took form in the American Philosophical Society. The 1771 *Transactions* of the Society carried reports by a number of colonial scientists on a transit of Venus across the sun that had occurred in 1769. In Philadelphia, where the observation took on the proportions of a community enterprise, David Rittenhouse, an ingenious clockmaker and builder of the celebrated orrery (a mechanical planetarium), was the principal contributor. European scientists hailed the Society's *Transactions* as evidence that American science had attained a surprising maturity.

## III   Cultural progress

### Education

The educational system of the colonies was largely English in origin. The idea of the public grammar school was already a century old before its introduction to North America in 1642, and English universities served as the models for the first (if not the later denominational) colleges in the New World. English pedagogy and textbooks, English schoolmasters and scholars, all enjoyed great prestige.

In the eighteenth century the introduction of secular subjects began to modify the religious emphasis in education. Yet social conformity as well as social usefulness remained an educational goal. Schools reflected the social cleavages that existed not only in the South, where class lines were especially sharply drawn, but also in the Middle and New England colonies. Rich children received a different kind of education from that received by poor children, who, if they were educated at all, were prepared solely for their limited stations in life. Even liberal-minded men in the mid-eighteenth century—revolutionists in the making—accepted these social distinctions as natural and proper. The Revolutionary decades saw a weakening of this two-class system, but traditional attitudes lingered.

The kind and quality of education in eighteenth-century America depended also on the section, the national origin of the settlers, their religion, and their closeness to settled areas. Education in the South, for example, where it was difficult to establish any kind of organized educational system for the scattered plantations, lagged behind that in the North.

Pauper schools gave rudimentary instruction to orphans and the children of the poor, but in general only the children of the rich were educated. Higher standards prevailed in the Middle colonies, where the dissenting Protestant denominations emphasized Bible-reading, but the amount and quality of education that most children received was limited to what their parents could afford.

Only in Massachusetts and Connecticut did education become a public responsibility. The Massachusetts school laws of 1642 and 1647 (see p. 42) meant, in effect, that all children must be taught to read. These standards—unique in the English-speaking world at the time—deteriorated as New England society became more decentralized and as educational control passed to the local authorities. By 1700, education was at a low ebb in New England, and illiteracy was prevalent on the frontier. But conditions rapidly improved. During the forty-year period from 1720 to 1760, a number of excellent semiprivate academies were established, and New Englanders once again could proudly claim to be the best-educated people in all North America.

In the cities, several interesting educational experiments were carried on in the eighteenth century. Philadelphia, Boston, and New York, besides having the best private academies, also had a number of private evening schools that offered practical courses ignored by classical academies. Such subjects as geography, navigation, bookkeeping, mathematics, and surveying had a high practical value in a commercial society. All classes of people attended evening schools, but the majority of students, of both sexes, came from middle-class homes.

A relatively small number of well-to-do students attended the seven colonial colleges that had been established by 1764. These and the private academies retained the European curriculum (Latin, Greek, Hebrew, and Science) and fostered aristocratic, conservative ideals.

**99**

*The rewards of learning: last alphabetical page from the 1727 edition of the New England Primer, and the "Promises" elicited from the young scholars.*

Religious training remained ostensibly the chief function of the colleges, but the liberal and rational influences of the age began to be felt as the century waned. Such eminently practical political leaders as Thomas Jefferson and James Monroe were trained at William and Mary College, the second oldest in British America. The College of Philadelphia became an advocate of *"every thing* that is useful, and *every thing* that is ornamental."* King's College (later Columbia University) advertised that while the teaching of religion was its principal objective, "it is further the Design of this College, to instruct and perfect the Youth in . . . The Arts of *Numbering* and *Measuring,* of *Surveying* and *Navigation,* of *Geography* and *History,* of Husbandry, Commerce and Government."

Naturally enough, the colleges had become the centers of the new science by the first quarter of the eighteenth century. True, no college professor ever matched the self-taught Benjamin Franklin or John Bartram in originality. But America's ablest astronomer, John Winthrop, taught at Harvard College, and David Rittenhouse, astronomer and mathematician, lectured at the College of Philadelphia, as did Dr. Benjamin Rush, the first professor of chemistry in America.

### Journalism and letters

Literacy, by European standards, was high in the colonies, but only a few Americans kept up with the new learning. A somewhat larger number read the newspapers. During Franklin's term as the Deputy Postmaster for the colonies (1753-1755), he succeeded in reducing postal rates for newspapers and in speeding up their distribution. But throughout the pre-Revolutionary period they remained too expensive for the poor. By 1765, nevertheless, twenty-five weekly papers were being published in eleven colonies. Most of the columns were filled with excerpts from English papers, but after the famous trial of John Peter Zenger in New York in 1735, greater opportunities opened up for independent reporting.

Zenger was charged with criminal libel for printing an unfavorable report about a crown official. He was defended by the eminent Philadelphia lawyer, Andrew Hamilton, who appealed to the jury to define libel in a way contrary to the current English rule. For the judges, the question was merely whether Zenger had published the offending articles; for Hamilton, whether the articles were true. The jury accepted Hamilton's advanced version of libel and held that since the articles were true, Zenger was not guilty as charged. Fifty years passed before the finding in this case became formal law, but the decision did encourage other journalists to speak out more freely.

A more popular medium than newspapers for spreading scientific and political information, especially to rural Americans, was the almanac, an old English institution. The first colonial almanac appeared in New England in 1639; by 1731, almanacs were being read in all the colonies. Pocket-sized and paper-bound, they served as calendars, astrological guides, recipe books, and children's primers. Sandwiched in between bits of practical information were jokes, poems, and maxims. The better almanacs (published by Nathaniel Ames and Benjamin Franklin) punctured superstition, provided simplified summaries of the new science, and presented tasteful selections from the best British authors. Franklin's *Poor Richard's Almanack,* first published in 1732, soon sold 10,000 copies a year.

Literature received more attention in the eighteenth century than in the seventeenth, although the Puritan suspicion of the secular imagination had not entirely relaxed. By the 1740s, Philadelphia had become the literary center of the colonies and the first city to manifest a literary self-consciousness. But even here, the coterie of young men who gathered around the educator and magazine editor William Smith became even more fettered by English literary conventions than their predecessors had been. Not one of them measured up to the gifted Puritan poet Edward Taylor, whose verse blended homely details of New England life with magnificent visions of God. None wrote with the urbanity, robustness, and wit of William Byrd II, or with the charm and lucidity of Franklin. Ardent young poets though becoming aware of their American-ness, expressed their emotions in the prescribed and "proper" poetic diction, singing of "swains" and "snowy lambkins" haunting the banks of the Schuylkill River. After 1750, the leading poets became absorbed in political issues and expended their talents on satire and polemics.

Literally as well as metaphorically, everyday Americans in this period had begun to speak a different language from the English. In the eighteenth century, English lexicographers and scholars like Dr. Samuel Johnson had pruned and refined Elizabethan English, but many of the barbarisms they eliminated persisted as good usage in the colonies. Surviving archaisms like *I guess, chump, flapjack, homespun, to hustle,* and many others came to be regarded as Americanisms. American speech also absorbed words from Dutch, French, German, and Spanish. New plants, animals, and birds tested the wit of the colonists, as did the peculiar American geography. *Pokeweed, bottomland, rolling country, backwoods, land office,* and *crazy quilt* all were colonial words that described new scenery, objects, and situations. Until the appearance of Philip Freneau's earliest poems in the 1770s, however, formal American writing remained derivative and imitative.

## Political ideas

The most important colonial writing in the eighteenth century and the most widely read was not the work of literary men but of theologians, scientists, and political theorists. Among the political writers were some of the most highly cultivated minds in the New World.

American political philosophy before the Revolution derived partly from colonial experience and partly from English and continental sources. Even during the seventeenth century, Puritanism nourished ideas of liberty, prog-

ress, and success. As rationalism gradually undermined old dogmas and as democratic tendencies grew more noticeable, Americans became receptive to ideas from abroad congenial to their own experiences. The leading imported idea was the doctrine of natural rights as formulated by John Locke in his *Two Treatises of Civil Government,* published in 1690, just after the Glorious Revolution (see p. 52). Locke's essays helped explode the divine-right theory of kingship which had brought the prestige of religion to the support of absolute political authority.

Philosophers before Locke had attacked the divine-right theory. Locke's distinction lay in his restatement of English constitutional ideas in their most persuasive and popular form. Government, he said (by which he meant king, parliament, or any other political agency), was responsible to the people, to the community it ruled. Its power was limited by constitutional traditions, popular conventions, and moral law deducible from the laws of nature. But what, precisely, were the laws of nature that governed man's political activities? It was one thing for Newton to work out fixed laws governing the heavenly spheres; quite another thing to demonstrate the existence of a natural order in society.

The early theorists of natural law tackled this problem by trying to identify man's elemental needs and faculties. How would man behave, they asked, if he acted solely in accordance with his *nature,* without social restraints of any sort? Of one thing they felt certain; in a natural state men would never consent to live under any form of government that did not protect life, liberty, and property. Hence, when men accepted government, they entered into a "social contract" with their rulers; in return for security and protection, they acknowledged the rulers' authority. But if rulers violated their part of the bargain, the people were released from the contract. Then they had the right to overthrow the government and establish a new one. These Lockeian ideas were easily digested by practical people. In business, contractual relationships were becoming more and more common, and society was familiar with the Puritan idea of a "covenant" between God and man.

102

Originally, Locke's sallies were directed against kingly government and were meant to justify Parliament's supremacy. But Locke phrased his theories in such general terms that when the time came the colonists found it easy to convert them into a challenge to Parliament itself. Other beliefs, widely held in the colonies, strengthened the natural-rights philosophy. The common-law rights of free-born Englishmen, for example, were closely identified with the natural rights of men. And these legal rights were sustained by two English authorities immensely influential in America: Sir William Blackstone, known through his *Commentaries on the Laws of England* (1765–1769), and Sir Edward Coke, the seventeenth-century English lawyer and scholar. The colonists quoted Blackstone to the effect that man's first allegiance was to a God whose will was but the universal law of nature, and that human laws in conflict with natural law were clearly invalid. The colonial pamphleteers cherished particularly this pronouncement by Coke:

*The law of nature is that which God at the time of creation of the nature of man infused into his heart, for his preservation and direction; and this is* Lex aeterna, *the moral law, called also the law of Nature. And by this law, written with the finger of God in the heart of man, were the people of God a long time governed before the law was written by Moses who was the first reporter or writer of law in the world.*

Ideas about natural rights seemed especially appropriate to a people who had in fact created government while still living in a state of nature. When these ideas were challenged in the developing conflict between the colonies and Britain, colonial pamphleteers increasingly used American experiences to defend them. John Wise based his support of the incipient rebels on the congregational principle of self-determination. When Jonathan Mayhew wrote his famous *Discourse Concerning Unlimited Submission and Non-Resistance to the Higher Powers* in 1750, he provided ammunition for the oncoming Revolutionary pamphleteers. Mayhew admitted that civil authority required obedience, that disobedience was morally as well as politically sinful. But when rulers pillage the public instead of protecting them, he said, they stop being emissaries of God and become "common pirates and highwaymen." To support a tyrant was to abet him in promoting misery. For Mayhew, the doctrine of the divine right of kings (with its corollary of nonresistance) was "altogether as fabulous and chimerical as transubstantiation; or any reveries of ancient or modern visionaries." The form that a government took was less important than the need for it to have popular support. If government derived from God, as the absolutists said, it was because God moved the people to organize it.

Here was a reasonable and religious basis for popular assemblies that made sense to the learned and the unlearned alike. A century and a half of colonial history, as a conservative Swedish observer noted in 1775, had created a new kind of political animal in North America:

*The chief trait in the character of an American is an immoderate love of liberty, or rather license. . . . And this enthusiasm rules in the breasts of all from the highest to the lowest. Education, manner of life, religion, and government—all contribute to it. Parents exercise no authority over children, beyond letting them for the most part do what pleases them. Everyone can maintain himself without trouble, for here there is room enough, and wages are high. No one, therefore, knows oppression or dependence. All are equally good; birth, office and merits do not make much distinction. Freedom of conscience is unlimited, without the least control by secular law, and church discipline means nothing. The English method of government is in itself quite mild, and is all the less able, in this remote part of the empire, to exercise a reasonable strictness. The reins of government lie so slack that they seldom are noticed, and the hand that guides is never seen.*

This observer continued:

*The result of all this is that the people neither know nor will know of any control, and everyone regards* himself as an independent Prince. One can grow weary of continually hearing and reading about noble liberty. Many, as stupid and shameless, regard all other na- tions as slaves. Their imagination constantly sees appa- ritions coming to steal away that goddess of theirs. All the enterprises of the government arouse suspicion. The most reasonable regulations are invasions of their rights and liberties; light and necessary taxes, robbery and plunder; well-merited punishment, unheard-of- tyranny.

## For further reading

Merle Curti, *The Growth of American Thought* (3rd ed., 1964), a comprehensive work, and vol. 1 of V. L. Parrington, *Main Currents in American Thought* (3 vols., 1927), afford useful introductions to the mature colonial mind. Max Savelle, *Seeds of Liberty* (1948), and Clinton Rossiter, *Seedtime of the Republic* (1953), are outstanding intellectual histories with emphasis on political ideas. Modern introductions to the religious history of the period will be found in S. E. Mead, *The Lively Experiment: The Shaping of Christianity in America* (1963), and W. S. Hudson, *Religion in America* (1965). L. J. Trinterud, *The Forming of an American Tradition* (1949), is outstanding on Presbyterianism. The liberal reaction and its opponents is well presented in Conrad Wright, *The Beginnings of Unitarianism in America* (1955). Chadwick Hansen, *Witchcraft in Salem* (1969) is suggestive.

Perry Miller, *Jonathan Edwards* (1949), and S. C. Henry, *George Whitefield, Wayfaring Witness* (1957), are good on the revivalists. Alan Heimert and Perry Miller, eds., *The Great Awakening, Documents Illustrating the Crisis and Its Consequences* (1967), provides the best general survey. On the relation of the religious revival to slavery and the blacks, see the discussion in D. B. Davis, *The Problem of Slavery in Western Culture* (1965), and W. D. Jordan, *White Over Black* (1968). R. B. Perry, *Puritanism and Democracy* (1944), is good on religion and politics. On deism, see G. A. Koch, *Republican Religion: The American Revolution and the Cult of Reason* (1933), and Herbert Morais, *Deism in Eighteenth Century America* (1934).

The impact of the Enlightenment is well presented in the general works cited at the head of these Readings. Its relevance to the life of the Negro is examined in detail in Davis, *The Problem of Slavery in Western Culture,* above. Numerous works by and on Benjamin Franklin help give substance to Enlightenment thought: A. O. Aldridge, *Benjamin Franklin: Philosopher and Man* (1965); Carl Van Doren, *Benjamin Franklin* (1938); I. B. Cohen, *Franklin and Newton* (1956); Franklin's *Autobiography* (first published 1868); and I. B. Cohen, ed., *Benjamin Franklin* (1953), an anthology. For a critical estimate see D. H. Lawrence, *Studies in Classic American Literature* (1953). Brooke Hindle, *The Pursuit of Science in Revolutionary America 1735-1789* (1956), is a scholarly monograph. Maurice Cranston, *John Locke* (1957), is a readable modern biography; and by John Locke, *Two Treatises of Civil Government* (1690), is fundamental for political thought. Caroline Robbins, *The Eighteenth-Century Commonwealthman* (1959), is an indispensable study "of English Liberal Thought from the Restoration of Charles II until the War with the Thirteen Colonies." Adrienne Koch, ed., *The American Enlightenment: The Shaping of the American Experiment and a Free Society* (1965), is a useful anthology.

Paul Monroe, *The Founding of the American Public School System* (2 vols., 1940), is a standard work. Robert Middlekauff, *Ancients and Axioms, Secondary Education in Eighteenth-Century New England* (1963), is excellent. On higher education, see Frederick Rudolph, *The American College and University* (1962); Richard Hofstadter, *Academic Freedom in the Age of the College* (1955); and S. E. Morison, *Harvard College in the Seventeenth Century* (1936).

On popular culture, see Sidney Kobre, *The Development of the Colonial Newspaper* (1944), and vol. 1 of F. L. Mott, *A History of American Magazines* (5 vols., 1930-1968). Richard McLanathan, *The American Tradition in the Arts* (1968), provides a fresh view. See also Oliver Larkin, *Art and Life in America* (1949). On colonial literature see the work of V. L. Parrington, above, and M. C. Tyler, *A History of American Literature 1607-1765* (1949). Worth reading for quick surveys are the first chapter of Marcus Cunliffe, *The Literature of the United States* (1954), and an excellent essay on colonial writing in H. M. Jones, *Ideas in America* (1944). Robert Spiller *et al., Literary History of the United States* (3 vols., 1948), contains scholarly treatments by specialists in colonial literature.

# FREE AND INDEPENDENT STATES

In 1763, when the French and Indian War ended, France seemed ruined. Although she was not beyond recovery, as William Pitt warned with characteristic insight, even few Frenchmen expected that she would soon be able to resume the imperial contest. Britain, by contrast, appeared to be at the peak of her imperial glory; yet her North American mainland colonies were to rebel against her "tyranny" much earlier than the French would turn on the absolutist Bourbons, and indeed they would win their independence with French aid.

Few changes in national fortunes have come about so swiftly and with so little apparent incitement. Indeed, on both sides of the ocean reasonable men found the revolutionary movement in America incomprehensible—and who could blame them when rebel spokesmen talked of little but preserving *English* liberties? Ambrose Serle, civilian secretary to Lord Richard Howe, the British naval commander in America during the early years of the fighting, declared that "The Annals of no Country can produce an Instance of so virulent a Rebellion, of such implacable madness and Fury, originating from such trivial Causes as those alleged by these unhappy People." Serle's description hardly characterizes the eight dreary years of spasmodic warfare nor the scattered instances of violence that preceded them; but even if it did, the Revolution was effected less by popular "virulence" than by learned argument, "the energies of well-weighed choice"; less by "those mad tumultuous actions which disgraced many of the great revolutions of antiquity" than by the force of continental aspirations.

Scotch-Irish and German colonists and members of other minority groups, ethnic or religious, although they often had as little sympathy for the English in America as they had for the mother country, sometimes were won over to the conflict by rebel leaders. When in 1775 a North Carolina convention elected delegates to the Continental Congress (see p. 120), Andrew Miller, a loyalist merchant, asked the westerners in the colony to pay no part of their expenses, "as they had no share in the Nomination. . . . It is not in Character, to dispute the power of Parliament when we say we are not represented, and yet quickly Submit to so unequal a Representation in a body formed by ourselves." Occasionally ethnic-group participation was gained by promises of attention to such frontier complaints, more often by the westerners' own generalized expectations of equality of opportunity with those of English descent in the future.

Had more of the 450,000 Negroes in the mainland colonies on the eve of the Revolution been aware of England's predominant role in the eighteenth-century slave trade and of Parliament's role in forcing captive blacks on ambivalent colonies for the benefit of commercial carriers (see p. 62), they might have loved the English even less than they loved their masters. As it was, tens of thousands of them responded to British promises of freedom in return for abandoning the fields and joining the fighting on the loyal side, and even greater numbers left with the British at the end of the war or were taken beyond the boundaries of the victors by their loyalist owners. At the same time, about 5000 Negroes, free and slave, largely from northern colonies, joined the rebels from time to time when reluctantly permitted to do so by American leaders, no doubt in the hope of securing that liberty and equality which, it was said, the fighting was all about.

Popular support of the fighting proved no stronger in the colonies than in the distant mother country. By December 1776 the 16,000 men Washington had taken under his command eighteen months earlier (see p. 122) had dwindled to 2400 bitter-enders; and frequently in succeeding years it seemed that the British might be near victory for want of opposition and the rebels near disintegration for want of pay.

Popular apathy toward the war may have given the large number of loyalists in the colonies encouragement to persist in their opposition to the rebellion despite personal harassment; and the more so since many of them believed that only the authority of the mother country could maintain political stability in an America of antagonistic commonwealths, each swelling with violent foreigners on the Indian frontiers and unruly mobs in the cities, neither class to be trusted with English liberties. Yet the challenge of British authority and loyalist sentiment from the top, and of rural squatters and urban workers from the bottom, only deepened the commitment of such conservative rebel leaders as John Adams of Massachusetts, Franklin of Pennsylvania, and Washington of Virginia to the necessity of ridding English liberties of the "systems of civil and priestly hierarchy" under which they had become corrupted in the mother country and of defending their purity here.

As early as the 1750s, Franklin in England had found "an extream corruption prevalent among all orders of men in this rotton state." Somewhat later, Adams observed of the mother country that, "Corruption, like a cancer . . . eats faster and faster every hour, . . . until virtue, integrity, public spirit, simplicity, and frugality, become the objects of ridicule, and . . . foppery, selfishness, meanness, and downright venality swallow up the whole society." "Every American of fortune and common sense," he said, "must look upon his property to be sunk downright half of its value" the moment "an absolute subjection" to the Parliament of such a society "is established."

The heart of the rebellion lay in the threatened infection of America with the pox that in colonial opinion had killed English liberties at home. As John Dickinson of Pennsylvania put it in 1768, the critical question was "not, what evil *has actually attended* particular measures,—but what evil in the nature of things, is *likely to attend* them." The colonials, their friend Edmund Burke told the Commons seven years later, "auger misgovernment at a distance and snuff the approach of tyranny in every tainted breeze."

Reminiscing long after American independence had been won, John Adams asked, "What do we mean by the Revolution? The War? That was no part of the Revolution. It was only an Effect and Consequence of it. The Revolution was in the minds of the people, and this was effected, from 1760 to 1775, in the course of fifteen years before a drop of blood was drawn at Lexington." He meant, of course, the educated people of "principle and property," not the "turbulent and changing" rabble "of no importance"; the "friends of order," not its foes.

And yet, despite the leaders' detestation of "Christian White Savages" on the frontiers, Franklin's epithet, the political Revolution became a social revolution of a new and lasting kind. It created not a purified England but an open America, one characterized not by virgin leaders but (forgetting the *red* "savages") by virgin lands. Thomas Jefferson identified the emerging American vision when he talked of our "Empire for Liberty." He would preserve it for English "yeomen"; but it had already engaged the imagination of other Old World subjects and for more than a century would continue to offer them a fresh start.

## I  Onset of British mismanagement

### Giving offense to the merchants

Rumblings of serious trouble in America were heard even before the French and Indian War ended. From the start of the war, colonial merchants, with characteristic disregard for British policy, had sold supplies to the enemy on the North American mainland and had carried on (illicit) business as usual with enemy islands in the West Indies. In 1760 Pitt's ministry had ordered colonial governors to make a more vigorous effort to enforce the standing customs regulations. To carry out the governor's orders in Massachusetts, the principal center of illicit trade, royal customs collectors applied to the Superior Court of the colony for writs of assistance allowing them to call upon constabulary aid in searching the premises of proud merchants suspected nevertheless of smuggling.

Writs of assistance had been in common use for a long time, both in Britain and America (see p. 53). Authorized by acts of Parliament, they had to be renewed each time a new sovereign came to the throne. Thus when George II died in 1760, new writs had to be authorized in the name of George III, and the Massachusetts merchants seized on this opportunity to denounce the whole practice. As counsel they engaged the eccentric young

Boston lawyer, James Otis, of an old Massachusetts family long in the King's service. Otis nevertheless had personal scores to settle with Chief Justice Thomas Hutchinson, under whose name the writs were to be issued.

Early in 1761, when Otis appeared in court to protest some writs Hutchinson had drafted, he delivered one of the most momentous speeches yet heard in North America. John Adams, who was on hand, recalled years later: "Otis was a flame of fire! . . . he hurried away everything before him. American independence was then and there born." Although the speech itself has been lost to history, we know that Otis rested his case not on legal technicalities but on broad Lockeian principles. In arguing that an act of Parliament contrary to natural law must be regarded by the courts as void, he laid down the grounds of opposition to Parliament to which the colonists were to return again and again. Parliament had no legal right, he said, to violate natural law either in Britain or America. Fundamental human rights could not be infringed by legislation.

Otis lost his case and the writs in this instance were issued. But other colonies soon joined in the protest against their legality; and despite the pleas and threats of imperial customs commissioners, judges often refused to grant them, thereby depriving the authorities of police power.

## Mishandling the West

British interference with colonial commerce during the French and Indian War angered Americans especially in New England, New York, and Pennsylvania. Britain's taking Canada from France at the end of the war gave colonial leaders in all thirteen commonwealths greater freedom and more frequent occasions to vent their anger. So long as France owned Canada, Americans had been drawn toward the mother country by the menace of an alien neighbor. The expulsion of France removed this menace, but subsequent

107

Benjamin Franklin Collection, Yale University Library

*George III at his accession, from an engraving after the painting by Joshua Reynolds. "He was tall, strongly sexed, had bulging eyes, a thick nose, loose, full lips, and a nature inclined to activity and adventure. Everything was done to stamp out this natural character."*

British administration of Indian affairs in particular quickly presented new dangers all along the frontier.

During the war, fearful of British expansionism, most of the tribes had become allies of the French, and with the British victory they had grown extremely restive. Probably no one could have satisfied all the clashing interests on the frontier. The established fur traders in the colonies as well as in Canada wanted the West permanently reserved for the Indian hunters and for the animals that bore the precious pelts. The newly influential land speculators, on the other hand, were urging settlers to go west, and wanted the frontier made safe for them. Both sides had powerful friends in

British politics. Colonial land speculators were particularly active in Pennsylvania and Virginia, and their claims often conflicted with one another's as well as with those of rivals in Britain. Benjamin Franklin represented a group of wealthy Pennsylvanians interested in lands along the Ohio. One of the Virginia enterprises was promoted by George Washington, whose Mississippi Company, formed as recently as 1763 as a successor to the old Ohio

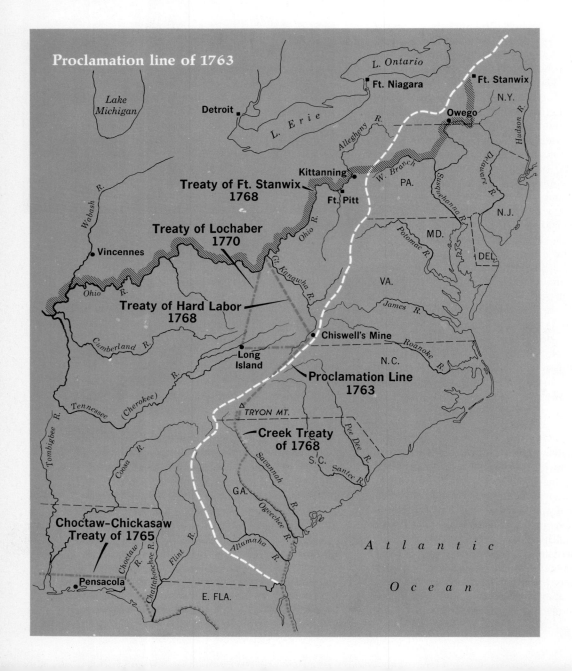

Proclamation line of 1763

Company (see p. 79), had its eye on thousands of acres at the junction of the Ohio and Mississippi rivers. Further complicating matters was the fact that with French power gone, British fur traders were cheating the Indian hunters and middlemen without remorse.

While the London government struggled to piece together a western policy for America, the aroused braves decided to look after themselves. Goaded by friendly Gallic traders who talked persuasively of the return of the French to North America, the red men, under the Ottawa chief, Pontiac (hence the name, "Pontiac's Conspiracy") went into action in May 1763. Pontiac had planned a concerted attack on British forts with the objective of sweeping the entire white population into the sea. By the end of June his followers had destroyed seven of the nine British garrisons west of Niagara. So desperate had the British become by July 1763 that they employed infected blankets to "send the *Small Pox*" among the "disaffected tribes." Thousands of braves soon died of the disease and by September 1764 most of the West had been pacified by such germ warfare and more conventional means.

Soon after news of Pontiac's Conspiracy reached London, the King, with the advice of the Privy Council, in October issued the Proclamation of 1763, intended as a temporary measure to give Britain time to work out a permanent western policy. This Proclamation set boundaries for three new crown colonies: Quebec, East Florida, and West Florida. Virtually all other western territory from the Alleghenies to the Mississippi, and from Florida to 50° north latitude, was reserved for the time being for the red men. Fur traders, land speculators, settlers, all were excluded.

Yet no proclamation issued thousands of miles away could keep speculators and frontiersmen out. Many colonials must have agreed with George Washington when he urged in effect that the Proclamation of 1763 be disobeyed: "I can never look upon that proclamation in any other light . . . than as a temporary expedient to quiet the minds of Indians. . . . Any person, therefore, who neglects the present opportunity of hunting out good lands, and in some measure marking and distinguishing them for his own (in order to keep others from settling them), will never regain it." Washington practiced what he preached, and he and others maintained agents in the Ohio Valley to stake out claims.

Opposition to the Proclamation of 1763 grew so strong that within a few years the British revised their western policy, making a series of treaties with the Indians to give the speculators room. One such treaty was made with the Choctaws and Chickasaws in 1765 to set the boundary of the Floridas. Three more followed in 1768: one with the Creeks at Pensacola, which affected the borders of South Carolina and Georgia; one with the Cherokees at their village of Hard Labor, which affected the boundary of western Virginia; and one with the Iroquois at Fort Stanwix in New York, which defined and in some places extended that colony's northern boundary. By the Treaty of Lochaber in 1770, the Cherokees, for a price, accepted a line even farther west than that set at Hard Labor.

Every extension of the boundary line touched off new bursts of speculation. In 1768 the first actual settlers beyond the Blue Ridge barrier occupied the Watauga Valley of North Carolina. In 1769, having made his first trip west two years before, Daniel Boone traversed the future "Wilderness Road" from the Holston River, through the Cumberland Gap, into Kentucky (see map, p. 110). Here he spent two years exploring the river valleys north to the Ohio, and in 1775, spurred on by Richard Henderson's land enterprises (see p. 145), he guided the first group of permanent settlers to the blue grass region. Unfortunately for the British, the deeper the Americans moved into the West and away from the old centers of power the more determined on self-government did they become.

### The planters' disenchantment

Britain's restrictive western policy was especially hard on the planters of the South. By concentrating on their one money-making crop, the Chesapeake tobacco planters in particular had depleted the soil of both tidewater and piedmont. Cheap lands farther west seemed their only salvation. "The greatest estates we have in the colony," Washington wrote in 1767, were established "by taking up ... at very low rates the rich back lands which were thought nothing of in those days but are now the most valuable lands we possess." Washington and others had already begun to shift from tobacco to wheat growing in anticipation of moving inland.

Land policy was only one source of planter discontent with British rule. British merchants served as middlemen, at exorbitant commission fees, for everything the southerners bought abroad as well as for everything they sold. In addition, British shipowners charged high rates for carrying the planters' produce and purchases across the ocean. As their returns from the depleted lands dwindled, the southerners' debts mounted. Jefferson once estimated that Virginia planters owed at least £2 million to British merchants and observed that these debts "had become hereditary from father to son, for many generations." When the planters tried to pay their debts in American paper currency, such a howl of protest arose from the British merchants that Parliament passed the Currency Act of 1764 forbidding this practice and warning that a burdensome penalty would be laid on any colonial governor who signed a paper-money bill.

The Virginians' discontent became a broad

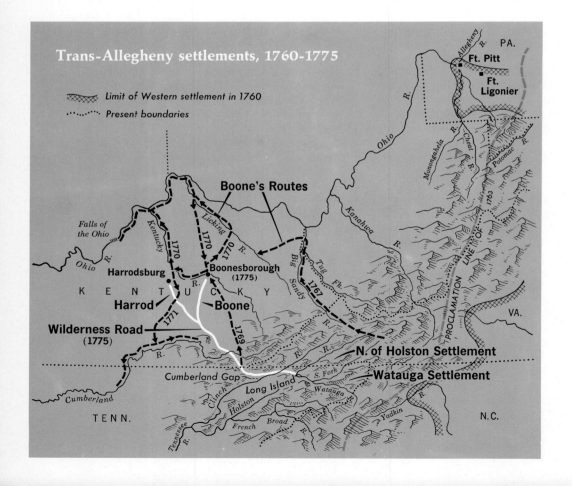

Trans-Allegheny settlements, 1760-1775

Limit of Western settlement in 1760

Present boundaries

colonial issue as a result of the "Parson's Cause" of 1763. This dispute over how the clergy of the established church were to be paid first brought Patrick Henry to notice. Traditionally, the Virginia clergy's salary was stated in pounds of tobacco; but when a tobacco shortage in 1758 drove prices far above their usual level, the assembly passed the Twopenny Act which allowed taxpayers to meet their obligation to the clergy at the rate of 2 cents for each pound of tobacco due, even though tobacco had soared to 5.5 cents a pound. On complaint of the clergy to the Episcopal Bishop of London, the King in 1759 disallowed the Twopenny Act. Not content with this victory, several Virginia clergymen sued for a year's back pay. In one of these suits, which came to court in 1763, young

Henry represented the Virginia tax collectors. In an inflammatory speech to the jury, he cried that the King, by disallowing the Virginia law of 1758, had "degenerated into a tyrant, and forfeits all rights to his subjects' obedience." The opposing attorney called this "treason," but Henry knew his strong language was safe in a country made up largely of dissenters. The jury awarded only one penny in damages to the churchman who had brought the case, and Henry's victory made him famous.

In 1764 the frontier region in which Patrick Henry lived voted him into the House of Burgesses. From then on he was an effective spokesman for Virginia religious dissenters and the common people generally. Since Virginia herself was so predominant a power in the South, her hurts and her heroes furthered her neighbors' as well as her own preparation for cooperating with rebellious colonists to the north.

## II   A passion for self-government

### Taxation the great issue

The most divisive problem raised by the French and Indian War was taxation. Britain's long, costly struggles for empire had boosted tax rates to such staggering heights that British landowners by 1763 were turning over about a third of their income to the government. Now the British had to face the cost of garrisoning their expanded possessions. In North America alone, it was calculated that 10,000 troops were needed; and Parliament felt that the colonies should share the cost, which after all went largely to pay for their protection. The British government felt especially justified in its stand by the manifest good thing the northern colonists in particular had made of the war. "You cannot well imagine," a visitor wrote from Boston in 1760, "what a land of health, plenty and contentment this is among all the ranks, vastly improved within these ten years. The war on

this continent has been equally a blessing to the English subjects and a Calamity to the French."

The colonists, however, for all their affection for the mother country and their avowed loyalty to the Crown, had long since learned to manage their home finances without British interference and now began to demand that the British solve their financial crisis without troubling America. For one thing, the colonies had worked up a war debt of their own of £2.5 million which they would have to pay and service. In addition, by Pitt's estimate, British merchants, under the mercantilist tendency of trade, made profits of no less than £2 million a year on colonial commerce, and such profits seemed to Americans, and to Pitt himself, to be "tax" enough. The very prosperity that made the colonials seem fair game to the British, moreover, had given them, in the words of Lieutenant-Governor Hutchinson of Massachusetts, "a higher sense" of their "grandeur and importance," and stiffened their stand against Parliament's financial innovations and in support of their own scholarly ideas. These ideas themselves grew in scope as the conflict deepened.

### The novelty of the Sugar Act

The task of coping with the vast new problems of imperial government and finance after the French and Indian War fell first upon the ministry of George Grenville, which lasted from 1763 until 1765. In April 1764, the new ministry took its first financial plunge by imposing on the American colonies what became known as the Sugar Act. By this measure Grenville hoped to raise £45,000 a year. Instead he raised the spirit of revolt.

A duty of 6 cents a gallon on the importation of foreign molasses essential to the distilling of Yankee rum had been imposed on the colonies in 1733 but was weakly enforced. The new act halved the duty but made it clear that it would be collected to the penny. Duties on many other essential imports were raised at the same time. To insure collection, suits over the payment of the new duties and charges of smuggling on other grounds as well were removed from the regular colonial courts, where Americans usually were let off by friendly juries, to the hated admiralty courts, where there were no juries. This provision excited American merchants even more than the ruin they saw in store for them because of the Sugar Act's direct interference with the whole range of colonial commerce.

But what aroused Americans most of all were the ominous implications of the official title of the act—the Revenue Act—and the preamble which elaborated its purpose to tax the colonists directly. Heretofore charges placed upon the colonials had been explained and excused as a legitimate part of imperial administration. The Sugar Act was the first law ever passed by Parliament with the avowed objective of raising money in the colonies.

The Currency Act, passed in the same month as the unprecedented Sugar Act, worsened the situation. Faced with one measure designed to draw money from America and another to forbid expansion of American currency, many groaned under the heavy hand of empire. The town of Boston, preparing instructions for its representatives in the general assembly at this time, asked an ominous question: "If taxes are laid upon us in any shape without ever having a legal representation where they are laid, are we not reduced from the character of free subjects to the miserable state of tributary slaves?" James Otis wrote a thundering pamphlet in which he declared: "No parts of his Majesty's dominions can be taxed without their consent." The Massachusetts House of Representatives authorized a committee of correspondence to write to other provinces about the issue. In Boston, New York, and elsewhere, merchants and mechanics pledged themselves not to buy or use certain British goods. The Sugar Act spawned the idea of nonimportation, which soon became so effective a revolutionary weapon.

### The Stamp Act Congress

When Grenville announced the Sugar Act, he served notice that another revenue measure was being prepared. This was the Stamp Act, passed by Parliament in March 1765, to go into effect in November. Grenville had even higher hopes for this act than for the Sugar Act, for he expected it to bring in £60,000 a year. Every time a colonial wanted a legal document, or a license, newspaper, pamphlet, almanac, playing cards, or dice, this act required that he purchase a stamp for it ranging in value from a half-penny to £10.

One section of the Stamp Act especially alarmed the dissenting clergy, who were to become among the most influential of the rebels. This was the section that required stamps on "every skin or piece of vellum or parchment, or sheet or piece of paper," as the act said, issuing from any court, including courts "exercising ecclesiastical jurisdiction within the said colonies." There were, as yet, no courts in the colonies "exercising ecclesiastical jurisdiction"; but there was a justifiable fear, growing since 1763, that the Church of England might gain the authority to set them up under the bishop it was urging for America. When the Stamp Act seemed to assume that these courts, and this centralized religious authority, would be imposed, it galvanized the resistance of the many colonials whose whole tradition was based on congregational self-determination. The Stamp Act provided further that all violators were to be tried in the same hated juryless admiralty courts in which smugglers were brought to account, and heavily fined if found guilty. The Sugar Act had struck mainly at merchants. The Stamp Act hit every articulate and influential person in the colonies—lawyers, printers, editors, tavern owners, and dissenting preachers. "One single act of Parliament," said James Otis of the Sugar Act, "set the people a-thinking in six months, more than they had done in their whole lives before." That was in New England. The fatal flaw of the Stamp Act was that it set people *talking* everywhere. The Stamp Act, in fact, set people to acting as well as talking. In response to this Act, colonial leaders began to develop the revolutionary machinery by which they ultimately separated from Britain.

No sooner had news of the Stamp Act reached America than the Massachusetts House of Representatives, in June 1765, resolved to call a full-scale intercolonial congress, the first ever to be convened on American initiative, to meet in New York City in October, to combat it. In the intervening months the Sons of Liberty, secret organizations often led by men of wealth and standing, were formed in most port cities to intimidate stamp agents and others insufficiently rebellious. In August 1765 a Boston mob burned the records of the admiralty court, ransacked the home of the comptroller of the customs, and then entered, looted, and wrecked the elegant Hutchinson mansion, stealing or destroying everything down to the last shirt. Even before November 1, when the

Stamp Act was to go into effect, every stamp agent in the colonies had been badgered into resigning or promising not to execute his commission.

When the Stamp Act Congress met in New York in October 1765, nine colonies were represented. Of the four absentees, Virginia, Georgia, and North Carolina had failed to send delegates only because their royal governors would permit none to be selected. The fourth missing colony was New Hampshire.

It was at the Stamp Act Congress that Christopher Gadsden of South Carolina proposed that "there ought to be no New England man, no New Yorker, known on this continent, but all of us Americans." This Congress's moderate "Declaration of Rights and Grievances" began by acknowledging "all due Subordination" not only to the Crown, but also "to that August Body the Parliament of Great Britain." At the same time it sharply advanced the American position by stating, "That the people of these Colonies are not, and from their local Circumstances cannot be, Represented in the House of Commons in *Great Britain;* That the only Representatives of the People of these Colonies, are Persons chosen therein by themselves, and that no Taxes ever have been, or can be Constitutionally imposed on them, but by their respective Legislatures." The Declaration closed by asserting "the Right of ... these Colonies to Petition the King, or either House of Parliament ... to procure the Repeal" of the Stamp Act as well as "any other Acts of Parliament, whereby the Jurisdiction of the Admiralty is extended" or the "American Commerce" is restricted.

The Stamp Act Congress was followed by signed agreements among hundreds of merchants in each of the major ports not to buy British goods until repeal of the hated law and the other objectionable trade regulations had been effected. When the Stamp Act went into force in November 1765, merchants almost everywhere suspended business in protest. When they resumed business by the end of the year, they did so without using stamps, and not a single one ever was sold in America.

By then Grenville had been relieved of his ministry, more for boring the young King who had developed "a kind of horror of the interminable persistency of his conversation," than for overburdening the Americans. The new ministry under the Marquis of Rockingham faced not only opposition in America but pressure also from merchants at home, who were feeling the pinch of the American boycott.

Parliament repealed the Stamp Act on March 17, 1766. Few British leaders, however, were willing to admit that it had been repealed because, as Pitt put it, "it was founded on an erroneous principle." To make it clear that repeal was not a renunciation of revenue-raising powers, the legislature passed, along with the repeal, the Declaratory Act, which asserted that Parliament had the full right to make laws "to bind the colonies and people of America . . . in all cases whatsoever."

Parliament, unfortunately, did more. On Lord Amherst's departure from Canada in 1763, General Thomas Gage had risen to Commander-in-Chief of the few thousand British troops still holding western posts. On his elevation, Gage, something of a social lion, moved from Montreal to more cosmopolitan New York City, and in March 1765 within a few days of adopting the Stamp Act, Parliament had passed a Quartering Act requiring the colonies to supply barracks for Gage's men and other materials heretofore furnished by the British army. Compliance lagged. When the Stamp Act Congress made New York appear to have become the center of rebellious activity, Gage called in more of his men to join him in the city. Chiefly to house them, Parliament, in 1766, passed a second Quartering Act requiring the colonies to supplement barracks where necessary with accommodations for the troops in public inns, alehouses, unoccupied buildings, and even private barns.

New York's legislature and the city's residents both resisted the new law. In August 1766, almost four years before the Boston Massacre (see p. 116), redcoats and rebels clashed, and Isaac Sears, the leader of the city's Sons of Liberty, was wounded. A larger clash on the same issue, known as the Battle of Golden Hill, took place in New York in January 1770, with no fatalities but with numerous casualties among the Sons of Liberty and the sons of Britain.

The Declaratory Act's assertion of power in London and the mobilization of "standing armies" in the colonies augured ill for the future despite the rejoicing with which repeal of the Stamp Act was hailed.

### Townshend Acts and the clarification of ideas

About four months after the repeal of the Stamp Act the Rockingham ministry fell and Pitt was called upon to form a new cabinet. But Pitt, now Earl of Chatham, soon became so ill that he was forced to retire temporarily. Control then fell to the clever Chancellor of the Exchequer, Charles Townshend, whose fiscal measures turned the Americans from resistance to revolution, a turn Pitt might have averted.

Townshend had been led by American arguments in 1765 and 1766 to believe that the colonials would accept revenue-raising acts presented not as "internal taxes" but as traditional "external" trade regulations. Accordingly, in June 1767, on his recommendation, Parliament passed the Townshend Acts imposing new *import* duties—on glass, lead, paints, paper, and tea. Such thinking did not impress American spokesmen, but the extraordinary thoughtlessness of other provisions of the Townshend Acts did. To insure collection of the new duties, the Acts reasserted the power of imperial courts in the colonies to issue writs of assistance. Provocative as this assertion was, worse lay ahead, for the Acts also provided that violators of the new regulations be tried in the hated admiralty courts.

Resentment was heightened further by the Acts' creation of a new Board of Customs Commissioners whose job it was to spy out every petty violation and even to invent violations under technicalities. The crowning insult was the provision that the salaries of the

King's new appointees be paid out of the fines and judgments levied against violaters convicted in the admiralty courts. The final section of the Townshend Acts hit specifically at New York for noncompliance with the Quartering Act of 1766. After October 1, 1767, all legislative functions of the New York Assembly were to be suspended.

Even before the customs commissioners reached Boston in November, colonial merchants had revived the nonimportation agreements that British merchants found so costly the year before. Colonial spokesmen, at the same time, were honing up their ideas. Starting in December 1767 the moderate John Dickinson published in the *Pennsylvania Chronicle and Universal Advertiser* his series of *Letters from a Farmer in Pennsylvania to the Inhabitants of the British Colonies,* in which he assailed the Townshend Acts as unconstitutional. He denounced Parliament's treatment of the New York Assembly in particular as a threat to the liberties of all the colonies.

*I regard the late act[s, Dickinson wrote] as an* experiment made of our disposition. *It is a bird sent over the waters, to discover, whether the waves, that lately agitated this part of the world with such violence [meaning the Stamp Act], have yet* subsided. *If this adventurer gets footing here, we shall quickly find that it be of the kind described by the poet.—*
　"Infelix vates."
　*A direful foreteller of future calamities.*

We must not sacrifice "a single iota" of our privileges, Dickinson asserted. We must defend them, *"peaceably—prudently—firmly—jointly."* "Tho' your devotion to *Great Britain* is the most affectionate," he concluded, "yet you can make PROPER DISTINCTIONS, and know what you owe to *yourselves,* as well *as to her."*

By 1768, Franklin's "distinctions," for one, had been made. After mulling over the question of "internal taxes" and "external duties,"

he said, he found it "difficult to draw lines" between them,

*and if the Parliament is to be the judge, it seems to me that establishing such a principle of distinction will amount to little. The more I have thought and read on the subject, the more I find myself confirmed in opinion, that no middle ground can be well maintained. . . . Something might be made of either of the extremes: that Parliament has a power to make all laws for us, or that it has a power to make no laws for us; and I think the arguments for the latter more numerous and weighty, than those for the former. Supposing that doctrine established, the colonies would then be so many separate states, only subject to the same king, as England and Scotland were before the union.*

These last bold words laid bare the direction the colonial argument was taking—that the colonists should become completely independent of Parliament and united to Britain only by their loyalty to the Crown. Such distinguished American lawyers as James Wilson of Pennsylvania, John Adams, and Thomas Jefferson already shared this view.

Algernon Sidney, the seventeenth-century republican who opposed both the absolutism of Charles I and the dictatorship of Cromwell—and with James Harrington and John Locke was most quoted by the American rebel philosophers—once wrote: "Peace is seldom made, and never kept, unless the subject retain such power in his hands as may oblige the prince to stand on what is agreed." Sidney had followers in eighteenth-century England as well as in America who willingly conceded that history, the British constitution, and the rights of man all supported the colonial argument against having their money taken from them, as they put it, by a legislature in which they had no voice. Parliament itself, however, until too late, offered in rebuttal only the sophistry of "virtual representation." True, said the government defenders, Americans were not directly represented in Parliament. But neither were the people of Manchester, Birmingham, and other growing industrial cities in England represented by men of their own choosing. Yet they willingly paid taxes levied by members elected elsewhere in the kingdom who "virtually represented" them—and the colonials should profit from *that* example.

Americans failed to be impressed with this argument. To them, 3000 miles from London, "virtual representation" by men who never saw them from one year to the next was no representation at all. To their friend Pitt, "virtual representation" was "the most contempt-

116

ible idea that ever entered into the head of man." His friend Camden told Parliament, "virtual representation ... is so absurd as not to deserve an answer."

## III  The nesting of rebellion

### To the "Boston Massacre"

Dickinson's *Letters* were reprinted in many colonial newspapers and distributed in pamphlet form. In February 1768, on behalf of the Massachusetts legislature, Samuel Adams already the acknowledged leader of the "popular party" in the House of Representatives to which he had been elected in 1766, wrote a circular letter to be sent to the other colonies restating Dickinson's points.

Sam Adams's letter drew from the newly created office of Secretary of State for America instructions to all colonial governors to see to it that their assemblies treated it with "the contempt it deserves," even if they had to dissolve the assemblies to enforce this policy. The Secretary's order came too late to stop the assemblies of New Hampshire, New Jersey, and Connecticut from openly endorsing Massachusetts's stand. Virginia, meanwhile, issued her own circular letter in support of it. Governor Francis Bernard, Shirley's successor in Massachusetts in 1760, had been specifically admonished to dissolve the legislature should it fail to rescind Adams's letter. On June 30, 1768, the Massachusetts House of Representatives voted 92 to 17 not to rescind. Next day Bernard dissolved the House.

Certain to be provocative at any time, Bernard's act at this juncture proved peculiarly ill-timed. Earlier in June, John Hancock's sloop *Liberty* had attempted to land a cargo of wine on Boston's wharf without paying the duty. To improve their chances of success, her officers had locked a wharf official in the sloop's

cabin. When the customs commissioners ordered *Liberty's* seizure, crowds began to assault other wharf officials and to menace their homes, leading the commissioners to demand protection by British troops. Rumors of their coming ran through Boston daily until, in fact, at the end of September 1768, two well-equipped infantry regiments dispatched by Gage arrived, the general following soon.

The presence of redcoats in Boston now, as in New York earlier, was ample incitement to riot, and it is remarkable that serious violence was averted for eighteen months. One cause of friction was competition for jobs between Yankee laborers in the port and redcoats seeking work in off-duty hours. A fistfight over this issue on the afternoon of March 5, 1770, raised tension to a peak and that night, the "victualling houses" having done good business, the "Boston Massacre" took place. Ten British soldiers, goaded by an unruly crowd, fired at their tormentors despite their officer's efforts to restrain them, and killed five while wounding others.

John Adams defended the soldiers in court against a murder indictment. The civilian dead, he said later, were among "the most obscure and inconsiderable [men] that could have been found upon this continent." They were not even genuine Bostonians, but outsiders looking for trouble. "And it is in this manner," he told the trial jury, that "this town has often been treated; a Carr from Ireland, and an Attucks from Framingham, happening to be here, ... sally out upon their thoughtless enterprises, at the head of such a rabble of negroes, &c, as they can collect together."

Adams's plea won acquittal from the Boston jury on the murder charge. Two soldiers, found guilty of manslaughter, were released after minor punishment. But the "massacre" itself became a favorite theme for oratory. At the same time, nonimportation progressed in the South as well as in the North. By 1770, every colony but New Hampshire had agreed to participate in enforcement, thereby leaving few loopholes for evasion by Americans as yet unaccustomed to working together. That year, colonial trade with the mother country fell off by a third.

Frederick, Lord North, who became Prime Minister in March 1770, could not help but realize that the Townshend Acts were costing more than they would ever bring in, and he promptly called on Parliament to repeal all the duties except that on tea. This *one* must contin-

ue simply to maintain the principle of parliamentary power. Parliament complied in April, without yet having learned of the Boston Massacre. Against the urging of the Sons of Liberty, most Americans, on hearing of Lord North's apparently conciliatory step, let nonimportation drop. It had to be acknowledged, however, that the British had so far failed to force the colonials to yield a regular revenue, even for their own protection, while the Americans had failed to win their point on the unconstitutionality of Parliament's efforts.

**117**

### The spearhead of revolt

"Happy are the men, and *happy the people who grow wise by the* misfortunes of

*This view, by Paul Revere, of "The Bloody Massacre" in Boston, and its many variants are regarded as major revolutionary propaganda pieces, focusing colonial rancor on the British. The pen and ink diagram at the left, showing what actually occurred, is said to have been used at the trial of the British soldiers.*

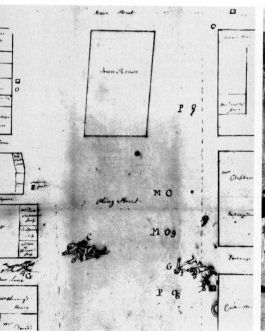

others," said one of the rebel philosophers. To attain such wisdom, John Adams admonished his friends, "Let us . . . read the histories of ancient ages; contemplate the great examples of Greece and Rome; set before us the conduct of our British ancestors, who have defended for us the inherent rights of mankind against foreign and domestic tyrants and usurpers." Others, led by John's cousin Sam, were more impatient. "I doubt whether there is a greater incendiary in the King's dominion," Governor Hutchinson said of him as early as 1771.

While tension abated following repeal of the Townshend measures and merchants and others went about their business, British administration of the ports and the courts also continued its abrasive course. Ships were stopped and searched, their officers abused, their owners hailed before admiralty judges, warehouses entered with constabulary aid. Many like John Hancock, disenchanted by the rumor that Sam Adams "led him by the nose," learned to endure the painful British presence, hoping only that nothing worse would befall them. Adams, writing tirelessly for the *Boston Gazette* and other Boston newspapers, at the same time made the most of every petty incident, regretting only that none was sufficiently combustible to feed the flame of rebellion. He also wrote letters to correspondents in other colonies to keep patriot spirits high. "If it were not for two or three Adamses," Hutchinson reported to London in 1771, "we should do well enough. We have not been so quiet these five years." Later letters announcing the decline of Adams's "popular party," a fact confirmed by Sam's much narrowed margin of victory on being reelected to the provincial House of Representatives in 1772, came like the music of sirens to Lord North's ministers. Adams himself felt confident that Hutchinson's "quiet" would sooner or later lull the British into playing his game, and in fact he found his opening sooner than expected.

Late in 1771, Boston learned that henceforth the royal governor was to be paid by the Crown, not the colony. In September 1772 the rumor of a similar change in the method of paying judges was confirmed. This was the

The Metropolitan Museum of Art, Bequest of Charles Allen Munn, 1924

*Sam Adams, the great incendiary,
by John Norman.*

"FINISHING STROKE," cried the Boston Sons of Liberty in October; Americans will become "as complete slaves as the inhabitants of Turkey or Japan." In November, on Adams's motion, a sharply divided Boston Town Meeting appointed an official "committee of correspondence . . . to state the rights of the Colonists and of this Province in particular, as men, as Christians, and as Subjects; and to communicate the same to the several towns and the world." "All Men," Adams now asserted, "have a Right to remain in a State of Nature as long as they please; And in case of intollerable Oppression, Civil or Religious, to leave the Society they belong to, and enter into another."

The *Gaspee* incident, June 9, 1772 advanced Adams's intercolonial campaign. That day the British customs schooner, *Gaspee*, a thorn in the flesh to Rhode Island merchants in Narragansett Bay, ran aground near Providence while pursuing a local vessel. As night fell, eight boatloads of men led by prominent local businessmen attacked the stranded revenuer, removed her crew, and burned her. Aware that Rhode Island courts would never punish the offenders even if caught, the King, on learning of the affair, named a special commission to find the perpetrators and ship them to England for trial. Although Rhode Islanders utterly frustrated the commission, the plan to try colonials in England jarred Americans all the way to Virginia and Charleston. By February 1774 every colony but North Carolina and Pennsylvania had formed committees of correspondence to keep one another informed on further breaches of their natural rights. Thus, Hutchinson lamented, "was the Contagion which began in Boston" diffused. The committees, Sam Adams boasted, turned people from "picking up pins, and directed their View to great objects."

*To the breaking point*

Perhaps the irreversible urge to revolution began in May 1773, when Parliament passed the incredibly provocative East India, or Tea, Act. No ordinary commercial organization, the East India Company was a gigantic monopoly to which Parliament had entrusted even the government of India. Like the British government itself, the company now was shot through with corruption and mismanagement. Trembling on the brink of bankruptcy, it demanded that Parliament bail it out. The warehouses of the East India Company in England were bulging with 17 million pounds of tea. The Tea Act granted the company the right to ship this tea to America and to sell it there through its own agents. Cheap tea for colonial consumers was one thing. Cheap tea at the expense of colonial importers was another.

By December 1773 East India Company tea had reached Boston, where it sat under the protection of British troops. To rid themselves of it, patriots under Sam Adams's direction hit on the device of disguising themselves as Indians, boarding the tea ships, and throwing the tea into the harbor. This feat, famous as the "Boston Tea Party," was performed on December 16.

The North ministry could not ignore so defiant an act, nor could friends of the colonies in Parliament condone it. To punish the Americans, Parliament early in 1774 passed a series of measures called in the colonies Coercive, or "Intolerable," Acts, which killed whatever hope of reconciliation remained: (1) The Port of Boston was to be closed until the East India Company and the British customs had been reimbursed for their losses. (2) Any British official indicted by Massachusetts courts for capital offenses committed while enforcing British laws would be tried at home, away from hostile colonials. (3) In Massachusetts, the King or his governor was given power to fill by appointment many offices heretofore elective; and no town meeting could be held without the governor's permission, and then only on business he approved. (4) A new Quartering Act was imposed on all the colonies.

With characteristically poor timing, Parliament also picked May 1774 to pass the Quebec Act. By recognizing certain features of French law, this act gratified the former Canadian subjects of France. But these features included trials without juries and political equality for Catholics—two items which especially alarmed the alerted Protestants of neighboring Massachusetts. More objectionable still to the rest of the colonists, the act enlarged the Province of Quebec to include territory north of the Ohio and east of the Mississippi where Massachusetts, Connecticut, and Virginia all had claims.

To voice their united opposition to these Acts and take steps in self-defense, the Massachusetts House of Representatives asked the colonies to send delegates to Philadelphia in September 1774. All but Georgia complied. Delegates of the remaining twelve, all named by extralegal conventions to perform acts now unthinkable for regular state legislatures and governors, made up the First Continental Congress.

Work began in Philadelphia with the proposal of the conservative Joseph Galloway of Pennsylvania that a grand colonial council be set up to share power with Parliament on colonial matters. But, spurred on perhaps by false rumors that General Thomas Gage (recently appointed governor of Massachusetts) had bombarded Boston and that New England had taken up arms, the Congress rejected Galloway's scheme by a single vote and resolved on more drastic action.

A meeting of delegates in Massachusetts towns had just adopted the "Suffolk Resolves," which advocated two bold measures: (1) that the colonies raise their own troops; and (2) that they suspend all trade with Britain, Ireland, and the British West Indies. The

*"The Alternative of Williamsburg," from* London Chronicle, *January 26, 1775, showing reluctant Virginians signing up for the Association under duress. On gibbet, upper right, hang barrels of feathers and tar, each inscribed: "A Cure for the Refractory, which proved very effective in securing signatures."*

The Metropolitan Museum of Art, Bequest of Charles Allen Munn, 1924

Continental Congress endorsed these proposals and companies of "minutemen" soon began to drill on the village greens. To insure that the boycott of British trade be complete, Congress organized a "Continental Association," with local enforcement committees in each colony. These committees were empowered to publish the names of all violators as "enemies of *American* liberty," the better to expose them to public attack. The enforcement committees soon became, in fact, virtual local governments, and few dared to provoke their enmity.

The First Continental Congress may rightly be described as the first national government in America. "By assuming the powers of legislation," wrote a Tory critic of the Association and other congressional acts, "the Congress have not only superseded our provincial legislatures, but have excluded every idea of monarchy; and not content with the havoc already made in our constitution, in the plentitude of their power have appointed another Congress to be held in May."

Before adjourning on October 26, 1774, the First Continental Congress did in fact agree, unless their grievances had been fully met, to reconvene on May 10, 1775. The date proved to be none too early. Unnerved by the gathering of minutemen around Boston, General Gage, on April 19, 1775, sent 700 troops to destroy the large amount of munitions and supplies that the colonists appeared to be collecting in Concord, about 20 miles north. Boston patriots, in turn, sent Paul Revere, William Dawes, and Dr. Samuel Prescott to arouse the minutemen along the way, and at Lexington green, 5 miles short of Concord, the redcoats encountered a line of armed farmers and townsmen. Eight minutemen fell here, and the British moved on. Revere and Dawes were halted by the British before reaching Concord, but Dr. Prescott got through in time to warn the minutemen there to get their supplies away, which they did. Frustrated at Concord, Gage's men turned back toward Boston; but by then thousands of minutemen lined the road and shot down the redcoats as they passed. By the time they reached Boston the British had suffered 273 casualties. Ninety-three Americans had been killed or wounded.

There remained many men on both sides who were hoping, still, to avert war. But as the news spread of the fighting and the dead, the colonials looked anxiously to the forthcoming Philadelphia meeting for leadership in the crisis.

**Boston and vicinity, 1775**

North Bridge
Concord
**British Route**
April 19, 1775
Lexington
Medford
Bunker Hill
Breed's Hill
Cambridge
Charlestown
Charles R.
**Boston**
M A S S.
Roxbury
Dorchester Heights

## IV Patriots and Loyalists

*Failure of conciliation*

When the Second Continental Congress convened hastily in Philadelphia in May 1775, all thirteen colonies were to be represented, but distant Georgians did not arrive until September. The delegates made up a distinguished if divided group. Sitting among them were the men who were to become the first three Presidents of the United States. Few of them, nevertheless, could have imagined that they would remain in session almost continuously for fourteen years.

It was clear at the outset that Congress would support the action Massachusetts had taken, yet there was no formal resolve that the Continental Congress create a Continental army. The existence of an intercolonial fighting force was recognized only in an offhand announcement that Congress would "adopt" the army then congregating around Boston, for "the general defense of the right of America." Despite some Yankee military aspirations, moreover, the delegates by a nearly unanimous vote, agreed on the selection of Washington the Virginian as commander-in-chief of the army they adopted.

Many in the Second Continental Congress still hoped that Washington, as general, would

find little to do. On July 6, 1775, Congress voted a Declaration of the Causes and Necessity of Taking up Arms: "Our cause is just," they confidently declared. "Our union is perfect." Then came an open threat: "Our internal resources are great, and, if necessary, foreign assistance is undoubtedly attainable. . . . The arms we have been compelled by our enemies to assume, we will . . . employ for the preservation of our liberties, being with one mind resolved to die free men rather than live slaves." But there was also a note of hope: "We have not raised armies with ambitious designs of separating from Great Britain, and establishing independent States."

At this time, too, Congress adopted the "Olive Branch Petition," the work of its most cautious members. This document begged King George to keep Parliament from further tyrannical measures so that a plan of reconciliation could be worked out. On receiving it in August, however, the incautious King himself brushed it aside. In a proclamation he stigmatized the Americans as rebels and warned all loyal persons to abstain from assisting them.

Still, there remained conciliators in Britain too. In March 1775 Edmund Burke, in one of his great speeches, urged Parliament to meet American demands and surrender the right to

*General George Washington, 1779,*
*after Charles Willson Peale's portrait.*
*In background left is said to be the first*
*correctly engraved American flag.*

tax. "An Englishman," he exclaimed, "is the unfittest person on earth to argue another Englishman into slavery." Lord North himself persuaded Parliament to offer last-ditch concessions that might have helped in 1765 but in 1775 were too late.

By the time the North plan of conciliation reached Philadelphia, the Battle of Bunker Hill, the bloodiest engagement of the entire war, had been fought. The main battle actually took place on Breed's Hill, overlooking Boston, where American militiamen had gathered soon after the surviving redcoats had returned from Concord. On June 17, 1775, General Gage, strengthened by fresh troops, decided that he would drive the patriots off. He did manage to dislodge them, but at a frightful cost. The Americans lost almost 400 men; Gage lost more than 1000—over 40 percent of those he had moved into battle. Two weeks later, General Washington arrived at Cambridge, outside Boston, to take command.

By this time, too, fighting had begun farther north. Early in May 1775, in an effort to gain control of Canada, Ethan Allen, from future Vermont, captured the British posts at Crown Point and Ticonderoga in New York. On May 29, Congress approved an address to their "fellow-sufferers" in Canada, inviting them to join the rebellion; but the Canadians' "sufferings" had been assuaged by the Quebec Act of 1774, and their loyalty was not to be shaken.

When the British, in turn, organized a force in Canada to invade New York, Washington decided to try to forestall them. In September 1775 Benedict Arnold set out for Quebec from Cambridge with about 1000 of Washington's men, and early in December he was joined below the town by a smaller contingent under Richard Montgomery, which had already taken Montreal. On New Year's Eve, 1775, Arnold and Montgomery made their assault, and it ended in Montgomery's death and Arnold's defeat. Arnold's force kept Quebec isolated through the bitter winter; but with the arrival of British reinforcements in the spring, he was forced to retire to Ticonderoga. The venture only sharpened British concern for Canada's safety, and coming as it did just after Congress had rejected Lord North's last effort at conciliation, it also prompted George III to build up his forces there for the fight to the finish against the rebels to the south.

### The Declaration of Independence

Since the average Englishman had no heart for the fight against the colonials, the mother country was obliged to hire foreign mercenaries. Almost 30,000 "Hessians," as they were called after the German principalities of Hesse-Kassel and Hesse-Hanau from which many of the foreign mercenaries came, ultimately served with the British army in America.

Colonial propagandists and America's sympathizers in Parliament were quick to exploit this move, which stiffened the will of those

Americans who had already declared for separation. The number of such Americans was raised early in 1776 by a pamphlet called *Common Sense,* issued anonymously in Philadelphia in January. Since more than 120,000 copies were quickly sold and each found many readers, its author, Thomas Paine, an Englishman of Quaker origins who had arrived in Philadelphia in 1774, was soon smoked out. "There is something very absurd," Paine said, "in supposing a Continent to be perpetually governed by an island." And he added: "Freedom hath been hunted round the globe. . . . England hath given her warning to depart. O receive the fugitive, and prepare in time an asylum for mankind."

Such preparation was indeed under way. On April 6, 1776, the Congress had opened American ports to the commerce of all nations except Britain. This, in itself, placed America independent of Britain, as many in Congress realized when they debated the step. A month later Congress advised such colonies as had not already done so to form new state governments. Then on July 2, 1776, after nine hours of debate the day before had helped bring certain reluctant delegates around, Congress adopted Richard Henry Lee's "Resolution of Independence":

RESOLVED, *That these United Colonies are, and of right ought to be, free and independent States, that they are absolved from all allegiance to the British Crown, and that all political connection between them and the State of Great Britain is, and ought to be, totally dissolved.*

The adoption of this resolution was the great step, but in order to help enlist the support of foreign powers one more step seemed desirable. As Jefferson put it, "a decent respect to the opinions of mankind requires that they should declare the causes which impel them to the separation." On July 4, having made numerous changes in Jefferson's draft of this declaration of causes, Congress finally ordered it "authenticated and printed," and

"proclaimed in each of the united states & at the head of the army."

One of Congress's great goals was unanimity before the world; but not until July 19 was it possible to give the declaration its lasting title: "The Unanimous Declaration of the Thirteen United States of America." In order that unanimity be attained, what John Adams called Jefferson's "vehement philippic against negro slavery" had to be struck out, "in complaisance," as Jefferson noted at the time, "to South Carolina and Georgia. . . . Our northern brethren," he added, "also I believe felt a little tender under these censures; for tho' their people have very few slaves themselves, yet they have been pretty considerable carriers of them to others."

There was no difficulty, however, about the ringing opening phrases of the Declaration, "these truths" we hold "to be self-evident." Many years later, John Adams was to belittle Jefferson's achievement, holding that the Declaration merely repeated what men had been saying all along. But Jefferson replied that this was exactly what he had intended to do. The Declaration, Jefferson said, was "to be an expression of the American mind. . . . All its authority rests on the harmonizing sentiments of the day."

Although most of their quarrels had been with acts of Parliament, the list of grievances the Congress subscribed to in the Declaration was directed at "the present King of Great Britain." Had the delegates made their case against Parliament, they might have implied that they still could be persuaded to remain loyal subjects of the King. By attacking George himself, they served notice that they accepted no British authority whatever.

The "self-evident" truths in the preamble to the list of grievances were meant to justify this revolutionary step in terms of the doctrine of natural rights, including the right of revolution, to which John Locke had given its classic formulation in defending the Glorious Revolution of 1688 in England (see p. 52). By 1776 Locke's ideas had become virtually axiomatic in America. What they meant was that all men share equally in certain basic *political* rights, which government must not invade. "Governments long established," the Declara-

**124**

tion acknowledged, "should not be changed for light and transient causes." But in America, Britain's "invasion" involved "a long train of abuses and usurpations" which showed an intention to place the colonists "under absolute Despotism." This a free people had more than a right to oppose; they had a duty to rebel against such tyranny.

The Declaration of Independence, when it stated that "all men are created equal," might not have seemed to Congress to venture beyond the conventional political equality of free citizens. But even before the Declaration was made men were deeply troubled by the discrepancy between the institution of slavery and the rebels' bold avowals about liberty as their goal. The Association of 1774 and other nonintercourse proposals of the time, explicitly named the slave trade as one to be boycotted to make unmistakable the aversion to it. When in May of the following year, the question of using slaves as soldiers came up in Massachusetts, it was decided that their enlistment would be "inconsistent with the principles that are to be supported," and they were rejected. When the British, that November, began to make overtures to the slaves to enlist against their masters, however, Americans recognized the danger and altered their stand. Most of the slaves among the 5000 Negroes who served with the American revolutionary army were freed on enlistment. In his attack upon slavery in the early drafts of the Declaration, moreover, Jefferson included bondmen among those whose "sacred rights of life and liberty" had been violated by His Royal Majesty, George III.

Like all great political documents, the Declaration of Independence instantly took on a life of its own, consistent with the hopes and aspirations of all men under fetters, not merely white men in the America of 1776. Manumission in the South, abolition in the North, during and after the Revolutionary War itself, gained momentum from the self-evident truths of the Declaration of Independence. In 1789, when the French rebelled against Bourbon absolutism, the Declaration helped light the way for their leaders. In our own time, among colonial peoples abroad and the repressed at home, the Declaration has con-

tinued to serve the cause of revolution and of social as well as political equality.

*American "Tories"*

The Continental Congress, of course, found enemies at home as well as abroad, many of whom, often after agonizing indecision, concluded that they must remain loyal to the Crown, come what may. Nor were such "Loyalists"—or Tories, as the Whig patriots branded them—limited to those in the colonies who had a great stake in the preservation of the Empire. Many ordinary citizens proved slow to shift their allegiance from its traditional foundations to the rising revolutionary elite around them. "Damn the Rebels," shouted one vehement farmer in western Massachusetts. "I wish I had the Keys of Hell, I would turn on all the damned Rebels and kick them along. ... I wish they were all Scalped: damn the Congress to hell." Some ordinary Americans, indeed, embraced the Crown with new fervor rather than support the hated *colonial* aristocrats. In North Carolina, the Regulators, as such back-country Tories were called, even took up arms against the seaboard patriots. Growing patriot intolerance swayed still others toward loyalty to the King, who at least had the sanction of royalty for his impositions.

In the war of words that preceded the Declaration of Independence, Tory spokesmen held their own against the arguments of the patriots. True, they sometimes indulged in violent statements of aristocratic prejudices. The Maryland Anglican Jonathan Boucher, even harked back to ancient and outmoded arguments like the divine right of kings: "Unless we are good subjects," wrote Boucher, "we cannot be good Christians." Others, however, invoked legal and philosophical notions that commanded wide respect. One group of New York Loyalists drew up an imitation "Declaration of Independence" in which the preamble repeated almost the exact words of Jefferson, including his statement of the natural right of revolution. But when they came to their bill of grievances, they artfully substituted the actions of the Continental Congress for those of the King, enumerating *them* as evidence of "a long train of the most licentious and despotic abuses." And indeed there were many such.

While Loyalists waited confidently for the hand of British authority to smite their foes, Whigs organized "Tory committees" which drove many from their homes and communities, confiscated their estates and personal property, and saw to the imprisonment of hundreds. Few Loyalists, however, lost their lives. American Whigs who lived long enough to learn of the horrors of the French Revolutionary terror sometimes remarked on the rela-tive mildness of their own earlier behavior toward the counterrevolutionaries. Clearly, some kind of repression was in order. As Washington asked in 1775, "Why should persons, who are preying on the vitals of the country, be suffered to stalk at large, whilst we know that they will do us every mischief in their power?"

The British forces never used the full potential of Tory support, but Loyalists did provide them with provisions and munitions and serve them as spies, informants, soldiers, and propagandists among wavering neighbors. Some Loyalists quickly fled behind British lines to enjoy the comfort of British protection, especially in New York City and Philadelphia. Thousands moved for good to England or Canada, where they were warmly welcomed. Years later the British government spent about £3 million in compensating Loyalists for their losses.

## V  War for independence

### Opposing camps

Loyalist warnings that Britain possessed enormous military advantages in the looming war were well founded. A divided population of about 2.5 million, with no army or navy and no true central government, was ranged against an imperial power of 10 million persons, the mistress of the seas, with thousands of trained officers and troops.

Yet Britain suffered many strategic disadvantages to which the United States was to grow accustomed in the twentieth century. She had to wage the war across 3000 miles of ocean, on unfamiliar terrain, much of it trackless forest. As one of her officers put it, the difficulty of moving supplies into the interior "absolutely prevented us this whole war from going fifteen miles from a navigable river." In contrast, the Americans became swift and mobile, adept at swooping down for short skirmishes, pecking away at the enemy's supply lines, and taking cover in the woods.

This sort of "guerrilla warfare," a term to be applied to other colonial conflicts later on, left British officers bewildered. In Lord George Germain, the Colonial Secretary, they had an intelligent and meticulous organizer who fully appreciated the difficulties "of opposing an enemy that avoids facing you in the open field." Germain gave his commanders in America wide latitude in planning their maneuvers under the new conditions. One of their failings was a contempt for the American "yokels" that often led to careless actions. Even at Yorktown the redcoats surrendered gracelessly, preferring to bow before the trim French forces instead of the ragged Yanks. The morale of the British troops was further weakened by faltering home-front support.

On their part, most Americans tended to underestimate their own difficulties. The same jealous attachment to their liberties that had made them quick to resist the assaults of Parliament, now made them slow to accept the tight organization and discipline needed to

126

carry on a war. Raising an army was hard enough; whipping it into a responsive force was harder; and keeping it active in the field became all but impossible. Although some 300,000 persons may have taken up arms in the rebel cause, the largest army Washington ever pieced together at one time amounted to a little over 20,000 men. Usually he had fewer than 5000, most of them state militia accustomed to marching under friendly officers elected by themselves and resentful of outside commanders. Most soldiers, concerned with families and farms back home, were reluctant to sign up for more than a few winter months, and few were ready to reenlist. With the Continental army sadly in need of professionals, Washington gladly welcomed such foreign sympathizers as Baron Friedrich W. A. von Steuben of Prussia, Count Casimir Pulaski of Poland, and the Marquis de Lafayette, a twenty-year-old volunteer from France. Von Steuben in particular proved the kind of drillmaster raw troops most needed.

As long as the war lasted, Washington plagued Congress with requests for fighting men. The delegates were powerless but to pass his demands on to the states. No one was satisfied with the results. Yet Congress's record was not as poor as often painted. The new nation, heretofore largely dependent on the mother country for its manufactures, was always hard put to feed, clothe, arm, and pay the relatively few soldiers it could put in the field at any time. Washington's army was desperately small. And yet the country could not have supported a much larger one.

The story of the wartime economy is similar. Congress lacked not only the power to tax, but also—given the origins of the Revolution—the inclination to do so. Moreover, much of the taxable specie in the country— English guineas, Spanish pieces of eight, Dutch florins, and, for that matter, household silver—had gone with the Loyalists. Specie loans, foreign and domestic, were slow in coming and were used up with disheartening swiftness. Thus the war was financed mainly with paper money and a whole Pandora's box of IOU's, both of which depreciated rapidly.

The almost universal speculation that accompanied the rise of commodity prices, ex-

pressed in terms of the depreciated currency, angered Washington more deeply than almost any other problem of the Revolution. At the same time, rising prices served to induce legitimate producers among farmers, miners, and manufacturers to increase their output greatly. Profits soared; but so did the quantity of goods available to the Continental army. Robert Morris expressed the philosophy of the wartime entrepreneurs, a philosophy that did not cost them the good opinion of their friends: "It seems to me that the present opper't'y of improving our fortunes ought not to be lost, especially as the very means of doing it will contribute to the service of our country."

### From Long Island to Saratoga

On being dislodged from Breed's Hill in June 1775, patriot forces successfully occupied Dorchester Heights overlooking Boston. There, Washington armed his men with cannon laboriously hauled down from Fort Ticonderoga early in 1776. Confronted by this force, the British General, Sir William Howe, who had supplanted General Gage, decided in March 1776 to evacuate Boston for Halifax, Nova Scotia. From there he planned an assault on New York City, which, with its heavy Loyalist population and fine harbor, he hoped to make his headquarters. Washington expected this move, and in April he rallied as many soldiers as he could and marched them off to protect the city. By July, however, Howe had landed 10,000 men on New York's Staten Island, a force which by early August had grown to 32,000. Sensing that it would be risky to concentrate his troops in the city itself, Washington now fortified Brooklyn Heights on Long Island, hoping thereby to gain control of Manhattan as Dorchester Heights had given him control of Boston. But this time, on August 27, Howe attacked and defeated the rebels on Long Island. Two days later Washington crossed back to Manhattan, where he was chased northward to White

Plains. Beaten here again he fled to Hackensack, New Jersey to reform his ranks.

By now Washington had his strategy firmly in mind. "We should on all occasions avoid a general action," he told Congress, "or put anything to the risque, unless compelled by a necessity, into which we ought never to be drawn." Conforming to this strategy, when Howe in December 1776 attacked Washington in Hackensack, the rebel commander sped to Trenton, New Jersey, and then across the Delaware River into Pennsylvania. From here, realizing that Howe's troops must be spread thin, Washington counterattacked brilliantly. On the stormy Christmas night of 1776 he recrossed the Delaware, surprised the sleepy Hessians at Trenton, killed their commander, and took almost 2000 prisoners. Washington followed up this victory with another near Princeton, January 3, 1777. Before retiring for the winter near Morristown, he had cleared the British out of New Jersey.

Before his Trenton offensive, Washington had written to Congress that he must have more men, or "I think the game will be pretty much up." After his successes at Trenton and Princeton, he again dared hope for success. These hopes soared with the defeat of "Gentleman Johnny" Burgoyne at Saratoga, New York, in October 1777.

Burgoyne had worked out an elaborate plan to divide and conquer the rebels. With a large force from Canada he himself would push southward along Lake Champlain. At the

**127**

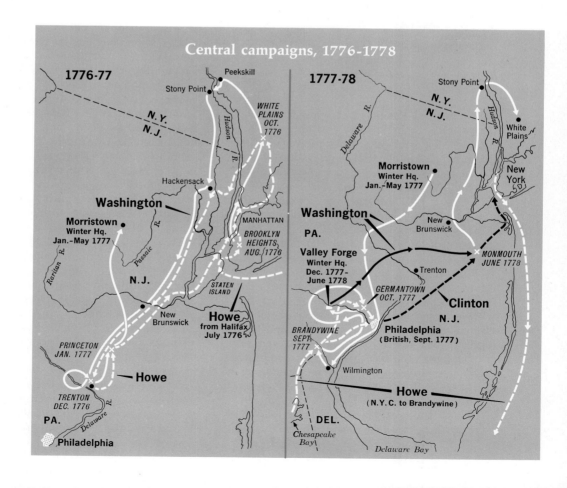

Central campaigns, 1776-1778

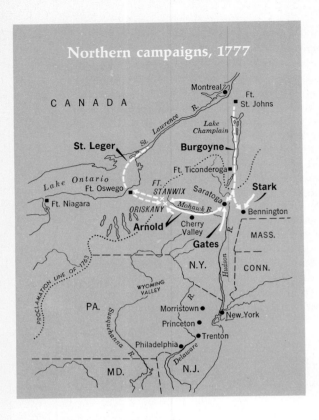

Northern campaigns, 1777

lolled in the lap of Philadelphia's grateful Loyalist society. Although tempted by fewer attractions than Howe, St. Leger was also lost to Burgoyne. On August 22, after Benedict Arnold by a clever ruse deprived him of his Indian contingents at Fort Stanwix, St. Leger, battered in earlier engagements on the way, decided to return to Fort Oswego.

Of the three British armies essential to Burgoyne's campaign, only one remained to him—his own. Blissfully unaware of his predicament, "Gentleman Johnny" started southward from Canada on June 17, with his wine, his fine clothes, his camp-following women, and almost 8000 redcoats.

Misfortune dogged Burgoyne at almost every step, and of a kind that he and his men most detested. Impromptu bands of "country yokels," materializing suddenly, riddled his proper formations and as suddenly dissolved. On August 11, at Bennington, a group of Green Mountain Boys led by John Stark fell fiercely upon a force of 700 men whom Burgoyne had sent out to forage, and destroyed them entirely. A few days before, Burgoyne had received the dismal news of Howe's Philadelphia enterprise, but he pushed on to the vicinity of Saratoga, where on September 19 he was checked at the battle of Freeman's Farm. Overwhelmingly outnumbered now, he was met by Gates and Arnold at Bemis Heights on October 7. While Gates was arguing in his quarters with a captured British officer about the merits of the Revolutionary cause, Arnold led a magnificent assault. On October 17, 1777, Burgoyne surrendered his battered army, the remnants of which were shipped back to England, pledged not to serve again in the war.

Arnold's victory was an eye-opener to the redcoats. One captured officer wrote:

*The courage and obstinacy with which the Americans fought were the astonishment of every one, and we now become fully convinced, they are not that contemptible enemy we had hitherto imagined them, incapable of standing a regular engagement.*

same time, a smaller force under Colonel Barry St. Leger would march eastward through the Mohawk Valley from Fort Oswego on Lake Ontario. Still a third force, under General Howe, was to move northward up the Hudson Valley from New York City. Converging on Albany, the three armies would crush any American opposition, proceed to control New York and cut New England off from the south. Then the rebel states could be picked off one by one.

But Burgoyne reckoned without General Howe who, with Germain's permission, aimed first to occupy Philadelphia, the rebel capital, before moving north. Washington was determined to check Howe if he could, but after defeating the patriots at Brandywine Creek on September 11 the British leader secured Philadelphia two weeks later. When Franklin, in Paris, heard that Howe had captured Philadelphia, he dissented. "No," he said, "Philadelphia has captured Howe." And so it was. Deserting Burgoyne, the pleasure-loving Howe

Burgoyne's dramatic defeat, in turn, electrified all Europe.

## The force of the French alliance

From the start of the Revolution, European governments had looked with mixed pleasure and concern at Britain's plight. On the one hand they yearned to see the island kingdom humbled and the balance of power restored; on the other, they feared the example of American success among their own people, at home and in their overseas possessions.

As early as November 1775, Congress began to play upon Europe's hopes and fears by sending Silas Deane to France. Deane was successful in gaining secret assistance in the war both from France and Spain. After the Declaration of Independence, Congress dispatched Arthur Lee, then serving secretly in London, and the renowned and engaging Franklin, to assist Deane in Paris in negotiating a formal alliance. Franklin charmed the French, but they did not capitulate until they had learned of Burgoyne's surrender.

Following Burgoyne's defeat, in order to check Franco-American negotiations, Lord North's government offered to suspend all laws passed since 1763 concerning America, and appointed a commissioner to seek to end the war on these terms. News of North's offer spurred the French to conclude their treaty of alliance with the rebels on February 6, 1778. Congress summarily rejected North's offer; nothing short of independence would now do. On March 4, 1778 the delegates ratified the French treaty, "the essential and direct end" of which was "to maintain . . . the liberty, sovereignty, and independence absolute and unlimited of the United States."

In case of war between Britain and France (Britain did declare war in June 1778), the treaty stipulated that the United States and France "make it a common cause," and neither party was to make peace without consulting the other. The French generously con-sented not to interfere if the Americans could conquer Canada and Bermuda. Not to be outdone in generosity at Britain's expense, the Americans gave the French *carte blanche* in the British West Indies. In a separate commercial treaty the two nations granted one another favorable trade terms.

The American war for independence now was transformed into a renewal of the old European struggle for empire in North America. In 1779 France induced Spain to join the conflict, and New Orleans thus became available as a base in the war at sea. At the end of 1780, Britain went to war with the Netherlands to stop her from trading with the United States. Britain was also harassed by the Russians, who hampered British shipping in the Baltic. Elsewhere, the French navy began to contest British sovereignty of the seas, while American privateers, operating safely now off the French coast, played havoc with British vessels even in the English Channel. As early as September, 1779, John Paul Jones, in a French man-of-war renamed *Bonhomme Richard* in honor of Ben Franklin, fought his famous battle off the English coast with the British warship *Serapis*. Although *Bonhomme Richard* was sunk in the meeting, Jones and his men successfully boarded *Serapis* and took her to port in France.

It was during this engagement, when invited to surrender by the heavier British vessel, that Jones is said to have replied, "I have not yet begun to fight." Jones's subsequent exploits had no military effect on the progress of the cause. Nor, for some time, did the French treaty. Rebel success was delayed in part because, so divided were the states, so poor the people, they could not long sustain the buoyant spirit of Saratoga and the French alliance; and in part because the French, belatedly concerned for the safety of their West Indian possessions, were slow in making their critical naval contributions to America's final victory.

## Nadir of the cause

After his defeat at Germantown, Washington had taken his battered bitter-enders to nearby Valley Forge where they endured their well-known winter ordeal. Howe's pleasures in Philadelphia at the same time were wearing thin, and he soon asked to be relieved of "this very painful service." Howe's dilatoriness made it easy for Germain to accede to his request, and in May 1778 he was supplanted as head of the British forces by General Henry Clinton. Clinton's orders were to evacuate Philadelphia and to prosecute a vigorous new campaign in New York.

Vigor was no more Clinton's strong point than Howe's. After a few discreditable meetings between his forces and the rebels, Clinton managed to reach New York from Philadelphia at the end of June and, except for one expedition to South Carolina in December 1779, here he remained until the end of the war. Washington himself followed Clinton to New York and again encamped at White Plains to keep an eye on the enemy. In the meantime, Loyalist and Indian bands terrorized frontier settlements in the Wyoming Valley in Pennsylvania's eastern interior and in Cherry Valley in central New York.

While the principal armies played their waiting game in the East, Virginia's own forces under George Rogers Clark undertook to destroy the Indians assisting the British in the West. His principal target was Colonel Henry Hamilton, the hated English commander at Detroit, known as the "Hair Buyer" for paying his Indian auxiliaries for American scalps. Late in February 1779 Clark found Hamilton at the old French town of Vincennes and forced him to surrender. The Virginian never reached Detroit, but his remarkable exploits with fewer than 200 men lifted the Indian pressure from settlements in future Kentucky and western Virginia. By August 1779, other rebel forces had also neutralized the Indian menace in the East.

Success against Britain's Indian allies could not offset the slide in numbers and morale of Washington's main army in New York. Unpaid, ill-clothed, miserably fed, this army grew ever more restive as it watched Congress's inability to stem the inflation that forced up the cost of war supplies on the one hand, and on the other the high life of civilian profiteers. Late in 1779, Washington took this army to winter quarters in Morristown, New

Jersey, where its sufferings outdid even those at Valley Forge. Desertions soared, and before camp was broken in the spring of 1780, Washington had to quell an armed mutiny of Connecticut regiments.

The British tried to make capital of the rebels' plight by offering handsome bribes to alienated officers. Their best catch was the brilliant Benedict Arnold, long conscious of real and imagined snubs. Arnold's plot to gain command at West Point in the summer of 1780 and to turn the fortress over to the British collapsed when the enemy agent, Major John André, was caught behind rebel lines with incriminating evidence and hanged as a spy. On learning of André's fate, Arnold, on September 25, 1780, fled to a British warship on the Hudson and fought the rest of the war on their side.

Back in 1778, in the so-called Conway Cabal, a group in Congress had given serious consideration to supplanting Washington with a more manageable commander. Under the changed circumstances of 1780, a new congressional delegation set out for Morristown in April empowered, as they said, to offer him "a kind of dictatorial power, in order to afford satisfaction to the army." As Washington ignored the Conways, so he rejected the desperate alternative. "He has strange notions about the cause," General Nathanael Greene told the visitors, "and the obligation there is for people to sacrifice fortune and reputation in support thereof."

## To Yorktown

The final battles of the war were fought in the South, where Clinton believed Loyalist support to be strong. Soon after he had taken over from Howe in 1778, Clinton planned an attack on Savannah, Georgia, which was successfully carried out in December that year. From Savannah, Georgia was overrun. One year later, Clinton personally led an expedition against Charleston from New York, and on May 12, 1780, the town fell and with it over 5000 men, 300 cannon, and four ships. Clinton then returned to New York, leaving Lord Cornwallis in charge. On August 16, 1780 Cornwallis won a smashing victory at Camden, South Carolina.

With Georgia and South Carolina firmly held (despite the partisan warfare of South Carolina guerrillas like the daring "Swamp Fox," Francis Marion), the British commanders now turned to North Carolina, but here the tables were rudely turned. At King's Mountain, on October 7, 1780, an army of 1100 Tories was shot up by back-country patriots.

Then, General Daniel Morgan's victory at Cowpens on January 16, 1781, and a severe engagement at Guilford Courthouse in March, at last persuaded Cornwallis to abandon the state and move on to Virginia. Here, Cornwallis believed that British ships would assure the evacuation of his troops, if necessary. But he was unaware of a French fleet on the way, and also of the approach of Washington's force from the north. Pinned down finally between the French fleet and a combined French-American army of 16,000 men, Cornwallis had to yield.

The British surrender at Yorktown, October 19, 1781, virtually ended hostilities. Lord North, on learning the news, cried out again and again, "Oh God! it is all over!" In March

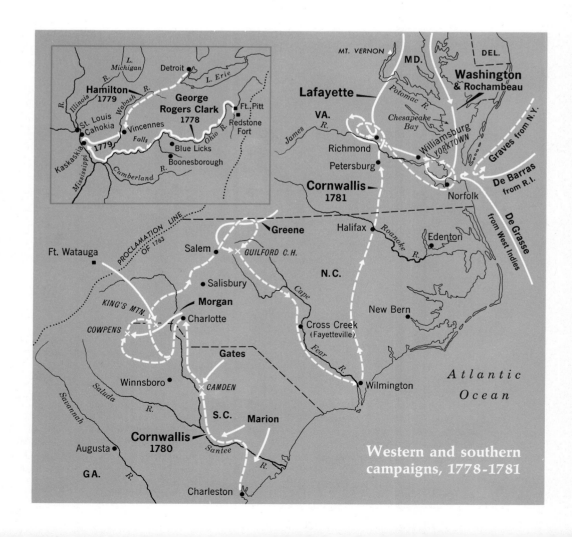

Western and southern campaigns, 1778-1781

1782 he resigned in favor of the Marquis of Rockingham, and his long and disastrous ministry came to an end.

132

## The Treaty of Paris

The American peace commissioners, Franklin, John Jay, and John Adams, sent by Congress to Paris in 1782, had to proceed with delicacy in their negotiations. Congress, as the treaty of 1778 seemed to require, had instructed them to consult with the French negotiators on matters of diplomacy. Yet as Jay observed, "We can depend upon the French only to see that we are separated from England, but it is not in their interest that we should become a great and formidable people, and therefore they will not help us to become so." Jay and his colleagues knew, too, that Spain had never approved of American independence and that she opposed the Mississippi River boundary the envoys were seeking. Since it seemed certain that France would support Spain, the three Americans ignored their instructions and reached a preliminary independent agreement with the British delegation that gave them the territory they coveted up to the Mississippi shore. In return, the Americans renounced all claims to Canada. Vergennes, the French foreign minister, was chagrined by these behind-the-scenes deals, but the adroit Franklin managed to soothe him and even to extract another fat loan for the United States.

The Treaty of Paris between the United States and Great Britain was signed September 3, 1783, and ratified in Philadelphia, January 14, 1784. By its terms, (1) Britain recognized American independence; (2) America obtained all the territory bounded by the Mississippi River on the west, the 31st parallel on the south (the line agreed upon if Britain ceded Florida to Spain, which she did), and the Great Lakes on the north; (3) Britain acknowledged America's right to the Newfoundland fisheries, but (4) retained the privilege with America of navigating the Mississippi. The United States agreed (5) to impose "no lawful impediment" to the recovery by British creditors of private debts due them but, (6) consented only to "recommend" that the states restore Loyalist property.

The American negotiators had done well. Although the treaty left many important issues unresolved, many commercial agreements uncertain, and some boundaries dangerously inexact, American independence had become a recognized fact, and a princely domain had been acquired for the new nation to grow in. An epoch had begun, a New Jersey delegate in Congress observed. "It opens a new scene to Mankind, and is big with inconceivable Effects in the political and I hope in the moral world."

## For further reading

E. S. Morgan, *The American Revolution: Two Centuries of Interpretation* (1965), is a good introduction to the various views on the origins and character of the break with Britain. Morgan's *The Birth of the Republic 1763-1789* (1956) is a statement of his own view. L. H. Gipson, *The Coming of the Revolution 1763-1775* (1954), is an authoritative short version of the later volumes of his 13-volume *The British Empire Before the American Revolution* (1936-1967). Merrill Jensen, *The Founding of a Nation* (1968), reflects modern scholarship on the period 1763-1776. E. B. Greene, *The Revolutionary Generation 1763-1790* (1943), is a social history, which should be supplemented by the more analytical J. T. Main, *The Social Structure of Revolutionary America* (1965). Eric Robson, *The American Revolution 1763-1783* (1955), is a succinct discussion of imperial problems by an English scholar. John Shy, *Toward Lexington, The Role of the British Army in the Coming of the American Revolution* (1965), is an illuminating work. On the great event involving the army, set in a broad context, see H. B. Zobel, *The Boston Massacre* (1970).

Three books by Sir Lewis Namier remain important on British politics in the revolutionary period despite certain recent criticisms of them: *England in the Age of the American Revolution* (1930); *The Structure of Politics on the Accession of George III* (1957 ed.); and *Personalities and Powers* (1955). Richard Pares, *King George III and the Politicians* (1953), is in the Namier tradition. Herbert Butterfield, *George III and the Historians* (1957), presents a dissenting view. The older view of party conflict which Namier attacked but which has regained interest is presented in G. O. Trevelyan, *The American Revolution* (4 vols., 1898-1907; reduced to one useful volume by Richard Morris, 1964). O. A. Sherrard, *Lord Chatham and America* (1958), vol. 3 of Sherrard's life of William Pitt, is excellent.

Bernard Bailyn, ed., *Pamphlets of the American Revolution,* vol. 1, 1750-1765 (1965), is a fruitful anthology with a penetrating introduction on the colonial response to British measures. Bailyn's *The Ideological Origins of the American Revolution* (1967), elaborates this introduction. In this vein see also H. T. Colbourn, *The Lamp of Experience: Whig History and the Intellectual Origins of the American Revolution* (1965), and G. S. Wood, *The Creation of the American Republic 1776-1787* (1969). Max Beloff, ed., *The Debate on the American Revolution 1761-1783* (1949), combines British and American documents. Carl Bridenbaugh, *Mitre and Sceptre: Transatlantic Faiths, Ideas, Personalities and Politics 1689-1775* (1962), is authoritative on the Anglican threat to religious liberty and its role in the revolutionary movement. A. M. Schlesinger, *Prelude to Independence: The Newspaper War on Britain 1764-1776* (1958), is a good introduction to the efforts to engage the public. Thomas Paine, *Common Sense,* is available in M. D. Conway, *The Writings of Thomas Paine* (4 vols., 1894-1896), and in numerous other editions. C. L. Becker, *The Declaration of Independence* (1922), is the outstanding study of that document. The background for it and many other related subjects is fully revealed in J. P. Boyd, ed., *The Papers of Thomas Jefferson,* vol. I, 1760-1776 (1950).

Special studies of British action and colonial reaction include C. B. Currey, *Road to Revolution, Benjamin Franklin in England 1765-1775* (1968); T. C. Barrow, *Trade and Empire: The British Customs Service in Colonial America 1660-1775* (1967); A. M. Schlesinger, *Colonial Merchants and the American Revolution 1763-1776* (1918); Carl Bridenbaugh, *Cities in Revolt, Urban Life in America 1743-1776* (1955); E. S. and

H. M. Morgan, *The Stamp Act Crisis: Prologue to Revolution* (1953); B. W. Labaree, *The Boston Tea Party* (1964); Clarence Alvord, *The Mississippi Valley in British Politics* (2 vols., 1916); and J. M. Sosin, *Whitehall and Wilderness: The Middle West in British Colonial Policy 1760-1775* (1961). J. R. Alden, *The South in the Revolution 1763-1789* (1957), ably covers that section's participation. G. M. Wrong, *Canada and the American Revolution* (1935), is authoritative. R. B. Morris, ed., *The Era of the American Revolution* (1935), is an outstanding collection of essays.

In addition to certain biographically oriented works cited above, the following lives of leading figures are of value: D. S. Freeman, *George Washington* (6 vols., 1948-1954), completed by J. A. Carroll and M. W. Ashworth (vol. 7, 1957); Marcus Cunliffe, *George Washington, Man and Monument* (1959); Carl Van Doren, *Benjamin Franklin* (1938); Gilbert Chinard, *Honest John Adams,* (1933), and *Thomas Jefferson* (1929); Dumas Malone, *Jefferson and His Time* (4 vols., 1948-1970); J. C. Miller, *Sam Adams* (1936); R. D. Meade, *Patrick Henry* (2 vols., 1957, 1969); and Esther Forbes, *Paul Revere and the World He Lived In* (1942). W. H. Nelson, *The American Tory* (1961); Wallace Brown, *The King's Friends* (1965); and P. H. Smith, *Loyalists and Redcoats* (1964), are good studies.

H. S. Commager and R. B. Morris, eds., *The Spirit of "Seventy-Six"* (2 vols., 1958), is a superb anthology of participant accounts on battlefronts and home fronts. S. E. Morrison, *John Paul Jones* (1959), offers an admirable introduction to the war at sea. Especially useful on the military phases of the war are Howard Peckham, *The War for Independence* (1958); J. R. Alden, *A History of the American Revolution* (1969), and from the British side: Piers Mackesy, *The War for America 1775-1783* (1965). See also G. A. Billias, ed., *George Washington's Generals* (1966), and *George Washington's Opponents* (1969); and G. S. Brown, *The American Secretary: The Colonial Policy of Lord George Germain 1775-1778* (1963).

S. F. Bemis, *The Diplomacy of the American Revolution* (1935), is a scholarly account. American relations with France are well presented in E. S. Corwin, *French Policy and the American Alliance* (1916). R. B. Morris, *The Peacemakers: The Great Powers and American Independence* (1965), is the indispensable study of the Peace of Paris. On the effects of the Revolution in Britain, see R. Coupland, *The American Revolution and the British Empire* (1930). The financing of the Revolution is ably dealt with in Clarence Ver Steeg, *Robert Morris* (1954), and E. J. Ferguson, *The Power of the Purse: A History of American Public Finance 1776-1790* (1961). On the Continental Congress, see Lynn Montross, *The Reluctant Rebels* (1950), and E. C. Burnett, *The Continental Congress* (1941).

# A MORE PERFECT UNION

In December 1776, Tom Paine published the first number of *The American Crisis,* which opened with the famous words: "These are the times that try men's souls." During the war Paine published about a dozen more *Crisis* essays on current issues—how to treat Tories, what to do with Loyalist and western lands, the need for *federal* taxation—issues that seriously divided the "united colonies." The last *Crisis* appeared on April 19, 1783, the eighth anniversary of Lexington and Concord, when America's triumph had been all but formally signed and sealed. " 'The times that tried men's souls,' are over—," Paine began his valedictory, "and the greatest and completest revolution the world ever knew, gloriously and happily accomplished. . . . So far as my endeavours could go," the pamphleteer reminded his public, "they have all been directed to conciliate the affections, unite the interests, and draw and keep the mind of the country together." Then he underscored his transcendent theme:

> We have no other national sovereignty than as United States. . . . Individuals, or individual states, may call themselves what they please; but the world, and especially the world of enemies, is not to be held in awe by the whistling of a name. Sovereignty must have power to protect all the parts that compose and constitute it; and as UNITED STATES we are equal to the importance of the title, but otherwise we are not.

Paine's words fell sweetly on the ears of many patriots. Yet perhaps even more Americans wondered whether union was desirable now that independence had been won. Their experience with the mother country made

134

them only the more suspicious of any new centralizing agency that might interfere in their local affairs, and indeed of local government itself and its nosing into their private lives. So far as these Americans were concerned, government meant snooping tax-collectors, mortgage-foreclosing courts, hamstringing regulations, and little else—and the less of it the better.

Some of the men who drew up the new state constitutions that followed the Declaration of Independence understood this attitude, and the weak Articles of Confederation of 1777 are a monument to it. By 1787, however, even many localists had grown disillusioned with their failing central administration and had come around to Paine's high view of a sovereign nation.

## I   First state constitutions

### The fundamental law

Although the American colonies, of course, were older than the American nation, the independent *states* that eventually formed the Union were themselves set up following the advice or actions of the revolutionary central government known as the Second Continental Congress.

Even before the Declaration of Independence, this Congress had advised four provinces troubled by the "convuls'd state" of their affairs under makeshift revolutionary administrations to draw up permanent constitutions that "shall best conduce to the happiness and safety of their constituents in particular, and America in general." With the adoption of the Declaration of Independence by the Congress in July 1776, the legal basis on which most of the colonies had been governed—their royal charters—was swept away, and the remaining provinces had to follow the lead of the first four. Rhode Island and Connecticut, simply by deleting all reference to the king, were able to go along under their old corporate charters. By 1780, all the other states had written new instruments of government.

In most of the states, the revolutionary provincial congresses, self-conscious tribunes of the people, drew up and adopted the new constitutions without troubling to consult the voters. Massachusetts, however, set an example that was later followed by the others when they came to rewrite their basic law, and by the Republic itself when the Great Convention of 1787 wrote the fundamental law of the land.

In Massachusetts, when the provincial congress asked the people for power to draw up the new state constitution, the majority conferred it, but the people of the town of Concord objected. As much as they loved liberty *under* government, they cherished even more the principle of individual liberty *against* government. In resolutions published in October 1776, the Concord town meeting declared: "We Conceive that a Constitution . . . intends a System of Principles established to Secure the Subject in the Possession & enjoyment of their Rights and Privileges, against any Encroachments of the Governing Part." If the provincial congress makes the constitution, argued the Concord meeting, what is to prevent it from unmaking it? If the fundamental law has no sanction superior to that of ordinary legislation, what will protect our liberties? Concord demanded that a special "Convention . . . be immediately Chosen, to form & establish a Constitution."

The Massachusetts provincial government ignored Concord's novel proposal and drafted a new constitution. But the Concord notion spread, and when the provincial congress presented its work to the people in 1778 they rejected it by a five-to-one majority. Recognizing that the principal objection to the constitution was indeed its authorship, the provincial congress voted in June 1779 to embrace the Concord idea. By March 1780, under the leadership of John Adams, a specially elected convention completed a new framework of government which the voters approved in June. Even the state constitutions written and adopted by the provincial congresses elsewhere set forth at the outset a "bill" or "declaration" of "unalienable" or "natural" or "inherent" rights, of which the "Governing Part," as the Virginia Constitution said, "cannot by any compact deprive or divest their posterity."

These rights included: "acquiring, possessing, and protecting property"; freedom of worship, speech, and assembly; moderate bail, prompt hearings, trial by jury, and punishments to fit the crime; protection from general search warrants and from liability to serve in or support standing armies. Above all, "when any government shall be found inadequate or contrary to [the people's wishes] . . . a majority of the community hath an indubitable, unalienable and indefeasible right to reform, alter or abolish it." To reduce the likelihood of revolutions, elections must be "free, . . . frequent, certain, and regular." And in such elections, all "men having sufficient evidence to permanent common interest with, and attachment to the community, have the right of suffrage."

Conservatives for some time found it easy enough to live with these gaudy generalizations. Yet the "Bills of Rights" gave the populace, in the language of the times, "a standing law to live by." Without the promise of such a Bill of Rights they almost certainly would have rejected the new federal Constitution of 1787 (see p. 156). Reformers, moreover, eventually used the leverage afforded by the liberal language of these bills to abolish imprisonment for debt, provide free schools, prohibit the use of public funds for favored religious sects, promote free expression in the press, reform the courts, improve the jails, liberalize the qualifications for officeholding, and broaden the franchise. They turned the principle of liberty against the "governing part" into the pursuit of equality with the governing parties, employing government itself to remove the barriers to liberty defined as opportunity (see Chapter Ten).

Such reforms often were slow in coming, and sometimes disappointing in their practical results. Among the earliest reforms based explicitly on the Bills of Rights in the constitution-making period itself were the gradual abolition of slavery north of Delaware and (at least for the time being) the removal of many restrictions on manumission, especially in Virginia.

The Bill of Rights of the first Vermont constitution of 1777 (see p. 144) straightforwardly abolished slavery, and when Vermont after entering the Union in 1791 drew up a new constitution two years later, the abolition provision was carried over. In Massachusetts, a court decision in 1783 used the Bill of Rights to justify fining a slaveholder on the charge of assaulting and shackling a runaway. Thereafter slaves began to leave their masters, and in the census of 1790 Massachusetts was the only state to report no slaves. New Hampshire soon was in the same position. Between 1780 and 1804, all the states from Rhode Island to

New Jersey put abolition in process by legislation freeing children of slave mothers once they had reached a certain age, ranging from eighteen to twenty-eight.

In the northern states the slave population was relatively small and the number of free Negroes grew but slowly. In Virginia, after private manumission was eased in 1782, the number of free Negroes jumped from 2000 to almost 13,000 in 1790, and to 30,500 in 1810. In Maryland the legislature rejected easing bills, but the restrictions there had been comparatively mild. In 1790 more than 8000 free Negroes lived in Maryland, and thereafter their number multiplied as rapidly as in Virginia. Farther south, although abolition and manumission were often mentioned in connection with the struggle for liberty, progress was slight.

The Negro freed by abolition or manumission, by legislation or by courts, seldom entered the free world the law prescribed. In the North as well as in the South, as the numbers of free Negroes grew, their social fetters multiplied. As a result, they seemed to become incorrigible public problems and costly public charges. Sometimes the very laws designed to open up the world of opportunity for the whites explicitly closed that world to the blacks and hardened their pariah status.

### The framework of government

Soon after the new state constitutions were written, Congress had them collected and printed for general distribution, and numerous editions were required to meet the demand at home and abroad. The Bills of Rights, setting forth the "higher law" of nature from which the supreme law itself derived its validity, aroused the greatest interest. This interest has survived the test of time. The Bills of Rights have been the most enduring parts of the constitutions, and along with the Bill of Rights of the federal Constitution have figured most prominently in constitutional issues since raised and resolved.

For the most part, the actual framework of government prescribed in the new state constitutions followed colonial forms. Usually the legislature consisted of two houses, both elected, although Pennsylvania experimented by having only a single house. "The oftener power Returns into the hands of the people the Better," the manifesto of a Massachusetts town meeting declared in 1778. As the terms of legislators in many of the new states indicate, "rotation in office" had already become one of the political shibboleths of the age. In ten states the lower house was elected for twelve months; in Connecticut and Rhode

137

*Title page of French translation of John Adams's "Defence," first published in 1787 to tell the world of the new state constitutions written by representatives of the people and establishing "balanced government."*

Private collection

# DÉFENSE
DES
## CONSTITUTIONS
AMÉRICAINES,
OU
*De la nécessité d'une balance dans les pouvoirs d'un gouvernement libre.*

Par M. JOHN ADAMS, ci-devant Ministre Plénipotentiaire des États-Unis près la cour de Londres, et actuellement Vice-Président des États-Unis, et Président du Sénat.

Avec des Notes et Observations de M. DE LA CROIX, Professeur de Droit Public au Lycée.

*All nature's difference keeps all nature's peace.*
L'opposition de toute la nature tient toute la nature en paix. POPE.

TOME PREMIER.

A PARIS,
Chez BUISSON, Libraire et Imprimeur, rue Hautefeuille, No. 20.
1792.

*John Adams in 1788 (left),*
*with the French philosophe Montesquieu*
*(1689–1755), one of the strongest*
*influences on the American's thought*
*about the separation of powers.*

Island for but six; only in South Carolina did representatives serve as long as two years. At the same time, the aristocratic principle was not entirely lost sight of. In New York and Virginia, for example, the upper house was to be elected for four years, in Maryland for a solid five.

The state constitutions varied widely in their interpretation of Bill of Rights provisions that the suffrage be granted to all men "having sufficient evidence to permanent common interest with, and attachment to the community." In five states (Pennsylvania, North Carolina, Delaware, New Hampshire, and Georgia) virtually all adult male taxpayers could vote. Virginia gave the vote to all who owned 25 acres of settled land. In more con-

servative states, considerably higher property requirements for suffrage were retained; and in some, like South Carolina, New Jersey, and Maryland, even higher property-holding requirements were established for members of the legislature.

A second political shibboleth, deriving from Montesquieu's attack on "despotism" in his *The Spirit of Laws* (first published in France in 1748 and widely read in the colonies), was the "separation" and "balance" of powers. Article XXX of "Part the First" of the Massachusetts constitution of 1780 was most explicit on this point:

> *In the government of this commonwealth, the legislative department shall never exercise the executive and judicial powers, or either of them: the executive shall never exercise the legislative and judicial powers, or either of them: the judicial shall never exercise the legislative and executive powers, or either of them: to the end it may be a government of laws and not of men.*

138

Almost two hundred years of independent political practice in America (not to speak of an even longer history in England, and in America under English rule) have failed to clarify in any absolute way where legislative, executive, and judicial power begins and ends. Separated in theory, these departments of government have always been dependent on and usually at war with one another. "Balance," indeed, seems to imply interference just where "separation" suggests independence.

The most important single change in the new constitutions was the drastic reduction in the power of the executive, especially in money matters. The power of the purse was universally retained in the legislature and in three states—Virginia, South Carolina, and New Jersey—it was assigned exclusively to the lower house. Conservatives, democrats, and moderates alike, moreover, all explicitly stripped the executive of the absolute veto power, and in all but two states—Massachusetts and New York—of any veto power whatever. Only in New York did the governor retain a certain limited control over the date and duration of legislative sessions; elsewhere the constitutions specifically set forth when the legislature should convene and left the houses themselves free to make their own rules and elect their own officers.

The degradation of the executive was capped by the mode of his election and the nature of his tenure. In New England and New York the voters elected the governor; but from New Jersey southward—in eight states— he was elected by the legislature itself.

In nine states the governor's term was limited to but twelve months. Most states, moreover, applied the policy of rotation in office with peculiar severity to the governorship, frequently denying him the opportunity of a second term without a lapse of years.

The courts no more than the executive escaped the pervasive power of the legislatures. Every state constitution provided that the legislature "have full power and authority to erect and constitute judicatures," to use the words of the Massachusetts document. In Connecticut, Rhode Island, and South Carolina the legislature alone named the judges; and in no state was the legislature without some voice in their appointment and removal.

In 1787, while addressing the Great Convention in Philadelphia, James Madison said: "Experience in all the States has evinced a powerful tendency in the legislature to absorb all power into its vortex. This was the real source of danger to the American Constitutions; and suggested the necessity of giving every defensive authority to the other departments that was consistent with republican principles." In later years, constitutional conventions in all the states undertook to rectify this gross imbalance among the "separated" departments. But not until regular political parties developed and the governor became the head of his party in the state was he able to assert executive leadership and overcome the fruitless factionalism of what even Jefferson denounced as "legislative tyranny."

## II  A "firm league of friendship"

### The first federal constitution

In July 1775, ten months before the revolutionary instructions to form permanent governments went out to the states, Benjamin Franklin disclosed to certain members of the Second Continental Congress a draft of "Articles of Confederation and Perpetual Union" under which a permanent national government might also be set up. Franklin's friends found that too many delegates "were revolted" by the idea of creating a permanent government while some lingering hope of conciliation with Britain remained; and indeed, nearly two and a half years passed before Congress's own draft was sufficiently advanced to be submitted to the states. John Dickinson of Pennsylvania, the principal author of the new document, undertook to establish a viable national government without weakening the individual commonwealths. This, of course, was difficult to accomplish. Dickinson's name for his government, "a firm league of friendship," strongly suggests that where conflict of authority arose, the states, not the new government, would triumph.

Only too aware of the defects of its offspring, Congress in its letter to the states in November 1777, asking formal approval, apologized for the "uncommon embarrassment and delay" in framing the Articles and solicited the most generous consideration of their form, "as that alone which affords any tolerable prospect of general ratification." Franklin's draft offered membership in "our Association" to "any and every Colony from Great Britain upon the Continent of North America," including the islands of the West Indies. He even opened the door to Ireland. Congress's aspirations were more sober. It ordered the Articles translated into French so that "the inhabitants of Canada, &c." might subscribe.

Under the Articles, each state elected and paid the salaries of its delegates and reserved the right to recall them. In the single-chamber legislature voting was to be by state, with each state having but one vote no matter how populous and rich it was or how many delegates it sent. Important legislation required a two-thirds majority of the states, a margin made more difficult to attain by the provision nullifying a state's vote if its delegation were evenly split. The administration of such laws as could be passed was hamstrung by the provision making the only executive a "committee of the states" consisting of one delegate from each state. Nor could the Articles be amended except by the unanimous consent of the states.

The Articles gave the new government considerable powers: Congress might (1) make war or peace and fix state quotas of men and money for the national army; (2) make treaties and alliances; (3) decide interstate disputes, limit state boundaries, and admit new states;

(4) borrow money and regulate standards of coinage and weights and measures; and (5) establish post offices. But such basic perquisites of sovereignty as levying taxes, raising troops, and regulating commerce were denied it.

The framers of the Articles, having made every concession they could to the states' freedom of action, expected quick approval by state governments. One last concession to Virginia, however, aroused the suspicion of Maryland and other "landless" states and delayed ratification for almost four more years. This concession stated that "no state should be deprived of territory for the benefit of the United States."

Seven "landed" states led by Virginia, on the basis of their original charters or on other grounds, laid claim to territory extending either to the Mississippi or all the way to the Pacific. By the Quebec Act of 1774 (see p. 119), Britain had overridden these claims; and Maryland now argued that since the Revolutionary War was a common effort, the territories claimed by the landed states should be "considered as common property." New Jersey and Delaware soon aligned themselves with Maryland.

As the costs of the war mounted, these landless states became increasingly alarmed at the high taxes they would be forced to levy, whereas the landed states would be able to pay their shares out of land sales. The landless states also were troubled by the likely growth in population and power of the others. Their own people, they said, would be lured by low taxes to the western territories of the landed states, thereby making such states predominant in any central government. Speculators in some landless states added their voices to those of their representatives. Before the Revolution, such speculators had purchased millions of acres from Indians in areas claimed especially by Virginia. If Virginia's claims were allowed to stand, their own claims surely would be invalidated in favor of Virginia speculators.

The deadlock over ratification of the Articles held until February 1780. Finding, because of the weight of taxes, "a violent inclination in most of the States to appropriate all the western Lands to the use of the United States," New York, a landed state, proposed at that time "especially to accelerate the federal alliance," to tender its lands to Congress. Connecticut soon followed suit. When Virginia at last yielded in January 1781, Maryland withdrew its objections to the Articles. In Feb-

ruary, Congress named March 1 as the day to proclaim the start of the new government. The Second Continental Congress then became the formal ruling body of "The United States of America," the "Stile," as the Articles said, "of this confederacy."

### Weakness in foreign affairs

"As to the future grandeur of America," wrote the influential Englishman, Josiah Tucker, Dean of Gloucester, at the close of the Revolution, "and its being a rising empire under one head, . . . it is one of the idlest and

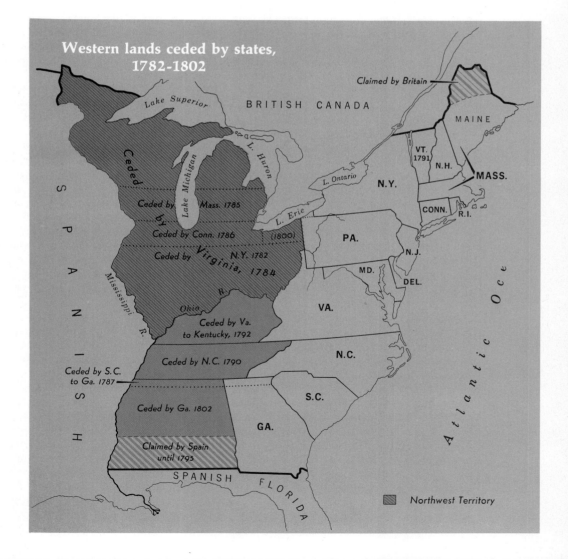

**Western lands ceded by states, 1782-1802**

Claimed by Britain

BRITISH CANADA

Lake Superior

L. Huron

L. Ontario

L. Erie

Ceded by Mass. 1785

Ceded by Conn. 1786 (1800)

Ceded by Virginia, 1784 N.Y. 1782

Ohio R.

Ceded by Va. to Kentucky, 1792

Mississippi R.

Ceded by N.C. 1790

Ceded by S.C. to Ga. 1787

Ceded by Ga. 1802

Claimed by Spain until 1795

SPANISH FLORIDA

SPANISH

MAINE

VT. 1791

N.H.

MASS.

N.Y.

CONN.

R.I.

PA.

N.J.

MD.

DEL.

VA.

N.C.

S.C.

GA.

Atlantic Oce

Northwest Territory

most visionary notions that ever was conceived even by writers of romance. . . . A disunited people till the end of time, suspicious and distrustful of each other, . . . [the Americans] will be divided and subdivided into little commonwealths or principalities . . . [with] no centre of union and no common interest."

If, after 1783, Congress looked to the magnificent gains of the peace treaty and the surge of spirit on the attainment of independence to strengthen its hand, it was once more proved wrong, the far-seeing Tucker right. It had, in fact, been all but impossible for Congress to get enough delegates together even to ratify the peace treaty. When this step at last could be taken in January 1784, it came too late to get the signed document to Britain within the six months stipulated to make it operative. The British, however, contented themselves with jibes at their former subjects and permitted the treaty to go into effect two months late. The treaty signing in January, moreover, seemed almost a signal for the formal abdication of the American government. January 14 to 16, 1784, were the only three days in a period of four months when nine states or more were represented in Congress. Sometimes the number fell as low as three.

Only because a fanatical little group "were unwilling to familiarize the idea of a dissolution of the federal government" did efforts to build a "peace establishment" proceed. The results were discouraging. American spokesmen were especially concerned over the figure a headless government cut in "a world of enemies." "Whatever little politicians may think," wrote Charles Thomson, the "perpetual secretary" of Congress, in September 1784, "a government without a visible head must appear a strange phenomenon to European politicians and will I fear lead them to form no very favourable opinion of our stability, wisdom or Union."

According to the peace treaty the British were to surrender their military and fur-trading posts in the Northwest "with all convenient speed." But the British clung to the posts in order to protect the rich Canadian fur trade until, as they hoped, the new nation would collapse. To hasten this collapse they egged on the Indians against American settlers whom Congress was powerless to keep off Indian lands. They used force, moreover, to deny Americans use of the Great Lakes.

Spain, an ally of France in the Revolutionary War, proved to be as much an enemy as Britain to the new nation once the war was over. In a separate treaty in 1783, Spain had received East and West Florida from Britain. Here she promptly established forts of her own, from which she proceeded in 1784 to make treaties with the Indians of the region obliging them to join in the harrassment of American interlopers. Congress's inability to force Spain to desist cost the government support in the South and Southwest just as weakness against the British had cost it support in the Northwest.

Even more damaging to the standing of Congress were the efforts of John Jay, the Confederations's Secretary for Foreign Affairs, to negotiate a commercial treaty with Spain in 1785. Spain had played on westerners' discontent by suggesting that they secede from the United States. As bait, she offered the use of the Mississippi and New Orleans, privileges Britain had agreed to in the peace treaty but which Spain insisted had not been hers to grant. Despite his early exhilaration over the prospects of continental empire (p. 132), Jay, an urbane New Yorker, had come to fear that the development of the West would only "fill the wilderness with white savages . . . more formidable to us than the tawny ones which now inhabit it." With this prejudice in mind, he concluded his long negotiations with Spain by agreeing that, in exchange for favorable commercial treatment of American ships in Spanish ports elsewhere, the United States would surrender claims to use of the Mississippi for twenty-five years. Although seven states, most of them in the commercial north, supported Jay's agreement, nine were needed to ratify it, and the treaty died. This failure added the Northeast to the ranks of those discontented with the new government and further alienated westerners and southerners shocked by Jay's proposal to Spain.

British (and for that matter, Spanish) recalcitrance over the West was hardened by American failures involving other international issues. The peace treaty, for example, declared that no legal impediments should hinder creditors on either side from collecting old debts. Actually the great bulk of the debts were owed by the ex-colonials, and although Congress urged the new states themselves to honor the treaty provision, it had no power to prevent their passing legislation to frustrate the British instead. Not until 1802 did the United States settle private debts incurred by Americans before the Revolution by agreeing to pay the sum of £600,000 to British creditors.

In accordance with the terms of the peace treaty, Congress also made "earnest recommendation" to the states to restore confiscated Loyalist property to its former owners. But most states chose to ignore this recommendation, and even after the war patriots continued to confiscate Loyalist lands without being punished by the courts. The treaty also permitted Loyalists to return for twelve months to try to recoup their losses, but many who came back received only tar and feathers for their pains. Years later, Britain awarded £3,300,000 to about 5000 Loyalists for property lost in America.

### Financial debility at home

Besides international problems arising from the treaty of peace, Congress was faced after 1783 by domestic problems growing out of independence. Bereft of the power to lay and collect taxes, it had to face its predicament without the sinews of sound finance. Worse, with no money to pay the Continental troops, Congress was physically menaced by its own army, which, sharing the almost universal lack of confidence in the government, refused to disband without first receiving its due compensation. In June 1783, apprised that the Philadelphia militia would not raise a single musket against mutinous

Pennsylvania regiments, and having no force of their own with which to "hazard the authority of government," the few delegates in attendance hied themselves to the hamlet of Princeton, New Jersey. "The great Sanhedrin of the Nation," jeered the unpaid Pennsylvania officer, Major John Armstrong, "with all their solemnity and emptiness, have . . . left a state, where their wisdom has long been question'd, their virtue suspected, and their dignity a jest."

Many other claims arising from the war poured in upon Congress. Above all there was the back interest, not to speak of the principal, to be paid on the public debt. Robert Morris, named Secretary of Finance in 1781, urged Congress to establish a national tariff so that it would no longer have to beg states for funds; he also proposed a land tax, a poll tax, an excise on distilled liquors. But none of these measures would the delegates enact. When Congress in 1782 then requested $10 million from the states for the next year, they bestowed less than $1.5 million.

In January 1783, his patience exhausted, Morris decided to quit. When no successor could be found he was prevailed upon to remain until the army had been paid. In June, Washington got the troops to go home, even though they were not to be paid for some months to come, and even then not in cash but in warrants to western lands from which the Indians were determined to bar white settlers. A loan from Holland enabled the government to limp along for a time; but when Morris finally left in September 1784, the treasury was empty as usual.

Morris's efforts, however, were not wholly in vain. In 1781, at his suggestion, Congress chartered the Bank of North America, the first commercial bank in the nation, with a paid-in capital of $400,000, to be located in Philadelphia. This bank eventually lent millions to the government and saw it through some of its most critical situations, but most of the bank's business was with private entrepreneurs. Like other American institutions under the Confederation, this bank—and others modeled after it in New York and Massachusetts in 1784—performed strongly even while the government itself declined.

## Congress and the private economy

Historians still disagree about how dark or how bright general economic conditions actually were during the Confederation years from 1783 to 1787. But it is certain that specific areas were hurt by the postwar depression.

American shipowners were especially hard hit by the loss of their favored position in the trade with Britain and the British West Indies. When Congressional envoys tried to get Britain to reopen the West Indian trade in particular to American goods and American ships, they were laughed out of court. The loss of British trade was only in part offset by the new trade opened up with China in 1784, and by increased trade with Baltic nations, France, and other continental countries.

American luxury importers soon grew as discontented as American shipowners. Just after the war, American importers had a taste of prosperity when colonials starved for English finery went on a buying splurge. But the market for luxuries was small and the splurge quickly petered out. Newly risen American manufacturers, in turn, who had had the American market for coarse goods so largely to themselves during the Revolution, also suffered from postwar foreign competition. From Congress they demanded protective tariffs to keep foreign goods out and subsidies to support their own industrial expansion—neither of which Congress could provide.

There was, of course, a brighter side. Most Americans were subsistence farmers who did not depend on Congress for their well-being. Even those who most loudly railed against Congress, moreover, often found ways to help themselves while Congress languished. Philadelphia, New York, and Baltimore merchants profited as usual from illicit West Indian trade. Public creditors, though unpaid by Congress and angry over this, apparently still had funds enough to sponsor new business ventures; for the years immediately following the war saw unprecedented activity in canal and bridge building, river and road improvement, house building, land transactions, and banking. The resumption of immigration to America and the rapid growth in the number and size of families, moreover, provided grounds for optimism about the future of the private economy. In Pennsylvania in 1784 Washington found a "spirit of enterprise [which] may achieve almost anything." In New York he noted a "temper, genius, and policy" directed single-mindedly toward capturing trade. Washington advised Virginia to adopt the commercial spirit. Otherwise, she "must submit to the evils" of commercial competition "without receiving its benefits."

## Congress and the frontier

In writings about American history, the term "frontier" is usually employed to describe the West in an early phase of its development. This is as it should be; the history of the frontier is essentially the history of the westward movement of population. But this use of the term obscures the opening and progress of the "northern frontier" of Vermont, New Hampshire, and Maine.

Unlike Maine and New Hampshire, Vermont was a wholly landlocked territory, and the last part of the northern frontier to be penetrated by white settlers. Both New York and New Hampshire claimed the territory, but not until 1769 did migrants from either state venture to build permanent homes there. After Ethan Allen's victory for the rebel states at Fort Ticonderoga in 1775 (see p. 122), he and his brother Levi tried to get the Governor of Canada to guarantee Vermont's independence in exchange for their future neutrality in the war. Failing here, the Allens, in 1777, when about 30,000 persons had settled in Vermont, set up an independent government. After the war, when the population had reached about 80,000 and many wanted to join the Union, Ethan and Levi swore "at all risks, . . . that Congress shall not have the parcelling of [Vermont] lands to their avaricious Minions." Congress did nothing for the unionists and not until 1791 did Vermont become the fourteenth state.

Far to the southwest other individualists also were staking out land for independent settlements. During the 1770s, James Robertson and John Sevier, two Virginia speculators, took settlers into the region of the Watauga and Holston Rivers. In 1784, when North Carolina ceded her old claims in this region to Congress, the Wataugans, now 10,000 strong and aware that Congress could do nothing for them that they could not do better themselves, set up the independent state of Franklin, with Sevier as governor. In 1788, North Carolina rescinded her cession and reclaimed Franklin, but the next year she returned the territory to Congress. The Watauga country later became part of Tennessee.

Another private state was staked out by James Robertson in 1780 in the vicinity of Nashville in the Cumberland Valley, and still another in future Kentucky by Judge Richard Henderson's Transylvania Company in 1775. Robertson's government lasted but two years. During the Confederation period, Henderson's satrapy was torn by strife between settlers who wanted to join Spain in order to gain commercial privileges on the Mississippi and those who wanted to remain part of the United States. During these years, ten conventions were held in Kentucky by settlers seeking statehood, and on three occasions Virginia herself supported their demands. While Congress did no more than it had done about Vermont, future Kentucky, like Vermont, burgeoned.

The organization of the southwestern frontier was so haphazard and disorderly that Washington, after a visit there in 1784, warned Congress "that scarce a valuable spot within a tolerable distance of [the Ohio River] is left without a claimant." He urged Congress, in developing the land above the Ohio obtained in the peace treaty, to follow the Yankee tradition of orderly survey and sale. Once the cessions of the landed states were complete and the Indian title "quieted," Congress followed Washington's advice. The first effective measure for developing the North-

west Territory was the Land Ordinance, written by a committee headed by Jefferson and enacted by Congress in 1785.

The Land Ordinance reserved no less than one-seventh of the Northwest Territory "for the use of the continental army." It also reserved four lots in each township for the United States, and one lot "for the maintenance of public schools." Except for a small sector retained by Connecticut as its "Western Reserve," the rest of the Northwest Territory was to be surveyed into townships of 36 sections, each section 640 acres, or 1 square mile, in area. The minimum purchase, at auctions to be held at convenient locations, was to be one section; the minimum price, $1 per acre in cash. Congress hoped that good land would command a better price. But sales were disappointing even at the minimum. The requirement of $640 in cash shut out most settlers and $1 an acre discouraged speculators.

After the first seven ranges of townships surveyed had failed to produce the revenue desired, Congress yielded to the proposals of speculators who offered 9 cents an acre for some 1.5 million acres beyond these ranges. Having made their huge purchase, these speculators, organized as the Ohio Company, prodded Congress to get the government of the new territory in order so that settlement could proceed. Congress responded by adopting the Northwest Ordinance of 1787, probably its most important piece of legislation.

Under this Ordinance, the Northwest Territory was to be set up as a single unit with a governor appointed by Congress. When 5000 free male inhabitants had settled in the Territory those who owned at least 50 acres apiece were to elect a territorial legislature whose acts would be subject only to the governor's veto. The voters would also send a nonvoting delegate to Congress. No less than three and no more than five states were to be carved out of the Territory, and the boundaries of three future states were tentatively laid out.

When a potential state had 60,000 free inhabitants, it was to be admitted to the Union on an equal footing with the original states. The Northwest Ordinance required, in addition that "the people and states" in the Territory, adopt "articles of compact" with the "original states" which shall "forever remain unalterable, unless by common consent." These articles in effect set forth the first *federal* Bill of Rights, similar to those in the first state constitutions, and with the momentous provision prohibiting slavery in the Territory and in all the states to be carved from it.

It has been persuasively argued (the actual negotiations presumably were secret) that the southern delegates in Congress accepted this provision in return for the incredible three-fifths rule in the Constitution permitting five slaves to be counted as three persons in apportioning representation in the new national legislature. Congress, in New York, enacted the Northwest Ordinance in July 1787, just when the Great Convention was sweltering in Philadelphia over the issue of representation (see p. 151), and such a compromise may have been worked out.

Following adoption of the Ordinance, the Ohio Company sent out a small group of pioneers in December 1787, and the next spring they established the village of Marietta at the junction of the Ohio and Muskingum rivers. A second group, sent out by the New Jersey speculator, John Cleves Symmes, to a tract he also had purchased from Congress, laid the foundations of Cincinnati in 1788. Eight years

later Moses Cleveland led a band of pioneers to Connecticut's Western Reserve, where they built the town of Cleveland on Lake Erie.

### Final shocks

Besides the Northwest Ordinance and the opening of settlement in the Northwest Territory, Congress could boast of few achievements during the postwar years. Even in the Northwest, pioneers were left almost entirely to their own resources in combating the Indians, the British, and the Spanish. Frontier violence and threats of violence, meanwhile, stifled the demand for land and added speculators to the ranks of the grumblers as their holdings failed to appreciate in value.

Only the established small farmer in the older sections of the country appeared content. So long as British, French, and Continental forces remained mobilized in America and needed his stores and supplies he prospered, and conditions grew even better when cheap British imports started to come in right after the war. By 1785, however, he too found trouble. The foreign troops had been withdrawn, the American army had been disbanded, and the farmer's markets had shrunk.

*Fort Harmer on the Ohio River, 1790, showing the new settlement of Marietta across the stream.*

Historical Society of Pennsylvania

146

Discontent deepened when impatient wartime creditors of the states persuaded them at this time to pay at least some back interest by taxing the farmers' lands more heavily and requiring payment in specie. This sudden reversal of fortune led the farmers and the harassed small retailers who depended on their trade to demand relief. They agitated especially for legal tender paper money and for "stay laws" to delay foreclosure of farms where mortgage payments were in arrears.

In many states farmers won concessions. Seven states issued some form of paper money, often with good effect. But in New England in particular, creditors and conservatives in the seaboard commercial towns usually managed to avoid paper money and also to shift a disproportionate part of the tax burden onto the inland farmers. By 1786 conditions had grown so bad in New Hampshire that the militia had to be called out to disperse a mob of respectable farmers who had surrounded the legislative meeting house in an effort to coerce the members to issue paper money. It was in Massachusetts, however, where, according to estimates in the early 1780s, farmers already were taxed as much as one-third of their income, that conservatives experienced their deepest shock. Here the legislature not only failed to heed the farmers' demands for relief, but levied higher specie taxes on them as well. To evade the farmers' protests, on July 31, 1786 the legislature adjourned until the following year. This cowardly act precipitated the uprising known as Shays' Rebellion.

Thirty-nine at the time, Daniel Shays typified the thousand men who became his followers. A poor farmer in western Massachusetts, he had enlisted in the revolutionary army in time to see action at Bunker Hill. "A brave and good soldier," as a subordinate described him after the war, he had won early promotion to sergeant; but the four years he had to wait for a promised commission to captain embittered him. After a year in this exalted position, he was mustered out in 1780 and returned home to await payment for his long service to his country. His farming went badly, his army compensation was delayed, his obligations accumulated, and "the specter of debtors' jail always hovered close by."

An articulate rebel, Captain Shays became a spokesman for his neighbors when the western counties became agitated over their worsening economic straits. Some of these counties were too poor to send delegates to the legislature in far-off Boston; and in some towns no men were to be found who could meet the property qualifications to sit in the General Court. Deprived of any voice in the state government, the debtor leaders resorted to the time-honored device of county conventions. Here men from neighboring towns would gather at the county seats on a basis of personal equality and give voice to their political feelings by means of published resolutions and petitions to the legislature.

After the legislature adjourned in July 1786, having ignored the petitions of the disfranchised, more and more county conventions met. Shays and other leaders repeatedly warned the members to "abstain from all mobs and unlawful assemblies until a constitutional method of redress can be obtained." But popular discontent overrode such advice, and mobs soon attacked civil courts where foreclosure proceedings by the hundreds were scheduled. After forcing the suspension of many civil court sessions, the mobs attacked the criminal courts to prevent trials of the rioters. When they next menaced federal arsenals, the government no longer could postpone action.

By October 1786, Shays had somehow become the focus of the whole movement and the rebels who rallied to him soon became the targets of state forces hastily gathered by General Benjamin Lincoln at the behest of Governor James Bowdoin. Fighting between Shays' forces and Lincoln's continued from mid-January to the end of February 1787, when the Rebellion finally was crushed and Shays fled to Vermont. A number of his straggling followers, captured during the fighting, were freed by the legislature in June. The bitterness that followed in the wake of this uprising emerged in the subsequent elections, when the aging John Hancock defeated Bowdoin for governor. No reprisals of an enduring kind, however, were imposed on Shays or his followers, and the Massachusetts legislature held off the harsher taxes that were on its agenda and instead passed laws exempting household goods and workmen's tools from confiscation for debt.

News of Shays' Rebellion shocked already aroused conservatives in all the states who were depressed by the persistent ineptitude and decline of Congress, the discontent of the army, the vulnerability of government to mob action. Washington himself described Congress as "a half-starved, limping" body "always moving upon crutches and tottering at every step." Others voiced even lower opinions. But the Confederation crisis was soon to be over and the nation more soundly launched.

## III   "To form a more perfect Union"

### The strength of leadership

In the early 1780s most American leaders recognized that the new nation was going through a "critical period." Some had grown so discouraged about the entire national experiment that they advocated deliberately breaking up the Union. "Some of our more enlightened men," wrote Benjamin Rush in 1786, "have secretly proposed an Eastern, Middle, and Southern Confederacy, to be united by an alliance, offensive and defensive." Those, on the other hand, who still hoped to preserve the Union—"even respectable characters," as Washington said—"speak of a monarchical form of government without horror," with Washington himself as monarch. "What a triumph for our enemies," exclaimed the General, "to verify their predictions! What a triumph for the advocates of despotism to find we are incapable of governing ourselves, and that systems founded on the basis of equal liberty are merely fallacious! " Washington, steadfast in his nationalism and republicanism, would tolerate neither destructive alternative. Even before the Articles of Confederation had been ratified, he and others were advocating their improvement to strengthen, not to destroy, the Union; to prove the possibility of republicanism, not to discredit it. Such men carried the day, but not without revolutionary steps of their own.

As early as 1780, Alexander Hamilton had asked for a new and more energetic government to press the war forward. In 1782 the New York legislature and in 1785 the Massachusetts legislature passed resolutions calling for conventions to supplant the Articles, but nothing came of them. Finally a strong movement for a new form of government emerged from the efforts of practical men to achieve what the Articles could not—that is, a more satisfactory regulation of interstate commerce. Early in 1785, delegates from Maryland and Virginia met at Alexandria in an attempt to settle differences between the two states over navigation of the Potomac River and Chesapeake Bay. The delegates moved on to Washington's home in Mount Vernon, where they extended their sessions so that delegates from neighboring Delaware and Pennsylvania could attend. Finally, these discussions resulted in a recommendation to the Virginia legislature that it call a general meeting of all the states, to take place at Annapolis, in September 1786.

Only five states responded to the Virginia call, but one of them was New York and among its delegates was the indefatigable Hamilton, whose ideas had long since soared beyond mere commercial accomodations. To attempt much more with but five states represented, however, appeared impractical, and at Hamilton's suggestion, after agreeing that the New Yorker write the report of the meeting,

148

the Annapolis convention adjourned. In his report, Hamilton stressed the numerous hamstringing defects of the Confederation, and he closed with a call for a new convention to meet in Philadelphia the following May to amend the Articles.

By the time of Hamilton's report, Shays' Rebellion had aroused concern among the rich and wellborn for their very property and lives; and the state legislatures responded to his proposal far more positively than they had to Virginia's a few months earlier. All save Rhode Island, indeed, eventually sent representatives to Philadelphia, and on the whole their best men. John Adams, John Jay, and Thomas Jefferson were absent on other duties at this time. Sam Adams was not named a delegate; Patrick Henry, appointed by Virginia, refused to attend. Otherwise the cream of the country was there, led by Benjamin Franklin and James Wilson from Pennsylvania; James Madison, Edmund Randolph, and Washington from Virginia; and Hamilton from New York.

Of the seventy-four men named to the Convention only fifty-five actually attended. Their average age of forty-two attests to the youthfulness of the group. Revolutionary army officers were conspicuous among them, and twenty-seven belonged to the Society of Cincinnati, an organization formed to look after officer interests. A mere eight were signers of the Declaration of Independence. In an age when few Americans went to college, a majority of the delegates were college graduates. Lawyers predominated, but businessmen and planters were numerous. Only William Few of Georgia, a man well versed in politics, could be said to represent the plain farmer class.

The second Monday in May, the 14th, was the date set for the meeting, but following the leisurely fashion of the age, not until the 25th did representatives from seven of the thirteen states, the majority needed to begin the Convention's business, reach Philadelphia. On that day the twenty-nine delegates present

unanimously elected Washington presiding officer. Next, uneasy about the populace and the clamorous press, they voted unanimously to keep their discussions secret. Debate then took place on their purpose in coming together, with some maintaining that they must adhere to the letter of their instructions simply to "amend" the Articles. But others, lest they "let slip the golden opportunity," as Hamilton said, took a freer view. When Edmund Randolph of Virginia announced that he was not "scrupulous on the point of power," Hamilton backed him, and the Convention went on to supplant, not amend, the Articles.

On May 30, Randolph disclosed something of the revolutionary temper of the leaders by offering these resolutions:

*1. That a union of the states merely federal will not accomplish the objects proposed by the Articles of Confederation—namely common defense, security of liberty, and general welfare.*

*2. That no treaty or treaties among the whole or part of the states, as individual sovereignties, would be sufficient.*

*3. That a national government ought to be established, consisting of a supreme legislative, executive, and judiciary.*

The delegates promptly agreed to put off debate on propositions 1 and 2; but sitting as the *"Committee of the Whole* on the state of the Union"—not on the state of the Articles— they directly applied themselves to the summer-long task of shaping an instrument of government conforming to proposition 3.

### Philosophic guidelines

Although the Convention spent a good deal of time settling differences among the delegates, in their general philosophy and on a great number of specific objectives they were in substantial agreement. Almost without exception practical men of affairs, if pressed most of them would have subscribed to the comment of John Rutledge of South Carolina during a warm discussion of the slave trade: "Religion & humanity had nothing to do with this question—Interest alone is the governing principle with Nations." At

149

**150**

the same time, as thoughtful and exceptionally well-educated men, they realized, when not too closely involved, that considerations of "interest alone" usually led nowhere but to warfare. Thus their overriding aim was to temper interest with reason, to bring human nature under the discipline of the optimistic philosophy of the Enlightenment, so that "civilization," a term then just coming into general use, might be improved and conflict avoided.

The delegates permitted themselves to be optimistic about constructing a suitable government—one, in Washington's words, with a "liberal and energetic Constitution," yet "well guarded and closely watched to prevent encroachments"—because they expected their profound pessimism about human nature to impel them to leave nothing undone to control it.

Human nature, they believed, was universally fallible. "Men," said Hamilton in a characteristic generalization, "are ambitious, vindictive, and rapacious." Madison agreed. Vice, he argued, could not be checked with virtue; vice must be checked with vice:

*Ambition must be made to counteract ambition. The interest of the man must be connected with the constitutional rights of the place. It may be a reflection on human nature that such devices should be necessary to control the abuses of government. But what is government itself, but the greatest of all reflections on human nature? If men were angels, no government would be necessary.*

The delegates generally acknowledged that the people must have a voice in government. But they felt they knew from history and experience that the people could be stampeded into following demagogues, dictators, and plunderers of the rich. Hence, the people's role must be limited. Although largely men of property who distrusted democracy, the delegates harbored no illusions either about the benevolence of the rich. Even a wealthy aristocrat like Gouverneur Morris of Pennsylvania acknowledged that "wealth tends to corrupt the mind," and that rich men as well as poor would use power to their own advantage if given the opportunity. Thus the greed and

pride of the rich, like the gullibility and passions of the poor, must also be held in check.

The delegates were as reluctant to entrust power to interests as to individuals or social classes. They believed that a landed interest, a slaveholding interest, a creditor interest, a commercial interest, if it could seize control of government, would tyrannize over the rest of society. And the danger would be even greater if several interests were to join forces in a phalanx that could control the nation.

In meeting this problem, the advocates of a stronger constitution turned to a *federal* republic rather than a consolidated one, looking to political selfishness among the parts to offset power grabs by material interests working in concert.

The concept of offsetting interests in *politics* was as old as Aristotle. In the eighteenth century, it gained great force as an instrument of *government* through the works of the French Enlightenment philosopher, Montesquieu. True to the mechanistic spirit of the age, Montesquieu offered along with classical political propositions modern means of applying them. His most powerful instrument, of which we have spoken in connection with the constitutions of the new American states (see p. 138), was the system of checks and balances. John Adams stated the argument succinctly:

*A legislative, an executive, and a judicial power comprehend the whole of what is meant and understood by government. It is by balancing each of these powers against the other two, that the efforts of human nature toward tyranny can alone be checked and restrained, and any degree of freedom preserved in the constitution.*

American practice and American conditions offered the delegates still another opportunity to introduce balance into the new national government, which they grasped. In the provincial and state legislatures, the lower house usually served as the "democratic branch" elected by a broad suffrage. In the new national legislature, most delegates agreed, there must also be two houses, the "democratical" one to check and in turn be checked by a second, representing the wealthier and more aristocratic elements. John Adams declared that there could be "no free government without a democratical branch in the constitution"; and fearful though most delegates were of "pure democracy," none, not even Hamilton, would contradict him. A few delegates feared that a two-house legislature, by pulling in opposite directions, would be incapable of effective action. But advocates of bicamerialism pointed out that a strong and independent executive could prevent this.

Naturally, the convention did not agree unanimously, even on these general principles. Some delegates were so concerned lest state power be eclipsed that they could not enter sympathetically into the proceedings; others, certain that the establishment of a national sovereignty would swallow up traditional personal liberties, earned reputations merely as obstructionists. Hamilton himself stood on the extreme conservative side and believed that concessions to the people made the Constitution "a frail and worthless fabric." Although he later urged ratification of the document for all its faults, in Philadelphia, it was said, "the gentleman from New York has been praised by everybody, . . . supported by none."

John Adams more felicitously expressed the spirit of the Founding Fathers and the spirit of the age when he observed that "the blessings of society depend entirely on the constitutions of government." Buoyed by that faith, the delegates in the Great Convention, often sorely tried by controversy despite their congeniality in philosophy, managed to balance out contending claims and complete their enduring instrument.

### Compromise in the Convention

One of the most divisive controversies in the Great Convention was that of the relative power to be granted large and small states. This issue became doubly menacing because it arose at the very outset.

Once the delegates had agreed to venture beyond the idea of amending the Articles, they took up Edmund Randolph's so-called "Virginia Plan" for a new government structure especially attractive to the large states. Randolph proposed a two-house "National Legislature" with membership in both houses allotted among the states in proportion to their free population. Members of the upper house were to be elected by the members of the lower, who were themselves to be elected by the people. The whole "National Legislature" was then to elect the "National Executive" and the "National Judiciary." This proposal, by so obviously violating the principle of the separation of powers, aroused general disapproval. But it particularly alarmed the small-state delegates who feared that their commonwealths would be overwhelmed in the popularly elected house and that some states might win no representatives at all in the second house.

To protect themselves the small states immediately offered a plan of their own, presented to the Convention by William Paterson of New Jersey and known since as the "New Jersey Plan." According to this plan Congress was to remain a single house, as under the Articles, and all states would continue to have one vote apiece. The delegates quickly rejected this futile proposal and used the Virginia Plan as the preliminary model from which to construct the final document.

Rejection of Randolph's specific proposals for the makeup of the new national legislature brought the issue of large and small state representations immediately to a head. The debate, indeed, grew so long and sharp in the hot Philadelphia summer that at one point the small state delegations, threatening, as a Delaware member put it, to "find some foreign ally, of more honor and good faith" than his large-state colleagues, were on the verge of going home. And even so thoughtful a delegate as James Wilson of the large state of Pennsylvania, agreed that, "if they will have their own will, and without it, separate the union, let it be done."

152

Catastrophe was averted at this juncture by the appointment of a special committee, headed by Elbridge Gerry of Massachusetts, to restudy the whole issue of representation. Early in July this committee at last brought in a compromise scheme devised largely by Franklin: There would be a two-house legislature, with membership in the lower house apportioned according to population, thus satisfying the large states, and with membership in the upper house equal for all states, thus satisfying the small ones. This arrangement, adopted only after much further debate, provided the basis for the "Great Compromise" of the Constitution and determined the general character of the two bodies that were soon named the House of Representatives and the Senate.

The two-house plan enabled the delegates to establish the lower house as the people's branch. The members of this house were to be elected by all voters in each state who were eligible to vote for "the most numerous branch of the State Legislature." The upper house, whose members were to be chosen, more restrictively, by state legislatures, was expected to be more friendly to property and more conservative in other ways.

The Great Compromise quickly spawned two new issues which divided the free and slave states and again found rival delegations threatening to leave. The first of these concerned the "direct taxes" the new government was empowered to levy. The Convention agreed that such taxes should be apportioned among the states according to population, just as representation was to be apportioned in the lower house. But the slave states wanted their Negroes, if they were counted at all in apportioning taxes, to be given less weight than free men. The North wanted Negroes to be given less weight only in apportioning congressional representation. In the debate, the proportion "three-fifths" was proposed many times. But Wilson of Pennsylvania "did not well see on what principle the admission of blacks in the proportion of three-fifths could be explained. Are they admitted as Citizens? Then why are they not admitted on an equality with White Citizens? Are they admitted as property? Then why is not other property admitted into the computation?" Wilson, nevertheless, talked now of "the necessity of compromise," and the others yielded on the three-fifths rule, directing that for both direct taxes and representation, five blacks were to be counted as equivalent to three whites.

Delegates from the commercial North urged that the new government be granted full power to regulate interstate and foreign commerce and to make treaties which the states must obey. The Convention readily agreed on these points. But the South, fearful of being outvoted in the new Congress, demanded, as the second of the two new issues, that commercial regulations and all treaties require the consent of a two-thirds majority of the Senate rather than a simple majority. The southerners were concerned about taxes on exports, for they were heavily dependent on selling tobacco and other staples in competitive world markets. But of even greater concern to them was the slave trade. Gouverneur Morris said, "he did not believe that those [southern] states would ever confederate on terms that would deprive them of that trade."

To conciliate the South, the Convention negotiated its third major compromise. The Constitution would prohibit all taxes on exports. It would also guarantee that for at least twenty years there would be no ban on "the migration or importation of such persons as any of the states now existing shall think proper to admit;" and that any "person held to service or labor in one State . . . escaping into another, . . . shall be delivered up on the claim of the party to whom such service or labor may be due." By these provisions, prohibition of the slave trade was delayed and slaves seeking freedom were frustrated, even though many delegates hated slavery sufficiently, in the words of Paterson of New Jersey, to have "been ashamed to use the term 'Slaves' & had substituted a description." "The thing," as Lincoln said later, "is hid away in the Constitution, just as an afflicted man hides away a wen or cancer which he dares not cut out at once, lest he bleed to death."

Finally, the South won the provision requiring a two-thirds vote in the Senate for the ratification of all treaties. In exchange for these concessions, the northerners won their point on a simple congressional majority for acts regulating commerce.

Once the decision on a single executive, a President, was made (p. 154), the method of his election, while never as heated an issue as those of representation and slavery, presented one last test of the compromising spirit. After many arguments—especially between the centralists, who wanted the President elected directly by the people, and the state sovereignty men, who wanted him chosen by the state legislatures—the Convention devised the elaborate electoral-college plan (Article II, Section 2). This plan left the method of choosing presidential electors up to the legislature of each state, and thereby mollified the state sovereignty men. The centralists were consoled by the virtual apportionment of the electors by population. Each state was to have as many electors as it had representatives and senators.

The delegates, even the most national-minded ones, believing that the electors in each state would normally vote first for citizens of their state, expected that no candidate would receive the majority of ballots required for election. In that case, or in case two candidates, each with a majority, were tied, they stipulated that the election be decided in the House of Representatives where each state, regardless of population, would cast but one vote. This gave the small states equal standing with the large in ultimately choosing the President from among candidates whom the large states, because of their preponderance of votes in the electoral college, would in effect nominate.

This complex scheme was based on the assumption that each state would constitute its own party. The emergence of national parties early in American history nullified the framers' elaborate machinery. The two-party system eventually made it possible for voters throughout the country to choose electors pledged to one of a few leading candidates. Electors, nevertheless, retained the privilege of exercising personal choice in the electoral college, and when third and fourth party movements developed in succeeding centuries, major party machines sometimes courted them in close campaigns.

## Toward sovereign power

Government under the Confederation had two fatal flaws. Congress enjoyed neither the power of the purse nor the power of the sword. Although distracted at the outset by problems of apportioning power to the states and the people, the delegates with few exceptions had come to Philadelphia principally to remedy these flaws by endowing a new national government with such sovereign strength.

Every delegate but Gerry of Massachusetts voted to give the new national government the power to levy and collect taxes and tariffs. The clause granting Congress the power to pay the debts of the United States passed unanimously. No one opposed giving Congress the power to coin money and "regulate the value thereof," nor the power to borrow money on the credit of the United States, nor the power to regulate commerce among the states or with foreign nations and Indian tribes.

When Madison complained of the "mutability of the laws of the states," he had most particularly in mind state laws that made credit more risky, investment more hazardous, long-term business planning more uncertain—the principal culprit in all instances being state issues of paper money. The delegates so strongly subscribed to Madison's position that virtually unanimously they forbade the states to issue "bills of credit," that is, paper money; to make anything but gold and silver legal tender for the payment of private or public debts; to interfere with the obligations of contracts; to tax imports or exports in commercial wars with one another.

The Constitution's provisions for the sovereign power of the sword went further to reassure the business community. The new government alone was enabled to "provide for

154

the common defence"; "to declare war"; "to raise and support armies"; "to provide and maintain a navy"; "to provide for calling forth the militia to execute the laws of the Union, suppress insurrections and repel invasions"; and, more broadly, to provide for the "general welfare of the United States." To insure, moreover, that sovereignty would not be impaired by technicalities, the framers added the famous "elastic clause," enabling Congress "to make all laws which shall be necessary and proper for carrying into execution the foregoing powers."

A third flaw in the Confederation had been the absence of an independent executive. To remedy this defect, the Constitution created a President—a single responsible executive elected, as we have seen, independently of Congress. The President was to be Commander-in-Chief of the army and navy, and of the state militias when called into federal service. His power of appointing federal officers was extensive, and only for his higher aides was the consent of the Senate required (the power of dismissing such aides, though not specifically mentioned, was later held to be included). The President could make treaties with foreign nations with the consent of two-thirds of the Senate. He could call Congress into extraordinary session, and could veto acts of Congress—although his veto could be overridden by a two-thirds vote in both houses. In the future, of course, the effectiveness of presidential leadership grew even beyond the expectations of the framers, partly because of the dynamic qualities of certain individual leaders, but also because of the development of the American party system and the vast extension of presidential patronage.

A fourth flaw of the Confederation was its lack of a judiciary independent of state courts. This fault the Constitution remedied by providing for a national judicial system. At the head of the system stood the Supreme Court of the United States: It could decide cases on appeal from lower federal courts, which Congress was empowered to establish, and from state courts in cases involving the Constitution, the laws of the United States, or treaties with other nations.

The Constitution made no specific provision for "judicial review" of federal legislation—that is, the power of the federal courts to declare acts of Congress unconstitutional and void—but the Supreme Court itself under Chief Justice John Marshall later clarified this issue (see p. 187). Article VI, Section 2, of the Constitution did make it plain that any state acts or laws that encroached on the supreme powers of Congress must be found unconstitutional by the federal courts.

Thus, the Philadelphia Convention erected a government that could act with speed, strength, and dignity. By the Tenth Amendment (in force after 1791) the states were permitted to retain all powers not specifically delegated by the Constitution to the new federal government. But in the exercise of the powers it received, the new government was supreme.

## Building for the ages

If the framers sought primarily to substitute a strong central government for the weak Articles, they also hoped to create a government, as Madison put it, "for the ages." Their success in this respect rests in part on certain features they introduced and on others unforeseen by them, that proved at least as important.

From the framers' point of view, the Constitution's built-in checks and balances were its best safeguards and the best safeguards of the Republic. Constrained by them, no Chief Executive could become a man on a white horse. And no transient surge of popular feeling, reflected in the legislature, even in its "democratical branch," could lawfully unseat the President or overturn the courts.

A second source of the Constitution's lasting strength is the amending process. The futility of trying to amend the Articles by the required unanimous consent of the states had hastened their demise. The easier amending process in the Constitution was at first sparingly used—but only after the promised first ten amendments constituting the much desired federal Bill of Rights had been adopted. Patrick Henry had opposed the movement for the Constitution and would fight its ratification in Virginia. Once he had lost this fight, the amending process alone reconciled him to the new system. "I will be a peaceable citizen," he said. "My head, my hand, and my heart shall be at liberty to retrieve the loss of liberty, and remove the defects of that system in a constitutional way."

A third somewhat less tangible source of the Constitution's long life lies in the general terms in which the document is written—no accident, but a result of the framers' classical training and universal way of thinking. Statesmanship required that they leave important powers to the jealous states. Having done this, they wrote down the prerogatives of the sovereign national government so broadly that essential powers could be retrieved when changes in national life made it imperative that they be exercised on the national level.

Among the nonconstitutional sources of the Constitution's long life we may note the two-party political system that developed early in the United States and tended to sponge up a host of divisive issues; the enlargement of the role of the Cabinet and the strength it added to the administrative powers of the executive; the committee system in the House and Senate, which, though often obstructive, nevertheless gave order and insight to legislation; and the bureaucratic civil service, which preserved professional continuity (sometimes, indeed, against the public wish, if not the public interest) in spite of the frequency of elections and the constant turnover in political leaders.

The Constitutional Convention, for all its conservatism, set up what was surely by worldwide standards a radical government, a democratic nation among aristocratic ones, a republic among oppressive monarchies. Under the Constitution, said John Marshall, who rose as a new leader during the ratification controversy in Virginia, "It is the people that give power, and can take it back. What shall restrain them? They are the masters who give it, and of whom their servants hold it."

For all its stress on private property, which, in the eighteenth century was thought to be the best foundation for public responsibility, the Constitution stipulated no property qualification for office, not even that of President. It also required "a compensation—to be ascertained by law, and paid out of the Treasury of the United States" for all elective posts, so that the poor as well as the rich might hold them. In the instrument itself, before the Bill of Rights was appended, the Constitution forbade religious tests for any federal position. It provided that "for any speech or debate in either House," senators and representatives "shall not be questioned in any other place," thereby assuring their fullest freedom of expression. It also guaranteed trial by jury for all crimes, "except in cases of impeachment"; and forbade suspension of "the privilege of the writ of habeas corpus" except in times of invasion or rebellion.

## Ratification

The Constitutional Convention was in session from May 25 to September 16, 1787. Of the fifty-five delegates who took some part in the deliberations, forty-two stayed to the end, and thirty-nine signed the document. The other three, Gerry of Massachusetts, and Randolph and Mason of Virginia, refused to go along, their reasons accumulating as the sessions drew out. These refusals gave warning of the storm ahead when the Constitution would be offered to "we the people" for approval. But the signers were not to be diverted from their course by fear. The day after the Convention itself adopted the Constitution, a copy was sent to Congress, largely out of courtesy, and with a letter that did not mince words. "In all our deliberations on this subject," said the signers, "we kept steadily in our view that which appeared to us the greatest interest of every true American—the consolidation of the Union—in which is involved our prosperity, felicity, safety, perhaps our national existence." They petitioned Congress for no vote. Nor would they apply to the state legislatures for confirmation. In keep-

155

ing with their revulsion from existing governments, in the Constitution itself they asked only the assent of nine special conventions like their own.

156 While the election of delegates to these conventions was in progress, the Constitution began to be discussed and debated throughout the country. Rufus King, a member of the Massachusetts ratifying convention, summed up the feelings of the opposition, though he did not share them, when he wrote to Madison in January 1788: "An apprehension that the liberties of the people are in danger, and a distrust of men of property and education have a more powerful effect upon the minds of our opponents than any specific objections against the Constitution."

But the Constitution's critics, named "Anti-

federalists" by the Constitution's friends, did offer plenty of specific objections: There was no Bill of Rights; state sovereignty would be destroyed; the President might become king; the standing army would be everywhere; only the rich and wellborn could afford to hold office; tax collectors would swarm over the countryside; the people could not bear to be taxed by both state and national governments; commercial treaties would sell out the West and the South; debtors would no longer be able to defend themselves through recourse to state paper money and state stay laws. In March 1787, Washington had remarked that "A thirst for power [has] taken fast hold of the states individually; . . . the many whose personal consequence in the control of state politics will be annihilated [by a national government] will form a strong phalanx against it." But it was not merely the local lions who felt themselves menaced by the proposal. Many honest citizens shrank from so drastic an innovation.

*"Done in Convention by the unanimous consent of the States present the seventeenth day of September in the year of our Lord one thousand seven hundred and eighty seven, and of the independence of the United States of America the twelfth. In witness whereof we have hereunto subscribed our names." (From the painting by Albert Herter.)*

Brown Brothers

At the outset, nevertheless, ratification went along smoothly. Between December 7, 1787, and January 9, 1788, five states ratified, and the conventions of three (Delaware, New Jersey, Georgia) did so without a single opposing vote. A fourth state, Connecticut, ratified by 128 to 40. In Pennsylvania alone among the first five was controversy heated. By staying away, opponents of the Constitution tried to prevent the legislature from forming the quorum it needed before it could vote to call a ratifying convention. The Federalists then seized enough of their opponents and forcibly dragged them into the chamber to make up a quorum. In the Pennsylvania ratifying convention itself the Federalists won handily, 46 to 23.

In Massachusetts, the sixth state to ratify, the contest was close. Its convention debated from early January to early February, but Federalist leaders maneuvered ingeniously to win over such popular opponents as John Hancock and Sam Adams, and placated many opponents by promising to support amendments guaranteeing popular liberties. Finally, Massachusetts voted for the Constitution, 187 to 168.

In Maryland and South Carolina ratification went smoothly and won easily. In New Hampshire, the opposition was powerful, and after a first convention failed to reach a vote, a second convention ratified on June 21, 1788, by the narrow margin of 57 to 46. Technically speaking, the new government could now go into effect, for nine states had accepted it. But no one believed that it could function without Virginia and New York, and in these two states the outcome remained doubtful.

In Virginia, an extraordinarily thorough and brilliant review of the issues took place, with the opposition led by the scholarly George Mason and the inflammatory Patrick Henry. Washington's influence and the knowledge that he would consent to serve as first president was responsible for the unexpected conversion of Edmund Randolph, who had refused to sign the Constitution. The promised

157

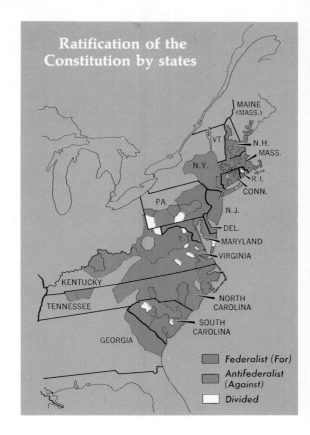

**Ratification of the Constitution by states**

Legend:
- Federalist (For)
- Antifederalist (Against)
- Divided

addition of a Bill of Rights further softened the opposition. Four days after New Hampshire had ratified, Virginia fell in line, 89 to 79. By arrangement between Madison and Hamilton, couriers were quickly dispatched with the good news to New York, where a very close struggle was in process.

In New York, Hamilton led the Federalist fight in support of ratification, Governor Clinton the opposition. Well aware of Clinton's strength, Hamilton, assisted on a few occasions by John Jay and more elaborately by Madison, began to write articles in the press supporting the Constitution. Later published as *The Federalist,* these articles provide the best commentary on the Constitution by its contemporary advocates. But they did not create a landslide for the Constitution in New York. More important in the vote here was the news of Federalist success in New Hampshire and Virginia, for it changed the issue

158

from helping to form a new union to joining one that seemed almost certain to be established. Once again, the promise of amendments constituting a Bill of Rights overcame some opposition. Having agreed to support such amendments, the Federalists finally won on July 26 by 30 to 27.

Rhode Island and North Carolina were so hostile to the Constitution that they did not join the Union until after the new government was in operation. North Carolina, by a wide margin, decided to join in November 1789. Rhode Island held out until May 1790, when Congress had in view a bill placing her on the footing of a foreign nation. Even then Rhode Island decided to enter only by the narrowest of margins.

Over fifty years ago, the distinguished historian Charles A. Beard tried to show that the vote for and against the ratification of the Constitution took place along class and sectional lines. Speculators, men with large holdings in public securities, and other investors favored the proposal, Beard wrote, while the frontiersmen, small farmers, and debtors opposed it. The bitter struggle that raged over the Constitution, he argued, was won by the Federalists against the wishes of the majority largely because so many of the opponents were disfranchised and because the Federalists were better organized, better educated, and more aware of their interests.

This materialistic view shocked many in Beard's day, and ever since it has arrayed historians in opposing camps. Few subjects have so aroused students of American politics; and the subject refuses to die because of its great interest, on the one hand, and the elusiveness of the data, on the other.

Beard's own most significant contribution to

the discussion of the adoption of the Constitution was his pursuit of new sources in support of his hypothesis. Since he used these sources carelessly, his conclusions have been subjected to more abuse than his materialism alone might have stirred up. In more recent times, historians and political scientists, less concerned with Beard's materialism, have themselves come to the problem with new ideas and have pursued new data in support of them. The structure of politics and the behavior of voters and leaders has interested them more than the structure of the economy and the behavior of businessmen of different sorts.

The Beardian literature, pro and con, is enormous, intricate, and available. On the basis of it, but on the basis of politically oriented research as well, we may present another picture which, in any case, tallies more closely with what the Founding Fathers themselves appear to have thought they were undertaking. That is, that the Constitution was conceived, drawn up, and promoted by an extraordinary generation of political leaders who had no false modesty about their own abilities, as few leaders did in their day; that, for all the controversy their work stirred up, these leaders had persuaded the politically active public to make a drastic change in the structure of their government without violence, without bloodshed, without coercion; and finally that these leaders were given an ample opportunity to show that the Constitution which had been won on paper could be made to work.

## For further reading

Allan Nevins, *The American States During and After the Revolution 1775-1789* (1924), although superseded on many points by more recent scholarship, remains the most substantial account of state

politics in the "critical period." A survey of the recent scholarship is available in the chapters on Charles Beard in Richard Hofstadter, *The Progressive Historians: Turner, Beard, Parrington* (1968). On state-constitution making see R. J. Taylor, ed., *Massachusetts, Colony to Commonwealth, Documents on the Formation of Its Constitution* (1961); Richard McCormick, *Experiment in Independence: New Jersey in the Critical Period 1781-1789* (1950); R. L. Brunhouse, *The Counter-Revolution in Pennsylvania 1776-1790* (1942); and Dumas Malone, *Jefferson the Virginian* (1948). Other relevant biographies of the Founding Fathers are Irving Brant, *James Madison* (6 vols., 1941-1961), and Broadus Mitchell, *Alexander Hamilton* (2 vols., 1957-1962). *Rebels and Democrats* (1955), is best described by its subtitle, "The Struggle for Equal Political Rights and Majority Rule during the American Revolution." R. A. Rutland, *The Birth of the Bill of Rights 1776-1791* (1955), covers the subject in the states, the Constitutional Convention, and the ratifying process. Here, as elsewhere, W. D. Jordan, *White over Black* (1968), is illuminating; see especially Parts Three and Four. E. C. Burnett, *The Continental Congress* (1941), is the indispensable study of the national government in the "critical period." On the central issue of public finance, see E. J. Ferguson, *The Power of the Purse, A History of American Public Finance 1776-1790* (1961).

The old but influential work by John Fiske, *The Critical Period of American History 1783-1789* (1888), still merits serious consideration. Merrill Jensen, *The New Nation: A History of the United States During the Confederation 1781-1789* (1950), develops the idea that conditions in this period were not as bad as proponents of a new constitution claimed. His work derives from C. A. Beard's outstanding scholarly monograph *An Economic Interpretation of the Constitution of the United States* (1913). Beard's principal critics include R. E. Brown in *Charles Beard and the Constitution* (1956), and Forrest McDonald, *We the People: The Economic Origins of the Constitution* (1958). Criticisms of the critics include Lee Benson, *Turner and Beard: American Historical Writing Reconsidered* (1960), and J. T. Main, *The Anti-Federalists, Critics of the Constitution 1781-1788* (1961). On the social impact of the Revolution, besides the works by E. B. Greene and J. T. Main cited in Chapter Five, see J. F. Jameson, *The American Revolution Considered as a Social Movement* (1926).

R. A. East, *Business Enterprise in the American Revolutionary Era* (1938); and E. J. Ferguson, *The Power of the Purse . . . 1776-1790* (1961), are outstanding on the economy. On land sales and speculation see P. J. Treat, *The National Land System 1785-1820* (1910). Excellent on the early land companies is T. P. Abernethy, *Western Lands and the American Revolution* (1937). On early western settlement, see F. S. Philbrick, *The Rise of the West 1754-1830* (1965); B. W. Bond, Jr., *The Civilization of the Old Northwest* (1934); and A. P. Whitaker, *The Spanish-American Frontier 1783-1795* (1927). For background on the Northwest Ordinance and slavery, see Staughton Lynd, "Slavery and the Founding Fathers," in Melvin Drimmer, ed., *Black History, A Reappraisal* (1968). M. L. Starkey, *A Little Rebellion* (1955), is excellent on Shays' revolt. A good shorter account is R. B. Morris, "Insurrection in Massachusetts," in Daniel Aaron, ed., *America in Crisis* (1952).

The best text of the Constitution, with an analysis of each clause and summaries of Supreme Court interpretations, is E. S. Corwin, *The Constitution of the United States of America* (1953). The classic commentary on the Constitution is *The Federalist,* written in 1787-1788 by Hamilton, Madison, and Jay. The definitive modern edition is by J. E. Cooke (1961). Richard Henry Lee, *Letters from the Federal Farmer* (originally published in 1787 and 1788 and available in Forrest McDonald, ed., *Empire and Nation* (1962), became the Antifederalist equivalent of the Federalist papers. Cecelia Kenyon, ed., *The Antifederalist* (1966), is an outstanding anthology. The spirit of the Constitution and its makers is best presented in Max Farrand, ed., *Records of the Federal Convention* (4 vols., 1911-1937). For its reception by the ratifying conventions see Jonathan Elliot, ed., *The Debates in the Several State Conventions on the Adoption of the Federal Constitution* (5 vols., 1836-1845). Perhaps the best brief book on making the Constitution is R. L. Schuyler, *The Constitution of the United States* (1923). See also Max Farrand, *The Framing of the Constitution of the United States* (1913). J. A. Smith, *The Spirit of American Government, A Study of the Constitution: Its Origin, Influence and Relation to Democracy* (1907), foreshadowed Beard's, *An Economic Interpretation of the Constitution . . .* (above).

On judicial review, R. K. Carr, *The Supreme Court and Judicial Review* (1942), is brief and clear. Other leading studies include C. G. Haines, *The American Doctrine of Judicial Supremacy* (1932); and C. A. Beard, *The Supreme Court and the Constitution* (1912).

On ratification in the states besides Elliot's *Debates* (above), see F. G. Bates, *Rhode Island and the Formation of the Union* (1898); R. L. Brunhouse, *The Counter-Revolution in Pennsylvania* (above); L. I. Trenholme, *The Ratification of the Federal Constitution in North Carolina* (1932); S. B. Harding, *The Contest over Ratification of the Federal Constitution in the State of Massachusetts* (1896); and for Virginia, vol. I of A. J. Beveridge, *The Life of John Marshall* (4 vols., 1916-1919).

# FEDERALIST NATIONALISM

March 4, 1789, was the date set for the new Congress to assemble in New York City. But as late as March 30, a quorum of neither representatives nor senators had completed the rough journey to the capital. "The people will forget the new government before it is born," moaned Fisher Ames of Boston, the conservative who had defeated Sam Adams for Congress. By April 1, however, the House of Representatives was ready to convene, and by April 6 the Senate had its quorum and could join the House in examining the ballots of the presidential electors. Washington, with 69 votes, was chosen President, and John Adams, second in the balloting with 34 votes, was named Vice-President. After a triumphal journey from Mount Vernon, Washington arrived in New York on April 23, 1789. One week later, with the sun shining on the gaily decorated streets, he was inaugurated.

The leaders of the first Congress were determined to make a good impression as well as to make good. John Adams, for example, as President of the Senate, a body which Gouverneur Morris hoped would "show us the might of aristocracy," was so insistent upon dignified titles and procedure that the Antifederalists soon dubbed him "His Rotundity." Such preoccupation with decorum made Congress seem almost ridiculous at first, especially to "back parts" members who cared very little for the trappings of authority in a democratic country; but the need for getting down to more serious business soon sobered it up. The Constitution made few suggestions on punctilio or procedure, but it was clear enough on objectives, and the times were making their own urgent demands.

New York was the capital of what was still a weak nation—one beset by foreign and domestic debts, surrounded by enemies, harassed on its borders by hostile Indians, on the sea by bold pirates, and in foreign ports and even upon the high seas by unfriendly navies. Nor was there to be any real measure of unity at home.

## I The new government at work

### First Federalist measures

"Few who are not philosophical spectators," President Washington wrote at the outset of his administration,

*can realize the difficult and delicate part, which a man in my situation has to act. . . . my station is new, and, if I may use the expression, I walk on untrodden ground. There is scarcely an action, the motive of which may not be subject to a double interpretation. There is scarcely any part of my conduct which may not hereafter be drawn into precedent.*

Much has been made of the "furious pace" with which Alexander Hamilton in particular worked to get the new government off the ground. One reason for Hamilton's administrative zeal may have been that Washington had allowed a precious five months to elapse before commissioning the new Secretary of the Treasury on September 11, 1789. In taking other steps the first President acted with similar deliberation, and the first Congress, once it had adopted and submitted to the states the promised amendments to the Constitution creating a federal Bill of Rights (see p. 157),

(see p. 157),

followed his example. These amendments, the first ten, were ratified by the required three-fourths of the states by December 1791. When few other measures passed through Congress with the unanimity of these amendments, Washington grew concerned. When some legislation reopened sectional rifts he viewed the future with dismay.

The new government's most urgent need was for money to meet its day-to-day expenses, and more important, as Madison put it, "to revive those principles of honor and honesty that have too long lain dormant" by paying the national debt. Madison, the acknowledged leader in the House of Representatives and the President's closest advisor, hoped to raise the necessary funds principally by a modest tariff bill which he submitted to the House even before Washington was inaugurated. By touching "such articles . . . only as are likely to occasion the least difficulty," Madison expected prompt enactment of his measure. With lobbying and log-rolling tactics that became notorious later on, however, manufacturers combined to hold up the bill until each obtained special protection for his products.

162

The claims of competing economic interests would have been settled sooner had not Madison conceived of his tariff as a weapon in the new nation's commercial war with Britain as well as a money-raising bill. Once the Revolution ended, Britain, as we have seen (p. 144), had deprived Americans of their extensive prewar commerce with the British West Indies, while in her home ports she treated American goods and ships as she treated those of other nations with whom she had no commercial treaties. Nor, rightfully skeptical of enforcement here, would she make commercial treaties with the Confederation Congress. In an effort to compel her now to restore the old privileges and grant new ones, Madison, in his tariff bill, asked for higher duties on goods entering American ports from countries without treaties with the United States, such as Britain, and lower duties on similar goods from countries with treaties, such as France. He also asked for higher duties on goods entering in foreign ships, and higher port charges on such ships.

These discriminatory proposals presented welcome opportunities for oratory by restored Loyalists, renascent monarchists, and others whose "habitual affection for England" had revived or regained respectability during the critical period in America. Even though Madison, the author of these proposals, was a Virginian, they also galvanized the never really dormant suspicion of the commercial North in the agrarian South, where planters simply wanted cheap and plentiful shipping under any flag to carry their staples overseas. Yankee, Yorker, and Quaker merchants, in turn, also opposed Madison's commercial warfare, preferring friendliness to hostility as the policy most likely to move Britain to restore normal trade relations between the new nation and the old.

As finally enacted in July 1789, Madison's tariff, placing duties averaging 8.5 percent on the value of certain listed imports, made no reference to countries with or without commercial treaties with the United States. At the same time, for the benefit of American carriers, it provided lower duties on goods imported in their ships than on those arriving in foreign ships. A second act passed later in the month set lower tonnage duties on American ships entering American ports than on foreign ships.

Explicit discrimination against Britain had been rejected; yet so sensitive was London to America's every independent step that as soon as the government there learned of the differentials in favor of American carriers, it dispatched Major George Beckwith, an officer familiar with America and American leaders through his experiences in the Revolution, to serve as a secret agent in New York. Besides working to remove these tariff and tonnage differentials, Beckwith was to uncover and report on American attitudes toward all other outstanding problems with Britain and to bend these attitudes toward London's own policy.

Beckwith soon penetrated the highest ranks of the new national government, his path smoothed by the active Anglophiles now in it. He became especially close to Hamilton, whose love for everything English matched his love for power and soon led him deliberately to mislead Washington himself in order to further his own favorite policy of a permanent alliance with Britain involving far more than commercial reciprocity. Hamilton, indeed, using the code number 7, secretly became Beckwith's principal source of information and misinformation, asserting as fixed American policy at critical junctures positions he then undertook to impose upon the President by falsifying the nature of Beckwith's mission as well as his communications.

No Anglo-American alliance was made in this period, and no commercial treaty was negotiated with Britain until Jay's Treaty of 1794, which Hamilton characteristically helped bend toward London's desires (see p. 175). His secret activities did not go unsuspected; had they actually been uncovered, his own national career would have been checked at the outset, an event that would have had more far-reaching consequences than the Tariff Act.

While the House was occupied with debate on the tariff, the Senate began work on what was to become the Judiciary Act of September 24, 1789. This act helped cement the federal system by spelling out the procedure by which federal courts could review and, if necessary, declare void, state laws and state court decisions involving powers and duties delegated by the Constitution to the federal government. It also specified that the Supreme Court be manned by a Chief Justice and five Associate Justices. The system of federal courts was to be completed by three circuit courts and thirteen district courts. Attached to each district court were to be United States attorneys and their deputies to serve as federal prosecutors, and United States marshals and their deputies to serve as federal police. One of the duties of these marshals and deputies, with numerous special assistants, was to take the first federal census in 1790, as provided in the Constitution.

The executive had been one of the weakest links in the old Confederation. Yet the three executive departments created under the Ar-

ticles of 1781—Foreign Affairs, Treasury, and War—continued unchanged for months under the new government. Not until July 1789 did Congress create the new Department of State to manage foreign relations. The new War Department was set up soon after; the Treasury, not until September. An act of February 1792 stipulated that there should be "one Postmaster General," but this official remained in the Treasury Department until 1829. The Judiciary Act of September 24, 1789, created the office of Attorney-General, but the Department of Justice was not established until 1870.

While Congress busied itself with these basic measures, the President gave his most serious attention to the appointments he knew he must make to fill the positions Congress was creating. Washington wanted to surround himself with the best men available, but other considerations carried great weight in his thinking. It is impossible to exaggerate Washing-

163

*James Madison, advocate of legislative independence (left), and Alexander Hamilton, advocate of executive energy, both portraits by Charles Willson Peale.*

Thomas Gilcrease Institute, Tulsa, Oklahoma

The New-York Historical Society, New York City

*General Henry Knox. On becoming
Secretary of War, he inherited an army
of 672 officers and men. When Congress
in 1790 cut private's pay from $4
to $3 a month, it was said that none would
come in but men "purchased from prisons,
wheel barrows, and brothels."*

ton's awareness of the tenuousness of the thread that held the states together, or his care not to give offense to local sensibilities in filling even minor posts. "A single disgust excited in a particular state, on this account," he wrote, "might perhaps raise the flame of opposition that could not easily, if ever, be extinguished. . . . Perfectly convinced I am, that if injudicious or unpopular measures should be taken by the executive under the new government, with regard to appointments, the government itself would be in the utmost danger of being utterly subverted by those measures."

Washington also was reluctant to appoint an opponent of the Constitution to any office, however insignificant, when a sympathizer

could be found. Finally, he gave preference, when he could, to men whose measure he personally had taken during the heat of the Revolution. General Henry Knox of Massachusetts, Washington's chief of artillery and one of the army's most outspoken opponents of the old Congress, became the first Secretary of War. To Edmund Randolph of Virginia, one of Washington's wartime aides-de-camp, went the Attorney-Generalship. The Treasury seems to have been reserved for the Middle states, with Hamilton of New York, another of Washington's military aides, the designee. John Jay of New York, in charge of foreign affairs for the old Congress, continued to direct them until April 1790, when Thomas Jefferson of Virginia took over and Jay became the first Chief Justice of the Supreme Court.

The Constitution made no provision for a presidential Cabinet, but early in his administration Washington established the practice of taking action only on matters that had been referred to him by the Secretaries of the three departments or the Attorney-General. Gradually, he began to consult these Secretaries on questions that arose outside their departments. In the spring of 1791, in anticipation of a journey to the South that would keep him from the capital for an extended period, Washington wrote to each of the three Secretaries that, should "any serious and important cases arise during my absence," they should consult together on them. While holding himself in readiness to return to the capital in an emergency, he also admonished them to take whatever "measures . . . may be legally and properly pursued without the immediate agency of the President," and "I will approve and ratify" them. Thereafter, the Secretaries did meet from time to time. After the crisis in foreign affairs in 1793, arising from the wars of the French Revolution (see p. 172), such meetings, which Washington himself had begun to call, became regular events. In this way the Cabinet became a permanent cog in the federal machinery.

## Hamilton's funding program

The Constitution stipulated that the President "shall from time to time give to the Congress information of the state of the Union, and recommend ... such measures as he shall judge necessary and expedient." But on Hamilton's insistence, which fell in nicely with Congress's determination to control money matters, the act creating the Treasury Department gave the Secretary of the Treasury the right to advise Congress directly on finance. Near the end of the first session, Congress asked the Secretary to prepare financial reports for the new session to begin in December 1789. Hamilton had his first report, "for the Support of Public Credit," ready in January 1790. In December he submitted his report on a national bank, and in 1791 he advised the Second Congress on the value of a mint and the fostering of manufactures.

While many of his colleagues floundered amidst the perplexities of an infant republic in an age of almost universal monarchy, and the new Congress rang with a multiplicity of counsels, most of them in the voice of inexperience, Hamilton grasped the strategic opportunity for what he called the "Executive Impulse." Thirty-four years old at this time, he had been close to great men and great events for more than twelve years and was now at the height of his faculties. Even his enemies in Congress acknowledged "the force of his genius." During his first years as Secretary of the Treasury, Hamilton frequently sat with House committees to help them frame the legislation required by his "advice." He also became conspicuous on the floor of Congress, whipping Federalist forces into line behind his measures. The saturnine Senator from Pennsylvania, William Maclay, observed:

*Nothing is done [in the House] without him. ... Mr. Hamilton ... was here early to wait on the Speaker, and I believe spent most of his time running from place to place among the members.*

At the Constitutional Convention, Hamilton had observed that "the views of the governed are often materially different from those who govern." He was determined to array "those who govern" behind the new administration. But even among those who govern, he made an additional differentiation. Early in his report on the public credit, he noted a rise of over 80 percent in the market value of public securities during the past year, most of it in the past two months, simply in anticipation of his recommendations. "It cannot but merit particular attention," he added directly, "that among ourselves the most enlightened friends of good government are those, whose expectations are highest." None nursed higher expectations of the new government than the speculators in public securities.

Besides Hamilton himself, the speculators had a great friend at court in the person of William Duer, the New York wartime profiteer who was Hamilton's client in his private law practice. Within but three days of his own appointment as Secretary, Hamilton had named Duer Assistant Secretary of the Treasury. Even then Duer had in hand an elaborate scheme for speculating in heavily depreciated public securities, the initial success of which—depending on advance knowledge of Hamilton's program among insiders and ignorance of it among other security holders—was reflected in the dramatic rise in security prices of which Hamilton had boasted.

In his report on the public credit, Hamilton made three major recommendations: (1) that the foreign debt, of almost $12 million, including arrears of interest, be repaid by means of a new bond issue; (2) that the domestic debt, made up of many kinds of Revolutionary securities valued in 1789 at about 25 cents on the dollar, be exchanged at its face value, plus back interest, for additional new bonds amounting to some $40 million; (3) that the remaining state debts, totaling about $21 million, be assumed by the federal government and refunded on a similar basis.

No one could deny Hamilton's assertion in his report, that "the debt of the United States ... was the price of liberty. The faith of America has been repeatedly pledged for it," he added, "and with solemnities, that give particular force to the obligation." His assertion that funding the debt by "a punctual performance of contracts" with the current holders of public securities would "cement more closely the union of the states," was another proposition.

166

Congress adopted Hamilton's proposal for refunding the foreign debt with very little debate or division. Despite his pertinacity on its behalf, his program for the domestic debt found much tougher going. Included in the issues to be refunded were certificates with which the Revolutionary veterans had been paid. Large amounts of such certificates along with other issues, were scattered through the hinterland, and many speculators dispatched fast boats and coaches loaded with cash to beat the news to the back country, where their agents bought up for a song securities that were soon to soar further in value. Most of the speculators were northern capitalists already well-schooled in Duer's schemes and in command of cash and credit when new opportunities offered. Many of them were members of Congress, so primed to vote for Hamilton's program that a rising group of Antifederalists led by Madison in the House raised the cry of corruption. The cash and credit of southern planters were more likely to be tied up in land and slaves and in obligations to British merchants. Even among planters "who governed" in their states and ranked high in the counsels of the new nation, few were able to compete with Yankees and Yorkers in such security manipulation.

As an alternative to Hamilton's plan, Madison and his followers proposed to discriminate between the original holders of the securities representing the domestic debt and those who purchased them later on speculation. The latter, the Antifederalists held, should not be permitted to profit at the patriotic public's expense. "Discrimination," however, proved too cumbersome a proposition to work out in time. Madison's hastily written bill failed, and Hamilton's plan won.

With the funding of the foreign and domestic debts approved, albeit with scandals that divided many from Washington's administration even among "enlightened & discriminating" men in the North, there remained the further question of the debts the states had accumulated in the revolutionary cause. Certain states, especially in the South, had paid off substantial portions of such obligations; others, led by Massachusetts, the storm center of the Revolution, had paid none. With federal securities at their peak in value now, Hamilton's friends among the speculators buzzing around Federal Hall, the Capitol building in New York, had turned to the deeply depreciated state securities to make their latest killing. Hamilton, as they knew, viewed the war debts incurred by the states as a responsibility of the nation which victory in the war had preserved. They wondered, nevertheless, how far he would go in endangering national unity by pressing this position upon reluctant southern legislators. Their wonder was deepened by the crucial consideration that no money had as yet been appropriated for funding even the approved foreign and federal debt. They realized that the entire funding program might collapse if the assumption of state debts was urged too obdurately upon rebellious congressmen who could kill appropriations for any funding at all.

Southern intransigence on the subject of assumption, aroused by the fact that mainly northern debts would be assumed, was fed by the additional fear that in paying for assumption Congress would preempt the remaining tax sources of the nation, thereby endangering the fiscal standing of the states and state rights themselves. Thus, when assumption came up for a House vote in April 1790, southerners ganged up to defeat it by two votes. By taking the lead in mobilizing the opposition, Madison deepened his breach with Washington and the administration but at the same time strengthened his political position in his own state.

Like Hamilton and the speculators, nevertheless, Madison was unwilling to see the whole funding program, and hence the credit of the new nation, founder on the question of assumption. Jefferson, recently returned from France to take up his duties as Secretary of

State, agreed with him. On recognizing that Hamilton was irretrievably committed to assumption, they finally yielded in June in exchange for objectives of their own. The subject of the permanent "residence" of the new government deeply agitated Congress at the same time as the funding program. New York and Philadelphia both wanted it. When, after numerous failures to reverse the House vote on assumption, Hamilton at last proposed to Madison and Jefferson that in exchange for their support of the whole funding program he would undertake to swing enough northern votes behind the proposition to locate the permanent capital in the South, the deal was made.

By the time assumption passed late in July, Hamilton and his followers had already carried out their part of the bargain by sponsoring the measure which made Philadelphia the capital for ten years, starting late in 1790, and designated a site on the Potomac to be ready in 1800 as the permanent seat of the government. In 1791, the commissioners for the development of the new "Federal City" let it be known that the capital would be named for the first President.

## Hamilton's bank

It is "a fundamental maxim, in the system of public credit of the United States," Hamilton said, "that the creation of debt should always be accompanied with the means of its extinguishment." But in practice Hamilton undertook to supply only the means for paying the interest, not the principal, of the debt. He had no intention of eliminating the bonds that served the moneyed class as a source of income and as collateral for further speculation.

The annual interest on all the new bonds averaged about $2 million for the period 1791–1795 and came to nearly half the government's total expenditures for these years. Although the American carrying trade benefited from the tariff differentials of 1789 and from

opportunities for neutral shipping once the wars of the French Revolution began in 1793 (see p. 172), the customs duties failed to provide even this small amount. Thus, besides successfully urging an increase in the tariff, Hamilton made two more proposals. Both were adopted, but not without further factional and sectional strife.

Hamilton's first proposal called for a Bank of the United States, modeled explicitly on the Bank of England, with a capital of $10 million, one-fifth to be subscribed by the government, the rest by private capitalists. The Federalists, opposed on principle to government paper money, planned to have the Treasury issue only minted gold and silver. Consequently, Hamilton argued, a commercial bank was needed to supply notes that would serve as currency in business transactions. This bank would also assist the government by lending it money to meet its short-term obligations and by serving as a depository for government funds. Finally, by providing personal loans, the bank would make it easier for individuals to pay their taxes.

"This plan for a national bank," objected Representative James Jackson of Georgia, "is calculated to benefit a small part of the United States, the mercantilist interests only; the farmers, the yeomanry, will derive no advantage from it." But Hamilton's bill passed the House, 39 to 20. Thirty-six of the favoring votes came from the commercial North, 19 of the opposing votes from the agrarian South. In February 1791 the Bank of the United States was chartered for twenty years with headquarters in Philadelphia, and in December it opened. Ultimately, eight branches were established in port cities from Boston to New Orleans.

In the House debate on the bank bill, Madison had argued that a national bank would be unconstitutional. The Constitutional Convention, he insisted, had expressly rejected the proposition that the federal government be empowered to charter companies. When the bill was sent to Washington for his signature, he asked Jefferson and Hamilton as well as Attorney-General Randolph for their opinions on its constitutionality. Jefferson supported Madison. But Hamilton argued that since the

**167**

government had been delegated the power to regulate currency, it had the "implied power" to establish a bank to issue currency. Randolph equivocated on the constitutional problem, and it seems that Washington himself never resolved it. He rejected Jefferson's and Madison's "strict interpretation" of the Constitution in favor of Hamilton's "broad interpretation"; but his decision was not based on constitutional reasoning. Washington's administrative credo required him to give his support, when in doubt on an issue, to the Cabinet member whose office was most closely involved. On these grounds Hamilton won his bank.

### Excises and insurrection

Hamilton's second proposal for raising money, excise taxes on various commodities, including distilled liquors, was enacted quietly enough in March 1791 but soon raised a storm.

Opposition to the excises was strong in the South, where whiskey was held essential to men working in the hot climate. The most violent resistance to Hamilton's measure, however, occurred in western Pennsylvania, where government efforts to collect the excise were resisted with gunfire. Here, as on other frontiers, to save transportation costs on bulky grain, farmers often converted it into whiskey, which indeed became a medium of exchange. A tax on whiskey thus was viewed as a tax on money itself. There were also deeper reasons for resentment. In *The Federalist* Hamilton had acknowledged that "the genius of the people will ill brook the inquisitive and peremptory spirit of excise laws." How right he was became clear as early as September 1791, when opponents of the excise, meeting in Pittsburgh, resolved that "it is insulting to the feelings of the people to have their vessels marked, houses . . . ransacked, to be subject to informers," and so forth.

One of the most objectionable features of the excise was the provision requiring those prosecuted for infractions to stand trial in federal courts, the nearest one to the Pittsburgh district, for example, being 300 miles away in Philadelphia. Besides obliging farmers to halt

all work to attend court, the cost of the trip itself was equivalent to a heavy fine. In June 1794, Congress attempted to mitigate this "great popular grievance" by permitting state courts to exercise jurisdiction in excise cases which arose more than 50 miles from the nearest federal court. Far from being received as a concession, however, this act was looked upon as inflammatory, for its application was specifically withheld from "distillers who had previously to its enactment incurred a penalty." To make matters worse, in May 1794, the federal court in Philadelphia had issued writs against seventy-five western Pennsylvania distillers returnable in that court but had delayed until July to serve them. When federal marshals came west with the writs, a mob attacked them shouting, "The Federal Sheriff is taking away men to Philadelphia!"

Hamilton interpreted the uprising that followed against all federal collectors in the disaffected area as a rebellion against the United States, and he prevailed upon Washington early in August 1794 to order the mobili-

*Oath of submission signed by a score or more of the rebels, September 11, 1794, after suppression of the Whiskey Insurrection at the storm center of the resistance, Pittsburgh in Allegheny County.*

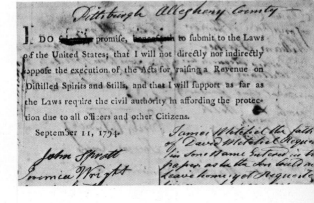

zation of 13,000 militiamen to crush the farmers. Hamilton, naturally, rode west with the troops, whom Washington himself journeyed out to inspect at Carlisle. Although they found no organized opposition, the militia rounded up about a hundred men. Two of them were later convicted of treason and sentenced to death, but Washington eventually pardoned them.

In the year of the so-called Whiskey Insurrection, receipts from the excise on distilled liquors fell lower than ever and the cost of collection, including the cost of the military display, naturally skyrocketed. But Hamilton, having already devised excises on additional essentials like salt and coal, and boots and shoes, to eke out the interest on the government debt, persisted in the "experiment" of collection to prove to the skeptical capitalists of the world that a republic could coerce its citizens where financial responsibility was at issue.

## The first Federalist crisis

Hamilton's blueprint for converting the United States into a powerful industrial nation was his celebrated Report on Manufactures, which he sent to Congress in December 1791. This Report argued the value of industry to the community, and the need for protective tariffs, subsidies, and other aids while industry was in its infancy. Congress gave the Report a cold reception. The Secretary's own manufacturing enterprise, set up in 1791 to show the validity of his theories, also soon collapsed (see p. 228).

The merchants in whose hands the money of the country was concentrated were to remain cool to industrial enterprise for another quarter of a century. For longer than that they opposed protective tariffs, which they felt only taxed and troubled trade. Along with farmers, who also felt burdensomely taxed, many merchants grew increasingly suspicious of Hamilton as more and more of the country's funds were tied up in speculation in the Secretary's new securities. When in the spring of 1792, "the prince of the tribe of speculators," Hamilton's bosom friend Duer, failed and went to a debtor's cell, much of the onus fell on Hamilton himself. Since Duer's bankruptcy left others unable to meet their obligations, many businessmen were ruined. The farmers at the same time were having difficulties of their own, for excellent harvests in Europe had reduced both the demand and the prices for American exports.

To make matters worse, the Federalist administration was having international troubles. In the Southwest, Spain continued to contest the Florida border as defined in the Treaty of Paris and to keep the Mississippi at New Orleans closed to American shipping. In the Northwest, Britain persisted in using military power to help Canadian fur trappers against American entrepreneurs. Neither Spain nor Britain tried to restrain the Indians in their territories from systematically molesting American frontiersmen. Coupled with the failure of Washington's own efforts to deal with the Indians on American territory, this situation was doubly depressing to settlers on the borders who had looked to a strong central government for protection against repeated Indian raids. After Governor Arthur St. Clair of the Northwest Territory in 1791 lost most of his 2000 ill-equipped and untrained men by desertion even before encountering any Indians against whom they had been mobilized, and the rest of his force was trapped and compelled to flee for their lives, Washington stormed: "Here in this very room, I warned General St. Clair against being surprised." The explanation of the President's fury by John C. Fitzpatrick in his biography of Washington helps us understand the plight of the poor and poorly respected nation:

*The Commander-in-chief of the Continental Army ... knew by bitter experience what it meant to collect, arm and equip a force, only to have it annihilated, the man-power wasted, and all the time and expense for naught.... It took two years to gather another army.*

Not until 1794, in the Battle of Fallen Timbers, did General "Mad Anthony" Wayne subdue the northwestern tribes, and not until

1795, by the Treaty of Fort Greenville, did these tribes yield most of their Ohio land to the United States. At about the same time, private action by John Sevier and James Robertson in the Kentucky region quieted the southwestern tribes. But the Treaty of Fort Greenville came too late for the Federalists to retrieve the political support that earlier failures on the northwestern frontier had cost them. And for the accomplishments of Sevier and Robertson in the Southwest, the Federalists won no credit at all. The awareness that a substantial opposition party was beginning to form only served to intensify a sense of crisis in Federalist ranks.

The Federalist crisis was no figment of a later generation's imagination. In 1792, Daniel Carroll, one of the commissioners for the development of "Federal City," explained Congress's delay in making appropriations for the new capital as arising from a strong suspicion that the government was about to be dissolved. In February 1793, Oliver Wolcott of Connecticut, who was to succeed Hamilton in the Treasury two years later, observed that if the funding and assumption policies did break up the Union, "the separation ought to be eternal." In 1795, the Reverend John Pierce, on observing the grandiose new state capitol at Hartford, Connecticut, wrote that it "excites the suspicion ... that it is contemplated by some to make this a Capitol [of New England], should there be a division of the Northern from the Southern States."

Washington interpreted such signs as dire omens. He found the government during his first administration "encompassed on all sides with avowed enemies and insidious friends," and he proposed to deliver a "valedictory address" in 1792 to impress upon the nation "that we are *all* children of the same country." It was only to reinforce this impression that he yielded most reluctantly to demands that he accept a second term instead. During this term little occurred to allay his fears and much, indeed, to increase them.

## II The crucible of party politics

### Consolidating Republican opposition

Hamilton's ambition for America was higher than that of most of his followers, and his vision far exceeded theirs. Yet his agrarian opponents outstripped him in both ambition and vision. Hamilton had no respect for the men who were opening up the vast reaches of the new country. He despised farmers and looked upon westerners as troublemakers. In his plan to unify the nation, he assigned inferior roles to both groups. Within a decade after the new government was launched, however, the majority who lived on the land were to show that they counted for more than the minority in the cities and that votes counted more than wealth.

We cannot assign specific dates to the beginnings of political parties in America. During the colonial period so-called "factions" came and went, with as little continuity as Washington hoped the factions of his own time would have. The issue of the Constitution again divided the country into what became known as Antifederalists and Federalists, and during the first years of the new government factional leaders tried to strengthen the opinions and mobilize the votes of the opposing groups. The Federalists at first enjoyed many advantages. Above all, they had a strong, clear program and, in Hamilton, a resourceful, energetic, and uncompromising leader. In Washington himself they had a personal symbol of great prestige. Most of the well-educated, wealthy men in the country were Federalists, as were most newspaper editors, clergymen, and other makers of public opinion. Hamilton demonstrated, too, that the

Federalists controlled the army and were quite willing to make use of it. A ready-made network of chambers of commerce, units of the Society of Cincinnati, and other going organizations worked for Federalism on the local level, and the party quickly developed a grassroots patronage system to reward local party workers with sinecures.

Even in the First Congress, Federalist leaders caucused and corresponded on platforms, candidates, and campaigns as though they were members of an organized machine. Ideals of party loyalty and the mechanics of party corruption had not yet made much headway, nor had the idea of office as a source of personal gain become the hallmark of the political profession. Yet the Federalists well understood the gratifications and emoluments of power.

The men who opposed the Federalists showed a preference for the prerogatives of the states as against the national government as conducted under the Constitution by Hamilton and his friends. In the contest for national power this preference seemed to be a weakness that the Federalists could exploit. Yet even during the campaign for ratification of the Constitution many of the voters had shown their concern over the aggrandizement of the national administration under the new framework of government, and little of this concern had been allayed by Federalist legislation. Far from uniting the states and the people, indeed, Hamilton's program served only to magnify existing sectional and class antagonisms.

Jefferson, as much as Hamilton, sought stability and dignity for the new government, but he believed that men "habituated to think for themselves"—American yeomen, in short—were much easier to govern than men (usually city dwellers, he thought) who were "debased by ignorance, indigence, and oppression." By 1791 Jefferson was convinced that Hamilton and his "corrupt squadron" menaced the country, and he wrote Washington to say so. More than that, he began to

exert systematic pressure on the Treasury Department—pushing his own nominees for every new opening, while at the same time trying to strip the department of many functions. In none of these stratagems did Jefferson succeed; but they at least kept the Treasury on the defensive. Having accomplished this much, Jefferson, with Madison's support, worked out a plan to save the United States in his own way. Basic to his program was getting the people to use their great privilege of the franchise. He sought to get out the vote by explaining what individuals could do for themselves if each flexed his political muscle.

"If left to me to decide whether we should have a government without newspapers, or newspapers without a government," Jefferson once wrote, "I should not hesitate for a moment to prefer the latter." He had disapproved of the secrecy of the Constitutional Convention, and to upset what he believed to be the plot of the Convention victors he now sought the best available editor to inform the people of their peril. This man proved to be the poet Philip Freneau, Madison's classmate at Princeton. In October 1791 Freneau issued the first number of the *National Gazette,* the new Antifederalist paper in Philadelphia. Freneau so quickly took the play away from John Fenno, the editor of the Hamiltonian *United States Gazette,* that Hamilton felt obliged to enter the newspaper battle himself.

If Jefferson was the philosopher of agrarian politics, Madison, strategically situated in Congress where issues were argued and supporters mobilized, soon emerged as "the great man of the *party.*" Serious party work began as early as the winter of 1791–1792, when Madison wrote a number of articles for the *National Gazette* in which he gradually developed the position of "the Republican party, as it may be termed." Thereafter, influential allies, local lieutenants, grass-roots clubs, and candidates who could afford the time and money to campaign and hold office were all arranged for. Besides Jefferson and Madison, those enlisted under the new banner included Governor George Clinton of New York, who, in opposition to General Schuyler, Hamilton's rich father-in-law, controlled the upstate vote; and Aaron Burr of New York City (Clinton had recently helped Burr defeat Schuyler for the Senate), whose followers in the Society of Tammany, a drinking club and benevolent association, were numerous. The brilliant young Swiss, Albert Gallatin, who had settled on the western Pennsylvania frontier, soon joined the Virginia and New York leaders, while intellectual, professional, and literary luminaries in all the other states filled out the Republican officer corps.

The Republican party was too young to run a presidential candidate in 1792, and in any event its leaders preferred Washington to any other man. The Federalists, in turn, were far from ready to risk going on without him. Once more the reluctant general was elected unanimously; the Republicans, however, had the satisfaction of throwing a scare into the Vice-President, John Adams. Their candidate, Governor Clinton, carried Virginia and New York, together with North Carolina and Georgia. All told, Clinton polled 50 electoral votes to Adams's 77.

### Republicanism abroad and at home

During Washington's first administration, party lines had been drawn over financial issues and violence on the frontier. In his second administration, problems of foreign policy, as Colonel Higginson of Massachusetts said, "not merely divided parties, but moulded them; gave them their demarcations, their watchwords, and their bitterness." Some of these problems were carry-overs from the war with Britain; but the French Revolution, which began just a few weeks after Washington first took office in 1789, was the source of most of the trouble.

At first, most Americans welcomed the French Revolution. In 1790, when Lafayette sent the key to the Bastille to Washington, the President acknowledged it as a "token of victory gained by liberty over despotism." Within a year, however, the Hamiltonians had aligned themselves with Edmund Burke's condemnatory *Reflections on the Revolution in France,* while the Jeffersonians championed Tom Paine's libertarian response, *The Rights of Man.* The execution of Louis XVI in January 1793 disgusted most American conser-

vatives, and the Jacobin "reign of terror" that followed confirmed their deepest misgivings about excessive democracy. In the meantime, the French wars against the continental monarchs, who had combined to end the threat of republicanism, had begun in 1792, and early in 1793 they spread to Britain and Spain.

For weeks, westerly gales kept news of the executions and the wars from reaching America. When all the news flooded in at once, in April 1793, it strengthened the Hamiltonians in their stand against France. The Jeffersonians, on the other hand, held to their hatred of monarchs and monarchy and voiced their confidence in the people of France against the autocrats of Britain.

It was not long before the conflict in opinion was deepened by issues of foreign policy. The French treaty of 1778 (see p. 129) provided that the United States must defend the French West Indies in case of an attack on France herself, and also that American ports must receive prizes captured at sea by French privateers and men-of-war. The Girondists, who ruled revolutionary France in 1792, assumed that this treaty remained in force, as indeed it did under international law; and they sent "Citizen" Edmond Genêt as envoy to America to see that it was carried out. Genêt had other instructions as well. He was to organize expeditions from America to detach Louisiana and Florida from Spain, and to outfit American privateers to prey upon British shipping. These enterprises were to be financed with American funds made available by a speedup in American payments on the old French loan. Genêt had one more project: to organize Jacobin clubs in America to advance the cause of Liberty, Equality, and Fraternity—just at the time when Jefferson himself had begun to sponsor Republican political clubs of his own.

Genêt, an attractive and enterprising young man, landed in Charleston, South Carolina, a pro-French stronghold, on April 8, 1793. After a warm welcome, he went right to work without even bothering to present his credentials to the government in Philadelphia. By the time he finally arrived at the capital, the President, after consulting Jefferson and Hamilton, had issued his Neutrality Proclamation of April 22, making it clear that the United States would not participate in the French wars. Jefferson had defended the Girondist position that the treaty of 1778 was with the French nation, no matter what its government might be. He also argued that since only Congress could declare war, only Congress could proclaim neutrality, and a presidential proclamation of neutrality was unconstitutional. Jefferson felt, too, that if such a proclamation were issued, Britain should be forced to make certain commercial concessions in return. Hamilton, on the contrary, held that the French treaty had died with the French king, and that neutrality in any case was the only feasible American policy. Jefferson, having made the arguments that supported his position, did not persist in opposing the practical step, and Washington's proclamation followed.

By this time, Genêt had already commissioned enthusiastic Charleston ship captains as French privateers to prey on British shipping; he had also organized a South Carolina military adventure against Spain in Florida, and had induced George Rogers Clark and other Kentuckians to float down the Mississippi and dislodge the Spanish from New Orleans, a mission dear to Kentuckian hearts. The warmth of Genêt's reception had convinced him that the people were with him, whatever the government might do. Thus when Washington received Genêt with forbidding coldness and gave him to understand that the government would no longer tolerate his operations, let alone abet them under the old treaty, Genêt decided to ignore the President and proceed with his revolutionary work.

Even Jefferson was put out by this persistence, and when Genêt, contrary to Washington's express warnings, permitted *Little Democrat*, a prize ship converted into an armed vessel, to sail as a privateer, Jefferson voted with the President and the rest of the Cabinet

to ask for Genêt's recall. By then, Genêt's group had fallen out of favor at home and, fearing for his life, the young envoy decided to remain in America. He married Governor Clinton's daughter and retired to a country estate on the Hudson.

The repercussions of this affair in the American government were less romantic. Washington's Neutrality Proclamation had reflected the President's determination, at almost any price, to keep the infant nation at peace. Jefferson shared this determination, but his apparent sympathy with Genêt's early activities led the President to read the most sinister meaning into the conduct of his Secretary of State and not least of those "self-constituted societies," as Washington called the new Republican grass-roots clubs Jefferson sponsored. "It is not the cause of France, nor I believe of liberty, which they regard," he wrote in October 1793, but only the "disgrace" of the new nation under Federalist rule. By the end of the year Washington accepted Jefferson's resignation from the Cabinet after many months of indecision.

In October 1794, Attorney-General Randolph wrote to the Chief Executive, "I never did see an opportunity of destroying these self-constituted bodies, until the fruits of their operations were disclosed in the [Whiskey] insurrection of Pittsburg. . . . They may now, I believe, be crushed." To which Washington promptly replied, "My mind is . . . perfectly convinced that if these self-constituted societies cannot be discountenanced they will destroy the government of this country." In his address to Congress on the Whiskey Insurrection in November 1794, Washington accused such societies of "disregarding the unerring truth that those who rouse cannot always appease civil convulsion." The evidence against the Republican societies was slender indeed. Madison called the President's attack on them, "perhaps the greatest error of his political life." Jefferson added that, "the attempt which has been made to restrain the liberty of our citizens meeting together . . . has come upon us a full century earlier than I had expected. . . . The tide against our constitution is unquestionably strong, but it will turn." The progress of the revolutionary struggle abroad soon deepened Jefferson's own suspicions of politics at home as well as his confidence in the Republican future.

*Profits and problems of neutrality*

By greatly increasing the belligerents' need for food and other materials, and at the same time occupying belligerent commercial vessels in noncommercial duties, the war in Europe opened the way for a boom in the carrying trade of neutrals. As a leading maritime nation, the United States was among the greatest gainers. Since the French, particularly, had only a small fleet, painfully vulnerable to British attack, they desperately needed neutral assistance. Early in the war, France at last surrendered her monopoly of the French West Indian trade and opened the islands' ports to American ships and American produce—a turn of events that gave great impetus to American commerce.

The British, determined to monopolize world shipping and especially to keep the late rebels down, retaliated quickly. Trade, according to them, was simply an arm of war. They resurrected the "rule of the War of 1756," which held that trade barred to a nation in peacetime could not with impunity be opened to it during hostilities. This applied with special force to the French West Indian trade. In November 1793 they decreed that *all* shipping to or from the French colonies would be subject to British seizure. American ships by then had swarmed into the Caribbean to serve the French islands, and the British seized about 300 United States vessels, abused their passengers, and forced many of their sailors into the British navy.

Even so, American trade thrived. Many ships were captured, but many more slipped through with profits that more than compensated for the risks involved. Ship losses served as an additional stimulus to the shipbuilding industry. By 1794, however, the British had become so brazen that even Federalists expected war. The United States insisted that neutral ships made neutral goods, but the British enforced the right to search for enemy supplies anywhere in any ship. The United States insisted that a blockade, to be effective, must be enforced by actual patrols of the closed ports. But the British simply announced "paper blockades" and undertook to enforce them on the oceans wherever they found a vessel presumably bound for a forbidden harbor. Foodstuffs, the United States insisted most firmly, could not be classified as contraband. But the British did not hesitate to capture ships sailing with food for France and her allies.

Painful as Federalist shippers found these British measures, it was the Republicans who made the most of them by labeling them monarchist affronts to the American flag. Recalling how effective commercial retaliation had been against the British in the great days of the Revolution, the Republicans now demanded an embargo to keep British ships out of American ports and American ships off the seas, where they were subject to British seizure.

As if to keep American memories fresh, the British in Canada chose this time to incite the Indians to raid the Ohio country, where thousands of farmers were settling. The British also made it clear that they still had no intention of relinquishing their armed posts on American territory, which were giving assistance and encouragement to the Indians. Public opinion, aroused over the hot issues of trade and territory, forced the Republicans' embargo through Congress early in 1794. It was to remain in effect for one month, but at its expiration it was extended for two months more.

*Jay's Treaty*

When the British, in March 1794, sought to end the embargo by revoking the harshest of their rules for neutrals, the Federalists decided to try to gain additional concessions through diplomacy. In April, Washington named John Jay his special envoy with instructions to get the British (1) to surrender

"Stop the Wheels of Government".

*A Federalist view of Congressman Albert Gallatin in 1796, when he argued that the House, by withholding appropriations, could in effect veto the Jay Treaty and, as the Federalists charged, "stop the wheels of government." The guillotine is a Federalist reminder of the dangerous implications of Gallatin's French-speaking ancestry.*

**175**

have always preferred a connexion with you, to that of any other country, *we think in English,* and have a similarity of prejudices and predilections." Thereafter, Hamilton had let nothing pass to Britain's disadvantage. In 1794, while Jay was still at sea on his voyage to England, Washington received a proposal from Sweden and Denmark, two of the northern neutrals Jay was to consult if he failed to gain British concessions. They suggested just what Jay was instructed to suggest to them—that all three nations unite in combating British assaults on neutral shipping. Washington naturally inclined toward a proposal so similar to his own, and Edmund Randolph, Jefferson's successor as Secretary of State encouraged its adoption. Hamilton, nevertheless, managed to dissuade him, arguing that far from strengthening Jay's hand, such action would only make the British the more difficult to deal with. Hamilton, moreover, promptly told George Hammond, the British minister in New York, of Washington's decision; and Hammond lost little time in conveying this information to the British negotiators, thereby short-circuiting Jay's bargaining power. The result was an uphill fight for the American envoy and a very unsatisfactory agreement.

By the Treaty of London (completed in November 1794 and henceforth known in America as Jay's Treaty), the British agreed again to evacuate their Northwest posts and by 1796 had done so. But Jay had to barter away a great deal in return. The British could still carry on the fur trade on the American side of the Canadian border with Indians hostile to advancing American settlement. This concession almost nullified the surrender of the posts and deeply displeased westerners suspicious of Jay ever since his negotiations with Spain in 1784. As for the British paying for captured ships, settlement of this issue was left to a future joint commission which would determine what, if anything, was owed. On the rights of neutrals, Jay failed altogether, while his efforts to gain commercial concessions proved as futile. The jewel of the British empire, so far as American merchants were concerned, was the British West Indies. For

their military posts in the Northwest, (2) to pay for American ships that had been captured illegally, and (3) to respect the American position on the rights and privileges of neutrals. Jay was also to negotiate the best commercial treaty he could. Failing to get the British to agree on all these points, Jay was to try to get the northern countries of Europe to agree jointly with the United States to enforce neutral rights.

Jay had a good case, and the British needed American friendship. But Hamilton nullified these advantages. As early as October 1789, he had told Major Beckwith, his secret contact reporting on American affairs (see p. 162): "I

176 the privilege of visiting Indies ports (a privilege limited to small American ships of no more than 70 tons), American cargoes of molasses, coffee, cocoa, sugar, and cotton—the only worthwhile British West Indian commodities—had, under the treaty's terms, to be carried directly to American ports. World trade in these commodities was denied American merchants, but the British could continue to carry them anywhere, including American ports. The Senate forced the removal of this provision before it would ratify the treaty.

Jay's whole agreement was so unsatisfactory that Washington hesitated a long time before sending it to the Senate. The Senate, in turn, made every effort to hide the terms from the people lest the call for war against Britain become too strong to withstand; but there were leaks. When the Senate on June 25, 1795, by the slenderest possible two-thirds majority ratified the treaty, the public outcry was as violent as expected. In the months following, "Sir John Jay" was hanged in effigy throughout the country. One zealot caught the spirit of the whole people when he chalked up in large letters on a Boston street wall: "DAMN JOHN JAY! DAMN EVERY ONE WHO WON'T DAMN JOHN JAY!! DAMN EVERY ONE WHO WON'T SIT UP ALL NIGHT DAMNING JOHN JAY!!!"

In the Congress that met in December 1795, the question was asked whether the House of Representatives, by failing to vote appropriations required under the agreement, could in effect reject the treaty even though the Senate had accepted it. The House voted 57 to 35 that it had the constitutional right to reject treaties by withholding funds, but it went on to approve the appropriations in April 1796 by a vote of 51 to 48.

## Pinckney's Treaty

In June 1795, while the Senate was considering Jay's Treaty with Britain, Spain withdrew from the British coalition against France and made peace with the revolutionary government there. This step made her fearful of British reprisals which might take the form of attacks on her empire in America. She also feared attacks from American frontiersmen. When Britain and America concluded Jay's Treaty, Spain's fears for her empire grew, and she decided to try to win American friendship to offset Britain's enmity. After several proposals failed to lure Thomas Pinckney, the American minister who had gone to Madrid on Spain's invitation in 1794, Pinckney was able to write home in August 1795 that the King of Spain was now prepared "to sacrifice something of what he considered as his right, to testify to his good will to us."

Pinckney proceeded to negotiate the Treaty of San Lorenzo, usually called Pinckney's Treaty, which the Spanish signed in October 1795 and the United States Senate unanimously approved in March 1796. This agreement settled the northern boundary of Florida at the latitude of 31 degrees. Much more important, Spain consented to open the Mississippi "in its whole length from its source to the ocean" to American traffic and to allow Americans the free use of the port of New Orleans for three years, after which time the arrangement could be renewed.

## III   John Adams's administration

### Election of 1796

Washington had been so serious about not running for President again in 1792 that he had asked Madison and others to draw up ideas for his "valedictory" to the nation. Early in 1796 he resurrected these papers and turned them over to Hamilton (who had followed Jefferson out of the Cabinet after Republican victories in the congressional elections of 1794) with a request for a new draft. Nothing could deter Washington now from leaving his high office. He looked with deepest dismay, he said, on the "baneful effects of the spirit of party," but at the same time he took keen satisfaction in many of his accomplishments.

Washington did not deliver his Farewell Address in person; he simply published it in the newspapers on September 17, 1796, a date so close to the presidential elections that it stirred the keenest resentment among opposition leaders, who felt that his delay in announcing his decision handicapped them in mounting an effective campaign. They felt, also, that his strictures on party spirit were attacks on them and not equally on the governing party.

Washington noted as a "matter of serious concern that any ground should have been furnished for characterizing parties by *geographical* discriminations—*Northern* and *Southern, Atlantic* and *Western.*" In much of his address he urged upon the country the need for preserving "the unity of government which constitutes you one people." Only toward the end did he discuss foreign affairs; nowhere was there an admonition against all "entangling alliances." Washington actually said:

> The great rule of conduct for us in regard to foreign nations is, in extending our commercial relations to have with them as little political connection as possible.... It is our true policy to steer clear of permanent alliances with any portion of the foreign world.... Taking care always to keep ourselves ... on a respectable defensive posture, we may safely trust to temporary alliances for extraordinary emergencies.

The party strife that Washington deplored was nearing its peak when he retired. Debate in the House over Jay's Treaty had continued well into 1796, and Washington's own decision intensified the conflict by opening up the highest office to the rising political machines. The Federalists had considered Jay as a candidate, but the furor over the treaty killed his chances. Widespread satisfaction with the Treaty of San Lorenzo, on the other hand, made Thomas Pinckney a plausible choice. In the end, the Federalists brought out a ticket of John Adams of New England and Pinckney of South Carolina. The Republicans named Jefferson as their standard-bearer, and Aaron Burr of New York for Vice-President.

Hamilton and Adams had long since grown cool toward each other, and Hamilton went to great pains to maneuver Pinckney into the presidency. But his elaborate scheme backfired. Not only did Adams, with 71 votes, win the presidency, but Jefferson, with 68 votes, was second in the balloting and defeated Pinckney for the vice-presidency.

Americans now take the transition from one presidential administration to another as a matter of course. In 1796 the public was experiencing the first transfer of presidential power from one man to another, and its anxiety was deepened by the fact that a leader of Washington's stature was about to retire. The President, writes Leonard D. White, in his history of Federalist administration, "had already determined to demonstrate to the world the supreme achievement of democratic government—the peaceful and orderly change of the head of the state in accordance with the voice of the people." John Adams himself was moved by the historic event to write to his wife on his inauguration: "All agree that ... it was the sublimest thing ever exhibited in America."

### John Adams's foreign policy

No one in the United States had written more than John Adams about man's nature. But, as Jefferson shrewdly observed, in practice Adams was "a bad calculator" of the "motives of men." He made the mistake of retaining in his Cabinet such second-rate Hamiltonians as Secretary of State Timothy Pickering and Secretary of the Treasury Oliver Wolcott, who had surrounded Washington toward the end when even the great general himself could not induce able administrators any longer to forego private business for public service. Worse, by being absent from his post more often, perhaps, than any President in history, Adams inadvertently gave these Hamiltonians free rein.

In later years, after his retirement, Adams counted as one of his major accomplishments that he, like Washington, had kept the United States at peace with France. Hamilton's anti-French friends in Adams's virtually autonomous Cabinet, however, carried the administration to the brink of all-out hostilities despite the President.

The French had taken less kindly than the Spanish to Jay's Treaty; interpreting it as a British diplomatic victory, they intensified their attacks on American ships bound for British ports. By the time of Adams's inauguration in March 1797, the French had captured about 300 American vessels and had manhandled their crews. In the meantime, Washington had recalled the Francophile minister, James Monroe, and sent Charles C. Pinckney to replace him. After he had been in France the two months allowed to foreigners, the French police notified Pinckney that unless he got a permit to remain they would arrest him. Pinckney fled to Amsterdam in a rage. When news of Pinckney's treatment reached Philadelphia, Adams (now President) had to face up to Federalist demands for war with the brutal French.

Adams withstood such demands, but without querying the French government he decided as one of his first presidential moves to send a three-man mission to Paris to persuade the French to end their raids on American shipping. When Talleyrand, then Foreign Minister of France, refused to negotiate until the Americans had given a bribe of $250,000 to three subordinates, the mission collapsed.

In their reports home the American envoys had referred to Talleyrand's three subordinates as X, Y, and Z. When the reports became public, an uproar broke out among the partisans of both parties over the so-called XYZ dispatches, during which someone is said to have cried, "Millions for defense, but not one cent for tribute." Congress did vote millions for the expansion of the army and navy in 1798 and 1799; it also created a separate Navy Department and repealed all treaties with France.

To the chagrin of Hamilton, who was aching to lead it into battle, the new army materialized very slowly. Adams himself saw little use for it in fighting for the freedom of the seas and was most reluctant to burden the country with needless military costs. The new Navy Department, on the other hand, promptly pushed to completion three well-armed frigates then under construction, produced twenty other ships of war, and unleashed hundreds of American privateers to prey upon the French. In 1798 and 1799, an "undeclared naval war" raged with France in which American ships, operating mainly in the Caribbean, took almost a hundred French vessels, and suffered serious losses themselves.

Hamilton's friends in the Cabinet and Congress, meanwhile, were pushing the expansion of the army with such zeal that many suspected a plan to use it against domestic as well as foreign enemies. Their suspicions were confirmed in February 1799, when troops were sent once more to western Pennsylvania to put down a rebellion led by John Fries against the collection of new taxes just levied to pay for the army itself. The Hamiltonians even induced Washington, only a few months before his death, to take nominal command of the army once more, a step that helped persuade Adams, much against his inclination, to name Hamilton as next in command and effectively in charge. But Adams would go no farther, refusing even to ask Congress to make the war with France official.

News that France was relenting in her attitude in the face of Adams's naval policy confirmed the President in his hopes for peace. The same news only drove the Hamiltonians to desperation. When, early in 1799, Adams named a new three-man commission to reopen negotiations with Talleyrand, Hamilton's friend, Timothy Pickering, still Secretary of State, went so far as to delay the sailing of two of the three commissioners not already in Europe. The three Americans finally assembled in France early in 1800 and found that the best they could get from her was confirmation of the principle that "neutral ships make neutral goods." An indemnity for losses already suffered on the high seas in violation of this principle proved to be out of the question.

When the Hamiltonians learned in September that the American envoys had agreed to peace on these meager terms, they launched their fiercest attack yet on John Adams. Hamilton himself gave the signal in a "fatal tirade" against the President early in October, in which he referred to Adams's "extreme egotism," "terrible jealousy," and "violent rage," and proceeded to question even "the solidity of his understanding." This attack so shattered the Federalist party that, as one former leader said to another, "We have no rallying-point; and no mortal can divine where and when we shall again collect our strength. . . . Shadows, clouds, and darkness rest on our future prospects."

### Alien and Sedition Acts

At the time of Adams's election, Madison had written to Jefferson: "You know the temper of Mr. A. better than I do, but I have always conceived it to be rather a ticklish one." One thing Adams quickly became "ticklish" about was the Republican taunt that he was "President by three votes." Other partisan attacks on him and his administration aroused him, early in the summer of 1798, to strike out at his detractors. Adams felt especially imposed upon by the Swiss, Albert Gallatin, who on Madison's retirement from Congress in 1797 had become Republican leader of the House; by the English radical, Thomas Cooper, who had come to America in 1794 and soon proved himself a vigorous Republican pamphleteer; and by a number of recently arrived French intellectuals, including the chemist, Pierre A. Adet, the botanist, André Michaux, and Victor Du Pont, all of whom Adams suspected of engaging in espionage. Many undistinguished but noisy French Jacobins who had fled the repression of the Direc-

*Boston troops reviewed on the Common on President Adams's birthday, October 19, 1799. Charles Bullfinch's State House, completed that year, is at upper right.*

tory after 1795 also set up a clamor against Adams. Most offensive of all, perhaps, to Anglophile Federalists, were the defeated fighters for Irish freedom, who chose this time to carry their insatiable hatred of Britain to the United States.

Nor did Adams forget American-born Republican journalists. Outstanding among them was Franklin's grandson, Benjamin Bache, known as "Lightning-rod Junior," whose Philadelphia *Aurora* had supplanted Freneau's *National Gazette* in 1793 as the leading Republican paper.

Adams might easily have overcome his pique had not the most violent men of his party in June and July, 1798, pushed through Congress a series of measures known as the Alien and Sedition Acts. Angered as he was, the President grasped the weapons so gratuitously presented. The first of these measures was a Naturalization Act, which raised the residence requirement for American citizenship from five to fourteen years and would have meant permanent disfranchisement for many. The second, the Alien Act, empowered the President in peacetime to order any alien from the country and to jail for not more than three

180

years those who refused to go. The third, the Alien Enemies Act, permitted the President in wartime to jail enemy aliens at his pleasure. No arrests were made under either alien act, but they did frighten hundreds of foreigners from the country.

The fourth measure was the Sedition Act. Its key clause provided severe fines and jail penalties for anyone speaking, writing, or publishing "with intent to defame . . . or bring into contempt or disrepute" the President or other members of the government. Its intent to gag the Republican opposition until after the next presidential election is evident in the provision continuing the act, "in force until March 3, 1801, and no longer."

Matthew Lyon, an outspoken Irish-born Republican congressman from Vermont, while campaigning for reelection against a "government" man, was the first to be jailed under the Sedition Act. Jefferson protested that Lyon was treated the same as the vilest criminals of the day. "I know not which mortifies me most," he remarked on learning of Lyon's fate, "that I should fear to write what I think, or my country should bear such a state of things." Lyon's constituents backed him to the hilt. During his four-month jail term they reelected him to Congress.

Many others, most of them Republican editors, followed Lyon to jail and Republican papers had to shut down. With few exceptions the trials were travesties of justice dominated by judges who saw treason behind every expression of Republican sentiments. Grand juries for bringing in the indictments and trial juries for rendering the monotonous verdict of guilty were hand-picked by Federalist United States marshals in defiance of statutes prescribing orderly procedure. The presiding judges often ridiculed the defendants' lawyers and interrupted their presentations so outrageously that many threw up their hands and their cases, leaving the accused to the mercy of the courts. The courts, at the same time, fell sharply in the estimation of the people.

In January 1798, the states had ratified the Eleventh Amendment to the Constitution excluding "the judicial power of the United States" from becoming involved in any suit "against one of the United States by citizens

of another State, or by citizens of any foreign state." This amendment had grown out of a Supreme Court verdict against the state of Georgia in *Chisholm* v. *Georgia* in 1794, a case in which the state had been sued by a British creditor. The amendment was a blow to the federal court system which stirred John Marshall a few years later to heroic efforts to restore the standing of the judiciary (see p. 187). His task was made all the harder by the conduct of the courts in Sedition Act cases.

Madison called the Sedition Act "a monster that must forever disgrace its parents." He and Jefferson both recognized it as the start of the Federalist campaign for the elections of 1800, and they quickly set in motion a broad-gauged attack on the whole Federalist philosophy. Their offensive took the form of a series of resolutions for which their allies won the approval of the legislatures of Kentucky and Virginia in November and December 1798. The resolutions were then circulated among the rest of the states.

Jefferson wrote the Kentucky Resolutions, Madison those adopted in Virginia. Both sets attacked the Hamiltonian "broad interpretation" of the Constitution and developed the state-rights position later used to justify nullification and secession. In Jefferson's words, "the several states composing the United States of America, are not united on the principle of unlimited submission to their general government"; that government, in Madison's terms, is but a "compact to which the states are parties." The Kentucky Resolutions held that, as parties to the "compact," the states had the right to declare what measures went beyond their agreement and were "unauthoritative, void, and of no force," and to decide what remedies were appropriate. Madison, in the Virginia Resolutions, said that the states *together* might "interpose" to check the exercise of unauthorized powers. Jefferson, in his Kentucky Resolutions, went further: he held that the legislature *of each individual state* had this right.

No interpretation of the intent, purpose, or action of the Great Convention of 1787 could have been more far-fetched than that expressed in these partisan Resolutions. But Madison and Jefferson at least had a liberalizing goal absent from later state-rights movements in pressing their argument this far. At the time of Washington's condemnation of the "self-constituted" Republican societies, Madison had written, "the censorial power is in the people over the government, and not in the government over the people." In the Kentucky Resolutions, Jefferson said that the Alien and Sedition Acts, by employing the loosest construction of the Constitution to impose the tightest tyranny, soured "the mild spirit of our country and its laws."

## Election of 1800

While the XYZ affair and other affronts by France had cost the Francophile Republicans some strength in the country, their prospects for the presidential campaign of 1800 were brightened by the sharp split in Federalist ranks between the Adams men and the Hamiltonians.

For the campaign of 1800 the Republican caucus named Jefferson and Burr. The Federalists were so divided that no caucus of their leaders was possible. By devices difficult to disentangle, the ticket of Adams and C. C. Pinckney finally was made public; but once again, as in 1796, the central drama revolved around Hamilton's determination to defeat Adams by means of his own running mate. No one was willing to go along with Hamilton's strategy, however, and what was worse, the Republicans, as many Federalists expected, polled enough votes to make the maneuver meaningless. The electoral college voted 65 for Adams and 64 for Pinckney; Jefferson and Burr each received 73 votes.

The Republicans triumphed in a campaign that one writer describes as "a havoc of virulence." But worse was to come. Burr had no pretensions to the presidency at this time; but many Federalists, especially those from commercial New England and New York, saw in his tie vote with Jefferson an opportunity to raise to the presidency, "a friend of the Constitution . . . a friend of the commercial interests . . . the firm and decided friend of the *navy.*" The *Washington Federalist,* which carried these words in January, 1801, went on to say: "The *Eastern* States have had a President and Vice President; So have the *Southern*. It is proper that the *middle* states should also be respected. . . . Mr. Burr can be raised to the Presidency without any *insult* to the feelings of the Federalists, the friends of Government."

According to the Constitution, the House would have to decide between the two Republicans. There the voting was to be by states, not individual representatives, and nine states (out of the sixteen) were needed to win. The first ballot in the House was taken on February 11, with the results that Jefferson had forseen: he carried eight states, Burr six, and two were undecided. And so it went for a feverish week during which thirty-five ballots were taken.

While the deadlock persisted, Federalist strategists, whose party still retained a majority in Congress, began to think in terms of having the Senate "appoint a Presidt. till another election is made," as Monroe reported to Jefferson. Jefferson replied on February 15: "We thought best to declare openly and firmly, one & all, that the day such an act passed, the Middle States would arm, & that no such usurpation, even for a single day, should be submitted to."

The deadlock finally was broken on February 17 on the thirty-sixth ballot. *"This was done,"* Jefferson wrote, in italics, *"without a single vote coming over."* He went on to explain the intricacies of the strategy by which, by voting blanks, certain Federalist congressmen took their states out of Burr's camp. "Their vote [none whatever having been cast directly for the Republicans] showed," Jefferson added, "what they had decided on, and is considered a declaration of perpetual war."

The next Congress put an end to this kind of problem by sending the Twelfth Amendment to the states, which ratified it by September 1804. This amendment provided that, henceforth, "The electors ... shall name in their ballots the person voted for as President, and in distinct ballots the person voted for as Vice-President."

The transfer of power from the Federalists to the Republicans had been much more foreboding than the transfer of the presidency from Washington to Adams in 1796. Yet it had been accomplished peaceably after all, and henceforth an organized opposition was to be permitted its own free voice and aspirations to power, without any taint of treason or disloyalty.

Although the Republicans in 1800 captured the presidency and control of both the House and the Senate, the country's first great shift in political power was not quite complete. Just before adjourning in March 1801, the retiring Federalist Congress gave Adams a new judiciary act which relieved Supreme Court and district court justices from riding to the circuit courts, created a whole new group of circuit court judges, and increased the number of district court judges. Adams filled these lifetime jobs and other new judicial posts with Federalist sympathizers. Most important, he named his interim Secretary of State, John Marshall, as Chief Justice of the Supreme Court. Adams was the last Federalist President. After him, as the country became more Republican and expansive, his party became sectional and narrow. Yet for more than thirty years of Republican political rule, the new Chief Justice continued to hand down old-line Federalist, nationalist, interpretations of the law.

But even Marshall had his fears. On the morning of Jefferson's inauguration, he wrote of them to C. C. Pinckney: "The Democrats are divided into speculative theorists & absolute terrorists. With the latter I am disposed to class Mr. Jefferson." A few months later, the Boston merchant, George Cabot, described by Marshall's biographer Albert J. Beveridge as "the ablest, most moderate and far-seeing of the New England Federalists," wrote: "We are doomed to suffer all the evils of *excessive* democracy through the United States. ... Maratists and Robespierrians everywhere raise their heads. ... There will be neither justice nor stability in any system, if some material parts of it are not independent of popular control."

Jefferson himself was more sanguine. Two days after his inauguration he wrote to John Dickinson:

*What a satisfaction have we in the contemplation of the benevolent effects of our efforts, compared with those of the leaders on the other side, who have discountenanced all advances in science as dangerous innovations, have endeavoured to render all philosophy and republicanism terms of reproach, to persuade us that man cannot be governed but by the rod, etc. I shall have the happiness of living and dying in the contrary hope.*

## For further reading

J. C. Miller, *The Federalist Era 1789-1801* (1960) is a good modern introduction to the Federalist period and rich in bibliography. H. J. Ford, *Washington and His Colleagues* (1921), and J. S. Bassett, *The Federalist System* (1906), are worthwhile older surveys. C. G. Bowers, *Jefferson and Hamilton* (1925), is a colorful account with an Antifederalist bias. Good reading on the Federalist side are vols. II and III of A. J. Beveridge, *The Life of John Marshall* (4 vols., 1916-1919). E. S. Maclay, ed., *The Journal of William Maclay* (1928), provides lively comment on the First Congress by an Antifederalist senator. His views may be compared with those of an arch-Federalist from Massachusetts in Seth Ames, ed., *Works of Fisher Ames* (2 vols., Boston, 1854).

The first volume of the distinguished series on administrative history by L. D. White, *The Federalists* (1948), is comprehensive. The following works are useful on Federalist precedent making: R. V. Harlow, *The History of Legislative Methods in the Period before 1825* (1927); E. S. Corwin, *The President: Office and Powers 1787-1948* (1948); and H. B. Learned, *The President's Cabinet: Studies in the Origin, Formation and Structure of an American Institution* (1912).

The best approach to Hamilton's thinking is through his *Papers,* now being edited by H. C. Syrett and J. E. Cooke: as of 1972, 17 volumes have been issued, reaching to December 1794. J. C. Miller, *Alexander Hamilton* (1959), is probably the fairest biography. It should be supplemented by J. P. Boyd, *Number 7, Alexander Hamilton's Secret Attempts To Control American Foreign Policy* (1964). See also Broadus Mitchell, *Alexander Hamilton* (2 vols., 1957, 1962). Bray Hammond, *Banks and Politics in America: From the Revolution to the Civil War* (1957), and the later chapters of E. J. Ferguson, *The Power of the Purse, A History of American Public Finance 1776-1790* (1961), put Hamilton's economic program in context. The biographies of Washington and Madison, cited in Chapter Five, and of Jefferson, cited in Chapter Eight, are essential for the Federalist period and early party rivalry.

Richard Hofstadter, *The Idea of a Party System: The Rise of Legitimate Opposition in the United States 1780-1840* (1969), traces the gradual acceptance of party competition. Joseph Charles, *The Origins of the American Party System* (1961), is a penetrating short account. Valuable also are W. N. Chambers, *Political Parties in a New Nation, The American Experience 1776-1809* (1963), and W. N. Chambers and W. D. Burnham, eds., *The American Party Systems: Stages of Development* (1967). C. A. Beard, *The Economic Origins of Jeffersonian Democracy* (1915), may be supplemented by N. E. Cunningham, Jr., *The Jeffersonian Republicans: The Formation of Party Organization 1789-1801* (1957). E. P. Link, *Democratic-Republican Societies 1790-1800* (1942), examines sources of early Republican strength.

Foreign affairs in the Federalist period, and their inescapable impact on party development, are dealt with in Felix Gilbert, *To the Farewell Address, Ideas of Early American Foreign Policy* (1961); Alexander De Conde, *Entangling Alliance: Politics and Diplomacy under George Washington* (1958), and *The Quasi-War: The Politics and Diplomacy of the Undeclared War with France 1797-1801* (1966); P. A. Varg, *Foreign Policies of the Founding Fathers* (1963); C. D. Hazen, *Contemporary American Opinion of the French Revolution* (1897); L. S. Kaplan, *Jefferson and France* (1967); and S. F. Bemis, *Jay's Treaty* (1923) and *Pinckney's Treaty* (1926). The frontier and foreign policy are covered thoroughly in A. P. Whitaker, *The Spanish-American Frontier 1783-1795* (1927), and *The Mississippi Question 1795-1803* (1934), and in F. S. Philbrick, *The Rise of the West 1754-1830* (1965). L. D. Baldwin, *Whiskey Rebels: The Story of a Frontier Uprising* (1939), is a readable account.

Gilbert Chinard, *Honest John Adams* (1933), and Page Smith, *John Adams* (2 vols., 1962), are good biographies of the second President. Authoritative works on his administration include M. J. Dauer, *The Adams Federalists* (1953), and S. G. Kurtz, *The Presidency of John Adams: The Collapse of Federalism 1795-1800* (1958). Adams's illuminating marginal comments on books by his contemporary philosophers are presented in Zoltán Haraszti, *John Adams and the Prophets of Progress* (1952). Adrienne Koch and William Peden, eds., *The Selected Writings of John and John Quincy Adams* (1946), is more conventional. J. C. Miller, *Crises in Freedom: The Alien and Sedition Acts* (1951), and J. M. Smith, *Freedom's Fetters* (1956), are good on the origins and impact of these early attempts at repression of opinion. L. W. Levy, *Legacy of Suppression: Freedom of Speech and Press in Early American History* (1960), is useful for background on issues raised by the Sedition Act. Morton Borden, *The Federalism of James A. Bayard* (1955), is especially good on the election of 1800.

# THE JEFFERSONIAN "EMPIRE FOR LIBERTY"

Of all the great figures among the Founding Fathers, Thomas Jefferson was at once the most approachable and the most aloof. The rustic dress he affected, and his casual pose even on solemn public occasions, furthered the illusion of informality in his manner. Senator Maclay of Pennsylvania left us a characteristic picture of Jefferson in 1790, on his taking up his duties as Secretary of State:

*His clothes seem too small for him. He sits in a lounging manner, on one hip commonly, and with one of his shoulders elevated much above the other.... His whole figure has a loose, shackling air. He had a rambling, vacant look, and nothing of that firm collected deportment which I expected would dignify the presence of a secretary or minister. I looked for gravity, but a laxity of manner seemed shed about him.*

Jefferson tended to underscore this impression as he grew older. In 1804, for example, Augustus Foster, secretary of the British Legation in Washington, in describing the President's dress in detail, did not omit his "yarn stockings, and slippers down at the heels," and concluded that he looked, to the life, "very much like . . . a tall, large-boned farmer."

Yet Maclay, while commenting that Jefferson's face had "a sunny aspect," felt constrained to add that he "has rather the air of stiffness in his manner." And Foster, noting that Jefferson appeared "good natured, frank, and rather friendly," remarked also that "he had somewhat of a cynical expression of countenance." "The people," writes Albert Jay Nock, one of Jefferson's most perceptive biographers, "could have quite taken him to their hearts if they had not felt, as every one felt in his presence, that he was always graciously but firmly holding them off."

Jefferson took the Republican victory in 1800 much more seriously than some historians have taken it since. "The revolution of 1800," he said, "was as real a revolution in the principles of government as that of 1776 was in its form." Later in life, after a full generation of Republican rule, Jefferson wrote: "The Federalists wished for everything which would approach our new government to a monarchy; the Republicans to preserve it essentially republican."

Fundamental to Jeffersonian aspirations was what came to be called America's "continental destiny." Jefferson and his hand-picked Republican successors in the White House, James Madison and James Monroe, were determined to keep the United States free of involvement in European monarchical rivalries. The phrase so much heard in discussions of American foreign policy—"no entangling alliances"—originated with Jefferson himself.

Yet the Republicans had this still higher goal: to keep Europe and her conflicts out of America, both hemispheres if possible, North and South. To them, our "continental destiny" was to create, as Jefferson said, a self-sufficient "empire for liberty" throughout the New World.

Unfortunately for the Republicans, their goals occasionally clashed. To keep Europe out of America meant in fact to have to evict her from areas in the New World she long held. This, as we have seen in our discussion of the French Revolution, sometimes meant of necessity getting involved in European power struggles. How little heart the Jeffersonians had for such involvement is shown in their abysmal conduct of the War of 1812, itself a product of the rivalry between Britain and France. Yet this war and its immediate aftermath only drove the Republicans the harder to achieve splendid isolation—for the whole western world, as the Monroe Doctrine of 1823 showed.

## I  Jefferson as President

*Republicans take office*

The narrowness of the Republican victory over the Federalists, and the latter's desperate maneuvers during the struggle with Burr in the House, brought home to the new President even more strongly than before the deep political division in the country. Jeffer-

son's inaugural address in March 1801 is often described as a bid to heal this division:

*Let us, then, fellow citizens, unite with one heart and one mind. . . . Every difference of opinion is not a difference in principle. . . . We are all Republicans, we are all Federalists. If there be any among us who would wish to dissolve this Union or to change its republican form, let them stand undisturbed as monuments of the safety with which error of opinion may be tolerated where reason is left free to combat it.*

**186**

Yet Jefferson's "hopes [that] we shall be able to restore union to our country," were always constrained by his realization of what failure to do so might mean. "The clergy, who have missed their union with the State," he wrote in May 1801, "the Anglo men, who have missed their union with England, and the political adventurers who have lost the chance of swindling & plunder in the waste of public money, will never cease to bawl, on the breaking up of their sanctuary." Such men, whose tactics during the contest with Burr had opened "upon us an abyss, at which every sincere patriot must shudder," remained beyond the pale of his approaches. "They are

*Unusual pencil sketch of Jefferson in 1799, by B. H. Latrobe, one of the architects of the Capitol.*

From the collections of the Maryland Historical Society

invincibles," he wrote, "but I really hope their followers may ... be brought over.... The bulk of these last were real republicans, carried away from us by French excesses. ... A moderate conduct throughout, which may not revolt our new friends and may give them tenets with us, must be observed." The "invincibles," meanwhile, were to feel the President's wrath when occasion demanded, however warm his talk of tolerance.

In naming his Cabinet, Jefferson could hardly be expected to choose Federalists—even if any of the "Anglican monarchical aristocratical party," as the Republican press characterized the opposition, could be found to serve his administration. Of the five Cabinet positions, nevertheless, Jefferson gave two to New England, where Federalism was most intransigent. A New Englander also got the Postmaster-Generalship, not yet of Cabinet rank. The two most important Cabinet posts went to the two most important Republicans after Jefferson: James Madison became Secretary of State; and Albert Gallatin, Secretary of the Treasury. In filling the hundreds of other federal jobs, Jefferson conceded that "some [removals] must be made." But "they must be as few as possible, done gradually, and bottomed on some malversation or inherent disqualification."

To this general principle Jefferson maintained one overweening reservation, which he put in some of his harshest language. The "midnight appointments" which John Adams had "crowded in with whip and spur" when he was aware "that he was making appointments not for himself but his successor ... I consider ... as nullities, and will not view the persons appointed as even candidates for their office, much less as possessing it by any title meriting respect." Adams's "filling all offices ... with the bitterest Federalists, and providing for me the alternative either to execute the government by my enemies, ... or to incur the odium of such numerous removals ... as might bear me down," was an "outrage on decency" that "should not have its effect."

One such Adams appointment created the occasion for the famous case of *Marbury* v. *Madison* and Jefferson's subsequent war on the judiciary. Adams had signed William Marbury's commission as justice of the peace in the District of Columbia so late that it could not even be delivered to him before Jefferson took office. Madison (the Secretary of State in those days was charged with certain domestic duties as well as the conduct of foreign affairs) now refused to deliver Marbury's commission. Marbury in turn asked the Supreme Court to issue a writ ordering Madison to hand it over. The Court, by the Judiciary Act of 1789, had the power to do as Marbury asked. But John Marshall, in his decision in *Marbury* v. *Madison* (1803), refused to exercise it. He held, indeed, that Marbury, despite the Judiciary Act, had no case at all.

The Constitution, Marshall argued, stated explicitly in what actions the Supreme Court had original jurisdiction, and Marbury's complaint was not among them. Only an amendment to the Constitution could extend the Court's jurisdiction to it. That being so, Marshall continued, the provision in the Judiciary Act of 1789 that granted the Supreme Court the authority to issue such writs as Marbury sought was unconstitutional.

In 1792, without having aroused any significant discussion, a United States circuit court in Pennsylvania had declared a federal statute unconstitutional, so Marshall's decision did not set a precedent. What made the decision memorable was Marshall's firmness in confronting Jefferson's state-rights theory of the Kentucky Resolutions with grand *ex cathedra* proclamations of his own which have stood the test of time.

The Constitution, said Marshall, was law, to be enforced by *courts;* it was, moreover, the *supreme law* to which even federal legislation must conform to be valid; and in conflicts over the meaning of the Constitution as law, or over the validity of legislation under it, "it is emphatically the province and duty of the judicial department"—and not of the states or the popularly elected legislature—"to say what the law is."

That the power of judicial review should be placed uniquely in the Supreme Court, by an irremovable Federalist so early in the first Republican administration, and, gallingly, in a case in which the administration was nominally the victor, taunted Jefferson into taking up his war on the "despotic branch." For if Federalist judges, the Republicans reasoned, could check legislation simply by declaring it unconstitutional, the legislature must have some means to counteract them. Congress, the Republican legislators now held, had these means in the power of impeachment.

The most conspicuous victim of the impeachment policy was the vulnerable Supreme Court Justice Samuel Chase, who had a habit of entertaining juries with anti-Republican harangues before sentencing Republican victims. Chase had been especially nasty in cases involving the Sedition Act. The House impeached him for misconduct in 1805, but he escaped conviction in the Senate. The Republicans did not try this maneuver again. Instead, they looked to the growing popular approval of their program to bring the courts into closer harmony with the election returns.

*Republicanism in spirit and substance*

It is fitting that Jefferson should have been the first President to begin his term in the rude capital on the Potomac. He himself had suggested the layout of Pennsylvania Avenue, and on many other details had advised the Frenchman, L'Enfant, who planned the city of Washington. An Irishman, James Hoban, designed the White House, and an Englishman, B. H. Latrobe (with the assistance of the American, William Thornton), designed the Capitol.

Adams's Alien Act offered poor hospitality to such men. Jefferson, once he had named his advisers and manned his administration, began by allowing this "libel on legislation" to lapse, and distinguished foreigners were welcomed to the country once more. Next he freed all who had been jailed under the Sedition Act and recommended to Congress the return of all fines collected under it. He also urged the restoration of a five-year residence requirement (instead of the Naturalization Act's fourteen-year requirement) for foreigners who wanted to become American citizens. Congress acted favorably on both his suggestions.

Having thus righted matters of the spirit, Jefferson turned to matters of the purse. He admonished Secretary of the Treasury Gallatin to keep the finances so simple "that every member of the Congress and every man of any mind in the Union should be able to comprehend them." In his first "state of the Union" message, which he sent to Congress in December 1801, instead of delivering it "from the throne," as Washington and Adams had done, he recommended that Congress require annual accountings from the Secretary of the Treasury, something Hamilton would have taken as a personal affront. Jefferson himself halted expansion of the navy, reduced the size of the army, dismembered the diplomatic corps, and cut out costly presidential social affairs. By such good management, he believed, Congress could save enough to repeal the hated excise immediately and still speed up payments on the public debt and save millions in interest.

Another Jeffersonian economy move was entirely unlooked for in New England and must have surprised everyone who thought the President a poor custodian of national honor. This was Jefferson's "Barbary War."

Jefferson's economies in the naval and military establishments were prompted in part by the theory, a favorite of his, that every foreign nation felt such a vital interest in American trade and the use of American ships and harbors that none would dare risk war. But this blanket proposition failed to cover such outlaw nations as Morocco, Algiers, Tunis, and Tripoli, whose rulers were in league with the Barbary pirates that preyed on Atlantic and Mediterranean shipping and at the same time demanded tribute from European powers. Britain, who paid tribute herself, often connived with the pirates to keep other nations from encroaching on her trade. When the United States became an independent nation, American shipping proved a particularly attractive target. During their administrations, Washing-

ton and Adams had sweetened pirate treasuries with $2 million, but valuable ships, cargoes, and men were still being lost.

In May 1801 Tripoli suddenly demanded higher American payments and Jefferson, deciding that it might be cheaper to check the extortion by taking the offensive himself, ordered a navy squadron to sew up the pirates in their home ports. For a navy "supported" by an economy-minded administration, however, such action was more easily ordered than achieved. The war against Tripoli in particular dragged on until 1805, when the Pasha, threatened with the loss of his throne from other quarters, sued for peace. The United States continued to pay tribute to the pirates until 1816, but after 1805 at lower rates than other nations.

### Jefferson and the West

Late in 1801 Jefferson wrote: "The increase of [our] numbers during the last ten years we contemplate not with a view to the injuries it may enable us to do others, . . . but to the settlement of the extensive country still remaining vacant within our limits."

To encourage settlement of the public lands, Congress in 1796 and 1800 had lowered both the minimum acreage a pioneer had to buy and the actual cash he had to put down. In 1804 Jefferson got Congress to reduce requirements to the point where, for a down payment of only $80, a man could get title to a quarter section of 160 acres. These measures speeded up the settlement of the Northwest Territory, out of which Ohio (admitted to the

Sketches from the journal
of Sergeant Patrick Gass, who accompanied
Lewis and Clark on their entire journey:
(left) Lewis and Clark hold a
council with the Indians; (right) Clark
and his men shooting bears.

Union in 1803) was the first state to be formed.

Jefferson also tried to promote settlement in the Southwest, where conflicting claims involving state and federal interests in huge tracts near the Yazoo River (now in Mississippi but then owned by Georgia) had been blocking development since 1789. When Georgia finally ceded her western lands to the federal government in 1802, Jefferson set up a commission to resolve the conflicting claims, and in 1803 Georgia and Jefferson accepted its recommendations. In the House of Representatives, however, John Randolph of Virginia led the fight against compensating certain of the Yazoo claimants as the commission had proposed, insisting that the precious rights of the sovereign state of Georgia had been forfeited, with Jefferson's connivance, for the benefit of corrupt speculators. On these grounds he successfully opposed payment for more than ten years, and split the Republican party in the process. Randolph was supported by the diehard state-rights Republicans whose philosophy Jefferson himself had buttressed with the Kentucky Resolutions of 1798. Jefferson, however, was to prove no stickler for state rights or for a narrow interpretation of the Constitution where America's expansion was concerned, and the majority of the Republican party clung to his leadership.

In 1810 in the case of *Fletcher* v. *Peck,* John Marshall upheld the contract initially made with Georgia by the successful Yazoo claimants even though a later Georgia legislature had rescinded it. This decision strengthened the position of the Yazoo stockholders and

finally, in 1814, with Randolph out of Congress for the time being, Congress awarded them $5 million. Within five years, Alabama and Mississippi, both made up of territory ceded by Georgia, were admitted as states.

Jefferson had far larger plans for the West, looking, as he said, "to distant times, when our rapid multiplication will expand itself" to "cover the whole northern, if not the southern, continent, with a people speaking the same language" and "governed . . . by similar laws." After some early misadventures over transcontinental exploration, Jefferson early in 1803 persuaded Congress to make a secret appropriation to be used to send Meriwether Lewis and William Clark on an expedition to the Pacific. Lewis and Clark successfully completed their mission by 1806, thereby demonstrating the feasibility of overland transportation across the country and establishing an American claim to Oregon. In 1806 Zebulon Pike was sent to explore the Southwest.

The appropriation for Lewis and Clark was secret because their mission would traverse foreign territory. But even before they were properly under way much of the country they did cross had become part of the United States through the Louisiana Purchase.

### The Louisiana Purchase

Spain, with Jefferson's blessing, held Louisiana—or New Orleans, as the whole western country was often called—from 1762 to 1800. "Till our population can be sufficiently advanced [in numbers] to gain it from them piece by piece," Jefferson thought, it could not "be in better hands." It is not hard, therefore, to imagine the President's anxiety on learning early in 1802 from Rufus King, the American minister in London, that by a secret treaty in October 1800, the insatiable

Napoleon, compensating Spain with territory elsewhere, had retrieved Louisiana for France.

Napoleon intended to develop Louisiana into a source of food for the French West Indies, thus ending their dependence on the United States. But he could not proceed with this plan until he had secured his position in Europe. In Santo Domingo, moreover, a stubborn slave insurrection led by the Negro General Toussaint L'Ouverture, who claimed to have liberated the island from France, threatened to spread to the rest of the French West Indies and ruin Napoleon's whole vision of a new American empire. Once Napoleon had quieted Europe with the Peace of Amiens in 1802, he sent 20,000 men to crush Toussaint

and then occupy the port of New Orleans. But this campaign failed.

When Jefferson first learned of the treaty by which Napoleon had reacquired Louisiana, he warned the French that their action might "completely reverse all the political relations of the United States" and drive us into the arms of England. "There is on the globe one single spot," he added, "the possessor of which is our natural and habitual enemy. It is New Orleans, through which the produce of three-eighths of our territory must pass to

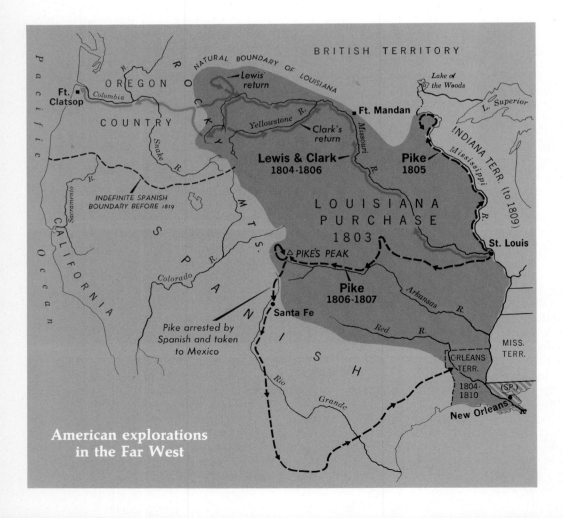

American explorations
in the Far West

market, and from its fertility it will ere long yield more than half of our whole produce and contain more than half of our inhabitants." In May 1802, Jefferson had instructed Robert Livingston in Paris to try to get France to put a price on New Orleans (and on the Floridas, which Jefferson mistakenly assumed had also passed into French possession). Before Livingston could make much progress, Jefferson learned that in October 1802, the Spanish *intendant* still in charge at New Orleans had been instructed by France to suspend the American right, under Pinckney's Treaty (see p. 176), to deposit cargoes there. Nothing could more strongly have confirmed French enmity. "The agitation of the public mind" over this step, Jefferson wrote in January 1803, "is extreme." He continued with an analysis of American opinion:

> In the western country [the agitation] is natural, and grounded on honest motives; in the seaports it proceeds from a desire for war, which increases the mercantile lottery; in the Federalists generally, and especially those of Congress, the object is to force us into war if possible, in order to derange our finances; or if this cannot be done, to attach the western country to them as their best friends, and thus get again into power.

Jefferson was determined that "nothing but dire necessity, should force us from the path of peace." To quiet the agitation for war he won from Congress an appropriation of $2 million to be used by James Monroe who sailed in March 1803 to assist Livingston in Paris. Monroe's instructions were to offer up to $10 million for New Orleans and the Floridas. If France refused to sell and persisted in keeping New Orleans shut to American commerce, Monroe and Livingston were to suggest to Britain that she join the United States in the event of a new war with Napoleon. By the time Monroe arrived in Paris, he found his elaborate instructions obsolete. A staggering offer of the whole Louisiana Territory for $15 million had been made to Livingston, and on

April 30, 1803, the two Americans closed the deal.

To negotiate such a "noble bargain" was one thing; to obtain the money for it quite another. One difficulty was that the Constitution did not delegate power to the federal government to purchase territory. Jefferson was so troubled on this point that he suggested an amendment to make the treaty legitimate. But warned that delay might cause Napoleon to renege, Jefferson swallowed his scruples and pushed the treaty through. In November 1803, the Senate ratified it, 26 to 5, and the House appropriated the needed money, 90 to 25. On December 20th, the United States formally took possession. The next year, two territories were made of the Purchase, to be administered as under the terms of the Northwest Ordinance of 1787. Under these terms, Louisiana, with its present-day boundaries, became a state in 1812.

Florida had not been included in the deal, since Spain had never actually yielded it to France. But Jefferson was not discouraged. "If we push them strongly with one hand, holding out a price in the other," he said, "we shall certainly obtain the Floridas, and all in good time."

The method if not the results of the Louisiana Purchase troubled the Randolph Republicans in the South. But the strongest reaction came from Federalists in New England who expected their influence in the nation to be utterly destroyed by the acquisition of this enormous new territory. So distraught were some of the northerners that they proposed to leave the Union; desperately, they turned for help to Aaron Burr, Jefferson's alienated Vice-President, who was then running for governor of New York. If victorious, Burr was to take his state into a new northern confederation with New England, and thereby escape from the "Virginia dynasty." Hamilton helped defeat Burr, and the projected confederation collapsed. Embittered by this and other offenses, real and imaginary, Burr challenged Hamilton to a duel in which Hamilton was killed, July 11, 1804.

Although he bore the brand of Hamilton's murderer, Burr completed his term as Vice-President. Yet his political future was nonexistent, while his private future was boxed in by debt, and he appeared to have little choice but to take refuge, like many other discredited Americans, in the depths of the West. Here he quickly paved the way for new and profound suspicions of his conduct involving alleged plots and plans both to detach Louisiana and other American territory from the United States (treasonable activity, if true), and to make war on Spain over Florida and Mexico (a high misdemeanor, since Spain was a power formally at peace with the United States).

Jefferson kept close watch on Burr's activities, and following a report of his "deep, dark, and dangerous conspiracy" from General James Wilkinson, the military commander in the West, early in 1807 he issued a proclamation for Burr's arrest. Burr was soon apprehended and on March 30 was brought before the United States Circuit Court at Richmond, presided over, of all people, by John Marshall.

Arraigned at first on lesser charges, Burr was indicted for treason on June 24. On August 3 his trial, one of the most memorable criminal prosecutions in American history, began. On Marshall's instructions to the jury, "as unconvincing as he was labored," Burr was acquitted and Jefferson, Marshall's real target, defeated. In the opinion of Edward S. Corwin, one of the most eminent of constitutional historians, "Marshall's conduct of Burr's trial for treason is the one serious blemish on his judicial record." In extenuation, it may be said that the President's own conduct in hounding his party enemy had been ferocious.

Jefferson's disappointment deepened when Burr, in a second trial, was acquitted of the high-misdemeanor charge as well.

## II    Trials of a neutral

### Freedom of the seas

John Randolph of Roanoke, reflecting in his old age on the first three years of Jefferson's reign, when he himself, booted and spurred and flashing a horsewhip, rode herd on the Republicans in the House, said: "Never was there an administration more brilliant than that of Mr. Jefferson up to this period. We were indeed in the 'full tide of successful experiment.' Taxes repealed; the public debt amply provided for . . . ; sinecures abolished; Louisiana acquired; public confidence unbounded." Even in New England the congressional elections of 1802–1803 showed the surge of Republican strength. And the next year the schemes of Burr's Yankee conspirators so weakened the Federalist party there that in the presidential election of 1804 Jefferson carried every Yankee state but Connecticut and every other state in the Union but Delaware. The new Vice-President was George Clinton, to whom, in Burr's place, Jefferson had entrusted the distribution of Republican patronage in New York.

Jefferson's first administration had coincided more or less with the first years of peace in Europe since the French Revolution, and he had made the best of the interval. His second administration had hardly begun when the country was plunged once more into the maelstrom of the Napoleonic Wars, and Jefferson was obliged to defer his domestic plans. By 1805 Napoleon's military victory at Austerlitz had given France control of much of the European continent, and Nelson's naval victory at Trafalgar had given Britain control of the seas. This apparent stalemate led only to a relentless war of attrition, with disastrous results for neutral carriers, especially those of the United States.

The first new blow was the decision of a British court in the case of the ship *Essex* in 1805. In 1800, a British court had ruled that American ships could carry goods from the French West Indies to France provided the goods were first landed on American shores, duty-free. This decision had given a strong impetus to the so-called reexport trade, which by 1805 accounted for more than half of America's booming neutral commerce. In the *Essex* case, however, the British court revoked the earlier decision and now held that French colonial goods could be sent to France only if a duty had been paid on them in America and only if other evidence proved that the goods had not been meant for France in the first place. Any ship unable to produce such evidence to Britain's satisfaction became vulnerable to British capture.

Britain also stepped up her attacks on other American commerce, and the impending termination of the twelve-year commercial agreement made at the time of Jay's Treaty in 1794 threatened to leave American shipping more imperiled than ever. To remedy the situation, Congress, at Jefferson's urging, passed a nonimportation act in 1806 prohibiting the landing in the United States of any British goods that could be purchased elsewhere or manufactured at home. With this as a club (the act was not enforced until later), the President sent William Pinkney to join Monroe, who was now the regular minister in London, in an effort to make a new commercial treaty and otherwise put an end to the British aggression.

As a result of new victories on land, Napoleon soon lifted the pace of his own activities on the sea. In November 1806, he issued his Berlin Decrees, nominally closing the entire European continent to Britain, her goods, and her friends, and blockading the British Isles. When Pinkney and Monroe negotiated a treaty in London, the British stipulated as a condition of enforcement that the United States must resist these Berlin Decrees. But Jefferson rejected such dictation and did not even submit the treaty to the Senate. In 1807, Napoleon added the Milan Decrees to the Berlin Decrees, ordering the confiscation of all ships, especially neutral ships, that had visited any British port or might be bound for one.

Britain responded with a series of "orders-in-council." The major orders, in January and November 1807, stated that "all ports and places of France and her allies or of any country at war with His Majesty," were blockaded and that neutral ships that sailed toward them did so at their peril.

### Impressment, embargo, nonintercourse

Between 1804 and 1807, the United States lost hundreds of ships to the British alone. She also lost many men to the British practice of stopping ships on the high seas to search for and take off alleged deserters from the British navy, the practice known as impressment.

The British navy, a harsh institution enormously expanded to fight Napoleon, was characteristically short of men. This shortage was intensified by competition from American shipowners and the United States government, both attracting thousands of British sailors in American ports to sign on American vessels for higher pay and better working conditions. The United States frigate *Constitution* with a crew of 419 in 1807, listed only 241 who claimed American citizenship and 149 who admitted to being English. To the British, who believed that "Once an Englishman, always an Englishman," this was intolerable. In June 1807, the new United States frigate *Chesapeake,* suspected by the British of having a certain deserter on board, was sailing off Norfolk, Virginia, outside the 3-mile limit, when the British warship *Leopard* came up and demanded the right of search. *Chesapeake's* captain demurred, and minutes later *Leopard* opened fire. *Chesapeake,* her new guns ill-mounted, and her decks cluttered with as yet undistributed gear, suffered twenty-one casualties before being boarded by *Leopard's* officers. They found the deserter they were after and along with him took three Americans who had served in the British navy.

To almost everyone, it seemed, this attack meant war. But the President had more patience than most, and also a policy of his own, called "peaceful coercion," which he presented to Congress in December. To save ships and men from capture, and thereby save the country from incendiary insults, Jefferson planned to keep American ships off the high seas altogether. Thus deprived for a time of American goods and American carriers, he reasoned, the warring powers of Europe would be forced to recognize neutral, and American, rights. Congress in the so-called Embargo Act of December 27, 1807, voted this policy and even banned exports over land.

The Embargo Act meant ruin not to Britain and France but to American commerce and American ports. In spite of ship losses that ran into the hundreds, American commerce had doubled between 1803 and 1807. Under the Embargo Act it came to a standstill, and the industries associated with it, such as shipbuilding and sailmaking, also shut down.

Fourteen months of embargo were enough even for many of the Republicans, and on March 1, 1809, three days before Jefferson's retirement, he was forced to sign an act repealing the measure. He also approved a strong substitute—a Nonintercourse Act proscribing trade with England and France but keeping it open with other countries. If either England or France would cancel its orders or decrees against American shipping, then the ban would apply only to the other.

### The Republican succession

As early as 1805, Jefferson had written: "George Washington set the example of voluntary retirement after eight years. I shall follow it. And a few more precedents will oppose the obstacle of habit to anyone after a while who shall endeavor to extend his term. Perhaps," he added, anticipating what actually occurred in 1951, "it may beget a disposition to establish it by an amendment of the Constitution."

One year later, clearly having failed to keep Europe out of American affairs and the United States free of Europe's quarrels, Jefferson found himself "panting for retirement." His withdrawal as a candidate, as in the case of Washington in 1796, only heightened the ambitions of the different leaders. The Republican congressional caucus reflected the disunity in the party, while leaders outside the caucus strained the party fabric further by en-

dorsing independent candidates of their own, such as Monroe and Clinton. Jefferson remained influential enough, however, to keep the nomination in the power of the caucus and to win that body over to his favorite, James Madison. Since the embargo fiasco had helped resurrect the Federalist party, Madison faced a real fight for the presidency.

In 1807 every New England state but Connecticut had a Republican governor. By the summer of 1808, after six months of embargo, every New England governor had been turned out in favor of a Federalist. Federalist representation in the House, moreover, was to double between 1807 and 1809. For the presidential campaign of 1808, without the formality of a caucus, the revived party made a demonstration of its national, not merely New England, character by renaming its ticket of 1804—Charles C. Pinckney of South Carolina for the presidency and Rufus King of New York as his running mate. This ticket carried Maryland, North Carolina, and Delaware as well as all New England but Vermont. All told, Pinckney and King each garnered 47 electoral votes. Madison won with 122, while Clinton won the vice-presidency with 113.

"Our lawyers and priests," Jefferson once wrote, "suppose that the preceding generations held the earth more freely than we do; had a right to impose laws on us, unalterable by ourselves." Jefferson supposed quite the contrary. He believed that "the earth belongs to the living not to the dead," that each generation must make its own laws. When, in 1809, he turned over to his friend and protégé, James Madison, all the problems his embargo had failed to solve, he saw an exciting new generation on the threshold of power in the United States and optimistically awaited the future that lay in its hands.

Benjamin Franklin, John Hancock, Washington, and Patrick Henry had died in the 1790s. Between 1803 and 1806, Sam Adams, Hamilton, and Robert Morris had followed them to the grave. Ready to take their places were men like Henry Clay, the idol of the

West; John C. Calhoun, the idol of the South; and Daniel Webster, the idol of New England—all youthful enough never to have been British subjects, all eager to build a great American empire of their own. The oldest of the new group, at forty-two, was Andrew Jackson, North Carolina-born, who, one fine day in his early twenties, it is said, loomed on the Tennessee frontier astride a grand horse and equipped with dueling pistols and fox hounds, all picked up during a spree in Charleston financed by a legacy from an Irish relative. "Knowing little about jurisprudence but a great deal about making his own way," Jackson promptly set up as a lawyer to seek his fortune among the influential and well-to-do of Nashville.

The earlier generation of leaders had won independence and established a nation. It was the role of the new generation to overcome, if they could, the persistent problems of contempt abroad and sectionalism at home, to infuse the people with a national spirit and foreign nations with respect.

Unfortunately James Madison, fifty-eight years old when sworn in as fourth President in March 1809, was not quite the man for the crises he inherited. "Our President," Calhoun observed during Madison's first term, "tho a man of amiable manners and great talents, has not I fear those commanding talents which are necessary to control those about him." Madison was perhaps most poorly equipped for executive positions. In congresses, conferences, and conventions the weight of his intellectual equipment was most telling. In political infighting and cloakroom bargaining he was no match for Hamilton among the older generation nor for Clay among the younger. At the very outset of his presidential term, he lost control of his Cabinet and even the privilege of making his own selections.

The lack of unity in the administration was aggravated by the sectional controversies carried over from Jefferson's time. Under Madison such controversies grew so acrimonious that even a war failed to unite the country.

## III   The War of 1812

*The urge to war*

Driven from the sea by Jefferson's embargo, northern businessmen after 1807 began to take a greater interest in manufacturing, especially in cotton spinning, wool carding, and the weaving of cloth. In the South, meanwhile, cotton growing, which had been made practicable in many new areas by Eli Whitney's invention of the cotton gin in 1793, was further stimulated by northern demand for the staple. These pregnant changes in the American economy, which were to have such profound consequences at home in later decades (see Chapter Nine), were not lost on British industrialists and exporters. In order to keep for themselves the American market for manufactured goods, they began pressing their own government, as Jefferson had hoped they would, for concessions to American carriers.

At the same time, many nostalgic Englishmen still had not forgiven their American cousins for the Revolution and lived for the day when the American flag would be wiped off the seas. Their policy was to keep at a high level the pressure of impressments and captures that had forced Jefferson so to offend New England, especially since, in their opinion, this policy would also hasten the destruction of Napoleonic France. Foreign Minister George Canning, though himself a leader of the anti-American diehards, recognized the merit in the tolerant position of the other camp sufficiently to send diplomatic emissaries to America, if only to quiet discontent at

195

home. Since such emissaries were empowered to offer little, their presence only rubbed Madison and his advisers the wrong way and worsened Anglo-American relations. By 1810 Madison had required the British to recall the last of their representatives from Washington, while he called home the American minister in London. These steps closed all channels of diplomatic communication between the two nations. Napoleon and the ubiquitous Talleyrand, meanwhile, played their own game with Madison and Congress, leading them early in 1811 to restore nonintercourse with Britain, to the consternation of New England, with no real gains from France.

Popular disgust with administration fumbling in foreign affairs was recorded in the elections of 1810 and 1811, in which the voters unseated most of the Eleventh Congress. The replacements arriving in Washington in November 1811 included bristling young men from the frontiers. Little concerned with Europe's attacks on American ships, except as affronts to the American flag, these newcomers hoped to extend American territory at embattled Europe's expense.

On the southern frontier, Spain still held the Floridas, long a haven for runaway slaves, marauding pirates, and hostile Indians. By 1810, most of the permanent settlers on the rich lands of West Florida were Americans. Bemoaning Spain's inability to protect them from the Indians, they revolted that year and asked to be annexed by the United States. Madison, as eager as Jefferson to acquire new territory, had connived with the rebels and in October 1810 agreed to their request. Early in 1812 an armed American expedition set out to take weakly defended East Florida as well, but when Spain threatened war and New England threatened secession if war came, Madison was obliged to recall the troops. Such "treachery" set the southerners, in turn, to marking time.

On the frontier in the Ohio and Mississippi Valleys, the trend of events was even more aggravating. Here, between 1801 and 1810, the Indians had been tricked by treaties they ill understood into granting more than 100 million acres of prime land to the United States, and they were promptly driven off their old preserves. In 1811, Tecumseh, the great Shawnee chief, decided a stand must be made. While he was away mobilizing the tribes, Governor William Henry Harrison of Indiana Territory, one of the harshest negotiators of Indian treaties, attacked the leaderless Shawnee at Tippecanoe Creek and burned their village of Prophetstown. Finding the ruins on his return, Tecumseh swore the survivors to eternal war, and many would-be settlers soon were fleeing for their lives.

Frontiersmen long believed that the British in Canada had been arming Tecumseh and egging him on. As they viewed Tippecanoe as a victory over the British as well as the Indians, they also saw Tecumseh's revenge as part of a British plot; and they now cried for the conquest of all Canada to drive the British from "Our Continent," and for the conquest of all Florida, lest Spain be used as a cat's-paw for Britain's return.

Among the frontiersmen who brought this cry to Congress in November 1811 were Calhoun of upland South Carolina, whose grand-

*Tecumseh, by unknown artist.*

Field Museum of Natural History

mother had been scalped by Cherokees; Felix Grundy of Tennessee, who had lost three brothers in Indian raids; and their leader, "Harry of the West," Henry Clay of Kentucky. The easterners promptly branded them "War Hawks."

Taking advantage of political enmity among older members of the decaying Republican party, Clay's friends quickly elected him Speaker of the House; he then used the Speaker's prerogative to name them chairmen of the major committees. Soon Clay and his backers had before the House bills for a big army and an enlarged navy, to let the world know, as Clay said, that "we could fight France too, if necessary, in a good cause—the cause of honor and independence." Such pressure, coming on top of the failure of diplomacy and the continuation of affronts at sea, Madison found difficult to withstand.

Two events in particular played into the hands of the war party. One was the encounter in May 1811 between the American frigate *President*, a formidable forty-four-gun man-of-war, and the British twenty-gun corvette *Little Belt*, mistaken by *President's* captain for the much more formidable Britisher *Guerrière*, known to be very active in impressment raids off New York harbor. Believing she had spotted *Guerrière* off Sandy Hook, *President* gave chase. When her prey refused to identify herself, *President's* captain ordered her bombarded. Nine British were killed and twenty-three wounded. *President* suffered no casualties for the good reason that *Little Belt*, her victim, could offer small resistance. Madison's government tried to settle British claims amicably in return for assurances of freedom of the seas. But the British refused to be pressured in this manner, and the American public was just as happy. The pounding of *Little Belt* was hailed as a great triumph in the United States and helped dissolve any lingering fears of "the mistress of the seas."

A few months after the *Little Belt* affair, disclosure of the notorious "Henry Letters" further inflamed America's warlike ardor.

These letters included reports of a Canadian secret agent, John Henry, on the extent of disunion sentiment in New England. British interest in this subject enraged many Americans and brought the pressure on Madison to a peak. On June 1, 1812, he reluctantly sent a message to Congress asking for war on Britain, and by the 18th both House and Senate complied. "I verily believe that the militia of Kentucky are alone competent to place Montreal and Upper Canada at your feet," boasted Clay during the House debate. Congress must have believed him, for when it adjourned it had voted no new taxes and only a few new men to carry on the war it declared.

The maritime sections of the Middle states as well as of New England voted against the war mainly because they knew that their ships would bear the brunt of the fighting and their commerce the brunt of the cost. The South, which had lost its European tobacco market because of Napoleon's Continental System and which was losing cotton sales because the British could no longer sell their manufactured cotton textiles across the Channel, supported the war. Except in upper New York State and part of upper Vermont, where relations with Canada were close and where trade across the border was profitable, the war had the vociferous support of the exposed frontier. Some doubted, however, that western deeds would prove as brave as western words. "When a man rises in this House," said Representative Stow of New York in January 1812, "you may almost tell how ardent he will be, by knowing how far distant he lives from the sea."

In his war message Madison had named impressment as the most important cause of the war. He said nothing of Canada and Florida and little of the Indians. But how all were tied up together was made clear in a letter written the previous March by the frontiersman Andrew Jackson:

*We are going to fight for the reestablishment of our national character, ... for the protection of our maritime citizens impressed on board British ships of war, ... to vindicate our right to a free trade, and open market for the productions of our soil now perishing on our hands because the mistress of the ocean has forbid us to carry them to any foreign nation; in fine, to seek some indemnity for past injuries, some security against future aggression, by the conquest of all the British dominions upon the continent of North America.*

### Strategy on land and sea

Confusion in American minds over the nature and objectives of the war muddied preparations at the outset and strategy thereafter.

Money, men, ships, and supplies had all to be provided. Yet early in 1811, Congress had allowed the Bank of the United States to die at the expiration of its twenty-year charter, just when it was to be needed most. Despite the urging of Secretary of the Treasury Gallatin, Congress put off the consideration of new taxes until 1813, and throughout the war taxes were reluctantly voted and expertly evaded; loans were optimistically authorized and niggardly subscribed. Not until six months after war had been declared, moreover, did Congress appropriate money to enlarge the navy. The army faced a different problem. Early in 1812 Madison was authorized to accept 50,000 volunteers for a year's service. But in six months scarcely 5000 signed up. A little later the President was authorized to call out 100,000 state militia, but few of those who took up arms would follow their officers across the borders of their own states.

The army probably was no worse than its generals deserved. "The old officers," observed the rising Winfield Scott at the outset of hostilities, "had very generally slunk into either sloth, ignorance, or habits of intemperate drinking." The newer ones, mainly political appointees, included a few good men, Scott acknowledged. But most were "coarse and ignorant"; or, if educated, were "swaggerers, dependents, decayed gentlemen, and others unfit for anything else." Admittedly it would have been difficult for anyone to uncover talent in the army as it was then constituted. But Madison magnified the difficulty by permitting "the advisory Branch of the appointing Department," as he called the Senate, to dictate to, overrule, and intimidate the executive departments.

Canada, it was universally agreed, was the only "tangible" place to engage the British, but New England, the logical base for an invasion of Canada, opposed the whole war and withheld its militia. The South proved to be no more enthusiastic, fearing that the acquisition of Canada would put slaveholders at a great disadvantage in the government in the future. The West agreed with Jefferson that "the cession of Canada . . . must be a *sine qua non* at a treaty of peace." But for all its hunger for Canada, the West in turn would not tolerate the withdrawal of troops to the north from the garrisons guarding the western frontier against the Indians.

To conquer Canada, Montreal, the main port of entry for British assistance, had first to be taken and held. But checked by such antipathy at home from making a quick and concerted push on Montreal, the United States at the opening of the war tried three timid and uncoordinated forays against Canada, scattered over almost a thousand miles of border. The first of these, in July 1812, found General William Hull not only failing to penetrate Canada but being forced to yield Detroit to the brilliant Canadian General Isaac Brock, who had infiltrated his rear from Niagara. In 1814 Hull was sentenced to death by a court-martial for cowardice and neglect of duty but was allowed to escape the penalty because of his record in the Revolution.

The second American foray took place early in October and cost the Canadians General Brock's life. Captain John Wool led an American detachment across the Niagara River and took Queenston Heights, where New York militia were to join him and push on. But New York's militiamen refused to cross their state line and stood by while Canadian reinforcements mowed down Wool's men. As disgraceful was the third foray in November, this one directed against Montreal itself from Plattsburg on Lake Champlain in New York. Here militia under General Henry Dearborn marched north 20 miles, decided that was far enough from home, and marched back again.

Before 1812 was over, a new American force under General William Henry Harrison was frustrated in its efforts even to regain Detroit. Canada thus proved somewhat less "tangible" than had been supposed. Far from occupying it—it "will be a mere matter of marching," Jefferson had said—the Americans after six months of fighting found their own frontier pushed back to Ohio.

At sea, a more satisfactory story was unfolding. Statistically, the American navy was no match for the enemy, yet in the opening months of hostilities American ships recorded startling victories over British men-of-war in single-ship engagements. The winter of 1812-1813 found most of the American navy back in harbor, where the British, intensifying their blockade of American ports south of New London, Connecticut (they left friendly Rhode Island and Massachusetts ports alone), succeeded in bottling it up for the rest of the war. But they could not discourage American privateers, who, all told, captured more than 800 British merchantmen, most of them after 1813.

## Withstanding the British regulars

Only a week after the American declaration of war, the Czar of Russia had joined Britain in the struggle against Napoleon. One of his first moves was to try to make peace between his new ally and her old colonies in order to free Britain for the greater war on the Continent. Madison, who, in the looming election of 1812 hated to have to head a "war party," sent Gallatin and Senator James A. Bayard to join John Quincy Adams, the American minister in Russia, as soon as he heard of the Czar's plan. But the British spurned the Americans and the war went on. In the election, De Witt Clinton of New York, named by the "peace party" among the Republicans and supported by the Federalists, carried every northern state except Pennsylvania and Vermont. Madison, however, added to the votes of those two states the solid support of the South and West, and won.

Perhaps it was the war party's political victory which inspired more successful efforts in the field. The first step seemed to be to regain Detroit, and General Harrison and others agreed that control of Lake Erie was essential to success here. The task of clearing the Cana-

**199**

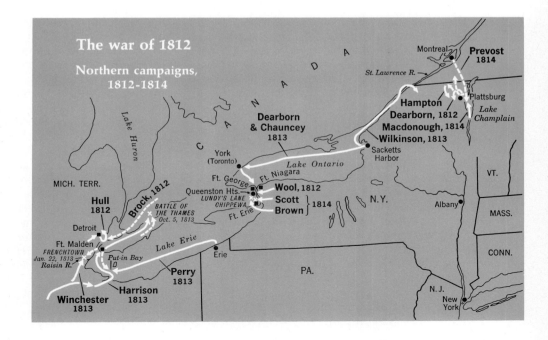

The war of 1812
Northern campaigns, 1812-1814

dians from the lake was given to young Captain Oliver Hazard Perry. By August 1813, Perry's laboriously constructed lake fleet was ready, and on September 10, he found the British squadron in Put-in-Bay at the western end of the lake. At the end of the engagement, Perry reported to Harrison, "We have met the enemy and they are ours."

Harrison followed up immediately, pursuing Canadian General Henry Proctor, who had abandoned Detroit on Perry's victory. Harrison caught and defeated Proctor at the battle of Thames River on October 5. Tecumseh, who had earlier gone over to the British, was killed in this engagement and his Indian forces ceased to be a factor in the war. To the east, on Lake Ontario, Captain Isaac Chauncey, in collaboration with General Dearborn, raided York (now Toronto), burned the Parliament houses (thus giving an excuse for the later burning of Washington), and fled.

In April 1814 Napoleon abdicated and Britain was eager for a general peace, but not before putting the American upstarts in their place. In May she extended the blockade of Atlantic ports to northern New England and strengthened it elsewhere, steps that permitted the harassment of American seaboard cities all the way to Maine and the incitement of slave insurrections in and around southern ports. On one such adventure, emanating from Chesapeake Bay, a force of British regulars supported by a British fleet began a march on Washington. The hastily mobilized defenders, led by the incompetent General William H. Winder, were routed at Bladensburg, leaving Washington open to the invaders. On August 24, in retaliation for the exploit at York, the British set fire to the Capitol and the White House. The failure of an assault the next month against Baltimore and Fort McHenry prompted the British to withdraw from the area on October 14.

The burning of the government buildings was of little military importance, but, as Leonard D. White writes, it marked "probably the lowest point ever attained in the prestige of the presidency." Before the burning, Secretary of War Armstrong had rejected Madison's warnings that a British attack was imminent and had taken no measures to prepare

for it. When Madison took the city's defense on his own shoulders, Armstrong washed his hands of the capital and rode off to Maryland. Unfortunately for Madison, his tactics were disastrous. After the debacle, the President wrote to Armstrong that "threats of personal violence had . . . been thrown out against us both." He warned the absent Secretary to stay away from the troops, and explained by saying that "I had within a few hours received a message from the commanding general of the Militia informing me that every officer would tear off his epaulets if Gen'l Armstrong was to have anything to do with them."

Only after further delay did Madison demand Armstrong's resignation; and only after still more procrastination did he appoint Monroe, virtually on the latter's demand, as Secretary of War.

Of greater military significance than the burning of Washington was a three-pronged attack that the British directed successively against Niagara, Lake Champlain, and New Orleans, starting in the summer of 1814. All phases of this attack failed. At Niagara, in July, new vigorous American commanders, General Jacob Brown and his subordinate, Winfield Scott, fought the British to a standstill. A month later, 10,000 veterans of Wellington's Napoleonic campaigns under Sir George Prevost arrived at Montreal ready to march south toward Lake Champlain. Their objective might have been to detach northern New York and New England and restore them to the British Empire. Whatever their purpose, they were foiled in the battle of Plattsburg Bay in September.

Plattsburg Bay was the last battle before the Treaty of Ghent officially ended hostilities (see p. 202). But it was not the last battle of the war. In the Southwest, Andrew Jackson had been campaigning more or less on his own against the Indians, and after routing the Creeks at the battle of Horseshoe Bend in Alabama in March 1814 (see map), he compelled them to yield by treaty many thousands of acres of excellent land. The vigor of

Jackson's actions brought him full command in the southwestern theater and the responsibility for checking the British attack in that sector—the third prong of their comprehensive assault. Aware that the British might use Pensacola in Spanish Florida as a base, Jackson invaded the area and burned the town. Then he marched to New Orleans and was ready for the British when they arrived.

The battle between General Sir Edward Pakenham's 8000 veterans of the Napoleonic wars and a ragtail collection of militiamen, sailors, and pirates under Jackson took place January 8, 1815, two weeks after the Treaty of Ghent had been signed but more than a month before news of the signing had reached Washington. The British lost more than 2000 men in this needless encounter. American ca-

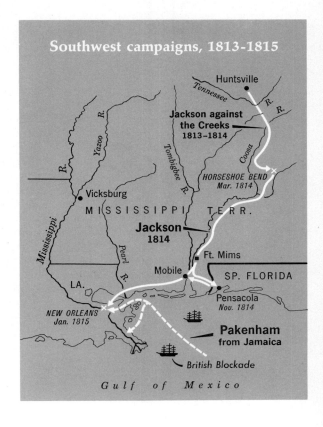

*Southwest campaigns, 1813-1815*

*Broadside giving Bostonians news of the signing of the Treaty of Ghent.*

The New-York Historical Society, New York City

sualties numbered twenty-one. Jackson himself went on from this triumph to become the country's most popular hero since George Washington.

### The Hartford Convention

If Prevost, before Plattsburg Bay, had hoped to detach New England from the United States and restore it to Britain, many New Englanders, men already soured by the whole tendency of Republican diplomacy, would have wished him luck. Besides Republican diplomacy, Republican expansionism, especially in the West, had also stirred the deepest misgivings in Yankee hearts. As early as January 4, 1811, during the opening stages of the debate over the admission of Louisiana as a state, the Massachusetts congressman, Josiah Quincy, told the House of Representatives that favorable action would make it "the duty of some to prepare definitely for a separation—amicably if they can, violently if they must." Once "Mr. Madison's War" began, New England decided to have as little to do with it as possible, except insofar as it feathered her nest.

Until near the war's end, the British blockade left the friendly ports of Massachusetts and Rhode Island alone, and through them funneled imported iron and other essential goods for which Yankee merchants made the rest of the country pay through the nose. Yankee farmers and manufacturers at the same time grew rich selling supplies to the Quartermaster of the army their sons refused to serve. The specie New Englanders thereby drained from the other sections they either hoarded or invested in British bonds. Between 1811 and 1814 the banks of Massachusetts alone quadrupled their hoards of Spanish milled dollars and the other hard currency of the country. Yet of $40 million in long-term bonds floated by the federal government in this period, New Englanders subscribed less than $3 million.

The Hartford Convention of December 1814, "this mad project of national suicide," in John Quincy Adams's words, marked the climax of Yankee intransigence. Half of New England felt accursed by the profiteers in their midst. The profiteers felt accursed by Mr. Madison's war "against the nation from which we are descended." Reminded by their clergy of "Israel's woes in Egypt," where the Jews "had been the most opulent section," they re-

solved like Moses' followers, "to dissolve . . . their union."

The Hartford Convention met on a call from the Massachusetts legislature to all the New England states. When the participants assembled on December 15, it was found that only Massachusetts, Rhode Island, and Connecticut had sent formal delegations, with enough moderates among them to smother the hotheads. Secession was postponed. Yet even the demands of the moderates on Congress exposed the workings of the sectional virus. One amendment proposed in the Convention's Report would eliminate the "three-fifths" clause of the Constitution, thereby depriving the South of that part of its representation based on slaves. Another would limit the presidency to one term and prohibit the election of successive Presidents from the same state, i.e., Virginia. Others would require a two-thirds majority in each house for the admission of new states, the "interdiction of commercial intercourse" with foreign nations, and declarations of war.

The members of the Hartford Convention threatened to meet again for sterner measures if Congress rejected the moderates' proposals; but they were saved from themselves when the end of the war followed closely on the end of the meeting.

## IV  "Our continent" diplomacy

### The Treaty of Ghent

Britain had launched her military offensive in the summer of 1814 partly to gain a better position from which to dictate terms at the war's end. When her peace commissioners formally met the Americans for the first time in the Belgian town of Ghent in August 1814, they confidently awaited reports of new victories and confronted Madison's negotiators

with the most exacting demands. Besides Gallatin, Bayard, and John Quincy Adams, who had been in Europe for more than a year, the American group included Henry Clay and his unstable satellite, Jonathan Russell. Although the British got nowhere in the end, their terms were well calculated to set the Americans at one another, especially Clay the westerner and Adams the Yankee, whose temperamental differences sharpened their sectional ones.

The British opened by demanding western territory to provide for an Indian buffer state between the United States and Canada and to give Canada herself access to the Mississippi. They seemed determined, at the same time, to concede nothing on maritime matters, including New England's privilege (granted in 1783 but withdrawn in 1812) to fish in Newfoundland and Labrador waters.

Britain's extravagant claims to the American West angered Clay, but not nearly so much as Adams's willingness to concede them if necessary in order to recover New England's fishing privileges. These privileges Clay, in turn, was ready to trade away for territorial demands of his own, consistent with the War Hawks' grand war aims. Although Gallatin kept the negotiations from foundering on the Americans' fierce antagonism toward one another, neither he nor his colleagues could force the British to yield on a single demand.

The British also disagreed violently among themselves. But the Duke of Wellington eventually warned *their* expansionists that the cost of a more conclusive victory in America would be greater than the British people would bear. The British reversals at Niagara and Plattsburg Bay seemed to confirm his opinion, and the British expansionists backed down. Britain at this time had begun to fall out with her recent allies at the Congress of Vienna where Napoleon's fate and that of his erstwhile empire were being decided. Her difficulties there made it all the more urgent for her to make peace if she could with the United States and perhaps eventually to seek her support in a new balance of power.

The British retreat at Ghent reminded the American negotiators that their own principal purpose was simply to make peace. On Christmas eve both sides at last agreed. The Treaty of Ghent, ratified by the Senate in February 1815, left most issues just as they were at the war's start but also provided for commissions to settle questions of boundaries, fisheries, and the terms of commercial intercourse. Few were optimistic about the future. Adams char-

acterized the treaty as, "an unlimited armistice, . . . hardly less difficult to preserve than . . . obtain." Clay on his part averred that "the real cause of British aggression" had been "not to distress an enemy, but to destroy a rival." And he added:

*That man must be blind to the indications of the future, who can not see that we are destined to have war after war with Great Britain, until, if one of the two nations be not crushed, all grounds of collision shall have ceased between us.*

Although devoid of funds, Congress voted in March 1815 to set up a standing army of 10,000 men, to enlarge appropriations for West Point, and to spend $8 million for warships. New wars, as it turned out, were averted, but many "grounds of collision" kept the threat of renewed hostilities alive.

### The course of Anglo-American relations

While the world had had enough of fighting during the wars of the French Revolution and the Napoleonic age, with the spread of the industrial revolution trade wars grew in intensity. "It was well worthwhile," Henry Brougham told Parliament in defending Britain's post-Ghent policy of dumping manufactures in the United States at bargain prices, "to incur a loss on the first exportation in order, by the glut, to stifle in the cradle those rising manufactures in the United States which the war has forced into being." Clay had rivalry of this sort in mind when he spoke of Britain's determination to crush America; and when petitions poured into Congress demanding that British trade aggression be checked, he led the fight for the first avowedly protective tariff in the nation's history.

This tariff, adopted in April 1816, had solid support in all parts of the country. When it failed to stem the tide of imports, Clay said it was not because of real defects in the measure, nor because of smuggling, "which has something bold, daring, and enterprising in it," but because of Britain's "mean, barefaced, cheating, by fraudulent invoices and false denominations." While the British forced themselves into United States markets, moreover, by the commercial treaty at last worked out between the two nations in July 1815, they insisted on keeping Americans out of the precious British West Indies, whose trade remained closed to foreigners, indeed, until Jackson forced it open in 1830.

The "armistice" of Ghent, meanwhile, soon spawned those "future controversies" that Adams had foretold. Article I of the treaty, for example, required that "any slaves . . . taken by either party . . . during the war, . . . shall be restored without delay." Americans claimed that no fewer than 3600 slaves taken in the Chesapeake region and around New Orleans were held on Royal Navy ships at the time of ratification of the treaty. These, they said, must be paid for. The British demurred; and only after arbitration by the Russian Czar in 1826, did the British pay $1,200,000 to settle such claims.

The silence of the treaty on impressment, in turn, quickly led to new incidents, as the British continued to search American vessels even on the Great Lakes for deserters. When Madison learned that the British were building new frigates in Canada for lake service, he proposed to Foreign Secretary Lord Castlereagh that construction be stopped and that both nations agree to keep naval ships off these waters. Castlereagh, as eager as the President to avoid a costly arms race, welcomed Madison's suggestion. In April 1817 Charles Bagot, the British representative in Washington, and Richard Rush, Madison's Acting Secretary of State, worked out their famous agreement under the terms of which neither

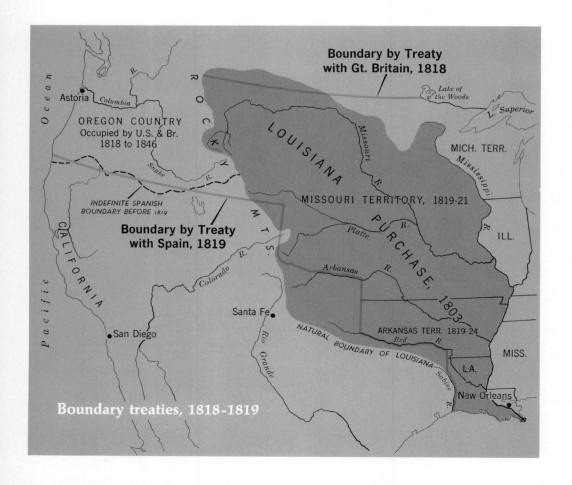

Boundary treaties, 1818–1819

country would maintain more than four small armed vessels on the Great Lakes. Except for certain technical changes, the Rush-Bagot settlement was still in force 150 years later.

The successful demilitarization of the Great Lakes was a good omen for the settlement of the other boundary issues left to commissions by the treaty. By 1818 four separate commissions had worked out the permanent boundary between the United States and Canada as far west as the "Great Stony [Rocky] Mountains." The peaceful settlement of the line this far was exceedingly gratifying to those concerned with America's "continental destiny." Knowledge of geography beyond the mountains was still vague, and Britain and the United States agreed to occupy the "Oregon Country" jointly. When settlement was extended to this region in the 1840s, America's "continental destiny" had become an obsession with many, and joint occupation became intolerable enough to inspire new talk of war (see Chapter Twelve).

### Weakening the grasp of the Spanish and the Indians

The apparent improvement in Anglo-American relations that resulted from the peaceful negotiations over the Canadian boundary was endangered by events on the Spanish and Indian frontiers even before these negotiations were concluded. Trouble had first occurred in the badlands between American West Florida and Spanish East Florida. When violence in this wild region seemed to endanger settlers moving into Georgia after the war, the state asked the federal government to wipe out the disturbing elements. Early in 1817, General Andrew Jackson got the nod, or so he believed, to perform this service; and in his usual manner he performed it thoroughly, burning Indian villages and hanging Indian chiefs. Jackson also arrested, court-martialed, and executed two Britishers—an old Scottish trader, Alexander Arbuthnot, and a young adventurer, Robert

Ambrister—who, he believed, had stirred up Indian discontent. He then marched on the Spanish in Pensacola, where the Seminoles had found a haven, ejected the governor, installed his own garrisons, and claimed the territory for the United States, as he had promised he would do "in sixty days."

Many Britishers demanded war over the execution of Ambrister and Arbuthnot, to no avail; while Spaniards, outraged over the invasion of their territory, made blustering gestures of their own. Peace was kept; but Jackson's adventure gave Spain just "the push" Jefferson believed she needed to make her realize that she had better sell Florida to the United States before uncontrollable Americans simply took it. In 1819, with the United States "holding out a price in the other hand," as Jefferson had also suggested, Spain closed the deal. In the Adams-Onís Treaty of February 1819, she surrendered her remaining claims to West Florida, and ceded East Florida. In exchange, the United States agreed to assume, up to $5 million, the claims of American merchants who had lost ships and cargoes to Spain during the Napoleonic wars.

The Adams-Onís Treaty went beyond the Floridas to establish the boundary between the United States and Mexico all the way to the Pacific (see map). Secretary of State John Quincy Adams was disappointed in not gaining Texas in the bargain. The absorption of all North America by the United States, he said in 1819, was "as much a law of nature . . . as that the Mississippi should flow to the sea." But American interest in Texas was only just awakening, and Adams, finding little support, did not press the issue.

The boundary agreements with Britain and Spain sharpened the definition of the Republic's vast inland empire. But the Indians there had still to be subjugated or expelled before land-hungry white men could settle in it. Tecumseh's death had deprived the northern tribes of their leader, and Britain's retirement from the Great Lakes area had removed their only remaining friend. The Indians' plight encouraged the United States, more thoroughly to cow the braves, to embark on an ambitious fort building program in this region. To discourage them, at the same time, from seeking

205

any new allegiance with Canada, the government added a string of trading centers at which they could buy goods below cost. This stick-and-carrot policy gradually made the Indians in the Northwest Territory more tractable, and they at last agreed, in a series of new treaties, to move beyond the Mississippi.

In the Southwest, the red men had been overawed by Jackson's wartime victories and his ruthless subsequent assaults. Now the government offered them (in what was regarded as a humane move) the choice of taking up agriculture on the lands where they lived or of moving west. To the chagrin of the whites, most of the Indians preferred farming to abandoning their homes, and not until Jackson became President in 1829 were they forcibly ejected from their lands.

### The Monroe Doctrine

In 1800, although she had yielded her exclusive claim to the Oregon country to Britain and Russia, and her vast territory of Louisiana to France, Spain still owned an immense New World empire ranging through nearly 100 degrees of latitude from Upper California to Cape Horn. Portugal, in turn, owned in Brazil a land soon to cover half of South America. Twenty-five years later, Spain's New World empire had been reduced to Cuba and Puerto Rico; Portugal's to nothing.

The immediate cause of this shattering collapse was Napoleon's successful invasion of Portugal in 1807 and of Spain in 1808. The Portuguese king and his family fled to Brazil and ruled there until called home in 1821, when the king's son was left behind to continue the monarchy in their New World land. Independence under the Portuguese heir was established in Brazil by 1823.

The Spanish Bourbons suffered a less happy fate after Napoleon had placed his brother Joseph on their throne in 1808. The Spanish empire was the personal possession of the Bourbons, and when the emperor fell, the colonies refused allegiance to the usurper. Revolts against the new administration began in Spanish America about 1810 and 1811, and the independence of the last of the new separate states was completed in 1824, when the Spanish viceroy of Peru capitulated. After Napoleon's downfall in 1814 and the restoration of the Bourbons, Spain made a serious effort to regain her New World lands. But she was successfully defied by such Latin-American patriots as José de San Martín, founder of Argentina; Simón Bolívar, founder of Venezuela; and Bernardo O'Higgins, dictator of Chile.

The restoration of the Bourbons in Spain in 1814, besides heightening the revolutionary spirit in Spanish America, soon led to repression and revolution at home. By 1822 the "Holy Alliance," set up by the Congress of Vienna especially to combat the republican spirit in Europe, was ready to suppress the Spanish revolt. When, in 1823, France, the instrument of the Holy Alliance, did in fact invade Spain, Britain and the United States both believed that the invasion might easily reach across the Atlantic to suppress the revolutions in Spanish lands here. That spring, Canning, again Britain's Foreign Secretary, "unofficially and confidentially" suggested to Richard Rush, now American minister in London, that their two countries declare to the world, for the benefit of France, that "we conceive the recovery of the [American] colonies by Spain to be hopeless." Canning innocently suggested further that they state that "we could not see any portion of them transferred to any other Power with indifference."

Canning's proposal was forwarded to Washington, where it arrived in October 1823 and immediately became the subject of debate in the Cabinet and of profound consideration by the retired Republican patriarchs, Jefferson and Madison. Jefferson, acknowledging that "Great Britain is the nation which can do us the most harm of any one," advised that "with her on our side we need not fear the whole world." He recommended accepting Canning's proposal. Madison concurred.

When the new Latin American countries first sought United States recognition, Henry Clay had demanded as a point of honor that the North American republic embrace the

*any interposition ... by any European power in any other light than as the manifestation of an unfriendly disposition towards the United States.*

new antimonarchy rebels. And more than honor was involved. Britain, from the first, had lent money to the Latin American revolutionaries and was using their friendly disposition toward her to get in on the ground floor for trade and investment. It was high time, Clay thought, for the United States to combat the advantages already gained by the most hateful monarchy of all. Fearful of upsetting Spain while negotiations over acquiring Florida were in progress, Congress demurred and only later extended recognition to some of the new nations.

Now, in 1823, Secretary of State John Quincy Adams feared that Canning's proposal for *joint* protection of the rebel countries was an attempt to head off future American acquisition of any territory still held by Spain—particularly Cuba. He urged that the United States should act in the Western Hemisphere alone. President Monroe yielded to Adams's arguments, and in his annual address to Congress in December 1823 he used the words later called the "Monroe Doctrine":

> *The political system of the allied powers [of Europe] is essentially different ... from that of America.... We owe it, therefore, to candor and to the amicable relations existing between the United States and those powers to declare that we should consider any attempt on their part to extend their system to any portion of this hemisphere as dangerous to our peace and safety. ... With the governments who have declared their independence and maintained it, and whose independence we have ... acknowledged, we could not view*

Latin America was not the only area of the Western Hemisphere in which European aggression worried Monroe's government. The Russians had been in Alaska for decades. In 1821, the ambitious Alexander I issued a decree declaring that "the pursuits of commerce, whaling, and fishery, and of all other industry on all islands, posts, and gulfs, including the whole of the northwest coast of America, beginning from Behring Straits to the 51° of northern latitude ... is exclusively granted to Russian subjects." Nothing could have aroused Secretary Adams more; and he immediately advised the American minister in Russia that "the United States can admit no part of these claims." Monroe, in turn, added "as a principle," in his message to Congress, that the American continents "are henceforth not to be considered as subjects for future colonization by any European powers." The following April the President learned that the Czar had agreed on 54°40′ as his southern boundary in North America.

Once Monroe had made his remarks (they were not known as the Monroe Doctrine until many years later), interested Latin Americans queried Secretary Adams on how the United States would implement the new policy in case of real need. For all his chauvinism, Adams had to admit that his government would fall back upon the British Navy, still mistress of the seas. Yet, Monroe's message served at least to remind European reactionaries that the time had come to recognize the United States as a new force in world politics.

## V  The test of national unity

### *"Era of Good Feelings"*

In the Republican caucus of 1816, the Randolph state-rights coterie pressed the presidential candidacy of William H. Craw-

ford of Georgia, but Crawford himself did not oppose Monroe's nomination, and with Madison's support, Monroe became the Republican standard-bearer. His Federalist opponent was Rufus King of New York, whose selection was

208

dictated by the desire of those New Englanders who still dominated the Federalist party to make it appear less sectional in character than it was. Monroe found the election easier to win than the nomination. He received 183 electoral votes to 34 for King, the last Federalist candidate in history, who carried only Massachusetts, Connecticut, and Delaware.

Born in 1758, Monroe early in life had become an admirer and follower of Jefferson. Later on he fancied himself a worthy competitor of Madison's. Lacking both the imagination of the "Sage of Monticello" and the intellectual energy of the scholar of Montpelier, he was slower than either in divesting himself of his narrow localism. Yet, by refusing to join the die-hard state-rights men he kept himself available for regular Republican preferment. Monroe twice served as Governor of Virginia; on the national scene, the vigor of American military activity in the last phases of the War of 1812 reflected credit on his performance on taking over the War Department and helped him to win both the coveted nomination and the election in 1816.

Monroe had suffered many defeats during his long political career, some of them humiliating. Yet these setbacks failed to dampen his ambition or lower his self-esteem. Unlike many men jealous of power, he felt strong enough to surround himself with able associates. Indeed, his Cabinet probably was the strongest since that of Washington's first administration. After some early shuffling, it boasted such luminaries as Crawford himself, Calhoun, and John Quincy Adams, a choice that helped appease the Yankees.

Shortly before his inauguration in March 1817, Monroe had been invited to visit New England by the editor of the *North American Review,* a journal that had been so determinedly Federalist during the war that it was often referred to as the "North Unamerican," but which was now ready to bury the hatchet. Monroe accepted the invitation and made a triumphal journey through the northeastern states. His visit was topped by a cordial reception in Boston, where, soon after, the *Columbia Sentinal* published the article "Era of Good Feelings," in which it noted with pleasure "all the circumstances . . . during the late Presidential Jubilee." By 1817, the Republicans had indeed shown so much concern for manufactures and a protective tariff, for an army and a navy, even for chartering a national bank, that the old issues seemed no longer to stand in the way of sectional reconciliation. Virginia and Massachusetts appeared to have made peace at last; and indeed Monroe was reelected in 1820 with but one electoral vote (from New Hampshire) cast against him.

### Boom, bank, and bust

The apparent conversion of the Republican agrarians to policies favorable to American commercial, industrial, and financial growth had been effected by the War of 1812. In 1813 Jefferson himself acknowledged that "manufactures are as necessary to our independence as to our comforts." Once the war ended, most of the "war babies" among American factories succumbed to British competition despite efforts at tariff protection. Britain's own postwar boom, however, soon promoted an unprecedented nonindustrial boom in the United States. The spurt in British textile manufacturing brought with it an enormous demand for southern cotton to feed her tireless machines. The end of the war also reopened European markets for southern tobacco. Poor European harvests in 1816 and 1817 added to the demand for American grain. Such agricultural exports strongly supplemented the hard money Americans needed to pay for their record postwar imports of manufactures.

The boom in agriculture quickly inspired a boom in land speculation, especially in the West and Southwest, where population soared. By 1820, Ohio had become more populous than Massachusetts; and the entire West, with about 2,200,000 settlers, had more people than New England. Land, naturally, was in great demand, and the 300 or more state and "private" banks that had been established after the First Bank of the United States went out of existence in 1811 were available to help speculators sell it and settlers to buy. By 1817, such banks had issued $100 million in paper money, much of it unnegotiable even in neighboring communities. The Second Bank of the United States, established by Congress in 1816 to help the government meet its obligations during the intense money shortage caused by the boom, itself at first fostered the speculative tendencies.

Like the first national bank, the Second Bank of the United States was chartered for twenty years as the sole depository for government funds. Its capital, reflecting the growth of the country, was placed at $35 million, three and a half times that of the earlier bank. Of this sum, the government was to subscribe one-fifth, private capitalists the remainder. Five of the bank's twenty-five directors were to be appointed by the President of the United States; the rest by American stockholders. Foreign stockholders, who became numerous, were to have no voice in the bank's affairs. The Second Bank had the right to establish branches in different parts of the country. Foreseeing competition, however, influential local bankers had persuaded some states to write into their constitutions provisions against "foreign banks," that is, branches of the national bank, doing business within their borders.

Ill-managed from the first in the places where it was permitted to do business, the Second Bank proceeded to justify local fears by outdoing even the state banks in the lavishness of its loans. These loans, moreover, made in the form of national bank notes that had national circulation, were more acceptable as currency than the notes of most local banks. In retaliation, injured local bankers soon got their states to try to tax out of existence both the branches and the notes of "the monster."

In the summer of 1818, when the postwar boom was at its height, the Second Bank was at last ready to try deflationary measures to control speculation. But its sudden contraction of credit simply prevented many people from keeping up payments on their speculative debts. Before the year 1819 was over, for this and other reasons, the whole boom collapsed and the bank had become as unpopular with the public as it had been from the start with local financiers.

Actually, the economic collapse was worldwide. The revival of European agriculture after the Napoleonic wars and the weakening of the postwar textile boom combined to create a glut both of wheat and cotton in world markets. But the depression was most severe in the United States and most devastating in the West.

The crisis prompted a number of states to abolish the useless and degrading practice of punishing debtors with imprisonment and to pass liberal bankruptcy laws and laws easing the settlement of contracts. Congress also came to the aid of the West with a new land act in 1820, which permitted a settler to buy an 80-acre homestead for $100 in cash. The next year it added a relief act to assist land purchasers who had run afoul of the credit provisions in earlier land acts.

### The nationalism of John Marshall

Against this background of local self-assertion, economic crisis, and heightened conflict between debtors and creditors, John Marshall issued a series of historic Supreme Court decisions. We have already observed how, following his appointment in 1801, he sustained in *Marbury* v. *Madison* (1803) the Court's power to declare acts of Congress unconstitutional, and how, in *Fletcher* v. *Peck* (1810), the Marshall Court upheld the obligation of contracts against unilateral state interference.

The question of contracts gave Marshall the occasion for two resounding decisions in 1819 which alarmed state-rights men. The first of these came in *Dartmouth College* v. *Woodward,* which raised this issue: Could the royal charter granted to the college in 1769 and later acknowledged by the New Hampshire legislature, be altered by the legislature without the college's consent? In a decision at least as interesting to business corporations chartered by state legislatures as to colleges, Marshall decided that a charter was a contract between two parties, neither one of whom alone could change it, and on that account certain actions taken unilaterally by the legislature were unconstitutional. In his second decision in 1819, in *Sturges* v. *Crowninshield,* Marshall declared a New York bankruptcy law unconstitutional for seeking to relieve a debtor of his contractual debts.

In cases other than those involving contracts, Marshall's court no less than thirteen times set aside state laws as contrary to the federal Constitution. One of the most far reaching of such cases was *McCulloch* v. *Maryland,* also decided in 1819. The state of Maryland was one of those that had attempted to tax the Baltimore branch of the Second Bank of the United States out of existence. But, said Marshall in finding the Maryland tax law unconstitutional, "the power to tax involves the power to destroy." If the states were permitted to nullify acts of Congress by attacking its agencies, they could "defeat and render useless the power to create." This, Marshall could not tolerate. In broad language Marshall then asserted the constitutionality of the act creating the bank: "Let the end be legitimate, let it be within the scope of the Constitution, and all means which are appropriate, which are plainly adapted to that end, which are not prohibited, but consist with the letter and spirit of the Constitution, are constitutional." This, one of the most famous sentences in American constitutional law, laid the foundation for as broad an interpretation of the implied powers of Congress as Hamilton could have wished.

Finally, in the case of *Gibbons* v. *Ogden* (1824), Marshall spoke out on the power of Congress to regulate commerce. New York had granted Robert Fulton and Robert R. Livingston a monopoly of steam navigation in state waters, and Aaron Ogden had bought from them the right to operate a ferry between New York and New Jersey. When Thomas Gibbons set up a competing ferry under a federal coasting license, Ogden tried to invoke the state-sanctioned monopoly to restrain him from running it. The original grant by New York encroached upon the exclusive right of Congress to regulate interstate commerce, but

Marshall did not rest content simply with throwing out the New York monopoly. He went on to construe the term "commerce" so broadly as to include in it commerce "among the several states" that may venture into the interior of any state. No state could act on such commerce when its acts intruded on the powers of Congress.

It is frequently stated that Marshall, while the Republicans dominated the legislature and the executive, handed down Federalist law from the fortress he held for thirty-four years in the Supreme Court. But it is closer to the truth to say that, once his war with Jefferson had ended, Marshall gave all his energies to extending national power, just as Jefferson gave his to extending the national domain. Both were expansionists; the work of one complemented that of the other. Together they gave Americans of the oncoming Jacksonian era the limitless space and legal spaciousness within which they might seek their destinies unencumbered by local monopolists.

### The Missouri Compromise

One notable feature of the economic growth of the country was the orderly admission of new states to the Union. After Ohio in 1803 and Louisiana in 1812, there followed, after the war, Indiana in 1816, Mississippi in 1817, and Illinois in 1818. This gratifying procession was rudely interrupted by the controversy over the admission of Missouri which reopened the dormant issue of the extension of slavery. This "momentous question," Jefferson wrote in 1820, "like a fire-bell in the night, awakened and filled me with terror."

Slavery had been forbidden in the Northwest Territory in 1787. Thus the first momentous conflict over the "peculiar institution" occurred just beyond, in the so-called Upper Louisiana Territory, whose settlers first applied for admission to the Union under the name of Missouri in 1818. No problem arose until Representative James Tallmadge of New York, on February 13, 1819, shocked the

South by offering an amendment to the Missouri "enabling act" which would prohibit the introduction of additional slaves into the new state. He proposed, further, that all children born of slaves in that region be freed when they reached the age of twenty-five.

The Tallmadge Amendment passed the House promptly by a narrow margin, reflecting the predominance of northern strength in that chamber, which itself reflected the greater population of the free states. The story in the Senate was different. Even though the free states outnumbered the slave states 11 to 10 at the time, a number of northern senators who had been born and brought up in the South voted with the large minority of southern senators and helped defeat the Tallmadge Amendment, 22 to 16.

The deadlock carried over to the next session of Congress, which opened in December 1819. Now, along with Missouri's petition for admission as a slave state, came Alabama's

Collection, Corcoran Gallery of Art

*The House of Representatives at candle-lighting time for an evening session, detail of Samuel F. B. Morse painting, 1821–1822.*

application also. There was no issue about admitting Alabama as a slave state, and she was accepted as such on December 14. Alabama became the twenty-second state and established the balance between slave and free states at eleven each. Missouri, as a twelfth slave state, benefiting from the three-fifths

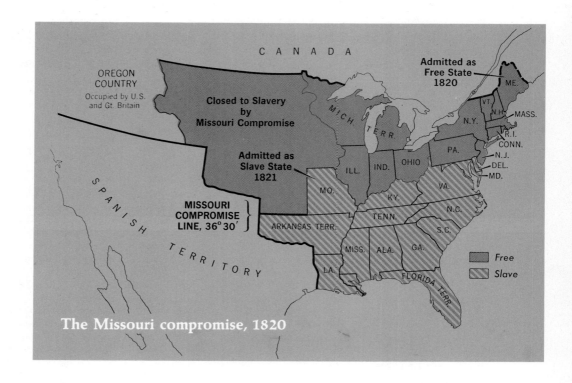

The Missouri compromise, 1820

rule in counting slaves in the apportionment of representation in the House, would also give the South a virtual veto in the Senate of all legislation enacted by the preponderantly northern House.

The northern majority in the House insisted on keeping Missouri closed to slavery. When the northeastern part of Massachusetts applied for admission to the Union as the independent state of Maine, however, some members of Congress, led by Henry Clay, grasped the chance to break the deadlock. Many in Maine did not relish their role as "a mere *pack-horse* to transport the odious, antirepublican principle of slavery into the new State of Missouri, against reason and the . . . great fabric of American liberty." But the compromisers were not to be diverted by such objections.

In a series of measures known as the "Missouri Compromise," they arranged for the temporary preservation of the balance of power in the Senate by admitting Missouri as a slave state and Maine as a free one. The most significant provision of the Compromise permitted slavery in Missouri, but prohibited it "forever . . . in all territory ceded by France to the United States . . . which lies north of 36°30' . . . not included within the limits of [that] state." President Monroe hesitated to sign the compromise measures, indeed he was prepared to veto them, on the ground that the

Constitution nowhere gave Congress the power to exclude slavery from a territory. But the unanimous urging of his Cabinet overcame his scruples and he signed the Missouri Compromise on March 6, 1820.

When Congress took up the matter of approving Missouri's new state constitution, as required by the admitting process, new trouble arose. This constitution provided that the state should never emancipate slaves without the consent of their owners; worse, it contravened the equal privileges and immunities clause of the federal Constitution by absolutely prohibiting the entry of free Negroes into the state.

Through the efforts of Henry Clay, Congress finally accepted the state constitution, but not before the so-called Second Missouri Compromise had been hammered out. This new compromise required the state legislature to guarantee that it would never deny any of the privileges and immunities of citizens of the United States inside the borders of Missouri. There the slavery issue rested for a generation, but the Missouri controversy intensified sectionalism and gradually undermined the spirit of nationalism that the war generation had labored so hard to bring about.

## For further reading

Much the best approach to Jefferson is to read his own writings. The most satisfactory comprehensive edition is that by P. L. Ford (10 vols., 1892-1899). Good one-volume editions include Bernard Mayo, ed., *Jefferson Himself* (1942), and Adrienne Koch and William Peden, *The Life and Selected Writings of Thomas Jefferson* (1944). L. J. Cappon, ed., *The Adams-Jefferson Letters* (2 vols., 1959), is invaluable. The great modern edition of *The Papers of Thomas Jefferson,* edited by J. P. Boyd, had reached to 1791 (vol. 18) by 1972.

The standard modern biography of Jefferson is Du-

mas Malone, *Jefferson and His Times* (4 vols., 1948-1970). The standard older biography, valuable for its many original writings quoted at length, is H. S. Randall, *The Life of Thomas Jefferson* (3 vols., 1865). Two one-volume biographies merit special mention: A. J. Nock, *Thomas Jefferson* (1926), and Gilbert Chinard, *Thomas Jefferson* (1939). Adrienne Koch, *Jefferson and Madison, The Great Collaboration* (1950), might be read most profitably with L. W. Levy, *Jefferson and Civil Liberties, The Darker Side* (1963). D. J. Boorstin, *The Lost World of Thomas Jefferson* (1948), and R. B. Davis, *Intellectual Life in Jefferson's Virginia*

212

1790-1830 (1964), help recreate the intellectual environment. The Jeffersonian heritage is emphasized in C. M. Wiltse, *The Jeffersonian Tradition in American Democracy* (1935), and M. D. Peterson, *The Jefferson Image in The American Mind* (1960). N. K. Risjord, *The Old Republicans, Southern Conservatism in the Age of Jefferson* (1965), is a valuable special study.

Henry Adams, *History of the United States during the Administrations of Jefferson and Madison* (9 vols., 1889-1891), is a classic; abridged versions are available in paperback. Good introductions to modern scholarship are N. E. Cunningham, Jr., *The Jeffersonian Republicans . . . 1789-1801* (1957), and *The Jeffersonian Republicans in Power . . . 1801-1809* (1963); W. N. Chambers, *Political Parties in a New Nation, The American Experience 1776-1809* (1963); and J. S. Young, *The Washington Community 1800-1829* (1966). L. D. White, *The Jeffersonians* (1951), maintains the high level of his related works on government administration. Malcolm Rohrbough, *The Land Office Business: The Settlement and Administration of American Public Lands 1789-1837* (1968), is excellent. On the Federalists in this era see J. M. Banner, Jr., *To The Hartford Convention: The Federalists and the Origins of Party Politics in Massachusetts 1789-1815* (1970); D. H. Fischer, *The Revolution of American Conservatism* (1965); and Shaw Livermore, Jr., *The Twilight of Federalism . . . 1815-1830* (1962).

On the war with the judiciary, besides vol. III of Beveridge's life of Marshall, see C. G. Haines, *The Role of the Supreme Court in American Government and Politics 1789-1835* (1944); and E. S. Corwin, *John Marshall and the Constitution* (1919). J. E. Bakeless, *Lewis and Clark* (1947), is good. Outstanding on the Louisiana Purchase is E. W. Lyon, *Louisiana in French Diplomacy 1759-1804* (1934). T. P. Abernethy, *The Burr Conspiracy* (1954), covers this exploit well.

Major issues in foreign affairs under Republican rule are well covered in three books by Bradford Perkins: *The First Rapprochement: England and the United States 1795-1805* (1955); *Prologue to War . . . 1805-1812* (1961); and *Castlereagh and Adams . . . 1812-1823* (1964). L. M. Sears, *Jefferson and the Embargo* (1927), and W. W. Jennings, *The American Embargo 1807-1809* (1921), are useful older books on Jefferson's attempt at "peaceful coercion."

J. W. Pratt, *Expansionists of 1812* (1925), develops the idea that the origins of the war had less to do with freedom of the seas than with American hunger for Canada. A. L. Burt, *The United States, Great Britain, and British North America* (1940), takes issue with

Pratt's thesis. The quest for national prestige as a factor in bringing on the war is examined in three works: Reginald Horsman, *The Causes of the War of 1812* (1962); R. H. Brown, *The Republic in Peril: 1812* (1964); and N. K. Risjord, *The Old Republicans* (above). Michael Lewis, *A Social History of the Navy 1793-1815* (1960), provides rich background for British impressment practices. The issue as seen by Americans is presented in J. F. Zimmerman, *Impressment of American Seamen* (1925). H. A. De Weerd, ed., *The War of 1812* (1944), extracts the military parts of Henry Adams's history of the Jefferson and Madison administrations (above). An outstanding modern account is H. L. Coles, *The War of 1812* (1965). The Canadian side is presented in J. M. Hitsman, *The Incredible War of 1812* (1966). On the war at sea, A. T. Mahan, *Sea Power in Its Relations to the War of 1812* (2 vols., 1919), is most important. On the diplomacy of the war and the peace, see S. F. Bemis, *John Quincy Adams and the Foundations of American Foreign Policy* (1949). F. L. Engleman, *The Peace of Christmas Eve* (1962), is more closely focused on the Treaty of Ghent. On the Hartford Convention, besides the Henry Adams and Banner works above, see S. E. Morison, *Harrison Gray Otis* (1969), and George Dangerfield, *The Era of Good Feelings* (1952). The latter, and Dangerfield's *The Awakening of American Nationalism 1815-1828* (1965), are perceptive as well on many other issues of the postwar period. F. J. Turner, *The Frontier in American History* (1920), and *Rise of the New West* (1906), are essential classics on this period.

Irving Brant, *James Madison* (6 vols., 1941-1961), is a comprehensive modern biography. S. K. Padover, *The Complete Madison* (1953), is less complete than it sounds, but offers a selection of Madison's writings. Harry Ammon, *James Monroe* (1971), is excellent. On internal conflicts of Monroe's administration, see the old biography by Carl Schurz, *The Life of Henry Clay* (2 vols., 1887); C. M. Wiltse, *John C. Calhoun, Nationalist 1782-1828* (1944); and Marquis James, *The Life of Andrew Jackson* (1-vol. edition, 1938).

Dexter Perkins, *A History of the Monroe Doctrine* (1955), is the standard account. For the British side, see C. K. Webster, *Foreign Policy of Castlereagh 1815-1822* (1925), and H. W. V. Temperley, *The Foreign Policy of Canning 1822-1827* (1925). R. A. Humphreys and John Lynch, *The Origins of the Latin American Revolutions 1808-1826* (1965), provides a good introduction to this subject.

An excellent account of the western Panic of 1819 is in vol. IV of Beveridge's life of Marshall. A more intensive treatment is M. N. Rothbard, *The Panic of 1819* (1962). On the Court in this era, besides Beveridge, see Corwin and Haines, above. Glover Moore, *The Missouri Controversy* (1953), is scholarly.

# SECTIONAL STRAINS IN ECONOMIC GROWTH

The War of 1812 is often called America's "second war of independence," and there is much justice in that designation. When the war ended in 1815, all of forty years had passed since Lexington and Concord. In those years the United States acquired territory far larger than all western Europe, and she was soon to extend her holdings and her claims across the continent she coveted. After 1815, with France bled white in the Napoleonic struggles, with Spain forced to recede inward upon her troubled self, and with Britain soon to be preoccupied with the extension of her "second empire" eastward not westward, the United States became freer to organize her energies for the unwavering pursuit of wealth and welfare that was to become her hallmark in the virtual world she called her own.

Although hostile Britain still reigned in Canada, hostile Spain to the South and Southwest, and hostile aborigines in the open spaces between them, and although haughty monarchs overseas continued to view the United States as a pawn in their own power game, American involvement in foreign affairs gradually yielded to domestic questions. Among these, sectionalism overshadowed all others.

Many issues, open or covert, obvious or obscure, lent their weight to pulling the country apart. Heaviest of all, perhaps, were those arising from the spectacular surge in economic growth, once the people turned to the discovery and development of their vast endowment in natural resources. Alexis de Tocqueville, in his rightfully famous *Democracy in America* (1835) and in his letters home during his visit to the United States, made the usual observations about the contrast in enterprise between the free North—"everything is activity, industry; labor is honored"—and the slave South—"you think yourself on the other side of the world; the enterprising spirit is gone." Yet the South too enjoyed a strong westward and economic surge which, like that of the North, added to the strength of union. But the Civil War disclosed the greater force of the sectional rivalry that had begun to rend the young nation, as we have seen, from the first moment of her independent existence.

# I  Enterprise and empire

## The grip of tradition

In 1815, and indeed for several decades thereafter, the majority of white Americans in the South as well as in the North still lived on family farms, with all but a few of their needs supplied by the husbandry of men and boys, the spinning, stitching, baking, and brewing of women and girls. These people, or their forebears, had come to America in search of personal freedom based on economic independence. Although by their mere zealous occupation of the land they were the true emissaries of empire, they remained relatively unconcerned about economic enterprise or growth. Cultivating the land and husbanding its yield was to them a complete and gratifying way of life, which left them isolated from the ups and downs of the world and worldly affairs.

The fish of the sea supplied another great natural resource from which many Americans continued to eke out a fiercely independent existence long after the Revolution. In 1821, Timothy Dwight, reporting on his travels through New England, said of the fishing ports south of Boston: "The whole region wears remarkably the appearance of stillness and retirement; and the inhabitants seem to be separated in a great measure, from all active intercourse with their country." Fishermen in these ports went out, typically, like farmers, only for the day. Each had his own boat and brought back his catch for his family, though he might sometimes barter a surplus for grain, clothing, or equipment. At more active fishing centers like Newburyport and Beverly, and on Cape Cod, fishermen showed greater enterprise. Their voyages were longer and better organized. But here too the rule was that each man supplied his own gear and provisions in return for a share of the catch. The fisherman always preferred going out "on his own hook," a phrase that originated with these Yankees.

One specialized fishing occupation—whaling—ranked very high in value of product until kerosene supplanted whale oil as an illuminant after the Civil War. Until the War of 1812, just about every New England port had its whaling fleet, but after the war, Nantucket and New Bedford, Massachusetts, almost monopolized the industry. After 1820, New Bedford became the whaling center of the world, with perhaps a third of the international fleet. "New Bedford is not nearer to the whales than New London or Portland," wrote Emerson, "yet they have all the equipments for a whaler ready, and they hug an oil-cask like a brother."

The concentration of whaling activities in New Bedford added to the efficiency of operations; otherwise, whaling remained a conservative industry in which the only significant changes since colonial times were that voyages grew longer, captains crueler, and crews— paid, like fishermen, a share of the catch— more ruthlessly exploited. Rebellious hands, when they did not mutiny or desert, often found themselves abandoned on some foreign shore by the captain, who thus avoided paying them their shares. On return voyages, crews were made up of men from every primitive island and backwater of civilization. Even Fiji islanders, and Polynesians like the harpooner Queequeg in Melville's *Moby Dick,* could be seen walking the streets of New Bedford after a whaler had put in.

In lumbering, as in farming, fishing, and whaling, few innovations were made in the first third of the nineteenth century. The industry grew, of course, but until the railroads added their own huge demand for wood for fuel, ties, and rolling stock, lumbering re-

*License No. 23 to Josiah Jennings*
*to graze one cow on Boston Common for the*
*year 1829.*

The Henry E. Huntington Library and Art Gallery, San Marino, Calif.

No. 23   Mr. *Josiah A Jennings*
           **To the City of Boston, Dr.**
For a License for one COW to go upon the Common for the year 18 *29* agreeably to an Ordinance of the City Council,   $ 5
         *Received payment, May 21 1829.*
                                    City Clerk.

mained the occupation of uncompromisingly individualistic loggers, who supplied timber to widely scattered and independently owned saw mills.

The Indians had taught the first settlers how to grow corn, harpoon whales, and girdle and kill trees before felling them. For more than two centuries, these basic techniques of farming, fishing, and lumbering spread unchanged as the country gradually expanded. Enterprises that specialized in making such other commodities as flour, leather goods, and ironware usually were organized locally and conducted according to time-tested methods by generation after generation in the same family. Such enterprises offered a living and a way of life; until vast new markets were opened up by improved transportation, they continued to characterize the American economy, even if they did not portend its future.

### Fur trade and China trade

No one in early nineteenth-century America was more isolated than the fur trapper and trader; but unlike the other primary occupations, the fur trade soon gave a new direction to American life, a new method to

Foreign "factories," or trading
stations, in Canton, China, about 1840;
American factory with flag, center.

furs) among the wealthy mandarins of North China, where tastes were elegant, winters frigid, and dwellings unheated.

New Englanders, especially, were attracted to the sea otter because it gave them a commodity to export in exchange for the tea, silk, spices, handsome willowware china, and cheap cottons ("nankeens") of the Orient, so much wanted at home. By the early 1800s the sea otter neared extinction. Profits from Chinese imports, however, had proved even greater than those from the sale of furs in China, and when the sea-otter supply failed, approximately at the outbreak of the War of 1812, ship captains began to carry Hawaiian sandalwood to the Orient, where it was used for incense in the joss houses. Even the most upright Yankee traders also began to smuggle opium from the Dutch East Indies and neighboring islands into China to pay for the tea, but the American opium traffic always remained a small fraction of that carried on by the British East India Company, which forced immense quantities of India opium into China with cannon and bayonet.

The fur market in China had attracted land trappers and traders as well as sea captains, and following the return of Lewis and Clark from their trailblazing expedition across the continent in 1806 (see p. 189), mountain men in quest of pelts and skins began to exploit the upper Missouri, the Yellowstone, the Green and other northwestern rivers, and the Colorado and the Gila in the southwestern desert. The farther trappers and traders reached out from their Mississippi base at St. Louis, however, the greater difficulty they found in carrying on their business. One reason for this was the hostility of the Plains Indians, with whom, it seemed, only large and well-armed expeditions could safely deal. Of more lasting importance was the fact that time and distance cost money; only well-financed organizations could send trappers and traders into far-off regions for a year or more.

American business, and a new spirit to the American economy.

Fur—mink, otter, lynx, fox, and the ubiquitous beaver, as well as the coarser bear, wolf, deer, rabbit, muskrat, "coon," and "possum"—had been one of the first staples exported by the colonies. The finer pelts were used in hats, cloaks, and robes; the coarser ones, in blankets for man and beast. The Indians, who did most of the actual trapping, traded their valuable furs for tinsel, shoddy, and drink. Consequently, from the start, profits had been large and competition keen. As early as 1700, overtrapping had depleted the fur-bearing animals in some areas, and in the next fifty years French traders from Canada and Spanish traders from Mexico, as well as the English colonists, had forced their way a thousand miles inland, far in advance of settlement.

Two thousand miles beyond even the farthest inland fur-trading post in the Mississippi Valley were the sea-otter waters off the Oregon coast. Sea captains from New England and New York, turning to the China trade immediately after the Revolution, discovered an eager market for the strikingly beautiful sea-otter skins (as well as for other domestic

**218**

It was the New Yorker John Jacob Astor, by 1800 the city's leading fur merchant and one of its most creative businessmen, who most successfully met the new conditions. His instrument was the American Fur Company, chartered by New York State in 1808 for twenty-five years and capitalized at $1 million. As Astor's friend Washington Irving wrote, the entire "capital was furnished by [Astor] himself—he, in fact, constituted the company." He had simply played up the "sagacious and effective" idea that a group of responsible capitalists was behind the venture to justify his demand for a monopoly of the western fur trade.

New York refused to grant Astor the monopoly he petitioned for; in September 1810, nevertheless, he sent out his first expedition by sea to set up a trading post at the mouth of the Columbia River in Oregon, and in October he sent an overland expedition west from St. Louis. By the time the cross-country party arrived in Oregon early in 1812, the sea-going contingent had already landed and begun to build the settlement of Astoria.

Canadian fur traders eyed Astor's maneuvers with growing hostility, and on the outbreak of the War of 1812 they decided to put an end to the American company. Information that a British warship was headed toward the settlement convinced Astor's men that resistance would be futile, and in January 1813 they sold out to the North West Company, a Canadian enterprise, for $58,000. For a generation thereafter, the Canadians succeeded in barring American trappers and traders from Oregon and maintaining their own monopoly of the region's fur.

But they did not succeed in stopping Astor. Once the War of 1812 was over, his American Fur Company set out to capture the fur trade east of Oregon. In 1816, at Astor's urging, Congress passed a law forbidding foreigners (i.e., Britishers) from engaging in the fur trade of the United States, except when licensed as employees of American traders. Subsequently, he induced Governor Lewis Cass of Michigan Territory to issue licenses almost exclusively to his men.

Until the 1830s Astor's Company averaged about $500,000 a year in profits. Then styles in Europe suddenly changed. "It appears that they make hats of silk in place of beaver," Astor observed during a European trip in 1834. By then, the fur reserves of the entire continent had been depleted. The most natural resource to be exploited by the new business methods, the fur-bearing creatures were the first to go.

The fur trade estranged and trampled on the Indian, taught him to drink "firewater," and armed him with guns and ammunition. At the same time, it opened the path of empire "to that ocean," as Lewis and Clark said of the Pacific in 1805, "the object of all our labours, the reward of all our anxieties." Across that ocean it nurtured the China trade and related Christian missionary activity, an active commerce in Philippine sugar, hemp, and indigo, and the start of continuous American settlement in Hawaii. It also made Astor the first American millionaire.

### The Santa Fe Trail

Less dramatic than the fur trade, and involving far fewer men and far less capital, was the trade across the Santa Fe Trail. Spain had established the isolated outpost of Santa Fe in the desert of New Mexico early in the seventeenth century, and had supplied it most laboriously from Vera Cruz, 1500 miles away. Early American efforts to trade at Santa Fe were frustrated by Spain's rigid colonial policy, which sternly excluded foreigners. Soon after Mexico won her freedom from Spain in 1821, however, she opened Santa Fe to her northern neighbor, a step she later regretted and reversed. In 1825 the United States Army surveyed the Santa Fe Trail, westward from Independence, Missouri (see map, p. 300). Thereafter, for twenty years, caravans of American farm wagons trekked across it, hauling all sorts of goods from the East and from Europe to be exchanged at fabulous profits for Spanish gold and silver.

The arrival of the caravan each year was a great event in the Spanish town. Gradually, some Americans settled in Santa Fe, and others, attracted by the fertile land bordering the eastern stretches of the trail, staked out farms along the way. When Santa Anna, the Mexican leader, closed the trail in 1844, Americans viewed his act as interference with their rights and "destiny." The Santa Fe trade never engaged more than two or three hundred persons a year. But, like the fur trade, it opened a new path across the continent, lured American businessmen into new country, and led to a political and territorial claim that eventually would be made good by the Mexican War (see Chapter Twelve).

## II   Rise of the Middle West

### Early settlers

Well to the east of fur trappers and traders, but traveling over trails they had marked through the wilderness, moved frontier families like that of Abraham Lincoln. Thomas Lincoln, the President's father, was the typical itinerant pioneer of the early nineteenth century, part backwoodsman, part farmer, part handyman-carpenter. Thomas had been born in the western Virginia hills in 1778. Four years later found the Lincolns in Kentucky, where Thomas grew up "a wandering laboring boy," altogether without schooling. In 1806, he married the illiterate Nancy Hanks, who bore their son Abe in 1809. The Lincolns and the Hankses rarely stayed put for long, and by 1816 the whole tribe had reached Indiana, where they "squatted" the first year. "We lived the same as the Indians," one of the Hankses said years later, " 'ceptin' we took an interest in politics and religion." Then they managed to build a typical log cabin, without floor, door, or window. A roof stuffed with mud and dry grass afforded the only protection from rain. This cabin remained their home for a decade before they pushed on to Illinois.

By 1816, more than a million people had trampled over the Lincolns' trail to set up households in the West. Most of them traveled on foot, their possessions on their backs, in wheelbarrows, or saddled to a few scrawny cows transformed into beasts of burden. Travelers from abroad noted the characteristic bluish complexion of these settlers, many of whom suffered from forest fever, milk sickness, and especially swamp-bred ague (malaria). Fertile land could be had for the taking, or at a very low price per acre, but life was hard. "The rugged road, the dirty hovels, the fire in the woods to sleep by, the pathless ways through the wilderness, the dangerous crossings of the rivers"—why, asked the Englishman, William Cobbett, in 1817, did pioneers put up with all this? "To boil their pot in gipsy-fashion, to have a mere board to eat on, to drink whiskey or pure water, to sit and sleep under a shed far inferior to English cowpens, to have a mill a twenty miles' distance, an apothecary's shop at a hundred, and a doctor nowhere." Few Englishman, Cobbett confessed, could survive such conditions. But Americans, as Jefferson said, found it "cheaper to clear a new acre than to manure an old one." So on into the West they moved.

Congressman Peter B. Porter of Buffalo, New York, described the western country and the plight of the pioneers in 1810:

*There is no better place where the great staple articles for the use of civilized life can be produced in greater abundance or with greater ease, yet as respects most of the luxuries and many of the conveniences of life the people are poor. . . . The single circumstance of want of a market is already beginning to produce the most disastrous effect, not only on the industry, but on the morals of the inhabitants. Such is the fertility of their land that one-half of their time spent in labor is sufficient to produce every article which their farms*

*Dalzell's clearing, at Piqua*
*on the Miami River in Ohio, 1831,*
*showing early buildings*
*and fencing in original drawing*
*by T. K. Wharton.*

*are capable of yielding, in sufficient quantities for their*
*own consumption, and there is nothing to incite them*
*to produce more. They are therefore naturally led to*
*spend the other part of their time in idleness and*
*dissipation.*

These pioneers used up their capital instead of augmenting what little capital they may have had. Even their boys, adept from childhood with rifle and rod, "lit out for the tall timber" on their own.

### "King Cotton" and the West

After 1815 western prospects improved rapidly. Subjugation of the Indians, the British departure from their western military posts and the Great Lakes, and the disintegration of Spanish rule on the Gulf Coast all opened new lands to American settlement. The federal government aided pioneers by showing more tolerance of squatters and by liberalizing land-sale policies. Two epochal developments then broadened the market for western produce and afforded cheap access to this market. The first was the phenomenal rise of "King Cotton" in the neighboring South (and large-scale sugar growing in Louisiana). The second was the introduction of the steamboat on western waters.

Commercial cotton growing gained its first great impetus in the South after 1790 when British East Indian indigo virtually destroyed the market for the American product, which for two generations had been the staple of South Carolina and Georgia planters (see p. 66). Between 1790 and 1793 the indigo planters turned their land to cotton to such an extent that annual production rose from 3000 to 10,000 bales. Most of this cotton was of the fragile long-staple variety, the finest kind, which alone could be cleansed of its oily black seed at reasonable cost. In America, however, long-staple cotton seemed to be limited by its apparent climatic and soil requirements to the sea islands off the South Carolina and Georgia shore and the adjacent coastal plain extending into Spanish Florida. The other type of cotton, the coarser short-staple green-seed boll, could be grown on almost any soil provided the warm season were long enough. Its single drawback was the difficulty of removing the seed. One woman worker could clean but a single pound a day.

Cotton became King in the South after 1793 when Eli Whitney, a young Massachusetts Yankee with a formidable mechanical bent who had gone to Georgia to tutor a planter's family while preparing for a law career, invented his engine for cleaning the green-seed plant. Although soon beset by infringements on his simple mechanism and by patent suits, by 1794 Whitney had many "gins" at work, and short-staple cotton production spread at a rate probably unmatched by any other product of the land. One worker operating a single gin by hand could clean not one but fifty pounds a day. Rapid improvements in Whitney's and other gins, and the application of power to the machine, soon multiplied its productive capacity forty to sixty times. By

1800 about 75,000 bales of cotton went to market, most of it now the short-staple variety. On the eve of the War of 1812, this figure had soared to over 175,000 bales, nearly three-fourths of the crop being accounted for by South Carolina and Georgia, largely in the piedmont sections of these states. Virginia and North Carolina accounted for most of the balance.

Within a few years, however, piedmont land was used up as tidewater land had been earlier. The piedmont, a traveler said in 1820, presented a scene of "dreary and uncultivated wastes . . . half-clothed negroes, lean and hungry stock, houses falling to decay, and fences wind-shaken and dilapidated." Turning their backs on this disheartening scene, cotton planters pushed west into Alabama and Mississippi. By 1830, the combined population of these states exceeded 400,000, even though the large planters had bought up many small farms in the best cotton-growing areas. Sections of Tennessee, Arkansas, and Florida suitable for cotton planting also became heavily settled, as did the Louisiana sugar country.

The rising traffic at New Orleans reflects the rapid growth of the new regions. In 1816 only 37,000 bales of cotton were shipped from this Mississippi port. By 1822, the figure was 161,000 bales, and by 1830, 428,000. Most of this cotton found its way to English textile factories, although some went to the Continent and increasing amounts to New England mills.

Until the beginning of the nineteenth century, South Carolina had exported considerable quantities of wheat and corn as well as rice, indigo, cotton, and hides; and other southern states had exported horses, mules, and swine. Such diversity now disappeared. As an English visitor observed in 1826, "every other object gives place to cotton."

A year later, a traveler wrote of his visit to Louisiana:

*Corn, sweet potatoes, melons and all northern fruit, with the exception of apples, flourish here; though the planters find the great staples, cotton and sugar, so much more profitable than other kinds of cultivation that many of them calculate to supply themselves with provisions almost entirely from the upper country.*

The Cotton Kingdom's growing need for food and work animals gave the slack western-

*The Mississippi at New Orleans, showing forest of masts in booming port, etching after drawing on the spot by Basil Hall, 1829.*

ers the impulse they needed to lay down their rods and guns and to think seriously about farming. As markets and prices improved, western farmers hungered for more land and went into debt to acquire it. As land speculation spread, debt mounted, forcing the farmer to concentrate almost as single-mindedly as the planter on cash crops to meet financial obligations. Southern specialization in cotton spurred western specialization in grain and meat and mules. The marvelous Mississippi River system conveniently tied the two sections together, and the steamboat tightened the knot.

## III  Growth of intersectional commerce

### Transportation problems

In colonial America the ocean had afforded the easiest means of communication and trade. As farms and plantations spread along the eastern rivers, they too began to carry their share of people and goods. The progress of settlement in the West brought the Mississippi River system into the transportation network, and the steamboat made it the foremost inland carrier of all. The first steamboat on the western waters was *New Orleans,* built in 1811 by Robert Fulton, four years after his success with *Clermont* on the Hudson. As he had in New York, Fulton promptly won a monopoly of the carrying trade of the West which lasted, except for the competition of interlopers, until 1824, when John Marshall, in his momentous decision in *Gibbons* v. *Ogden,* dealt the death blow to monopolies on interstate waters. By 1830, nearly 200 steamboats plied the western rivers.

Keelboat rates between Louisville and New Orleans had been about $5 per hundred pounds of freight. By 1820, steamboat rates for this trip had fallen to $2 per hundred pounds, and by 1842 competition had driven them down to 25 cents, still a profitable price since technological improvements had so greatly increased the carrying capacity and operating efficiency of the vessels. Western staples now were sped down to the levees of New Orleans for shipment overseas or for distribution by coastal vessels to the rest of the South and Southwest and even to the Northeast. Commodities from abroad or from the Northeast also were funneled into the booming port for transshipment inland.

The Mississippi system, however, was less hospitable than it seemed. The river itself and

Mississippi River system about 1830

most of its tributaries teemed with snags, hidden banks, floating trees, whirlpools, and eddies, while pirates infested the entire system. Seasonal floods often swept both boat and boatmen to destruction. Summer droughts pinched the river channels into narrow ribbons, stranding many vessels in the shallow water. So pernicious, indeed, was this hazard that most Mississippi traffic came to be bunched on the floodtides of spring and fall. This tactic eased the problems of navigation but raised new problems of marketing. During the floodtide seasons, produce now glutted the New Orleans wharves. Since storing the incoming crops was costly, and since in any case grain spoiled quickly in the humid air of the Mississippi basin, shippers were obliged to accept the catastrophically low prices buyers offered.

The difficulties of road transport, if anything, presented greater challenges than those on the rivers. From the earliest times, many Americans chose to settle far from neighbors on land several miles from water routes. And yet somehow they had to travel to grist mills, tobacco warehouses, cotton gins, forges, country stores, county courts, and to the rivers themselves. As time went on, a crude network of roads spread across the sparsely settled countryside, often following old Indian trails and the paths of trappers and traders through dense forests. Only a few such roads, bristling with tree stumps, had been made wide enough to accommodate wagons or carts. Spring floods and fall rains transformed them into muddy quagmires, while winter cold froze them into malevolent ruts.

As early as 1806, Congress chartered the "National Highway" to be built with federal funds, the greatest road-building enterprise of the early years of the Republic. Not until 1811, however, did the first crews begin to cut the road westward from Cumberland, Maryland. By 1818 it had been pushed to Wheeling, Virginia, on the Ohio River. The failure of Congress to provide additional money checked construction here, but work was re-

sumed in 1825 and by midcentury the road reached Vandalia, Illinois, its westernmost point.

The National Highway, paved with stone over much of its course and with sturdy stone bridges over the rivers in its path, became an efficient carrier, "the path of empire" for millions of Americans on the move westward. Other useful roads included the privately financed Lancaster Turnpike, built in 1794 at a cost of $465,000 across the 62-mile stretch from Philadelphia to Lancaster, Pennsylvania. At first only a dirt road, after many accidents caused by holes, rocks, and floundering horses, the Lancaster pike was reconstructed on the principles worked out by the Scottish engineer John L. McAdam (1756–1836). These principles dominated paved-road building in America as in England until asphalt supplanted the "macadamized" road in the automobile age. "It is the native soil," McAdam wrote, "which really supports the weight of traffic." But to do so effectively, the soil must be "preserved in a dry state." In order to keep it dry, a covering impenetrable to rain must be placed over it. "The thickness of a road should only be regulated by the quantity of material necessary to form such an impervious covering, and never by any reference to its own power of carrying weight." This covering was to be made of small stones carefully broken into the right size, often along the road-building site itself.

Tolls collected along the Lancaster pike more than paid for the cost of the enterprise, which proved profitable enough to encourage the construction of similar roads elsewhere. By 1825, private companies, mostly in New England and the Middle states, built more than 10,000 miles of turnpikes, by no means all of them paved. The best of such roads cost from $5000 to $10,000 per mile, and state and local governments often helped defray the cost to the companies by buying their stock and by granting them the proceeds from the sale of government bonds. Most turnpikes, however, remained modest enterprises, and their short stretches of road did little to improve the sorry network of country paths. Their high tolls for the transportation of heavy agricultural produce, moreover, discouraged shippers always hard pressed for coin. By the 1830s, management and maintenance of privately operated turnpikes had become so costly, and returns so scanty, that thousands of miles of such roads either were abandoned or turned over to the states.

224

## The canal boom

Turnpikes, clearly, would not enable New York, Philadelphia, Boston, and the other eastern seaports to compete with New Orleans for the growing trade of the West. These cities turned instead to canals to link up the great waterways with which nature had endowed the American continent. But canals were even harder and more expensive to build than turnpikes. They cost not $5000 but $20,000 a mile; some cost as much as $60,000 and $80,000 a mile. They took not a year or two but seven to ten years to build. Thus they presented new problems in finance and management as well as in engineering.

In 1816 only three American canals ran as far as 2 miles, none as far as 30 miles. All

told, the country boasted 100 miles of such artificial waterways. As early as 1810, the New York State legislature had appointed a committee to investigate the feasibility of digging a canal to the West, and in 1816 De Witt Clinton again raised the issue. So convincing were his arguments that even his political opponents voted for his project—a canal to connect the Hudson River with Lake Erie, a breathtaking 363 miles distant.

Construction of the Erie Canal began in 1817, and by 1823 a 280-mile stretch was in operation from Albany to Rochester. The tolls that came pouring in from the traffic on this part of the canal helped finance the final leg to Buffalo, completed in 1825. In 1823, New York had also opened the Champlain Canal, connecting the Hudson River and Lake Champlain to the north. In 1825, returns from both projects exceeded $500,000, and over the next nine years the Erie paid back its total original cost of $7 million. Two figures tell the story of the Erie's success: It reduced freight rates between Albany and Buffalo from $100 to $15 a ton, travel time from twenty to eight days.

*The western end of the*
*Erie Canal, etching after drawing*
*at the scene by Basil Hall, 1829.*

Lilly Library, Indiana University

Spurred to action by New York's dramatic success, Boston, in 1825 induced the Massachusetts legislature to consider building a canal into the interior, but the hilly Massachusetts terrain disheartened the promoters. When Boston did gain entry to the West in 1842, it was by way of three railroads strung across Massachusetts to the eastern terminal of the Erie Canal at Albany. In 1826, Philadelphia won state approval for yet another scheme to tap the West, an undertaking even more ambitious than the one Boston had abandoned. This system included a main canal and railroad tracking, and was completed to Pittsburgh in 1834 at a cost of more than $10 million, all of it supplied by the state.

In 1827, Baltimore joined in the race for western business, announcing plans for the Chesapeake and Ohio Canal. Maryland's legislature thought the project visionary and refused to finance it, but work began with private and federal funds. The state legislators turned out to be right, for construction of the canal ground to a halt at the broad southern mountains. In 1828, a private corporation began to lay track for the B & O Railroad, the first successful line in America. But many years passed before the B & O reached the Ohio River in the 1850s.

Westerners became as energetic as easterners in seeking ways to promote East-West trade, for they soon discovered that their rich soil could produce more wheat and corn, and that their corn could fatten more hogs, than southern market's could absorb. Moreover, westerners had grown weary of trying to cope with the hazards of river transportation. In the 1820s they turned a sympathetic ear to Henry Clay's program for high tariffs and "internal improvements"—the first to promote the growth of eastern factory towns, the second to provide the means for opening towns to western produce. "Internal improvements" would also mean that manufactured goods could be shipped more cheaply from the East than by way of New Orleans. Congress never adopted Clay's program, but even without federal assistance Ohio and other western states soon embarked on their own ambitious canal and railroad projects.

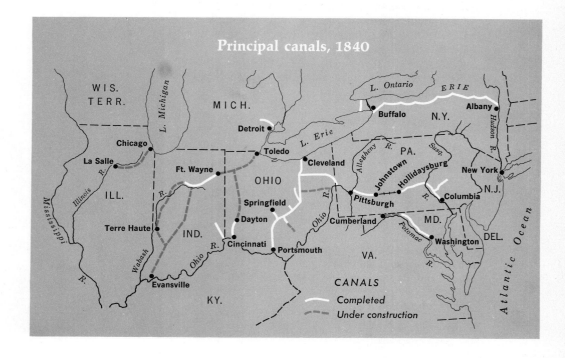

Principal canals, 1840

CANALS
— Completed
- - - Under construction

By 1840, some 3326 miles of canals, most of them in the North and West, had been built in the United States at a cost of $125 million. Private investors could supply only a small fraction of this sum. Federal and state subscriptions to the securities of private canal companies accounted for part of the balance, while more than half the total was provided directly by the states out of revenues or through the sale of state bonds abroad, mainly in England.

Generations of economic historians have made so much of the issue of public financing of transportation enterprises such as roads, canals, and railroads in an avowedly private, capitalist, economy, that they have stretched "ideological laissez-faire" from fetish to myth. Private capitalists always employed the instrumentalities at hand, even if they were those of the state, including armies and navies as well as public tax, tariff, and credit powers. This hardly made them (or the politicians involved) socialists; and in the early nineteenth century, especially in expanding America, little concern was expressed over the issue in these terms. Economic rewards, public as well as private, gained first consideration; and impact of the canals, the first enterprises to engage large-scale public financial participation, proved as salutary as expected. The South remained a valuable and growing customer of the West, and the Ohio and Mississippi River systems continued to be heavily used. But the West's connection with the North and East became ever stronger as the canal system developed in these sections and as slavery spread below the Mason-Dixon line.

Travel over canals was much cheaper than over turnpikes, but for four months of the year the northern canals stood frozen solid. Railroads soon freed shippers from the uncertainties and limitations of weather and from the medieval pace of oxen and tow horses. By 1840, 3328 miles of railroad had been built in the United States, almost exactly equal to the canal mileage. But only about 200 of these railroad miles could be found in the West. For some time after 1840, rivers, canals, and turnpikes remained the principal channels of inland commerce.

226

## New York City's spectacular rise

In the competition for western trade, as the East gradually outstripped the South, in the East itself New York City quickly pulled ahead of her rivals, Boston, Philadelphia, and Baltimore. Nature greatly aided New York. She boasted a far larger hinterland market than Boston; the Hudson and Mohawk Rivers gave her a far more serviceable water route west than either Philadelphia or Baltimore enjoyed; and she lay ideally situated for the coastal trade, Boston being too far north, Philadelphia and Baltimore each too far upstream

Prints Division, New York Public Library

for easy access from the ocean. All these advantages in domestic trade combined to make New York the best warehousing site for transatlantic exchange as well. Yet competition remained keen for a long time, and New York won her eventual supremacy through the enterprise of her businessmen.

The promotion and construction of the Erie Canal, of course, was the New Yorkers' most rewarding accomplishment; but even before canal digging began, they had made attractive innovations. One was a modified auction system for disposing of imports. Most American ports held auctions at which the common practice was for traders to offer imports for

sale and then to withdraw them if bids proved unsatisfactory. In New York City, after 1817, merchants were guaranteed that the highest bid would be accepted and that their purchases would be delivered promptly at the price named. This change drew merchants to New York from all over the country; and where merchants congregated, shippers were bound to land their goods.

Another New York innovation was a transatlantic packet service with vessels running on regular schedules, "full or not full." Heretofore, ocean commerce waited upon the whims of the weather and the convenience of ship captains. New York's Black Ball Line, first in the world to operate on the new basis, dispatched *James Monroe* from New York, January 5, 1818, in the teeth of a snowstorm that would have been regarded as a valid excuse for delay by any ordinary vessel.

Even after the Black Ball Line began operations, irregularity of sailings continued to characterize most ocean shipping. The American merchant marine carried cargo around the world to the Levant, the Baltic states, Africa, and the East Indies, as well as to the West Indies, South America, western Europe, China, and India. In an age without wireless communication, shipowners could not tell when a vessel might sight its home port, what it might be carrying, or what ports of call it might have touched. The shipowners of Boston in particular thrived on this old-fashioned worldwide carrying trade. Nevertheless, the so-called Atlantic Shuttle grew steadily in importance as cotton exports soared and the United States offered expanding markets for Old-World manufactures. And New York became most important among Shuttle ports. By 1828, New York's share of the American merchant marine almost equalled that of Philadelphia, Boston, and Baltimore combined.

*Waterfront at South Street,*
*between Maiden Lane and Wall Street,*
*New York City, 1828,*
*where most Atlantic Shuttle packets docked*
*and their owners carried on their business.*

228

As dependable auctions and dependable sailings brought businessmen and goods flooding into New York, the city's need for an adequate export staple to balance its trade grew acute. Western produce pouring into the city over the Erie Canal helped some, but in the 1820s New York's ambitious shippers began to sail right into New Orleans, Mobile, and other southern ports to pick up cotton to carry to Britain and the Continent. There they exchanged the cotton for manufactures and other goods, which they brought back to New York for distribution in the city and in the interior. Eventually they also took over the shipping of imports directly to the cotton ports themselves.

So successful were the New York merchants in this new trade that by 1830 it was estimated that 40 cents of every dollar paid for raw cotton went north—almost exclusively to New York—to cover freight charges, insurance, commissions, and interest. In 1837, a convention in the South—called to promote the revival of direct trade with Europe—reminded southern merchants, "You hold the element from which [the New York merchant] draws his strength. You have but to speak the word, and his empire is transferred to your own soil." But the word was not spoken. Two years later a similar convention declared that "the importing merchants of the South [had become] an almost extinct race, and her direct trade, once so great, flourishing, and rich, [had] dwindled down to insignificance."

## IV The industrial revolution

### Difficult beginnings

The expansion of commercial agriculture in the West, the rapid growth of western population, and the growing accessibility of western markets—all gave a strong impetus to the development of eastern industry. The concentration on cotton planting in the South also made it a market for the coarse textiles worn by slaves and other workers, and for other manufactures that it could have produced itself. Until western and southern markets were opened, however, factory industry had difficulty getting started in America.

Back in 1791, in his Report on Manufactures to Congress, Alexander Hamilton had written, "The expediency of encouraging manufactures in the United States . . . appears at this time to be pretty generally admitted." But he was too optimistic. In the first decades of the new nation's life, America had neither surplus capital to invest in factories nor surplus labor to man them. In 1791, Hamilton himself helped organize the Society for Establishing Useful Manufactures, a corporation capitalized at $1 million chartered by New Jersey. In the next few years, this corporation founded the city of Paterson, erected numerous buildings to house its works, smuggled in skilled British mechanics, and began manufacturing yarn, cloth, hats, and other commodities. By 1796, however, both the works and the town were moribund. A few similar undertakings suffered a similar fate. Cautious financiers chose to keep their money in the fruitful and accustomed paths of trade, shipping, and land speculation. The Federalist swells of northern cities with their English commercial connections, and the Republican planters of the South with their English commercial credit, scorning goods manufactured at home, demanded English woolens, linens, china, cutlery, furniture, and tools.

The first successful full-time factory in America was the cotton-spinning plant of Almy & Brown, Providence merchants. Under the direction of an experienced Englishman, Samuel Slater, this factory began operations at Pawtucket in 1791. Nine children, working for wages of 12 to 25 cents a day, tended its seventy-two spindles under full-time supervision. Slater's, of course, was a tiny affair, and only Almy & Brown's well-established market connections kept the company afloat.

After the outbreak of the Napoleonic wars in Europe in 1799, Americans found it increasingly difficult to obtain British manufactures. To supply their needs, Slater's mill expanded operations and many hopeful imitators started up to enjoy a share of the market. Few of these enterprises were capitalized at more than $10,000; since their managers were inexperienced in keeping accounts, handling money and men, and exploiting markets, conservative banks would simply have nothing to do with them. They drew their labor from the poorest farm families in the area, often employing both the parents and their small children. The thread they spun was given out to home weavers to make into cloth. But Almy & Brown complained in 1809 that "a hundred looms in families will not weave as much cloth as ten . . . under the immediate inspection of a workman." Once the long war was over, most of the wartime mills shut down. The shining exception became one of the most profitable enterprises in early business annals and laid the foundations for the industrial revolution in the United States.

### Entry of big capital

This exception was the Boston Manufacturing Company of Waltham, Massachusetts, incorporated in 1813 by Francis Cabot Lowell, Patrick Tracy Jackson, and Nathan Appleton, leading New England merchants. The Boston Manufacturing Company was as distinct a step forward in its day as Slater's mill had been twenty-two years before. The organizers, who had already demonstrated their ability to manage hazardous, large-scale enterprises, invested liberally in the new company. In the first six years, they poured $600,000 cash into it and held as much or more in reserve for operating and emergency expenses. They built the first completely integrated cotton-manufacturing plant in the

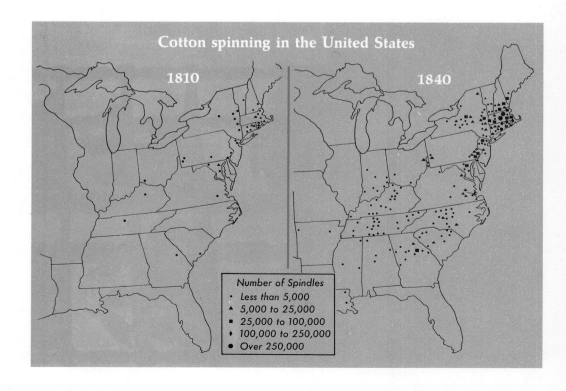

**Cotton spinning in the United States**

1810    1840

*Number of Spindles*
· Less than 5,000
▲ 5,000 to 25,000
■ 25,000 to 100,000
♦ 100,000 to 250,000
● Over 250,000

world; all operations were under one roof, from the unbaling of the raw cotton to the dyeing and printing of the finished cloth. They even established their own selling agencies, instead of depending on local jobbers as earlier companies had done.

The scale on which it operated and its carefully integrated production methods enabled the Boston Manufacturing Company to eliminate middlemen and unsupervised domestic workers and to reduce the time spent in carrying goods from place to place for successive processing steps. The managers made their system even more economical by introducing power looms and power spindles and by giving constant attention to other improvements, from the design of waterwheels and power-transmission systems to the fastness of dyes.

In another innovation, these New England merchants devised a scheme for attracting and holding workers. Instead of employing children and their parents from the immediate neighborhood, the Boston Manufacturing Company took on young women ranging in age from eighteen to twenty-two, and sheltered and fed them in newly constructed houses that made up a company town. Here, under the sharp eyes of the organizers, religion was cultivated, educational opportunities

were made available in leisure hours, and cleanliness and hygiene were insisted upon. All these devices, calculated to attract sturdy, ambitious, hardworking young women from respectable farm families, succeeded in doing just that. Absenteeism was low and industrial discipline easily imposed. Although the Boston Manufacturing Company began operations in 1816 when the flood of British imports sank many struggling American mills, it proved an immediate and lasting success. In 1817, it earned a dividend of 12.5 percent for its stockholders; thereafter, despite the Panic of 1819, annual dividends rose even higher. By 1822, dividends totaling 104.5 percent had been paid to the original investors.

### Corporations and industrial progress

In 1823 Harrison Gray Otis of Boston wrote: "There has been a curious 'revival' in the spirit of men ... which is quite remarkable. Two years ago our sun had sunk never to rise again.... All is now reversed and [manufacturing] stocks as well as spirits have risen inordinately. ... It is amazing to see what is done by the puff on one hand and the panic on the other." The opening up of the West and the expansion of the Cotton Kingdom in the South spurred the general business up-

230

*The mills of Lowell. The falls, with a drop of over 30 feet, supplied the needed power.*

Prints Division, New York Public Library

turn. The revolutions against Spain in Latin America opened up the first foreign markets for American manufactured goods. After 1826, more and more such goods found their way to China to help pay for the tea that Americans drank in ever larger quantities.

All these changes were reflected in the expansion of the firms that had survived the depression and in the large numbers of new textile corporations that set up in business during the 1820s and 1830s. Some of these new companies were organized and chartered by the same group that had started the Boston Manufacturing Company. Between 1821 and 1835, these men, often referred to as the "Boston Associates," opened nine new companies in Massachusetts and southern New Hampshire, each specializing in a particular textile product on a large scale. More important, during and after the depression these men founded insurance companies and banks to maintain and concentrate their supply of capital, real-estate companies to take over the best factory sites, and water-power companies to control dams and dam sites and to harness the power of the great rivers. After 1823, Lowell on the Merrimack supplanted Waltham on the Charles as their main operating center.

The corporation had first been used as a legal device for securing a monopoly by means of a special charter. Astor employed it next as a symbol of prestige. The turnpike and bridge companies used the corporate form mainly as a means of accumulating capital through the sale of inexpensive shares to numerous subscribers. By the time the canal and railroad companies were being formed, the idea of limited liability had become well established in law and finance. Limited liability meant that the owners of corporation stock were liable for the obligations of the company only to the extent of their own investment, regardless of how large their personal fortunes might be. This protection helped to attract the capital required for costly, long-term projects.

The Boston Associates used the corporate form for all these purposes and for certain new purposes of their own. In their hands, the corporation became a device by which a few able men, through the ownership of only a fraction of the total stock, could direct the activities of many and varied businesses. The corporate form also made it possible for them to reside in Boston while actual operations were conducted in distant mill towns under the supervision of hired professional managers. Since corporate securities could be more easily disposed of than investments in partnerships or single-owner businesses, corporate enterprises also could look forward to a long life, uninterrupted by the death or withdrawal of investors.

The cotton-textile industry became the proving ground for these new business techniques. It was the first mature American industry to be geared not to the individual craftsman but to the machine, to be financed not by the owner alone or by his bank but by the accumulated private savings of numbers of people, and to be managed by hired professionals accountable to capitalists living in the great financial centers.

### The early labor movement

The corporation gave a tremendous impetus to American economic and social progress, but almost from the outset it revealed a seemingly inherent tendency toward harshness in human relations. Before Samuel Slater set up his first mechanized spinning plant in 1791, America had had many "spinning houses" and "spinning schools," the first of which appeared in Jamestown, Virginia, as early as 1646. These schools were opened to provide useful employment for the children of the poor. Slater's factory was modeled on these public institutions, and the children who worked for him were not abused. Many of Slater's imitators, however, proved less charitable. By 1810, few of the little spinning corporations scattered through southern New England retained any aspects of philanthropy.

A more striking deterioration in working and living conditions blighted the factories and factory towns of the Boston Associates and their imitators, especially after scrupulous founders turned direct management over to

231

outsiders whose efficiency was checked in Boston through the medium of financial reports. Here is the way an observer in Lowell described the factory routine there in 1846:

> *The operatives work thirteen hours a day in the summer time, and from daylight to darkness in the winter. At half past four in the morning the factory bell rings, and at five girls must be in the mills. A clerk placed as a watch, observes those who are a few minutes behind the time, and effectual means are taken to stimulate punctuality. This is the morning commencement of the industrial discipline (should we not rather say industrial tyranny?) which is established in these Associations of this moral and Christian community. At seven the girls are allowed thirty minutes for breakfast, and at noon thirty minutes more for dinner, except during the first quarter of the year, when the time is extended to forty-five minutes.*

Some years earlier, in 1840, the reformer Orestes Brownson described the plight of Lowell girls who presumably had gone to work just long enough to accumulate a dowry or to add to the family income until they married:

> *The great mass wear out their health, spirits, and morals without becoming one whit better off than when they commenced labor. The bills of mortality in these factory villages are not striking, we admit, for the poor girls when they can toil no longer go home to die.*

Such conditions became particularly prevalent after the Panic of 1837, when corporate managements cracked down on factory superintendents whose accounts showed too much red ink. But even before that panic, conditions had become so bad in some of the cotton factories that the girls were driven to strike. In February 1834 a thousand or more Lowell girls walked out in protest against a 15 percent wage cut. "One of the leaders," reported the *Boston Transcript,* "mounted a stump, and made a flaming . . . speech on the rights of women and the iniquities of the 'monied aristocracy' which produced a powerful effect on her auditors, and they determined to 'have their way, if they died for it.'" Actually, the girls went back to work in a few days at the reduced wages—all but the leaders, who were discharged.

Other abortive strikes occurred in the 1830s, but the girls in the New England textile mills and the mill workers in other parts of the country lacked unions, funds, leadership, and organizational experience, and their pathetic rebellions almost always ended in failure.

One of the weapons the corporations used against strikers was the law itself. Until the decision of the Massachusetts Supreme Court in the case of *Commonwealth* v. *Hunt* in 1842, strikers were subject to prosecution for criminal conspiracy under the common law. The pretext for such prosecution lay in the idea that all labor combinations were organized to injure some person or persons. Judge Roberts made this point perfectly clear in a famous decision in a Pittsburgh labor trial in 1815:

> *In many cases of conspiracy the means employed have a semblance of being lawful. They are frequently such as would be lawful in an individual. For instance, you have a right to have your boots, your coat, or your hat made by whom you please. . . . But should you combine and confederate with others, to ruin any particular shoemaker, tailor, hatter, or other mechanic, or tradesman by preventing persons from employing him, this would be unlawful and indictable.*

In Judge Roberts's terms labor organizations were illegal conspiracies per se; their mere existence menaced both employers and the workers who did not join up. This remained the prevailing attitude until Chief Justice Lemuel Shaw of the Supreme Judicial Court of Massachusetts ruled in 1842 that labor unions, even though they "may have a tendency to impoverish another, that is, to diminish his gains and profits," might nevertheless "be highly meritorious and public spirited." But even Justice Shaw left a wide opening for employers by declaring that if the objective of labor unions "be carried into effect . . . by falsehood or force, . . . it may be stamped with the character of conspiracy." He permitted the supposition, however, that labor unions as such may be "to say the least, innocent," and granted them legal standing for the first time in American history.

Yet this improvement in the legal climate served chiefly to demonstrate that economic and social conditions, not the law, really underlay the workers' weakness. For a long time, the factory labor force simply remained too small in number to make much headway in an agrarian society that knew little and cared less about the problems of factory life.

Although little progress was made in organizing American industrial workers until the 1930s, the craft unions had a much longer history. The crafts themselves—shoemaking, horseshoeing, carpentry, bricklaying, tailoring—reached far into the past. By the eighteenth century they were carried on by independent artisans who bought their own raw materials, fabricated them for their own customers, and set their own prices. Sometimes they employed journeymen who traveled from farm to farm to make shoes, repair houses and barns, and do other jobs beyond the capacity of the farm family. Below the journeymen ranked young apprentices, whose families contracted them out to artisans for as long as twenty years.

By the beginning of the nineteenth century, improvements in transportation had opened much larger markets to the artisans, some of whom gave up their handwork to become "merchant capitalists"—that is, businessmen who gathered up larger orders than one artisan and a few helpers could fill and who employed artisans and journeymen to work

for them. Others who had never been artisans also entered the different crafts as merchant capitalists. By the 1820s, competition among them had become so keen, they were forced to cut their craftsmen's wages. The craftsmen were further embittered by the loss of their independent status, and complained in addition that their specialized skills were being broken up into simpler tasks too often given to less well-trained workers who further depressed wage rates.

In protest against these conditions the first unions were formed in America. The Philadelphia shoemakers had organized as early as 1792, but not until the middle 1820s did other craftsmen, in defiance of the conspiracy law, turn to united action. In New York, Philadelphia, and other large centers, the craft unions combined in citywide organizations; and in 1834 six of these combinations joined forces in a "National Trades' Union." In the next three years craft union membership rose from 26,000 to 300,000. In these years, the unions conducted at least 175 strikes, many of them called to win improvements in working conditions, not merely to keep them from growing worse. In 1828, the Philadelphia unions organized the American Working Men's party to seek, by political means, such improvements as the ten-hour day for themselves and free public education for their children.

The business collapse of 1837 crushed the early craft-union movement. Some of the crafts, especially those in construction industries or in specialized fields like printing, maintained a semblance of organization even in the worst years; but the crafts subject to rising competition from factory production tended to disappear, along with their unions and merchant capitalists.

## For further reading

Roger Burlingame, *The March of Iron Men* (1938), an admirable social history of American technology before the Civil War, provides an excellent introduction to the subject of this chapter. More conventional, but scholarly and comprehensive, is G. R. Taylor, *The Transportation Revolution 1815–1860*

(1951). Taylor's book is part of a ten-volume *Economic History of the United States,* edited by Henry David and others. Two other volumes of this work are relevant here: C. P. Nettels, *The Emergence of a National Economy 1775-1815* (1962), and P. W. Gates, *The Farmers' Age: Agriculture 1815-1860* (1960). Brief presentations will be found in the early chapters of T. C. Cochran and William Miller, *The Age of Enterprise, A Social History of Industrial America* (1942). D. C. North, *The Economic Growth of the United States 1790-1860* (1961), is a careful appraisal of causes, which should be compared with Stuart Bruchey, *The Roots of American Economic Growth 1607-1861* (1965). For contemporary material on economic aspects, see G. S. Callender, ed., *Selections from the Economic History of the United States 1765-1860* (1909).

Besides Gates, cited above, essential material on northern agriculture will be found in C. H. Danhof, *Change in Agriculture, The Northern United States 1820-1870* (1969). On southern agriculture see L. C. Gray, *History of Agriculture in the Southern United States to 1860* (2 vols., 1933); Stuart Bruchey, ed., *Cotton and the Growth of the American Economy 1790-1860* (1967); and works cited for Chapter Thirteen. On the cotton gin see Jeannette Mirsky and Allan Nevins, *The World of Eli Whitney* (1952).

Herman Melville, *Moby Dick* (1851), is a great American novel that provides much fascinating and authentic whaling lore. For this and related subjects see also S. E. Morison, *The Maritime History of Massachusetts 1783-1860* (1921). H. M. Chittenden, *The American Fur Trade of the Far West* (2 vols., 1902), while dated, remains the best comprehensive account. Bernard DeVoto, *Across the Wide Missouri* (1947), is excellent on the climax and decline of the trade. The best business biography of the main figure in the fur trade is K. W. Porter, *John Jacob Astor* (2 vols., 1931). Besides Morison, above, the following are illuminating on the China trade: K. W. Porter, *The Jacksons and the Lees, Two Generations of Massachusetts Merchants 1765-1844* (2 vols., 1937); and Tyler Dennett, *Americans in Eastern Asia* (1922). On the Santa Fe Trail see Josiah Gregg, *Commerce of the Prairies* (1954 ed.), and Paul Horgan, *The Centuries of Santa Fe* (1956).

L. D. Baldwin, *The Keelboat Age on Western Waters* (1941), is a good introduction to river transportation before the age of steam, which is authoritatively dealt with in L. C. Hunter, *Steamboats on the Western Rivers* (1949). J. A. Durrenberger, *Turnpikes* (1931), is a scholarly work on the toll roads. A popular work on roads, their builders and users is W. C. Langdon, *Everyday Things in American Life 1776-1876* (1941).

Useful older books on the controversy over laissez-faire and public assistance to transportation enterprises include Louis Hartz, *Economic Policy and Democratic Thought, Pennsylvania 1776-1860* (1948); Oscar and M. F. Handlin, *Commonwealth, A Study of the Role of Government in the American Economy, Massachusetts 1774-1861* (1947); and J. N. Primm, *Economic Policy in the Development of a Western State: Missouri 1820-1860* (1954). Carter Goodrich, *Government Promotion of American Canals and Railroads 1800-1890* (1960), reflects a scholar's lifetime study of this subject. See also his "Internal Improvements Reconsidered," in *Journal of Economic History* (June 1970, pp. 289-311), in which he ably reviews the recent literature. Works cited include R. E. Shaw, *Erie Water West: A History of the Erie Canal 1792-1854* (1966); H. N. Scheiber, *The Ohio Canal Era: A Case Study of Government and the Economy 1820-1861* (1968); and M. E. Reed, *New Orleans and the Railroads: The Struggle for Commercial Empire 1830-1860* (1966). For more on railroads, see Chapter Fourteen. Also, vol. II of Joseph Dorfman, *The Economic Mind in American Civilization* (5 vols., 1946-1959).

R. G. Albion, *The Rise of New York Port 1815-1860* (1939), is a brilliant work, which may be supplemented by Albion, *Square Riggers on Schedule* (1938). More modest but illuminating is J. W. Livingood, *The Philadelphia-Baltimore Trade Rivalry 1780-1860* (1947). R. R. Russel, *Economic Aspects of Southern Sectionalism 1840-1861* (1924), ably recounts the slave section's efforts to reclaim the cotton trade.

C. F. Ware, *The Early New England Cotton Manufacture* (1931), presents all phases of America's first modern industry in scholarly fashion. An illuminating special study is Vera Shlakman, *Economic History of a Factory Town* (1935). J. S. Davis, *Essays on the Earlier History of American Corporations* (2 vols., 1917), is authoritative. See also E. M. Dodd, *American Business Corporations until 1860* (1954), and J. W. Cadman, Jr., *The Corporation in New Jersey 1791-1875* (1949). Volume I of V. S. Clark, *History of Manufacturers in the United States* (3 vols., 1928), is very informative on industrial developments. On preindustrial developments, R. M. Tryon, *Household Manufactures in the United States 1640-1880* (1917), is invaluable. The best account of the early labor movement is in vol. I of J. R. Commons and others, *History of Labor in the United States* (4 vols., 1918-1935). On technology and the enterprising spirit, see W. P. Strassman, *Risk and Technological Innovation* (1959); H. J. Habakkuk, *American and British Technology in the 19th Century* (1962); and also such more widely ranging books as Siegfried Giedion, *Mechanization Takes Command* (1948); and Jacques Ellul, *The Technological Society* (1967).

# Democracy and its discontents

—*Business operations! what is business, as you term it, sir,*
*to the affections, to the recollections of ancestry, and to the solemn*
*feelings connected with history and tradition?*
—*Why, sir, in the way of history, one meets with but few incumbrances*
*in this country. . . . A nation is much to be pitied*
*that is weighed down by the past [and] constantly*
*impeded by obstacles that grow out of its recollections.*
*(James Fenimore Cooper, Home As Found, 1838)*

*But I trust that . . . the intelligence pervading the masses, and, above*
*all, the high degree of morality and virtue which distinguishes the American above*
*all other nations . . . will be proof against the temptations*
*of a handful of political sceptics; and that the country . . . selected*
*by Providence for the noblest experiment tried by man, will fulfil its mission*
—*which is not only the civilization of a new world, but the practical*
*establishment of principles which heretofore have only had an ideal existence.*
*(F. J. Grund, The Americans in Their Moral, Social, and Political Relations, 1839)*

*A free press, universal suffrage, elections of perpetual recurrence,*
*multifarious legislation, open courts of justice,*
*numberless voluntary associations—while they change the character of enjoyment,*
*are nevertheless inexhaustible funds of it.*
*(C. J. Ingersoll, "An Oration Delivered . . . July 4, 1832")*

*Our flag, yet flying in advance of the convoy of Nations, is regarded*
*by those who follow, as their light and guide: if shallows,*
*rocks, or mutiny, destroy us, the region of our stranded wreck is one which no*
*political Columbus will dare hereafter to explore.*
*(J. A. Hillhouse, "An Oration . . . in Commemoration of . . . General Lafayette," 1834)*

STUDY FOR "THE STUMP SPEAKER," from the George Caleb Bingham Sketchbook,
1847. (St. Louis Mercantile Library)

"PROCESSION OF VICTUALLERS OF PHILADELPHIA," March 15, 1821, celebrating slaughter of prize cattle; aquatint by Joseph Yeager. (Samuel T. Freeman & Co., Philadelphia)

*Equality of conditions . . .
encourages trade, not directly, by
giving men a taste for
business, but indirectly
by . . . expanding in their minds
a taste for prosperity.
(Alexis De Tocqueville,
Democracy in America, 1835)*

*Stay, mortal, stay! nor heedless thus
Thy sure destruction seal;
Within that cup there lurks a curse.
Which all who drink shall feel.
("One Glass More"
in The Mountain Minstrel, 1847)*

"ONE GLASS MORE" at the elegant bar—Temperance, not Prohibition, drawn on stone by A. Fay, 1854. (The New-York Historical Society, New York City)

BINGHAM, "THE COUNTY ELECTION," 1852 (The Boatmen's National Bank of St. Louis)

*How should freemen spend
their time, but looking after their
government, and watching that
them fellows as we gives offices to,
does their duty,
and give themselves no airs.
(Quoted by Mrs. Frances Trollope, in
Domestic Manners of the Americans,
1832)*

*Had America every attraction under
heaven that nature and social enjoyment
can offer, this electioneering
madness would make me
fly it in disgust. It engrosses every
conversation, it irritates
every temper, it substitutes party spirit
for personal esteem.
(Mrs. Frances Trollope,
Domestic Manners of the Americans,
1832)*

"SINCE ROWDYISM RULES THE DAY, I cannot vote with safety to my person," says gentleman on left at riotous election scene: 1844 election caricature. (The New-York Historical Society, New York City)

"STORMING OF THE CASTLE OF CHAPULTEPEC, September 13, 1847," drawn for *The Pictorial Brother Jonathan* in 1848. (The New-York Historical Society, New York City)

*Go, blind worm, go,*
*Behold the famous States*
*Harrying Mexico*
*With rifle and with knife!*
*(R. W. Emerson,*
*"Ode, Inscribed to W. H. Channing,"*
*1847)*

*We need never have white slaves*
*in the South,*
*because we have black ones.*
*Our citizens, like those of Rome*
*and Athens, are a privileged class.*
*(George F. Fitzhugh,*
*Sociology for the South, 1854)*

SLAVE AUCTION, Richmond market, 1856. (Schomburg Collection, New York Public Library)

When two steamboats
happen to get alongside each other,
the passengers will encourage
the captains to run a race. . . .
The races are the causes
of most of the explosions, and yet
they are still constantly
taking place.
*(F. A. von Gerstner,
Report From the United States
of North America, 1839)*

Another destructive railroad
"accident" at Burlington, N.J.;
the murder in this case chargeable
to the directors, who could not
spare from their immense receipts
the cost of a double track,
and to the conductor
of the demolished train.
*(The Diary of George Templeton Strong,
August 1855)*

In America, the country itself
is ever on the change, and in another
half century those who view
this portrait of the Mississippi
will not be able to recognize
one twentieth part of its
details. Where the forest now
overshadows the earth, and affords
shelter to the wild beasts, corn fields,
orchards, towns, and villages,
will give a new face to the scene . . .
*(John Rowson Smith,
Description of Banvard; Panorama
of the Mississippi River, 1847)*

(Top) "MIDNIGHT RACE ON THE MISSISSIPPI," by Currier and Ives. (Prints Division, New York Public Library)

(Middle) "MURDER" ON CAMDEN AND AMBOY RAILROAD, August 29, 1855, drawn on the spot immediately after the accident; lithograph by John Collins. (Library of Congress)

(Bottom) "WESTWARD THE COURSE OF EMPIRE TAKES ITS WAY," drawn by C. Inger after fresco in Capitol in Washington by Emanuel Leutze, 1860. (Courtesy Kenneth M. Newman, Old Print Shop, New York City)

# GENERAL JACKSON AND PRESIDENTIAL POWER

When James Monroe left the White House in 1825, the age of the Founding Fathers had clearly ended. The new nation at last had won that standing and respect abroad which gave her the security she needed to direct the energies of her people toward the immeasurable opportunities beckoning at home. These opportunities were grasped with a will in all parts of the country; their rewards had already fostered that strong leveling tendency which was to culminate in broad democratic reform while they enlarged hemispheric ambitions.

The Jeffersonians, the levelers and expansionists of the early national period, built their power by urging "the people," especially the people who had won a stake in the land, to vote. The philosophy that goes by the name of Jeffersonian Democracy assumed that nature had endowed the common man, the yeoman farmer, with enough good sense to vote for those among his betters who manifestly had his best interests in view. While the so-called first party system developed out of the antagonism of the Jeffersonian Republicans to the Anglophile Federalists, Republican as well as Federalist deference to the gentry in this period made it preeminently one of "personal faction" political organization, a characteristic that itself grew more pronounced as the Federalist party declined and left the field to contentious Republican aspirants.

In the new age, governed by the philosophy called Jacksonian Democracy, one's "betters" in the older states seemed to have retreated to the backwaters of power or to have been swallowed up in the strong surge toward equality, which open economic opportunity had favored. The Jacksonians, so-called, in these as in the newer states of the West, urged the people to seek office as well as to vote. Careers in politics, as in business and the professions as well as on the land, were now to be opened to talent no matter how coarse the garb it might be clothed in.

Few men were more coarsely clothed than "Old Hickory" himself. When friends in Tennessee hinted to the general early in the 1820s that he was "by no means safe from the presidency in 1824," he replied: "No, sir, I know what I am fit for. I can command a body of men in a rough way; but I am not fit to be President." But after the people elected him to the highest office in 1828, he conceded they knew a good man when they saw one.

Jackson's heroic past became irresistible to the new breed of career politicians, who, as one of them put it in 1823, "always bow to a 'rising sun,' and stand prepared to dance round the 'golden calf.' " Once in office, moreover, the general's high and mighty posture only embellished his reputation with the populace. Congress, the Supreme Court, the National Bank; the Indians, the British, and the French; the "interests" of the North, the "nullifiers" of the South, the "internal improve-

ments" men of the West—all were to feel the sting of his wrath.

Jackson's zeal in searching out enemies of the people and his rhetoric in demolishing them helped the politicians keep their idol in the public eye and consolidate the Democratic party. Unfortunately for them, the President also helped unite his opponents who soon borrowed Democratic methods to defeat Jackson's handpicked heir. In the election of 1840, when the Whigs aligned Jackson's enemies in all sections behind another old hero, General William Henry Harrison, the full strength of "Jacksonian Democracy" for the first time really showed itself at the polls.

The Whigs very name reflected their determination to associate this party of the successful business class with the defenders of liberty and democracy in the Revolution. By transcending personal and sectional loyalties in selecting their standard-bearer, they strengthened the national character of the second two-party system. By extending the reach of the presidency, Jackson himself had given this system a lasting national focus, which also helped mitigate for a time the irreconcilable sectional antagonisms.

## I  Rise of the common man

### The democratic impulse

On July 4, 1826, the fiftieth anniversary of the Declaration of Independence, the Jacksonian historian-to-be, young George

Bancroft of Massachusetts, said in a commemorative address:

*We hold it best that the laws should favor the diffusion of property and its acquisition, not the concen-*

Library of Congress

*"Old Hickory" in 1829,
in engraving by J. B. Longacre
from this artist's drawing from life.*

*tration of it in the hands of the few to the impoverish-
ment of the many. We give the power to the many in
the hope and to the end, that they may use it for their
own benefit.*

At the time Bancroft spoke, a greater proportion of American citizens than ever before
had acquired the right to vote, and to vote for
candidates named by themselves. Between
1816 and 1821, six new states (all but Maine
in the West or Southwest) entered the Union
with constitutions that required no property
qualifications for voting. But it was the older
states, not those on the then moving frontier,
that had set the precedent and offered the
example.

The Vermont constitution of 1777, although
containing other restrictive conditions, was the
first explicitly to free the right to vote from
property-holding or taxpaying qualifications,
and this constitution remained intact when
Vermont entered the Union in 1791. Kentucky in 1799, New Jersey in 1807, Maryland
in 1810, Connecticut in 1818, then successively liberalized the franchise. Connecticut became a model for such northern states as
Maine, Massachusetts, and New York. As the
New York *National Advocate* said in August
1821, "In Connecticut they disarmed the poorer classes by taking them into the body politic." New York followed suit that year (with
further liberalizing constitutional amendments
in 1826), after Maine and Massachusetts had
acted in 1819 and 1820.

The South, generally, lagged behind the
North and the West, and Virginia, despite the
Jeffersonian tradition, lagged behind the rest
of the South. In 1852 she became the last state
in the Union to surrender the property test.
Only a few years earlier, Louisiana significantly broadened the franchise by reducing her
heavy taxpaying qualification. Elsewhere in
the slave states, prompted in large part by the
argument of Senator Morgan of Virginia, the
more liberal example of Maryland already had
been followed. "We ought," said Senator
Morgan in 1829, "to spread wide the foundation of our government, that all white men
have a direct interest in its protection." What
Morgan meant specifically was protection
against slave revolts.

Besides Virginia and Louisiana, the only
state that did not achieve virtual white male
suffrage by 1840 was Rhode Island. Here, the
state government still functioned under the
colonial charter of 1663 according to which
freeholders alone, now making up less than
half of the adult males in the state, could vote.
When the state government in 1841 rejected a
proposed new constitution liberalizing the
franchise, the reformers elected a governor of
their own, Thomas W. Dorr. The official regime responded by declaring the Dorr party in
rebellion, imposing martial law, and calling
out the militia. Both sides then appealed to
President John Tyler, who felt obliged under

the United States Constitution (Art. IV, Sec. 4) to promise "protection" to the regular government "against domestic violence." After a Dorrite assault on the state arsenal failed (the extent of the "Dorr War"), Dorr surrendered. In 1844 he was tried and sentenced to life imprisonment, but the next year his sentence was withdrawn. In 1843, meanwhile, the official regime saw the light and accepted a new constitution liberalizing the franchise.

The democratic spirit of the country failed to carry over to one significant class of the population—the free blacks. As late as 1820, free Negroes were permitted by law to vote equally with whites in northern New England, in New York and Pennsylvania, and even in such southern states as Tennessee and North Carolina. This right, however, usually had arisen only from omissions in the law and was subject to every abuse until the law itself was tightened. As a delegate to the Pennsylvania constitutional convention of 1837 said on his way to the assemblage that would disfranchise the free blacks, "the people of this state are for continuing this commonwealth, what it always has been, a political community of white persons." By then, the free Negro's right to vote survived only in New England north of Connecticut. In Connecticut, after 1818, past black voters could continue to vote, but newly freed Negroes were disfranchised. In the other states where they once enjoyed the franchise free Negroes had been deprived of it, usually by the very same article which for the first time provided virtually full manhood suffrage for whites. No state entering the Union between 1819 and the Civil War permitted free blacks to vote.

Loss of the franchise, moreover, was only one of the lengthening list of free Negro disabilities in the free as in the slave states. Consigned to miserable alley slums, confined by curfews, beyond the pale of the judicial and educational systems, barred from all but the most menial urban occupations and from the land as well, he was "cast upon the world," as an Oregonian said even of his own distant commonwealth in the 1850s, "with no defense; his life, liberty, his property, his all, are dependent on the caprice, the passion, and the inveterate prejudices of not only the community at large but of every felon who may happen to cover an inhuman heart with a white face." By then, many western states would not even allow free blacks in.

For the "political community of white persons," on the other hand, even more significant perhaps than the legal extension of the suffrage was the heightened interest of the common man in exercising that right on the national level. While proportions running up to 70 percent of the electorate had voted earlier in hot local contests, presidential elections until 1828 seemed to have left most voters cold. Even in 1824, when Jackson himself first was a candidate, only 356,000 votes were counted, a mere 27 percent of those eligible, compared with 1,155,000 (or 56 percent) in 1828. In the following twenty years the number going to the polls rose by 250 percent, far more than the rise of those who had been enfranchised.

One reason for the voters' new interest was the gradual emergence of a new two-party system after 1824 and sharper party differences on issues. Another was the voters' enlarged participation in actually naming the candidates.

The old system of nominating presidential candidates had been perfected by the "caucus," or meeting, of Republican congressmen in Washington, a system that kept the inner clique in power. Its success was prolonged by the availability of eminent members of the Virginia dynasty, who triumphed more or less easily over opponents put forward by scattered personal factions in key states. Rising politicians, however, hated "king caucus," and, as we have seen (p. 194), even opposed Jefferson over Madison's nomination in 1808. The first genuine break in the caucus system came in 1824 when sectionalism at last made it impossible for the Republicans to smooth over their differences, and four major candidates solicited electoral support. Credit for initiating the modern method of nominating candidates by means of national conventions made up of delegates "fresh from the

243

people" goes to a short-lived minor party, the Anti-Masons, who held the first such convention in 1831. The new major parties, Democrats and Whigs, adopted the innovation in time for the election of 1832.

Still another institution gave way before the demand to bring government closer to the people. This was the old system under which, in most states, presidential electors had been chosen by the state legislatures. By 1828, every state but Delaware and South Carolina had substituted for this system the popular election of members of the electoral college, thereby giving a powerful impetus to popular participation and theatrical innovations in the presidential canvass. Jackson, as he often reminded his opponents, thus became the first President who could claim to have been elected directly by the voters, a claim not altogether justified since those named by the people to the electoral college retained personal discretion on just how they would cast their ballots.

Governors also began to be popularly elected, and property qualifications for that office and others were swept away. Finally, by the 1840s, state judges were being elected rather than appointed—an innovation that would have startled even the more democratic of the Founding Fathers.

The Democratic impulse in the Jacksonian era did not, of course, bring many backwoodsmen in coonskin caps to Congress, nor many plain lumberjacks, fishermen, journeymen, and even farmers to high political office. A man still needed a decided standing in his community, a distinct level of achievement, or at least a certain eloquence, to aspire to and win preferment. Jackson himself, of course, had shed most of his rough ways and rough companions on the way to the pinnacle. Certain writers have attempted to discredit the democratic movement on this account, and on account of the disfranchisement of black voters, as more form than substance. Yet white Americans gained a greater degree of participation in public decisions than any other people in the world, a success self-serving elites might find dangerous and deplore, yet one that placed certain healthy constraints upon them.

## Jackson's first candidacy

Tennessee, admitted to the Union in 1796, was one state in which party politics had never impinged on the personal-faction domination of a few rich and powerful men, beginning with John Sevier. In the early 1820s the ruling clique long dominated by John Overton, perhaps the richest man in the state, found itself challenged; and Overton, with two friends, Senator John Henry Eaton and William B. Lewis, Eaton's one-time brother-in-law and Andrew Jackson's neighbor at the Hermitage, sought ways to retrieve their position. The best way was to uncover a strong presidential candidate, and there proved to be none stronger, although they did not realize it at the time, than the Hero of New Orleans, most recently in the public eye via his characteristic violent forays in Florida.

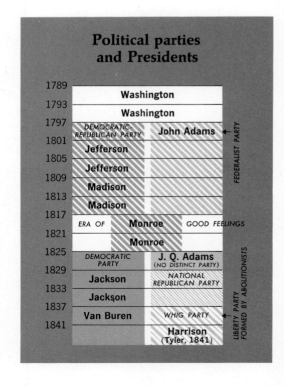

**Political parties and Presidents**

|  | | |
|---|---|---|
| 1789 | **Washington** | |
| 1793 | **Washington** | |
| 1797 | DEMOCRATIC-REPUBLICAN PARTY | **John Adams** |
| 1801 | **Jefferson** | |
| 1805 | **Jefferson** | |
| 1809 | **Madison** | |
| 1813 | **Madison** | |
| 1817 | ERA OF | **Monroe** GOOD FEELINGS |
| 1821 | | **Monroe** |
| 1825 | DEMOCRATIC PARTY | **J. Q. Adams** (NO DISTINCT PARTY) |
| 1829 | **Jackson** | NATIONAL REPUBLICAN PARTY |
| 1833 | **Jackson** | |
| 1837 | **Van Buren** | WHIG PARTY |
| 1841 | **Harrison** (Tyler, 1841) | |

FEDERALIST PARTY

LIBERTY PARTY FORMED BY ABOLITIONISTS

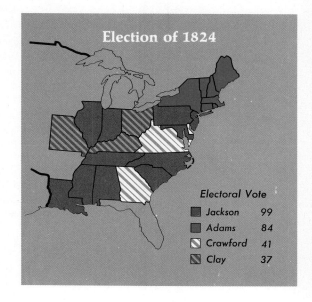

Election of 1824

Electoral Vote

| | | |
|---|---|---|
| ■ | Jackson | 99 |
| ■ | Adams | 84 |
| ▨ | Crawford | 41 |
| ▨ | Clay | 37 |

As early as July 1822, the Overton camp had seen to the placing of this item in the *Nashville Whig:*

*GREAT RACING !!! ... The prize to be run for is the Presidential Chair.... There have already four states sent their nags in. Why not Tennessee put in her stud? and if so, let it be called* Old Hickory.

A day or two later, Tennessee's lower house, adequately primed, unanimously endorsed the general, and the campaign gained further momentum when the state legislature in 1823 elected Jackson to the United States Senate.

Like virtually everyone else's in frontier Tennessee, Jackson's party affiliation was Jeffersonian. But among the Jeffersonians, his law practice and land speculations as well as his personal bent placed him on the side of the "land barons" or "nabobs," and against the "leather shirts." Jackson shared with other westerners the willingness to judge men by their attainments, not by their social backgrounds. If this helped his backers to present him as the champion of the common man, well and good.

Jackson's opponents in 1824 were William H. Crawford of Georgia, the caucus candidate, who suffered a stroke during the campaign and was not a serious contender; Henry Clay, now Speaker of the House; and Secretary of State John Quincy Adams, of whom Jackson had written when his own boom began, "I am told Mr. Adams is at present the strongest in the state."

Clay and Adams, although far apart in origins and temperament, both subscribed to Clay's celebrated "American System." Clay pictured an industrial East providing a growing home market for southern cotton and western grain and meat, and an agricultural West and South providing an expanding market for eastern factory goods. For the East he would supply protective tariffs; for the West and South, "internal improvements" such as canals and railroads to reduce transportation costs. Transactions between the sections were

to be facilitated by a stable credit system underwritten by a national bank. This plan, said Clay, would "place the confederacy upon the most solid of all foundations, [that] of common interest."

Jackson's national policies were less clear, even to himself. When pressed he said he was for a "judicious" tariff, which only caused Henry Clay to explode, "Well, by —, I am in favor of an injudicious tariff!" Yet the Hero of New Orleans did not disappoint the politicians. In the election of 1824 he won 153,500 popular votes to Adams's 108,700, Clay's 47,100, and Crawford's 46,600. In the electoral college, however, his 99 votes fell considerably short of the required majority, and the contest was thrown into the House of Representatives. Here Clay, having polled the lowest *electoral* total, was eliminated under the terms of the Twelfth Amendment. Of the top three, Crawford fell away for health reasons, leaving the contest to Jackson and Adams. Clay, a power in the House, had no love for Jackson. "I cannot believe," he said, "that killing 2500 Englishmen at New Orleans qualifies [him] for the various difficult and complicated duties of the Chief Magistracy." After a private talk with Adams, Clay swung his supporters to the Yankee. Thanks largely to Clay's influence, Adams was elected.

One of Adam's first presidential acts was to name Clay his successor as Secretary of State, tantamount, in the opinion of the age, to naming him as his successor as Commander-in-Chief. The Jackson men lost little time in charging that a "corrupt bargain" had been made at the Clay-Adams talk. Even had a bargain been made, there need have been nothing corrupt about it between men so sympathetic to one another's program. But "bargain and corruption" became the Jacksonians' slogan for the 1828 campaign, which they opened as soon as they learned of their defeat in 1824.

## John Quincy Adams in office

The alleged "deal" was not the only issue that haunted Adams in the White House. A sensitive and high-minded man, he regretted having to accept the presidency with, as he said, "perhaps two-thirds of the whole people adverse to the actual result." Adams, nevertheless, was not to be deterred by popular symptoms from launching a program he considered right for the country. In his first annual message to Congress he displayed both his stubborn courage and his political ineptitude by making a sweeping argument for a strong national government vigorous in the use of its powers for national improvements directed from the top. Warned by Henry Clay and all but one of the rest of his Cabinet that, at a time when state-rights feelings were rising and sectional jealousies were strong, it was all but suicidal for a President—and a minority President at that—to launch upon such a course, Adams at least conceded that his program was a "perilous experiment." Congress under the Constitution, Adams argued in his message, had the power to "provide for the common defense and general welfare." The "common defense" seemed a clear enough obligation; the "general welfare" a remarkably elastic one. Adams proposed to stretch the latter to justify establishing a national university, financing scientific expeditions, building astronomical observatories, reforming the patent system, and developing a national transportation system. To refrain from exercising the general-welfare clause in

the grand manner, he said, would be "treachery to the most sacred of trusts." Adams's further suggestion that it would be shameful for Congress to be "palsied by the will of our constituents" was simply to seal the doom of his experiment from the outset.

A dozen years later, Adams explained that "the great effort of my administration" was to apply "all the superfluous revenue of the Union into internal improvement."

*With this system in ten years from this day the surface of the whole Union would have been checkered over with railroads and canals. It may still be done half a century later and with the limping gait of State legislature and private adventure. I would have done it in the administration of the affairs of the nation.*

Adams continued this explanation with an analysis of the defeat of his program:

*When I came to the Presidency this principle of internal improvement was swelling the tide of public prosperity, till the Sable Genius of the South saw the signs of his own inevitable downfall in the unparalleled progress of the general welfare in the North, and fell to cursing the tariff and internal improvement, and raised the standard of free trade, nullification, and state rights.*

In fact, many in the Middle states and the Midwest, with their own "mass of local jealousies," joined with the South in rejecting Adams's proposals. At the same time, many self-made men (Clay first coined this term to describe the rising manufacturers of Kentucky) were ranged on Adams's side.

Adams's comprehensive program for centralized economic and cultural development, and his failure to push it through, encouraged his state-rights opponents everywhere to mobilize their own machines behind the pleasingly vague and perfectly popular Jackson. Adams's additional setbacks in Indian and foreign relations made their task all the easier. The President's efforts to preserve the lands of the Creek and Cherokee Indians in Georgia, against the violent resistance of the state, its speculators, and its potential frontier settlers, proved most humiliating in their outcome. This confrontation led to the case of *Worcester* v. *Georgia* (1832), which was to provide the occasion for Jackson's major victory over the Supreme Court.

Adams was no more successful in diplomacy. When the United States was invited in 1826 to attend a congress of Latin-American republics in Panama to discuss hemispheric questions, in his eagerness to accept the President tactlessly named delegates without first consulting the Senate. His eagerness arose from his hope to lay the foundations there for the elimination of Spain from Cuba and the island's ultimate acquisition by his own country. His Senate enemies, however, led by Martin Van Buren of New York and John Randolph of Virginia, after attacking the Latin Americans as "an ignorant and vicious people," held up appropriations for the delegates' expenses, and none ever reached Panama.

A more discouraging blow to national prestige was Adams's failure, in negotiations with Foreign Secretary George Canning, to get the British to permit American ships, at long last, to engage in direct trade with their West Indian islands. Canning, in fact, would end up imposing even more drastic restraints on American commerce.

### Jackson's election

By the time of the congressional elections of 1826 Adams's program had gained for his followers the name of National Republicans, while his opponents became known as the Democratic Republicans, designations that helped clarify national party allegiances. In these elections, for the first time in the history of the country, as Adams himself ruefully acknowledged, but far from the last, a President lost his majority in Congress after two years in office.

On convening in December 1827 under Jacksonian leadership, the newly elected legislature made its single purpose the advancement of the general's presidential prospects in 1828. When the Jacksonians showed their mettle by winning the Speakership of the House, Senator John Tyler of Virginia observed, "the opposition party constitutes the *administration*. Upon it rests the responsibility of all legislative measures." Even Adams's Vice-President, Calhoun, although still a nationalist, went over to the Jacksonians. On agreeing to become their vice-presidential candidate, Calhoun very likely expected the 61-year-old Jackson not to run for a second term and to leave the succession to him.

The Jacksonian strategy was to woo support in all key or questionable states by means of legislative handouts. Beyond that, the Jacksonian press so blackened Adams's name that this austere Yankee intellectual was made to seem "a very compost of European vices" and unfit for high office. Such attacks were continued during the 1828 campaign itself, when Jackson's supporters also introduced a rough-and-tumble carnival spirit into the presidential contest that persisted in later years. They paraded with hickory sticks to symbolize the toughness of Old Hickory, and brandished hickory brooms to suggest the need for sweeping the rascals out.

Adams condemned the resort to abusive smears, but he had backers who outdid the Jackson men in scurrility. They went so far as to brand Jackson an adulterer on a trivial technicality over his wife's divorce from her former husband almost forty years earlier. Mrs. Jackson suffered intensely from such publicity, and when she died shortly after the election, Jackson never forgave "those vile wretches who have slandered her" and, in his opinion, killed her.

Jackson's efforts to deal with issues in the campaign probably cost him more votes than his opponents' tactics. The principal issue was the protective tariff on manufactured goods that Congress had adopted in 1824. This act gained the support of the industrial middle states and the Old Northwest, which continued to look to eastern cities for markets for its agricultural surplus. New England, with big

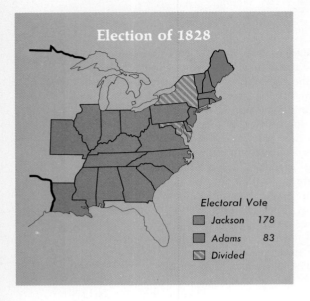

Election of 1828

Electoral Vote
Jackson 178
Adams 83
Divided

Because it raised the general level of the duties, southerners branded the Tariff of 1828 "the tariff of abominations." But because it failed to protect woolen manufactures while it raised duties on raw wool and other raw materials, the Tariff of 1828 also distressed certain northern industrialists. By embracing the principle of protection, Jacksonians may have sought support among manufacturers in the forthcoming elections; but by writing a bill which manufacturers might help defeat, they may also have hoped for southern backing. If such was their plan it failed, for the bill passed, abominations and all.

With the help of large grants of federal lands made by his lieutenants in Congress to politically doubtful states, Jackson survived the backfiring of the tariff scheme. As the Hero of New Orleans, the righteous victim of the Adams-Clay "corrupt bargain," the most visible old soldier in the country for four solid years, he polled 647,000 votes. The surprise, if any, was that Adams, with 508,000 votes, was far from routed. In the electoral college Jackson won, 178 to 83. Despite the tariff catastrophe he carried the entire South. Only New England, Delaware, and New Jersey voted against him.

manufacturers of her own, yet still heavily committed to commerce, had split on the measure. The cotton South, in turn, which had surrendered its hopes for manufacturing, overwhelmingly opposed it. From this alignment Jackson's lieutenants hoped to make more political hay. Their means was the Tariff of 1828, whose object, as John Randolph said, was to encourage "manufactures of no sort but the manufacture of a President of the United States."

## II  Old Hickory in the White House

### The head of the government

Jackson's inauguration attracted to Washington an immense crowd which seemed to think, as Daniel Webster said, that "the country is rescued from some dreadful danger." The people surged through the still unpaved streets and pressed into the White House as if to make themselves equally at home as their hero.

In the White House the new chief was busily engaged with his friends in naming the official functionaries of his administration. Martin Van Buren emerged as Secretary of State. John McLean of Ohio, Adams's Jacksonian Postmaster-General, was retained in his post and the post itself soon was raised to Cabinet level. One disappointed big fish said of the rest of the Cabinet that it reflected "The Millennium of the Minnows." But Jackson's principal advisers, besides Van Buren, were in his private, not his public, Cabinet.

In addition to William B. Lewis and Andrew Jackson Donelson, the young nephew of the

President's wife, whom he had raised, Jackson's "Kitchen Cabinet" numbered such trusted western newspaper editors as Duff Green, Francis Preston Blair, and Amos Kendall, a late convert. Whatever these men or Jackson may have thought about the urgent new issues in national politics—the tariff, internal improvements, the bank, land and Indian policy—they all shared Old Hickory's feeling about the presidency. Jackson's enemies wondered whether the arbitrary old general would turn out to be a tyrant, whether republican government was safe in his hands. Initially National Republicans, such men eventually came together as Whigs in defiance of "King Andrew I." Jackson did not, in fact, become a tyrant. But the first principle of his two administrations was the congenial one of executive supremacy: The President alone, elected by all the people, was the chief instrument of their will, as interpreted by himself.

Jackson's policy toward the executive civil service was consistent with his independent view of his high office. The President shocked the Adams men by discharging about 900 jobholders from among the 10,000 he found on the payroll. Actually, his party chieftains, having made many commitments in two campaigns, wanted many more heads to roll, many more places to fill; but Jackson restrained them. The Adams press made a great noise about the new "reign of terror," and the grim "purge" that was bloodying Washington's streets; but in the long run it was the President's gratuitous defense of the "spoils system," rather than the particular replacements, that so firmly associated his name with it. Earlier Presidents had removed opposition partisans from office without raising many eyebrows. Jackson was the first to make the "spoils system" seem a social and moral as well as a political "reform."

The political aspect Jackson covered in his inaugural address. Conveniently closing his eyes to the deals made by his own promoters, he noted as "inscribed" by the recent election, "in characters too legible to be overlooked,

the task of *reform*, which will require particularly the correction of those abuses that have brought the patronage of the Federal Government into conflict with the freedom of elections."

The social aspect Jackson dealt with in his first annual message to Congress in December 1829. In this message he proposed "a general extension of the law [passed in 1820] which

**249**

In the War of 1812, Jackson's soldiers named him Old Hickory after "the toughest thing they could think of." This cartoon, used against him in the 1828 campaign, seems to document the observation of one of his friends, when an opponent expressed doubt over a threat by Jackson: "I tell you, . . . when Jackson begins to talk about hanging, they can begin to look for the ropes."

*"Jackson is to be President, and you will be HANGED."*

limits appointments to four years," thereby furthering "that rotation which constitutes a leading principle in the republican creed, giving healthful action to the system." Such a law, he continued, in a style that was to become characteristic of his presidential pronouncements, would nullify the prevailing idea that "office is . . . a species of property, and government . . . a means of promoting individual interests, . . . an engine for the support of the few at the expense of the many." Jackson was ready to exclude judges, Cabinet officers, and diplomats "of the highest rank" from this egalitarian rule. Otherwise, "the duties of public offices" are "plain and simple," and plain and simple men could best perform them in the people's interest.

The moral aspect Jackson dealt with in his "Outline of Principles," according to which his heads of departments were to examine the "moral habits" of incumbents and to fire those lax in "private or public relations."

The four-year law Jackson urged was not enacted; but he and his successors did so well without it in distributing "the loaves and fishes" to loyal party workers that the reform of Jackson's "reforms" eventually became the leading issue in American politics.

## "The legitimate sphere of State sovereignties"

In his relations with Congress and the courts the new Chief Executive proved no less aggressive than in his attitude toward the "unfaithful" officeholders he inherited.

Earlier Presidents had been largely content to administer the laws passed by Congress. But Jackson grasped the constitutional power given the executive to participate in making (or better, unmaking) the law as well as executing it. In his two terms Jackson vetoed more legislation than all former Presidents together. This would appear a remarkable record for one so openly attached to popular government; but Jackson, especially after losing the election of 1824 in the House, had come to regard Congress, in his usual vein, as the home of "aristocratical establishments" like the national bank, and his own office as the only popular bulwark against such "inter-

ests" as the new industrialists. In his inaugural address he promised that, "in administering the laws of Congress, I shall keep steadily in view the limitations as well as the extent of the Executive power." He did not necessarily mean the limitations of his own power, only the limitations on Congress in requiring the Executive to do what he did not wish to do. Jackson's vetoes usually were based on the specific constitutional point of unwarranted congressional invasions of state rights.

One of Jackson's most famous vetoes killed the Maysville Bill of 1830, which would have required the federal government to subscribe to the stock of a private corporation promoted to build an "internal improvement" in Clay's state of Kentucky. Because the Maysville road would lie wholly within a single state, Jackson's stand was easier to take. He knew also that he would be strongly supported in such states as New York and Pennsylvania which had helped assure his election victory and which, having developed transportation systems at their own expense, were determined to keep the federal government from helping to construct competing systems farther west. He could expect support, too, from the South Atlantic states, increasingly committed to slavery and hence to the principle of state rights, the strongest constitutional bastion of slavery. These states were also increasingly opposed to protective tariffs, which supplied the bulk of federal funds for internal improvements.

Jackson, in his two administrations, approved unprecedented appropriations for river and harbor improvement bills and similar pork-barrel legislation sponsored by worthy Democrats in compensation for local election support. On the basis of this record a case has been made for the old general's genuine sympathy for federal aid to internal improvements of a national character and hence for the exceptional nature of the Maysville veto, influenced, it is said, by strategic party considerations. But Jackson was eternally at pains to disavow any such interpretation and to make it clear that he believed federal aid to internal improvements of any sort an unconstitutional invasion of state prerogatives.

In his first annual message, President Jackson told Congress that "the mode . . . hitherto adopted" for the "improvement of inland navigation and the construction of highways . . . has been deprecated as an infraction of the Constitution." He went on to propose, "that the most safe, just, and federal disposition which could be made of the surplus revenue would be its apportionment among the several states." He then proceeded to draw the general moral:

*The great mass of legislation relating to our internal affairs was intended to be left where the Federal Convention found it—in the State governments. Nothing is clearer, in my view, than that we are chiefly indebted for the success of the Constitution under which we are now acting to the watchful and auxiliary operation of the State authorities. This is not the reflection of a day, but belongs to the most deeply rooted convictions of my mind. I can not, therefore, too strongly or too earnestly, for my own sense of its importance, warn you against all encroachments upon the legitimate sphere of State sovereignties.*

In his Maysville veto message, Jackson reminded Congress that "the act which I am called upon to consider has, therefore, been passed with a knowledge of my views on this question." Such disrespect was intolerable to Old Hickory, and the veto stuck.

In asserting his independence of the Supreme Court also, Jackson put states rights first. His most famous stand against the Court came in 1832, following John Marshall's decision in *Worcester* v. *Georgia,* concerning Georgia's claims to sovereignty over Cherokee lands.

In 1803, as we have seen (p. 189), after Georgia ceded her western lands to the United States, the federal government agreed to quiet Creek and Cherokee title to the region. Federal action, however, was slow; and as cotton growing spread in the state, the planters' patience ran out. The planters had the full sym-

pathy of Georgia's militant governor, George M. Troup, who in 1826 ordered a state survey of Creek lands with an eye to their prompt sale and settlement. When President Adams threatened to halt the survey with federal forces, Governor Troup said he would resist force with force. Civil war was averted only by the Creeks' capitulation to the inevitable and their decision to move beyond the Mississippi.

The Cherokees, like the Creeks, had embraced the white man's ways, set up farms and factories, erected schools, and published a newspaper. In 1827, they decided to form an independent state on the American model. They also adopted a constitution under which this state would be governed. Georgia responded by nullifying all federal Indian laws and ordering the forcible seizure of Cherokee lands. When her courts next tried and convicted a Cherokee of murder, the Supreme Court of the United States ordered the conviction set aside; but Governor Troup and the state legislature ignored the federal government's "interference" and executed the prisoner. By then, Jackson had become President; and it was well known in Georgia, as elsewhere, that his concern for the red men was as cold as his sympathy for the planters was warm.

Unlike Adams, Jackson did nothing to assert federal authority over Georgia in Indian affairs. The Cherokees, however, did have friends who sought an injunction in the Supreme Court forbidding the extension of Georgia law over Indian residents and Georgia's seizure of Indian lands. In 1831, John Marshall, in the case of *Cherokee Nation* v. *Georgia,* denied the long-standing rule that the Indians were tantamount to "foreign nations" with whom the United States made treaties which federal courts were empowered to enforce. The Indians, he said, were "domestic dependent nations," who could not sue in United States courts. He denied the injunction, but he asserted, nevertheless, that the United States alone, and no single state, had sovereignty over the red men and over the disposition of their lands.

In 1832, Marshall had an opportunity to strengthen this opinion in the case of *Worces-*

The Virginia Museum of Fine Arts, Glasgow Fund, 1956

*John Marshall in 1834*
*in the Rembrandt Peale portrait.*

ter v. *Georgia.* One Samuel Worcester had been convicted by Georgia for occupying Cherokee land without having first obtained a state license to do so. Marshall reversed the conviction and went on to say that the Cherokee nation was a legitimate political community, with clearly defined territories, where "the laws of Georgia can have no force, and which the citizens of Georgia have no right to enter" without Cherokee consent. Georgia herself boycotted the Court's proceedings. It was after this case that Jackson is reported to have exclaimed, "John Marshall has made his decision, now let him enforce it."

Unfortunately for the Cherokees, the Jacksonian House of Representatives tabled the enforcement order introduced to restrain Georgia from evicting the Indians. This meant that no federal troops would be made avail-

able to support Marshall's decision, and the spoliation of the Indian lands continued. By 1835, only a remnant of red men still retained their lands, and after the subjugation of the Florida Seminoles (1835–1842) millions of fertile acres were thrown open to white occupation. The Indians meanwhile made their trek westward over what became known, and rightly so, as the "trail of tears." A fourth or more of the red men died on the journey; officials overseeing them robbed them of their funds; what they had left went for burial rites. Of the Cherokee removal in particular, Emerson cried out that "such a dereliction of all faith and virtue, such a denial of justice, and such deafness to screams for mercy were never heard of in time of peace . . . since the earth was made."

### The Webster-Hayne debate

While the head of the government in the White House was asserting his leadership of the whole nation and of all the people, the heads of the sections in Congress were clarifying their differences and sharpening their defenses. Many issues divided the slave from the free states, and the free West from the free East. And if agreements like the Missouri Compromise of 1820 from time to time cemented over sectional breaches, new developments in the rapidly expanding country broke them open again. Two of the most persistently disruptive issues were public land policies and protective tariffs, and the Webster-Hayne debate in winter of 1830 plumbed the sectional depths of both.

For a generation, pioneers had pressed for cheap government land and for protection of squatters who staked out such land before it was surveyed and put on the market. The squatter who had improved his land during his illegal tenure demanded, in particular, the right to buy it at the minimum rate of $1.25 an acre when it finally came up for sale. This right became known as "preemption," and while it was permitted for short periods in the

1830s, not until 1841 was it enacted for an unlimited period for male *citizens* (meaning whites only) and for aliens having declared their intention of becoming citizens.

Many westerners, for whom Senator Thomas Hart Benton of Missouri became the spokesman, went further. As early as 1824 Benton had proposed that the price of unsold government land be gradually reduced to 75 cents an acre and then to 50 cents. If no buyers appeared even then, the land should be given away. This proposal came to be known as "graduation," and it was the first formally to place a higher value to the nation as a whole on the work of the pioneer in opening up the country than on land-sale receipts to the Treasury.

Easterners regarded Benton's plan as one more scheme to tap their labor supply and force wage costs up; they also saw the quickening of western development as a further threat to their political strength in the nation. On the other hand, it was obvious that the continuation of land sales at the established prices would bring into the Treasury money enough to invalidate one of their principal arguments for high tariffs—the need for additional revenue to pay off the national debt and support government services. In an effort to eat their cake and have it too, some easterners offered the policy of "distribution"— keep up the price of land and the tariff, and distribute the surplus revenue among the states to help them improve public education and business morality. When nothing came of this, they resorted to the rather desperate pro-

*City of Washington, 1833.*

posal that the West be closed to settlement altogether.

In December 1829, Senator Samuel A. Foot of Connecticut offered a resolution to this effect, urging specifically that public-land surveys be stopped for a time and that future sales be limited to lands already on the market. Senator Benton, speaking for the West, promptly and angrily denounced Foot's resolution as a manufacturer's plot. Spokesmen for the slave South, in turn, supported Benton in the hope that they could thereby aggravate the growing differences between the free East and the free West. The South's purpose was to lure the West away from the protective-tariff phase of the "American System," so much desired by eastern manufacturers.

Senator Robert Y. Hayne of South Carolina presented the South's case, but his most divisive remarks were derived from an antitariff essay published anonymously by Vice-President Calhoun in 1828 under the title of *Exposition and Protest.* According to Calhoun, the Tariff of 1828 reduced the South to serfdom to northern industrialists. "The tariff is unconstitutional and must be repealed," Calhoun wrote. "The rights of the South have been destroyed, and must be restored, . . . the Union is in danger, and must be saved." No free government, Calhoun argued, would permit the transfer of "power and property from one class or section to another." The tyranny of the majority could be met by the constitutional right of each state to nullify an unconstitutional act of Congress.

It was Hayne's introduction of Calhoun's nullification theory into his argument against Foot's resolution that moved Daniel Webster of Massachusetts in January 1830 to reply to the South Carolinian. Senate debate was prolonged, but Webster, stirred to make an especially noble effort by Hayne's provocative references to the New England Federalists' disloyalty to the Union during the War of 1812, had the last word.

The Union, said "God-like Daniel," was not a mere compact among state legislatures; it was "the creature of the people." They had erected it; they alone were sovereign in it. It was for the Supreme Court, not for states, to decide whether laws passed by Congress were in keeping with the Constitution. If a single state had that right, the Union was dissolved. Webster closed his speech, which ran no less than four hours, with what Senator Benton called "a fine piece of rhetoric misplaced," a vision of two Americas. One was a land "rent with civil feuds, or drenched . . . in fratricidal blood"; the other, a republic "now known and honored throughout the earth, still full high advanced, its arms and trophies streaming in their original lustre." He ended with the famous words: "Liberty *and* Union, now and forever, one and inseparable."

Senator Foot's resolution was lost sight of in the hubbub over the greater issues his proposal had reopened only a decade after the Missouri Compromise. Once the debate ended on January 26, the first question everyone asked

*Daniel Webster in his prime, by Matthew Brady.*

was, where does Jackson stand? Two days later, publisher Duff Green, of the Kitchen Cabinet, was thought to have let the cat out of the bag, when he declared in his *United States Telegraph:* "The doctrine contended for by General HAYNE is too well understood and too firmly established . . . to be shaken." This opinion surely did no violence to Jackson's views as we have presented them up to this point of his administration. But still he kept his peace. A month passed before Webster and Hayne would release their polished-up speeches to the press, a period during which pressure for a presidential statement mounted. Many Jacksonians accused Webster of hazardous demagoguery in attacking so fiercely the straw man of disunion. But once again, the man in the White House would go his own way. When he finally made up his mind to talk, he confronted not Hayne, the spokesman, but John C. Calhoun, the philosopher behind the spokesman.

## Nullification

The doctrine of nullification was a curious lure for the South to choose to capture the heart of the West. Beyond the coastal tier of the thirteen original commonwealths, each of which had asserted its own independence of Britain, all the new states had been created by the national government of the United States. None had ever known independence; each had grown and flourished in and with the Union. Where they stood on the issue of nullification finally became clear enough to Jackson himself. And where the Union was involved he was with them. He was for state rights; about that there was to be no mistake. But he was for state rights *within* the Union. There was to be no mistake about that either.

In April 1830, when the leading Democrats gathered at a Jefferson birthday dinner, Old Hickory looked Calhoun in the eye and proposed this toast: "Our Union—it must be preserved!" Before news of Jackson's toast was released, Hayne prevailed upon the President to soften it by inserting the word, "Federal" before "Union." But "Federal" or not, Calhoun was unrepentant. To Jackson's words, he rose to reply: "The Union—next to our liberty, the most dear." In the following months, old personal grudges and new personal conflicts brought a clean break between the two men, which profoundly influenced sectional and party rivalries. One had to do with the President's discovery that Calhoun, when Secretary of War in 1818, had favored punishing Jackson for his conduct in the Seminole War (see p. 205). The Vice-President tried to explain the incident away in a letter to Jackson, but the latter remained unforgiving. When Calhoun next attributed his misfortune to Secretary of State Van Buren's prying, the President viewed this as a low blow at his trusted friend.

Other incidents, some trivial but telling, speeded Calhoun's fall and Van Buren's rise, and the decline of South Carolina and the South generally in the counsels of the administration in favor of New York, along with Pennsylvania and the rapidly growing states of the free West. The shift in allegiance of New York and South Carolina in particular demonstrated the persistence of personal power and personal perils in party politics even while party machines matured.

Calhoun still had a few volleys of his own to fire, but unfortunately for him, when he found another occasion to press not only his defiance but his doctrine, Jackson chose the same occasion to show who was boss. The tariff once more provided the decisive issue; and on it the South went largely with Calhoun, the free East and the free West with the President.

Receipts from existing duties had become so high by 1830 that the national debt had been almost entirely paid off. Jackson believed protective (as against revenue) tariffs to be as unconstitutional as appropriations for internal improvements, and in his message to Congress in December 1831, he urged the legislature to revise the Tariff of 1828 downward. If he hoped to appease the South by this proposal, he also sufficiently modified the requested reductions so as not to antagonize the industrial Northeast. In July 1832, Congress passed a tariff bill that met Jackson's specifications. It hardly satisfied Calhoun, however, and the Vice-President rushed home from Washington to mobilize southern opposition.

The doctrine of nullification was reasserted. This time, moreover, South Carolina moved to put Calhoun's theories into action. A legislature overwhelmingly favorable to nullification was elected. This legislature then ordered the election of delegates to a special state convention which, on assembling in November 1832, adopted by a vote of 136 to 26 an ordinance of nullification declaring the 1828 and 1832 tariffs void. The convention also ordered the legislature to prohibit the collection of the duties in state ports after February 1, 1833; and asserted that the use of federal troops to collect the duties would be followed by secession.

Jackson, more assertive than ever after his recent smashing success in the election of 1832 (see p. 260), replied on December 10 with his ringing Nullification Proclamation:

*I consider ... the power to annul a law of the United States, assumed by one State, incompatible with the existence of the Union, contradicted expressly by the letter of the Constitution, unauthorized by its spirit, inconsistent with every principle on which it was founded, and destructive of the great object for which it was formed.*

Jackson warned that the laws of the United States compelled him to meet treason with force.

In February 1833 the Senate passed a "Force Bill" empowering the President to use the army and navy if South Carolina resisted federal customs officials. While the Force Bill was being debated in the House, Henry Clay sponsored a new tariff bill calling for gradual reduction of the 1832 duties. South Carolina leaders having learned that other southern states repudiated nullification and that a vigorous Unionist faction inside their own borders would continue to fight it, anxiously awaited the decision on these two measures.

On the day (March 2) that the Force Act

became law, Jackson also signed Clay's Tariff of 1833. This tariff provided for a gradual reduction of duties until, by July 1, 1842, none would be higher than 20 percent. It also lengthened the list of commodities that could be imported duty free. Even Calhoun, who had resigned as Vice-President in order to be named a member of the Senate by the Carolina legislature, voted for this bill. After its enactment, South Carolina showed her satisfaction by withdrawing her nullification ordinance. At the same time, she adopted a new ordinance nullifying Jackson's Force Act. Since that act was no longer needed, Jackson wisely ignored this face-saving step.

### "Shirt-sleeve" diplomacy

Old Hickory was as adamant in asserting American rights in foreign relations as he was in projecting the rights of the Chief Executive at home. He appointed diplomats, moreover, on the same basis as domestic spoilsmen, and their "shirt-sleeve" methods, at a time when diplomatic protocol was most strict, caused many a shock abroad.

It was Jackson's own handling of two long-standing issues, however, that brought the most satisfying results. By using the velvet glove approach, he at last persuaded Britain to open the British West Indian trade to American ships on the same basis that American ports would be opened to British ships engaged in the West Indian trade. This matter was settled in October 1830. By using the iron fist approach the following year, he also persuaded the French to agree to pay up American claims for ships and cargoes lost to them during the Napoleonic wars. When the French delayed making the actual payments, Jackson recommended that Congress vote reprisals on available French property. This recommendation was accompanied by such harsh words that the French demanded a formal apology. But Jackson retorted: "The honor of my country shall never be stained by an apology from me for the statement of truth and the performance of duty." The British at last undertook to mediate the dispute and the French eventually paid in full.

Jackson, fearful of northern opposition to the enlargement of southern slave territory, proved less vigorous and less provocative in his relations with Mexico over the issue of Texas independence, even though he personally favored both the initial independence of the Lone Star State and her eventual annexation by the United States.

## III   The bank war

*Party preparations for 1832*

The defection of Calhoun and his destructive state-rights followers from the Democratic Republicans inspired National Republican leaders to try to corral them in a new coalition to overthrow Jackson's "presidential tyranny." The strength of this coalition eventually was to be found in the Whig party, largely Adamsite in its willingness to use national political instrumentalities for the development of the country's business system, yet overready to unite for campaign purposes with all others who might help tap the rising democratic sentiment of the common people to which Jackson had so successfully appealed.

As the election of 1832 neared, influential National Republicans saw their best bet to be an alliance with a meteoric third party—the Anti-Masonic party—which had recently won considerable success in Van Buren's own state of New York. Masonry, with its fraternalism and colorful rites and costumes, had long attracted colorful personalities, best of all Jackson himself. At the same time, the fact that such a large proportion of established political leaders and judges were Masons suggested that Masonry ("a horrid, oath binding system" its enemies called it for the secrecy of its proceedings) constituted a kind of officeholding clique and a gigantic conspiracy against the common man. Moreover, many associated Masonry with free thought and found it a threat to Christianity. Others, aroused by the rumor that alcohol was used with abandon in

Masonic ceremonies, embraced anti-Masonry almost as a temperance crusade.

Murder itself was made to appear a Masonic crime when in 1826 a body washed ashore from Lake Ontario was rather uncertainly identified as that of a former member of the society in Batavia, New York who had earlier threatened to expose its secrets and was never seen again. The finding of this body, in fact, first inspired local politicians to use the intensified anti-Masonic "enthusiasm" to form the Anti-Masonic party, which in the fall elections in New York in 1827 carried several western counties and sent fifteen members to the state assembly. In several other states Anti-Masons also gained office.

Among those most determined to use anti-Masonic sentiment against Jackson was the hard-boiled Rochester, New York editor and political boss Thurlow Weed, who hoped to put Henry Clay in the White House in 1832. Embarrassingly enough, Clay too was a Mason. Moreover, he had as little use for Weed as for Jackson. Weed and his henchmen, Clay said in 1830, were "in pursuit of power . . . without regard to the means of acquiring it." The Anti-Masons at last found a candidate in the aged William Wirt of Maryland (he too a Mason), who accepted the party's nomination at its national convention in Baltimore in September 1831 simply to enhance his chances when the National Republicans made their selection.

The Anti-Masons adopted the convention system of nominating national candidates—

the first in the nation to do so, as we have said—because they had no body of national officeholders to form a caucus. They made the most of the new mode by stressing its democratic nature compared with Jackson's "dictatorship." Not to be outdone, the National Republicans held a convention in Baltimore in December and passed over Wirt for Clay. The Democrats, as the Jacksonians now formally called themselves, could hardly fail to follow suit. At their first convention in Baltimore in May 1832, by acclamation they named Old Hickory and Van Buren.

At the National Republican convention, Jackson was taken to task for his positions on internal improvements, Indian removal, and the tariff. But the principal target was his administration's unfriendly attitude toward the Second Bank of the United States. As it turned out, the bank question overshadowed all other issues in the 1832 campaign.

### President Jackson versus President Biddle

For ten years prior to the election of 1832, the Second Bank had been managed by the able Philadelphian Nicholas Biddle. A reformed Federalist, Biddle had been appointed a director of the bank by President Monroe in 1819. In 1824 and 1828 he voted for Jackson himself. On becoming president of the bank in 1823, Biddle had intensified the deflationary policies that his predecessor had introduced during the Panic of 1819 (see p. 209). Not only was Biddle cautious about issuing notes of his own bank; by refusing to accept at face value the notes of state and local banks that had issued more paper than their specie reserves warranted, he also forced an element of caution upon such banks that they and their clients came to resent. Resentment lay deepest in the West, which, because it was growing faster than the rest of the country, felt most keenly the disregard of its financial needs by Biddle's watchdog policies.

The Second Bank, in addition, had become an enormous institution with such far-reaching powers over the private economy and privileged custodianship of government funds that its enemies apparently rightfully could denounce it as a monopoly, or "monster." No

one attacked the bank more vigorously on this score than the Democratic Senator from Missouri, Thomas H. Benton. In February 1831 Benton introduced a resolution against rechartering the bank and declaimed for several hours on its threat to democracy. He also skillfully exploited egalitarian feelings against the bank: "It tends to aggravate the inequality of fortunes; to make the rich richer and the poor poorer; to multiply nabobs and paupers; and to deepen and widen the gulf which separates Dives from Lazarus." The Senate rejected Benton's resolution, but he had given a strong impetus to anti-bank sentiment.

Benton's fear that the bank was "too great and powerful to be tolerated in a government of free and equal laws" reflected a widespread conviction that this great agency, aside from its economic force, was corrupting political life. Senators and congressmen received financial favors from the bank, as did many newspapermen. In the bank's defense it could be argued that most of the loans made to politicians and editors were sound enough and that it would have been suicidal to refuse to do business with such influential persons.

Many of the old Republican school, moreover, had never accepted the bank's constitutionality. Among these Jackson himself ranked high. "You know my opinion as to the banks," he wrote William B. Lewis in 1820, "that the Constitution of our State, as well as the Constitution of the United States, prohibited the establishment of banks in any state." Thereafter Jackson seemed so often to have changed his mind that he became an enigma to Biddle, who desperately needed to understand him. In November 1829 Biddle had an interview with the old soldier in which Jackson set forth his old philosophy. Jackson handsomely acknowledged the bank's services to the government, but he added:

*I think it right to be perfectly frank with you—I do not think that the power of Congress extends to charter a Bank out of the ten mile square [District of Columbia]. I do not dislike your Bank any more than all banks. But ever since I read the history of the South Sea Bubble I have been afraid of banks.*

Jackson added: "I have read the opinion of John Marshall [on the Second Bank's constitutionality in *McCulloch* v. *Maryland*, 1819], . . . and could not agree with him."

Jackson's first annual message to Congress was under consideration among his advisers at the time of the Biddle interview. They urged him not to rock the boat, to say nothing about the bank. But Jackson could not restrain himself. "My friend," he told one of them, "I am pledged against the bank." When the time came to submit this message in December, Jackson remained silent on the bank almost to the end. Then he said it was not too soon for the issue of rechartering the bank in 1836 to be submitted "to the deliberate consideration of the Legislature and the people." To assist them in their deliberations, he added: "Both the constitutionality and the expediency of the law creating this bank are well questioned by a large portion of our fellow-citizens." Two years later, in his message to Congress in December 1831, the President reaffirmed his views of the bank "as at present organized."

Jackson himself, underestimating popular support for his position, would have preferred to keep the Second Bank out of the 1832 campaign, and his Secretary of State and Secretary of the Treasury were busy talking to Biddle's friends about certain renewal after the election if application were put off. But Webster and Clay, grossly overestimating public support for the bank, urged Biddle to take the offensive against Old Hickory and petition Congress for a new bank charter now. Biddle, increasingly confused in the political maelstrom, at last yielded to such seemingly authoritative advice, and on July 3, 1832, as forecast, the recharter bill passed both houses. Jackson, bedridden for the moment, grimly observed to his heir apparent: "The Bank, Mr. Van Buren, is trying to kill me, *but I will kill it.*"

In his veto message of July 10, Jackson did not fail to note at the start that the recharter

The Historical Society of Pennsylvania

*Nicholas Biddle in 1837,*
*in engraving from painting by Thomas Sully.*

bill had come to him on the Fourth of July, and that he had considered it, "with that solemn regard to the principles of the Constitution which the day was calculated to inspire." He also considered it a monopoly operating to the advantage of the privileged few and open to the danger of control by foreign owners of its stock, a negligible possibility. His closing remarks were well suited to the coming election:

*Distinctions in society will always exist under every just government. Equality of talents, of education, or of wealth cannot be produced by human institutions; . . . but when the laws undertake to add to these natural and just advantages artificial distinctions . . . to make the rich richer, and the potent more powerful, the humble members of the society—the farmers, mechanics, and laborers—who have neither the time nor the means of securing like favors to themselves,*

*have a right to complain of the injustice of their
Government.*

260

Daniel Webster hastily prepared a brilliant
and eloquent reply to Jackson's message—"a
state paper," he said, "which finds no topic
too exciting for its use, no passion too inflammable for its address and its solicitation."

Biddle himself thought so little of Jackson's
"manifesto of anarchy" that he had it circulated as pro-bank propaganda. But Jackson
swept the election with 687,000 votes to Clay's
530,000. In the electoral college it was Jackson
by 219 to 49. Jackson, moreover, interpreted
his triumph as a mandate to press on with his
war against Biddle's "Hydra of corruption."

In this war Jackson at first held the support
of the speculative business and banking interests. If their politicking on the local level was
as unspeakable as Biddle's on the national
one, it was also unmentionable. The President
also gained support from hard-money conservatives like the "Locofocos" in New York,
who got their name from the "locofoco"
matches they used when party regulars shut
off the lights after losing control of a Democratic party meeting. As the bank war grew
warmer, however, and its consequences more
apparent, the country's business leaders in all
sections rallied to Biddle, while the ranks of
the Jacksonians became strained. Jackson
triumphed. But his victory was to prove costly
to the country as a whole.

### To the Panic of 1837

Jackson's opening shot in the renewed battle with Biddle was to order the
removal of government deposits from the Second Bank's branches on the grounds that
Biddle's policies no longer insured the safety
of the public's funds. He then ordered that
these deposits and all new government revenue
be placed in selected state institutions
that became known as Jackson's "pet banks."
These orders were more easily issued than
carried out. The Secretary of the Treasury
alone had the power to withdraw government
deposits, and Jackson's Secretary was a friend
of the bank. Such obstacles did not long deter
Old Hickory. He fired two Secretaries of the

Treasury until he found in Roger B. Taney of
Maryland the man who would do his bidding.
Late in 1833 Taney began the removal of the
deposits, and by the end of the year twenty-
three state banks had been named to receive
federal funds.

Even though his bid for a new charter had
been defeated, Biddle did not take this new
assault on his bank with complacency. If the
bank was to be forced to close, it must begin
to call in loans and limit new business. After
the federal deposits had been removed, Biddle
embarked on this policy with zeal. His object
was to create a business panic so widespread
that public opinion would force Jackson to reverse his stand on the charter. For some
months in 1833 and 1834, a panic indeed
seemed imminent. But once again Biddle miscalculated the political effects. To petitioners
who began to press Jackson for help, the President insistently replied, "Go to Nicholas
Biddle." In time, segments of the conservative
business community, profoundly alienated by
Jackson's high-handed political maneuvers in
the Treasury, did appeal to Biddle to relent,
and finally he gave in.

Relief over Biddle's capitulation turned the
near panic into a soaring boom, especially in
the South and West, where land was most in
demand. Speculation was further stimulated
by the inflationary practices of the "pet
banks," which used the windfall of federal
deposits as reserves for many ill-considered
loans. By throwing millions of acres of public
land on the market at this time, the administration itself encouraged much ill-considered
borrowing.

The land boom quickly heightened the demand for internal improvements, leading to
reckless investments in turnpikes, canals, and
railroads. Many such projects were financed
in part by foreign capitalists who would not
risk their money in private American corporations but were willing to purchase state
bonds, backed by state revenues, which many
states now issued to support internal improvement schemes. The optimistic state programs

were spurred on in the summer of 1836 when it became clear that the federal government was about to distribute to the states most of the $35 million Treasury surplus that had accumulated from tariff revenues and public land sales. Distribution began in time to sustain the boom, but before payments could be completed the surplus evaporated. Responsibility for this turn of events rested largely on another administration measure, Jackson's "Specie Circular." Issued July 11, 1836, this Circular required that all land purchased from the federal government after August 15 be paid for in silver or gold. Settlers, as distinguished from speculators, were allowed to use bank notes for an additional four months provided their purchases were under 320 acres.

This drastic reversal of policy soon checked land sales and sent prices plunging. In the spring of 1837, after Jackson had left office, stock and commodity prices also broke, and soon the Panic of 1837 was on in earnest. Like other panics, that of 1837 was worldwide and had worldwide as well as American causes and effects. Especially hard hit were British investors in American securities and British banks engaged in financing American trade, mainly trade in cotton. Their calls on American merchants forced many to the wall.

The failure of Biddle's bank, which had been operating since 1836 under a Pennsylvania charter, helped deepen the depression that followed the panic. After suspending activities twice, beginning in the fall of 1839, the bank was finally turned over to trustees for liquidation in 1841. Biddle was charged with fraud but subsequently acquitted. In 1844, at fifty-eight, he died a broken man.

## IV Jackson's legacy

### The concept of the presidency

When the voters went to the polls in 1836 to choose Jackson's successor, the boom was still alive, and the surface prosperity helped sustain Old Hickory's popularity. He had checked the nullifiers, routed Biddle's "monster," and in foreign affairs had forced Britain as well as France to knuckle under. The principal complaint against him was that of "executive usurpation," as his enemies called it. No less an authority on the Constitution and the office of the Chief Executive than E. S. Corwin remarks that Jackson's presidency was "no mere revival of the office—it was a remaking of it."

In his own day, Henry Clay most bitterly attacked the "revolution, hitherto bloodless," as he told the Senate in December 1833, after Jackson's firing of Treasury Secretaries who would not do his bidding, "but rapidly tending toward . . . the concentration of all power in the hands of one man." In 1834, at Clay's instigation, the Senate gave Jackson a taste of his own medicine by adopting, 26 to 20, the following unprecedented resolution:

Resolved, *That the President, in the late Executive proceedings in relation to the public revenue, has assumed upon himself authority and power not conferred by the Constitution and laws, but in derogation of both.*

Jackson responded promptly with an eloquent "Protest," which the Senate refused to enter in the journal of its proceedings. On their part, Jackson's supporters in the Senate waged a ceaseless battle for almost three years to have the censure resolution expunged from the record, and at last, in January 1837, they had their way. During the debate, Clay again expressed the resentment of many of his fellow senators over what they regarded as Jackson's aggrandizement of his rights:

*The Senate has no army, no navy, no patronage, no lucrative offices, nor glittering honors to bestow. . . .*

*How is it with the President? . . . By means of principles which he has introduced, and innovations which he has made in our institutions, alas! but too much countenanced by Congress and a confiding people, he exercises uncontrolled the power of the state. In one hand he holds the purse and in the other brandishes the sword of the country! . . . He has swept over the government like a tropical tornado.*

Others voiced similar judgments. "I look upon Jackson," wrote Chancellor Kent of New York, "as a detestable, ignorant, reckless, vain and malignant tyrant. . . . This American elective monarchy frightens me. The experiment, with its foundations laid on universal suffrage and our unfettered press, is of too violent a nature for our excitable people." In the Senate, Webster roared out this protest: "The President carries on the government; all the rest are sub-contractors." Such sentiments were exaggerated, but the transformation complained of had, in fact, occurred.

### The second two-party system

Early in 1835, even in Jackson's home state of Tennessee, steps were taken in the legislature to name a favorite son for the presidency the next year in order to divert Old Hickory's obvious leaning toward the "foreigner," Van Buren. To nip this apostasy in

the bud, Jackson arranged for the Democrats to hold their second national convention in Baltimore as early as May 1835; and when this convention nominated "Little Van" unanimously, it made the charge of the President's autocracy the more telling.

Jackson's enlargement of presidential power, although so sharply condemned by Clay and Webster, drove his rivals to attempt to strengthen the national character of their own emergent party, known as Whigs from the 1834 congressional elections onward. In this effort, the Whig leaders eventually were forced themselves to turn to national military heroes—men like William Henry Harrison (1840), Zachary Taylor (1848), Winfield Scott (1852)—to gloss over the sectional coalitions that alone made national parties possible. But it took a little time for the brilliant civilian politicos to sacrifice personal ambition to national party needs. For the 1836 campaign, fearful of a two-sided contest with Jackson's favorite in a boom year, they decided instead to try to leave the ultimate choice of President, as in 1824, to the national legislature, an arena of sectional rivalry, rather than to the growing national electorate.

The Whig leaders leaned so far in this direction, in fact, that they renounced a national convention in favor of random sectional endorsements: Webster by the Massachusetts legislative caucus; Willie P. Mangum by South Carolina (his reward for having voted against the Force Bill of 1833 in the Senate where he represented North Carolina); Supreme Court Justice John McLean, an opponent of Jackson's removal of reluctant Secretaries of the Treasury during the bank war, who withdrew in August 1836 after being named by his home legislature in Ohio; and Hugh L. White, the anti-Jackson Democrat named by the one-party Tennessee legislature. True to their tradition, Whig converts from the Anti-Masonic party held the only Whig presidential convention—in Harrisburg, Pennsylvania in December 1835—where they nominated William Henry Harrison.

## Election of 1840

**Electoral Vote**

Harrison 234
Van Buren 60

262

In the popular canvass, all the Whigs together gained 739,700 votes, Van Buren 765,500. Little Van's electoral college majority, 170 to 124, kept the decision out of Congress. Webster carried only Massachusetts; Mangum only South Carolina. Of the whole array, "Old Tippecanoe," William Henry Harrison, did much the best, so well, indeed that he came on to defeat Clay for the nomination at the Whigs' first national convention in 1839, and to defeat Van Buren himself in the election the next year. Clay made a good deal of "union and harmony" in sacrificing himself to General Harrison at the 1839 convention under pressure from Thurlow Weed; but Democratic embarrassment during the depression of the late 1830s rather than Whig solidarity contributed most to Harrison's election triumph.

### "Tippecanoe and Tyler Too"

Soon after Van Buren took office in March 1837, the business panic was in full swing and the President received plenty of advice on how to reverse the trend. Most of this advice centered on the Specie Circular, which business leaders claimed "had produced a wider desolation" than a recent cholera epidemic. Easy-money Democrats urged the President to recall the Specie Circular but to continue the pet-bank system. The financially conservative Locofocos proposed that the government go even farther than the Circular in its hard-money crusade. They also demanded that Van Buren remove public funds from all banks, so that federal fiscal operations might no longer be "embarrassed by the doings of speculators."

The President favored the Locofoco approach to banks and throughout his administration sought to create an "Independent Treasury" where government specie and other funds would be placed in depositories around the country and used to pay obligations in cash. The first Independent Treasury Bill was presented to Congress in September 1837 and got a cool reception not only from Whigs but

from Democrats sympathetic to state-banking interests. Van Buren persisted until, in 1840, significant shifts having been made in the Democratic alignment, an Independent Treasury Act squeaked through. The administration margin was supplied by Calhoun and his southern followers, who had returned to the Democratic fold from the Whig party to which Calhoun's feud with Jackson had driven them.

The "divorce of bank and state," as the Independent Treasury victory was called, marked the high-water mark of Locofoco influence in the Democratic party but did little for economic recovery, and as the election of 1840 drew near, Whig leaders scented victory. Clay, defeated for the nomination on the bank issue in 1832 and by-passed in 1836 for strategic reasons, now hoped to gain the elusive prize. This time, however, he failed to receive the support of Webster, who looked upon him as a rival. With little hope of winning the nomination himself, Webster backed Harrison; and with Thurlow Weed's support at the Whig convention in Harrisburg in December 1839, he put Harrison across. John Tyler of Virginia was named the general's running mate, with the hope of strengthening Whig chances in the South. The Democrats, at their convention in Baltimore in May 1840, renominated Van Buren; but since Jackson's retirement they had become so divided that they were not able to agree on a candidate for Vice-President and were forced to leave the choice to the states.

With the slogan, "Matty's policy, 50 cts. a day and soup; our policy, $2 a day and roast beef," the Whig campaigners made much of the hard times under the Democrats. At the same time they focused their attack on the President's luxurious tastes. A campaign document, on the "Royal Splendor of the President's Palace," pictured Van Buren in the White House as a slothful and effeminate oriental potentate sampling French cookery from golden plates and resting after the turtle soup on a "Turkish divan." By contrast, the Whigs made almost too much of the stern simplicity of Old Tippecanoe. When a Baltimore newspaper taunted the Whigs by saying that Harrison would be perfectly satisfied with a log cabin and a good supply of cider, his managers capitalized on the intended slur and picked up the log cabin as a party symbol. "It tells of virtues," Thurlow Weed declared, "that dwell in obscurity, of the privations of the poor, of toil and danger." The log cabin, this "emblem of simplicity," was as foreign to Harrison's gentlemanly origins and habits of living as Van Buren's Turkish divan, but the symbol helped elect him. The record 2,412,000 votes cast (60 percent more than in 1836), represented an extraordinary 78 percent of those eligible. Of these votes, Harrison won 53.1 percent. His electoral college count was 234 to Van Buren's 60.

Having surrendered the nomination to a popular hero who gave their party national stature, such Whig stalwarts as Clay and Webster planned to run the administration once it took office, and in fact during his single month as President Harrison humbly yielded to them. Of Clay, a New York newspaper correspondent had this to say at the time: "He predominates over the Whig Party with despotic sway. Old Hickory himself never lorded it over his followers with authority more undisputed, or more supreme."

When Harrison died on April 4, 1841 and Tyler became President, the situation changed drastically. Tyler was a Whig only because he had followed Calhoun out of the Democratic party after the break with Jackson in the early 1830s. A veteran of the Virginia legislature and of both houses of Congress, he had had many opportunities in the past to disclose his strong antitariff views, his antagonism to Biddle's bank, his distaste for federal aid to internal improvements. Beyond these issues, he sided with Calhoun on nullification. The Whigs had named him for the vice-presidency in order to attract southern anti-Jackson support; but with the example of Jackson before him, as President this state-rights enthusiast was to be no cipher.

On one matter Clay and Tyler were able to agree: Congress passed and the President signed in 1841 a measure repealing Van Buren's Independent Treasury Act. But when Clay pushed farther, he and his colleagues were unceremoniously rebuffed. In August 1841 Congress actually passed a bill creating a new national bank. When Tyler returned it with a firm veto, the Whigs, in September, adopted a new bank bill designed to satisfy Tyler's constitutional scruples. When Tyler vetoed this bill too, about fifty Whig congressmen met in caucus and read Tyler out of the party. Moreover, with the exception of Secretary of State Webster, who was busy with the negotiations that eventually led to the Webster-Ashburton Treaty (see p. 294), all the Cabinet members resigned. Tyler promptly named a new Cabinet which was southern with two exceptions. When Webster himself resigned in 1843 after completing his diplomatic work, he was soon replaced by Calhoun—further evidence of the Whig administration's new Democratic party orientation, and confirmation of that party's having become the standard-bearer of the slaveocracy.

## For further reading

Maurice Duverger, *Political Parties* (1954), offers a good modern introduction to these organizations. Richard Hofstadter, *The Idea of a Party System* (1969), is an analytic study of "The Rise of Legitimate Opposition in the United States 1780-1840." R. P. McCormick, *The Second American Party System* (1966), is indispensable for "Party Formation in the Jacksonian Era," state by state. Among older works still of interest are H. J. Ford, *The Rise and Growth of American Politics* (1898), and vol. II of M. Ostrogorski, *Democracy and the Organization of Political Parties* (2 vols., 1902).

Chilton Williamson, *American Suffrage, from Property to Democracy 1760-1760* (1960), provides a reliable survey. M. D. Peterson, ed., *Democracy, Liberty, and Property* (1966), is a comprehensive anthology of the work of "The State Constitutional Conventions of the 1820s." On the Negro and the franchise, see L. F. Litwack, *North of Slavery, The Negro in the Free States 1790-1860* (1961). Enlightening state studies include Lee Benson, *The Concept of Jacksonian Democracy: New York As a Test Case* (1961); H. R. Stevens, *The Early Jackson Party in Ohio* (1957); and C. G. Sellers, *James K. Polk, Jacksonian 1795-1843* (1957), on Tennessee.

On particular parties, in addition to McCormick (above), see Charles McCarthy, *The Anti-Masonic Party* (1902); E. M. Caroll, *Origins of the Whig Party* (1925); A. C. Cole, *The Whig Party in the South* (1913); G. G. Van Deusen, *Thurlow Weed, Wizard of the Lobby* (1947); R. V. Remini, *Martin Van Buren and the Making of the Democratic Party* (1959), and *The Election of Andrew Jackson* (1963); and R. G. Gunderson, *The Log Cabin Campaign* (1957). L. D. White, *The Jacksonians: A Study in Administrative History 1829-1861* (1954), is outstanding on the spoils system and its effects. On the types of men appointed to high office in the early republic, see S. H. Aronson, *Status and Kinship in the Higher Civil Service . . . in the Administrations of John Adams, Thomas Jefferson, and Andrew Jackson* (1964).

George Dangerfield, *The Era of Good Feelings* (1952), and *The Awakening of American Nationalism 1815-1828* (1965), provide well-written analyses of American life and politics leading to the election of Jackson. S. F. Bemis, *John Quincy Adams and the Union* (1956), is standard on the sixth President. F. J. Turner, *The United States 1830-1850* (1935), provides a classic introduction to Jacksonian democracy and its aftermath. G. G. Van Deusen, *The Jacksonian Era 1828-1848* (1959), is a modern survey. The following offer varied points of view: E. C. Rozwenc, ed., *Meaning of Jacksonian Democracy* (1963); Arthur Schlesinger, Jr., *The Age of Jackson* (1945); Joseph Dorfman, *The Economic Mind in American Civilization 1606-1865* (2 vols., 1946); Walter Hugins, *Jacksonian Democracy and the Working Class* (1960); Richard Hofstadter, *The American Political Tradition* (1948); and Marvin Meyers, *The Jacksonian Persuasion: Politics and Belief* (1957).

Marquis James, *The Life of Andrew Jackson* (1938), is excellent reading. See also J. S. Bassett, *The Life of Andrew Jackson* (2 vols., 1925). Most useful on Van Buren besides Remini (above) is Holmes Alexander, *The American Talleyrand* (1935). Clement Eaton, *Henry Clay and the Art of American Politics* (1957), is sound and short. C. M. Fuess, *Daniel Webster* (2 vols., 1930), is standard. See also R. N. Current, *Daniel Webster and the Rise of National Conservatism* (1955). C. M. Wiltse, *John C. Calhoun, Nullifier 1829-1839* (1949), is a good introduction to the man and his thought. W. W. Freehling, *Prelude to Civil War* (1966), provides the most intensive study of, in the words of its subtitle, "The Nullification Controversy in South Carolina 1816-1836." See also, Charles Sellers, *Andrew Jackson, Nullification, and the State-Rights Tradition* (1963). T. H. Benton, *Thirty Years' View* (2 vols., 1854-1856), is a good inside account. On Tyler, see Robert Seager II, *And Tyler Too* (1963).

On land and Indian policy, see R. G. Wellington, *The Political and National Influence of the Public Lands 1826-1842* (1914); Grant Foreman, *Indian Removal, The Emigration of the Five Civilized Tribes of Indians* (1932); and F. P. Prucha, *American Indian Policy in the Formative Years: The Indian Trade and Intercourse Acts 1790-1834* (1962).

A good short introduction to the bank war (which is also treated in virtually all the Jacksonian books cited above), is G. R. Taylor, ed., *Jackson versus Biddle* (1949). Bray Hammond, *Banks and Politics in America: From the Revolution to the Civil War* (1957), is the most elaborate study. T. P. Govan, *Nicholas Biddle, Nationalist and Public Banker 1786-1844* (1959), gives Biddle's side. On the bank itself see R. C. H. Catterall, *The Second Bank of the United States* (1903), and W. B. Smith, *Economic Aspects of the Second Bank of the United States* (1953). R. C. McGrane, *The Panic of 1837* (1924) is illuminating.

# AMERICA IN FERMENT

Reflecting on "Fenimore Cooper's White Novels" in his book *Studies in Classic American Literature,* the English writer D. H. Lawrence asked the telltale question, "Can you make a land virgin by killing off its aborigines?" Toward the close of the nineteenth century, Americans were to grow less and less certain of the answer to this question; but the generation that came to manhood in the Age of Jackson had few if any doubts. Its greatest spokesmen salved the national conscience. Ours, said Emerson, "is a country of beginnings, of projects, of vast designs and expectations. It has no past; all has an onward and prospective look." "We," said Melville, "are the pioneers of the world; the advance guard sent on through the wilderness of untried things, to break a new path in the New World that is ours. In our youth is our strength; in our inexperience our wisdom."

Americans in this self-conscious age took ever greater pride in distinguishing their "system," as they came to call it—open, expansive, an Eden for its fortunate citizens, a model for the world's oppressed—from the closed system of declining Europe. And even before they had fulfilled what they long believed to be their rightful "destiny" to occupy the whole continental range from ocean to ocean (see Chapter Twelve), their pretensions worked on Europe's fears. As early as 1824, following the bold assertions of the Monroe Doctrine, no less a personage than Prince Metternich of Austria, the reigning head of the Holy Alliance formed to repress Europe's own republican tendencies, pointed the finger at the formidable new foe:

*These United States of America, which we have seen arise and grow, and which during their too short youth already meditated projects which they dared not then avow, have suddenly left a sphere too narrow for their ambition. . . . In their indecent declarations they have cast blame and scorn on the institutions of Europe most worthy of respect. . . . In fostering revolutions wherever they show themselves, in regretting those which have failed, in extending a helping hand to those which seem to prosper, they lend new strength to the apostles of sedition and reanimate the courage of every conspirator.*

And yet questions beyond that posed by D. H. Lawrence remained to prod an ambitious people. Granted the virginity of the land and the rightness of their possession of it, what would Americans make of their wealth? Would they succeed, as Horace Mann put it in 1842, in "converting material wealth into spiritual well-being"? The question of the character of the civilization which was to encompass the globe, if Americans had their way, kept the nation, and not merely its intellectuals, artists, and reformers, in ferment.

## I  The American temperament

### A restless society

All observers agreed that Americans worked harder, ate faster, moved around more, and relaxed less than Europeans. In America, Tocqueville wrote in 1835,

*a man builds a house in which to spend his old age, and he sells it before the roof is on, . . . he brings a field into tillage, and leaves other men to gather the crop, he embraces a profession and gives it up, he settles in a place, which he soon afterwards leaves, to carry his changeable longings elsewhere.*

Nothing seemed finished in America. "Improvement," both personal and collective, was a national preoccupation. People were on the move, in transit, going from somewhere to somewhere better. The symbol of the young republic might have been the locomotive that never ceased its labors, or the steamboat that moved up and down the rivers—and frequently blew up.

### An optimistic society

In 1823 an anonymous writer listed some of the reasons for America's glorious prospects: "an extensive seacoast, abundantly provided with capacious ports and harbors"; "magnificent rivers" providing the means for a "lucrative internal trade"; a tremendous waterpower potential; "every variety of soil and climate," which made for self-sufficiency; "a capacity for raising cotton to supply the demand of the whole world"; a population "active, energetic, enterprising, and ingenious"; the most liberal, and most cheaply administered government in the world; the absence of a nobility of drones; "abundant room for all the superfluous population of Europe."

**268**

America, set aside for a heavenly experiment, now looked forward to a golden age. In the words of one contemporary (1828):

*A moral influence is withdrawing their subjects from the old and worn out governments of Europe and hurrying them across the Atlantic, to participate in the renovated youth of the new republic of the west; an influence which, like that of nature, is universal, and without pause or relaxation.*

Faith in the American future had actually sprung up before the Revolution, but after 1820 all signs seemed to confirm the prospects

*Merchant William Paulding's*
*"Lyndhurst" in Tarrytown, New York,*
*"an immense edifice of white or gray marble,*
*resembling a baronial castle,*
*or rather a Gothic monastery," to quote*
*the astonished diarist Philip Hone,*
*designed by architect Alexander Jackson Davis*
*in 1838 with instructions to ignore costs.*

Metropolitan Museum of Art, Harris Brisbane Dick Fund, 1924

of "indefinite perfectibility," while Americans prepared themselves for the "golden day."

## A commercial society

American society was primarily a business society.

*It will require but little reflection to satisfy us [wrote a spokesman for the mercantile and banking interests in 1838] that the resources of this country are controlled chiefly by the class which, in our own peculiar phraseology, we term "the business community"— embracing all those who are engaged in the great occupation of buying, selling, exchanging, importing and exporting merchandise, and including the banker, the broker, and underwriter.*

Every American, declared the editor of a well-known commercial periodical, was in some sense a trader. The physician traded his "benevolent care," the lawyer his "ingenious tongue," the clergyman "his prayers." One principle motivated the commercial classes, another explained, a principle that enabled them to enrich the country as well as themselves:

*Whether it be called avarice or the love of money, or the desire of gain, or the lust of wealth, or whether it be softened to the ear under the more guarded terms, prudence, natural affection, diligence in business, or the conscientious improvement of time and talents—it is still money-making which constitutes the great business of our people—it is the use of money which controls and regulates everything.*

But even America's severest critics usually agreed that there was something large and even heroic in this pursuit of wealth. Public opinion regarded making money as an "engine" of benevolence as well as a good in itself. Merchants, like the public-spirited Abbott Lawrence of Boston, shared this view and supported humanitarian and cultural enterprises.

## An idealistic society

In spite of their insistence on the practical and the useful, even those Americans most triumphant in business competition felt the spiritual leavening of their conquests. In February 1853, his fortune having soared to $11 million, Cornelius Vanderbilt wrote to his friend Hamilton Fish: "I have a little pride as an American to sail over the waters of England and France, up the Baltic and through the Mediterranean, without a reflection of any kind that it is a voyage for gain." When, later that year, "old Cornele" set out in his magnificent steamer *North Star,* constructed in the most extravagant way so "as to be a credit to our *Yankee Land,*" his fellow tycoon James Gordon Bennett of the *New York Herald* hailed the expedition. "Although it is solely a personal matter," Bennett said, "it partakes somewhat of a national character," one calculated to display "the refinement of those whose enterprise, industry and genius have placed them at the head of the social scale."

Lesser Americans, with the world still to conquer, were themselves susceptible to every sort of evangelical appeal. This was preeminently the age of "Causes." Tocqueville found a "fanatical and almost wild spiritualism" rampant in America, and surmised that religious enthusiasm was probably natural in a society "exclusively bent upon the pursuit of material objects." A people who made so great a virtue of common sense, Tocqueville believed, were most prone to "burst the bonds of matter by which they are restrained" and "soar impetuously towards Heaven."

## A violent society

Critics of American society had been quick to include the American penchant for the gun and the bowie knife in their canards. Men who lived beyond the reach or protection of law were all potential criminals or victims, and stories from the hinterlands (real or invented) all too frequently told of stabbing and shootings, of ambuscades, river piracy, and deadly feuds. By the 1840s, violence in eastern cities had also become prevalent enough to attract public notice. New York, Boston, and Philadelphia slums already provided a lurid background for crimes that seemed to justify Jefferson's view of cities as boils and carbuncles on the body politic.

Prostitutes, thieves, and murderers might be explained, if not condoned, as the inevitable consequence of human wickedness or social injustice, but tolerance for lynch law did not meet with comparable disapproval. The animus behind lynchings or mobbings in northern cities or southern plantations was identical. "The victim," as David Brion Davis says, "was . . . often the representative of a scapegoat group whose very existence infuriated a mob of righteous men." Undeterred by what one apologist of mob violence called the "sickish sensibility of mawkish philanthropy," they whipped, burned, hanged, tarred, exiled, or shot those they deemed dangerous or subversive—gamblers, Mormons, abolitionists, Roman Catholics, and blacks, among others.

## Democracy and equality

*In our government [declared an orator in 1840], we recognize only individuals, at least among whites; and in social life, the constant effort to do away with the castes produced by difference of fortune, education, and taste. The motto upon the flag of America should be "Every man for himself." Such is the spirit of our land, as seen in our institutions, in our literature, in our religious condition, in our political contests.*

Democracy meant (to many, if not to all) social as well as political equality. To paraphrase Tocqueville again, men pounced "upon equality as booty" and clung to it "as some precious treasure."

Freedom-hungry immigrants, who were particularly impressed by American egalitarianism, swelled the ranks of democracy. A new citizen wrote German friends in the late 1830s:

*Our President walks across the street the same as I do—no Royal Highness or Majesty would ever do that.*

*They do not even call him "Mister." . . . When talking to the President you say simply: "How are you, President?" and he answers: "Thank you, how are you?"*

270 Yet while the industrial revolution progressed, the growth of an urban population weakened republican simplicity and intensified social distinctions. Conservatives grew especially concerned about the new immigrants and felt that American privileges were being granted too promiscuously. Although it is impossible to chart the fine gradations of rank and repute among native Americans, successful planters, business leaders, bankers, and lawyers still seemed to occupy the top rungs of society. Clergymen, physicians, and teachers, too, if patronized by the influential, might claim high standing. Below these privileged groups ranged the rest of the white citizenry, with subtle distinctions among themselves.

But no fixed and artificial barriers prevented men from rising rapidly. No class outside the South demanded special respect from another, and persons of different degrees mingled indiscriminately in business and travel. Despite the fears of conservatives the American people embarked on no wildly revolutionary course. Wrapped up in his individual daily progress, the citizen usually abided by the "empty phantom of public opinion," which was "strong enough to chill innovators and to keep them silent and at a respectful distance."

### Individualism and cooperation

Much has been made, and correctly, of the pre-Civil War era as the heyday of individualism. But this was also a time of cooperation, of voluntary, not coercive "association." When Tocqueville visited America he was immensely impressed by the fact that citizens of "the most democratic country on the face of the earth . . . carried to the highest perfection the art of pursuing in common the object of their common desires."

For the American to pool resources, both material and intellectual, and to throw in his lot with his neighbors and community, simply seemed the most sensible thing to do much of the time. A society of "lone wolves" would not have survived. Businessmen who joined together in companies in all the major lines of enterprise well understood this. Citizens hungry for culture set up libraries, art associations, mutual improvement clubs. Immigrants formed societies with their fellow countrymen. Charitable, reform, fraternal, and benefit organizations proliferated naturally in a democracy where there was no ruling class with a tradition of social responsibility. "Many can accomplish what one cannot," said one organizer, defending his trespassing on individualism. But he was quick to add this qualification: "We mean to receive as much as we give, and we ask others to join us on that principle."

### In the American grain

But if Americans poured their energies into countless organizations pulling in many directions at once, what was it, if anything, that held their society together? Many observers during the 1830s and 1840s were disturbed by the diffuseness of American activity, by the "lack of a common skeleton." Emerson, in 1847, noted America's "immense resources," but he was also struck by America's "village littleness." America, he concluded, "is great strength on a basis of weakness."

A major weakness in a country of churches was sectarian rivalry. Americans seemed to be the most religious of peoples and yet the one most afflicted by denominational discord. The United States had always provided a fertile soil for new sects, but in the 1830s and 1840s the splintering of dissenting churches, with each group claiming possession of the authentic faith, reached a peak of frequency and ferocity. The Baptists and Methodists, the fastest-growing denominations of the day, were most susceptible to schisms, but new cults sprang up everywhere and the competition for the souls of immigrants pouring into the Mississippi Valley was frequently unchristian.

Doctrinal differences created a good deal of friction, but the false pride of those who considered themselves socially superior to others, even in the sight of God, deepened religious conflict. Presbyterians, Congregationalists, Episcopalians, and Unitarians differed in theology and in church organization but drew their membership largely from the well-to-do. Baptists, Methodists, Campbellites, and Universalists were held to be socially a cut lower, while the immigrant and Free Negro churches lined the bottom.

Most Protestants, though they fought among themselves, shared a common hatred of the Roman Catholic church. Even to sophisticated ministers like Lyman Beecher, the father of Harriet Beecher Stowe and president of Lane Seminary in Cincinnati, Catholicism still smacked of the sinister rites of the Inquisition and of political autocracy. The gullible readily swallowed crude fictions about Catholic atrocities and sensational "exposés" of Catholic depravity. Sometimes Catholics were insulted and attacked, their churches burned.

Anti-Catholic prejudice deepened after 1830 when immigration began to rise. Between 1830 and 1850, 2.5 million newcomers arrived, many of them Catholics from Ireland and Germany. In 1830, there were 500 Catholic priests in the United States and about 500,000 communicants. By 1850, 1500 priests served 1,750,000 of their faith. In addition, the Roman Catholic church had established seminaries, schools, colleges, monasteries, convents, hospitals, and other parochial institutions. A Catholic press, starting with the *United States Catholic Miscellany,* in 1822, also had come into being, along with a Catholic Tract Society, founded in Philadelphia in 1827 to combat Protestantism and to propagate the religion of Rome.

Yet the general acceptance of democracy, private property, and Christian faith seemed somehow to give a national character to the "American grain." Even in religion, powerful clergymen like the great revivalist Charles Grandison Finney (1792-1875) had begun in the 1820s to preach a "social gospel" by which they strove to redeem entire communities, not merely errant individuals. Many of them now equated sin with social selfishness, and indifference toward socially benevolent enterprises like Sunday Schools, Home Missions, and temperance crusades as a sign of a "backslidden heart." Not all religious leaders went along with Finney's advanced notions, yet his social Christianity gave religious belief a relevance that helped rescue it from sectarian self-destruction.

Lawyers performed a lay role analogous to that of the liberal ministers. The great figures of the antebellum period—Webster, Clay, Jackson, Calhoun, Stephen A. Douglas, and Lincoln, to name only a few—all were lawyers. As the principal orators of an oratorical age, they became the official celebrants of civic occasions like Fourth of July anniversaries, victorious battle commemorations, birthdays and funerals of national leaders, and other unifying public events. Tocqueville believed the lawyers of America formed "the most cultivated circle of society. . . . If I were asked where I place the American aristocracy, I should reply without hesitation, that it . . . occupies the judicial bench and the bar."

The model of the lawyer in this age was Daniel Webster, to his contemporaries a remarkable natural phenomenon like Niagara Falls. No one declaimed about the Pilgrim Fathers or Bunker Hill more movingly or evoked the spirit of nationalism more powerfully. Emerson like others eventually tired of Webster's paeans and periods as well as of his conservatism. "He believes in so many words," the Concord philosopher once said, "that government exists for the protection of property. He looks at the Union as an estate, a large farm, and is excellent in the completeness of his defence of it." Yet to young Emerson, Webster's reply to Hayne in 1830 symbolized "the beauty and dignity of principles." How well Webster's reputation survived is perhaps best suggested in the vitriolic assaults upon him as a kind of god gone wrong when but two years before his death he accepted the Fugitive Slave Law of 1850 as part of the Compromise made in the hope of saving the Union.

## II Writers and society

*Precursors of a national literature*

"Men of genius," according to a Boston critic in 1820, were "outlaws" because, "for the most part, they want that getting-along faculty which is naturally enough made the measure of man's mind in a young country, where every one has his future to make." And yet during the next three decades the United States experienced an intellectual flowering scarcely equaled by any other generation in American history. In 1802, when Washington Irving began to write, America had no literature and hardly a reading public. When he died, a year before the Civil War began, Emerson, Thoreau, Hawthorne, Poe, Melville, and Whitman had already struck off their masterpieces.

The achievements of these writers seem all the more remarkable when we consider the unpromising environment from which they sprang. Besides the prevailing hostility to genius in general there was the specific hostility to literature, and more particularly to American literature. After the Revolution, patriots had called for a national literature that would reflect the dawning greatness of the new nation, but such American poets as Timothy Dwight and Joel Barlow, who planned mighty epics, turned out only pale and unreadable imitations of English literary forms and deferred to English standards of taste. Among the would-be writers of this period, only the poet Philip Freneau (1752–1832) and the imaginative Philadelphia novelist Charles Brockden Brown (1761–1810) possessed more than a minor talent. For the few Americans with literary interests the easily obtainable works of such popular British authors as Sir Walter Scott, Bulwer-Lytton, and Charles Dickens crowded native writers out.

American authors understood their neglect. Washington Irving (1783–1859) was only one of a long line of American writers who felt the need of Europe, where the necessary romantic background was available.

*I longed [Irving said] to wander over the scenes of renowned achievement,—to tread, as it were, in the footsteps of antiquity,—to loiter about the ruined castle,—to meditate on the falling tower,—to escape, in short, from the commonplace realities of the present, and lose myself among the shadowy grandeurs of the past.*

American writers also had to reckon with the religiously inspired distrust of literature as Satan's snare. Fiction, it was said, "pampers and bloats the intellect with unwholesome food, and enfeebles and demoralizes all future exertions of the mind."

Yet the better-known American writers overcame or ignored these cultural handicaps and managed to attract a following of their own. Irving, an urbane New Yorker, was the first professional man of letters to win wide popularity at home and applause abroad. Irving lived much in Europe and wrote his best books about it. When still in his twenties, however, he wrote and published in America his *History of New York* (1809), a rousing burlesque of the early Dutch and later backwoods democrats, that had the whole country laughing. Irving's *History* ranks second in popularity among his works only to *The Sketch Book* (1819–1820), an instantaneous success in Britain as in the United States, in which he made Rip Van Winkle and Ichabod Crane luminous American characters in the rural and village setting of his native state.

Irving's friend and contemporary William

Cullen Bryant (1794-1878) grew up in the Berkshire Hills of Massachusetts, but he made his career in New York City as poet, newspaper man, and reformer. No lisping imitator of British sentiment, Bryant wrote of his native habitat in a way that won Emerson himself. It was Bryant, Emerson noted, who "subsidized every solitary grove and monument-mountain in Berkshire or the Katskills . . . every water fowl and woodbird . . . so that there is no feature of day or night in the country which does not, to the contemplative mind, recall the name of Bryant."

An even more illustrious member of the New York group was the novelist and moralist James Fenimore Cooper (1789-1851). In Europe, where he lived and wrote for a number of years, Cooper truculently defended the government and institutions of his native land. In America, he berated his countrymen for bad manners, chauvinism, contempt for privacy, slavish submission to public opinion. Cooper's upbringing among the landed gentry of New York did not block his early sympathy with Jacksonian America. If his "democracy" soured in the last years of his life, his thoughtful depiction of republican government, *The American Democrat* (1838), remains one of the best political essays ever written by an American.

What first brought Cooper fame both in Europe and at home were his early "white novels," especially *The Pilot* (1823), a forerunner of many masterly tales of the sea. Of deeper interest today is the celebrated "Leatherstocking" series: *The Pioneers* (1823), *The Last of the Mohicans* (1826), *The Prairie* (1827), *The Pathfinder* (1840), and *The Deerslayer* (1841)—the romance of the white hunter Natty Bumppo among the Indians of the woods, the lakes, and the open country. Natty, in his first incarnation, was but a composite of some of the types Cooper had known during a boyhood spent in a pioneer settlement in New York. In successive appearances, however, he grew into a mythic figure, a kind of forest philosopher-king mediating between white men and red, and immune both to the viciousness of civilization and the barbarism of the frontier. Cooper had by no means exhausted his talent after completing his wilderness saga, but he lost a good part of his audience when he turned from romance to social censure.

A surer gauge of American taste in this early period of American literature is the phenomenal success of the New England poet Henry Wadsworth Longfellow (1807-1882). Born in Portland, Maine and educated at Bowdoin College, Longfellow, like Irving and Cooper, had his years in Europe where he went to prepare himself to become a professor of modern languages, first at Bowdoin and later (1836) at Harvard. Sitting in his Cambridge study, Longfellow composed volume after volume of mellifluous verse that made him famous throughout the world. *Hyperion* (1839), *Evangeline* (1847), *Hiawatha* (1855), and *The Courtship of Miles Standish* (1858) delighted the largest audience, perhaps, that any American poet ever commanded. His sentimentality, his didacticism, his optimism, and his antiquarianism satisfied popular taste. If his Hiawatha smacked more of Cambridge, Massachusetts, than of the shores of Gitchie Gumee, and if the brawny "Village Blacksmith" was a Whig dream of a docile and respectful workingman, poems like "A Psalm of Life" expressed without irony the aspirations of middle-class America.

> Let us, then, be up and doing,
>    With a heart for any fate;
> Still achieving, still pursuing,
>    Learn to labor and to wait.

Longfellow and his Boston and Cambridge associates belonged to the coterie of writers who contributed to what Van Wyck Brooks called, following the self-satisfied Yankees' own estimate of themselves, "The Flowering of New England." The emphasis placed by historians on this regional renaissance has partially obscured the intellectual and artistic activity of other sections, notably New York. Yet, New England's "golden day" was real enough. No other region contained such a hive of industrious writers. Much of their cul-

273

ture was thin and bookish, and the great reputations once enjoyed by James Russell Lowell, Oliver Wendell Holmes, and John Greenleaf Whittier have deservedly shrunk. But the cumulative output of New England between 1830 and 1850 remains impressive, and the great names live on: Francis Parkman and William H. Prescott, historians; Ralph Waldo Emerson and Henry David Thoreau, essayists and poets; Nathaniel Hawthorne, writer of romances and tales.

## Edgar Allan Poe

One Bostonian who did not relish Boston's appreciation of itself was Edgar Allan Poe (1809–1849). Although born in the "hub of the universe," a city he sarcastically referred to in later life as "Frogpond," Poe regarded himself a Virginian. After the death of his actor parents during his infancy, he grew up in Richmond where his foster-father John Allan was a substantial merchant. He attended the University of Virginia until Allan's stinginess and Poe's own gambling debts forced him to leave. His subsequent career included a two-year hitch in the army, a nomination to West Point in 1830, and dismissal for gross neglect of duty in 1831. Two volumes of verse, *Tamerlane* (1827) and *Al Aaraaf* (1829), preceded his becoming a professional man of letters after the West Point fiasco.

Nothing could seduce Poe from this "most noble profession," as he once referred to it, but he spent the rest of his short life in the American Grub Street, writing and editing brilliantly for inferior men, and publishing poems, stories, and critical essays that brought him little. In his most productive year, 1843, Poe earned $300. His impoverished term with the literary Bohemians of Philadelphia, Baltimore, and New York aggravated his natural instability. In 1836 he had married his thirteen-year-old cousin, Virginia Clemm. "I became insane," he wrote after her death ten years later, "with long intervals of horrible sanity." In 1849, Poe was found lying unconscious in a Baltimore street and died in delirium at the age of forty.

Poe was no apostle of progress. He had no taste for middle-class truths, and democracy displeased him. As a literary critic he performed a tremendous service by attacking American provincialism in cruel reviews of bad books. His own poetry and fiction contained most of the weaknesses he detected in his inferiors: theatricality, bombast, and sentimentality. But in stories like "The Fall of the House of Usher," "The Imp of the Perverse," "The Black Cat," "The Man in the Crowd," and "The Premature Burial"—tales of murderers, neurotics, the near-insane—his vulgarity was redeemed by an extraordinary intelligence and intensity. The owner of the black cat who sorrowfully cuts out the eyes of his pet, the brother who entombs his sister alive, the lover who pulls out the teeth of his mistress while she sleeps in a cataleptic trance, all live in a tormented world far removed from Emerson's optimistic America, if not our own. Yet Poe's very exoticism proved a tonic for the democratic culture he rejected, and his work profoundly influenced later poets and critics in Europe and America.

## Emerson and transcendentalism

The most universal literary figure of his generation was Ralph Waldo Emerson (1803–1882). Boston-born and Harvard-educated, he entered the ministry like his father and grandfather before him, but he resigned his pastorate in 1832 because he found church formality meaningless. Thereafter, he devoted himself to writing and lecturing. *Nature* (1836), which presented in condensed form most of the themes of his later works, was followed by two volumes of essays (1841, 1844), *Poems* (1847), *Representative Men* (1850), *English Traits* (1856), and *The Conduct of Life* (1860).

Half Yankee and half yogi, Emerson contained within himself the warring tendencies of his age. Part of him belonged to the practical American world of banks and railroads, and no one celebrated more enthusiastically than he (see his essays on "Wealth," "Power," and "Napoleon") the deeds of powerful individualists. At the same time, Emerson was a mystic and an idealist who looked upon the external world as a passing show and detected an unchanging reality behind it. This shrewd and canny man declared himself to be "part and particle" of God and rejoiced in the unsettling effect his theories had on his countrymen.

Like many other Boston intellectuals of his day, Emerson rebelled against the coldness of the Unitarian faith, which while repudiating the harsh Calvinist doctrine of human depravity and a vengeful God, became passionless in the process. Emerson wanted to revive old-time Puritan fervor without the rigidities of Puritan theology. Quakerism, with its doctrine of the inner light, its gentleness, and its hu-

*Transcendentalism's positive thinker, Ralph Waldo Emerson of Boston.*

manitarianism, moved him deeply, and he was drawn to any philosophy that broke down the barriers between mind and matter. In Emerson's youth, the philosophy of the English materialist John Locke was still much in vogue. Locke had held that ideas did not arise spontaneously in the mind but that they were implanted there by the impressions of the external world acting through the senses. This meant that spirit was subordinate to matter. Emerson's own disposition told him otherwise, and he found support for his idealism in the works of certain continental and Scottish philosophers, oriental poets and sages, and in English romantic poetry.

Transcendentalism, the philosophy associated with Emerson and his sympathizers, was not a systematic faith; it had no creed and could not easily be defined. To some, the word "transcendentalist" covered "all those who contend for perfect freedom, who look for progress in philosophy and theology, and who sympathize with each other in the hope that the future will not always be as the past." To the journalist and critic Orestes Brownson, the only common bond shared by the transcendentalists was opposition "to the old school":

> They do not swear by Locke, and they recognize no authority in matters of opinion but the human mind, whether termed the reason with some of them, or the soul with others. They have all felt that our old catechisms need revision, and that our old systems of philosophy do not do justice to all the elements of human nature, and that these systems can by no means furnish a solid basis for a belief in God, much less in Christianity. Some of them . . . ignore all philosophy, plant themselves in their instincts and wait for the huge world to come round to them. . . . Some of them reason . . . others merely dream.

Although vague in its outlines, transcendental doctrine was nobly formulated in Emerson's essays and lectures, in which he announced to his fellow Americans that they, too, could speak to God directly without churches and creeds. He urged them to be self-reliant, to get their experience at first hand. Every object in the physical world had a spiritual meaning, and those capable of seeing

275

that material things were the symbols of spiritual truths might best understand nature's purpose. The ability to communicate with God, or the "Over Soul," was everyone's gift; but only a few poets, scholars, and philosophers (Emerson called them men of "Reason") had developed this inborn capacity. From them, others might learn that only the idea is real, that evil is negative (the mere absence of good), and that a kindly destiny awaited them.

These thoughts Emerson expressed in fresh and audacious language. Even in his most abstract utterances, he used simple concrete words and homely illustrations:

*The world of any moment is the merest appearance. Some great decorum, some fetish of a government, some ephemeral trade, or war, or man, is cried up by half mankind and cried down by the other half, as if all depended on this particular up or down. The odds are that the whole question is not worth the poorest thought which the scholar has lost in listening to the controversy. Let him not quit his belief that a popgun is a popgun, though the ancient and honorable of the earth affirm it to be the crack of doom.*

To an audience of levelers, Emerson urged each man to stand up against public opinion, be an individual:

*What I must do is all that concerns me, not what the people think. . . . It is easy in the world to live after the world's opinion, it is easy in solitude to live after our own; but the great man is he who in the midst of the crowd keeps with perfect sweetness the independence of solitude.*

A number of Emerson's contemporaries tried to live according to his precepts: Henry David Thoreau as the transcendental adventurer of Walden Pond, Walt Whitman as the democratic poet, Theodore Parker as the minister-reformer, and others.

### Thoreau

Henry David Thoreau (1817–1862), like Emerson, his friend and mentor, was a graduate of Harvard and a resident of Concord, Massachusetts. "He declined," Emerson later wrote of him, "to give up his large ambi-

tion of knowledge and action for any narrow craft or profession, aiming at a much more comprehensive calling, the art of living well." Thoreau gave all his time to self-cultivation and self-exploration, and meticulously entered the results in his literary medium, the diary-like record of his experiences.

In *A Week on the Concord and Merrimack Rivers* (1849), *Civil Disobedience* (1849), and especially *Walden; or, Life in the Woods* (1854), Thoreau expressed his tart and unconventional conclusions about literature, religion, government, and social relations. Many of the reformers were his friends, but he distrusted their work and meant to keep himself free from what he called "greasy familiarity." Good fellowship he once described as "the virtue of pigs in a litter, which lie close together to keep each other warm." "Not satisfied with defiling one another in this world," he wrote, "we would all go to heaven together."

Like most transcendentalists, Thoreau was an unblushing egoist, but he wrote about himself, he said, because he knew no one else so well. Moreover, his accounts of how he discovered the miraculous in the common contained suggestions for those who led "lives of quiet desperation." He asked a generation geared to practicalities, what do the practicalities of life amount to? The wealth of the world, he said, is less a reward than one true vision.

*The ways by which you may get money almost without exception lead downward. . . . There is no more fatal blunderer than he who consumes the great part of his life getting his living . . . you must get your living by loving. . . . It is not enough to tell me that you worked hard to get your gold. So does the Devil work hard.*

Thoreau advised his countrymen to simplify their private lives and to simplify their government, too. He regarded the state as a threat to true independence. Abolitionist, naturalist, poet, and rebel, and a down-to-earth but subtle writer—he attracted no great notice while he lived. In our day, *Walden* is justly considered a literary masterpiece, and its author—who discovered a universe in Concord—is regarded as one of the most original minds of the New England renaissance.

## Walt Whitman

The poet whose arrival Emerson had predicted in his essay "The Transcendentalist" (1842) was soon to appear. Emerson had written:

*We have yet had no genius in America, with tyrannous eye, which knew the value of our incomparable materials, and saw, in the barbarism and materialism of the times, another carnival of the same gods whose picture he so admires in Homer. . . . Banks and tariffs, the newspaper and the caucus, Methodism and Unitarianism, are flat and dull to dull people, but rest on the same foundations of wonder as the town of Troy and the temple of Delphi, and are as swiftly passing away. Our log-rolling, our stumps and their politics, our fisheries, our Negroes and Indians . . . the northern trade, the southern planting, the western clearing, Oregon and Texas, are yet unsung. Yet America is a poem in our eyes; its ample geography dazzles the imagination, and it will not wait long for metres.*

The "genius" Emerson demanded was Walt Whitman (1818-1892), born on Long Island and a lifelong New Yorker. During his formative years, Whitman worked as schoolteacher, printer, carpenter, journalist, publisher, editor. When *Leaves of Grass,* his first volume of poems, appeared in 1855, its undisguised references to the body and sex caused Whitman to be denounced as the "dirtiest beast of his age." The most friendly review, save the three reviews he wrote himself, described his verse as "a sort of excited compound of New England transcendentalism and New York rowdy." Emerson was the only eminent writer who instantly discerned Whitman's freshness and found (as he wrote to the poet) "incomparable things, said incomparably well."

Whitman's poems, like Emerson's essays,

embody the idea of progress, celebrate the innate goodness of man, and idealize nature; they insist on the spiritual reality underlying the material world. But Whitman looked more to the people than to his own soul for inspiration. Other poets, he said,

*have adhered to the principle, and shown it, that the poet and the savant form classes by themselves, above the people, and more refined than the people, I show that they are just as great when of the people, partaking of the common idioms, manners, the earth, the rude visage of animals and trees, and what is vulgar.*

This belief prompted him to write poems about Negroes and Indians, carpenters, coach drivers, sailors, and trappers, felons and prostitutes, and above all, himself:

*I celebrate myself, and sing myself,*
*And what I assume, you shall assume,*
*For every atom belonging to me as good belongs*
*    to you.*

In his poems, Whitman imagined ranks, races, and civilizations commingling, and it was to be America's mission, he held, to promote this final fellowship of peoples. At home he saw much in his generation to displease him. His optimism was severely tested by the Civil War, and his faith in America's manifest destiny was shaken by the events after 1865 (see *Democratic Vistas,* 1871), but he did not despair:

*Do I contradict myself?*
*Very well then I contradict myself,*
*(I am large, I contain multitudes.)*

Whitman died believing that in the people there existed "a miraculous wealth of latent power and capacity."

## Naysayers

Emerson, like Whitman, made many trenchant criticisms of American society, but, like the New Yorker, his optimism never flagged. Some of his fellow writers, however, were less sure.

Nathaniel Hawthorne (1804-1864) was one

who could not slough off the pessimistic doctrines of his Puritan forefathers on the irretrievable fall of man. The son of a Salem shipmaster, Hawthorne attended Bowdoin College with the more sanguine Longfellow and grew up to be a robust, masculine person who held government jobs and enjoyed human contacts. He was not the recluse he has sometimes been painted, but his ideas went against the grain of his age. In his tales and sketches, and in his novels—*The Scarlet Letter* (1850), for example—Hawthorne painted a somber moral landscape where men and women were devoured by vices they were constrained to keep secret, but which he exposed. These terrible facts of life mocked the claims of progress. In his works, schemes for human renovation ("Earth's Holocaust," "The Celestial Railway") come to nought; reformers, scientists, and secret

*Heir of the Puritans,*
*Nathaniel Hawthorne of Salem.*

probers are changed into monstrous villains thwarted in their search for perfection (*The Blithedale Romance,* "Ethan Brand," and "Rappaccini's Daughter").

Hawthorne's New York friend Herman Melville (1819-1891) also clung to the idea of original sin. After his father's bankruptcy, Melville endured the humiliations of genteel poverty which were only deepened by teaching school. In 1841 he quit city life and sailed on a whaling ship to the South Seas. Three years of adventuring in the Pacific provided materials for his two best-selling books, *Typee* (1846) and *Omoo* (1847). His reputation declined after he stopped writing light-hearted sketches of Polynesian life and turned to public as well as to his private conflicts.

An ardent nationalist and celebrator of "the great democratic God," Melville nevertheless cautioned against a freedom that sanctioned barbarism. He pronounced slavery "a blot, foul as the craterpool of hell," and predicted that "These South savannahs may yet prove battlefields." A somber observer of the war he envisaged, he wrote in *Battle-Pieces* (1866) some of the noblest poetry on this tragic episode.

In rejecting transcendental optimism, Melville reacted even more strongly than Hawthorne against Emerson's blandness. Evil, for Melville, resided not merely in the tainted heart, that "foul cavern," as Hawthorne called it; evil hung over the world like a curtain. In *Moby Dick* (1851), his finest novel, Melville struck through the "pasteboard mask" of life to confront this eternal menace. Ahab, a Yankee whaling captain, the doomed hero of the novel, spends himself in pursuit of Moby Dick, a gigantic white whale that symbolized the beauty, the wickedness, and the mystery of nature. The pursuit fails; Ahab dies. If man were half-divine, as the transcendentalists insisted, according to Melville he nonetheless faced a tragic destiny. God remained unknowable, progress an illusion; the seeker was only led on and deceived by what he saw and thought.

278

## III Plastic and performing arts

*Painters and sculptors*

The division in American society between those preoccupied with "stern realities" and those who would keep the arts uncontaminated by "dirty facts" was felt by the would-be painter and sculptor even more than by the writer. The Bible forbade the making of images and likenesses that dignified man rather than God. To many sturdy democrats, moreover, the fine arts seemed particularly aristocratic, products of "corrupt and despotic courts, the flatterers of tyranny," as even the refined *North American Review* described them in 1825.

In an environment in which no utility could be found for the "meager productions of the pencil, the brush or the chisel," it is not surprising that Samuel F. B. Morse turned to invention after spending half his life struggling as an artist, or that many American artists began their careers in the more practical roles of artisans and mechanics. The celebrated sculptor Hiram Powers (1805-1873) worked in a Cincinnati organ factory and made wax statues before turning to art as a career. His mechanical ingenuity as well as his ability to model "busts remarkable for their perfect resemblance" accounted for Powers's early reputation. But his most popular work, the "Greek Slave"—the statue that won him international fame—reveals only his adoption of popular notions of ideal form devoid of the fruits of his practical past.

Powers's work pleased the critics of the 1830s who only praised art that raised "the mind above the sordid interest of a merely material life." Artists were invited to contemplate native forests, rivers, and sunsets, which "inspired the soul of man with visions of the ideal, the beautiful, the immortal." The English painter Thomas Cole (1801-1848) became famous in America in this period for his romantic renditions of Hudson River and Catskill Mountain scenes dominated by "sweeping effects of storm cloud and streaming light to suggest the brooding presence of the Eternal." Asher Durand (1796-1886) and Thomas Doughty (1793-1856), American contemporaries of Cole in the Hudson River school, painted scenic wonders in the same grand mode. By 1860, a realistic school of landscape painters had emerged who caught the character of the horse Indians and early settlers on the Great Plains. Among the best were George Catlin (1796-1872) and Alfred Jacob Miller (1810-1874).

A few iconoclasts, notably the architect Horatio Greenough (1807-1883), tried to break down the unhappy distinction between the beautiful and the useful:

*The men who have reduced locomotion to its simplest elements, in the trotting wagon and the yacht America [Greenough wrote], are nearer to Athens at this moment than they who would bend the Greek temple to every use. I contend for Greek principles, not Greek things. If a flat sail goes nearest the wind, a bellying sail, though picturesque, must be given up. The slender harness, and tall gaunt wheels, are not only effective, they are beautiful for they respect the beauty of a horse, and do not uselessly tax him.*

But views like these remained unpopular during the Jacksonian period.

A change in the national attitude toward the fine arts could be observed after 1840, when patronage in the larger cities offered new hope to talented painters, sculptors, and architects. In the two decades before the Civil War, New York City, Philadelphia, and Boston, competing with each other for culture as

*"Distribution of the American Art
Union Prizes," December 25, 1847. Founded
in 1839 in New York City,
the American Art Union helped develop
nationwide interest in American
artists by its annual Christmas night
distribution of prizes and by other means.*

for trade, built up their "academies" and "athenaeums." Artists began to exhibit their work in private and public galleries, while new schools of design appeared along with magazines devoted to the fine arts. Although the artist's standing did not change much in the country as a whole, his rising prestige in rich metropolises and his growing confidence in the prospects of authentic native expression suggested a hitherto unsuspected cultural vitality.

The ordinary citizen, meanwhile, continued to derive more enjoyment from "a carnival of wild beasts" and from artistic phenomena like the huge panoramas, unwound from rollers, that presented with painstaking accuracy the Mississippi River or historical scenes like the landing of Lafayette. The depiction of native scenes sometimes attained lasting artistic merit, as in the works of John James Audubon (1785-1851) and the famous team of Currier and Ives. By fusing science and art, Audubon produced meticulous studies of American bird and animal life. Currier and Ives, meanwhile, flooded the country with gay lithographs of forest and farm, railroads, sleigh rides, and skating and boating scenes. Artists like William S. Mount (1807-1868), David G. Blyth (1815-1865), and George Caleb Bingham (1811-1879), the painter equivalents of the humorists and writers of tall tales, caught the atmosphere of minstrel shows, rowdy electioneering, and western river life.

### Drama and music

If moralists had stern reservations about literature and the plastic arts, they felt even more strongly about the theater. Dramatic productions, as one of them declared, "lead the minds of youth from serious reflection." Lay-preachers assailed the "vagabond profession" and the indecency of "displays of half-clad females." The most damning criticism of the theater was that it unfitted "mankind . . . for the common concerns of life."

But the theater seemed more vital than the fine arts and despite objections it flourished. Audiences heard and applauded everything from Shakespeare to the broadest farce. While New York remained the dramatic center, cities in every section supported theaters, and stars like Edwin Forrest, James K. Hackett, and Fanny Kemble won national reputations. Most popular of all were toe dancers like the ravishing Fanny Elssler, burlesque and popular opera, and E. P. Christy's celebrated minstrel show.

Coming into vogue in the early 1820s, minstrelsy expropriated and formalized characteristic strains of black folk culture that had been flowing freely through the popular consciousness long before white entertainers in blackface commercialized them. Both foreign and American observers often referred to the haunting chants and songs of the black man, his humor, his skill in extracting music and rhythms from primitive banjos, bones, and tambourines. Bayard Taylor, poet and traveler, asserted in 1849 that "Ethiopian melodies well deserve to be called, as they are in fact, the national airs of America. They follow

280

the American race in all its migrations, colonizations, and conquests."

Many white minstrels who incorporated Negro tunes and themes into their comic or sentimental songs had heard them in the South and Southwest. The comic dances that figured in minstrel shows also derived from the shuffles, shakedowns, and jigs of the slave compounds. Friends of the Negro then and later interpreted the "comic nigger" of blackface as a racial slur and preferred the Spiritual as a truer and more dignified expression of Negro character. Yet blackface humor was double-edged—self-parody in part, but also covertly "putting on ol' massa." The jaybird, turkey, crow, frog, bulldog, and fox enacted fables bearing closely on master-slave relations, with the master not infrequently discomfited. Denatured versions of slave songs by popular songwriters of the day like Dan Emmett and, later, Henry C. Work, failed to capture the force and incisiveness of the originals sung at black camp meetings. But even the act of borrowing undercut the supposition of black inferiority. Perhaps it was not accidental that the appeal of minstrelsy coincided with the spread of emancipation sentiment, or that Walt Whitman should see in the influence of musical Negro dialects on English speech the possible basis for a native grand opera.

Foreigners might comment on the "barbarity" of American music, but between 1820 and 1860, along with the perfection of minstrelsy, instrumental and choral performances improved. Artists from abroad successfully toured the country, and local musical societies in New York, Boston, and elsewhere offered orchestral and choral programs to appreciative if uncritical audiences. The ingratiating ballads of Stephen Foster (1826–1864), one of the first of a long line of northerners to romanticize the "sunny South," also were sung across the land; and opera, introduced about 1825, had some success in a few of the larger cities. Hymn writers like Boston's Lowell Mason (1792–1872), composer of "Nearer My God to Thee" and "From Greenland's Icy Mountains," evoked a more genuine response and grew rich from the sales of their songs.

### Newspapers and magazines

"The influence and circulation of newspapers," wrote an astonished visitor to the United States about 1830, "is great beyond anything known in Europe. . . . Every village, nay, almost every hamlet, has its press." From 1801 to 1833, the number of newspapers rose from 200 to 1200, most of them weeklies. The larger cities boasted numerous daily papers, and competition grew ferocious. New York City alone in 1830 had 47 papers, only one daily among them claiming as many as 4000 subscribers. Enterprising editors reduced the price of their papers to a penny and sought to lure readers by featuring "robberies, thefts, murders, awful catastrophes and wonderful escapes."

Benjamin Day's *New York Sun* pioneered in the new sensationalism, but Day's rival, James Gordon Bennett of the *Herald,* soon surpassed him. Bennett played up the news value of New York society (he headlined his own marriage), and developed circulation techniques quickly copied throughout the country. New printing presses and improved delivery methods helped meet the rising demand.

The press, one reader pointed out, served as a kind of gutter that carried away "all the wanton vagaries of the imagination, all the inventions of malice, all the scandal, and all the corruptions of heart in village, town, or city." Yet newspapers did more than pander to low tastes. Mercantile interests, religious denominations, and political parties sponsored their own papers, and each editor rode his private hobby horse. The best editors explained and interpreted pertinent issues, sometimes making demands upon their readers that few modern editors would attempt.

Magazines also sprang up by the dozens in the middle decades, but few survived for long. With no generally accepted literary standards to rely upon, always in danger of offending the prudish, and yet aware of the "vulgar" preferences of their public, harassed magazine editors had no way to turn. Delinquent subscribers probably were most responsible for the high mortality of periodicals, but the penny newspapers and cheap imprints of pirated English books also reduced their audience. A few metropolitan monthlies or quarterlies gained national audiences—*The North American Review* (Boston), *The Knickerbocker Magazine* (New York), *Graham's Magazine* (Philadelphia), and *The Southern Literary Messenger* (Richmond). They printed pieces by Cooper, Poe, Bryant, Hawthorne, Holmes, and Longfellow, and by lesser figures, but provided only a meager outlet for American talent.

The female audience had its choice of *The Ladies Magazine,* edited by Sarah Josepha Hale, and *Godey's Lady's Book,* with which the former merged in 1836. *Godey's* did more than dictate fashions and rule over morals and manners. Miss Hale, literary editor of the magazine for many years, is best known as the author of "Mary's Lamb," but she published and reviewed intelligently the productions of leading American writers, paid for poems and articles (a significant innovation), and between 1837 and 1849 increased her magazine's circulation from 10,000 to 40,000. The success of *Godey's* and its imitators indicated that American women—the principal consumers of books and magazines—would soon dominate the cultural life of the nation. Their interest was indispensable, but they imposed a kind of petticoat tyranny over American letters narrowly defining the limits of propriety.

## IV   Education: formal and informal

### In lower schools

The religious spirit that had such a powerful effect on literature and the arts in America was felt even more strongly in education. What American leaders wanted was a "baptized intelligence." Most Americans favored Bible teaching in the schools because, as the famous Presbyterian minister Lyman Beecher expressed it, the Bible gave no sanction "to civil broils, or resistance to lawful authority, but commands all men to follow peace, and to obey magistrates that are set over them, whatever the form of government may be."

But despite the lip service paid to Christian, democratic, and practical education, crusaders for free public schools faced an apathetic and often hostile populace. Men who could afford to educate their children in private academies saw no reason why they should be taxed to educate children of the poor. Administrators of private and parochial schools, farmers, and non-English-speaking groups joined the conservatives in fighting the free-school movement. But the advocates of free public schools had strong arguments. Every class would benefit, said one free-school publicist in 1832:

> The man who is poor must see that this is the only way he can secure education for his children. The man in moderate circumstances ... will have his children taught for a less sum than he pays at present. The rich man, who will be heavily taxed, must see that his course secures to the rising generation the only means of perpetuating our institutions, and the only guarantee that his children will be protected.

The leaders of the free-school movement—men like Horace Mann in Massachusetts, Henry Barnard in Connecticut, and Calvin Stowe in Ohio—hammered away with these arguments in widely circulated reports and articles based on thorough investigations, and finally won their battle. By 1860, most northern states had installed a tax-supported school program. But education on all levels continued to suffer from low salaries, poor equipment, primitive pedagogy, unmanageably large classes, and a short school term.

Throughout the period, educational reformers suggested a variety of schemes to raise the educational level but usually met stiff opposition. In defense of the critics, it must be acknowledged that many quacks flourished in the profession, and "painless" methods for acquiring a quick education were in vogue. At the same time, the quality of education did improve enough for foreigners to comment on the exceptional literacy of the American public. The graded school with orderly upward progress made higher standards easier to impose; and improved teaching made the high standards easier to achieve.

Formal teacher training came about largely through the work of Horace Mann, who established the first so-called normal schools for the preparation of teachers, and Henry Barnard, one of the founders of the American Association for the Advancement of Education (1855) and editor of the influential *American Journal of Education*.

Private academies were providing elementary and secondary education for girls by the 1840s. In 1833, Oberlin became the first coeducational college; in 1858, the University of Iowa, the first coeducational state university. For the most part, girls' seminaries concentrated on the ornamental attainments. The learned woman, or "blue-stocking," was considered a monstrosity, "an unsexed woman" who "does not fill her true place in the world. . . . It is thought more creditable," a writer said in 1833, "for a young woman . . . to be sentimental [rather] than learned—to *appear* than to *be*." Yet schools like Miss Emma Willard's Troy Female Seminary and Catherine Beecher's Hartford Female Seminary did attempt to provide a substantial intellectual diet for their students.

Public high schools were rare until 1840, but during the next two decades the number increased substantially, especially in Massachusetts, New York, and Ohio. Such schools offered a more practical kind of education than private schools and were open to both girls and boys.

### In colleges and universities

The number of so-called American colleges grew from 16 in 1799 to 182 in 1860. In these years 412 others started and died. Colleges, said a prominent educator in 1848,

*rise up like mushrooms on our luxuriant soil. They are duly lauded and puffed for a day; and then they sink to be heard of no more. . . . Our people, at first, oppose all distinctions whatever as odious and aristocratical; and then, presently, seek with avidity such as remain accessible. At first they denounce colleges, and then choose to have a college in every district or county, or for every sect and party—and to boast of a college education, and to sport with high sounding literary titles—as if these imparted sense or wisdom or knowledge.*

The multiplication of colleges resulted in part from the difficulties and expenses of travel, but sectarian rivalry and local pride were probably the principal causes. Each important denomination and many minor ones supported one or more colleges that hoped to rekindle the spirit of piety, most of them hardly more than dressed-up academies which students might enter at fourteen or fifteen. So-called universities were hardly more than large colleges. Most professional schools in this period, law and medical schools in particular, were independent institutions.

College and university curriculums varied little throughout the country. Latin, Greek, mathematics, science, political economy, and moral philosophy offered a solid enough program, but teaching by rote was as common as in lower schools. Before the Civil War, a few notable professors found time to write and experiment, but in general the college atmosphere offered little stimulation. With sectarianism rampant and political issues explosive, no American college could live up to Jefferson's dream of a higher institution based "on the illimitable freedom of the human mind."

### Through self-help

Philosophers of democracy like Franklin and Jefferson had insisted that only an

284

educated electorate could sustain a republican government. Many, too busy or too old to go to school, continued to believe them. One institution designed to meet adult needs, especially in the towns and cities, where groups could easily come together for study, was the mutual-improvement, or -benefit, society.

An even more popular informal educational institution was the lyceum, which grew out of the proposals of an Englishmen, Lord Henry Brougham. In his *Political Observations Upon the Education of the People* (1825), which went through more than thirty editions in five years, Brougham called for a system of public lectures on the arts and sciences, the formation of discussion societies, the establishment of libraries for workingmen, and the publication of cheap books. His admirers in America, spurred on by a New Englander, Joseph Holbrook, soon put his recommendations into practice.

By 1835, lyceums could be found in fifteen states, their activities coordinated by a national lyceum organization. By 1860, no less than 3000 lyceums had been set up, mainly in New England, New York, and the upper Mississippi Valley, where public-school sentiment was strong. The lyceums sponsored talks on every conceivable topic, with scientific and practical subjects arousing the greatest interest. Eminent men like Emerson addressed lyceum audiences on such themes as "Wealth" and "Power," and others of stature discoursed on the issues of the day.

The lyceums had their faults. They often "confounded knowledge of useful things with useful knowledge." The education they offered was likely to remain superficial and remote from the interest of the very classes for which it was theoretically designed. Yet lyceums helped bridge the gulf between the learned minority and the community and fostered the ideal of culture in a predominantly commercial society.

## V    Reformers

### Temperance and humanitarianism

The spirit of reform of which the free-school and lyceum movements were reflections pervaded America during the antebellum years. Most reformers were religious people, motivated by evangelical zeal to promote pet projects, many of them eccentric, such as seeking salvation through dress and diet practices or the abandonment of money. But reform had its less visionary side as well. During the 1830s and 1840s, a number of men and women devoted their lives to stamping out specific social evils or to supporting defensible social innovations: temperance in the consumption of alcohol; treatment of the insane and the criminal; education for the deaf, dumb, and blind; equality for women; world peace; and the abolition of slavery.

Until abolitionism aroused the country after 1830, the "temperance" movement was the most intense reform enterprise. What caused the rising consumption of liquor is hard to say, but the social scapegoats most frequently pointed to were the excessive mobility of the American population, the attendant breakup of families and disruption of community life, the loneliness and fatigue of the farmer, and the long hours of the industrial worker newly arrived in the impersonal city from the country or from another country. In 1820, census takers would not list distilling as a separate industry since almost everyone in rural areas engaged in it. In the cities, saloons were numbered in the thousands.

The agitation against drinking had been given a strong impetus by the publication in 1805 of Dr. Benjamin Rush's *Inquiry into the*

*Effect of Ardent Spirits upon the Human Mind and Body.* But whereas Rush attacked drinking as bad for the health, the temperance reformers stressed its moral viciousness. This approach was promoted after 1810 by Lyman Beecher and his fellow evangelical preachers, who—with the support of Bible and Tract Societies and missionary boards—soon induced millions to take the pledge as "teetotalers." In 1826 the American Temperance Society was organized in Boston to coordinate the activities of hundreds of local groups.

One surviving example of teetotaling propaganda is Timothy Shay Arthur's *Ten Nights in a Bar-Room.* But the temperance crusaders went beyond persuasion to legislation. The first Prohibition law was enacted in Maine in 1846, and within five years twelve other states, all in the North, had adopted some kind of liquor-control law. Many who supported such legislation were opposed to total Prohibition, and their quarrels with the teetotalers eventually weakened the movement. Yet the campaign against "demon rum" probably reduced the consumption of alcohol. It also offered a training ground for supporters of other reform movements.

One of the most salutary of these was the crusade for humane hospital treatment of the insane and feebleminded, led by Dorothea Lynde Dix (1802–1887). In her *Memorial to the Legislature of Massachusetts* (1834), the result of painstaking investigation, Miss Dix depicted conditions in asylums throughout the state as medieval in their barbarity. To the popular mind, insanity was a hideous moral regression into animality, and Miss Dix found its victims whipped, caged, and neglected as if they were indeed dangerous beasts. In her fact-strewn and quietly effective summary, she omitted nothing: "The condition of human beings, reduced to the extremest states of degradation and misery, cannot be exhibited in softened language or adorn a polished page." Before she died in 1887 Miss Dix played an important part in establishing mental hospitals in more than thirty states.

## Communitarians

In the early stages of the industrial revolution in America as in Britain and France, the condition of the workers often seemed so oppressive that leading industrialists themselves thought there must be some alternative to the barbarism around them, and substitutes for private capitalism won respectable and even conservative consideration. Cooperatives and, indeed, entire new cooperative communities were proposed by the most thoroughgoing. Before the militant abolitionism of William Lloyd Garrison heightened feelings and hopes on the slave issue in the 1830s, the idea of black communities as an alternative to black bondage also attracted followers.

It became fashionable to debunk the early nineteenth-century communitarians as escapists and nitwits, even as the precursors of twentieth-century totalitarianism. But in pointing out the obvious limitations of the utopian mentality, one need not throw out the baby with the bath water. Early American communities, both religious and secular, were efforts to improve society, not escape it. The communitarian believed in social harmony rather than in class warfare, in voluntary action rather than in compulsion.

The two most controversial community experiments in this period were inspired by Robert Owen, a successful manufacturer and industrial reformer from New Lanark, Scotland, and Charles Fourier, a French socialist.

Owen came to America in 1825 to found a community at New Harmony, Indiana, on a site he had purchased from a group of German communitarians known as the Rappites. A number of gifted European scholars came to Owen's utopia, and for a time the community offered the best education in the country, but the rank and file had more than their share of human frailties. According to Timothy Flint, a missionary and novelist, New Harmony attracted

*the indolent, the unprincipled, men of desperate fortunes, moon-worshippers, romantic young men ... those who had dreamed about earthly Elysiums, a great many honest aspirants after a better order of things, poor men simply desiring an education for their children.*

286

A good many visitors wondered even in 1825 whether Owen's ideas could "keep alive that spirit of liberty and self-respect for one's own opinion, that so peculiarly belongs to the American people." Owen's experiment did indeed fail after two years, hastened to its end more by its founder's intolerance of common practice than by his main purpose: the establishment of a rational system of society. Owen's denunciation of "MARRIAGE," as one along with "PRIVATE OR INDIVIDUAL PROPERTY" and "absurd and irrational SYSTEMS OF RELIGION" in his "TRINITY of the most monstrous evils that could be combined to inflict mental and physical evil," got him into most trouble. No instance of licentiousness was ever authenticated at New Harmony, but this did not save Owen from being classed by his critics with "whores and whoremongers," nor his community from being branded as "one great brothel."

The collapse of New Harmony in 1827 speeded the demise of Nashoba, the black community set up by the Owenite Englishwoman Frances Wright in 1826 in Shelby County, Tennessee. Ironically, Nashoba was situated on 300 acres once forcibly taken from the Chickasaw Indians. From 50 to 100 slaves were to be brought here, hopefully to earn enough money to purchase their freedom while learning the attitudes and skills needed to sustain it. Miss Wright, however, soon imposed on Nashoba a full-scale communitarian scheme open to whites as well as blacks. She also went further than Owen in attacking marriage and religion, and one of her lieutenants proceeded to publish in a popular magazine accounts of the free sexual relationships there. Miss Wright defended these. If "the possession of the right of free action," she said, "inspire not the courage to exercise the right, liberty has done but little for us." Nashoba did not long survive the assaults upon it; yet its end was happier than that of many other communities in that Miss Wright sailed with Nashoba's slaves in January 1830 to Haiti, where they were emancipated.

Owenism had threatened middle-class Americans with free thought and free love. The doctrines of Fourier seemed less dangerous, and during the 1840s were espoused by a talented and respectable nucleus: Albert Brisbane, Fourier's chief propagandist; Parke Godwin, reformer and critic; Margaret Fuller, feminist, famed conversationalist, critic, and one-time editor of *The Dial,* the organ of the transcendentalists; George Ripley, founder of Brook Farm; and many others. Most of them eventually gave up their early radicalism, but for some years they spread Fourier's theories across the country.

The Fourierists (or "Fury-ites," as their enemies called them) regarded private capitalism as wasteful and degrading. If men would only abandon the competitive way and gather in *phalanxes,* or associated groups, they could transform the world of work into a paradise. What particularly appealed to the Fourierists, many of whom were New England transcendentalists, was the emphasis that Fourier put on practical idealism and the dignity of the worker.

Between 1840 and 1850, Fourier's followers organized more than forty phalanxes in the United States. None was successful, but one at least became a lasting legend, the subject of Hawthorne's *The Blithedale Romance.* This was Brook Farm, organized by a group of transcendentalist intellectuals in 1841 and expressly converted to Fourierism in 1843–1844. More interested at first in the Oversoul than in their bank accounts, the Brook Farmers decided to demonstrate the possibility of combining the life of the mind with manual labor. ("After breakfast," Hawthorne noted in his diary, "Mr. Ripley put a four-pronged instrument into my hands, which he gave me to understand was called a pitch-fork; and he and Mr. Farley being armed with similar weapons, we all commenced a gallant attack upon a heap of manure.") The community, which never numbered more than 100, attracted about 4000 visitors a year. But its practical side proved less successful. In 1847 a fire ruined the already insolvent enterprise and it was abandoned.

Secular communities like Owen's and Fourier's may have failed because of the idiosyncrasies of their promoters. Yet Americans as a rule proved too individualistic to sink their glowing private prospects in such projects.

*Abolition*

From the 1830s on, one reform issue grew larger and more portentous until it overshadowed all others: the antislavery cause, or abolition. Its origins reached back to the late seventeenth century, when humanitarian Puritans like Samuel Sewall and Roger Williams spoke out against the ownership of human chattel. The Quakers had long fought the buying and selling of slaves by their coreligionists, and in the Revolutionary and post-Revolutionary eras liberals in every section deplored slavery as a mortal disease. It was this conviction that inspired the American Colonization Society, founded in 1817 with private, state, and federal support, to establish Liberia in 1822 as a colony for ex-slaves. Unfortunately for the proponents of colonization, hardly more than a thousand free Negroes were transported to Africa between 1822 and 1830, and the others showed little desire to emigrate. By 1860 no more than 15,000 American blacks had settled outside the country. The failure of the colonization plan and the ineffectiveness of those who backed gradual liberation encouraged radical abolitionists to start their campaign for immediate emancipation.

In 1831, William Lloyd Garrison began publishing *The Liberator*, the first outright abolitionist periodical. Its appearance marked the beginning of the great antislavery offensive. Garrison was a Massachusetts journalist, neurotic and wayward yet gentle and humorous, tolerant on occasion yet uncompromising in his cherished beliefs. As with many of his followers, abolition was only one of Garrison's causes. He was an ardent worker for women's rights and international peace, a fervent opponent of capital punishment and imprisonment for debt. But after 1830 slavery absorbed him. He denounced slavery not because it was inefficient or undemocratic or unjust, but because it was sinful. The Constitution, which guaranteed slavery, he called "the most bloody and heaven-daring arrangement ever made by men for the continuance and protection of a system of the most atrocious villainy ever exhibited on earth." And he publicly burned copies.

Garrison's vituperative attacks against the "Southern oppressors" did much to intensify antiabolition sentiment in the South, while his fanaticism frightened moderate antislavery people everywhere. His refusal to resort to political action also reduced his effectiveness. A different approach was taken by Theodore Dwight Weld of Ohio, who organized and directed the activities of the abolitionist societies in the Northwest. Weld preferred patient organization to flamboyant pronouncements, and his devoted followers, well versed in the techniques of revival meetings, converted thousands to the abolitionist cause. Before 1850, almost 2000 societies had been formed with a membership close to 200,000, and the talent and conscience of the North had rallied to the antislavery standard. John Greenleaf Whittier of Massachusetts became the bard of abolition, while Emerson, Thoreau, Whitman, Longfellow, and Melville all condemned slavery. Boston's eloquent Wendell Phillips thundered against it, as did reputable ministers like Theodore Parker and William Ellery Channing. Southerners like James G. Birney and the Grimké sisters renounced their slave property and joined the antislavery cause.

The abolitionists' strength lay in their unselfish dedication and their appeal to Christian principles. Their weakness lay in their reckoning insufficiently with the social barriers to be overcome by blacks once they were declared free. Since the abolitionists denounced slavery as a sin as well as a social evil, they concentrated upon arousing the conscience of the country, not only to break the slave's shackles but to welcome him to the open society. "To be without a plan," cried one of Garrison's followers, "is the true genius and glory of the Anti-Slavery enterprise!" In his discussions of slavery, even Theodore Weld once said he had "always presented it as preeminently a moral question, arresting the conscience of the nation. . . . As a question of politics and national economy, I have passed it with scarce a look or a word."

Such pronouncements reflected the abolitionist's conviction that the appeal to conscience must not be allowed to fail. If it failed, all would be lost. Practically all abolitionists abhorred the idea of violent revolution by the slaves, a fact seldom recognized in the South; nor did they envisage or want—as James Russell Lowell wrote in 1848—a civil war over slavery. Lowell did not, however, rule out the possibility:

*No one can deplore more sincerely than we do an armed appeal for justice. But still more deeply do we lament the cause of it. Starvation and slaughter are both bad, but while you tolerate the one you are creating the necessity for the other. Are the atrocities of men driven to insurrection so horrible as the fact that society has allowed them to become capable of their commission. If violence be not the way of obtaining social rights, neither is it capable of maintaining social wrongs.*

Once the Civil War started, most abolitionists preferred to let the South go in peace in the hope that slavery would wither sooner there if the section were isolated from the rest of the world. As the war progressed, abolitionists gradually altered their stand and were in the forefront of those who helped convert the war into a struggle for emancipation (see p. 437). When emancipation finally did come, the abolitionists themselves had worked out a constructive program for weaning the ex-slave to full citizenship. But all that was in the future.

In the mid-1830s even in the North, public opinion stigmatized the abolitionists as a band of misguided bigots whose activities on behalf of a people hopelessly inferior would destroy the Union if left unchecked. New York, Boston, Philadelphia, Cincinnati, as well as Richmond and Charleston—towns and cities in every section—were swept by anti-Garrison riots and mobbings, in defiance, or with the connivance, of the local authorities. Garrison was dragged through the streets of Boston by an angry mob of "genteel ruffians," as he called them, and with the not so secret connivance of the "higher" classes; George Thompson, an English abolitionist, was howled down and threatened with bodily harm; Elijah Lovejoy, an antislavery editor in Alton, Illinois, was murdered by a mob in 1837.

Despite the stern repression of the abolitionists in the North and the constant assurances given to southern leaders that the majority of people in the free states detested the ideas of *The Liberator,* the South grew ever more uneasy (see Chapter Thirteen). It demanded penal laws against antislavery terrorists and threatened economic reprisals if they were not silenced. Southern postmasters confiscated suspected abolitionist literature. Southern fears of slave insurrection and resentment against atrocity stories in abolitionist propaganda made the South magnify the strength of the antislavery movement in the North. The intemperate response of the southerners only increased northern antislavery sentiment. As the sectional conflict deepened, the dream of the millennium that had stirred the hearts of the reformers in the 1830s and 1840s faded.

## For further reading

Alexis de Tocqueville, *Democracy in America* (1835), is a work of genius on the period of this chapter. G. W. Pierson, *Tocqueville and Beaumont in* America (1938), adds considerably to the understanding of Tocqueville's work. A. F. Tyler, *Freedom's Ferment: Phases of American Social History to 1860*

(1944) is good on many topics. See also E. D. Branch, *The Sentimental Years 1836–1860* (1934). V. L. Parrington, *The Romantic Revolution in America 1800–1860* (1927) retains many merits. D. B. Davis, *Homicide in American Fiction 1798–1860* (1957), and Fred Somkin, *Unquiet Eagle: Memory and Desire in the Idea of American Freedom 1815–1860* (1967), are suggestive studies of social violence and literary reflection.

On individual writers, see Kay House, *Cooper's Americans* (1965); R. L. Rusk, *The Life of Ralph Waldo Emerson* (1949); J. W. Krutch, *Henry David Thoreau* (1948); A. H. Quinn, *Edgar Allan Poe* (1941); Mark Van Doren, *Nathaniel Hawthorne* (1949); Newton Arvin, *Herman Melville* (1950); and G. W. Allen, *The Solitary Singer: A Critical Biography of Walt Whitman* (1955). D. H. Lawrence, *Studies in Classic American Literature* (1923), is available in full, along with other penetrating literary studies, in the superb anthology, Edmund Wilson, ed., *The Shock of Recognition* (1943). F. O. Matthiessen, *American Renaissance* (1941, is a brilliant interpretation of America's literary flowering. Lewis Mumford, *The Golden Day* (1926), is also revealing. R. W. B. Lewis, *The American Adam* (1955), treats of innocence in American literature; Leo Marx, *The Machine in the Garden* (1964), of innocence under pressure.

O. W. Larkin, *Art and Life in America* (1949), covers the history of painting and sculpture. See also Richard McLanathan, *The American Tradition in the Arts* (1968), an illuminating study with emphasis on the period before the Civil War. Neil Harris, *The Artist in American Society: The Formative Years 1790–1860* (1968), is a searching analysis. Horatio Greenough's essays are conveniently collected in H. A. Small, ed., *Form and Function* (1957). On popular arts see A. H. Quinn, *A History of the American Drama from the Beginning to the Civil War* (1923); and J. T. Howard, *Our American Music* (1946). C. M. Rourke, *American Humor* (1931), is full of insight. F. L. Mott, *American Journalism: A History of Newspapers in the United States* (1950 ed.), *A History of American Magazines* (5 vols., 1930–1968) are standard.

The literature on education is more extensive than exhilarating. Relevant for this chapter are Paul Monroe, *Founding of the American Public School System* (1940). Merle Curti, *The Social Ideas of American Educators* (1935); and L. H. Tharp, *Until Victory: Horace Mann and Mary Peabody* (1953). The history of colleges is well presented in Frederick Rudolph, *The American College and University* (1962). See also, Richard Hofstadter and W. P. Metzger, *The Development of Academic Freedom in the United States* (1955). Carle Bode, *The American Lyceum, Town Meeting of the Mind* (1956), is the best account.

Books on specific reform movements include J. A. Krout, *The Origins of Prohibition* (1925); Albert Deutsch, *The Mentally Ill in America* (1937); Charles Nordhoff, *The Communistic Societies of the United States* (1875); Lindsay Swift, *Brook Farm* (1899); A. E. Bestor, *Backwoods Utopias* (1950); and W. H. and J. H. Pease, *Black Utopia: Negro Communal Experiments in America* (1963). Religion and reform are treated in Perry Miller, *The Life of the Mind in America, from the Revolution to the Civil War* (1966); W. R. Hutchinson, *The Transcendentalist Ministers—Church Reform in the New England Renaissance* (1959); T. L. Smith, *Revivalism and Social Reform in Mid-Nineteenth Century America* (1957); and C. S. Griffin, *Their Brothers' Keepers, Moral Stewardship in the United States 1800–1865* (1960).

P. J. Staudenraus, *The African Colonization Movement 1816–1865* (1961), is a scholarly monograph. Of the many studies of antislavery and abolitionist activities, the most comprehensive is D. L. Dumond, *AntiSlavery: The Crusade for Freedom in America* (2 vols., 1961). See also Martin Duberman, ed., *The Antislavery Vanguard, New Essays on the Abolitionists* (1965); Louis Filler, *The Crusade Against Slavery 1830–1860* (1960); G. H. Barnes, *The Anti-Slavery Impulse 1830–1844* (1933); and Truman Nelson, ed., *Documents of Upheaval, Selections from William Lloyd Garrison's* THE LIBERATOR *1831–1865* (1966). S. M. Elkins, *Slavery* (1959), offers a critique of the abolitionist approach. J. M. McPherson, *The Struggle for Equality, Abolitionists and the Negro in the Civil War and Reconstruction* (1964), while covering a later period, is valuable for insights into the abolitionists' program. See also readings cited for Chapter Thirteen.

# MANIFEST DESTINY

The struggle for power among the older sections of the country during the reign of Old Hickory did not obscure the beckoning opportunities in regions still to be encompassed in America's "empire for liberty."

Throughout the 1820s and 1830s, Americans were very much on the move not only into new states in the Louisiana Purchase but also deep into foreign territory beyond, all the way to the Pacific Coast and even to Pacific islands. Within little more than a quarter of a century thereafter, the unbroken expanse of the United States had been extended to its present limits, the annexation of Hawaii had been proposed, and the purchase of Alaska completed. Canada to the north and Cuba to the south, meanwhile, fed a craving for full hemispheric sovereignty that was curbed only with increasing difficulty once the slogan "Manifest Destiny" seemed to give the impetus of inevitability to America's explosive course.

The phrase Manifest Destiny became identified with expansionism only after 1845, but the idea of celestial design it embodied was much older. According to this idea, the "Father of the Universe," or the "Great Architect," had set aside the American continents and their island environs "for the free development of our yearly multiplying millions." No physical barrier, no foreign force, least of all what they often considered the sinister absolutism of the European system, could thwart the providential mission of the American people to extend *their* system across this hallowed land.

In this vein, Lewis Cass of Michigan told his fellow senators in February 1847:

*In Europe ... men are brought too much and kept too much in contact. There is not room for expansion. Minds of the highest order are pressed down by adverse circumstances, without the power of free exertion. ... I trust we are far removed from all this; but to remove us further yet, we want almost unlimited power of expansion. That is our safety valve. The mightiest intellects which when compressed in thronged cities, and hopeless of their future, are ready to break the barriers around them the moment they enter the new world of the West, feel their freedom, and turn their energies to contend with the works of creation; converting the woods and the forest into towns, and villages, and cultivated fields, and extending the dominion of civilization and improvement over the domain of nature.*

Practical politicians in charge of America's day-to-day diplomatic and military policies in the 1840s promoted more tangible objectives than the propagandists. They hoped to dominate northern Pacific waters and Oriental trade, which they saw (and later generations continued to see) as the legitimate extension of the American West itself. The whole grand stretch of the Pacific Coast of North America afforded but three good locations for the necessary port facilities: the Strait of Juan de Fuca, leading into Puget Sound and then to disputed Oregon country; breathtaking San Francisco Bay inside Mexico's Californian Golden Gate; and the Bay of San Diego farther south, "as fine a bay for vessels under three hundred tons," said an American captain in the 1820s, "as was ever formed by Nature in her most friendly mood to mariners." American spokesmen from all sections of the country were in agreement on grasping these few fine anchorages and thereby keeping out rival powers, especially the rival who too proudly called herself Mistress of the Seas.

Much has been made in recent years of the force of these tangible objectives in effecting America's unparalleled expansion in this period, as against the vague vaporings of the Manifest Destiny enthusiasts. But it is safe to say that these tangible objectives themselves gained in realism, as they gained in grandeur, for being promoted in the heady atmosphere of divine purpose.

## I   Confrontations on the Canadian border

*Seeds of suspicion*

The westward surge of the American people and their star-spangled prognostications that their flag would soon wave from Patagonia to the North Pole only strengthened official British opinion (along with that of the rest of monarchical Europe) that the Yankees were a nation of bullies and braggarts who must be carefully watched and closely constrained.

Among the watchers in the 1830s and 1840s

were the swarms of British travelers who made quick tours of the upstart land and reported it as dirty and swaggering and as shamelessly dollar-conscious as they thought it before they left home. These tours culminated in the visit of the famous "Boz," the still youthful Charles Dickens, in 1842, and the publication two years later of his novel, *Martin Chuzzlewit.*

Dickens's discontent with the United States was aggravated by his personal resentment against American publishers who pirated his enormously popular works. Deeper down he shared his countrymen's revulsion against the American states for repudiating their debts to British creditors after the Panic of 1837. The soaring (Dickens said "spurious") spirit of American democracy—"we are a model of wisdom, and an example to the world, and the perfection of human reason, and a great deal more to the same purpose, which you may

hear any hour in the day"—also angered many John Bulls, especially after Britain's First Reform Act of 1832 showed the force of the democratic spirit abroad. The American defense of slavery and assaults on abolitionists, after Britain had led the world in emancipating blacks in bondage in her colonies in 1833, hardened disenchantment with the American brand of liberty.

If Americans were to be watched and vilified within their gates, they were to be constrained at the nearest vantage point outside, their Canadian border. The British, if possible, thought even less of their Canadian subjects than they did of the restless old rebels to the south, and for Canada itself as a paying colony they had learned to entertain the meagerest expectations. Yet Canada had her uses, "above all," wrote the future Colonial Secretary E. G. Stanley, in 1824, "in case of [a third]

*San Francisco and the Bay, 1851,*
*by S. F. Marryat.*

The New-York Historical Society, New York City

war with the United States (no improbable future contingency)." In such an event, Stanley added, Canada "furnishes ample assistance in men, timber and harbours for carrying on the war, and that on the enemy's frontier." How seriously Britain took the American menace is evidenced, beginning late in the 1820s, by her spending millions of pounds (after the Canadians themselves refused to be taxed for the purpose) to build the inland Rideau Canal as an alternative to the St. Lawrence waterway in case control of the latter ever fell to American invaders. The British spent millions more rebuilding the strategic citadel of Quebec.

### The Caroline affair

In the late 1830s and early 1840s three confrontations gave John Bull and Brother Jonathan welcome cause for honing up the weapons to be used beyond the war of words, if words failed. The first of these is known as "the Caroline affair."

In November and December 1837, inspired to a degree by the advance of the "great experiment" below the border, insurrections flared up against the Crown in lower and upper Canada. Loyal forces quickly suppressed these uprisings, but not before certain Americans had rallied to the rebels' cause. On the night of December 29, 1837, Caroline, a small American steamer engaged in ferrying supplies to the insurgents, lay moored on the New York side of the Niagara River. A party of loyal Canadian volunteers rowed across, routed Caroline's crew, set her afire, towed her out, and watched her sink. During the scuffle one American was killed.

The United States promptly demanded an apology for the British "invasion" of American territory. But the British replied that Caroline, by abetting the criminal conspiracy in Canada, had become fair game. They were on less tenable ground for having taken direct action without first formally protesting to American officials and giving them a chance to discipline their own citizens—an oversight

which reflected the lifelong contempt of British Foreign Secretary Lord Palmerston for American claims to nationhood.

While Anglo-American relations worsened over other issues, the Caroline deadlock continued until 1840 when New York authorities arrested Alexander McLeod, one of the Canadian participants in the raid on the vessel, and charged him with murder and arson. Palmerston now acknowledged that the raid had been officially planned to forestall American aid to the insurrectionists and demanded McLeod's release on the ground that any actions he may have taken were done under orders. McLeod's execution, Palmerston warned, would mean war.

New York's Governor William H. Seward insisted that McLeod face trial in the state courts, though he promised Secretary of State Webster that if convicted McLeod would be pardoned. Fortunately, McLeod was acquitted. Lest similar incidents occur, Webster, with presidential support, drafted a measure establishing federal jurisdiction in all cases involving aliens accused of committing acts under the direction of a foreign government. Congress passed this measure in August 1842.

### The "Aroostook War"

The Rideau Canal was not the only military-inspired transportation project in Canada during these troubled times. The freezing of the St. Lawrence had hampered the movement of troops in putting down the Canadian insurrections of 1837, and the next year the British decided to build a road from St. John on the Bay of Fundy in New Brunswick to Montreal and Quebec. In February 1839 work began in the rich Aroostook River valley where the conflicting claims of the State of Maine and the province of New Brunswick had grown ever more loudly asserted as the value of the timber in the valley soared. When "foreign" lumberjacks now once more entered the disputed area and began felling trees for the road project, the hastily mobilized Maine militia chased them out.

The "Aroostook War" was a bloodless affray; but Congress confirmed the gravity of the border situation by appropriating $10 million for war purposes and authorizing President Van Buren to enlist 50,000 volunteers. As it turned out, neither money nor men were needed, for in March 1839, General Winfield Scott, Van Buren's emissary, succeeded in smoothing things over at the scene. Scott, however, could not eliminate the source of the trouble, which lay in the rankling vagueness of the frontier line and soured Anglo-American relations until the Webster-Ashburton Treaty of 1842.

### The Creole incident

The *Creole* case of 1841 is related to the Canadian border only because it so strained Anglo-American relations on another touchy subject that it made border issues more difficult to settle. This subject was the slave trade.

In her attempts to destroy the slave traffic, especially after the emancipation of 1833, Britain had made treaties with many nations giving her navy even in peacetime the right to stop and search suspected merchantmen under all flags. Palmerston boasted that Britain had enlisted in the fight against the slave trade, "every state in Christendom which has a flag that sails on the ocean, with the single

exception of the United States of North America." This was not entirely true; France, like the United States, had resisted Britain's assumption of holier-than-thou authority. But it suited Palmerston to point the finger, and with some justice, for slave ships often escaped search and seizure simply by running up the Stars and Stripes in time.

The American brig *Creole* was carrying about 130 slaves from Virginia to New Orleans in October 1841, when the blacks mutineed and took over the vessel. They then sailed her to the British port of Nassau in the Bahamas and went ashore. One white passenger had been killed in the mutiny. Despite the protests of *Creole's* owners to local authorities and the efforts of American officials to reclaim the slaves, those not held for the killing were permitted to live in the Bahamas as free men. British affronts to the flag in the slave trade heightened American indignation over the *Creole* affair.

### The Webster-Ashburton Treaty

Behind each confrontation between Britain and her mettlesome former colonies throughout the nineteenth century lay the growing commercial and industrial rivalry of the two nations. This rivalry inspired Palmerston, the curmudgeon, to prick every Yankee pretension. His insults and attacks finally sickened even his own people and his colleagues in the Cabinet, and when he fell with the Melbourne ministry in 1841, both nations breathed sighs of relief. Soon after, Lord Aberdeen, as the new Foreign Secretary, and Webster, the American Secretary of State, arranged to meet in an attempt to improve Anglo-American relations. Aberdeen showed his goodwill by accepting Washington as the scene of negotiations and by appointing as his special envoy Lord Ashburton, the husband of an American heiress.

The principal subject of the Webster-Ashburton talks was the Canadian-American border. Webster ultimately compromised on

**Maine boundary settlement, 1842**

the Maine boundary issue and reached an agreement that gave the United States approximately 7000 of the 12,000 square miles in question. The two diplomats also agreed on the still inaccurately surveyed boundary along northern Vermont and New York and westward to Minnesota and Ontario.

Webster enlarged the discussions by raising the question of the *Creole* incident, but Ashburton merely promised that henceforth British colonial authorities would not interfere with American vessels "driven by accident or violence" into British ports. The Americans, on their part, agreed to assist the British in patrolling the African coast and suppressing the slave runners. Ashburton also refused to eat humble pie over the *Caroline* affair. He merely "regretted" that "some explanation and apology for this occurrence was not immediately made," and Webster had to make the best of the word "apology."

Extremists in Britain and America protested that their respective countries had suffered a diplomatic defeat in these negotiations, but the Webster-Ashburton Treaty, signed on August 9, 1842, was a model of compromise that paved the way for other peaceful settlements during the next two decades. Anglo-American relations were further improved in 1846 when Sir Robert Peel's government repealed the British Corn Laws and Polk's administration (see p. 301) pushed the Walker Tariff through Congress. The British measure opened her ports more freely to American wheat; the low duties in the Walker Tariff opened American markets more freely to British manufactures.

Canadian sentiment for annexation to the United States, however, continued strong, as did American sentiment (except in the South) for satisfying the Canadian feeling. The repeal of the Corn Laws particularly, by ending the favorable position enjoyed by Canadian wheat in Britain, fed the hopes of annexationists in Canada and in the United States, for Canadian growers now longed for free entry into the American market by means of the union of the two lands.

## II The Lone Star State

*Limitations on southern expansion*

The Manifest Destiny of Texas, and of the even more inviting warm empire beyond, had become far closer to realization by the time of the Webster-Ashburton Treaty than the destiny still reserved in optimistic American minds for Canada largely because of the land hunger of the South.

In the North, after the removal of the Sauk and Fox tribes in 1833, emigrants from Illinois, Indiana, Ohio, and Kentucky had begun to spill into the newly opened Iowa and Wisconsin country. By 1840, some 75,000 settlers had established themselves on the rich farmlands here, and smaller numbers, including lumbermen and trappers, were pushing into Minnesota. The small southern farmer, as well as the planter, had no such vast tracts at his disposal. By 1840, much of the best land on the southern Gulf plains was occupied by big planters and was being worked by slave gangs. After the admission of Arkansas in 1836, the only remaining prospective slave state under the provisions of the Missouri Compromise was the territory of Florida.

Immediately to the west of the last southern settlements lay the "permanent Indian frontier," established in the 1820s in much of present-day Oklahoma and Kansas, to hold forever, it was said, the displaced woods Indians of the East as well as the numerous hostile tribes native to the region. As late as the 1860s this Indian reserve was known as "the Great American Desert" and had little appeal to slaveholders whose "peculiar institution,"

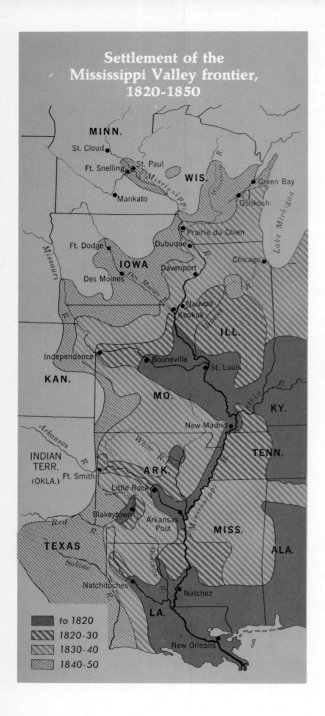

**Settlement of the Mississippi Valley frontier, 1820-1850**

to 1820
1820-30
1830-40
1840-50

independent of shaky Mexican regimes. Beyond Texas lay Mexico's vague and vaguely held California empire whose charms had so long and so lavishly been reported by far-ranging mountain men and mariners. Both Texas and California had ultimately to be fought for, but their fall to the United States seemed destined nonetheless.

### The Lone Star Republic

In 1819, when she obtained Florida from Spain, the United States had surrendered her dubious claim, based upon the carefree geography of the Louisiana Purchase treaty, to the Mexican province of Texas in the state of Coahuila—much to the disgust of later frontier politicians, who kept harping on "our former limits." American traders and military adventurers nevertheless continued the illicit commercial relations they had already established with the Mexicans despite Spain's many warnings. When Mexico, with the assistance of such traders and fighters, won her independence from Spain in 1821, she promptly put American commerce on a legitimate footing and invited additional Americans to settle in Texas and develop its resources.

Connecticut-born Moses Austin, who obtained a land grant from the Mexican government in 1820, pioneered the American colonization of Texas. Moses Austin died in 1821 and could not develop his tract, but in 1823 Mexico validated the grant for his son Stephen, who carried through the first colonization program.

Mexican officials had hoped that the settlement of Texas by white Americans would protect their country from Indian raids and from possible aggression by the United States. But they soon realized they had miscalculated. Between 1820 and 1830, about 20,000 Americans with approximately 2000 slaves had crossed into Texas, largely from the lower Mississippi frontier. Most of them were law-abiding people, but rougher elements, particularly in eastern Texas, soon made the Mexi-

in any case, was barred by law if not by nature from its northerly portion.

South and west of the Indian range stretched Texas, recently become precariously

cans subscribe to John Jay's old complaint that white frontiersmen were more troublesome than red Indians. The Texans, on their part, soon began to champ at their lack of self-government. In 1826, after a settler named Haden Edwards quarreled with the authorities over land titles, his brother Benjamin proclaimed the Republic of Fredonia and staged a rebellion that the Mexicans easily put down.

Offers by the United States to purchase Texas in 1827 only served to deepen Mexico's anxiety over Yankee expansionism. Mexico had complaints about Yankee independence as well. American settlers in Mexico had failed to become Catholics, as they were required to do by the terms of their invitation. They had ignored a Mexican prohibition against the slave trade by substituting a thinly disguised indenture system. Some, moreover, had slipped over into territory reserved by law for Mexicans.

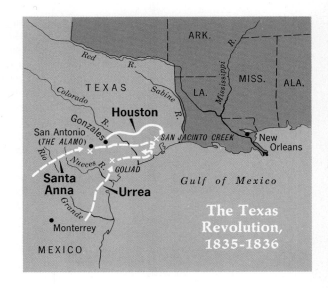

The Texas Revolution, 1835-1836

*Annihilation of Texas defenders of the Alamo, woodcut from Davy Crockett's Almanac, a publication devoted mainly to the humorous exploits of the Tennessee frontiersman and congressman. Crockett, who died here, is the central figure.*

In 1830 the Mexican government sent troops to occupy Texas, called a halt to further American immigration, and passed other restrictive measures, including the abolition of slavery itself. This change in policy angered the American Texans already aroused by the government's refusal to separate Texas from the state of Coahuila. In 1832 General A. L. de Santa Anna emerged as Mexico's strong man, instituted a centralist program, and three years later abolished all local rights. Early in 1836 he led an army of 6000 into Texas to bring the rebellious Americans to book. Confronted with Santa Anna's threat to exterminate them, Americans in Texas declared their independence on March 2, 1836, set up a provisional government under a constitution that sanctioned slavery, and appointed Sam Houston Commander-in-Chief of the few hundred men mobilized at Gonzales. Santa Anna already had the Alamo mission in San Antonio under siege and when it fell on March 6 he massacred the 187 defenders, including the commander William B. Travis and such legendary figures as Davy Crockett and Jim Bowie. Three weeks later more than 300 were massacred at Goliad on surrendering to the Mexican General José Urrea.

Such brutal attacks led Houston to beat a steady retreat eastward until he reached the vicinity of San Jacinto creek. Here, on April 21, 1836, he suddenly turned on his unprepared pursuers. Fired up by the cry, "Remember the Alamo," Houston's force routed Santa Anna's army and took the dictator captive. On May 14, Santa Anna signed a treaty pledging Texan independence and fixing a vague boundary between Texas and Mexico. Although the Mexican Congress promptly repudiated the treaty, it could do nothing to reverse it.

### Annexation effected

Sympathy for the Texas insurrectionists had been strong in the South and also in the Northwest, where their cause was identified with the struggles of the underprivileged. As one Ohio supporter declared in 1835, "The Texans are mostly composed of ... men whom misfortunes have driven from our country; men who have gone there at the instance of the invitation of the Mexican Government, ... to retrieve their shattered fortunes, and procure bread for their suffering families."

Support for the Texans' cause, however, was less enthusiastic in the Northeast, especially among Whig party leaders, who viewed the Texans' request to enter the Union after they defeated Santa Anna as a slaveowners' plot. From five to seven states, it was pointed out, might be carved from the huge Texas domain, thus insuring southern control of Congress. Opponents of annexation protested so vehemently that President Jackson held off even recognizing the Lone Star Republic until just before he left office in 1837. Van Buren also withstood growing annexationist pressure, a policy that was to cost him dearly during Tyler's administration when his enemies in the South sought to unseat him as the titular head of the Democratic party and thereby improve Calhoun's chances for the White House. In this strategy southern expansionists received enthusiastic support from western political leaders.

Denied admission to the United States and menaced by unforgiving Mexico, the Lone Star Republic sought protection elsewhere. Britain in particular liked the idea of an independent Texas that would export cotton and import British manufactured goods on a free-trade basis. Britain also opposed slavery, and Foreign Secretary Aberdeen declared in December 1843 that "with regard to Texas, we avow that we wish to see slavery abolished there, as elsewhere." But slavery in Texas did not keep Britain from seeking permanent relations with her.

That Texas might link herself with Britain, a dark prospect to northern businessmen, was even more alarming to slaveowners who felt that the abolition of slavery in Texas under British pressure would encourage Negro insurrections in the slave states. Sam Houston, now President of Texas, played upon American fears until the annexationists were ready to do almost anything to bring Texas into the

Union before Britain succeeded in keeping her permanently out.

President Tyler himself worked tirelessly to gain credit for annexation before his successor took office. In April 1844 he submitted a Texas statehood treaty to the Senate drawn up by Calhoun, whom he had just appointed Secretary of State. Unfortunately for him, Calhoun attached to the treaty a little disquisition on the beauties of slavery (in response to Aberdeen's avowal to abolish it) that insured the Senate's rejection of the arrangement, 36 to 16. But Tyler was not finished. In February 1845, after Polk's election on an expansionist platform, he persuaded Congress to effect annexation by a joint resolution that required only a majority vote, not the two-thirds majority needed for treaties. Such a resolution barely won Senate approval, 27 to 25; and in October, Texas accepted its terms, which explicitly permitted slavery under the Missouri Compromise. When, on December 29, 1845, Texas became the twenty-eighth state, Mexico recalled her minister from Washington.

## III   Manifest Destiny in the Far West

### The future of Oregon

The future of Oregon as well as the future of Texas had reached a critical point as Americans rallied to their party standards for the presidential campaign of 1844.

Distant though it was from the mainstream of European and American politics and business, Oregon country since the eighteenth century had been the scene and subject of competition among France, Spain, and Russia, as well as Britain and the United States. Early in the nineteenth century France and Spain had surrendered their claims to the region; and in 1824, the Russians, expanding southward from Alaska, had agreed to fix their own southern boundary at 54° 40' (see p. 207). This left Britain and the United States free to settle ownership of the remainder of Oregon between themselves.

After John Jacob Astor's Pacific Fur Company was forced out of Oregon in 1812, American interest in the region lay dormant until the 1830s. In 1832 and again in 1834, Nathaniel J. Wyeth, a merchant of Cambridge, Massachusetts, sent several expeditions to the region. Although financial failures, they served to call attention once again to the feasibility of the overland route to the Northwest that had first been explored by Lewis and Clark. Accompanying Wyeth to Oregon in 1834 was the first band of Methodist missionaries led by Jason Lee. The great fertility of the soil in Oregon's Willamette Valley so captivated these men that its cultivation quickly took precedence over conversion of the Indians. By 1844, the home church in the East washed its hands of the enterprise, but the settlement in Oregon flourished. In the meantime, other denominations had followed the Methodists' lead. Marcus Whitman established a Presbyterian mission near Fort Walla Walla in 1836, and in 1840 the Jesuits sent out Father De Smet to build a Catholic mission.

The Protestants made so little headway with the Indians of the region that Marcus Whitman, his wife, and twelve others in his mission were massacred in 1847 by a disgruntled tribe. Father De Smet, in turn, found his principal difficulties to be with French-Canadian priests who, with British support, resisted American competition for souls. Missionary reports and letters, however, published regularly in the missionary press, kept attention on Oregon's agricultural possibilities. By 1843, "Oregon fever" was sweeping across the Mississippi Valley frontier, and in May that year the first large migration, a thousand strong under Peter H. Burnett, set out on the Oregon Trail from Independence, Missouri.

Hard on their arrival, American leaders in Oregon, in the face of aroused Canadian opposition, organized a provisional government, while expansionists back east began to thunder about America's right to the territory. Nor were they to be satisfied with a boundary at the 49th parallel, which had been the limit of American claims in earlier discussions with Britain. As the Democrats put it, in their campaign slogan for 1844, "54°40' or fight."

### Election of 1844

American bombast in the capital, brashness in Texas, and bumptiousness on the Pacific Coast naturally made expansion the leading issue in the impending national elections. By opposing the annexation of Texas, Van Buren had forfeited his chance of renomination by the Democrats. A majority in the convention favored him, but the Calhoun men invoked the rule requiring the vote of two-

thirds of the delegates for the nomination, a number Van Buren could not muster. In his place they finally named James K. Polk of Tennessee, who readily supported the aggressive platform plank, "the reoccupation of Oregon and the reannexation of Texas." When his followers cried "54°40' or fight," Polk did not attempt to quiet them.

Swiftly disposing of Tyler, the Whigs at last chose as their standard-bearer their idol, Henry Clay; but once more the times were against him. Clay earlier had openly opposed the annexation of Texas, on which the Whig platform itself remained silent. The more he hedged in the campaign, the worse off he became, and Polk, clearly a "dark horse" against the glamorous "Harry of the West," won. Polk's electoral margin was 170 to 105; his

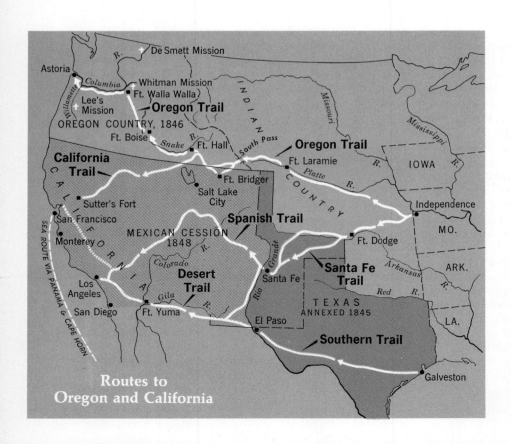

**Routes to Oregon and California**

popular margin, 1,337,000 to 1,299,000. While Clay carried Ohio, Tennessee, and his home state of Kentucky, all the new states west of the Appalachians went for Polk. The Democrats enlarged their House majority and gained a majority in the Senate.

The election results were widely interpreted as a mandate for expansion, not least by Polk himself. Yet his triumph was hardly decisive, and some saw in the convention support for Van Buren, and in the closeness of the popular vote in the election, signs that expansionism as much as slavery would endanger national unity.

### A peaceful solution

Although indeed a "dark horse," Polk was not so obscure as the Whig campaign dig—"Who is James K. Polk?"—was meant to suggest. A well-tempered veteran of state politics in Tennessee, before his elevation to the White House Polk had served fourteen years in the House of Representatives in Washington, the last four (1835–1839) as Speaker. As President, Polk remained the solid Democrat he had always been. He opposed protection, and in 1846 signed the Walker Tariff which put the country back on low duties for revenue only. He opposed a national debt and meant to keep it low enough to be serviced (and reduced when possible) by the revenues available. He opposed banks and restored Van Buren's Independent Treasury System for handling federal funds. He gave nullifiers no comfort. Above all, he was as expansionist and isolationist as Jefferson.

In his inaugural address in March 1845, Polk asserted "the right of the United States to that portion of our territory which lies beyond the Rocky Mountains. Our title to the country of the Oregon," he said, "is 'clear and unquestionable,' and already are our people preparing to perfect that title by occupying it with their wives and children." In his first annual message to Congress in December 1845, Polk proceeded to stretch the Monroe

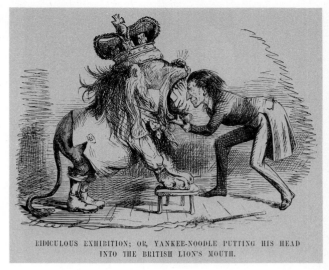

RIDICULOUS EXHIBITION; OR, YANKEE-NOODLE PUTTING HIS HEAD INTO THE BRITISH LION'S MOUTH.

*Punch,* London

*Punch (of London) view
of American temerity in challenging
John Bull over Oregon, 1846.*

Doctrine by making two assertions that are often called the Polk Doctrine: (1) "The people of *this continent* alone have the right to decide their own destiny." (2) The United States cannot allow European states to prevent an independent state from entering the Union.

While war with Mexico over Texas still threatened, war with Britain over Oregon would be foolhardy. Polk was responsible enough to realize this and found a way, after the election was over and the 54°40′ slogan had served its purpose, to back down from it. He had been reliably advised that Oregon above the 49th parallel was ill-suited to agriculture. Below the 49th parallel, he said, lay "the entrance of the Straits of Fuca, Admiralty Inlet, and Puget's Sound, with their fine harbors and rich surrounding soils." A concession to Britain on the boundary, moreover, might speed America's effort to secure the even more valuable California ports.

While Polk was coming around to accepting the 49th parallel, where Britain three times earlier had suggested dividing Oregon, Britain herself now found reasons to try once more.

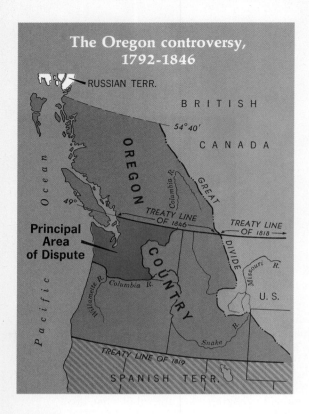

**The Oregon controversy, 1792-1846**

RUSSIAN TERR.

B R I T I S H

54°40'

CANADA

OREGON

Ocean

GREAT

Columbia R.

49°

TREATY LINE OF 1846

TREATY LINE OF 1818

**Principal Area of Dispute**

COUNTRY

DIVIDE

Missouri R.

U.S.

Pacific

Willamette R.

Columbia R.

Snake R.

TREATY LINE OF 1819

S P A N I S H   T E R R.

North America, one group moved west to escape the thralldom of American government. This group was the Mormons.

In 1823, Joseph Smith, a visionary from Vermont, claimed to have been led by angels to a hill near Manchester, New York, where "there was a book deposited, written upon gold plates," and "two stones in silver bows ... deposited with the plates." The "possession and use of these stones," Smith wrote, "were what constituted Seers in ancient or former times; and ... God had prepared them for the purpose of translating the book." As God's helper, Smith used the stones in revealing the Book of Mormon, a composite of mythology and prophecy which recalled an ancient legend that the Indians were descendants of the lost tribes of Israel and which enjoined Smith's followers to convert them from their heathenish ways.

On the basis of his revelation, Smith in 1830 founded the Church of Jesus Christ of Latter-day Saints and published his book. Along with other Messianic movements of the times, Mormonism spread into the Western Reserve in Ohio, and there, at Kirtland, the distinctive pattern of Mormon community living—markedly similar to the seventeenth-century New England settlements centered on the church—first took shape.

Thereafter trouble dogged the Mormons. Following the Panic of 1837 financial difficulties in Ohio drove them to the frontier in Missouri; but within a year, scorned as a sect of thieving Yankee abolitionists and heretics, they were harried back across the Mississippi to Nauvoo, Illinois. Here they found peace until, following Joseph Smith's own example, the practice of plural marriages spread. Whether these marriages were "sealed for a time," that is, consummated in this life, or "sealed for eternity," that is, to be consummated in Heaven, or both, this practice alienated the monogamists of the sect and infuriated the non-Mormon inhabitants.

When the anti-Smith faction among the Mormons attacked him in their newly estab-

She was finding it increasingly difficult to keep unruly American elements out of Oregon. At the same time, the depletion of fur-bearing animals along the Columbia River gave her justification for getting out herself. These circumstances suggested the resumption of negotiations, and on June 15, 1846 a treaty was signed. The line drawn along the 49th parallel to Puget Sound and from there to the Pacific through the Straits of Juan de Fuca was simply an extension of the Canadian-American boundary that had been fixed in 1818 as far as the Rockies. The territory north of the Columbia River, though clearly British by right of settlement, fell into the American sphere. Britain retained Vancouver Island and navigation rights on the Columbia.

*The Mormons in Utah*

While thousands of Americans from the North and the South were moving west to "perfect," as Polk said, American title to

lished newspaper in 1843, Smith and his friends smashed their press. For this offense, the civil authorities threw him and his brother Hyram into jail. Soon freed, they were jailed again on a related charge and in 1844 were shot dead in their cell by members of an aroused mob. Joseph Smith's murder almost killed the Mormon movement. At the same time, it provided the Mormon church with a martyr in whose name a new leader might rally its forces. Such a leader appeared in the person of Brigham Young, a loyal follower of Joseph Smith, who became the new "Lion of the Lord."

In 1842, Smith had envisaged a Mormon homeland "in the midst of the Rocky Mountains" and had even dispatched some of his followers to "investigate the locations of California and Oregon, and hunt out a good location, where we can ... build a city in a day, and have a government of our own." Forced out of Illinois after the Prophet's assassination, in the winter of 1846 the Mormon host led by Young began its tortuous exodus westward. On June 24, 1847, the first wave of Mormons entered the Salt Lake Valley—a Zion isolated on a barren Mexican plateau remote from the lands of the gentiles. Here, encircled by mountain and desert, the Mormon leaders created a theocracy superbly organized for survival.

The Salt Lake community was cooperative rather than competitive. Since its very existence depended on controlling the limited water supply brought in by the mountain streams, Young devised an irrigation system that distributed water equitably to the whole settlement. Between 1847 and 1857, he and his advisers laid out ninety-five communities in which they closely regulated life. The Mormon state of Deseret (Congress later changed the name to Utah) probably was the most successful communitarian project in American history.

Remote as the "Saints" were, they soon found there was no escaping the American environment. Within two years the Mexican War brought Young's community once more under United States jurisdiction. Furthermore, the Mormon state lay athwart one of the routes to California and inevitably became involved in the American push to the Pacific.

### On to California

California had been loosely held by Spain since the middle of the eighteenth century, when she opened a number of Franciscan missions, protected by small garrisons, for the double purpose of converting Indians and preventing British and Russian penetration down the California coast. In theory, these missions were temporary establishments set up to teach the Indians agriculture and household arts, and the Franciscans did succeed in Christianizing and training thousands of red men. After completing this task, the Franciscans were expected to move on to new fields and allow the regular clergy to take over. The mission lands would then be broken up and distributed to private owners. But who was to decide when each move was to be made? Anticlericals hungered for the lands from the start; and when Mexico won her independence from Spain early in the 1820s, officials and land speculators pressed for distribution of mission property. By 1834 half the mission lands had passed into private hands, and the other half was soon lost to landsharks. At the outbreak of the Mexican War in 1846, the Indians had hopelessly degenerated and few signs of the missions remained.

During the preceding twenty-five years, Yankee whalers from Nantucket and New Bedford had stopped at the California ports of Monterey and San Francisco, and New England traders had sailed there and further south to exchange everything from Chinese fireworks to English cartwheels for hides and tallow. Year by year these visitors left behind them deserters and adventurers, their number soon augmented by emigrants from the Oregon and Mississippi frontiers.

Richard Henry Dana, Jr., whose classic *Two Years Before the Mast* (1840) contains the best account of California life in the 1830s, succumbed to the elegance and pride of the Mexicans encountered by Yankee mariners, but he also saw the sources of their defenselessness against the interlopers. He found the Mexicans "an idle people" incapable of making anything, bad bargainers, and suspicious of foreigners. "Indeed," he wrote, "as far as my observation goes, there are no people to whom the newly invented Yankee word of 'loafer' is more applicable than to the Spanish Americans." For the interlopers themselves, the most helpful figure on the coast was Thomas O. Larkin, who settled in Monterey in 1832 and later became a confidential agent of the American government. His counterpart in the interior was Captain John A. Sutter, who built a fort in the Sacramento Valley in 1839 and set up a small trading empire.

Although California had not been an issue in the 1844 campaign, it soon became identified in the popular mind with Oregon. No one was more eloquent in its praises than the witty Larkin, who described the pleasures of "hunting wild Deer and dancing with tame Dear." By the summer of 1845, talk about a mighty nation extending from sea to sea had become commonplace, and expansionists warned Polk to take over California before the British did. Polk himself aired plans for a transcontinental railroad to link the Golden Gate with the Mississippi Valley. San Francisco, all agreed, was the great prize, twenty times more valuable, thought Daniel Webster, than the whole of Texas. San Diego harbor, in turn, according to many observers, would outweigh Oregon.

The United States, alas, had no claim to California except desire. During Jackson's and Tyler's administrations, government efforts to buy California only deepened Mexican hostility. In 1842 an American naval officer, Commodore Thomas ap Catesby Jones, mistakenly informed in Peru that the United States and Mexico were at war and that the British were planning to seize California, sailed into Monterey and captured the city. On discovering his mistake, he promptly apologized to the Mexicans, but the significance of this assault was not lost.

In 1845, on learning that the government of General Herrera was in such straits that it might be persuaded at last to sell California, President Polk hurriedly sent a representative, John Slidell, to Mexico City with still another offer to buy. By then, however, United States and Mexican forces had begun to make military passes at each other over Texas, and the recently installed Mexican regime would not even receive Slidell. Nothing could be done with the Mexicans, his envoy now wrote Polk, "until they shall have been chastised."

The canny Larkin had a plan by which the United States would encourage a "spontaneous" rebellion of Spanish-speaking Californians favorably disposed to annexation. Nothing came of this scheme, but its feasibility was indicated by a genuinely spontaneous revolt of other Americans north of San Francisco Bay where, on July 5, 1846, they set up an independent state with its own bear flag. On learning of the formal outbreak of war between the United States and Mexico, these rebels disestablished the "Bear Flag Republic" and joined the American forces.

## IV  War with Mexico and its consequences

### A short and fruitful war

With Texas wrenched from her and California obviously slipping away, Mexico, if only to save face, had to take a stand against her neighbor to the north. Her opportunity came early in 1846, when, on hearing from Slidell of the failure of his mission, Polk ordered General Zachary Taylor to occupy disputed territory on the southern boundary of Texas. Taylor had carried out his orders by the end of March. Such a show of force, thought Polk, might bend the Mexicans toward reconsidering their refusal to negotiate. Failing that, it might cause an incident to serve as an excuse for a declaration of war.

Mexico responded to Polk's strategy by sending up troops of her own, and on April 25, 1846 they clashed with Taylor's men. Polk had already prepared a war message and on May 11 he sent it to Congress. The shedding of American blood on what the United States claimed to be its own soil put Congress in a mood to act without lengthy debate, and on May 13, with but few dissenters, the legislature did the President's bidding.

The size of his congressional majorities may have raised Polk's hopes for bipartisan support of the war, but they were soon dashed. His refusal openly to declare his war aims (the seizure of New Mexico and California) encouraged southern as well as northern Whigs to attack his entire Mexican policy. By forcing an unwilling people into war, said northern Whigs, Polk was simply "attempting to consummate a scheme for the extension and strengthening of slavery and the Slave Power." Some southern Whigs themselves feared that the acquisition of new territories would intensify old sectional controversies and destroy their party. But if the Whigs publicly castigated Polk, they did not obstruct the war; indeed, they quickly made all the political capital they could out of the triumphs of two Whig generals, Zachary Taylor and Winfield Scott.

The war's promotion of the presidential aspirations of such Whig heroes caused many Democrats, in turn, to see party suicide in the conflict. The Van Buren Democrats, furthermore, opposed to Polk's expansionism from the outset, gave verbal support to the war only to keep up a show of patriotism. The Calhoun Democrats were no happier. They also asked the further question—would not the debts piled up by the war encourage the protectionists to renew their demands for high tariffs on manufactures?

Moral and political dissatisfaction with the war became most evident in the Northeast where such New England antislavery spokesmen as Emerson, Parker, and James Russell Lowell castigated Polk's adventure. The most populous part of the country, the Northeast supplied only 7900 recruits for the army. Some 20,000 southerners and 40,000 westerners enlisted, however, and the war was quickly won.

Taylor captured Monterrey, Mexico, on September 24, 1846, and defeated a Mexican force of 15,000 men under General Santa Anna at Buena Vista on February 23, 1847. General Scott, appointed next to lead an expedition against Mexico City, the enemy capital, overcame tough resistance on landing at Vera Cruz and went on to take Mexico City on September 14, 1847. Further west, an army under Colonel Stephen W. Kearny, starting from its base at Fort Leavenworth, Kansas, captured Santa Fe and pushed through to California. Commodore Robert F. Stockton and a battalion of troops under General John C. Frémont had already proclaimed the annexation of California in August 1846, but the Mexican rebels who had been fighting among themselves settled their differences and in September drove the Americans from southern California. When Kearny arrived at San Diego in December, he joined with American naval units under Stockton and with Frémont's men to reestablish American rule. By January 13, 1847, all Mexican forces in California had surrendered.

When news of the victories at Buena Vista and Vera Cruz reached Washington, Polk decided to try to arrange a peace with the Mexican leaders. For this mission he chose the State Department's Spanish-speaking chief clerk, Nicholas P. Trist. Trist was instructed to demand the Rio Grande boundary and the cession of New Mexico and California, and was authorized to offer to pay American claims against Mexico and an additional sum of $15 million. The last provision was presumably meant to salve the American conscience by giving the annexations the character of a purchase.

Almost immediately after Trist arrived at Vera Cruz, he quarreled with General Scott, who resented the appearance of a State Department clerk whose authority exceeded his own. The two men soon became fast friends, however, to the alarm of the President, who, like other Democrats, had come to regard Scott as a serious political rival. When Trist's negotiations with Santa Anna broke down and the temporary armistice ended in August 1847, Polk ordered his emissary back to Washington.

The President and his Cabinet now began to consider a prolonged occupation of Mexico, the annexation of New Mexico and California without compensation, and a levy on the people of Mexico to pay the costs of occupation. There even was serious talk of permanently annexing all Mexico, an objective, strangely enough, opposed by southerners of both major parties. Antislavery men, they felt, would insist on keeping the annexed country free. Some, like Calhoun, also feared that the American government would become more centralized than ever in the effort to administer a conquered empire. Trist himself sympathized with these objections.

The rise to power of a moderate party in Mexico prompted Trist to ignore his instructions to return, and without authorization he pressed on with his negotiations. On February 2, 1848 he signed the Treaty of Guadalupe Hidalgo. In it he secured the Rio Grande

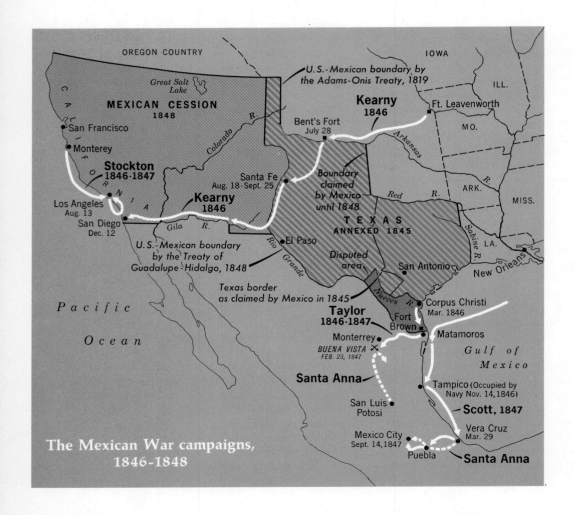

The Mexican War campaigns, 1846-1848

boundary, Upper California, including the much-desired port of San Diego, and New Mexico. He agreed that the United States would assume Mexican obligations to Americans up to $3.25 million and would pay Mexico $15 million.

Astonishing as Trist's independent behavior was (Polk called him "an impudent and unqualified scoundrel"), the President nevertheless accepted the treaty and sent it to the Senate for approval. After all, it conformed to Trist's original instructions. Moreover, prolonged negotiations would surely raise vehement criticism in Congress, especially in the House, where the Whigs held a majority. The Senate on March 10, 1848, approved Trist's work by a vote of 38 to 14, most of the opposition coming from those who wanted all Mexico. The Treaty of Guadalupe Hidalgo added a magnificent 500,000 square miles to the continental domain of the United States. Although Trist failed to acquire a strategic 54,000 square miles along the southern New Mexico border, a strip of land that offered the best route for a railroad to the Pacific through the South, this oversight was corrected by the Gadsden Purchase of 1853 for $10 million.

### The "free soil" election

As American soldiers stormed into Mexico, Ralph Waldo Emerson wrote in his journal: "The United States will conquer Mexico, but it will be as the man who swallows the arsenic, which brings him down in turn. Mexico will poison us."

The symptoms of poisoning were swift to appear. As early as August 1846, David Wilmot, a free-soil Democrat from Pennsylvania, offered an amendment to an appropriation bill in the House, proposing that, "neither slavery nor involuntary servitude shall ever exist in any part" of the territory that might be acquired from Mexico. The House adopted the amendment; the Senate defeated it. But that was far from the end of the matter. The "Wilmot Proviso" was persistently added to

bill after bill in Congress and was hotly debated there and in the country generally. At the same time, the admission of Iowa and Wisconsin to the Union was pending; Minnesota was soon to apply for statehood; and even Oregon Territory was readying its petition. For all these inevitably free states to enter the Union while the South at the same time was to be deprived of slave states in the new territory won largely by her sons was an intolerable prospect to many southern spokesmen. But growing numbers of northerners saw in slavery an unmitigated evil that at least must be contained where it was.

Did Congress, indeed, have authority, to determine whether or not slavery might exist in territory obtained by the United States? Southerners who first raised this question replied that since the Constitution recognized and protected property in slaves, owners of such property could not lawfully be discriminated against by being prohibited to carry such property wherever they went, even across the Missouri Compromise line. But antislavery northerners replied that ever since 1789, when it confirmed the clause in the Northwest Ordinance of 1787 that excluded slavery from the Northwest Territory, and especially in adopting the Missouri Compromise in 1820, Congress had exercised its prerogatives over property and territory as the Constitution (Art. IV, Sec. 3) plainly said it could.

A third position on the issue of extending slavery to the territories now appeared. This was "squatter sovereignty," or "popular sovereignty," a doctrine hopefully set forth by Lewis Cass of Michigan and Stephen A. Douglas of Illinois. They argued that there was a long-established precedent in America for communities to act as the best judges of their own interests. Let the new territories be set up with the question of slavery left open, and then permit the people to decide for themselves. Plausible enough, this doctrine nevertheless left disastrously vague precisely when a territory should decide the momentous question—after slaves had already been brought in or before, if free settlers had come before slaveowners? By leaving resolution of the question open to zealots of both camps, popular sovereignty also left it open to violence, which in fact broke out a few years later in Kansas.

By 1848 the issue of the extension of slavery to new territories had become so poisonous that both major parties, in preparing for the presidential campaign, shunned it. On taking office in 1845, Polk had pledged himself to but one term, and for the 1848 election the "regular" Democrats, at their convention in Baltimore, nominated Lewis Cass, who ran on a platform that ignored slavery altogether. The "regular" Whigs, at their convention in Philadelphia, hoped to silence talk of all issues by nominating the "hero of Buena Vista," General Taylor.

The watchword of the "regulars" in both parties was "party harmony." But they reckoned without determined antislavery northern Democrats—in New York and New England they became known as "Barnburners," because they were said to be willing to "burn down" the Democratic "barn" in order to get rid of the proslavery "rats." The regulars also reckoned without the "conscience," as against the "cotton," Whigs. In August 1848 antislavery Democrats and Whigs, who had bolted from their regular party conventions, met in Buffalo with other antislavery leaders and formed the Free Soil party, with the slogan, "Free soil, Free speech, Free labor, and Free men." They named as their standard-bearer Martin Van Buren, who had won their sympathy as he had lost that of the Democratic regulars, by his clear stand against the annexation of Texas.

The 1848 election itself aroused little popular enthusiasm. Neither Taylor nor Cass appealed particularly to his respective party, and Van Buren—despite his forthright repudiation of slavery—could not live down his reputation as a slippery fox. Moreover, he had no nationwide machine behind him. Horace Greeley thought that Cass was a "pot-bellied, mutton-headed cucumber," but he supported Van Buren only as a lesser evil. Webster, after some hesitation, gave Taylor a cold endorsement. In the balloting, Taylor won 1,360,000 votes to Cass's 1,220,000. The Free Soilers polled only 291,000 votes, but they absorbed enough Democratic support in New York to give that state's electoral vote to Taylor, and enough Whig support in Ohio and Indiana to give those states to Cass. The Free Soil party also elected nine congressmen to a divided House where they might hold the balance of power. Most important, the Free Soilers had demonstrated the potential strength and disruptive power of a purely sectional party. Henceforth, there could be no slurring over of the slavery

*The "hero of Buena Vista," with his bloody sword, atop a hill of Mexican skulls, in an anti-Whig campaign cartoon of "the available candidate," 1848.*

The New-York Historical Society, New York City

issue. Southern extremists now had fresh grounds on which to convince the moderates and Unionists in their states that a southern party must be formed to combat northern aggression against the "peculiar institution."

### Compromise of 1850

Sectional tensions relaxed for a moment when the news of gold in California spread across the nation early in 1848. Americans of every class and occupation dropped whatever they were doing and headed for the Pacific Coast. Men from all over the world joined them. To Henry Thoreau the gold rush was a shocking reflection of American materialism. The "world's raffle," he called it. He added, "What a comment, what a satire on our institutions! ... Is this the ground on which Orientals and Occidentals meet?"

By 1849, California had an unruly population of over 100,000, and an inadequate military government to cope with it. Polk had retired before a deeply divided Congress could decide California's future. Taylor, the new President, recommended, on appeals from California leaders, that California, and New Mexico and Utah as well, draw up constitutions and decide without congressional direction whether or not slavery should be excluded. Congress, however, was in no mood to let the new President run things. This was especially true of proslavery spokesmen whose fears over antislavery decisions in the Far West were soon confirmed by the action of all three territories in writing constitutions which forbade slavery. These spokesmen, amidst talk of the certainty of secession, now prepared to take an uncompromising stand in Congress on all sectional issues. Should slave depots be banned in the District of Columbia? Should the Fugitive Slave Law be tightened? Must Texas, a slave state, yield part of its western land to the proposed free territory of New Mexico? Southern unity in defense of slavery had never been so strong.

President Taylor's reaction to the heightening crisis was simply to ask Congress, in December 1849, to avoid "exciting topics of sectional character." At a time when senators and representatives carried Bowie knives and Colt revolvers, Taylor's request was tantamount to abdication. Clearly the South had no intention of allowing California to enter the Union as a free state unless it received important concessions. The South would secede rather than accept the Wilmot Proviso.

Fortunately there remained more realistic leaders than the President, yet men who put the Union first and the section second. Their spokesman was Henry Clay, seventy-three years old now, but still a powerful and persuasive orator who understood the truly desperate mood of the South. On January 29, 1850 Clay offered the following resolutions in the Senate: (1) that California be admitted as a free state; (2) that the territorial governments set up in Utah and New Mexico decide for themselves whether slavery should be permitted or abolished; (3) that the western boundary of Texas be fixed so as to exclude "any portion of New Mexico"; (4) that in return for this concession, the United States would assume that portion of the public debt of Texas contracted before annexation; (5) that slavery within the District of Columbia would not be abolished without the consent of Maryland and the District's residents, and "without just compensation to the owners of slaves within the District"; (6) that slave trading be prohibited in the District of Columbia; (7) that a stricter fugitive slave law be adopted; and (8) that "Congress has no power to promote or obstruct the trade in slaves between the slave-holding States."

The battle for the Compromise of 1850 was one of the most hotly contested in congressional history. Arrayed against Clay were (1) the angry and suspicious President Taylor, firm in his conviction that California must be admitted to the Union without any reservations and prepared to treat even moderate and Union-loving southerners as traitors if they protested; (2) fiery secessionists like Jefferson Davis (Mississippi), Robert Barnwell Rhett (South Carolina), and Louis T. Wigfall (Texas)—contemptuous of compromise; (3) extreme antislavery men and radical free soilers

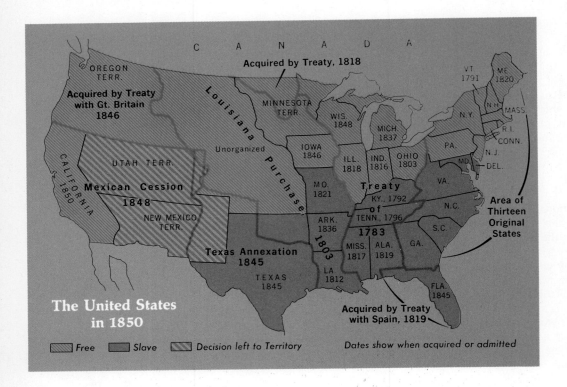

C A N A D A

OREGON TERR.

Acquired by Treaty
with Gt. Britain
1846

Acquired by Treaty, 1818

Louisiana Purchase

MINNESOTA TERR.

WIS. 1848

MICH. 1837

Unorganized

IOWA 1846

ILL. 1818

IND. 1816

OHIO 1803

PA.

VT. 1791

ME. 1820

N.H.

MASS.

N.Y.

R.I.

CONN.

N.J.

MD. — DEL.

CALIFORNIA 1850

UTAH TERR.

Mexican Cession
1848

NEW MEXICO TERR.

MO. 1821

Treaty
of
1783

KY., 1792

TENN., 1796

VA.

N.C.

Area of
Thirteen
Original
States

ARK. 1836

1803

S.C.

Texas Annexation
1845

MISS. 1817

ALA. 1819

GA.

TEXAS 1845

LA. 1812

FLA. 1845

The United States
in 1850

Acquired by Treaty
with Spain, 1819

| Free | Slave | Decision left to Territory | Dates show when acquired or admitted

like William H. Seward (New York), Salmon P. Chase and Joshua Giddings (Ohio), and Charles Sumner (Massachusetts), who stood pat on the Wilmot Proviso and placed the law of Congress, and the Constitution, below the "Higher Law"—the law of God—under which slavery could never be justified.

But Clay's resolutions were broad and conciliatory enough to win over reasonable men, North and South, and devout Unionists in every section. Among the staunchest of the Unionists stood Webster, who, in a moving speech in the Senate on March 7, 1850, brooked the wrath of his fellow Yankees by supporting even Clay's proposal for stricter enforcement of the Fugitive Slave Law. Nor were expressions of their wrath slow in coming. Theodore Parker, the Boston clergyman, said of the irretrievably tarnished hero: "I should think he must have been begotten in sin, and conceived in iniquity; ... the concentration of the villainy of whole generations of scoundrels would hardly be enough to fit a man for a deed like this."

Webster himself had underestimated northern revulsion against returning fugitive slaves and free-soil hatred of the whole plantation system. But for the moment at least, his efforts strengthened the Unionists' position to which other eloquent men rallied. Outstanding among them was Stephen A. Douglas, who brought many in Congress around to the view that the Southwest was unsuitable for slave labor. After the aged Clay had been forced to retire from the fray exhausted, Douglas whipped through the five separate measures that made up the Compromise of 1850. His cause was helped by the sudden death of President Taylor early in July and the ascent of Vice-President Millard Fillmore, a free soiler who nevertheless supported the Compromise.

Under the provisions of the Compromise of 1850, California entered the Union as a free state, and the western boundary of Texas was fixed where it is today, at the 103rd meridian. Texas received $10 million for giving up her claims to New Mexico. Two new territories,

The Granger Collection

New York Public Library

## CAUTION!!

### COLORED PEOPLE
OF BOSTON, ONE & ALL,
You are hereby respectfully CAUTIONED and advised, to avoid conversing with the
### Watchmen and Police Officers of Boston,
For since the recent ORDER OF THE MAYOR & ALDERMEN, they are empowered to act as
# KIDNAPPERS
AND
## Slave Catchers,
And they have already been actually employed in KIDNAPPING, CATCHING, AND KEEPING SLAVES. Therefore, if you value your LIBERTY, and the *Welfare of the Fugitives* among you, *Shun* them in every possible manner, as so many *HOUNDS* on the track of the most unfortunate of your race.
### Keep a Sharp Look Out for KIDNAPPERS, and have TOP EYE open.
*APRIL 24, 1851.*

*(Left) Frederick Douglass in 1854, at age 25.*
*(Right) Having failed*
*to save seventeen-year-old Thomas Sims,*
*a runaway Georgia slave,*
*from being returned to his master*
*after his capture in Boston on April 3, 1851,*
*the Reverend Theodore Parker wrote*
*this placard to be posted around*
*the city by the Vigilance Committee*
*organized to fight the Fugitive Slave Act.*

New Mexico and Utah, were created, with the proviso that the question of slavery be left for the people to decide in their constitutions at the time of their becoming states. Slave trading, but not slavery, was prohibited in the District of Columbia. Finally, a strong Fugitive Slave Law was passed, with many northern congressmen abstaining from voting.

Several northern states, beginning with Vermont in 1850, virtually nullified the Fugitive Slave Law by enacting new "personal liberty laws" enabling alleged fugitives to have legal counsel, jury trials, and other means of defending their freedom. Northern Negroes themselves also took up the defense of fugitives. Blacks, they said, had for too long been characterized as meek and yielding. "This reproach must be wiped out," declared Frederick Douglass, "and nothing short of resistance on the part of the colored man, can wipe it out. Every slavehunter who meets a bloody death in his infernal business, is an argument in favor of the manhood of our race."

### Election of 1852

The nation as a whole, nevertheless, exulted when news of the Compromise became known, and in the first presidential election after the Compromise the national yearning for sectional tranquility and moderation seemed to persist. In this election, in 1852, Franklin Pierce, the Democratic candidate, easily defeated General Scott, now the Whig candidate, running up a popular plurality of 214,000 votes and a margin of 254 to 42 in the

311

electoral college. The Free Soil candidate, John P. Hale, won only half as many votes as Van Buren in 1848, as northern Democrats in particular returned to the fold.

But in the long run the issue of slavery and its extension could not be compromised, and civil war loomed as the Manifest Destiny of the nation all the more certainly as the Manifest Destiny of continentalism was pursued. An ominous sign of trouble ahead was the breaking up of the Whig party following the deaths of Webster and Clay in 1852. The party, said Schuyler Colfax in Indiana, "seems almost annihilated by the recent elections." Once-loyal southern Whigs felt that this was precisely what any party deserved that accepted the guidance of antislavery men like Seward.

The Democrats still stood as a great national party, to which, indeed, many southern Whigs were now drawn. The rest of the Whigs would soon form the backbone of a new *northern* party to be called the Republican party. Politics, moreover, was not the only realm of sectional division. The slave South had become profoundly conscious of its differences from the burgeoning free North and West in all phases of life. These sections, in turn, developed a sense of their own individuality which grew clearer and stronger as the South felt impelled to stress its distinctive culture.

## For further reading

On the critical subject of British and Canadian relations, see H. C. Allen, *Great Britain and the United States* (1955); A. B. Corey, *The Crisis of 1830-1842 in Canadian-American Relations* (1941); and D. F. Warner, *The Idea of Continental Union, Agitation for the Annexation of Canada to the United States 1849-1893* (1960).

An excellent review of the expansionist period may be found in R. A. Billington, *The Far Western Frontier 1830-1860* (1956). Albert Weinberg, *Manifest Destiny* (1935), is comprehensive on the expansionist spirit. H. N. Smith, *Virgin Land* (1950), is an imaginative study of Americans' conception of the destiny of the West. Three books by Frederick Merk reflect a lifetime of study: *Manifest Destiny and Mission in American History: A Reinterpretation* (1963); *The Monroe Doctrine and American Expansionism 1843-1849* (1966); and *The Oregon Question* (1967). N. A. Graebner, *Empire on the Pacific* (1955), stresses the commercial side of expansionism. F. P. Prucha, *The Sword of the Republic: The United States Army on the Frontier 1783-1846* (1969), is authoritative. Bernard DeVoto, *The Year of Decision* (1943), is a fine popular history of the events of 1846.

E. C. Barker, *Mexico and Texas 1821-1835* (1928), offers a good account of the beginnings of American interest; W. C. Binkley, *The Texas Revolution* (1952),

carries the narrative further along. Stanley Siegel, *A Political History of the Texas Republic 1836-1845* (1956); and E. D. Adams, *British Interests in Texas* (1910), are informative on special subjects. More comprehensive older works include G. L. Rives, *The United States and Mexico 1821-1848* (2 vols., 1913), and two books by J. H. Smith, *The Annexation of Texas* (1911), and *The War with Mexico* (2 vols., 1919). A. H. Bill, *Rehearsal for Conflict: The War With Mexico 1846-1848* (1947), is a good short account.

C. J. Brosnan, *Jason Lee: Prophet of the New Oregon* (1932), and C. M. Drury, *Marcus Whitman, Pioneer and Martyr* (1937), supply the missionary background. Francis Parkman's classic, *The California and Oregon Trail* (1849), is better known through modern editions called *The Oregon Trail*. D. O. Johansen and C. M. Gates, *Empire of the Pacific: A History of the Pacific Northwest* (1957), is among the best general accounts. See also J. W. Caughey, *California* (1970).

Wallace Stegner, *The Gathering of Zion: The Story of the Mormon Trail* (1964), is a stirring account. L. J. Arrington, *Great Basin Kingdom: An Economic History of the Latter-day Saints 1830-1900* (1958), is best on the material side of Mormon history. T. F. O'Dea, *The Mormons* (1957), is a detached and informative discussion of Mormon history and doctrine. Fawn Brodie, *No Man Knows My History: The Life of Joseph Smith*

(1945), and Preston Nibley, *Brigham Young, the Man and His Work* (1936), are illuminating.

Allan Nevins, *Ordeal of the Union* (2 vols., 1947), is excellent on the politics of this period. W. E. Dodd, *Expansion and Conflict* (1915), remains valuable. J. H. Silbey, ed., *The Transformation of American Politics 1840-1860* (1967), is an anthology revealing underlying forces in party realignments. T. C. Smith, *The Liberty and Free-Soil Parties in the Northwest* (1897), is still useful. J. T. Carpenter, *The South as a Conscious Minority* (1930), and A. O. Craven, *The Growth of Southern Nationalism 1848-1861* (1953), are good on the slave section's position. Holman Hamilton, *The Compromise of 1850* (1964), offers a scholarly analysis.

Strong Negro comment on the Compromise and on the events preceding it will be found in the pertinent sections of Herbert Aptheker, ed., *A Documentary History of the Negro People in the United States* (1951).

Numerous biographies supply invaluable background: C. G. Sellers, Jr., *James K. Polk: Jacksonian 1795-1843* (1957) and *James K. Polk: Continentalist 1843-1846* (1966); Holman Hamilton, *Zachary Taylor* (2 vols., 1941, 1951); R. J. Rayback, *Millard Fillmore* (1959); F. B. Woodford, *Lewis Cass* (1950); G. F. Milton, *Eve of Conflict: Stephen A. Douglas and the Needless War* (1934); G. M. Capers, *Stephen A. Douglas* (1959); A. J. Beveridge, *Abraham Lincoln* (2 vols., 1928); U. B. Phillips, *The Life of Robert Toombs* (1913); and the lives of Clay, Calhoun, and Webster cited in Chapter Ten. Of the biography of Calhoun by C. M. Wiltse, the volume most relevant to this chapter is *John C. Calhoun, Sectionalist 1840-1850* (1951).

# A SOUTHERN NATION

The challenge of the South, the persistent discrepancies between its values and its condition, its longings and its impotence, is older than the Union. These discrepancies grew especially harsh after 1820 when industrialism under a regime of free labor captured the spirit of the country and the Western world while the South with its slaves clung only the more compulsively to plantation and subsistence agriculture.

For a time, while open land lasted in the South and industrialism elsewhere often was convulsed by its own growing pains, southern spokesmen successfully deluded themselves with dreams of grandeur sweetly nourished by the elevation slavery gave even to the crudest planter's ego and by the immense role of King Cotton in the industrial revolution itself. The growing differences, and the growing rivalry, between the slave states and the rest of the country in this period evoked enough interest to multiply the number of inquisitive visitors to the South, and her leaders remained confident enough to let them in. Many of them learned, indeed from troubled southerners themselves, that nineteenth-century cotton, like eighteenth-century tobacco, was in fact keeping the South a colony, not a kingdom, one characteristically producing raw materials for the enrichment of distant carriers and processors. They found, also, that slavery was making the section a pariah in a democratic age, one shunned by most immigrants to the country. The increasingly hostile reports of these visitors, their savage exposure of the dream of white excellence built upon black thralldom, caused the South as early as the 1830s to turn ever more self-consciously

314

inward, to ravel up the many and varied strands of her culture, and with fierce intransigence to see to the defenses of her "peculiar institution" and its fruits.

Richard Hildreth, the New England historian, visited the South late in the 1830s and in 1840 published his book, *Despotism in America; or An Inquiry into the Nature and Results of the Slave-Holding System in the United States*. Within the "great social experiment of Democracy" in America, he found in the South, "another experiment, less talked about, less celebrated, but not the less real or important, to wit, the *experiment of Despotism*. . . . The Southern States," he wrote, "are Aristocracies; and aristocracies of the sternest and most odious kind."

Hildreth saw only two classes in the southern aristocracies, the privileged planters and all lesser whites who aspired to planter status, on the one hand, and their "hereditary subjects, servants and bondsmen," on the other. "Extremes meet," he added. "Ferocity of temper, idleness, improvidence, drunkenness, gambling—these are vices for which the masters are distinguished, and these same vices are conspicuous traits in the character and conduct of slaves."

This was the image of Dixie also drawn in the abolitionist tracts of the day. Some southerners undertook to expose the excessive simplicity of the image and thereby discredit and destroy it. The section's most aggressive defenders, however, following the lead of Calhoun, preferred an equal simplicity and meeting of extremes the better to convey an alternative image of their own. In January 1838, Calhoun told Congress:

*This agitation [against the slave system] has produced one happy effect at least; it has compelled us in the South to look into the nature and character of this great institution, and to correct many false impressions that even we had entertained in relation to it. Many in the South once believed that it was a moral and political evil; that folly and delusion are gone; we see it now in its true light, and regard it as the most safe and stable basis for free institutions in the world.*

Calhoun continued:

*It is impossible with us that the conflict can take place between labor and capital, which makes it so difficult to establish and maintain free institutions in all wealthy and highly civilized nations where such institutions as ours do not exist. The Southern States are an aggregate, in fact, of communities, not of individuals. Every plantation is a little community, with the master at its head, who concentrates in himself the united interests of capital and labor. . . . These small communities aggregated make the State [in which] labor and capital [are] equally represented and perfectly harmonized. The blessing of this state of things extends beyond the limits of the South. It makes that section the balance of the system; the great conservative power, which prevents other portions, less fortunately constituted, from rushing into conflict. . . . Such are the institutions which these deluded madmen are stirring heaven and earth to destroy, and which we are called on to defend by the highest and most solemn obligations that can be imposed on us as men and patriots.*

Recent historians have returned to the view that the structure of southern society before the Civil War was in fact more complex than Hildreth's hell or Calhoun's heaven. All au-

315

thorities now concede that aristocratic planters were few, that many slaves enjoyed adequate creature comforts. They add that the "poor white trash," once lumped indiscriminately with all nonslaveholding whites, made up but a small minority reduced by disease to what subsistence they could scratch from otherwise unwanted land, eked out by fish and game; and that the statistically "average" southerner was an independent "yeoman" farmer who

316

*Calhoun in the perceptive portrait attributed to G. P. A. Healy.*

Henry Gourdin Young and Frick Art Reference Library

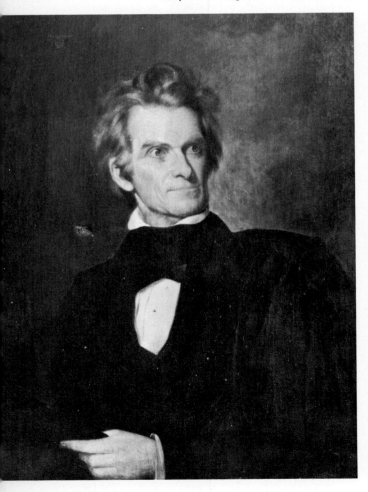

worked his own quarter section, more or less, with the help of his family, sometimes laboring side by side with one or a few Negro "hands." This independent yeoman is especially celebrated in the work of Frank L. Owsley, whose influential studies of *Plain Folk of the Old South* are devoted to making the slave section seem in fact an agrarian utopia. Other historians have rediscovered the Creoles of Louisiana and neighboring states, the mountaineers of Appalachia and the Ozarks, the "crackers" of the piney woods. Still others recall that the South had its professional class, doctors, lawyers, editors, teachers, and its urban and even its industrial centers.

And yet, as the Civil War forcibly reminds us, the simpler picture probably remains the more valid and realistic one. Creoles, crackers, and mountaineers, commercial and industrial workers, trained professionals—all were but marginal groups in the Old South. The average yeoman, moreover, decided neither his own fate nor the fate of his section. It was the planter, in an increasingly unfriendly universe, and his "niggers" bereft of their manhood, who set off the South from the rest of the country and from more and more of the world. The old Virginians knew this and regretted it. As the hateful system spread itself, the romantic fiction of Old Dominion cavaliers helped cloak the crude violence of frontier life. The "Great Revival" in religion, from which abolitionism itself took fire, also burned through the South and Southwest and spawned many lasting reforms, especially against whiskey drinking and its attendant degradation. To many northerners newly admitted to the "mighty Baptism of the Holy Spirit," no greater sin could be found in Christendom than pride of pigment, property in men, the enslavement of one Christian brother by another. To many southerners, the word of the Lord placed the black sons of Ham in everlasting bondage. Fundamentalism in religion reinforced the slave foundations of southern life.

# I White people of the South

## Dixie Land

No one knew the South as "Dixie" until Dan Emmett, a blackface minstrel out of Mount Vernon, Ohio, sang the new song of that name in a New York City theater in 1859. Two years later the band played "Dixie" at Jefferson Davis's inauguration as President of the Confederacy, and thereafter it became the unofficial anthem of the southern republic. Just where the term "Dixie" came from remains obscure. One of the dubious derivations is one of the most suggestive—that is, that "Dixie" was a corruption of the name of Jeremiah Dixon who surveyed the Mason-Dixon line. The Mason-Dixon line helped settle the boundary between Pennsylvania and Maryland in the 1760s. Its extension westward, roughly along the Ohio River, also helped settle the northern boundary of Dixie. Above that boundary slavery had been put well on the way to extinction around the turn of the nineteenth century. Below that boundary slavery existed in all the sixteen states and neighboring territories. Dixie was the land of slavery. It was also, as the song says, "the land of cotton."

There are many parts of the South where the growing season is too short for cotton, where the weather is too cold for rice, where it snows every winter and even beasts need sheltering barns. Yet the characteristic and distinguishing feature of the southern climate is the prevailing heat—*90° in the Shade* Clarence Cason titled his moving book on the South published in 1935, one of the early works of our time to expose the fiction and frailties of the utopian legend.

If the weather drew the characteristic southerner outdoors, the terrain and what it held helped keep him there. All across the Cotton Kingdom stood the densest forests in the world; as late as 1860 a large part of the slave's labor was given to clearing new land to let the sunshine in as well as to prepare fields for cultivation. The forest rewarded the hunter with ample and varied game. The Kingdom was also exceedingly well endowed with navigable streams to carry cotton and other staples to export centers, and with thousands of smaller brooks and creeks and rivulets, lakes and ponds, to feed the marshes and water the earth. These waterways rewarded the fisherman with ample and varied fare. "His leisure," writes W. J. Cash in *The Mind of the South* (1941),

*left the Southerner free to brood as well as to dream— to exaggerate his fears as well as his hopes. And if for practical purposes it is true that he was likely to be complacently content with his lot, and even though it was the lot of white-trash, it is not yet perfectly true. Vaguely the loneliness of the country, the ennui of long burning empty days, a hundred half-perceived miseries, ate into him. . . . Like all men everywhere, he hungered after a better and a happier world.*

A more concrete ambition also stirred the southerner's soul, like that of enterprising businessmen everywhere in America. The Cotton Kingdom was not extended in a single generation from South Carolina to Texas by men content to brood and dream at home. No better cotton land existed anywhere than in the Red River Valley of northern Louisiana and Texas. A typical Red River planter, accosted one day on a steamboat by a representative of the Education Society selling a "Bible Defence of Slavery," shouted: "Now you go to hell! I've told you three times I didn't want your book. If you bring it here again, I'll throw it overboard. I own niggers; and I calculate to own more of 'em, if I can get 'em, but I don't want any damn'd preachin' about it."

Yet white society in the South was more homogeneous than in the North, more conservative in its ways, less exposed to social and intellectual ferment. To the novelist John De Forest, who lived with the "Southrons" immediately after the Civil War, they seemed as different from New Englanders as Spartans from Athenians. "They are more simple than us," he wrote, "more antique, more picturesque; they have fewer of the virtues of modern society, and more of the primitive, the natural virtues." The violence of white southern life has perhaps been exaggerated, but the "Arkansas toothpick" (as the Bowie knife was sometimes called) became one of the principal instruments for settling differences in the rougher sections, and even in the older and more settled regions the code of honor prevailed.

The history of the Tillmans of South Carolina is a saga of violence. Benjamin Ryan Tillman, the first, an industrious but lawless planter, gambled as hard as he worked, killed a man in 1847, and died of typhoid fever two years later, aged forty-six. His wife, Sophia, a commanding woman, bore him three daughters and seven sons. Thomas the eldest, was killed in the Mexican War. The second, George Dionysius Tillman, might have served as the hero of a Faulkner novel (Faulkner speaks of the "glamorous fatality" of southern names). This erratic young man spent a year at Harvard, read law, and served in the state legislature. On two occasions, he fought and wounded his opponent; shortly after, he killed a third man during a card game, fled the country, filibustered in Cuba, and returned in 1858, repentant, to spend two luxurious years in the local jail. A third son was killed by two brothers whose family he had insulted; a fourth was slain in some domestic quarrel. Despite such open violence, travelers found Dixie hospitable and friendly until the virus of suspicion spread.

### The southern castes

In 1850, approximately 6.2 million white people or nearly 1.25 million white families (taking five persons per family on the average as authoritative writers like U. B. Phillips do) lived in Dixie. Of such families between a third and a fourth, no more than 350,000 all told, owned slaves, many of them only one or two, most of them under six. Above a third of the slaveholding families owned from 6 to 20 slaves, placing the larger owners among them, according to Phillips, on the threshold of the planter class or in the category of comfortable townspeople. Such families owned no less than 40 percent of all slaves and no doubt aspired to more. A mere 8000 planters owned 50 or more slaves, 250 owned 200 or more, and only 11 in the entire South owned 500 or more. The cotton kings, whose vast holdings and splendid mansions figure so prominently in southern romances, never amounted to more than 1 percent of the white population.

No doubt a conspicuous number of the large-planter caste lived the high life of saber-rattling, fire-breathing "cavaliers." But they were likely to be more worrisome than wonderful even to their own families. In their youth, sons of the well-to-do often were sent West with the hope that they might settle down under the cares of plantations of their own. Many did; but many more only found broader scope for recklessness and violence to match the rough and somber environment. Those who, like our Red River planter, were determined to develop their priceless natural endowment, spent many years in crude surroundings. The saw mill itself came late to Alabama, Mississippi, and Louisiana, and even in the 1840s and 1850s wealthy planters continued to live in "two pen" log houses, with only crevices between the unhewn logs to let in the light along with the rain and the wind.

In the older South many of the gentry lived well, and some extravagantly. But most of them also bore the cares that went with ownership of property and had little time to enjoy more than the simple pleasures of rustic society: hunting, horse racing, card playing, visiting, and perhaps an annual summer pilgrimage to the mountains or the sea to escape the heat.

Susan Dabney Smedes's reminiscent account of her father, Thomas S. G. Dabney of Virginia and Mississippi (*A Southern Planter,* 1887), conveys the *beau ideal* of the highest caste. Humane, upright, generous, and courteous, Dabney was most deeply concerned with sick slaves, the price of cotton, and unreliable overseers, subjects too unliterary for southern romancers, but the meat of plantation diaries and account books, with their records of hazards, anxieties, and disappointments. "Managing a plantation," Mrs. Smedes observed (as Calhoun did, in a significantly larger context), "was something like managing a kingdom. The ruler had need of great store, not only of wisdom, but of tact and patience as well." Nor did the planter's wife escape irksome domestic duties.

To the two-thirds of the southern white families who owned no slaves one should add those who worked their small holdings side by side with a black helper or two to find the true proportion of "plain folk" in the antebellum South. The farms of these "average" yeomen might be discovered tucked away among the large plantations in the cotton and tobacco country, but they predominated in the upland South—in eastern Tennessee, western North Carolina, northern Georgia, Alabama, and Mississippi. Here, while some produced the southern staples, most of the plain folk grew subsistence crops—grains and cereals, sweet potatoes, sorghum cane—or raised livestock. The plain folk also included the storekeepers, the mechanics, and other artisans in southern villages and towns.

Seen through the candid but critical eyes of Frederick Law Olmsted, the Connecticut Yankee who traveled through the southern hinterlands in the early 1850s, yeoman living standards seemed distinctly below those of northern farmers. And yet, though Olmsted complained of wretched cooking, vermin-filled beds, and rude manners, he also noted

319

Library of Congress

*A yeoman "plantation" in central Florida. Lithograph from sketch on the scene in 1838 by Francis Comte de Castelnau, an able French naturalist who toured Amérique du Nord in that year.*

that the yeomen in general presented a picture of a sturdy, hospitable people. "If you want to fare well in this country," he was told in northern Alabama, "you stop to poor folks' housen; they try to enjoy what they've got while they ken, but these yer big planters they don' care for nothing but to save." Riding through an area of thin sandy soil, "thickly populated by poor farmers," Olmsted reported:

*The majority of dwellings are small log cabins of one room, with another separate cabin for a kitchen; each house has a well, and a garden enclosed with palings. Cows, goats, mules and swine, fowls and doves are abundant. The people are more social than those of the lower country, falling readily into friendly conversation. . . . They are very ignorant; the agriculture is wretched and the work hard. I have seen three white women hoeing field crops today. A spinning-wheel is heard in every house . . . every one wears home-spun. The negroes have much more individual freedom than in the rich cotton country, and are not infrequently heard singing or whistling at their work.*

Among such farmers, as one who grew up in Mississippi reported, "people who lived miles apart, counted themselves as neighbors, . . . and in case of sorrow or sickness, or need of any kind, there was no limit to the ready service" they rendered one another.

The "bottom sill" of southern white society, the so-called poor white trash, perhaps as much as the Negro himself, were the victims of slavery. Such was the conclusion of one embittered southerner, Hinton Rowan Helper, a Negro hater who turned abolitionist to save the South from itself. In his sensational and propagandistic book, *The Impending Crisis of the South: How to Meet It* (1857), he made slavery "the root of all the shame, poverty, ignorance, tyranny and imbecility of the South." Although Helper's widely publicized

analysis distorted the southern picture, it contained some uncomfortable truths about white people that were hardly answered by calling its author a "miserable renegade."

On the "poor whites," the discerning Olmsted wrote:

> They are said to "corrupt" the negroes, and to encourage them to steal, or to work for them at night and on Sundays, and to pay them with liquor, and to constantly associate licentiously with them. They seem, nevertheless, more than any other portion of the community, to hate and despise the negroes.

## II  Life of the southern Negro

### The black population

Slavery took root in the South because black Africans provided a cheap and available labor force to cultivate staple crops. When Congress closed the slave trade in 1808, southerners owned about 1,160,000 slaves. Between 1808 and 1860, smugglers brought in approximately 270,000; but most slaves carried to the newly opened lands in the Southwest were bred from slave populations of the older states. Between 1830 and 1850, Virginia alone exported close to 300,000 Negroes, South Carolina about 170,000. On the eve of the Civil War about 3,800,000 slaves lived in Dixie, a mere 250,000 free Negroes. In some plantation counties and parishes, slaves made up three-fourths and even higher proportions of the population (see map, p. 329).

The heaviest concentration of slaves and of cotton could be found in the prize lands of the South: in the "Black Belt" that stretched across central Alabama into northwest Mississippi; in the flood plains of the Mississippi River; and in parts of southern Texas that drained into the Gulf of Mexico. Compared to 350,000 engaged in tobacco in 1850, and

150,000 in rice, no less than 1,815,000 of the 2,500,000 slaves engaged in agriculture in 1850 were occupied with cotton. By then the Black Belt had become the world's greatest cotton-growing region; and here it was that the slave system could be studied in its most mature form. Relations between master and slave of necessity became more impersonal on large plantations than on small ones, and discipline more severe. Well-run plantation "factories," self-sufficient units producing corn, peanuts, and livestock in addition to cotton, were serviced by slave carpenters, masons, and weavers, as well as field hands.

Few free Negroes lived in the South's agricultural regions, but among them were some who themselves had become large planters and slaveowners. Such Negro "kings" were especially conspicuous on the frontier in Mississippi, Alabama, and Louisiana before the period of "ultraism" in white supremacy following upon the onset of the abolitionist crusade; and they appear to have been treated as gentlemen among gentlemen. In the cities, too, free Negro businessmen owned slaves whom they hired out for all sorts of urban tasks.

In the first quarter of the nineteenth century, slaves made up at least 20 percent of the urban population of the South; in places like New Orleans and Richmond they were more numerous; and in Charleston, South Carolina, they outnumbered whites. Thereafter the slave population of southern cities declined. By 1848 it was said that "slavery exists in Louisville and St. Louis only in name." Two reasons were offered by contemporaries for the falling off in urban slaves: "The first is a dense population . . . the next is the intelligence of slaves." To be remunerative, city slaves had to be hired out singly or in small numbers, not in gangs under overseers. Thus, flight or mere disappearance could be more easily effected, and with skills learned as a slave a Negro could make a living as a free man.

Even so, at the outbreak of the Civil War, approximately 500,000 slaves were living in southern cities and towns as servants or artisans or were engaged in such nonagricultural pursuits as cutting wood for steamboats, lumbering, mining, iron manufacturing, and construction.

### The slave's world

"The first black men in the American midlands—not counting a few who were brought in chains to work the salt mines—were fugitives and wanderers. They came thrashing the wilderness grass like frightened animals," write Arna Bontemps and Jack Conroy in their book on Negro migrations, *Any Place But Here,*

*and at night they cast their aching, exhausted bodies on the ground and slept. In the morning they rose up, filled their lungs with the free air of God's country, and swore it was different from the air of bondage. The difference, they reasoned soberly, was exactly the difference between night and day. . . . The air made the difference. That's why folks always talked about going North and breathing the free air.*

*The Charleston waterfront
in 1831, from painting by S. Barnard.*

No one knows how many slaves took the path of the so-called underground railroad toward freedom, nor how many died before reaching their goal. Estimates range as high as 100,000 successful refugees, most of them moving out after the onset of the abolitionist campaign in 1830. That they moved singly or in pairs, seldom in larger and more vulnerable groups, appears well established. Brave blacks lit out when they could without much concern for preparation. Many, of course, fled from impending punishment for real or asserted violations of the slave code. If fortunate, they found shelter, food, and guidance—mainly from blacks who had earlier made good their escape or who had been born free in the North and who used their freedom to help others retrieve their humanity. But religious and humanitarian whites also worked on the "liberty line."

As we know from the history of emancipation and Reconstruction, even when freed perhaps a majority of southern Negroes stayed put on the land they knew. Running away may have been many a slave's dream; the storm over enforcement of the fugitive slave provision of the Constitution (Art. IV, Sec. 3) and the Fugitive Slave Act of 1850 supports the conclusion that flight was one of the principal actions that made the slave such a "troublesome property" to the master. At the same time, the small proportion of actual refugees to the distant free states of the North (as distinct from the much larger number who simply fled oppression on particular plantations) suggests that freedom remained more a dream than a drama. With the intensification

*Resurrection of Henry "Box" Brown, runaway slave shipped from Richmond in wooden box addressed to William Johnson, Arch Street, Philadelphia, and marked "this side up with care." The journey took twenty-six hours.*

*shrinking from the snaky contact. Now why is this? You do not so treat the man who deals in corn, cattle or tobacco.*

of the sectional struggle and the southern defense of slavery in the 1840s and 1850s, flight became a more frequent occurrence while repression and punishment also grew harsher.

In the Cotton Kingdom, the heart of the slave's world, and in less well organized areas of the South, as we have said, certain bondsmen escaped the drudgery of the field gang; and the lot of others might vary according to their age and sex, the character and disposition of their masters, and their own temper and personality. Yet all slaveowners in the nineteenth as in the eighteenth century were bound by the system under which black men and women were their chattels in an environment of violence and mutual fear and dread. House servants usually found life easier than field hands; but the death of a humane master might result in his servants' being put out to the land when least prepared for its burdens. Some gifted slaves were rewarded with positions of trust and responsibility and responded with loyalty and devotion to their masters for affectionate treatment. Yet even the kindliest slaveholder, either as buyer or seller, sometimes felt obliged to break up black families, which themselves had no standing under the law.

Of all the institutions of slavery, the slave market was perhaps the most distressing, for white and black alike. Lincoln, in 1854, reminded the South that "the great majority" there, as in the North, "have human sympathies, of which they can no more divest themselves than they can of their sensibility to physical pain." The one who tried those sympathies to the utmost was "a sneaking individual, of the class of native tyrants, known as the 'SLAVE-DEALER.'" Lincoln went on:

*He watches your necessities, and crawls up to buy your slave, at a speculating price. . . . Your children . . . may rollick freely with the little negroes, but not with the "slave dealer's" children. . . . It is common with you to join hands with the men you meet; but with the slave dealer you avoid the ceremony—instinctively*

On some plantations where the "task" system was employed, a slave might complete his assigned work by early afternoon and spend the rest of the day as he chose. Progressive planters sometimes gave their slaves incentive payments and also encouraged them to cultivate truck gardens and to raise pigs and chickens for their own consumption or for sale. Holidays and entertainments alleviated the drudgery on some plantations, and where work became too exacting slaves developed their own slowdown techniques. Yet such situations were exceptional, even in the upper South where the "institution" is said to have been less vicious than elsewhere in the United States.

Frederick Douglass, a house servant who had been taught to read and write, yet who fled from slavery in Maryland in 1838 and gave the rest of his life to the pursuit of freedom and equality for other blacks, spoke from experience when he wrote of slavery as "perpetual unpaid toil; no marriage, no husband, no wife, ignorance, brutality, licentiousness; whips, scourges, chains, auctions, jails and separations; an embodiment of all the woes the imagination can conceive."

The poet Paul Laurence Dunbar of Dayton, Ohio, son of a fugitive slave and friend of Douglass, wrote in "Life":

*A crust of bread and a corner to sleep in,*
*A minute to smile and an hour to weep in,*
*A pint of joy to a peck of trouble,*
*And never a laugh but the moans come double:*
*    And that is life!*

On the characteristic Black Belt plantation, the field hand's routine hardly varied from day to day and year to year, only a break on July 4th and at most a week at Christmas relieving the tedium. The day's work ran, as the saying went, from "can see, 'til can't" with ten to fifteen minutes at noon to eat the lunch ration of cold bacon. The assigned "task" in the harvest season would be a certain weight

The Bettman Archive

The Bettman Archive

New York Public Library

(Top left) Slaves at work picking cotton
for primitive presses in the fields that
baled the bolls for easy shipment.

(Center) Harvesting and ginning cotton.
Lithograph by Oertel, about 1830.

(Bottom left) Typical slave quarters of the 1850s
in the eastern plantation states.

(Below) Slaves, after all, did relieve
the life of the whip, hunger, and broken
families. This sketch of slaves
dancing to music was drawn from life by Lewis
Miller in Lynchburg, Virginia, August 1853.

Virginia State Library

of cotton to pick. On the Red River plantation where Solomon Northrup, a free Negro kidnapped and enslaved, worked for twelve years, those who failed to "tote" their quotas to the gin house were thrashed; those who exceeded their quotas under the whip in the field were assigned an extra measure thereafter. In his log cabin, open to the wind and rain, Northrup slept on "a plank 12 inches wide and 10 feet long," with a "stick of wood" for a pillow and a coarse blanket for his bedding.

Slave gangs like Northrup's worked the long day under the eye of the overseer whose job it was to get out his own crop quota. Obviously it was to the slaveholder's advantage to protect his slave property against excessive work and barbarous punishment; but it required the nicest judgment to maintain a balance between laxness and severity in the management of involuntary workers, and overseers with such judgment were hard to come by. The lash, applied by the overseer himself or his black "driver" (a slave assigned as a kind of foreman to keep the hands on the job), was more commonly resorted to than other inducements.

Abolitionists sometimes exaggerated the brutalities of slavery, but they did not have to invent stories of routine whippings, brandings, mutilations, and murder. Documented evidence also abounds, were it needed, to lay to rest claims that "fetters on black skins don't chafe." Thousands stood sunk in unalleviated depression and despair. Many tried to buy their freedom. Failing this, even many of those most kindly treated attempted flight. Others, to escape forced labor, would mutilate themselves, feign sickness and stupidity, devise many other stratagems, and sometimes openly rebel.

Allusions to "horrible and barbarous massacres" plotted by blacks go back to the early colonial period. The first widely publicized nineteenth-century slave rebellion was the "Gabriel conspiracy" in Henrico County, Virginia in 1800. More than a thousand slaves allegedly were implicated in this proposed march on Richmond, which was betrayed by two black informers and thwarted by a violent rainstorm. Gabriel and about thirty followers were hanged as a lesson to others. In 1822, Denmark Vesey, a Charleston freedman, organized another large rebellion, one also betrayed by slaves and resulting in about thirty executions. By far the most sensational slave revolt was that engineered by the black Virginia preacher Nat Turner, in 1831, with the intention of killing every white person in Southampton County. Believing himself divinely appointed, Turner led a two-day rampage that ended with the death of fifty-seven whites and about a hundred blacks. Tracked down after a desperate manhunt, Turner and twenty followers were taken and executed.

Turner's was the last of the organized slave revolts. The reports of suppression and bloody reprisals carried a disheartening message across the black South, while, with the spread of abolitionist propaganda after 1830, the white South sharpened its alertness and strengthened its defenses. Riding night patrols was one task even irresponsible planters took more seriously, whiskey often bucking them up against the terrors of darkness. In the towns and cities, police costs "for the purpose of 'keeping down the niggers'," as one traveler reported, made up the largest municipal budget item. Olmsted wrote that in nearly every southern city he visited, "you come to police machinery such as you never find in towns under free governments: citadels, sentries, passports, grapeshotted cannon, and daily public whippings ... for accidental infractions of police ceremonies."

"Free people of color," along with abolitionists, came increasingly under suspicion in the South, while many black preachers among the slaves were silenced. The religious language, indeed, in which rebel exhorters addressed their followers convinced many planters that Bible reading, in fact any reading, had become incendiary, and slave improvement in letters lapsed. Yet many slaves persisted in study and in individual strikes for freedom despite the growing hostility of their environment.

## III   The plantation system

### Minor southern staples

The southern economy lagged behind that of the North for some reasons that had nothing to do with slavery. The North had a more invigorating climate, more varied natural resources, better harbors. But it was the single-crop system, the gang-labor system, the slave system, that kept the South from making the most of its own natural endowment.

The first southern agricultural staple was tobacco, and the first slave-labor plantations were devoted to growing the leaf in the tidewater regions of Virginia and Maryland. After 1800, tobacco culture spread westward across the upper South, and by midcentury this newer area was raising more tobacco than the old. In the 1850s, however, Virginia, North Carolina, and Maryland made such a spectacular comeback in tobacco production that seven of the ten leading tobacco counties in the entire country lay in these three states. The source of their new prosperity was the discovery in 1839 by a slave, Stephen, employed as an overseer and blacksmith on a North Carolina plantation, of a way of curing a type of tobacco, the "Bright Yellow Tobacco," that grew better on the poor sandy soil of the Roanoke Valley and inland Maryland than on the worn-out soil of the tidewater. Great plantations once again became the rule in the Old Dominion and her neighbors, and the grim business of breeding slaves for the Southwest declined. But compared to cotton, tobacco remained a minor southern crop, and the tobacco revival did not bring general prosperity even to the three leading states. In 1860, only 36 percent of Virginia land and 27 percent of land in North Carolina was "improved," compared to 68 and 61 percent for New York and Pennsylvania.

Although the chief beneficiaries of the Bright Tobacco boom were large slaveholders, tobacco was also grown by many small farmers. Small farmers were the main producers of another minor crop, hemp, which became a staple in Kentucky and Missouri. Only rich planters, on the other hand, could embark on the production of rice and sugar, the South's two other important minor staples. In 1860, indeed, not even the Gulf states of the Cotton Kingdom could match the rice regions of South Carolina and Georgia (much more limited in area, of course) in the relative density of their slave populations and the scale of their plantations. The only estate of more than 1000 slaves in the entire South was in the South Carolina rice country. Rice was also grown in lowland regions of Louisiana, Texas, and Arkansas.

Cane-sugar planting gained a strong impetus after 1822, when steam engines were introduced to crush the cane. The cost of machinery for a sugar plantation might run as high as $14,000, and harvesting of cane called for intensive periods of the hardest labor by slave gangs. Only owners of large plantations in the rich delta lands of Louisiana and the alluvial soil regions of southeastern Texas and coastal Georgia could afford the cost of sugar-milling equipment, but even they could compete with the more favorably situated West Indian producers only because of the tariff on imported sugar.

### The Cotton Kingdom

As early as 1820, the South's cotton crop had become more valuable than all its other crops combined. By 1835 the Cotton Kingdom itself had spread more than a thousand miles from South Carolina and Georgia all the way to Texas and ranged some six or seven hundred miles up the Mississippi Valley. In 1859, the South grew a record cotton crop of 5,387,000 bales, two-thirds of it in the Gulf states. That year cotton accounted for two-thirds of the *nation's* exports.

With a little capital, small acreage, and a few slaves, a cotton farmer could still make a profit. Cotton could survive rough handling when shipped to market, and it did not spoil when stored—important considerations where poor transportation and warehousing caused marketing delays. Much of the American cotton crop, even on the frontier, was in fact grown by small farmers; yet cotton, with its huge market and great adaptability to slave-gang labor, was the ideal staple for the big planters who spread over the virgin lands of the Southwest. By 1860, slave-gang planters grew more than 93 percent of the Mississippi crop.

Where land was plentiful and cheap and labor dear, the essence of good plantation management was high production per slave, not per acre. Under effective overseers and gang bosses, the more slaves a planter had, the greater his margin of success was likely to be. It was this circumstance that helped put such great pressure on overseers and on slaves. Large-scale operations gave big planters other advantages as well. Necessities that they could not grow or make on the plantation they could purchase in large quantities at wholesale rates. They could also market their crops more efficiently. Wealthier planters, moreover, were more likely to be interested in conserving the soil, more willing to experiment with new agricultural techniques.

### Profits and penalties of the plantation system

Those who argue—as many did in the South as well as the North before 1860, and as many continue to argue today—that slave labor was more costly in cotton growing

*Georgia riverfront plantation wharf with cotton bales ready for loading, in lithograph from de Castlenau sketch made on the scene in 1838.*

New York Public Library

than free labor would have been and that slavery would have disappeared eventually if left alone, have tended to make a mere bookkeeping problem of a profound social issue. It is true that only exceptional cotton plantations earned large profits, even on the virgin soil of the Gulf area. It is also true that such profits as were earned were menaced by high slave mortality and the cost of maintaining aged slaves and slave children. Despite efforts to quicken their incentive, moreover, slaves proved to be reluctant workers, while solicitude for their welfare proved insufficient to prevent them from misusing tools and damaging equipment, often willfully. To make matters worse, the cost of prime male field hands jumped in the 1840s and 1850s from $1000 to $1200 or more, forcing the planter to tie up larger amounts of capital in slave labor. But few were motivated on that account to aban-

don slavery, any more than Queen Victoria was motivated to abandon monarchy because of the rising cost of soldiers.

If slavery was in fact an economic disadvantage to the cotton South, it need not bear all the responsibility for southern economic backwardness. Even in antebellum days men like Edmund Ruffin of Virginia argued that southern soil exhaustion, for example, was only indirectly connected with the unchanging routines of slave gangs. Soil exhaustion, they said, was primarily the result of shortsightedness, itself encouraged by the easy availability of new land; and of ignorance, promoted by widespread white illiteracy and indifference to technology. But even these men acknowledged that the plantation system itself discouraged widespread education even in agricultural processes and that slavery induced an indifference to technological innovation.

Would slavery have persisted after the lands suitable for staple crops had been used up? Many southerners and northerners believed that nature had confined slavery to a

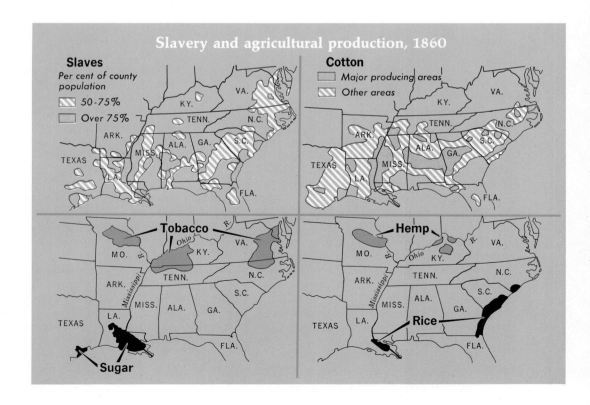

Slavery and agricultural production, 1860

restricted area and that the institution on that account would not outlast the century. Lincoln and others in the North who, in the political arena, so strongly opposed the extension of slavery to new territories (see Chapters Twelve and Fifteen) obviously did not share this belief; nor did those in the South who so pertinaciously opposed restrictions on free expansion of the institution. It has been argued, moreover, by Lewis C. Gray, the leading historian of antebellum agriculture in the South, that further railroad building would have brought fresh lands into easy reach of the migrating planter, and that industry might well have absorbed the surplus slave population. Although slaves, as we have seen, did in fact work in southern industries and in other urban occupations, the growing need to defend the slave system and the plantation system from attack by the industrial North drained such incentive as there might have been among the great planters really to develop a dynamic industrial regime in their own area. The need to justify the slave system and the plantation system in its own terms, indeed, helped dissipate the profits that were made on the land and turned the proud Cotton Kingdom into a disenchanted colony of industrial and commercial Britain and the North.

## Colonial status of the Kingdom

Southerners were perfectly familiar with the invidious contrasts drawn even by their own spokesmen between the busy, contented North—enterprising, public-spirited, prosperous—and indolent, poverty-stricken Dixie. Many of them nevertheless feared the effects of factories in an agrarian slave society. Some felt (though there was evidence in southern factories to the contrary) that slaves working in a factory were already half-free; others believed that blacks were incapable of mastering machinery. Many still harbored the distrust of cities that Jefferson had expressed so vividly in his *Notes on Virginia*.

In spite of such doubts and apprehensions, a favorable attitude toward manufacturing developed during the 1820s and early 1830s when tariff controversies made the South acutely conscious of its dependence on northern industry. Factories, it was said then, would furnish employment for hitherto unproductive poor whites, and help keep southern wealth at home.

Not until the 1840s, however, did such arguments, vigorously presented by the Charleston businessman William Gregg, in his book *Essays on Domestic Industry* (1845), begin to take hold. Gregg did more than write. He set up factories and factory towns on the model of the Lowell mills he had gone north to study. Poor white families, not slaves, ran his machines. Nor did he offend the planters by demanding tariff protection for the coarse textiles he manufactured, since foreign cloths did not compete with his. Falling cotton prices in the 1840s, and economic stagnation in his own state in particular, laid the ground for a friendly reception to new economic ideas. Gregg's program also was applauded by the growing number of southern nationalists (already looking ahead to southern independence) who wanted a strongly industrialized South when the great day arrived. Another influential group backed the industrial program for precisely opposite reasons: They hoped that factories would make the South prosperous and that prosperity would remove the chief cause of animosity between the sections.

Yet little came of Gregg's work. Between 1850 and 1860, the number of industrial workers in the South rose only from 165,000 to 190,000. On the eve of the Civil War, the South was producing less than 10 percent of the nation's manufactured goods. In 1860, the Lowell mills alone operated more spindles than all the cotton-spinning factories of the South combined.

The South showed an even greater aversion to commerce than to manufacturing, with even stiffer penalties for producers of staple crops that had to be marketed abroad. At the numerous commercial conventions held in the South between 1830 and 1860, the southern imagination was fired with rhetorical visions of teeming cities, happy artisans, and bustling marts, all the rewards of recapturing the cotton-carrying trade from New York and New England. But recapture never passed the rhetorical stage.

## Roots of southern loyalty

"It may seem a paradox, and yet it is true," declared a North Carolinian in 1853, "that a community of planters may grow rich while they are impoverishing and depopulating their country." Slavery discouraged diversity in agriculture, accelerated the flow of southern yeomanry to the free-soil states, and created an illusory prosperity based on long-term credit, and ownership of land declining in fertility and of slaves rising in cost.

The personal penalties that slavery imposed upon many slaveowners, though less obvious and less physically trying than those on blacks, were often almost as disastrous. A few slaveowners publicly acknowledged their spiritual discomforts, as the following extract from the will of a North Carolinian who emancipated his slaves makes clear. He gave four reasons for his action:

*Reason the first. Agreeably to the rights of man, every human being, be his or her colour what it may, is entitled to freedom. . . . Reason the second. My conscience, the great criterion, condemns me for keeping them in slavery. Reason the third. The golden rule directs us to do unto every human creature, as we would wish to be done unto. . . . Reason the fourth and last. I wish to die with a clear conscience, that I may not be ashamed to appear before my master in a future World.*

And yet after 1830 the allegiance of the vast majority of southerners to the slave system and the plantation system only deepened. Their attachment to the "peculiar institution," of course, varied according to class, region, and occupation, but the following consider-

ations help to explain why slavery received such overwhelming support in the decades preceding the Civil War:

1. FEAR OF BECOMING A WHITE MINORITY   The extremely heavy concentration of slaves in parts of the South created a serious problem in race relations. Antislavery northerners, southern spokesmen declared, living in states where blacks comprised only a tiny fraction of the population, had no inkling of what it was like to live in South Carolina or Mississippi communities where blacks often far outnumbered whites.

2. THE NEGRO UNFIT FOR FREEDOM   It was widely held in the South that the Negro would only be harmed by abolition, a belief strengthened by reports about the deteriorating condition of free Negroes in the North. Everywhere in the free states, even in the centers of abolition, as we have seen, blacks were abused and discriminated against politically, economically, and socially, and then blamed for their low condition as though the reasons were congenital.

3. ANTI-NEGRO SENTIMENTS OF WHITE LABORERS   White workers in southern cities, like most northern workingmen, did not want slavery abolished. Black competition, whether slave or free, threatened their livelihood, while working alongside blacks demeaned their social position. Race prejudice was particularly strong among immigrant groups, like the Irish, who performed menial jobs too dangerous for high-priced slaves.

4. THE SOCIAL AMBITIONS OF SMALL PLANTERS   Small planters, linked to the gentry either by kinship or common interest, felt that their chances of rising in the world would be jeopardized by abolition. They, and many yeoman farmers too poor to own slaves, looked forward to the time when they would be masters of larger plantations.

5. THE "POOR WHITE" COMMITTED TO RACIAL INEQUALITY   Finally, the impoverished southern whites, disease-ridden and shiftless, fanatically supported slavery as a way of preserving what little status they had. When the time came, they fought for slave property and for a slaveowning class that looked upon them with contempt.

## IV The mind of the South

*Limitations on the reform spirit*

To the Bostonian Henry Adams, the southerners he met at Harvard between 1854 and 1858 seemed incredibly archaic, sunk in a simplicity beyond the comprehension of the most unsophisticated New England student. "Strictly, the Southerner had no mind; he had temperament," Adams wrote later in his celebrated *Education*. "He was not a scholar; he had no intellectual training; he could not analyze an idea, and he could not even conceive of admitting two."

Adams's sweeping generalizations were provincial enough. Calhoun, a brilliant but doctrinaire analyst, was one of a number of acute thinkers in the South who reasoned only too well. But the claim of impassioned proslavery men that the South had erected a superior culture on a slave base was no less mistaken. Intellectual novelties were not welcomed in the antebellum South, and the arts won little encouragement; as education and literacy lagged compared to the North, old ways and old ideas strengthened their hold, and intellectual pursuits were confined to a tiny minority. In the southern mind, all "isms"—feminism, transcendentalism, Fourierism, and the rest—quickly became tinged with abolitionism, and rightly enough, since northern abolitionists like Garrison, Theodore Parker, Theodore Weld, and Horace Greeley *were* drawn to the whole range of reform programs. Feminism in particular outraged the southern ideal of womanhood. Some southern mavericks—notably the aristocratic Grimké sisters, Angelina and Sarah, of Charleston—turned abolitionist or succumbed to other enthusiasms, but they were made to suffer for their independence and often driven north.

Yet the humanitarian influences and reform spirit that coursed through the country in the 1830s and 1840s did not leave the South untouched. Criminal codes were humanized at least for whites, prisons improved, and treatment of the insane made more scientific. Dorothea L. Dix was one Yankee reformer whom the South loved for her work on behalf of the mentally ill. Her visit to Tennessee and North Carolina in 1847–1848 brought immediate action, and the asylum that was opened in Raleigh, North Carolina in 1853 bore her name. During the same period, schools for the deaf patterned after northern models were established in a number of southern states. Perhaps the most enthusiastically supported reform movement in the prewar South was the temperance cause. Backed by religious and political leaders, temperance societies sprang up everywhere to the accompaniment of parades and petitions and the publicized testimony of reformed drunkards.

*Antislavery sentiment
and the proslavery argument*

Like slavery itself, antislavery sentiment arose early in the South. In the eighteenth century, William Byrd II of Virginia expressed the widely held view that slaves in the colony "blow up the pride and ruin the industry of the white people." In the Revolutionary period, many southern leaders saw the incongruity of slavery in a Republic dedicated to the principles of the Declaration of Independence, although they did little about it. A later generation of southerners dominated the American Colonization Society, headed by George Washington's nephew and dedicated to transplanting freed slaves overseas. In Virginia, abolition was seriously argued in 1829, when tobacco planting was at a low point and a new state constitution was being drafted, and again in the legislature of 1831-1832, on the heels of Nat Turner's insurrection.

Since 1793, nevertheless, when Whitney's cotton gin gave the South a strong new reason for expanding the slave system, southern attitudes toward slavery had grown in illiberality. Awareness of antislavery sentiment in Europe and Latin America, and the spread of abolitionism in the North, only hardened southern attitudes until, in the 1830s, the proslavery forces in the section launched a counterattack. Their initial targets were southerners opposed to slavery, and then the northern emancipationists. The Bible and the Constitution as well as political science, biology, and classical requirements for high culture—all were arrayed in favor of the "peculiar institution." Slavery, they held, fostered the classical form of democracy with all the Greek virtues, as distinct from the "mongrelized" industrial democracy of the North.

George Fitzhugh's *Sociology for the South; or The Failure of Free Society* (1854), and *Cannibals All! or Slaves Without Masters* (1857) brought together all the familiar arguments of the day. Following Calhoun's prized lead, Fitzhugh claimed that in the South capital and labor were not divorced. The fierce exploitation of one class by another, as in the cannibalistic laissez-faire economy of the North, was blessedly absent here. Northern capitalism, Fitzhugh declared, led to the impoverishment of the masses not their enrichment, to social revolution not democracy and liberty. No such dangers threatened the South.

Fitzhugh and his coterie sought to win northern conservatives over to support the slave system, but his extreme views, presented in his exuberant style, backfired. Slavery, known as a curse and a menace, became the scapegoat for all else that underlay the slave section's desperation. It grew as convenient for the northerner to ascribe soil exhaustion, illiteracy, and economic instability to slavery alone as it did for the southerner to attribute the social and economic backwardness of his region to greedy northern middlemen and to high tariffs.

### Education

The extension of the suffrage just before the abolitionist campaign got under way went farther in the North than in the South (see p. 242), but even in the slave section it raised the specter of an "ignorant and debased" electorate. Public education, nevertheless, remained almost nonexistent. Even a Horace Mann would have made little headway in the thinly populated rural areas of the South, where rich planters resisted taxation for public schools while those who would have benefited from them felt they bore the stigma of charity. Some 2700 private academies could be found in the South by 1850, more than in New England and the Middle states together. But students were few and the quality of education fell below northern standards. The 1850 census showed 20 percent of southern whites illiterate as against 3 percent in the Middle states and 1 percent in New England.

Southern higher education compared more favorably with that in the North but, even after abolitionism had soured them on northern ideas, southern families who could afford it continued to send their sons up to Yale, Princeton, Harvard, and the University of Pennsylvania rather than to their own state universities and denominational colleges. At the same time, a greater percentage of young southerners than northerners was receiving college training. In 1860, for example, when the northern population was 2.5 times that of the white population of the South, each section counted about 26,000 college students. Most southern colleges were less richly endowed than those in the North. But the University of Virginia, South Carolina College, and briefly, Transylvania, measured up to the standards of the best above the Mason-Dixon line.

As antinorthern sentiment intensified in the 1840s and 1850s, southern leaders made strenuous efforts to throw off the intellectual yoke of the Yankees. It was particularly gall-ing for southern students to be given northern texts. One book, for example, described slavery as "that stain on the human race, which corrupts the master as much as it debases the slave." Agitation against importing poisonous alien doctrines, however, apparently did not halt the sale of northern books nor keep many southern students from northern schools.

### Religion in the South

The political and religious liberalism so marked in the Jeffersonian South declined after 1825 when the skeptical spirit fostered by the Enlightenment among the aristocracy gave way to the fundamentalism of the common man. The religious revivals of the early 1800s converted thousands to the Methodist and Baptist faiths, and ministers of such evangelical denominations now assumed a powerful influence over the raw democracy. Moral reform went hand in hand with intellectual intolerance. From southern pulpits came denunciations of infidelity and alcohol, while the atheist, the Deist, the Unitarian (all often lumped together) were branded subversive. In 1835, a North Carolina constitutional convention voted to exclude Jews, atheists, and skeptics from public office. Six years later, a Georgia court held the testimony of Universalists (who did not believe in hell-fire) invalid.

Intellectual repression was by no means confined to the South. Heresy hunts and anti-infidel crusades occurred in the North and West at the time, under the same auspices. But in the South the skeptical minority now kept silent. Jefferson himself had tried to obtain a professorship at the University of Virginia for the free-thinking Dr. Thomas Cooper. He failed, but Cooper served as president of South Carolina College between 1821 and 1834, when his attacks against the clergy and against Biblical literalism became too extreme to be condoned, even though he sympathized with the South on slavery and state rights. In Kentucky, Presbyterians ousted the liberal Unitarian Horace Holley from the presidency of Transylvania University in 1827, and soon after Unitarianism practically disappeared from the South. Episcopal and Presbyterian churches survived among tidewater gentility; but elsewhere those described by the frontier preacher as "profane sinners, downright skeptics, and God-defying wretches" were converted or silenced.

### Southern writers

No literary flowering occurred in the South in any way comparable to New England's during the antebellum period, even though a number of talented writers published fiction, poetry, and essays of high quality. Even Edgar Allan Poe, often considered the South's greatest writer, was, as we have seen, born in Boston, while his literary domain was the landscape of the mind, not the section.

Southern, like northern, writers had to combat the national indifference to literature and contempt for the writer, but conditions peculiar to their section magnified their problems. So long as the older and better-educated families dominated southern culture, literary tastes and standards were those of cultivated amateurs who believed professional writing to be unsuitable for gentlemen. They enjoyed biography and history and shared the national enthusiasm for British authors, but they gave little practical encouragement to their own. The "highbrows" of Charleston, according to the poet Paul Hamilton Hayne, who grew up among them, were great devotees of the classics but read little else. They might admire their distinguished townsman, the novelist William Gilmore Simms, but they did not buy enough of his books to please him. "The South," Simms wrote to a friend in 1847, "don't care a d—n for literature or art."

When, for patriotic reasons, southern writers published in the South, their books sold poorly. Well-written magazines like the *Southern Literary Messenger* might praise their works, but only the approval of northern periodicals had cash value. Southern writers resented their dependence on northern publishers, periodicals, and critics who, they felt, puffed Yankee mediocrities while ignoring southern genius. Without northern publishers and audiences, however, such popular writers as Poe and Simms would have fared even more poorly than they did. Simms's conclusion about his countrymen seems just: "We are not, in fact, a reading people. We are probably, at best, only the pioneers for those, who will atone to letters and the arts hereafter, for our grievous neglect."

As sectional animosities deepened, southern writers found themselves in a dilemma. According to the Charleston poet Henry Timrod, any truthful account of the South antagonized northern readers, while southern readers were quick to detect any lapse in local pride. Writers were expected to fight with their pens to uphold the southern gospel against such intellectual incendiaries as Emerson.

**335**

*His mind [declared a critic in the* Southern Literary Messenger] *is like a rag-picker's basket full of all manner of trash. His books are valuable, however, for the very reason they are no earthly account. . . . We of the South require something better than this no-system.*

*Idealization of the plantation home, a setting near Charleston, South Carolina, residence of "Colonel George Buckingham," from the frontispiece of Robert Criswell's book, "Uncle Tom's Cabin" contrasted with Buckingham Hall (1852).*

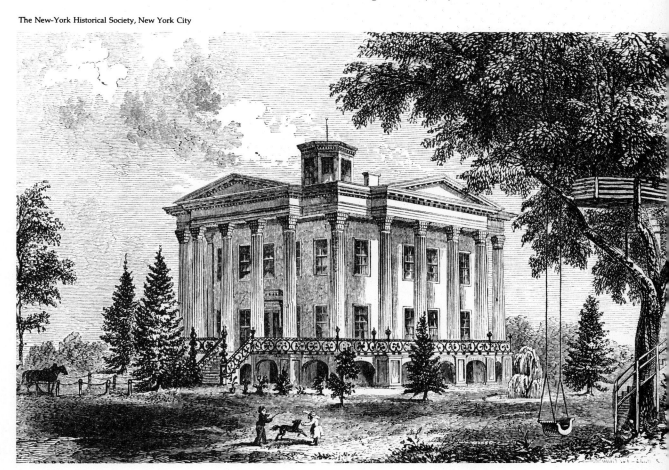

*Your fragmentary philosopher, of the* Emerson *stamp, who disturbs the beliefs of common folk . . . is a curse to society.*

**336**

In the light of these peculiar circumstances, what can be said of the literary achievements of the Old South? Taken as a whole, southern writers did not depict the agrarian society as accurately or as fully as they might have. Nowhere is slavery or the slave treated meaningfully. Simms, the section's most prolific novelist, contributed his full share of wooden heroes, whose lips curl and whose eyes flash, and of doll-like ladies who speak in stilted phrases. But at least his low-life characters, his traders, tavern keepers, and poor whites, are real. He was the only southern novelist before the war who wrote convincingly of the yeomanry and the riffraff. His novels, loose and careless in style, nevertheless capture the violence and gustiness of the southern frontier. His fondness for brutal detail makes him seem at times a precursor of the twentieth-century school of southern naturalists.

The plain people of the South are also graphically portrayed in the sketches of southern humorists, journalists, doctors, sportsmen, lawyers. Poe praised as masterpieces of reporting Augustus Baldwin Longstreet's colorful descriptions of rural Georgia. The Cumberland Mountain country inspired another frontier humorist, George Washington Harris.

## For further reading

F. B. Simkins, *A History of the South* (1963), and W. B. Hesseltine, *The South in American History* (1960), are useful surveys. Clement Eaton, *The Growth of Southern Civilization 1790-1860* (1961), deals more comprehensively with the period of this chapter. C. S. Sydnor, *The Development of Southern Sectionalism 1819-1848* (1948), and A. O. Craven, *The Growth of Southern Nationalism 1848-1861* (1953), contain richly documented analyses of southern life.

E. D. Genovese, *The Political Economy of Slavery* (1965), is a broad analysis of the southern economy. See also his *The World the Slaveholders Made* (1970). L. C. Gray, *History of Agriculture in the Southern United States to 1860* (2 vols., 1933), the standard work, may be supplemented with the chapters on the South in P. W. Gates, *The Farmer's Age: Agriculture 1815-1860* (1960). For other aspects of southern economic life see Broadus Mitchell, *William Gregg, Factory Master of the Old South* (1928); R. E. Russel, *Economic Aspects of Southern Sectionalism 1840-1861* (1924); and U. B. Phillips, *A History of Transportation in the Eastern Cotton Belt* (1908). Illuminating "Sources and Readings" will be found in Stuart Bruchey, *Cotton and the Growth of the American Economy 1790-1860* (1967), and H. D. Woodman, *Slavery and the Southern Economy* (1966).

F. L. Olmsted's indispensable record of his travels in the South is presented in the excellent modern edition by A. M. Schlesinger, *The Cotton Kingdom* (1953). H. R. Floan, *The South in Northern Eyes 1831-1861* (1958), is a useful monograph. Other revealing glimpses of southern life may be found in F. B. Simkins, *Pitchfork Ben Tillman* (1944); J. H. Franklin, *The Militant South 1800-1861* (1956); and Everett Dick, *The Dixie Frontier* (1948). F. L. Owsley, *Plain Folk of the Old South* (1949), has been most influential in emphasizing the yeoman as against the plantation tradition. The lasting costs of this emphasis are examined in W. H. Nicholls, *Southern Tradition and Regional Progress* (1959).

Modern reading on slavery must begin with W. D. Jordan, *White Over Black* (1968). J. H. Franklin, *From Slavery to Freedom: A History of American Negroes* (1967), is the standard account. Two works by August Meier and E. M. Rudwick are also recommended: *From Plantation to Ghetto* (1966), an authoritative short survey, and *The Making of Black America* (1969), a comprehensive anthology. Allen Weinstein and F. O. Gatell, eds., *American Negro Slavery: A Modern Reader* (1968), also offers informative selections. Two older works by U. B. Phillips, *Life and Labor in the Old South* (1929), and *American Negro Slavery* (1918), should be contrasted with K. M. Stampp, *The Peculiar Institution: Slavery in the Ante-Bellum South* (1956).

Frederic Bancroft, *Slave Trading in the Old South* (1931), is excellent on the domestic slave trade. H. D. Woodman, "The Profitability of Slavery: A Historical Perennial," *Journal of Southern History,* XXIX, No. 3 (August 1963), affords a documented survey of studies of this subject from the 1840s to the 1960s.

L. P. Jackson, *Free Negro Labor and Property Holding in Virginia 1830-1860* (1942), is one of the few scholarly works on the free black. R. C. Wade, *Slavery in the Cities, The South 1820-1860* (1964), is a scholarly monograph touching on this subject. Frank Tannenbaum, *Slave and Citizen, The Negro in the Americas* (1947), and S. M. Elkins, *Slavery, A Problem in American Institutional and Intellectual Life* (1959), afford comparisons with the institution in other American lands. Herbert Aptheker, *American Negro Slave Revolts* (1943), is perhaps too comprehensive; H. Aptheker, ed., *A Documentary History of the Negro People in the United States* (1951) is the fullest anthology of the Negro's own words from colonial times to 1910. Larry Gara, *The Liberty Line* (1961) places the "underground railroad" in perspective. Benjamin Quarles, ed., *Narrative of the Life of Frederick Douglass, An American Slave, Written by Himself* (1960), is a moving document.

W. J. Cash, *The Mind of the South* (1941), is a pene-

trating study of illusion and reality. W. R. Taylor, *Cavalier and Yankee: The Old South and American National Character* (1961), probes the conflict of attitudes that helped bring about the Civil War. F. P. Gaines, *The Southern Plantation* (1924), confronts southern romanticism with certain aspects of realism. Other challenges to southern thinking are examined in R. G. Osterweis, *Romanticism and Nationalism in the Old South* (1949), and J. T. Carpenter, *The South as a Conscious Minority* (1930). Clement Eaton, *Freedom of Thought in the Old South* (1940), is broader than its title suggests. E. L. McKitrick, ed., *Slavery Defended: The Views of the Old South* (1963), is a valuable anthology of proslavery apologists. This subject is dealt with in W. J. Jenkins, *Pro-Slavery Thought in the Old South* (1935), and Harvey Wish, *George Fitzhugh: Propagandist of the Old South* (1943). H. C. Bailey, *Hinton Rowan Helper, Abolitionist-Racist* (1965), is a penetrating study of the author of *The Impending Crisis of the South and How to Meet It* (1857), the most controversial contemporary account of slavery and the southern white population. J. B. Hubbell, *The South in American Literature 1607-1900* (1954), is comprehensive. Edmund Wilson, *Patriotic Gore, Studies in the Literature of the American Civil War* (1962), is masterly analysis of expression in both sections. The *Letters of William Gilmore Simms* (1952-1955), are full of interesting material on the southern writer. S. L. Gross and J. E. Hardy, eds., *Images of the Negro in American Literature* (1966), is a revealing collection of essays.

# THE EXPANSIVE NORTH

At the end of 1854, after a decade of unprecedented expansion, a brief depression befell the American economy. The stock market crashed, tens of thousands of factory workers were thrown out of work, prices of western produce tumbled, and land values collapsed. The depression was short-lived, but the recovery that began in 1855 raised the speculative fever to such a pitch that a new and more resounding crash occurred in 1857. All sections of the country suffered except the South, and all sectors of the economy were depressed except the culture of cotton. "The wealth of the South," announced that section's leading economist, J. D. B. DeBow of New Orleans, "is permanent and real, that of the North fugitive and fictitious."

Never was thinking more wishful or more wrong. The South's economy, though prosperous, lacked the vitality and variety of the North's; and the ups and downs in northern production reflected the dynamism of industry that would soon make the United States the richest country in the world. Perhaps we should speak of industrial*ism* rather than of industry alone, for it was the *spirit* of machine production that was at work—a spirit that was to pervade commercial agriculture and steamboating and railroading as well as the factories.

In the 1850s, the North was almost unanimous in the belief that the country's growth would proceed apace even if the South should desert the Union. In the North in the 1850s, writes Allan Nevins in *Ordeal of the Union,* "the underlying forces of the industrial revolution were simply irresistible." Among them he notes the country's natural resources, the surge of immigrants into the labor force, the energy and inventiveness of the people, the flow of capital from California gold mines and from abroad, government friendliness to industrial objectives as shown in tariff policies, low taxes, and subsidization of transportation. All these, Nevins writes, "combined like a chain of bellows to make the forge roar."

## I  Peopling the "Middle Border"

Mechanized agriculture first became widespread in the United States on the free family farms of the northern prairies and the eastern edges of the unforested Great Plains. This fertile country, Hamlin Garland's "Middle Border," stretched from upper Indiana and Illinois northward to central Wisconsin and Minnesota, and westward through Iowa and upper Missouri to the eastern townships of Kansas and Nebraska. Even more than the southern coastal plains, this level, lush terrain invited the large-scale corporate type of farming that characterizes much of the area in the twentieth century. At the outset, however, most of its settlers were independent small farmers from the neighboring states to the east or immigrants from the British Isles and the continent of Europe.

Driven by debt during the worldwide depression of the early 1840s, tens of thousands of farm families in the Ohio Valley and the country bordering Lake Erie and Lake Michigan sold their cleared and cultivated homesteads to newcomers with capital. Drawn by the government's liberalized land policy (see p. 253) to try again on the distant frontier, they settled there in such numbers that Iowa became a state in 1846, Wisconsin in 1848. Minnesota had grown large enough for statehood by 1858, and the admission of Kansas was delayed until 1861 for political reasons, not for lack of population. Nebraska and even the Dakotas to the north also were becoming inhabited.

During this period, economic distress, accompanied by political repression and religious persecution, had spread across Europe once again. Among the worst sufferers were the Irish Catholics, who were especially hard hit by the potato crop failure and the famine that followed in 1845 and 1846. In the decade that ended with the business Panic of 1854, about 1,300,000 Irish had fled the Emerald Isle for the United States. Their love of the Old Country ran deeper than that of the Ulstermen of the eighteenth century, yet for all their attachment to the "old sod," they usually were too poor even to move inland from the coastal cities in which they landed. Some of them did travel west as laborers with canal- and railroad-building crews. Second in numbers to the Catholic Irish were the 940,000 Germans who arrived during this decade to augment the German population long

339

here. The decade's immigrant Englishmen, Welshmen, and Scots numbered about 375,000. A few thousand Scandinavians also came, the heralds of a large migration later in the nineteenth century, along with small contingents of Dutch, Swiss, Belgians, French, and Czechs.

All told, between 1844 and 1854 almost three million immigrants braved the Atlantic crossing to America. Although some of the thousands who were crowded into cotton ships on the return voyages from British and Continental ports remained in New Orleans where they were landed, most of the newcomers shunned the land of cotton. A majority of the immigrants were young, unmarried adults, who immediately swelled the working force of the free section. Others came as before in family groups, among them independent, outspoken middle-class businessmen, lawyers, doctors, scientists, and journalists, who brought new skills, new learning, and new leadership to western cities like Cincinnati

and St. Louis. More numerous than these urban settlers were rural "reading families," readily identified by their bookish preparation for life in the New World. Such families were devoted to the Bible and often were led to America by their Old-Country pastors. By 1860 they were 30 percent of the population of Wisconsin and Minnesota and almost as numerous in other Middle Border states.

So determined were these religious newcomers to preserve their old way of life in the wilderness that they sometimes segregated themselves in a "New Germany," a "New Norway," or a "New Bohemia." But many soon caught the vision of a brighter future, and their commitment to the homeland and to the past grew dimmer with the passing years. So long as the cotton planters kept their labor system to themselves, away from the Lord's

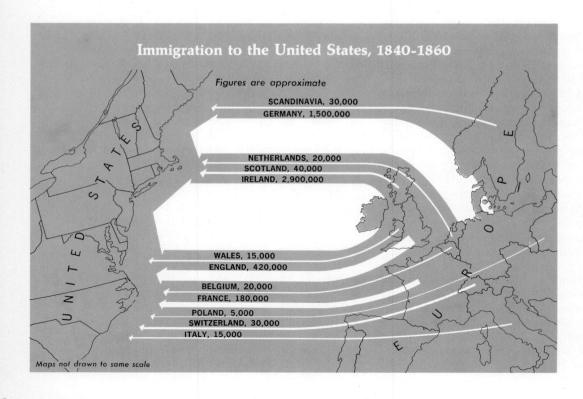

**Immigration to the United States, 1840-1860**

Figures are approximate

SCANDINAVIA, 30,000
GERMANY, 1,500,000

NETHERLANDS, 20,000
SCOTLAND, 40,000
IRELAND, 2,900,000

WALES, 15,000
ENGLAND, 420,000

BELGIUM, 20,000
FRANCE, 180,000

POLAND, 5,000
SWITZERLAND, 30,000
ITALY, 15,000

UNITED STATES

EUROPE

Maps not drawn to same scale

free soil, these western pioneers as a rule opposed meddling with the institution of slavery. Their own labor supply came from their large families; they kept their sons and daughters on the land, and invested in machines to multiply their productivity. The religious mysticism and pseudoscience of the times fed the belief that iron poisoned the earth, and some of these settlers were as wary of iron and steel implements and machines as of abolition. But they could not long withstand the competitive force of innovation.

## II The agricultural revolution

### Breaking the sod

For most of the decade and a half before the Civil War, the settlement of the free West ran well ahead of the railroads. Pioneer families traveled on foot, in wagons, and in boats on the rivers and the Great Lakes. Groups of families sometimes settled a particular region, but even here, the whole territory being so vast, farms often were a day's travel or more apart. One reason for choosing isolated sites was the settler's habitual suspicion of intruders. More important was his hope of adding more land to the quarter section with which he usually started.

Having prayerfully picked his land and registered it at the nearest land office, a farmer would build a one-room log cabin or, in treeless country, a hut made of slabs of sod and a barn of the same material. Meanwhile, he would turn his few sheep, cows, and oxen out to graze on the wild buffalo grass and fence them off as best he could from the kitchen vegetable garden, the care of which became one of the many responsibilities of his wife. Once he had fenced in his main fields, at a cash outlay of $1 or $1.25 an acre, he would begin the laborious round of cultivation.

His first discovery would be that the plow he carried with him from the East, though it took two men to handle and four oxen to pull, could hardly scratch the heavily matted virgin soil. So at a further cost of $1.75 to $2.50 an acre, he would hire professional "breakers," teams of men with huge plows drawn by six to twelve oxen, to cut the first shallow furrows on the prairies and the plains. In following seasons, the farmer and his family would be able themselves to plow and plant the land first broken by the professionals.

An acre or an acre and a half a day—perhaps 40 acres of a 160-acre quarter section in the planting, and harvesting, season—was the most the pioneer could hope to put under

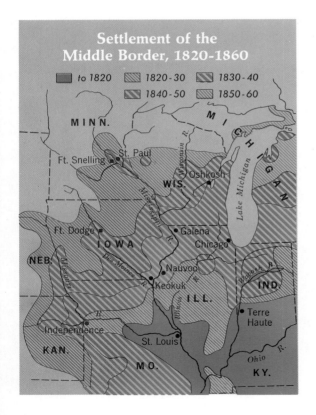

Settlement of the Middle Border, 1820-1860

to 1820   1820-30   1830-40
1840-50   1850-60

MINN.
MICHIGAN
Ft. Snelling   St. Paul
Wisconsin R.
Oshkosh
WIS.
Lake Michigan
Ft. Dodge   Galena
IOWA   Chicago
NEB.   Missouri R.
Des Moines R.
Nauvoo   Wabash R.
Keokuk   IND.
ILL.
Terre Haute
Independence
St. Louis   Ohio R.
KAN.
MO.   KY.

cultivation with his available ox-power and equipment. But men who had moved their families to the prairies and the plains with the idea simply of reestablishing an independent way of life based on self-help and Christian charity were quite satisfied to do as well as this. In the belief, cherished in the United States, that the tiller of the soil was of all creatures closest to God—a belief that had given a Christian base to the Jeffersonian ideal of a democracy of farmers—they tended to resist rapid changes that promised nothing more than greater material reward for their labors.

And yet the sheer fertility of the Middle Border's soil, superficially cultivated though it was by backward methods and outmoded tools, soon inundated the pioneers with surplus crops. Many of them welcomed the opportunity to market their produce for cash and to buy more land. Every farmer, or at least every farmer's wife, aspired to move on from the crude log cabin or musty sod hut to a neat frame dwelling with proper furniture and a touch of color in a table covering, a window curtain, or a picture on the wall. Such "improvements" required money, and until the crash of 1857 money was crying to be made. The crash, indeed, reminded many of how deeply they had sunk into the sin of covetousness, and in 1858 a new sweep of revivalism in the West recalled backsliders—for a time at least—to religion and church.

### Expanding markets

For all the Christian traditionalism of the "New Germanys" and the "New Norways," and the terrifying isolation of the American settlements, the prairie farmers in this Age of Progress were in fact the vanguard and support of a worldwide business surge. In Europe, industrialism was spreading, cities were growing rapidly, tariffs on agricultural imports were coming down, the exchange of currencies was being simplified. Accompanying these social changes were the revolutions, famines, and wars that cast so many immigrant families onto American shores in search of asylum and a fresh start. These circumstances taken together created a lively de-

National Portrait Gallery, Washington, D.C.

*A contemporary Japanese woodcut depicting Commodore Matthew Perry, at the time of his visit to Japan, as the Yankee equivalent of a shogun.*

mand for foodstuffs which the virgin American West, manned so largely by the immigrants themselves, could quickly supply.

Nor was the business ferment restricted to Europe. After 1844, American ships and the vessels of other nations enjoyed new rights in the treaty ports of China; in 1854, Commodore Matthew Perry, with a fine show of American naval power, opened up the "Hermit Kingdom" of Japan to American trade; in 1856, Siam (modern Thailand) broadened the privileges accorded twenty years before to United States exporters; and all this stirring in the Pacific warmed American interest in Hawaii. The Orient never became a market for the produce of American farms nor for more than a minute fraction of the products of American factories; yet Oriental trade contributed its mite to American aspirations toward world power. It helped transform the American merchant marine into the world's largest fleet and its home ports into booming metropolises where, as in the great cities of Europe, landless multitudes clamored to be fed.

In the West itself farmers were finding markets at frontier forts, among the loggers who had recently opened up the north woods of Wisconsin and Minnesota, and among the lead miners who, after the 1830s, extended their operations from Galena, Illinois, into neighboring Wisconsin and Iowa. Gold-mining camps farther west had also begun to look to the nearest farmers for flour and meal.

From the beginning of the westward movement, corn was always the frontier farmer's first marketable crop. Easily converted into fattened hogs (which were commonly turned loose in the corn fields to "hog down" the ripened ears), corn could be made to walk to market when other transportation was lacking. Corn also served as suitable winter feed for beef cattle, which could be walked even farther than hogs. For human consumption, corn was distilled into a potable and package-able "likker," or it was eaten off the cob, baked into bread, and prepared in many other ways. In the famine years of the late 1840s, even the hungry Irish brought themselves to eat American corn; but they and other Europeans never developed a taste for it, and little corn was exported. In the United States, on the other hand, corn bread and corn-fed pork made up the bulk of the national diet. American corn production reached 838 million bushels in 1859, an increase of 40 percent in ten years, and the Middle Border states accounted for most of the gain.

Wheat was far more selective than corn in soil and climate, and even in suitable latitudes it grew best on land that had already produced a corn crop. In 1849, Pennsylvania, Ohio, and New York were the leading wheat states. By 1859, though the country's total wheat production had soared 75 percent to a record 173 million bushels, each of these three states produced less wheat than it had a decade earlier. Illinois, Indiana, and Wisconsin had moved to the head of the wheat states; and in succeeding decades, reflecting the momentum of the westward surge of wheat growing, first Iowa, then Minnesota, then Kansas, and then the Dakotas entered the ranks of the leaders.

Acre for acre, wheat paid better than corn, over which it had advantages both in marketing and production. Unlike corn, wheat was eaten all over the world. Less bulky than corn in relation to value, it could bear high transportation costs more easily, and it also with-

343

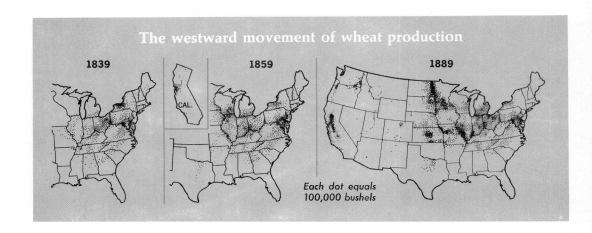

The westward movement of wheat production

1839    1859    1889

CAL.

Each dot equals
100,000 bushels

stood shipment more successfully. Finally, on the open prairies and plains, where land was plentiful and hired labor scarce, wheat production responded magnificently to improved tools and labor-saving machinery.

344

### Mechanized farming

The western farmer's first need in the way of equipment was a new plow. Back in 1837, John Deere, an Illinois blacksmith, had produced the first American steel plow, and by 1858, after making many improvements on his original design, he was manufacturing 13,000 a year. Light enough for a strong man to sling over his shoulder, the Deere

*The McCormick reaper-mower, 1857, with lettered and numbered parts and directions for putting them together.*

plow nevertheless was the first to cut deep, clean furrows in the prairie sod. Nor did it take bovine strength to draw it, and the weaker but faster-moving horse began to supplant the ox on western farms. So great was interest in plow improvement that by the time of the Civil War 150 varieties of plows were on the market, and experimenters were working on steam-powered "plowing engines" that could cut as many as six furrows at once.

Even more striking improvements were being made in machines especially designed for wheat growing. Cyrus Hall McCormick of Virginia (in 1834) and Obed Hussey of Ohio (in 1833) had patented practical steel-tooth reapers in the early days of the westward move-

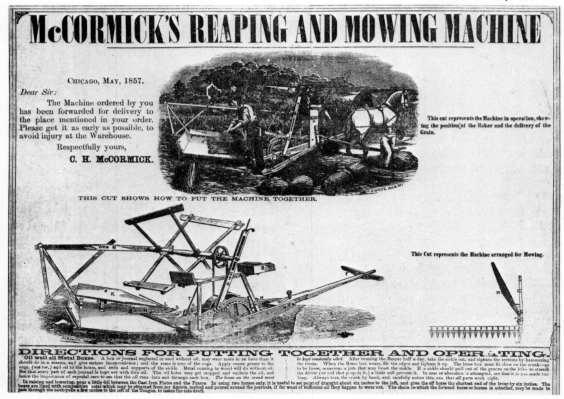

ment. With McCormick's horse-drawn machine a single man could do the work of five men equipped with scythes. Sales lagged, however, until McCormick (while Hussey languished in the East) moved his plant to Chicago in 1848 and hurried his demonstrators off to the western frontier. Ten years later, by means of the "American System," as admiring Europeans had begun to call the manufacture of standardized parts (not to be confused with Henry Clay's "American System" of domestic exchange and finance), McCormick was producing 500 reapers a month and still falling behind the demand. The standardized parts were packed and shipped directly to the farmer, along with printed instructions on how to assemble them.

At first, entire neighborhoods had to be mobilized to harvest the vast quantities of wheat the new reapers could cut down. But in the 1850s progress was being made in the design of mechanical wheat binders, which in the next decade would eliminate much of the harvesting army. In the 1850s, mechanical threshers already were in use.

In 1800, the average American farmer spent about $15 to $20 for his tools. By 1857, *Scientific American* was recommending that every farmer with 100 acres of land should have machinery worth about $600. Although many wheat farmers got along with less, by the time of the Civil War, about $250 million was invested in farm implements and machines, an average of about $120 for each farm in the country. On the extensive wheat farms of the prairies and the plains, the average investment was much higher.

### Farming as a business

Once the western farmer had committed himself to machinery, he found his life greatly altered. The most disturbing change came from his discovery that he was suddenly in the grip of forces over which he had little control. His principal machines, for example, such as reapers and threshers, could speed the

production of wheat but could be used for little else when the wheat market fell off, as it did in 1854. The fact that he usually purchased these machines on credit further narrowed the farmer's range of choice, for his debt eventually had to be paid in cash, and wheat, the specialty of the new machines, was also the cash crop *par excellence*. Falling wheat prices simply forced him to grow more wheat than ever in order, at lower prices, to get as great an *aggregate* cash return as before. But increasing his wheat production often meant breaking or buying new land, either of which would plunge him still more deeply into debt. Then he would need still larger wheat crops in order to acquire the cash to maintain payments on his larger obligations.

The continuous round of specialization, mechanization, and expansion in the free West gave a momentum to wheat production that was a priceless boon to the world. Other aspects of wheat growing on the prairies and the plains, however, were hardly boons to the farmer. In some years, frost, hail, and other visitations far more severe than in the East destroyed much of the crop before it could be harvested. Even in the best growing seasons, moreover, the servicing of broad new markets seemed to involve an endless spiral of new charges. The steps between the wheat grower and the ultimate urban consumer, for example, seemed to multiply disastrously with distance. All along the line, weighers, graders, storage-elevator operators, rail and water carriers, warehouses, local haulers, insurers, moneylenders, and speculators—the whole urban apparatus of finance and distribution—mysteriously placed a hand on the farmer's fate, and worse, in the farmer's pocket.

The worldwide collapse of prices in 1857 staggered the wheat farmer. His debts went unpaid, the threat of foreclosure and indeed foreclosure itself soured his prospects, and his mind turned once more to the free frontier. In 1858, western wheat farmers began attending meetings other than religious revivals, and from these meetings arose broad denunciations of conspiratorial "trading combinations," monopolistic elevator and railroad operators, and grasping moneylenders. The farmer's special place in God's plan received renewed publicity, and farmers were urged to "assert not only their independence but their supremacy" in society. Vague proposals also began to be made for farm cooperatives and for state and federal control of railroads and other big businesses.

Out of it all, before the Civil War, came a stronger demand for two specific programs. One, a favorite among educational and agricultural reformers, was for agricultural colleges to educate farm youth in the science of agriculture and to afford them broader educational opportunities as well. These colleges were to be set up by the federal government and financed by federal land grants. The second demand, with a far broader backing among farmers, was for free homesteads—free of payment and free of slaves—on the remainder of the public domain. Over southern opposition, Congress enacted a land-grant college bill in 1859, only to have President Buchanan veto it. In June 1860 he vetoed a homestead bill that would have made western lands available at 25 cents an acre. In the elections later that year, the farmers of the West, crying the slogan "Vote Yourself a Farm," helped carry the country for Lincoln, even though they were aware that his policy of no extension of slavery to the territories could carry the nation to war.

### The agricultural revolution in the East

Right up to the outbreak of the Civil War southern planters remained active customers of the western farmers, but the great bulk of western grain and meat flowed to the Northeast. So great did this volume become that the agricultural revolution in the West forced upon the East an agricultural revolution of its own.

Let the West "supply our cities with grain," William Buckminster of Massachusetts had said in 1838:

*We will manufacture their cloth and their shoes. [Our farms] shall find employment in furnishing what cannot so well be transported from a distance. Fresh meats, butter, hay, and the small market vegetables must be supplied by the farmers of N. England.*

What Buckminster had foreseen developed with a rush in the following twenty years—not only in New England but also on the more friendly soil of other eastern states. Two foodstuffs that he failed to enumerate became the most profitable of all—milk and fruits.

Dairying, once a routine chore in most households, had become big business by 1850. In that year, the Harlem Railroad brought about 25 million quarts of milk into New York City. Every other sizable city in the East had developed its own "milk shed," a nearby expanse of pasture land where carefully bred and carefully tended herds of cows were reared especially for milk production.

Fruit orchards were as common as pastures in the East. But after 1840, the growing of apples and peaches was expanded and brought under scientific care. Strawberries, blackberries, and many varieties of melons added interest and nourishment to the urban American's diet. The tin canister, or the "tin can," an English invention for packaging perishables, became widely used by American fruit and vegetable merchants in the late 1840s, greatly enlarging their market.

A revival of scientific farming in the East furthered the agricultural revolution in that section. An earlier scientific farming movement, restricted largely to gentlemen farmers, died out in the 1830s. But after 1845, when success hinged increasingly on special knowledge and up-to-date processes, eastern dirt and dairy farmers took a keen interest in information about climate, soils, fertilizers, methods of cultivation, and the idiosyncrasies of different crops. Agricultural associations, fairs, magazines, books, courses, and schools multiplied in the East in the 1840s and 1850s.

Railroad and water routes linking the East and the West encouraged each section to produce its own specialties. Railroads and water routes *in* the East and especially in New England so covered the land that farmers in this section could specialize in perishables with the assurance that their produce would be speeded to city consumers.

346

## III   Peak of water transportation

### Revival of foreign trade

When the Civil War began, the railroad dominated the economy of the free North and exercised a powerful influence on the welfare of the entire nation. But the railroad had to fight for ascendancy while other avenues of exchange and other forms of transport helped to build up the country.

One of the most important commercial developments of the 1840s and 1850s was the revitalization of America's foreign trade. During the depression that followed the crash of 1837, foreign trade had fallen to a point well below the level even of the early years of the Republic. In 1843, combined imports and exports were only $125,250,000, a trough never touched in the preceding thirty years. Then began an almost continuous rise to a record $687,200,000 in 1860. In almost every year during this period, imports exceeded exports. Eighty percent of the half-billion dollars in gold taken from the California mines before 1857 was sent abroad to make up the difference. The rapidly increasing export of western wheat and flour helped keep the imbalance within reasonable limits.

The revival of foreign trade had a tremendous effect on immigration. Without the vast fleets of merchantmen that plied the Atlantic between Europe and America, the millions of newcomers to the United States in the late 1840s and in the 1850s could never have found passage to the New World. Seventy-five percent of American commerce, and an even greater proportion of the immigrant traffic, was carried in American sailing ships.

The average westward crossing by sail from Liverpool, England, to New York took about thirty-three days. Steamships, which had been used in ocean commerce since 1838, could make this crossing in the 1850s in ten to fifteen days, but they remained undependable and excessively costly to operate. As late as 1899, all ocean steamships carried sails for auxiliary or emergency power. By 1860, only a tiny fraction of the world's ocean commerce had been captured by steamships, most of them British.

### Surge of domestic commerce

In the fifteen years before the Civil War, American domestic commerce far surpassed even the record foreign trade both in volume and rate of growth. The vitality of foreign trade itself contributed significantly to this development, for the mere collection at American ports of commodities for export created a great deal of business for home carriers. Similarly, the need to distribute to the interior the increasingly voluminous imports landed at a few great coastal cities added to the demand for domestic transportation.

But domestic commerce was far more than an adjunct of foreign trade. As the American population grew—and it grew with phenomenal rapidity in the free North in the 1840s and 1850s—the home market naturally expanded. As different regions began to specialize in particular commodities, the need for exchange among them increased. Exchange itself was made easier by the gold being mined in California and by the improved credit facilities of the expanding banking system. Between 1851 and 1860, money in circulation in the United States, including specie and banknotes, rose 9 percent per capita. But the importance of this increase to trade was even greater than this figure indicates, for the telegraph and the railroads were now speeding up business transactions and accelerating the collection of bills.

*The clipper* Flying Cloud, *in 1852.*

This meant that the actual money in circulation could be used many more times in a single year than heretofore; and, since the amount of money itself was rising rapidly, the whole pace of domestic commerce quickened. Between 1843 and 1860, while American foreign trade grew five and a half times, domestic trade grew ten times. By 1860, domestic carriers were hauling goods worth at least fifteen times the combined value of exports and imports, or about $10 billion worth a year.

### The clipper ship era

Before the railroad boom of the 1850s, domestic commerce was almost monopolized by water carriers; and of these carriers the oldest and for a long time the most successful were the coastal sailing ships. In 1852, the value of goods carried by American coastal vessels (the coastal trade was closed by law to foreign ships) was three times the value of goods hauled by the railroads and canals combined.

The most glamorous period of coastal commerce was the era of the clipper ship, the boldest commercial sailing vessel ever built. The designers of the clippers, among whom Donald McKay in East Boston, Massachusetts,

was the unchallenged master, drew out the ordinary three-masted packet ships to extraordinary lengths and then reduced the ratio of beam to length so drastically that traditional shipbuilders were dazed. The result was the most graceful hull that ever took to the sea. The hulls were topped with the tallest masts available and the largest spread of canvas ever to challenge a captain's courage. The captains themselves were selected from among the most relentless "drivers" of the day.

The first genuine clippers were built early in the 1840s in an attempt to shorten the seemingly endless voyage to the Orient, but the clippers really came into their own with the growth of California gold mining after 1850. Since the clippers' designers had sacrificed cargo space for speed, their owners had to charge higher rates for their limited cargoes than most shippers could afford. To the California adventurers, however, money was no obstacle and speed was all-important. Conventional sailing ships arriving at San Francisco in the summer of 1850 from Boston and New York had averaged 159 days for the journey around the Horn. The next summer, *Flying Cloud* arrived from New York after a voyage of 89 days, 21 hours, a record that stood until she herself reduced it by 13 hours three years later. It was for this run that most of the great clipper ships were built.

Unfortunately for the clippers, they were beaten at their own game just about the time they seemed to have perfected it. Even before the gold rush to California, New York steamship operators had organized an alternate route by which the trip to the West Coast could be completed in five weeks or less, as against the clippers' best time of three months. This route involved an Atlantic run to Panama, a portage across the Isthmus, and then a Pacific run north again in another steamship to American ports. At first this route was meant to serve the settlers of Oregon, but by the time the initial voyage was made, in January 1849, news of the California gold discoveries had swept across the country, and San Francisco became the main destination.

The difficulty with this short cut to the West Coast was the Panama portage, a nuisance that discouraged many travelers and made the handling of heavy freight impossible. Even so, enough profit was made by the New York entrepreneurs to attract the interest of Cornelius Vanderbilt, the richest man in the country, who had made his fortune as a ship operator. In 1851, Vanderbilt launched a competing line to the West Coast, using a Nicaragua instead of a Panama portage. In 1855, Vanderbilt, in turn, was challenged by still other New Yorkers bold enough to try to dislodge him from Nicaragua by supporting William Walker in his successful effort to take over the government of that country. Vanderbilt promptly retaliated by hiring agents to raise a force among neighboring Central American states with which to overwhelm Walker's government. The conflict between the two camps effectively closed the Nicaraguan route.

Events in Panama, meanwhile, greatly improved the competitive position of the original steamship operators. There, in 1855, after many engineering difficulties had been overcome, an efficient railroad was opened across the Isthmus. This railroad and its affiliated steamships virtually monopolized traffic to the West Coast until 1869, when the first transcontinental railroad was opened across the United States. Long before that, many of the surviving clippers, their magnificence quite tarnished, had sunk to the status of tramps sailing random routes with random cargoes under alien flags.

### The steamboat crisis

The early success of coastal shipping can be attributed in large part to the great volume of goods brought down to Atlantic and Gulf ports over the navigable rivers with which the United States was so lavishly endowed. Most of the river traffic moved through the Ohio and Mississippi River systems, which profited both from the expansion of staple agriculture in the free Northwest and the extension of cotton culture into the Southwest. The bulk of river commerce, as in earlier decades, was increased by an immense traffic in passengers, many of them immigrants heading west, but most of them native Americans characteristically on the go.

If the coastal trade suffered from having to traverse great distances over roundabout routes, the river trade soon suffered from the inflexibility of the main streams. Rivers could not be relocated to accommodate the inland settlers. River commerce reached its peak about 1851; but even then, so great had the total of domestic commerce become that the rivers carried but one-twentieth of it. By 1851, the upstart canals and the rising railroads each carried goods worth three times those transported on all the rivers of the country. The relative share of rivers in the commerce of the West, where other means of transportation were less developed than in the East, was no doubt much greater; but the fight to maintain this share proved less successful each year.

In order to compete with the railroads and canals, river men began cutting their rates to the bone. That was bad enough, but as they engaged in fierce competition among themselves for a worthy share of the traffic saved by rate cutting, they also saddled themselves with suicidal rising costs. Never was western steamboat travel so swift, so luxurious, so gilded with gaudy inducements as it was in the mid-1850s; but the river men themselves grew only more and more depressed. In days gone by, riverboat racing had been one of the joys of competition and had lent sparkle and spirit to river life. But now the grim competitors sought literally to knock one another out, and collisions, explosions, and fires took a sharply rising toll of property and lives.

### Completing the canals

When canals between East and West first were built, river men hoped that the artificial waterways would serve as feeders to hungry river craft, just as the rivers fed the coastal carriers. And in many eastern states the canals did perform this function. None, of course, performed it better than the Erie Canal, which poured a flood of western commodities into boats standing ready at Albany to carry them down the Hudson River to New York harbor.

And yet in the long run the Erie, in concert with the Ohio canals and others completed in the West before 1837, took trade away from the western rivers. By 1838, Buffalo, at the Erie's western end, was receiving more grain and flour annually than New Orleans. And once western canal construction had begun in the 1840s (there was little more canal building in the East after 1837), virtually every project was aimed at swinging more and more of the western trade away from the Mississippi system toward the North and the East. Perhaps the most dramatic shift was brought about by the completion in 1848 of the Illinois and Michigan Canal, linking Chicago on Lake Michigan with La Salle on the Illinois River. This river, which joined the Mississippi north of St. Louis, quickly siphoned off so much Mississippi traffic that by 1850 Chicago had soared to greatness as a port even though the city was still without a single railroad connection.

Much of the canal-boat traffic originated right in the vigorous market towns that sprang up along the canal routes. By reversing the direction of southbound traffic on the Ohio, the Illinois, and the northern Mississippi, the canals transformed these once-proud rivers into humble feeder streams. In the fifteen years before the Civil War, a struggle for control of western commerce occurred between the Mississippi River system and the Great Lakes—a struggle that paralleled the rivalry of the free states and the slave for control of the West itself. By the 1850s, the canals had swung the victory irrevocably to the Lakes. Two canals, one of which was foreign-built and neither of which was in any way associated with the great north-south river system, added to the Lakes' supremacy. The first was the Welland Canal, which circumvented Niagara Falls. Built by the Canadian government, this canal joined Lake Erie with Lake Ontario, and thence by way of the St. Lawrence River connected the Northwest with the East at Quebec. In the late 1850s, vessels laden with western goods were voyaging from Chicago all the way to Liverpool, England, over this route.

The second Great Lakes canal was the Saulte-Ste. Marie, popularly known as the Soo Canal. This one was needed to bypass turbulent St. Mary's Falls, which blocked the passage of ships between Lake Superior and Lake Huron. After two years of incredible construction feats under the guidance of engineer Charles T. Harvey, the Soo was opened in April 1855, just in time to catch the massive flow of iron ore from the Marquette range of northern Michigan to the mills of Pittsburgh, Cleveland, and Chicago. Northern wheat also found a convenient outlet through the Soo.

The value of goods carried by Great Lakes vessels, estimated at $150 million in 1851, quadrupled in the next five years. This increase reflected the growth of the canals that diverted traffic away from the South, but it also reflected the rise of the western Great Lakes country itself as a power and a prize.

## IV  Triumph of the railroad

### Railroads in the East

The striking extension of the canal system in the late 1840s and the 1850s serves to remind us that the railroad was not so obvious an improvement over other means of inland transportation as might be supposed. Practical steam locomotives had been invented in England and the United States years before 1829, when their commercial feasibility was first established, and problems of roadbed construction, track, scheduling, and safety continued to harass railroad operators. By 1860, nevertheless, Americans had built a railroad network of 30,000 miles—one of the marvels of the world. In that year, American passenger trains sped along at more than 20 miles an hour, though only at mortal peril to travelers, while freight trains averaged about 11 miles an hour.

Of the 3328 miles of railroad track in the United States in 1840, a meager 200 miles lay rusting in the West, mute testimony to the debts and disappointed hopes of Michigan, Indiana, and Illinois (see p. 226). The rest of the mileage was shared almost equally by the Northeast and the old South. No railroad linked the two sections, and neither section had succeeded in thrusting a line across the Appalachians to the Ohio or Mississippi Valley. Pennsylvania, with about one-third of all the northern mileage at this time, was the nation's leader. But most of Pennsylvania's track lay in the northeastern part of the state, where small lines, privately built, had begun to haul anthracite to barges on nearby rivers and canals. The state government was so determined to protect its canal system to the West that even when the legislature did grant a charter to the privately financed Pennsylvania Railroad Company in 1846 permitting it to build a line from Harrisburg to Pittsburgh, it required the new company to pay the state's canal administration 3 cents for each ton-mile of freight hauled.

Second to Pennsylvania in railroad mileage in 1840 was New York State, most of whose lines lay in the Albany-Troy-Schenectady region at the eastern end of the Erie Canal and westward roughly parallel to the canal itself. Until 1851 New York, as eager as Pennsylvania to protect its canal investment, forbade railroads to carry freight except when the Erie Canal was frozen over or otherwise closed to navigation. In 1840, New York City had only one tiny railroad, the New York and Harlem, which connected the metropolis with the independent town of Harlem 7 miles to the north.

Boston's thriving capitalists, always on the lookout for new investment opportunities, did not allow Massachusetts to lag for long in railroad construction. By 1850 almost every town in the state with 2,000 persons or more was served by trains. Boston became the hub of the whole New England railroad network; and, more important, rail connections with the Welland and Erie Canals now made her a vigorous competitor for western trade. To further this trade, in the late 1840s Boston capitalists under the leadership of John Murray Forbes began investing heavily in railroads in distant western cities.

Baltimore was as free as Boston from the prior claims of a state canal system to western traffic. In 1842 the promoters of the Baltimore & Ohio Railroad began gathering new capital with an eye to pushing their track over the mountains to Wheeling, Virginia, on the Ohio River. The B & O reached Wheeling in 1853.

The enterprise of Boston and Baltimore in extending railroads westward jolted Pennsylvania and New York out of complacent confidence in canals. The Pennsylvania Railroad was opened from Philadelphia to Pittsburgh in December 1852, months before the B & O itself reached Wheeling. Five years later, the Pennsylvania Railroad bought out the state canal system and the short railroad lines the state had built to feed the canals with traffic. Henceforth, the Pennsylvania Railroad was to dominate the transportation structure of the commonwealth and much of its economic and political life.

New York City gained its first western rail connection in 1851 when the Hudson River Railroad was opened all the way to the Erie Canal at East Albany. Two years later, under the direction of Erastus Corning, an iron manufacturer and former mayor of Albany, the seven independent railroads strung from Albany to Buffalo were consolidated into the New York Central Railroad. In conjunction with the Hudson River Railroad, the Central could offer a continuous water-level route from New York to the West. A few years later, a second New York railroad, the Erie, was opened all the way from Jersey City to Buffalo, thereby becoming the fourth great

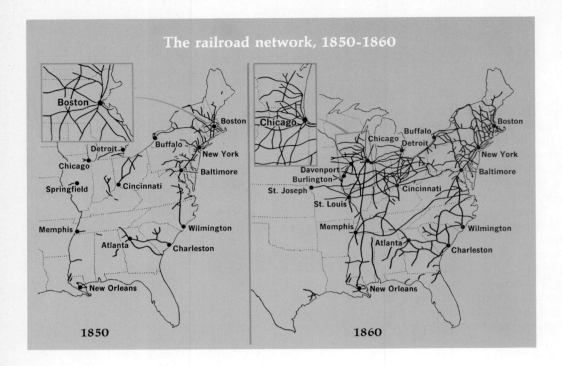

The railroad network, 1850-1860

1850

1860

eastern road in competition for east-west traffic.

By March 1852 some 10,800 miles of railroad (about three times the mileage of a decade earlier) had been completed in the United States, and an additional 10,900 miles were under construction. Most of the completed roads either lay in the Northeast or connected that section with waterways beyond the Appalachians. With few exceptions these railroads originated in great cities and ran through hundreds of miles of populous and productive territory; clearly they promised to return ready profits to investors. Although most of the roads were assisted by state and local governments, they could be and largely were financed by the sale of corporation stock to private investors.

### Railroads in the West

Most of the railroads built during the 1850s were in the West—in Ohio, Indiana, Illinois, Missouri, Michigan, Iowa, and Wisconsin. By 1860, these states, with 11,000 miles of track, had more railroads than the Middle states and New England combined.

Western roads faced entirely different conditions than those in the East, for private investment capital was scarce beyond the mountains, distances great, population sparse, and corporation stock difficult to market.

Before 1850, the federal government had given about 7 million acres of the national domain to road and canal companies in thinly settled areas. The recipients of these grants could sell or mortgage the land for the cash they needed for construction and for operational expenses in the first few years. Congress made the first land grant for railroad construction in 1850, for the benefit of a system of railroads to run north and south from Chicago to Mobile, Alabama. Actually, Congress granted the land to the states that would be crossed by the railroads (except Tennessee and Kentucky, where the federal government owned no land) with the understanding that the states in turn would give the land to the companies chartered to build and operate the lines. All told, the first grant ran to 3,736,000 acres, 2,500,000 of them in Illinois, the only state to complete its part of the new system.

In the legislation authorizing this land grant, Congress had provided for a 200-foot-

*Grain elevators at Illinois Central depot
in Chicago, 1858, where prairie
wheat was stored awaiting shipment
east and abroad. Chicago exports and imports
at this time accounted for approximately
one-fourth of American foreign trade.*

wide right-of-way, and had also relinquished the even-numbered sections (640 acres) of land to a depth of 6 miles on each side of the line. The federal government retained the intervening odd-numbered sections for sale at a later date. This grant served as the model for later grants of western lands, though some railroads were to receive their lands directly, instead of by way of the state governments.

By 1860, Congress had granted 18 million acres in 10 states for the benefit of 45 different railroads. With these lands as collateral, the roads were able to market first-mortgage bonds through Wall Street investment bankers to American and foreign investors. During the 1850s, indeed, the issues of such bonds became so voluminous that many New York mercantile firms, especially those with connections abroad, gave up handling goods and became investment bankers specializing in the distribution of railroad securities. The invention of the first-mortgage bond and the development of investment banking were as important as iron and steel in speeding the development of the western railroads. In this connection the Illinois project was pivotal.

In 1851, the Illinois state legislature became the scene of a heated contest among financial interests struggling for possession of the federal land grant and for the privilege of constructing the new north-south railroad. The victors were a group of New York capitalists allied with the Bostonian John Murray Forbes, who called their company the Illinois Central. By 1858 Chicago at last was linked by rail with the Mississippi at Galena to the west and Cairo to the south. Forbes had interests in other western railroads, among them the Michigan Central, which linked Chicago with Detroit. Two years later, Chicago was reached by the Lake Shore and Michigan Southern, which paralleled the Michigan Central across the state.

The next step was to push the rails across the Mississippi. By 1856 Forbes and his associates had combined and constructed various lines to form the Chicago, Burlington & Quincy Railroad, the first to penetrate the state of Iowa from the east. By tying this line to the Michigan Central, and by making arrangements between the Michigan Central and Corning's New York Central, Forbes by 1856 was able to offer service all the way from New York City to Burlington, Iowa.

In 1851 Chicago had not a single railroad connection with another city. By 1856, it had become the nation's largest railroad center. Almost 2500 miles of track radiated out from Chicago into the East, the South, and the West, tapping the traffic of 150,000 square miles. By 1860, a total of 5000 miles of track extended Chicago's connections from the Atlantic all the way to the Missouri River at St. Joseph, Missouri. The Mississippi River by then had been bridged in twelve places, nine of them served by roads connecting with Chicago, a mere three with St. Louis.

All over the West the railroad knocked out the canal systems and decimated river traffic. Railroad trains were faster than canal barges or steamboats. Moreover, railroad spurs could be laid directly to factory doors and warehouses. The competitive practices of railroad managers hastened their triumph. Where they encountered water rivals, the railroads cut rates below cost to capture the available traffic. They recouped losses on such runs by charging all the traffic would bear at noncompetitive terminals.

And yet two waterways survived railroad competition. One was the Great Lakes route, over which heavy freight like wheat and iron ore could still be carried more efficiently by boat than by freight trains. The second was the Erie Canal. The continued use of these two waterways reflected the massive volume of the east-west trade, which needed every carrier available to meet the demands of the rising population of the western farms and the eastern cities. As for the east-west railroads themselves, the census of 1860 reported the following: "So great are their benefits that, if the entire cost of railroads between the Atlantic and the western States had been levied on the farmers of the central west, their proprietors could have paid it and been immensely the gainers."

## V  Advance of northern industry

### Industry and the Union

"Could the Union endure?—that," writes Allan Nevins, "was the anxious, all-pervading question that faced the politicians" of the 1850s. "Could a truly national utilization of the country's resources be achieved?— that was the major question confronting business leaders." Steamboat and clipper-ship operators, canal and railroad builders, had done everything they could to further such "truly national utilization." But by drawing the East and the West closer together, they seemed only to broaden the chasm between the free states and the slave. The spread of manufacturing in the free states, and the south-ern states' continued concentration on cotton growing and other staples, made even clearer the profound differences in their ways of life.

In the 1850s southern businessmen—merchants, land speculators, manufacturers, and railroad promoters—sometimes saw that their section's future lay in joining the "truly national" development of the country. Rich planters themselves sometimes invested in northern lands, mines, and railroads. But such southerners, among the last to yield to their section's secessionist agitators, remained but a corporal's guard in an overwhelmingly agrarian society, saved, according to its spokesmen, from demeaning industrial and commercial pursuits.

Northern businessmen, on their part, valued their southern business connections. Almost without exception they deplored the abolitionist campaign in their own section and were among the last to yield to the cry for war once the South had left the Union. Yet few northern businessmen, uncoerced, would restore to embittered New Orleans or St. Louis the commerce that New York and Chicago had captured by enterprise and energy. Fewer still would grant the slaveocracy the first transcontinental railroad or the western lands it would traverse. Southerners might take part in the country's development, and welcome. But they could not be allowed to forestall it or fence it in.

## Industry and the land

And yet even in the North the roar of industry had only begun to be heard. As late as 1860, the richest northerners, with few exceptions, were merchants rather than industrialists. Among them ranked H. B. Claflin, who had built up a large wholesale drygoods business on the modern principle of mass sales at low unit profits; A. T. Stewart, one of the creators of the American department store; and Charles L. Tiffany, who made his fortune selling jewelry and silverware to other rich merchants. Ex-China traders like John Murray Forbes and importers like George Griswold, Jonathan Sturges, and Morris Ketchum, not industrialists, also supplied much of the early enterprise and capital for railroad building. The limits of industrial progress in the United States before 1860 are indicated by the urgent missions the North itself had to send to Europe at the outbreak of the Civil War to purchase arms and woolen cloth for uniforms. These purchases, like the imports brought in before the war, were paid for largely by the export of the vast agricultural surpluses, whose value even during the years of "irresistible" industrial progress grew at a faster rate than the value of manufactured goods.

The first fairly accurate census of American manufactures was taken in 1850. The results proved doubly dramatic, for they showed (1) that the annual output of American industry had just passed $1 billion in value, and (2) that this figure was a few million dollars more than the value of all agricultural products, including cotton. In the next ten years, as the Census of 1860 showed, American manufacturers had pushed their production almost to $2 billion. (The exact figure was $1,885,862,000.) Yet by 1860, agriculture seems to have regained the lead it had lost ten years earlier, for agricultural commodities were now valued at $1,910,000,000.

The growth of manufacturing and the growth of agriculture, of course, reinforced each other. As the industrial cities filled up, their landless populations provided expanding markets for farm produce; and as the number of farms increased, farm families provided an expanding market for domestic manufactures. Yet it is remarkable how closely related to the land large segments of American manufacturing still remained. One of the great industries of 1860 was the making of lumber from the virgin forests that still covered much of the nation's land. Lumber production that year was evaluated by the census at $105 million, about equal to the value of cotton-textile production itself. Far higher than either in value were the flour and meal produced by the milling industry, whose output in 1860 the census put at nearly $250 million. The distilling of spirits, the brewing of beer, the tanning of leather, and the packing of meat also were growing rapidly.

All these industries were represented in the cities of the East, but it was the factories of the West that produced the largest volume. The scale of their operations, moreover, was not their only modern characteristic. By the 1850s, many lumber mills had begun to *specialize* in the production of barrel staves or shingles or railroad ties, and to use single-purpose machines for the work. Specialization and mechanization appeared in other industries as well, particularly meat packing, which, in addition, developed to a high degree the modern principle of marketing by-products. The hams and shoulders of hogs, for example, were packed as meat. The rest of the flesh then was rendered into oil for sale as a lubricant and shortening. The hog's bristles went into brushes, the blood into chemicals, the hooves into glue. What remained of the animal was then ground into fertilizer.

Another modern feature of meat packing was the use of inclined tables down which each carcass would slide past a stationary worker responsible for removing a particular part. This "continuous-flow" method remains one of the principles of modern assembly-line technique in many industries, even those run by computers. One of the leading industries of the West was the manufacture of agricultural machinery, in which mass production based on the assembly of standardized metal parts was perhaps more advanced than in any other industry in the world.

### Progress in invention

At the 1851 "world's fair" held at the Crystal Palace in London, few exhibits won greater admiration than the display of American farm devices. Everything from road scrapers and sausage stuffers to currycombs and hayrakes "bore off the palm" for their ingenuity, utility, and cheapness. Few of these inventions were ever patented, and we know hardly any of the inventors' names.

Nonagricultural inventions remained far fewer than agricultural ones, but they helped swell the number of patents issued by the United States Patent Office each year after it was opened in 1790. In 1835, a record number of patents, 752, were issued; in 1860, 4700 were granted. Most, no doubt, went to the actual inventors of the devices, but some went only to those who commercialized their ideas.

One of the great inventions of the nineteenth century was the electric telegraph, for which Samuel F. B. Morse, the painter, received the first American patent in 1840. But Morse's contribution to the telegraph, which was perfected for commercial use in the United States in 1844, had more to do with promotion than with mechanics. Back in 1831, Joseph Henry, one of America's most brilliant scientists and later the first director of the Smithsonian Institution in Washington, rang a bell by an electric impulse transmitted over a mile of wire. This accomplishment was based on knowledge of electricity that had taken a century to accumulate—knowledge with which Morse had scarcely a nodding acquaintance. In 1837, Henry made his idea available to an English inventor, Charles Wheatstone, who proceeded to furnish his homeland with practical telegraph service. The principal American contribution to telegraph operation was the "Morse Code," but Morse himself designed neither the apparatus nor the alphabet, for which much of the credit belongs to his partner, Alfred Vail.

It was Morse, however, who prodded Congress into contributing financially to the telegraph's development in 1843. With government money, Morse staged the famous tableau on May 24, 1844, in the Supreme Court Chambers in Washington, when he sent the message "What hath God wrought?" to Vail in Baltimore, who then returned it. This demonstration aroused public interest in the telegraph, and companies began bidding for the rights to use it. By 1860, 50,000 miles of telegraph wire had been strung in the United States, and the next year a transcontinental service was opened.

In England, the telegraph was first used to control railroad traffic, an application that came later in the United States. The first use to which Americans put the telegraph was the transmission of business messages and public information. Its effect on the newspaper business was enormous. The "penny press" already dominated American journalism, and printing machinery had been developed that could produce 1000 newspapers an hour. But with news telegraphy the demand for newspapers rose so sharply that presses were wanted that could turn out at least 10,000 papers an hour. This resounding volume was achieved in 1847 by the cylindrical press developed by Richard March Hoe. Further improvement in presses and other printing equipment enabled publishers to keep pace with the public's appetite for "hot news," advertising, and printed entertainment.

356

Two industrial patents merit special notice: (1) the vulcanization of rubber; and (2) the sewing machine. "India" rubber (most of which came from South America, though the East Indies supplied some) had a unique imperviousness to rain, snow, and mud, but when exposed to heat it melted, grew sticky and collapsed. Finally, after years of effort, Charles Goodyear, a stubborn, sick, impoverished Yankee, hit on just the right mixture of raw rubber, chemicals, and heat that would yield a stable product at all ordinary temperatures. Goodyear patented his process, called "vulcanization," in 1844. A profitable rubber-goods industry was quickly developed by men licensed by Goodyear, but the inventor himself died in 1860 leaving debts of $200,000.

Before the automobile, rubber was used mainly in the boot and shoe industry—one that soon gained further impetus from the sewing machine patented by Elias Howe in 1846. Howe's invention aroused little interest in America until 1851, when Isaac Merritt Singer entered the picture. Singer, a clever inventor in his own right, made many improvements on Howe's original machine, but his largest contribution to its success was his in-

vention of installment selling, an idea he made popular through mass advertising. Having worked up an impressive demand for sewing machines, Singer proceeded to mass-produce them by assembly-line methods. By 1860, a total of 110,000 sewing machines had been manufactured, largely for home use but for factories as well. Almost all boots and shoes now were factory-sewn. The sewing machine also made factory-sewn clothing practical, cheap, and popular.

The perfection of new machines often led to the development of entirely new industries—some for the manufacture of the new devices, others for their employment. In the older industries, such as the manufacture of cotton and woolen goods spectacular new inventions were no longer to be looked for. Even so, a continuous round of invention greatly speeded up production and turnover. Acceleration of the industrial pace was more marked in cotton-goods manufacture than in woolens. But in both, new machines like the Crompton loom, which permitted the weaving of patterns, and new applications of chemistry, which led to improved dyes of many colors, added to the variety of factory-made

357

*A Crompton loom, showing woven patterned woolen cloth.*

cloth. Middle-class consumers now had a wide range of styles and qualities to choose from at prices importers no longer could match. Women became increasingly conscious of fashion, and began to feel that they had to follow the annual shifts in style if they were to keep up with the Joneses. By 1860, the cotton-goods industry ranked second only to grain milling in value of product. This category, of course, included the value of the raw materials. In "value *added by manufacture*," the cotton-textile industry ranked as the nation's leader.

## The iron industry

The whole cycle of invention from the simple steel plow to the Hoe press and the sewing machine gave a powerful impetus to the American iron industry. New reapers and threshers, rakes and seed drills, were fabricated from iron and steel parts. By 1860, about 3500 steamboats had been built for the western rivers alone, all of them requiring boilers made of iron sheets—as well as boilers to replace those that blew up. The hulls of the clipper ships were themselves reinforced with iron forms. The telegraph was strung entirely with iron wire until copper began to replace it in the 1860s. By 1846, John A. Roebling, the future builder of the Brooklyn Bridge, had begun to use wire rope in bridge suspension. Four years later, James Bogardus, an imaginative New Yorker, erected the world's first completely cast-iron building. Cast iron buckled under strain; but when wrought-iron beams began to be rolled for building construction, the skyscraper was in the offing. The first wrought-iron building was New York's Cooper Union, designed by F. A. Petersen and erected in 1854. In machinery for the manufacture of textiles and for other industries, and for machines that made machines, iron was indispensable.

By far the biggest single user of iron in the 1850s was the railroad—for rails, locomotives, wheels, axles, and hundreds of other parts of equipment and rolling stock. The railroads, moreover, ran by far the most extensive machine shops in the country, which not only made parts and repairs but also turned out their own iron and steel tools and machinery.

In the refining of iron ore and the manufacture of iron products, as in so many other industrial processes, heat is the key element. One of the fundamental changes in iron manufacture after 1840 was the rapid shift in fuel from wood and charcoal (half-burned wood) to anthracite and coke (half-burned soft coal). Far greater temperatures could be attained with these new combustibles, and the rate of production was boosted to ever higher levels. A second great change was the widespread use of rolling mills, in place of the hand forge, for shaping iron forms. Improvements in iron-making were reflected in a fourfold increase in the production of pig iron between 1842 and 1860, when annual volume stood at 920,000 tons.

Dramatic as all these developments seem, the American iron industry in the 1850s developed very slowly in comparison with progress abroad. In 1860, the United States mined less iron ore and manufactured less pig iron than Britain had twenty years earlier. Britain's coal production in 1860 was five times that of United States mines, and even little Belgium mined 60 percent as much coal as Americans did. In 1856, Abram Hewitt, America's leading iron manufacturer, observed: "The consumption of iron is a social barometer by which to estimate the relative height of civilization among nations." But America's consumption of iron merely suggested that the country had a long way to go to catch up with other industrial nations of the day.

Certain scattered incidents underline the immaturity of the industrial spirit. In 1829, drillers had brought in an oil gusher in Kentucky; but it only terrified and angered the workmen, who had been looking for salt. Two years later, Joseph Henry had worked out the essentials of the electric dynamo; but many decades were to pass before his "philosophical toy," as he called his electromagnetic machine, found practical employment. In 1847, William Kelly, a Kentucky ironmaster, had discovered the essential process for the mass production of steel; but scarcely anyone was apprised of his discovery until an Englishman, Henry Bessemer, successfully sought American patents in 1856 for a similar process and the machinery for its use. Even so, another fifteen years passed before Bessemer steel was produced in large commercial quantities in the United States.

## Industrialism and society

By 1860, invention and industry had begun to transform the face of America and the character of its people. But the majority of farmers and the commercial elements in the cities misjudged—and with good reason—both the force and the imminence of the revolution that was taking place Three years before, in 1857, the country had suffered a severe business panic. But there had been panics in the past, notably in 1819 and 1837, so there was nothing particularly remarkable in the occurrence of yet another one. Still, the crash of 1857 had certain peculiarities that

should have given a hint of the extraordinary changes in the United States in the preceding twenty years.

By 1857, the number of factory workers in the country had risen to 1.3 million, and together with construction workers they made up an industrial labor force of almost 2 million persons, nearly three times that of 1837. Unemployment following the crash thus was far more widespread than ever before.

Even when fully employed and receiving regular wages, the members of the new industrial proletariat endured the worst working and living conditions yet found in white America. Bad as working conditions had become, living conditions in the segregated slums of industrial cities were worse. Housing alone was so miserable that many workers preferred to put in the long hours in the factories, sheltered and among friends, than to spend their

*"The Dry-Goods Epidemic,
Broadway at Three P.M." late October 1857,
two months after the business panic,
showing bargain hunters at aptly named
O.L.D. Pinchpence's emporium.*

The New-York Historical Society, New York City

time at home. Under these circumstances, the crash, depriving hundreds of thousands of work, proved unprecedentedly brutal.

Other telltale features of the crash of 1857 were not so apparent to contemporaries. In the 1850s, as in the 1830s, large amounts of money and great reserves of credit had been drawn to land speculation, and the bursting of the bubble only confirmed conservatives in their belief that fools were parted from their fortunes as before. By 1857, however, over-investment in productive facilities had become as important as overinvestment in land in bringing about the stringency of funds that led to the crash and deepened the depression that followed. By then more than $1 billion had been invested in manufacturing and another billion in railroads, two-thirds of it during the seven years just preceding the crash.

Many such investments were made possible only by the marketing of stocks and bonds—and speculation in corporate securities introduced still another new element into the business system which was to grow in importance. Securities often were bought with mere token down-payments eked out with high-interest loans from New York banks. These banks, in turn, often paid interest to depositors, among whom so many other banks were included that, in the late 1850s, 70 percent of the entire country's bank reserves were on deposit in New York City. In times of financial emergency, country banks sought to withdraw some of their funds from the metropolis. To satisfy their country bank depositors, the New York banks would have to call in the loans made with the country deposits. Such calls were almost certain to embarrass city security speculators and drive many of them into bankruptcy. Their failures, in turn, would leave their creditor banks insolvent or nearly so.

On August 24, 1857, the New York branch of the Ohio Life Insurance and Trust Company, Ohio's leading bank, was forced to close its doors after discovering that its treasurer had embezzled most of its funds. The parent bank in Ohio soon failed, causing runs on many New York banks. By October 13 all but one of these had closed, as had most of the banks in the country.

Fortunately, industrialists and financiers learned valuable lessons from the latest financial breakdown. In the 1850s, as we have said, most leading businessmen still were merchants, many of whom hoped, like the diarist Philip Hone, to earn enough by 40 to retire to the good things of life. But the representative businessmen with the future on their side now were industrial corporation executives, often administrators for absentee owners or scattered stockholders. Confronted with the high daily toll of overhead costs, they became alert to rapid changes in technology, markets, and sources of raw materials, and sensitive to the nuances and rumors of the money markets. Such men no longer looked for profits in the lucky voyage or the fortunate speculation or the simple soundness and progress of the country. Profit would come henceforth from strict attention to management, from cautious financing, careful bookkeeping, enhancement of labor productivity, adaptability to changing markets. Profits promised to grow enormously beyond the dreams of speculative avarice; but they were likely to be made up of mountains of pennies and fractions of pennies, which were just as likely to disappear unless constant attention was given to such insignificant sums.

The lure of speculation did not die; unsettled conditions during the Civil War, and the expansion of the country after the war ended, created a speculator's paradise. But American industrialists had learned something of the industrial discipline; and the North, and ultimately the nation, were the stronger for it.

# For further reading

Most of the books on economic history suggested for Chapter Nine are important for this chapter as well. On the northern economy, in addition, we may recommend here, Allan Nevins, *Ordeal of the Union* (2 vols., 1947), especially vol. II. On American material well-being, E. W. Martin, *The Standard of Living in 1860* (1942), is informative.

The writings of Hamlin Garland on the Middle Border are full of interest. The reader may start with *A Son of the Middle Border* (1917). Merle Curti and others, *The Making of an American Community* (1959), presents a thoroughgoing examination of life in a frontier Wisconsin county, 1840–1880. Leo Rogin, *The Introduction of Farm Machinery . . . in the United States During the Nineteenth Century* (1931), C. H. Danhof, *Change in Agriculture, The Northern United States 1820–1870* (1969), and the early chapters of A. G. Bogue, *From Prairie to Corn Belt: Farming on the Illinois and Iowa Prairies in the Nineteenth Century* (1963), are especially illuminating.

For the immigrants, M. L. Hansen, *The Atlantic Migration 1607–1860* (1940), is indispensable. A more general account is Carl Wittke, *We Who Built America* (1967). The background for the German immigration of the mid-nineteenth century is well depicted in Mack Walker, *Germany and the Emigration 1816–1885* (1964). For the Irish, see George Potter, *To the Golden Door* (1960), and Cecil Woodham-Smith, *The Great Hunger* (1962). For the British, see W. S. Shepperson, *British Emigration to North America, Projects and Opinion in the Early Victorian Period* (1957).

On American trade the best general survey is E. R. Johnson and others, *History of Domestic and Foreign Commerce of the United States* (2 vols., 1915). Roger Pineau, ed., *The Japan Expedition 1852–1854: The Personal Journal of Commodore Matthew C. Perry* (1969), is illuminating on the opening of the "hermit kingdom." J. K. Fairbank, *Trade and Diplomacy on the China Coast* (1953), is excellent on the "opening of the treaty ports 1842–1854." The leading works on the clippers are A. H. Clark, *The Clipper Ship Era 1843–1869* (1910), and C. C. Cutler, *Greyhounds of the Sea* (1930). W. J. Lane, *Commodore Vanderbilt* (1942), is an outstanding biography. See also I. D. Neu, *Erastus Corning, Merchant and Financier, 1794–1872* (1960). L. C. Hunter, *Steamboats on the Western Rivers* (1949), is invaluable.

An excellent introduction to railroad history is F. A. Cleveland and F. W. Powell, *Railroad Promotion and Capitalization in the United States* (1909). More technical are R. W. Fogel, *Railroads and American Economic Growth* (1964), and Albert Fishlow, *American Railroads and the Transformation of the Ante-Bellum Economy* (1965). A. D. Chandler, Jr., *Henry Varnum Poor: Business Editor, Analyst, and Reformer* (1956), stresses the role of management in railroad development. For contemporary material see Chandler, ed., *The Railroads* (1965). Thorough on the theme indicated by their titles are L. H. Haney, *A Congressional History of Railways in the United States to 1850* (1908) and *A Congressional History of Railways in the United States 1850–1887* (1910). The major work on New England railroads is E. C. Kirkland, *Men, Cities and Transportation 1820–1900* (2 vols., 1948). See also A. M. Johnson and B. E. Supple, *Boston Capitalists and Western Railroads* (1967); and H. H. Pierce, *The Railroads of New York: A Study of Government Aid 1826–1875* (1955). On railroads and western lands see P. W. Gates, *The Illinois Central Railroad and Its Colonization Work* (1934). T. C. Cochran, *Railroad Leaders, 1845–1890: The Business Mind in Action* (1953), fulfills the promise of its subtitle.

On industry and technology see Chapter Nine. E. C. Mack, *Peter Cooper, Citizen of New York* (1949), and Allan Nevins, *Abram S. Hewitt, with Some Account of Peter Cooper* (1935), are informative on the iron industry. Waldemar Kaempffert, ed., *A Popular History of American Invention* (2 vols., 1924), is comprehensive. Thomas Coulson, *Joseph Henry, His Life and Work* (1950), is excellent. R. L. Thompson, *Wiring a Continent: The History of the Telegraph Industry in the United States 1832–1866* (1947), is useful on one of the major applications of Henry's work. D. H. Calhoun, *The American Civil Engineer, Origins and Conflict* (1960), is a substantial study. On the conditions of labor see Norman Ware, *The Industrial Worker 1840–1860* (1924). On banking and the money market, see M. G. Myers, *The New York Money Market* (1931); and *Henry Varnum Poor* by A. D. Chandler, Jr., referred to above. The best account of the ups and downs of economic life is W. B. Smith and A. H. Cole, *Fluctuations in American Business 1790–1860* (1935). G. W. Van Vleck, *The Panic of 1857* (1943), offers a readable analysis.

# UNION SEVERED

At the beginning of the 1850s North and South, like two bellicose nations, warily eyed each other. Responsible statesmen, of whom there were too few in either section, tried desperately to find ways of reconciling sectional differences, but powerful forces seemed to defeat their every effort.

The most divisive force, of course, was slavery. Northern abolitionists, and growing numbers of others in the North, looked upon slavery as a sin, one all the worse for its menace to the Union. To southerners, slavery had become the keystone of their civilization, the agency of their material well-being. If all the world was right about slavery and had put it on the road to extinction, all the more tenaciously would the South, and a few outlying centers of the institution like Cuba and Brazil, defend it.

While abolitionists in the North and fire-eaters in the South heated the atmosphere, businessmen and promoters and the ordinary citizens of both sections continued to follow the main chance—to settle the land, to speculate, to seek profits from supplying goods and services to one another—overlooking sectional differences or sectional aims when possible. But they could not go far along their own paths without encountering the sectional combatants. In the promotion of railroads, the organization of territories, the settlement of disputed areas such as Kansas, businessmen plunged ahead, although encountering sectional strains at every step. Others in the North and the South, full of the sense of their own righteousness and often heedless of the slave himself, also held their own fatal course.

In the past, political leaders had been able

to mediate between the sections whenever the slavery issue threatened the Union. The compromises in the Constitutional Convention of 1787, the Missouri Compromise, most recently the Compromise of 1850, all managed to mend the tears in the national fabric. In the next decade compromise after compromise was attempted, even as late as 1861. But the bonds of the Union had become too frayed, the opposition of North and South too sharply honed by ambition and argument, and all compromise efforts failed.

## I   The slave issue overwhelms Pierce

### Hunting fugitives

The Democrat Franklin Pierce of New Hampshire took office as the fourteenth President of the United States on March 4, 1853. A "vain, showy, and pliant man," as an observer said, Pierce quickly showed those qualities which made his administration quail before the contesting forces, free and slave.

Most Americans in 1853, including the President, still hoped that the Compromise of 1850 would stifle the agitation over slavery once and for all. But they hoped in vain. Northerners gagged particularly on the Compromise provision requiring the return of fugitive slaves to their owners. Actually, the number of slaves who managed to escape remained infinitesimal, making the southern outcry against northern cooperation with such refugees appear all the more extreme and unregenerate. Even those northerners who disliked blacks as much as they respected property, now began to condemn slavery as a stench to the whole nation and to look forward to the time, as Lincoln put it later, when "the hateful

institution, like a reptile poisoning itself, will perish by its own infamy."

The person who single-handedly did more than any other American to deepen hatred of slavery was the novelist Harriet Beecher Stowe. A New Englander who had lived close to slavery in the border city of Cincinnati, Mrs. Stowe began to write *Uncle Tom's Cabin* soon after the Fugitive Slave Law was adopted and published it in 1852. Her hope was that once the South recognized the sinfulness of the "peculiar institution," the Negroes would be freed. She felt no special malice toward southerners, only toward slavery. The villain of her novel, Simon Legree, was a Yankee who became a harsh and morbid plantation owner. Her most eloquent spokesman against slavery was a humane southern planter. Mrs. Stowe's novel sold 300,000 copies in its first year, and its stage version became a smash hit. One young southerner, after reading the novel in 1853, observed that it

*greatly tended ... to influence one-half of the nation against the other, to produce disunion and to stir up a*

363

*civil war. . . . Can any* friend *of the human race, or any* friend *of the Negro desire such an issue?*

With northern resistance to the Fugitive Slave Law quickened by *Uncle Tom's Cabin,* slaveowners pursuing runaways into free states often were glad to get home safely without their quarry. In Chicago, Detroit, Boston, and elsewhere, federal officers trying to reclaim fugitive slaves were menaced by mobs.

*(Left) An early poster advertising*
Uncle Tom's Cabin *in various editions,*
*including one in German*
*for the strong antislavery immigrants of 1848.*

*The Beecher family, with father*
*Lyman seated, young Henry Ward Beecher*
*standing at far right, and Harriet Beecher*
*Stowe seated second from right.*

## The Ostend Manifesto

Northern incitement and protection of runaways, few though they were, provoked planters to seek countermeasures. A vociferous minority demanded nothing less than the reopening of the African slave trade to replenish the work force. A more influential group, supported by Pierce himself, sought the acquisition of Cuba, Spain's slave-packed "pearl of the Antilles."

Cuba, like the rest of the Western Hemisphere, had been eyed by American expansionists for decades. In 1848 President Polk offered Spain $100 million for the island but was turned down. Three years later, although alarmed by two filibustering expeditions from the American mainland launched by Cuban rebels against Spanish rule, Spain once more rejected purchase offers. In 1854, a naval incident at Havana in which, on a mere technicality, Spanish officials seized an American merchant vessel, gave Pierce an excuse to press the question still again, amid loud sabre rattling.

Before sitting down with Spanish representatives this time over the incident and the island, Secretary of State William L. Marcy asked Pierre Soulé, the American minister in Madrid, to discuss the problem of Cuba with James Buchanan, the American minister in London, and John Y. Mason, the American minister in Paris. The three diplomats met at Ostend in Belgium, and on October 15, 1854, sent a confidential dispatch to Marcy recommending that the United States offer $120 million for Cuba. If the offer was rejected, they added, "by every law, human and divine," the United States "shall be justified in wresting [the island] from Spain," on the ground that Spain's control of it gravely endangered "our internal peace and the existence of our cherished Union."

Marcy, of course, felt as these diplomats did. What he wanted from them was not such an incendiary avowal of his own plans, but an estimate of how the European powers would react to them. When Pierce's enemies in the House of Representatives insisted on the publication of the confidential dispatch, what became known as the "Ostend Manifesto" was out of the pot. Free soilers denounced it vigorously—Horace Greeley's *New York Tribune* called it a "Manifesto of Brigands"—and Marcy had to repudiate it.

Quite possibly enough public support could have been mustered by the Pierce administration to annex Cuba had not Congress, some months before the Ostend Manifesto, passed a momentous measure which, in the words of a New York paper, "has forever rendered annexation impossible." This was the Kansas-Nebraska Act, which, by reopening the question of slavery in the western territories, strengthened northern determination to check the spread of slavery anywhere, *"come what may,"* as Greeley said.

## The Kansas-Nebraska Act

Nebraska country, a veritable empire ranging west of the 95th meridian all the way to Oregon Territory and north to the Canadian border, stood athwart the aspirations of the contending older sections of the country for two reasons: (1) Its southern part bordered the slave state of Missouri, but slaveholders were forbidden to extend slavery there by the Missouri Compromise of 1820; (2) this segment and the area north of it to the Great Bend of the Missouri River, which now forms the eastern boundary of the State of Nebraska, also lay just beyond the "Permanent Indian Frontier" (see p. 295). Here, in the words of Stephen A. Douglas (the italics are his), the Indians, by treaty, had been guaranteed "perpetual occupancy, *with an express condition that* [the land] *should never be incorporated within the limits of a territory or state of the Union."* This "barbarian wall," Douglas continued, "was to have been a colossal monument to the God terminus saying to christianity, civilization and Democracy, 'thus far mayest thou go, and *no* farther.' "

As early as the congressional session of 1843-1844, "with a direct view of arresting the further progress of this savage barrier to the

366

extension of our institutions," Douglas, then a freshman member of the House of Representatives from Illinois, had introduced the first bill to break the Indian treaties and organize the Territory of Nebraska. "From that day to this," Douglas wrote in December 1853, when he had risen to the chairmanship of the Committee on Territories in the Senate, "I have taken care always to have a bill pending when Indians were about to be located in that quarter." Others, meanwhile, led by Senator David R. Atchison of Missouri, who vowed he would see Nebraska "sink in hell" before allowing it to be organized as a free territory, also had bills at hand to forestall any measure aimed at keeping slavery out.

Much else had risen besides Douglas by 1853, including his own aspirations to the presidency and the fever of the sectional conflict. The sectional conflict itself was intensified by the rivalry between North and South for the first transcontinental railroad.

By 1853, Douglas had become the leading spokesman for the construction of the first transcontinental over a northern route that would link the Pacific coast with his beloved Chicago, where he owned much real estate. But he was not selfish about that. "Continuous lines of settlement," he said then,

*with civil, political and religious institutions all under the protection of law, are imperiously demanded by the highest national considerations. . . . No man can keep up with the spirit of this age who travels on anything slower than the locomotive, and fails to receive intelligence by lightning. We must therefore have Rail Roads and Telegraphs from the Atlantic to the Pacific, through our own territory. Not one line only, but many lines. . . . The removal of the Indian barrier and the extension of the laws of the United States in the form of Territorial governments are the first steps toward the accomplishment of each and all of those objects.*

For these purposes, Douglas reported his fourth and fateful Nebraska bill in the Senate on January 4, 1854.

Douglas's report was deliberately vague and crafty. He specifically undertook to apply in Nebraska—part of the Louisiana Purchase north of 36°30'—the "popular sovereignty"

provisions applied in the Mexican cessions of Utah and New Mexico by the Compromise of 1850 of which he was so proud (see p. 311). He would not, however, expressly repeal the Missouri Compromise, which specifically forbade slavery in Nebraska but not in Utah and New Mexico. Some "eminent statesmen," Douglas's report said, thought the Missouri Compromise was unconstitutional. But the Committee on Territories was "not now prepared" to make recommendations "as to the legal points involved." If they never came up, so much the better. On one unfortunate provision of the Compromise of 1850, nevertheless, the committee was prepared to make a recommendation: that in Nebraska, as in all other territories and states, the Fugitive Slave Law must be enforced.

Douglas's tactic has been called "astute." But the committed spokesmen of the contending sections lost little time in making the "legal points" Douglas so conspicuously passed up; and they did so in an especially incendiary manner because of the committee's shilly-shallying on freedom while standing firm on the return of fugitive slaves.

Douglas's report of January 4 ordinarily would have been only a routine step by which to place his Nebraska bill before the Senate in preparation for a full-dress debate at some future date. But by the time debate began on January 30 his bill had already been bitterly argued in and out of Congress and had been so fatally altered under sectional pressure that Douglas himself is said to have predicted that in its latest form it would raise "the hell of a storm."

Three critical alterations were made in the bill, two of them outright victories for the slave section, and the third, one which the South hoped to turn to advantage.

As originally written it seemed that the bill did not necessarily deprive Congress of its constitutional power to "make all needful Rules and Regulations respecting the Territory . . . belonging to the United States," including those respecting slavery. If, as the bill said, the constitution of a new state in the territory permitted slavery, Congress appeared still to have the power to accept or reject this constitution during the admission procedure. Under unyielding pressure from Senator Atchison and his southern colleagues, who perceived this loophole, Douglas was forced to correct what he lamely called this "clerical error" in the bill. His correction explicitly took the power over slavery from Congress and gave it, "in the Territories and in the new States to be formed therefrom, . . . to the people residing therein, through their appropriate representatives." This change left Nebraska open to slaveholders, regardless of Congress or of the Missouri Compromise.

Once he had thus enlarged the area of application of the principle of "popular sovereignty," whose ambiguities had already become anathema to many in the North, Douglas was next forced specifically to concede, in the bill, that the Missouri Compromise was henceforth to be "inoperative and void."

Douglas's third concession revolved around the railroad issue. It was clear to all that Congress at this time would help build no more than one transcontinental line. A government-sponsored survey in 1853 had shown that a southern route along the Mexican border offered the fewest physical obstacles to such a line. The Gadsden Purchase from Mexico, in fact, had been made explicitly for possible railroad use (see p. 307). Atchison's prosouthern group in Missouri, at the same time, advocated a central route originating in St. Louis. They would not even consider supporting any transcontinental, including their own, which passed through territory forever closed to slavery. Fearful of their strength, and fearful that the southern part of Nebraska bordering Missouri would indeed fall to slavery, a group of Iowa congressmen urged Douglas to divide Nebraska into two territories to insure the passage of the transcontinental through the free valley of the Platte in the more northerly part. Douglas had said of the whole of Nebraska, "in that climate . . . it is worse than

folly to think of its being a slaveholding country." Although skeptical of the Iowans' fears concerning slavery in this region, he felt constrained to concede their request as he had conceded those of their enemies. His bill was altered to divide Nebraska into two territories, Nebraska and Kansas. And Kansas was immediately marked for slavery by the South.

These three alterations in fact make up the substance of the Kansas-Nebraska Act as finally passed on May 30, 1854. The first transcontinental was itself to remain a will-o'-the-wisp for ten more years. But the law was readied for the belated extension of slavery into new country and for another dislodgment of the aborigines from it.

In the Senate, which was less subject than the House to political storms, the Kansas-Nebraska Act passed, 37 to 14. In the House, which in 1854 was up for election, the bill had much harder going before it squeaked through, 113 to 100. Every one of the 45 northern Whigs in the House voted against the bill. This group received the support of almost half the northern Democrats, thereby fracturing the principal *national* party, on whose unity Douglas himself had staked his own future as well as that of the Union. A solid bloc of southern Democrats and half the northern Democrats, on the other hand, together with the majority of the *southern* Whigs, had put the measure across. Thus the Whig party was split as well.

It took southerners outside of Congress a little time to grasp the value of their coup. One paper declared that the Kansas-Nebraska Act was "barren of practical benefit." Once the "mad ferocity" with which many in the North began to assault the measure struck home, however, southern truculence in its favor mounted. The repeal of the Missouri Compromise, in particular, sent a thrill of excitement through the northern people. Lawyer Lincoln wrote in his third-person autobiographical sketch that by 1854, "his profession had almost superseded the thought of politics in his mind, when the repeal of the Missouri Compromise aroused him as he had never been before." Perhaps the most influential attack, written while Douglas's draft was still undergoing alteration but not widely pub-

367

lished until after the act's adoption, was the "Appeal of the Independent Democrats in Congress to the People of the United States," the work mainly of Senators Salmon P. Chase of Ohio and Charles Sumner of Massachusetts but also signed by other members. The Appeal, one of the first stimulants for the formation of the Republican party, branded the Kansas-Nebraska Act a

*criminal betrayal of precious rights; . . . part and parcel of an atrocious plot to exclude from a vast unoccupied region immigrants from the Old World and free laborers from our own States, and convert it into a dreary region of despotism, inhabited by masters and slaves.*

That they did not intend to let this "betrayal" pass is clear from their other statements. "They celebrate a present victory," said Chase when the act passed the Senate, "but the echoes they awake will never rest till slavery itself shall die." The Act, said Sumner, "puts Freedom and Slavery face to face, and bids them grapple. Who can doubt the result?"

When Douglas attempted to speak in defense of his act, even in his home base in Chicago, he was hooted off the platform by members of his own party and menaced by crowds in the streets.

## "Bleeding Kansas"

The Kansas-Nebraska Act failed its first test in the new Territory of Kansas. Under the theory of "popular sovereignty," did a new territory have the power to prohibit or legalize slavery before framing its constitution and before seeking statehood? According to Douglas, it did. According to southern spokesmen, it did not. No territory could decide this question, southerners said, until it became a state. So long as it was still a territory it could not keep slaves out. As settlers moved into Kansas, the issue quickly passed beyond debate.

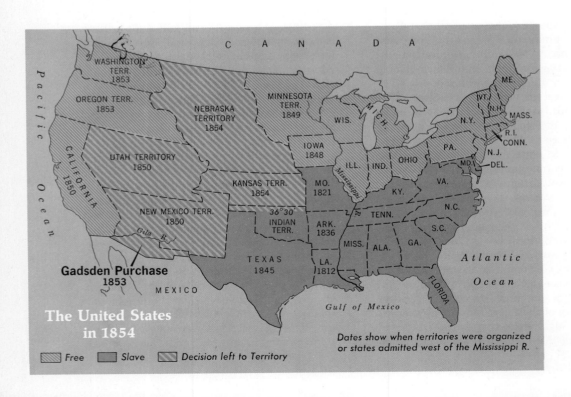

**The United States in 1854**

Dates show when territories were organized or states admitted west of the Mississippi R.

Free   Slave   Decision left to Territory

Most of those who settled in Kansas after the organization of the territory were slaveless farmers from adjacent states. Along with them, as in all other frontier settlements, came the characteristic body of rovers and opportunists bent on bleeding the newcomers. As a cover for their unsavory activities, they were no doubt callous enough to keep the controversy over slavery boiling. Others also helped turn Kansas into a battleground. To "beard oppression in its very den," as they said, the New England Emigrant Aid Company and similar associations organized in the North between 1854 and 1855 financed the migration of more than a thousand right-thinking Yankees to Kansas to see that the new settlers voted correctly when the issue of free soil or slavery came up, and to participate in the vote themselves. To support their mission, boxes of "Beecher's Bibles" were sent to them. Henry Ward Beecher, a vigorous antislavery clergyman, had preached that rifles might have stronger effect than the Bible on the proslavery camp, and he was believed.

To forestall these Yankee "serfs," "paupers," and "cutthroats," as they called them, hot-headed Missourians—"bar-room rowdies," "blacklegs," and "border ruffians," said the Yankees, returning the compliments—as well as hundreds from Alabama, Georgia, and South Carolina, also poured into Kansas, determined to pack the first Kansas territorial legislature with proslavery men.

On election day, March 30, 1855, slightly more than 2000 Kansans were registered to vote, but over 6000 ballots were cast, most of them by Missourians who had come into Kansas for this day only. Andrew H. Reeder, a Pennsylvania Democrat who had been appointed governor of the Kansas Territory by Pierce, tried to disqualify eight of the thirty-one members who had been elected irregularly, but Pierce refused to back his governor and eventually recalled him. Over Reeder's vetoes, the new legislature adopted a series of savagely repressive laws that, among other punishments, prescribed the death penalty for aiding a fugitive slave. But free soilers in Kansas were not intimidated. In the fall of 1855 they met in Topeka and drew up their own constitution. In January 1856, they elected their own legislature and Charles Robinson as governor.

With two rival administrations, Kansas was ripe for war. And in May 1856, while Pierce procrastinated, war came. At that time a force of proslavery men led by a United States marshal raided the Kansas town of Lawrence in search of some free-soil leaders who had been indicted for treason by the proslavery legislature. Fortified by alcohol, the raiders burned down the hotel, destroyed homes, and smashed free-soil printing presses.

This celebrated "sack of Lawrence," blown up to horrendous proportions by northern newspapers, took two lives and spawned a bloodier sequel. John Brown, of Osawatomie, Kansas, a fanatical abolitionist who was soon to become better known, gathered six followers, rode into the proslavery settlement at Pottawatomie Creek, and wantonly hacked five men to death. He acted, so he said, under God's authority. But his sacred vendetta started a guerrilla war in which over 200 persons were killed.

Violence over Kansas, moreover, had already spread from the territory to the very halls of Congress. On May 19, 1856, shortly after the "sack of Lawrence," but before news of the incident reached Washington, Charles Sumner of Massachusetts rose to speak in the Senate in favor of the free-soil constitution of Kansas. His speech, lasting all of two days, flailed away at the "harlot slavery" and especially at the "murderous robbers" of Missouri, "hirelings picked from the drunken spew and vomit of an uneasy civilization." But Sumner aimed his choicest epithets at Senator Andrew P. Butler of South Carolina and drove Butler's nephew, Preston Brooks, congressman from South Carolina, to avenge his uncle, his state, and his section. Two days after his speech, as Sumner sat at his desk in the Senate chamber, Brooks beat him repeatedly over the head with a cane and injured him so severely that Sumner remained an invalid for three and a half years. The assault on Sumner by "Bully" Brooks, together with the news from Kansas,

The New-York Historical Society, New York City

The New-York Historical Society, New York City

*The assault on Senator Sumner
by Congressman Brooks, May 22, 1856,
and the report of it the next day
in the* New York Herald, *received by magnetic
and printing telegraph.*

# THE LATEST NEWS.

## BY MAGNETIC AND PRINTING TELEGRAPHS.

### Assault on Senator Sumner in the Senate Chamber.

WASHINGTON, May 22, 1856.

About half past one, after the Senate adjourned, Col. Preston S. Brooks, M. C., of South Carolina, approached Senator Sumner, who was sitting in his seat, and said to him—

Mr. Sumner, I have read your speech against South Carolina, and have read it carefully, deliberately and dispassionately, in which you have libelled my State and slandered my white haired old relative, Senator Butler, who is absent, and I have come to punish you for it.

Col. Brooks then struck Senator Sumner with his cane some dozen blows over the head. Mr. Sumner at first showed fight, but was overpowered. Senator Crittenden and others interfered and separated them.

Mr. Keitt, of South Carolina, did not interfere, only to keep persons off.

Senator Toombs declared that it was the proper place to have chastised Mr. Sumner.

The affair is regretted by all.

The stick used was gutta percha, about an inch in diameter, and hollow, which was broken up like a pipe-stem.

About a dozen Senators and many strangers happened to be in the chamber at the moment of the fight. Sumner, I learn, is badly whipped. The city is considerably excited, and crowds everywhere are discussing the last item. Sumner cried—"I'm most dead! oh! I'm most dead." After Sumner fell between two desks, his own having been overturned, he lay bleeding, and cried out—"I am almost dead—almost dead!"

came unfortunately just when preparations were being made for the presidential campaign in 1856.

*A new party alignment*

The breakup of the Whig party, evident before the election of 1852, was hastened along by defeat in that campaign. The sectional strife of Pierce's administration, in turn, undermined the other great national party, the Democrats, and sent politicians scurrying for new homes. The first of the new parties, the short-lived American party, raised its standard in 1852. It took its name from its opposition to Catholic immigrants and other foreign groups who were pouring into the country and especially into the free North. Politicians in both sections were drawn to it because they thought that the issue of immigration might deflect the nation from the issue of slavery. But they were soon proved wrong.

The American party was so concerned over its "Americanist" bias that it placed its members under secret regulations requiring them to pretend they "knew nothing" when pressed for information. Thus they soon became known as the "Know-Nothings." The spell of cabalistic handclasps and mystifying passwords no doubt added to the party's ranks. But the party drew strong enemies as well. One of them was "Abe" Lincoln. Slower than most to disown his long Whig allegiance, Lincoln wrote in 1855:

*I am not a Know-Nothing. That is certain. How could I be?... Our progress in degeneracy appears to me to be pretty rapid. As a nation, we began by declaring that 'all men are created equal.' We now practi-*

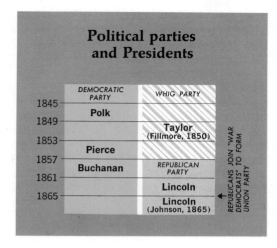

**Political parties and Presidents**

| | DEMOCRATIC PARTY | WHIG PARTY | |
|---|---|---|---|
| 1845 | | | |
| 1849 | Polk | | |
| 1853 | | Taylor (Fillmore, 1850) | REPUBLICANS JOIN "WAR DEMOCRATS" TO FORM UNION PARTY |
| 1857 | Pierce | | |
| 1861 | Buchanan | REPUBLICAN PARTY | |
| 1865 | | Lincoln | |
| | | Lincoln (Johnson, 1865) | |

ern Know-Nothings moved to the new Republican party.

371

The Republican party came into being almost spontaneously in 1854. No single leader or group can claim sole credit for its organization, but one firm principle brought its members together: the determination to keep slavery out of the territories and the conviction that Congress had the right to do so. Besides the Know-Nothings, Free Soilers, of course, flocked to Republican ranks, as did "conscience Whigs"—those, that is, whose dislike of the extension of slavery was so strong that they had refused to join their party's condemnation of the Wilmot Proviso (see p. 307). Northern Democrats who rejected all further compromise with the South also joined, as did outright abolitionists, and a considerable number of German immigrants, who might have been deterred by the Know-Nothing contingent but whose taste for free land proved stronger than their distaste for teetotalers and nativists.

Although the Republicans opposed the extension of slavery, it is doubtful that more than a small minority of them had any humanitarian interest in the well-being of the Negro. North or south, he remained outside the pale of the enterprise and individualism that was making the land of opportunity such an expansive force within the Union, such a looming power in the world. What most Republicans wanted was free soil, not freed slaves; the advancement of the common white man, rather than the welfare of the black.

*cally read it "all men are created equal except negroes." When the Know-Nothings get control, it will read "all men are created equal except negroes and foreigners and Catholics." When it comes to this I should prefer emigrating to some country where they make no pretense of loving liberty—to Russia, for instance, where despotism can be taken pure, without the base alloy of hypocrisy.*

When, in 1854, the American party's national convention voted to support the Kansas-Nebraska Act, most of its southern following joined the Democrats, while many northeast-

## II Buchanan's ordeal

*Election of 1856*

Franklin Pierce actively sought renomination for the presidency in 1856 and, to improve his chances as the conventions approached, he made complaisant gestures toward the South, as we have seen, in Kansas as well as Cuba. Unfortunately for him these

backfired and even many southern Democrats no longer could stomach him. National Democratic leaders, at the same time, dared not back Douglas, whose successes, as in the adoption of the Kansas-Nebraska Act, proved even more damaging to the party than Pierce's failures. Instead, they turned to a veteran of forty inconsequential years in politics, the conservative Pennsylvanian, James Buchanan. As minister to Britain, Buchanan had the advantage of having been out of the country during Pierce's administration and thus distant from party squabbles. For their first presidential campaign, the Republicans, in the Whig tradition, placed their hopes upon a military hero—General John C. Frémont, the glamorous Georgia-born son-in-law of the Jacksonian Democrat Thomas Hart Benton. The expiring American party named ex-President Millard Fillmore as its standard-bearer.

Although "Old Buck" soon came to be despised as a "Doughface," a northern man with southern principles, this combination of characteristics helped the efficient Democratic machine put him across with 174 votes in the electoral college to Frémont's 114 and Fillmore's 8. Buchanan's popular vote of 1,833,000, however, came to only 45 percent of the ballots cast. Nor did the sectional character of the vote augur well for the country. New England, stung by the Kansas-Nebraska Act and increasingly hostile to slavery, voted overwhelmingly (61.7 percent) for Frémont. Frémont also won New York. Had he captured Pennsylvania and Illinois, the Republicans would actually have taken the election. Hence what solace the South found in the Democratic party's victory hardly compensated for the extraordinary Republican show of strength.

### The case of Dred Scott

Buchanan was in office only a few days when faced with the first great crisis of his administration. The trouble arose over the Supreme Court decision in the case of *Dred Scott* v. *Sandford,* which confirmed the southern contention that Congress had no right under the Constitution to exclude slavery from the territories.

Dred Scott, a slave, had been taken by his master in 1834 from Missouri to the free state of Illinois, and from there to Wisconsin Territory where he stayed until his return to Missouri several years later. The antislavery group who backed his suit for freedom hoped to prove that Dred Scott's sojourn in free Illinois and in a territory where slavery was illegal under the Missouri Compromise had made

him a free man. By a complicated route the *Dred Scott* case reached the United States Supreme Court in May 1856 but was not decided until March 6, 1857.

The Supreme Court might simply have dismissed this case on the grounds that Scott was not a citizen of Missouri or of the United States and hence was not entitled to sue in a federal court. Or, falling back on an earlier Supreme Court decision, *Strader* v. *Graham* (1850), they might have ruled that Scott's residence in a free state only suspended his slave status temporarily. But the Court knew that Buchanan was expecting the judiciary to resolve the thorny issue of slavery in the territories, specifically in war-torn Kansas territory, with which neither the executive nor legislative departments had had any lasting success. Buchanan had even gone so far as to notify Justices Catron and Grier of his expectations; and on receiving their agreement, he had stated in his inaugural address two days before the decision: The issue of slavery in Kansas "is a judicial decision which legitimately belongs to the Supreme Court of the United States before whom it is now pending, and will, it is understood, be speedily and finally settled."

No fewer than eight of the nine justices on the Supreme Court wrote separate opinions on different aspects of the *Dred Scott* case. In speaking for the Court for more than two hours, Chief Justice Taney spent half his time arguing that since Negroes had been viewed as inferior beings at the time the Constitution was adopted, its framers did not intend to include them within the meaning of the term "citizens." Therefore, the right of citizens of different states to sue in the federal courts could *never* apply to a former slave or descendant of a slave.

Only two justices would concur in Taney's rank racial concepts and *ex parte* perversions of history. But these two and four others joined Taney in a majority finding that Scott, even had he become free, had reverted to slavery on his return to the slave state of Missouri and had no right to sue in a federal court.

Five justices, conforming to the President's wishes, joined the Chief Justice in plunging further. The slave, they said, is property, pure and simple. According to the Fifth Amendment to the Constitution, "No person shall be ... deprived of life, liberty, or property without due process of law." The prohibition against taking slave property into the territories they found to be a violation of this clause. "No word can be found in the Constitution," Taney observed, "which gives Congress a greater power over slave property, or which entitles property of that kind to less protection than property of any other description." Thus Congress had no right under the Constitution to exclude slavery from the territories and the Missouri Compromise was, and always had been, unconstitutional.

The Kansas-Nebraska Act, as we have seen, had already declared the Missouri Compromise "inoperative and void." If, as the Court now held, the attempt of the Compromise to legislate slavery out of the territories was also unconstitutional, then the fundamental objective for which the Republican party had been formed was unconstitutional. Even the Douglas Democrats were troubled by the decision, for if slaves were property untouchable by law under the federal Constitution, Douglas's program for "popular sovereignty" on the slavery question in the territories was dead.

In June 1857, as part of his continuing campaign against Douglas's "popular sovereignty" position, Lincoln said of the *Dred Scott* decision:

*If this important decision had been made by the unanimous concurrence of the judges, and without any partisan bias, and ... had been in no part, based on assumed historical facts which are not really true; or, if ... it had been before the court more than once, and had there been affirmed and re-affirmed through a course of years, it then might be, perhaps would be, factious, nay, even revolutionary, to not acquiesce in it as a precedent.*

*But when, as it is true, we find it wanting in all these claims to the public confidence, it is not resistance, it is not factious, it is not even disrespectful, to treat it as not having yet quite established a settled doctrine for the country.*

### The Lincoln-Douglas debates

The baleful issue of slavery in the territories was most comprehensively examined during the contest for the Illinois senatorial seat in 1858. In July that year, the rising Republican candidate, Abraham Lincoln, challenged his Democratic opponent, "the little giant," Stephen A. Douglas, to a series of joint debates. Before the Lincoln-Douglas debates began, however, two events in 1857 and 1858 soured the hopes of the South as much as the *Dred Scott* decision had sweetened them.

The first of these was the business panic of August 1857. The sudden collapse of the free economy did allow southern spokesmen to point with pride to the comparative stability and success of the slave system. But the depression that followed aligned all the more strongly with the antislavery Republican party (1) free businessmen (and the workers they employed), who favored the Republican plank for high tariffs to stimulate free industry and industrial employment; and (2) free farmers, who endorsed the Republican plank for free homesteads. As fearful of high tariffs and free land as of the Republican party itself, southerners thus grew all the more determined to preserve for their section, if only for political advantage, all the western territories not yet lost to slavery.

The second event was the state constitutional convention at Lecompton, Kansas, in October 1857. Here, proslavery delegates named in a rigged election not only wrote a constitution explicitly guaranteeing slavery, but prudently, from their point of view, refused to permit the whole body of voters to ballot on it. Under severe pressure they did offer the electorate a proposition which restricted the entry of new slaves but which protected slave property already in the state. The dominant antislavery voters abstained from balloting on this proposition and the proslavery party thereby carried it.

Governor Robert J. Walker, a Buchanan appointee, demanded of the President that all Kansas be allowed in an honest election to vote on the Lecompton Constitution. But Buchanan, leaning heavily in the direction of southern Democratic strength, affirmed the validity of this document and laid it before Congress as the one on which admission of Kansas as a state should be determined. Walker immediately resigned. Senator Douglas fought the entry of Kansas on Buchanan's terms, but the bill accepting the Lecompton Constitution won in the Senate. In the House, "Douglas Democrats" in favor of honest "popular sovereignty" joined with Republican congressmen to defeat it.

374

*The rare daguerreotype by Mathew Brady of Stephan A. Douglas at the outset of his political career.*

The stalemate was broken in May 1858, when Congress passed the English Bill offering Kansas statehood immediately, together with a federal land grant should her voters decide to accept the Lecompton Constitution, or continuing territorial status should they reject it. Given the chance, Kansans overwhelmingly rejected the Lecompton Constitution, 11,812 to 1926. Here the matter rested until 1861, when Kansas entered the Union as a free state.

The Illinois state Republican convention that was to nominate Lincoln to run for the Senate against Douglas met in Springfield, June 16, 1858. Lincoln's lank frame, careless dress, and seamed yet sensitive (and still clean-shaven) face were not so well known as they soon would be, but in Illinois he already was a popular figure, a prosperous lawyer and Whig leader who had served a term in the United States House of Representatives. In his speech accepting the senatorial nomination, he observed that the slavery issue had grown worse each year. "In my opinion," he said, "it will not cease until a crisis shall have been reached and passed. 'A house divided against itself cannot stand.'"

This "House Divided" speech was carefully studied by Douglas and furnished the basis for his attacks on Lincoln in the seven debates that followed. Douglas, who admired Lincoln personally, stigmatized him during the debates as a sectionalist whose "house divided" philosophy would end in "a war of extermination." Why, Douglas asked, did the Republicans say that slavery and freedom could not peaceably co-exist? Lincoln replied that his party did not propose to interfere with slavery where it existed, nor did he wish to enforce social equality between black and white, as Douglas alleged. But, in keeping with the Republican program, he flatly opposed any further extension of slavery.

In the debate at Freeport, Illinois, Lincoln asked Douglas a momentous question: "Can the people of a United States territory, in any lawful way, against the wish of any citizen of the United States, exclude slavery from its limits prior to the formation of a State constitution?" To answer this question, Douglas either had to abandon his popular sovereignty concept or defy the *Dred Scott* decision. If the people could not exclude slavery, popular sovereignty meant little. If they could exclude it, popular sovereignty was as much in conflict with the *Dred Scott* decision as the Republican principle of congressional exclusion. Douglas answered that the people of a territory could take this step, in spite of the *Dred Scott* decision. Slavery could not exist for a day, he explained, if the local legislature did not pass the necessary laws to protect and police slave property. Therefore, merely by failing to arrange for slavery, a territorial legislature, without formally barring it, could make its existence impossible.

Douglas's realistic answer broadened the opposition to him in the South and widened the split in the Democratic party, as Lincoln anticipated. Douglas won the senatorial election in the Illinois state legislature despite Lincoln's popular plurality, since inequalities in apportionment permitted Douglas men to dominate. But the war between Douglas and Buchanan's administration left the Democratic party, and the Union, more divided than ever.

## John Brown's raid

The most portentous event in the sectional struggle was John Brown's raid on the federal arsenal at Harpers Ferry, Virginia, Sunday, October 16, 1859. Brown and his seventeen men actually captured the arsenal with millions of dollars worth of arms, and that night he sent a detachment to take nearby planters, with some of their slaves, as hostages. This mission accomplished, he awaited news of the slave uprisings he hoped would follow. "When I strike the bees will swarm," Brown had told Frederick Douglass and others.

By dawn, Monday, instead, news of his own exploit had spread across the countryside and hastily gathered militia counterattacked. Dangerfield Newby, a free Negro—his wife and seven children still slaves in Virginia—was the first of Brown's raiders to die. Brown's two sons also were mortally wounded that day, along with others. Before the day ended, Brown and his survivors had been trapped in the arsenal. Exaggerated stories of the adventure by now reached Washington, and Buchanan quickly ordered the nearest federal troops to the scene. He also dispatched Colonel Rob-

375

*An item in the apotheosis of John Brown:*
*A Currier and Ives lithograph of 1863*
*from the painting by Louis Ransom, showing*
*Brown's compassionate gaze on the slave*
*mother and her child who blocked his passage*
*to the scaffold.*

Library of Congress

ert E. Lee and Lieutenant J. E. B. Stuart from the capital to take charge, with Lee in command. On Tuesday, October 18, having rejected Brown's truce terms, Stuart led the attack on the arsenal and soon regained it, capturing Brown and five others prisoners, leaving ten of Brown's men dead.

Eminent northern reformers, while they did not incite Brown to violence, had known of his project and provided him with money and weapons, ostensibly intended for antislavery partisans in Kansas. Such collaboration only aggravated the fury of the reaction in the South where vigilante groups now beat up and banished anyone suspected of antislavery sympathies, while dangerous books were publicly burned. Governor Wise of Virginia did nothing to calm the excitement in his state. In New York, Boston, and elsewhere, meanwhile, huge meetings organized by northern conservatives attacked Brown and his methods. Seward, Lincoln, Douglas—men of all parties—joined in the condemnation. But when Wise rejected the plea of Brown's relatives and

friends that the raider was insane and ordered him hanged, he insured Brown's martyrdom.

Brown's bravery and dignity on the scaffold touched millions who had abhorred his deeds. "One's faith in anything is terribly shaken," a conservative New Yorker confided in his journal, "by anybody who is ready to go to the gallows condemning and denouncing it." The deification of John Brown that followed was partly the work of writers like Emerson and Thoreau, who converted a brave monomaniac into an "angel of light." "A fervid Union man" of North Carolina, as he described himself, reflected the southern response in these words: "I confess the endorsement of the Harpers Ferry outrage . . . has shaken my fidelity and . . . I am willing to take the chances of every probable evil that may arise from disunion, sooner than submit any longer to Northern insolence and Northern outrage."

## III  No compromise

### Lincoln's election

John Brown's raid came in the midst of the clash between Republicans and southern Democrats that lasted from March to May 1859, before the Congress elected in 1858 could agree on a Speaker. The compromise choice, William Pennington, a nondescript old Whig from New Jersey and a newcomer to the House, soon distinguished his elevation to the post by many laughable examples of total ignorance of procedure. Less laughable, during the contest congressmen often rose to speak armed with pistols as protection against assault by fellow members.

In April 1860 the Democratic national convention assembled at Charleston, South Carolina, the heartland of secession sentiment. Southern extremists had resolved to insist on a plank in the party platform declaring that

neither Congress nor a territorial government could outlaw slavery or impair the right to own slaves. Northern Democrats, hoping to nominate Douglas without irretrievably alienating the southerners, expressed willingness to accept the *Dred Scott* ruling; yet they stood equally firm for popular sovereignty. "We cannot recede from this doctrine," a Douglas spokesman insisted, "without personal dishonor." When it became evident that the extremists' plank would fail, most delegates from eight southern states withdrew. Their departure made it impossible for Douglas to get the two-thirds of the ballots needed to win the nomination, and the convention adjourned.

On June 18 the Democrats reconvened in Baltimore. When the southern delegates bolted once more, this convention went ahead to nominate Douglas on a popular-sovereignty platform. Ten days later the southerners met

Library of Congress

*Lincoln in February 1860,*
*Brady's first portrait of the*
*President-to-be.*
*"Honest Abe" attributed his election*
*success in some part to the wide*
*distribution of Brady's photo.*

independently in Baltimore and chose John C. Breckinridge of Kentucky, himself a moderate, to represent their position on slavery in the territories. With two Democrats in the field, the last unionist bond—a great political party with support North and South—had broken.

377

The Republicans, buoyed up by the Democratic fiasco at Charleston, met in Chicago on May 16. Their front-runner was William H. Seward of New York. But Seward had a perhaps undeserved reputation as an irreconcilable because he once had spoken of the "irrepressible conflict" between North and South. The unsavoriness of his backer, the political boss Thurlow Weed, and the rowdy actions of Weed's henchmen at the convention also handicapped him. Two other possibilities were Salmon P. Chase of Ohio and Edward Bates of Missouri; each had his own limitations, which opened the way for Lincoln. Strongly supported by the powerful Illinois and Indiana delegations and acceptable to both East and West, six weeks before the convention Lincoln had assayed his chances in a letter to a friend: "My name is now in the field; and I suppose I am not the *first* choice of a very great many. Our policy, then is to give no offense to others—leave them in a mood to come to us, if they shall be impelled to give up their first love." This strategy paid off when Pennsylvania and Ohio switched from Seward; on May 18 Lincoln was nominated.

The Republican platform, while making a shrewd appeal to powerful economic interests, also sounded a high moral tone. It included planks for a protective tariff, free homesteads, a Pacific railroad, and the rights of immigrants. "The normal condition of all the territory of the United States," it said, "is that of freedom, . . . and we deny the authority of Congress, of a territorial legislature, or of any individuals, to give legal existence to slavery in any territory of the United States." Practical politicians knew that to win the election Pennsylvania and either Illinois or Indiana would have to go Republican. The tariff was a bid to the iron interests in Pennsylvania; Abraham Lincoln was a lure to Indiana Hoosiers and the men of Illinois. But a resolution (passed over powerful conservative opposition) calling for a reaffirmation of the Declaration of Indepen-

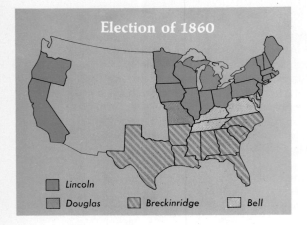

## Election of 1860

Lincoln
Douglas
Breckinridge
Bell

dence indicated the idealism of the rank-and-file Republicans if not of the convention managers.

The campaign was further complicated by the nomination of John Bell of Tennessee, a fourth candidate, by the new Constitutional Union party composed largely of old-line Whigs in the border states. This party called upon the people "to recognize no political principle other than the Constitution of the country, the Union of the states, and the enforcement of the laws."

The 1860 election presented the remarkable picture of a divided nation simultaneously carrying out two separate contests for the presidency: one between Breckinridge and Bell in the South, the second between Lincoln and Douglas in the North. Ten slave states did not even place Lincoln on the ballot. Of his 1,866,000 popular votes, he won a meager 26,000 in the entire South. Douglas, although acknowledged as a candidate, also ran poorly there. In the North, at the same time, neither Breckinridge nor Bell found support.

Although sectional loyalties proved decisive in the 1860 election, the significant unionist vote in the South must not be overlooked. Bell, the unionist candidate, won Kentucky, Tennessee, and Virginia and only barely lost Maryland and Missouri. Nevertheless, although Lincoln gained a decisive majority in the electoral college, he carried less than 40 percent of the popular vote, and none could deny that a sectional candidate had become President of the United States.

### The deep South moves out

Southern leaders had repeatedly warned after Lincoln's nomination that a Republican victory would be followed by secession—for, as the governor of South Carolina put it, the election of a sectional northern candidate would "ultimately reduce the southern states to mere provinces of a consolidated despotism, to be governed by a fixed majority in Congress . . . fatally bent upon our ruin."

Such expectations perhaps best answer the question: Why did the South move out? To understand secession, too, it must be realized that few in the South anticipated its melancholy aftermath. It was by no means certain that the North would go to war to keep a reluctant South in an unhappy Union. And if war came, why should not the South win, and quickly? Many southerners imagined that the will to fight in the crass commercial civilization of the North would be weak. For success they also looked to the sympathy of foreign aristocrats, the commercial power of "King Cotton," and the help of the many prosoutherners above the Mason-Dixon line.

Secession also had positive lures. No longer would the South be drained of its resources by taxes and tariffs that chiefly benefited the North and tribute to northern banking and shipping interests. Perhaps the slave trade would be reopened. Cuba, Santa Domingo, Mexico, even territories in Central America, beckoned enterprising planters.

On December 20, 1860, South Carolina at last took the initiative to bring such thinking to fruition. A convention formally repealed the state's ratification of the Constitution and withdrew from the Union. By February 1, 1861, six other commonwealths—Mississippi, Florida, Alabama, Georgia, Louisiana, and Texas—had followed her example.

The urge to secede, however, had proved far from universal even in the deep South. In almost every case the momentous step was taken over articulate opposition, ready to give

Lincoln a chance to show whether he would really enforce the Fugitive Slave Act and meet other southern demands. But the whirlwind tactics of the fire-eaters overwhelmed the "cooperationists," as the southern moderates were called. Pockets of Unionism persisted in the lower South. Texas Germans, Alabama and Georgia mountaineers, and small farmers in Louisiana parishes all cleaved to their federal loyalties. Yet by the spring of 1861 the majority of southerners of all classes were ready to leave the Union. On February 4, 1861, with seven states having seceded, but with Texas absent, delegates from six states met at Montgomery, Alabama, to form a new government, which they called the Confederate States of America, to adopt a new flag, the "Stars and Bars," and to write a new constitution.

### A federal vacuum

Secession, having begun promptly with Lincoln's victory, took place while Buchanan still occupied the White House. Thus, at the moment of greatest urgency, the country had a "lame-duck" president, one without the will or the power to make commitments. Although Buchanan declared that secession was unconstitutional, he also argued that Congress had no power under the Constitution to prevent it!

While Buchanan vacillated, border-state men in particular, aware that if secession were followed by war their land would become a battleground, still sought to avert disaster.

The most seriously considered proposals were those put forward by Senator John J. Crittenden of Kentucky two days before South Carolina's formal departure from the Union. Crittenden offered these constitutional amendments: (1) Slavery was to be barred in the territories north of the Missouri Compromise line, 36° 30'. (2) It was to be permitted and protected south of that line. (3) Future states were to come in as they wished, slave or free. (4) The Fugitive Slave Law was to be enforced and compensation to be paid by the federal government when enforcement failed because of the action of northerners. (5) The Constitution was never to be amended so as to authorize Congress to interfere with slavery in any state or the District of Columbia.

This comprehensive program failed to win either northern or southern support. Southern leaders would not accept it unless it was endorsed by the Republican party. Lincoln himself, though he favored enforcement of the Fugitive Slave Law and would accept an amendment protecting slavery where it then existed, wholly opposed any compromise on excluding slavery from the territories. To a friend in Congress he wrote: "Entertain no proposition for a compromise in regard to the extension of slavery. The instant you do they have us under again: all our labor is lost, and sooner or later must be done over."

The second compromise effort was made by Virginia. On the very day the Confederacy was being organized in Montgomery, Alabama—February 4, 1861—a peace convention called by Virginia assembled in Washington. Twenty-one states, free and slave, dutifully sent representatives, but the best they could offer were the discredited Crittenden proposals.

## IV The final failure

### Lincoln's inaugural

When, on March 4, 1861, Abraham Lincoln stood up to take the oath of office,

secession was an accomplished fact. A Southern Confederacy had been formed and important federal properties had fallen into rebel hands. Yet a far greater territory than the then existing Confederacy remained very much at issue. The upper South—Virginia, Maryland, North Carolina, even Delaware—was riven by conflict as individuals, families, neighborhoods, and entire regions wrestled with their awful alternatives. Farther west, in the more authentic border states of Tennessee, Kentucky, Arkansas, and Missouri, genuine battles were fought before allegiance to North or South could be established. In all these states the President's inaugural address had been almost too long awaited, and his words when received were pounced upon like Nevada nuggets and minutely assayed for their true value.

Early in his oration Lincoln stressed the perpetuity of "the more perfect Union" established by the Constitution. Then followed his sharpest words to the rebels: "No State upon its mere motion can lawfully get out of the Union; . . . acts of violence . . . against the authority of the United States, are insurrectionary or revolutionary, according to circumstance. . . . The mails, unless repelled," Lincoln added, "will continue to be furnished in all parts of the Union."

The President was as conciliatory as his office and his nature allowed. As Chief Executive, he said, he was bound to enforce federal regulations, including those requiring the return of fugitive slaves, in all the states. He even went so far as to say that he had no objections to a proposed constitutional amendment guaranteeing that "the Federal Government shall never interfere with the domestic institutions of the States"—including slavery. Other constitutional obligations, on the other hand, required that he "hold, occupy, and possess the property and places belonging to the Government, and to collect the duties and imposts" in every American port. But in performing these acts, "there needs be no bloodshed or violence; and there shall be none, unless it be forced upon the national authority." Near the end of his address, Lincoln reminded the intransigents: "In your hands, my dissatisfied fellow-countrymen, and not in mine is the momentous issue of civil war."

But Lincoln could not stop on a note of

iron, and added this famous, eloquent paragraph:

*I am loath to close. We are not enemies, but friends. We must not be enemies. Though passion may have strained, it must not break, our bonds of affection. The mystic chords of memory, stretching from every battlefield and patriot grave to every living heart and hearthstone all over this broad land, will yet swell the chorus of the Union when again touched, as surely they will be, by the better angels of our nature.*

Few if any inaugural orations in United States history bore the burden of Lincoln's first. Few if any played so deliberately for time. In the terrible economic crisis of 1933, Franklin D. Roosevelt caught the public mood when he declared in his inaugural address, "In their need [the people of the United States] have registered a mandate that they want direct, vigorous action." But Lincoln, though pressed by zealots of every political creed, electrified the nation by putting action off:

*My countrymen, one and all, think calmly and well upon this whole subject. Nothing valuable can be lost by taking time. If there be an object to hurry any of you in hot haste to a step which you would never take deliberately, that object will be frustrated by taking time; but no good object can be frustrated by it.*

## Sumter falls

And yet there was action, precipitate action indeed, required of the President himself. In defiance of Buchanan's threat to meet force with force, the Confederacy in the early months of 1861 had seized federal forts, post offices, and custom houses throughout the South without reprisal from the then Commander-in-Chief. Only Fort Sumter in Charleston harbor, and three forts off the coast of Florida, now remained in federal hands. On March 5, the day after his inauguration, Lincoln was given a letter from Major Robert Anderson, in charge at Sumter, reporting that he could hold the fort only with the immediate aid of 20,000 men, a large naval force and ample provisions.

Anderson, in effect, recommended evacuation. But if Lincoln retreated, as his advisers suggested, he would have taken the first step toward recognizing the power if not the legality of the Confederacy. If, on the other hand, he attempted by force to strengthen Sumter, he would be made to appear the aggressor. Lincoln moved in a way that involved neither of these alternatives. He notified South Carolina authorities that he would attempt to provision Sumter peacefully. "If such attempt be not resisted," he wrote Governor Pickens, "no effort to throw in men, arms, or ammunition will be made."

Lincoln's decision shifted the burden to Confederate authorities. If they permitted Sumter to be provisioned, the fort would stand indefinitely in the mouth of one of their few good harbors, a threat to their prestige throughout the world. If they attacked a peaceful expedition bringing food, *they* would have fired the first shot.

When requested by the Confederate general, Pierre G. T. Beauregard, to surrender Sumter before the supply ships arrived, Major Anderson promised to evacuate by April 15, unless relieved or ordered to remain. But the Confederacy dared not risk so long a delay. Anderson was given until 4 A.M. April 12 to capitulate. At 4:30 A.M. the batteries on the Charleston shore began their 34-hour bombardment. Lincoln's provisioning flotilla lay in the vicinity of the fight, but without the support of *Powhatan*, the navy's most powerful warship, which had failed to escort the supply vessels as a result of official bungling, no provisions could be landed. When Anderson at last ran down the flag on the afternoon of April 13, Sumter was virtually consumed in flames, her ammunition spent. Only then did the federal ships approach, with Confederate permission, to take off the defenders. Remarkably, not a man had been hit on either side

during the engagement. But a war that was to overshadow even Napoleon's campaigns in casualties had begun.

Before Sumter, northern opinion had divided sharply on the proper response to secession. Abolitionists like Garrison thought it futile to enforce union "where one section is pinned to the residue by bayonets." For once, the business community, still suffering the effects of the Panic of 1857 and concerned over collecting southern debts and holding southern markets, fully agreed with abolitionist policy to let the "erring sisters go in peace." But bellicose voices also spoke out. "If South Carolina is determined upon secession," warned the *New York Times,* "she should take the plunge with her eyes open. She must face the consequences—and among them all, the most unquestionable is war." Detestation of disunion was especially widespread in the Northwest, where freedom for white men on the land was the very watchword of the Lord, and the free use of the Mississippi from its source in Minnesota to its mouth below New Orleans the foundation of economic life. No section uttered "Amen" more appreciatively to Lincoln's March 4 dictum, "Physically speaking, we cannot separate."

After Sumter, peace partisans still were heard here and there in the North. But with the Confederacy branded before the world as the aggressor, it became easier than before to portray hostilities as a *defense* of the Union. Lincoln's call on April 15 for 75,000 three-month volunteers met with overwhelming response everywhere. Walt Whitman in Manhattan, whose *Drum Taps* establish him as the Union poet of the war, caught the new surge of spirit:

Forty years had I in my city seen soldiers
   parading,
Forty years as a pageant, till unawares
   the lady of this teeming turbulent city,
Sleepless amid her ships, her houses,
   her incalculable wealth,
With her million children around her, suddenly,
At dead of night, at news from the south,
Incens'd struck with clinch'd hand
   the pavement.

*Thomas Nast caught the spirit
of the flag-waving throngs cheering
on New York's Seventh Regiment
as it marched down Broadway, April 19, 1861.*

*A shock electric, the night sustain'd it,
Till with ominous hum our hive at daybreak
   pour'd out its myriads.*

*From the houses then and the workshops,
   and through all the doorways
Leapt they tumultuous, and lo! Manhattan
   arming.*

### The upper South and the Border decide

It is sometimes said that South Carolinians, aware that a Confederacy without Virginia would be a tragic sham, hastened the bombardment of Sumter to force the Old Dominion's hand in taking up arms to defend the South against the expected retaliation from the North. Yet as late as April 13, three months after it was called together, Virginia's "secession convention" still refused to vote for disunion, despite constant urging from hotheads farther south. Then, on April 14, Lincoln framed the fateful proclamation declaring that "combinations too powerful to be suppressed" by ordinary means existed in the seven Confederate states, and calling "forth the militia of the several States of the Union, to the aggregate number of seventy-five thousand, in order to suppress such combinations." On April 15 this proclamation was received with hosannas throughout the North. Throughout the upper South and the border states it came like the toll of death. Should Virginia and the rest answer the President's call and yield their militia to the Union cause? Should they stand by while the deep South was invaded by southern men and arms?

382

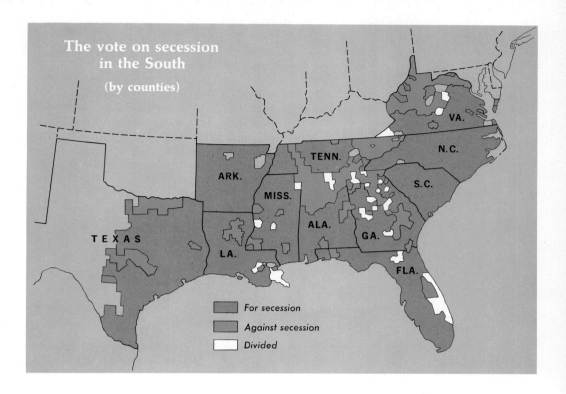

The vote on secession
in the South
(by counties)

VA.

TENN.

N.C.

ARK.

S.C.

MISS.

ALA.

TEXAS

GA.

LA.

FLA.

For secession

Against secession

Divided

More than Lincoln's election, more than his inaugural, more even than the attempt to provision Sumter, Lincoln's proclamation of April 15 sealed the issue of war and peace. On April 17 the Virginia convention at last passed its ordinance of secession 88 to 55. One week later it leagued the Old Dominion with the Confederacy and put its armed forces at the service of the Stars and Bars. On May 21, the provisional Confederate government named Richmond its permanent capital and prepared to move from Montgomery in June. On May 23 a referendum in Virginia (which by law should have preceded secession) sanctioned all those steps. And only then did the President acknowledge all hope gone: "The people of Virginia have thus allowed this giant insurrection to make its nest within her borders; and this government has no choice left but to deal with it where it finds it." Only then were the federal mails cut off from Confederate routes. Secession was now complete in Virginia, even to the point where the western counties were organizing to secede themselves from the new Confederate state.

On April 19 Lincoln had supplemented his proclamation calling out the militia with an order to the navy to blockade the ports of the first seven Confederate commonwealths. On April 27 he extended the blockade to Virginia and North Carolina. The Supreme Court was later to rule that the war legally began with these blockade orders, which officially recognized that a state of "belligerency" existed between two powers. Lincoln himself never accepted this idea; he never recognized the Confederacy as a nation, nor secession as anything but "insurrection."

Virginia ranks among the Confederacy's greatest conquests, one enhanced by the satellites and stragglers that now quickly took the same path. In March an Arkansas convention had rejected secession but on May 6 approved it. In North Carolina on May 20 a convention called by the legislature unanimously voted to secede. In Tennessee, the governor and legislature took the state into the Confederacy even before the people ratified this decision on June 8.

Unionist regions, nevertheless, could still be

found in the upper South and on the border. Like the western Virginians, the yeomen of eastern Tennessee would probably have rejoined the Union had Confederate troops not prevented them. Four indecisive slave states, moreover—Kentucky, Missouri, Maryland, and Delaware—were retained by the Union. Maryland's strategic position forced Lincoln to take strong unconstitutional measures against prosouthern agitators there, and with the show of federal force the secessionist spirit in Maryland subsided. Rich and populous Kentucky maintained a precarious neutrality until

September 1861, when the legislature voted to remain loyal to the Union. Kentucky volunteers for the Confederates numbered about 35,000; approximately 75,000 fought with the Federals. In Missouri the division between prosouthern and pronorthern supporters flared up into a small civil war, but only 20,000 Missourians fought with the South as against 100,000 who joined the Union armies.

## For further reading

The most comprehensive survey of events in this chapter is to be found in Allan Nevins, *Ordeal of the Union* (2 vols., 1947), vol. II, and *The Emergence of Lincoln* (2 vols., 1950). A. O. Craven, *The Growth of Southern Nationalism 1848-1861* (1953); David Potter, *The South and the Sectional Conflict* (1968); and H. C. Hubbart, *The Older Middle West 1840-1880* (1936), are rich in sectional materials. A. O. Craven, *Civil War in the Making 1815-1860* (1959); H. H. Simms, *A Decade of Sectional Controversy* (1942); and Bruce Catton, *The Coming Fury* (1961), offer differing explanations of the sectional schism. D. L. Dumond, *Anti-Slavery Origins of the Civil War* (1939), is a short and incisive analysis, elaborated in his *Anti-Slavery: The Crusade for Freedom in America* (2 vols., 1961). Volume VI of Edward Channing, *A History of the United States* (6 vols., 1905-1925); and vols. I and II of J. F. Rhodes, *History of the United States 1850-1877* (7 vols., 1906), should not be neglected because of their age.

R. W. Johannsen, ed., *The Letters of Stephen A. Douglas* (1961), and G. M. Capers, *Stephen A. Douglas, Defender of the Union* (1959), are illuminating on American expansionism. See also Basil Rauch, *American Interest in Cuba 1848-1855* (1948). Nevins's account of the Kansas-Nebraska issue in *Ordeal* (above) should be supplemented by J. C. Malin, *John Brown and the Legend of Fifty-Six* (1942), and *The Nebraska Question 1852-1854* (1953); and P. W. Gates, *Fifty Million Acres: Conflicts over Kansas Land Policy 1854-1890* (1954). C. V. Woodward's essay on John Brown in Daniel Aaron, ed., *America in Crisis* (1952), is excellent. Edward Stone, ed., *Incident at Har-*

*pers Ferry* (1956), is a good collection of contemporary material on Brown's last act.

The rise and role of the Republican party are well described in many books cited above. Valuable special studies include A. W. Crandall, *The Early History of the Republican Party 1854-1856* (1930); J. A. Isely, *Horace Greeley and the Republican Party 1853-1861* (1947); and Eric Foner, *Free Soil, Free Labor, Free Men: The Ideology of the Republican Party before the Civil War* (1970). More particularized emphasis will be found in R. F. Durden, *James Shepherd Pike: Republicanism and the American Negro 1850-1882* (1957); H. L. Trefousse, *The Radical Republicans, Lincoln's Vanguard for Racial Justice* (1969); and M. F. Holt, *Forging a Majority, The Formation of the Republican Party in Pittsburgh 1848-1860* (1969).

On the sectional crisis and the Democratic party see R. F. Nichols, *The Democratic Machine 1850-1854* (1923), *Franklin Pierce* (1931), and *The Disruption of American Democracy* (1948); and P. G. Auchampaugh, *James Buchanan and His Cabinet on the Eve of Secession* (1926). For the Know-Nothing movement see W. D. Overdyke, *The Know-Nothing Party in the South* (1950); Sister M. E. Thomas, *Nativism in the Old Northwest 1850-1860* (1936); and R. A. Billington, *The Protestant Crusade 1800-1860* (1938). T. B. Alexander, *Sectional Stress and Party Strength* (1967), illuminatingly examines congressional roll calls in the crisis years. J. H. Silbey, ed., *The Transformation of American Politics 1840-1860* (1967), is a short anthology of contemporary partisan expression. The following biographies help fill out the party situation: David Donald, *Charles Sumner and the Coming of the Civil War* (1950);

G. G. Van Deusen, *William Henry Seward* (1967); and C. B. Going, *David Wilmot, Free-Soiler* (1924).

C. B. Swisher, *Roger B. Taney* (1935), is good on Dred Scott, as is Nevins's analysis in *Ordeal* (above). Valuable background material will be found in Charles Warren, vol. II, *The Supreme Court in United States History* (2 vols., 1922).

A. J. Beveridge, *Abraham Lincoln 1809-1858* (2 vols., 1928), and Carl Sandburg, *Abraham Lincoln, The Prairie Years* (1-vol. ed., 1929), are classic studies. Lincoln's emergence is well presented in D. E. Fehrenbacher, *Prelude to Greatness, Lincoln in the 1850's* (1962), and J. G. Randall, *Lincoln the President, Springfield to Gettysburg* (2 vols., 1945), part of a full-scale biography. The Lincoln-Douglas debates are printed in full in P. M. Angle, ed., *Created Equal* (1958). A stimulating analysis is J. V. Jaffa, *Crisis of the House Divided* (1959). R. H. Luthin, *The First Lincoln Campaign* (1944) is authoritative.

D. L. Dumond, *The Secession Movement 1860-1861* (1931); U. B. Phillips, *The Course of the South to Secession* (1939); G. H. Knoles, ed., *The Crisis of the Union 1860-1861* (1965); and R. A. Wooster, *The Secession Conventions of the South* (1962) cover the South's departure. Ollinger Crenshaw, *The Slave States in the Presidential Election of 1860* (1945), adds an important link to the story. For Lincoln's role, see David Potter, *Lincoln and His Party in the Secession Crisis 1860-1861* (1942). K. M. Stampp, *And the War Came: The North and the Secession Crisis 1860-1861* (1950), analyzes the northern position in general. R. N. Current, *Lincoln and the First Shot* (1963), deals in detail with the Sumter alternatives. For a private view of the crisis, *The Diary of George Templeton Strong* (4 vols., 1952), splendidly edited by Allan Nevins and M. H. Thomas, is recommended.

# CIVIL WAR

*Beat! beat! drums!—blow! bugles! blow!*
*Make no parley—stop for no expostulation,*
*Mind not the timid—mind not the weeper or prayer,*
*Mind not the old man beseeching the young man,*
*Let not the child's voice be heard, nor the mother's*
*    entreaties,*
*Make even the trestles to shake the dead where they*
*    lie awaiting the hearses,*
*So strong you thump O terrible drums—so loud you*
*    bugles blow.*
(Walt Whitman, "Beat! Beat! Drums! " 1861)

A Confederate general, writing when the Civil War was over, said: "Aggrieved by the action and tendencies of the Federal Government, and apprehending worse in the future, a majority of the people of the South approved secession as the only remedy suggested by their leaders. So travelers enter railway carriages, and are dragged up grades and through tunnels with utter loss of volition, the motive power, generated by fierce heat, being far in advance and beyond their control."

Secession, whether or not a majority in the South did in fact approve it, led directly to the war. It was not to be so easy to sever the Union as southern leaders might suppose—to tear away a third of its occupied land, to set artificial barriers against the course of its rivers, to defy its sovereign laws, to thwart at one stroke its grand continental aspirations and its great experiment in republican government. The South was not to be allowed to depart in peace.

And yet, from the start of the war a pall seemed to lie on both combatants. The Civil War became the deadliest war ever fought on this continent. Nevertheless, it was amazingly slow in gaining direction, agonizingly slow to those on both sides whose most fervent wish was that, once begun, the fighting might soon be over.

And when it was over, little indeed seemed to have been secured by the slaughter. Not that, in the judgment of history, nor even in the judgment of the times, it was in vain. Lincoln made that clear in the Gettysburg Address: "from these honored dead we take increased devotion to that cause for which they gave the last full measure of devotion—that

... this nation, under God, shall have a new birth of freedom—and that government of the people, by the people, for the people, shall not perish from the earth." The war pointed the way "for us the living," as Lincoln said, to dedicate themselves to "the unfinished work which they who fought here have thus far so nobly advanced." And yet "the living" were to stride but a very short distance forward with this task, and then only to turn back; and their descendants for a century would leave the "unfinished work" untouched.

## I  Enemies face to face

### The question of manpower

In April 1861, about 22 million persons lived in loyal states and territories. Nine million (5.5 million whites and 3.5 million blacks) lived in "Secesh" country. But Union superiority in manpower was not so great as the gross figures suggest.

Half a million persons, scattered from Dakota to California, could make no substantial contribution to Union strength. On the contrary, every year during the Civil War, Union regiments were sucked into the Wild West to wage a desperate war against the Indians.

Hundreds of thousands of Americans in loyal border states and millions more in southern Ohio, Indiana, and Illinois, moreover, favored the Confederacy and worked or fought for southern independence. Indeed every north-

ern state furnished men for the southern cause. Many southerners, of course, clung to the old flag and the Union. "Old Fuss and Feathers," General Winfield Scott, the ancient head of the armed forces of the United States at the outbreak of hostilities, was one Virginian who had no need to search his soul, as did Robert E. Lee, to decide where his allegiance lay. He "had fought 50 years under the flag," Scott told Senator Douglas, "and would fight for it, and under it, till death." Such instances can be multiplied many times, but there is little doubt that more Federals than Confederates "crossed over."

Certain other considerations, when it was seen that the North really meant to fight, may also have tempered southern discouragement in the face of apparently overwhelming Union numbers. One was superior officer personnel.

Confederate Museum

Cooper-Hewitt Museum of Design,
Smithsonian Institution

*Private, Georgia Volunteers,*
*April 1, 1861 (left), and young Union*
*soldier by Winslow Homer.*

For twenty years before Lincoln's inauguration, a southern clique headed by General Scott ruled the army. Under this regime, many northern West Pointers, including Sherman and Grant, found little opportunity for advancement and resigned their commissions early in life for civilian careers. Virtually all the young officers pushed up the ladder by Scott were southerners, and most of them, unlike Scott, embraced the Confederate cause.

A second comfort to the South was its confidence in cotton, largely produced by slaves. Secession leaders expected to exchange their famous staple for all the foreign manufactures they needed without sacrificing fighting men to factory work. A third consideration reinforced the second. The South's vaunted military tradition—which meant, practically speaking, that white men of all classes were trained from childhood to the horse, the hunt,

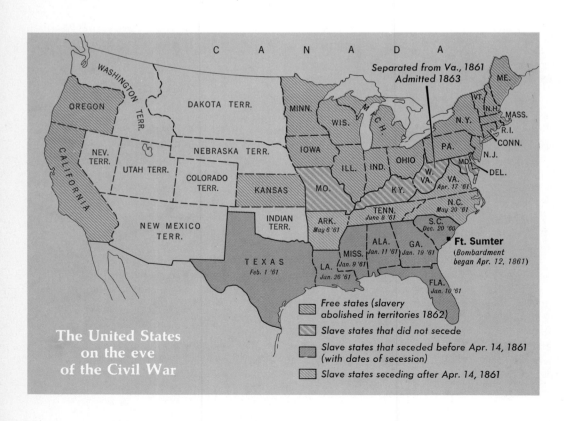

**The United States on the eve of the Civil War**

Separated from Va., 1861
Admitted 1863

Ft. Sumter
(Bombardment began Apr. 12, 1861)

S.C. Dec. 20 '60
N.C. May 20 '61
VA. Apr. 17 '61
TENN. June 8 '61
ARK. May 6 '61
ALA. Jan. 11 '61
GA. Jan. 19 '61
MISS. Jan. 9 '61
LA. Jan. 26 '61
FLA. Jan. 10 '61
TEXAS Feb. 1 '61

Free states (slavery abolished in territories 1862)

Slave states that did not secede

Slave states that seceded before Apr. 14, 1861 (with dates of secession)

Slave states seceding after Apr. 14, 1861

and the use of firearms—had left southern women with the drudgery of running the small family farms and even some large plantations. When the men went off to "hev a squint at the fighting," the women redoubled their efforts in raising dirt crops, cattle, and swine.

A fourth, and the most important, consideration was strategic. Throughout the fighting, the men in gray defended short "interior" lines against invaders who were forced to traverse and protect long avenues of communication and to attack on a broad periphery. The Confederacy, moreover, had no need to divert "effectives" to such tasks as garrisoning captured cities and holding subjugated territory. "Owing to the character of the conflict," concludes the historian Edward Channing, "instead of two or three Northern soldiers for every Southern one, there should have been five or six at least."

By the end of the war, from its 1.5 million white men of fighting age, the South had enlisted about 900,000. Thousands of slaves performed fatigue duty and other tasks for the services, but no blacks except such as might pass for whites were armed. Rebel forces reached their numerical peak at the start of 1864 with some 480,000 in uniform.

From its 4 million white men of fighting age, the Union enrolled approximately 2 million, nearly half of them toward the end of the war. In addition, after 1862, about 200,000 Negroes, most of them former slaves from border states or occupied Confederate territory, were enlisted in the Union army (and to a small extent in the Union navy), many of them forcibly and under discriminatory conditions in pay and quarters. Segregated in their own regiments, mainly under white officers who resented such assignments, they nevertheless performed hearteningly well in the opinion of those who had their capacity for freedom in mind.

In a short war, northern numerical superiority would have availed little. As the war drew itself out, and as generals were found with the determination to take advantage of the disparities in their favor, northern numerical strength became a psychological as well as a physical weapon. During the closing years of the conflict, Union armies, massed at last against critical strongholds, suffered terrible casualties but seemed to grow stronger with every defeat. By the same token, Confederate frustration as well as Confederate losses sapped the southern will to fight.

### The question of machines

The fact that the Civil War stretched over years instead of months magnified every other material advantage of the North—in money and credit, factories, food production, transport. It took precious time to redirect the free economy of the North to the requirements of the battlefield, especially as these requirements were persistently underestimated because of wishful thinking about the likely duration of the war. But the South, with its intense concentration on cotton growing even at the expense of foodstuffs, found it more difficult than the North to convert to a war footing. Abominable roads and poorly built railroads which by-passed many strategic centers magnified every difficulty.

As the war lengthened, southern troops suffered miserably from short rations and ragged clothing, especially the paucity of shoes. Yet the Confederacy was never so lacking in basic materials of war—small arms, artillery, ammunition, and horses—that it could not carry out whatever actions its strategy or its predicament required. Every rural home in the South had its weapons, and some estimates place as high as 5 million the number of such private arms available for the cause. Large quantities of munitions also were garnered from captured federal forts and federal positions. To these were added imports run through the blockade (see p. 383). Under the brilliant administration of its chief of ordnance, Josiah Gorgas, a Pennsylvanian who had long since adopted the sentiments of his Alabama wife, the Confederacy also developed its own munitions plants to supplement the output of the giant Tredegar Iron Works in Richmond.

General Beauregard put the South's situation most clearly:

390

*No people ever warred for independence with more relative advantages than the Confederates; and if, as a military question, they must have failed, then no country must aim at freedom by means of war. . . . The South . . . would be open to discredit as a people if its failure could not be explained otherwise than by mere material contrast.*

Beauregard placed most of the blame for the South's defeat on the failure of President Davis and the civilian command to follow up strategic victories in the field with bold and comprehensive campaigns. Lee's wartime correspondence confirms this charge.

## II  Civilian commands

### The Confederate Constitution

When the delegates from the first seceding states met at Montgomery, Alabama, in February 1861 to draft a frame of government for the new southern republic, they had hoped, by not departing too greatly from the familiar federal document, to attract their as yet uncommitted neighbors in the upper South and on the "border." Because so many southerners remained more firmly opposed than ever to surrendering state rights to a central government, certain weaknesses so successfully fought in 1787 nevertheless crept into the Confederate version. Its very preamble declared that it was established, not by "We, the people," but by "the people of the Confederate states, each state acting in its sovereign and independent character."

While the Confederate Congress was granted power "to . . . provide for the common defense," no mention was made of promoting the "general welfare." "The judicial power of the Confederate States" was placed in a Supreme Court and certain lower tribunals. But no Supreme Court ever was set up. The old federal district courts, indeed, continued to sit in the Confederacy, often under their old judges who applied the old rules and precedents, each as he saw fit. The President's term, optimistically, was extended to six years; but whatever advantage in stability was sought by this change was vitiated by the provision barring his reelection. With little politi-

cal leverage or allegiance, the Confederate President soon became a lame-duck.

The new constitution contained provisions designed to make it a weapon as well as a vehicle of government. Of course, it "recognized and protected . . . the right of property in negro slaves." Yet it explicitly prohibited "the importation of negroes . . . from any foreign country." As a sop to Virginia and other slave-breeding states not yet in the Confederacy, it excluded the slave-holding states of the United States from this prohibition. But as a manifest threat to such states, it empowered the Confederate Congress, when it wished, to include in the ban "any State not a member of . . . this Confederacy."

### Jefferson Davis's administration

In Montgomery, the Constitutional Convention named Jefferson Davis of Mississippi provisional President and Alexander H. Stephens of Georgia provisional Vice-President. Neither man sought nor wanted his job, but in the first Confederate elections in November 1861, the voters confirmed the Convention choices.

Like so many Mississippians, Jeff Davis was born out of the state, in Kentucky. A West Pointer of the class of 1828, at heart he was a soldier hungry for honor in the field. In 1846, he had resigned his seat as a Democratic congressman to lead his regiment of Mississippi Rifles in one grand stand at Buena Vista. This exploit convinced him perhaps more than it did the Mexicans that he was born to generalship, an opinion that was to be of no help to Confederate officers. Davis's strong southern chauvinism soon linked him with the anti-Douglas wing of the Democratic party. But he was no fire-eater and, while sympathetic to secession, he had hoped that the South could take the plunge united and not be harried into the fatal step piecemeal by headstrong individual commonwealths like South Carolina.

Ill health may have accounted for Davis's testiness as President. But his frequent quarrels with subordinates also arose from their incompetence and even hostility. Vice-President Stephens, especially, although he stayed home in Georgia most of the time, was a thorn to his commander-in-chief. A wizened little scholar wracked by rheumatism and neuralgia, Stephens yearned only for the solitude of the study. As a stickler for state rights, he complained on every exercise of presidential power that Davis was becoming a despot with Bonapartist ideas of grandeur. Saddest of all, Stephens had been certain from the start that not even a Bonaparte could establish a free Confederacy, and his pessimism became contagious.

Davis's Cabinet scarcely made up in strength for the Vice-President's weakness. Fourteen different men filled the six Cabinet posts during the life of the Confederacy. Such turnover alone would have forced the President to lean increasingly on the few familiar figures about him; and of these Judah P. Benjamin, a brilliant New Orleans lawyer who served through the whole ill-fated administration, first as Attorney-General, then as Secretary of War, and finally as Secretary of State, was by far the ablest. Benjamin's task was made none the lighter by the ceaseless slander of his character by newspapers and legislators. His determination to make the Confederacy face up to the grim reality of its financial, economic, and diplomatic predicament earned him the appellation "the hated Jew."

The Confederate Congress, more stable in

*Jefferson Davis and his second wife, Varina Howell Davis, whom he married in February 1845. He seemed to her, she said during the inauguration ceremonies, "a willing victim, going to his funeral pyre."*

personnel than the Cabinet, was no more responsible. Three distinct congresses held office during the life of the Confederacy. Many men served in all three, and as conditions worsened they came to grate so on one another's nerves that the more truculent brandished guns and knives, in addition to the traditional horsewhips and canes, to cut short distasteful harangues. As federal forces occupied "Secesh" territory, irresponsibility increased, for many legislators found themselves representing lost constituencies which could not vote them out.

Davis was especially hard pressed by state-rights enthusiasts who saw almost no justification for a central government at all. The South's military genius, moreover, was paraded daily in the legislative halls where Davis's strategy came under ever harsher scrutiny. Military reverses, of course, raised the fever of the malcontents to delirious heights, to which the famed oratorical genius of the Old South proved equal. Such reverses also heightened congressional opposition to Davis's program for mobilizing the South.

## Lincoln as President

By temperament and character, Lincoln was far better fitted than Davis for presidential responsibility. Patient as a possum, tolerant, flexible, and crafty, Lincoln had a genius for giving men enough rope to hang themselves. If they escaped the noose, so much the better.

Throughout his term, the President was savagely handled by most newspapers and abused by politicians of his own and other parties. Nor was he popular with the electorate. But Lincoln took the verbal abuse, it seemed, with a kind of wry satisfaction in his critics' scratching for barbs. Even to men who knew him longest he remained something of a mystery, enlivening meetings with the earthiest kind of stories and yet melancholy, aloof, in counsel with his inner self. His law partner, William H. Herndon, considered him a "sphinx . . . incommunicative—silent—reticent—secretive—having profound policies—and well laid—deeply studied plans."

Lincoln seldom acted until he felt that the groundswell of public opinion would sustain him, a point he reached by a process of divination to which his contentious associates contributed much by their discussions, but how much and in what way precisely they could not tell. Nor was he always right, especially in simply taking time. Lincoln's procrastination in getting on with the fighting encouraged the ambitious egotists around him—Secretary of State Seward, for example, and Secretary of the Treasury Chase—each to strive to assume "a sort of dictatorship for the national defense" in order to fill the vacuum they found in presidential power. But all learned sooner or later, as Seward acknowledged after an early brush with the railsplitter's own ego, that "the President is the best of us. There is only one vote in the Cabinet and it belongs to him. Executive ability and vigor are rare qualities, but he has them both."

In 1861 the federal government was honeycombed with secessionists. No President, not even Jackson, cleaned house so indiscriminately. Few, on the other hand, chose replacements with such care. Lincoln labored so painstakingly in selecting loyal Republicans that idealistic critics accused him of frittering away his time with low politics while the nation was splitting apart. His justification was that patronage was the cement of the Republican party, which alone held the North together.

"The Inside Track," from Vanity Fair, March 2, 1861, showing Thurlow Weed addressing the President-elect: "Trust to my friend Seward—Trust to us. We'll compromise this little difficulty for you. Gentlemen from the country are often egregiously swindled by unprincipled sharpers. TRUST TO US!"

The New-York Historical Society, New York City

### Disunity within the Union

Extremes sometimes met in opposition to Lincoln's administration. Many dedicated abolitionists, for example, were dedicated pacifists as well. In addition, they had preached disunion as vigorously as Calhoun. Their argument, that by sloughing off the slave section the Union itself would be purified (a goal somewhat different from their most widely advertised one), fed on the fond hope that in an isolated South slavery would wither away. Now these abolitionists demanded that the rebels be allowed to depart in peace, slaves and all. "Peace" was also the goal of many northern Democrats, often called Copperheads, who spared Lincoln no abuse but who saved their heaviest fire for the abolitionists themselves.

As the war proceeded and congressional support for emancipation grew, partly as a result of continued abolitionist agitation, most abolitionists eventually embraced the fight to the finish. Many, indeed, came to fear an early end to the conflict lest it lead to a compromise peace, with the "peculiar institution" still intact in the South. As the Confederacy's chances declined, on the other hand, the Copperheads grew shriller in their demands for compromise and more active in obstructing Union enlistments, while encouraging northerners to fight for the slave power. In the closing years of the war, rumors were rife of traitorous plots by secret Copperhead societies, but these groups, largely made up of the ill-educated and untrained, never constituted an effective fifth column.

As abolitionists gradually came around to conceding the rightness of the fighting, they also threw their support to the faction within the Republican party most in sympathy with emancipation as the objective of the war. This faction became known as the "Radicals." The "Regulars," or "Conservatives," sought only to suppress the "insurrection" and to restore the Union for the white men regardless of the freedom and progress of the black.

Lincoln, who never ceased to fear offending the slaveholders of the loyal border states, likewise never disavowed his Conservative leanings. But he also kept in touch with the Radicals to whom he harkened at least as patiently as to others. The Radicals, who fought not only to free the slaves but to impose the "permanent dominion" of free institutions on the slaveocracy, were less patient with him. By their cannonading criticism of Lincoln's "sickly policy of an inoffensive war" they early earned the epithet "Vindictives," which was not unacceptable to them.

The Radicals boasted a formidable array in both houses of Congress, led in the Senate by Sumner of Massachusetts, Wade of Ohio, and Chandler of Michigan, and in the House by the most vindictive Radical of all, Thaddeus Stevens of Pennsylvania, chairman of the regal Ways and Means Committee. Born and bred on the Vermont frontier, Stevens had made his career in Pennsylvania, where he owned extensive iron works. There, in 1837, he refused to sign the new constitution, to the writing of which he had contributed a great deal, because the convention had rejected his demand that blacks as well as whites be given the suffrage. He had seen much of slavery in those parts of Maryland that adjoined his Pennsylvania haunts, and he early denounced it as "a curse, a shame, and a crime." A lawyer as well as a businessman, Stevens defended fugitive slaves without a fee and usually secured their freedom. The Civil War crowned a political career notable for its ups and downs. After the war Stevens's determination that the slaveocracy should never rise again made him for a time the most powerful figure in the country (see Chapter Seventeen).

### Lincoln's "dictatorship"

Lincoln allowed nearly a whole year to pass after the first shocking act of secession before he would acknowledge, and even then not fully, that the awful chasm between the two sections could be closed only by the dead of both. He hated bloodshed. Determined to get the war over as expeditiously as possible, he nevertheless was reluctant even to begin the fighting. As late as December 3, 1861, he told Congress: "I have been anxious and careful that the inevitable conflict ... shall not degenerate into a violent and remorseless revolutionary struggle."

Lincoln nevertheless lost no time in readying the Union for survival. Between April and July 1861, with Congress cooling its heels at home (against the wishes of many members who wanted their special session to begin in March when Lincoln was inaugurated, and not in July, as he had designated), Lincoln earned the epithets "despot," "tyrant," "dictator" more justly than any other president.

On May 3, without presidential precedent or legislative authority, Lincoln issued a call for forty regiments of three-year *United States* volunteers to supplement the *state* militia he had called out in April. On no firmer constitutional grounds, he ordered a rapid expansion of the fleet for blockade service. The Constitution states: "No money shall be drawn from the Treasury, but in Consequence of Appropriations made by Law." Without any law, Lincoln ordered Chase to scratch for funds to pay for the new army and navy, and Chase obliged.

More widely opposed than these military and monetary stratagems were Lincoln's trampling of traditional safeguards of personal rights. Neither private letters nor telegrams were safe from federal prying eyes, and holders of passports questionable in any respect were subject to detainment and inquisitions at major ports. Military commanders in particular were empowered to make summary arrests without warrants and "in the extremest necessity," in Lincoln's words, to suspend the writ of habeas corpus. Under this edict and even harsher later ones, at least 15,000 Americans were jailed; and despite Lincoln's characteristic clemency, many remained in jail until the war's end and without ever having been faced with their accusers or informed of the charges against them.

But even these high-handed measures were mild compared with Lincoln's militancy in Maryland, Kentucky, and Missouri, where the most anguished cries of dictatorship arose.

These border states (along with Delaware) had refused to follow Virginia into the Confederacy. But (unlike Delaware) they denied the federal government the use of their state militias, as called for on April 15, and instead declared their individual *"armed neutrality."*

Each of these states had immense strategic importance. Maryland virtually surrounded Washington and, with Virginia gone, could make the national capital the captive of the Confederacy. Baltimore, Maryland's leading port and railroad center, was also Washington's main link with the outside world. Kentucky, in turn, controlled the use of the Ohio River. Missouri, with Kentucky, controlled the use of the Mississippi. "An arming of those states," Lincoln told Congress in July, "to prevent the Union forces passing one way, or the disunion the other, over their soil ... would be disunion completed, ... for under the guise of neutrality it would tie the hands of Union men and freely pass supplies ... to the insurrectionists, which it could not do as an open enemy. [Moreover], it recognized no fidelity to the Constitution, no obligation to maintain the Union."

Maryland, because of its proximity to Washington, was the first of the "neutrals" to feel Lincoln's heel. After a riot in Baltimore on April 15, 1861, between Massachusetts troops bound for Washington and secessionist-minded citizens, Lincoln sent a force into Maryland under General Benjamin F. Butler with orders to take all necessary measures to forestall the state authorities from arming the people against the Union, "even, if necessary, to the bombardment of their cities." Butler, a notorious "problem on two legs," soon roughly rounded up and jailed the mayor of Baltimore, nineteen members of the state legislature, and other citizens. Butler engaged in so much other inflammatory activity that Lincoln felt obliged to recall him. But Lincoln did not undo the General's work; and Maryland, especially the secessionist eastern sector, was held to the Union side throughout the war chiefly by uninvited Union forces.

"I hope I have God on my side," Lincoln said, "but I must have Kentucky." By the time Kentucky formally declared her neutrality on May 24, 1861, Simon Bolivar Buckner, the commander, had molded the state militia into an effective army of sixty-one companies. Buckner's Confederate sympathies already had aroused suspicion, and another Kentuckian, a former naval lieutenant, William Nelson, went to ask Lincoln for permission to organize and arm a countervailing loyal force. Nelson's mission was successful; under cover of night, he soon had 10,000 "Lincoln rifles" distributed among his "home guard." By June 1861, Union sentiment in the Kentucky legislature was so strong that funds requested by Buckner were voted for Nelson instead. By then, too, Lincoln had ordered the establishment of a Union recruiting camp at Danville, Kentucky, to offset camps the Confederates were setting up on Kentucky's border in Tennessee.

The delicate balance held in Kentucky until September 4, 1861, when General Leonidas Polk, unnerved by the growing unionism Lincoln had patiently nourished, ordered his rebel forces to occupy the strategic town of Columbus on the Mississippi. When Polk's men moved in, the recently commissioned Ulysses S. Grant swung over from Cairo, Illinois, to occupy Paducah, Kentucky, on the Ohio River. Jefferson Davis tried to recall Polk's forces and retrieve his hasty step. But it was too late. Kentucky declared her allegiance to the Union

(although a separate convention of Confederate volunteers voted in November to join Kentucky to the South), and was held thereafter, but only at great cost.

Unlike Maryland, which had a Unionist governor, and Kentucky, which had a Unionist legislature, Missouri's government was wholly Confederate in temper. Here Lincoln went so far as to sanction the establishment of a revolutionary Union government which, throughout the great war, carried on a local civil war with the secessionist regime it had unseated. Thousands were killed in the Missouri fighting even before the first battle of Bull Run in July 1861.

In still a fourth area, western Virginia, traversed by the Baltimore & Ohio Railroad, Washington's principal link with the West, Lincoln early took advantage of Union sentiment to create a Union bulwark. His agent here was General George Brinton McClellan, who, in June 1861, drove Virginia state forces from the western mountain passes and restored service on the B & O which those forces had disrupted. Local civil war persisted in Virginia until 1865; but the western counties—and after 1863, the new state of West Virginia as such—remained a firm part of the Union-held border stretching from the Atlantic to the Mississippi.

McClellan reported his successes in western Virginia in such resounding language that he became the first Civil War soldier to win official citation by Congress. After the Union rout at Bull Run it was to this officer, largely on his literary performance, that the country turned three times for victory—each time to suffer twinges of regret.

## III   "Forward to Richmond!"

### First Battle of Bull Run

Lincoln's principal military adviser in the early months of the war was the General-in-Chief of the United States Army, Winfield Scott—"magnificent as a monument and

nearly as useless," as an ungenerous critic described him in 1861. Born in 1786, Scott was a year older than the Constitution. But difficult as he sometimes found it to keep his eyes open, he was one of the few who had been wide awake to the fact that the Union must prepare for a long struggle. Scott, moreover, was perfectly clear-headed about the uses to which he would put the many months he wanted. Clamp a vise of steel on the border states, he said; master the whole course of the Mississippi; screw down the blockade on every rebel port on the Atlantic and the Gulf. Then, when the enemy had begun to writhe under pressure, speed his inevitable end by marching in the overpowering armies for whose preparation all earlier steps would have gained the necessary time.

Lincoln's early success in thwarting the neutrality of the border states provided a favorable start in carrying through Scott's plan on land. The early success of Secretary of the Navy Gideon Welles in making Lincoln's "paper blockade" of April 19 effective further improved prospects on the water. In a few months all but a few rebel seaports were closed in, and the South's foreign trade had been cut at least 80 percent.

Jefferson Davis, as revolted as Lincoln by bloodshed and reluctant to surrender the fantasy that the South would be permitted peacefully to sever the Union, had a war plan of his own that played right into Scott's hands.

The South, Davis said, had seceded to get away from, not to conquer, the North. He saw a perfect "natural frontier" stretching along the Mason and Dixon Line onward to the Black Hills of the Dakotas. Plant along this sweeping border, within which the Confederacy would have ample room for growth, a forest of impregnable forts. Then look to the naval power of Britain and France—hungry as these countries must quickly become for the cotton that was King of the Universe—to unlock southern ports, free southern trade, and protect independent southern commerce.

As early as March 16, 1861, almost a month before Beauregard's bombardment of Fort Sumter, Davis, in one of his first steps as President, had sent three commissioners to Europe to carry out his "cotton diplomacy." Their initial goal was to arrange for massive munitions and supplies needed immediately by the Confederacy. How Lincoln's own commissioners foiled this mission, except in one significant respect (see p. 405), may have been a straw in the wind. Far more than cotton,

with which she had filled her warehouses in anticipation of the war, Britain in particular in 1861 needed wheat. Wheat could be purchased elsewhere, but the Union's ability to pay with massive wheat exports for the munitions and supplies her own envoys ordered in large quantities in the early years of the war made it difficult for Davis's agents to do business.

In the end, the Civil War was to be fought out as the confrontation of Davis's defensive plan, full of holes from the start though it was, and Scott's aggressive "anaconda," painfully slow though it proved to mount.

Both strategies, however, had their enemies from the outset. Many Confederate leaders, General Beauregard among them, urged a relentless Confederate offensive without delay. This camp banked on the supposed superior valor of southern troops and on the less satisfying realization that if the South did not win quickly she was not likely to win at all.

The most popular Union plan seemed to count on just such rebel strategy as Beauregard proposed. In June 1861 the main rebel army under Beauregard himself was stationed at Manassas Junction in Virginia, a critical railroad crossing between Washington and Richmond. Wipe out this army, sweep triumphantly down to the rebel capital, and crush the insurrection in one stroke—that was the siren plan to which Lincoln himself, nursing his own fantasy of a "ninety-day war," remained for some time trustingly drawn.

Each morning during the week preceding the return of Lincoln's Congress to Washington for its special session, Horace Greeley flaunted on the editorial page of his nationally read *New York Tribune,* "Forward to Richmond!" Then, on July 4, the day Congress opened, the *Tribune* cried: "Forward to Richmond! Forward to Richmond! The Rebel Congress must not be allowed to meet there on the 20th of July. By that date the place must be held by the National Army."

Thereafter, Radical demands mounted for "action—crushing, irresistible, overwhelming." A touch of hysteria magnified the pressure. The Confederacy, everyone said, was gathering a rebel host for its own assault on Washington. "Why don't they come? " was the anxious question on every tongue. At last, on July 16, with the "three-months men" nearing the end of their service, General Scott, on Lincoln's authorization, ordered General Irvin McDowell to move.

McDowell's 30,000 were green as saplings, but Beauregard's force, estimated at 24,000, was as little seasoned. As McDowell marched southward, Beauregard probed northward to meet him on suitable terrain. By July 20 he had settled in on the southern side of the little stream of Bull Run, and there, the next morning, the Federals found him. By noon a Union triumph seemed certain. Then General Thomas J. Jackson's "stonewall" stand in one sector, followed by a succession of counterattacks, their fury embellished by the "rebel yell," first heard here, halted the Union offensive.

In the afternoon, Confederate reinforcements under General Joseph E. Johnston arrived from the Shenandoah Valley where the rebels were to maintain a force for most of the war like a gun at Washington's back. McDowell, disappointed at not receiving reinforcements of his own, soon deemed it the better part of valor to retire. Some of his men, their three-months' service over, kept going all the way to New York, New Hampshire and Maine, where they first had volunteered.

"Give me 10,000 fresh troops, and I will be in Washington tomorrow," Stonewall Jackson is reported to have stated after Bull Run. But President Davis clung to his defensive plan and Washington, if indeed it was in mortal danger, was saved.

### "All quiet on the Potomac"

In his opening message to the new Congress on July 4, 1861, Lincoln had reviewed the record of his autonomous four months. "Of all that which a President might

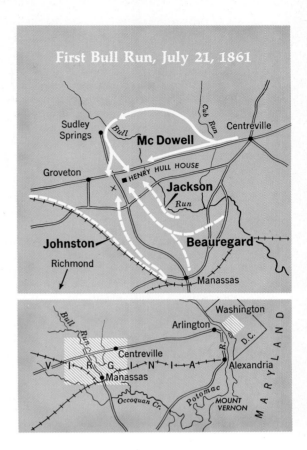

First Bull Run, July 21, 1861

constitutionally and justifiably do in such a case," he said, "everything was forborne without which it was believed possible to keep the government on foot." But three days later, when a joint resolution was introduced seeking to validate the President's extra-legal acts in Congress's absence, the majority laid the resolution aside. Even those members who sympathized with Lincoln's conduct refused to sanction, *post facto,* an invasion of their powers when they themselves deliberately had been left out in the cold. Congress would not even vote Lincoln the men and money he requested, "the legal means for making this contest a short and decisive one," until after the debacle of Bull Run. Only on August 5, the day before the session closed, and then merely as a rider to an army pay bill, would both houses vindicate Lincoln's military steps. His suspension of habeas corpus never was approved.

On August 6, the last day of the session, the Radicals pushed through Congress a portentous measure of their own which Lincoln, fearful of driving the South to vengeful retaliation, said he "had some difficulty in consenting to approve." This was the so-called First Confiscation Act (a second was to be passed in July 1862; see p. 407), making it the duty of the President to seize all property used in aiding the insurrection. Hateful as it was to the Radicals to identify Negroes as property, the act nevertheless included as subject to forfeit all slaves employed in building fortifications and in other military and naval work. Lincoln did sign the measure. "This government will be preserved," cried Congressman Hickman of Pennsylvania in approval, "and the gallows will eventually perform its service."

But the rebels had to be caught before they could be hanged. Immediately after Bull Run, Lincoln relieved McDowell, created a new Division of the Potomac, and placed McClellan, then a cocky thirty-four years of age, at its head. "All tell me that I am held responsible for the fate of the nation," the new commander wrote to his wife. A few days later, with his characteristic flourish, he added the telltale plan: "I shall carry this thing *en grande* and crush the rebels in one campaign." Under the paralyzing pull of Richmond, on the one hand, and the paralyzing fear for Washington's safety on the other, the "anaconda" policy was on its way toward official oblivion. By November 1, Scott himself, outgeneraled in the struggle for power in the capital, retired. McClellan, who had his hand in everything, including the overthrow of his old chief, was elevated to Scott's place. At the same time, this general's officious buzzing about in nonmilitary affairs, against the background of the prolonged inactivity of the army he was readying, soon caused confidence in him, and indeed in Lincoln on his account, to curdle.

McClellan's orders were, in the vicinity of the anxious capital, to forge the Army of the Potomac into a mighty sword and with it to bring the rebels to their knees. He was, in fact, a masterly organizer and conditioner. His failing was his pride in smart execution of the drill, his exasperating reluctance to risk his beauties in battle. By the time Congress reconvened for its regular session on December 2, 1861, McClellan was still grandly housed in Washington, still marching his men, and beginning to tax even Lincoln's patience. "Forward to Richmond!" was forgotten by the press and the people. "All Quiet on the Potomac" became the derisive slogan of the day.

Little more than two weeks after Congress reconvened, the Radicals, their ranks augmented in the legislature by the apparent indolence of the executive, succeeded in establishing a Joint Committee on the Conduct of the War, with wide powers of investigation. It was the "bounden duty" of Congress, they said, to scrutinize "executive agents," including generals who made a practice of returning fugitive slaves and were otherwise retrograde on "the Negro question." McClellan, well-known for his "softness" on slavery, soon became the Committee's pet target and hence doubly Lincoln's concern. Radical suspicions grew that he was in fact more unwilling than ready to fight the rebels, a view the President, although still dreading the onset of a war to the finish, dared not allow to be confirmed.

At last, on January 27, 1862, his patience spent, Lincoln issued General Order No. 1, naming Washington's Birthday, February 22, as "the day for a general movement of the land and naval forces of the United States against the insurgent forces." But even this unmistakable command went unheeded by McClellan. "In ten days I shall be in Richmond," he boasted on February 13. But not until April did he move.

## Coming to grips in the West

While Washington remained preoccupied with the long quiet on the Potomac, the war was far from quiet in the West, where subordinate Union officers had taken things more or less into their own hands. Regular Confederate forces held on in southwestern Missouri until March 1862, when General Samuel R. Curtis chased them into Arkansas and on March 8 defeated them at Pea Ridge. In southeastern Missouri, General John Pope drove the rebels from New Madrid on March 13, and from heavily fortified "Island No. 10" in the Mississippi on April 7, opening the great river all the way to Memphis.

In neighboring Kentucky, Confederate General Albert Sidney Johnston, having seized Bowling Green in mid-September 1861 and made it his headquarters, labored all fall to firm up a line across the southern range of the state from the Mississippi almost to Virginia. If he could not advance farther into Kentucky, Johnston, if he were lucky, planned at least to protect Tennessee and the heartland of the deep South she guarded.

Johnston's campaign failed. The eastern anchor of his line at Mill Springs, near the Cumberland Gap, fell to Union General George H. Thomas in January 1862. On February 6, Commodore Andrew H. Foote, directing a flotilla of gunboats under Grant's command, took Fort Henry on the Tennessee River, while on February 16 Grant's and Foote's combined operation took nearby Fort Donelson on the Cumberland. The loss of Fort Henry cut Johnston's communications between Bowling Green and his western anchor at Columbus and prompted him to quit his Kentucky line. Donelson's loss prevented him from taking a stand even in Tennessee. It was at Donelson that Grant made the demand on Johnston's subordinate, Simon Bolivar Buckner, which caught the fancy of the North: "No terms but immediate and unconditional surrender."

In his *Personal Memoirs* Grant wrote, "immediately after the fall of Fort Donelson the way was opened to the National forces all over the Southwest without much resistance." The way was closed because no "one general who would have taken the responsibility had been in command." Grant himself was relieved of duty March 4, and while his army was broken up for tactical operations here and there (including those of Pope in southeastern

Missouri), "the enemy," Grant added, gained time "to collect armies and fortify his new positions."

During the month following Donelson, Albert Sidney Johnston thus was left free to lead his men across the whole of Tennessee to the strategic railroad center of Corinth, Mississippi. Trailing along behind, Union General Don Carlos Buell mopped up in Tennessee. When Grant resumed command on March 17, he found most of his force at Pittsburg Landing on the Tennessee River, just above Tennessee's southern boundary opposite Corinth. Before pushing south once more against Johnston, Grant decided to await Buell's arrival. But Johnston took the offensive himself before Buell showed up.

On April 6, Johnston led the attack on Grant's exposed encampment at Shiloh, southwest of Pittsburg Landing, and with the advantage of surprise pushed the Federals back

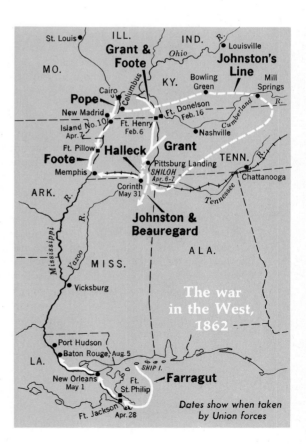

The war in the West, 1862

Dates show when taken by Union forces

to the Tennessee River. There Buell's vanguard appeared and helped stiffen Union resistance. Johnston was killed the first day, and on the next, the combined armies of Grant and Buell drove off the shaken rebels, now led by Beauregard. General Henry W. ("Old Brains") Halleck, recently put in command of the Department of the West, soon appeared to take personal charge of pressing the Union counteroffensive into Corinth. But he procrastinated for weeks as usual, and while his strength persuaded Beauregard, at the end of May, to abandon Corinth, the rebels got away again with their army intact.

Neither side could take much satisfaction from the bloody Shiloh engagement (the Federals lost 13,000 of 60,000 men; the Confederates almost 11,000 of 40,000), yet it gave each a healthier respect for the other. When Grant saw that the rebels here "not only attempted to hold a line farther south, . . . but assumed the offensive and made such a gallant effort to regain what had been lost, then, indeed," he wrote in his *Memoirs*, "I gave up all idea of saving the Union except by complete conquest." Robert E. Lee, in turn, still cooling his heels in Richmond as a presidential adviser, warned Davis that unless he outdid himself to hold the lower Mississippi and keep the Confederacy from being split, Grant's "complete conquest" would not be far off.

Lee's warning was underscored soon after Shiloh by more decisive Union operations farther west. At the end of April a Union fleet led by Captain David G. Farragut smashed through Confederate fortifications below New Orleans and forced that great Mississippi port to surrender. Baton Rouge fell soon after to a force under General Butler. In the meantime, Foote's formidable flotilla had come pushing down the Mississippi to Memphis where it destroyed a Confederate fleet. Between Memphis and New Orleans only Vicksburg, Mississippi, and Port Hudson, Louisiana, now blocked Union control of the mighty river, the outermost border of the "anaconda" plan.

## The Peninsular Campaign

Union operations in the West early in 1862 received only the barest notice in

Library of Congress

Washington, where protection of the capital and preparation of the *"en grande"* assault on Richmond were the main concerns.

Lincoln, who had taken to studying books on military strategy to compensate for the manifest inadequacy of his advisers, had formed very definite opinions about how Richmond might be taken. In short, he was for a new frontal attack, which would have the advantage of keeping the Army of the Potomac between the Confederates and Washington itself. Largely because he had not been consulted about it, McClellan opposed Lincoln's plan. The Confederate capital, the general argued, should be approached by way of the peninsula formed by the York River (on the north) and the James River (on the south). The peninsular plan involved a hazardous combined sea-and-land operation dangerously distant from Washington. To the normal difficulties of such an operation were added in this instance Confederate control of the Norfolk navy yard at the mouth of the James. At Norfolk, moreover, lay the Confederate iron-clad *Virginia,* the former United States frigate *Merrimac,* which only a month before McClellan began his campaign had fought to a standstill the Union cheese-box-on-a-raft, the redoubtable *Monitor.*

Flag Officer Andrew Foote's gun
and mortar boats on the Mississippi pounding
strategic Island No. 10, April 1862,
thereby helping to clear the river
of rebel installations.

401

Could McClellan rely on Union naval support while *Virginia* menaced Chesapeake Bay? Lincoln thought not. Thankful, however, that McClellan at last proposed to move, Lincoln let him have his way. But Lincoln insisted that the general surrender to the President his overall command, retaining leadership only of his new Army of the Potomac, and that he leave behind under other generals a part even of this army to guard the capital.

The first contingents of McClellan's force—all told, 110,000 strong—were landed successfully on the peninsula on April 4, 1862. Yorktown, the first Confederate stronghold on the way to Richmond, might have been overrun in a day. McClellan, still fearful of a new Bull Run, took a month to level and enter the town. Almost another month was lost while the general, vainly awaiting expected reinforcements, was led slowly up the peninsula by wily "Joe" Johnston, who had a rendezvous with reinforcements of his own. What kept McClellan's reinforcements away was Stonewall Jackson's brilliant foray up the Shenandoah Valley, where, as Lincoln had anticipated, he menaced Washington from the rear. Having unnerved the Union capital sufficiently to force Lincoln to keep even a stronger army there than he had planned, Jackson

dashed back to the main front to lend his strength to Johnston.

Before Jackson arrived, McClellan had been drawn to within five miles of Richmond where, on May 31, he narrowly averted disaster at Seven Pines. "Joe" Johnston was badly wounded in this battle, and McClellan might have taken advantage of the Confederates' ill luck to press on. Instead, he left 25,000 men under General Fitz-John Porter in the vicinity of Richmond and returned with the rest to his base at the town of White House, some 20 miles to the east. Here he waited once again, in expectation of the still more men he had requested to oppose the vast host that he imagined stood before the Confederate capital. While McClellan waited, on June 1 Lee at last

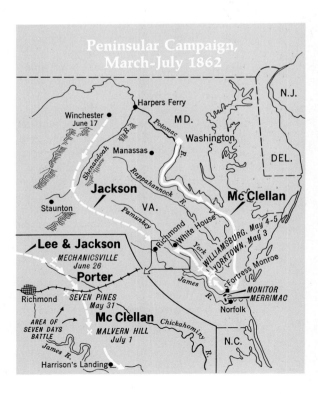

James F. Gibson photo, Brady Collection, Library of Congress

*Union horse artillery at Fair Oaks,*
*Virginia, site of the Battle*
*of Seven Pines—where, when the fighting*
*ceased, a Massachusetts soldier observed*
*that the earth had "the damp, mouldy*
*odor" of blood.*

was returned to the field as the wounded Johnston's replacement. On taking charge, he gave his troops the name "The Army of Northern Virginia," his only command until Davis, in February 1865, named him General-in-Chief of all the forces of what by then had become "The Lost Cause."

Lee possessed the capacities as well as the appearance of a hero. His many admirers regarded him as the greatest military genius of the war. His soldiers themselves came to look upon him as a man "above his race" who "communed with the angels of Heaven." Some military historians have argued that Lee was so concerned with defending his native state that he never developed a coordinated overall strategy. But Virginia's front for too long was all he was vouchsafed and he used it, with his forays into the North itself (see pp. 403, 409), as the most effective means of relieving Union pressure elsewhere. Other writers point to Lee's failure to provide adequate supplies for his armies, which kept him from exploiting his victories; his habit of giving too much independence to his generals in

the field; and his practice, at the same time, of taking on staggering burdens of staff work that he should have delegated to subordinates. So long as he could draw on brilliant corps commanders, however, Lee's confidence was rarely misplaced. In the later stages of the war the caliber of his junior officers declined.

On learning how McClellan had split his army, Lee immediately formed a plan to send a small force "looking numerous and aggressive" to intimidate the susceptible general, while he himself moved in to crush Porter. This accomplished, Lee hoped to outflank McClellan and cut his main force to pieces.

Unfortunately for Lee, Porter and McClellan were prepared. Lee's "eye" in spying out McClellan's position was his dashing cavalry chief, "Jeb" Stuart. It was Stuart's nature to improve any opportunity for showmanship. In a marvelous manifestation of contempt for the enemy—and of foolish disregard of risk for his own cause—for three days (June 12–15, 1862) he drove his worthies completely around the idling Federals and, unscathed, brought Lee the wanted information. His exploit also alerted the Union invaders. McClellan regrouped his forces and surprised the Confederates with his mobilized strength. Having done this much, however, he turned again to the strategy of retreat. In the Seven Days' Battle, between June 26 and July 2, McClellan inflicted very heavy losses on Lee's advancing troops, but his own sorry objective was Harrison's Landing on the James River where the Union navy, if necessary, could evacuate his men.

## Second Bull Run and Antietam

Lincoln visited McClellan at Harrison's Landing on July 9 and called off the whole Peninsular Campaign. He also named "Harry" Halleck commander of all the Union armies. In McClellan's place as commander of the Army of the Potomac, Halleck placed the rash and boastful John Pope. These men, in accordance with Lincoln's own direct overland strategy, were ordered to try to take Richmond at last. But Lee disclosed the full scope of their inadequacies when he routed Pope in the momentous Second Battle of Bull Run, August 29–30, 1862.

This fresh setback left Union soldiers bitter and discouraged. "So long as the interests of our country are entrusted to a lying braggart like Pope," one of them wrote home, "we have little reason to hope successfully to compete with an army led by Lee, Johnston, and old 'Stonewall' Jackson." In June 1862 McClellan had been on Richmond's threshold, three strong Union armies appeared to have control of the Shenandoah Valley, and western Virginia was in Union hands. Now, at the end of August, as Douglas S. Freeman says, "the only Federals closer than 100 miles to Richmond were prisoners . . . and men . . . preparing to retreat." In desperation, Lincoln again entrusted McClellan with temporary command of the disorganized army in the East. "If he can't fight," Lincoln said, "he excels in making others ready to fight."

Lee meanwhile, characteristically pressed the attack, hoping for the first time to penetrate the North. Across his path lay the refurbished federal arsenal at Harpers Ferry, Virginia, with 10,000 men, and munitions and supplies much needed by his own ragged and hungry ranks. If he could take the arsenal and move from there into Maryland, he might win new recruits in this and other border states with which to move on to Pennsylvania. France and Britain then might recognize the southern republic and actively intervene on her behalf. McClellan at the same time would be driven to defensive activity with a still demoralized force backed by a disheartened citizenry.

But Lee's plans again miscarried. On September 15, 1862, Stonewall Jackson with 25,000 men did take Harper's Ferry and all they wanted there. They also learned that McClellan had got wind of this adventure in time to have smashed Lee's divided army. But for two days McClellan did nothing. When he

403

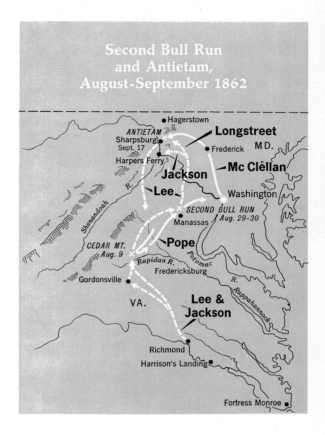

*Union dead along Hagerstown Pike, Antietam, Maryland, September 1862.*

Alexander Gardner photo, Brady Collection, Library of Congress

404

did attack Lee on September 17 at Antietam Creek, he almost engulfed the far outnumbered rebels. But by then, Jackson had returned to help check the Federal momentum, and Lee's battered army was permitted to slip away. According to one of his antagonists, McClellan lacked "that divine spark which impels a commander, at the accepted moment, to throw every man on the enemy and grasp complete victory."

Antietam has been called a defeat for both armies. But the Union, at least, had repulsed an invasion on which the South had spent perhaps too much. "Our maximum strength has been mobilized," Jefferson Davis told his Secretary of War after the battle, "while the enemy is just beginning to put forth his might."

## IV The civilian response

### Confederate ways and means

The brutal, inconclusive engagement at Antietam was an appropriate symbol of the course of the entire war, and naturally the civilian fronts bent under the aimless slaughter. To check mounting criticism in the Confederacy, Davis, in February 1862, prevailed upon his Congress to enact the first Confederate law granting the executive the power to suspend the writ of habeas corpus and to impose martial law. But so intense had state-rights sentiment become in the South that no sooner were Davis's critics locked up under Confederate authority than state authorities released them. Southern editors were frequent victims of the regime. Yet criticism would not be stilled.

The military stalemate was even more acutely felt by those charged with maintaining the resources and manpower of the fighting forces. As early as April 1862, the Confederate Congress was obliged to enact the first conscription act in American history, calling up for three years' service all white men eighteen to thirty-five. Later acts raised the age limit to fifty. But anyone could escape the draft by paying for a substitute, and occupational exemptions were numerous. Evasion, moreover, had the support of certain state-rights governors who ran their commonwealths like private satrapies.

The poor showing reflected in southern draft statistics veils the true serviceability of the conscription acts. "Conscript" became such a brand of opprobrium that many youths hastened to volunteer before their age group was called, and they more than the conscripts themselves maintained Confederate military manpower. On the other hand, the draft acts' official sanction of the purchase of substitutes seemed to confirm the disheartening slogan, "a rich man's war and a poor man's fight." Desertions soared to well over 100,000—only a third, perhaps, of Union desertions, but much more keenly felt.

Symptoms of economic difficulties could be detected in the South even during the first year of the war. Loans in specie were virtually impossible to make in a country where wealth was traditionally tied up in land and slaves. By 1862 the Confederacy was trying "produce loans" by which planters were expected to pay in cotton and other commodities for Confederate bonds. But these loans had two drawbacks. Many planters would not surrender their commodities for government paper; and when they did, the government found it as difficult as its citizens to transform commodities into cash.

The Confederacy had little better luck with taxes and, like other governments frustrated in the quest for gold, it began to print paper money in 1861. By 1864 a Confederate paper dollar was worth, on average, a cent and a half in specie. Prices naturally soared, thus encouraging speculation and hoarding. Food became especially hard to obtain; and widespread famine, made more difficult to fight by the breakdown of transportation, sapped Confederate morale even more than setbacks in the field.

### Failure of southern diplomacy

Confederate difficulties at home were aggravated by the collapse of southern diplomacy abroad, after some early successes.

The ruling classes in Europe had no love for slavery, but as aristocrats they would have been pleased with the failure of the "American experiment" in democratic government. Their attitude was reflected in the decision of Britain and France early in 1861 to recognize the Confederacy as a belligerent power if not as a sovereign government. Britain, moreover, made warlike gestures at Lincoln's administration in November 1861, after a Union cruiser stopped the British mail steamer *Trent* on the high seas and removed Mason and Slidell, two Confederate diplomats, on their way to London and Paris. War was averted when Secretary of State Seward heeded British representations and released the two rebels. But Britain followed up the *Trent* episode by dispatching 8000 troops to Canada.

Confederate hopes for foreign military assistance, sanguine after the *Trent* affair, were scotched by the check Confederate forces received a year later at Antietam. When Lincoln, moreover, took this occasion to announce an Emancipation Proclamation (see p. 408), the surge of Union sentiment among foreign middle- and working-class elements made it even more unlikely that foreign rulers would risk discontent at home by again backing the wrong horse in America. Early in November 1862, the British government rejected the last French approach to intervene in the war and thereafter resisted all Confederate pleadings as well.

Britain's willingness to build sea raiders for the Confederacy, however, seemed to invalidate her official policy of nonintervention. International law permitted neutrals to build nonnaval craft for belligerents, but it forbade such craft to be "equipped, fitted out, or armed" for fighting. British shipbuilders evaded this restriction by allowing apparently inoffensive hulls to "escape" to obscure and unpoliced ports, there to take on guns and munitions. All told, eighteen such "brigands of the sea" (*Alabama* was the most successful of them) preyed on northern shipping. Union threats in 1863 to loose a "flood of privateers" against Britain's nominally neutral trade had the desired effect. No new Confederate raiders were launched; but the American merchant marine did not recover until World War I from the blows of those already at sea.

By 1863 an air of caution had taken hold in France as well, where Napoleon III had dreams of reinstating a monarchy in Mexico, to which the Confederates might look for help. Maximilian of Austria, a puppet of Napoleon's, actually was placed at the head of Mexico's government soon after French army units had taken over Mexico City in June 1863. But thereafter he received scant French support, and when Maximilian was captured and executed by Mexican rebels in June 1867, the French acquiesced quietly in his extinction.

### The North in wartime

The conduct of the war, of course, was the overwhelming civil as well as military responsibility of Lincoln's government. Yet the Republican party had also made many civil commitments that had nothing to do with the war, and many party leaders were eager to meet these commitments while the South was out of the Union.

Thus the Republican Congress soon enacted the following measures: (1) In 1861, to satisfy the protectionist interests, it passed the Morrill Tariff, which raised duties to their 1846 levels, from which they soared steadily during and after the war. (2) In 1862 Congress voted to build the long-debated transcontinental railroad over a central route and to help finance it with lavish grants of public lands and generous cash loans. (3) In 1863, with revisions in 1864, Congress created a national banking system congenial to northern capitalists.

Nor did Republican leaders neglect their free-soil supporters. The Homestead Act passed in May 1862 made available to adult "citizens of the United States" (meaning whites), and to those who declared their intention of becoming citizens, 160 acres of the public domain. The land itself was free of charge, but prompt "settlement and cultivation" of the land was required by the act. Only men who had borne arms against the United States were explicitly excluded. Farmers also benefited from the Morrill Land Grant Act of July 1862, the result of a long campaign led by Jonathan B. Turner, an Illinois educational and agricultural reformer. This act donated public lands to the states and territories to support colleges where agriculture, and mechanical arts, and military science became the staples of the curriculum.

After a short depression in 1861–1862 caused by the loss of $300 million in uncollectible southern debts and uncertainty about the war, the North enjoyed a substantial boom. Historians have questioned the role of the war in stimulating general economic growth in the North; but it cannot be denied that the splurge of government war buying in particular gave a great impetus to the expansion and mechanization of agriculture, the production of shoes and other apparel, and the manufacture of munitions. "Shoddy" millionaires made fortunes foisting off on the government much useless material. Other millionaires of the future—Rockefeller, Carnegie, Mellon, Morgan—all laid the foundations of their huge fortunes in wartime business activity.

Wartime prosperity had its harsh aspects, of course. Industrial wages, for example, rose far more slowly than living costs, causing much hardship in cities where food speculators flourished. Families living on fixed incomes were especially hurt by the wartime inflation. Yet few northerners suffered the privations that became all but universal in the Confederacy.

Despite the boom, Lincoln's government had a difficult time financing the war, partly because it failed to realize how long the war would last. Secretary of the Treasury Chase's monetary doctrines did not help matters.

Chase distrusted debt and paper money, but when the heavy excise taxes and even the income tax imposed in 1861 at his behest failed to provide the needed revenue, he was compelled to resort to both. After early failures, by 1863 he had sold $500 million in bonds to almost a million persons. Chase's later campaigns proved less successful, and since, in any case, the government needed more revenue than could be raised by borrowing, in 1862 Chase was obliged to begin printing paper money. That year and the next, the Treasury issued certificates soon known as "greenbacks," to the amount of $450 million. Unsupported by gold, these certificates nevertheless were made legal tender for domestic debts. By the summer of 1864, when Union armies were still in straits, greenbacks had fallen to their low of 39 cents on the gold dollar. Thereafter, when Union bonds began to sell well again, no more paper money was issued, and the greenbacks' value rose.

Despite the sizable emigration from Europe to the North during the war, shortages of manpower hurt the Union military effort at certain junctures almost as much as they hurt the Confederacy. By March 1863 conscription could no longer be put off, and that month, almost a full year after the Confederacy's measure, Congress voted the first Union draft. Far from helping the manpower situation, the wording of the act lit a torch to inflammable social discontent. One of its provisions permitted a man to escape military service simply by paying $300 to the authorities, leaving them with the responsibility of finding substitutes ready to serve for a bounty. Clearly the poor were going to be saddled with the rich man's duty in a struggle, it seemed, only to elevate the black worker.

Minor riots protesting the discriminatory measure occurred in numerous towns. In Boston, several would-be rioters were shot dead after stoning troops there. Democratic Governor Horatio Seymour of New York helped turn the protest in New York City into a violent disturbance of major proportions by de-

406

nouncing the constitutionality as well as the unwisdom of the draft on the eve of the first drawing of the names, July 11. On July 12, the city's papers printed the names of early draftees, and the next day, and for three days following, mobs reaching 50,000 in number so terrorized New York that federal troops had to be withdrawn from the battlefield to quell the violence. The leading perpetrators were poor Irish-American workingmen, themselves heavily discriminated against for their Catholicism. Some of them were striking longshoremen whose jobs the city's free Negroes had filled, and black homes and churches became their principal targets. Fires roaring out of control are estimated to have destroyed buildings worth $1.5 million. At least a dozen people were killed and hundreds wounded in the melee. As in the Confederacy, the Union draft furnished comparatively few soldiers. But by prompting tens of thousands of young men to enlist voluntarily to avoid the brand of "conscript," it helped build up the fighting forces.

## The progress of emancipation

If Lee, before Antietam, and again before Gettysburg (see p. 409), yearned to end the war's slaughter by breaking the North's morale through invasion, Lincoln, as the dreary reports from the battlefields indicated no release from the dreadful stalemate, yearned to end it through political action. That, no doubt, is what he meant when he said that "military necessity" required the Emancipation Proclamation of January 1, 1863. "Military necessity" was a phrase that the pertinacity of the abolitionists themselves first made popular and palatable as the proper ground for emancipation. It also offered, in Lincoln's eyes, perhaps the only constitutional justification for the Proclamation. But he used the phrase for more than merely expedient or technical reasons.

From the day he took office Lincoln had "struggled," as he said, against every kind of

pressure, religious, journalistic, political, personal, to declare the slaves free without compensating their owners and without undertaking to "colonize" freed Negroes outside the country. Even had he sympathized with such demands, the sensitivity of slaveholding border states within the Union, not to speak of northern sentiment in general, would have constrained him to hold back. "On the news of General Frémont having actually issued deeds of manumission" in Missouri in August 1861, Lincoln declared, "a whole company of our volunteers threw down their arms and disbanded."

As the fighting spread in the border states and in the South itself, and increasing numbers of blacks sought the security of Union lines, generals in the field still were left more or less to their own discretion in dealing with them until in March 1862 Congress adopted "an additional article of war" forbidding officers, on pain of dismissal from the service, from using any of their men to return fugitive slaves to their owners. In August 1862 the War Department issued the first specific authorization for the recruitment of fugitive slaves as soldiers. This authorization, although of very limited application, was accompanied by the request that it "must never see daylight because it is so much in advance of public opinion."

Following the First Confiscation Act of August 1861, Congress also added more steps to the ladder of freedom independent of the armed forces. In April 1862 it passed and Lincoln signed a measure abolishing slavery in the District of Columbia. Under this act, former owners were to be paid, on the average, $300 per slave. In June that year Congress, with Lincoln's consent, also abolished slavery in United States territories, with no compensation granted. In July, Congress adopted the so-called Second Confiscation Act, providing for the conviction for treason of all persons engaged in rebellion, "or who shall in any way give aid ... thereto," and including as among its penalties the stipulation that "all slaves" of such persons "shall be forever free of their servitude." Lincoln prepared a veto message on a technicality; but when Congress removed it, he signed the Act.

By then Lincoln had already failed in his own first effort as Chief Executive to use emancipation as an instrument to end the war and restore the Union. This effort was made in March 1862, when he proposed to Congress that both houses adopt a joint resolution offering to "any state which may adopt gradual abolishment of slavery, . . . pecuniary aid . . . to compensate" it for the "change of system." His object was to wean the border states from their attachment to the "institution." In his message to Congress, Lincoln explained his thinking:

> The leaders of the existing insurrection entertain the hope that this government will ultimately be forced to acknowledge the independence of some part of the disaffected region, and that all the slave States north of such part will then say, "the Union for which we have struggled being already gone, we now choose to go with the Southern section." To deprive them of this hope substantially ends the rebellion, and the initiation of emancipation completely deprives them of it as to all the States initiating it.

In Congress, border state votes helped defeat Lincoln's proposal. When his personal appeal to such states' leaders to free their slaves and save the Union failed, Lincoln, as a last peaceful recourse, decided to admonish the slave states to return to the Union or see their slaves freed. For this purpose he immediately began work on his so-called preliminary emancipation proclamation, which he was prevailed upon by the Cabinet to withhold from the public at least until word from the battlefield improved. He was unwilling to wait beyond Antietam in September 1862, and on September 22 he read to the Cabinet a new draft of a proclamation, which the papers published the next day.

In this preliminary plan Lincoln said that at the next meeting of Congress in December he would recommend the enactment "of a practical measure" offering to *all* slave states not then in rebellion against the United States and having "voluntarily adopt[ed] immediate, or gradual abolishment of slavery within their limits," the same type of "pecuniary aid" as he had offered the border states in March. He also promised to continue his efforts to "colo-

nize persons of African descent, with their consent." On January 1, 1863, the September proclamation went on, he would designate which states still were in rebellion, and in them, "all persons held as slaves . . . shall be then, thenceforward, and forever free," with no compensation whatever. Moreover, "the military and naval authority" of the United States would make no effort to suppress any attempts slaves may then make to effect their freedom; on the contrary, this authority would do whatever necessary to shelter the slaves' efforts.

Conservatives in the North, sick of the military stalemate and fearful that any tampering with slavery would only prolong the South's resistance, registered their disapproval of the preliminary emancipation proclamation in the fall elections of 1862, when the Democrats cut deeply into the Republican majority in the House and won the governorship in New York. The Radicals, on the other hand, deplored Lincoln's tortuous and tolerant maneuverings and demanded that he get on with the "revolutionary struggle" he abhorred.

Lincoln, nevertheless, held to his deliberate course. Following the elections, in accordance with his announced plan, he urged Congress in his second annual message on December 1, 1862, to adopt an amendment to the Constitution providing that each slave state which abolished slavery "any time before the 1st day of January, 1900, shall receive compensation from the United States"; but only those not in rebellion against the United States on January 1, 1863, might participate in this offer. In line with the election returns, Congress rebuffed the President. More than that, a Radical congressional delegation proceeded to the White House to demand a Cabinet reshuffling which, according to Lincoln's friend, Senator Browning of Illinois, was to transform that body into a thoroughly Radical unit to run the war from the Executive Department the way the Committee on the Conduct of the War, in Congress (see p. 398), wanted it run. Lincoln managed to turn the tables on his visitors, effected the resignation of the Radical leader Chase from the Cabinet, and cried, "Now I can ride!"

On January 1, 1863, the "full period of one hundred days" of grace since his September announcement having expired with no takers among the rebellious commonwealths (they, in fact, viewed the proclamation as little short of an invitation to slave revolts and a servile war), Lincoln issued his final Emancipation Proclamation:

> I, Abraham Lincoln, . . . in time of actual armed rebellion against the . . . United States, and as a fit and necessary war measure for suppressing said rebellion, do . . . order and declare that all persons held as slaves within . . . states and parts of states wherein the people . . . are . . . in rebellion . . . are and henceforward shall be free. . . . And I hereby enjoin upon the people so declared to be free to abstain from all violence, unless in necessary self-defense. . . . And I further declare . . . that such persons . . . will be received into the armed service of the United States.

*Negro troops under General Wild freeing slaves in North Carolina. Woodcut from Harper's Weekly, January 23, 1864.*

The proclamation neither freed any slaves nor shortened the war. But it insured the death of slavery when the war was won.

## V  To Appomattox

### The long road to Gettysburg

After Antietam, observing that McClellan had the "slows," Lincoln replaced him with General Ambrose E. Burnside, who quickly proved at Fredericksburg in December 1862 that he was far worse than his predecessor. In January 1863, Lincoln replaced Burnside with General Joseph Hooker. "My plans are perfect," announced "Fighting Joe" in the spring of 1863, "and when I start to carry them out, may God have mercy on General Lee, for I will have none." Hooker decided to feign a movement that would draw Lee from his strong Fredericksburg entrenchments. This tactic worked well, but when Hooker early in May caught up with Lee at Chancellors-

ville, he, like so many of his predecessors, lost his nerve and once again almost lost his army.

Victory at Chancellorsville cost Lee 12,000 men. Worse, it had taken the life of his flaming field commander, Stonewall Jackson. Worse still, Lee thought he now saw the path open to an invasion of the North itself and to final victory. When Davis refused to withdraw men from the western theater to support his grand assault, Lee decided to plunge ahead with the nearly 75,000 men in his Virginia command. "General Lee," one of his lieutenants said at this time, "believed that the Army of Northern Virginia, as it then existed, could accomplish anything." He was wrong.

Lee began his fateful march toward Harris-

burg, Pennsylvania, on the strategic Susquehanna River, June 3, 1863. Hooker, unchas-
tened, thought he detected in Lee's departure
yet one more, one more chance to move on
Richmond. But Lincoln, grown wiser with the
years, undertook to set him straight: "Lee's
army, not Richmond, is your true objective
point. If he comes toward the upper Potomac,
follow on his flank and on his inside track,
shortening your lines while he lengthens his."
By June 29 Lee's advance corps had reached a
point a mere 10 miles from Harrisburg—the
deepest penetration of the war. Concerned,
now, about the lengthening of his communications, Lee began to look for favorable ter-

rain onto which to lure and confront the
"Yanks." By then Hooker had been replaced
by "the old snapping turtle," General George
Gordon Meade, who was making his own
plans to invite attack on favorable ground.
Both generals were to be disappointed. On
June 30 some of Lee's foragers encountered
Meade's most northerly watch at the cross-
roads town of Gettysburg, Pennsylvania, and
on July 1 the Battle of Gettysburg began.

The setting was almost perfect for a fight to
the death, and when, on July 3, the Federals
on Cemetery Ridge had broken Pickett's famous last charge, the great battle had ended.
"Call no council of war. . . . Do not let the
enemy escape," Lincoln wired Meade. But
Meade called a council while Lee made good
his retreat. "Our army held the war in the
hollow of its hand," Lincoln said later, "and
would not close it."

Many months after the memorable battle,
the bodies of thousands who there "gave their
lives" still lay unburied. The degrading sight
led to a call for a national cemetery in their
honor. It was at the dedication ceremonies for
this cemetery, on November 19, 1863, that
Lincoln delivered the Gettysburg Address,
promising "that these dead shall not have died
in vain."

### Grant takes command

On July 4, 1863, on the heels of the
victory at Gettysburg, came the thrilling report of as great a Union triumph in the West.
After a year of struggle, Grant had taken
Vicksburg, "the Gibraltar of the Mississippi."
Four days later Port Hudson, the last Confederate stronghold on the river, surrendered.
Then it was that Lincoln wrote his memorable
words: "The Father of Waters again goes
unvexed to the sea."

Grant's victory in the western theater focused the attention of the entire nation on
this West Point graduate, a veteran of the Mexican War who had resigned his army cap-
taincy in 1854 the better to support his family.

410

PENNSYLVANIA

Harrisburg

Chambersburg • Lee

Waynesboro • GETTYSBURG
July 1-3

Hagerstown — Meade

Potomac R.

W. VA. MARYLAND
Martinsburg •
Lee • Frederick •

Harpers
Ferry

Fredericksburg
to Gettysburg,
1863

• Winchester Leesburg •

Shenandoah R.

• Front Royal — Hooker
June
Washington
Alexandria • D.C.

VIRGINIA

• Manassas

• Warrenton

Rappahannock R.

BRANDY STA.
June 9

Aquia Cr.

Potomac R.

Jackson Hooker
May 1-4
CHANCELLORSVILLE
Lee Burnside
Rapidan R. Dec. 13, '62
FREDERICKSBURG

Grant possessed no glamor, but he would soon reveal his own brand of greatness. His "art of war" best sums up his military theory: "The art of war is simple enough. Find out where your enemy is. Get him as soon as you can. Strike at him as hard as you can and keep moving on."

After Vicksburg, one Confederate army and part of the Confederacy itself were isolated west of the Mississippi. But another Confederate army commanded by General Braxton Bragg was still operating in central Tennessee. In September 1863, under Grant's orders, General William Rosencrans began to pursue Bragg in earnest, but after being outmaneuvered at Chickamauga, Rosencrans's army found itself bottled up in nearby Chattanooga. To raise the siege, Grant called on Union armies from the East and the West, and on November 25 these combined forces won a spectacular victory at Chattanooga, thereby splitting the Confederacy north and south as well as east and west.

On February 26, 1864, Congress revived the highest office in the army, the post of lieutenant-general. On March 1 Lincoln elevated Grant to that rank, and on March 9 Grant arrived in Washington for the first time in his life to meet the President.

His commission as supreme commander of all Union forces received, Grant got right down to work on the victory program. In the West his forces held all important communication centers and could lay waste the interior of the Confederacy from Mississippi to Virginia. In the East, back in the vicinity of Fredericksburg, Lee had rebuilt the army he had been allowed to salvage at Gettysburg into a formidable force, once again capable of menacing Washington. Grant's plan was for the Army of the Potomac, itself rebuilt and now directly under himself and Meade, so to occupy Lee's army that it could not link up with any other rebel force—and to bleed it daily in the bargain. While the Army of the Potomac thus was to cling to the Confederacy's leg, as it were, Sherman's army was to push eastward from Tennessee into Georgia and take Atlanta, skinning the Confederacy's body as it went. Franz Sigel, at the same time, was to operate in the Shenandoah Valley and protect Washington from that direction; while still another army, under "Ben" Butler at Fortress Monroe, was to repeat McClellan's peninsular maneuver and strike at Richmond, which Lee was to be kept from defending.

The first reports of Grant's campaigns were disheartening. Throughout May 1864, the Army of the Potomac, under Meade and Grant himself, engaged Lee in murderous but indecisive battles on the route to Richmond from the North. The enormous federal casualties in the Wilderness and at Cold Harbor—Grant is said to have lost a colossal 55,000 men in this first month of his campaign—aroused strong resentment in the Union, and newspapers began to speak of the general as "the butcher." But Lincoln stood by him. "I have just read your dispatch," he wrote to Grant after Cold Harbor. "I begin to see it. You will succeed. God bless you all." Grant himself, however, had begun to have second thoughts. On June 12, he decided to disengage his army from Lee's, to swing down to the peninsula, and with Butler's assistance to get at Richmond once more from the South. Butler botched his orders sufficiently for the rebels to block Grant at Petersburg, 20 miles below Richmond, long enough for Lee to move his own forces to this front. Nine months later, in March 1865, Grant's siege of Petersburg still was on.

In July 1864, to help lift this siege, Lee sought to reenact Stonewall Jackson's old diversion of 1862: to menace Washington by way of the Shenandoah Valley. But when Grant placed his top cavalryman, General Philip Sheridan, in command in the valley on August 7, his orders were: "Nothing should be left to invite the enemy to return. . . . If the war is to last another year we want the Shenandoah Valley to remain a barren waste." By March 1865 Sheridan had carried out these orders with the thoroughness of a Sherman. "A crow would have had to carry its rations," he said, "if it had flown across the valley." Sheridan then joined Grant for the Richmond campaign.

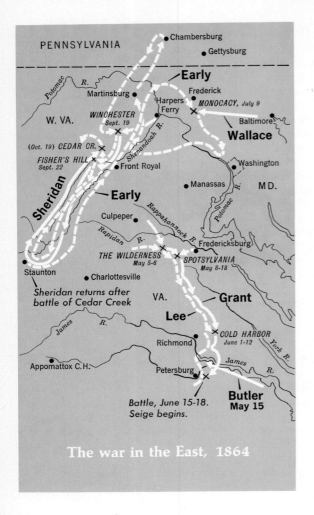

The war in the East, 1864

Since May 1864 Sherman himself, with three veteran armies in the West, had been slowly forcing the redoubtable Joseph E. Johnston toward Atlanta. On September 3 Sherman wired Washington, "So Atlanta is ours, and fairly won." On November 16, having left Atlanta, as he said, "smouldering and in ruins," Sherman and his "bummers" began their "picnic" march to the sea. "To realize what war is," Sherman said, "one should follow in our tracks."

### The end in sight

Sherman's victory at Atlanta in September 1864 had more than military signifi-

cance. Early in the year the politicians had begun to prepare for the presidential elections in November, and Lincoln, for the good of the Republican party, had been urged not to seek renomination. By the time of the party convention at Baltimore in June, however, his Radical opponents had failed to agree among themselves on a candidate and his loyal backers put him across. To bolster the ticket they named the "War Democrat," Andrew Johnson of Tennessee, for Vice-President. In fact Lincoln and Johnson ran under a "Union party" label.

When the Democrats met at Chicago in August, a hodgepodge (to quote Gideon Welles) of "Whigs, Democrats, Know-Nothings, Conservatives, War men and Peace men, with a crowd of Secessionists and traitors to stimulate action," promptly chose General McClellan as their nominee after the bid of Governor Seymour of New York fizzled out. The "war failure" plank in the Democratic platform declared that hostilities should cease and that the "Federal Union of the States" should be reestablished on the old basis. This was nothing less than an armistice offer. McClellan, after serious soul searching, decided to reject this plank and to commit himself to continuing the war. At the same time, some of Lincoln's advisers had begun to press him to make peaceful overtures to Richmond. Then came the stirring news of Atlanta's fall and a revival of confidence, not only in Lincoln's generals but in the President himself. In November Lincoln won a smashing victory. With 55 percent of the popular vote, he outdistanced McClellan in the electoral college, 212 to 21. Victory, not negotiated peace, now became the military theme as well.

While Sherman and his men were gouging their way through Georgia, George Thomas and his subordinate, John Schofield, had been left to clean up in the West. Their objective was the Confederate Army commanded by General John Bell Hood, who had replaced "Joe" Johnston just in time to yield Atlanta to Sherman. Having saved his army then, Hood

412

lost little time turning back to try to regain Tennessee, but on December 15 Thomas annihilated him at Nashville in one of the most crushing defeats of the war. Five days later Savannah on the Georgia coast fell to Sherman. By his own estimate, Sherman's invasion had cost Georgia some $100 million in military resources, $80 million of it "simple waste and destruction."

From Savannah, in February 1865, Sherman headed north toward the "hellhole of secession," South Carolina, where, as he said, "the devil himself could not restrain his men." By February 17, the "pitiless march" had brought him to Columbia, South Carolina's capital, and soon, whether by accident or design, one of the most beautiful cities in the country was consumed in flames. Charleston, outflanked by Sherman, was occupied the next day by Union forces blockading the harbor after the defending rebels had fled. Sherman, meanwhile, pounded on into North Carolina, where on February 22 Wilmington, the very last of the Atlantic ports of the blockade runners, was evacuated, like Charleston, by the rebel defenders and taken by Union harbor contingents.

On March 19 Sherman's progress was checked at Bentonville, North Carolina, by a considerable force commanded, once again, by Joseph E. Johnston, whom Lee had restored to service. Johnston yielded Bentonville to Sherman's larger army after a fight, but the contact with the Confederates convinced Sherman that it would be best to leave Richmond and Lee to Grant and Sheridan while he kept the capable Johnston away.

Gettysburg, Vicksburg, Atlanta, the humili-

**413**

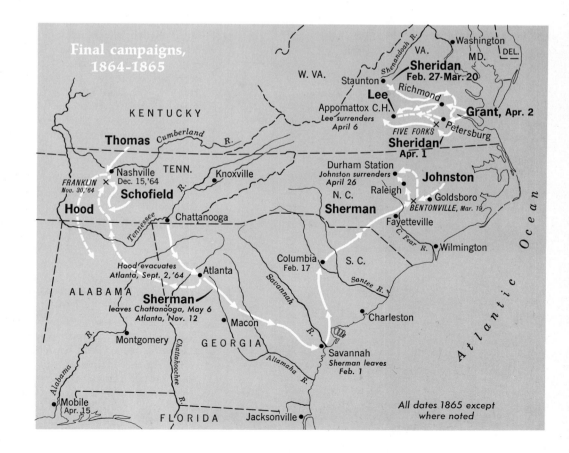

Final campaigns, 1864–1865

GAF Corporation

*Grant after Vicksburg*
*in the Mathew Brady photograph*
*which captured the worn look*
*of the determined campaigner.*

*Lee leaving the McClean farmhouse,*
*in the drawing by A. R. Waud, April 1865.*

Library of Congress

ating failure of cotton diplomacy, the bruising wall of the blockade—none of these had quite managed to dissipate the Confederacy's material capacity for war. But before Sherman's devastation the southern spirit drooped. As early as September 1864 Davis acknowledged that "two thirds of our men are absent . . . most of them absent without leave." Soon after, he began negotiations for a peace conference on terms capable of "firing the Southern heart." But no such terms remained. On March 25, 1865, the Confederacy took the fateful step of recruiting men "irrespective of color," slaves "who might volunteer to fight for their freedom." But even this measure as finally passed offered the Negro nothing and came far too late to lift Lee's sinking heart.

By then, although he had lost opportunity after opportunity to crack Petersburg's defenses, Grant had made progress. The once nearly even opponents numbered now 115,000 "blues" to 54,000 "grays." The time had come for Lee to pull out of his hateful trenches while he still had so formidable a force, try to join up with Johnston in North Carolina, and carry on the war from there.

Under cover of darkness on April 2, the Confederate exodus began. On April 3, while Davis and his government fled from their capital, exposed at last by the evacuation of the Petersburg front, contingents of Grant's army poured into Richmond. Grant and Sheridan themselves pursued Lee. On April 7, his path to North Carolina irretrievably sealed off, Lee asked for terms. On April 9, impeccable in a new uniform, he met the mud-spattered Grant in the McClean farmhouse at Appomattox Court House, a village some 95 miles west of Richmond. "Give them the most liberal terms," Lincoln had ordered Grant. "Let them have their horses to plow with, and, if you like, their guns to shoot crows with. I want no one punished." Grant complied.

On April 26, Johnston surrendered his army to Sherman at Durham Station, North Carolina. On May 10, the fleeing Davis was caught in Georgia and imprisoned for two years.

414

Brady-Hardy Collection, Library of Congress

*Lincoln's funeral
on Pennsylvania Avenue, Washington, D.C.*

### Lincoln's death

When news of Richmond's fall reached Washington on April 3, the city exploded with joy, and for the next eleven days the holiday mood continued. Then, on April 14, Good Friday, a fanatic, John Wilkes Booth, shot Lincoln as the President sat in his box at Ford's Theatre in Washington watching a performance of *Our American Cousin*. At 7:20 the next morning Lincoln died.

The victorious President had charged the nation to act "with malice towards none, with charity for all." He had acknowledged the guilt of the North as well as the South for "the bondsman's two hundred and fifty years of unrequited toil." At first Robert E. Lee would not credit the news of Lincoln's death. Then, on that Sunday, he told a visitor that he had "surrendered as much to [Lincoln's] goodness as to Grant's artillery." Now Lincoln and "goodness" were removed, with what consequences Herman Melville foretold when he wrote in "The Martyr":

*He lieth in his blood—
    The father in his face;*

*They have killed him, the Forgiver—
    The Avenger takes his place. . . .*

*There is sobbing of the strong,
    And a pall upon the land;
But the People in their weeping
    Bare the iron hand:
Beware the People weeping
    When they bare the iron hand.*

## For further reading

The best modern study of the Civil War era is that by Allan Nevins. In addition to the volumes cited for Chapter Fifteen, see *The War for the Union: The Improvised War 1861-1862* (1959), *War Becomes Revolution 1862-1863* (1960), and *The Organized War 1863-1864* (1971). J. F. Rhodes, *History of the United States, 1850-1877* (7 vols., 1906) remains invaluable for many special subjects. A shorter scholarly survey is J. G Randall and David Donald, *The Civil War and Reconstruction* (rev. ed., 1961). See also David Donald and others, *Divided We Fought* (1956), a pictorial history with excellent text on military events. The strong national feeling in the North is well documented in G. M. Frederickson, *The Inner Civil War: Northern Intellectuals and the Crisis of the Union* (1965). J. C. Andrews, *The North Reports the Civil War* (1955), and *The South Reports the Civil War* (1970), are exceptionally revealing. M. M. Boatner III, *The Civil War Dictionary* (1959), is an invaluable reference work.

Northern industrial potential is measured in E. D. Fite, *Social and Industrial Conditions in the North during the Civil War* (1910). J. C. Schwab, *The Confederate States of America* (1901), covers financial and industrial matters in the South. See also F. E. Vandiver,

*Ploughshares into Swords: Josiah Gorgas and Confederate Ordnance* (1952). Thomas Weber, *The Northern Railroads in the Civil War 1861-1865* (1952), and R. C. Black III, *The Railroads of the Confederacy* (1952), are scholarly accounts. Ralph Andreano, ed., *The Economic Impact of the American Civil War* (1962), and D. T. Gilchrist and W. D. Lewis, eds., *Economic Change in the Civil War Era* (1965), present stimulating essays on the war and industrial growth. E. P. Oberholtzer, *Jay Cooke, Financier of the Civil War* (2 vols., 1907), is good on bond sales. R. P. Sharkey, *Money, Class & Party, An Economic Study of Civil War and Reconstruction* (1959), offers a more general financial analysis.

Clement Eaton, *A History of the Southern Confederacy* (1954), is the best general survey. See also C. P. Roland, *The Confederacy* (1960). A. D. Kirwan, ed., *The Confederacy* (1959), is a "social and political history in documents." A. H. Stephens, *Recollections* (1910), offers a remarkable inside view by the Confederate Vice-President. On the Confederate President and his administration, see Hudson Strode, *Jefferson Davis* (2 vols., 1955, 1959); and R. W. Patrick, *Jefferson Davis and His Cabinet* (1944). F. L. Owsley, *State Rights in the Confederacy* (1925), is valuable.

Of the many books on Lincoln as President, Carl Sandburg, *Abraham Lincoln: The War Years* (4 vols., 1939), remains preeminent. The following also are recommended: J. G. Randall, *Lincoln: the President* (4 vols., 1945-1955)—the last volume completed by R. N. Current after Randall's death; and B. P. Thomas, *Abraham Lincoln* (1952), a one-volume life. R. P. Basler, ed., *The Collected Works of Abraham Lincoln* (9 vols., 1953-1955), offers information and insights not available elsewhere. David Donald, *Lincoln Reconsidered* (1956), is suggestive. On Lincoln and his Cabinet, see *The Diary of Gideon Welles* (3 vols., 1911); David Donald, ed., *Inside Lincoln's Cabinet: The Civil War Diaries of Salmon P. Chase* (1954); and B. P. Thomas and H. B. Hyman, *Stanton: The Life and Times of Lincoln's Secretary of War* (1962).

Lincoln's troubled relations with his party are discussed in T. H. Williams, *Lincoln and the Radicals* (1941); H. J. Carman and R. H. Luthin, *Lincoln and the Patronage* (1943); and H. B. Hesseltine, *Lincoln and the War Governors* (1948). Copperheadism is described in Wood Gray, *The Hidden Civil War* (1942), and F. L. Klement, *The Copperheads in the Middle West* (1960). J. G. Randall, *Constitutional Problems under Lincoln* (1926), offers a rigorous examination. The role of the abolitionists during the war is presented in J. M. McPherson, *The Struggle for Equality, Abolitionists and the Negro in the Civil War and Reconstruction* (1964). F. M. Brodie, *Thaddeus Stevens* (1959), and David Donald, *Charles Sumner* (1961), are outstanding on

the leading Radicals. J. H. Franklin, *The Emancipation Proclamation* (1963), is the leading monograph on that document. The diplomatic aspects of the war are covered in the general war histories. See also F. L. Owsley, *King Cotton Diplomacy* (1931), and M. B. Duberman, *Charles Francis Adams* (1961), on the Union minister in London.

A vast literature exists on the military aspects of the Civil War. Moving and authoritative accounts of the Union army in the East may be found in four books by Bruce Catton: *Mr. Lincoln's Army* (1951); *Glory Road* (1952); *A Stillness at Appomattox* (1954); and *This Hallowed Ground* (1956). Also recommended are Catton's *Centennial History of the War* (3 vols., 1961-1965) and K. P. Williams, *Lincoln Finds a General: A Military History of the Civil War* (4 vols., 1949-1956). A classic account of the campaigns is *The Personal Memoirs of U. S. Grant* (2 vols., 1885-1886). See also Lloyd Lewis, *Captain Sam Grant* (1950), and its sequels by Bruce Catton, *Grant Moves South* (1960) and *Grant Takes Command* (1969). W. T. Sherman, *Memoirs* (2 vols., 1886), may be supplemented by Lloyd Lewis, *Sherman, Fighting Prophet* (1932). D. S. Freeman, *R. E. Lee, A Biography* (4 vols., 1934-1935) and *Lee's Lieutenants* (3 vols., 1942-1944), are authoritative. An outstanding one-volume life is Clifford Dowdey, *Lee* (1965). Dowdey and L. H. Manarin, eds., *The Wartime Papers of R. E. Lee* (1961), is a rich collection.

For the ordinary man's role in the war, see H. S. Commager, ed., *The Blue and the Gray: The Story of the Civil War as Told by Participants* (2 vols., 1950); and B. I. Wiley, *The Life of Johnny Reb* (1943) and *The Life of Billy Yank* (1952). On the war and the Negro see Benjamin Quarles, *The Negro in the Civil War* (1953); D. T. Cornish, *The Sable Arm: Negro Troops in the Union Army 1861-1865* (1958); B. I. Wiley, *Southern Negroes 1861-1865* (1938), and W. L. Rose, *Rehearsal for Reconstruction* (1964).

Wartime Washington is colorfully described in Margaret Leech, *Reveille in Washington 1860-1865* (1941), and C. M. Green, *Washington, Village and Capital 1800-1878* (1962); wartime Richmond, in A. H. Bill, *The Beleaguered City: Richmond 1861-1865* (1946). Southern civilian life is presented in B. I. Wiley, *The Plain People of the Confederacy* (1943), and C. H. Wesley, *The Collapse of the Confederacy* (1937). The reader should not miss Walt Whitman's *Drum-Taps* (1865) and *Specimen Days* (1875), and Herman Melville's *Battle-Pieces and Other Aspects of the War* (1964 ed.).

PART TWO

*A world power*

Detail of watercolor by Henry Reuterdahl showing the United States
Fleet passing through the Straits of Magellan on tour around the world,
1907-1909. (Courtesy, United States Naval Academy Museum)

# THE RECLAIMED SOUTH

Most of the wars of the nineteenth century, once the great Napoleonic struggle had ended, were limited wars for limited objectives, waged by professional forces, between nations that rarely questioned one another's sovereignty. The wars between the United States and Mexico and the United States and Spain (1898) were such wars. The American Civil War also began as a war for limited objectives, but with the question of sovereignty at its very heart. And it soon engaged an entire people in a struggle for survival. For the Confederacy to succeed, the Union had to be destroyed. For the Union to survive, the Confederacy had to be obliterated. The Union survived. The men in blue, said one disillusioned southerner late in 1865, "destroyed everything which the most infernal Yankee ingenuity could devise means to destroy; hands, heart, fire, gunpowder, and behind everything the spirit of hell, were the agencies which they used."

Two days after Appomattox, three days before his assassination, Lincoln, on April 11, 1865, said of the South:

*Unlike the case of a war between independent nations, there is no organized organ for us to treat with. No one man has authority to give up the rebellion for any other man. We must simply begin with, and mould from, disorganized and discordant elements.*

Lincoln's view of the realities of the southern situation was consistent with his whole theory of secession, rebellion, and reclamation. Lincoln held from the outset that the Union was indestructible and that states could not break away from it even though their people might rebel. Rebellious citizens could be restored to citizenship by presidential pardon and then could set about manning new governments in states which themselves had never been defunct. This view became the foundation of Lincoln's program for reconstruction by the *executive* department.

In designing his program, Lincoln calculatingly closed his eyes to one overwhelming fact: the war, besides devastating parts of the South, had washed away the slave foundations of southern society. The Radicals knew this very well; in fact its accomplishment had been their central objective. After the war, they aimed to rebuild southern society around the equality of freedman and white, come what may. Lincoln's Radical Secretary of the Treasury, Salmon P. Chase, stated it clearly to the President: "It will be, hereafter, counted equally a crime & a folly if the colored loyalists of the rebel states shall be left to the control of restored rebels, not likely, in that case, to be either wise or just, until taught both wisdom and justice by new calamities." According to Radicals in Congress, the rebel states had forfeited all connection with the Union and were reduced to the status of territories. In seeking statehood once again, they came under the jurisdiction, not of the executive but of the *legislative* department in whose hands territorial affairs lay.

Lincoln, an ex-Whig, had not forgotten the strength this nationalist party had found among business leaders and professional men in the Old South. By his policy of "malice toward none; charity for all," as he said in his second inaugural in March 1865, he hoped to draw surviving southern Whigs to the Republican standard. By entrusting the freedman's fate to these new "Republicans," the party would be strengthened nationally. If he could swing his old project of black colonization overseas, a project he never surrendered (see p. 424), so much the better. The Radicals, on the other hand, saw the southern Negro vote as the only means of gaining that section for the Republicans and insuring their party's national character and strength. To protect the freedman from southern pressure, the Radicals also tried to develop an educational program to nourish his mental independence and a land program to support his economic liberty.

The failure of Radical Reconstruction is no indication that Lincoln's alternative was preferable. The evidence is overwhelming that the South's attitude toward the ex-slave was as unregenerate just after the war as it was after Radical Reconstruction was formally abandoned in 1877. A Virginia judge reported the observation of a friend of his in 1866: "Sooner than see the colored people raised to a legal and political equality, the Southern people would prefer their total annihilation." Radical Reconstruction postponed the legal and political annihilation of the freedman for a decade, and it laid the legal and political foundation for the improvement of his condition when he found his own leaders in the twentieth century.

# I The conquered section

The Civil War ravaged the fighting families of the North as well as the South; and it was difficult even for the most conciliatory Unionist to forget for long "the patriot hosts that had fallen on fearful battlefields." Yet the North, as Whitman stated it, had its great compensation:

*The ship is anchor'd safe and sound, its*
*    voyage closed and done,*
*From fearful trip the victor ship comes in*
*    with object won;*
*        Exult, O shores, and ring, O bells!*

The North had more mundane compensations as well. Wartime prosperity, to be sure, did not extend to all lines of business. The cotton textile industry, for example, broke down; the merchant marine and the shipbuilding industry suffered losses from which they did not recover until the wars of the twentieth century; railroad building was sharply retarded. Yet it seemed to contemporaries and it seems to us that the $4 billion in direct wartime expenditures gave a fillip to enterprise, an impetus to industrialization. Victory, moreover, brought its own reward. As John Sherman wrote in 1865 to his brother, General William T. Sherman, "The close of the war with our resources unimpaired gives an elevation, a scope to the ideas of leading capitalists, far higher than anything ever undertaken in this country before. They talk of millions as confidently as formerly of thousands."

Direct Confederate expenditures for the war exceeded $2 billion, and expenditures by the individual rebel states added many millions more to the total cost. But in the defeated South, in contrast with the victorious North, these outlays became an utter loss. A few southerners managed to accumulate capital during the war—some by running cotton through the northern blockade or by preying profitably on Yankee shipping, others by demanding gold or goods from their neighbors instead of Confederate paper money in payment for food, clothing, and farm supplies. But most southerners were impoverished. The planters' $2.5 billion investment in slaves had vanished. Their land, worth $1.5 billion in 1860, was evaluated at but half that amount ten years later. The section's $1 billion in banking capital had been wiped out; and worse, the credit system on which the staple planters had been dependent for all essential purchases was paralyzed. At the end of the war, each of the boys in blue went home at government expense with about $235 in his pocket and with every hope of returning to the fruitful land, to business, or to school. The boys in gray turned homeward with their pockets empty, their prospects grim. Some of Lee's soldiers, writes Dixon Wecter, "had to ask for handouts on the road home, with nothing to exchange for bread save the unwelcome news of Appomattox."

Fighting occurred only in relatively few sections of the South, but these were devastated. Writing in September 1865 of Columbia, South Carolina, a traveler said it was "a wilderness of ruins." Nor had rural areas escaped. Five years after the war an English traveler described the Tennessee Valley country:

*The trail of war is visible throughout the valle, in burnt-up gin-houses, ruined bridges, mills, and factories ... and in large tracts of once cultivated land stripped of every vestige of fencing. The roads, long neglected, are in disorder, and ... in many places ... impassable.*

Southern river ports and coastal harbors were put out of commission. Levees were destroyed or neglected, and floods washed out miles of farm land.

But the South lost even more in nonmilitary damage.

*Weak their hearts from too much sorrow,*
*Weak their frames from want and toil . . .*

So ran the lament of southern women left with responsibility for land, buildings, tools, and machinery when even boys ran off to fight. Every third horse and mule had died, wandered off, or been taken by Union or Confederate foragers, so that after the war men and women often harnessed themselves to the old plows to prepare fields for planting. Southern factories, in turn, frequently forsaken for want of materials to make even simple repairs, fell into irretrievable decay.

In the disorganization of southern life, few suffered more than the ex-slaves. As early as 1862 Radicals in Congress had talked seriously of establishing blacks who had sought the shelter of Union lines on land captured by Union forces. Subsequently, on taking over conquered territory, certain Union generals had made land available to ex-slaves on easy terms. Many of the black farmers did well, but little came of the aspirations of the black masses. Eventually, thousands of Negroes were corralled in Union "contraband camps," so flimsy, filthy, and crowded that death from epidemics, exposure, and crime soon claimed one of every four inmates.

When the Emancipation Proclamation of January 1, 1863 sharply focused attention on the plight of freed Negroes, Congress began to consider bills to establish a bureau for their care. Not until March 1865, however, did Congress create, as part of the War Department, the so-called Freedmen's Bureau to operate for but one year after the end of the war. This agency was authorized to issue "provisions, clothing and fuel . . . for . . . desti-tute and suffering refugees and freedmen." It was also empowered to assign up to 40 acres of abandoned or confiscated land in the Confederacy at a fair rent "to every male citizen, whether refugee or freedman."

At first, the Freedmen's Bureau did nobly. But once the full flush of liberty struck the former slaves, the rate of migration soared and the Bureau became so hard-pressed merely to sustain life that the land program languished. In the summer of 1865, more than 20,000 blacks flocked into Washington, D.C. Greater numbers congregated in Charleston, New Orleans, Memphis, and other southern cities. Their resources sorely diminished by the war, these cities could do little for the newcomers but increase the number and size of their already overtaxed "contraband camps." During the first two postwar years in some camps a third of the freedmen died.

White farmers and planters often fared little better than the blacks. Famine struck many parts of the South as early as 1862, and by 1865, the statewide systems of relief set up during the war years in all the Confederate commonwealths had collapsed in the general ruin. In the first four years after the war the Freedmen's Bureau alone issued almost 21 million rations, 6 million of them to impoverished whites.

Perhaps the heaviest blow to the South was the moral cost of war and defeat. The losses in youth and talent hurt beyond measure. Among the survivors, purpose, morale, and aspiration drooped. In Georgia, in 1865, one reporter noted that "aimless young men in gray, ragged and filthy, seemed, with the downfall of the rebellion . . . to have lost their object in life." "These faces, these faces," cried a visitor to New Orleans in 1873: "One sees them everywhere; on the street, at the theater, in the salon, in the cars; and pauses for a moment struck with the expression of entire despair."

The war crippled all social agencies in the South. Church buildings were demolished, their congregations scattered. Schools and colleges simply ceased to exist. Policemen, sheriffs, courts, judges—the instruments of law enforcement—could scarcely be found. Heart-

421

less bands led by ex-Confederate guerillas like Jesse and Frank James roamed the countryside, refusing to give up the war against the victors and their society.

**422**

Not until 1877 did the South produce a cotton crop as large as that of 1860, and not until 1879 did cotton exports to Britain reach the level of 1859. Much is sometimes made of postwar southern industrialism in smoothing the "road to reunion." Yet as late as 1900, the so-called industrialized New South actually produced a smaller proportion of American manufactures than did the Old South in the year 1860.

## II  Presidential reconstruction

### Lincoln's commitment

Many of those who, like Lincoln, closed their eyes to the inescapable challenge of the slaveless South were encouraged to do so by the official Union objective in the war, to which Lincoln himself adhered to the end of his life. This objective was set forth as follows in the Crittenden Resolution adopted by the House on July 22, 1861, with but two dissenting votes:

*This war is not waged . . . for any purpose . . . but to defend and maintain the supremacy of the Constitution and to preserve the Union, with all the dignity, equality, and rights of the several States unimpaired; and . . . as soon as these objects are accomplished the war ought to cease.*

Three days after the House acted, the Senate, with but five dissenting votes, adopted the virtually identical Johnson Resolutions. True to the Crittenden criteria, Lincoln in 1862, when much of Tennessee, Louisiana, and North Carolina had fallen to Union arms, hastened to appoint military governors to shepherd these states back to the shelter of the Constitution, as prescribed in Art. IV, Sec. 4 (see Appendix), and nothing more.

One of Lincoln's shining virtues was his flexibility; and many of those who mourn his passing at the very moment when reconstruction of the South had to be undertaken in earnest see in his loss the cause of subsequent extremism in North and South alike. Lincoln showed his flexibility in December 1863, when Arkansas and certain other rebel states seemed on the verge of capitulation and a more general reconstruction program was required. On December 8 he issued his Proclamation of Amnesty and Reconstruction, which became known as Lincoln's "ten percent plan." By then, under mounting Radical pressure, Congress had passed the Second Confiscation Act and other antislavery measures (see p. 407), and the President had issued the Emancipation Proclamation. Lincoln adapted the terms of his new proclamation to these *political* realities.

The "ten percent plan" excluded from participation in southern politics all high military and civil officers of the Confederacy or its states and any others who had attempted to return black prisoners of war to slavery. To all other Confederates who would take an oath of loyalty to the Constitution and swear to "abide by all acts of Congress passed during the existing rebellion with reference to slaves, . . . and faithfully support all proclamations of the President . . . having reference to slaves," a general amnesty would be granted by the President and confiscated property other than slaves would be restored. As soon as 10 percent of a state's *1860 electorate* had taken the oath and sworn allegiance to the Union, that state, having thereby gained Executive recognition, could proceed to write a new constitution, elect new state officers, and send members to the United States Congress. The House and Senate, of course, would retain their constitutional privilege of seating or rejecting such members.

Other provisions of this Reconstruction Proclamation, at the same time, disclose how *inflexible* Lincoln was to remain on the *social* realities of the emancipation measures. The "ten percent" proclamation, for example, assured the states to which it applied "that any provision" they may make "in relation to the freed people of such State, . . . which may yet be consistent with their present condition as a laboring, landless, and homeless class, will not be objected to by the national Executive." The proclamation backed down still further: "It is suggested as not improper," Lincoln said, that "subject only to modifications made necessary" by emancipation, "in constructing a loyal State government, . . . the general code of laws, as before the rebellion, be maintained." This was nothing short of an invitation to the reconstructed states to adopt such inflammatory "Black Codes" as those they did exact in 1865 and 1866 (see p. 426).

Two further observations on Lincoln's proclamation are in order: (1) He was at pains to reassure all states that had remained loyal to the Union that the congressional antislavery measures and the Emancipation Proclamation did not yet apply to them. (2) He was also at pains to notify these and the rebel states that Congress could repeal or modify its antislavery measures and that the Supreme Court could nullify them and the Emancipation Proclamation as well.

To make congressional repeal more difficult, Supreme Court nullification impossible, and emancipation itself more general, Radicals in Congress now sought an amendment to the Constitution which would forever abolish slavery throughout the United States. The failure of a joint resolution for this purpose to pass in a Congress in which the South was wholly unrepresented only confirmed Lincoln's skepticism about northern concern for the freedman's welfare.

The proposed amendment promptly became a leading issue in the presidential campaign of 1864, the Republican platform committing the party to "such an amendment as shall terminate and forever prohibit [slavery] . . . within the limits of the jurisdiction of the United States." Yet in August 1864, during the campaign, Lincoln told a conservative critic, "If Jefferson Davis wishes to know what I would do if he were to offer peace and reunion, saying nothing about slavery, let him try me."

Lincoln interpreted his reelection by a large majority in November 1864 as a demand for the amendment, and in the lame-duck Congress that met in December his effective logrolling helped win approval of the proposal on January 31, 1865, when it was sent to the states. Yet a mere three days later, Lincoln, according to his old Whig friend, Alexander H. Stephens, told a peace delegation headed by the Confederate Vice-President, that in his opinion the Emancipation Proclamation freeing the slaves of the South "was a war measure, and . . . as soon as the war ceased, it would be inoperative for the future. It would be held to apply only to such slaves as had come under its operation while it was in active exercise." At that time, at least 3 million blacks were still in bondage in the South.

The Thirteenth Amendment was ratified in December 1865 by the required twenty-seven states, including eight formerly of the Confederacy, which Congress, for other purposes, did not even recognize as states. The leading Radical in the Senate, Charles Sumner of Massachusetts, believed that the unprecedented second section of the Thirteenth Amendment—"Congress shall have power to enforce this article by appropriate legislation"—meant that Congress could enfranchise the ex-slave if, in its judgment, the Negro required the right to vote in order to preserve his freedom. Not many, as yet, even among the Radicals, went along with the Senator.

In his last public address on April 11, 1865, Lincoln dallied with the idea "that the elective franchise" might be "now conferred on the very intelligent" among the colored men, "and on those who serve our cause as soldiers." But for "the great mass of Negroes," as Kenneth M. Stampp writes, "he never abandoned his hope that they could be persuaded to leave the country." One of Lincoln's last efforts at overseas colonization was one of the most disastrous. This occurred early in 1864 when he won the reluctant approval of the government of Haiti to allow certain northern promoters to settle hundreds of freedmen on an island off the Haitian coast. A virtual return to slave conditions under the most ruthless exploitive methods killed half the victims before the rest were brought home.

### The congressional response

Very early in the war, Senator Sumner observed that "Mr. Lincoln's administration acted in superfluous good faith with the Rebels." As the war proceeded, Sumner found few reasons to change his mind; and as the

*"I'm not to blame for being white, sir!"*
*—one of numerous contemporary caricatures of Sumner's pro-Negro inclinations.*

Library of Congress

end neared, he meant to see to it that Lincoln's policy did not cost the Union the fruits of victory. His alter ego in the House, Thad Stevens of Pennsylvania, had championed the black man all his life and was determined that his ideas of social equality, though advanced even for the North, be forced upon the proud planters.

*The whole fabric of southern society [Stevens declared] must be changed. . . . The Southern states have been despotisms, not governments of the people. . . . If the South is ever to be made a safe republic let her lands be cultivated by the toil of the owners or the free labor of intelligent citizens. This must be done even though it drive her nobility into exile. If they go, all the better.*

Surely the crimes of the South, said Stevens, "are sufficient to justify the exercise of the extreme rights of war—'to execute, to imprison, to confiscate.'" And Sumner added his insistent voice: "If all whites vote, then must all blacks. . . . Without them the old enemy will reappear, and . . . in alliance with the Northern democracy, put us all in peril again."

If Lincoln had a reconstruction plan for restoring the southern states but none for elevating southern blacks, Sumner and Stevens had a plan for the blacks but none that they openly championed at first for the southern states. Their principal early goal was to *slow down* political reconstruction so that southern congressmen would not soon reappear in Washington and exert political influence. In this objective they had the support of many conservative Republicans fearful that northern and southern Democrats would close ranks as before the war and overturn Republican economic legislation.

The Radical leadership did not offer an alternative to Lincoln's "ten percent" plan of December 1863 until July 4, 1864, when Congress, on the last day of the session, adopted the Wade-Davis bill. This bill would have made reconstruction of the South by southerners impossible. It required a *majority* of citizens, not just 10 percent, to swear loyalty to the Union before an acceptable state government could be established in a seceding state. This majority, moreover, had to swear not only that it would be loyal in the future but that it had been consistently and continuously loyal in the past. The bill also prescribed that new state constitutions in the South must abolish slavery, repudiate state debts, and disfranchise ex-Confederate leaders.

The Radical strategists hoped by this bill to commit the Republican party to the Radical reconstruction program in the 1864 presidential campaign. Lincoln attempted to forestall them by permitting the Wade-Davis bill to die by a pocket veto and issuing a proclamation justifying his action. Lincoln said rebel states might follow Wade-Davis provisions if they wished, but he refused to make them mandatory. The Radicals replied with the Wade-Davis Manifesto of August 1864: "The President, by preventing this bill from becoming a law, holds the electoral votes of the Rebel States at the dictation of his personal ambition. . . . A more studied outrage on the legislative authority of the people has never been perpetrated."

Most Radical leaders supported Lincoln in the 1864 campaign because they did not want to smash the Republican party machinery which they hoped soon to control. Once the election was over, they resumed their own bent. In January 1865, as we have seen, they adopted the Thirteenth Amendment (p. 423). In February, Congress refused to admit members from Louisiana which Lincoln had declared "reconstructed" under his "ten percent" plan. On March 3, it created the Freedmen's Bureau. The next day, Congress went home, with the Radicals determined to keep up the steam in their boilers.

### Andrew Johnson carries on

When Lincoln died on April 15, 1865, Andrew Johnson, fifty-six years old, be-

came President. Born, like Lincoln, into the direst poverty, Johnson never succeeded in outgrowing his self-pity. Early in his political career this attitude had taken the form of aggressive dislike for the nobby cotton planters, and a good deal of Johnson's almost unbroken success at the polls in nonslaveholding eastern Tennessee may be attributed to his ability as a stump speaker in rousing the poor farmers against the plantation class. Of all southern senators in 1861, Johnson alone refused to abandon his seat. While still a senator, in March 1862, he was appointed by Lincoln as military governor of Tennessee, and under his regime this state became a kind of laboratory for Lincoln's reconstruction policy. Johnson's success here earned him the nomination of the Republican (Union) party for the vice-presidency in 1864, even though he had been a Jacksonian Democrat all his life.

During the 1864 campaign, Johnson made himself attractive to many Radicals by his characteristic denunciations of rebel leaders. They have "ceased to be citizens," he cried on one occasion. They have become "traitors." Within ten days of Lincoln's death, Senator Chandler of Michigan declared Johnson "is as radical as I am and as fully up to the mark." "Johnson, we have faith in you," exclaimed the jubilant Ben Wade of Ohio.

Others, however, suspicious of Johnson's southern background and political past, held back. Congressman George W. Julian of Indiana, an old abolitionist, recalled that early in the war, Johnson had been as energetic a Negro colonizer as Lincoln. Julian acknowledged Johnson's hatred of the planters; but he recognized that as one of the yeoman class he was also "as decided a hater of the negro . . . as the rebels from whom he separated." Julian also feared the state-rights bent of Johnson's Jacksonian philosophy.

Julian's suspicions proved justified even sooner than he anticipated. Early in May 1865 the new President recognized Lincoln's "ten percent" governments in Louisiana, Tennessee, Arkansas, and Virginia. He next appointed military governors in the seven states that had not yet complied with Lincoln's "ten percent" plan. On May 29 he offered executive amnesty to all citizens of these states except high Confederate military and civil officers, and others worth more than $20,000. These people had to make personal application for amnesty to the President. The "whitewashed" electorate—that is, those who benefited by the amnesty offer—were then to elect members to a constitutional convention in each state, which would abolish slavery, rescind the state's secession ordinance, adopt the Thirteenth Amendment, repudiate the state war debt, and call an election for a new state government. The suffrage for this election was to be determined by each state rather than by Congress. The Negro, clearly, would not get the ballot in the South any more than he had obtained it in most states in the North.

By the winter of 1865, all the seceding states but Texas had complied with Johnson's terms, and their sincerity was confirmed by the reports of investigators Johnson had sent to find out if the South actually did accept the judgment of arms. One investigator, however, Carl Schurz, the German-American leader who had become one of the organizers of the Republican party in Wisconsin and a general in the Union army, dissented. Schurz found that "there is as yet among the southern people an *utter absence of national feeling* [Schurz's emphasis] ... and a desire to preserve slavery in its original form as much and as long as possible." Johnson received this report with "great coldness," but few deny today that of all Johnson's emissaries, Schurz was the one who was right and that southern extremism was plainly evident even before Radical Reconstruction began.

For all his yeomen animosity to the southern Old Guard, Johnson no doubt also had a sneaking admiration for them and perhaps a certain servility in their presence. His personal grants of amnesty, in any case, exceeded all bounds, and with heroes of the "Lost Cause" made suddenly available, the whitewashed voters proceeded to elect them to high national, state, and local offices. Other candidates, a correspondent from Alabama informed Johnson, were cried down as "traitors to the South." A widespread reluctance to renounce the rebel debt was accompanied in some states by a determination to resist taxation for

redemption of the Union debt. While ratifying the Thirteenth Amendment as required, Johnson's reconstructed states almost as a unit warned Congress to keep hands off "the political status of former slaves, or their civil relations," to quote the South Carolina legislature. In the "Black Codes" adopted in 1865 and 1866 by all the reconstructed states but Tennessee, the freedman's "political status" was nullified simply by being ignored.

## Black Codes

Some revision, of course, of the old slave codes of the South was required by the slave's sudden liberation. In making such revisions, the new southern legislatures studied British practice following emancipation of the slaves in the West Indies, and northern legislation for free Negroes. Adopted, as Mississippi's first Reconstruction governor said, only "under the pressure of federal bayonets," the new Black Codes were as illiberal as Lincoln had suggested would be suitable for laws governing a "laboring, landless, and homeless class" (p. 423).

The Black Codes "opened the courts" to the freedmen. Although still universally forbidden to serve on juries, even in cases involving whites, they could now swear out affidavits in criminal cases, sue and be sued in civil actions, and appear as witnesses and otherwise give testimony. Marriages among colored persons were to be sanctified under law, but interracial marriages carried sentences up to life imprisonment for both parties. Negroes could make wills and pass on personal property. Their children could go to school; and their apprenticed children were to be protected from abuse by the state.

Nowhere, at the same time, could blacks bear arms, vote, hold public office, assemble freely. In some states they could work at any jobs and quit jobs freely. Most states, however, forbade them to work as artisans, mechanics, and in other capacities where they competed with white labor; and they could not leave jobs except under stated conditions. Moreover, as the Mississippi code put it, the law "shall not be construed as to allow any freedman, free negro or mulatto to rent or lease any lands or tenements." The code of a Louisiana parish stated: "Every negro is required to be in the regular service of some white person, or former owner, who shall be held responsible for the conduct of said negro."

The vagrancy provisions were the most oppressive. In Georgia, for example, the law said that "all persons wandering or strolling about in idleness, who are able to work and who have no property to support them," might be picked up and tried. If convicted, they could be set to work on state chain gangs or contracted out to planters and other employers who would pay their fines and their upkeep for a stated period.

The Black Codes, said the Radical Schurz, are "a striking embodiment of the idea that although the former owner has lost his individual right of property in the former slave, 'the blacks at large belong to the whites at large.'"

## III Congress and the South

### The storm breaks

When Congress met in December 1865, it was faced with Johnson's executive coup and the South's disquieting response to it. As their first countermove, the Radicals set up the Joint Committee of Fifteen—six senators and nine representatives—to scan the qualifications of the men elected in the southern states and to review the whole presidential reconstruction plan that had brought such "traitors" to the threshold of Congress. These men were never permitted to take their seats. Without them, Congress proceeded early in 1866 to enact a bill continuing the Freedmen's Bureau, which was gradually becoming an instrument of Radical policy. Johnson, believing that the future care of the freedmen had better be left to the state legislatures, vetoed the bill. The Radicals overrode the veto in the House, but failed in the Senate.

In March 1866 Johnson vetoed a civil-rights bill which forbade states to discriminate among their citizens on the basis of color or race, as they had in the Black Codes. By now a sufficient number of conservative senators were ready to join the Radicals in defense of congressional prerogatives if not of Radical

principles, and both houses overrode the President. A few months later, in July 1866, the Radicals pushed through a second Freedmen's Bureau bill over Johnson's veto.

The supreme test developed over the Fourteenth Amendment, perhaps the most far-reaching one ever added to the Constitution. When the Radicals introduced this amendment in June 1866, they were concerned over the constitutionality of coercing the states under the Civil Rights Act and the danger that another Congress might repeal this act. A civil-rights amendment would set the constitutionality issue at rest and also make repeal more difficult. The amendment's importance, however, derives more from other considerations at the time it was proposed and from later interpretations.

The amendment's opening section for the first time defined citizenship in the United States as distinct from citizenship in a state. By identifying as citizens "all persons born or naturalized in the United States," it automatically extended citizenship to American-born blacks. It also forbade any state to abridge "the privileges and immunities" of United States citizens, to "deprive any person of life, liberty, or property, without due process of law," and to "deny to any person within its jurisdiction the equal protection of the laws."

The second section of the amendment did not give the Negro the vote, as many Radicals hoped it would, but penalized substantially any state for withholding it. This penalty, however, was never imposed either in the South or the North, where only six states allowed Negro voting at this time; and it became archaic with the passage of the Fifteenth Amendment (see p. 432).

The third section disqualified from federal or state office, unless Congress specifically lifted the disqualification by a two-thirds vote, all Confederates who before the war had taken a federal oath of office. Finally, the amendment guaranteed the Union debt and outlawed the Confederate debt and any claims for compensation for loss of slaves.

The Fourteenth Amendment had a stormy history before it finally was ratified in July 1868. Many years later the use of the word "person" in the first section of the amendment was interpreted by the federal courts as applying to such "legal persons" as business corporations as well as to Negroes, who were the only persons the framers of the amendment had in mind. It thus supplied the legal grounds for the courts to declare unconstitutional state regulation of railroads and trusts. Still later, the phrase in Section 1 prohibiting the denial of "equal protection of the laws" supplied the legal grounds of the Supreme Court's school integration decision in 1954.

At the time the Fourteenth Amendment was proposed much of its importance lay in the hope of many in the South as well as in the North that it provided "the final condition of restoration," as a Boston paper put it, that it was in effect a lasting "treaty of peace" reestablishing the Union. The leading Radicals, however, thought it too full of compromises and hoped to stiffen its provisions later

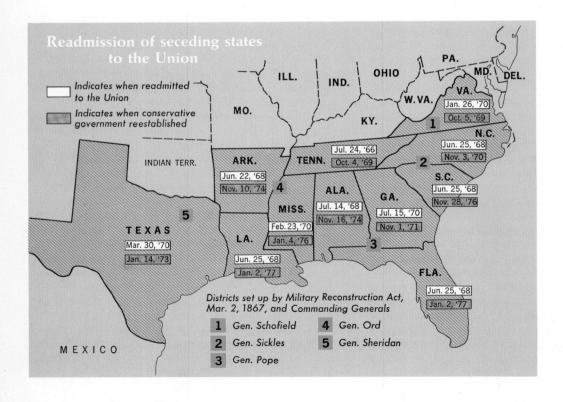

Readmission of seceding states to the Union

Indicates when readmitted to the Union

Indicates when conservative government reestablished

Districts set up by Military Reconstruction Act, Mar. 2, 1867, and Commanding Generals

1 Gen. Schofield    4 Gen. Ord
2 Gen. Sickles      5 Gen. Sheridan
3 Gen. Pope

on. Speaking in favor of the amendment in Congress, Stevens said, "Forty acres of land and a hut would be more valuable to [the freedman] than the immediate right to vote." But Stevens acknowledged even of the indirect suffrage provisions of the Fourteenth Amendment, "I believe it is all that can be obtained in the present state of public opinion."

Susan B. Anthony and other agitators for woman's suffrage at this time, arguing that by their contributions to victory in the Civil War women at last had earned the franchise, fought valiantly to have the word "male" deleted from the voting provisions of the Fourteenth Amendment (and soon to have the word "sex" added to "race, color, or previous condition of servitude" in the Fifteenth Amendment). But Radical leaders believed that merging women's rights with Negro rights would weaken the chances of both, and they withstood the women's campaign.

The Radicals demanded that southern states ratify the Fourteenth Amendment to regain representation in Congress. Johnson advised the states not to ratify, and by mid-February 1867, all but Tennessee—that is, ten of the eleven ex-Confederate states—had followed his advice. Legally, the amendment was dead. At the time of the adoption of the Thirteenth Amendment, Congress had agreed that the eleven as yet unreconstructed states should be counted as part of the Union for purposes of ratification, making thirty-seven states in all. The same thirty-seven were to vote on the Fourteenth Amendment, which could thus be defeated (according to the constitutional provision requiring approval by three-fourths of the states) by ten commonwealths. For good measure, Delaware and Kentucky, in addition to the ten ex-Confederate states, had also rejected the amendment by this time, making twelve rejections in all. When the last of the southern rejections had arrived, James A. Garfield of Ohio declared: "The last one of the sinful ten has at last with contempt and scorn flung back into our teeth the magnanimous offer of a generous nation. It is now our turn to act."

### Radical revolutionary measures

The Fourteenth Amendment was rejected in most of the ex-Confederate states while the congressional elections of 1866, the first national elections since the close of the war, were taking place. The amendment had drawn the issue clearly between the President and Congress, and from August 28 to September 15 Johnson made a "swing around the circle," visiting key cities on behalf of candidates who favored his policy. Many people considered such campaigning unseemly for a President, and all the more so in Johnson's case, since he was often indiscreet. The more he talked, the more the Radicals made fun of him. Their own campaign was aided by violence in the South, which reached a peak in New Orleans on July 30 over Radical efforts to force Negro suffrage on the state of Louisiana. Blacks and whites clashed and forty-one persons were killed.

The Radicals used such incidents to pound home the intransigence of the ex-rebels. As if to underscore the need for vigilance, Union veterans completed the organization of the Grand Army of the Republic just before the elections, and in November 1866 the GAR held its first national encampment in Indianapolis. The Radicals made a big play for the soldier vote and the big business vote. Stung by the South's rejection of the Fourteenth Amendment, they sought so sweeping a victory that they might impose even sterner measures and carry them by the two-thirds majorities required to upset presidential vetoes. Nor were they disappointed. They carried the Senate with 42 Republican seats to 11 for the Democrats, the House 143 to 49.

So convincing was the Radicals' victory that even before the new Congress met they were able to marshal all the votes needed to proceed with a virtual revolution in the government. Ordinarily, the new Congress would not convene until December 1867, unless called into special session by the President.

429

430

But on January 22, 1867, the old Congress took it upon itself to call the new Congress into session on March 4, the day the old Congress was required by law to adjourn. Having insured Congress's uninterrupted presence in Washington, the Radicals moved to concentrate all power in congressional hands.

Their initial and most comprehensive measure was the so-called First Reconstruction Act, passed over Johnson's veto on March 2, 1867 (supplementary Second, Third, and Fourth Reconstruction Acts elaborated its language and filled out its enforcement machinery). By the terms of this Act, all existing southern state governments except that of Tennessee, which had been accepted back into the Union in 1866, were declared illegal. The South was organized into five military districts, each under a general to be named by the President. Each general was to have an armed force at his command to help him maintain martial law if necessary. The general's main task was to call a new constitutional convention in each state, the delegates to be elected by universal adult male suffrage, black and white. Although the Fourteenth Amendment had been dead for nearly a month, the act explicitly cited its provisions to indicate those in the "said rebel states" who were to be excluded from serving as or voting for delegates.

Once manned, the new conventions would proceed to establish state governments in which Negroes could vote and hold office. Once in operation, these governments were to ratify the arbitrarily revived Fourteenth Amendment as a condition for their return to the Union and the acceptance of their representatives by Congress.

By June 1868 all but three states—Mississippi, Texas, and Virginia—had been "reconstructed" by Congress in time to participate in the presidential elections that year, though in some of them armed forces remained to protect Republican rule for as long as ten years more. In July 1868 Secretary Seward announced the completion of ratification of the Fourteenth Amendment, but only after Congress a week earlier by a joint resolution wholly unsanctioned by the supreme law of

the land had declared the amendment part of the Constitution. The three recalcitrant states were readmitted in 1870. In that year, Georgia, whose reconstruction had been suspended because of the expulsion of black members from her legislature, was also readmitted for the second time.

The Radicals' next step was to protect their program from the Supreme Court. In the case of *ex parte Milligan* (1866), which arose over Lincoln's suspension of habeas corpus in Indiana during the war, the Supreme Court had held that if military rule "is continued *after* the courts are reinstated, it is a gross usurpation of power." When the First Reconstruction Act was passed southern courts were open, and by establishing military rule the act deliberately defied this decision. When, in *ex parte McCardle*, the constitutionality of the First Reconstruction Act was challenged, the Radicals attached a rider to a minor bill, withdrawing appellate jurisdiction from the Court in habeas corpus matters. Johnson vetoed the whole bill, but the withdrawal provision was then passed over his veto, in March 1868. The Court had already put *ex parte McCardle* on its schedule but, against the judgment of two justices, the majority yielded to the Radicals, allowed the case to be quashed, and the First Reconstruction Act survived.

Having successfully defied the Supreme Court, the Radicals next set about eliminating the Executive. Two measures had been passed at the same time as the First Reconstruction Act, in March 1867, with this end in view. The first, the Tenure of Office Act, declared that the President could not remove federal officers who had been appointed with the consent of the Senate without first getting the Senate's consent to their removal. The second, the Command of the Army Act, forbade the President to issue orders to the army except through the General of the Army, General Grant. These measures left the President at the mercy of Radical officeholders and divested him of his constitutional role as Commander-in-Chief. But the Radicals were not satisfied.

After almost a full year of investigation in 1867, the House Judiciary Committee, in November, though failing to draw up any list of Johnson's "high crimes and misdemeanors," had voted by a bare five-to-four majority to recommend to the whole chamber that the President be impeached and haled before the Senate for trial. The committee's grounds were simply that the President's offenses were all referable "to the one great overshadowing purpose of reconstructing the ... rebel States in accordance with his own will, in the interests of the great criminals who carried them into rebellion." This charge proved too vague for the whole House to swallow, and in December 1867 it rejected the committee's recommendation 57 to 108. By attempting to remove Secretary of War Stanton, the remaining Radical in his Cabinet, and thereby also to test the validity of the Tenure of Office Act, Johnson soon gave his congressional enemies a second chance.

On February 21, 1868, Stanton was formally removed. Three days later, a new impeachment resolution came before the House, this one reported out not by the Judiciary Committee, but by the Committee on Reconstruction, of which Stevens was chairman. Once more no bill of particulars was leveled at the Chief Executive; yet the House now voted for impeachment, 126 to 47, and only then promised the Senate in due time "to exhibit particular articles of impeachment ... and make good the same." By March 2, eleven "particular articles" had been drawn up, all but one of them referring to the Tenure of Office Act. The exception was the notorious "Butler article," number 10, which charged Johnson with "inflammatory, and scandalous harangues" calculated to bring Congress into disgrace, but which mentioned no law that had thereby been violated.

The trial did not seriously get under way in the Senate until March 13, and it quickly be-

came "a solemn theatrical fiasco," to use the words of James Schouler. An effort was even made to implicate Johnson in Lincoln's assassination; and while most of the other charges had no better foundation, Johnson escaped conviction only by the barest margin. When on May 16 and again on May 25, seven Republicans showed their determination to desert the Radical leadership, the Radicals' game was up. These seven, together with twelve Democrats, made nineteen against Johnson's removal. Thirty-five voted for it, one short of the two-thirds needed to carry.

### Election of 1868

Although they had done everything possible to destroy the presidency before the election of 1868, the Radicals were determined to secure the office for themselves that year. Their medium was to be General Grant, who had no known political allegiances, nor for that matter any known political ambitions, but who had served the Radicals well in the controversy over Stanton's removal and on his war record appeared a certain winner. At the Republican convention in Chicago in May, Grant was nominated on the first ballot. Johnson sought the Democratic nomination, but that party's convention in New York City in July, after twenty-two ballots, designated the untainted if unappealing northerner, former New York Governor Horatio Seymour.

In the campaign the Democrats sought to divert attention from their rebel past and Reconstruction backsliding by making an issue of cheap money. In 1866 Congress had passed a measure providing for the gradual retirement of the wartime greenbacks whose dollar value always remained below that of gold; and in the next two years almost $100 million worth had been withdrawn from circulation, much to the disappointment of many businessmen as well as farmers. Seeking the support of western farmers in particular, who were emotionally attached to the Republican party for its free soil commitments but who wanted cheap money with which to meet their fixed mortgage obligations and other debts, the Democrats in their platform advocated the

431

reissue of these greenbacks by using them to retire war bonds that did not specifically require repayment in gold. The leading proponent of this "soft money" plank was an early aspirant for the 1868 Democratic nomination, George H. Pendleton of Ohio, and it became known as the "Ohio idea."

The Republicans scotched the Ohio Idea in the West by reminding the farmers, in difficulties though they were because of the falling off of the war-time demand for foodstuffs and fibers, that redemption of war bonds in anything but gold smacked of rebel repudiation of a sacred debt contracted to preserve the Union. At the same time, the Republicans promised businessmen that they would extend redemption "over a fair period" so as not to disturb the business credit structure and that, when the time came, all bondholders would be paid in gold.

Having dealt with the persistent problem of the money supply in an expanding economy, the Radicals proceeded to keep before the voters the main political issue—Radical Reconstruction versus Democratic dishonor. The "bloody shirt," which had done valorous service in the 1866 campaign, again was waved with vigor. The Democratic party, cried Republican spellbinders, was the standard-bearer of rebellion, Negro repression, and financial repudiation. "In short," cried Oliver P. Morton, the Radical governor of Indiana, in a typical "bloody shirt" foray, "the Democratic party may be described as a common sewer and loathsome receptacle, into which is emptied every element of treason North and South, and every element of inhumanity and barbarism which has dishonored the age."

Such tirades served as the staple of Republican oratory for a generation. Practical Republican electioneering, meanwhile, was handled by the Union League clubs which had been organized in the North in 1862 to spread Union propaganda. Gradually they extended their wartime activity to captured southern territory. By 1868, more than eighty chapters of the League were operating in South Carolina alone, where estimates indicate that most of the state's blacks were enrolled as members. "I can't read, and I can't write," one Negro said. "We go by [League] instructions."

Yet the Republican campaign did not overwhelm the opposition. In 1868, against a weak opponent, Grant was elected with a popular plurality of a mere 310,000. Had the Union League not helped deliver the votes of about 700,000 freedmen in the seven hastily reconstructed southern states, Grant might have had no plurality at all.

The part that Negroes played in winning the election—or rather the fact that Negroes in certain states such as Louisiana and Georgia had been prevented from casting what might have been much-needed Republican votes—led Radicals to attempt to strengthen the Fourteenth Amendment's protection of black suffrage. When Congress convened early in 1869, it promptly passed the Fifteenth Amendment: "The right of citizens of the United States to vote shall not be denied or abridged by the United States or by any State on account of race, color, or previous conditions of servitude." This amendment was declared ratified in March 1870.

"The agitation against slavery," *The Nation* magazine declared at this time, "has reached an appropriate and triumphant conclusion." But many retained doubts about *The Nation's* own conclusion. During the congressional debate on the Fifteenth Amendment, Oliver P. Morton, now in the Senate, accurately forecast the future:

*This amendment leaves the whole power in the States just as it exists now except that colored men shall not be disfranchised for the three reasons of race, color, or previous condition of slavery. . . . Sir, if the power should pass into the hands of the Conservative or Democratic population of those southern States, if they could not debar the colored people of the right of suffrage in any other way they would do it by an educational or property qualification . . . and thus this amendment would be practically defeated in all those States where the great body of colored people live [see p. 447].*

## IV Day of the carpetbagger

### Revisions in the Radical camp

When Grant accepted the Republican nomination in 1868, he wrote, "Let us have peace." Many men, recalling his magnanimous surrender terms to Lee, thought that the severity of Radical Reconstruction might now be softened. The death of Stevens in August 1868, the defeat of Ben Wade for the Senate later that year, and Sumner's decline soon after (see p. 437) gave substance to this hope.

But Grant's administration was easily dominated by such surviving Radicals as Senators Zachariah Chandler of Michigan, Simon Cameron of Pennsylvania, and Roscoe Conkling of New York. Untinged by the abolitionist

*"The fate in store for those great pests of Southern society—the carpet-bagger and scallawag—if found in Dixie's Land after the break of day on the 4th of March [1869]." Contemporary Mississippi cartoon.*

Culver Pictures Inc.

idealism that had marked the Stevens-Sumner leadership, these men had ample partisan reasons—chief among them the wish to protect wartime tariff, railroad, and banking legislation from attack by returning southerners—for keeping ex-Confederates disfranchised and colored voters in Republican ranks. In the defeated section they had the help of Radical "carpetbaggers" who had begun to go South right after the war to show what northern "brains and sinew" could accomplish. After passage of the First Reconstruction Act in March 1867, with military protection, they virtually took charge of politics. In the seven states reconstructed in 1868, ten of fourteen United States senators, twenty of thirty-five congressmen, and four governors were carpetbaggers. The others, with few exceptions, were "scalawags"—southerners who rode to office on Radical coattails. The few exceptions were blacks.

### Carpetbaggers as reformers

Many carpetbaggers, especially the early ones, were genuine reformers who tried to help freedmen become useful citizens, economically independent and legally the equal of whites. Often enough their objectives were not in conflict with those of the self-seekers who came later, and under carpetbag rule political and social advances were made in the South by both races.

Many such gains grew out of provisions in the new southern state constitutions written by the "black and tan" conventions, as southerners branded the assemblages called by the Radical generals. These constitutions gave the Negro the franchise and the right to hold office even before the Fifteenth Amendment

Library of Congress

*The first Negro United States senator,
H. R. Revels of Mississippi, at far left,
elected to Jefferson Davis's seat
in 1870, with the first Negro
representatives in the Forty-first
and Forty-second Congresses.*

was ratified. They also eliminated property qualifications for voting and officeholding among whites as well as blacks, more fairly apportioned representation in state legislatures and in Congress, and abolished imprisonment for debt and other archaic social legislation. Above all, for the first time in many southern states, they provided for public schools—for whites and blacks.

Next to giving Negroes the vote, nothing offended the South more than Radical efforts to give them schooling. The slogan "Schooling ruins the Negro" expressed the general belief. As early as July 1865 Carl Schurz had noted instances of Negro schools being burned and of teachers and students being threatened. Yet by 1877, 600,000 blacks were enrolled in southern schools; and several colleges and universities, including Fisk, Howard, and Atlanta, and the Hampton Institute in Virginia, had been established by the Freedmen's Bureau and northern philanthropic agencies. Night schools for adults also flourished.

The ballot, though at first misused, was a notable step forward for the freedman. Officeholding, though also abused, was another significant advance, but it was less widespread than the term "black reconstruction" might imply. Only in South Carolina, in 1868, did black legislators outnumber whites, 88 to 67, but the sessions were not controlled by the blacks. In other state legislatures, Negroes made up sizable minorities, but white politicians dominated. One mulatto, P. B. S. Pinchback, became lieutenant-governor of Louisiana. Several Negroes became congressmen and two became United States senators. Others gained administrative posts, in which they did well.

*Corruption and reaction*

Many southern leaders actually found little fault with the Radicals' tariff, railroad, and money policies, and felt that the Republicans could trust the South sufficiently to give its spokesmen a voice in national affairs once again. Southern whites also felt that by 1868 they had made every concession that a vanquished nation (as they thought of themselves) ought to have been asked to make by the victors in the late war. The South had repudiated the Confederate debt, renounced secession as a constitutional device, and accepted the Thirteenth Amendment abolishing slavery. When the Radicals began to court the Negro vote to insure protection for their national legislative program, southerners balked at what they called "barbarization of the South," and prepared, if not to resume the war, at least to promote violence and terror to thwart the Radicals' plan.

The mere existence of the carpetbag governments within their borders seemed insulting and shameful to many southerners. Carpetbag corruption made the affront even harder to bear, even though it was not as bad as painted. Between 1868 and 1874, the bonded debt of the eleven Confederate states grew by

434

over $100 million. But this enormous sum was not itself evidence of crime. To raise money, the southern states had to sell bonds in the North, where southern credit was so poor that investors often demanded a 75 percent discount from a bond's face value. Thus for every $100 worth of bonds sold, a southern state might actually realize only $25. Many of the social and humanitarian reforms of the Reconstruction legislatures, moreover, were costly, as was the relief extended to the starving and homeless of both races.

Nevertheless, much of the debt was corruptly incurred, though not necessarily by carpetbaggers. A large part of it arose from the sale of state bonds to back southern-sponsored railroad enterprises that never built a mile of track. Carpetbaggers were more likely to busy themselves with more traditional forms of graft, such as taking large contracts for themselves for public construction or printing and then failing to supply what the contracts called for. Public funds also were spent for personal furniture, homes, carriages, jewelry, liquor, leather goods, and other amenities. But such conspicuous corruption probably cost the least.

Taxes to pay for carpetbag government expenditures and to service the rapidly growing debt fell most heavily on the oppressed planters, who before the war had been able to pass taxes on to other groups in their section. Such discriminatory taxation, along with the public debt, aroused the ire of former southern leaders. The majority of the people most bitterly deplored the flamboyant or slovenly dress, the posturing of the new political leaders, black and white, and the bizarre legislative sessions. Rubbed into the unhealed sores of the war, this kind of "reconstruction" completed the moral rout of the South. The poet Sidney Lanier said during this period in a letter north, "Perhaps you know that with us of the young generation in the South, since the war pretty much the whole of life has been merely not dying."

To combat carpetbag rule and the Negro vote on which it rested, thousands even of the most respectable elements in the South banded together in the Ku Klux Klan, the Knights of the White Camelia, and other secret groups. Between 1867 and 1869, hooded or otherwise incognito, they roamed the land, shot, flogged, and terrorized blacks and their supporters, burned homes and public buildings, assaulted Reconstruction officials, and, under the guise of keeping order (which, indeed, often needed keeping), perpetrated other acts of violence dedicated to the maintenance of white supremacy. After 1869, some of these white organizations engaged in such random pillage and murder that respectable elements abandoned them in horror. But the organizations themselves persisted.

### Radical reprisals and retreats

The Radical leadership in Congress did not permit the activities of the violent white organizations to go unchallenged. In May 1870 Congress passed a Force Act designed to strengthen the protection of Negro voting by imposing heavy fines and jail sentences for offenses under the Fourteenth and Fifteenth amendments. This act also gave federal courts controlled by carpetbaggers, rather than southern state courts, original jurisdiction in all cases arising under these amendments.

In spite of the Force Act, the Democrats made substantial gains in the congressional elections of 1870, and by the following year southern whites had recaptured the state governments of Tennessee, Virginia, North Carolina, and Georgia. Attributing these successes to violence, the Radicals next forced through Congress the Ku Klux Klan Act of 1871. This act gave federal courts original jurisdiction in all cases arising out of conspiracies or terrorism against freedmen. It also empowered the President to suspend habeas corpus in any terrorized community, to declare martial law, and to send troops to maintain order.

Within a short time, about 7000 southerners were indicted under these two acts, and although few were convicted or even tried, the personal harassment served to smother white

435

political activity. In October 1871, to convince remaining skeptics that the Radicals still meant business, President Grant declared nine counties of South Carolina, where the Klan was especially active, to be again in rebellion and placed them under martial law. An investigation by a congressional committee presently placed its seal of approval on the President's militancy.

The South Carolina episode marked the peak of forceful repression of southern whites. In May 1872 Congress passed a liberal Amnesty Act which restored voting and office-holding privileges to all white southerners with the exception of a few hundred of the highest surviving Confederate dignitaries. In that year, the Freedmen's Bureau, protector of Negro rights, was permitted to expire.

No doubt the presidential election coming in the fall of 1872 led the Radicals to make these concessions. Testimony offered at the few trials of persons indicted in South Carolina and elsewhere under the Force Act and the Ku Klux Klan Act had cast doubt on the efficacy of the Radicals' program. The severe political and social disabilities fastened upon the southern states seemed clearly to have retarded their recovery. Evidence inadvertently publicized by the congressional committee's own report supported the trials' disclosures. To many in the North it now appeared that carpetbaggers were using the black vote simply to sustain their own corruption and oppression. Increasingly disgusted by Radical excesses in their own section—now roundly condemned under the unedifying epithet, "Grantism"—they were ready to call a halt to such excesses in the South. By buoying up the white South while jettisoning the blacks, the tarnished general's Radical backers hoped to preserve Grantism in Washington a while longer.

## V  Radical Republicanism in the North

*Grantism*

On observing the Washington scene early in 1869, young Henry Adams, grandson and great-grandson of Presidents, remarked that "the progress of evolution from President Washington to President Grant was alone evidence enough to upset Darwin." An organism as simple as U. S. Grant "should have been extinct for ages."

In fact, Grant, as President, was no throwback but very much a product of his time. A failure in business himself, he became infatuated with business success. In Washington, he frequently was entertained by Henry Cooke, whose business it was to report to his financier brother, Jay, what he could learn at the nation's capital. Fond of the horseracing at Saratoga Springs, New York, Grant, in the summer of 1869, accepted the use of Commodore Vanderbilt's private railroad car to travel there. He once described Jim Fisk as "destitute of moral character"; yet, as President, he saw nothing wrong in enjoying the hospitality of the Erie looters while making them privy to the country's financial affairs.

Grant's political appointments were hardly likely to keep the President's businessman associates from using the information they garnered. In making his appointments, the President, understandably, turned first to his old army friends. Grant's White House staff, his "Kitchen Cabinet," it was said, had "nothing but uniforms." His regular Cabinet, in turn, with three exceptions, was made up of men who frightened people by their obscurity. The three exceptions were Secretary of State Hamilton Fish, who served through Grant's two administrations; and Secretary of the Interior Jacob D. Cox, and Attorney-General Ebenezer Hoar, both of whom gave way in little over a year to more pliant souls.

Traditionally, United States senators had the last word on appointments from their states. Grant, and his former military aide and now White House secretary, Colonel Orville E. Babcock, ignored this tradition and placed the President's and the Kitchen Cabinet's relatives and friends in the fattest jobs. This practice quickly cost Grant any chance he had for the support of such senators as Sumner and Schurz. Alienated also were some of the less-principled patronage mongers in Republican states like New York and Pennsylvania, who resented being shortchanged by men as dishonest as themselves. Schurz became a leader of the movement for federal civil-service reform to place federal jobholding on a merit basis, with candidates selected by objective examinations, but little came of it for many years. When Secretary of the Interior Cox tried to staff his department with men chosen on merit, Grant promptly replaced him with Columbus Delano, a former Ohio congressman skilled in dispensing patronage for party ends.

Even worse than Grant's handling of major appointments and patronage was the way he allowed himself and his great office to be used by the corruptionists around him. One of the most unsavory incidents occurred only a few months after his inauguration. This was "Black Friday," September 24, 1869, when Grant's long overdue action in releasing $4 million in government gold to New York banks broke a gold corner that Fisk and Jay Gould had planned by earlier persuading the financially innocent President not to release any government gold that fall. Fisk and Gould were foiled, but not before many speculators and others who needed gold in their business transactions had been ruined.

Black Friday occurred in the midst of negotiations over the annexation of Santo Domingo (now the Dominican Republic), for which other Grant cronies had won his pledge "privately to use all his influence." An island rich in minerals, timber, and fruit, Santo Domingo had won its independence from Spain in 1865. Among those who now hungrily eyed the island were a couple of discreditable Massachusetts promoters who, like so many of the kind, got Orville Babcock's ear. On visiting Santo Domingo late in 1869, Babcock was able to negotiate a treaty of annexation. When Attorney-General Hoar denounced Babcock's treaty making as illegal, Grant removed Hoar from office. When Charles Sumner, Chairman of the Senate Foreign Relations Committee, then denounced the entire "deal," the Senate defeated Babcock's treaty in 1870. Grant's senatorial friends retaliated the next year by stripping Sumner of his committee post and practically reading him out of the Republican party.

## Lobbies and legislation

Grant, no doubt, was simply used by the corruptionists, many of them men or representatives of men who had made fortunes on war contracts but in Grant's eyes had also contributed handsomely to winning the war. Now they were sustaining the postwar boom. To those who would point a finger, moreover, Grant could reply that he had inherited a government already far gone in corruption. The competition for war contracts and the battles for other wartime legislation covering protective tariffs, land grants, and the money system had made lobbying a full-time occupation whose practitioners often prowled the floor of House and Senate to keep their legislators in line.

Few political plums were more valuable than the tariff, which by 1870 had become "a conglomeration of special favors." The railroads also shared in congressional handouts. The last federal land grant for railroad building was made in 1871, by which time the total distributed to the roads directly or through the states came to 160 million acres, valued conservatively at $335 million. The roads also had received lavish government loans. After the Union Pacific and Central Pacific Railroads had obtained their loans, Congress annually considered legislation that would have provided for their eventual repayment. The transcontinentals fought such measures stubbornly and successfully, often distributing company shares among the legislators "where they will do us the most good." The famous scandal of 1867–1868 involving the Crédit Mobilier, the construction company that built the Union Pacific, destroyed many political reputations.

Nor were northern financiers left out of the "Great Barbecue," as Grant's regime has been called. In March 1869, in fulfilling Republican campaign promises made the year before, both houses of Congress adopted a resolution pledging the government to redeem the entire war debt in gold or in new gold bonds. This pledge, and the laws soon passed to carry it out, sent the value of war bonds soaring and brought substantial profits to speculators. These laws, it should be said, proved salutary as far as the government's credit was concerned. Forced during the war to offer interest as high as 6 percent, the victorious national government was soon able to borrow for as little as 2.5 percent. Yet the new laws permitted the Secretary of the Treasury to issue new bonds more or less at his pleasure, and Wall Streeters openly charged that Secretary of the Treasury George S. Boutwell frequently made moves "conspicuously more advantageous to certain 'friends of Government' among speculators . . . than to men engaged in legitimate business."

### Grant's second term

The worst of the corruption in Grant's first administration was not disclosed to the public until after the 1872 presidential campaign. In that campaign, the "Liberal Republican" movement led by the disenchanted Radical Carl Schurz of Missouri tried to unseat the Regulars' general by running candidates of "superior intelligence and superior virtue," on a platform stressing civil-service reform. Unfortunately for the Liberal Republicans, their ranks soon were infiltrated by victims of the Radical grafters, political hacks who had lost out in contests for patronage, and others simply out for revenge. Many northern Democrats also joined the movement, hoping thereby to cast off the treasonous label of their party and win their way back to power.

At the Liberals' Cincinnati convention in May the irreconcilable differences in this motley array forced the delegates to name a compromise presidential candidate, the aging Horace Greeley, a perverse choice. As befitted a man who had long been an abolitionist, Greeley remained an outspoken Radical. Worse, he was a staunch high-tariff man. Worse still, as editor for more than thirty years of the *New York Tribune* he had taken so many contradictory political positions that he was universally known as a crackpot.

If Greeley's nomination was a misfortune for the Liberal Republicans, it was a tragedy for the Democratic party. This party's only chance to regain national power was to support Grant's opponents. Yet Grant's opponents had nominated the man who in 1866 had publicly branded Democrats, "the traitorous section of Northern politics." The Democrats eventually swallowed their pride and at their convention in Baltimore in July named Greeley as their own standard-bearer. This move made the election contest easy for Grant, who had been nominated without opposition at the regular Republican convention in Philadelphia in June. The General won by a majority of 763,000 and carried all but six states.

During the campaign Roscoe Conkling told a receptive New York audience: "If the name and the character of the administration of Ulysses S. Grant have been of value to the nation, no one knows it so well as the men who represent the property, the credits, the public securities and the enterprise of the country." These men truly were in debt to the Republican party, and as a group became its strongest backers over the years. Yet even many of them had begun to grow restless over the ceaseless exactions of the Radical Republicans who now controlled the party, Conkling himself, from his stronghold in the New York City Customs House, being a particularly nasty article. The outright scandals of the administration soon soured many more Republicans and fostered the Democratic revival. The first major Grant scandal, the Crédit Mobilier affair, broke while the 1872 campaign still was in progress. After the business crash of 1873, each new revelation struck with added force, and once the Democrats captured the House in 1874, revelations and prosecutions snowballed.

Two affairs hit close to Grant personally. One was the uncovering of the "Whiskey Ring" in St. Louis, which had defrauded the government of millions of dollars in internal revenue charges. Deeply involved in this, as in other frauds, was Grant's ubiquitous assistant secretary, Orville Babcock, whom the President saved from imprisonment only by incessantly interfering in his trial. The second affair led to the impeachment of Grant's third Secretary of War, W. W. Belknap, who since his appointment in 1870 had been "kept" by traders in Indian Territory under his jurisdiction. When his impeachment appeared imminent, Belknap had taken the precaution to offer his resignation to the President, which Grant, with characteristic loyalty to his betrayers, accepted "with great regret."

While his cronies were undermining Republican strength in the North, Grant, by persisting in the forbearance evident before the election of 1872, was helping to enhance Democratic strength in the South. In particular, he refused any longer to call upon the army for additional support for troubled Republican regimes. Encouraged by Grant's turnabout, southern leaders in states still under carpetbag rule became more determined than ever to "redeem" their states through their own efforts.

In communities where Negroes were a majority or nearly so, these efforts revolved around the so-called Mississippi Plan which operated openly with full white support and thus proved more effective than the covert Klan. The aim of the Mississippi Plan was to force all whites into the Democratic party while at the same time forcing blacks to desist from political action. Where persuasion failed, violence was used against both groups by

such well-armed, paramilitary enforcement agencies as Rifle Clubs, White Leagues, and Red Shirts. Whites who resisted were driven from their homes and their communities. Recalcitrant black sharecroppers, in turn (see p. 444), were denied credit by southern merchants, evicted from the land, denied other employment, assaulted, and murdered. Many blacks themselves had had their fill of northern domination, and some proved willing to cooperate with their new masters. After the Panic of 1873 depressed northern business, capitalists looking south for investment opportunities also aided the "redeemers."

**439**

As the election of 1876 neared, the national administration began to have second thoughts about revived Democratic strength. To counteract it, the House, in February 1875, passed a new Force Bill to protect Negro voters, but the Senate rejected it. At the same time, the

*"The Union as it was" (1874),*
*wood engraving after Nast cartoon depicting*
*plight of southern blacks at the hands*
*of white "redeemers."*

Library of Congress

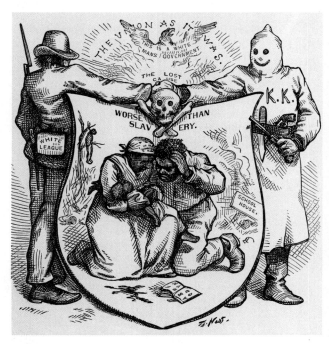

440

Senate joined the House in adopting a new Civil Rights Act which Grant signed on March 1. This act recognized "the equality of all men before the law," and imposed stiff penalties for denying any citizen "full and equal enjoyment of ... inns, public conveyances, ... theaters, and other places of public amusement." Penalties also were placed on the denial of equal rights to serve on juries.

Eight years later, in the momentous *Civil Rights Cases* of 1883, the Supreme Court declared much of the Civil Rights Act unconstitutional, ruling that the federal government had no jurisdiction over discrimination practiced by private persons or organizations. Later on,

the Court sanctioned state segregation laws requiring separate public facilities for whites and blacks. In *Plessy* v. *Ferguson* in 1896, the Court decided that the Negro's equal rights under the Fourteenth Amendment were not abrogated if the separate facilities on railroads were themselves equal. In *Cumming* v. *County Board of Education* in 1899, the Court extended the philosophy of "separate but equal" to schools. These decisions ruled until the desegregation decisions of the 1950s and 1960s.

## VI    Extension of white supremacy

### Republican southern strategies

The approach of the national nominating conventions in 1876 found the Grand Old Party, as the Republicans had taken to calling themselves, split more deeply than ever over the issue of corruption because of the rising Democratic challenge. The "Stalwarts," the hard-core political professionals closest to Grant, wanted the general to run for still a third term. These men put politics first; if business wanted favors, it would have to continue to come to them and pay up. The "Halfbreeds"—the name given in contempt by the Stalwarts to those Republican reformers who had not deserted to the Liberal Republicans in 1872—lined up behind the "Plumed Knight," Congressman James G. Blaine of Maine.

Unluckily for the Halfbreeds, Blaine's candidacy was undermined by the dramatic disclosure early in 1876 of his own shady relations with the Union Pacific Railroad while serving as Speaker of the House during the preceding five years. Blaine, his astuteness as a campaigner acknowledged by all, might still have won the nomination had he not blundered in denouncing the Stalwarts as "all desperate bad men, bent on loot and booty." When the Republican convention met in Cincinnati in June, Conkling and the old guard exacted the penalty. Balked in their attempts to renominate Grant, they backed Rutherford B. Hayes, the reform governor of Ohio.

The Democratic surge in the South, meanwhile, and vicious repression that underpinned it, accented the sectional differences in that party not only on "the Negro question," but on such other national issues as money policy, the tariff, and federal subsidies for internal improvements. But hunger for the spoils of the presidency, long denied them, led the Democrats to close ranks at their June convention in St. Louis behind Samuel J. Tilden, a rich corporation lawyer and hard-money man who had won a national reputation for incorruptibility as a reform governor of New York. Tilden's strongest claim on the nomination was his success, in 1872, in sending "Boss" Tweed, the notorious head of Tammany Hall, the leading Democratic club in New York City, to the penitentiary. During the preceding three years, the Tweed Ring had looted the city government of no less than $100 million.

The unprecedented presidential scandals,

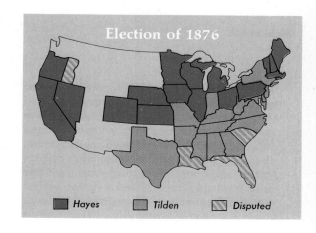

Election of 1876

■ Hayes    ☐ Tilden    ⧄ Disputed

the unmatched severity of the business depression of the mid-1870s, and the rising demand for reform all seemed to work so to the Democrats' advantage that Hayes privately forecast his defeat. No one was certain, however, how the "redeemed" white South would vote. Many of the new southern leaders were former Whigs to whom Lincoln had looked so optimistically. They had never been at home in the Democratic party, into which secession and war had forced them. As harbingers of a new industrialized and business-minded South, they found Republican economic policies attractive, and they especially resented the failure of northern Democrats to support land grants and other federal aid to southern railroads.

The attitudes of the Whiggish southern Democrats were not lost on Hayes's political managers, who felt it urgent to create a white southern Republican wing to offset the losses the party had suffered through corruption in the North and repression of Negro voters in the South. Once he had gained the nomination, on the other hand, Hayes went along with those Republicans whose "southern strategy" remained damning the Democrats, old and new. Indeed, as the canvass waxed in the hot summer, Hayes took the lead in promoting another "bloody shirt" campaign. "Our strong ground," he advised Blaine, "is the dread of a solid South, rebel rule, etc., etc. I hope you will make these topics prominent in your speeches. It leads people away from 'hard times,' which is our deadliest foe."

First reports of the election results seemed definite enough. The Democratic candidate, Tilden, had a plurality of 250,000 votes, and the press proclaimed him the new President. But Republican strategists suddenly awoke to the fact that returns from Louisiana, Florida, and South Carolina, three states where carpetbagger control was still supported by the army, had not yet come in because of election irregularities. Tilden needed but a single electoral vote from these states to win; Hayes thus needed every one. Although both parties had

resorted to the most barefaced skullduggery, evidence available now indicates that Tilden deserved Florida's four electoral votes and Hayes the others. In 1876, however, Congress had to determine promptly which of the double sets of returns from the three states should be accepted, the Democratic count or the Republican.

Amidst renewed talk of insurrection, the two parties agreed to the extraordinary device of deciding the election by turning the problem over to a commission of five representatives, five senators, and five Supreme Court justices. One of the justices, David Davis, presumably was independent in politics; the remaining fourteen members of the commission were equally divided between Democrats and Republicans. Unfortunately for Tilden, Davis quit the commission before it met and was replaced by a Republican justice. The Republican majority of eight then voted unanimously for Hayes.

One step that helped placate the aroused South was the pledge exacted from the Stalwarts by their "southern compromise" party colleagues to vote the federal subsidies to southern railroads, so persistently petitioned for not only by southern ex-Whigs but by northern railroad leaders who would participate in the subsidies by participating in the railroad construction. In exchange, southern leaders, Democrats though they nominally were, and Democratic though the new House of Representatives was to be, agreed to vote for the Republican James A. Garfield as Speaker—a position through which the whole course of legislation could at that time be controlled. Garfield himself became more palatable to the Democrats because of Hayes's change of tune toward the ex-rebels once he was named victor in the election at the price of favors to the South.

In his inaugural speech in March 1877, Hayes spoke out clearly on the need for a permanent federal civil service beyond the reach of Stalwart thieves and grafters and hungry party hacks. To show that he meant business, he courageously named Schurz Secretary of the Interior. With the aid of his able Secretary of the Treasury, his fellow Ohioan, the Halfbreed John Sherman, Hayes also succeeded in dislodging Conkling's minions from the New York Customs House, although not for long. Besides Schurz and Sherman, Hayes's Cabinet included William M. Evarts of New York, Andrew Johnson's Attorney-General as Secretary of State; and David M. Key of Tennessee, a high-ranking former Confederate officer and a Democrat, as Postmaster-General. "Hayes has sold us all out," cried John A. Logan, Illinois's counterpart of Conkling, on learning of these choices. Another midwestern Stalwart, Senator Timothy O. Howe of Wisconsin, declared that the new Cabinet "may give peace to the State of Louisiana, but it is quite likely to breed war within the Republican party."

Very soon after the inauguration it became clear to the South that Hayes's administration would fail to fulfill its promise of railroad subsidies. One reason for the Republican defection on this score was the failure of southern leaders in the House to deliver enough Democratic votes to give the promised speakership to Garfield. Thus the compromise by which the talk, at least, of the resumption of armed conflict was quieted, broke down almost at its first test.

Hayes, nevertheless, persisted in his new course. By the end of April 1877 he had withdrawn the last federal troops from the South, and with their departure the last Radical state governments collapsed. In September 1877, accompanied by Evarts and Key, he set forth on a good-will tour of the South. En route they were joined by former Confederate General Wade Hampton, just elected Governor of South Carolina by the "straight-out" Democrats, chiefly by suppressing the black vote. "The majority of the people of the South—the white people of the South—" Hayes now said in a speech at Nashville, Tennessee, "have no desire to invade the rights of the colored people." On his return to Washington, the President observed of his journey: "Received everywhere heartily. The country is again one and united." A few months later, in January 1878, the *New York Herald* reported him as saying that the race issue was dead, and if Republican spokesmen did not soon furl the bloody shirt, the party would be rejected by the people in both sections.

As the depression dragged out, Hayes gained more and more support for "killing our southern brethren with kindness" from the northern business community hungry for a revival of intersectional trade and the peaceful development of southern resources with northern capital. Less than a year after his southern tour, nevertheless, the President was obliged to reverse his course once more and return to his old campaign position. He had adopted his southern policy, he said on November 13, 1878, "with an earnest desire to conciliate the southern leaders." Now, "in fact, I am reluctantly forced to admit that the experiment was a failure. The first election of importance held since it was attempted has proved that fair elections with free suffrage for every voter in the South are an impossibility under the existing conditions of things."

The elections Hayes referred to were those of November 1878, which saw the Republican party in the South, without troop support, routed by the redeemers. A Senate investigation of the elections reported that in Louisiana alone the Democrats had committed more than forty political murders.

Once again dominant in Congress, moreover, southern Democrats, with northern party support, immediately began an assault on the Fourteenth and Fifteenth Amendments protecting Negro suffrage. But Hayes fought them off, vetoing bill after bill seeking, among other objectives, to force the removal of federal marshals assigned to supervise southern elections. "To establish now the state rights doctrine of the supremacy of the states and an oligarchy of race," he told members of his own Civil War regiment at this time, "is deliberately to throw away an essential part of the fruits of the Union victory."

Although Hayes's performance and protest were too little and too late, Negro voting survived for a generation in many parts of the South because of the white oligarchs' need for it (see p. 446). In the meantime, the revived southern leadership confounded Republican Radicals, Liberals, and Halfbreeds, each in their own way seeking to make the South solidly Republican, by making the South solidly Democratic.

## The economic undertow

While the Radicals tried to reconstruct the Union by extending to the southern states the familiar political privileges of freedom, failure of the Radicals to buttress political with economic gains gave southerners themselves a better opportunity to reconstruct their *section* by restoring the familiar economic disabilities of slavery. The Radicals' failure, in particular, to distribute land to the freedmen left the national government with no instrument but force to protect the political rights of its charges. When the policy of force was given up, the bitter fruits of the freedmen's economic dependency were harvested.

The economic plight of the South and its people, colored and white, was worsened by many other federal policies, although a few were ameliorative. One of the first economic needs of the South after the war was the restoration of markets and transportation, and here the federal government lent a helping hand. Within weeks of Appomattox all restrictions on the exchange of commodities between the former belligerents were withdrawn

and the blockade of Confederate ports was terminated. Soon after, the federal government returned southern railroads to their owners—many of them in better condition than before the war. River transport was at least as important to the South as railroads, but twenty years of Republican rule were to pass before the South got a fair share of river and harbor improvement funds, and many navigable streams long remained unusable for commerce.

The South's need for capital was as urgent as that for markets and transport. Many planters had hoped to raise the money with which to restore land, buildings, and equipment to their former productivity by selling at the very high prices of 1865 the stores of cotton that they had built up during the war, presumably for export. But these hopes were quickly dashed. Ordered, at the end of hostilities, to confiscate all Confederate government assets, federal Treasury agents indiscriminately raided private as well as public warehouses and kept much of their loot. The Treasury eventually paid some 40,000 southerners $30 million for their losses, but this was only a fraction of what was taken and in any case came too late to help in the first postwar years. Confiscatory federal taxes further depleted southern capital. In three years following the war, a so-called revenue tax on cotton alone took $68 million from the South—far more than the total amount spent on relief and reconstruction by all northern agencies.

Before the war, most of the large southern plantations had been heavily mortgaged. After the war, creditors, hard-pressed themselves, began demanding payment of interest and principal. Fear of imminent foreclosure stirred some planters to an unwonted show of activity, but the federal confiscation and confiscatory taxes checked them. Some southern planters fended off the day of judgment by selling off part of their land in order to finance cultivation of the rest. Others leased out acreage for money rent. But obviously there was not money enough available to sustain these expedients for long. The upshot was the reenactment of the familiar routine of the prewar South, by which planters paid no wages for labor while their workers paid no rent for land. Instead, each was to share in the *forth-coming* crop. That was the rub.

In order to get this crop into the ground both parties to the arrangement had to borrow. Since they had no other security, they had to give a first lien on what they hoped to produce. Only against this *forthcoming* collateral would the supply merchant advance the required seed, fertilizer, and equipment, as well as food and clothing. For his own stock-in-trade, the local merchant had to seek credit from northern suppliers. Risks in the South were so great that these suppliers demanded high prices for the goods they sold directly and high interest for the credit they extended. In addition, oppressive fees were charged for transportation, insurance, and other commercial services. All these charges the merchant passed on to the landlords and croppers whose liens he held. The merchant also added his own profit and perhaps a generous tithe to reward himself for his literacy at the expense of borrowers who could not read his books. Under this regime, the South became more firmly chained to northern creditors, while the cropper was enslaved to the merchant.

The South drifted the more deeply into the sharecropping and crop-lien systems because they offered a solution to the problem of labor as well as capital. Immediately after the war, many planters tried to hold on to their newly freed workers by offering them keep and cash. To protect the Negroes from being packed off as soon as the crops were in, the Freedmen's Bureau insisted, often over objections of the suspicious freedmen themselves, that the working arrangements be confirmed by written contracts. In the hope that the Negroes would stay at least until the harvest was over, the planter usually was willing to sign. The Black Codes, in turn (see p. 426), made it dangerous for the ex-slave to wander. A typical contract stipulated that the planter pay wages of $10 to $12 a month, less the cost, determined by the planter, of "quarters, fuel, healthy and substantial rations." In exchange, the freedman agreed "to labor . . . faithfully . . . six days during the week, in a manner customary on a plantation."

The wage system failed on the plantations largely because, as before, there was too little money. For what money there was, moreover, the planter usually found good prior uses. "The freedmen have universally been treated with bad faith," wrote General W. E. Strong from Texas in 1866, "and very few have received any compensation for work performed." The Negro himself often did not help matters. Emancipated, he quickly learned to resent working "in a manner customary on a plantation."

Sharecropping gradually stabilized labor relations in the cash-poor South. It also helped preserve the plantation system. Under sharecropping, the land was divided into many small "holdings" which gave the illusion of small independent farms, and indeed did represent a significant upward step for freedmen relieved of the gang labor of the slave system. But many small holdings together actually formed parts of single plantations, which, through foreclosures, gradually fell to the supply merchants or their own creditors. These businessmen helped liquidate the survivors of the old planter caste, but they themselves gained much gratification from becoming great landowners.

During the late 1860s and early 1870s, the cotton crop never reached the prewar levels of 3.5 to 4 million bales and prices held at 15 cents a pound or more. Under the sharecropping system, with its emphasis on the single cash crop, overproduction soon became the rule and cotton prices tumbled. By 1890, the South was growing 8.5 million bales, and the price had fallen to 8.5 cents. In 1894, production reached a record high of 10 million bales, and the price sank to a record low of 4.5 cents. Falling prices and mounting debts sapped whatever spirit of enterprise had survived the social conflicts and legalized abuses of the time.

### White farmers in the "New South"

At the outbreak of the Civil War, eight times as many blacks as whites had been employed in growing cotton, most of them concentrated on the newer plantations of the rich Gulf plain and the Mississippi Valley. After the war, many of these blacks had become sharecroppers and continued to work these once excellent lands. Their lingering servility, in turn, recommended them to the landowner and the merchant. White croppers were likely to be "ornery." "White labor," said an Alabama planter in 1888, "is totally unsuited to our methods, our manners, and our accommodations." Another in Mississippi said, "Give me the nigger every time. . . . We can boss him, and that is what we southern folk like."

The devastation of the war, however, also soon caught up with the yeoman white farmer. He too needed credit from the local merchants to get his land back into production and his home and barns repaired. And, as in the case of the croppers, the merchants dictated that the white farmers also grow little but cotton. At first, the white farmers might give the merchant a lien on their forthcoming crops. As debts mounted, the merchant demanded a mortgage on the farmer's land as well; and as the cotton market deteriorated, the merchant ultimately foreclosed. Some white farmers managed to beat the trend and became large landowners and even merchants. But most of them went under.

The independent white farmers had learned early to look on sharecropping as a Negro institution, but most were forced to accept it—"like victims of some horrid nightmare," said the imaginative Tom Watson of Georgia, "powerless — oppressed — shackled." Those who refused to give up their independence were relegated to the poorest land, from which their offspring began drifting to the towns. By the 1880s, many white farmers had lost virtually everything but their pride of race. It was to restore employment and ambition to white farm youth that the idea of the "New South" was born—a South in which black "hands" would "keep their place" growing staples in the hot sun while whites found remunerative work in textile and to-bacco factories, iron and steel mills, and other industrial enterprises.

The movement to save the South through industrialism took on the guise of a crusade. After 1880, white doctors, preachers, lawyers, professors, and a veritable army of old generals and colonels gave their names and reputations, their energy and their capital, to the mission. The textile industry, already restored, continued to grow most rapidly, but during the depression of the mid-1880s, southern iron began to compete successfully with Pittsburgh's, the North Carolina tobacco manufacturing industry responded optimistically to the new fad of cigarette smoking, and a bit later the cottonseed-oil manufacturing industry spurted upward. Another and more important goal of the crusade was to draw northern capital southward. It was to this goal that Henry Grady, publisher of the powerful *Atlanta Constitution*, gave most attention. Invading the North to recruit capital, management, and men, Grady told the barons of the New England Club in New York: "We have wiped out the place where Mason and Dixon's line used to be. . . . We are ready to lay odds on the Georgia Yankee as he manufactures relics of the battle-field in a one-story shanty and squeezes pure olive oil out of his cotton-seed, against any down easterner that ever swapped wooden nutmegs for flannel sausages in the valleys of Vermont."

In the 1880s northern capital had good reason for looking hopefully to the South. "The South," Chauncey M. Depew, the railroad lawyer and politician, told the Yale alumni, "is the Bonzana of the future. We have developed all the great and sudden opportunities for wealth . . . in the Northwest States and on the Pacific Slope. . . . Go South, Young Man." There were other inducements, such as the promise of long hours of labor at moderate wages. An Alabama publicist in 1886 offered this additional security: "The white laboring classes here are separated from the Negroes . . . by an innate consciousness of race superiority. This sentiment dignifies the character of white labor. It excites a sentiment of sympathy and equality on their part with the classes above them, and in this way becomes a wholesome social leaven."

*Wealthy northerners promenading
in St. Augustine, Florida, during a winter
season in the eighties, reflecting
"the road to reunion" promoted by big-
business wealth in the North
and big-business aspirants in the South.*

Grady thinks that 'Plenty rides on the springing harvest!' It rides on Grady's springing
imagination. . . . In Grady's farm life there are
no poor cows . . . lands all 'Rich—Richer—Richest.' Snowy Cotton, rustling corn. In reality—barren wastes, gullied slopes—ruined
lowlands. . . . Gin houses on crutches. Diving
down in the grass for cotton." In notes for a
speech which Grady's *Constitution* would not
print, Watson jotted down: " 'New South'
idea. If it means apology, abject submission—
sycophancy to success—perish the thought. . .
Shame to Southern men who go to Northern
Banquets and Glory in our defeat. . . . Unpa-
ternal, patricidal."

### A closed society

While the Supreme Court's decision
in the *Civil Rights Cases* of 1883 opened the
way for social segregation under the law in
the South, and the "separate but equal" decisions extended the legality of such segregation
to educational institutions (see p. 440), Negro
voting in many parts of the South survived
the end of Radical Reconstruction in 1877 and
the violence of the white supremacists. One
reason for this was the heavy concentration of
Negroes in the old plantation districts; another
was that, in many localities where they did
not actually make up a majority of the electorate, they were sufficiently numerous to hold
the balance of power when white voters split,
as they often did on important local issues.
When these splits occurred, even though their
own interests might be closer to those of the
small white farmers, the Negroes usually were
courted with success by the ruling conservatives, or Bourbons. Perhaps the successors to
the old masters indeed knew how to manage
their colored hands. In any case, their tactics,
when they wanted the black vote, also included economic intimidation in the form of
threats of loss of land, credit, or jobs; and
economic and other inducements such as
bribes and fiery libations. When intimidation
and inducement failed, open resort was had to

Unfortunately for the promoters of the New
South, as late as 1900 fewer than 4 percent of
the people in the important textile state of
South Carolina were as yet engaged in manufacturing, while 70 percent remained in agriculture. The ratios in the rest of the South
were little different. And what did the white
industrial family gain? "Their power," writes a
critic of the factory owners, "was peculiarly
Southern. Unconsciously copying the planters,
they established their workers in villages
which resembled the slave quarters of old." In
return for this "benevolence" they received a
"feudal obedience."

And as for the agrarian South? In 1888,
young Tom Watson wrote in his journal: "Mr.

Raleigh News and Observer

*Front-page cartoon by Norman E. Jennette*
*from* The News and Observer, *Raleigh,*
*North Carolina, July 4, 1900,*
*depicting fear of Negro rule in the state.*

crude election frauds. All these expedients came to be used against vulnerable whites as well.

In the late 1880s and early 1890s, when agricultural depression caused discontented staple farmers to organize in the Populist movement and to pit their strength against conservative business and political leaders, it seemed possible in the South that poor white and black farmers might join together politically to unseat the Bourbons. Populist leaders like Tom Watson now began to preach cooperation among poor croppers regardless of race. Only in North Carolina, however, were the Populists able, by joining with the Republicans still to be found there, to defeat the Bourbon Democrats. In 1894 the Populists won control of the state legislature, captured a majority of the state's congressional seats, and elected both United States senators. In 1896 they retained control of the state legislature and also won the governorship. Most black voters supported them in these elections and they rewarded hundreds of such voters with government jobs.

North Carolina promptly became the target of the entire South, which rallied to the support of the Democratic party in the state and helped it violently to dislodge the biracial Populists in the election of 1898. Elsewhere in the South black support of the hated Bourbons, even at the peak of Populism's highly emotional appeal, only intensified the white farmers' antipathy toward the Negro, and their racism and resentment of Bourbonism both ran amuck.

In order to restore some stability to white unity after they had thwarted the Populist challenge, the Bourbons displayed a growing willingness to sacrifice what remained of those Negro prerogatives which had served themselves so well. They were the more strongly motivated to do this by their own profound revulsion from the corruption and violence that increasingly marred southern elections as differences among white voters widened. By appealing, at the same time, to

the small farmers' deepened commitment to white supremacy, the Bourbons hoped to induce the white farmers to sacrifice some of their own prerogatives for the cause, thereby offsetting Bourbon losses in black voting strength.

The small farmers proved very reluctant to be induced; yet, after making some genuine concessions, sometimes simply by legislation, sometimes by constitutional amendments, but most frequently by wholly new constitutions, the Bourbons carried the day after all. Their concessions included such Populist demands as railroad regulatory commissions and paid public appraisers of corporation property so that it might more rewardingly be taxed. But the stormiest issue was the central one of the suffrage, and the broadest concessions were made here. These took such forms as the notorious "understanding" tests, "grandfather" clauses, "veterans" privileges, and "good character" provisos, all to be administered by Democratic registration boards and similarly "discreet" election officials. As the Chairman of the Judiciary Committee of the Louisiana Constitutional Convention of 1898, Thomas J. Semmes, said of the grandfather clause adopted there, by this means "... every white man ... although he may not be able to read and write, although he does not possess the property qualifications, may, notwithstanding, if he register himself pursuant to this ordinance of the Constitution, be thereafter entitled to vote."

**448**

Such were the sieves—and there were others, such as long residence requirements and disqualifications for the pettiest of crimes, that were especially effective against peripatetic and sufficiently provoked Negroes—that were to trap the black aspirant but let the white man through. Because these measures "did not on their face discriminate between the races," as they were forbidden to do by the Fifteenth Amendment, but rather "swept the circle of expedients" remaining, the Supreme Court, in the case of *Williams* v. *Mississippi*, April 25, 1898, ruled that such means were "within the field of permissible action under the limitations imposed by the Federal Constitution."

Nevertheless, there were catches for the whites as well. One of them was the time limit often placed on the escape provisions. As Semmes said of the white man's grandfather clause, "If he doesn't choose to register between now and the last of September next, he loses the privilege conferred upon him, and thereafter he can only vote provided he possesses the qualifications which I have just mentioned—the property or education. That is the temporary clause." The property qualifications, in turn, were uniformly high, while the education clauses could be enforced stringently enough to discourage respectable illiterates from exposing their limitations in schooling to their neighbors. Another effective catch was the poll tax usually imposed by the new regulations. This tax was cumulative from year to year. Since little effort would be made to collect it, it often mounted up. The only penalty for nonpayment might be the loss of the right to vote, a loss the more stoically borne as the amount soared.

The small farmers had been so certain that any means of disfranchising the Negro under the Fourteenth and Fifteenth Amendments would necessarily disfranchise themselves that they vigorously fought even the calling of the new constitutional conventions. So certain were the Bourbons, in turn, that the escape clauses for the whites would prove unsatisfactory to these farmers that, except in Alabama, they declared the new fundamental laws adopted without submitting them to referendums. Both groups were proved right. In state after state, following Mississippi's example of 1890, as the new suffrage laws were adopted, Negro voting virtually ceased, white voting also fell off, and small Democratic oligarchies gained control of political machinery. Such control insured Bourbon domination of most social institutions in the South and kept them lily white.

By returning their friends to Congress year after year, the Bourbon Democrats also gained extraordinary power in major House and Senate committees, where seniority ruled and the life and death of legislation often was at stake. This was especially true during Democratic administrations, which they themselves helped elect by delivering the "Solid South" to the party.

## For further reading

The best introduction to the Reconstruction period is K. M. Stampp, *The Era of Reconstruction 1865-1877* (1965). R. W. Patrick, *The Reconstruction of the Nation* (1967), and J. H. Franklin, *Reconstruction After the Civil War* (1961), are able surveys. J. G. Randall and David Donald, *The Civil War and Reconstruction* (1961), is a comprehensive study with special emphasis on constitutional issues. Donald, *The Politics of Reconstruction 1863-1867* (1965), is illuminating on early policies. R. N. Current, ed., *Reconstruction*

1865-1877 (1965), and J. P. Shenton, ed., *The Reconstruction, a Documentary History 1865-1877* (1963), are useful short anthologies. W. J. Cash, *The Mind of the South* (1941), is as stimulating on this period as on others. P. H. Buck, *The Road to Reunion 1865-1900* (1937), is a unique study of influences tending, with too little success, to reunite the sections. W. E. B. Du Bois, *Black Reconstruction in America 1860-1880* (1935), is a classic by a leading Negro intellectual. Robert Cruden, *The Negro in Reconstruction* (1969), is illuminating if less ambitious. Otis Singletary, *The Negro Militia and Reconstruction* (1957), gives a glimpse of the violence of the times. J. W. De Forest, *A Union Officer in the Reconstruction* (1948 ed.), is a revealing report. Much valuable material on this subject will be found in Herbert Aptheker, *A Documentary History of the Negro People in the United States* (1951).

Reconstruction really began in the Confederacy with the movement of northern forces southward. The Lincoln biographies by Sandburg, Randall, and Thomas; and R. P. Basler, ed., *The Collected Works of Abraham Lincoln* (9 vols., 1953-1955), cover much of his program. Early reconstruction efforts are examined in W. L. Rose, *Rehearsal for Reconstruction, The Port Royal Experiment* (1964), and Joel Williamson, *After Slavery, The Negro in South Carolina during Reconstruction 1861-1877* (1965). J. E. Sefton, *The United States Army and Reconstruction 1865-1877* (1968), is a comprehensive monograph. W. S. McFeely, *Yankee Stepfather, General O. O. Howard and the Freedmen* (1968), is a good modern account of the Freedmen's Bureau. H. A. White, *The Freedmen's Bureau in Louisiana* (1970), is an illuminating case study. E. L. McKitrick, *Andrew Johnson and Reconstruction* (1960), is a comprehensive account. LaWanda and J. H. Cox, *Politics, Principle and Prejudice 1865-1866* (1963), emphasizes Johnson's role in efforts to restore the Democratic party in the North.

T. H. Williams, *Lincoln and the Radicals* (1941), offers a starting point for the study of Stevens, Sumner, and company. F. M. Brodie, *Thaddeus Stevens* (1959), and David Donald, *Charles Sumner and the Rights of Man* (1970), are leading biographies. J. M. McPherson, *The Struggle for Equality, Abolitionists and the Negro in the Civil War and Reconstruction* (1964), is an outstanding monograph on certain sources of Radical thinking. Illuminating monographs on the Fourteenth Amendment include J. B. James, *The Framing of the Fourteenth Amendment* (1956), and Jacobus tenBroek, *The Antislavery Origins of the Fourteenth Amendment* (1951). William Gillette, *The Right to Vote, Politics and the Passage of the Fifteenth Amendment* (1965), covers that measure. Paul Lewinson, *Race, Class and Party, A History of Negro Suffrage and White Politics in the South* (1932), is an able study. S. D. Smith, *The Negro in Congress 1870-1901* (1940), is a thorough scholarly account. V. L. Wharton, *The Negro in Mississippi 1865-1890* (1947), is a model study; among other such special accounts the following may be noted: A. A. Taylor, *The Negro in Tennessee 1865-1880* (1941). and G. B Tindall, *South Carolina Negroes 1877-1900* (1952).

Allan Nevins, *Hamilton Fish: The Inner History of the Grant Administration* (1936), is the definitive account. See also Matthew Josephson, *The Politicos 1865-1896* (1938). E. D. Ross, *The Liberal Republican Movement* (1919), and C. M. Fuess, *Carl Schurz, Reformer* (1932), cover this third-party venture.

Four outstanding works by C. V. Woodward offer the best introductions to the demise of the Reconstruction spirit: *Reunion and Reaction* (1951), *Origins of the New South 1877-1913* (1951), *Tom Watson, Agrarian Rebel* (1938), and *The Strange Career of Jim Crow* (1966 ed.). V. O. Key, Jr., *Southern Politics in State and Nation* (1949), is a brilliant study of the "redeemers" legacy. R. W. Logan, *The Negro in American Life and Thought, The Nadir 1877-1901* (1954), is a detailed study of the abandonment of Radical goals, north and south. For the Negro reaction see August Meier, *Negro Thought in America 1880-1915* (1963). S. P. Hirshon, *Farewell to the Bloody Shirt: Northern Republicans & the Southern Negro 1877-1893* (1962), and V. P. De Santis, *Republicans Face the Southern Question—The New Departure Years 1877-1897* (1959), are outstanding on party strategies. On sharecropping and related subjects, see the relevant chapters in F. A. Shannon, *The Farmers Last Frontier: Agriculture 1860-1897* (1945). Theodore Saloutos, *Farmer Movements in the South 1865-1933* (1960), is excellent on organized protest and self-help. R. B. Nixon, *Henry W. Grady: Spokesman of the New South* (1943), is a useful introduction to the industrial spirit. A. W. Tourgée, *A Fool's Errand* (1879); L. H. Blair, *A Southern Prophecy, The Prosperity of the South Dependent upon the Elevation of the Negro* (1889; modern ed., 1964); and Arlin Turner, ed., *The Negro Question, A Selection of the Writings on Civil Rights in the South by George W. Cable* (1958 ed.), foreshadow some modern ideas.

# LAST LAND FRONTIERS

Only about half of the United States, geographically speaking, had been seriously engaged in the sectional conflicts of the 1850s, in the Civil War, and in the issues of Reconstruction. As late as 1860, except for Texas, not a single state had been set up on the vast plains beyond the Mississippi Valley, roughly between the 95th and 104th parallels. Farther west, in the forbidding mountain country of the Rockies and the Sierras, and in the Great Basin between these ranges, political organization had hardly begun.

News of the great events of the Civil War often failed to reach the men who roamed this distant wilderness, nor were they much concerned with the battle reports. Yet their own battles, formal and informal, helped force open the way for the millions from the older sections of the country and the old countries of Europe who would soon follow across the trails of these pioneers.

Before the last land frontiers were brought within the framework of the big business system that was to make the United States a powerful newcomer among the world's great nations, the Wild West led an extraordinary life of its own—a life that entered profoundly into the American spirit and mythology. Even before the Civil War ended, the pattern of cowboys, rustlers, and roundups, warpaths and council fires, wide-open mining towns, and posses and sheriffs, had imposed itself on the vast open spaces of the West. After the war, this pattern became so firmly implanted in the American consciousness that to this day it remains a TV staple.

Yet the Wild West had a very short life. By

1890, all of it, except for future Utah, Arizona, New Mexico, and Oklahoma, had been cut up into states of the Union. Railroads had long since spanned the continent and opened connecting lines in the new mining, ranching, and farming areas. Mining, cattle raising, and even farming had come conspicuously under the control of great corporations financed by eastern and foreign capital. By 1890, the Indian wars were over; the army had been withdrawn from the western forts; the frontier era itself was officially declared closed.

## I  Conquest of the plains

*The land and the people*

In the 1540s the Spaniard Coronado had described the enormous western plains as "uninhabited deserts," a description that persisted for more than three centuries. When, in 1820, following western boundary settlements with Britain, Major Stephen H. Long returned from his explorations of the region, he called the plains worthless for an agricultural people, and his phrase "Great American Desert" henceforth appeared on all maps of the West. As late as 1856 the *North American Review,* referring to elaborate surveys that had been made for transcontinental railroads, said: "We may as well admit that . . . whatever route is selected, . . . it must wind the greater part of its length through a country destined to remain forever an uninhabited waste."

The uncharted vast expanse of the plains, which extended well into Mexico and Canada, lay as boundless and unbroken as the ocean and offered hardly a hollow for cover. Trees for fuel, houses, fences, or shade were almost completely lacking. Only the lightest rains fell here, but violent hail storms and crushing falls of snow as dry as sand periodically assaulted the region, driven by winds that surged to gale velocity. Sucked dry in their passage over the snow-crowned western mountains, these winds brought extremes of heat and cold to the plains, and alternately parched and froze the few rivers on their surface.

For white men whose outlook had long been conditioned by the forests, rivers, rainfall, and rolling hills of western Europe and eastern America, here was a country to be shunned. Most of those who journeyed to the woodlands and watercourses of Oregon and California, starting with the forty-niners and ending with the first passengers of the transcontinental railroads twenty years later, avoided the "desert" altogether. Some went by clipper ship around the Horn. Others sailed to Panama, made the portage across the Isthmus, and sailed again up Pacific coastal waters. So strewn were the plains with wrecks of conveyances, carcasses of cows and oxen, and burial piles of loved ones of those who attempted to cross the "desert" by wagon train, that Mark Twain exclaimed of one region in Nevada, "The desert was one prodigious graveyard."

Yet the arid, treeless plains, like the high mountain ridges and the clear mountain streams that the western trappers plied, teemed with life. Hundreds of millions of jack rabbits and "prairie dogs" (really rodents) fed on the prevalent grass; tens of millions of wolves and coyotes fed on the rabbits and the "dogs." Most picturesque and most significant were the immense buffalo herds. "Of all the quadrupeds that have lived upon the earth," wrote W. T. Hornaday, a leading nineteenth-century naturalist, "probably no other species has ever marshalled such innumerable hosts as those of the American bison."

The American buffalo herd in the 1850s and 1860s has been estimated at 12 to 13 million head. The Plains Indians lived off the buffalo. Its flesh provided their food, its skin their clothing, its hide the sheltering cover of their tepees. Their daily life revolved around the buffalo hunt, and their ritual and worship were dedicated to its success.

For centuries the Plains Indians had hunted the buffalo on foot, yet the herds multiplied. In the sixteenth century, Spaniards brought the horse to the American continent, and during the next 200 years hundreds of thousands of horses wandered northward from Mexico. The horse greatly increased the Plains Indians' hunting range, and, by carrying them to lands that belonged to other tribes, had intensified tribal warfare. A mounted Indian was also a much more efficient hunter than one on foot, and the buffalo herds now steadily diminished. As time went on, tribal wars for possession of the precious beast became more frequent and bloody. To survive, the Indians grew more nomadic, more violent, and more hostile to trespassers of any kind or color.

George Catlin, who spent a decade in his middle years painting pictures of Plains Indians, said of the Comanche tribe:

*I am ready, without hesitation, to pronounce the Comanches the most extraordinary horsemen that I have seen yet in all my travels. . . . Comanches . . . on*

The New-York Historical Society, New York City

*their feet [are] one of the most unattractive and slovenly-looking races of Indians; . . . but the moment they mount their horses, they seem at once metamorphosed, and surprise the spectator with the ease and elegance of their movements. [The Comanche's] face even becomes handsome, and he gracefully flies away like a different being.*

Other riders of the plains—the Sioux, Cheyenne, Pawnee, Blackfeet, and Crow—were nearly as proficient horsemen as the Comanches. A little to the south, the rather less nomadic but equally fearsome Osage, Kiowa, Iowa, Omaha, and related tribes also took well to the horse and the hunt. In the Southwest, on the more authentic desert of Arizona and New Mexico, rode the formidable Navajos and Apaches. These Indians gradually developed a short bow, no more than two and a half or three feet across and superbly adapted to shooting from horseback. They also carried a quiver of a hundred barbed arrows, a long spear, and (in warfare) a circular shield fashioned from the hide of buffalo neck. These shields were so carefully smoke-cured and hardened they could deflect bullets that struck at an angle.

"We were surprised, incredulous, almost offended," reported visitors to Kansas in 1854, "when a young officer . . . deliberately asserted that our mounted men, though armed

*"Herd of Bison, Near Lake Jessie"*
*(in Griggs County, North Dakota)*
*by John Mix Stanley, 1853. "One of the few*
*pictures still extant," writes Robert Taft,*
*"made by an actual observer of the*
*enormous number of the buffalo on the*
*western plains before the day*
*of the railroad."*

453

with revolvers, were in general not a match in close combat, for the mounted Indians, with their bows and arrows." Riding outside (not atop) his horse, with both hands free, one to feed and the other to release his bow, and shooting under the neck or belly of his mount while remaining virtually invisible himself, the Indian would circle madly, frighten ill-trained army horses with his curdling yells, and thus render "any certain aim with the revolver impossible, while his arrows [were] discharged at horse and man more rapidly than even a revolver [could] be fired." At 30 yards, an Indian fighter galloping at full speed is said to have been able to keep six or eight arrows in the air and on the target, each delivered with sufficient force for the entire shaft to penetrate the body of a buffalo.

Not all the Indians of the West were as fierce and efficient as the fighting tribes of the plains and the "desert." In the poor but protected areas of the Colorado Plateau and the southern Great Basin, for example, agricultural and essentially peaceful tribes, such as the highly civilized Hopi and Zuñi, built their pueblos into the Basin's cliffs and cultivated fields sometimes as far as 20 miles from their homes. To the north and west, in the upper regions of the Great Basin and on the Columbia Plateau, lived such primitive tribes as the Utes, Shoshones, Bannocks, and Snakes, who never took up agriculture but eked out a thin diet of occasional bear and elk by eating reptiles, rodents, vermin, grasshoppers, and, as Mark Twain said, "anything they can bite." Still farther west lived the "Digger Indians" of California, who subsisted on roots, tubers, and seeds that they dug out of the earth. Mark Twain found them "the wretchedest type of mankind I have ever seen." Completing the Indian population were the sad remnants of the Five Civilized Tribes of the East, forcibly removed to Oklahoma country, and other "woods Indians" who had been driven west. Both groups soon fell prey not only to government neglect but also to the "horse" tribes, as implacably opposed to their presence as to that of the encroaching whites.

In 1860, about 225,000 Indians shared the "desert" and the mountain region—providentially reserved, as Zebulon Pike had said half a century earlier, for "the wandering and uncivilized aborigines of the country"—with the buffalo, the wild horse, the jack rabbit, and the coyote. But the white man, and for that matter, the black, could not be excluded altogether. In 1860, about 175,000 whites and a sprinkling of blacks—probably 90 percent of them male—lived in future Dakota country, Montana, Idaho, Wyoming, Colorado, New Mexico, Arizona, Utah, and Nevada. Civil War deserters and free Negroes from the North and South soon increased their number. Except for the 25,000 Mormons settled in Utah, they, like most Indians, kept on the move. They prospected for precious metals, hunted buffalo, trapped marten and beaver, drove cattle and sheep, guided and sometimes misguided emigrant trains bound for California and Oregon, scouted for the army, hauled overland freight and mail, gambled, drank, and wenched when occasion offered, and traded and fought with the red men. Some of them, like Kit Carson and Jim Bridger and the less well-publicized ex-mountain men like the Irishman Thomas Fitzpatrick and mulatto Jim Beckwourth, were as free on a horse and as sharp on a trail as the best of the braves.

### Removing the Indians

Commenting years later on the disease that had wiped out the Wampanoags and other tribes in Massachusetts within a decade after the arrival of *Mayflower,* Cotton Mather said: "The woods were almost cleared of those pernicious creatures, to make room for a better growth." From the very beginning of white settlement in North America, the paganism of the natives served to justify Christian violence.

The white migration to Oregon in the 1840s, the surveys for transcontinental railroads starting in 1853, the organization and settlement of the Kansas-Nebraska region in 1854, and the Colorado Gold Rush of 1859 all joined to convince the western Indians of "the fatal tendency of their new environment." If further evidence were needed, the attitude of the United States government furnished it. Demands from traders, travelers, and explorers for protection against Indians striving to protect their own lands and way of life prompted the army in the 1840s and 1850s to establish a line of forts on the plains. In 1851, the policy of maintaining "one big reservation" on the whole expanse of the "desert" ended, and treaties were made with Plains Indians chieftains obliging them (if they could) to force their own braves, for sheer survival, onto reservations that (1) deprived them of their traditional hunting grounds, and (2) crowded them onto the lands of other tribes who resented their presence.

In the meantime, the administration of Indian affairs, which had previously been a function of the army, was given in part to the Bureau of the Interior, created in 1849. The discontent among the Indians caused by the new reservation policy was fanned into rebellion by the corruption and maladministration of this new department. Many of its officials made fortunes supplying reservation Indians with shoddy of all sorts, by cheating them of their lands, and by selling them forbidden liquor. Westerners often took part in the Bureau's dealings with the Indians and naturally supported it.

The army, at the same time, reluctant to yield any of its power to civilian politicos, found supporters of its own among western merchants who made a good deal of money off the army garrisons and wanted the troops to stay. Between corrupt administrators and touchy soldiers, the red men were either starved on the reservations or killed in the open country. In the 1850s, one western settler wrote:

> It was customary to speak of the Indian man as a Buck; of the woman as a squaw.... By a very natural and easy transition, from being spoken of as brutes, they came to be thought of as game to be shot, or a vermin to be destroyed.

The treaties of 1851 and after progressively shrank the Indians' lands and permitted the government to build roads and railroads across Indian preserves. As in the past, such treaties often were made only with nominal Indian leaders and rump groups. Most Indians never were consulted; if they raised their voices in protest, they were ignored. But it proved one thing to set aside Indian reservations and another to force the red men onto them and to keep them there. Trouble was constantly brewing. In 1862, when regular army units were recalled from the plains for Civil War service and were replaced by inexperienced recruits, the earliest of the Indian wars on the plains broke out.

That year a small band of Sioux youths murdered five whites near a reservation in the vicinity of New Ulm, Minnesota. To forestall retaliation, the Sioux, under Little Crow, took to the warpath, killed hundreds of settlers, and burned their farmhouses. The militia finally overwhelmed them and thirty-eight braves were hanged in a ghoulish public ceremony. Running conflict between the eastern Sioux and the army continued until late in 1863, the year of Little Crow's death. The Sioux lands in Minnesota were confiscated, and the remnants of the tribe moved elsewhere.

Two years later, in an attempt to satisfy the miners' demands for better access to supplies and civilization, the government tried to build a good wagon road along the Bozeman Trail from Fort Laramie, Wyoming, north to isolated Bozeman and Helena, Montana. This road would have cut across the choicest hunting grounds of the western Sioux. Red Cloud, chief of the western tribes, led his warriors in

unremitting harassment of the work. "Every straggler was cut down, every wagon train bringing in supplies raided, every wood-cutting party attacked." To protect the project, the army started three forts along the trail. In December 1866 a wood train approaching one of them was set upon by the Indians. To see the caravan through and to relieve the unfinished fort, a small force under Captain W. J. Fetterman was ordered to the scene. Red Cloud's braves dissolved into the wilderness and Fetterman foolishly led his men after them. The Indians quickly ambushed Fetterman's forces and massacred all eighty-two of them, including the rash captain. Inflamed by their success, the Sioux increased the frequency and violence of their assaults, and in the next few months forced the abandonment of the Bozeman Trail project. They also forced

**455**

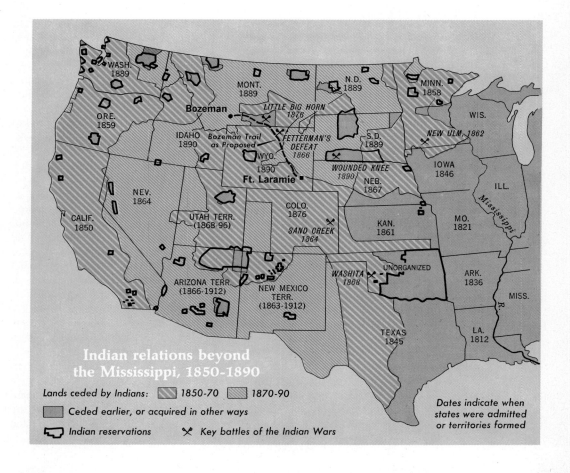

Indian relations beyond the Mississippi, 1850–1890

Lands ceded by Indians: 1850-70  1870-90

Ceded earlier, or acquired in other ways

Indian reservations        Key battles of the Indian Wars

Dates indicate when states were admitted or territories formed

a disconcerted country to rethink its approach to the red men. "Our whole Indian policy," observed *The Nation* after the "Fetterman massacre," "is a system of mismanagement, and in many parts one of gigantic abuse."

456

To the south, meanwhile, warfare with the Cheyenne and Arapaho tribes had been raging since 1861, when miners claimed their Colorado lands. This phase of the Indian wars came to a climax in 1864, when a force under Colonel John M. Chivington butchered about 450 men, women, and children in a temporary Cheyenne encampment at Sand Creek. The Indians, under their chief, Black Kettle, had tried every means to surrender peacefully, first by raising an American flag and then the traditional white flag. But Chivington's native lust had been set aflame by a telegram from his superior, General S. R. Curtis, United States army commander in the West: "I want no peace till the Indians suffer more." And suffer they did. A white trader, witness to the slaughter, reported that the Cheyenne "were scalped, their brains knocked out; the men used their knives, ripped open women, clubbed little children, knocked them in the head with their guns, beat their brains out, mutilated their bodies in every sense of the word." Such savagery fed upon itself, and Indian-army warfare in the Southwest grew more and more brutal until 1868. In that year, at Washita in Oklahoma, an army contingent under Colonel George A. Custer (he had lost his title of Major-General when the volunteer army was disbanded following Appomattox) defeated a band of Cheyenne and Arapaho warriors. Black Kettle was killed here and his braves thus the more easily subdued.

Scores of other battles took place between the army and the Indians and between Indians and marauding white civilians. But the Sioux and Cheyenne wars convinced a parsimonious Congress that the cost of subduing the Indians was too great and that the rate of subjugation was too slow. Thus, in 1867 peace commissioners were sent to convince the tribes to move to selected reservations, one in the Black Hills of Dakota, the other in present-day Oklahoma. By 1868, treaties to this effect were forced upon the war-weary Indians. General Sherman wrote:

*We have now ... provided reservations for all, off the great roads. All who cling to their old hunting grounds are hostile and will remain so till killed off. We will have a sort of predatory war for years—every now and then be shocked by the indiscriminate murder of travelers and settlers, but the country is so large, and the advantage of the Indians so great, that we cannot make a single war end it.*

As Sherman predicted, conflict became constant. Between 1869 and 1875 over 200 pitched battles were waged between the army and the Indians. The nature of these conflicts may be deduced from a statement of General Francis A. Walker, Commissioner of Indian Affairs, in 1871: "When dealing with savage men, as with savage beasts, no question of national honor can arise. Whether to fight, to run away, or to employ a ruse, is solely a question of expediency." On the reservations, meanwhile, a new civilian Board of Indian Commissioners, created in 1869, tried to convert the Plains Indians to agriculture on inadequate land. By ekeing out the pitiful crops with bonuses, annuities, and other doles, these commissioners made the Indians increasingly dependent, and pauperization completed their moral undoing.

In the 1870s, violence continued to flare as the Indians were kept on the new reservations only with great difficulty, and as the whites, with equal difficulty, were kept off them. Moldy flour, spoiled beef, and moth-eaten blankets made up the typical fare supplied to the reservation Indians by the commissioners. The Sioux in Dakota were further enraged by the encroachment on their reservation of Northern Pacific railroad crews and by the influx of gold prospectors in the Black Hills in 1874. In 1876 war broke out again. It was during this conflict that Colonel Custer made his famous "last stand" against Crazy Horse and Sitting Bull in the Battle of the Little Big Horn, June 25, 1876. The Sioux annihilated Custer, but shortages of ammunition and food forced them to scatter. An ill-timed attack on a wagon train gave away the location of the largest group of braves, and their capture in October 1876 ended the war. Sitting Bull fled to Canada but, facing starvation, returned in 1881.

In Oregon, the Nez Percé tribe, whose religious leaders urged them to drive out the whites, took to the warpath against encroaching miners in 1877. Until they succumbed to starvation and disease, the Nez Percé, under Chief Joseph, led 5000 government troops on a wild chase over Oregon and Montana. In the 1880s, the Apaches in New Mexico went on a prolonged rampage until their chief, Geronimo, was captured in 1886.

What finally destroyed the Indians was the extermination of the buffalo herd. The building of the Union Pacific in the late 1860s cut the herd in two and left the southern bisons at the mercy of every railroad worker, miner, adventurer, and traveler. Since a stampeding herd was capable of overturning a train, buffalo hunting became a regular feature of railroad building. "Buffalo Bill" Cody made his reputation by killing some 4000 buffalo in eighteen months as a hunter for the Kansas Pacific Railroad. In 1871, the fate of the buffalo was sealed when a Pennsylvania tannery discovered that it could process buffalo skins into commercial leather. Hides, hardly worth retrieving before, suddenly became worth $1 to $3 apiece. Between 1872 and 1874, the annual carnage of buffalo averaged 3 million head, and by 1878 the southern herd had been wiped out. In 1886, when the National Museum wanted to mount some buffalo, it found only about 600 of the northern herd left, deep in the Canadian woods.

When Columbus discovered America, probably a million aborigines lived on the continent, north of Mexico. These natives were grouped in more than 600 distinct tribes, few of which numbered more than 2000 persons. With the coming of the horse, small groups of Plains Indians began to break off from the western tribes to hunt independently, and only once a year, in summer, did they reunite for tribal ceremonies which grew into a deca-

dent agglomeration of activities known, inaccurately, as the Sun Dance. This ritual lasted about a week and offerings were made to the buffalo. Fearful of the warlike spirit heightened by these religious activities and of the battle strength represented by the congregation of the surviving Indian bands, the government in 1884 prohibited the Sun Dance and other religious meetings. In 1890, nevertheless, the Sioux went ahead with the dance on their reservation. When troops appeared, the braves fled. The troops followed and, in the "battle" of Wounded Knee, massacred the half-starved remnants of the once fierce tribe. By then, barely 200,000 Indians remained in the United States.

Three years before Wounded Knee, in 1887, Congress had passed the Dawes Act, which defined the government's basic Indian policy until 1934. This act broke up tribal autonomy even on the reservations. It divided up reservation land and gave each family head 160 acres to cultivate. After a probation period of twenty-five years, he was to be granted full rights of ownership and citizenship in the United States. In 1924, the United States granted citizenship to all the Indians in the country.

The Dawes Act, a dramatic reversal of former Indian policy, was the result of widespread humanitarian opposition to the extermination policy that had been conducted by the army and the Interior Department. A highlight of the humanitarian campaign was the publication in 1881 of *A Century of Dishonor* and in 1884 of the novel *Ramona,* both by the prolific Massachusetts versifier and writer of children's books, Helen Hunt Jackson. The first, a scorching indictment of traditional governmental policy toward the red men, is no longer read except by scholars. *Ramona,* a kind of *Uncle Tom's Cabin* of the Wild West, has survived as a popular romance about the last days of Spanish rule in California.

Despite Mr. Dawes and Mrs. Jackson, the reversal of the traditional Indian policy by the Dawes Act did the Indian little but harm. In dividing the land as the act provided, the poorest territory was usually given to the red men, the best sold to white settlers. Even where the individual Indian obtained good

458

land, inexperience with ownership and with legal matters left him vulnerable to the same kind of sharp practice that had marked the making of tribal treaties. Again and again, braves were tricked into selling their best holdings. More disastrous still, they had neither the tradition nor the incentive to cultivate the land they retained. Many became paupers. The few exceptions included the handful of Indians who held onto their oil-rich Oklahoma lands and became millionaires.

The Indian Reorganization Act of 1934 again reversed Indian policy. Under men like John Collier, who had lived much of his life among the Navajos, the Office of Indian Affairs succeeded in restoring tribal landholding and tribal incentive on a wide scale. Collier's administration turned the "vanishing Americans" into one of the fastest-growing groups in the United States. By 1970 their number, including Eskimos, had risen to about 700,000.

Indian troubles, however, were far from over. During World War II, about 25,000 Indians served in the armed services, and the experience of many of them off the reservations led them to promote the accelerated assimilation of red men in white society. Westerners in Congress, led by Senator Arthur

Watkins of Utah, picked up this line for reasons of their own. At their urging, Congress in 1953 adopted two unfortunate measures. One, a joint resolution, set forth the legislature's intent, once and for all, to terminate federal responsibility for the surviving tribes as soon as feasible. The second, a step in the direction of this intent, gave the states authority over criminal and civil issues on the reservations independently of tribal leaders. The prompt termination of certain reservations threw the Indians on them into turmoil, causing the affected tribes immense losses in jointly held property and business enterprises and the individual Indians losses of homes, public services, and security. Many of them were thrown on state welfare rolls, thereby saddling the affected commonwealth with large new costs, difficult to meet. The "Great Society" programs of the 1960s undertook once more to alleviate the Indians' worsening situation and to restore purpose and incentive to their lives, but the "fatal tendency of their environment" clearly persisted.

## II  Prospectors and ranchers

### Mining country

The plains and mountains of the West, as we have seen, far from being desert wastes, pulsated with plant, animal, and human life. The thirty years after the Civil War were to reveal that this territory was also rich in agricultural and mineral wealth, the enormous extent of which has even yet to be appraised fully. The most productive of the earth's wheat lands, once the secret of cultivating them had been discovered, stretched across the Dakotas and eastern Montana. In the most westerly parts of these states, in large areas of Wyoming, Colorado, and Texas, and even in sections of Nevada, Utah, and Ari-

zona, seemingly boundless grazing lands lay ready to feed the cattle and sheep that would supply most of America's and the world's beef, mutton, hides, and wool. Other parts of the plains and the mountains held some of the world's largest and purest veins of copper and iron ore, some of the world's most extensive deposits of lead and zinc, and valuable seams of coal. Beneath the earth in Texas (and elsewhere in the West, as time proved) lay incredible reserves of crude petroleum and natural gas.

For centuries, nature had developed and stored these riches. But for generations the forest-oriented nation had even less use for them than did the Indians who roamed the western lands. Americans had plenty of land elsewhere; since wood remained abundant in the older settled areas, the demand for coal as a fuel and for iron in construction was small. Copper was virtually wasted on a people with little use, as yet, for electric wire. The supply of Pennsylvania petroleum, which was burned almost exclusively as an illuminant rather than a fuel, was more than adequate for a nation still awaiting the automobile. In the mid-nineteenth century, traditional channels of investment continued to reward American capital well enough, and men of means were content to leave to prospectors with little standing and less credit the job of searching out new wealth. And the prospectors cared little about the future requirements of organized society; they followed, unflaggingly, only the most ancient of lures—the precious metals, gold and silver.

The early prospectors for gold in California had a fine code and fine camaraderie. "Honesty was the ruling passion of '48," one of them wrote. "If an *hombre* got broke, he asked the first one he met to lend him such amount as he wanted until he could 'dig her out.' The loans were always made and always paid according to promise." A year later, however, the California crowds had thickened:

Hordes of pickpockets, robbers, thieves, and swindlers were mixed with men who had come with honest intentions. . . . Murders, thefts, and heavy robberies soon became the order of the day. A panic seized that portion of the diggers who had never before been out of sight of "marm's chimbly." . . . But men were to be found who had ridden the elephant of this world all their lives and well knew the course we had to pursue under the change of affairs. Whipping on the bare back, cutting off ears, and hanging soon became matters of as frequent occurrence as those of robbery, theft and murder.

Conditions grew steadily worse in California during the 1850s as the fabulous discoveries at Sutter's Fort and elsewhere in the San Joaquin and Sacramento valleys were thorough-ly staked out and some of the best locations began to run thin. In a single decade, miners extracted hundreds of millions of dollars in gold from these hills and streams, much of it by the crudest placer-mining methods. All a man needed was a shovel to throw "pay dirt" into a washing pan, a little water in which to swirl the dirt so that the mud and gravel separated from the grains of gold, and some kind of tool to scrape the grains from the bottom of the pan. The "cradle," an improvement over the crude washing pan, had cleats to catch the gold, so that it could be rocked with one hand while dirt and water were fed in with the other. The "sluice box" offered a still more efficient method. A long wooden box, called a "long Tom," with openings at one end and cleats at the other, was placed so that the flow of a fast-moving stream could be diverted through it. The miner then shoveled dirt into the box, let the water carry it away, and collected the gold that was caught. With these methods a man could take $50 a day from a rich area.

By the late 1850s, the pickings in California had become slender; plenty of gold remained, but it was buried under enormous deposits in hills that had to be blasted away, or was locked in tough veins of quartz that had to be tunneled and worked with costly equipment and teams of men.

Blasting and quartz-mining required more capital and business ability than most of the prospectors had. Those who managed to strike it rich usually gambled away their "dust" or squandered it in other ways. When surface gold ran out, a few took up more stable occupations; some became miners for corporations, and others even became farmers. Tens of thousands made "prospectin'" a way of life. Distance and inaccessibility meant nothing to them. Chinese, Australians, South Americans, Africans, and Europeans—all had come to California. Soon they were taking Californians back with them to prospect in their home countries. Gold fever was a disease from which thousands suffered all over the world. Few ever got over it, and fewer still became rich. But taken together, the prospectors gave a strong impetus to the wealth of nations and the flow of trade.

459

Even on the way to California in 1848 a pair of adventurers, Captain John Beck of Oklahoma country and W. Green Russell of Georgia, had seen signs of gold around the South

**460** Platte River in northeastern Colorado. In 1858, having sold out in California, they decided to look further into Colorado's possibilities and in July staked out the first claim in the Pike's Peak region near present-day Denver. Soon eastern newspapers were full of news of other Colorado strikes, and by the end of 1858 the cry "Pike's Peak or Bust" echoed through the land. By June 1859 over 100,000 "yondersiders" from California and "greenhorns" from Kansas and points east had made the trek to Colorado. Tall stories kept the gold bugs coming, but the truth soon became known: There was gold around Pike's Peak but very little of it. When the trek homeward began, the wagons carried the slogan "Pike's Peak and Busted." Some of the prospectors, as in California, stayed on to try their hand at farming and grazing and to lay the foundations for Colorado's future economy.

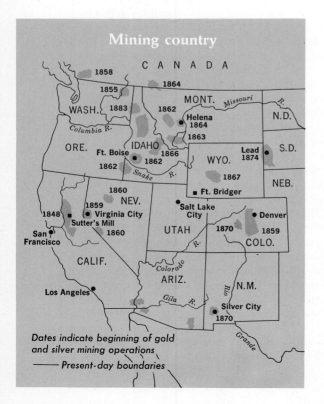

Mining country

Dates indicate beginning of gold and silver mining operations

—— Present-day boundaries

In May 1859 John H. Gregory made a new Colorado strike in an area west of Denver that became known as Gregory Gulch. By June, the 5000 people there in new Central City were much more richly rewarded than those at Pike's Peak. One of them, George Pullman, the future builder of Pullman cars, is said to have got the idea for his sleepers from the miners' double-decked bunks. The mines around Boulder to the north were opened soon after those at Central City. In the early 1870s, rich beds of silver were successfully worked near Leadville, and a bit later gold was found in the region of Cripple Creek. Such discoveries, coupled with the growth of Denver as a commercial center, spurred the campaign for statehood, and in 1876 Colorado was honored with admission to the Union as the "Centennial State."

In the spring of 1859 the fabulous Comstock Lode on Mount Davidson in western Nevada was struck, and by summer 20,000 men—with their horses and mules, their picks, shovels, and pans, their whiskey, cards, and camp-following women—swarmed into the wild country and established never-to-be-forgotten Virginia City. This "wondrous" place, said a visitor, looked "as if the clouds had suddenly burst overhead and rained down the dregs of all the flimsy, rickety, filthy little hovels and rubbish of merchandise that had ever undergone the process of evaporation from the earth since the days of Noah."

In four years, about $15 million, more of it silver than gold, was taken from the Comstock Lode alone, but this was only "placer" pickings. By ancient Mexican "reducing" methods, still universally used in the early 1860s, it cost $50 to get $200 in silver from a ton even of high-grade ore, and even then the yield was but 65 percent. In the decade after 1868, new methods cut costs to $10 per ton and raised the yield to 85 percent. Four men made the most of these methods: John W. Mackay and his partners, James G. Fair, James C. Flood, and William S. O'Brien. All told, they took $150 million from Comstock.

A Prussian immigrant, the well-trained engineer Adolph Sutro, also saw new business possibilities in Mount Davidson. With capital collected largely in Europe, in 1869 he began construction of the famous Sutro Tunnel to supply drainage, ventilation, and transport for the deep Comstock mines. On its completion in 1877, Sutro's tunnel proved a milestone in engineering history. It came too late, however, to reward its builder. By 1877, Comstock miners had penetrated deeper than the tunnel, and in any case had taken the cream off the Lode, no less than $306 million.

The discovery of the Comstock Lode in 1859 set others looking for deposits nearby, and by 1861 Nevada had several settlements and a population larger perhaps than it has ever been since. Organized as a territory in that year, Nevada became a state in 1864.

In 1860, the cry of "Gold!" on the reservation of the Nez Percé Indians in present-day Idaho brought 15,000 miners into that country. By 1863, the Territory of Idaho, with Boise as its center and with Montana and much of Wyoming included in it, was carved from old Washington territory. The Boise district alone claimed as many as 25,000 hopefuls—a number that soon fell off sharply. The census of 1870 reported only 15,000 in all of Idaho Territory, which by then had been somewhat reduced in area. Not until 1890 did Idaho become a state.

In the Southwest, where the Spanish had lived for centuries, deposits of precious metals had long been known, but not until 1862 did prospectors turn their serious attention to the gold and silver of Arizona and New Mexico. By 1863, Arizona had grown populous enough to become a territory. The lasting monument to its placer-mining history is the reputation to this day of Tombstone, one of the most violent towns of the epoch.

The era of the prospectors' West was drawing to a close when, in 1874, the rumors of gold on the Sioux reservation in the sacred Black Hills of South Dakota were confirmed. These somber mountains, their pine-clad

461

Denver Public Library Western Collection

*Main Street, Helena, Montana ("Last Chance Gulch"), 1872.*

slopes rising to great rounded domes above the desolate northern plains, loomed as a heartening reminder to white men that the earth was not everywhere a flat, inhospitable, shelterless expanse. Yet the Black Hills had been made unapproachable by the ferocious Sioux. The United States army also was as determined to keep the wild braves incarcerated in their reservations here as it was to exclude white intruders. Prospectors themselves were happy to give the region a wide berth so long as the mountain country farther west afforded them opportunities. Yet stories of Indians with bags of nuggets, of army officers concealing their knowledge of outcroppings lest their troops desert, and of a few desperate men who worked a stake and ran, kept the lure of the Hills alive.

*An old trail, a bold trail,*
  *The old French trappers knew,*
*A far trail and a war trail*
  *Through the land of the fighting Sioux;*
*A rough trail, once a tough trail,*
  *Where oft the war-whoop thrills,*
*The gold trail is a bold trail*
  *As it bears to the far Black Hills.*

By October 1876 the army despaired any longer of keeping the irrepressible prospectors

462

out of the Black Hills and opened the Sioux reservation to all who cared to chance the Indians' vengeance. Fifteen thousand prospectors poured in almost at once, and the army under Colonel Custer did what it could to protect them (see p. 456). In the winter of 1876, the richest veins were discovered around Deadwood Gulch, and Deadwood, South Dakota, soon outdistanced Tombstone as the toughest of the "badman" towns. All told, the Black Hills mines yielded $287,500,000.

Henceforth, big business came increasingly to dominate the development of the Wild West. In 1881 the first far western copper seam was discovered in "the richest 'hell' on earth," conventionally known as Butte, Montana. By the end of the decade—sparked by the booming demand for copper wire, a far more efficient carrier of electric power than iron or steel—annual copper production had passed that of gold in value; by 1900, it neared that of gold and silver combined. The production of another mundane metal, lead, also increased with the growing use of electric storage batteries. Missouri remained the main source of lead, but after 1880 sizable quantities from the Leadville district of Colorado and the Coeur d'Alene district of Idaho became available. In 1901, in time for the commercialization of the automobile, "Black Gold" roared onto the western scene from the fabulous gushers of the Spindletop fields in Texas, establishing the oil industry of that state. Like the silver of Mount Davidson, exploitation of these new metals and minerals required heavy investment in plant and machinery, and it was not long before financiers like Henry H. Rogers and the Rockefellers of New York, the Guggenheims of Philadelphia, and the Mellons of Pittsburgh dominated the economy of the "desert."

Although the mining country was wide open and offered a haven to every kind of refugee from society, it early developed its own legal code. This code applied not only to personal crimes but also to such matters as claims, assays, and water rights. Enforcement was difficult, however, and in the 1850s and early 1860s Congress was pressed to extend federal justice to the West. In 1866 Congress simply declared that the mining country was

free to all, "subject to local customs or rules of miners in the several mining districts." This attitude put a premium on vigilantism. But the settlement of the West eventually brought about the establishment of more formal government agencies, which were strengthened by improved communication facilities.

And yet it was these very facilities that offered the last opportunity to western desperadoes. Before the railroad penetrated the Wild West, freight was hauled to the mining camps and other settlements by trains of "prairie schooners" run by express companies like Russell, Majors, and Waddell, and Wells Fargo. The overland mail was also carried by these companies and, in the short but exciting period of 1860-1861, by the Pony Express, a project of William H. Russell, who was determined to show that mail could be carried profitably to the West Coast without a government subsidy. By April 1860, Russell had set up 190 stations about 10 miles apart between St. Joseph, Missouri, and San Francisco. At these stations 500 of the strongest and fastest horses available stood ready. At each stop the mail pouches were switched to a fresh pony and whisked away. The Pony Express kept eighty riders in the saddle, forty racing west and forty returning, all of them light-weight lads specially clothed to reduce wind resistance to a minimum. Until they were supplanted by the transcontinental telegraph in October 1861, the Pony Express riders made the 2,500-mile run between St. Joseph, Missouri, and San Francisco in the incredible time of ten days.

Before the completion of the transcontinental railroads, express and mail holdups occurred with regularity in the West. Thereafter, the headline "Great Train Robbery" became a standard feature of western news. But in 1881, even this phase of wild western life was brought under control. In that year, the railway and express companies joined the Governor of Missouri in placing such a high price on the heads of Jesse and Frank James that one of their own men shot Jesse in the back for the reward. In Oklahoma country in the 1890s, the notorious Dalton brothers reenacted some of the bloodiest of the Jameses' exploits, but by then the West had generally become a safer if not a saintlier place.

### The cattle kingdom

The violence of the mining camps and mining towns kept the more staid and settled members of American society out of the western country for a long time. The violence of the trail, the range, and the cow town kept them off the Great Plains. In the cattle kingdom as in the mining country, the population was almost wholly male, but the monotony was relieved in the towns by the usual coveys of obliging women. Tombstone and Deadwood had nothing on Dodge City, Kansas, the "Cowboy's Capital," where twenty-five men are said to have been killed during the town's first year.

Western-style ranching and cowpunching came into American life with the annexation of Texas in 1845. Long before, Mexicans had designed the bit, bridle, saddle, and spurs, the lariat, chaps, and five-gallon hat of the traditional cowboy; for centuries they had broken broncos, grazed calves, roped steers. But they were too careless to use the branding iron. When Americans from Missouri, Mississippi, Alabama, and Tennessee began to trickle into Texas in the 1820s, many of them simply put their brands on what they deemed to be wild herds and set themselves up as cattle kings. Other Americans, meanwhile, were grasping horses and cattle that had broken away from the Mexican herds to wander northward. In this way the range-cattle industry in Kansas and Nebraska began. The northern ranchers supplied beef and fresh horses to emigrants going farther west and to mining camps and railroad crews. Compared with the herds of Texas, however, the northern herds were tiny.

In the 1850s, some of the more enterprising Texas ranchers undertook to drive their cattle westward to the Colorado and California markets or northward to Illinois. But these drives proved uneconomical. Both herds and herders fell easy prey to the Indians, while the surviving steers reached their destination maimed and lame and too thin and tough to command a price sufficient even to cover costs. While the cattlemen awaited the opening of more accessible markets, their herds multiplied. By the time of the Civil War, nearly 5 million longhorns, all of them owned but most of them unbranded "mavericks," taxed even the almost limitless Texas range.

As soon as the war ended, Texas ranchers began looking with renewed interest for markets. When they learned that $3 or $4 Texas steers would command as much as $40 a head in the north, they decided to try the cross-country drive once more. They were the more encouraged to risk this now by the westward extension of the railroads. Before 1865 the ranchers had to drive their cattle all the way to the abattoirs in the big market cities. In the spring of 1866, the first of the "long drives" to a railroad town—Sedalia, Missouri, on the Missouri Pacific—began. Sedalia had just been connected with Kansas City, and Kansas City with St. Louis. Big markets themselves, these thriving Missouri cities would serve as distributing points to metropolitan markets elsewhere.

By the fall of 1866, some 260,000 Texas steers had hit the trail for Sedalia, a venture quickly beset with unanticipated difficulties. The trail to Sedalia wound through unfamiliar forests, which made the longhorns of the open range stampede. The trail also crossed over new Missouri farm land, where protesting "nesters," as the cowboys called the settlers, came rushing out with guns and other weapons, which they were not loath to employ. Moreover, most of the horse Indians, though nominally on their reservations, still roamed the plains. In the end, only a few Texas steers ever reached Sedalia. Those that did, however, brought $35 a head, a price that encouraged many ranchers to try again the next year.

By then an enterprising Illinois meat dealer, Joseph G. McCoy, realized that he could make a fortune if he could establish a convenient meeting point for northern buyers and Texas and western breeders. After scouting around,

McCoy chose Abilene, Kansas, on the Kansas Pacific, which (with the Hannibal and St. Jo Railroad and other lines) connected Abilene with Chicago. At Abilene McCoy built a hotel, and barns, stables, pens, and loading chutes. In 1868 Abilene received 75,000 head of cattle. Within three years this number had multiplied nearly ten times.

As the Kansas Pacific was extended westward across Kansas, new cow towns nearer the cattle range were used. Ellsworth, Kansas, which succeeded Abilene, received over a million head between 1872 and 1875. Next came fabulous Dodge City, to which another million head were driven between 1876 and 1879. On the Union Pacific route, first Cheyenne and then Laramie became important cattle railheads.

The "long drive," a romantic chapter in the history of the West, actually held little glamor

The cattle kingdom

for its human participants. The cowboys usually set out in groups of six, working for $24 to $40 a month. Equipped only with cow ponies, lassos, and six-shooters, for two months of grueling travel they tried to keep safe and under control a thousand head of hungry, thirsty, touchy steers. P. A. Rollins, a veteran of the drive, wrote: "It was tiresome grimy business for the attendant punchers, who travelled ever in a cloud of dust, and heard little but the constant chorus from the crackling of hoofs and of ankle joints, from the bellows, lows, and bleats of the trudging animals."

Since even the drive to the nearest railhead did grown steers ready for market little good, it became the practice in the 1870s to drive Texas yearlings to the northern range in western Kansas and Nebraska and in Colorado, Wyoming, Montana, and the Dakotas—the area where the buffalo herds were being obliterated. With the buffalo went the Indians' food supply, and with the food supply went the Indians themselves. Now northern "feeders" could buy young longhorns and other breeds and fatten them free on the lush grass of the public lands until they were ready for market at four to five years of age. As time went on, the best cows and bulls were culled from the herds, and breeds were constantly improved. The open-range cattle industry came into its own after 1878, when the business depression of the midseventies had run its course and beef prices revived.

Like the isolated mining centers, the range too was forced to make its own laws. Here the vital need was for water, and "range rights" along a stream became the most precious part of a cattleman's ranch. Local regulations had the force of law in determining the extent of each man's or company's "range rights," but claims often had to be backed up with the six-shooter. Even where the ranchers respected one another's territory, the cattle did not. Here again rules had to be established for recording brands and for disposing of "mavericks." Since ranches might cover as many as

30 or 40 square miles, they could not be policed efficiently and rustling became common.

The enforcement of rude justice was one of the main objectives of the numerous stock-growers' associations organized on the plains in the 1870s. Eventually, these groups developed hidden governments in the territories cut from the range. One of their more important business objectives was to forestall competition by making it difficult for newcomers to become members and by making it dangerous for them to operate without joining up. This objective grew out of awareness of the speed with which the range, endless though it seemed, might be disastrously overstocked.

In spite of all the stock growers' efforts, news soon leaked out about how $5 steers could be transformed into property worth $45 to $60 a head, with only the investment of four years of free grazing. New ranchers flocked to the range like prospectors to the mines, and when the anticipated profits materialized, large investors set up corporations further to enlarge activities. Profits of 40 to 50 percent became common in the early 1880s, but by 1885 the range finally grew over-crowded, and the disastrous winter of 1885–1886, followed by a blistering summer, destroyed most of the feed and cattle. The steers that found their way to market were of such poor quality that beef prices crashed, despite the intense shortage.

It was at this time, too, that sheep herders began to cross the range in large numbers.

Their flocks, which tainted the water and made the atmosphere noxious to cows and cowboys alike, ate not only the grass but the roots themselves, leaving in their wake wide swaths of barren range. To add to the stock growers' misery, farmers began homesteading the plains and fencing in the open range. Many farmers kept herds of their own on fenced fields where they could control breeding more carefully and regulate the feed. The beef they produced was superior to any grown on the open range. In 1882 range beef commanded $9.35 per hundred pounds in Chicago; by 1887 the price had fallen to $1.90. By then, the cowboys were singing mournfully:

*I little dreamed what would happen*
  *Some twenty summers hence*
*When the nester came with his wife and kids,*
    *His dogs and his barbed-wire fence.*

The West had indeed changed. One open-range cowboy working on a fenced-in ranch had this to say in the late 1880s:

*I remember when we sat around the fire the winter through and didn't do a lick of work for five or six months of the year, except to chop a little wood to build a fire to keep warm by. Now we go on the general roundup, then the calf roundup, then comes haying—something that the old-time cowboy never dreamed of—then the beef roundup and the fall calf roundup and gathering bulls and weak cows, and after all this a winter of feeding hay. I tell you times have changed.*

The end of the open range brought an end to the last frontier.

## III  Frontier farmers

*Settling the land*

"These fellows from Ohio, Indiana, and other northern and western states," an old trail driver complained in the 1870s, "—the 'bone and sinew of the country,' as politi-cians call them—have made farms, enclosed pastures, and fenced in water holes until you can't rest; and I say D—n such bone and sin-ew!" Although the cattlemen were then on the verge of their greatest boom, revolution-ary agricultural developments were to make

465

that boom their last. Perhaps the most important of these developments was the perfection of barbed-wire fencing, first patented by three different inventors in 1874. One cattleman expressed the feelings of all when he wished that the "man who invented barbed wire had it all around him in a ball and the ball rolled into hell."

Although the Homestead Act of 1862 had opened the public domain in the West to free settlement by American citizens and by those who declared their intention of becoming citizens, much of the best land had been appropriated before homesteaders could get to it. Certain other circumstances, having to do with both the law and the land itself, further restricted the act's usefulness. For example, the quarter section (160 acres) offered by the act though suitable for the Mississippi Valley and lavish for New England (the two areas from which most of the proponents of the measure came), was either too large or too small for the arid, treeless plains. For the small settler, the cost of breaking enough of the 160 acres to get a paying crop, plus the cost of irrigation, buildings, equipment, taxes, and hired help, was prohibitive. In 1871 the Department of Agriculture estimated that wood fencing alone for such a farm would cost $1000. On the other hand, for the large farmer or farming corporation willing to use the costly new machinery so well fitted to the broad expanse of the plains, a mere quarter section hardly justified the investment.

Belated recognition of these problems prompted the passage of the Timber Culture Act of 1873. On the theory that trees brought rain, this act offered an additional quarter section to the settler who would put at least 40 acres of it into forest. Far too few settlers complied with the provisions of the act, and it was repealed in 1891.

Two other measures, passed ostensibly to stimulate settlement of the West by farmers, actually worked to keep them out. One was the Desert Land Act of 1877. This act allowed a settler to occupy 640 acres on payment of 25 cents an acre; the settler could win clear title to the land in three years for an additional payment of $1 an acre, provided he could prove he had irrigated the plot. Thousands of farmers agreed to try to irrigate the land, but the job proved too difficult and most of them gave up long before the three years had expired. The Desert Land Act was really a ruse of cattlemen to win private title to the once open grazing range. They registered thousands of acres in cowboys' names and then, to prove that they had irrigated the land, they got the cowboys to testify that they "had seen water on the claim."

The second measure was the Timber and Stone Act of 1878, an attempt by the lumbermen to wrest public lands for themselves. This act offered a maximum of 160 acres of rich timber land—land "unfit for cultivation"—in California, Nevada, Oregon, and Washington, at $2.50 an acre, "about the price of one good log," as R. A. Billington has commented. Since even aliens who had done no more than file their first citizenship papers were eligible for these grants, a land-office business was set up right in the waterfront courthouses. In return for on-the-spot bonuses ranging from $10 to $50, thousands of alien seamen were induced to register claims and then to sign them over to lumber-company agents.

All told, between 1862 and 1900, 80 million acres were registered under the Homestead Act, and this figure includes many dummy registrations used by speculators to accumulate large holdings. During the same period, railroads and land companies, as well as states receiving grants of federal land for educational purposes under the Morrill Act of 1862, sold at least five or six times as much land. These sellers charged from $2 to $10 an acre, a fair enough range for the best sites near transportation and markets. Railroads and land companies, eager to sell, often were willing to give purchasers credit for equipment with which to develop the land as well as for the land itself.

By 1868, when the Union Pacific Railroad (see p. 478) was nearly ready for passengers, it placarded Kansas and other states on the edge of the frontier with advertisements calling its lands "Better than a Homestead." Thereafter every land-grant railroad opened a land department and a bureau of immigration. In the 1870s, the Union Pacific and the Burlington Railroads each spent over $1 million in advertising their lands abroad, often in spectacular fashion. Other railroads and land companies followed suit, many of them opening London offices with agents scouring the Continent for settlers. Western states with land to sell and steamship companies engaged in carrying immigrants to the New World also actively courted settlers abroad.

These land sales and immigration campaigns proved remarkably successful. According to the 1880 census, 73 percent of Wisconsin's population was of foreign parentage, 71 percent of Minnesota's, 66 percent of the Dakotas', and 44 percent of Nebraska's. In the following two years, "American fever" rose to epidemic proportions in western and central Europe. In 1882 alone, the record year for immigration to the United States in the entire nineteenth century, almost 650,000 foreigners debarked in American ports. Large numbers of these newcomers remained in the teeming coastal cities, and many others got no farther west than the mills of Pittsburgh and Cleveland (see Chapter Twenty-one). But hundreds of thousands of them found their way to the farmlands of the plains. Between 1860 and 1900, the land held by American farmers more than doubled, from 407 to 841 million acres, and the proportion of land under cultivation rose from 40 to almost 50 percent.

Not to be neglected in this connection was the flight of "cotton belt" blacks from northern Louisiana and neighboring southern states in the 1870s to Homestead Act land and other plains areas. "The fiat to go forth is irresistible," said the report of one of the secret black committees of "plantation laborers." With "justice a mockery, and the law a cheat, the very officers of the courts being themselves the mobocrats and violators of the law, the only remedy left the colored citizen . . . is to emigrate."

This movement, under the leadership principally of the Negro Henry Adams, of Shreveport, Louisiana, in the rich Red River district, culminated in 1879 in the "great exodus" to Kansas, "the State made immortal by Old John Brown," as the governor said at this time in welcoming the first contingents. A few months earlier, the state's Republican Senator, John James Ingalls, is reported to have stated:

*I do not think there is any class prejudice or any feeling of hostility to the colored people that would prevent their being cordially welcomed as an element of our population. We have an area of about 81,000 square miles, comprising 55,000,000 acres of arable land, not more than one-tenth of which has been reduced to cultivation. The remainder is open to settlement under the Homestead Act, . . . and I am inclined to think we could absorb 100,000 of these people without serious injury or inconvenience.*

Henry Adams claimed that just about that number were organized and ready to abandon their native South, and it is estimated that perhaps half that number actually departed for Kansas within a few months in the spring and summer of 1879. Another 5000 or so also left for Iowa and Nebraska.

Unfortunately for the emigrants, as their number swelled, their reception chilled, until the same Kansas officials who first welcomed them (with an eye, as it turned out, to their votes for the Republican ticket) sent emissaries south urging no more to come. Most of those who had completed the journey, moreover, failed to slake their thirst for land. "Hopeless, penniless and in rags," as one observer of the exodus noted, they had no means with which to set up farms and no philanthropic agencies to turn to. Some eventually found jobs as laborers building railroads or mining coal, while women took in washing or became domestics. Others joined the westward drift of the frontiersman, living from hand to mouth.

There were exceptions, however. One of the eleven Negro settlements made in Kansas in 1879 survives to this day in Nicodemus, Graham County, where, besides all the human disabilities of race prejudice, the migrants also overcame the harsh natural difficulties of plains farming.

467

### Plains agriculture

Before any of the new settlers of the plains could transform the country into farmland, they had many obstacles to overcome. Not even rude log cabins could be built on the treeless plains; the first shelters were dank and dark sod huts. The lack of wood made it difficult to heat such dwellings in a region that covered some of the coldest parts of the United States. The first settlers burned dried buffalo dung. They next turned to hay, to be burned in special stoves designed to consume it slowly. But nothing proved satisfactory until the railroads brought coal to the plains.

The aridity of the region, which increased as one moved westward, offered even greater difficulties, especially to families at a distance from the infrequent rivers. By 1880 mechanical well-digging equipment was in use, but even when wells could be dug the necessary 200 or 300 feet, there remained the problem of getting the water to the surface. Windmills that harnessed the power of the strong prevailing breezes promised to provide an answer, but before windmills became cheap enough for the average farmer he had solved the wa-

Library of Congress

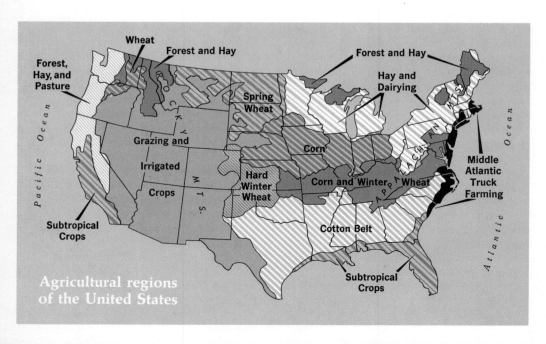

**Agricultural regions of the United States**

Wheat

Forest and Hay

Forest and Hay

Forest, Hay, and Pasture

Hay and Dairying

Spring Wheat

Grazing and Irrigated Crops

Corn

Corn and Winter Wheat

Hard Winter Wheat

Middle Atlantic Truck Farming

Subtropical Crops

Cotton Belt

Subtropical Crops

Pacific Ocean

Atlantic Ocean

Harvesting wheat on a huge "bonanza farm"
in the state of Washington.
Halftone reproduction from Harper's Weekly,
August 29, 1891.

**469**

that several furrows could be cut at once. The next step was to mechanize the sulky and thereby increase the number of plowshares that could be pulled. Other innovations accompanied those in the plow. By 1874 grain drills had been designed to mechanize planting. In a region battered by hail storms, wind storms, and sudden frosts, a farmer's production was most sharply limited not by how much he could plant but how much he could harvest. The "cord binder," perfected about 1880, greatly speeded up the harvesting process. This device permitted two men and a team of horses to harvest 20 acres of wheat a day. Old-time eastern farmers dared not plant more than 8 acres of wheat a season; by 1890 one plains farmer with a cord binder could count on harvesting 135 acres.

But there had to be a revolution in the grain industry before such a wheat harvest became worthwhile. Eastern wheat farmers grew soft-kernel winter wheat, traditionally milled by grinding the husks between two millstones. They usually planted the crop in September or October, let it grow during the winter, and harvested it in June or July. The first farmers in Wisconsin and Minnesota found that the early winters there killed the tender seed before it could sprout. On the open plains, the winters proved even more severe. Moreover, the moisture needed for soft winter wheats was lacking here.

Spring wheat, planted in May and harvested before the first frosts, had been known to farmers before 1860. But the known varieties lacked hardiness and, worse, their tough husks could not be milled economically. In the 1860s, after a long journey from Poland via Scotland and Canada, a new type of hard spring wheat appeared on the plains, and by the end of the decade a new process for milling the hard grain had been brought over from Hungary. This process employed a series of revolving rollers instead of the old mill-

ter problem in other ways. One recourse, still widely used though undependable and costly, was "dry farming." With this system, a field is harrowed after each precious rainfall in order to retard evaporation. The turned-over mud thus forms a mulch to store water upon which roots continue to feed long after the rain has ended.

Scarcity of water was but one of many problems in cultivating the virgin land. The tough sod of the plains, like the tough sod of the prairie, resisted the old-fashioned eastern plow. John Deere's steel plow, perfected for prairie farming before the Civil War, was a great improvement, but only for those who could afford its high price. In 1868, James Oliver of Indiana began making innovations in the chilled-iron plow which by 1877 had become a cheap, versatile, and efficient tool. Plowshares soon were being mounted on sulkies, with a number of them in a line, so

stones. In 1872 or 1873, settlers from the Crimea introduced into Kansas a hard *winter* wheat known as "Turkey Red." This too became commercially manageable through the new milling process, which itself was steadily improved.

Both hard wheats became profitable and popular among millers and bakers, and plains farming forged ahead. In 1879 Illinois, the leading wheat state for twenty years, still held first place; by 1899 it had fallen out of the first ten, now led by such hard-wheat states as Minnesota, the Dakotas, Kansas, California, and Nebraska. Oklahoma and northern Texas had also become large wheat producers.

During the 1870s, plains farmers grew more and more insistent that the ranchers fence in their cattle; the ranchers, in turn, urged the "nesters" to move away or else bear the high cost of fences to keep the range cattle out. The sharp hostility between the two groups led to open gun fights, but cheap fencing, not guns, eventually won the plains for the farmers.

Joseph F. Glidden, one of three independent holders of the barbed-wire patent, set up the first barbed-wire factory in DeKalb, Illinois, in November 1874. Two years later, 3 million pounds of such wire were sold at about $20 per hundred pounds. Four years later annual sales had zoomed to 80 million pounds, and the price had fallen to $10 per hundred. By 1890, the price per hundred was down to $4, and much of the arable land of the plains had been fenced in.

Once a disastrous series of grasshopper invasions of the plains ended early in the 1870s, everything conspired to make the new wheat country the El Dorado the advertisements pictured. After 1875 Europe suffered one crop failure after another. Widespread hardship there was deepened by the Russo-Turkish War of 1877-1878, which closed Russia's ports and thus cut off Europe's main source of grain. All the improvements in American farm technology coincided with the new needs of the European market—a market that was to continue to expand as western Europe turned from farming toward industry, with populous manufacturing cities that had to be fed. The future of wheat growing on the plains appeared all the rosier because for eight consecutive years after 1877 the region enjoyed such plentiful rainfall that many believed its characteristic aridity had passed.

While American agricultural production soared, the seemingly limitless demand kept prices high. From 1866 to 1875, the average annual price of a bushel of wheat was $1.24. In the next decade the average price was still 92 cents. Such prices encouraged expansion, mainly by farmers mortgaging their land to the limit in order to raise money to acquire more land before the next fellow claimed it. The banks and their optimistic managers themselves encouraged this practice.

Wiser heads, however, knew that the West was riding for a fall. Overproduction in the United States by the mid-1880s, the entry of India and Australia into the world wheat market, the revival of Russian wheat exports, all were ill omens. Yet just as buffalo had drawn the Indian to the virgin West, as gold had drawn the prospector, and grass the rancher, so wheat had drawn the commercial farmer. He alone had come to stay.

## For further reading

R. A. Billington, *Westward Expansion* (1967), has informative and admirably organized sections on each of the themes discussed in this chapter. See also, T. D. Clark, *Frontier America: The Story of the West-ward Movement* (1959). Billington, *The Far Western Frontier 1830-1860* (1956), and Bernard DeVoto, *Across the Wide Missouri* (1947), supply illuminating background material. DeVoto considered *The Life and*

Adventures of James P. Beckwourth, as told by the old mountain man to T. D. Bonner (1856), the work that best captured the frontier spirit. W. P. Webb, *The Great Plains* (1931); J. C. Malin, *The Grassland of North America* (1948); and Isaiah Bowman, *The Frontier Fringe* (1931), add greatly to our understanding of the relationship between the natural environment and social life. Thurman Wilkins, *Clarence King* (1958); and Wallace Stegner, *Beyond the Hundredth Meridian: John Wesley Powell and the Second Opening of the West* (1954), are interesting biographies of men who first assayed far western natural resources. Good regional studies include O. O. Winther, *The Great Northwest* (1950); H. R. Lamar, *The Far Southwest 1846-1912* (1966); J. C. Caughey, *History of the Pacific Coast* (1933); and H. E. Briggs, *Frontiers of the Northwest: A History of the Upper Missouri Valley* (1940). Robert Taft, *Artists and Illustrators of the Old West 1850-1900* (1953), is well illustrated and contains a great deal of useful information on the region as well as on its lively art.

A moving account of Indian life is found in J. C. Collier, *Indians of the Americas* (1947). More conventional short surveys include J. R. Swanton, *The Indian Tribes of North America* (1953), and W. T. Hagan, *American Indians* (1961). W. C. Macleod, *The American Indian Frontier* (1928), is an older analysis well worth study. F. G. Roe, *The Indian and the Horse* (1955), is outstanding. Wayne Gard, *The Great Buffalo Hunt* (1959), does justice to its subject. J. P. Dunn, *Massacres of the Mountains* (1886), is a comprehensive contemporary account of the Indian wars. C. C. Rister, *Border Command: General Phil Sheridan in the West* (1944), and R. G. Athearn, *William Tecumseh Sherman and the Settlement of the West* (1956), deal with the army's role. H. H. Jackson, *A Century of Dishonor* (1881), is a passionate indictment of Indian policy. L. G. Priest, *Uncle Sam's Stepchildren: The Reformation of United States Indian Policy 1865-1887* (1942), is a scholarly account. H. E. Fritz, *The Movement for Indian Assimilation 1860-1890* (1963), examines this ambiguous subject.

Outstanding modern studies of the mining country include R. W. Paul, *Mining Frontiers of the Far West 1848-1880* (1963), and W. S. Greever, *The Bonanza West: The Story of the Western Mining Rushes 1848-1900* (1963). Useful also is W. J. Trimble, *The Mining Advance into the Inland Empire* (1914). C. H. Shinn, *The Story of the Mine* (1896), tells the story of the Comstock Lode. Shinn's *Mining Camps: A Study in American Frontier Government* (1885) is solid. Mark Twain, *Roughing It* (2 vols., 1872), is the great writer's stirring account of Nevada days. H. P. Walker, *The Wagonmasters, High Plains Freighting from the Earliest Days of the Santa Fe Trail to 1880* (1966), is excellent on prerailroad transportation. See also Arthur Chapman, *The Pony Express* (1932), and L. R. Hafen, *The Overland Mail 1849-1869* (1926).

Sound general works on the cattle kingdom include Lewis Atherton, *The Cattle Kings* (1961); E. S. Osgood, *The Day of the Cattleman* (1929); E. E. Dale, *The Range Cattle Industry* (1930); and Louis Pelzer, *The Cattlemen's Frontier* (1936). Eugene Gressley, *Bankers and Cattlemen* (1966), is illuminating on its special phase. On the cowboy, see P. A. Rollins, *The Cowboy* (1922); J. F. Dobie, ed., *A Texas Cowboy* (1950); and Philip Durham and E. L. Jones, *The Negro Cowboys* (1965). J. B. Frantz and J. E. Choate, *The American Cowboy: The Myth and the Reality* (1955), offers a modern appraisal. Enlightening on the badmen and the coming of law and order to the West is Wayne Gard, *Frontier Justice* (1949).

F. A. Shannon, *The Farmer's Last Frontier: Agriculture 1860-1897* (1945), is a scholarly analysis somewhat updated by G. C. Fite, *The Farmer's Frontier 1865-1900* (1966). On the attempted Negro "exodus" to the Great Plains, see Herbert Aptheker, *A Documentary History of the Negro People in the United States . . . to 1910* (1951), and R. W. Logan, *The Negro in American Life and Thought: The Nadir 1877-1901* (1954). On the distribution and sale of the western domain, useful accounts may be found in R. M. Robbins, *Our Landed Heritage* (1942), and B. H. Hibbard, *A History of the Public Land Policies* (1924). A scholarly study of land policy in the twentieth century is E. L. Peffer, *Closing of the Public Domain* (1951). H. R. Lamar, *Dakota Territory 1861-1889: A Study of Frontier Politics* (1956), is a good introduction to statehood preliminaries. On pioneer farm life, Everett Dick, *The Sod-House Frontier 1854-1890* (1937), and Mari Sandoz, *Old Jules* (1935), present detailed and dramatic stories. Very revealing also are the novels of Ole Rölvaag, especially *Giants in the Earth* (1929), and Willa Cather's *O Pioneers!* (1913) and *My Antonia* (1918).

# AN INDUSTRIAL POWER

In 1890, the superintendent of the United States census made one of the most unnerving announcements in American history:

*Up to and including 1880 the country had a frontier of settlement, but at present the unsettled area has been so broken into ... that there can hardly be said to be a frontier line. In the discussion of its extent and its westward movement, etc., it can not, therefore, any longer have a place in the census reports.*

For almost 300 years the open spaces of the North American continent had stood as evidence to the world of free opportunity in American society. Now civilization had cut through the forests, traversed the prairies and the plains, scaled the formidable crests of the western mountains, and altogether encompassed the primeval wilderness of the stone-age braves. An epoch in American life had ended, one that, as Frederick Jackson Turner, the most influential historian of the frontier, insisted, had made the strongest impact on the American character and tradition and one that helped most clearly to distinguish the American from the European way of life.

To some Americans, the announcement by the superintendent of the census, unnerving though it was, hardly came as news. As early as 1881, the *New York Tribune* printed a letter from a correspondent who wrote that America's resources had all been claimed, and who advised: "The nation has reached a point in its growth where its policy should be to preserve its heritage for coming generations, not to donate it to all the strangers we can induce to come among us." The following year, in response to organized agitation in many parts of the country, Congress took its first tentative steps toward sealing the ports of the United States against foreign settlers. The business community had begun to consolidate as well as to expand its enterprises, to nurse as well as to nourish its creative urge.

Yet the United States survived the closing of the land frontier by breaching new frontiers of science, technology, and business management. In fact, the American people were to make the resources of the country yield wealth and riches far beyond the dreams even of the most optimistic prospectors and promoters of the past. The conquests on the new frontiers pushed the United States to world industrial supremacy and much of the world toward a hungering for "Americanization."

## I   The vogue of materialism

In January 1840, from his job with the bankers E. W. Clark & Co. in Philadelphia, young Jay Cooke wrote home to his brother Pitt in Ohio: "Among our customers are men of every age and of every position in society. . . . Through all the grades I see the same all-pervading, all engrossing anxiety to grow rich. . . . This is the only thing for which men live here." During the Civil War, inducements to enterprise became stronger than ever in the free section, and the vogue of materialism ever more pronounced. "Such opportunities for making money," wrote Judge Thomas Mellon of Pittsburgh in 1863, "had never existed before in all my former experience." That year his oldest son James, then a young lawyer in Milwaukee, had written home asking for permission to enlist. The Judge ordered, "Don't do it. It is only greenhorns who enlist. Those who are able to pay for substitutes do so, and no discredit attaches." And he added: "I had hoped my boy was going to make a smart, intelligent business man and was not such a goose as to be seduced from his duty by the declamations of buncombed speeches." The judge carried the day, and indeed he soon resigned from the bench to return to business himself.

Many northern spokesmen regarded their victory in the Civil War as proof that their industrial civilization was superior to the South's agrarian economy, and once the South had been reclaimed for the Union they became outraged by the defeated section's unwillingness to embrace the victor's philosophy and goals. In October 1866 James Russell Lowell wrote in the *North American Review:*

*Is it not time that [southerners] were transplanted at least into the nineteenth century, and, if they cannot be suddenly Americanized, made to understand something of the country which was too good for them?*

At about the same time, Governor John A. Andrew of the Bay State insisted that southerners must never be admitted to the counsels of the Union, "until their ideas on business, industry, money making ... were in accord with those of Massachusetts."

474

The extraordinary popularity in America of the English philosopher Herbert Spencer (1820–1903), coinciding as it did with the spectacular postwar economic growth of the North, helped make the triumph of materialism complete. Spencer had been raised in the tradition of English nonconformism with its radical resistance to the authority of the state. Such formal education as he gained, at the same time, had introduced him to the world of science. His nonconformist background prepared him for a wholehearted attachment to laissez-faire economics. Yet his scientific education led him to give such economics, which had been ethical and humanitarian in orientation, a naturalistic and hence a deterministic bent. "Morality," Spencer wrote as early as 1851, "is essentially one with physical truth." When, eight years later, Charles Darwin published his epochal work—*On the Origin of Species by Means of Natural Selection or the Preservation of Favored Races in the Struggle for Life,* to give it its full title—Spencer and his followers had at hand all the "physical truth" they needed to make laissez-faire economics seem both incontrovertible and sacrosanct.

The "Social Darwinists," as Spencer's followers became known, transformed Darwin's "struggle for life" into the system of unregulated business competition; the inevitable "survival of the fittest" they found manifested in the way such complex industrial organisms as John D. Rockefeller's Standard Oil "trust" swallowed up smaller, weaker creatures. The progress of society demanded that trusts and their makers be left entirely to their "natural" proclivities. Just as nature worked untrammeled in "selecting" her elite, so society moved most rapidly toward perfection when it allowed its elite free play.

The leading American Social Darwinist, the Yale professor William Graham Sumner, said early in the 1880s:

*The millionaires are a product of natural selection, acting on the whole body of men to pick out those who can meet the requirements of certain work to be done. . . . They get high wages and live in luxury, but the bargain is a good one for society. There is the intensest competition for their place and occupation. This assures us that all who are competent for this function will be employed in it, so that the cost of it will be reduced to the lowest terms.*

To "the survival of the fittest," Sumner added, "we have only one possible alternative, and that is the survival of the unfittest. The former is the law of civilization; the latter is the law of anticivilization."

When the millionaire steel magnate Andrew Carnegie first read Spencer, he recalled in his *Autobiography,* "Light came as in a flood and all was clear." Earlier, Carnegie had noted for his own guidance:

*Man must have an idol—the amassing of wealth is one of the worst species of idolatry—no idol more debasing than the worship of money. . . . To continue much longer overwhelmed by business cares and with most of my thoughts wholly on the way to make more money in the shortest time, must degrade me beyond the hope of permanent recovery.*

But reading Spencer helped resolve Carnegie's doubts. "Not only had I got rid of theology and the supernatural, but I had found the truth of evolution. 'All is well since all grows better' became my motto, my true source of comfort." Others were not so fortunate.

## II Completing the railroad network

*Competition and consolidation*

After the Civil War, as earlier, Americans moving westward often ran ahead of the railroads, which continued to be built largely in populous areas that promised the most traffic. Even the completion of the transcontinentals in the late 1880s left hundreds of settlements distant from transportation and communication facilities until the coming of the automobile and the motor truck.

In 1865 approximately 35,000 miles of railroad track served the country. By the time of the Panic of 1873 this figure had been doubled. About 5000 miles of new track had been laid in the South, most of the remainder in the East and the Old Northwest where trunk lines were being extended to the Mississippi Valley and a network of feeder lines opened up. Virtually all the new construction was privately financed through security issues sold mainly on the New York Stock Exchange. None of it enjoyed land-grant benefits, and little of it received any other kind of formal government assistance.

As important as railroad building in the older areas was the consolidation of independent lines into large companies that offered coordinated service over wide areas. Cornelius Vanderbilt, the New York shipping magnate who began investing in railroads in 1862, became one of the great consolidators and operators of the postwar period. By 1869, through a series of stock manipulations, the Commodore, as his shipping friends called him, had bought control of the New York Central, running across the state between Albany and Buffalo, and the two more or less parallel lines that connected it with New York City, giving him a through route from the great Atlantic port to the West.

In the midst of his New York Central negotiations, Vanderbilt had tried to capture the Erie Railroad, which loomed as a competitor to his new combination. He was foiled by the agility of the Erie management, led by the unscrupulous Daniel Drew and his wily lieutenants, Jay Gould and Jim Fisk. The "Erie War," one of the *causes célèbres* of the postwar decade, started in 1866. For more than a year the opposing sides battled for the road in the securities market, in the courts, where each sought injunctions obstructing the operations of the other, and in the state legislature, where each tried to saddle investigating committees with cooperative politicians. The unconcealed corruption to which the contestants resorted helped open the eyes of the public to the political malignancy of the new business forces.

His failure to acquire the Erie may have soured the aging Vanderbilt on further expanding his railroad holdings; but prodded by his son, William H., in 1870 he acquired the Lake Shore and Michigan Southern, which gave the New York Central system a magnificent, wholly owned route to Chicago. In the same year the Vanderbilts entered into working agreements with other roads that extended their operations all the way to Omaha, Nebraska.

More than just empire builders, the Vanderbilts were among the ablest railroad managers of their time. Under their direction, the Central's lines were double-tracked with sturdy rails, while roadbeds, bridges, and embankments were reconstructed to provide greater safety and comfort even with the faster engines the Central used. In 1871 the Commodore opened the first Grand Central Terminal in New York City, from which passenger trains made the 965-mile run to Chicago in the then incredible time of twenty-four hours. Two years earlier he had built a downtown freight depot which may have supplied the occasion for the coining of the "Robber Baron" legend. During construction of the depot, a huge bronze pediment was set in place atop the structure on which in sculptural low relief were strewn cogwheels, anchors, and other symbols of Vanderbilt's career, "with a colossal Cornelius looming up in the midst of the chaos." This event prompted Godkin to comment in *The Nation*:

476

*There in the glory of brass, are portrayed in a fashion quite good enough, the trophies of a lineal successor of the medieval baron that we read about, who may have been illiterate indeed; and who was not humanitarian; and not finished in his morals; and not, for his manners, the delight of the refined society of his neighborhood; nor yet beloved by his dependents.*

In the 1870s the Pennsylvania Railroad, guided by its masterful vice-president, Thomas A. Scott, also built and bought up numerous lines to gain wholly owned routes from Philadelphia to Chicago and St. Louis. In 1871 the Pennsylvania at last gained access to New

*Cornelius Vanderbilt on the pediment of his downtown freight depot in New York City, 1868.*

Brown Brothers

York City by acquiring most of the railroads that ran across New Jersey. The Baltimore & Ohio, meanwhile, although it had extended its track from Baltimore to Cincinnati, failed to make a New York City connection and fell far behind the Pennsylvania, the New York Central, and even the Erie in the cutthroat trunk-line competition of the postwar decades. In this competition cities like Chicago, Cleveland, and New York, served by rival railroads, were courted royally with low rates and fine service. Cities like Pittsburgh, where the Pennsylvania had a monopoly of the traffic, were treated, as Allan Nevins says, "with outrageous insolence."

Once northern railroad building had passed its peak in the 1880s, capital from that section and abroad turned to the South. Between 1880 and 1890 nearly 25,000 miles of track were laid below the Mason-Dixon line, realizing a rate of growth almost twice that of the country as a whole. Here too consolidation accompanied expansion—as much for speculative purposes as for service—and it was not long before a few companies controlled most of the railroad properties. One of the most aggressive of these was the Richmond Terminal Company, headed after 1888 by John H. Inman. Unfortunately for the South, Inman soon led this company toward receivership, from which it was rescued on very stiff terms by J. P. Morgan in 1893 and reorganized with other lines into the Southern Railway system.

### First transcontinentals

Much more spectacular than railroad building in the older sections was the construction of the first transcontinentals, chartered during the Civil War—the Union Pacific to build across the continent westward from Omaha, and the Central Pacific, to build eastward from Sacramento. To both companies Congress made unprecedentedly large land grants. In addition, for each mile of track laid, the companies were to receive loans secured by first-mortgage bonds held by the govern-

*can get 2 per cent a month for our money here," and they would not think of going into a speculation that would not promise that at once.*

ment on the security of their lands and rising in amount with the difficulty of the terrain to be crossed. In return, these roads, like others that received government assistance, were required to carry the mail at low rates and to be on call for the movement of troops.

Despite all the fanfare over their charters and land grants, both companies quickly experienced difficulty in raising money with which to begin the actual construction that would make them eligible for the government loans. Having failed to dispose of more than a few shares of stock in all San Francisco, Charles Crocker of the Central Pacific, early in 1863, went to Virginia City, Nevada, the gold-mining El Dorado. This is what he reported:

*They wanted to know what I expected the road would earn. I said I did not know. . . . "Well," they said, "do you think it will make 2 per cent a month?" "No," said I, "I do not." "Well," they answered, "we*

The Union Pacific, promoted mainly by eastern capitalists, had little better luck in New York, Boston, or elsewhere, and by the end of 1863 the whole enterprise was on the verge of collapse. The next year the railroads' lobbies persuaded Congress to double the land grant for each road. More than that, Congress agreed that its loans should be secured now only by a second mortgage, and that the roads themselves could issue first mortgage bonds up to the amount of the government's bonds, backed by completed 20-mile sections of track. These provisions doubled the amount of bonds available to the roads; but not even the new well-secured first-mortgage bonds could find a market among private capitalists except when sold at an average discount of 12.5 percent.

The Union Pacific and the Central Pacific were not built by the railroad corporations, but by separate construction companies.

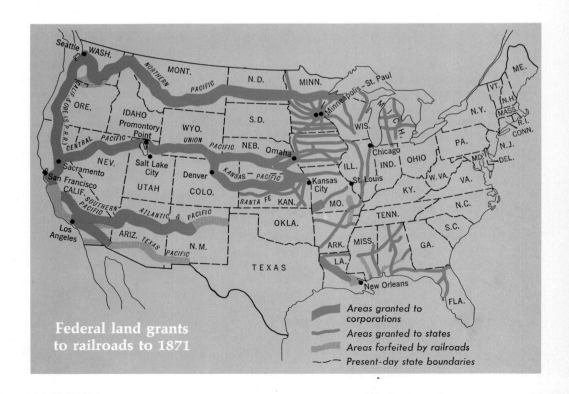

**Federal land grants to railroads to 1871**

Areas granted to corporations

Areas granted to states

Areas forfeited by railroads

- - - Present-day state boundaries

*The High Secrettown Trestle*
*of the Central Pacific Railroad in the Sierra*
*Nevada Mountains of California, in 1877,*
*in a remarkable photograph taken at the time,*
*showing the hand tools and human and animal*
*labor with which the Chinese coolies*
*had to work. Pick and shovel, wheelbarrows,*
*and one-horse dump carts made up*
*the earth-moving equipment of the day.*

These companies were handsomely paid by the railroads for their work; and since they were largely owned by the directors of the railroads they served, it was through them rather than through the provision of railroad service across still largely uninhabited terrain that the promoters of the first transcontinentals made their fortunes. Part of these fortunes also found their way into the pockets of congressmen and senators who looked after the railroads' legislative business, and few legislative reputations remained untainted.

The transcontinentals' engineering problems had been at least as trying as the financial ones, and though both roads had to be almost completely rebuilt some years later, the feat of crossing the broad plains and the forbidding mountain ranges remains one of the great engineering accomplishments in history. All told, the Crédit Mobilier, the imagi-

native and ambiguous name of the Union Pacific construction company, which also gave its name to one of the major political scandals of the Gilded Age, laid 1086 miles of track, most of it the work of Civil War veterans and Irish immigrants. The Central Pacific, its construction crews manned largely by Chinese, laid 689 miles. In the spring of 1869 the two lines approached one another, and on May 10 they were joined by golden spikes at Promontory Point, near Ogden, Utah.

## Contest for the Great West

Before the Panic of 1873, three other transcontinentals were chartered and enriched by the federal government—the Northern Pacific in 1864, the Atlantic and Pacific in 1866, and the Texas and Pacific in 1871. Of the three, only the Northern Pacific reached the coast, and its arrival was long delayed. By 1872, the other two, along with their land grants, had fallen under the control of the Central Pacific's "Big Four"—Crocker, Leland Stanford, Collis P. Huntington, and Mark Hopkins. In an effort to dominate all California railroading, this group also acquired the Southern Pacific Railroad, a company that had been chartered in California in 1865 to connect the ports of San Francisco and San Diego. After 1876, they began pushing the Southern Pacific eastward through the two best mountain passes, at Needles in California and Yuma in Arizona, thereby controlling the strategic access routes to California as well as the lines within the state. In planning their monopoly, however, the Big Four reckoned without the ubiquitous Jay Gould and others as unscrupulous as themselves.

After selling out his Erie securities for millions in cash on the eve of the Panic of 1873, Gould soon began buying up the depressed securities of the Union Pacific. Having won virtual control of this great transcontinental by 1878, he proceeded to buy up other western roads, including the shaky Kansas Pacific, which paralleled the Union Pacific from Denver east to Kansas City. By threatening to extend the Kansas Pacific west from Denver to Salt Lake City, where it would find the Central Pacific ready to carry its cars all the way to California, Gould early in 1880 forced the directors of the Union Pacific to buy the Kansas Pacific from him. He had bought into the Kansas Pacific at under $10 a share; he sold out at over $90. Gould also foisted on the Union Pacific many of his other western roads.

While he was milking the Union Pacific, Gould began quietly selling off his own stock in the company at the high prices that prevailed until the true state of the road's finances became known. At the same time he

pushed his way into Huntington's Southern Pacific. His weapon was a pasted-up system of southwestern roads, the key parts of which tied Dallas and Kansas City to St. Louis, where they met the Pennsylvania and other trunk lines running all the way to the Atlantic. Since 1877, Gould had been extending one of these roads, the Texas and Pacific, westward across Texas from Dallas to El Paso, soon to become the *eastern* terminal of Huntington's Southern Pacific. Faced with the threat that the Texas and Pacific might cut off his path through Texas, Huntington hastened to make a traffic-sharing and rate-fixing agreement with Gould in 1881. From that time Gould played an increasingly important role in the development of the Southern Pacific's power in California. His own system, meanwhile, dominated the Southwest east of California. By 1890, he controlled about 9000

479

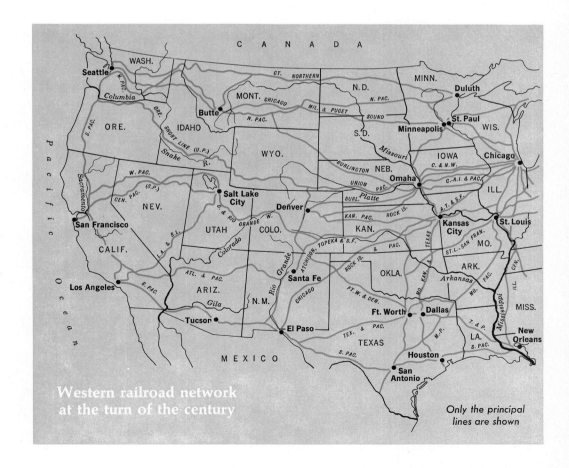

Western railroad network
at the turn of the century

Only the principal
lines are shown

miles of railroad in the Southwest, nearly half the total mileage of the section, and held the shippers of his domain in bondage.

480

In 1886, the remaining major system in the southwest, the Atchison, Topeka and Santa Fe, had also been captured by Huntington and Gould, and within two years had been consolidated with others to make connections with far-off Chicago. By then the Santa Fe, chartered initially with the modest aim of connecting Atchison, Kansas with the state capital at Topeka, had grown into a 7000-mile system. More striking was the fact that 2000 of these miles had been built between 1886 and 1888, not to meet any transportation needs but simply to saturate strategic railroad territory.

Huntington and Gould had come to consider the entire West Coast, if not indeed the entire West, as their private empire. Far to the north, however, they were confronted with vast transcontinental enterprises they could not quite control. One of these was the Northern Pacific, which in 1864 received the most lavish of all federal land grants, running to some 40 million acres. Even so, its promoters failed to attract adequate construction capital. Only after Henry Villard captured the Northern Pacific in 1881 was it pushed onward to Portland, Oregon, and then, by 1883, to Tacoma, Washington.

An educated German who had come to America in the 1850s, Villard found his way into finance through promotional journalism. In the middle 1870s, he had become attracted to the Oregon region, and with European capital proceeded to develop its resources and transportation. His grandiose ideas for the development of the Northwest, however, soon taxed his finances to the utmost, a situation only worsened by the attention he had drawn to Oregon country among more knowledgeable and more strongly financed giants. The New York bankers, Drexel, Morgan and Company, at one point backed Villard's rivals in Oregon. Huntington and Gould also became his enemies. In the background, moreover, loomed James J. Hill, who had his own ideas about the Pacific Northwest and how to build and run railroads.

Hill had come to St. Paul from Canada as a young man in 1856, and at the end of twenty years had risen no higher than a transportation agent handling the transshipment of Mississippi River cargo between the United States and Canada. He had also become something of a town character—"that Hill," as he was called—with all his talk about the future of the Northwest. Hill's chance came after the crash of 1873 had left the optimistically named St. Paul and Pacific Railroad—it ran only about 200 miles west from St. Paul—in bad shape. After biding his time, Hill with his

*"The Curse of California,"*
*from the* Wasp *of San Francisco,*
*August 19, 1882, showing Stanford*
*and Crocker in the eyes of the*
*railroad octopus.*

Courtesy, The Bancroft Library, University of California, Berkeley

tall talk won the support of Canadian financiers in acquiring this road in 1878. In 1889 it took the name Great Northern. By then, with little government assistance, Hill and his backers had pushed construction 2775 miles west through Minnesota, North Dakota, and Montana, and up to Winnipeg in Canada. In 1893 the Great Northern, on a route north of Villard's line, reached Puget Sound.

In 1883, when Villard reached the West Coast, Hill had written: "I think the time is at hand when railway property generally will be tested by its capacity to pay net earnings. . . . I think the Northern Pacific will have its greatest trial when . . . its finances are no longer sustained by sales of bonds, but all payments must be made from earnings." Hill was right. From the start, he insisted on constructing Great Northern track and roadbed with the best materials. He also chose to build around mountains rather than over them. Not only did this approach greatly reduce construction costs, an objective abhorred by the construction-company type of promoter whose purpose was to spend as much as possible, but it also reduced operating costs once a road was built. The Great Northern's long trains and heavy trainloads, which neither the track nor the mountainous routes of other western roads could carry, became the wonder of the railroad world. The proof of Hill's policies came in 1893 when the Great Northern alone among the transcontinentals survived the business crash that year.

During the next decade, Hill acquired the Northern Pacific, which had been financially reorganized with the aid of J. P. Morgan and Company in 1898. With Morgan's collaboration in 1901, Hill also won control of the Chicago, Burlington & Quincy, the best entry to Chicago from the west. The Burlington acquisition touched off a bitter fight between Hill and Edward H. Harriman, as thorough a railroad man as Hill himself, who the year before, at Collis Huntington's death (Gould had died eight years earlier) acquired 45 percent of the stock of the Southern Pacific. Harriman's

backer was Jacob H. Schiff, head of Morgan's principal banking rival, Kuhn, Loeb and Company, with as strong financial connections on the European continent as Morgan had in Britain. Harriman also enjoyed the financial confidence of the Rockefeller Standard Oil crowd, always on the lookout for likely outlets for its millions. Thus was the stage set and the parts assigned—Kuhn, Loeb; Rockefeller; Harriman; and the National City Bank versus Morgan; Hill; and the First National Bank—for one of the epic financial contests of the twentieth century, with control of the western, and indeed the national, railroad network as the prize.

After a titanic Wall Street battle that ruined many unoffending investors but settled nothing, the antagonists, in November 1901, finally decided to merge their interests. For this purpose they formed the Northern Securities Company. In 1904 this company was broken up by a Supreme Court decision that was one of the highlights of "Teddy" Roosevelt's regime, but the contestants quickly made less vulnerable financial arrangements to keep from killing one another off. By then, the American railroad grid of about 200,000 miles had been virtually completed. There was nothing like it anywhere else in the world, but to say that Americans took complete satisfaction in it and its management would grossly misrepresent the case.

### Railroads and the public

While Hill was giving the railroad men of the Far West lessons in railroad construction, management, and responsibility— lessons they were reluctant to learn—some of the roads in the older sections, as we have seen, had begun to mend their lines and their ways. The most far-reaching of the improvements in service before the crash of 1893 stemmed from the steel rail. As late as 1880, only 30 percent of American trackage boasted steel rails. By 1890 the proportion had climbed to 80 percent; by 1900 virtually to 100 percent. Steel rails could bear ten or fifteen times the weight of iron rails and still last twenty times as long. The heavier and faster locomotives and larger freight and passenger cars they could carry assured safer and more reliable service run on shorter schedules.

A related development was the double-tracking and quadruple-tracking of thousands of miles of busy routes in the West as well as in the East. Many roads in all sections of the country also laid new track to extend their service to a growing list of cities and towns. By 1887 about 33,000 American communities had gained regular train service. Unfortunately, all but 2700 of them as yet were reached by but a single line, one certain to take advantage of its monopoly position to charge what the traffic would bear.

After 1875, moreover, "through service" between distant metropolises at last began to achieve the smoothness and coordination that had merely been promised earlier. In addition, clean and often elegant dining cars were added to many long-distance passenger trains and sleepers were continuously improved. Terminals and stations, once open sheds or mere platforms, were becoming carefully planned architectural showpieces on the model of Vanderbilt's terminal in New York City for roads that had begun to take pride in their names and emblems.

Yet none of these improvements seems to have muffled the cry for railroad regulation and reform, especially after the Panics of 1873

and 1884 had forced many speculators and speculative roads to the wall. Railroad rate and dividend policies came most bitterly under attack from shippers and investors. When the railroads fought the growing agitation by spending large sums to make political friends and employ the best legal talent, they made additional enemies. "War," said the English commentator James Bryce in the 1880s, "is the natural state of an American railway towards all other authorities." In this war, as the reformers complained, the railroads enlisted "the ablest [attorneys] in the United States, all of them paid out of the people's money." Such open flouting of the people's government, such open corruption of all the channels of political practice, would have been enough in itself to raise the protest against the railroads, even by distinterested citizens, to irresistible levels. Reform and regulation, nevertheless, also won the backing of many railroad men themselves who had come to look upon the national government as the only power that could save them from their own disastrous competitive and financial practices (see Chapter Twenty).

## III Enterprise in industry

### Spirit of the age

Railroad expansion and the railroad improvement, of course, had a great deal to do with the surge of northern industry after the war. Actual railroad construction expanded the market for all kinds of goods ranging from iron and steel for rails to meat and blankets for construction crews. Railroad financing, in turn, helped familiarize the public with investment procedures that industrial corporations could also use in selling securities in the growing money markets of the country. Railroad financing also drew large

amounts of foreign capital to America. With such capital available for railroad building, industrialists like Carnegie, Armour, and Rockefeller could use their profits to expand their own enterprises and to exploit profitable by-products, fully confident that others would supply the carriers to haul raw materials to their factories and factory output to market.

But railroad development itself only strengthened the spirit of optimism and enterprise that dominated the northern economy after the war. "Everybody and everything's goin' places," observed an Indiana farmer in the late 1860s. In 1869, David A. Wells, Special

Commissioner of Revenue in the federal government, reported:

*Within the last five years, more cotton spindles have been put in operation, more iron furnaces erected, . . . more steel made, more coal and copper mined, more lumber sawed, . . . more houses and shops constructed, more manufactories . . . started, and more petroleum collected, refined, and exported than during any equal period in the history of the country.*

And the country was still only midway through the industrial boom that would reach a peak in the early 1870s. The Panic of 1873 called but a temporary halt to northern progress.

*John D. Rockefeller in 1872.*

The New-York Historical Society, New York City

## The Standard Oil nexus

Nowhere was the spirit of enterprise more evident than in the newest industry of all, the production and refining of petroleum. In the 1850s whale oil, then the world's chief commercial illuminant, had become so scarce that its price edged toward $2 a gallon. Seepages of surface petroleum had been detected in many parts of the world for centuries and as "rock oil" it had gradually gained a reputation as a medical cure-all. Some chemical pioneers had also begun to refine petroleum into kerosene, to design lamps for burning it conveniently, and to promote it as a cheap illuminant.

What no one knew was how to find enough petroleum to meet the rising demand for it both for its alleged medical properties and for the kerosene to be derived from it. Then, in 1857, a young New York lawyer, George H. Bissell, and his associates sent E. L. Drake to the neighborhood of Titusville, Pennsylvania, to make the first deliberate attempt to drill for oil. Drake, a railroad conductor on the New Haven Railroad, had only two qualifications: availability and pertinacity. Adorned with a hastily purchased "colonelcy" to give the operation a semblance of army-trained engineering experience, Drake began work the next year. His novel enterprise encountered great scorn and difficulties until, in August 1859, "Drake's Folly" gushed in.

Twentieth-century drillers sometimes go down two miles and more for oil. Drake most laboriously got down to 69.5 feet, and his first well yielded 20 barrels of crude oil a day. By 1864 wildcatters, as oil prospectors were called, had covered the Titusville district with so many oil derricks that annual production exceeded 2 million barrels. By 1872, the oil fields covered 2000 square miles in Pennsylvania, West Virginia, and Ohio, and annual production had soared to 40 million barrels. Of this massive total, John D. Rockefeller's Standard Oil Company was already refining no less than one-fifth.

Born in 1839 in Richford, New York, Rockefeller, aged twenty-six in 1865, had already accumulated a wartime fortune of $50,000 in a

483

484

grain and meat partnership in Cleveland. Two years earlier he had invested in a small Cleveland oil refinery to which he was now ready to devote all his time. He dissolved the old partnership and set up a new one with Samuel Andrews, a man experienced in oil refining.

Rockefeller saw early that an efficient refinery could be built for as little as $50,000 and that an industry into which entry was so cheap and easy must be intensely competitive. In order to outdo all rivals, he and Andrews started with $200,000. Moreover, they built their first refinery not at the oil fields, where skilled labor and bank credit were scarce and markets distant, but in the rising city of Cleveland, where Rockefeller had become well known. In 1867 they added Henry M. Flagler as a partner and won additional backing from Stephen V. Harkness, a rich Ohio brewer and distiller. In 1870 these men and John's brother, William Rockefeller, organized the Standard Oil Company with a capital of $1 million. These funds supplied the wherewithal for a triple attack on the competition, which was located mainly in the oil region and in Cleveland, Pittsburgh, and New York.

*First,* Rockefeller spent heavily to make his plants the most efficient in the country so that he could undersell all competitors and still make sizable profits. Often enough, he would sell his products well below cost in selected markets in order to ruin a competitor—the practice known as "cutthroat competition." To recoup his losses he would then charge more than ever once he had the market to himself.

*Second,* with his volume of business soaring, Rockefeller demanded that the railroads grant him lower freight rates than his competitors. Railroad rates nominally were required by law to be public and equal, but Rockefeller sought his advantage by requesting secret rebates from the regular charges. Since Cleveland was a city in which carrier competition was intense, the railroads felt obliged to comply with his request to hold his business.

Having by these means eliminated almost all competition in Cleveland, Rockefeller, in 1872, took the *third* step to bring the industry elsewhere to book. This step involved him in the notorious South Improvement Company

which Tom Scott of the Pennsylvania Railroad had organized in 1870 with the grandiose idea of curtailing the harsh rate competition among railroads by bringing as many rival lines as possible under one management, his own. Scott had done little with his scheme before 1872, by which time Rockefeller had developed similar "pooling" ideas to eliminate the cutthroat competition that continued to plague the oil industry. Many of the refineries in Pittsburgh, New York, and other centers had already been shaken by Rockefeller's competitive tactics. What Rockefeller needed was a club to brandish at the holdouts. No better bludgeon could have been invented than discriminatory freight rates on oil shipments, which a railroad pool such as the one Scott had in mind could enforce.

The South Improvement scheme as finally worked out in January 1872 included the Erie, the New York Central, and the Pennsylvania railroads and their affiliates on the one hand, and Standard Oil leaders on the other. It involved a series of steps: (1) The South Improvement Company was to be reorganized as an oil company headed by Standard Oil chiefs; (2) the railroads were to be permitted to double their charges for hauling crude oil and oil products; (3) the South Improvement Company alone was not to be charged the increase; (4) more than that, the South Improvement Company and not the railroads was to receive—as "drawbacks"—most of the increase paid by Standard's competitors; (5) the railroads were to report daily to the South Improvement Company on all shipments made by competitors, informing the company of the amount, quality, price, and destination of the oil involved; (6) to keep tabs on these reports, the South Improvement Company was to have access to the railroads' books. In exchange, the railroads would receive a small part of the rate increases and the promise that the South Improvement Company would distribute its patronage as evenly as practicable over the heretofore rival railroad lines.

When word of this bold scheme leaked out

the Standard publicly abandoned it, but Rockefeller got his secret rebates and drawbacks from some of the more vulnerable lines after all. By 1879, he held about 95 percent of the refining capacity of the country and had captured almost the entire world market for his products. By then the oil pipeline was well on the way to supplanting the railroad tank car as the principal oil carrier, and before long the Standard had used its enormous power to gain a virtual monopoly of pipeline transportation.

A few years later, Rockefeller observed:

*This movement [toward monopoly] was the origin of the whole system of modern economic administration. It has revolutionized the way of doing business all over the world. The time was ripe for it. It had to come, though all we saw at the moment was the need to save ourselves from wasteful conditions. . . . The day of combination is here to stay. Individualism has gone, never to return.*

Rockefeller was not the only one in the oil industry to employ sharp tactics. Samuel Downer, a leader in refining before Rockefeller so outdistanced the field, once said to Henry Flagler: "Flagler, I am opposed to the whole scheme of rebates and drawbacks—without I'm in it!" Those refiners who could exert enough pressure on the railroads were "in it."

An even more daring and original move late in the 1880s protected and extended the Standard's position. Crude oil production in Pennsylvania and neighboring regions hit its all-time peak in 1882, and industry leaders began to worry that the whole business would soon dry up. So alarmed did they become that within a few years John D. Archbold, Rockefeller's closest and most trusted associate, quietly began to sell off his Standard stock at 75 cents on the dollar. In 1885, a huge new oil field was discovered near Lima in western Ohio, and a second just across the Indiana border. The crude produced here, however, was so contaminated with odoriferous sulphur that it became known as "pole cat oil" or "skunk

juice." In 1887, when Lima-Indiana oil seemed unmarketable because of its stench, Rockefeller decided that a way could surely be found to eliminate this fault. By threatening to go it alone if need be, he forced the Standard Oil directors to organize the Ohio Oil Company and hire a team of chemists to make its products saleable. The chemists made short work of the problem, leaving Standard Oil in a position to monopolize the new fields and the new markets in the Mississippi Valley and beyond.

Rockefeller remained nominal president of Standard Oil until the "trust" was dissolved by court order in 1911. As early as 1882, however, seven years after he had been brought into the organization, Archbold had become the company's chief administrative officer. Archbold "believed in a large executive committee," writes Allan Nevins in his life of Rockefeller, "and insisted that it hold daily meetings to present a variety of points of view. . . . He reserved his judgment until the end, and usually based it upon a consensus of opinion." But the Standard's Executive Committee itself was simply the peak of a whole pyramid of committees that gradually became common in large corporate structures. By 1887, the first year for which the information is complete, the Standard had a salary committee, a proxy committee, and committees for manufacturing, export trade, lubricating oil, transportation, cooperage, case and can, and domestic trade. In later years some committees were disbanded, others added.

Rockefeller put his finger on the security of the committee system when he said that in mobilizing so many people, "the conservative ones are apt to be in the majority, and this is no doubt a desirable thing when the mere momentum of a large concern is certain to carry it forward."

## Bessemer and open-hearth steel

Before the Civil War, steel had been a rare and costly metal which could be made only in quantities of 25 to 50 pounds by processes that took weeks to complete. In 1847, William Kelly of Kentucky had discovered a simple method by which tons of excellent

486

steel could be produced in a matter of minutes; but nothing much was heard of his discovery until ten years later, when Kelly contested the application of an Englishman, Henry Bessemer, for an American patent on a process similar to his own and on an efficient "converter." Patent controversies soon were straightened out, yet as late as 1867 only 2600 tons of what has since become known as Bessemer steel were produced in the United States.

In 1872, fresh from his long experience in railroading and the building of steel railroad bridges, Andrew Carnegie entered the steel-making industry, but he put off adopting the Bessemer process. "Pioneering doesn't pay a new concern," he said: "we must wait until the process develops." A trip to England the next year convinced Carnegie of the practicality of the new method, and on his return he organized a new firm, Carnegie, McCandless & Company, and built the biggest steel mill in the world, the J. Edgar Thomson Steel Works, near Pittsburgh, shrewdly named after the president of the Pennsylvania Railroad. On intimate terms with Thomson, Tom Scott, and other railroad kings, Carnegie ignored the depression of the succeeding years and "went out," as he said, "and persuaded them to give us orders." By 1879 American steel production had risen to 930,000 tons, three-fourths of it in the form of steel rails, almost all of them manufactured by the Carnegie company.

By 1890 American steel production had taken another spectacular leap to an annual figure of over 4 million tons. By then, three other giant steel enterprises had arisen in the South and West, but the "Pittsburgh district" continued to dominate the industry. Carnegie, in turn, was acknowledged to have had "almost absolute control" of the business there until he sold out in 1901 to the billion-dollar United States Steel Corporation formed that year, which—with the Carnegie empire as its base—became the world's leading steel producer.

Carnegie's success sprang in part from his ability as a salesman. But he also had a grasp of big business management that far outstripped that of his competitors. Other steel men (like the wildcatters in oil) often lived off their profits in the grand style, but Carnegie, like Rockefeller, plowed back his own and his company's earnings into the expansion, integration, and modernization of the enterprise. Before he retired in 1901, Carnegie had acquired immense holdings in the fabulous Mesabi ore lands in Minnesota, from which as much as 85 percent of America's entire iron ore needs in the first half of the twentieth century were to come. He also bought up Pennsylvania coal fields and scattered limestone quarries, and the coke business of Henry Clay Frick, taking Frick himself, an excellent manager, into partnership.

Ore, coal, limestone, and coke are the basic raw materials for the manufacture of steel; to insure their regular delivery to his plants, Carnegie also invested heavily in ore ships and railroad cars. Beyond all this, Carnegie was one of the first to employ a full-time chemist to study and control the tricky metallurgy of steel in order to produce a more uniform and satisfactory product. He introduced sound cost accounting and developed a successful incentive pay system for executives and workers alike.

At about the time Kelly and Bessemer had discovered the Bessemer process, other inventors were developing the open-hearth method, which had two important advantages over Bessemer. The open-hearth furnace could attain a higher temperature than the Bessemer converter; yet it was easier to draw samples from it for testing during production. The greater heat broke down the raw materials more thoroughly than a Bessemer converter could, and the easy testing gave the worker greater control in recombining these materials or mixing them with alloying metals.

As experience with steel grew, and as metallurgy furnished more precise explanations for faults and accidents, the quality of steel improved. Bessemer steel was especially satisfactory for steel rails. But when steel came into greater demand for other uses—in skyscraper construction, high-speed machinery, the manufacture of automobiles—the finer open-hearth steels grew more popular. By 1910 United States steel production exceeded 26 million tons, two-thirds of it open-hearth.

### Advances in the use of electricity

Among the many new management problems in the giant enterprises emerging in the postwar years were such sheer mechanical ones as communication and data control. Such simple mechanical devices as the typewriter, first used in business in 1867, and the adding machine, made practical by 1888, helped resolve such problems. They also set in motion the mechanization of the office that was to make such huge strides when electronic equipment became common after World War II.

More fundamental in the nineteenth century were the expansion of the electric telegraph and the development of the telephone. By 1878 Western Union owned 195,000 miles of telegraph lines and controlled 80 percent of the telegraph business. In 1881, at a cost of nearly $25 million, the company proceeded to buy out its two principal competitors. This accomplished, President Norvin Green of Western Union assured his stockholders that, while "competition may be a popular demand, . . . successful competition with your Company is improbable if not actually impossible." Within two years, nevertheless, a strong new rival loomed. This was the Commercial Cable Company, partly owned by John W. Mackay, the Comstock Lode millionaire. A disastrous rate war with Western Union began in 1886, but both companies soon were ready to call quits and, while they did not merge, they agreed to end rate competition.

In 1876 Alexander Graham Bell patented the telephone he had invented the year before, and the next year Western Union, which first scorned Bell's invention as an "electrical toy," decided it had better enter the field. Backing a rival patent by Elisha Gray, it organized the American Speaking Telephone Company

# EDISON'S LIGHT.

## The Great Inventor's Triumph in Electric Illumination.

## A SCRAP OF PAPER.

## It Makes a Light, Without Gas or Flame, Cheaper Than Oil.

## TRANSFORMED IN THE FURNACE.

## Complete Details of the Perfected Carbon Lamp.

## FIFTEEN MONTHS OF TOIL.

## Story of His Tireless Experiments with Lamps, Burners and Generators.

## SUCCESS IN A COTTON THREAD.

## The Wizard's Byplay, with Bodily Pain and Gold "Tailings."

## HISTORY OF ELECTRIC LIGHTING.

The New-York Historical Society, New York City

*The first news story of the incandescent bulb, New York Herald, December 21, 1879, indicating the "wizard" status the great inventor had already attained.*

*"What will he grow to?"—a forecast
of the threat of electricity to coal and steam,
from* Punch *of London, June 1881.*

was the development of long-distance telephone service, beginning in 1884. To expand this business, the Bell directors set up a new corporation, the American Telephone and Telegraph Company. In 1900, AT&T became the overall holding company of the entire Bell system, with a capitalization of $250 million. In that year, 1,350,000 Bell telephones were in use in the United States. Service still cost New Yorkers $240 a year for a private phone, and AT&T's profits became the envy of industry.

While Bell and others were improving the telephone, Thomas A. Edison was experimenting with electric lighting. In 1879 he perfected a reasonably priced incandescent bulb and three years later built the first central electric power station, the Pearl Street station in New York City, from which he distributed *direct* current to the eighty-five buildings soon wired to receive it. Direct current, which Edison believed the only current commercially feasible, could be transmitted great distances only at great cost. With the use of transformers, *alternating* current could take direct current from a power plant, cheaply step up the voltage many times for distant transmission, and then step it down again for ordinary purposes.

In collaboration with William Stanley, George Westinghouse, the inventor of the railroad air brake and other devices, developed the first generators and transformers to make alternating current practical. Before it could be used for mechanical power, however, a suitable motor had to be devised. Such a motor was perfected in 1888 by Nikola Tesla, a Serbian immigrant. Soon after he bought up Tesla's patent, Westinghouse made alternating current famous by using it to light up Chicago's World Fair in 1893.

Electric power revolutionized American business and American life even more than cheap steel did; but the great era of electricity was to be the twentieth century. In the nineteenth century, the United States as well as the rest of the world still looked to water and steam for power.

and proceeded to use all its political influence to block the Bell Company from winning franchises in local communities. The Bell Company, under the direction of Theodore N. Vail, was not awed by its great rival and proceeded to sue Western Union for patent infringement. Bell's case was so good that Western Union settled out of court in 1879 and sold Bell the 56,000 telephones it had set up in fifty-five cities, along with its franchises there.

During the 1880s the Bell Company was further beset by rivals, all of whom it ultimately bought out at a total cost of $225 million. Patented improvements in the telephone instrument and in wires and transmission thereafter kept the company almost invulnerable to competition. One of its major innovations

# IV Cycles, science, and consolidation

## Panic of 1873

By 1860, $1 billion had been invested in American industry, and the factories and shops that made up the industrial community produced goods that year valued at about $1.8 billion. By 1890, the capitalization of industry had soared to $6.5 billion, and annual output approached $10 billion in value. These are simply crude indices of the transformation of the United States in a short thirty years from an essentially agrarian nation to one of the leading industrial powers of the world. In the refining of crude oil, the manufacture of steel, the packing of meat, the making of lumber, the extraction of gold, silver, coal, and iron, the United States had surpassed all rivals. In specialties like hardware, machine tools, and small arms and ammunition, she retained the leadership assumed before the Civil War, while her pianos as well as her locomotives ranked with the world's best.

In any age, this would have been a towering performance. In an age wedded to bigness, it made an impression so profound that few, even in the doldrums of the middle 1870s, cared to challenge business leadership. Americans had much to complain of in this early age of industrial advance, and their most frequent complaint was of hard times. Yet there was little questioning of the "system." In the nineteenth century, and even up to the Great Crash of 1929, depressions continued to be viewed simply as the results of errors of judgment, and recovery was expected as soon as the rituals of liquidation and reorganization could be performed. Thus instead of destroying hope, depressions paid dividends for faith. They presented opportunities to expand and modernize plants at lowest cost, to corner raw materials at bottom prices, to capture customers with attractive schedules of rates and deliveries. It was in the seventies that Rockefeller organized his oil monopoly, that Carnegie built his first great steel plant, that Armour and Morris raised their meat-packing empires, that the Comstock Lode was exploited, and that Boston capitalists began to finance Bell's telephone.

Signs of trouble during the first postwar boom had become apparent as early as 1871, when the number of business failures reached 3000. By 1872 more than 4000 additional firms had collapsed. A clue to their difficulties may be found in the fact that during the boom period from 1868 to 1873 the volume of American bank loans had grown seven times as fast as bank deposits. The Panic of 1873 began on September 8, when the New York Warehouse and Securities Company went into bankruptcy, carrying many of its creditors down with it. The greatest shock came ten days later with the failure of Jay Cooke and Company, the most famous banking house in the country. On September 20, the New York Stock Exchange, "to save [Wall] Street from utter ruin," suspended all trading for ten days. Shock then gave way to profound depression as railroads halted construction, mills closed down, and trade languished. As late as the year 1877, over 18,000 business firms failed.

In the mid-1870s unemployment and privation found levels never before plumbed in American history, and together they brought unprecedented violence in labor relations (see p. 493). Family tragedies also multiplied as business and professional men in the thousands, like unskilled workers in the millions, were obliged to seek public charity. But those who understood the normal rhythms of capitalist ups and downs did well. "So many of my friends needed money," Carnegie explained later about the years 1874–1878, "that they begged me to repay them. I did so and bought out five or six of them. That was what gave me my leading interest in this steel business."

490

## Mechanization and rationalization

Once the depression of the 1870s had run its course, such a resurgence of industrial production followed that the prices of most commodities fell rapidly. This state of affairs put a premium on the use of the most efficient machinery to keep production costs down; it also forced manufacturers to rethink the processes by which many commodities were being produced. Engineering, heretofore largely limited to problems of transportation such as bridge construction and railroad surveys, was now brought into the factory. Even before the Civil War, firearms and farm machinery companies had speeded up production by manufacture of interchangeable parts which could be quickly and systematically assembled, while the meat packers had exploited continuous-flow methods. In the 1870s and after, both the manufacture of interchangeable parts and their assembly along a continuous line became common techniques in many new industries. Their highest refinement before the age of space and electronics came in the making of automobiles which could hardly have developed into a mass-market business without such mass-production methods (see Chapter Twenty-six).

By furthering the rapid mechanization of factories and the simplification of workers' tasks, science made it possible for businessmen sharply to reduce production costs. Yet there was a catch. So high was the initial investment required to build and equip modern plants that economies of production could be realized only when plants operated at or near capacity. If plants produced fewer items than they were geared for, the cost of each item rose remarkably. On the other hand, if plants ran at capacity, their volume became so great that the markets were flooded and prices sank. Every source of hope for enlarged markets in the postwar era—the opening of a new railroad line, a boom in immigration, a burst of exports, a rise in the tariff—promoted expansion and mechanization. But each new development soon ran its course and left behind idle plants and equipment—usually purchased with borrowed money on which interest had to be paid, come what may.

This situation became a constant hazard of American business life in the 1880s. As the *Bulletin* of the American Iron and Steel Association said in 1884, "Indeed it might almost be rated the exception for half the works in condition to make iron to be in operation simultaneously." Even in the manufacture of bread, the vice-president of the National Millers Association pointed out that year, "large output, quick sales, keen competition, and small profits are characteristic of modern trade." He added:

> We have the advantage in our business of always being in fashion. . . . But our ambition has overreached our discretion and judgement. . . . The thousand-barrel mill of our competitor had to be put in the shade by a two-thousand-barrel mill of our own construction. . . . As our glory increased our profits became smaller, until now the question is not how to surpass the record, but how to maintain our position and how to secure what we have in our possession.

One outcome of the competitive struggle in highly mechanized industries was the growing number of family firms and other independent companies forced to shut down. A second was the defensive movement toward industrial pools and trusts somehow to bring order out of the chaos of tooth-and-claw competition and assure satisfactory profits.

Long known to manufacturing industries as well as to railroads, pools or pooling agreements administered by trade associations were essentially secret arrangements among competitors to restrict output, maintain prices, and divide markets. Usually created in emergencies, they quickly collapsed when the emergency passed or deepened. "A starving man . . . will get bread if it is to be had," said James J. Hill, "and a starving railway will not maintain rates."

Pools enabled independent entrepreneurs to retain a semblance of individuality and to express it if need be. When pools failed, they often were supplanted by trusts, of which the first in this epoch was that organized by Rockefeller in 1879 and reorganized in 1882. "Its success," said a New York legislative committee that investigated Standard Oil in 1888, "has been the incentive to the formation of all other trusts or combinations."

In forming a trust, the stock of the companies involved is turned over to a group of trustees agreed upon by the combining firms. In exchange for such stock, trustee certificates are issued. Ownership of the stock remains in the original hands, but management of the enterprises represented by it is concentrated in the hands of a single board of trustees. In the decade after the founding of the Standard Oil Trust, there appeared the Cottonseed Oil Trust, the Salt Trust, the Whiskey Trust, the Sugar Trust, and others. Not all were strictly "trust" arrangements, but the tag was pinned to any large combination whose objective was to restrain cutthroat competition. Judge George C. Barrett of the New York Supreme Court said of the Sugar Trust:

*It can close every refinery at will, close some and open others, limit the purchases of raw material, artificially limit the production of refined sugar, enhance the price to enrich themselves and their associates at the public expense, and depress the price when necessary to crush out and impoverish a foolhardy rival.*

### The Panic of 1893 and banker control

Pools and "trusts" seemed to be the answer to cutthroat competition abroad as well as in the United States. In Germany in particular, the *cartel,* essentially a large pooling arrangement with more or less severe penalties for backsliders, became the accepted means of regulating production, marketing, and prices. In Europe, such arrangements usually had the overt sanction of the state. In the United States, where free competition was the accepted path to progress, the government for a long time was forced to give tacit sanction to consolidations of every sort while at the same time seeming to impose restraints on monopolistic tendencies. The Sherman Anti-Trust Act of 1890 (see p. 518), the first admonitory federal measure, reflected the growing public opposition to the "artificially" raised prices and "artificially" closed opportunities that the trusts brought about. Competition, however, grew more intense than ever after the passage of the Sherman Act and especially after the Panic of 1893, when once again thousands of industrial firms became insolvent, banks shut down, and one railroad of every six went into receivership.

This panic began in February 1893, when the Philadelphia & Reading Railroad, with negotiable assets of a mere $100,000 and short-term debts of $18 million was forced into bankruptcy. As the business collapse snowballed and unemployment soared, the federal government for the first time was bombarded with demands for direct relief but to no avail. Pressure on government grew the more intense because of prophets of doom even among the nation's most conservative leaders. No earlier panic had elicited such fears of revolution. In 1894 Francis Lynde Stetson, perhaps the leading corporation lawyer in the country and J. P. Morgan's personal attorney, warned President Cleveland, "We are on the eve of a very dark night, unless a return of commercial prosperity relieves popular discontent."

At the same time, just as the Panic of 1873 had given Carnegie and Rockefeller great opportunities for expansion at bargain rates, so the Panic of 1893 gave Morgan and a few other investment bankers their opportunity to consolidate economic control in their own hands. Their first objective was to bring order out of the chaos in railroad finance. By 1904, 1040 distinct railroad lines had been consolidated into six huge combinations with an aggregate capital of $10 billion, each in turn allied to either the Morgan or the Kuhn, Loeb interests.

Success in railroad consolidation turned these bankers to manufacturing and to public utilities serving the rapidly growing cities (see Chapter Twenty-one). The return of prosper-

**492**

ity in 1898 made it all the easier for them to market the securities of new combines, many of them formed, indeed, merely to make banking profits from the flotation of new stocks and bonds. The strong movement toward consolidation following the Panic of 1873 had produced in twenty years only twelve great industrial trusts, with an aggregate capital under $1 billion. By contrast, Morgan's United States Steel Corporation, formed in 1901, alone boasted a capitalization of almost $1.5 billion. In 1904, John Moody, in his classic study *The Truth About the Trusts,* listed no less than 318 new industrial combinations with an aggregate capital of $7.25 billion. They controlled 5288 separate plants. Moody also listed 111 public utility combinations, all but 14 of them organized after 1893. They controlled 1336 plants with an aggregate capital of $3.7 billion.

There was still more to the story. The power of the House of Morgan, and that of its competitors in the investment banking business, arose from their ability to supply the wherewithal for growing and groping companies. Once they had raised money for such companies from investors who acted largely on their confidence in the bankers themselves, the bankers felt the necessity to place their own men on the companies' boards of directors and thereby take a direct hand in management. In this way, the bankers' economic power, and Morgan's especially, spread far from the financial community to the heart of the big-business system.

A second feature of the Morgan method became the banker's control of, or close alliance with, not only American users of capital but the growing American institutional sources of it. These institutions included commercial banks, the trust companies that administered large estates and other properties, and the immense life insurance companies whose premium collections from millions of small policyholders mushroomed during Morgan's heyday. Thus the bankers' influence spread far from the big-business community and eventually extended virtually over the entire population.

"With a man like Mr. Morgan at the head of a great industry," his friend John B. Claflin told a group of bankers assembled to honor the financier in 1901, "as against the old plan of many diverse interests in it, production would become more regular, labor would be more steadily employed at better wages, and panics caused by overproduction would become a thing of the past." Economic instability arising from the vagaries of politics would also be guarded against. "As the business of the country has learned the secret of combination," said the *Bankers' Magazine* in 1901, "it is gradually subverting the power of the politician and rendering him subservient to its purposes. . . . That [government is not] entirely controlled by these interests is due to the fact that business organization has not reached full perfection."

## V  Conditions of labor

### The factory world

Accompanying the transformation of American business life in the postwar decades was a 300 percent rise in nonagricultural employment, compared with a rise of but 50 percent in the number engaged on the farms. By 1890, more than 4,600,000 persons worked in American factories, and another 3 million were divided equally between construction industries and transportation.

In the 1870s and 1880s the fierceness of business competition, as we have said, depressed the prices of essential commodities. At the same time, wages paid unskilled nonagricultural workers remained virtually fixed at

$1.25 to $1.50 a day. Skilled workers were paid at least twice that. Since such fixed money wages could buy more and more goods as prices fell, it would appear that industrial labor was constantly improving its situation. In fact, industrial workers, skilled and unskilled, often were harder hit than the expropriated independent businessmen.

The workers' plight arose from the same conditions that underlay the trust movement and was worsened by that movement. Translated into the workers' terms, the inability of fiercely competitive firms to keep their costly machinery going the year round meant that although his daily rate of pay remained unchanged, the number of days he worked fluctuated violently. Few industrial workers, none among the unskilled, had job security. After trusts or giant corporations came into control in many industries, moreover, and shut down the less efficient plants, they made no provision for workers displaced. Under such conditions, some areas became blighted by more or less permanent unemployment and by the exodus of younger workers to more likely places.

One of the conditions making periodic unemployment a certainty in some industries was the tendency to keep factories in operation for excessively long hours when demand was high. Workweeks ranging from sixty to over eighty hours were common; and the seven-day week was the rule in steel and paper mills, oil refineries, and other highly mechanized plants. Advances in technology, in turn, accelerated the pace of industrial production, and where this occurred the worker was expected to keep up. Rapidly operating machines greatly increased the physical danger of factory work, while long hours and fatigue ran up the toll in accidents, injuries, and deaths. Another consequence of advancing technology was that the machines did more and more of the skilled work, draining much of the personal satisfaction from labor and leveling proud craftsmen to the status and pay of menials.

### The great railroad strike of 1877

Work in railroad transportation was freer of constant supervision than in factories but had its own overpowering hazards. These took such a heavy toll in accidents that sound life-insurance companies rejected railroad workers outright as bad risks. It was principally to establish some means of protection for their families that the railroad workers set up their early labor organizations in the postwar decades. Significantly, these were called "Brotherhoods" and "Orders," not unions. Their members paid "premiums," not dues. Their constitutions made no reference to collective bargaining, little to working conditions. Their main goal, as the Brotherhood of Locomotive Engineers put it, was "post-mortem" security.

As in the factory, the hazards of railroad work may be grouped under the speedup and the stretchout, accentuated in railroading by such technological advances as steel rails, steel-plate boilers, and faster engines, and such managerial advances as the consolidation of lines. For the men on the roads these changes simply added up to the necessity of carrying heavier and heavier loads at faster and faster clips over greater and greater distances. Engineers might be forced to remain at the throttle for twenty to forty hours of uninterrupted service, with firemen keeping up steam and brakemen staying constantly on the alert. "Our railroads are barbarizing our Trainmen as rapidly as possible," wrote Robert Harris, President of the Burlington, in 1877, "by keeping them unceasingly at work." The sheer physical exhaustion of railroad toil, moreover, was in no way relieved by rising pay. On the contrary, since labor costs made up nearly 65 percent of railroad operating costs, and since railroad competition was often cutthroat, pay scales were likely to be slashed as the work itself became most taxing and most dangerous.

Working conditions on the railroads grew so bad during the depression of the 1870s that in 1877 spontaneous strikes spread terror across the country. The stage had been set by local railroad strikes earlier in the depression

494

and by strikes in other industries, notably the "Long Strike" among the anthracite coal workers in Pennsylvania, one marked by exceptional brutality on the part of Pinkerton detectives hired by the coal operators. This strike lasted from January to June 1875, when hunger forced the miners to capitulate and accept a 20 percent wage cut.

By 1875 many of the anthracite coal mines had come under control of the Philadelphia & Reading Railroad, largely occupied in carrying coal to factories and homes in Philadelphia and to coaling ships in Philadelphia port. The Philadelphia & Reading had shown the way in breaking the coal strike; it was also responsible for working up its violent sequel.

For some years before the strike of 1875 the coal regions had been plagued by murders, beatings, and other savagery, widely attributed by authorities to "Molly Maguires," a name taken over from the authentic Molly Maguires of Ireland, one of a number of secret societies formed there in the 1840s to terrorize landlords and prevent evictions. A few months after the coal strike, twenty-four men, most of them members of the broken miners' union, were picked up by the police in the anthracite region, charged with the Molly Maguire atrocities, held until tried early in 1876, and then uniformly convicted as charged. Ten of the twenty-four were summarily hanged, the rest jailed. The evidence that convicted the men had been supplied by one of the Reading road's Pinkertons, James McParlan, and supported by other men criminally involved themselves but granted immunity in exchange for their testimony. This evidence remains inconclusive to this day. The purpose behind the arrests and the trials, however, is clear: to smear labor generally with accusations of "riot, sabotage, arson, pillage, assault, robbery, and murder"; and this purpose seemed to have been achieved. Early in 1877, the *Commercial and Financial Chronicle* boasted that "Labor is under control for the first time since the war."

As the impending railroad strikes would soon show, the *Chronicle* underestimated both the popular hatred of "the James boys in frock coats" who ran the roads and the depres-

sion-fed discontent of the men who moved their trains. At the same time, the strikes revealed how the "Molly Maguire" accusations may well have undermined popular patience with labor violence.

One of the railroad workers' major complaints by mid-1877 was the corporations' practice of blacklisting all who dared join even the timid brotherhoods and orders. Another sore point was the high prices charged at the railroad hotels where men away from home had to put up. Discontent deepened when the roads ordered greater numbers of "doubleheaders"—that is, trains of approximately twice the normal number of cars without added trainmen. The last straw was the announcement late in the spring of 1877 of further wage cuts.

The leaderless revolt began on July 16, when the firemen on the B & O quit work. On July 22 the *Baltimore Sun* commented:

*There is no disguising the fact that the strikers in all their lawful acts have the fullest sympathy of the community. The 10 per cent reduction after two previous reductions was ill advised. . . . The singular part of the disturbance is in the very active part taken by the women, who are the wives and mothers of the firemen. They look famished and wild, and declare for starvation rather than have their people work for reduced wages.*

By July 19, the strike had spread to Pittsburgh, where the local militia actually fraternized with the men of the hated Pennsylvania Railroad and fought on their side even after federal troops had arrived. From the Pennsylvania the strike spread along the Erie and New York Central, all the way to St. Louis. Coal miners, stevedores, farmers, small businessmen, and thousands of unemployed all joined in demonstrations sympathetic to the workers' cause. Less desirable friends also pitched in, and soon the looting, burning, murder, and mayhem that respectable elements foresaw became general. As the strike disintegrated into a nationwide melee, public opinion turned away in horror from the just cause of the original strikers.

By August 2, after hundreds of strikers and others had been killed and thousands injured, railroad service was forcibly restored on all lines, but not the *status quo ante*. According to one authority, the railway strikes of 1877 "involved the largest number of persons of any labor conflict in the nineteenth century." To a contemporary, "it seemed as if the whole social and political structure was on the very brink of ruin." To preserve themselves, and by that token to preserve the country, railroad leaders now demanded that National Guardsmen in the states be trained specifically to combat "labor violence" with greater discipline and dispatch; and many states did in fact appropriate large sums for the expansion of their Guards and for building and equipping new armories. The railroads and many other corporations also more actively enrolled Pinkertons in private armies of their own. Detectives were used to ferret out union members, who were promptly fired. New employees now were forced to sign "yellow-dog" contracts obliging them to shun union activity.

On their part, the railroad workers grew more militant, and certain factions forsook the brotherhoods to join the broadly based Knights of Labor and even such militant political organizations as the Workingmen's Party in California and the national Greenback Party. When the engineers' Brotherhood did strike against the Burlington Railroad in 1888, members of the Knights' faction signed on as strikebreakers in retaliation for Brotherhood scab activity against them during a conflict with the Reading shortly before. By the time of the Burlington strike the men in the railroad shops and yards had organized independent craft unions and some steps were taken to coordinate their activities with those of the train service brotherhoods. But railroad labor was to remain torn even during the great Pullman strike of 1894 (see p. 498), while the an-

The New-York Historical Society, New York City

*Army cavalry charging the crowd at the Halstead Street viaduct, Chicago, July 26, 1877, during the great railroad strike.*

tagonism of the white-collar public to strikes and violence hardened.

### National unions and black workers

The national labor organizations of the antebellum years all had collapsed in the Panics of 1837 and 1857. After the Civil War a number of new efforts were made to organize labor nationally, of which two (before the advent of the AFL in 1886) are worth noting. These were the National Labor Union formed in Baltimore in 1866, and the Noble Order of the Knights of Labor formed in Philadelphia three years later. Although, as we have said, relatively few Negroes had entered the industrial labor force during the early postwar decades, the race issue sharply confronted these new unions and industrial workers generally. Two basic questions faced white workers and union leaders: (1) Should black workers be organized or left to swell the ranks of "an industrial labor reserve" compelled to work for minimum wages and to serve as strikebreakers; (2) if organized, should black workers be invited to join with white workers, or should they be in segregated unions?

The National Labor Union drew delegates from many local labor organizations and from a medley of reform groups interested in labor's welfare. In 1872 it grew ambitious enough to form a Labor Reform party and to run a candidate in the presidential election. Most of its other efforts were as impractical as this one, however, and although at one time it claimed a membership of nearly 650,000, it failed to survive the Panic of 1873.

Their political aspirations made the leaders of the National Labor Union as conscious of the Negro's vote as of his potential competition with white workers. "Their strength at the ballot box," said one spokesman, "would be of incalculable value to the cause of labor." "There is no concealing the fact," said another, "that the time will come when the Negro will take possession of the shops if we have not taken possession of the Negro." The leaders, here as elsewhere, however, had trouble with their followers: "We find the subject [of attracting black labor] involved in so much mystery, and upon it so wide a diversity of opinion amongst our members," said a committee of the organization in 1867, "that we believe it is inexpedient to take action on the subject" at this time. No specific action was taken before the demise of the National Labor Union, which, its leaders acknowledged, was speeded by racial discord.

As miscellaneous in its membership and as unfocused in its goals was the Noble Order of the Knights of Labor, organized in 1869 but of little consequence until Terence V. Powderly, a Scranton, Pennsylvania, machinist became "Grand Master" in 1878. The Knights' principal aim was to unite the whole country—except for liquor dealers, lawyers, gamblers, and bankers—into one big union to engage in the production and distribution of goods on a cooperative rather than a capitalistic basis. An energetic organizer, Powderly traveled all over the country recruiting enthusiasts for the cooperative idea, and established more than thirty cooperative enterprises. Although Powderly opposed strikes and violence, a successful strike of certain unions affiliated with the Knights against Jay Gould's Missouri Pacific Railroad in 1885 forced Gould to rescind a wage cut and rehire hundreds of union men he had fired. This victory so raised the Knights' standing that within a year membership had grown from about 100,000 to more than 700,000. Nearly 70,000 were Negroes.

Under Powderly's direction, the Knights organized black as well as mixed locals both in the South and the North. In the North, Pinkertons were employed to impede the Knights' progress. In the South, Knights organizers, like their political counterparts, were assaulted by vigilantes and lynch mobs, often with the assistance of law enforcement officers. The latter usually had the law on their side, since state governments had enacted statutes declaring it a conspiracy for persons to join together to alter contracts between workers and masters, even if only oral.

The American Federation of Labor, given its modern form in 1886 by the "business unionists" led by Samuel Gompers, was an entirely different kind of national labor organization than the National Labor Union or the Knights. Its members were not workers as such, but national craft unions affiliated together. The AFL imposed certain standards on its members. It insisted on their collecting regular dues to provide themselves and the Federation (which took a share) with strike funds in advance of need. It required members to hire full-time organizers. It undertook to settle all issues of jurisdiction that arose when two or more member unions tried to organize workers in similar fields, and it sought to protect its members from raids by non-affiliated rivals.

The AFL, after an early flirtation with socialism and other political panaceas, gave up what political aspirations it may have had and showed only lukewarm interest in reform legislation. Its dominating aim was to force business to engage in collective bargaining with member unions on such everyday issues as wages, hours, and working conditions. An essential goal was the establishment of the "closed shop"—that is, a shop that would agree to employ only AFL members.

Between 1886 and 1892, the AFL gained the affiliation of unions with some 250,000 members. Few of these were Negroes, for few blacks had ever been admitted to the craft unions that made up the Federation. Only among the miners in the new organization were black workers to be found in meaningful numbers. Gompers's lasting position was made clear in his annual report of 1890, when he reiterated the "necessity of avoiding as far as possible all controversial questions." Certain questions did arise from time to time about AFL unions whose constitutions explicitly excluded blacks, but these were handled simply by representations from the national leadership which were ignored with impunity.

Not until World War I did black workers begin to emerge from the marginal "reserve" to become "a regular element in the labor force of every basic industry," to quote Spero and Harris in their history of *The Black Worker*. And not until the effective closing of American ports to white immigrant labor in the 1920s could black workers move by the millions from the still predominantly agrarian South to the industrial cities, slums, and ghettos of the North. But even then, except among miners and longshoremen, the advantages of union organization were almost totally denied them for a generation.

## Haymarket, Homestead, Pullman

Within a year after its successful strike against Gould's Missouri Pacific, the Knights of Labor found good reason to believe that nonviolence was the best policy after all. On May Day, 1886, Knights of Labor unions and other groups sponsored a massive demonstration to promote the eight-hour day. In Chicago, where an independent strike against the McCormick Harvester Company was in progress, the Knights' demonstration was followed by outdoor meetings addressed by anarchists. At a meeting in Haymarket Square on May 3, a bomb thrown at the police killed an officer. Seven more policemen and four civilians died in a riot that followed. The bomb thrower never was found, but seven of the eight anarchists rounded up and accused of murder were sentenced to death. Four of the seven were executed and one committed suicide. The sentence of the other two soon was changed to life imprisonment, and six years later, accusing the sentencing judge of "malicious ferocity," Illinois Governor John P. Altgeld gained lasting fame by unconditionally pardoning them.

The Haymarket riot outraged the general public, and although the Knights of Labor had had nothing to do with it, skilled workers within the organization began to desert in large numbers. The organization suffered also from growing internal dissension, and in a few years it shrank almost to extinction.

Labor violence also impeded the early progress of the AFL. One of the feathers in Gompers's cap was the contract he negotiated with the Carnegie Steel Company in 1890. The Homestead strike a mere two years later, however, cost the AFL dearly. This strike was incited by the Carnegie Steel Company itself when, with Carnegie in Europe, President Henry Clay Frick tried to cut wages. The Amalgamated Association of Iron and Steel Workers, an AFL member, refused to accede to Frick's proposal, and on July 1, 1892, Frick anticipated a walkout by closing down the huge Homestead plant and hiring 300 Pinkertons to protect it. When the Pinkertons arrived by barge on July 6, they were over-whelmed by an army of angry workers. Frick then requested the governor of Pennsylvania to call out the state militia to preserve order. Only after five months did the workers begin to go back to their jobs on company terms. By then they had lost more than the strike. Public sympathy had been with them at first; but when an anarchist who had nothing to do with the strike tried to assassinate Frick, unionist sentiment declined.

The second great strike of the 1890s began two years later at the Pullman Company town near Chicago but soon spread to most of the western railroads. With the onset of the depression in 1893, the Pullman Company began discharging workers and cutting the pay of those kept on. When in May 1894, the workers asked for some reduction in company rents and store prices, they were refused and their negotiators summarily fired. The workers then walked out and appealed for help to the American Railway Union, which many of them had joined. This was the union of all levels of railroad workers that Eugene V. Debs had begun to organize in August 1893, when he found the individual railroad craft unions inadequate to fight the roads. On Pullman's refusal to arbitrate with Debs late in June 1894, 120,000 railroad workers joined the Pullman strikers and the western roads were paralyzed. By July 1, Debs thought he had won the strike. The railroads' "immediate resources were exhausted," he wrote, "and they were unable to operate their trains." All this was accomplished with "no sign of violence or disorder."

The very next day, however, the outlook changed. The General Managers Association, an employer organization representing all the railroads terminating in Chicago, had earlier appealed to Attorney-General Richard Olney for federal troops to get the trains rolling. Olney, a former railroad lawyer, was more than willing to oblige. When restrained for the time being by President Cleveland, he proceeded, on July 2 and 3, to get a series of "blanket" injunctions in federal courts in states affected by the strike enjoining the union and "all other persons whomsoever" to desist from virtually every kind of activity im-peding railroad operation, even "persuasion" of workers to quit their jobs. With the federal injunctions issued, Olney, by July 3, had gathered the first of thousands of federal marshals in the Chicago area to see that the injunctions were obeyed.

The marshals' presence soon provoked a crowd to the first violence in the strike. An exaggerated report of this affair moved Cleveland to send in federal troops, beginning on July 4. Mobs of workers responded by burning railroad cars and cargoes. Incensed by federal troops in his state without invitation from the governor, as the Constitution required, Governor Altgeld now poured in his own militia and by July 10 there were 14,000 soldiers in Chicago and on the railroads' right of way. In twenty states the national guard had been mobilized, and many American Railway Union members were arrested.

On July 10, moreover, Debs himself and three other union officers were indicted for conspiracy in restraint of trade under the Sherman Anti-Trust Act (see p. 518) and on other grounds. Under this indictment they were arrested and then released on bail. A week later they were picked up once more, this time on charges of contempt of court for disobeying the original federal injunctions. The harassment of the union leaders soon disorganized the strikers and their boycott of the railroads collapsed. The American Railway Union itself disintegrated, and such Pullman workers as the company would rehire soon straggled back to work under the old conditions. In December, the United States Circuit Court convicted Debs of the contempt charge and sentenced him to six months in jail. This sentence was upheld in May 1895 by the Supreme Court in the case of *In re Debs*.

The decision in this case had momentous consequences for organized labor. Heretofore, many injunctions had been issued and sustained in labor cases but only on the grounds of strikes being *criminal* conspiracies against the public under the common law. These grounds were wholly unsatisfactory to employers who were forced to proceed through long and uncertain jury trials to make the criminal charges stick. By then, strike damage probably was complete and the strike over. In the *In re Debs* case the Supreme Court placed labor injunctions under equity, not criminal, proceedings, permitting civil courts to issue them in order to *forestall* a public nuisance or *prevent* damage to property.

This new doctrine gave employers a remedy against strikes and boycotts at their outset. Even if an equity injunction were indefensible or merely temporary, it usually was enough to kill organized labor action before labor leaders could get the injunction set aside or quashed. On the other hand, if they chose to ignore such injunctions they became immediately vulnerable to the full penalties for contempt of court regardless of the legality or illegality of any strike activity. Henceforth, blanket injunctions became the most widely used and effective weapons against strikes and other militant union activity until outlawed by the Norris-LaGuardia Anti-injunction Act of 1932.

The Homestead strike and the Pullman strike disclosed the chasm that was opening up between big corporate business on the one hand and the mass of workers on the other. Yet for all the prominence given to labor warfare and labor organization, the vast majority of workers in the factories remained unorganized and docile. By 1898, their number had soared to more than 17 million. Of this vast number, a mere 500,000 were in unions.

## Syndicalism of the IWW

One of the most vigorous early efforts to enlarge the ranks of organized labor was the formation in Chicago in 1905 of the Industrial Workers of the World—the menacing "Wobblies"—under the leadership of "Big Bill" Haywood of the Western Federation of Miners. Like the AFL, the Wobblies believed in direct economic action to improve the workers' condition. Unlike the AFL, their direct action was of the revolutionary "syndi-

calist" brand. Like the old Knights of Labor, the IWW wanted to abolish the wage system; unlike the Knights and their bent toward co-operatives, the Wobblies meant to gain their economic ends by the violent abolition of the state and the creation of a nationwide industrial syndicate directed by the workers.

In their most active period, the Wobblies claimed over a million members, 100,000 of them Negroes concentrated in the lumber industry in Louisiana and Texas and among the longshoremen of such northern ports as Philadelphia and Baltimore. Most of the white Wobblies were to be found among the migratory workers of the West engaged in fruit growing and mining as well as lumbering and dock work. But the Wobblies also moved east, especially into the oppressive textile industry where, in 1912, they won one of the bloodiest strikes in labor annals, in Lawrence, Massachusetts. This success marked the peak of Wobbly influence. In 1913 they had a hand in the strikes of textile workers in Paterson, New Jersey, and of rubber workers in Akron, Ohio; but both strikes ended as total failures.

Under the growing pressure of patriotism and conformity after the entry of the United States into World War I in 1917, the IWW came increasingly under vigilante attack and federal prosecution and waned as a force in the labor movement.

## The industrial immigrant

In the decades after the Civil War, with the new industrial giants like Rockefeller and Carnegie as their models, American farm boys swarmed into the cities with the expectation of working just a few years in the factories before scaling the heights of enterprise on their own. In Europe a similar movement from rural to urban life was under way, of which the migration of millions to the cities of the United States was but a part (see Chapter Twenty-one).

The belief in individual opportunity no doubt accounted for much of the indifference of American workers to unionization drives. Another source of resistance was the introduction of foreigners to factory work. Each new influx—first the Irish, then the Germans, then the Italians, Poles, Hungarians, and others from central and southeastern Europe—tended to start at the bottom only to be pushed upward as less experienced newcomers arrived. Gradually the native American workers monopolized the top of the "blue shirt" hierarchy and found it distasteful to unite with the immigrants in common action against common grievances. Most immigrants, in turn, shrank from the unions and clung to their own communities and churches.

European immigration to the United States reached its nineteenth-century peak in 1882, when almost 640,000 newcomers were admitted. Immigration was not resumed on a rising scale until the turn of the century, and in the decade that ended with the outbreak of World War I in 1914 it broke all earlier records. By that time the immigrants came largely from areas that had sent few persons to the United States during the nineteenth century. The year 1882 thus is a kind of watershed between the "old immigration" from western Europe and the "new immigration" from central and southeastern Europe.

The old immigration had its quota of illiterates and unskilled, who supplied much of the labor for American factories and for mining and construction crews; but it also included millions of farmers and large numbers of artisans, businessmen, and professional men, who often moved on to the rising cities of America's "inland empire." The new immigration was made up of poorer people, less well educated, most of whom remained in the port cities in which they landed or nearby factory towns. By 1910 such immigrants, along with Negroes migrating from the South, made up two-thirds of all workers in twenty-one major branches of American industry. The conditions of their life often made them hostile to American institutions. This hostility, in turn, was reciprocated by Americans over whom the irresistible tide of immigration swept.

The earliest federal measure to restrict immigration was passed in May 1882, in response to long-standing demands of West Coast agitators to exclude the Chinese, who first came in large numbers in the 1860s to help build the Central Pacific Railroad. This act forbade Chinese to enter the United States for a decade; in 1902, another act made this exclusion permanent.

The spread of Darwinian ideas about the "hereditary character of pauperism and crime," as one social worker put it in 1880, lay behind the growing middle-class agitation against indiscriminate European immigration. At the same time, organized labor began to urge immigration restriction on the grounds that American jobs be held for American workers. In 1885 the Knights of Labor persuaded Congress to forbid the importation of contract laborers after Hungarians and Italians had been brought in under contract the previous year to be used as strikebreakers. Businessmen also joined the agitation for immigration restriction after measuring the gains of having an unrestricted supply of new workers against the costs of such "foreign ideas" as socialism, anarchism, and the like, with which all immigrants were supposed to be infected. Not until well into the twentieth century, however, was general restriction successfully imposed by Congress (see Chapter Twenty-six). Until that time, the United States seemed to have prospered as no other nation in history under the policy of free entry that had been hers since the Revolution and that had settled the colonies long before independence.

## For further reading

E. C. Kirkland, *Industry Comes of Age, Business, Labor and Public Policy 1860-1897* (1961), offers a comprehensive examination of the American economy of the period. Other general accounts of value include I. M. Tarbell, *The Nationalizing of Business 1878-1898* (1936); T. C. Cochran and William Miller, *The Age of Enterprise* (1942); and L. M. Hacker, *The World of Andrew Carnegie 1865-1901* (1968). D. A. Wells, *Recent Economic Changes* (1890), is a most illuminating contemporary account. Sigmund Diamond, ed., *The Nation Transformed: The Creation of Industrial Society* (1963), and F. J. Jaher, ed., *The Age of Industrialism in America* (1968), are contrasting anthologies. Matthew Josephson, *The Robber Barons* (1934), reflecting more of the spirit of the 1930s than the 1880s, nevertheless remains useful. Ray Ginger, *Age of Excess, American Life from the End of Reconstruction to World War I* (1965), ably places business enterprise in its social context. See also, S. P. Hays, *The Response to Industrialism 1885-1914* (1957), and R. H. Wiebe, *The Search for Order 1877-1920* (1967).

Richard Hofstadter, *Social Darwinism in American Thought* (1955 ed.), is a comprehensive analysis. See readings cited for Chapter Twenty-two. E. C. Kirkland, ed., *The Gospel of Wealth and Other Timely Essays by Andrew Carnegie* (1962), affords a good selection of Carnegie's writings. A more elaborate anthology is Moses Rischin, ed., *The American Gospel of Success* (1965). See also, Richard Weiss, *American Myth of Success, From Horatio Alger to Norman Vincent Peale* (1969). Joseph Dorfman, *The Economic Mind in American Civilization 1865-1918* (1949), vol. III of a five-volume work, is illuminating.

W. J. Lane, *Commodore Vanderbilt* (1942), is best on "Old Cornele." A lucid account of the "Erie War" appears in C. F. Adams, Jr., and Henry Adams, *Chapters of Erie and Other Essays* (1886). C. F. Stover, *The Railroads of the South 1865-1900* (1955), ably covers the ground. Three books by Julius Grodinsky are outstanding on railroad management: *The Iowa Pool* (1950); *Jay Gould, His Business Career 1867-1892* (1957); and *Transcontinental Railway Strategy 1869-1893* (1962). Other works on transcontinentals include R. R. Riegel, *The Story of the Western Railroads* (1926); Oscar Lewis, *The Big Four* (1951); Stuart Daggett, *Chapters on the History of the Southern Pacific* (1922); and R. W. Fogel, *The Union Pacific Railroad, A Case in Premature Enterprise* (1960). For details of railroad manipulation and consolidation see E. G. Campbell, *The Reorganization of the American Railroad System 1893-1900* (1938). Two books by W. Z. Ripley merit special study: *Railroads: Rates and Regulation* (1912) and *Railroads: Finance and Organization* (1915).

Gabriel Kolko, *Railroads and Regulation 1877-1916* (1965), breaks some new ground on management as well as reform. T. C. Cochran, *Railroad Leaders 1845-1890: The Business Mind in Action* (1953), admirably fulfills its subtitle. A. D. Chandler, Jr., *The Railroads* (1965), is an illuminating anthology of primary sources.

H. F. Williamson and others, *The American Petroleum Industry 1859-1899* (1959) and *The American Petroleum Industry 1899-1959* (1963), are the best accounts. Allan Nevins, *John D. Rockefeller* (2 vols., 1954 ed.), remains useful on the man and his colleagues. I. M. Tarbell, *The History of the Standard Oil Company* (one-vol. ed., 1950), is excellent on the spirit of the early oil men. J. F. Wall, *Andrew Carnegie* (1970), supersedes all earlier biographies. See also, Peter Temin, *Iron and Steel in Nineteenth-Century America* (1964). Matthew Josephson, *Edison* (1959), is the best biography. See also H. C. Passer, *The Electrical Manufacturers 1875-1900* (1953). R. N. Current, *The Typewriter and the Men Who Made It* (1954), adequately covers that subject.

Rendigs Fels, *American Business Cycles 1865-1897* (1959), is an outstanding analysis. On Morgan and the other bankers see G. W. Edwards, *The Evolution of Finance Capitalism* (1938), and F. L. Allen, *The Great Pierpont Morgan* (1949). John Moody, *The Truth About the Trusts* (1904), is indispensable.

J. R. Commons and others, *History of Labor in the United States* (4 vols., 1918-1935), is the standard work. A first-rate short survey is J. G. Rayback, *A History of American Labor* (1959). N. J. Ware, *The Labor Movement in the United States, 1860-1895* (1929), deals largely with the Knights of Labor. T. V. Powderly, *Thirty Years of Labor* (1889) and *The Path I Trod* (1940), are autobiographical accounts by the Grand Master of the Knights. On the AFL see Samuel Gompers, *Seventy Years of Life and Labor* (2 vols., 1925), and Philip Taft, *The A. F. of L. in the Time of Gompers* (1957). On Debs, see Ray Ginger, *The Bending Cross* (1949). W. G. Broehl, Jr., *The Molly Maguires* (1964), is excellent. On the great railroad strike, see R. V. Bruce, *1877: Year of Violence* (1959). Henry David, *History of the Haymarket Affair* (1936), is justifiably the standard account. On the Homestead strike, see Leon Wolff, *Lockout: The Story of the Homestead Strike of 1892* (1965). *The Autobiography of Big Bill Haywood* (1929); and P. F. Brissenden, *The I.W.W.* (1919), cover the Wobblies and their leader. On the industrial immigrant, see readings for Chapter Twenty-one.

# NATIONAL POLITICS IN THE GILDED AGE

CHAPTER TWENTY

In his famous *Education,* Henry Adams wrote of national politics in the Gilded Age: "One might search the whole list of Congress, judiciary, and executive during the twenty-five years 1870 to 1896 and find little but damaged reputations. The period was poor in purpose and barren in results."

The verdict of history may be less harsh or at least less one-sided than this contemporary assessment. Callous and corrupt, politics was also critical and creative. Henry Adams's quarter century witnessed the political abandonment of the Negro, the political pauperization of the Indian, the heyday of bossdom, of the spoils system, of the pension grabbers, of the protective tariff lobby. But these years also encompassed the Granger and Populist movements, the beginnings of the merit system in the civil service and of public regulation of big business. Narrow though they may have been in concept and truncated though they became in action, these movements nevertheless reflected a public willingness to check promiscuous power.

In attempting to explain the voters' apathy during the presidential campaign of 1884, President Garfield's Attorney-General, Wayne MacVeagh, wrote in *The Century* magazine on the eve of the elections that year:

*The truth ... will be found to be that the average American citizen cares very little about politics at present, because the government under which he lives touches his life very rarely, and only at points of very little importance to him. From his rising up until his lying down, the vast aggregate of his interests and his activities are entirely beyond its scope, and there is hardly any serious interest of his life which is affected by it.*

Yet MacVeagh himself was one of the many Americans who long since had turned with anger and action against the advantage taken of public apathy by the Stalwart party machines. In the next generation there were to be enough insurgents like him to topple the Stalwarts from power.

# I   Regulars and reformers

## Pursuit of party loyalty

The poverty of political issues following the failure of the Reconstruction settlement of the mid-1870s (see p. 441) is suggested by the success of the Republican party in living for decades off the issues of the fading past. Fully exploiting the advantages of being the party of Lincoln, of the Civil War victory, and of the Union, Republican managers continued to wave the Bloody Shirt for another quarter of a century. The brutality of the Democratic "redeemers" in many southern states made it only the more reasonable for Republican leaders to point to *them* as the ones who really were keeping the wounds of the rebellion open and the questions of slavery, race, and unconstitutional government alive. Even moderate organs like the Springfield (Illinois) *Daily Republican* said of the first elections in the South after the removal of federal troops in 1877: "The whites are committing outrages which no cloak of charity can be stretched to cover." Referring to Carl Schurz, one of the first of the Liberal Republicans to advocate a conciliatory policy toward the ex-rebels, the Stalwart boss of Wisconsin, Elisha W. Keyes, declared at this time: "Give me the 'Bloody Shirt' in preference to 'Carl Shirt.'"

As the party of high tariffs for industry, liberal aid to railroads, and, for the greater part, sound money, the Republicans also gained the financial support of large numbers of businessmen. The eastern and western wings of the party clashed from time to time over economic issues, but before the party confronted the voters in national elections divisions in the ranks usually were resolved by national leaders. The party also was riven by feuds between the Stalwart regulars and the more flexible Halfbreeds (see p. 440), and between these groups together and the more idealistic Liberals, or Independents, later derided by the others as "Mugwumps" (after an Indian word signifying insufficiently disciplined chiefs). But the national leaders usually managed to compromise philosophical as well as geographical differences before each quadrennial contest.

The Democrats, despite the treason label plastered on them by their rivals, offered strong opposition in national elections almost to the turn of the century. The political violence of the southern Democrats, so irresistible a target for Bloody Shirt fulminations elsewhere, insured that the South would stand solidly Democratic in national contests. In northern industrial cities, moreover, where Irish bosses in particular proved able organizers of the rapidly multiplying immigrant population, the Democrats developed powerful political machines. The Democrats gained less support from northern industry than the Republicans. Yet they were not without substantial business backers, especially among northern merchants and commercial bankers who most keenly felt the constraints on trade of tariff and railroad abuses and who also were likely to have southern business ties. The Bourbon Democrats of the South and of the more southerly parts of the Middle West often joined hands with the political representatives of these eastern commercial and financial interests to hold down for the most part the less conforming sections of their party in the distant West. Nor did they harm their political standing nationally when, for a share of the spoils, they voted in Congress with the business politicos of the North to gain mutually desired objectives or repulse mutually detested opponents. In the Senate particularly, conservatives frequently crossed party lines.

The Democrats lost the presidency when Lincoln was elected in 1860 and regained it only temporarily (and only with Mugwump support) with Cleveland's two victories in 1884 and 1892. Yet the two parties showed almost equal postwar strength in numbers. In no election from 1876 to 1896 was the winning side's share of the popular vote greater than 50.8 percent. In two elections, 1876 and 1888, the Republican candidate won with fewer popular votes than his Democratic rival. In the thirteen Congresses elected between 1870 and 1894, the Democrats controlled the House nine times. Such balanced voting put the politicians on their mettle. "The source of power and the cohesive force" in American political parties, James Bryce wrote in 1888, "is the desire for office, and for office as a means of gain." Office came with election victories, and with the national contests so closely fought party loyalty was held at a premium.

### Divided counsels of reform

Conservatives could more readily dominate the major parties because their opponents were more divided than themselves. Advocates of such special panaceas as Henry George's "single tax" (see p. 559) aroused intellectual interest in the cities but had little political impact even there. Monetary reformers who sought the cure-all for rural economic ills in currency inflation won larger political followings than the single-taxers, but only in isolated sections of the country. The Grangers (see p. 513), who advocated more varied solutions to the farmers' problems, actually gained some political victories, but again these were regional, notably in a few midwestern states, and short-lived. Much Granger strength, moreover, was sapped by internal controversies over relations with such other reform groups as labor unions.

All reformers were confronted by the spectacular development of the nation's resources and the prevailing doctrines of Social Darwinism and laissez-faire, which counseled unqualified freedom for the forces at work. Yet the nation had become an industrial power with government assistance to private industry, and reformers complained most bitterly of the abuse of political power on a national scale by its industrial as well as its party beneficiaries. In the Gilded Age these complaints were most effectively voiced by the Republican Independents; yet the fragmentation in reform ranks was only heightened by Independent fears that most other reformers were dangerous radicals. Independent spokesmen included E. L. Godkin, editor of *The Nation;* George W. Curtis, editor of *Harper's Weekly;* and Henry and Brooks Adams, the disenchanted scions of two former Presidents, who felt shut out of their rightful heritage of power by vulgarians.

In many respects the Independents were more conservative than the Regulars. They especially despised the parvenu plutocrats and the masses of immigrants who worked for them. In politics, the bosses who did these plutocrats' business and the patronage system that kept the bosses in power came under their sharpest attack. Charles Francis Adams, father of Henry and Brooks, expressed the Independent creed when he said, "the great and everlasting question" in all conduct was that simply of right and wrong. It was axiomatic, he added, that "the first and greatest qualification of a statesman . . . is the mastery of the whole theory of morals which made the foundation of all human society."

As the Liberal Republicans of 1872 were among the first of their party to abandon unlettered freedmen to the mercies of cultivated ex-rebel leaders, so the Independents of the 1880s were among the first of their party to advocate shutting the nation's ports to untutored immigrants who appeared to threaten Anglo-Saxon Protestant leadership. Moorfield Storey, Senator Charles Sumner's secretary as a young man and a leading Massachusetts Independent later on, caught his faction's characteristic disillusion with Reconstruction and distaste for immigration in his essay "Politics as a Duty and as a Career" (1889):

> The immigration of every year adds to the mass of poverty and ignorance in our country. The foreigners who seek our shores know little of our society, our methods, our history, or the traditions of our government. Their prejudices, their habits of thought, their entire unfamiliarity with American questions—in a word, their whole past, unfit them to take an intelligent part in our political contests, yet in a few years they become citizens and their votes in the ballot-box count as much as our own. . . . [They] are to-day the most dangerous element in our body politic. When our reconstruction acts gave the right of suffrage to the colored race in the South, the strain proved too great, and while the forms of free government have been preserved, its essential principles have been violated. If the control of the government passes into the hands of the ignorant, civilization is in danger, and intelligence is forced to regain the supremacy even by revolutionary methods if necessary.

Rising young politicians like Henry Cabot Lodge and Theodore Roosevelt—both sympathetic to reform—suspected the social snobbery and political ineffectiveness of the Independents and saved their political careers by refusing to join those who jumped from the Republican camp to support Grover Cleveland, the reform Democrat, in 1884. TR called the jumpers "those political and literary hermaphrodites." The Stalwarts referred to them as "man milliners" of politics. Moorfield Storey acknowledged in the 1890s that "the position of Independents has not been made too pleasant for a number of years. They are the subject of constant attack and sneer." Yet as Mugwumps they did help raise the tone of party politics, at least in the populous Northeast. Their articulateness incommoded if it did not improve the Regulars of both parties. Moreover, they denounced foreign wars as bitterly as they denounced foreigners, and attacked business imperialism as stridently as business plutocracy.

## II  Republican presidential years

### Hard times and monetary policy

When Rutherford B. Hayes won the Republican nomination for President in June 1876, the depression of the seventies neared its lowest point and unrest had become widespread. At the same time, Democratic repression of southern Negroes following Grant's removal of federal troops in many southern states had grown in violence. With the return of southern Democrats to power, as we have seen, the question of whether the Republican party could best achieve national, and majority, status by conciliating white southerners or dragooning the black vote remained a divisive issue in party ranks until the 1890s, when the rapid growth of an industrial population in the older Middle West, the heartland of Republicanism, and the rapid settlement of the Great Plains by Republican farmers convinced party bosses that they had gained the allegiance of a majority of the nation regardless of southern whites or blacks. But even then, other issues besides white and black, North and South, had to be dealt with successfully if the party were to keep winning elections. Among the most persistent issues were those arising from the ups and downs of the business cycle, especially the hard times accompanying the "downs."

Not until the twentieth century would the federal government assume direct responsibility for the welfare of individuals in depression years. Still, there were traditional political steps to be taken to reverse the downward course of the economy. Most popular with the vast majority of depression debtors, especially long-term debtors like western farmers with mortgages, was an inflation of the money supply to cheapen the currency and raise prices. Creditors normally took the opposite view, preferring that debts owed them be paid in currency at least equal in value in gold to that available at the time debts were incurred. The changing status of greenbacks issued during the Civil War intensified the inflationary-deflationary conflict.

Of the $450 million in greenbacks issued, almost $100 million had been retired by 1868 (see p. 431) and the rest had risen significantly in value from the wartime low of 38 cents in terms of the gold dollar. In 1869, in *Hepburn* v. *Griswold,* the Supreme Court decided belatedly that Congress could not simply declare paper money like greenbacks legal tender when it had no gold behind it—as Congress had done in 1862 and 1863 when it first created the new currency. This decision sent the value of the greenbacks fluttering downward. Then, in 1871, the Court reversed itself. In the Legal Tender cases *(Knox* v. *Lee*

and *Parker* v. *Davis),* it said Congress could declare paper money legal tender.

Congress, meanwhile, further muddied the currency picture. Early in the depression, the legislature yielded to debtor pressure with a bill restoring enough greenbacks to circulation to raise their face value to $400 million. President Grant, however, vetoed this bill. Then, in 1875, Congress passed the Resumption Act which Grant signed.

This complex measure, a compromise between debtors and creditors, freed national banks created under the laws of 1863 and 1864 from the limitations on the amounts of banknotes they could issue. It required the Treasury, at the same time, to retire greenbacks equal in face value to 80 percent of new bank currency until the amount of greenbacks in circulation was reduced to $300 million. By providing for the substitution of banknotes for most of the retired greenbacks, this provision did little harm to the inflationary cause. The Resumption Act also put off until January 1, 1879 the date on which the Treasury must resume redeeming for gold, on presentation by the holders, all government legal tender notes like the greenbacks still in circulation. The question of whether such additional greenbacks must then be retired, or whether the Treasury might reissue them within the $300 million limitation was left unclear. The distant date for resumption and the obscurity of the greenbacks' future actually forced the value of greenbacks down in 1875 and 1876, to the debtors' advantage.

After Hayes took office in 1877, however, inflationists found reason to grumble. Hayes had strongly backed the Resumption Act of 1875 when he was governor of Ohio. In 1877 his Secretary of the Treasury, John Sherman, began to build up government gold reserves for the retirement of greenbacks beginning in 1879, as the Act required. Sherman's first recourse was the sale of government bonds for coin. Since the public had little coin, this forced him to negotiate with banking syndicates and money brokers, both in ill repute with debtors. Despite unfavorable public opinion, Sherman persisted and soon disposed of about $95 million in bonds. The accumulation of additional gold supplies was made easier by the favorable balance of trade the United States enjoyed because of bumper wheat crops exported to Europe.

As news of Sherman's success spread, greenbacks rose in value until they reached par with gold two weeks before January 1, 1879, the resumption deadline. Content with the solid backing of $200 million in gold in the Treasury, few then bothered to redeem their greenbacks, which long remained at par, the creditors' goal. When debtor farmers now began an agitation for more greenbacks, their campaign was supported by the Greenback party, which had reached its high point in 1878 with the election of fourteen congressmen. But with the passing of the long depression of the seventies, both the Greenback party and the greenback agitation declined.

However another cheap-money movement—that for the unlimited coinage of silver—had begun to gather strength during Hayes's administration and to grow in political importance until its culmination in the depression of the nineties. This movement had the support of silver-mining interests as well as farmers.

In 1834 Congress had fixed the ratio of silver to gold in the dollar at 16 to 1—that is, there was to be sixteen times as much silver by weight in the silver dollar as there was gold in the gold dollar. Until 1849 this ratio adequately reflected the market value of the two metals. Then gold came pouring in from the mines of California and other parts of the West, and its value in terms of silver declined. Owners of silver found it more profitable to sell it on the open market as a metal than to present it to the mint for coinage. No one protested, therefore, when Congress adopted a new law in 1873 ending both the minting of silver dollars and the legal tender status of the existing supply. Of course, when the western silver mines began in the depression seventies

to yield their own enormous wealth, silver quickly fell in value in terms of gold and it became worthwhile again to offer it to the mint. On discovering the law against silver coinage, the inflationists now charged that a sinister group of bankers had engineered the "Crime of '73" and demanded its repeal. The first test for the silverites came in November 1877, when Richard ("Silver Dick") Bland of Missouri introduced a bill in the House for the unlimited coinage of silver at 16 to 1. The silver dollar at this time was worth about 89 cents and was falling, and bankers advised Hayes that passage of the Bland bill would amount to debt repudiation. Capitalists, they warned, would never again buy government bonds for gold if silver became legal tender. The President believed them, but he knew that Congress would override a veto.

Hayes was rescued from this dilemma when the Bland bill was quietly emasculated in the Senate by Iowa's smooth-talking William Allison. The amended Bland-Allison bill (passed in 1878 over Hayes's veto) substituted limited for unlimited coinage of silver. It required the Treasury to buy not less than $2 million and not more than $4 million of silver every month. These silver purchases neither drove gold out of circulation nor raised prices. And so the matter rested for twelve years.

### Hayes and labor

As the depression of the seventies waned, Hayes, though unfairly, gained an antilabor as well as an antidebtor reputation. During the great railroad strike of 1877, when four state governors begged the President for federal troops, he felt it his constitutional duty to oblige. Only once before, during Jackson's administration, had federal forces intervened in a struggle between private industry and its employees and Hayes, despite the nationwide fears of revolution raised by the railroad strike and the tremendous dependence of his party on railroad support, took this step with misgivings. He shared none of the antilabor vindictiveness of those who applauded him.

Hayes's veto in 1879 of a bill restricting the number of Chinese passengers on ships bound for the United States was also widely

508

interpreted as an antilabor gesture. Besides helping to build the transcontinental railroads, Chinese immigrants worked in western gold and silver mines where whites resented their willingness to accept lower wages and exist on shorter rations than themselves. Race prejudice deepened in the West with the anxieties of the depression years. During these years, Chinese workers also were shipped across the breadth of the continent to serve as strikebreakers in such industrial states as Massachusetts. When Bloody Shirt oratory wore thin from time to time, opportunists like "Blaine of Maine" grasped the "Chinese labor invasion" as a campaign issue, promising to check it for the benefit of the American working man. Hayes also disapproved of the Chinese labor invasion, but he felt that the restriction bill of 1879 violated the spirit of the Burlingame Treaty of 1868 with China, which gave Chinese unlimited immigration rights. Workingmen's parties in the West condemned him, but Hayes followed the correct diplomatic procedure of negotiating a new treaty with China in 1880 that gave the United States the privilege of regulating or suspending Chinese immigration. In 1882, Congress suspended Chinese immigration for ten years, a period extended by subsequent legislation until, in 1902, Chinese exclusion was made permanent.

*Garfield, standing, right center,
making his influential speech
at the Republican Convention in Chicago,
June 2, 1880, in an "instantaneous
photograph taken by C. D. Mosher
while the Convention was in session."*

Library of Congress

### Election of 1880

When the reformer Hayes announced soon after his nomination that he would serve only one term, the Stalwarts, and especially Roscoe Conkling of New York, lost no time in reviving the pliable Grant for the campaign of 1880. Slipshod management at the Republican national convention in Chicago in June 1880, however, cost the Stalwarts their chance to put Grant over. At the same time James A. Garfield, the veteran Ohio congressman, so brilliantly managed the campaign of his fellow Ohioan, Senator John Sherman, that he won even the support of the Grant men as the "dark horse" to break the deadlock that developed between Sherman and Blaine. To appease the Stalwart faction, the convention then rallied behind Conkling's chief patronage-monger in New York, Chester A. Arthur, as Garfield's running mate. The candidates chosen, the delegates proceeded to frame a platform boldly declaring for veterans' pensions and Chinese exclusion, blandly expressing pride in the party's monetary accomplishments, and pussyfooting on civil-service reform, the protective tariff, and other meaningful issues.

Three weeks later the Democrats met in Cincinnati and shrewdly named as their standard-bearer one of the heroes of the Battle of Gettysburg, Winfield Scott Hancock of Pennsylvania. Hancock was described as "a good man weighing 250 pounds." Futile politically, he nevertheless came close to winning. Garfield squeaked into office with a plurality of only 9464 votes out of almost 9 million cast. His large electoral majority—214 to 155—was the result of narrow victories in two pivotal states, Indiana and New York, which had been carried by Republican party discipline and plenty of hard cash.

After the election, Conkling and his friends expected recognition for their pains, but the new President, who had reached the top after a brilliant Civil War career and an arduous apprenticeship in the House, was a man of some delicacy who had an instinctive dislike for the coarse-grained professionals. He broke with Conkling immediately after his inauguration by giving the most lucrative patronage post in the United States, Chester Arthur's old position as the Collector of the Port of New York, to an anti-Conkling Republican.

Pressure on behalf of Conkling's prerogatives by other senators did not budge Garfield, and by holding up all other New York appointments he forced a balky Senate to confirm his own man. Conkling and the junior senator from New York, Thomas C. Platt, then took the extraordinary step of resigning their Senate seats. Their strategy was then to go to Albany to win vindication from the state legislature. But the New York legislators shilly-shallied and finally refused to reelect them. This startling denouement marked the beginning of the end for the Stalwarts.

Blaine, rewarded with the prestigeful post of Secretary of State, was more than pleased with Garfield's firm conduct and looked forward to an auspicious administration. This hope was dashed in July 1881, when Garfield was shot down as he entered the Washington railroad depot by a deranged job-seeker, Charles Guiteau. As the assassin fired, he exclaimed, "I am a Stalwart and Arthur is President now." Garfield died two months later. Although President Arthur dutifully filled his Cabinet with Stalwarts, his administration saw the beginning of civil-service reform that eventually sucked out the marrow of Stalwart rule.

### The "chief evil"

Civil-service reform was not merely one issue among many. As the Maryland patrician Charles Bonaparte said in 1879, the aim of civil-service reform was to correct the "chief evil" of the day, from which all others stemmed—"the alliance between industrialists and a political class which thinks like industrialists." Civil-service reform would unseat such vandals and put in their place "gentlemen . . . who need nothing and want nothing from government except the satisfaction of using their talents," or at least "sober, . . . middle class persons who have taken over . . . the proper standards of conduct."

Even veteran politicos who owed a great deal to machine support had grown thoroughly sick of the "hungry applicants for office . . . lying in wait . . . like vultures for a wounded bison." Until Garfield's martyrdom, however, what Conkling liked to call "snivel-service" reform had languished. The first significant step toward the merit system of appointment to public office was taken with the Pendleton Act of 1883. This act gave three civil-service commissioners, to be named by the President, authority to draw up practical competitive examinations. The act forbade assessing federal employees for campaign funds or firing them for political reasons. It required that within sixty days Treasury and postal employees be classified in civil-service categories and permitted the President to extend the coverage. During Arthur's administration about 12 percent of federal employees, compared to 85 percent in the mid-twentieth century, were classified.

The Pendleton Act, by depriving the parties of funds from public employees, forced party

509

## Political parties and Presidents

| | DEMOCRATIC PARTY | REPUBLICAN PARTY | |
|---|---|---|---|
| 1868 | | Grant | |
| 1872 | | Grant | LIBERAL REPUBLICAN MOVEMENT |
| 1876 | | Hayes | |
| 1880 | | Garfield (Arthur, 1881) | |
| 1884 | | | |
| 1888 | Cleveland | | |
| 1892 | | B. Harrison | RISE OF THE POPULIST PARTY |
| 1896 | Cleveland | | |
| 1900 | | McKinley | |
| | | McKinley (Roosevelt, 1901) | |

leaders to turn more and more to big business for the wherewithal for campaigns—a consequence not foreseen by the reformers. Shrewd party managers like "Matt" Quay of Pennsylvania, "Tom" Platt of New York, and "Mark" Hanna of Ohio thus were soon representing their big-business clients as efficiently as hired lawyers. And so were the candidates they chose. By 1889, as William Allen White put it:

*A United States senator ... represented something more than a state, more even than a region. He represented principalities and powers in business. One senator, for instance, represented the New York Central, still another the insurance interests. . . . Cotton had half a dozen senators. And so it went.*

## III   Regulation and protection

### The Democrats return

Although Chester A. Arthur conducted himself creditably in office, he could not throw off the taint of his earlier associations as far as the reformers were concerned, while his independence as President displeased the old guard. Consequently, the Republican convention in 1884 passed him by in

favor of the perennial aspirant James G. Blaine. Since Blaine was an easterner and a Halfbreed, without a war record, the delegates balanced the ticket by nominating John A. ("Black Jack") Logan of Illinois, a midwesterner, a good Stalwart, and a dashing political general.

Blaine had most of the attributes that make for a successful presidential candidate, including political shrewdness derived from many years in the House. But his House years had also marked him inescapably with the blemishes of the age which deprived him of his

The World, *October 30, 1884,*
*reports Blaine's disastrous "royal feast."*

New York Public Library

*This Republican cartoon,*
*September 27, 1884, "Another Voice*
*for Cleveland," purports to show*
*the Democratic candidate "tormented"*
*by the revelation of his fathering a child*
*out of wedlock. But to the Republican*
*taunt, "Ma, ma where's my pa?"*
*the Democrats replied:*
*"Gone to the White House, Ha, Ha, Ha!"*

highest ambition. During his political career he had grown rich without any visible means of income and had withstood all efforts to uncover the sources of his wealth. E. L. Godkin expressed the reformers' view when he said that Blaine had "wallowed in spoils like a rhinoceros in an African pool." Godkin now followed Schurz out of the Republican party once more. With such selfless Mugwumps as university presidents Charles W. Eliot of Harvard and Andrew D. White of Cornell and pastor Henry Ward Beecher, they supported the Democratic nominee Grover Cleveland.

Blunt and honest, his solid build and bulldog features truly reflecting his character, Cleveland had attracted notice as a reform mayor of Buffalo and as governor of New York. His hard-nosed defense of sound money and property rights earned him industrial and banking support. But issues remained secondary in the scurrilous campaign.

Shortly before election day, the Democrats capitalized on two episodes that seriously damaged Blaine's candidacy. In pledging support for Blaine, the Reverend Samuel D. Burchard, a spokesman for a New York delegation of clergymen, observed that the Democratic party's "antecedents have been rum, Romanism, and rebellion." Apparently Blaine was not listening when these fatal words were uttered. But a Democratic reporter was, and he quickly informed Irish voters that Blaine had not rebuked the minister for his insulting allusion to their drinking habits and religion. On the same day, Jay Gould and other "money kings" tendered a lavish testimonial dinner to the Republican candidate which was described in the Democratic press as "The Soft Soap Dinner" or "The Royal Feast of Belshazzar Blaine."

In the balloting, Blaine lost New York by 1149 votes, and New York turned out to be decisive in the electoral college where Cleveland squeaked through, 219 to 182. His popular plurality was only 23,000 out of 10 million votes cast, but it was enough to bring the Democrats back to the White House after a quarter of a century.

Even more than the Republican Presidents of the day, Cleveland had to face up to the problem of jobs for his patronage-starved party. His position was complicated by the support he had received from the Mugwumps, whose pet theme was the extension of the merit system. Within a year, Carl Schurz wrote to the President with a bluntness Cleveland knew he deserved: "Your attempt to please both reformers and spoilsmen has failed." Cleveland, however, did earn one success. The old Tenure of Office Act permitted Republicans in the Senate to obstruct Cleveland's appointments to positions that required that body's approval by refusing to acknowledge his right to dismiss Republican holdovers. By appealing to the people, Cleveland forced Congress, in June 1886, to repeal the Tenure of Office Act, thereby restoring to the Chief Executive the power to function through men of his own choosing.

Cleveland's conception of government was almost entirely negative. He especially disliked what he called "paternalism." Early in 1887, in vetoing an act to distribute seeds in drought-stricken Texas counties, he used a phrase which returned to haunt him during the depression of the nineties: "The lesson should be constantly enforced that though the people support the Government, the Government should not support the people." In the cause of destroying paternalism, he also foiled "pension grabs" by veterans and tariff grabs by industry, and even retrieved 81 million acres of the public domain from railroads that had failed to meet the terms of their land grants. Cleveland also fought federal regulation of business in the public interest. But he lost that fight to public pressure.

### Drive for railroad regulation

Certain historians in recent years, through intensive analyses of railroad statistics in relation to economic statistics in general, have attempted to reduce the importance usually assigned to railroads, especially to trunk or interstate railroads, in nineteenth-century America. Yet there can be no denying the importance contemporaries attached even to the promise (or the retraction of the promise) of rail service to distant markets or sources of supply. As for the public standing of railroad presidents, there is ample evidence to support this appraisal by James Bryce in *The American Commonwealth* (1888):

*No talents of the practical order can be too high for such a position as this; and even the highest talents would fail to fill it properly except with a free hand. . . . When the master of one of the greatest Western lines travels towards the Pacific on his palace car, his journey is like a royal progress. Governors of States and Territories bow before him; legislatures receive him in solemn session; cities and towns seek to propitiate him, for has he not the means of making or marring a city's fortune?*

Bryce continued:

*Although the railroad companies are unpopular, and although this autocratic sway from a distance contrib-*

*utes to their unpopularity, I do not think that the ruling magnates are themselves generally disliked. On the contrary, they receive that tribute of admiration which the American gladly pays to whoever has done best what every one desires to do. . . . I doubt whether any congressional legislation will greatly reduce the commanding positions which these potentates hold as the masters of enterprises whose . . . influence upon the growth of the country and the fortunes of individuals, find no parallel in the Old World.*

While perhaps accurately assaying contemporary bedazzlement by great railroad builders and their enterprises, Bryce may have underestimated the fear also bred by their regal power and the determination of *New* World citizens to constrain it. Two years before Bryce wrote, a Senate committee headed by the solid Republican Regular Shelby M. Cullom of Illinois concluded that "Upon no public question are the people so unanimous as upon the proposition that Congress should undertake in some way the regulation of interstate commerce." Given the prevailing bad odor of government regulation in a free society wedded to private advancement, this was a remarkable conclusion.

The "people" most directly encountered railroad management when paying for transportation service; and one of the principal sources of their discontent was railroad rate policy. In the late 1870s and throughout the 1880s, it is true, *average* railroad freight rates were steadily pummeled down by the fierce competition for traffic. The trouble, as we have seen, was that *average* rates included suicidally low ones for railroads at junctions where two or more lines crossed and murderously high ones for shippers at monopoly points where the roads made up for their losses at competitive points. This situation satisfied no one, least of all the railroads, which were under severe pressure for special consideration from all sides. The most ill-favored shippers were those situated at monopoly points along railroads that terminated at competitive points. Such shippers often were required to pay more for short hauls along a small portion of the road than shippers at the terminals paid for long hauls over the road's entire length.

Discriminatory carrying charges, which acted like special taxes on unfortunately located farmers in particular, were reflected further in the decline of land values where shipping costs were highest. In one rich farming area in New York State served only by the New York Central, the railroad's high short-haul charges contributed to a decline in land values of 20 to 25 percent in 1879 alone. Thus some of the most prosperous and conservative farmers in the state joined the hue and cry against the carriers. Rebates and other special favors to powerful shippers like Standard Oil also angered those inequitably treated. The secrecy by which rebating had to be carried on burdened even those who profited from it; those discriminated against often were forced to the wall by the practice.

Railroad dividend policies likewise made the carriers few friends. Dividends, of course, were not unrelated to the rates by which dividends were earned. In the 1870s, for example, the New York Central maintained regular annual dividend payments of 8 percent of invested capital. But "invested capital" often was but a euphemism for grossly watered stock. The New York Central's actual investment in its right-of-way, roadbed and track, rolling stock, and terminal facilities was valued at $20 million in 1879. But William H. Vanderbilt, who reputedly held nearly 80 percent of Central stock, insisted on his 8 percent return on the full $90 million worth of stock actually issued—and on manipulating rates for outraged New York shippers to see that this dividend was maintained.

In the early 1880s, rash railroad managements sometimes paid out as dividends money they had not earned. Persistence in this policy could lead only to insolvency. When roads went bankrupt, as they frequently did, investors cried that they had been cheated. The unsavory ways in which many leading railroads had won their charters, land grants, loans, and other privileges from Congress and from state and local governments added many disinterested persons to the roll of enemies.

The first railroad regulatory commission was set up in Massachusetts in 1869. It had no punitive powers but only the right to investigate railroad abuses and make its findings public. Despite fierce railroad opposition, fourteen states had set up railroad commissions by 1880, and some had taken more severe measures. City manufacturers and distributors, and their banker allies, sometimes initiated the fight for railroad regulation, but the most persistent action was that of the Patrons of Husbandry, which began organizing farmers into local "Granges" in 1867. A year after the Panic of 1873, the Grangers boasted 1.5 million members, principally in Iowa, Wisconsin, Minnesota, and Illinois. Here they won legislation setting statewide maximum rates for railroad traffic and maximum charges for the use of grain elevators, where farmers had to store their staple while awaiting shipment.

Railroad management quickly fought "Granger legislation" in the courts. Rate fixing by public bodies they particularly attacked as legalized confiscation. In 1876, in *Munn* v. *Illinois,* the most important of the Granger cases to reach the Supreme Court, a majority of the bench found against the railroads and grain elevators. Owners of property "in which the public has an interest," said the Court, must "submit to be controlled by the public for the common good."

It soon became clear, however, that attempts by single states to regulate corporations chartered by other states and carrying on most of their business across state borders must fail. Pressure for federal regulation mounted in the early 1880s as railroad securities slumped on the stock exchanges. By 1886, 108 roads with 11,000 miles of track, nearly 10 percent of the entire railroad system, had sunk into receivership, and the *New York Times* warned that plungers like Jay Gould might gather up such financial wrecks into a "great confederation of railroads" that would bear down on the public and their government with consolidated force.

513

How railroad management itself was determined to gain some advantage from the clamor for reform is made clear in an editorial, June 6, 1885, in the influential *Commercial and Financial Chronicle* of New York. After summarizing shippers' complaints on rates and service that we have mentioned, and stockholders' complaints on dividend policies and "speculative directors and managers," this editorial states:

*The railroads too, now look to the Government to help them out of their difficulties. They want to see to it that no road does business for less than cost, ... that pools and combinations be legalized, that the building of parallel and competing lines be prohibited in the future, and that solvent roads be in some way protected against the competition of bankrupt roads.*

"In a word," the *Chronicle* concluded,

*merchants want to be protected against the railroads, the railroads want to be protected against themselves, and investors against both. And they all cry for the same soothing syrup—legislative enactment.*

Two events in 1886 made it virtually impossible for the federal government to postpone action any longer. The first was the report, in January, of Cullom's Senate committee, already referred to (p. 512). The second, in October, was the Supreme Court decision in the *Wabash* case. This decision sucked much of the strength from *Munn* v. *Illinois* by forbidding any state henceforth to set rates even within its borders on railroad traffic entering from or bound for other states.

The Interstate Commerce Act, reluctantly signed by President Cleveland on February 4, 1887, derived largely from the findings of the Cullom committee. This act forbade higher rates for noncompetitive short hauls than for competitive long ones and rebates to favored shippers. It also prohibited railroad self-regulating practices, such as agreements to pool traffic and maintain high rates. What it did not do was to provide means for enforcing its restraints.

Cleveland showed his good faith by appointing highly qualified men to the Interstate Commerce Commission set up to administer the act. During the first three years of the Commission's existence the railroads, on their part, seemed to be "conforming promptly" to Commission requests, as the agency said in 1888. Glaring inequalities in rates were scaled down, sincere efforts were made to line up "like kinds" of freight for equal treatment; other adjustments sought to soften traditional abuses.

The honeymoon, however, ended quickly enough. The "cease and desist" orders the commissioners were empowered to issue could be made to stick only by court action, which the railroads became very adept at delaying. In the end, moreover, the railroads almost always won. In the first ten years of its existence, 90 percent of the Commission's orders on rate charges were overruled by the judiciary. Of the sixteen cases heard by the Supreme Court between 1887 and 1905, it upheld the carrier in fifteen. In the process the Court demolished Commission pretensions to setting "reasonable and just" rates on its own initiative.

In 1890, the Commission noted the continuing "general disregard" of the prohibitions against rebating and began vigorous prosecutions. The roads responded not only with obstructionist tactics but with a concerted attack on the Commission itself. Wiser heads, however, saw a little farther than railroad managers and advised them, even as early as 1892, along lines that history, at least for a generation, would justify. In that year the corporation lawyer Richard S. Olney, soon to become Cleveland's Attorney-General, wrote to a railroad friend:

*My impression would be that, looking at the matter from a railroad point of view exclusively, it would not be a wise thing to undertake to abolish the Commission. ... The Commission, as its functions have now been limited by the Courts, is, or can be made of great use to the railroads. It satisfies the popular clamor for a government supervision of railroads, at the same time that such supervision is almost entirely nominal. Further, the older such a commission gets to be, the more inclined it will be found to take the business and rail-road view of things. It thus becomes a sort of . . . protection against hasty and crude legislation hostile to railroad interests. . . . The part of wisdom is not to destroy the Commission, but to utilize it.*

Time proved Olney right. Yet the Interstate Commerce Act was not a complete failure. It clearly affirmed the right of the federal government to regulate private interstate business, and it supplied a foundation upon which a system of increasingly effective regulation could be built in the twentieth century. By midcentury, indeed, effective regulation had been commonplace for so long that many believed that it had sapped the initiative and enterprise of railroad management.

### The great issue of "protection"

Although Cleveland was unimaginative and often shortsighted, his response to Democratic politicians who advised him to soft-pedal the tariff issue is a measure of his superiority to the other Presidents of his epoch: "What is the use of being elected or reelected, if you don't stand for something?" Following his own course, in December 1887, the President devoted his third annual message to Congress entirely to the tariff. "Our present tariff laws," he said, "the vicious, inequitable, and illogical source of unnecessary taxation, ought to be at once revised and amended."

Cleveland had no quarrel with advocates of protection who sought to nurse "infant industries" into "perennial vigor." Beginning with the wartime duties of 1864, however, as Frank W. Taussig, the leading tariff historian, put it, "protection ran riot." By 1887 no fewer than 4000 separate items were dutiable.

One of the protectionists' favorite themes was the patriotism implicit in high tariff duties. Reduction of the duties, they said, meant reduction of revenue and repudiation of the national debt. This argument was most successful, said an Ohioan in 1867, in winning and maintaining "a consistent and solid front"

for protection in the West. But Cleveland had an answer. Those who buy imports, he warned Congress, "pay the duty thereon into the public Treasury." This, he said, must be encouraged by keeping duties below a level that made imports prohibitive.

Cleveland was sophisticated enough to add an even more telling point often overlooked:

*The great majority of our citizens, who buy domestic articles of the same class [as dutiable imports] pay a sum at least approximately equal to this duty to the home manufacturer.*

The latter's price, Cleveland said, may sometimes be reduced by domestic competition "below the highest limit allowed by such duty. But it is notorious that this competition is too often strangled by combinations prevalent at this time, frequently called trusts. . . . The people can hardly hope for any consideration in the operation of these selfish schemes."

In response to growing public pressure, President Arthur in 1882 had appointed a bipartisan tariff commission to study tariff schedules and to recommend simplifying changes. Most of the experts on tariff making, however, were associated with the protected industries, and Arthur's commission reflected the dilemma that was to face others who would seek expert advice later on. Of all people, John Lord Hayes, the most effective tariff lobbyist of his generation and the spokesman for the woolen interests, was named chairman of Arthur's group. In addition, as Senator Nelson W. Aldrich pointed out, "there was a representative of the wool growers on the commission; . . . a representative of the iron interests; . . . a representative of the sugar interests; . . . and those interests were very carefully looked out for." Actually, this commission did a fair job, proposing reductions of some 20 percent in the general level of the duties. Once the commission's proposals reached Congress, however, they were disfigured.

Following Cleveland's tariff message of December 1887, the House early in 1888 was presented with the Mills bill, a measure reflecting deep study of industry's real needs and recommending the moderate reductions that mild revisionists like Cleveland demanded. The Mills bill passed the House with deceptively few changes. The elections of 1888 were nearing, and an appearance of satisfying the public clamor against industrial greed was more essential to congressmen than to senators with six-year terms. The lobbyists thus let House members soothe the electorate, while looking to the upper chamber with a confidence that was not misplaced—as very soon became clear.

On receiving the Mills bill, the Senate responded with the so-called Allison substitute, which called, as usual, for a general rise in the tariff. "I am satisfied," Joseph Wharton, the Pennsylvania iron and steel king, wrote to Senator Allison in July 1888, "that your aim is to report a bill . . . which can command the votes of such men as . . . have industrial interests." "We all know," Wharton added meaningfully,

*that the legitimate expenses of a general election are heavy, and that failure to provide for them sometimes*

*Parodying the real "Coxey's Army" (see p. 522), this cartoon by W. A. Rogers shows big-business petitioners for government aid in the form of tariff protection.*

The New-York Historical Society, New York City

*entails defeat. I am in a position to know that the success of appeals for funds among the steel rail men will be jeopardized if the party they are asked to support proposes a measure that looks to them nearly as fatal as that proposed by the other party.*

Other industrial spokesmen reached Allison with urgent reminders of satisfying "the people who have money to give for the success of Republican principles."

The "Allison substitute" was essentially a device to kill the Mills bill until after the presidential election of 1888; and the Senate thus debated the tariff to election day, when the Mills bill expired. In the meantime, the election machinery had begun to grind. For the "holy work" of protecting protection, Tom Platt, New York's "Begging Chief," besieged Wall Street. James P. Foster, of the protectionist Republican League, said, "I would put the manufacturers of Pennsylvania under the fire and fry all the fat out of them."

One of the protectionists' great bugbears was the surplus piling up in the Treasury from tariff revenues and other sources. If this surplus were not reduced by other means, the tariff level was sure to be attacked for fiscal reasons alone. But Congressman Samuel J. Randall, the Democratic high-tariff man of Pennsylvania, had an answer. Simply raise the duties out of sight. "No imports, no revenues," cried Randall. This policy, the tariffs' foes protested, might push prices out of sight too. But young Republican Congressman McKinley of Ohio replied to this charge. "Cheap," he said, "is not a word of hope; it is not a word of inspiration! It is the badge of poverty; it is the signal of distress."

## A Republican interlude

Cleveland was renominated by acclamation at the Democratic convention in St. Louis, in June 1888. The Republicans, gathering in Chicago two weeks later, found the cupboard bare of possible nominees after Blaine's decision not to run again. Seven bal-

516

lots were taken before the party put its stamp on Benjamin Harrison, a dreary corporation lawyer from the pivotal state of Indiana. As the grandson of President William Henry Harrison, he was hopefully dubbed "Young Tippecanoe."

Under the astute management of National Party Chairman Matt Quay, the Republicans waged a vigorous campaign. They charged that Cleveland's "free-trade" policy (as they insisted on labeling the mild reforms of the Mills bill) would ruin American manufacturing and betray the American worker to the "pauper labor of Europe." Even the Knights of Labor succumbed to this argument and endorsed Harrison.

Of great help to the Republicans in the last days of the campaign was a widely publicized letter written by the British minister in Washington to a Republican who had represented himself as an English-born American seeking advice on how to vote in the coming election. Which candidate, the correspondent asked, would be more friendly to England? The minister foolishly replied that Cleveland was to be preferred. Falling in so neatly with the Republican claim that reduced duties would play into the hands of British industrialists, this missive was peculiarly disastrous. It had the further effect of swinging many Irish-American votes, traditionally Democratic, to Harrison. Cleveland's popular vote topped Harrison's by more than 100,000, but Harrison won an electoral majority of 65. A switch of only 6500 votes in New York would have given Cleveland that state and the election. When Harrison solemnly proclaimed that "Providence has given us the victory," Matt Quay exploded: "Think of the man! He ought to know that Providence hadn't a damn thing to do with it." Quay added that Harrison "would never know how close a number of men were compelled to approach the gates of the penitentiary to make him President."

It was in Harrison's administration that the Senate became known as the "Millionaires Club," for the money the members brought in; and the whole legislature became known as the "billion-dollar Congress," for the money it handed out. To diminish the surplus the billion-dollar Congress in 1890 provided pensions for all disabled Union army veterans (whose votes had helped defeat the Democrats) even when their disability had no connection with the war. Pensions also were provided for the widows of veterans. The pension bite on the surplus rose from $98 million in 1889 to $156 million in 1893.

Later the same year Congress took care of the industrial contributors to the campaign with the McKinley Tariff, the highest and broadest thus far in American history. Understandably, Secretary of State Blaine feared that exporting nations hit by the new duties would refuse to buy American farm surpluses. As a club over such nations, Blaine induced Congress to place a "reciprocity" clause in the new tariff act giving the President authority to remove remaining items from the free list in retaliation against any discriminatory duties on American produce.

The McKinley Tariff raised havoc with Hawaiian sugar growers by placing competitive sugars as well as their's on the free list and at the same time giving American growers a bounty of 2 cents a pound. Other American farmers were courted by duties on eggs, potatoes, and similar products, of which only the minutest quantities ever were brought into the United States.

In return, further, for western votes on the McKinley Tariff, Congress in 1890 passed the Sherman Silver Purchase Act. This act authorized the Treasury to issue notes redeemable in gold or silver coin in exchange for greater amounts of silver than had been permitted under the Bland-Allison Act of 1878. Virtually a bounty to the silver-mining companies, the Silver Purchase Act was defended as an agrarian cheap-money measure, but it failed to satisfy inflationists who were pressing for unlimited silver coinage.

One more sop offered to the public was the Sherman Anti-Trust Act, which passed Congress in July 1890, with scarcely a murmur of dissent about its final form. Earlier, many states had enacted "anti-trust" statutes, which were no more effective against "trusts" char-

517

tered in other states than state regulation of interstate railroads had been. After the *Wabash* decision of 1886 cut the ground away from stronger state measures against private corporations, the demand for federal trust regulation grew stronger.

The Sherman Anti-Trust Act sounded severe. It made combinations in restraint of trade illegal, subjected perpetrators to heavy fines and jail sentences, and ordered that triple damages be paid to persons who could prove injury by such combinations. Few courts, however, sustained any of the actions brought under the measure.

One of the grave defects of the Sherman Act was its failure to protect nonbusiness "combinations" from attack under its terms. Senator James Z. George of Mississippi put this point most clearly when he said,

*The farmers and laborers of this country who are sending up their voices to the Congress of the United States, ... imploring us to take action to put down trusts, ... will find that they themselves in their most innocent and necessary arrangements, made solely for defensive purposes against the operation of these trusts, will be brought within the punitory provisions of this bill.*

The Senator's fears were justified. Although Republican and Democratic Attorneys-General alike refused to administer the new law with zeal, four labor unions soon fell afoul of its terms. Business combinations cited were likely to get off scot-free. Finley Peter Dunne, the political humorist, said of the Act, "What looks like a stone wall to a layman, is a triumphal arch to a corporation lawyer."

The Sherman Act did prompt certain groups of companies to alter their specific "trust" arrangements and to merge into huge monolithic corporations which, without having to act any longer in concert, succeeded in dominating their industries at least as thoroughly as the trusts had. In other industries, the holding-company device was employed. The holding company was an independent corporation which owned enough stock in other companies to control their policies effectively. Dodges such as these neutralized the Sherman Act for a short period; but in the

twentieth century political administrations and the courts gradually gave substance to the terms of the Act. Business consolidation and centralization continued apace; but antitrust legislation did serve as a brake on many combinations deemed adverse to the public interest. According to some midcentury analysts, indeed, it served as too tight a brake on combinations that might have afforded the consuming public many real economies of bigness.

## Election of 1892

Blaine had warned his crasser colleagues that the McKinley Tariff of 1890 "will protect the Republican party only into speedy retirement," and the congressional elections late that year proved him right. The Republicans lost control of the House, where the Democrats gained no less than 76 seats. This Democratic surge foreshadowed Harrison's eclipse in the elections of 1892. Running against Cleveland again, Harrison this time polled 5,176,000 votes. But Cleveland gained 5,556,000. Narrow though his margin was, it represented the most decisive presidential election victory since 1872. The electoral college count was Cleveland 277, Harrison 145.

Labor unrest, culminating in the Homestead strike against the Carnegie Steel Company in July 1892, added to Harrison's burdens. Republican leaders begged Carnegie and Frick to relent in their labor policies, but the industrialists were much less frightened by the idea of a Cleveland victory than by a labor-union victory. "I am very sorry for President Harrison," Frick wrote to Carnegie on learning of Cleveland's election, "but I cannot see that our interests are going to be affected one way or another by the change in administration." Carnegie replied, "Cleveland! Landslide! Well we have nothing to fear. . . . People will now think the Protected [Manufactures] are attended to and quit agitating. . . . Off for Venice tomorrow."

Conservative industrialists may have assumed indifference to the election results;

518

conservative politicians of both parties, however, had something new to think about; the showing of the People's party, familiarly known as the Populists, especially in the new wheat states beyond the 95th meridian. Organized in 1890, the party ran General James B. Weaver in 1892 in its first bid for the presidency. The general gained over a million votes, and his party succeeded in capturing four states.

## IV Rise and fall of Populism

### The farmers' plight

In 1887 Leonidas L. Polk, a North Carolina farm editor, expressed the views of farmers in all parts of the country when he wrote:

> There is something radically wrong in our Industrial system. There is a screw loose. . . . The railroads have never been so prosperous, and yet agriculture languishes. The banks have never done a better . . . business, and yet agriculture languishes. Manufacturing enterprises never made more money, . . . and yet agriculture languishes. Towns and cities flourish and "boom," . . . and yet agriculture languishes.

The cash-crop farmers were not always the best diagnosticians of their own ills, or for that matter of industry's condition, but no historian has doubted that their hardships were genuine. What is more, they suffered only slightly less in good times than in bad.

Broadly speaking, the farmers faced four major problems: (1) the high cost of transportation; (2) heavy taxes and tariffs; (3) falling prices; (4) the high cost of credit. Together, these made farming a second-class occupation, one that held few attractions for rural youths.

(1) Few enterprises had received more enthusiastic civic support than did the railroads of the West, and the farmers, understandably, felt that the railroads in return owed the community moderate freight and passenger rates. But the farmers' expectations, as we know, came to little. The farther west one moved, moreover, the worse conditions grew. In 1887, for instance, the ton-mile charge on the Pennsylvania Railroad east of Chicago was 95 cents; on the Burlington from Chicago to the Missouri River it was $1.32; on the Burlington west of the Missouri it jumped to $4.80. Railroad officials held that they had no choice but to charge high rates in sparsely populated regions. But farmers, as Frank Norris put it in his novel The Octopus (1901), likened the railroad to "a gigantic parasite fattening upon the lifeblood of an entire commonwealth."

(2) The burden of unfair taxes only made the burden of high railroad rates harder to bear. Before the corporate era, personal property consisted chiefly of land and livestock, on which it was relatively simple to assess a personal property tax. Railroads and other corporations created new kinds of personal property—stocks and bonds—which proved far easier to conceal from assessors. Since the railroads also pressed the politicians for tax exemptions or low rates on their own huge landholdings and other real property, taxes fell more and more oppressively on the middle-class farmer who could not, in the freely competitive market, pass them along to the consumer, as could many large industrial corporations whether parts of "trusts" or not.

The protective tariff constituted still another kind of discriminatory tax which was the more burdensome since, in the farmers' opinion, the tariff "mothered" the trusts. The trusts, they said, had the power to force down the prices they paid for raw materials produced on the farms and to force up without fear either of foreign or domestic competition the prices charged for farm machinery and other manufactures.

(3) Falling farm prices, of course, made heavy taxes seem all the more oppressive. The prices of staples began to sag in the 1880s. In the depression years of the nineties they hit bottom. Wheat brought $1.20 a bushel in 1881 and 50 cents in 1895; cotton, 10.5 cents a pound in 1881 and 4.5 cents in 1894. Of course, prices of nonfarm products fell too. But the fall in farm prices hit the grower particularly hard because he was a debtor with fixed *money* obligations. His intense concern with the currency stemmed from his determination to keep these obligations stable in terms of the amount of *commodities* needed to pay them. Their critics told the farmers they received low prices because they produced too much. But the only way the individual farmer could think of to make more money when prices were falling was to raise even bigger crops. The price decline, he said, reflected a cold-blooded Wall Street conspiracy to squeeze the settlers on the wide open spaces.

(4) The high cost of credit seemed only to confirm the western farmer's view of the eastern financial conspiracy. We have seen how the credit system helped force the landless southern farmer, and eventually the small southern landholder as well, into the vicious circle of sharecropping and the crop lien. Tenancy came later in the West, where land was more easily obtained and more easily mortgaged. But when mortgage money cost 15 percent or more a year, as it did in Kansas and states farther west in the 1880s, the day of foreclosure loomed.

### Origins of Populism

The roots of the People's party of the 1890s were firmly planted in American history, going back at least to Shays' Rebellion in 1786. Populism can be traced directly to farmer organizations—"Wheels," "Unions," and "Alliances"—that sprung up in the 1880s to supplant the Grange. By 1890 many of these had consolidated into two regional groups, the Southern Alliance, which claimed over a million members, and the somewhat smaller National Farmers' Alliance in the Northwest, mainly on the Great Plains.

The Alliances gave a strong stimulus to the social life and the thinking of their members. Like the Granges, they held picnics, conventions, and rallies to help overcome the isolation and bleakness of farm life. They disseminated agricultural information and tried to foster better business methods among their members. They sponsored economic and political discussions and established circulating libraries which enabled members to read books of social criticism like those of Henry George and Edward Bellamy (see Chapter Twenty-two). They helped circulate farm papers, such as the well-edited *National Economist* of Washington, D.C., and magazines of general discussion like the *Arena* of Boston. At one time perhaps as many as a thousand local newspapers were connected with the movement. One Alliance sympathizer wrote about the intellectual ferment that resulted:

*People commenced to think who had never thought before, and people talked who had seldom spoken. They discussed income tax and single tax; they talked of government ownership and the abolition of private property; fiat money, and the unity of labor; . . . and a thousand conflicting theories.*

In December 1889 all the major farm organizations met in St. Louis at separate sessions. Besides the Northern and the Southern Alliances, the presence of the Knights of Labor, the Farmers' Mutual Benefit Association, and the Colored Alliance suggested that all the forces of protest might join together. A number of issues, however, kept them apart. For one thing the Southern Alliance regarded secrecy as a distinct advantage, because so many of its members were mere tenants, not landowners, and thus more vulnerable to reprisals. But most northern representatives objected to it. Secondly, northern representatives resented southern insistence that black farmers be excluded from the consolidated membership, although southern spokesmen were willing to go so far as to leave to each state organization the right to decide on the eligibility of colored persons within its jurisdiction, so long as white persons only were eligible for the National Council. A third devisive issue arose over the question of creating a third political party. Certain northerners already were thinking of resorting to independent politics, but southerners found this difficult to contemplate, since they lived in a region dominated by the one-party system. An independent party would be far more difficult to launch, they felt, where politics was firmly controlled by a single entrenched party than where two major parties were in competition and a third party might attain the balance of power. Southern Alliance members also feared that third-party action, by dividing the voters of their region, would endanger white supremacy.

Despite organizational differences, the reform programs of the Northern and Southern Alliances proved to be very much alike, although northerners gave perhaps greater emphasis to the railroad issue, southerners to farm finances and farm credit. The most important proposal for solving the credit problem came from Dr. C. W. Macune, organizer of the Texas Alliance and editor of the *National Economist*. Macune suggested that the federal government set up a subtreasury office and warehouse in every county that offered for sale more than $500,000 worth of farm products annually. Farmers who placed nonperishable crops in these warehouses would receive as a loan Treasury notes in amounts up to 80 percent of the local market value of their stored crops. This loan was to be repaid when the crop was sold. Macune's plan, later incorporated into the agricultural programs of the 1930s, had the double advantage of allowing the farmer to hold his crop for the best price and of increasing the money supply.

Eastern conservatives laughed off the subtreasury plan and other Alliance proposals as "hayseed socialism," but they could not laugh off the political stampede behind them. Between 1887 and 1890, Southern Alliance men, working at first through the Democratic party,

elected three governors and won control of the legislatures of eight states. Northern Alliance candidates, in the major parties or in local "third parties" in the grain states of the Northwest, if less successful, still made impressive gains. It was in Kansas that the "third party" was first called the People's party, its members there becoming known as "populists," the foes of "plutocrats."

521

### The People's party

Although Southern Alliance members held back, by 1890 radical farmers of the Northwest went ahead with the third-party idea. The first step was a convention in Cincinnati in May 1891 which attracted relics of defunct parties like the Greenback party, other political has-beens, and visionaries and utopians, as well as Alliance leaders.

The Cincinnati convention postponed until 1892 the question of whether to start a national party, but the delegates drew up a People's party platform calling for unlimited coinage of silver; direct election of senators (who were still elected by state legislatures); nationalizing of banks, railroads, and utilities; prohibition of foreign ownership of land; and an eight-hour day. In February 1892, in St. Louis, the national People's party, including the Southern Alliance, was formally organized. After adopting the Cincinnati platform, the delegates called for a presidential nominating convention to meet in Omaha in July. It was at Omaha that the party chose James B. Weaver of Iowa as its candidate. The Omaha platform now made additional demands, including the subtreasury plan.

Populist leaders of the nineties bore such wild-sounding names as "Sockless" Jerry Simpson and David H. "Bloody Bridles" Waite, and their orators spoke with a vehemence that shocked many easterners. Yet the campaign of 1892 was far from the "lawless, irresponsible, incendiary" thing the eastern press described. Allan Nevins, Cleveland's biographer, says the 1892 campaign was "the cleanest, quietest, and most creditable in the memory of the post-war generation." In the balloting, as we have seen, Weaver received over a million votes, more than 8 percent of the total.

With the exception of the Republicans in 1856, no third party had done nearly so well in its first national effort, and shortly after the election Weaver confidently announced: "The Republican party is as dead as the Whig party was after the Scott campaign of 1852, and from this time forward will diminish in every State of the Union." A sober look at the distribution of the vote might have put a brake on Weaver's optimism. True, he had run strong in a few plains and mountain states and some southern states. But in such older agricultural states as Iowa, Wisconsin, and Illinois, and in the entire East, he received less than 5 percent of the votes. The Populists, in short, had shown strength enough in 1892 to worry the major parties but no more than that. The next year one of the worst depressions in American history began, and as discontent spread across the entire land it set the stage for another campaign in which Populism would alarm every conservative.

### Cleveland and the crash

Many Democrats placed the blame for the Panic of 1893 on Harrison's "billion-dollar Congress." Cleveland and other conservatives blamed the Silver Purchase Act, which, they said, destroyed business confidence. Even the withdrawal of foreign capital, they argued, had been prompted by fears that America was going off the gold standard. This move, indeed, seemed imminent by April 1893, when the Treasury's gold reserve dropped below $100 million.

Cleveland's first thought was to repeal the Silver Purchase Act, which permitted holders of silver certificates to exchange them for gold. For this purpose he called a special session of Congress in the summer of 1893. "Gold Democrats" and Republicans closed ranks against the inflationists in both parties and enacted the repeal in October. By then, however, a run on the Treasury was gaining momentum, and after the failure of other measures to stop it, Cleveland, in February 1895, was forced to borrow $62 million in gold from the Morgan and Belmont banking syndicate on terms decidedly unfavorable to the government. The inflationists denounced the

President as a tool of Wall Street. But the bankers, by bringing gold from Europe, succeeded in reversing the drain on the Treasury. With confidence restored, the government, in January 1896, floated another loan which ended this crisis.

Cleveland's resolute defense of the gold standard aggravated discontent in the West and South as much as it heartened eastern financiers, and it probably destroyed any hope of getting mass support for the tariff reform he had promised once again. The tariff act Congress did finally pass in August 1894, the Wilson-Gorman Tariff, Cleveland regarded as a disgrace to the party and it became law without his signature. This act did contain one provision that the Populists wanted, a 2 percent tax on incomes over $4000. But in 1895 by a 5-to-4 decision the Supreme Court cheered conservatives by declaring the income tax unconstitutional on the ground that "direct taxes" could only be apportioned among the states on the basis of population, not personal wealth.

As the depression deepened, the public mood grew ever more sullen. Thousands of unemployed roamed the country, sometimes in large gangs. Since the government offered no relief to the destitute, agitators proposed schemes of their own. In 1894, General Jacob S. Coxey, of Massillon, Ohio, a rich man himself, convinced frightened property holders that a revolution had actually begun. Coxey proposed that Congress authorize a half-billion dollar public works program. To dramatize his plan, he organized a march on Washington. Soon "armies" all over the country were heading for the national capital, but "Coxey's Army" of about 300 men was the only one to arrive. Police speedily dispersed it after arresting Coxey and a few of his lieutenants for stepping on the grass. Nevertheless, Coxey's march helped make unemployment a well-aired national issue, one on which the Populists hoped to capitalize in the elections of 1896. The silver issue, however, soon crowded out all others.

## Battle of the standards

The barrage of propaganda from western silver interests following Cleveland's repeal of the Silver Purchase Act in 1893 told very quickly on the farmers who had been demanding inflation for years and now began to see the "conspiracy" against silver as another example of Wall Street treachery. In 1894, when he published *Coin's Financial School,* William H. Harvey gave the silverites an ideal little handbook that reduced the complex subject of money to terms that farmers could grasp. It was also a model of Populist rhetoric.

A Virginian by birth, Harvey had experienced all the frustrations of his generation in a series of unsuccessful stabs at ranching, prospecting, and editing. Finally, with *Coin's Financial School,* he found his vocation. Profusely illustrated, and distributed in cheap editions, *Coin's Financial School* sold 300,000 copies the first year. Another 125,000 were given away by silver-mine owners during the campaign of 1896.

Harvey described the country as "distracted" by the hard times, with "the jails, penitentiaries, workhouses, and insane asylums ... full"; and "hungered and half-starved men marching toward Washington." Not always had the people suffered so. Up to 1873, under bimetallism, with gold merely "a companion metal enjoying the same privileges as silver," prosperity and growth had been the rule. Then came the demonetization of 1873. This act was

*a crime, because it has confiscated millions of dollars worth of property. A crime, because it has made ten thousands of tramps. A crime, because it has made thousands of suicides. A crime, because it has brought tears to strong men's eyes and hunger and pinching want to widows and orphans. A crime, because it is destroying the honest yeomanry of the land, the bulwark of the nation. A crime because it has brought this once great republic to the verge of ruin, where it is now in imminent danger of tottering to its fall.*

The "Crime of '73" had only been compounded by Cleveland's repeal of the Silver Purchase Act, which the Populists were already calling the "Crime of '93." The only solution was immediate resumption of free and unlimited coinage of silver.

More conservative men than Harvey agreed that it would be good to raise the price of silver and expand the currencies of the world. But they insisted that it would be disastrous for the United States alone to try to buy all the world's silver, and that the cooperation of Britain and others was essential. But Harvey repudiated the idea "that we must adopt for our money the metal England selects, and can have no independent choice in the matter." "If it is true," he declared, "let us attach England to the United States and blot her name out from among the nations of the earth." He went on:

*A war with England would be the most popular ever waged on the face of the earth. ...*

*The gold standard will give England the commerce and wealth of the world. The bimetallic standard will make the United States the most prosperous nation on the globe.*

Such silverite propaganda no doubt hurt the "Gold Democrats" most and contributed to a 42 percent rise, in two years, in the Populist vote. In the elections of 1894, when the Republicans won overwhelming control in the House, the Populists elected six senators and seven congressmen. Even more ominous for Democratic prospects, antiadministration rural Democrats in the South, men like "Ben" Tillman of South Carolina, viciously attacked Cleveland. "When Judas betrayed Christ," Tillman charged, "his heart was not blacker than this scoundrel, Cleveland, in deceiving the Democracy." He promised to take his pitchfork to Washington and prod the "old bag of beef in his old fat ribs."

## Election of 1896

Dissension among the Democrats naturally heartened the Republicans. At their national convention in St. Louis in June 1896 they showed their own solidarity by nominat-

524

ing for the presidency on the first ballot William McKinley of Ohio, sponsor of the high tariff of 1890 and the handpicked aspirant of his fellow Ohioan Mark Hanna, the shipping and traction magnate who was emerging as the Republican national boss. When the platform came up for discussion, however, Republican solidarity was shaken. Hanna wanted McKinley to straddle the money issue to keep silverite Republicans from bolting the party. But he yielded on a sound-money plank in return for needed eastern financial support in the campaign. "We are . . . opposed to the free coinage of silver," the Republican declaration read, "except by international agreement . . . and until such agreement can be obtained the existing gold standard must be preserved." On the adoption of this plank, silverite Republicans, led by Senator Henry M. Teller of Colorado, walked out.

The Democratic National Committee also favored the gold standard, but other Democrats, seeing a windfall in the Republican money plank, sought to draw Populist strength to themselves and win the election after all. At their convention in Chicago, which met shortly after the Republicans, the Democratic silverites routed the "goldbugs."

The Democratic platform was written largely by Governor John P. Altgeld of Illinois, whose pardon of the Haymarket rioters in 1893 and handling of the Pullman strike the next year had made him anathema to conservatives everywhere. This platform repudiated Cleveland's policies all along the line and came out flatly for *unlimited* coinage of silver at the ratio of 16 ounces of silver to 1 ounce of gold. A sharp debate preceded the adoption of the silver plank, but the issue was resolved once a 36-year-old Nebraskan, William Jennings Bryan, had spoken in its favor. The Democratic nomination was also resolved by this memorable speech, for Bryan's name suddenly was on every one's tongue, and he was voted the candidate on the fifth ballot.

Young as he was, Bryan, in 1896, was no Johnny-come-lately. A lawyer in Lincoln, Nebraska, he served in Congress from 1890 to 1894 as a vigorous member of the growing "silver bloc." Defeated for the Senate in 1894,

he became editor-in-chief of the influential *Omaha World-Herald,* and soon enhanced the reputation he had made in the House as an orator by embarking on the Chautauqua lecture circuit (see p. 571). When he made his convention speech, his friends were already working quietly for his nomination.

Bryan's speech was modest and dignified. "We are fighting in the defense of our homes, our families, and posterity," he said. He defended the principle of the income tax and denounced the Supreme Court's recent decision upsetting it; he challenged those who wanted to protect creditors against inflation by asking why debtors had not been protected against deflation in 1873; he declared firmly that money was by far the most important of the issues. "You come to us and tell us that the great cities are in favor of the gold standard; we reply that the great cities rest upon our broad and fertile prairies. Burn down your cities and leave our farms, and your cities will spring up again as if by magic; but destroy our farms and the grass will grow in the streets of every city in the country." Bryan closed with the striking image by which his speech has ever since been known:

*Having behind us the producing masses of this nation and the world, supported by the commercial interests, the laboring interests, and the toilers everywhere, we will answer their demand for a gold standard by saying to them: You shall not press down upon the brow of labor this crown of thorns, you shall not crucify mankind upon a cross of gold.*

Even before the election of 1896, many Populists had been sickened by the emphasis on silver and the neglect of the more radical reforms in the People's party platform. Henry Demarest Lloyd called the free-silver issue "the cowbird of the Reform movement. It waited until the nest had been built by the sacrifices and labour of others, and then it laid its eggs in it, pushing out the others which lie smashed on the ground."

When the Populists met at their convention in St. Louis in August 1896 they were forced to confront this sad dilemma: to wage a Populist campaign would be to split the silver vote and hand the election to the Republicans; to fuse with the Democrats in support of Bryan would mean their party's extinction. Most of the delegates approved of Bryan, but those southern Populists who boldly had joined the third-party crusade now strongly opposed fusion with the Democrats, most of them Bourbon Democrats in their section whom they had been fighting for years. The fusionists, however, could point out that the Democratic platform, besides demanding the unlimited coinage of silver, did attack Cleveland's deals with the bankers, did recommend stricter railroad regulation, and did support a constitutional amendment to make an income tax possible. Against the wishes of the diehards, the Populist convention nominated Bryan for President, but they could not stomach the Democratic vice-presidential candidate, Arthur Sewall, a rich Maine banker. In his place, they nominated the fiery Georgian Thomas E. Watson, once the staunchest third-party man in the South, who actively sought white and colored political unity.

The campaign of 1896 was one of the most dramatic in American history. Bryan, handicapped by two running mates who detested and contradicted each other, subordinated all issues to free silver. The redoubtable Hanna, in the meantime, was extracting millions for McKinley from monied interests eager to sink the silver ship. Bryan waged a whirlwind campaign, traveling more than 18,000 miles and delivering over 600 speeches, while McKinley remained securely anchored to the front porch of the family home in Canton, reading carefully drafted statements to delegations brought there by party leaders. "Nobody," the New York Republican boss Tom Platt had observed on the eve of the campaign, "can look at McKinley's record and read the flabby things he has said without perceiving that he

has no fixed opinions, but has been turned and twisted by changing public opinion." Given no chance to twist and turn, McKinley carried the day. His plurality of over 600,000 was the largest of any candidate since Grant defeated Greeley in 1872. McKinley won 271 electoral votes to Bryan's 176. Even such agrarian strongholds as Iowa, Minnesota, and North Dakota went Republican.

525

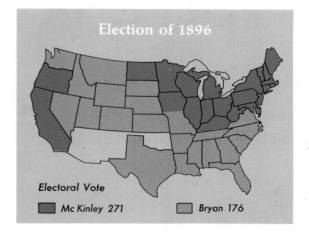

Election of 1896

Electoral Vote

McKinley 271    Bryan 176

No doubt the flood of propaganda, the pressure employers put on industrial workers, and the identification of Bryanism with anarchy and revolution had something to do with McKinley's success. But there were more obvious causes. Republicans argued, with much justice, that an inflationary price movement would leave wages behind and that workmen would be the losers. Urban workers failed to provide the mass support Bryan hoped for. Moreover, every middle-class American with savings invested in stocks, banks, or insurance was, in a small way, a creditor himself, and it was easy for him to see the point of the Republican argument that inflation would reduce the value of his holdings. McKinley won, according to the perceptive Kansas editor William Allen White, because "he could unite to a political solidarity the American middle class." This class itself had grown more distinctive and more self-conscious as plutocrats and proletarians themselves emerged at opposite poles of America's rapidly changing population.

### Republican "good times"

"God's in his Heaven, all's right with the world!" Hanna telegraphed McKinley when the returns were in. More revealing was the language of the *New York Tribune:* Bryan, cried the editor,

*the wretched, rattle-pated boy, posing in vapid vanity and mouthing his resounding rottenness . . . goes down with the cause. . . . Good riddance to it all . . . to the foul menace of repudiation and Anarchy against the honor and life of the Republic.*

It is doubtful that McKinley's election in 1896 restored prosperity, as the Republicans claimed, but Bryan's defeat surely raised the confidence of those who stood to gain most from sound currency and protective tariffs. The Republican administration quickly adopted the Dingley Tariff of 1897, which raised schedules even above those of the McKinley Tariff of 1890. Three years later, McKinley signed the Currency Act of 1900, which made the gold dollar the single unit of value and required all paper money to be redeemable in gold.

To the losers, at the same time, the results were disheartening. The Populist party was finished, while the espousal of silver had brought the Democrats their most severe defeat of many years, one all the more disastrous for leaving the party more divided than ever. Hundreds of thousands of agrarians must have sympathized with the defeated vice-presidential candidate Tom Watson, who doubted that "any soldier of the Southern Confederacy carried away from Appomattox a heavier heart than I took with me into my enforced retirement."

But history takes strange turns. The glee of the victors may have been justified; the despair of the losers was not. Soon the money supply was augmented by new flows of gold from the Klondike, South Africa, and Australia, and by enlarged United States production due to a new cyanide process for extracting gold from low-grade ores. Ironically, the inflation that the agrarian reformers failed to win through silver came through detested gold. Good harvests and good prices also became the rule. In the election of 1900, boasting of "Republican prosperity," McKinley again defeated Bryan, this time even more decisively than in 1896. The Republican slogan, "The Full Dinner Pail," seemed appropriate for the resurgent country.

At the same time, several of the radical planks in the Populist program that Bryan and the Democrats had neglected for silver in 1896 soon were enacted into law: the direct election of senators; the income tax; an improved national currency and credit structure; postal savings banks; and certain features of the subtreasury plan. Thus the doctrines of Populism outlived the party, while McKinley's victory did not long quiet the forces of protest. Their principal new target became the cities of the nation that had grown up without direction or goals in the iron age of industrial power.

## For further reading

The books by Cochran and Miller, Wiebe, and Ginger cited in the readings for Chapter Nineteen are also relevant to this chapter. H. W. Morgan, *From Hayes to McKinley* (1969), is a modern survey, which may be supplemented by J. A. Garraty, *The New Commonwealth 1877-1890* (1968); E. F. Goldman, *Rendezvous with Destiny* (1952); and Matthew Josephson, *The Politicos 1865-1896* (1938). James Bryce, *The American*

*Commonwealth* (2 vols., 1888), and vol. II of Moisei Ostrogorski, *Democracy and the Organization of Political Parties* (2 vols., 1902), are penetrating interpretations by foreign analysts. L. D. White, *The Republican Era 1869-1901* (1958), is outstanding on federal administration. Frances Carpenter, ed., *Carp's Washington* (1960), offers first-hand reporting on the Blaine era. Also good for political detail is C. M. Green, *Washington, Capital City 1879-1950* (1963).

G. T. Blodgett, *The Gentle Reformers: Massachusetts Democrats in the Cleveland Era* (1966), is a good introduction to the Mugwumps. M. A. DeWolfe Howe, *Portrait of an Independent, Moorfield Storey 1845-1929* (1932), is strengthened by contemporary letters. R. E. Welch, Jr., *George Frisbie Hoar and the Half-Breed Republicans* (1971), is excellent. Morton Keller, *The Art and Politics of Thomas Nast* (1968), is enhanced by fine reproductions of the cartoonist's work.

Useful biographies of the Presidents include Harry Barnard, *Rutherford B. Hayes* (1954); R. G. Caldwell, *James A. Garfield* (1931); Allan Nevins, *Grover Cleveland* (1932); H. W. Morgan, *William McKinley* (1963); and Margaret Leech, *In the Days of McKinley* (1959). On aspirants and others highly placed in politics, see D. S. Muzzey, *James G. Blaine* (1934); P. W. Glad, *The Trumpet Soundeth: William Jennings Bryan and His Democracy* (1960); P. E. Coletta, *William Jennings Bryan* (3 vols., 1964-1969); Herbert Croly, *Thomas Alonzo Hanna* (1912); and N. W. Stephenson, *Nelson W. Aldrich* (1930). The national Democratic party is well treated in J. R. Hollingsworth, *The Whirligig of Politics: The Democracy of Cleveland and Bryan* (1963); and H. S. Merrill, *Bourbon Democracy of the Middle West 1865-1896* (1953). D. W. Grantham, *The Democratic South* (1963), is a useful short study. Biographies of Populist leaders include C. V. Woodward, *Tom Watson* (1938); Martin Rudge, *Ignatius Donnelly* (1962); and F. E. Haynes, *James Baird Weaver* (1919).

Irwin Unger, *The Greenback Era ... 1865-1879* (1964), affords an excellent analysis of the money issue before the rise of Populism. Milton Friedman and A. J. Schwartz, *A Monetary History of the United States 1867-1960* (1963), is also useful. On patronage see Ari Hoogenboom, *Outlawing the Spoils, A History of the Civil Service Reform Movement 1865-1883* (1968 ed.). C. E. Rosenberg, *The Trial of the Assassin Guiteau*

(1968), goes beyond the patronage issue. D. J. Rothman, *Politics and Power, The United States Senate 1869-1901* (1966), a solemn statistical study, sometimes misses the spirit of the age. M. R. Dearing, *Veterans in Politics, The Story of the G.A.R.* (1952), is the story of a pressure group that succeeded. A sort of pressure group that failed is described in D. L. McMurry, *Coxey's Army* (1929).

The legislative background of federal railroad regulation is well presented in L. H. Haney, *A Congressional History of Railways in the United States 1850-1887* (1910). An authoritative analysis is W. Z. Ripley, *Railroads: Rates and Regulation* (1912). Lee Benson, *Merchants—Farmers—and Railroads* (1955), stresses the urban origins of the call for regulation. Gabriel Kolko, *Railroads and Regulation 1887-1916* (1965), emphasizes the frustration of regulation. The most comprehensive study of the Sherman Antitrust Act is H. B. Thorelli, *The Federal Antitrust Policy* (1955). Eliot Jones, *The Trust Problem in the United States* (1929), is good for background and consequences. I. M. Tarbell, *The Tariff in Our Times* (1911), covers tariff politics well.

F. A. Shannon, *The Farmer's Last Frontier 1860-1897* (1945), is the best introduction to agricultural problems after the Civil War. G. C. Fite, *The Farmer's Frontier 1865-1900* (1966), is more limited in coverage. S. J. Buck, *The Granger Movement* (1913), and J. D. Hicks, *The Populist Revolt* (1931), are good older accounts of farmer unrest and political action. See also R. B. Nye, *Midwestern Progressive Politics* (1951); F. D. Haynes, *Third Party Movements Since the Civil War* (1916); Richard Hofstadter, *The Age of Reform* (1955) and Hofstadter's introduction to the John Harvard Library edition of *Coin's Financial School* (1963), reprinted in Hofstadter, *The Paranoid Style in American Politics* (1965). For additional analyses of Populism, see, for example, Norman Pollack, *The Populist Response to Industrial America: Midwestern Populist Thought* (1962); W. T. K. Nugent, *The Tolerant Populists, Kansas Populism and Nativism* (1963); O. G. Clanton, *Kansas Populism* (1969); and R. F. Durden, *The Climax of Populism* (1966). G. B. Tindall, *A Populist Reader, Selections from the Works of American Populist Leaders* (1966), is a worthwhile anthology. G. H. Knoles, *The Presidential Campaign and Election of 1892* (1942), and S. L. Jones, *The Presidential Election of 1896* (1964), are exceptional studies. Valuable also are P. W. Glad, *McKinley, Bryan and the People* (1964), and Bryan's own account, *The First Battle* (1896).

# CITY LIFE

In Europe the idea of the city always implied a center of power and learning, of religion and art. The great city—Athens, Rome, Paris, London, Constantinople, Moscow—traditionally was a place of palaces, emperors, and aristocrats, of universities and cathedrals, of architects, sculptors, painters, poets, philosophers, scholars, doctors. In agrarian America, by contrast, the city was looked upon as a "problem" and little else. "When we get piled upon one another in large cities," Jefferson observed in 1787, "we shall become as corrupt as in Europe, and go to eating one another as they do there."

In the 1850s northern moralists already shuddered at the "immense accumulations of ignorance and error, vice and crime" to be found in the rapidly expanding towns. Thirty years later the Reverend Josiah Strong, in his widely read book *Our Country,* observed that "the city is the nerve center of our civilization. It is also the storm center." Among the "perils" to be encountered in city life—rather archaic ones they seem now—he noted Immigration, Romanism, Secularism, Intemperance, Socialism, and Wealth. "Each of the preceding perils" to the United States, he added, "is enhanced in the city."

As late as 1895 one commentator wondered over the readiness of farm youth to "leave the country where homes are cheap, the air pure, all men equal, and extreme poverty unknown, and crowd into cities" where they seemed to find "in the noises, the crowds, the excitements, even in the sleepless anxieties of the daily struggle for life, a charm they are powerless to resist." By then the growth of cities was looked upon as an irreversible force—to most Americans a force for evil. Yet the charm continued to exert itself. The very rich, like Mr. J. P. Morgan and his friends, would live nowhere but in the greatest city of all.

The rich elsewhere would aspire to New York mansions, while the very poor in the urban populations everywhere offered soul-satisfying causes to middle-class reformers, many of them of rural origins.

## I  Velocity of urban growth

### The surge in numbers

In 1840 only one-twelfth of the American people lived in cities of 8000 or more. By 1860 the proportion of city dwellers had grown to one-sixth, and by 1900 to one-third, of the population. In 1900 more than 25 million Americans were living in cities, most of them in the metropolises that had grown so lustily in the preceding fifty years. In 1850 New York City and independent Brooklyn together boasted a population of 1,200,000. By 1900 (after official consolidation in 1898) their population had soared to over 3 million. In the same period, again partly by the annexation of neighboring communities, Philadelphia grew from 560,000 to 1,300,000; Pittsburgh, Pennsylvania's second city, grew from 67,000 to 450,000. Most spectacular of all was the development of Chicago. A muddy trading post on the prairie in 1831, with twelve families and a meager garrison as its only inhabitants, Chicago had grown by 1850 to 30,000; by 1880, to 500,000. In the next twenty years, its population reached 1,700,000, placing if far

ahead of Philadelphia and second only to New York in size. No other city quite matched the speed of Chicago's rise, but striking in its own right was the sudden thrust forward of places that had scarcely existed in 1860. Denver, a small mining camp on the eve of the Civil War, had 134,000 persons in 1900. In the same period, Minneapolis grew from 2500 to 200,000; Los Angeles from 5000 to 100,000. Birmingham, Alabama, which had not even been founded until 1871, by 1900 had 38,000 inhabitants.

Two harbingers of the new industrial metropolis had begun to transform the urban landscape even before 1860: the steam railroad and the stationary steam engine. By the 1850s the rattle of the railway cars and the whistle of the locomotive had disrupted the solitude of rural towns and villages:

*To do things 'railroad fashion' [wrote Thoreau in Walden] is now the byword; and it is worth the while to be warned so often and so sincerely by any power to get off its track. There is no stopping to read the riot act, no firing over the heads of the mob, in this*

*case. We have constructed a fate, an Atropos, that
never turns aside.*

**530**

Thoreau's relentless railroad rushed into cities
whose economy and way of life had been attuned to the horse and the riverboat. It
grasped the most picturesque sites for rights
of way, freight yards, and depots, demolished
old landmarks, established the path and pace
of urban expansion. The velocity of railroad
growth and railroad service, in turn, forced
urban industry to shift rapidly from waterpower
to steampower, the more expeditiously to
meet the demand for manufactures from ever
larger and more distant markets. The railroad
also hauled in the coal from which steampower

was generated. The steam railroad and
steampower in factories combined to transform antebellum mill towns into soot-laden
cities with hundreds of new industries and
tens of thousands of new workers, thereby
multiplying their problems as well as their
wealth.

The rapid growth of American cities after
the Civil War was but one reflection of the
enormous increase in the scale and the pace of
American business enterprise. The expansion
of Pittsburgh and the development of Birmingham were both attributable directly to the
modernization and growth of the iron and
steel industry. Minneapolis rapidly attained
city status because of the surge in the grain
trade and flour milling. Chicago was first a

*The railroad crashing
through Main Street, as drawn for Harper's
Magazine, August 1885.*

New York Public Library

wheat port, next a railroad hub, then the meat-packing center of the world; her industry and trade so boosted business activity that she became the financial capital of the West as well. Chicago's credit facilities then attracted a great variety of new industries and new distributing enterprises, such as the Marshall Field store and the Sears, Roebuck mail-order house. Philadelphia and New York, still enlarging the commercial life that had been established early in their histories, also swelled with new industries, such as the manufacture of ready-to-wear clothing, enormously accelerated by the demand for uniforms during the Civil War.

In cities all over the country, moreover, opportunities were opening up in white-collar and service occupations as well as in industry. Between 1870 and 1910 the number of wholesalers grew approximately three and a half times, from 16,000 to 58,000; the number of retailers, from 376,000 to 1,106,000; the number of salespeople and clerks in stores, from 105,000 to 1,232,000; and the number of commercial travelers, from a mere 7000 to 164,000. Almost equally spectacular in growth was the number of domestics and of persons employed in laundries, restaurants, boarding houses and hotels, barbershops, real estate offices, and banks. All told, in 1910, about 7.25 million persons—not all of them, of course, white-collar workers—were employed in trade and service occupations, a figure almost four and a half times greater than that for 1870. If the 2.75 million persons engaged in transportation, urban and interurban, are included in the service category, the 1910 total for trade and service just about equals the totals for agriculture, and for manufacturing and mining combined.

### Sources of the new city population

A large proportion of the American urban population, of course, came from (one might better say fled) American farms. "There was a time, and not long ago," a South Da-

kota stock grower told the Industrial Commission in 1899,

*when to be considered a good farmer one had to be up with the whole family at 4 A.M., and to keep himself and them on the jump till 10 P.M. was considered especially commendable. . . . Many boys and girls are worked so hard on land that forever afterwards the thought of farming is distasteful to them.*

All the conditions that fostered the farmers' protest in the late nineteenth century contributed to the disenchantment with farm life, while the rewards of industry and finance—manifestly the forces of the future and the sources of great wealth—exerted their own allures. If hard work alone would not insure power and fortune, there was always the chance that a lucky break would smooth the way and transform one into a real-life Horatio Alger hero. The Alger stories had their greatest vogue in the 1870s and 1880s and sustained among the youths of those decades a belief in economic opportunity that faded for most of them only when they had grown to frustrated and impoverished manhood.

In Europe, at the same time, a similar movement from rural to urban life was under way, of which the migration of millions to the cities of the United States was but a part. Eventually this migration was to overwhelm the native-born urban families. By 1900, three-fourths of Chicago's population was foreign-born. The proportion of foreign-born in New York City was even higher. Greater New York's Italian population even in the 1890s equaled that of Naples, its German population that of Hamburg. Twice as many Irish lived in New York as in Dublin. Such a concentration of foreigners alarmed many native-born Americans, concerned—as one of them confessed in the 1890s—"at the prospect of adding enormously to the burden of the municipal governments in the large cities, already almost breaking down through corruption and inefficiency." And yet the real surge of the "new" immigration had hardly begun.

Certain inescapable statistics strongly suggest that "native" concern about the later immigration must have arisen as much from honest fears as from hypocrisy:

(1) Up to 1880 immigrants from the Austro-Hungarian empire and neighboring satellites in Central Europe never numbered more than 8800 a year; up to 1900, never more than 77,000 a year. Between 1900 and 1914, on the other hand, their number never fell below 100,000 annually, and in those fifteen years alone, more than 3.1 million Austro-Hungarians entered the United States.

(2) Up to 1880 immigrants from Italy never numbered more than 8700 a year; up to 1900, never more than 77,500 a year. Between 1900 and 1914, on the other hand, their number never fell below 100,000 annually, and in those same fifteen years, more than 3 million Italians entered the United States.

(3) Up to 1880 immigrants from Russia and related Baltic states never numbered more than 8000 a year; up to 1900 never more than 81,500 a year. Not until 1902 did their number exceed 100,000, and again not until 1914 did it dip under that figure. In the fifteen years 1900 to 1914, Russia and her Baltic neighbors sent more than 2.5 million persons to the United States.

(4) From the Balkan countries of eastern and southern Europe (and adjacent Asia)—for example, Rumania, Bulgaria, Greece, Turkey, and Syria—the aggregate number of immigrants to the United States before 1900 rarely exceeded 10,000 a year. Yet between 1900 and 1914, these countries sent out an annual average of nearly 60,000 and an aggregate for fifteen years of nearly 900,000 persons.

Thus, in a *single decade and a half,* at the start of the twentieth century, approximately 9.5 million exotic people (equal, almost to a man, to the 9.5 million who had come from the familiar United Kingdom over a period of a hundred years and more) engulfed the North Atlantic ports of the United States, most of them pouring into the port of New York, which many never left. Other peoples, of course, continued to arrive in northern cities in particular, including the advance guard of Negro migrants from the South (see p. 538), but they entered almost unnoticed in the flood of strangers—Magyars, Croats, and Ruthenians, Neapolitans and Sicilians, Serbs and Slovaks and near-Orientals, Roman Catho-

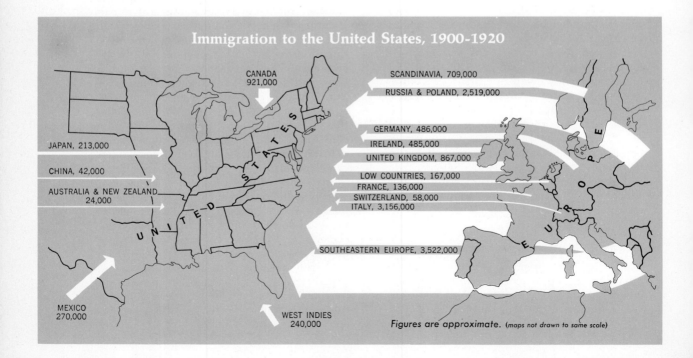

### Immigration to the United States, 1900-1920

CANADA 921,000

JAPAN, 213,000

CHINA, 42,000

AUSTRALIA & NEW ZEALAND 24,000

MEXICO 270,000

WEST INDIES 240,000

SCANDINAVIA, 709,000

RUSSIA & POLAND, 2,519,000

GERMANY, 486,000

IRELAND, 485,000

UNITED KINGDOM, 867,000

LOW COUNTRIES, 167,000

FRANCE, 136,000

SWITZERLAND, 58,000

ITALY, 3,156,000

SOUTHEASTERN EUROPE, 3,522,000

*Figures are approximate.* (maps not drawn to same scale)

lics, Greek Orthodox, Jews, and Muslims.

*These bringing with them unknown gods and
    rites,*
*Those, tiger passions, here to stretch their claws,*
*In street and alley what strange tongues
    are loud,*
*Accents of menace alien to our air,*
*Voices that once the Tower of Babel knew!*

"O Liberty," cried the genteel poet Thomas
Bailey Aldrich,

> *O Liberty, white Goddess! is it well*
> *To leave the gates unguarded?*

Fear of "the annihilation of the native American stock," whatever was understood by that phrase, proved groundless. Expert analysis of the nation's population in the 1920s revealed the remarkable fact that, despite the entry of considerably more than 35 million immigrants since the Revolution (a figure approximately ten times larger than the American population in 1783), 51 percent of the American people were descended from colonial families, and only 49 percent were foreign-born or descended from all the post-Revolutionary newcomers, including those from Great Britain. Again, in 1880, long before the massive migrations from eastern and southern Europe had begun, about 12 percent of the American population was foreign-born. Between 1890 and 1910, this figure rose to 15 percent, but by 1930 it was back to 12 percent, and declined thereafter.

Yet certain features of the massive "new" immigration, and not least its suddenly massive dimensions as well as its unusual concentration in great cities, make the turn-of-the-century alarm among the cities' growing middle and upper classes understandable. "We came not empty-handed here," wrote the immigrant poet Adam Dan, "But brought a rich inheritance." That, few Americans would deny. The trouble was, this inheritance suddenly had become far too rich for many to assimilate without uneasiness, and the immigrant soon became a more imposing scapegoat than ever for urban ills.

## II  The slough of city life

### Growth into decay

The full impact of sudden urban growth was not felt in America until the Progressive era early in the twentieth century. Yet even in the nineteenth century, American cities, for all their soaring wealth, suffered an accumulation of ills and evils exceeded only by those of the 1960s and 1970s, when decline, not growth, brutalized urban life. In the nineteenth century, city hardships were heightened by lack of knowledge and inexperience; but inattention, encouraged by the prevailing philosophy of laissez-faire, must also bear much of the blame.

Most city dwellers at best took only a half-hearted interest in civic projects that did not immediately affect their own pocketbooks or pleasure. "In this Garden City of ours," says one of the characters in Henry Blake Fuller's novel of Chicago, *With the Procession* (1895), "everyone cultivates his own little bed and his neighbor his; but who looks after the paths between? They have become a kind of No Man's Land and the weeds of rank iniquity are fast choking them up." The leaders of the older nineteenth-century metropolises, dominant merchants, lawyers, and bankers, were content to gaze with satisfaction on the rising value of the urban land they owned or managed, trusting to others less well off to look after themselves. Even the insatiable local politicians were left as free to prey as the tariff boodlers on the national scene. The industrialists who dominated the newer cities, in turn, viewed them simply as sites for the works and warrens for the workers. Distinct areas might be reserved for the industrialists and their families, and for their general managers, superintendents, and other ranking officials. For the rest of the populace, the meanest shelter and the meagerest public facilities were provided.

To accommodate the phenomenal surge in the city population, the rising profession of real-estate operators characteristically cut up city land into blocks of rectangular lots, divided by a gridiron of roads. The lots themselves were divided simply by lines on a layout, obliterating open space entirely. "The rectangular parcelling of ground," writes Lewis Mumford, "promoted speculation in land units and the ready interchange of real property; it had no relation whatever to the essential purposes for which a city exists."

Urban congestion rapidly fed upon itself. As sections of a city became thickly populated, more and more transportation arteries were directed there, and water, gas, and electrical utilities might be brought in. Increasing numbers of factories, most of them noisome, then came to take advantage of the new facilities. Eventually, neighboring residential regions were overrun, land values soared, and more and more intensive construction was undertaken to pay for higher taxes. Under such pressures, private dwellings that had accommodated single families were remodeled into tenements that housed eight or twelve families or else were destroyed to provide room for business structures. Living conditions deteriorated in such areas, and families that could afford to do so moved away, the richer ones into nearby suburban towns.

As strong as was the movement of population to the peripheries of the cities, the influx of newcomers from outside greatly exceeded it. Thus, while nineteenth-century growth had a decentralizing tendency, congestion continued rapidly to increase. The result was that land values grew higher every year, while to offset its rising cost land utilization became ever more intensive and hostile to human life. In the city, wrote the Reverend Strong, "Dives and Lazarus are brought face to face; here in

Library of Congress

sharp contrast are the ennui of surfeit and the desperation of starvation."

### Uses of political corruption

In *The American Commonwealth* (1888), James Bryce called American city government "the one conspicuous failure in the United States." Two years later, a prominent educator declared that American cities were "the worst [governed] in Christendom—the most expensive, the most inefficient, and the most corrupt."

While duly noting the problems of "recent immigrants untrained in self-government," and "cultivated citizens" so "sensitive to the vulgarities of practical politics" that they are "unwilling to sacrifice their time and tastes and comforts in the struggle," Bryce also listed other causes of the cities' malaise: (1) crooked and incompetent officials; (2) the "introduction of State and national politics into municipal affairs"; and (3) the control of local affairs by state legislatures unfamiliar, in the main, with the processes of city government and the needs of city dwellers.

In most American cities power resided in the mayor, in the single- or double-chambered city council, and in independent boards. These agencies determined how municipal funds should be raised and spent. They

*Lithograph of the Chicago gridiron, looking west from Lake Michigan, 1892.*

granted the franchises for street railways, let out contracts for laying sewers and paving streets, constructed public buildings, bought fire-fighting equipment, and contracted for other city services and supplies. Since most of these activities were entrusted to committees drawn from elected aldermen or council members with no training in city management, unscrupulous political bosses found it easy enough to place their henchmen in key positions where they could mulct city treasuries.

Boss Tweed's career in New York City became the prototype for all later political swindlers. In 1868 Tweed and his Tammany cronies installed John M. Hoffman in Albany as governor. The following year, by spending enormous sums to bribe state legislators (some senators were given as much as $40,000), Tweed got the legislature to pass and his governor to sign a new charter for New York City, which he used to make himself a virtual dictator.

Tweed's technique was delightfully simple. Everyone who worked for the city was required to pad his bill—at first only by 10 percent, later 66 percent, finally 85 percent. The padding was turned over to Tweed's gang. Thus, when Tweed built his notorious courthouse, whose final cost ran to many times the original estimate of $3 million, an item charged to the "repair" of fixtures ran to over $1,149,000 before the building was even completed. Forty chairs and three tables cost $179,000, thermometers $7500 apiece. The carpenter who got $360,000 was surpassed by "The Prince of Plasterers," as the *Times* called him, who drew over $2,870,000 for nine months' work.

When respectable citizens howled, Tweed insolently challenged them: "What are you going to do about it?" Nonetheless, the volume of criticism mounted, particularly in scathing editorials in the *New York Times* and in Thomas Nast's memorable cartoons in that paper and in *Harper's Weekly*. Tweed himself was sufficiently touched by these assaults to offer George Jones, part owner and publisher of the *Times,* $500,000 to shut up; but to no avail. He also sent a banker as emissary to Nast with an offer of $100,000 to go abroad to "study art." Mischievously, Nast worked the figure up to $500,000 before he replied: "I made up my mind not long ago to put some of those fellows behind the bars, and I am going to put them there." "Only be careful, Mr. Nast," replied the banker, "that you do not first put yourself in the coffin." But Tweed feared Nast more than Nast feared Tweed. His own followers, the Boss said, could not read, but they could "look at the damn pictures."

Tweed was ousted in 1871, and in 1876 he died in jail, friendless and penniless. A considerably cleaner Tammany regime followed under "Honest John" Kelly, but in the 1890s, when Tammany was bossed by Richard Croker, the whole cycle of corruption was repeated while lesser thieves plundered other cities.

If native Americans put the main onus for city corruption on ignorant immigrant hordes, the immigrant himself often proved wise enough to back the bosses who helped him survive in the new harsh surroundings the natives offered him. To speed the immigrant to the polls, the boss would often hasten on his naturalization proceedings. To insure that he voted correctly, the boss would also give him gifts at Christmas, find city jobs for him and his sons, encourage his ethnic customs, and mediate with the police and the courts when he or his children got into trouble.

Many immigrants carried with them to America feudal notions of government—especially the idea that aristocrats were bound to be the rulers—and could not think of themselves as active participants in public affairs even after they had become American citizens. Reform programs that sought to reduce taxes hardly touched the average immigrant's life, for he had no property to tax. Reforms to improve the efficiency of city administration only aroused his suspicion, for "efficiency" in government might well mean that he and his relatives would be dropped from the city payroll. Fearful of change, the immigrant disliked the very sound of "reform." And why not, since the typical upper-class reformer seemed to be attacking the very men to whom the immigrant felt most loyal—the bosses.

Reformers also had their troubles with the well-educated native voter taken in by politicians who cleverly exploited party loyalties. Many honest and respectable men, feeling that local reform movements would only besmirch their national party, chose to tolerate corrupt city and state machines that delivered the vote in national elections. The ties between politics and business, moreover, strengthened the tolerance of corruption arising from party affinities. Only when the exactions of the political rings became too outrageous did respectable citizens organize for "good government," and then only temporarily.

The so-called Dark Ages in American municipal history lasted through the 1880s. In 1894, local reform groups meeting in Philadelphia federated in the National Municipal League, which gave a continuous impetus to reform programs. Yet urban problems persisted and eventually worsened.

*Limited technical advances*

One further obstacle to good city government in the nineteenth century was widespread ignorance of how to make it work. The practice of municipal borrowing, for example, so rewarding to favored bankers and so much more gentle on taxpayers than paying cash for "improvements," led to the piling up of huge municipal debts which, even with the best intentions, sucked up enormous sums simply for interest and periodic refunding. There was as yet, moreover, no science of sewage disposal, of garbage collection, of water purification, of pollution control, of budget procedures to guide even the most circumspect administrators. Yet even in the city's "Dark Ages" some steps simply had to be taken to keep great cities functioning.

One of the worst problems was traffic congestion, especially at peak hours when millions of workers had to be carried to and from their jobs. The horsecar, with a maximum speed of 6 miles an hour, had sufficed for a simpler society, but no longer. As early as 1867 the steam-driven elevated railroad had been tried out in New York City and came into everyday use there during the seventies. Horsecar companies fought the new lines, with the support of citizens who complained of the soot and smoke and the hot ashes that dropped on pedestrians' heads. As time passed, elevated steam railroads were abandoned, but not because of the discomforts they produced. It simply became too expensive to construct elevated structures capable of supporting the heavy locomotives required to draw the lengthening trains at satisfactory speeds. Some other method had to be found to transport people forced by urban overcrowding to live farther and farther from their work.

The cable car, propelled by a moving underground chain, was used in San Francisco in 1873 and in Chicago ten years later. The most successful innovation, however, was the trolley car, developed by Frank Julian Sprague, whose pioneer system in Richmond, Virginia in 1887 demonstrated the practicality of electric traction in large cities. Since each of Sprague's trolleys carried its own electric motor and ran on the ground, both the stinking, clangorous, coal-burning steam locomotives and the dense network of heavy elevated track that cut off light and air could be dispensed with. Trolleys could be run singly or in trains; they could be switched easily on the ingenious tracking schemes Sprague devised to avoid clogging up the single- and double-track routes; and repair problems proved minimal. The elevated steam railroad operators fought the trolleys on every front but soon were forced to electrify their own surviving lines, while electric subways, operating in London since 1886, were introduced in Boston in 1897 and New York City in 1904.

Besides providing energy for urban transportation, electricity helped improve the lighting of city streets and structures. The development of the electric arc lamp for outdoor lighting in 1879 signalized the gradual disappearance of flickering gas lamps on main thoroughfares; and soon after, electric signs on buildings, in anticipation of the "Great White Way" of the modern city, lit up a few streets. Interior lighting by electricity also became commercially feasible in 1879, when Edison perfected the incandescent bulb. But gas was by no means driven out as an illuminant. In 1885, an Austrian, Auer von Welsbach, invented a conical gas mantle that produced an intense diffused light, and for many years the gas lamp was more widely used indoors than electric lights.

In dealing with such matters as water supply, waste disposal, and street cleaning, which had been handled relatively well in the past, American cities grew less and less conscientious. By 1870, the disposal of waste had reached a critical stage in the larger cities, where sanitation methods scarcely differed from those employed in the villages of a century before. Not one American city filtered its water, even though the indiscriminate dumping of sewage and garbage into streams often polluted the supply. The typhoid fever epidemics common in Chicago and Philadelphia in the last decades of the century could be traced to the drinking of contaminated water.

Between 1880 and 1900 cleaner streets, pur-

er water, and more efficient methods of fire fighting made the American metropolis more livable for many, yet it retained such ugly and brutal features that Europeans who visited the states at the end of the century often wondered whether their emigrating fellow countrymen might not better have remained at home. But Europe, of course, had its own grim rural poverty which was driving the most desperate into her own urban slums as well as overseas, slums seldom visited by those who could afford to travel and point a finger.

### The curse of urban housing

Many American cities, especially in New England and along the eastern seaboard, retained something of their provincial character until the Civil War, and even with the advent of the industrial age the vestiges of a simpler agrarian and commercial society was not entirely effaced. In such cities pleasant wooden houses, each set back from elm-lined streets on its own well-cared-for lot, could be found for many decades. Yet after 1865, the general appearance of the city changed as new architectural styles came in and as machine-made pressed brick displaced wood as the standard building material.

Not all the houses built in the next generation were the architectural absurdities some critics have declared them to be; the appearance of many streets and districts in the major American cities was by no means displeasing. Yet the urban landscape, as a whole, became dingier. Even the very rich, who with their armies of servants and their private equipages, escaped many of the trials of the poor, often lived in mansions situated near gasworks and slaughterhouses and breathed the same sooty air as the slum dwellers. In middle-class dwellings throughout the country, interiors were dark and crammed with overstuffed furniture peculiarly susceptible to dust. The bulk and clutter of Victorian living suited a generation that overate, whose women attached bustles to their dresses, and who lived what might be described as upholstered lives.

The very poor, comprising characteristically half and more of the metropolitan population, nearly the whole of many factory towns, lived under conditions that were scarcely endurable. The practice of leasing rows of abandoned middle-class houses in enveloping industrial districts for conversion into tenements had begun in New York City even before 1840. After 1865 such tenements spread over metropolitan America like a disease. Whole families, and sometimes more than one, lived in the airless closets of these houses—usually without sanitary facilities, lighting, or heat— and were victimized then as now by flourishing populations of rats and vermin.

The first tenements designed expressly to provide cheap lodging for working-class families were erected in New York in 1850. Driven by ever-rising land costs, their owners built on every available square inch and up to six stories in height, leaving no space for trees or grass, air or light. Soon entire districts were occupied by such barracks, into which swarmed the immigrant poor and the as yet not wholly segregated blacks, all paying extortionate rents. The profits extracted from such rookeries and from dark, damp basements, leaky garrets, outhouses and stables converted into dwellings, ran from 15 to 30 percent. Landlords then as later refused all pleas to repair or maintain their property and evicted occupants who could not or would not pay in advance.

In 1879 the "dumbbell tenement," so called because of the shape of its floor plan, was introduced as the model housing unit in New York City. Such structures provided fireproof stairways, a toilet at first for every two families, and an outside window for each room until doubling up cut off this limited opening for many. The solid rows of these five- or six-story buildings on 25-foot lots and extending 90 feet to the rear, which quickly degenerated through overcrowding into pesthouses as bad as the old tenements, simply postponed thoroughgoing tenement reform. By 1894 about 39,000 dumbbell tenement houses had been erected in New York City, and nearly half the city's population lived in them, most of their denizens lacking bathtubs, toilets, running water, and backyards.

Although New York's slums were the worst in the nation, wretched conditions prevailed elsewhere as well. Philadelphia constructed small two-story houses instead of tenements for its working-class population, but overcrowding produced the same hideous conditions. Other cities resorted to the wooden "three-decker" apartment building, first introduced in Boston during the 1840s, from where it spread west to Chicago, gaining in numbers per acre and numbers per room in the process.

## Toward the black ghetto

The major antebellum cities of the South all had sizable black populations, the free men among them often living in "proximity and confusion" with whites. Once set free, many plantation Negroes, like western farm boys later on, also headed for town. By 1900, it has been estimated, more than half the black people of Missouri, more than a third of those of Kentucky, lived in urban areas. These states, with Tennessee, by then also had supplied more than a third of Chicago's 30,000 Negroes, who in 1900 made up less than 2 percent of that city's people, compared with nearly 25 percent sixty years later. The older metropolises of New York and Philadelphia, with sizable antebellum Negro populations, counted about 50,000 blacks each in 1900. These cities trailed behind Washington, Baltimore, and New Orleans in numbers, and far behind such other southern cities as Memphis, Atlanta, Savannah, and Shreveport in the proportion of colored to white people. At the same time, while only about 20 percent of whites and blacks alike in the South were urbanized in 1900, almost 70 percent of the Negroes in the Northeast lived and worked in cities.

In the early postbellum decades the black populations of the older cities of the North, as of the South, often shared neighborhoods with whites, and even shared similar occupations. Significant numbers of them rose into the business and professional classes, to which their sons also aspired with success. As white ultraism spread in the South after 1890, the urban Negro's position declined, and "Jim Crow" laws and attitudes hastened segregation in housing and all other aspects of life. In the North at about the same time, as the number of white immigrants soared, the poorer blacks were among the first to be evicted and forced to outlying areas where black business and professional families eventually felt impelled to follow them to hold their trade. In such areas, as the black migration northward gained momentum, conditions worsened for both classes, the better-off Negroes frequently blaming their plight, as one of them put it, on the "worst class [of the] great stream of rural immigrants from the South." "All Negroes are not alike," said another in 1895. "There are various grades of colored people. . . . We are not to be judged by the street loungers and drunkards of our race."

Only housing of the most improvised sort was available to the evicted poor. Such housing bred its own misfortunes, which the cities' more prosperous citizens blamed on the blacks themselves. Stricter segregation, moreover, drew the black worker farther from the limited job opportunities open to him or to her, opportunities which shrank further from the growing competition of the immigrant poor.

Except as members of the "marginal labor reserve" available as strikebreakers, Negro men, prepared only for menial tasks and debarred by unions and other agencies from apprenticeship training, were by-passed as factory workers, one of the most rapidly growing segments of the labor force. It was once a mark of standing among the city rich to have black servants, male and female, as the cavalier planters once had slaves; and Negro men served as coachmen, valets, footmen, chefs. But as time passed, the glamour of such attendants wore off and male black employment declined. Negro nursemaids, housemaids, and other female domestic workers, however, remained in demand, at least until the new immigrants learned enough English to compete

Courtesy George Eastman House

*As many as thirty black families, sharing a single water tap and privy, lived in this alley tenement near Dupont Circle, Washington, D.C. Lewis Hine photograph from his group "Slum Dwellers," 1908.*

with them. Many such Negro women became the major, if not the only, breadwinners of their families, a situation which further undermined male morale and multiplied broken homes.

The proportion of Negro women to men in northern cities reflected their greater economic chances. In New York City around the turn of the century, there were 1000 Negro women to each 800 Negro men. The social worker Mary White Ovington wrote of this situation:

*In their hours of leisure, the surplus women are known to play havoc with their neighbors' sons, even with their neighbors' husbands, for since lack of men makes marriage impossible for about a fifth of New York's colored girls, social disorder results.*

Among "social disorders," illegitimacy ranked high, along with broken homes—heritages, not limited to segregated blacks, of city life in a highly mobile society.

540

Deepening urban segregation did encourage the Negro to develop or expand his own social institutions. Black business enterprises, churches, political clubs, charitable organizations, and similar units grew in number. At the same time, segregation heightened the likelihood of racial strife with other increasingly segregated groups, not least the native white population which deliberately segregated itself. Not enough is known of race riots in northern cities before World War I; but they surely caused widespread property damage; and while the number of victims compared to those killed by lynching in the South appears to have been small, hundreds of persons of both races died in them.

Not until the great migration of rural Negroes north during and after World War I, however, did the ghetto—the district marked off for black housing and hence for black life—take on the rigidity of later decades. "As late as 1910," writes Allan H. Spear in his study of *Black Chicago,* "Negroes were less highly segregated from native whites than were the Italian immigrants."

### The urban elite

The spread of metropolitan and factory-town decay in the postbellum decades depressed many observers, native and foreign alike. The astonishing growth in numbers and wealth among the urban middle and upper classes in the same period did not always lift their spirits. Prosperous merchants and planters of earlier generations had set modest standards of elegance and public virtue on incomes of $10,000 to $20,000 a year. Now, industrial magnates and railroad barons boasted incomes in the millions. So rapid was their ascent to power and privilege that few of them received any training in the social responsibilities of great wealth. Some millionaires like Rockefeller and Carnegie eventually followed the paternalistic pattern by building libraries, universities, research foundations, and other institutions where dividends took the form largely of public esteem. The great majority of the new rich held their investments more closely on a business basis, except for expenditures for "conspicuous consumption," usually dictated by the social ambitions of their wives.

"Conspicuous consumption" reached absurd heights in the cities during the "gay nineties," a characterization drawn from the follies of the rulers of the nation's business even while the business system was sunk in the deepest depression yet encountered. The follies of the rich made piquant newspaper copy that later returned to haunt them. At one party the guests, all on horseback, rode their mounts into a luxurious hotel. At another great dinner, cigarettes rolled in hundred-dollar-bills were passed out to the guests and smoked after the coffee. Harry Lehr staged a memorable dog dinner, at which his friends' dogs were invited to sup on rare dainties. Perhaps the most irritating single event was the notorious Bradley Martin ball, given at a cost of $369,000 during the severe depression winter of 1896-1897. The hostess appeared as Mary Queen of Scots, displaying among her ornaments a massive ruby necklace once worn by Marie Antoinette, and one of the guests, August Belmont, wore a $10,000 suit of steel armor inlaid with gold.

Theodore Roosevelt, then New York's police commissioner, saw all too well how such thoughtless extravagance would arouse the poor of the city, and growled sardonically, "I shall have to protect it by as many police as if it were a strike." Indeed, the indignation aroused by the ball persuaded the Bradley Martins to leave New York and take up permanent residence in England. Yet the extravagances went on.

By 1899 the depression had passed, and on New Year's Day, 1900, the *New York Times* declared in its lead editorial:

*The year 1899 was a year of wonders, a veritable annus mirabilis in business and production. . . . It would be easy to speak of the twelve months just passed as the banner year were we not already confident that the distinction of highest records must presently pass to the year 1900. . . . The outlook on the threshold of the new year is extremely bright.*

J. P. Morgan himself saw the New Year in while sitting isolated, as usual, playing solitaire. Describing the great banker and his family on the eve of the twentieth century and on the eve of his own marriage to Morgan's daughter Louisa, Herbert Satterlee writes:

*Mr. Morgan's house was just where he wanted it to be and it suited his mode of life. . . . He himself was in good health. His friends were nearby. The people in his social world were of his own kind, and the bankers and business men with whom he came into contact had, for the most part, the same standard of ethics and point of view that he himself had. New York was still a friendly, neighborly city and was a pleasant place in which to live.*

A few months later, Morgan built a temporary ballroom to accommodate the 2400 persons invited to Louisa's wedding. Most of the year he spent in Europe where, in the exasperated opinion of Roger Fry, curator of paintings at the Morgan-dominated Metropolitan Museum, he "behaved like a crowned head," going about buying the "gilt-edged securities" of continental art. The decades around the turn of the century, the golden age of millionaire collectors of companies, were also the golden age of millionaire collectors of masterpieces. In these decades, upper Fifth Avenue in New York City was lined by grandiose palaces of the rich that rivaled those of the titled families of Europe. High-priced architects like McKim, Meade, and White studiously reproduced ancient forms in limestone and marble, while their clients decorated the interiors with the sure things of Europe's artistic past and fraudulent reproductions of them.

541

*"Millionaires' Row," Fifth Avenue,
New York City, 1898, looking north, with
the John Jacob Astor mansion in foreground.*

The Byron Collection, Museum of the City of New York

## III   The halting voices of reform

### The humanitarians

Although Mr. Morgan found New York at the turn of the century a "neighborly city" and enjoyed it as such, it must have appeared excessively neighborly and less enjoyable to the 30,000 persons crowded into a

*Labor Day turnout
of the urban middle class on Main Street,
Buffalo, New York, 1900.*

Library of Congress

single New York East Side district of five or six blocks—notorious "District A," which boasted a greater density of population than any similar area anywhere in the world, even India or China. Mr. Morgan could isolate himself from this sore spot. At the same time, a number of urban reformers, philanthropists, and churchmen, moved by moral considerations and sometimes by fear of social revolution, sought to make life more livable for the slum dwellers. A few farsighted planners also tried to bring the country to the city.

The engaging vision of a garden city had been caught in 1858 when Calvert Vaux and the landscape architect Frederick Law Olmsted planned Central Park in New York. Philadelphia's Fairmount Park, opened in 1855, was considerably larger than Central Park, but Olmsted's and Vaux's ingenious and tasteful efforts to accommodate roads, lawns, and buildings to the topography ushered in a new era in landscape design. At first, many people complained that parks were aristocratic, un-American, and unbusinesslike, but this prejudice disappeared in later years. Between 1872 and 1895, Olmsted and his disciples laid out parks in Boston, Washington, Buffalo, and elsewhere. Although parks could hardly transform an industrial metropolis into an Eden, they at least preserved a vestige of nature in a world of iron and stone, and many poor people enjoyed them.

While landscape architects tried to beautify the city, social workers sought to aid the casualties of city life. The traditional view held that poverty and misfortune resulted from personal weakness, but by the 1870s urban reformers realized that the causes of poverty were complex. Illness, death of the breadwinner, low wages, or unemployment clearly made more paupers and criminals than lazi-

542

ness and alcoholism. The first step in poor relief often was simply to keep the distressed alive. During the depression of the 1870s the problem of indigency had grown so vast that private charities working independently could not cope with it. In 1877 Buffalo became the first city to coordinate its relief organizations. A decade later, twenty-five affiliated charities across the country had succeeded in eliminating much of the inefficiency of earlier social agencies.

By swelling the number of those most susceptible to political agitation and discontent, the slums, many believed, intensified the danger of social upheaval. Hoping to narrow the gulf between the privileged and the underprivileged, middle-class reformers opened settlement houses in the poorer districts to offer guidance, recreation, and companionship free of charge.

The idea of the settlement house—to bridge the gap between Disraeli's "two nations," the very rich and the very poor—originated in London in the 1870s. The opening of Toynbee Hall in the East London slums in 1884 provided a model for at least four such houses in the United States. Jane Addams (1860-1935), following a two-year sojourn in Europe beginning in 1887, when she visited Toynbee Hall, became the leader of the settlement movement in America. With her friend Ellen Gates Starr, in 1889 she converted the old Hull mansion in Chicago into a settlement house called Hull House. Women like Jane Addams, the municipal reformer Frederick Howe wrote condescendingly, saw the "city in the light of the home." Jane Addams herself put it differently:

*The settlement [she wrote] is an attempt to relieve . . . the overaccumulation at one end of society and the destitution at the other; but it assumes that this overaccumulation and destitution is most sorely felt in the things that pertain to social and educational advantages. It must be grounded in a philosophy . . . which will not waver when the race happens to be represented by a drunken woman or an idiot boy.*

In Boston, Cleveland, Pittsburgh, and elsewhere, college men and women soon put Jane Addams's philosophy to work. They formed clubs for boys and societies for wayward girls, transformed settlement houses into a combination day nursery, gymnasium, and employment bureau, and campaigned resolutely for improved sanitary regulations, better housing, and penal reform.

The scientific approach to social welfare did not slow down the crusade against intemperance and the saloon. On the contrary, this movement gathered greater momentum than ever after the heavy-drinking years of the Civil War. The Prohibition party, which ran its first national ticket in 1872, proved ineffective against the saloon interests and their stalwarts in both major parties. But a powerful new organization took shape in 1874 with the founding of the Women's Christian Temperance Union. Led by Frances E. Willard, a former educator whose creed was "No sectarianism in religion, no sectionalism in politics, no sex in citizenship," the WCTU propagandized against liquor and the people who made and sold it. Its stated policy was "mental suasion for the man who thinks and moral suasion for the man who drinks, but legal suasion for the drunkard-maker." No "suasion" seemed to work, however, for by 1898 only five states— Maine, New Hampshire, Vermont, Kansas, and North Dakota—were legally dry.

The women in the forefront of the temperance campaign were also to be found at the head of the campaign for women's suffrage, believed by many to be essential to the correction by legislation of all the growing evils of urban life. But this campaign also had to wait for fruition until women seemed to prove their mettle during World War I.

### The churches

The response of the churches to slums and poverty was at first halting and indecisive, for few ministers had any knowledge of lower-class life. When workingmen's demands for shorter hours and for government regulation of working conditions grew loud, one church leader reminded them: "Whatever you suffer here from injustice of others will turn to your account hereafter. Be quiet." But such advice could not withstand the exposés of urban and industrial conditions, and during the 1870s the churches began to modify their stand.

The Social Gospel movement, which burgeoned during the last quarter of the nineteenth century, was organized by socially conscious ministers of various denominations and rested on the conviction that man is born "in a sinful society, which fact is the cause of deep evil." Christ, the Social Gospelers asserted, came to "establish a new environment" as well as "to save rebellious men." Hence all Christians ought to be social reformers.

Some liberal clergymen went no farther than to advocate moderate reforms in wages, housing, and working conditions. The more radical, impatient with efforts to preserve the economic status quo, insisted that the nation's business system be reformed from the bottom up. Ministers like Washington Gladden, R. Heber Newton, Henry Codman Potter, and Walter Rauschenbusch boldly defended labor unions and wrote and preached against laissez-faire. Gladden's *Applied Christianity* (1886) and Newton's *The Morals of Trade* (1876) expressed the Social Gospel ideal that Christian solutions existed for all social problems. By the 1880s, theological seminaries were offering courses in social Christianity and social ethics.

Despite the manifest social need, the Social Gospel movement was confined to a minority of intellectuals. In general, churches like the Baptist and Methodist, whose membership consisted largely of artisans, shopkeepers, and farmers, preferred to keep the old emphasis on individual responsibility for sin. The fact that many of the newly rich were Baptist and Methodist laymen (John D. Rockefeller was a prominent Baptist elder, Daniel Drew a fervent Methodist) may also help to explain why their churches did not quarrel with society as they found it. Indeed, most of the influential American clergymen remained orthodox in economics even when liberal in theology.

Henry Ward Beecher (1813–1887), one of the most celebrated ministers of his day, preached a liberal theology congenial to his wealthy Brooklyn congregation. He also sanctified the cult of business success. Beecher condemned the eight-hour day, insisted that poverty was a sign of sin, and urged that strikers be put down with violence if necessary. Commenting in 1877 on the sharp wage cuts imposed on railroad workers, he observed:

> It is said that a dollar a day is not enough for a wife and five or six children. No, not if the man smokes or drinks beer. . . . But is not a dollar a day enough to buy bread with? Water costs nothing; and a man who cannot live on bread is not fit to live. What is the use of a civilization that simply makes men incompetent to live under the conditions which exist.

These sentiments were so deeply appreciated by Beecher's national following that not even the scandalous stories of his adulterous practices brought out in the Beecher-Tilton divorce trial in 1875 could extinguish the intense loyalty of his parishioners. The 112-day trial produced over a million words of testimony, providing titillating reading for millions. The case finally ended with a hung jury, and Beecher's Plymouth Church congregation considered that their beloved minister had been vindicated. But the country as a whole reached no such conclusion. The popular Kentucky editor "Marse Henry" Watterson labeled America's most influential clergyman "a dunghill covered with flowers."

Some Protestant ministers who, like Beecher, thought that the workingman could do without beer if not without bread, also thought he could do without God. That "the classes which are eminently nonintelligent or nonrespectable" should be "nonchurchgoers," said one, might be taken for granted. Others, however, had grown deeply apprehensive about the "unchurched masses," and sought ways to reclaim them. One device was the revival meeting where itinerant evangelists ignored economic and political issues and preached the "old-time" religion.

Among the most effective of the evangelists was Dwight L. Moody. In 1870 this former shoe salesman from Boston teamed up with the singer Ira D. Sankey to launch a mighty campaign for saving souls. Moody preached a simple but powerful message: abandon "the cold formalism that has crept into the Church of God" and persevere for Christ. Sankey chanted the tender old hymns "Saved by Grace," "Almost Persuaded," and "Safe in the Arms of Jesus" with such compelling sweetness that thousands were melted into grace. From Chicago, where Moody had evangelized successfully in "Little Hell" on the North Side, Moody and Sankey carried the question "Are you a Christian?" to England. Having silenced the scoffers there, they returned to every large city in the United States by storm. The Chicago Bible Institute for Home and Foreign Missions, founded in 1899, was only one of many monuments erected to them.

The evangelist spirit was more tangibly expressed in the Young Men's Christian Association, founded as the American offshoot of an English society in 1851, and the Young Women's Christian Association, founded in 1858. Both organizations dedicated themselves to "the physical, mental, social, and spiritual benefit" of men and women everywhere. By 1897 the YMCA had 263,298 members in the United States and the YWCA about 35,000. Another importation from England was the Salvation Army, organized by a Wesleyan Methodist, "General" William Booth. This army of Christians helped feed and shelter urban unfortunates. After the first American branch was opened in 1880, the Salvation Army's "slum brigades" marched out into the tenement areas and skid rows and brought comfort and relief to the neglected poor.

Better-off city dwellers, owing, it was sometimes suggested, to the hectic pace of urban living, sought another sort of spiritual balm— that provided by a remarkable woman, Mrs. Mary Baker Eddy. Her book *Science and Health* (1875) set forth the basic doctrines of the Church of Christ, Scientist, a sect that numbered 35,000 by 1900.

In brief, Mrs. Eddy taught that "Disease is caused by the mind alone" and that "Christian Science," the wisdom of God revealed to man by His Son Jesus Christ, alone could overcome it. "Mind," she boldly wrote, "constructs the body, and with its own materials instead of matter; hence no broken bones or dislocations can occur." Her message appealed with particular force to those Americans for whom science had come to have magical qualities.

The belated social activities of the dominant Protestant churches hardly touched the millions of Catholics in the United States—12 million by 1900, with millions more on the way—largely concentrated in the cities, and especially among the city poor. The Catholic clergy, unlike the Protestants, traditionally addressed themselves to the needs of the poor. Their organized efforts in America began in 1858 when Isaac T. Hecker, a Catholic convert formerly a member of the Brook Farm community, organized the Paulist Fathers to serve the impoverished New York Irish. After the Civil War, the Roman Catholic church enlarged its philanthropic activities and in its schools carried on an effective program to Americanize Catholic immigrants.

Roman Catholic success with the urban masses led certain Protestant leaders to suspect that the priests were plotting to capture the country, and it was not long before deep anti-Catholic fears, latent since the days of the Know-Nothings of the 1850s, surfaced once more. The American Protective Association, a secret society formed in 1887 to exploit the bigotry of the rural Middle West against the influence of Roman Catholicism in labor and politics, capitalized on these fears. The APA warned that a concealed army of 700,000 papal soldiers was ready to take over the government, even though at this very time Catholic leaders like Cardinal James Gibbons of Baltimore and Archbishop John Ireland of St. Paul were championing political democracy and accepting the separation of church and state. The irony of APA activities was that they appealed to farmers while the Catholics swarmed in the cities. APA leaders realized this; but when they sought to move into the cities, they attracted few men of stature and their organization quickly lost its impetus.

Protestant fears that the Catholic church might take possession of the nation, nevertheless, gradually stirred the Protestant clergy to imitate Catholic methods in the cities. "Too long," a Methodist Conference declared, "has Rome been allowed a practical monopoly of the humanitarian agencies of religion." During the post–Civil War decades, sectarian isolation gave way to nondenominational mission societies. The "institutional church" made its appearance—replete with club rooms, gymnasiums, youth organizations, and women's societies—in an effort to reach hitherto neglected slum dwellers.

## IV   Editors and architects

### Urban journalism

Even before the Civil War, writers and editors had discovered that crusades against civic corruption or private iniquity not only improved the moral tone of the public but also paid off in sales. In 1858 *Frank Leslie's Illustrated Newspaper* conducted a sensational campaign against New York milk producers accused of selling milk from diseased herds and succeeded in arousing such a public clamor that the state legislature in 1861 was forced to prohibit the sale of milk from cows nourished on the waste products of distilleries. A decade later, Thomas Nast's assaults on the Tweed Ring in *Harper's Weekly* trebled the *Weekly's* circulation. Henry and Charles Francis Adams's revelations in the *North American Review* of Jay Gould's financial piracies and W. T. Stead's lurid reports of Chicago wickedness in *If Christ Came to Chicago!* (1894) were other highly moral testaments that evoked a wide response.

Civic vice gave such a jolt to circulation that newspaper editors began to invent "causes" or to feature crime. Recent arrivals from the farm were particularly responsive to stories that fed their suspicions of life in the "wicked city." Reporters who were able to "crash" the lavish entertainments of the rich and to describe them from the inside or who could draw a tear by writing authentic reports of the sordid experiences of the poor brought a new individuality and a new glamour to newspaper careers. The new methods helped to enlarge daily newspaper circulation from 2.8 million in 1870 to 24 million in 1899. Increased revenue from subscriptions and sales, and above all from advertising, helped free editors from political pressure and enabled them to become powerful manipulators of public opinion.

Joseph Pulitzer, owner of the *St. Louis Post-Dispatch* and later of the *World* in New York City, exemplified the new type of publisher. Combining the crudest sensationalism with effective exposés, the *World* lived up to Pulitzer's promise to publish a "journal that is not only cheap but bright, not only bright but large, not only large but truly democratic that will expose all fraud and sham, fight all public evils and abuses." The *World* exploited all the inventions that were revolutionizing publishing in this period: improved newsprint made from wood pulp, the Linotype machine (1886), typewriters, telephones, and the telegraph. These improvements, put to sound use in spreading editorial coups, produced startling rises in circulation—from 20,000 to 40,000 within two months after Pulitzer took over in May 1883; 100,000 by the fall of 1884; and 250,000 by 1886.

Pulitzer's methods were quickly copied by publishers in other large cities and by ruthless competitors in New York. William Randolph Hearst, fresh from Harvard and backed by his father's gold-mining millions, even outdid Pulitzer in sensationalism in his *New York Journal.* One result of the fierce newspaper rivalry was "yellow journalism," a name derived from the yellow ink first used by Pulitzer in comics but soon made to stand for the lurid publishing he promoted. Conservative editors were quick to criticize yellow journalism, but the only effective answer was to produce a good newspaper that sold widely without it. Adolph S. Ochs proved that this could be done when he took over the moribund *New York Times* in 1896, cut its price to a penny, and revived its circulation by full and trustworthy coverage of foreign and domestic news.

When Congress, by an act of March 3, 1879, granted low postal rates to magazines, their circulation grew even more spectacularly than that of newspapers. *McCall's* (1870), *Popular Science* (1872), *Woman's Home Companion* (1873), *Cosmopolitan* (1886), *Collier's* (1888), and *Vogue* (1892) were only a few of the magazines that benefited from the new postal act. By and large, these publications, as well as old-established monthlies like *Harper's*, *The Atlantic*, *Scribner's*, and *The Century*, appealed to the literary tastes and the moral code of the middle-class urban reader. In the last decade of the century, magazines became more sensational in their methods and gave more attention to controversial current issues—a tendency that foreshadowed the muckraking magazines of the Progressive era. New techniques in printing and heavier subsidies from advertisers helped publishers lower magazine prices, so that by 1900, with the additional benefit of low mailing costs, hundreds of thousands of families could subscribe annually.

Cyrus H. K. Curtis's *Ladies' Home Journal*, founded in 1883, became the most spectacular magazine success, reaching a million in circulation by 1900. His brilliant editor, Edward Bok, filled the *Journal* with features designed to draw feminine readers avid for advice on how to bring up their children, decorate their homes, and preserve their health. Bok bought the fiction of the most popular American and English writers, and paid them well for their stories. Soon this "monthly Bible of the American home" had become a national force

which, among other accomplishments, influenced American domestic architecture, led a campaign to force municipal authorities to clean up their cities, and pioneered in the crusade against patent medicines.

### The new urban architecture

Much has been made of the ignorance and vulgar display of the "tastemakers" of the Gilded Age. We hear of the millionaire steel baron who, learning of a famous artist named Copley, told his secretary to get in touch with him "to paint the kids." Then there is the caricature of Henry C. Frick seated on his Renaissance throne under a baldacchino and immersed in a copy of the *Saturday Evening Post*. Anecdotes like these reveal the tastelessness of the nouveau riche, but they do not explain the bad architecture and painting of the Gilded Age or the failure of its genteel critics to appreciate the possibilities of art in an industrial era.

Realistic writers pictured the modern city as a kind of hell. The Chicago heroine of Hamlin Garland's *Rose of Dutcher's Coolly* (1895)

*looked out across a stretch of roofs, heaped and humped into mountainous masses, blurred and blent and made appalling by smoke and plumes of steam. A scene as desolate as a burnt-out volcano—a jumble of hot bricks, jagged cave-spouts, gas-vomiting chimneys, spiked railings, glass skylights, and lofty spires, a hideous and horrible stretch of stone and mortar, cracked and seamed into streets. It had no limits and it palpitated under the hot September sun, boundless and savage. At the bottom of the crevasses men and women speckled the pavement like minute larvae.*

Henry James, returning to New York City at the turn of the century after many years abroad, found everything "impudently new." He was struck by the "multitudinous sky-scrapers standing up to view, from the water, like extravagant pins in a cushion already overplanted." Over old Trinity Church a "vast money-making structure" loomed "horribly . . . with an insolent cliff-like sublimity." James clearly preferred the monuments of Europe.

And yet, in spite of all its ugliness and imitativeness, the Gilded Age saw some striking gains in American building. It took a different kind of imagination from that which James possessed to discover the originality and beauty in America's bridges, railroad stations, grain elevators, viaducts, warehouses, and office buildings. Brooklyn Bridge, conceived by John Roebling in 1869 and erected by his son Washington between 1869 and 1883, performed a practical function. It connected Manhattan Island with Long Island, carried tremendous loads, and eased ferryboat congestion. At the same time, its unadorned steel simplicity was breathtaking.

Many of the skyscrapers of the period revealed a similar functional beauty, fulfilling what a pioneer Chicago architect called the "ideals of modern business life, simplicity, stability, breadth, dignity." High ground rents made the maximum use of space in business districts imperative, and the vertical, soaring office building seemed to escape from the city's limited dimensions. Such buildings were made possible by the electric elevator, perfected in the 1880s, and by cheap steel, which replaced the customary bulky masonry walls or stone columns of business buildings with a light, strong "cage." James Bogardus, a New York architect, had designed buildings with supporting iron columns in 1847, but it was not until the 1860s that the needs of industrial America forced even architectural aesthetes, trained to regard iron as beneath the dignity of the artist, to work in steel and glass.

Henry Hobson Richardson (1838–1886), a great architectural innovator, borrowed boldly from traditional forms in designing his railroad stations, warehouses, and office buildings, but he stamped his personality on every structure. Richardson never promised that a finished building would conform to a client's "ideas of beauty and taste," but no businessman could quarrel with the huge seven-story granite Wholesale Store he designed in 1885 for the Chicago merchant Marshall Field. "Four-square and brown, it stands," wrote Richardson's contemporary, the architect Louis Sullivan, "in physical fact a monument to trade, to the organized commercial spirit, to the power and progress of the age, to the strength and resource of individuality and force of character."

Richardson, an audacious experimenter in masonry construction, died before steel-frame construction came into general use. But under his influence a group of architects—men like John W. Root, Daniel Burnham, William L. Jenney, and (in his early designs) Louis Sullivan—who helped rebuild Chicago after the fire of 1871, perfected the skyscraper and combined the beautiful and the purposeful in an exciting manner. City planning, or its lack, permitted the skyscraper to turn streets into canyons, shut out light and air, increase congestion. But at its best the building itself embodied what Horatio Greenough many years before had called "the principle of unflinching adaptation of forms to function."

### The dream city

In 1876 a centennial exposition at Philadelphia had convinced the world of America's technological, if not her artistic, maturity. "It is still in these things of iron and steel," William Dean Howells wrote then "that the national genius most freely speaks; by and by the inspired marbles, the breathing canvases, the great literature."

The World's Columbian Exposition, held in Chicago from May to October in 1893, did not fulfill Howells's prophecy, but the 21 million Americans who visited it did catch a glimpse of a white city rising miraculously from the shores of Lake Michigan. The Exposition is no longer regarded as the architectural awakening many once thought it. Nevertheless, as one observer noted, it was "the climacteric expression of America's existence."

The idea of a world's fair to commemorate the discovery of America was conceived by Congress in 1889. Washington, St. Louis, and New York all sought the privilege of housing the fair, and New York was so certain of success that investors actually bought up unoccupied land north of Central Park to serve as a site. But the Republican-dominated Congress, determined that the Tammany Democratic machine would get no such plum, awarded the honor to Chicago. Her enterprising business leaders raised the $10 million required by Congress, hired artists and designers to transform a marshland into a garden, and erected a temporary city of white plaster of Paris. An army of architects and others worked out the plans for housing more than 65,000 foreign and domestic exhibits, and a national commission representing the states joined forces with a local Chicago committee to direct the mammoth proceedings. The total cost of the Exposition came to approximately $60 million.

The landscape designer Frederick Law Olmsted and his assistant, Henry Codman, scored a brilliant success in laying out the grounds, but even their skill could not transform the Exposition into an artistic triumph. Two Chicagoans, John W. Root and Daniel H. Burnham, had been named to direct the construction of the buildings. But the sturdy Root, who, in the Richardson tradition, contemplated structures that suggested the purpose for which they were designed, died during the planning stage. A group of eastern classicists, dominated by Richard Morris Hunt and the (by this time) conservative firm of McKim, Mead, and White took over. They made a specious classicism the motif of the Exposition, and its glittering theatricality appalled sensitive observers. Only Louis Sullivan's Transportation Building broke with the past. The 9000 paintings hung in the Art Palace, the murals that glorified the arts and sciences, and the monumental sculpture that loomed everywhere showed hardly a trace of originality or a hint of the vital new art flourishing abroad. The classical buildings of the Court of Honor were destined to have a pernicious influence on the untutored American imagination and to produce a dismal progeny of pillared banks, town halls, and railroad stations.

On the positive side, the Exposition illustrated the virtues of planning, of unity, and of magnitude, a lesson that was not to be ignored. Howells rightly noted that the White City's importance lay not in its architectural banalities but in the idea of design it embodied, "the effect of a principle, and not the scraggling and shapeless accretion of incident." Critics might disagree about the artistic merits of the Exposition, but on one further point there was no dissent: The White City was an object lesson in how a well-managed city ought to be administered for the pleasure and convenience of its inhabitants. An electrified railway and electrically powered boats on the lagoons efficiently transported the hundreds of thousands of visitors. Sanitation squads cleaned up the day's debris every night, and adequate rest rooms were provided. Polite and considerate "Columbian Guards" suggested how a model police force should conduct itself. In contrast to Chicago proper, a jungle of disorder lying outside the gates of the Exposition, the White City was managed by the ablest men in Chicago. Inside, one visitor wrote, a man "could feel for once in his life that he was not liable to be snubbed by the police, nor bullied by car-conductors, nor brow-beaten by salesmen."

The Exposition began at the outset of a severe depression and ended as the depression deepened. Even before it closed, the temporary buildings had cracked and the laths had begun to show beneath the plaster.

## For further reading

Many of the books cited for Chapter Nineteen help put the subject of nineteenth-century urbanization in the context of the more general process of industrialization. The many studies of the decay of the city in our own time help illuminate some of the failures of the past.

Blake McKelvey, *The Urbanization of America 1860-1915* (1963), is a scholarly modern survey, rich in bibliography. C. M. Green, *American Cities in the Growth of the Nation* (1957), discusses specific cities and regions, as does George Leighton, *Five Cities: The Story of Their Youth and Age* (1939). A. M. Schlesinger, *The Rise of the City 1878-1898* (1933), touches on many social aspects of city living that have escaped more modern work. Useful studies of individual cities include C. M. Green, *Holyoke, Massachusetts* (1939), "a case study of the industrial revolution in America," as the subtitle says, and her two volumes on Washington, D.C., *Village and Capital 1800-1878* (1962) and *Capital City 1879-1950* (1963); B. L. Pierce, *A History of Chicago* (3 vols., 1937-1957), which carries the story to 1893 and may be supplemented by Lloyd Lewis and H. J. Smith, *Chicago: The History of Its Reputation* (1929); Lloyd Morris, *Incredible New York: High Life and Low Life in the Past 100 Years* (1951); and S. B. Warner, Jr., *The Private City: Philadelphia in Three Periods of its Growth* (1968).

Oscar Handlin, *The Uprooted* (1951), provides an excellent introduction to the urban immigrant. Much illuminating information will be found in the *Report of the Industrial Commission (1900-1902)*, especially in vol. 15. The work of a later federal commission, appointed in 1907, is summarized in J. W. Jenks and W. J. Lauck, *The Immigration Problem* (1912). The assumptions and findings of this commission are attacked, with much interesting argument, in I. A. Hourwich, *Immigration and Labor* (1912). P. U. Kellogg, ed., *The Pittsburgh Survey* (6 vols., 1910-1914), provides a thoroughgoing analysis of life in the steel city and its environs. More recent studies of the industrial side of city life include D. B. Cole, *Immigrant City: Lawrence, Massachusetts 1845-1921* (1963); and Gerd Korman, *Industrialization, Immigrants and Americanizers, The View from Milwaukee 1866-1921* (1967). W. C. Smith, *Americans in the Making: The Natural History of the Assimilation of Immigrants* (1939), is excellent. For some chinks in the process see Elin Anderson, *We Americans: A Study of Cleavage in an American City* (1937).

Illuminating introductions to the Negro in northern cities late in the nineteenth century will be found in such works as Robert Weaver, *The Negro Ghetto* (1948); St. Clair Drake and H. R. Cayton, *Black Metropolis* (1945), on Chicago; Allan H. Spear, *Black Chicago, The Making of a Negro Ghetto 1890-1920* (1967); and Gilbert Osofsky, *Harlem, The Making of a Ghetto, Negro New York 1890-1930* (1965).

Dixon Wecter, *The Saga of American Society, A Record of Social Aspiration 1607-1937* (1937), is a good introduction to the urban life of the elite. Ward McAllister, *Society as I Have Found It* (1890), is by the high factotum of the aspiring matrons of the day.

James Bryce, *The American Commonwealth* (2 vols.,

1888), offers an outstanding contemporary critique of city government. Lincoln Steffens, *The Shame of the Cities* (1904), is masterly, as are the chapters based on it in his *Autobiography* (1931). Z. L. Miller, *Boss Cox's Cincinnati* (1968), is a sophisticated modern study. On Tweed, see D. T. Lynch, *"Boss" Tweed, The Story of a Grim Generation* (1927). Other recommended works include W. B. Munro, *The Government of American Cities* (1913), and C. W. Patton, *The Battle for Municipal Reform: Mobilization and Attack 1875-1900* (1940). On urban public transportation and other utilities, see H. C. Passer, *The Electrical Manufacturers 1875-1900* (1953); and S. B. Warner, Jr., *Streetcar Suburbs* (1962).

R. H. Bremner, *From the Depths, The Discovery of Poverty in the United States* (1956), is outstanding. Robert Hunter, *Poverty* (1904), is an excellent pioneering study. Jacob Riis, *How The Other Half Lives* (1890), and *The Battle with the Slums* (1902), are famous contemporary accounts. James Ford, *Slums and Housing* (2 vols., 1936), is the standard study. The classic introduction to the settlement house movement is Jane Addams, *Forty Years at Hull House* (1935).

R. D. Cross, ed., *The Church and the City* (1967), offers a broad view of the church's part in urban reform. See also A. I. Abell, *The Urban Impact upon American Protestantism, 1865-1900* (1943), and *American Catholicism and Social Action* (1960); and Henry May, *Protestant Churches and Industrial America* (1949). The Social Gospel movement is the theme of C. H. Hopkins, *The Rise of the Social Gospel in American Protestantism, 1865-1915* (1940). Beecher's extraordinary career is sardonically chronicled in Paxton Hibben, *Henry Ward Beecher* (1927). T. L. Smith, *Revivalism and Social Reform in Mid-Nineteenth-Century America* (1957), shows the early penetration of revivalism in the cities. On the role of the Catholic church, in addition to Abell, above, see R. D. Cross, *The Emergence of Liberal Catholicism in America* (1967). The best treatment of anti-Catholic sentiment is in John Higham, *Strangers in the Land* (1955).

On the press, see F. L. Mott, *American Journalism* (1941), and *A History of American Magazines 1885-1905* (1957). On architecture, illuminating studies include Lewis Mumford, *Sticks and Stones* (1924), and *The Brown Decades* (1931); Wayne Andrews, *Architecture, Ambition, and Americans* (1955); and Christopher Tunnard and H. H. Reed, *American Skyline: The Growth and Form of our Cities and Towns* (1955). On the Exposition of 1893, see O. W. Larkin, *Art and Life in America* (1949).

# Pride and portents

*We lie midway between two old worlds and ought to absorb*
*the wealth and power of both. . . . We have been all along cringing before European*
*modes of thought and social views and should now begin to walk erect.*
*(Walcott Gibbs to F. L. Olmsted, November 6, 1862)*

*We see the principle of nationality under democratic forms asserting itself*
*with a grandeur of military strength, a unity of political counsel,*
*a dignity of moral power, before which the empires of Caesar, of Charlemagne*
*and of Napoleon dwindle into insignificance.*
*(The Nation, 1865)*

*Those whose faith in the American people carried them hopefully through*
*the long contest with slavery will not be daunted before many minor complexities*
*of Chinese immigrants or railway brigands or enfranchised women.*
*(Thomas Wentworth Higginson, Atlantic Essays, 1870)*

*We see by the vividest of examples what an absolute savage and pirate*
*the passion of military conquest always is, and how the only safeguard against*
*the crimes to which it will infallibly drag the nation that gives*
*way to it is to keep it chained for ever.*
*(William James in the Boston Evening Transcript, March 1, 1899)*

*The United States stands out as preeminently the "Land of Contrasts"*
*—the land of stark, staring, and stimulating inconsistency;*
*at once the home of enlightenment and the happy hunting ground of the charlatan*
*and the quack. . . . Always the land*
*of promise, but not invariably the land of performance.*
*(J. F. Muirhead, The Land of Contrasts, 1898)*

"LIBERTY ENLIGHTENING THE WORLD": preliminary sketch by Auguste Bertholdi,
1875. (The New-York Historical Society, New York City)

(Left) Negroes observing statue of "THE FREED SLAVE" at the Centennial Exposition in Philadelphia, 1876. (Right) "THE GREAT CORLISS ENGINE" in Machinery Hall at the Centennial Exposition. (Both, The New-York Historical Society, New York City)

Without doubt social differences
are facts, not fancies
and cannot be swept aside;
but they hardly need to be looked
upon as excuses for downright
meanness and incivility.
(W. E. B. Du Bois,
The Philadelphia Negro, 1899)

Yes, it is still in these
things of iron and steel that
the national genius most freely
speaks; by and by
the inspired marbles,
the breathing canvases, the great
literature; for the present
America is voluble
in the strong metals
and their infinite uses.
(W. D. Howells
on the Corliss engine, 1876)

Flames escaping
from drills, dazzling, crackling
motors, silent and dancing
rhythms of rods and pistons—
all these beat the cadences
of a new march. . . .
Once more man attempts
to understand man, in the midst
of force itself.
(Elie Faure on Rivera's
Detroit murals, April 1934)

Diego Rivera mural, "PART PRODUCTION AND ASSEMBLY OF MOTORS," 1934. (From the collection of The Detroit Institute of Arts, gift of Edsel B. Ford)

SOCIETY LADIES LUNCHING AT DELMONICO'S, New York City, 1902. (The Byron Collection, Museum of the City of New York)

*She is petted, and is permitted, or even*
*required, to consume largely and*
*conspicuously. . . . She is exempted, or*
*debarred, from vulgarly useful employment—*
*in order to perform leisure*
*vicariously for the good repute*
*of her natural (pecuniary) guardian.*
*(Thorstein Veblen,*
The Theory of the Leisure Class, *1899)*

*But where the ablest strength engages*
*with idealistic enthusiasm in the service*
*of the national economic problems, the nation*
*rewards what people do as done*
*in the name of civilization, and the love*
*of fame and work together spur them on more*
*than the material gain which they will get.*
*(Hugo Munsterberg,* The Americans, *1914)*

LEADERS OF FINANCE, THE BAR, AND SCHOLARSHIP comprising the Board of Directors of the Boston Public Library, 1894. (Library of Congress)

*It is impossible not to feel warmed, cheered, invigorated*
*by the sense of such material well-being all around one, impossible*
*not to be infected by the buoyancy and hopefulness*
*of the people. The wretchedness of Europe lies far behind;*
*the weight of its problems seems lifted from the mind.*
*(James Bryce,* The American Commonwealth, *1891)*

1776    1803

MIDDLE-CLASS RELAXATION, one of a series of sketches by C. S. Reinhart in *Harper's Magazine,* 1886. (New York Public Library)

*The typical immigrant is a European*
*peasant, whose moral*
*and religious training has been meager*
*or false, and whose ideas*
*of life are low.*
*(Josiah Strong,* Our Country: Its Possible
Future and Present Crisis, *1885)*

*Those dark and deadly dens*
*in which the family ideal was tortured*
*to death, and character*
*was smothered; in which children*
*were "damned*
*rather than born" into the world.*
*(Jacob A. Riis,*
The Battle with the Slum, *1900)*

IMMIGRANTS TO AMERICA, on S.S. *Westernland* about 1890, their faces indicating high hopes. (Museum of the City of New York)

"FIVE CENTS A SPOT"—Jacob A. Riis photograph of lodgers in a Bayard Street tenement, New York City, about 1890. (The Jacob A. Riis Collection, Museum of the City of New York)

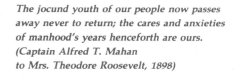

(Above) EXPLODING AMERICAN WORLDWIDE AMBITIONS, picked up in the French magazine *Le Rire* from *Life*, 1899. (Thames & Hudson, London)

(Right) THE CIVILIZER: TR and the navy implementing the "Roosevelt Corollary" in Latin America. *(New York Herald)*

*The jocund youth of our people now passes*
*away never to return; the cares and anxieties*
*of manhood's years henceforth are ours.*
*(Captain Alfred T. Mahan*
*to Mrs. Theodore Roosevelt, 1898)*

*We have invited our clean young men*
*to shoulder a discredited musket and do bandits'*
*work under a flag which bandits have been*
*accustomed to fear, not to follow;*
*we have debauched America's honor and blackened*
*her face before the world.*
*(Mark Twain, "To the Person Sitting*
*in Darkness," 1901)*

*Wrongdoing will only be stopped*
*by men who are brave as well as just . . .*
*who shrink from no hazard, not even the final*
*hazard of war, if necessary in order*
*to serve the great cause of righteousness.*
*(Theodore Roosevelt*
*to S. T. Dutton, November 24, 1915)*

(Center) CAPTURED FILIPINO GUERRILLAS, 1900. (Library of Congress)

(Right) AMERICANS IN PARIS, early in World War I, who volunteered to fight with the French, shown here off to training camp. (Paul Thompson photo, PHOTOWORLD)

# MINDS IN TRANSITION

In the realm of the mind, as in business and politics during the postwar decades, the consolidation of institutions, people, and purpose on a vast national scale became the dominant theme in American life. In the 1820s, President John Quincy Adams had offered a vision of national enterprise on all levels of endeavor to Congress and the public; but it passed harmlessly over the heads of the leaders of that age. Fifty years later the country, riven by civil war yet successfully reunited, became more receptive to ideas of nationhood. Technological advances in industry and communication, drawing upon transcontinental resources and markets, helped support and validate such ideas. The consciousness of power arising from all of these circumstances together also fed the idea of nationalism. Only a united America, when the time came, would be in a position to compete with the imperialist countries of the world for domination of far-off lands.

Even in the midst of the Civil War, a number of northern intellectuals called for a powerful and purposeful nation to supplant the "federation of loosely bound republics" so susceptible to ideas of secession.

*We need, in fine [one of them declared], a national policy which shall combine to a greater degree than any country has ever witnessed—a degree only possible in a strongly based republic—private enterprise and public cooperation with it. We have as a nation thus far avoided looking the great rising social problems of the age directly in the face. . . . But the day has come when, to maintain itself as a real republic, our Government must expand to suit the growing wants of the times. . . . We are passing through one of those* crises of expansion *for which no wisdom of the fathers of our Constitution could exactly provide.*

As the sectional South had feared, Union victory in the Civil War, among other events, gave great leverage to the proponents of "central direction" and the consolidated state. They called now for national universities, for an equivalent of West Point for civil servants, for a national academy of literature and art—in short, for institutions through which a national intelligentsia could enlarge its social role and social influence.

Great educators and editors of the Gilded Age, as we have seen in Chapter Nineteen, commended laissez-faire, economists and sociologists extolled the laws of competition, and popular ministers praised moneymaking as the highest form of public service. These defenders of economic orthodoxy drew on every realm of belief and knowledge to support their arguments, adapting even the new Darwinian ideas, so radical in many of their implications, to their conservative purposes. Yet a growing number of respected critics had begun to question and condemn business values and performance as indifferent if not inimical to the national interest. They also challenged the ideas of the Social Darwinists who, often independently of the national business community, had given a scientific gloss to its selfish ends. Many such critics became associated with the consolidated intellectual organizations formed by the postwar generation—for example, the American Historical Association (1884), the American Economic Association (1885), the American Psychological Association (1892)—to make an independent assessment of the changing nature of American civilization and to give an independent impetus to the direction it might henceforth take. Their work had a lasting impact on such twentieth-century developments as the Progressive Movement, the New Deal, and the later rationalizations of military power around the world.

## I  "Survival of the fittest" and scientific dissent

### Social Darwinism

When Charles Darwin published *The Origin of Species* in 1859, the age of the earth, the process of its formation, and the origins of its denizens had long been discussed by naturalists and other savants, but none reached such firm conclusions buttressed with such convincing evidence. Darwin argued that the species of life all around us, far from having been created by separate acts of God in seven days, had gradually evolved, over millions of years, out of lower orders of life through the operation of the principle of "natural selection." According to Darwin, all forms of life were engaged in an unceasing "struggle for existence" in a constantly changing natural environment. Although some species died, the fittest had lived—those whose physical adaptations had enabled them to survive under changing conditions—and had passed on to their offspring their favorable characteristics. Over long ages of time, cumulative adaptations had produced entirely new species, including mankind.

Darwin's idea outraged Biblical fundamentalists and offended some leading scientists as well, among them Louis Agassiz of Harvard. More remarkable, however, was the readiness of Americans to embrace the new views. Darwin's popularizers in the United States—men like the Harvard botanist Asa Gray and the historian and lecturer John Fiske—helped out. Such men found nothing antireligious in the belief that man was the product of a long evolutionary process. The Darwinian, said Fiske, "sees that in the deadly struggle for existence which has raged through aeons of time, the whole creation has been groaning and travailing together in order to bring forth that last consummate specimen of God's handiwork, the Human Soul."

But it remained for the English philosopher Herbert Spencer to reconcile scientific Darwinism with everyday American optimism. His "synthetic philosophy," as he called it, explained the new biology in moral terms easily appropriated by journalists and other publicists. The evolutionary process, he said, culminated in a state of existence where "evil and immorality must disappear" and a kind of genetically determined altruism prevail. For God, Spencer substituted the "Unknowable," thereby satisfying those many Americans who no longer interpreted the Bible literally yet clung to their faith in a supernatural agency.

By 1900 about 350,000 copies of Spencer's books had been sold in America, a fantastically high figure for sociological and philosophical works. Devoted disciples like Fiske and Edward Livingston Youmans spread the word further through magazine articles, popular books, and lectures. Harvard in 1869 and Yale, Johns Hopkins, and other universities in the 1870s adopted the Spencerian synthesis in teaching religion as well as biological and social sciences. Even the clergy was not immune.

In the 1880s, Henry Ward Beecher pronounced himself "a cordial Christian evolutionist," and acknowledged Spencer as his intellectual foster-father of many years standing. "Men have not fallen as a race," Beecher reminded his Brooklyn congregation, "Men have come up." For evidence he had only to turn to his parishioners, men certain of their high place in the scheme of things as evidenced by their possession of the good things of earth.

William Graham Sumner (1840–1910) of Yale, the most independent thinker among American Social Darwinists, stressed inevitability more than Spencerian optimism in the new thought. Sumner, like Darwin and Spen-

*From* The Hornet, *London, March 1871,*
*Charles Darwin as "A venerable orang-outang,*
*a contribution to unnatural history."*

Thames & Hudson, Ltd., London

cer, accepted the theory of the great English economist T. R. Malthus that population increase outstrips food supply, but he rejected the idea that progress arose out of the resultant struggle for existence. Reformers, in turn, he saw as meddlers engaged in an absurd attempt to make the world over. Unlike many professed Social Darwinists, Sumner was consistent in his hands-off philosophy, opposing even government handouts in the form of high tariffs to the "fittest" industrialists. Nor had he any sympathy for the racists and imperialists who glorified the Anglo-Saxon as the peak of evolutionary perfection and who cited Darwin to justify worldwide power for the benefit of "inferior peoples" (see Chapter Twenty-three).

### Dissenting voices

One of the most outspoken antagonists of Spencer and his American school of apologists for the established order was the largely self-taught sociologist Lester Ward (1841–1913). Ward faced a private struggle for existence and a hearing and did not obtain an academic post (at Brown) until he reached his sixties. His first major work, *Dynamic Sociology* (1883), sold only 500 copies in ten years.

A Darwinian as far as the origin and evolution of species went, Ward rejected the prevailing theory that "neither physical nor social phenomena are capable of human control." Science and "all the practical benefits of science," he asserted, "are the results of man's control of natural forces." He pointed out that nature untended was extraordinarily wasteful. Its value to mankind, he said, depended on its being governed by what he called "telic" forces (those originating in the human mind) as against blind "genetic" forces, which denied mind's role if not its existence altogether. Man's duty, then, in both the natural and the social sciences, according to Ward, was not to imitate nature but to dominate it. Far from assuring the survival of the fittest, competition often prevented it.

Ward emphasized the superiority of selective over natural breeding in animal and agricultural husbandry. Because he believed in social planning, he welcomed the intervention of government—"one of these artificial products of man's devising"—in social matters. A democratic government operating in the interests of all, he said, would permit a truer individualism by breaking up monopolies that manifestly strangled opportunity.

Ward's assault on Social Darwinism was supported by a group of thinkers—they might be called secular evangelists—whose most popular spokesman was the reformer Henry George (1839–1897). Spencerian philosophy, George said, sinned against the divinity of man by treating him like "a thing, in some respects lower than the animal." This philosophy also failed to explain why it was that some peoples progressed while others did not. George rejected as specious Spencer's talk of the "survival of the fittest." Progress, he said, depended on human association and social equality that unleashed man's creative powers. When inequality prevailed, association stopped and civilization declined.

What was the cause of inequality? George thought he had found the answer in California, where he went from his native Philadelphia in 1857. The frontier society of California, simple and equalitarian, had become transformed before his eyes into a wealthy and stratified society. As George put it, "The tramp comes with the locomotive, and almshouses and prisons are as surely the marks of 'material progress' as are costly dwellings, rich warehouses, and magnificent churches."

George felt that poverty accompanied progress because of the iniquitous system of private land ownership. The value of land, he said, was largely a matter of social accident. For example, land in metropolitan New York had grown so costly "not because of what its owners had done"; only "the presence of the whole great population" made it worth millions of dollars an acre. Since land grew in value because of the people who lived on it, George argued, the profit from it ought to return to the public in the form of a "single tax" on land values. He would leave the husk of ownership in private hands but would socialize the "kernel"—rent. George thought that the single tax on land would make other taxes unnecessary and would promote "the Golden Age of which poets have sung and high-raised seers have told us in metaphor!"

After George set down his theory in *Progress and Poverty* (1879), his ideas attracted worldwide attention. The book's appeal lay partly in its rhapsodic style and the skill with which George reduced economic complexities to everyday language and partly in its central theme that material progress without social justice led to despotism. George continued to develop this theme in later books. He narrowly missed being elected mayor of New York City in 1886. He ran again in 1897 but died five days before election day.

George's contemporary Edward Bellamy (1850–1898) also rejected the materialistic fatalism of the Social Darwinists, but, unlike George, he concentrated his attack on the competitive system itself. Bellamy's radicalism had something in common with the communitarian experiments of Fourier's American disciples in the 1840s and with the Social Gospel movement of the 1880s. In *Looking Backward*, his Utopian novel published in 1888, Bellamy offered a vision of an ideal society in the year 2000 whose beauty, tranquillity, and efficiency contrasted vividly with the smoky, striving, strike-ridden America of his day. The book's "Golden Age" dawned after the nationalizing of the great trusts and the "substitution of scientific methods of an organized and unified industrial system for the wasteful struggle of the present competitive plan."

The millions of Americans who read Bellamy's novel were delighted by its amiable tone and by the prospect of his immaculate, gadget-filled city of the future. Amazed by the impact of his book, Bellamy concluded that the American people might put his theories into practice. "Nationalism," as he called his system, was not a class movement. It rested on the idea that all people

*are victims in mind, body, or soul, in one way or another, of the present barbarous industrial and social arrangements, and that we are all equally interested, if not for ourselves, yet for our children, in breaking the*

*meshes which entangle us, and struggling upward to a higher, nobler, happier plane of existence.*

"Nationalist" clubs sprang up across the country. "Nationalist" magazines advocating such measures as public ownership of railroads and utilities, civil-service reform, and government aid to education sold widely. Before Bellamy's death, "Nationalism" had been absorbed by the agrarian reformers, but he had accomplished his purpose of familiarizing a large audience with the ideas of a Socialist order.

Bellamy and his coworkers deliberately avoided the word "socialism," for, as he wrote to William Dean Howells,

*In the radicalness of the opinions I have expressed I may seem to outsocialize the Socialists, yet the word socialist is one I could never well stomach. In the first place it is a foreign word itself and equally foreign in all its suggestions. It smells to the average American of petroleum, suggests the red flag with all manner of sexual novelties, and an abusive tone toward God and religion, which in this country we can at least treat with decent respect.*

Bellamy knew his public. American anarchists might protest that they were "simply unterrified Jeffersonian Democrats," and Socialists deny that they intended a violent overthrow of society. But the majority of Americans turned away and stayed away from these exotic systems.

## Orthodoxy challenged

The social ideas of such offbeat theorists as George and Bellamy found little support in the universities, where orthodox economics was firmly fixed in the Gilded Age. American students learned that inequality in wealth produced the incentives without which progress was impossible; that labor's wages depended on the number of men competing for jobs who shared in a "wage fund" that no artificial regulation could modify; and that competition was the only way for free individuals to satisfy their own needs and to work for "the greatest good of the greatest number." Only in an unregulated society could the natural economic laws function properly.

These sentiments, held by the leading academic social scientists, began to be challenged in the mid-1880s by a group of younger scholars, many of them trained in German universities. Economists like Richard T. Ely, John R. Commons, and Edward Bemis grew increasingly critical of laissez-faire and considered far more sympathetically than had their predecessors the idea that the power of the state might legitimately be used to improve society. Under the leadership of Ely, the younger economists and some liberal clergymen founded the American Economic Association in 1885. The AEA declared itself in favor of "the positive assistance of the state," and, while recognizing "the necessity of individual initiative in industrial life," it held that "the doctrine of laissez faire is unsafe in politics and unsound in morals."

Younger sociologists had also broken out of the Spencerian straitjacket by the 1890s. Such men as Albion Small, Charles H. Cooley, and E. A. Ross argued that individual personality was shaped by *social* institutions that were in turn amenable to social control. In *Sin and Society* (1907) Ross tried to show that new business conditions demanded a new code of ethics, one that required the soulless corporation to take full responsibility for its antisocial acts.

Although the younger social scientists differed in their economic and political programs, by and large they all distrusted a static view of the universe, absolute laws, and fixed conceptions. Society, they felt, was constantly changing and had to be examined as process

and growth. Consequently, they turned to the historical past in order to understand the present and looked for relevant facts in other disciplines that would help illuminate their own.

Foremost among the academic rebels was the economist Thorstein Veblen (1857-1929). Son of Norwegian immigrants, the Wisconsin-born Veblen had absorbed some frontier Populism before he completed his training at Yale, where he studied under Sumner, and at Johns Hopkins. His "predilection for shifty iconoclasm" (to use one of his own phrases), his unconventional personal life, intellectual arrogance, and heretical views blocked his academic advancement thereafter. A type of renegade whom he once described as "a disturber of the intellectual peace," Veblen pretended to survey society with scientific detachment, but his disguise, easily penetrated, failed to conceal the moralist and the critic of the "kept classes" of "pecuniary" society he was.

According to Veblen, millionaires were not, as Sumner had insisted, "a product of natural selection," nor were they socially useful. Captains of enterprise, he said, actually sabotaged the industrial machine, because their primary concern—unlike that of the engineer—was finance, not production. In his most widely read book, *The Theory of the Leisure Class* (1899), and in numerous other volumes, Veblen discussed the habits and thoughts of the rich as if they made up a primitive tribe he had discovered. In his analysis he introduced ethical, psychological, biological, and anthropological observations foreign to conventional economic studies. Although he asserted that only the "is" interested him, not the "right to be," he envisaged a community of "masterless" men organized under a technical elite. Veblen's ideas seemed merely whimsical in the early 1900s, but his influence grew during the 1920s and reached its peak after the Great Crash of 1929 disclosed the limitations of his favorite subjects.

**561**

## II  New lines of thought

*Philosophers: authoritarian and pragmatic*

What chiefly distinguished pre-Darwinian from post-Darwinian science, as Veblen pointed out, was the way in which the scientist looked at his facts. The Darwinian did not care whether his observations harmonized with old formulas, ideas, or fixed beliefs. He accepted evolution because he was less concerned (as the philosopher John Dewey remarked) "in what or who made the world" than in "what kind of world it is anyway." This, said Dewey, was "the intellectual transformation effected by the Darwinian logic." But the transformation did not occur immediately.

Before the Civil War, the prevailing philosophy in the United States was that known as Scottish or "common-sense" realism, a convenient adaptation of sophisticated Enlightenment rationalism to the needs of Protestant, mainly Calvinist, morality. This was the standard philosophy taught in the more liberal denominational colleges by such men as the Reverend James McCosh of Princeton, the Reverend Noah Porter, president of Yale, and their followers. It supposed that man possessed a God-implanted faculty which enabled him to arrive at truth. As Newton had authoritatively formulated the natural laws of the universe, so other men as authoritatively could formulate the natural laws of politics, economics, and ethics. What the Scottish realists most strenuously objected to in the Darwinists, as President Porter put it, was the way they removed leadership from enlightened moral arbiters and "reduce[d] all the phenomena of conscience and duty, all the obligations to law and order, all the restraints upon murder, robbery, and lust, to the relations of mechanism, and the affinities of matter."

In the 1870s and after, German idealism, particularly as developed by Hegel and his followers, made inroads upon the Scottish school. Hegel had seen the whole course of history as the working out of divine purpose according to certain general laws of change. But since Hegelians looked upon the present state of affairs as an inevitable stage in historical development, Hegelianism served as well as the Scottish philosophy to justify existing conditions. Its chief element of novelty lay in the fact that it taught reverence for social order as embodied in the National State and preached that the individual could be truly free only by subordinating himself to the advancement of his national government and the institutions of his society. William T. Harris, who became United States Commissioner of Education in 1889, was a leading American Hegelian.

Possibly the most influential and certainly the most readable of the American idealists was Josiah Royce (1855–1916), a brilliant Californian who taught at Harvard from 1882 until his death. Royce defended the idealistic belief in an absolute, unchanging mind pervading the natural universe, but unlike the more orthodox Hegelians he found a more active place for the individual. Royce preached a social ethic in which the greatest good was not to be found in aggregate national happiness but in harmony among the parts of society. He believed that through the principle of loyalty many individuals could be brought together into the unity of a single life, and he built a large part of his later philosophy around this theme of social cohesion.

Toward the end of the century a new school of philosophy appeared, the "pragmatists," as they came to be known, who repudiated all ideal or eternally fixed systems and evaluated ideas in terms of their evident consequences. The forerunners of pragmatism, Chauncey Wright and Charles Peirce, refreshingly bold thinkers, received small credit for pragmatism's development. Two other men, William James and John Dewey, as boldly extended pragmatic thinking into a philosophy of action.

William James (1842–1910), the brother of the novelist Henry James, detested the toadying determinism of Social Darwinism and all other systems of thought that left no place for luck or energy or mind. A splendid writer, James mocked Spencer's jaw-breaking definition of evolution, restating it as "a change from a no-howish untalkaboutable all-alike-ness to a some-howish and in general talkaboutable not-all-alikeness by continuous stick-togetherations and somethingelseifications." With wit and learning, he asserted "the right to believe at our own risk any hypothesis that is live enough to tempt our will." But if he rejected dictation he also rejected the "snarling logicality" of skepticism that paralyzed normal impulse or generous commitment.

In the late 1860s James went through a profound emotional crisis from which he emerged with an intense "will to believe," yet with a conviction that the purpose of thinking was "to help change the world." As a philosopher and psychologist at Harvard, he developed his case against the "awfully monotonous" Spencerian universe, wrote a brilliant exposition on the active role of the mind (*Principles of Psychology*, 1890), and later expounded his views on pragmatism. The pragmatist, James wrote,

*turns away from abstraction and insufficiency, from verbal solutions, from bad a priori reasons, from fixed principles, closed systems, and pretended absolutes and origins. He turns towards concreteness and adequacy, towards facts, towards action and towards power.*

Pragmatism regards theories as *"instruments, not answers to enigmas."* It "has no dogmas, and no doctrines save its method"—a method for arriving at truth.

When James declared that "the true is the name of whatever proves itself to be good in the way of belief, and good, too, for definite, assignable reasons," he laid himself open to the charge that pragmatism was only a high-sounding name for expediency—anything is good that works. But even if the charge were true, it was no less true that a working truth could more easily be defended than the established shibboleths of authority. "Mind," said James with daring, "*engenders* truth *upon* reality."

The charge of expediency also was leveled at John Dewey's "instrumentalism," a later version of the pragmatic philosophy, and one more vulnerable than James's because of Dewey's deeper commitment to instant action and application. Starting out as an idealist,

**563**

*William James in photograph by Alice Boughton, 1907. "Being susceptible to flattery, I am here," James told the famous photographer, who had asked for a sitting.*

Library of Congress

Dewey (1859-1952) had been converted to pragmatism in the 1890s after reading James, but he had less interest in proving truth than in using it, as the master suggested. The mind, Dewey said, "is at least an organ of service for the control of environment," and he called upon philosophers to stop speculating and searching and get to work:

*The effective control of [men's] powers is not through precepts, but through the regulation of their conditions. If this regulation is to be not merely physical or coercive, but moral, it must consist of the intelligent selection and determination of the environments in which we act; and in an intelligent exaction of responsibility for the use of men's powers.*

Like Ward, George, and other dissenters, Dewey became an early critic of laissez-faire and Social Darwinism in politics and business. More than others, he applied his ideas to education, which he felt must be intimately related to the rest of life and made into an instrument for social reform. Dewey conceived of the school as an institution through which the child would learn to criticize the customs and beliefs of society as a whole. The child would acquire this knowledge not by absorbing the conventional wisdom of his teachers, not by having his mind "disciplined" through traditional drills, but by developing a scientific approach to solving problems. Dewey wanted students to participate directly in the issues or situations that concerned them, to learn by doing. Nevertheless, he urged constantly that his own democratic values must permeate every aspect of educational training. In the early decades of the twentieth century, Dewey's "progressive" theories began to influence American education, and while the half century of controversy between his followers and pseudofollowers and their critics has simmered down, American schools and teaching were permanently altered by it.

### Law and social theory

The Darwinian influence undermined absolutism in law as in philosophy. The older generation of lawyers had acted as though the law were handed down from on high and held that judicial decisions followed inevitably from constitutions, statutes, and precedents. The man who perhaps did most to shake such conservatism was Oliver Wendell Holmes (1841-1935), son of the poet of the same name, and friend of his fellow Harvardian William James. Holmes did his work on the bench. For twenty years he served on the Massachusetts Supreme Court before being appointed to the United States Supreme Court in 1902. By the time of his retirement in 1932, he had become one of the most celebrated judges in the world.

To Holmes, law like life was part of the social process. Even the decisions of judges, he demonstrated in his book *The Common Law* (1881), arose as much out of human frailty, out of prejudices and preconceptions, as out of logic and embalmed authority. For this reason, he boldly challenged the prevailing faith in precedent and warned that the law must never lag too far behind concrete experience. "It is revolting," Holmes said, "to have no better reason for a rule of law than that so it was laid down in the time of Henry IV."

The fact that Holmes freely associated the law with the living did not make him indiscriminately liberal. Throughout his life he held in contempt those "stinking upward and onwarders" who claimed to be "on the ground floor with God." Unlike the lovers of causes he accepted injustice and suffering as two ineradicable elements of life. Yet in spirit he was an optimist who bravely made the best of a challenging if ultimately inscrutable universe. "Philosophy seems to me to sin through arrogance," Holmes once wrote to "Dear Bill" James. "The great act of faith is when a man decides he is not God."

Holmes once confessed that he hated facts: "I have little doubt that it would be good for my immortal soul to plunge into them, good also for the performance of my duties, but I shrink from the bore." Louis Dembitz Brandeis (1856-1941), a Boston Jew appointed to the Supreme Court by Wilson in 1916 against the concerted opposition of many eminent public figures, felt that without facts no just legal decision could be rendered. Brandeis agreed with his friend and colleague Holmes that the social beliefs of judges colored their judicial decisions; all the more reason then for assaulting their beliefs with objective economic and social information. Brandeis's long career as a "people's lawyer" before rising to the national judiciary convinced him that the law lagged behind realities and that its interpreters must understand the revolutionary social and economic changes wrought by the industrial transformation of the country in order to judge cases fairly. His most significant triumph as a lawyer came in the case of *Muller* v. *Oregon* (1908), in which the Supreme Court, on the basis of Brandeis's overwhelming evidence from physicians, factory inspectors, social workers, and other competent observers, upheld the Oregon ten-hour law for working women (see p. 618).

Even the supreme law of the United States, the Constitution itself, became an object of critical study. The political scientist Arthur F. Bentley concluded in his book *The Process of Government* (1908) that all law was the result of conflicts among interest groups and that constitutions were merely a special form of law. Another writer, J. Allen Smith, argued in *The Spirit of American Government* (1907) that the framers of the Constitution of the United States had intended not to realize democracy but to check it. In *An Economic Interpretation of the Constitution* (1913), the brilliant Columbia University professor of politics Charles A. Beard dared to confront the material interests of the framers of the sacrosanct document. Later historians riddled Beard's scholarship in this book and questioned or rejected his conclusions. Yet few deny the lasting value of his work in stripping away myths about the demigods at the Great Convention and disclosing how considerations of property profoundly shaped their ideas.

### The historians

The analogy between Darwinian ideas of the evolution of species and the historical evolution of social institutions was too obvious to be missed, and by the 1880s some historians had become convinced that history could be transformed into as exact a science as biology, once laws of social evolution had been ascertained. Spencer's apostle John Fiske pursued this line of thought, tracing for a large audience America's political development from its simple earliest stages to its later complexity. Academic historians under the influence of Herbert B. Adams of Johns Hopkins and John W. Burgess of Columbia, proud of their Anglo-Saxon heritage, were led to combine the evolution of species with the evolution of race, and both with the evolution (and improvement) of social institutions. In particular, they professed to see American democracy as the evolutionary outcome of political practices beginning with those of primitive tribes in German forests. Inspired by the racist views of English historians like E. A. Freeman and by the swelling expansionist sentiment at home, they made Anglo-Saxon blood the nesting place and nursery of freedom. "By that race alone," one of them wrote in 1890, freedom

had been preserved amidst a thousand perils; to that race alone is it thoroughly congenial; if we can conceive the possibility of disappearance among peoples of that race, the chance would be small for that freedom's survival.

To Frederick Jackson Turner (1861–1932), Wisconsin-born and Johns Hopkins-trained, the conquest of the American frontier also was part of the evolutionary process. But Turner argued in his immensely influential essay "The Significance of the Frontier in American History" (1893) that American democracy originated not in the German but in the American forests, "yet not among the Indians, its first denizens." According to Turner, the European settler eventually conquered the New World wilderness, but during his long

565

struggle (yet one exceedingly short on the evolutionary scale) the conqueror was forced either to adapt to new conditions or perish. Wrote Turner:

566

> The advance of the frontier has meant a steady movement away from the influence of Europe, a steady growth of independence on American lines. And to study this advance, the men who grew up under these conditions, and the political, economic, and social results of it, is to study the really American part of our history.

The closing of the frontier that Turner made so much of in 1893 had, he believed, dangerous implications for America. From the frontier had sprung the toughness, resourcefulness, individualism, and versatility that made the country great. Turner harbored misgivings about the new industrialized and urbanized civilization that overlay the once-savage wilderness, but he remained hopeful that America, because of its frontier heritage, would escape the social evils that plagued the tired civilization of Europe.

Optimistic faith might sustain a midwesterner like Turner, but to Henry Adams (1838-1918) and his brother Brooks—fallen descendants of Presidents marred by original sin—evolution, if anything, was working backwards, and nowhere more clearly so than in the United States. Throughout his life as political observer, journalist, professor, novelist, and traveler, Henry Adams had been fascinated by historical forces, and his meticulous and often brilliant account of Jefferson's and Madison's administrations and several historical biographies showed that he could write history very well. But as he grew older, his pleasure lay in demonstrating to his own satisfaction that history was not progress but degradation. In his famous autobiography, *The Education of Henry Adams* (1907), he maliciously observed that America's decline could be measured by contrasting Washington with Grant. In *Mont-Saint-Michel and Chartres* (1904), he compared the spiritual vitality of the Middle Ages, the age of unity symbolized by the cult of the Virgin, with the destructive violence of industrial civilization, the age of multiplicity symbolized by the dynamo. Drawing an intriguing analogy from physics, Adams concluded that the constantly accelerating dissipation of energy would ultimately end in the destruction of civilization and even calculated the dates of this debacle.

Brooks Adams shared his brother's pessimism but for a short time allowed his hopes to be stirred by the possibility of America's forging ahead in the competition among nations for world power. By 1912 he resumed the dour family outlook, agreeing with Henry that America could not adapt quickly enough to changing conditions. Her leaders, he said, lacked the will and imagination to convert the United States into a disciplined state.

## III  Ideas in education

### The higher learning

Beginning in the 1890s, American reformers complained about alleged plutocratic dictatorship over the universities, about professors being tried for economic heresies and fired for offending conservative founders or trustees. The reformers could cite the cases of the economist Richard T. Ely at Wisconsin, whose books were denounced as "utopian, impracticable or pernicious" by one of the state regents in an unsuccessful campaign to have him discharged; of Edward T. Bemis, ousted from the University of Chicago for attacking the railroads and the Gas Trust; of E. A. Ross, dismissed from Stanford for opinions offensive to the late founder's widow. In *The Theory of Social Revolutions* (1913),

Brooks Adams accused American universities of graduating narrow, half-educated specialists lacking the breadth of mind needed to administer a complex, centralized economy. Five years later, in *The Higher Learning in America*, Veblen pilloried the universities as temples of "intellectual quietism" run by "captains of erudition" for the production of salesmen.

Yet there was another side to the story. Forgotten by the critics was the far narrower sectarianism and intolerance that long marred many older colleges. Since 1860 American universities, as a rule, had grown larger and more bureaucratized in administration. At the same time, they improved steadily in quality, until in our own era, for better or worse, neither the economy nor the state could be run without them or their graduates.

Between 1860 and 1900, public and private donations helped finance the universities' growth. Within a decade of the Morrill Act of 1862 Wisconsin, Minnesota, California, Texas, Massachusetts, and New York had established land-grant colleges, many of them coeducational. Other colleges and universities were set up through private philanthropy. Ezra Cornell, for example, who made a fortune from the electric telegraph, founded Cornell, which opened in 1868. Vanderbilt University (1873) and Stanford (1891) were the beneficiaries of two railroad millionaires. Like the University of Chicago (1891), which received $34 million from the oil magnate John D. Rockefeller, they managed to outlast interference. The Johns Hopkins University (1876) bore the name of a wealthy Baltimore banker and railroad executive; Carnegie Institute (1896) in Pittsburgh, the name of the multimillionaire steel man.

Prewar colleges had confined themselves pretty much to nonutilitarian subjects—the classics, mathematics, and theology. The postwar institutions responded to the demand for business and technical education. The prestige of science had risen so high (another result of the Darwinian revolution) that such practical

additions to the curriculum as well as greater emphasis on research and a declining preoccupation with morals had to be accepted. By the end of the century, a number of American university scientists had won international reputations, among them Albert A. Michelson of the University of Chicago, who made important discoveries in molecular theory, and Josiah Willard Gibbs of Yale, whose work in theoretical physics paved the way for the theory of relativity.

Thanks to men like President Charles W. Eliot of Harvard, a new kind of university emerged in which undergraduates "elected" courses from a greatly expanded curriculum instead of being "compelled to an unwelcome task," while graduate schools grew in number and scholarly faculties were assembled. Between 1869 and 1900, Eliot also drastically reformed Harvard's medical and law schools, which became models for others. Premedical students, who had formerly obtained degrees with a minimum of course and clinical work, were now required to study three full years in medical school, to work in laboratories, and to take examinations. C. C. Langdell, dean of the Harvard law school, abolished the textbook and introduced a system whereby the law student gained his knowledge by examining specific cases.

Time showed that these innovations also had their limitations; Eliot's theories, for example, especially his "elective system," which permitted less serious undergraduates to choose unrelated subjects and to avoid difficult courses, provoked legitimate opposition. The founding of Johns Hopkins, in turn, gave a strong impetus to specialized research. Many of its faculty members had studied in Germany, and they proceeded to train a corps of teachers in the exacting methods of German university scholarship, which soon fell prey to pedantry.

Not all the changes in university and college life were intellectual or administrative. The introduction of organized sports like baseball and football aroused an almost fanatical concern with school rivalries. The poet T. S. Eliot later charged such contests with responsibility for the "decadent athleticism" of American life. By the 1890s intercollegiate football had become a mass spectacle attended by crowds of 30,000 or 40,000, and critics already protested its professional emphasis.

So far as educational opportunities went, women continued as "second-class citizens." Although much evidence to the contrary existed, many people continued to doubt women's intellectual or physical capacity to profit from college education. Would not the experience of higher learning, it was asked, open the "floodgates of a torrent of evils which should sweep away the loveliness and grace and essential charm of womanhood?" The founding of Vassar College at Poughkeepsie, New York in 1861 did much to dispel such antiquated notions. Matthew Vassar, an English-born brewer, believed that "woman having received from the Creator the same intellectual constitution as man, has the same right to intellectual culture and development." The course of study inaugurated at Vassar became as demanding as that of any male college of the day, and Vassar graduates quickly distinguished themselves among scholars, in the professions, and in social reform.

By 1880 most of the important midwestern universities admitted women, and women's colleges like Smith, Bryn Mawr, and Wellesley—founded shortly after Vassar—offered professional training. Despite diehard citations of example after example of breakdown and collapse among college women, the number enrolled as undergraduates rose from about 8000 in 1869 to more than 20,000 in 1894 and soared in the twentieth century.

### Gains in public education

By 1865 about 50 million acres of the public domain had been set aside for the support of common schools and colleges, and with the close of the Civil War the drive for a nationally supported system of education for all accelerated. The emancipation of 4 million slaves, according to one educator, had saddled the government with a special obligation. "Their former owners," he pointed out, "will not take the trouble to educate them. . . . Individual generosity, education societies, and partial taxation, will fail." Only the "impartial force of the general government" could do the

job. And besides the Negroes, there were the illiterate southern whites and millions of foreigners "averse to our national institutions." The United States, for its own safety and prestige, this educator held, must educate every child in the land.

Many decades elapsed before the federal government undertook "to wield the requisite power," but considerable advances in public education could be seen after 1865 in the lengthening of the school term, the higher dollar expenditure per pupil, the declining illiteracy rate, and the compulsory school-attendance laws. The old prewar academy that once monopolized American secondary education gave way after 1870 to the public high school. A broadened curriculum included history and literature, as well as vocational and commercial courses designed to prepare the child to meet the challenge of his environment.

Between 1870 and 1910, the number of public high schools grew from 500 to more than 10,000, and a high-school education had begun to be the normal expectation of great numbers of young Americans, especially white youths in towns and cities. In this forty-year period, the number of pupils attending public elementary and high schools each year rose from 6,871,000 to 17,813,000. The average number of days in the school year rose from 132 to 157, and per capita appropriations for education more than doubled. Illiteracy declined from 17 percent of the population in 1880 to 7.7 percent in 1910. Interest had also risen in schools for the very young. The first kindergarten was established in St. Louis in 1873, and within thirty years their number had grown to 3000.

### Schooling the Negro

Before the Civil War, a small minority of blacks (house servants and slaves of urban owners in particular) had learned to read and write, sometimes covertly. A much larger number had acquired mechanical skills.

*Booker T. Washington (bottom row, right),*
*with Tuskegee's philanthropic backers at the*
*twenty-fifth anniversary of his school*
*in 1906. Andrew Carnegie and Charles W. Eliot,*
*president of Harvard, stand together at*
*right end of second row. The others are*
*less well known today.*

Yet the vast majority, of course, remained field hands to whom schooling was virtually unknown. All the same, northern educators who journeyed to the defeated Confederacy in the early postwar years to set up improvised schools for freedmen found their charges, as a rule, avid for learning. Literacy, they fondly believed, a torch to lead them from intellectual darkness, would also light their path to economic, political, and social advances. Following the Emancipation Proclamation, education acquired almost a religious meaning for the ex-slave.

Conventional southerners, to be sure, had not welcomed Yankee schoolmarms come to implant alien and alienating notions in the minds of a susceptible people still regarded as "peculiarly" disadvantaged. In their eyes, the iron law of race condemned blacks to labor as hewers of wood and drawers of water. Learning, among such a caste, might become as addictive as liquor among Indians. Thus when federal troops departed from the South, the public-education structure erected by the Freedmen's Bureau disintegrated. After 1876, southern leaders countenanced the educational provisions still in the new state constitutions; but where schools continued to be provided for blacks, vocational training suitable to their "place" preempted the curriculum.

Northern philanthropists, themselves imbued with racist attitudes and discouraged by the slow progress of the blacks, went along with the southern conception of how to school the Negro, some of them because of their fear that white supremacist antagonism to anything better would jeopardize the educational future of whites as well as blacks. Such philanthropists thus funneled their contributions to vocationally oriented black "colleges," while Negro public schools foundered. By 1900 a mere 8000 black boys and girls were enrolled in public high schools in the entire South.

A northern clergyman in touch with the southern mind observed that "the less the negro talks about his civil rights, . . . the sooner he will attain to all the rights that justly belong to him," including schooling. Negro leaders, observing the mounting legal and violent repression of their people after 1876, also espoused this "accommodationist" philosophy. No one, indeed, subscribed to it more fully than the remarkable ex-slave Booker T. Washington.

Between 1872 and 1875, Washington, in his late teens, had attended the Hampton Normal and Agricultural Institute of Virginia, the experimental manual-labor school opened in 1868 under the direction of General Samuel C. Armstrong. When Washington opened his own normal school in 1881 at Tuskegee, Alabama, with funds supplied by an Alabama banker, he built upon the theories of his mentor Armstrong, who had recommended him to his backers. Washington could hardly help see that for an indeterminate future the southern black majority would be confined to agricul-

570

tural, domestic, or mechanical work. The best way to assure their welfare and the tolerance of the master caste, he reasoned, was to train them in such useful pursuits, leaving liberal education to the time when the indeterminate future had passed.

Washington's gospel naturally went down very smoothly among southern whites, "of the better class," as he always stipulated; and it is not surprising that they hailed his conciliatory speech to them at the Atlanta Exposition of 1895, at the very zenith of their legal and violent repression of blacks, as the "Atlanta Compromise."

Casting down your bucket among my people [he told his influential audience], helping and encouraging them ... to education of head, hand, and heart, you will find that they will buy your surplus land, make bloom the waste places in your fields, and run your factories. While doing this you can be sure in the future, as in the past, that you will be surrounded by the most patient, faithful, law-abiding and unresentful people the world has ever seen.

In his autobiographical writings later on, Washington pressed the same theme. "I was born in the South," he said, "and I understand thoroughly the prejudices, the customs, the traditions of the South. . . . These prejudices," he had learned, "are something that it does not pay to disturb," and he added: "the agitation of questions of social equality is the extremest folly." Yet he concluded, "I love the South"; and he did not veer from his conviction expressed in 1884: "My faith is that reforms in the South are to come from within" the section.

Today, Washington's docility is repudiated by the majority of Negroes everywhere in the United States. Even in his own day, militant black leaders resented his growing intolerance of persons or groups refusing him unqualified loyalty and support. Blacks needed the training he recommended; few denied that. But an exclusively vocational training, his opponents asserted, would never produce the leadership which might ultimately restore to the black man his legal rights and his manhood.

"Learn that it is a mistake to be educated out of your environment," a white northern businessman sympathizer of the Tuskegee institution advised blacks schooled in its philosophy. C. Vann Woodward, in *Origins of the New South,* well summarizes the "mistake" of being "educated" *within* that environment as well. "While at the end of the Civil War," he writes, "Negro artisans are said to have outnumbered white by five to one, they made up only a small proportion of the labor force in most crafts by 1890." Artisanship had become reserved as "white work" for boys off the farm. Woodward continues:

While in 1870 the [New Orleans] city directory had listed 3460 Negroes as carpenters, cigarmakers, painters, clerks, shoemakers, coopers, tailors, bakers, blacksmiths, and foundry hands, not 10 per cent of that number were employed in the same trades in 1904. Yet the Negro population had gained more than 50 per cent.

*Popularizing culture*

Commenting on the state of American culture in 1867, Thomas Wentworth Higginson, the Boston reformer and author, noted improvements over the past twenty-five years. More and better magazines were being published; the number of libraries had quadrupled; music and art had grown more readily accessible in larger cities. But these gains coincided with a decline in "an institution which once was more potent than all of these for the intellectual training of the adult American"— the old lyceum of the 1840s. "Take away the Lowell and Cooper Institutes," he concluded, "and all our progress in wealth has secured for the public no increase of purely intellectual culture through lectures."

Thirteen years later, in 1880, a second observer raised the question of what was to be done with all the many natively intelligent citizens "in whom the methods and tendencies of prehistoric thought are still dominant and almost unmodified by modern culture." Millions of Americans, he believed, who had the strangest notions of politics and science, became dupes for any crackpot panacea, any simplistic solution for complicated problems.

One way to counter this massive absence of intellectualism was to provide some form of popular education that would be the lyceum's equivalent. A highly successful venture in this direction began in western New York in 1874 with the establishment of the Chautauqua Assembly by an Ohio businessman, Louis Miller, and a Methodist bishop, John H. Vincent. Its original purpose was to train Sunday school teachers during the summer months, but like the lyceum movement, the Chautauqua soon expanded into wider fields. Before long, the Chautauqua Literary and Scientific Reading Circle had become a national society with study circles and a corps of eminent lecturers, including several Presidents of the era.

Perhaps most successful of all Chautauqua addresses, one that no doubt dismayed culture promoters like Higginson, was Dr. Russell H. Conwell's inspirational talk on how to get ahead, which he called "Acres of Diamonds." Conwell gave this lecture 6000 times, and his audiences never seemed to tire of his message or his spectacular oratory. "Get rich, young man," he declared, "for money is power, and power ought to be in the hands of good people. . . . I say you have *no right to be poor.*" Conwell never allowed his huge income from lecturing to accumulate. He gave much of it away to deserving young men and later founded Temple University in Philadelphia, whose president he remained until his death in 1925.

Other commercial "Chautauquas" soon appeared, and entrepreneurs capitalizing on the craving for self-culture also organized correspondence schools and published "libraries" of cheap books to be sold either by subscription or through department stores and mail-order houses. Middle-class women found an outlet for their cultural interests in the "literary" clubs later to be satirized by Edith Wharton in *The Custom of the Country.*

571

## IV  The writer and his world

### After Appomattox

Almost without exception the best-informed literary critics after Appomattox remarked on the lackluster state of American letters—what one magazine editor called in 1866 the "nerveless twaddle of petty authorship." E. P. Whipple, an influential essayist for Boston's *North American Review,* advised his readers to stick to the old literature and "at least avoid being swindled by the perishable shoddy of the mind" which wooed their attention "in the slop-shops of letters." Didactic versifiers, pale imitators of Tennyson, filled the magazines with their piddling stuff. "Do you call those genteel little creatures American poets?" Walt Whitman asked in 1871. "Do you term that perpetual, pistareen, paste-pot work, American art?"

Already partly visible by the 1870s, nevertheless, was a flush of fresh talent, soon to be followed by a stronger generation still. Old James Russell Lowell could declare in 1866 that he held "unchastity of the mind to be worse than that of the body . . . let no man write a line he would not want his daughter to read." The young new writers, many of them former newspaper men who had seen something of life, explored subjects hitherto largely excluded from polite literature: slums, crime, violence, divorce, miscegenation, political corruption, drunkenness, adultery. To be sure the "flimsy fabrications of shoddy"—romantic tales and do-good books—continued to flood the land. The genteel custodians of culture continued to pay homage to the "Iron Madonna," as the author Hjalmar H. Boyeson put it—the American Girl who "strangles in her fond embrace the American novelist." What Whitman called "ornamental confectionary" and "copious dribble" had not disappeared even by the end of the century, but at the same time a new realism had given a fresh vitality to literature.

572

## The escapists

The dividing line of the Civil War was sharpened by the death or withdrawal of the luminaries of the past. By 1865 Hawthorne and Thoreau were dead. Emerson, past his prime, retired more and more into himself, while Melville lived virtually forgotten in prisonlike anonymity. Of all the writers of the antebellum "Golden Day," only Whitman still sounded his "barbaric yawp over the roofs of the world."

Emily Dickinson (1830–1886), the one authentic poetic genius of the early postwar years, lived even more retired a life than the surviving old masters and gave the public but little of her work. A spinster recluse in Amherst, Massachusetts, for herself and her few friends she wrote verses burdened with the old-time themes of her Puritan forebears: love, death, God, and eternity, the rapture of sudden illumination, the symbolic meaning of the universe. Although her lines resemble Emerson's in their terseness and wit, her view of nature and of God was less benign, less optimistic than his. Nature's garden, so full of wasps and bees and snakes, caused "a tighter breathing / And zero at the bone." The "certain slant of light" she saw on winter afternoons oppressed "like the weight of cathedral tunes." Emily Dickinson's poetry was sometimes marred by coyness and sentimentality, but her best lyrics (among the finest in our literature) are distinguished by their diction and imagery. She could in the most remarkable way transmute the humble objects of her surroundings into symbols of eternity.

Emily Dickinson retreated into herself for private reasons. Other postwar writers, mostly country-bred and repelled by the industrialized and urbanized America of the victorious North, retreated to the past. Precisely when country people were severing their ties with the land, some writers of the "local-color" school, like Harriet Beecher Stowe and Edward Eggleston, retrieved the scenes and spiritual values of a pastoral America. Others, like Bret Harte, Joel Chandler Harris, Sarah Orne Jewett, and Mary N. Murfree, sought out the "native element" of their distinctive sections—the California mining country, the southern plantation, the New England village, the Kentucky and Tennessee mountains.

Theoretically, the local colorist did not rule out the city, as George Washington Cable's stories of New Orleans creoles attested. The local colorist Hamlin Garland wrote in 1894 that "St. Louis, Chicago, San Francisco, will be delineated by artists born of each city, whose work will be so true that it could not have been written by anyone from the outside. . . . To such a one, nothing will be "strange" or "picturesque"; all will be familiar, and full of significance or beauty." Yet in general, local colorists stuck to what they considered to be the authentic part of America—the village, the small town, the farm—and lovingly recorded variations in dialect, manners, and customs.

## Mark Twain

Mark Twain (1835–1910)—the pen name of Samuel L. Clemens—belonged by temperament to the local-color tradition and was regarded in his own day as a regional author, but he was a writer of far greater dimension than the others. In many respects, Mark Twain was the most revealing figure in postwar American literature, the one who best combined the virtues and defects of the society he analyzed far more caustically than many realize who simply honor his name. Born in Hannibal, Missouri, he had been reporter, river pilot, and popular lecturer before gaining his first literary success with *The Innocents Abroad* (1869), an uproariously funny account of a junket of his countrymen through Europe and the Near East.

Mark Twain wrote prolifically about everything from jumping frogs to Andrew Carnegie, but his best works, *The Adventures of Tom*

*Sawyer* (1876), *Life on the Mississippi* (1883), and *The Adventures of Huckleberry Finn* (1884), all derive from his riverboat days. It was his loyalty to the simple republican America of his boyhood that partly accounts for his rage over the betrayal of democratic ideals in the Gilded Age. "In my youth," wrote Twain, "there was nothing resembling a worship of money or of its possessor, in our region." It took people of the Jay Gould variety, he said, "to make a God of the money and the man":

> The gospel left behind by Jay Gould is doing giant work in our days. Its message is "Get money. Get it quickly. Get it in abundance. Get it dishonestly if you can, honestly if you must."

And yet Twain enjoyed "striking it rich" as much as anyone, speculated recklessly, and wrote always with an eye on his large audience. As he put it:

> I have never tried in even one single instance to help cultivate the cultivated classes. I was not equipped for it by native gifts or training. And I never had any ambition in that direction, but always hunted for bigger game—the masses.

In his own subtle way, however, Mark Twain was a moralist who looked upon mankind with exasperation because of its cruelty, credulity, and pigheadedness, and with compassion because it was not to blame. *Huckleberry Finn*, teeming with playful incident and touching drama, remains an assault upon social hypocrisy, false respectability, and the canons of success—all bound up in the "civilization" from which Huck is trying to escape. In renouncing civilization, Huck remains true to his natural goodness yet without denying human depravity or his kinship with the wicked. Mark Twain once wrote: "I am the whole human race without a detail lacking ... the human race is a race of cowards; and I am not only marching in that procession but carrying a banner."

## Realists and naturalists

William Dean Howells (1837–1920), a friend of Mark Twain, became the leader of the postwar school of self-conscious "Realists." Born and reared in Ohio, Howells had come to literature, as so many of his contemporaries had, through the printer's office and the newspaper. A campaign life of Lincoln earned him a consular appointment in Venice. After his return from Italy in 1865, he became subeditor and then editor-in-chief (1871–1881) of the *Atlantic Monthly* in Boston, and from 1886 to 1891 wrote his most influential criticism in the "Editor's Study" in *Harper's Monthly* in New York. Howells published at least forty works of fiction and many plays and critical works. By 1900 many of the younger writers considered him the dean of American letters.

"Realism," as Howells used the term, simply meant "the truthful treatment of commonplace material." The romanticism per-

573

*Mark Twain, at age thirty-eight, in 1873.*

Culver Pictures, Inc.

meating the popular literature of his day was immoral, in Howells' opinion, because it corrupted American taste and falsified life. He wanted fiction that maintained "fidelity, not merely to the possible, but to the probable and ordinary course of man's experience." Let fiction, he said,

574

*portray men and women as they are, actuated by the motives and passions in the measure that we all know; let it leave off painting dolls and working them by springs and wires; . . . let it not put on fine literary airs; let it speak . . . the language of unaffected people everywhere—and there can be no doubt of an unlimited future . . . for it.*

Howells practiced what he preached. His best-known, and probably his best, novels are *The Rise of Silas Lapham* (1885), the story of a self-made businessman, and *A Hazard of New Fortunes* (1890), which reflected his first-hand experience in New York of the mindless struggle for wealth, the paradox of Fifth Avenue luxury and East Side squalor, the degradation of the republican dream.

Although Howells's friend Henry James (1843–1916) could not find enough material for fiction in what he regarded as the bleak American scene, he allied himself, and properly, with Howells's camp. James was born in New York, but he spent a good deal of his youth in Europe. After a halfhearted attempt to study law at Harvard, he gave himself entirely to literature, and from 1875 until his death he did most of his writing abroad. Because he visited his native land so infrequently, and because so many of his novels and short stories have a European setting, many critics place James outside the main current of American literature. Actually, his international plots deal almost exclusively with Americans, and from his foreign vantage point he discerned much about the character of his countrymen that escaped fellow writers who remained too close to home.

Like Hawthorne, by whom he was profoundly influenced, James liked to place his Americans in what he called "morally interesting situations." He subjected his traveling businessman (*The American,* 1877), his sensitive and intellectually curious heiresses (*The Por-*

trait of a Lady, 1881), his artist heroes, hungry for culture (*Roderick Hudson,* 1876), to moral tests that they either passed or failed. America remained for him—with all its artistic sterility—a land of innocence and promise; Europe was beautiful but decadent. A superb technician and psychologist, James was also a social historian who faithfully recorded the moral gaps and strains that he detected in upper-class society.

As a result of the realists' efforts, the young writers who came of age in the last two decades of the century could experiment even more boldly than their predecessors in unvarnished truth. Although it no longer took courage to expose a society committed to railroads, stockyards, real estate, and Wall Street, the new literary school went much farther than the realists in uncovering seamy and brutal aspects of American life. "Naturalism," as the new movement was called, derived its inspiration from French novelists like Emile Zola, who believed that literature should be governed by the same scientific laws that guided the physiologist. Man's fate was determined by heredity and environment, by inward drives and external circumstances over which he had no control. Theoretically, the naturalist writer put down objectively what he saw, no matter how disgusting or shocking it might be.

In America, naturalists like Stephen Crane (1871–1900) and Frank Norris (1870–1902) never matched the frankness of the French school, but they dealt with themes from which Howells, who still kept his eye fixed on the young girl reader, flinched. In *Maggie, A Girl of the Streets* (1893), Crane wrote of the seduction and suicide of a New York slum girl; in *The Red Badge of Courage* (1895), he reproduced convincingly the animal fear of a young Civil War recruit under fire and his psychological recovery. In all his tales and sketches of derelicts and soldiers, of frightened, abandoned people, Crane suggests that men must confront an indifferent nature and without help from the supernatural.

Norris, a less able writer than Crane and more given to melodrama, disliked Howells's brand of realism because it smelled so much of the commonplace, "the tragedy of the broken tea cup." Norris had a fondness for huge supermen with "primordial" jaws clashing with titanic natural forces. Many of his books suffer from exaggerated violence and sensationalism, but in *McTeague* (1899), the story of a man's reversion to brutishness, he displayed a power new in American fiction. In his best-known novel, *The Octopus* (1901), Norris depicted an epic struggle between California wheat growers and the railroad. The apparent radicalism of this book was considerably diluted by Norris's message that wheat and railroad represented natural forces, each governed by the law of supply and demand. "Men have only little to do in the whole business," he said.

In Jack London (1876–1916), many of Norris's themes are repeated, especially the tendency to exalt the brutal while condemning the brutality of the social order. Born in 1876 and thrown on his own resources at an early age in the waterfront environment of Oakland, California, London became a hobo and a seaman, among other things, before settling down to write. His literary career lasted only eighteen years, but in its course he published over fifty books. Burnt out by his exertions and by the rage against life expressed in his work, he died at forty.

While he preached the despairing doctrine of man's subordination to the impersonal forces of nature, London nevertheless embraced the hopeful teachings of socialism. He never reconciled these ideas, but his work expressed one or the other sufficiently well to make him one of the most widely read writers of his time and one of the few American authors to gain recognition in Europe. Along with Mark Twain, he remains today one of the two or three most admired American writers in Soviet Russia. London's most interesting books are his autobiographical novel *Martin Eden* (1909) and *The Iron Heel* (1907), concerned with the fight to the death between the exploited classes and a plutocratic oligarchy. His greatest success, *The Call of the Wild* (1903), a book about pack dogs in the Yukon, glories in details of animal conflict.

The writings of Theodore Dreiser reflected a naturalism even more uncompromising than that of Crane, Norris, or London. But in Dreiser, the replacement of the good and the bad by the strong and the weak was accompanied by a deeper feeling for character and a profound, almost maternal, tenderness.

Born in Terre Haute, Indiana in 1871, one of thirteen children of German immigrant parents, Dreiser saw little but squalor and hardship during his childhood. After years of drifting from job to job, he spent several years as a newspaperman in Chicago, St. Louis, Cleveland, and Pittsburgh, observing at first hand the hard side of big city life. His experiences inspired him with the idea of treating a great American metropolis as realistically as Balzac wrote of Paris.

Dreiser's first novel and one of his best, *Sister Carrie,* was published in 1900 and then quickly withdrawn after the publisher's wife objected to its "indecency." Many critics concurred, condemning its clumsy style as well as its message. *Sister Carrie* tells of a young girl who comes to Chicago from a small western town and succumbs in succession to the blandishments of a vulgar but generous salesman and then to a restaurant manager. The best chapters of the book, one of the most remarkable sequences in American letters, trace the gradual deterioration of her second seducer, Hurstwood, who drifts toward complete ruin while Carrie, taking a grip on her own fortunes, becomes a successful actress.

Although Dreiser is always compassionate toward his characters, it is seldom clear whether he is complaining about harsh society or about the harshness of life itself. His characterization of a business tycoon patterned after the Chicago traction magnate Charles T. Yerkes, in *The Financier* (1912) and *The Titan* (1914), could be taken either as a naturalist's comments on the wastefulness of existence or Progressive protest against rapacious business. Dreiser's hero Frank Cowperwood has his image of life fixed in his mind when as a boy at an aquarium he watches a lobster devour a squid:

*Things lived on each other—that was it. Lobsters lived on squids and other things. What lived on lobsters? Men, of course! And what lived on men? he asked himself. Was it other men? ... He wasn't so sure about men living on men; but men did kill each other.*

Cowperwood grows up with the touch of Midas in his business dealings and the touch of Don Juan in his love life. In his pursuit of money and women, he is ruined once but boldly builds a new career. Dreiser maintains a mixed attitude of condemnation and approval toward his hero, but basically he condones Cowperwood. Like the less-successful organisms—like the squid that are eaten—Cowperwood is merely a product of nature.

### Persistence of romanticism

Although realists and naturalists tried to deal honestly with life and gained a following among liberals who would improve conditions despite nature's law, they failed to weaken the position of the sentimental school among the reading public. With love stories, cloak-and-dagger romances, and tales of exotic lands, the sentimentalists helped their middle-class audience, the largest in the world, avoid the raw society around them. Since most of their readers were protected women, they showed the least disposition to "trifle with the marriage relation." A love story, thought Francis Marion Crawford, should "foster agreeable allusions."

During the last three decades of the nineteenth century, the romanticists and the realists carried on a kind of journalistic warfare. The realists, said the romanticists (or the "pseudo-realists," as one critic called them), had "taught pessimism in every line of their work. They taught that marriage is a failure, that home is a brothel, that courtship is lewd, that society is an aggregation of animals." The romanticists, said the realists, purveyed flimsy juvenilia to adults who evaded the vital issues of the day. In practice, however, both schools made concessions to popular taste and interests.

Since romantic fiction outsold realistic novels four to one and dominated the best-seller lists every year, it is hardly surprising that the realists and naturalists injected a little exotic color, mysticism, and pseudoscientific information into their work. This was especially true of the younger naturalists—Crane, Norris, Dreiser, and London—who had rebelled against Howells's cult of drabness. They also concocted flamboyant "Horatio Alger" stories and sensational romances in which their supermen heroes triumphed over the "mongrel" races of the world and dominated the weak and the unfit. At the same time, the romantics could not wholly ignore the evident social turmoil that soon involved so many of their lady readers in social reform. By 1900 romantic fiction writers and realists were appearing together in the pages of the *Saturday Evening Post* and the *Ladies' Home Journal,* and it was not always easy to distinguish one from another.

## For further reading

Post-Civil War intellectual history is discussed fully in Merle Curti, *The Growth of American Thought* (1964); H. S. Commager, *The American Mind* (1950); and Richard Hofstadter, *Anti-Intellectualism in American Life* (1963). More specialized treatments of ideas between 1865 and 1920 include Richard Hofstadt-er, *Social Darwinism in American Thought* (1955); M. G. White, *Social Thought in America* (1949); Daniel Aaron, *Men of Good Hope* (1951); and Charles Page, *Class and American Sociology: From Ward to Ross* (1940). R. J. Wilson, *In Quest of Community 1860-1920* (1968), analyzes the impact of industrialization and Darwinism on five prominent social thinkers. Perry Miller, *American Thought: Civil War to World War I* (1954), is an excellent anthology prefaced by a first-rate introduction. Martin Green, *The Problem of Boston* (1966), examines America's cultural center from the "golden day" to its post-Civil War decline.

A. G. Keller, *Reminiscences (Mainly Personal) of William Graham Sumner* (1933), best conveys the flavor of the man, but Sumner himself must be read to be appreciated. Standard on their subjects are Samuel Chugerman, *Lester F. Ward* (1939); C. A. Barker, *Henry George* (1955); A. E. Morgan, *Edward Bellamy* (1944); and Joseph Dorfman, *Thorstein Veblen and His America* (1934). R. B. Perry, *The Thought and Character of William James* (2 vols., 1954), is an excellent biography containing many extracts from his letters. G. W. Allen, *William James* (1967), benefits from access to James family papers. Sidney Hook, *John Dewey* (1939), is admirable. Oliver Wendell Holmes best reveals himself in Max Lerner, ed., *The Mind and Faith of Justice Holmes* (1943), and in his remarkable correspondence: *Holmes-Pollock Letters* (2 vols., 1941), and *Holmes-Laski Letters* (2 vols., 1953), both edited by M. D. Howe. Howe's biography of Holmes, *The Shaping Years 1841-1870* (1957) and *The Proving Years 1870-1888* (1963), admirably places the man in his times, as does A. T. Mason, *Brandeis* (1946). August Meier, *Negro Thought in America 1880-1915* (1963), is an able work. H. H. Bellot, *American History and American Historians* (1952), is a useful survey. See also W. H. Jordy, *Henry Adams* (1952), and Richard Hofstadter, *The Progressive Historians: Turner, Beard, Parrington* (1968).

Frederick Rudolph, *The American College and University, A History* (1962), is a sound general account. See also Richard Hofstadter and W. P. Metzger, *The Development of Academic Freedom in the United States* (1955), and Hofstadter and Wilson Smith, *American Higher Education, A Documentary History* (2 vols., 1961). G. P. Schmidt, *The Liberal Arts College* (1957), contains a short and readable section on this period. Allan Nevins, *The State Universities and Democracy* (1962), and Willard Range, *The Rise and Progress of Negro Colleges in Georgia 1865-1949* (1951), are informative.

The expansion of primary and secondary schools is covered in Freeman Butler and L. A. Cremin, *A History of Education in American Culture* (1953), and A. E. Moyer, *An Educational History of the American People* (1967). Other pertinent studies include Merle Curti, *The Social Ideas of American Educators* (1935); Thomas Woody, *A History of Women's Education in* the United States (2 vols., 1929); H. K. Beale, *Are American Teachers Free?* (1936); Rush Welter, *Popular Education and Democratic Thought in America* (1962); and C. W. Dabney, *Universal Education in the South* (2 vols., 1936). Booker T. Washington, *The Future of the American Negro* (1899), is best on his thought; his autobiography, *Up from Slavery* (1901), also is valuable. See also Hugh Hawkins, ed., *Booker T. Washington and His Critics* (1962). The story of the Chautauqua movement is told in Victoria and R. O. Case, *We Called It Culture: The Story of Chautauqua* (1948).

The following works are especially illuminating on American literature between 1865 and the turn of the century: Jay Martin, *Harvest of Change, American Literature 1865-1914* (1967), for the cultural setting and major literary movements; Warner Berthoff, *The Ferment of Realism, American Literature 1884-1919* (1965), more distinctly literary and intellectual; Larzer Ziff, *The American 1890s, Life and Times of a Lost Generation* (1966), on the Edwardian period; Alfred Kazin, *On Native Grounds* (1942), a comprehensive literary history of our period; and Van Wyck Brooks, *New England: Indian Summer* (1940) and *The Confident Years 1885-1915* (1952), the final two volumes of his 5-vol. survey of *Makers and Finders*.

For Mark Twain's early years, Dixon Wecter, *Sam Clemens of Hannibal* (1952), is indispensable. For his mature years the same may be said of Justin Kaplan, *Mr. Clemens and Mark Twain* (1966). A. B. Paine, *Mark Twain's Letters, Arranged with Comment* (2 vols., 1917), and Charles Neider, *The Autobiography of Mark Twain* (1959), present his own views. Everett Carter, *Howells and the Age of Realism* (1954), discusses Howells and his contemporaries. Howells's work is authoritatively covered by E. H. Cady, *The Road to Realism* (1956) and *The Realist at War* (1958). The best introduction to Henry James is Leon Edel, *Henry James* (5 vols., 1953-1969). See also F. W. Dupee, *Henry James: His Life and Writings* (1956). C. C. Walcutt, *American Literary Naturalism: The Divided Stream* (1956), supplies helpful background. Kenneth Lynn, *Dream of Success* (1955), challenges some previously held notions about the naturalists. Thomas Beer, *Stephen Crane: A Study in American Letters* (1923), admirably discusses Crane in his cultural setting. John Berryman, *Stephen Crane* (1950), is perceptive; R. W. Stillman, *Stephen Crane* (1968), massive. A sample of London's writing is collected in P. S. Foner, *Jack London, American Rebel* (1947). There are stimulating essays on Norris, Crane, and London in M. D. Geismar, *Rebels and Ancestors: The American Novel 1890-1915* (1953). Informative biographies of Dreiser include R. H. Elias, *Theodore Dreiser, Apostle of Nature* (1949), and F. O. Matthiesson, *Theodore Dreiser* (1951). Ellen Moers, *Two Dreisers* (1969), is a brilliant study in terms of his two greatest novels.

# A WORLD POWER

For more than five hundred years before the age of space, the history of European man was the history of expansion overseas. To explain his impulse to explore and envelop new territories would be to explain his nature. Duty moved him as much as daring, the word of God as much as the spirit of adventure, power as strongly as trade, pride as strongly as profit. The quest for personal independence urged him on as irresistibly as the quest for knowledge. He was impelled to spread "civilization," but also to escape from it.

In this long history of expansion, the European discovery of America formed but a single chapter, the prologue, really, for more than three centuries of acute rivalry among European nations for New World dominance. By the eighteenth century, this rivalry, especially that between Britain and France (Spain and other pretenders to world power having fallen to the rank of secondary states), had spread to India and other parts of the Orient. Britain's victory over Napoleon in 1815 put her far ahead in the contest for empire, and the progress of the industrial revolution in the United Kingdom kept her beyond the reach of all comers for a hundred years.

But the industrial revolution also spread throughout Europe, and after the worldwide fall in prices following the international Panic of 1873, competition for world markets became increasingly intense. The wealth created by the new industrialism also gave a fresh impetus to imperial ambitions that had been banked since Waterloo. France, Belgium, Holland, Russia, and, belatedly, Bismarck's newly unified Germany, each now sought "a place in the sun." They were soon to be followed by Italy and newly westernized Japan. Latin America, the islands of the Pacific, the interior of Africa and China, indeed all the world, once again became the stage of the imperial drama. Out went western explorers, missionaries, travelers, traders, engineers, inventors, politicians, generals, and admirals, carrying with them Britain's "White Man's Burden," France's *mission civilisatrice,* rising Germany's *Kultur.*

Like Britain, many of the latecomers, once the growth of their own industrial systems had become stable and their profits modest, sought channels for more fruitful investment in the booming railroads and industries of the United States. By the 1890s the United States itself was ready to shoulder the "expansionist destiny" of the Anglo-Saxon race, to join "the Christian nations," as an American missionary said, who "are subduing the world, in order to make mankind free."

## I   Renewal of continental aspirations

*Mexico and the Monroe Doctrine*

Expansion, of course, was hardly a new idea in the United States in the 1890s. Even before the Revolution the American colonists had resisted the mother country's policy of restricting settlement to an area east of the Appalachians. Once independent, the United States spread westward across the continent with astonishing rapidity. Nor, since Jefferson's time, were Mexico to the south and Canada to the north ever more than momentarily beyond the horizon of America's aspirations.

Following her defeat by the United States in 1848, Mexico had been torn by factional conflict out of which she emerged, ten years later, with two governments locked in civil war. One was the government of Miguel Miramón,

supported by the church, the army, and the rich. The other was the government of the Zapotec Indian Benito Juárez, the government of "la reforma." When Juárez, in 1861, emerged victorious over Miramón, Lincoln welcomed him as the first civilian ruler of Mexico under a constitutional regime.

Juárez's administration promptly got into difficulties with European monarchies which had helped finance his enemies and which also made claims for damage to their property during the civil war. When Juárez, early in 1862, suspended payments on Mexico's debt and ignored the damage claims, Britain, Spain, and France sent troops to collect. On discovering that they were merely abetting Napoleon III of France, who aimed to take advantage of America's own involvement in civil war to reenter the New World mainland and establish a Catholic monarchy in Mexico, Britain and Spain quickly withdrew from the venture. Untrammeled by rivals, Napoleon proceeded with his plan. His troops defeated Juárez's forces in 1863, and following their success the French monarch installed his puppet, Maximilian of Austria, on the Mexican throne, backed by French military strength.

As the Union began to see victory over the South approaching in America's Civil War in 1864, certain northern generals proposed marching right into Mexico to throw the monarchists out. In April that year, the House of Representatives resolved never to "acknowledge any monarchical Government erected on the ruins of any republican Government in America under the auspices of any European power." When in 1866, General Grant and other Union officers urged President Johnson to evict the French by force, Johnson preferred the advice of Secretary of State Seward, who gently reminded Napoleon III of American proximity and concern and invited him to withdraw. Fearful of a reunited United States adjacent to Mexico and a newly aggressive Prussia on his European borders, Napoleon reluctantly consented. The last French troops left Mexico in the spring of 1867. Maximilian, grown enamored of his imperial role, attempted to reign without the French, but by June 1867 Juárez's forces had overthrown, courtmartialed, and executed him. Juárez then ruled until his death in 1872. This event was followed by five more years of discord in Mexican political life, out of which emerged the strong-man regime of the military hero and one-time Juárez follower Porfirio Díaz, who governed almost uninterruptedly from 1877 to 1911.

In his communications with Napoleon, Seward never mentioned the Monroe Doctrine, but it had become apparent to all Europe that the United States now had the strength to enforce her will in the western world, and indeed that Latin America could look to her for protection from overseas aggression. Henceforth, for the first time since its enunciation in 1823, the Monroe Doctrine became a genuinely effective instrument of American foreign policy.

## The Alaska Purchase

While avoiding armed conflict with foreign enemies, Andrew Johnson's administration carried through successful negotiations with foreign friends. Among these was Russia, one of the few European states which had not unofficially sided with the Confederates. In March 1867 the Russian minister in Washington offered to unload distant and costly Alaska, hoping, among other things, in light of the new power politics in Europe and the world, to build up the United States as a counterweight to Britain. Secretary Seward, an ardent expansionist, jumped at the opportunity. After a final all-night session with the Russians, he completed the deal at 4 A.M., March 30. That very morning the President astounded the Senate with a request for approval of the purchase treaty.

The opposition press promptly denounced "Seward's Folly." After persistent opposition in Congress as well, a remarkable three-hour speech by Charles Sumner, still chairman of the Committee on Foreign Relations, helped carry the project through the Senate on April 9. While stressing the value of sustaining Seward and thereby keeping Russian friendship, Sumner also pointed out that the purchase would have the effect of removing "one more monarch from this continent." The House proved an even more difficult hurdle; but a vigorous "educational" campaign by Seward, and a liberal infusion of cash by the Russians, finally won House consent, on July 23, for the appropriation needed to close the transaction. The final price was $7.2 million.

On completing the negotiations, Seward expressed the hope that Alaska would form the northern arm of a giant pincer movement to eliminate the British monarch along with the Russian by squeezing Canada into the American fold. "I know that Nature," he said, "designs that this whole continent, not merely these thirty-six states, shall be sooner or later, within the magic circle of the American Union."

*Hunger for Canada*

During the Civil War, Canada had afforded Confederate soldiers escaping from Union prisons, and active Confederate agents, a sanctuary from which to mount attacks on the northern frontier. Such attacks, of course, ceased with the end of the war, but in 1866 northerners were again reminded of the issues British control of Canada could raise. That year, the Fenians, or the Irish Revolutionary Brother-Republics, an organization of Irish-Americans in New York, began a series of assaults on Canada with the bizarre hope of capturing the country and holding it as a hostage until the British gave Ireland her independence. The Irish vote had become an important factor in northern politics, and how to retain it while discountenancing adventures of this sort presented a ticklish problem to Andrew Johnson's administration. But rather than yield to the temptation of supporting or even condoning Irish violence, the administration chose to give Great Britain a lesson in neutral conduct by taking stern measures against anyone who used American bases for foreign intrigues.

The failure of Secretary Seward's early postwar efforts to settle American claims against Britain arising from the depredations of such wartime sea raiders as *Alabama*—constructed in England for the Confederacy to prey on Union shipping—soon showed that the American lesson was wasted on United Kingdom leaders. At first, Britain refused even to receive Seward's claims, and resentful Americans began to eye the Fenian escapades as something worth joining if only to make Brit-

ain see the light. By 1869, however, Europe was in turmoil over Bismarck's expansionist policies on the Continent, and Britain, like others, wanted American friendship if these policies led to imperial competition and war. In January 1869 Britain and the United States signed the Johnson-Clarendon Convention for arbitrating all claims against each other.

This agreement had many defects, but it satisfied the administration as a peaceful solution of the question of the Confederate cruisers. Since it made no apology, however, for Britain's release of the cruisers nor any reference to the "indirect damage" they caused in prolonging the war, the Senate, under Sumner's leadership, rejected it in April 1869 by 54 to 1. Seward's claims, known by the overall name of the *Alabama* claims, had amounted to about $15 million. Sumner began to agitate for indirect claims of over $2 billion in addition, and he suggested that Britain's withdrawal from North America, leaving Canada ripe for American annexation, would go far toward paying the bill. Sumner's indirect claims only deepened Britain's disenchantment arising from the rejection of the Johnson-Clarendon Convention; at the same time, the worsening of the European situation prompted her to swallow her pride. New negotiations, begun in Washington in January 1871, resulted in the Treaty of Washington early in May, and before the end of the month the Senate approved it. In 1872 the arbitration tribunal set up by the treaty threw out America's indirect claims over the cruiser activity and awarded the United States $15.5 million.

But the United States continued to cast a hungry eye on Canada. In 1886 Theodore Roosevelt, just bursting upon the American political stage, told a Fourth of July audience that he looked forward to the "day when not a foot of American soil will be held by any European power." In 1891 "Jingo Jim" Blaine said he expected that Canada would "ultimately seek . . . admission to the union."

581

## II  Beyond continental frontiers

### A rising Pacific power

American ambitions did not end with North America nor at the water's edge. Commodore Matthew C. Perry in the 1850s thought it "self-evident" that the United States would have to "extend its jurisdiction beyond the limits of the western continent." At that time Cuba in particular attracted many southern expansionists. We may recall, too, how in 1869 President Grant's minions hungered for the annexation of Santo Domingo, again without success. Two themes were expressed then which would exert considerable influence later on. "The true interests of the American people," said the *Philadelphia Press,* "will be better served at this important period of our national history by a thorough . . . development of the immense resources of our existing territory than by any rash attempts to increase it." "We cannot have colonies, dependencies, subjects," the *New York Tribune* added, "without renouncing the essential conception of democratic institutions."

The construction of the transcontinental railroads after the Civil War strengthened the argument for concentrating on the development of domestic resources, but it also sharpened American appetites for Pacific outlets and islands, appetites first whetted by the settlement of Oregon and California in the 1840s and 1850s. Even in those early decades the United States had acquired "most-favored-nation" treaty rights in China giving American traders terms equal to those of any other country; and after Commodore Perry had forcibly opened Japan in 1854, Townsend Harris, the first American consul there, negotiated a treaty of friendship by which he became the chief advisor on international relations to the inexperienced Japanese government. In 1867 the United States Navy took possession of uninhabited Midway Island deep in the Pacific, but inability to dredge its harbor disappointed those who sought to use it as a way station for American ships. Soon after, Samoa in the southern Pacific and Hawaii in the northern Pacific involved the United States in epochal arrangements.

After the intensification of the China trade and the spread of Pacific whaling early in the nineteenth century, Samoa had become well known to mariners as a refuge for vessels caught in Pacific storms. By the 1830s ships of many nations had begun to make regular stops there for replenishment of supplies, and various religious denominations sent missionaries to cater to the spiritual needs of the crews as well as to convert the native Polynesians. After the opening of the first transcontinental railroad in 1869, Americans engaged in trade between San Francisco and Australia eyed Samoa's fine harbor of Pago Pago with the idea of making it into a coaling station for steamships. A treaty worked out for this purpose in 1872 died in the Senate, but in 1878, following a friendly visit to Washington the year before by a Samoan prince, a new treaty was negotiated and approved. While denying Samoans the privilege they sought of becoming a protectorate of the United States, this treaty obliged the United States to "employ its good offices" in adjusting differences between Samoa and other nations.

Shortly thereafter the treaty was put to a stern test. In the mid-1880s, Germany, already the leading economic power in Samoa, began to enlarge her activities at the expense of British and American interests. In 1889, dissatisfied with Samoan cooperation, the Germans replaced the reigning king with a more friendly native prince under their armed protection. The United States promptly supported the faction of the deposed ruler and, together with Britain, dispatched combat ships to the islands. A hurricane, blowing up at the appropriate moment and making rubble of all but one of the naval vessels in the vicinity, effectively put off hostilities. In the meantime, Britain and the United States agreed to attend a meeting with Bismarck in Berlin, and there, in June 1889, the three powers established a tripartite protectorate over Samoa.

German aggression in the islands had been checked; but friction among the three protecting nations persisted until 1899 when, by a new agreement, Samoa was formally divided between the United States and Germany, with Britain receiving compensation elsewhere in the Pacific. The United States acquired Pago Pago harbor and surrounding territory while Germany obtained the rest of the land.

Small though the Samoan issue was, Cleveland's Secretary of State, Walter Q. Gresham, saw its significance when he said in 1894, with manifest distaste, that it was "the first departure from our traditional and well-established policy of avoiding entangling alliances with foreign powers in relation to objects remote from this hemisphere."

### The question of Hawaii

The Hawaiian Islands, strategically a natural outpost of the North American continent, were much less remote from the United States than Samoa and had been engaged in relations with Americans for a longer time. New York and New England vessels in the China trade called at the islands in the 1790s, and in the following three decades Hawaiian produce as well as Hawaiian ports played a part in the fur trade. As early as 1820, Yankee missionaries had settled in the islands and proceeded to transform Honolulu into a pleasant replica of a New England town. After 1840 Hawaii became the center of South Pacific whaling, and by 1860, along with French, British, and other craft, about 400 American whalers had visited the islands. By then, many American citizens owned permanent homes in Hawaii, while many Hawaiians, after shipping on American vessels, found work in California and settled there.

After 1826 Hawaii became a focus of French Catholic missionary activity as well as French business enterprise—both objectionable to the entrenched Protestants, white and converted native alike. By 1840 France seemed on the verge of militant intervention in the islands to protect her religious and commercial interests. When nationals of other expansionist powers also threatened to supplant the stumbling Hawaiian government with a more efficient one of their own choosing, the United States was prevailed upon to take the first official step to preserve the islands' independence. In 1842 Daniel Webster, as Secretary of State, formally declared that the United States had a greater interest in Hawaii than any other country and would look with dissatisfaction upon any European power that sought "to take possession of the islands as a conquest" or to exercise "any undue control over the existing Government, or any exclusive privileges or preferences in matters of commerce." Rival foreign claims to Hawaiian ports and trade continued to agitate the islands, and a growing local faction sought outright annexation to the United States. In 1854 the Pierce administration accepted an offer from the Hawaiian king to negotiate an annexation treaty; but the king's death brought a change in local policy and the treaty project fell through.

After 1850 sugar growing supplanted whaling as Hawaii's main economic dependence, and problems of land tenure and labor supply were added to the earlier issues between the government and outside capitalists and among the outside rivals themselves. Until 1875 American sugar producers in the Louisiana area had succeeded in keeping Hawaiian sugar out of United States ports. That year, however, a reciprocity treaty between the United States and the islands (negotiated under

584

threats by Hawaiian growers to look to Britain for markets and political support) admitted Hawaiian sugar into the United States and American commodities into Hawaii, both duty-free. Political reciprocity also was involved. In exchange for a reassertion of Webster's old promise of America's "dissatisfaction" with any other nation's tampering with Hawaii's independence, the islands pledged themselves not to alienate any territory to foreign governments nor to extend to them the commercial privileges won by the United States.

Under the reciprocity treaty, Hawaiian sugar growing boomed, and with it flourished the rest of the business community engaged in financing sugar operations, hauling sugar products, supplying and maintaining machinery and tools, and in general satisfying the needs of a newly prosperous country. Native Hawaiians, however, grew increasingly restive as they saw more and more of their arable land controlled by white—mainly American-descended—planters, and themselves ever more deeply submerged under an influx of uncongenial Chinese workers.

Negotiations to renew the reciprocity treaty began in 1884, but the United States Senate would not approve a new agreement until 1887 when, in recognition of the rising strategic importance of Hawaii in the imperialist contest, it won an amendment granting the United States exclusive use of Pearl Harbor as a coaling station and repair base for naval vessels. In the same year, Hawaiian-born white businessmen, fed up with the corrupt and authoritarian regime of King Kalakaua, brought off a bloodless revolution forcing him to accept a new framework of government—the "Bayonet Constitution," Hawaiians called it—giving themselves control of the government and extending the franchise to white foreigners. Property qualifications, in turn, disfranchised most native citizens.

Strategically, politically, and economically, Hawaii was moving ever closer to the United States. But there was to be more violence before annexation was accomplished. In 1890, 99 percent of Hawaiian exports consisted of sugar for the American mainland. In that year Congress admitted other foreign sugars (as well as Hawaii's) duty-free but gave United States growers a bounty of 2 cents a pound. Hawaii's single-staple economy was sorely wounded by these measures. At the same time, nativist Hawaiians grew more and more antagonistic toward the discriminatory new constitution. Hawaiian discontent spread after 1891, when King Kalakaua died and was succeeded by his sister, Queen Liliuokalani, a resolute opponent of white rule. By 1893 "Queen Lil's" calculated disregard of constitutional restraints, and ultimately her efforts to throw off the constitution altogether, drove white businessmen into a second rebellion. They had the enthusiastic support of the American minister to Hawaii, John L. Stevens, who secured for them the protection of American troops landed from a cruiser.

Stevens promptly recognized the provisional government set up by the rebels, who lost no time in dispatching a five-man commission to Washington to negotiate a treaty of annexation. This treaty, sent to the Senate by the retiring President Harrison, who favored it, was held up by Democratic opposition, and was still under discussion when Grover Cleveland was inaugurated in March. Suspicious of Stevens's activities in Hawaii, Cleveland recalled the treaty from the Senate and sent a special commissioner to the islands to investigate the situation there. Secretary of State Gresham, in summarizing this emissary's report for Cleveland in October 1893, charged that Stevens, by his abuse of the authority of the United States, had done a great wrong to a "feeble but independent State." Cleveland tried to restore Queen Lil under a constitutional regime, but the provisional government held fast. In 1894 it wrote still another constitution, proclaimed the Republic of Hawaii, and confirmed Sanford B. Dole as its first President.

Realizing that he would have to use force to unseat the new government, Cleveland recognized it in August 1894, but he refused to accede to its urgent requests for annexation. In 1897, under McKinley, a new annexation treaty was worked out, but the Senate, reflecting popular discontent with imperialist adventures, rejected it. The public temper changed during the Spanish-American war when Hawaii's strategic value became more evident, and in July 1898, by a joint resolution, Congress approved a new treaty making Hawaii "a part of the territory of the United States,"—the first sizable part overseas. In August 1959, about seven months after Alaska was admitted to the Union, Hawaii became the fiftieth state.

## III   Economic and diplomatic militancy

### Blaine and Mahan

So intent were Americans after the Civil War on developing their domestic resources and home markets that the United States merchant marine, for almost a century among the largest in the world, was allowed to disappear almost entirely from the sea. Similarly, the United States navy, once as strong as the merchant marine, had shrunk by the 1880s to a small number of wooden sailing hulks worse than useless in an age of steel and steam.

Nevertheless, even in the most discouraging times, certain American spokesmen willingly shouldered the mantle of empire that Seward himself had inherited from the expansionist generation of the 1840s and 1850s. Among these men two ranked highest: James G. Blaine, Secretary of State in 1881 under Garfield and again from 1889 to 1892 under Harrison; and Captain, later Admiral, A. T. Mahan, the gifted propagandist who became the mentor of the later generation of imperialists.

An ardent admirer of Henry Clay as a young man, Blaine like Clay, as we have seen, became a perpetual aspirant for the presidency who never satisfied his ambition; but, like Clay once more, he used the power and prestige of lesser offices to push an aggressive and spirited diplomacy, especially in Latin America. Blaine strove not only to keep European governments out of this area but also to further American influence and commercial intercourse with the republics to the south.

Latin Americans still had strong religious and nationality ties with Spain and Portugal and strong commercial ties with Britain. In the 1870s Germany began to seek Latin-American outlets for her goods and capital. In an effort to deflect Latin-American trade and development toward the "Big Sister" to the north, Blaine in 1881 issued invitations to a Pan-American conference. Acceptances were still coming in when Garfield's assassination caused the meeting to be canceled. Back in office in 1889, Blaine revived his original scheme. That year, on his invitation, delegates from eighteen nations met in Washington and

*"The world is my market;*
*my customers are all mankind"*—
Y. Doodle. Front page of the Daily Graphic,
*New York, March 20, 1877.*

The New-York Historical Society, New York City

586

formed the Pan-American Union, but they accomplished little else.

Although Latin Americans persisted in buying largely from Europeans, they sold mainly in the United States, and mainly items that were duty-free. When the Latin-American delegates to the 1889 conference failed to grant tariff concessions to United States exports, Blaine showed his hand by threatening to retaliate with tariffs on Latin-American goods. The so-called reciprocity provision of the McKinley Tariff of 1890, which said the United States would reciprocate for favorable treatment and meant also that we would resist unfavorable treatment, was Blaine's weapon. Blaine's tactics induced few Latin-American countries to increase their trade with the United States or to reduce their hostility toward her.

As Secretary of State, Blaine also advocated a powerful new American navy. In 1881, with his approval, Secretary of the Navy William H. Hunt persuaded Congress to set up the Naval Advisory Board to agitate for larger naval appropriations. Though Blaine was soon out of office, this first step led to others. In 1883 Congress appropriated funds for the famous White Squadron of four new steel ships equipped with steam power and a full rigging of white sails. But these vessels constituted only a token navy, since they had no armor. The establishment of the Naval War College at Newport in 1884 gave further impetus to "big navy" propaganda. At Newport in 1886, just before he was made president of the College, Captain Mahan gave the lectures that eventually became the heart of his series of books on sea power in history. Such was the state of American opinion at this time that Mahan's classic-to-be, *The Influence of Sea Power upon History, 1660-1783*, went three years before finding a publisher in 1890.

During the nineties Mahan also published a series of magazine articles which were collected in a book entitled *The Interest of America in Sea Power* (1897). Here Mahan applied to American conditions the general principles outlined in his historical writings. Britain, he said, had grown great on sea power; the United States should profit from her example not simply by rebuilding her merchant marine and her navy but by adding colonies and naval bases throughout the world. Without colonies and bases, Mahan argued, ships of war would be "like land birds, unable to fly far from their own shores." In particular, the United States must have naval bases in the Caribbean to protect a potential isthmian canal and in the Pacific not only to guard and assist American commerce but also to take part in the coming great struggle between Western and Oriental civilizations.

Mahan's ideas were promptly taken up by a group of influential Republican Senators, including Henry Cabot Lodge and Albert J. Beveridge, and by Theodore Roosevelt, soon to become Assistant Secretary of the Navy. British navalists also took up Mahan, as did Kaiser Wilhelm II, who found in his writings additional arguments for the naval challenge Germany was already issuing to the United Kingdom.

Between 1883 and 1890, largely because of the work of Blaine and Mahan, Congress authorized the building of nine cruisers, and construction began on the first modern American battleship, *Maine*. Then came the Naval Act of 1890, the result of a report from a Naval Policy Board that Secretary of the Navy Benjamin F. Tracy had set up to investigate the whole naval expansion issue. Heretofore, to calm foreign anxieties over American naval expansion and modernization, the navy had been described officially as consisting of "seagoing coastline battleships." Now the fiction of coastline defense was officially abandoned, and the idea of a "navy second to none" emerged.

Tracy's Naval Policy Board acknowledged that the United States had "no colonies nor any apparent desire to acquire them," that its foreign trade was "carried in foreign vessels," and that its manufactures competed "with those of other nations in but few markets." But the Board also urged the construction of 200 modern warships. Although Congress did not go that far, it authorized the construction of so many battleships, cruisers, gunboats, and torpedo boats that by 1898 only Britain and France outranked the United States as a naval power. The expansionists also persuaded Congress to enact the Ocean Mail Subsidy Act of 1891 to resurrect the merchant marine. This act, by increasing federal payments for carrying overseas mail, encouraged the construction and operation of many new vessels.

Toward the end of the century, the position of the United States in world trade was greatly improved, as Blaine had hoped. American imports, valued at $462 million in 1870, almost doubled in the next thirty years, reaching $850 million in 1900; in the same period, American exports almost tripled, rising from $530 million to approximately $1.4 billion. The Panic of 1893, which shrank markets at home, greatly stimulated the quest of American businessmen for markets abroad and the quest of the imperialists for empire. Albert J. Beveridge put the case pridefully and aggressively in a speech delivered in April 1898:

> American factories are making more than the American people can use; American soil is producing more than they can consume. Fate has written our policy for us; the trade of the world must and shall be ours. . . . We will cover the ocean with our merchant marine. We will build a navy to the measure of our greatness. Great colonies governing themselves, flying our flag and trading with us, will grow about our posts of trade.

### The martial spirit

While the United States was girding her resources to serve the growth of foreign trade and world power, a series of diplomatic incidents triggered talk of war. Such talk did much to enliven the martial spirit that militant leaders wished to promote.

One incident arose over the old problem of United States fishing rights in Canadian wa-

ters. Friction over these rights had increased as a result of the other issues in Canadian-American relations during and after the Civil War, and while the Treaty of Washington of 1871 formally resolved some of the difficulties, American fishermen continued to be harassed and exploited by local authorities in Canada and Newfoundland. The Treaty of Washington permitted either party to terminate the agreement on two years' notice after ten years had passed. When the United States, accordingly, notified Canada in 1883 that it would terminate the treaty on July 1, 1885, Canada began taking American fishing vessels found in her waters after the latter date. "Wherever the American flag on an American fishing smack is touched by a foreigner," declaimed Henry Cabot Lodge, then a young congressman from Massachusetts, "the great American heart is touched." The *Detroit News* boasted in February 1887:

> We do not want to fight,
> But, by jingo, if we do,
> We'll scoop in all the fishing grounds
> And the whole Dominion too.

An informal arrangement with Britain, worked out through diplomatic channels by the Cleveland administration, ended the fishing controversy in the Atlantic, but another controversy over the seal fisheries in the Bering Sea area soon worsened relations once more. When rumors spread in 1890 that British warships were policing the region, war talk again was heard. "The thing to do," explained the *Sioux City Journal*, is to "shoot *any* British ship which is in those waters." Cooler heads again prevailed, and an arbitration treaty was ratified in February 1892.

A third episode occurred after a revolt in 1891 against the president of Chile, in which the United States had backed the president. When the rebels won, feeling against the United States ran high; and when, in October 1891, the captain of *U.S.S. Baltimore*, then in Valparaíso, permitted his crew to go ashore unarmed, a riot broke out among them and some Chileans in which two Americans were killed and others imprisoned. Chilean apolo-

587

588

gies were slow in coming, and President Harrison hinted that he might invite Congress to declare war. Other prominent people in the United States were bursting to take up the cudgels, among them Theodore Roosevelt, whose intimates thereafter were to taunt him as "the Chilean Volunteer." Just in time, a full apology arrived to calm American feelings, and Chile eventually agreed to pay $75,000 to the families of the dead sailors and to the men who had been injured in the fracas.

A more serious affair brought the United States closer to war in 1895. This incident involved disputed territory between British Guiana and neighboring Venezuela where gold was discovered in the 1880s. When Venezuela broke off diplomatic relations with Britain in 1887, the United States offered to act as mediator, but Britain rejected the proposal. The last American mediation effort was made in July 1895 by Richard Olney, Cleveland's Secretary of State. In a note to Lord Salisbury, the British Foreign Minister, Olney reminded him of the noncolonization clauses of the Monroe Doctrine and proceeded to invite Britain to leave America altogether. "Three thousand miles of intervening ocean make any permanent political union between a European and an American state unnatural and inexpedient," Olney wrote. Then he added these provocative words:

Today, the United States is practically sovereign on this continent, and its fiat is law upon the subjects to which it confines its interposition. Why? It is not because of the pure friendship or good will felt for it. . . . It is because, in addition to all other grounds, its infinite resources combined with its isolated position render it master of the situation and practically invulnerable as against any or all other powers.

Olney closed with a suggestion of "peaceful arbitration."

Salisbury took his time in replying. When he did, in November 1895, he rejected arbitration and proceeded to remind the United States that the Monroe Doctrine was not recognized in international law and did not apply to boundary disputes. Cleveland made the Olney-Salisbury interchange public in December, when he himself heightened feeling with

a message to Congress. In this message he asked for funds to finance a commission to determine the actual boundary between British Guiana and Venezuela, and then added the inflammatory assertion that "it will . . . be the duty of the United States to resist by every means in its power, as a wilful aggression upon its rights and interests" any efforts by Great Britain to grasp any territory that the United States, after investigation, found of right to be Venezuela's. He was fully aware, he said, "of all the consequences that may follow." But "there is no calamity which a great nation can invite which equals that which follows a supine submission to wrong and injustice and the consequent loss of national self-respect and honor, beneath which are defended a people's safety and greatness."

Congress cheered these fighting words and voted for the fact-finding commission. Twenty-six governors promptly pledged their support. If war came, said Theodore Roosevelt, he hoped he might "have a hand in it myself." "The bankers, brokers, and anglomaniacs generally," he moaned to his sympathetic friend Lodge, seemed to favor "peace at any price. . . . Personally I rather hope that the fight will come soon. The clamor of the peace faction has convinced me that this country needs a war."

Since the Venezuelan boundary dispute coincided with mounting silverite aspirations for action against the alleged center of the "gold power" (see p. 523), it was much more inflammatory than any of the earlier episodes. But the peace parties eventually won out both in the United States and Britain. Cleveland's proposal for a boundary commission gave Americans time to simmer down, since nothing could be done until such a commission reported. Britain, meanwhile, was growing increasingly restive over German rivalry, and increasingly concerned over American friendship on that account. In 1896, when faced with a serious outbreak of violence by the Boers in her colony of South Africa, Britain was reminded of German ambitions by a telegram of sympathy sent in January that year to the Boer leader by Germany's Kaiser Wilhelm. Thereafter, British leaders refused to be

drawn further into the Venezuelan dispute with the United States, which had become a power to be courted. In February 1897, at America's behest, Britain and Venezuela negotiated a treaty turning the boundary dispute over to international arbitration. In 1899 a final settlement was made.

## IV  The Spanish-American War

*Crisis over Cuba*

As the Venezuela issue faded, the young American inflammables found a new situation to exploit—the Cuban insurrection against Spain, which had begun in 1895.

When the Cubans rebelled against Spanish rule in 1868, Americans had looked on indifferently. This rebellion dragged out for ten sickening years. Then, having lost many men and spent large sums to crush the Cubans, Spain agreed to undertake serious reforms. The Cubans made two major demands: (1) emancipation of the slaves on the island; and (2) self-government for the island's inhabitants. Spain actually took another ten years before freeing the slaves, and she postponed granting autonomous government indefinitely, in the meantime saddling the devastated Cuban economy with all the costs of the ten years' struggle. She made the mistake, moreover, of giving amnesty to rebel leaders, perhaps to be rid of them. In any case, most of them exiled themselves to New York City where they agitated persistently for Spain's expulsion from the New World.

Spain's irresponsibility in Cuba soured her relations with the United States, but there were few serious incidents before 1895. By then, however, the world, the United States, and Cuba all had greatly changed. The aggressive activities of Britain, France, and Germany in the Western Hemisphere had made it increasingly likely that if Cuba were lost to decadent Spain a more vigorous power might attempt to claim her. France's efforts, starting in 1881, to build a canal across the Isthmus of

Panama intensified the threat of Europe in the Caribbean. In the United States, in turn, while expansionism, navalism, and empire building all were being pushed, interest in an American canal connecting the Atlantic and the Pacific as well as in coaling stations, strategic harbors, and protected bases had matured.

The changes in Cuba were as far-reaching as those elsewhere. After the emancipation of the slaves, large amounts of European and American capital had moved into the island, where modern business practices were introduced, especially in the production of cane sugar. At the same time, Europe had greatly enlarged its own sugar production, mainly beet sugar, and the United States gradually became Cuba's principal market and source of capital. An executive agreement with Spain in 1884 removing the American duty on Cuban sugar further stimulated production, pushing it to a record 1,050,000 tons in 1894. Events then suddenly conspired against Cuban prosperity. Europe's production of beet sugar became so great that the world price of sugar fell. The Panic of 1893 and the ensuing depression further weakened prices. Finally, the Wilson-Gorman Tariff of 1894 (see p. 522) restored a 40 percent duty on sugar. Raw sugar brought 8 cents a pound in Cuba in 1884. By 1895, the price had broken to 2 cents, and the Cuban way of life broke with it.

When insurrection started again in 1895, American interests were inevitably threatened. To quell the rebels, Spain sent over her best general and 200,000 men, but the Spaniards could not cope with the insurgent leaders and their guerrilla followers, who had taken to the hills. The rebels also embarked on the widespread destruction of property in order to exhaust government resources and thereby force the withdrawal of government forces. American property naturally was lost in the holocaust, much of it deliberately destroyed in an effort to drive the United States to intervene to protect her interests, and many Americans now renewed the old demand for annexation of the island.

In January 1896 Spain sent General Valeriano Weyler to Cuba as governor and military commander. Weyler did not hesitate to fight fire with fire, and soon earned the nickname "Butcher." Weyler made Cuba a country of concentration camps, into some of which he drove the guerrillas and into others the rest of the population. Since few could work, few could eat, and starvation and disease soon took 200,000 lives.

During all this time a junta, or council, of Cuban exiles in New York kept pressing for American intervention and Cuban autonomy. Joseph Pulitzer of the *New York World* and William Randolph Hearst of the *New York Journal,* meanwhile, started a spirited circulation battle, each trying to outdo the other in printing gory stories of Spanish brutality. Mahan, Roosevelt, Lodge, and others, their gaze as much on the Spanish Philippines as a stronghold of American empire in the Orient as on Spanish Cuba in the Caribbean, also whipped up the war spirit. Their concern over the eternal will-o'-the-wisp of a gigantic China trade was deepened just at this moment by the dramatic intensification of demands among the imperial powers of Europe for new "spheres of influence" in the collapsing colossus of the East (see p. 598). But President Cleveland refused to be stampeded by the junta, the journalists, or the jingoes. As to the public frenzy over Weyler's methods in Cuba, he feared, he said, "there were some outrages on both sides if the truth were known."

By March 1897, McKinley had become President on a platform calling upon the United States "actively [to] use its influence and good offices to restore peace and give independence" to Cuba. By then, "peace" and "independence" may have become contradictory goals, with "influence and good offices" insuf-

ficient to achieve either. In any case, in midsummer 1897 McKinley sent General Stewart L. Woodford to Madrid with instructions to let Spain know that American patience was wearing thin but that she still had time to introduce reforms in Cuba broad enough to quiet American if not Cuban anxiety. The fortuitous assassination of the hard-line Spanish premier, Cánavos del Castillo, just before Woodford's arrival, and his replacement by the liberal Práxedes Mateo Sagasta, made Woodford's mission easier, and in October the President received his report of proposed Spanish concessions sufficient to postpone further American action.

By the time of his first annual message to Congress, December 6, 1897, McKinley found that Spain had supplanted Weyler with a more humane general, that "the policy of cruel rapine and extermination . . . had been reversed," and that the Cubans had been offered autonomy under a liberalized Spanish sovereignty. And he urged upon the firebrands in and out of Congress that Spain "be given a reasonable chance to realize . . . the new order of things to which she stands irrevocably committed." It was in this speech, while discussing American choices in Cuba, that McKinley stated: "I speak not of forcible annexation, for that can not be thought of. That, in our code of morality, would be criminal aggression."

Early in 1898 two chance events combined to make presidential resistance to the jingoes increasingly difficult, if not impossible. On February 9, a letter stolen from the Havana post office by a rebel sympathizer fell into the hands of Hearst's *New York Journal.* In it, Dupuy de Lôme, the Spanish minister to the United States, characterized McKinley, after his message to Congress of December 1897, as "weak and a bidder for the admiration of the crowd, besides being a would-be politician who tries to leave a door open behind himself while keeping on good terms with the jingoes of his party." This was a private letter, but Hearst made it as public as possible. Spain disavowed any evil intent on her minister's part, and de Lôme himself resigned as soon as the letter was published.

The *Maine* tragedy followed in less than a week. The new battleship *Maine* had been sent to Havana in January 1898, when the American consul-general there cabled that American property and persons were increasingly in danger. Spain was assured that the ship's visit had no aggressive purpose, and when *Maine* arrived later in January, the Spanish General Blanco, Weyler's successor, entertained her officers and men. Then on February 15 *Maine* apparently hit a submarine mine, and two officers and 258 of her crew were lost.

An immediate official inquiry left the causes of the explosion uncertain, but to Assistant Navy Secretary Roosevelt it was "an act of dirty treachery" his Department should instantly avenge. The delay caused by the authorization of more thorough investigations terminated his allegiance to the administration; McKinley, he asserted at this time, had "no more backbone than a chocolate éclair." Among the messages, telegrams, and cables TR—in the absence of his chief, John D. Long—now fired off from the Navy Department to ship officers and to Congress itself was the famous one of February 25, to Commodore George Dewey, with his Pacific squadron off the China shore: "In the event of declaration of war Spain, your duty will be to see that the Spanish squadron does not leave the Asiatic coast, and then offensive operations in the Philippine Islands." But Dewey had already had such instructions the previous December; nor was he to be able to carry out his "offensive operations" until the following July.

The popularity, if not the legitimacy, of Roosevelt's attitudes and actions was reflected on March 8, when the President's request for $50 million for national defense was granted unanimously by both House and Senate. Although *Maine's* Captain Sigsbee had wired home right after the disaster that "Public opin-ion should be suspended until further report," it was not long before the cry "Remember the *Maine!*" ran through the country. When the report of the detailed investigation of the sinking leaked out in newspapers on March 27, the term "external explosion" (meaning the submarine mine for which Spain could not now be held responsible) captured the imagination of the people. America had suffered the "initial defeat!" "There is no stopping place now short of the absolute independence of Cuba," declared the *New York Times*. "It would have been as easy to end the war of the Revolution at Bunker Hill or the Civil War at Bull Run as to turn back now."

Peace, nevertheless, still counted many strong and well-placed partisans. Not least among them were the industrial giants of the country, the protectionist phalanx so committed to the Republican party, who saw the burgeoning business revival after the long depression of the nineties endangered by war costs and war taxes. Boss Hanna stood firmly with these party paragons. In the Senate, moreover, such Republican luminaries as Aldrich and Allison, and in the House, Czar Reed himself, led the peace factions. As for Major McKinley in the White House, "I have been through one war," he told a friend at this time. "I have seen the dead piled up, and I do not want to see another." Yet, no more than in the election of 1896 did he take to the rostrum. Even his leading defender among historians writes that "the chief personal weakness of his diplomacy was his silence. Fearful of being misunderstood or inflaming the issue, he remained silent during the whole long crisis."

Even a masterful leader might have found it impossible to reduce the war delirium of the American people; McKinley's efforts through diplomacy to divert Cuba and Spain from their war had no known effect. On March 27, just as the "external explosion" story of the *Maine* disaster broke, the President, after intensive consultation with his Cabinet, cabled Woodford in Madrid a series of demands on Spain. The most important one called for an armistice on the island until October 1, during which the United States would act as mediator between the contestants. The next day he

591

592

cabled the further stipulation that Cuban independence would be the only satisfactory outcome of the mediation. On March 31, Woodford was able to cable back that Spain, fearful of her own people in case of war with the United States, would make many concessions; yet fearful also for the survival of his government and even of the monarchy should Cuban independence be granted, Premier Sagasta refused to accept any armistice that the rebels did not ask for first.

With their hopes for American intervention rising every day, the rebels would make no such request; indeed, their demands upon Spain grew harsher as time passed. Spain, on her part, scrambled to find support and allies in Europe, but the German Foreign Minister, on April 5, expressed the attitude of most other nations when he told the Spanish ambassador: "You are isolated, because everybody wants to be pleasant to the United States, or, at any rate, nobody wants to arouse America's anger; the United States is a rich country, against which you simply cannot sustain a war."

When the Pope that same day agreed to suggest an armistice, thereby saving Spain the humiliation of yielding to an American ultimatum, Sagasta gratefully grasped the offer, and Woodford promptly cabled home Spain's consent to "immediate and unconditional suspension of hostilities, . . . to become . . . effective so soon as accepted by the insurgents." Woodford added on his own, "I believe that this means peace, . . . which must be approved at the bar of final history." On April 9, Woodford cabled the news that a "suspension of hostilities" had been proclaimed.

By then, prodded into a state of virtual prostration by the importunities of the public, the press, the Protestant clergy, expansionist Republican politicians, and their advisers among the "large America" intellectuals, McKinley had completed a despairing message to Congress. In it he cited the "disappointing reception by Spain" of his March 27 proposals, admitted that the "only hope of relief and repose . . . is the enforced pacification of Cuba," and asked for authorization "to use the military and naval forces of the United States" for this and related purposes.

Informed of Spain's capitulation of April 9, and fearful of its effect on the peaceable President, Senator Lodge rushed to the White House where he convinced McKinley that Spain's was a "humbug armistice." The proposed "enforced pacification of Cuba" by the United States could now at least have been postponed, the need to employ the "military and naval forces" averted. Under Lodge's influence, however, the President dispatched his message on April 11 exactly as written, adding only a face-saving paragraph at the end conveying "the latest decree of the Queen Regent" and asking Congress to give it "your just and careful attention." He fully exasperated that aroused body by closing with the fond hope that if Sagasta's submission found favor there, then "our aspirations as a Christian, peace-loving people will be realized."

McKinleyism has always meant Xenophobia, Protectionism, and Isolationism, the program his fellow small-town Ohioan, Warren G. Harding, would make famous as "normalcy" following his election in 1920 after the carnage of World War I. In his April 11 message to Congress, McKinley did not fail to make his personal position clear on the misplaced popular and political pressures upon him:

*The temper and forebearance of our people have been so sorely tried as to beget a perilous unrest . . . which has inevitably found expression from time to time in the National Legislature, so that issues wholly external to our body politic engross attention and stand in the way of that close devotion to domestic advancement that becomes a self-contained commonwealth whose primal maxim has been the avoidance of all foreign entanglements.*

Such sentiments, and the prayer for peace at the end, made it impossible for Congress to accept this message as the war message it hungered for. It lacked "that *ring*," one of the President's aides admitted. An aroused Republican senator, fearful for the future of his party, stormed into the State Department demanding of Secretary Day, "By —, don't your

President know where the war-declaring power is lodged? Tell him, by —, that if he doesn't do something Congress will exercise the power."

Very shortly thereafter, war resolutions were on the floor of both houses, their instant adoption delayed mainly by confusion over just what form the aspirations for Cuba should take. On April 17, in a sharp rebuff to the President whose prerogative it usurped, the Senate by 67 to 21 adopted the Turpie Amendment, recognizing the insurgent Republic of Cuba. McKinley was sufficiently aroused by this affront to promise a veto of any joint war resolutions if this amendment were included. The Senate rejected the threat; but the Republican leadership in the House eventually forced a compromise, agreeing to go along with the Senate war resolutions if the Turpie Amendment were withdrawn.

In their final joint resolutions of April 20, House and Senate, echoing the American Declaration of Independence, declared that "the people and the Island of Cuba are, *and of right ought to be*, free and independent." They demanded that Spain relinquish her authority in Cuba and withdraw her land and naval forces, and directed the President to use United States land and naval forces to see that Spain complied and Cuba was liberated. Without debate or roll-call vote, Congress added the famous Teller Amendment to these resolutions, disclaiming any American "disposition" to exercise sovereignty over the island once pacification had been accomplished and asserting the "intention" of the United States "to leave the government and control of the Island to its people." This renunciation, Senator Teller declared, was made in regard to Cuba alone, "whatever we may do as to some other islands," not excepting the Philippines.

Congress's disavowal of territorial aggrandizement in Cuba mollified McKinley sufficiently for him to sign the joint resolutions. Spain, on her part, on April 24, recalled her minister from Washington, gave Woodford his walking papers in Madrid, and declared war on the United States. Only the next day, April 25, did McKinley formally recommend to Congress, retroactive to April 21, that it declare a state of war to exist between the United States and Spain. A few weeks earlier, when urged to "dissuade" the inflammables in the House from their warlike course, Czar Reed himself was forced to admit: "Dissuade them! Dissuade them! You might as well ask me to stand in the middle of a Kansas waste and dissuade a cyclone."

### The splendid little war

The war with Spain was almost too cyclonically short and swift to suit those who craved an occasion for American might to resound across the world. The fruits of victory, at the same time, proved gratifyingly worldwide. They were not without their puckering sour taste, however, especially in the coveted Philippines where the first encounters for "Cuba Libre" took place.

On April 27 Commodore Dewey raised steam near Hong Kong and on the night of the 30th sailed into Manila Bay, where the

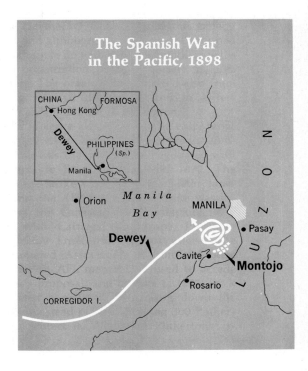

The Spanish War in the Pacific, 1898

next morning he blasted the antiquated Spanish fleet sitting there. News of the victory arrived in Washington May 7.

Dewey lacked the necessary men for further "offensive operations in Philippine Islands," and by the time the first reinforcements of 2,500 arrived on June 30, British, French, Japanese, and German men-of-war were swarming around the Philippines seeking to protect their nationals. The German force was much the strongest, and Dewey was suspicious of it, but it appears to have had no aggressive designs. By July 25 about 11,000 American troops had landed in the Philippines, under General Wesley Merritt. Supported by Filipino insurrectionists under Emilio Aguinaldo, whom Dewey had befriended and helped arm, Merritt took Manila on August 13.

By then the "splendid little war," as John Hay called it, had already come to a close in the West Indies. On April 29 a Spanish fleet under Admiral Cervera had sailed west from the Cape Verde Islands, destination unknown. American coastal cities panicked and demanded naval protection. A patrol fleet was established to satisfy eastern politicians, and the main American fleet under Admiral William T. Sampson and Commodore Winfield Scott Schley tried to find Cervera before he reached Cuba, where they decided he was headed. They did not locate him, however, until he was safely in Santiago harbor, where Sampson bottled him up. A military expedition was now planned to capture Santiago overland and force Cervera out under the American fleet's waiting guns.

On June 14 a poorly equipped expeditionary force of 17,000 men under General William R. Shafter finally left Tampa, Florida. Typical of this army was the First Volunteer Cavalry Regiment, the "Rough Riders," who had few horses. Shafter and his men reached the Cuban coast in the vicinity of Santiago on June 20 and took six days to disembark. A few more days passed before this army moved on toward the Cuban port. The Spaniards had 200,000 men in Cuba but only 13,000 in Santiago. And of these, because of problems of transport and supply, only 1700 could be mobilized to meet the Americans. The Spaniards were well trained and well armed, however. After a two-day battle, which saw Roosevelt on July 1 lead the Rough Riders up the elevation "we afterwards christened Kettle Hill" (it lay on a flank of San Juan hill which became famous for the Rough Riders' charge), the American attack petered out. "We are within measurable distance of a terrible military disaster," Roosevelt wrote Lodge.

Luckily for Shafter, the Spaniards were even more spent, and on July 3 Cervera decided to escape if he could. Sampson's fleet was awaiting this move but expected Cervera to try to sail away at night. When the Spaniard left in broad daylight instead, the surprised American ships became so snarled in their own tracks that Cervera almost got free. Overwhelming American firepower, however, finally destroyed his wooden ships. Of Cervera's men, 744 were killed or wounded. The American fleet suffered little damage and lost but one man killed and one wounded. On July 16 General Linares surrendered Santiago to the Americans. On July 25 a second Ameri-

594

The Spanish War in the Caribbean, 1898

can expeditionary force, commanded by General Nelson A. Miles, made a triumphant if belated march through Puerto Rico. By July 13 the Spanish government had already begun to seek a peace treaty, and on August 12 hostilities were declared over. Next day, Manila fell.

All told, the United States lost 5462 men in the four-months' war, but only 379 in combat. The rest died from disease and other causes. Spain's losses in the fighting were much higher, and in addition she lost the remnants of her once imposing New World empire. Confirmation of her loss was to be found in the peace treaty, on which formal meetings began in Paris on October 1. In December the treaty was signed. Ratification by the Senate, however, proved to be another matter.

### An imperial peace

When TR exclaimed at the time of the Venezuelan crisis of 1895, "this country needs a war," he probably gave voice to the only real justification that could be found for the adventure against Spain three years later. No question of American security or American honor was involved; and if there had been, Spain had cleared the way to satisfaction two weeks before war started. Perhaps an editorial in the *Washington Post,* read into the *Congressional Record* on the eve of hostilities, touched close to the core of the matter:

*A new consciousness seems to have come upon us—the consciousness of strength—and with it a new appetite, the yearning to show our strength. . . .*

*The taste of Empire is in the mouth of the people even as the taste of blood in the jungle. It means an Imperial policy, the Republic, renascent, taking her place with the armed nations.*

America's leading political wit, Finley Peter Dunne, put it perhaps more simply:

*"We're a gr-reat people," said Mr. Hennessy earnestly. "We ar-re," said Mr. Dooley, "We ar-re that. An' th' best iv it is, we know we ar-re."*

American ambiguity about the precipitating causes of hostilities no doubt helped muddle the nation's peace aims. Even in Cuba, Major James E. Runcie, an aide to the American military governor, General Leonard Wood, observed in 1900 that everything had to be done "as if the island had been captured the previous day." In his annual message to Congress, December 5, 1899, McKinley said of the Teller Amendment, "the pledge contained in this resolution is of the highest obligation and must be sacredly kept." At the same time, he added, Cuba must "be bound to us by ties of singular intimacy and strength." All abjurations of territorial aggrandizement elsewhere, on moral grounds, also were swept under the rug. Far from being the "criminal aggression" of his messages to Congress of December 1897 and April 1898, McKinley by July of the latter year was saying of the tempting territorial war gains, "We must keep all we get; when the war is over we must keep what we want."

Even while the war was in progress, on July 6, 1898, Congress adopted and McKinley approved the joint resolution annexing Hawaii to the United States. Two weeks later, in stating terms for an armistice in the war, McKinley demanded Puerto Rico and Guam. He stipulated, in addition, that the United States was to occupy the "city, bay, and harbor of Manila pending the conclusion of a treaty of peace." While the American negotiators at Paris worked on the treaty, American hunger for the Philippines kept growing. First it was only Manila; then, on September 16, the negotiators were instructed by the President to take nothing less than the island of Luzon. By October 26 the whole archipelago was being demanded. When Spain demurred, an ultimatum was issued on November 21, to which Spain capitulated. The continuing fear that Germany would seize the Philippines in her bid to become a Pacific power no doubt fed America's own expansive demands. McKinley also had a more palatable explanation ready. "There was nothing left for us to do," the President explained to a group of Methodist ministers after the United States had annexed the islands, "but to take them all, and to educate the Filipinos, and to uplift and civilize

Culver Pictures, Inc.

*John Bull to "a promising pupil,"*
*from* Life, *March 1899: "You're coming on*
*famously, Sam. You can bag your game*
*almost as well as I."*

and Christianize them, and by God's grace do the very best we could by them as our fellow men for whom Christ also died."

The final treaty, insuring the freedom of Cuba and granting the United States the Philippines (for a payment of $20 million), Puerto Rico, and Guam, was signed in Paris on December 10. In the debate on ratification in the Senate, the annexation of the Philippines became the principal issue. Many who had opposed the war from the start also opposed contaminating American democracy with the "little brown brothers" of this primitive outpost, just as they had opposed taking Catholic black Cubans into the Anglo-Saxon nest. Others voiced political rather than racist objections. In November 1898, the "little America" group formed the Anti-Imperialist League, which grew rapidly in numbers as the administration's expansionist policies developed. The League's supporters included some of the

leading thinkers and writers of the time. Opposed to them were the brash young men of the war party, flushed with victory and determined to enjoy its fruits.

On February 6, 1899, the Senate narrowly ratified the treaty by 57 to 27—only two votes above the required two-thirds majority. The decision might well have gone the other way were it not for the Filipinos themselves. On December 21, 1898, with the debate in the Senate at its peak, McKinley had ordered the War Department to extend the military occupation of Manila to the entire archipelago. This move promptly touched off armed Filipino resistance under Aguinaldo, whose well-known aspirations for Filipino independence had been made light of by Dewey and other officers in the islands. When the Senate learned of American lives lost in the fighting, enough votes were gained for annexation and for the treaty to squeak by.

The movement obstensibly begun to liberate the Cubans now quickly grew into a war to subjugate the Filipinos. "It shows how rapidly we are approaching an imperial form of government," wrote the Massachusetts anti-imperialist Moorfield Storey to his Senator, George F. Hoar, in January 1899, "that the President should undertake operations like this without the consent of Congress or without even consulting it." Two months later, after exercising his indignation for a year in numerous communications, the philosopher William James, in a letter to the *Boston Evening Transcript,* put forth his own "damning indictment" of this adventure and of the spirit that he believed had set it in motion:

*We gave the fighting instinct and the passion of mastery their outing . . . because we thought that . . . we could resume our permanent ideals and character when the fighting fit was done. We now see how we reckoned without our host. We see . . . what an absolute savage . . . the passion of military conquest always is, and how the only safeguard against the crimes to which it will infallibly drag the nation that gives way to it is to keep it chained forever.*

A few days following, James wrote in the *Transcript* once more:

> It is obvious that for our rulers at Washington the Filipinos have not existed as psychological quantities at all. . . . We have treated [them] as if they were a painted picture, an amount of mere matter in our way. They are too remote from us ever to be realized as they exist in their inwardness.

A certain amount of realization dawned, however, as Aguinaldo's islanders held off the Americans for three years in a conflict that cost more men and money than the war with Spain itself and found the United States forced to employ the same concentration-camp methods so bitterly condemned when used by the Spanish against Cuban guerrillas.

In Cuba itself, meanwhile, General Leonard Wood ruled as military governor until May 20, 1902, when the islanders were compelled to accept the restraints of the so-called Platt Amendment. This amendment to an army appropriation bill limited Cuba's treaty-making powers, her right to borrow money, and other prerogatives of sovereignty. Moreover, Cuba could not withhold lands wanted by the United States for coaling or naval stations, nor yield territory to any other power. Finally, the amendment permitted the United States at is own discretion to intervene in Cuba "for the protection of life, property, and individual liberty." The United States required the incorporation of the Platt Amendment in any constitution drawn up by Cuba and also stipulated that Cuba make a permanent treaty with the United States restating the amendment's terms. The Platt Amendment remained in force until 1934, when it and related treaties were abrogated by agreement. At that time the United States retained Guantánamo Bay and its shore area as a naval base.

## The public and the Court concur

In the midst of the public discussion of the new imperialism the election of 1900

took place. Unsympathetic to the treaty of peace, William Jennings Bryan, the Democratic candidate, had nevertheless secured some Democratic votes for it in the Senate partly to guard his party from the imputation of wanting the war renewed, and partly to carry the whole issue of overseas expansion into the campaign. McKinley's substantial victory was interpreted by many as a victory for the new course. When McKinley was assassinated a few months after his inauguration in 1901 and Theodore Roosevelt became Commander-in-Chief, the imperialist camp had reason to expect that expansionism would be further encouraged.

In May 1901, in the so-called *Insular cases,* the Supreme Court added its sanction to the assent of the executive and the people. In these cases, the Court held, essentially, that the Constitution did not follow the flag, that the rights of United States citizens did not automatically belong to the people of the territories. The *Insular cases* arose over the Foraker Act of 1900, under which the territorial government of Puerto Rico was set up. According to this act, Puerto Rican goods entering the United States were to pay duties for two years equivalent to 15 percent of the duties levied on similar products of *foreign* countries under the Dingley Tariff of 1897. If Puerto Rico was in fact part of the United States, duties on her goods, like duties on goods crossing state boundaries, were unconstitutional. The Court saved the duties by deciding, in language "not easily understood," as one constitutional historian put it, that Puerto Rico was "territory appurtenant . . . but not part of the United States," and that Congress could determine how much of the Constitution applied to the "native inhabitants." The Court's stand carried beyond mere duties on goods into the whole area of civil rights.

In 1903, even though Hawaii had been given formal territorial status in 1900, paving the way for eventual statehood, the Supreme Court also held that these islands had not been "incorporated" into the Union and that the native citizens thus had not become the equals of continental citizens of the United States. The case in question arose out of the denial of trial by jury to the Hawaiian people.

The Court decided that it was lawful to follow the existing criminal procedure in the islands instead of substituting that laid down for Americans by the Constitution. In reaching this decision, the Court differentiated arbitrarily between "fundamental rights," which could not be abridged, and "procedural rights," which could be. Trial by jury, it held, was a "procedural right" only.

These racist distinctions, however, were soon swept aside, and even the Filipinos were quickly put on the road toward self-government. The foundations were laid by the Philippine Commission appointed in 1900 with William Howard Taft at its head. By 1907, the

Filipinos had gained the right to elect the lower house of their legislature, and in 1916 the Jones Act gave them virtual autonomy over their domestic affairs. Some of this ground was lost during the 1920s, but in 1934 the Tydings-McDuffie Act provided for independence after ten years. The Filipinos agreed to the ten-year provision in 1936. After the islands were recovered from Japan during World War II, the Filipinos finally achieved independence, as planned, on July 4, 1946.

## V  Great nation rivalries

### The "Open Door" in China

Mahan's influential ideas about the inevitable twentieth-century struggle for the world between Western and Oriental civilizations had helped precipitate the United States into the Far East. But once established there, Americans soon found the major struggle to be with other Western powers, with the great prize the impotent and still passive country of China.

Here, around the turn of the century, as we have said, France, Germany, Britain, and Russia—along with Oriental Japan, to be sure—were staking out exclusive "spheres of influence." Should China become dismembered, American hopes for further trade with that country surely would be disappointed. The problem posed to the United States was to find a way to gain and maintain equal trading rights in China without risking war and without becoming a party to further partition. The situation became acute in 1898, when it appeared that the British were about to use some newly leased territory on the mainland opposite Hong Kong to smuggle imports into China without paying the Chinese tariff. If the other imperial powers were to follow this example, the Chinese government would soon

lose all its tariff revenues, and political as well as commercial chaos would result.

To meet this situation, McKinley's new Secretary of State, John Hay, in September 1899, sent his memorable "Open Door" notes to Britain, Germany, and Russia, and later to Japan, Italy, and France, inviting them to agree to three points: (1) No nation was to interfere with the trading rights or privileges of other nations within its sphere of influence. (2) Chinese officials were to be permitted to collect duties under existing tariffs, which granted the United States most-favored-nation privileges. (3) No nation was to discriminate against nationals of other countries in levying port duties and railroad rates.

Hay's proposals were not as modest as they seemed. While he did not ask the great nations to cease partitioning China, he did suggest that they forego much of the value of national spheres of interest. None of the powers would make the concessions asked for; yet Hay refused to accept their vague rejections. He saved himself from a fiasco by calmly announcing on March 20, 1900, that all had granted "final and definitive" consent to his request. Only Japan cared to challenge this audacious bluff.

Hardly had negotiations over the Open

Door notes been concluded when a group of fanatical Chinese nationalists, organized as the Order of Literary Patriotic Harmonious Fists and hence called by Westerners the "Boxers," rose up against foreigners in their country. Before they were put down by an international force to which the United States contributed 2500 men, they had killed hundreds of persons and destroyed much property, and only swift action by Britain and the United States now restrained the other imperial powers from retaliating by subjugating more Chinese territory.

Hay advised the imperial rivals at this time that American policy was to work to "preserve Chinese territorial and administrative entity" and to "safeguard for the world the principle of equal and impartial trade with all parts of the Chinese Empire." This announce-

ment went farther than the Open Door notes and also had more effect. Eventually, the nations participating in suppressing the Boxers accepted a money indemnity from China rather than new grants of territory. The United States' share of almost $25 million was larger than necessary to meet the losses she suffered, and she later returned the balance to China where it was used to help educate Chinese students in America.

*The Nation* called Hay's work "a splendid instance of American sagacity winning a peaceful victory." But what had made the settlement possible was the unwillingness of the European powers to start a new scramble for China that might touch off a general war.

### Relations with Japan

Few Americans took Mahan more seriously than Theodore Roosevelt, whose preachments about the importance of what he called "the soldierly virtues" frightened many

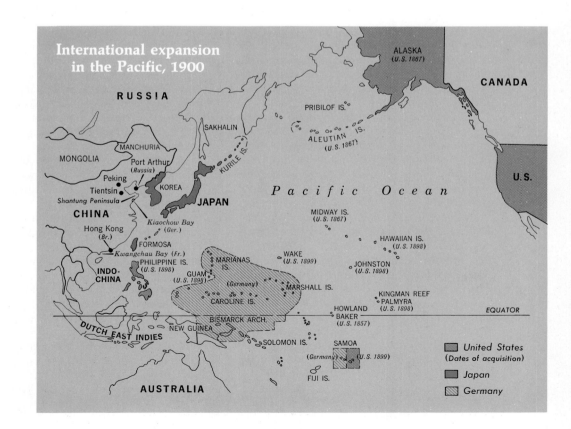

International expansion in the Pacific, 1900

when he ascended to the presidency at a robust forty-three in September 1901. Four years earlier he had said at the Naval War College, "The men who have dared greatly in war . . . are those who deserve best of their country."

But Roosevelt's first major international venture was delayed until after his reelection in 1904, and then it was as peacemaker not warmonger. Having thrashed the expansionist Russians in Manchuria in the Russo-Japanese War of 1904–1905, the Japanese in the spring of 1905, temporarily exhausted by their efforts, secretly asked the American President to mediate the conflict. Fearful of growing unrest at home that culminated in the Revolution of October 1905, the Russians were easily persuaded to agree, but Roosevelt would take no further steps until Japan, emerging as the dominant power in Asia, consented to respect the principles of the Open Door policy. When Japan yielded, the President invited her delegates and the Russians to meet at Portsmouth, New Hampshire, in August. Here, among other claims, the Japanese demanded a huge money indemnity to offset their war costs. When the Russians balked, Roosevelt warned the Japanese against pressing their demand, and they accepted some small territorial grants instead, along with Russia's promise to evacuate Manchuria.

The Japanese people had counted heavily on the Russian indemnity for tax relief and did not quickly forget the American's apparent responsibility for robbing them of it. The American people, in turn, soon showed their own reactions to Japan's victory. Prejudice against the Japanese had long existed on the West Coast in particular, and Japan's emergence as a great power now heightened anxiety about the "yellow peril." In October 1906 the San Francisco Board of Education ordered that the ninety-three Japanese children in the city be segregated in a separate school. News of this action stung Japanese racial pride and led a number of Japanese newspapers to call for drastic action. Roosevelt's fury over California's provocation was not lessened by his realization that the American federal system gave him no jurisdiction over California public schools. Only after denouncing

San Francisco's step in his annual message of 1906 as a "wicked absurdity" and bringing a great deal of pressure on local authorities did the President succeed in getting the action reversed. At the same time he promised Californians that the Japanese immigration which so alarmed them would be curbed. A series of notes in 1907 and 1908 made up the Gentleman's Agreement by which Japan promised to issue no more passports to workers seeking to emigrate to the United States.

Having mollified the Japanese, Roosevelt was anxious, as he wrote to a friend, "that they should realize that I am not afraid of them." In 1907, as a demonstration of strength, he decided to send the American fleet around the world on a practice cruise. Remarkably enough, Japan welcomed the visit of the fleet as a friendly gesture and for a time Japanese-American relations improved.

The Root-Takahira Agreement of November 1908 reflected the better feeling. An executive agreement, not a treaty, the terms bound only TR's administration and that then serving in Japan. Both powers agreed to maintain the status quo in the Pacific area, to uphold the Open Door in China, and to support by peaceful means that country's "independence and integrity." By saying nothing of Manchuria, however, the agreement seemed to concede Japan's special interest there. Indeed Roosevelt was courting Japan at the cost of retreating from Hay's Open Door principle. It was in the American interest, he wrote in 1910, "not to take any steps as regards Manchuria which will give the Japanese cause to feel . . . that we are hostile to them, or a menace—in however slight a degree—to their interests."

Roosevelt's Far Eastern policy was upset by his successor as President, William Howard Taft, and Taft's Secretary of State, the corporation lawyer Philander C. Knox. They favored a policy of pushing American investment and trade abroad, a policy that became known as "Dollar Diplomacy." Taft had an imposing explanation of it: "This policy has been characterized as substituting dollars for bullets. It is one that appeals alike to idealists of humanitarian sentiments, to the dictates of sound policy and strategy and to legitimate commercial aims." One of the troubles with Dollar Diplomacy was that those Americans who controlled investment dollars were as yet reluctant to invest them in far-off places. One of Taft's pet projects was to have American bankers finance China's purchase of Manchurian railroads, in which Russia and Japan both were interested. His effort only aroused the suspicion and animosity of Russia and Japan, driving together the two nations Roosevelt had sought to keep apart.

### The Panama Canal

Having become a world power with interests in the Pacific as well as the Caribbean, the United States began to look all the more urgently toward the construction of an isthmian canal to link these two great waters. Back in 1850, the United States and Britain had agreed in the Clayton-Bulwer Treaty that the two nations would enjoy equal rights in any such canal. Now, the United States pressed Britain to surrender her rights and at last in 1901, following her new policy of courting America as a friend in the concert of nations, Britain yielded. The Hay-Pauncefote Treaty that year gave the United States a free hand to build, control, and by implication to fortify an isthmian canal. The United States, on her part, promised to open the canal without discrimination to the commercial and fighting ships of all nations.

Two routes were possible for this canal—one through Panama in the Republic of Colombia; the other through Nicaragua. Across each route, indeed, different companies had already been at work for some time. But progress had been slow and costly, and the rivals now vied with one another in efforts to unload their enterprises on the United States. After much maneuvering and debate, the United States, in 1902, decided to use the Pana-

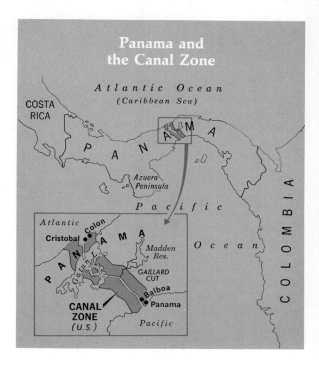

Panama and the Canal Zone

ma route, a triumph for the French New Panama Canal Company, which held the concession from Colombia. But Colombia herself had still to be heard from.

By holding the alternative of a Nicaraguan canal over the heads of Colombia's negotiators, Secretary of State Hay was able to drive a hard bargain with Tomás Herrán of Colombia in a treaty approved by the United States Senate in March 1903. A sum of $40 million had been earmarked earlier for the New Panama Canal Company, which was empowered by the treaty to transfer to the United States all its rights in Colombia. The treaty stipulated that $10 million cash and $250,000 annually were to be paid to Colombia itself for the rights to a canal zone 6 miles wide across the isthmus. In Colombia, however, a new revolutionary government had just taken over and expressed resentment over some of the treaty terms. Hay responded with such threats to Colombian proposals for altering these terms that, to preserve its own dignity, the Colombian Senate was obliged to reject the treaty in August 1903 by a vote of 24 to 0. Roosevelt then lost no time in announcing that the "black-mailers of Bogotá" must not be allowed "permanently to bar one of the future highways of civilization."

The *Indianapolis Sentinel* marked out the course that would be followed to break this impasse when it calmly observed in August 1903: "The simplest plan of coercing Colombia would be inciting a revolution in Panama . . . and supporting the insurrectionary government." Such thoughts concurred with Roosevelt's own and indeed with those of interested parties in Panama itself. Under the leadership of Philippe Bunau-Varilla, who had the crucial support of the United States Navy, these thoughts were brought to fruition at the end of October 1903. With the revolution a success, Washington promptly recognized a minister from the new Republic of Panama, and a treaty was signed at once giving the United States the desired strip of territory for the canal zone for the earlier stipulated $10 million and $250,000 a year.

Roosevelt has been much criticized for his complicity in the Panamanian revolution. He defended himself by remarking: "If I had followed traditional conservative methods I should have submitted a dignified state paper of probably 200 pages to Congress and the debate would be going on yet; but I took the Canal Zone and let Congress debate; and

while the debate goes on the canal does also." Roosevelt's high-handed behavior and remarks created many enemies for the United States throughout Latin America. Within a decade of the Panamanian revolution, however, the canal was completed, and on August 15, 1914, the first oceangoing steamship passed through it.

In the same year, the Wilson administration sought to placate Colombia and improve Latin American relations by apologizing to her for the part played by the United States in the Panamanian revolution and setting aside $25 million to be paid her to soothe her wounded feelings. Roosevelt's friends in the Senate would not abide this slur upon his conduct, and the treaty was shelved. In 1921, after Roosevelt's death, the treaty minus the apology at last passed the Senate by a vote of 69 to 19, and Colombia received its indemnity in full.

### In the Caribbean sphere

The Panama Canal, by giving the United States a great new enterprise to pro-

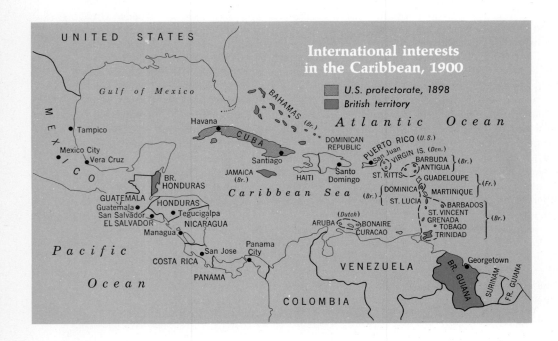

tect, broadened American involvement in the Caribbean. The political and financial instability of the smaller republics in the region posed an especially touchy problem. Practically all of their public financing had been done in Europe, and were any one of them to fail to pay interest due on its bonds some European state itching for imperialist expansion, like France in Mexico in 1863, might simply move in with the idea of staying indefinitely. To avert this danger, in his message to Congress on December 6, 1904, Roosevelt set forth what is known as the Roosevelt Corollary to the Monroe Doctrine:

> Chronic wrong-doing ... may in America, as elsewhere, ultimately require intervention by some civilized nation, and in the Western Hemisphere the adherence of the United States to the Monroe Doctrine may force the United States, however reluctantly, in flagrant cases of such wrong-doing or impotence, to the exercise of an international police power.

The first application of the Roosevelt Corollary came in 1905, when the Dominican Republic found itself unable to pay its debts. After an American show of force, the Dominican government was obliged to invite the United States to step in. The Dominican foreign debt was now scaled down and transferred from European to American bankers, while a percentage of customs collections was allocated to pay future interest and to reduce the principal of the new obligations. Cuba also drew the attention of the Roosevelt administration in 1906, when revolutionary disturbances prompted the administration to land troops to impose order. They were not withdrawn until 1909.

In Taft's administration, Secretary of State Knox persuaded American bankers to increase their interest in the debt of Honduras and to put capital into the National Bank of the Republic of Haiti. The most provocative instance of Dollar Diplomacy took place in 1911, when a revolution in Nicaragua led American bankers to take charge of that country's finances.

In 1912 American marines followed the bankers in to insure against further upheavals.

These almost routine displays of force naturally deepened Latin American hostility toward the United States, and when Woodrow Wilson succeeded Taft as President in 1913 he promised to rectify matters. The outbreak of World War I in 1914, however, made the American government more vigilant than ever in the Caribbean. In 1915 American marines entered Haiti in response to revolutionary disturbances and stayed until 1934. American forces also occupied the Dominican Republic again in 1916, and intervened once more in Cuba in 1917. By then Wilson had also become deeply embroiled in his painful adventure in Mexico.

### Wilson in Mexico

In May 1911 President Porfirio Díaz, dictator of Mexico since 1877, was overthrown by a revolutionary coalition led by the liberal idealist Francisco Madero. Unable to organize a new regime rapidly enough, the revolutionaries were themselves suppressed in February 1913 by General Victoriano Huerta, who coldly arranged Madero's assassination. Most European governments promptly recognized the Huerta regime, and American business interests, with large investments in Mexican industry, urged Wilson to do likewise. But Wilson, shocked by this official murder, refused on the ground that Huerta's was not a free government resting on the consent of the governed.

Wilson's departure from the historic American policy of recognizing all governments in power threw upon the United States the dubious responsibility of deciding which governments were pure and which were not. Confidence in his ability to see a pure government through also led Wilson to make a rash promise to Britain, which had a strong interest in Mexican oil, to protect her Mexican concessions if she would abandon Huerta, which she did. When Huerta's government failed to collapse as Wilson hoped it would, he offered to help the anti-Huerta Constitutionalist forces in Mexico under Venustiano Carranza. But Carranza wanted no support from unpopular

Yankees, and Huerta's regime stood up. Wilson now found himself unable to redeem the pledge he had made to Mexico and to the world that he would guarantee constitutional government in that country.

On April 9, 1914, an incident occurred that gave Wilson an excuse for direct intervention. One of Huerta's officers arrested the crew of an American vessel that had landed behind the government's lines at Tampico. Although the Americans were promptly released with expressions of regret, the commander of the American squadron demanded a more formal apology. This Huerta refused to make. Wilson took Huerta's action as an insult to the nation and asked Congress for authority to win redress by arms. Even before Congress could act, Wilson learned of a German steamer about to arrive at Vera Cruz with a load of ammunition for the Huerta government. In order to keep armaments that might be used against American forces out of the country, Wilson at once (April 21) ordered the navy to occupy the port, which it did in an action that cost 126 Mexican lives. Even Carranza's Constitutionalists were so angered by Wilson's occupation of Mexican territory that they threatened war.

At this critical point, the "ABC" powers—Argentina, Brazil, and Chile—offered to mediate, and Wilson welcomed this chance to crawl away from his difficulties. Mediation failed, but Huerta's regime, unable to secure arms from European nations busy strengthening their own forces, soon collapsed nevertheless. Carranza took over the presidency in August 1914, and a year later Huerta's best general, Francisco ("Pancho") Villa, took command of the opposition forces. Disorder spread, and in March 1916 Wilson sent General John J. Pershing across the border on a "punitive expedition" against Villa, who had repeatedly raided American territory and killed American citizens. Carranza himself replied to this "invasion" by mobilizing his army. Preoccupied as he was with the war in Europe, Wilson at last withdrew Pershing's forces and in March 1917 recognized Carranza's regime. Peace was maintained, but only after Wilson had aroused the lasting distrust of a people he meant to help.

## For further reading

P. T. Moon, *Imperialism and World Politics* (1926), remains among the best comprehensive works that places western imperialism in a world setting. W. L. Langer, *The Diplomacy of Imperialism* (1960), is indispensable for the period 1890 to 1902. G. F. Kennan, *American Diplomacy 1900-1950* (1951), has become an influential work, as has W. A. Williams, ed., *The Shaping of American Diplomacy* (1956), a well-edited anthology giving perhaps excessive emphasis to direct economic interests. Other general works of value include A. K. Weinberg, *Manifest Destiny* (1935); C. A. Beard, *The Idea of National Interest, An Analytic Study in American Foreign Policy* (1934); and J. A. S. Grenville and G. B. Young, *Politics, Strategy, and American Diplomacy: Studies in Foreign Policy 1873-1917* (1966).

Walter LaFeber, *The New Empire, An Interpretation of American Expansion 1860-1898* (1963), is a suggestive introduction in the W. A. Williams tradition. D. W. Pletcher, *The Awkward Years: American Foreign Relations under Garfield and Arthur* (1962), may be supplemented by A. F. Tyler, *The Foreign Policy of James G. Blaine* (1927). Other useful general accounts for this period include F. R. Dulles, *The Imperial Years* (1956); E. R. May, *Imperial Democracy, The Emergence of America as a Great Power* (1961); and such biographical studies as Margaret Leech, *In the Days of McKinley* (1959); H. F. Pringle, *Theodore Roosevelt* (1956 ed.), and *Life and Times of William Howard Taft* (2 vols., 1939); J. A. Garraty, *Henry Cabot Lodge* (1953); and C. G. Bowers, *Beveridge and the Progressive Era* (1932). A. T. Mahan, *The Influence of Sea Power upon His-*

tory 1660-1783 (1890), was the first of his long list of books. W. D. Puleston, *Mahan* (1939), is an informative biography. Mahan's influence on Roosevelt is well recorded in H. K. Beale, *Theodore Roosevelt and the Rise of America to World Power* (1956). Another strong influence was Brooks Adams, *America's Economic Supremacy* (1900), especially concerned with "the new struggle for life among nations." On this subject see also Richard Hofstadter, *Social Darwinism in American Thought* (1955). The role of religion in this struggle is well documented in the powerful contemporary tract, Josiah Strong, *Our Country* (1885). See also F. T. Reuter, *Catholic Influence on American Colonial Policies 1898-1904* (1967). Harold and Margaret Sprout, *The Rise of American Naval Power 1776-1918* (1939), and G. T. Davis, *A Navy Second to None* (1940), are excellent on American seagoing strength. Armin Rappaport, *The Navy League of the United States* (1962), is informative on big navy promotion.

On American policy in different regions, see S. F. Bemis, *The Latin American Policy of the United States* (1943); Dexter Perkins, *A History of the Monroe Doctrine* (1955); D. G. Munro, *Intervention and Dollar Diplomacy in the Caribbean 1900-1921* (1964); J. P. Treat, *Diplomatic Relations Between the United States and Japan 1895-1905* (1938); Tyler Dennett, *Americans in Eastern Asia* (1922); A. W. Griswold, *The Far Eastern Policy of the United States* (1938); Charles Vevier, *The United States and China 1906-1913* (1955); T. J. McCormick, *China Market, America's Quest for Informal Empire 1893-1901* (1967); and E. H. Zabriskie, *American-Russian Rivalry in the Far East* (1946). C. C. Tansill, *Canadian-American Relations 1875-1911* (1943), is a scholarly monograph. On the changing relations with Britain, see Bradford Perkins, *The Great Rapprochement: England and the United States 1895-1914* (1968). Theodore Morgan, *Hawaii, A Century of Economic Change 1778-1876* (1948), and S. K. Stevens, *American Expansion in Hawaii 1842-1898* (1945), cover the background of the fiftieth state. Interesting background on the forty-ninth state will be found in Hector Chevigny, *Russian America, The Great Alaskan Venture 1741-1867* (1965).

Walter Millis, *The Martial Spirit* (1931), captures the quality of the years preceding the Spanish-American War. J. E. Wisan, *The Cuban Crisis as Reflected in the New York Press 1895-1898* (1934), covers the journalism war. Frank Freidel, *The Splendid Little War* (1958), is the best modern account of the fighting. Theodore Roosevelt, *The Rough Riders* (1899), reveals the spirit of their leader. Orestes Ferara, *The Last Spanish War* (1937), conveys the Spanish point of view. C. H. Brown, *The Correspondents' War: Journalists in the Spanish-American War* (1967), is a rewarding study. H. W. Morgan, ed., *Making Peace with Spain* (1965), presents the diary of Whitelaw Reid, one of the American commissioners at Paris, September–December 1898.

J. W. Pratt, *America's Colonial Experiment* (1950), is excellent on America's postwar empire. D. F. Healy, *The United States in Cuba 1898-1902* (1963), and A. R. Millett, *The Politics of Intervention, The Military Occupation of Cuba 1906-1909* (1968), are definitive on the Platt Amendment and its implementation. Richard Hofstadter, "Manifest Destiny and the Philippines," in Hofstadter, *The Paranoid Style in American Politics and Other Essays* (1965), is valuable on the peace treaty and beyond. H. F. Graff, ed., *American Imperialism and the Philippine Insurrection* (1969), affords indispensable first-hand information on the struggle with Aguinaldo. Two books tell the story of the Panama Canal: Gerstle Mack, *The Land Divided* (1944), and D. C. Miner, *The Fight for the Panama Route* (1940). Many books cited for Wilson in Chapter Twenty-four deal with the Mexican intervention. Here we may note Harley Notter, *The Origins of the Foreign Policy of Woodrow Wilson* (1937); and C. F. Cline, *The United States and Mexico* (1953).

R. L. Beisner, *Twelve Against Empire, The Anti-Imperialists 1898-1900* (1968), is a valuable monograph. Some of the background for anti-imperialism will be found in W. M. Armstrong, *E. L. Godkin and American Foreign Policy 1865-1900* (1957); M. A. D. Howe, *Portrait of an Independent, Moorfield Storey 1845-1929* (1932); and Merle Curti, *Bryan and World Peace* (1931).

# TWENTIETH-CENTURY OPTIMISM

Most Americans would have agreed with Walter Hines Page, editor of the *Atlantic Monthly*, when he remarked in 1898 that "the adventurous spirit of our Anglo-Saxon forefathers" must plant American institutions "in every part of the world." Many others, at the turn of the century, felt as strongly the need to overhaul these institutions at home, if only the better to justify exporting them.

The preceding generation had devoted its energies to the quest for wealth on a continental scale. In this respect, at once meteoric and menacing, it outdid all past societies in the sheer magnitude of its achievements. The oncoming generation, profoundly disturbed by the evident recklessness, violence, and disorder of the Gilded Age, and by what Theodore Roosevelt in 1906 called "the dull, purblind folly of the very rich men, their greed and arrogance," set out to square accounts with history, lest "the Promise of American Life" be thwarted by its materialistic successes. *The Promise of American Life* was the title of Herbert Croly's exceptionally influential book, published in 1909. "An America which was not the Land of Promise, which was not informed by a prophetic outlook and a more or less constructive ideal," Croly wrote, "would not be the America bequeathed to us."

The abuses of the Gilded Age had led to violence and disorder among the poor as well as among the very rich. The great railroad strikes, Haymarket and anarchism, Homestead and the Pinkerton wars, the brutality of slums and skid roads in northern cities, the almost routine political murders in the South, the assassination of three Presidents between 1865 and 1901—all deeply impressed in their childhood and adolescent years the young men and women who were to lead the Progressive Movement in the twentieth century.

Yet theirs was not to be simply a "search for order," as some historians have suggested in recent years. Well beyond that, it was a quest for "improvement"—a constant theme in American life with deep roots in Puritan accountability, Enlightenment optimism, and the idea of "Civilization" which America, "the hope of humanity" in Turgot's phrase, was meant to bring to fruition. The boldest went farther still. "The average good American patriot," Croly wrote, "calls his country, not only the Land of Promise, but the Land of Destiny, . . . the continued prosperity of which is prophesied by the very momentum of its advance." But for "the higher American patriotism, . . . the better future which Americans propose to build is nothing if not an idea which must in certain essential respects emancipate them from their past. . . . The Promise can no longer remain merely an anticipation. It becomes in that case a responsibility."

No movement could have grown so nearly universal in its appeal as Progressivism had by 1912 without internal differences. Yet most Progressives shared similar goals. They hoped to offset plutocracy, waste, and corruption on the one hand, deprivation, alienation, and rebellion on the other, by restoring opportunities for the common man, broadening the distribution of income, rescuing the poor, purifying politics, and strengthening the state. Some of them put strengthening the state

first, the better to play the part of a world power that the nation had become.

Writing in 1930, Felix Frankfurter observed that "unlike almost all American prewar [pre-World War I] writers on politics (with the notable exception of Captain Mahan), Croly saw the American situation with its international implications." Croly himself wrote in 1909: "The Spanish war . . . and its resulting policy of extra-territorial expansion, so far from hindering the process of domestic amelioration, availed, from the sheer force of the national aspirations it aroused, to give a tremendous impulse to the work of national reform; . . . and it indirectly helped place in the presidential chair the man who represented both the national idea and the spirit of reform." He meant, of course, Theodore Roosevelt, who took the very name of his 1912 Progressive program, "the New Nationalism," from Croly's book. In July 1912, TR wrote the author: "If ever there should be a biography of me there is no one whom I should so like to have write it as you, because I think you understand, as no other literary man does, the kind of thing I am striving for in politics."

On the home front even the Negro, around the turn of the century, reawakened concern if not consideration. "Progressivism," as C. Vann Woodward put it in *Origins of the New South,* was "for whites only," and not only in the South. In the North, southern views of "the race problem" gained more sympathy than the race itself. In both sections blacks were admonished to leave to "silence and slow time" their progress toward turning white in skin color and "Germanic" in "blood

Courtesy of *Punch*, London

For Punch *of London the new century
opened with Father Time crying to heads of
state, "Make Your Game," and spinning
the wheel of fortune.*

and bone" (or so the hopeless requirements for admission into progressive humanity appeared to be). Yet the Negro, like others, grew less silent and less patient in this age. On grasping Negro leadership in 1896 from his post at Atlanta University, W. E. Burghardt Du Bois anticipated the Progressive "muckrakers" (see p. 613) by initiating scholarly and scientific studies of the actual condition of black life in America, compared to that of most whites. Nine years later, at a meeting at Niagara Falls, New York, he initiated the "Niagara Movement," which in 1906 issued this manifesto:

> We want full manhood suffrage and we want it now. . . . We want discrimination in public accommodations to cease. . . . We want the Constitution of the country enforced. . . . We want our children educated. . . . We are men! We will be treated as men. And We shall win!

Thereafter, Negroes took "slow time" by the forelock. Like other Progressives, in the words of the sociologist E. A. Ross, writing in 1901, they hastened "that gradual encroachment of society on private action which is registered in the progressive transformation of wrongs or torts into crimes."

## I The Progressive spirit

*The heart and soul of the movement*

No one can look back to the turn-of-the-century years, with the "Splendid Little War" so smashingly won, "Our New Prosperity" so suddenly arrived, and fail to be struck by the vitality of the Progressive spirit as well as the breadth of Progressive thought. National success seemed to make the many warts on society glower the more openly and accus-ingly, while national confidence put nothing beyond the reach of good will.

The impulse to reform society and strengthen the state became active around the turn of the century in Europe as well as in America, as the rapidly industrializing imperialist nations sought to ward off revolution at home while pursuing their objectives overseas. And some of the European stratagems rubbed off on American enthusiasts, especially those upper-class intellectuals who had gone to Bismarck's Germany in the 1870s and 1880s to complete their educations and returned with ideas of state socialism to offset the Marxist variety then coming to the fore. Yet the Progressive movement, just as it found indigenous targets, also discovered indigenous sources of attack and reconstruction.

One of the most persuasive of these was Social Christianity, once so deeply instrumental in abolitionism. Roosevelt, who (as one editor said) had a way of "slapping the public on the back with a 'bright idea,' " got to the heart of the matter when he declared that "the White House is a bully pulpit." To save mankind, many Progressives felt, they must save society first. In his book *Christianity and*

*Theodore Roosevelt proselytizing:
"The man who wishes to do good
in his community must go into active
political life."*

Brown Brothers

*the Social Crisis* (1907), the Progressive Protestant theologian Walter Rauschenbusch wrote: "It is true that any regeneration of society can come only through the act of God and the presence of Christ, but God is now acting, and Christ is now here." William Allen White, the tub-thumping Progressive journalist of Emporia, Kansas, put it this way: "In the soul of the people there is a conviction of past unrighteousness."

In his famous essay "What's the Matter with Kansas?" written during the 1896 presidential campaign, White had torn into the Populists:

> *That's the stuff! Give the prosperous man the dickens! Legislate the thriftless into ease, whack the stuffing out of the creditors. . . . Whoop it up for the ragged trousers; put the lazy, greasy fizzle, who can't pay his debts, on the altar, and bow down and worship him. . . . What we need is not the respect of our fellow men, but the chance to get something for nothing.*

Soon after, White met TR. "He sounded in my heart the first trumpet call of the new time that was to be," White records in his *Autobiography*. "It was youth and the new order calling youth away from the old order."

Women also played a powerful part in the Progressive movement. The spearhead of their campaign was the General Federation of Women's Clubs, which had been organized in 1889 to share "the joy of the vast intellectual wealth in us." Each member club was to provide a " 'resting place' from the regular absorbing activities of life." By the turn of the century, the General Federation had grown into a militant organization, especially in the fight for woman's suffrage and even for birth control. Its discovery of about 5 million women and nearly 1 million children under fifteen in the labor force as reported in the census of 1900 (about a fifth of all persons gainfully employed) broadened its interests. The new tone was well expressed in 1904 by suffragette Sarah P. Decker in her inaugural speech on becoming the federation's president:

> *Ladies, you have chosen me your leader. Well, I have an important piece of news for you. Dante is*

609

*dead. He has been dead for several centuries, and I think it is time that we dropped the study of his inferno and turned attention to our own.*

610 By then the State Federation of Women's Clubs in Illinois, assisted by the Cook County Child Saving League in Chicago, had led the successful campaign for the Illinois Child Labor Act of 1903. Under the slogan "Let us be our sisters' keepers," the campaign for improvement in women's working conditions also was well under way.

Businessmen, moreover, no more united in opposition to Progressivism than to imperialism, also found themselves touched by the new spirit. True, some businessmen, Roosevelt's pet targets, with their "green-grocer imaginations," defended the status quo as blindly as they battled their workers. "I entertain," wrote Croly, "an active and intense dislike" of their "optimism, fatalism, and conservatism." The number of businessmen who developed a social consciousness under Progressive prodding, at the same time, grew impressive. Reform movements enjoyed the support of moneyed men like Charles R. Crane, a backer of La Follette for the presidency who made his fortune in the manufacture of valves and fittings and served as vice-chairman of Wilson's finance committee during the 1912 campaign after La Follette's collapse. E. A. Filene, the leading Boston department store merchant, and Joseph Fels, the soap king, also became Progressive enthusiasts. William Kent, a Chicago real-estate operator and cattle-feed producer, became president of the Municipal Voters League and a member of the Illinois Civil Service Reform League. Among the most conspicuous were Samuel M. ("Golden Rule") Jones and Tom Loftin Johnson, oil millionaire and traction tycoon, respectively, the first a convert of Rauschenbusch, the second of Henry George, who emerged as model reform mayors of Toledo and Cleveland, Ohio.

Perhaps even more characteristic than the backing of such exceptional individuals was the support many businessmen gave to Progressivism because they felt that they had something to gain from particular Progressive measures. Rural, small-town, and midwestern bankers for example, took a more hospitable view of banking reforms than did the big bankers of the East, where the monetary resources of the nation were concentrated. As in the 1880s, many small merchants and shippers, at a competitive disadvantage because of persisting railroad favors to powerful interests, continued to seek stronger railroad regulation; while great railroad leaders like Alexander Cassatt, who became president of the Pennsylvania system in 1899, themselves backed antirebating and similar federal measures to help keep insistent favor seekers off their backs. In the newer public utilities engaged in supplying services to the cities, the most discerning executives themselves sometimes invited government regulation to short-circuit municipal-ownership proposals.

Nor could such men, even if devoid of social conscience, always remain impervious to the social ferment in the country, with big business one of its principal targets. For many years before the turn of the century they often employed well-spoken lawyers like Vanderbilt's Chauncey M. Depew to take a hand in party if not directly in national politics to help calm the waves of discontent. In the Progressive era, beginning with the hiring of the publicity agent Ivy Lee by the anthracite coal industry in 1906, they institutionalized the job of "public relations counsellor." During the next decade, Lee did face-saving jobs for the Pennsylvania Railroad, Standard Oil, and other beleaguered interests, sometimes persuading management actually to improve its social performance to make it easier for him to embellish its social image.

The effectiveness of business groups in selfishly using the Progressive spirit is sometimes called "the triumph of conservatism" in the Progressive era; but this phrase may perhaps even more appropriately be applied to the spirited revival of religious and moral imperatives in the Progressive movement, to which most elements of American society yielded, including such veterans of reform campaigns as eastern Mugwumps and western Grangers and Populists. Roosevelt again struck the right note when he wrote as early as 1899 of the possibility of "leading some great outburst of the emotional classes which should at least temporarily crush the Economic Man."

## Ideas in action

American "minds in transition," as we have called them (Chapter Twenty-two), as well as American hearts and souls, made fundamental contributions to twentieth century optimism. Since their purpose was not simply to effect changes in society but also to emancipate it from the past, as Croly said, Progressives naturally looked most optimistically for support among those willing to question fixed systems of belief, or "formalism" in philosophy. Nor did they have far to seek. One of their most gifted mentors was the Harvard psychologist and philosopher William James, who so dearly embraced "the will to believe" yet whose "pragmatism," as we have seen, marked a bold turning away from the unverified and often unverifiable abstractions of the conventional wisdom. In the study of law and political science, in economics, education, and the interpretation of history, Progressives also found turn-of-the-century thinkers at home and abroad who stressed timeliness over tradition, "process" over prescription, action over authority.

No intellectual liberation could have uncovered a more receptive disciple than the young Progressive orator and future senator from Indiana, Albert J. Beveridge, who declared in a speech in 1898: "The axioms applicable to thirteen impoverished colonies have been rendered obsolete by history. An echo of the past is not to stay the progress of a mighty people and their free institutions." William James in particular came to abhor Beveridge's violent imperialism, especially in connection with the subjugation of the Philippines (see p. 596), but he could not deny the contemporaneity of his thought.

The consuming concern of the pragmatists and the "process" thinkers, or institutionalists,

with the consequences of ideas led naturally to an unprecedented passion for the facts of life. The consuming concern of Progressives with the consequences of plutocratic rule, "by so many glorified pawn-brokers" in TR's words, led as naturally to an unprecedented passion for the facts of government. Who actually benefited from laissez-faire? Did government intervention really produce evil results? What convictions colored the minds of judges when they passed on the validity of legislation? Who put up the money for elections, and why? How did state and federal legislatures truly work? How, indeed, and to what ends, had the federal Constitution itself been contrived?

The enfranchisement of the minions of the plutocrats and their politicos, in turn, many of them "non-Aryans" unable to read or write English, led to deep questioning of the democratic process itself. In his book on the Negro *Following the Color Line* (1908), the muckraker Ray Stannard Baker wrote:

*The cause of all the trouble in the North is similar to what it is in the South. The underman will not keep his place. He is restless, ambitious, he wants civil, political, and industrial equality. In short, . . . we are coming again face to face in this country with the same tremendous (even revolutionary) question which presents itself in every crisis of the world's history:*

*What is democracy? What does democracy include? Does democracy really include Negroes as well as white men? Does it include Russian Jews, Italians, Japanese? Does it include Rockefeller and the Slavonian street-sweeper?*

After Frederick Winslow Taylor published his penetrating *Principles of Scientific Management* in 1911—it had been preceded by his more technical *Shop Management* in 1903—"efficiency" became the watchword of many Progressives who looked to "social engineering" by a trained and impartial elite at least to administer the "means" of government even if the people determined the "ends." Some, like the lawyer and judge Louis D. Brandeis, who enlarged the vogue of Taylor's work by applying its principles in a sensational railroad rate case in 1910–1911, preferred to leave even the determination of ends to those of "greatest ability and intelligence." Taylor had limited the implications of his theories to the factories; these elitist Progressives—the first generation in America fully conscious of the force of technology in consolidating power as well as creating wealth— wanted to extend "scientific management" to society as a whole. In this way they hoped to bring both their primary targets, the economically wasteful plutocracy and the politically warped proletariat, under beneficial control.

There remained to be considered what Beveridge called "the gifts of events"—America's new imperial possessions and their denizens. In his keynote speech in the fall of 1898 launching the by-election campaign in Indiana, he said: "The opposition tells us we ought not to rule a people without their consent. I answer, the rule of liberty, that all just governments derive their authority from the consent of the governed, applies only to those who are capable of self-government. ... The proposition of the opposition makes the Declaration of Independence preposterous, like the reading of Job's lamentations would be at a wedding, or an Altgeld speech on the Fourth of July." As to who was capable of self-government, the converted William Allen White, a few months later, declared in his *Emporia Gazette*, "Only Anglo-Saxons can govern themselves. ... It is the Anglo-Saxon's manifest destiny to go forth as a world conqueror." But White recanted later. "I read the popular pseudosciences of the day," he wrote in his *Autobiography* (1946), "such as *Anglo-Saxon Superiority* by Edmond Desmolins, ... and thought we were free to spout and jower and jangle, ... innocent of the fact that we were starting wars that would ... threaten all that we loved and wreck much that we cherished."

In his inaugural address in 1905, Roosevelt himself said, "We know that self-government is difficult, but we have faith that we shall not prove false to the memories of the men of the mighty past." Wilson, in turn, averred that, "every man who tries to guide the counsels of a great nation ... should feel that his voice is lifted upon the chorus and that it is only the crown of the common theme." By his own account, his "New Freedom" program promised "a Liberty widened and deepened to match the broadened life of a man in modern America, restoring to him ... the control of his government."

Yet neither the high priests nor the young acolytes of Progressivism and imperialism found it easy to shed the prejudices of their time and heritage. Even after the most violent decade of black repression in the old Confederacy in a generation, Roosevelt declared in 1912 that the Progressive party plan was "to try for the gradual re-enfranchisement of the worthy colored man of the South by frankly giving the leadership of our movement to the wisest and justest white men of the South." As for his views on self-government among people in America's spheres of interest abroad, we have only to recall Roosevelt's grasping of Panama from Colombia in 1903 and his corollary to the Monroe Doctrine in 1904.

Wilson's New Freedom, in turn, only broadened the gulf between blacks and whites. The first southerner to become President since Andrew Johnson (although elected as a New Jerseyite, he was born and brought up a Virginian), Wilson often stated that "the only place in the world where nothing has to be explained to me is the South." Segregation of the races in executive departments was begun by him as soon as he entered the White House, while by executive order separate eating and rest-room facilities, by race, were to be provided for all federal employees in Washington. In the South, Negroes in federal jobs were discharged or demoted as a matter of course. Nor would Baker's Russian Jews, Italians, Japanese, and Slavonians fare much better. Wilson wrote in 1901:

*Representative government has had its long life and excellent development not in order that common opinion, the opinion of the street, might prevail, but in order ... that some sober and best opinion might be created, by thoughtful and responsible discussion conducted by men intimately informed concerning the public weal, and officially commissioned to look after its safeguarding and advancement.*

And yet Roosevelt and Wilson, by acts as well as words, must be judged to be in the democratic vein compared to such other elitists of their time as Lodge and Root, Nicholas Murray Butler, John Hay, and Taft, all of whom gradually slunk away from Roosevelt's "wild ideas" (Taft's term) concerning the general welfare. And many other Progressives, especially in the West, subscribed to the view of the editor of *Public,* Louis Post of Chicago, when he said in 1906 that they "have been forced to the conclusion that the masses of the people are better to be trusted than any one class, however assertive of its superiority that class may be."

### The "Wisconsin Way" and the "muckrakers"

Croly's *The Promise of American Life* and Taylor's *Scientific Management,* of course, were but two of the large number of books and other publications early in the twentieth century that attracted the most intellectual political generation since that of the Founding Fathers. William Allen White's *The Old Order Changeth* and Walter Lippmann's *Drift and Mastery* both confronted the agrarian values of the past with the challenge of the industrial, urban present. The caustic analysis of the federal Constitution by such scholars as J. Allen Smith and Charles A. Beard raised a web-clearing storm that made the fundamental law itself more amenable to the winds of change. Brooks Adams's *The Theory of Social Revolutions* brought jurisprudence, courts, and judges under surveillance. Charles H. Cooley's *Human Nature and the Social Order* and his subsequent books, along with E. A. Ross's *Social Control* and later studies, carried sociology into the range of public discussion; while Franz Boas's attack on racism in *The Mind of Primitive Man* deepened the relevance of anthropology. Du Bois's *The Souls of Black Folk* helped humanize these and other fields in the emerging "social sciences," which also illuminated Thorstein Veblen's critique of business leadership in *The Theory of*

*Business Enterprise* and *The Instinct of Workmanship.* Other books on specific issues, such as Brandeis's study of the "Money Trust," *Other People's Money,* and C. R. Van Hise's *The Conservation of Natural Resources in the United States,* found wide and influential audiences.

A far-reaching Progressive practice was the publication of extensive government reports on social issues presenting expert testimony in depth. Precedents could be found for taking such testimony by legislative committees, but the Progressives enlarged and institutionalized the practice.

The first great federal investigation of this sort began in 1898, when Congress set up the Industrial Commission to study the relation of trusts to labor, immigration, agriculture, technology, and related subjects. Its report, in nineteen thick volumes, remains a mine of information; in the Progressive era it supplied much of the basic knowledge on the most vital social issues. The Armstrong investigation of the large insurance companies by the New York state legislature in 1905 and the Pujo investigation of the Money Trust by Congress in 1912 also removed much of the mystery from the machinations of high finance. The most intensive use of the legislative investigating function was made in Wisconsin under the governorship of Robert M. La Follette from 1901 to 1906. La Follette also first systematically brought to the service of the state government, as a "brains trust," the faculty of the state university. Reform governors in other states soon adopted the "Wisconsin Way."

The popular craving for inside information was sometimes satisfied by the sensational novels of Norris, Dreiser, and Upton Sinclair. Many more readers turned to the new muckraking magazines and books. It was TR, in a speech in 1906, who first pinned the label "muckrakers" on the young journalists who were exposing the sordid aspects of American society. "In Bunyan's *Pilgrim's Progress,*" he said, "you may recall the description of . . . the man who . . . was offered the celestial crown for his muck-rake . . . but continued to rake the filth on the floor." Roosevelt acknowledged that many of the revelations were

613

true, but argued that their effect was simply to deepen dangerous discontent which his own Square Deal and other programs could handle better. On their part, the muckrakers argued that the American people would not fight for reforms until they had been fired with indignation.

For many years reporters had written sordid stories of the kind that made the muckrakers famous. What was new after the turn of the century were the popular magazines that provided the muckrakers with research funds and nationwide audiences. Even such conservative magazines as the *Ladies' Home Journal* and the *Saturday Evening Post,* vehicles for colorful advertisements of new consumer goods for millions of middle-class families, were forced now to publish muckraking articles. What forced them was the competition of such new muckrake magazines as *McClure's,* named for its brilliant publisher, S. S. McClure, whose galaxy of young writers included Lincoln Steffens, Ida M. Tarbell, Ray Stannard Baker, and William Allen White. *Cosmopolitan, Everybody's, Arena,* and *Hampton's* all offered similar outlets to writers like Charles Edward Russell, David Graham Phillips, and Thomas W. Lawson.

Between 1903 and 1906, *McClure's* circulation rose from 370,000 to more than 750,000; *Hampton's* from 13,000 to 440,000; and most of the others matched this trend. Perhaps the muckrakers' most sensational accomplishment was Lincoln Steffens's series on Philadelphia, Pittsburgh, and other cities. When he collected these articles in his book *The Shame of the Cities* (1904), Steffens declared that his purpose had been "to sound for the civic pride of an apparently shameless citizenship." "The people are not innocent," he asserted. "That is the only 'news' in all the journalism of these articles."

Ida Tarbell's almost equally popular exposé of Standard Oil retold the story of the pitiless methods by which that huge combine had been built. Charles Edward Russell threw a searching light on the beef trust. Thomas Lawson, a reformed speculator, exposed Amalgamated Copper. Muckraking moved on to the national stage when the novelist David Graham Phillips wrote for *Cosmopolitan* a lively series of articles called "The Treason of the Senate."

The popular humorist Finley Peter Dunne, friend of many of the muckrakers, offered one view of their effect. Once, "Mr. Dooley" told his friend "Hinnissy," he had been able to enjoy magazine reading. "But now . . . what do I find? Ivrything has gone wrong. Th' wurruld is little better than a convict's camp. . . . It's a wicked, wicked horrible place, an' this here counthry is about the toughest spot in it. . . . It's slowly killin' me Hinnissy—or it wud if I thought about it."

## II  Progressivism in the cities and the states

*Humanitarianism and efficiency
in local politics*

By the turn of the century, efforts at municipal reform could boast a history of almost fifty years, yet "gold coast and slum," separated physically by but an avenue or two, otherwise still stood miles apart. The most glaring of the plutocrats' failures, the cities naturally ranked among the first objects of Progressive political attack, and humanitarians like Tom Johnson and "Golden Rule" Jones quickly showed how much could be accomplished simply by the time-honored practice of throwing the rascals out.

As one who had made his fortune in street railways in Indianapolis and Detroit as well as

Cleveland, Johnson had seen the franchise mill and other deplorable aspects of bossdom at first hand. In the 1880s he became a convert to Henry George's "single tax" idea and campaigned for George when he ran for mayor of New York in 1886. First elected mayor of Cleveland in 1901, Johnson won re-election three times, serving until 1909. To him, the success of democracy demanded public involvement. To keep the electorate continuously interested in its own welfare, he went so far as to acquire a huge circus tent accommodating 4000 to 5000 persons. This tent he moved from place to place in the city, holding huge public meetings where citizens could confront their officials in question-and-answer programs. At such meetings officials also had to confront the people; and Johnson's success lay in persuading presentable men to do the good work of city government. How well they did it can best be seen in Lincoln Steffens's accolade. The best-informed and severest critic of American city life named Johnson the "best mayor of the best-governed city in the United States."

In the neighboring city of Toledo Jones ruled from 1899 until his death in 1904. His work was carried on for eight more years by Mayor Brand Whitlock. Jones's interpretation of the "golden rule" went beyond reform to the reorganization of society on a "collective" basis, looking to the establishment of the "Co-operative Commonwealth, the Kingdom of Heaven on Earth." In Toledo he opened free kindergartens, free concerts, free playgrounds, and free golf courses. One of his major concerns became police work, so central to the derelictions of the poor. Here he substituted light canes for the heavy clubs carried by patrolmen, and checked the widespread system of arrests on suspicion and the jailing of presumed offenders without charging them. The principal point of attack by his enemies, in fact, became his alleged laxity in law enforcement. When they persuaded the state legislature in 1902 to create a police commission appointed by the governor to administer the Toledo police department, Jones fought this encroachment and won his case in the Ohio supreme court.

City commissioners appointed by corrupt state politicians could hardly be expected to improve urban management. At the same time, many Progressives were reluctant to rest their programs simply on the chance availability of good and energetic men. They sought institutional safeguards to support moral conviction.

An emergency in Galveston, Texas in 1900 seemed to point a way that with modifications became widespread. In September, that year, the politicians who made up the city council so botched the administration of relief and reconstruction following a savage hurricane that in its place, in 1901, the state was obliged to appoint a five-man commission of experts. This commission did so well in rebuilding the city, restoring its credit, and rehabilitating its services that Galveston retained it to run the government. Even without the incentive of such an emergency, Progressives in other Texas towns soon adopted the Galveston form. In 1907 it spread to Des Moines, Iowa and had such success that other midwestern municipalities followed the "Des Moines idea."

By 1914 over 400 American cities, most of them small or middle-sized, had adopted the commission form. By then, however, the administrative experts had proven themselves less than expert in politics itself. Moreover, the contradiction between Progressive objectives of greater democracy and citizen participation on the one hand and nonpartisan professional experts on the other could no longer be ignored. By 1914 most city commissioners were themselves required to run for office. Further modification of the commission idea in the direction of greater democracy followed another natural disaster, this one a flood in Dayton, Ohio in 1913. Under the system adopted there, political authority was vested in a small body of elected commissioners, who in turn appointed a professionally qualified city manager to administer the city departments. This system made it possible to combine expert management with democratic con-

615

trol, and by 1923 more than 300 cities had adopted it.

### The role of state governments

Legally, cities are creatures of the states, operating under charters or other limited grants of power from state legislatures. In order to protect municipal reforms from being undone by the political allies of unseated city bosses, urban Progressives naturally felt impelled to extend their attack to the state machines and the business interests they served.

Perhaps the innovation expected to be most salutary was the *direct primary.* Reformers hoped that this device, by leaving the choice of candidates to the people rather than to the party machines, would insure the selection of abler and more independent officeholders. By 1916 some form of the direct primary had been adopted by all the states except Rhode Island, Connecticut, and New Mexico. Several states also adopted the *initiative,* a reform that permitted the public to propose legislation, and the *referendum,* which enabled the voters to approve or reject measures passed by the legislatures.

The *recall* of public officers through popular votes, another reform device, received widespread support as a means of getting rid of unsatisfactory officials before their terms expired. The proposal to recall judges and thereby expose the judiciary to popular feeling especially aroused the ire of conservatives. But many judges were in bad odor for having invalidated social legislation, and seven states, all west of the Mississippi, actually passed laws providing for their recall. Nowhere, however, were these laws invoked. During the 1912 campaign Theodore Roosevelt boldly suggested, as an alternative to the recall of the judges, the recall of judicial decisions, and many of his old supporters feared he had lost his mind. Only Colorado adopted such a measure, and it was declared unconstitutional in 1921.

The kingpins of party machines in the states were their United States senators, much of whose power arose from their access to federal patronage. United States senators, according to the Constitution (Art. I, Sec. 3), were elected by the state legislatures. One of the reforms most in demand by Progressives was the direct election of senators by the people. The Seventeenth Amendment, passed by Congress in 1912 and ratified in May 1913, provided for this change.

Although the reformers succeeded in translating a great many of their political reforms into law, the results often disappointed them. The direct primary, for example, by depriving many aspirants for office of party funds, seemed to favor rich men over poor ones regardless of ability or commitment. Party bosses, moreover, soon proved adept at manipulating the political process despite the direct primary. The initiative and referendum in practice became cumbersome devices that often misfired. Recall was used only rarely. All too often, outbursts of reform lasted only a short time, rising or falling with the enthusiasm of one outstanding leader. The professional, full-time bosses usually outlasted the amateurs to return somewhat more careful perhaps but still powerful. Reformers consoled themselves with occasional victories which fed the thought that, were it not for the threat of reform uprisings from time to time, the machines might have done greater harm to the people.

Progressive political reforms in the states, as in the cities, naturally looked beyond progress in democratization to the substantive gains greater democracy might win. Railroads and other *public* utilities, their very name identifying their reliance on government grants of power as well as on political privilege and largesse, became the state reformers' principal targets.

One of the first, and perhaps the greatest, of the reformers on the state level was La Follette during his tenure as governor of Wisconsin from 1901 to 1906. Willing to fight fire with fire, La Follette's first step was to supplant his party's strong state machine with a Progressive machine of his own. With expert advice from his "brains trust," he proceeded to gratify his agrarian constituents by establishing an effective Railroad Commission headed by the chairman of the Transportation Department of the State University, B. H. Meyer. Within a few years, this commission brought other utilities besides railroads under its surveillance. In his *Autobiography,* La Follette writes of how his innovations disappointed many by not meeting "expectations by 'going after' the corporations." But the "object of our legislation," he adds, "was not to 'smash' corporations, but to drive them out of politics, and then to treat them exactly the same as other people are treated." One of his most useful measures was that of taxing railroad property the same as all other property, thereby reducing favoritism and special privilege to a minimum.

In Wisconsin as elsewhere, much reform legislation, while benefiting the state's citizens, also benefited the interests. Forced to reduce rates, for example, the railroads of the state found that the lower charges attracted much new traffic that more than made up for the lower unit fees. Prohibited from granting rebates, moreover, the roads found that they were able to retain for themselves the full income from rendering transportation service. The equalization of the tax load hit the railroads, and for that matter their political dependents, hardest; but as La Follette put it, this was "simply because equal taxation is always a hardship on those who had not been formerly paying their equal share."

His career as a state reformer in Wisconsin carried La Follette to the United States Senate in 1906 and to the verge of the Progressive presidential candidacy in 1912, perhaps his most humiliating experience (see p. 628).

One of the most extraordinary state reformers was William S. U'Ren of Oregon. An ex-blacksmith and former member of the Farmers' Alliance, U'Ren held but one minor political office. As a lawyer and newspaper editor, however, he became so influential that it was said in Oregon that the government was divided into four departments, "the executive,

judicial, legislative, and Mr. U'Ren—and it is still an open question who exerts the most power." U'Ren led the campaign in Oregon for the initiative, referendum, recall, and other political reforms. But more than that, his work became a model for others in neighboring far western states, California and Washington, where Progressives prospered perhaps longer than elsewhere.

### Progressive social legislation

Progressives had far greater success with social than with political reforms. Progressive women in particular, organized in Consumer Leagues, Charities Aid Societies, Child Labor Committees, and church organizations, as well as in the General Federation of Women's Clubs, turned in this direction. As with Progressive groups in other fields, their campaigns were based on solid study and research, widespread publicity, and the employment of trained lobbyists in state capitals and Washington. One outcome of their combined attack was the adoption of new child-labor laws or far-reaching amendments to old ones in forty-three states between 1902 and 1909. Following the adoption of the trailblazing New York Child Labor Act of 1903, the assemblyman who introduced the bill in the state legislature wrote to the Child Labor Committee in New York City that its passage "was due solely to the magnificent campaign waged by you. So thoroughly was the work done that all opposition was silenced through fear of opposing the intelligent public opinion that had been aroused."

Old statutes, going as far back as Connecticut's vague law of 1813, had dealt perfunctorily with child labor in the factories. In an investigation in 1901, the New York Child Labor Committee had found that of the 1.5 million children in the state between the ages of five and eighteen, nearly one-third were not in school. Of these, a mere one-tenth worked in factories. Among the rest who were employed, no laws whatever protected the numerous newsboys, bootblacks, peddlers, delivery and messenger boys, and other menials. The New York act of 1903 was designed to cover them.

Other states soon followed New York's example. A Delaware statute of 1909 was the first to declare outright that "no child under the age of fourteen years shall be employed or suffered to work in any gainful occupation." By 1914 every state but one had imposed a similar prohibition at least for factory work. Enforcement was made simpler in many states by laws requiring school attendance until the minimum working age. Other measures prohibited the employment of children at night and in dangerous occupations.

In 1916 Congress passed the Keating-Owen Act, which prohibited the shipment in interstate commerce of goods made in factories, mines, and quarries that employed children under specified ages. Two years later, in *Hammer* v. *Dagenhart,* the Supreme Court declared this act unconstitutional on the grounds that it invaded the police powers of the states and attempted to use federal control of interstate commerce to attain unrelated ends; but the states' acts survived.

Until 1908 the courts, while permitting state regulation of child labor as part of the police power, frowned on controls over working conditions of women as infringing their freedom of contract. Then, in 1908, in *Muller* v. *Oregon,* the United States Supreme Court reversed its long-standing negative position, most recently declared in the case of *Lochner* v. *New York* (1905), and validated Oregon's ten-hour law for women.

This reversal was another triumph for Progressive research, as reflected in the unconventional 112-page brief submitted by Louis D. Brandeis for the state. Brandeis offered the Court a mere two pages of the usual legal argument buttressed by "authorities." The rest of his brief consisted of historical, sociological, economic, and medical facts providing "some fair ground, reasonable in and of itself" on which the Court might find excessively long hours of work for women sufficiently injurious to "the public health, safety, or welfare" to warrant state limitations. Brandeis's social "facts" swayed even the most conservative justices, among them David J. Brewer, who had supported the *Lochner* ruling. In 1917, on the basis of a 1000-page brief modeled on Brandeis's, the Supreme Court, in

*Bunting* v. *Oregon,* upheld a ten-hour law for men. Numerous state laws were enacted on the basis of these decisions until 1923, when the Supreme Court, reflecting the return to "normalcy," again reversed itself and rejected hours legislation for women as well as men (see Chapter Twenty-six).

Insurance covering industrial accidents was another Progressive objective. Under traditional common-law rulings, the burden of all the hazards of industrial labor was placed upon the worker and his family. To collect compensation for disabling injuries or death on the job, dependents had to go to court—itself a costly and interminable undertaking—and prove that the victim had not willingly assumed the risks of his work, that neither he nor any fellow worker had contributed to negligence which may have caused the accident, and that the employer was solely to blame. Under Progressive pressure, states began to adopt public accident-insurance plans after 1909, and by 1920 all but five states had taken such action.

The Progressives also succeeded in establishing a certain amount of public responsibility for the support of children and old people. States had always provided public almshouses, but only occasionally did they offer relief at home. By 1911 state legislatures began to accept the idea that it was far better, where possible, to assist dependent children in their own domiciles than to place them in institutions. By 1913 eight states, and by 1930 all but four, had adopted mothers' assistance acts for this purpose, creating public agencies to grant financial aid to working mothers. Such acts helped widows with dependent children, as well as families left destitute by divorce, desertion, or the incapacity of the breadwinner.

In 1914 states began to provide home relief for the aged poor. Arizona led the way, although its supreme court found this first law unconstitutional. Urged on by the American Association for Old Age Security, thirteen states passed measures for this purpose during the 1920s. In most cases, persons sixty-five and over became eligible for pensions as high as $30 a month.

### Business resistance in the states

Progressive social legislation, especially legislation covering working conditions in business, hardly went unchallenged, especially by those made to foot the bill and otherwise imposed upon by bureaucratic interference. After 1900, old employer associations like the National Metal Trades and the National Founders, formed initially to combat unionization, turned their attention to politics as well. In 1902 and 1903 such new organizations as the Citizens Industrial Association of America and the Anti-Boycott Association joined the ranks. Coordinating all of their activities after 1903 was the National Association of Manufacturers.

At the NAM convention in 1909, President John Kirby, Jr. advised the members, "if you have a batch of bad bills before your legislature," do not hesitate to call upon our chief

*Lucy Burns, Editor of* The Suffragist, *in photo taken just before she went up in the airplane to scatter notices of a suffrage meeting in Seattle.*

Culver Pictures, Inc.

lobbyist, James E. Emery. "If he gets a chance at them I will promise you the bill is dead from that moment." That Kirby's was no empty promise is suggested by the testimony of a Mr. Hatch of Indiana:

*In the recent legislative session in Indiana we had . . . I think the largest list of malicious class bills ever presented. The general subjects might be classed under employer's liability, . . . fellow servants, our old friend anti-injunction, aesthetics and hygiene in factories, and everything of that kind, and we thought we were up against it; but through the insistent persistence of Mr. Emery we were able to prevent every one of these bills from going to the Governor.*

Business aggressiveness, especially in the increasingly sophisticated use of propaganda and pressure politics, contributed to the decline of Progressivism in the states. To satisfy aroused and enlightened voters, legislators often found they had no alternative but to enact reform measures. They did not, however, have to provide funds and machinery for enforcement. Progressive faith in legislation often was soured by enforcement failures. Progressive spokesmen like Lincoln Steffens and Upton Sinclair eventually became socialists; others, like Ray Stannard Baker and Ida Tarbell, hating socialism, became more conservative in their thinking.

### Woman's suffrage

Since the 1840s, a small advance guard under the leadership of Lucretia C. Mott, a graduate of Miss Emma Willard's famous Female Seminary in Troy, New York, had argued that women as well as men deserved the right to vote. Gradually other educated women were drawn to the cause. In 1869, stung by their failure to win the franchise under the Fourteenth Amendment, suffrage groups formed the American Woman Suffrage Association, with Lucy Stone and Julia Ward Howe of Boston at its head. A more radical contingent—favoring easy divorce laws and other social reforms as well as woman's suffrage—soon split off. This group, led by Susan B. Anthony and Elizabeth Cady Stanton, then organized the National Woman Suffrage Association. Efforts at reconciliation led to the formation of a Union Woman Suffrage Association, but this soon broke up and the American and the National associations carried on separately. By 1898 Wyoming, Colorado, Utah, and Idaho had given women full suffrage rights, and other states permitted them to vote for certain offices, such as school board members; but no federal amendment was passed, despite the agitation that was taking place throughout the nation.

The Progressive campaign for woman's suffrage picked up where the older organizations had shown the way. The role of women in effecting so many Progressive social reforms newly encouraged them to demand political rights for themselves. One of the strongest arguments for giving women the vote was their participation in the business of the country. By 1910 the number of American working women neared 8 million, many of them employed in offices and stores as well as in factories. Some had entered the professions of law and medicine, while their number in education, even on the college level, had soared.

Although Taft and Wilson, the candidates of the major parties, evaded it, woman's suffrage became an issue in the presidential campaign of 1912. The new Progressive party (see p. 629) supported it, while Roosevelt, its standard-bearer, who had heretofore given women little encouragement, now endorsed it. The election of Wilson, with his conservative southern views on the place of women in society, was a setback, but women went right on agitating and by 1914 they had won the franchise in eleven states.

Such limited gains dissatisfied many partisans, who now decided to concentrate on a federal amendment. To promote it they prepared a huge petition for Congress with 400,000 signatures and opened a lobby in Washington. Some women, like Mrs. Carrie Chapman Catt and Dr. Anna Howard Shaw, preferred the quiet techniques of gradual education and propaganda. Others, who followed the lead of Alice Paul, patterned their strategy after the English suffragists and engaged in dramatic demonstrations and picketing. Eventually, even Wilson was persuaded to give woman's suffrage some faint-hearted encourage-

ment. Women's role in World War I won the suffragists many new male supporters, and in June 1919 Congress, by a narrow margin, passed the Nineteenth Amendment giving them the vote. The amendment was ratified in August 1920, and women throughout the country took part in the presidential election that fall.

## Prohibition

While the fight for ratification of the Nineteenth Amendment was in progress, another proposed amendment came before the public. This was the Prohibition Amendment, the culmination of more than half a century of agitation for the prohibition of the manufacture and sale of alcoholic beverages.

Many women favored Prohibition. A recruit of dubious value to their cause was Carry A. Nation of Kansas, a 6-foot, 175-pound fanatic with a long family history of paranoia, whose first husband died of alcoholism just six months after their marriage in 1867. In 1890, when the "wets" of Kansas, encouraged by a favorable Supreme Court decision, opened a strong assault upon the state's "dry" laws, Mrs. Nation organized a branch of the Women's Christian Temperance Union there but had as little success with persuasion as the WCTU had elsewhere (see p. 543). Soon she embarked on her personal vendetta against the "joints" which, with strong encouragement from distillers, continued to operate more or less openly. Her weapon was her famous hatchet, used to smash saloon windows, furniture, fixtures, and supplies in many Kansas towns. In 1900 she turned her attention to such metropolises as New York, Washington, and San Francisco, wielding her weapon to such effect that she was arrested some thirty times, usually for "disturbing the peace."

With the formation of the Anti-Saloon League in 1893, the "drys" at last built up an agency strong enough to combat the saloon and distiller interests, and the machine politicians associated with them. The Progressive assault on the machines encouraged "temperance" advocates to feel that their hour had also struck, and with the Anti-Saloon League lobby keeping the pressure on both major parties, after 1907 state after state in the West and South fell into the "dry" ranks. The League's first national success came in March 1913, when Congress passed the Webb-Kenyon Act over President Taft's veto. This act prohibited the shipment of intoxicating liquors into any state, territory, or district where they were intended to be used in violation of local laws.

Encouraged by this victory, the "drys" introduced a Prohibition Amendment in Congress in December 1913, and such wartime conditions as popular resentment against German brewers and the need to conserve the materials used in distilling hastened its adop-

*W. E. Burghardt Du Bois.*

tion. The Eighteenth Amendment, passed by Congress in December 1917 and ratified in January 1919, went into effect in January 1920.

### Negro aspirations

Booker T. Washington's Tuskegee philosophy for schooling the Negro for service and silence, a failure in itself (see p. 570), became anathema to younger black leaders of the next generation. The whole spirit of the Progressive Movement involved opening the mind, not closing it; educating the public for change, not schooling it for subservience. New black leaders like Du Bois and William Monroe Trotter, who founded the Negro newspaper the *Boston Guardian* in 1901, shared this spirit. Of Du Bois in particular, the young black poet James Weldon Johnson wrote that his book *The Souls of Black Folk* (1903) brought about "a coalescence of the more radical elements, . . . thereby creating a split of the race into two contending camps."

Born in Great Barrington, Massachusetts, in 1868, Du Bois received his doctorate from Harvard in the very year of Washington's "Atlanta Compromise" address (1895). Until 1901, by then highly regarded as an authority on Negro social and industrial life largely because of his intensive research at Atlanta University, Du Bois did not openly attack the Tuskegee gospel, nor did he actively oppose the disfranchisement of the illiterate black farm worker. At the same time, he bitterly resented denial of the ballot, and of other elements of equality, to the educated Negro, "the talented tenth" destined to lead their people.

Between 1901 and 1903, Du Bois developed the set of sophisticated theses already implicit in his thinking but hitherto neither bluntly nor widely expressed: Negroes were at once black and American, inheritors of a national culture yet exhibiting the unique gifts of their race. Racial differences were beneficial; racial inequalities insufferable. Negroes required industrial disciplines but also the experience of a liberating education which Washington's philosophy denied them. Black advancement depended ultimately on civil equality. Protest, contrary to Washington's dictum, would gain what "accommodation" never could.

The Niagara Movement, launched by Du Bois and his intellectual black friends in 1905, included an education plank in its opening manifesto:

*Common school education should be free to all American children and compulsory. . . . We urge an increase in public high school facilities in the South, where the Negro-Americans are almost wholly without such provision. . . . We favor "an adequate and liberal endowment for a few institutions of higher education" by the federal government.*

But Niagara aims went well beyond this topic, stressing especially the need for unremitting agitation. "Through helplessness we may submit, but the voice of protest of ten million Americans must never cease to assail the ears of their fellows, as long as America is unjust."

The Niagara Movement, nevertheless, was destined to last but a short time. Internal differences, especially between Trotter and Du Bois, hastened its demise, while Washington worked persistently to undermine it. At the same time, the Movement led directly to the formation in 1909 of the National Association for the Advancement of Colored People (NAACP) by a determined group of white and black Progressives. Prominent among the former was Oswald Garrison Villard, publisher of the *New York Evening Post* and grandson of the abolitionist leader William Lloyd Garrison. Progressive women like Jane Addams and Lillian Wald, the outstanding settlement workers, also participated. As director of publicity and editor of the NAACP organ, *The Crisis,* Du Bois became its most militant spokesman. But the organization's most practical work from the start lay in its persistent legal action to protect Negro rights and promote Negro liberty.

By 1914 the NAACP boasted 6000 members in fifty branches across the country, but Washington continued to hold the allegiance of most blacks until his death the next year. Not until World War I and postwar migration of masses of southern blacks to northern cities did the NAACP develop the momentum which, until the 1960s, made it the most militant (but nonviolent) engine of black protest and progress. During the Progressive era itself the Negro made few gains.

## III   Progressivism and the GOP

### *The Republican Roosevelt*

A Republican by family tradition, TR nevertheless had always been offended by the mean pension and protectionist politics and GAR party patriotism of the Conkling, Hanna school. An aristocrat by temperament, in his political salad days he had flirted with Mugwumpery; but the blood of the heirs of the old Puritans had run too thin for him, and his love of power as well as his common touch kept him "regular" enough for McKinley to appoint him Assistant Secretary of the Navy just before the Spanish War. His feats as the Rough Rider added greatly to his popularity, and in the fall of 1898 he was elected governor of New York with full party support. He soon showed himself still so independent of the Republican machine, however, that the state boss, "Tom" Platt, determined that in the election of 1900 he would bury Roosevelt in the vice-presidency. This strategy worried Hanna. "Don't you realize," he cried, "that there's only one life between this madman and the White House?" In September 1901, when an assassin shot McKinley at Buffalo, the "one life" was removed from Roosevelt's path.

Not since the days of Jackson had the White House been occupied by a President so devoted to the energetic expansion of the role of the Chief Executive. But where Jackson assaulted what he was pleased to call the "aristocratical establishment" in the national legislature and used the national executive to strengthen the particularism of state rights, the Republican Roosevelt, like his cousin the Democratic Roosevelt of the New Deal, confronted the citadels of private power and used the prestige of the presidency to advance the nationalism of "we the people"—at least the people within the pale. Ironically, FDR made TR's nationalism—and internationalism—the trademark of the Democratic tradition for decades, while twentieth century Republicans after TR struggled to restore McKinleyism if not Jacksonianism.

### Big business and national power

Roosevelt's nationalism always retained strong elements of caution in confronting private power; "his bark," as the conservative Elihu Root discovered, was "worse than his bite." His nationalism also retained a strong element of paternalism toward the people. In virtually all his State of the Union messages to Congress, the question of the trusts took precedence over other subjects. In his very first such message he explained his attitude:

*An additional reason for caution in dealing with corporations is to be found in the international commercial conditions of today. . . . America has only just begun to assume that commanding position in the international business world which we believe will more and more be hers. . . . Under such conditions it would be most unwise to cramp or fetter the youthful strength of our Nation.*

Since certain trusts thus had to be coddled, federal social justice, Roosevelt insisted, must look after the welfare of the public.

To make "the malefactors of great wealth" (another Roosevelt phrase) realize nevertheless that a loose tether from Washington depended on good behavior, he lost little time before demonstrating how power had de-

parted from Wall Street. On March 10, 1902, he ordered Attorney-General Philander C. Knox to bring suit under the Sherman Antitrust Act to dissolve the Northern Securities Company. This company, as we have seen, had been created by the country's greatest bankers to combine the holdings of the country's greatest railroad barons. So stunning was Roosevelt's attack upon it that J. P. Morgan himself journeyed down to Washington to find out what the President had in mind. Two years later, in 1904, the Supreme Court by a 5 to 4 vote gave its verdict. The Northern Securities Company must be broken up. The company's rulers soon gained their consolidation goals by other means, but this did not tarnish TR's public or self-image. The decision, he said, was "one of the great achievements of my administration. The most powerful men in this country were held to accountability before the law."

The *Northern Securities* verdict was followed in 1905 by that in *Swift & Company* v. *United States* breaking up the Beef Trust. In this case the Court reversed its decision of ten years before in *U.S.* v. *E. C. Knight Company* disallowing the application of the Sherman Act to manufacturing enterprises. The Beef Trust prosecution was one of the earliest outcomes of TR's success in getting Congress, in 1903, to establish a Bureau of Corporations in the new Department of Commerce and Labor. In keeping with the characteristic Progressive belief in publicity as a deterrent to antisocial action, this bureau was authorized to investigate and disclose the affairs of interstate corporations. The Beef Trust litigation had been started on the basis of the bureau's information; and its success led the way to further prosecutions of such "evil" combinations as the Oil Trust and the Tobacco Trust. These actions had indecisive results; they did not halt the wave of consolidations, but they kept alive the threat that ruthless combinations would have to face up to the President.

Big labor, such as it was, stood no more exempt from Roosevelt's watchfulness than big business. This was demonstrated in October 1902, when workers in the Pennsylvania anthracite pits, most of them captive mines of the Morgan-dominated Reading Railroad, had been on strike for months against the long-term deterioration of conditions in the mines and in the company-owned mining towns. Led by the able John Mitchell of the United Mine Workers, the miners demanded improvement all along the line. The operators, headed by George F. Baer, the Morgan-appointed head of the Reading Railroad, stood immovable in their unwillingness to heed complaints. At one stage in the strike, Baer made the provocative observation that "the rights and interests of the laboring man will be cared for, not by the labor union agitators, but by the Christian men to whom God in His infinite wisdom had given control of the property interests of the country."

By October, with winter imminent and the nation's coal bins empty, coal riots had broken out in northern cities. When Roosevelt demanded that the strike be arbitrated, the operators refused until the workers went back to the pits. On their part, "having in mind our experience with the coal operators in the past," as Mitchell put it, the workers were determined to stay out until their demands were met. At last, on October 13, Morgan made a second trip to Washington, where he and the President were able to agree on an arbitration commission satisfactory also to Mitchell. Although the union failed to gain recognition as labor's bargaining agent in the coal industry, the mine workers won a nine-hour day, a 10 percent wage increase, and other concessions. A grateful public, moreover, was able to look forward to winter heat thanks to the Rough Rider.

When McKinley named Elihu Root Secretary of War in 1899, he did so because he believed the latter's competence as a lawyer best fitted him for the task of administering the country's new colonial possessions. But Root soon discovered from American disappointments in the Philippines that what a good colonial administrator needed most was a good army. "The real object of having an army," he wrote in his first annual report as Secretary, "is to provide for war." This may sound "like a truism," he added; but the army he inherited was "admirably adapted [only] to secure pecuniary accountability and economy of expenditure in time of peace." Roosevelt, of course, shared Root's view that a thorough reorganization of American land forces was needed, and on becoming President he kept Root on in the War Department and took the first steps to implement the many specific recommendations the Secretary had made during the previous two years. One such step was the establishment of the Army War College in Washington in November 1901 to provide advanced education and training for permanent officers of the new fighting army to come. Root's work, with TR's support, became the foundation on which the projection of military needs based on "all contingencies of possible conflict" began and on which expenditures for such "contingencies," with some interruptions, soared in peacetime.

## A "square deal" for the people

After he had ordered the prosecution of the Northern Securities Company in 1902, Roosevelt made his first tour of the states as President. On this trip the principal theme of his speeches was a "square deal" for all. The settlement of the coal strike in the workers' favor and the outcome of the *Northern Securities case* in the public's interest went far toward proving that Roosevelt meant what he promised. Thus, when the time came for the 1904 presidential campaign, TR was more popular than ever and won the Republican nomination at the national convention in Chicago in June without opposition. Such big capitalists as Harriman, Morgan, and the Rockefellers, finding Roosevelt's actions more discreet than his words, made such generous contributions to the Republican party that the Democratic charge of "blackmail" became the leading campaign issue. Judge Alton B. Parker, the Democratic candidate, proved uninspiring and colorless, and Roosevelt's huge majority—7,623,000 popular votes to 5,077,000—took even him by surprise.

President at last in his own right, Roosevelt now pursued a more comprehensive reform program on the national level. His major achievements lay in railroad regulation, protection of consumers, and conservation of natural resources.

By 1904 the Interstate Commerce Act of 1887 regulating the railroads had become virtually a dead letter largely because of the Supreme Court's narrow interpretation of the Interstate Commerce Commission's powers. In 1903, in response to pressure from the railroads themselves, Congress had passed the Elkins Act, making it illegal for railroads to depart from their published freight rates, and making shippers as well as railroads liable for punishment for infractions. This measure struck at the practice of rebating, which the railroad companies had come to regard as a major nuisance. The Elkins Act, however, failed to give the Interstate Commerce Commission any power to fix rates, which was what farmers and other shippers wanted most. Roosevelt now prodded Congress to strengthen and enlarge the commission's powers in this respect, and in response, in 1906, Congress passed the Hepburn Act.

Heretofore, the commission could order alterations in railroad rates, but the roads did not have to comply until the courts ordered them to do so. Under the Hepburn Act, the commission was authorized to set maximum rates when complaints from shippers were received and to order the roads to comply within thirty days. The roads might still go to court, but in the interim the new rates, not the old, were to be in force. The Hepburn Act also extended ICC jurisdiction to storage, refrigeration, and terminal facilities, and to sleeping-car, express, and pipeline companies. Within two years, shippers made more than 9000 appeals to the commission, and a great many rates were revised downward.

In his annual message to Congress in December 1905, Roosevelt asked for an act to protect consumers from undesirable adulterants and preservatives used in the food-packaging industry. His request was made on the basis of another characteristically Progressive action—investigations conducted by Dr. Har-

vey W. Wiley, a chemist in the Department of Agriculture, and by other scientists, which had shown that such adulterants and preservatives were being widely used in canned foods.

The packing interests naturally fought TR's proposal. They could not, however, withstand the force of public indignation aroused in part by Upton Sinclair's shocking novel of Chicago's meat-packing industry, *The Jungle*, published in 1906. In June that year, Congress passed the first federal meat-inspection law. In the same year, Congress responded to Samuel Hopkins Adams's muckraking exposure of the patent-medicine industry and its misleading advertising by enacting a Pure Food and Drugs Act. This law did not insure full protection to consumers, but it struck at some of the worst abuses and prepared the way for stricter regulation later on.

As an amateur naturalist and an outdoor man with a taste for natural beauty, Roosevelt took an early and intelligent interest in conservation. Under the Forest Reserve Act, which had been passed in 1891, he set aside almost 150 million acres of unsold government timber land in various parts of the country as a forest reserve. He also closed to public entry about 85 million additional acres in Alaska and the Northwest in order to give the United States Geological Survey a chance to study mineral and water resources in these areas before they were given away. He turned over the supervision of the national forests to the Secretary of Agriculture, who put a professional conservationist, Gifford Pinchot, in charge.

At home in tilting with capitalists for public favor, Roosevelt was less well equipped for grasping the economic implications of the capitalists' wars among themselves. One such war helped bring about the Panic of 1907, during which a number of New York banks went to the wall. Roosevelt naturally was eager to do something to forestall a long depression, not least because of his consciousness of the reputation of his regime. When industrialists and Wall Streeters thus advised him that business would recover sooner if he permitted the United States Steel Corporation to acquire control of the Tennessee Iron and Coal Com-

625

pany, a firm whose shaky securities were held by many precariously situated brokerage houses, Roosevelt nervously approved the combination. His act implied that at least during his administration the Steel Corporation would be immune from antitrust prosecution. Whether it implied, too, that he had saved the country from a business collapse is now doubtful. At any rate, business withstood the Panic, while financial authorities began to seek more fundamental ways to strengthen national finance. Their work led eventually to the Federal Reserve Act of 1913 (see p. 631).

## TR and Will

Roosevelt, awed for once by the stunning show of confidence on the part of the common man in the (then) youngest President in history, but one day after the election of 1904 made an impulsive commitment he was promptly to regret:

*On the fourth of March next I shall have served three and a half years, and this three and a half years constitutes my first term. The wise custom which limits the President to two terms regards the substance not the form. Under no circumstances will I be a candidate for or accept another nomination.*

Just because he so obviously thrived on power he felt obliged, at the moment of his triumph, to deny the Democratic assertions that his "supposed personal ambitions" would lead him to perpetuate himself in office.

As the 1908 campaign neared, Roosevelt nevertheless stood well enough with his party to name its next candidate: his friend William Howard Taft of Ohio, the first civil governor of the Philippines and Root's replacement as Secretary of War in 1904. He also stood well enough with the people to put Taft over. Having fared worse with a conservative candidate in 1904 than they had earlier with Bryan, the Democrats in 1908 returned to the "Great Commoner"; but Progressive reforms under Roosevelt left Bryan issueless, and Taft swept in with a vote of 7,679,000 to 6,409,000. His margin in the electoral college was 321 to 162.

The strains of abdication told on TR from the moment "Will" named his Cabinet, which represented virtually a complete housecleaning of his colleagues under the Rough Rider. Within days of Taft's inauguration in March 1909, Roosevelt set out to hunt big game in Africa; but letters from his son-in-law Nicholas Longworth and his "buddy" Henry Cabot Lodge, complaining of social coldness in the White House, also retailed the political news and soon convinced the traveler that his heir was a "flubdub." "Taft, Cannon, Aldrich and the others," TR replied to Lodge, "have totally misestimated the character of the movement which we now have to face in American life."

One means used by Roosevelt to hold the Republican party together while winning Progressive reforms was to evade the "Great Issue" of Protection. He evaded it so successfully that by 1908 the call for downward tariff revision, reflecting both urban and rural concern over the steadily rising cost of living, had grown loud enough to force Taft and the Republican platform writers to promise early action. To fulfill this promise, Taft called a special session of Congress for March 1909, and that is when his four-year ordeal began.

Taft may have been genuinely interested in lowering the duties. When proposals for downward revision were made in Congress, however, the Old Guard fought them as always. Moderate reductions were adopted in the House; but when Nelson Aldrich and his conservative friends in the Senate finished with the measure, as usual it not only failed to reduce the levies but actually raised them. Taft had done nothing to check Aldrich, and this betrayal of the platform pledge so incensed certain western senators—notably La Follette, Beveridge, Bristow of Kansas, and Dolliver and Cummins of Iowa—that they attacked their own party leaders in one of the most brilliant debates ever heard in the chamber. They lost the battle, but their insurgency shook the Old Guard to its foundations. When Taft, after signing the Payne-Aldrich Act, declared in a speech in Minnesota that it was the best tariff ever, he shocked the Republican rank and file as well.

Soon after the tariff fight in the Senate, insurgent House Progressives, chiefly Republicans, tried to unseat their Speaker, Joseph G. ("Uncle Joe") Cannon, the "hardboiled hayseed" of Illinois who hated "all this babble for reform." By long-standing House rules, the Speaker had the right to appoint a majority of the Committee on Rules, which dictated what legislation would (and would not) be presented for consideration. The Speaker also had sweeping powers of appointment over other committees, powers Cannon never hesitated to use to reward friends and punish enemies. The Senate itself soon learned that it was futile to buck Cannon's decisions, so his tyranny extended to the whole Congress. The White House under TR, moreover, realistically took Cannon's views into serious consideration before proposing legislation. Taft characteristically at first gave encouragement to the rebels and then unceremoniously gave way.

Cannon's days were numbered, however, when in March 1910 George W. Norris of Nebraska and other Republican insurgents, taking advantage of a parliamentary technicality, caught the Speaker by surprise, and in a thirty-six-hour session joined with Democrats led by Champ Clark of Missouri in adopting new rules. Henceforth, the entire House would *elect* the Rules Committee, from which the Speaker was now excluded. "The clock has struck for Uncle Joe," wrote the *Wall Street Journal.* "He has stood between the people and too many things that they wanted and ought to have, and the fact that he has stood off some things that they ought not to have won't save him."

The insurgents followed up this victory with new railroad legislation which went beyond Taft's wishes. In the Mann-Elkins Act of 1910, Congress empowered the Interstate Commerce Commission to suspend *general* rate increases (enlarging the power granted by the Hepburn Act to suspend specific increases) and to take the initiative in revising such rates. A Commerce Court was estab-

lished to speed up the judicial process by hearing appeals directly from the commission. These terms were substantially in line with Taft's desires. But the insurgents also pushed through a provision forbidding railroads from acquiring competing lines, and added another that put telephone, telegraph, cable, and wireless companies under the commission's control.

Furthermore the physical evaluation of railroad property as a basis for rate making, which was considered vital by the Progressives and which they had not been able to get into the 1910 bill, was enacted in 1913 during Taft's last months. The Physical Evaluation Act required the ICC to assess the value of all property owned by every company under its jurisdiction and specified the manner in which this assessment was to be made. Such valuations were to be taken as prima facie evidence of the value of the property. Now the commission could fix rates not on the basis of watered stock but on the true value of operating assets.

What may yet have remained of Republican unity was almost wholly destroyed by the conservation issue involved in the Pinchot-Ballinger affair. The trouble here began when the Chief Forester of the Department of Agriculture, Gifford Pinchot, heard from Louis Glavis, an investigator for the Interior Department, that Secretary of the Interior Richard A. Ballinger had agreed to let private interests take over the reserved coal lands in Alaska. Pinchot encouraged Glavis to appeal to Taft and himself issued a statement denouncing Ballinger. Taft chose to believe Gallinger's denials rather than Glavis's story and authorized Glavis's dismissal from the Interior Department. Pinchot carried on with the attack until he, too, was removed. Progressives in Congress now investigated the Interior Department and showed that Ballinger, though not found guilty of misconduct, had no sympathy with conservation policies. Taft himself was tarred with the same brush.

Taft did not disappoint the Progressives at every turn. Important Progressive measures passed during his tenure included the Sixteenth Amendment, which made the federal income tax constitutional, and the Seventeenth Amendment, providing for the direct election of United States Senators, both ratified in 1913. He also initiated about twice as many prosecutions under the Sherman Act in his one administration as Roosevelt had in two, an intensity of activity that TR need not necessarily have admired. Taft's two leading cases, against International Harvester and United States Steel, moreover, turned out to be worse than failures. The Steel prosecution, coming after Roosevelt's virtual guarantee of immunity to the corporation, dashed all hope for reconciliation between TR and Will; the Harvester action alienated the company's promoter and director, the former Morgan partner George W. Perkins, who was to become one of Roosevelt's leading backers in 1912. No doubt, prosecutions like these, together with the natural reluctance to invest in an apparent loser, explain some of the difficulties of Taft's regular Republican supporters in raising 1912 campaign funds.

### The Bull Moose party

After a triumphal tour of Europe on his way back from Africa, Roosevelt reached New York City in June 1910 and was enthusiastically greeted. Less pleasant was the news from the West. Here, in the heartland of insurgency, the strife in Republican ranks had broken into open warfare over Taft's using the full power of presidential patronage to build up conservative strength in anticipation of the congressional elections later in the year. At first, Roosevelt refrained from any move that would publicize his estrangement from the President. But as the campaign warmed up he grew restive, and in August he set out on a swing through the West for a rousing series of speeches on the "welfare state" and the "New Nationalism."

On August 31, at Osawatomie, Kansas, TR delivered his most striking talk. His espousal of the popular recall of state-court decisions nullifying social legislation and his accusation that the federal judiciary was obstructing the popular will shocked conservatives everywhere. He said many other stirring things as well: "The object of government is the welfare of the people." "This New Nationalism ... demands of the judiciary that it shall be interested primarily in human welfare rather than in property." "Property shall be the servant not the master of the commonwealth." "The ... essence of any struggle for healthy liberty has always been, and must always be, to take from some one man or class of men the right to enjoy power, or wealth, or position, or immunity, which has not been earned by service to his or their fellows."

Neither Taft's tactics nor Roosevelt's talks did the party much good in the 1910 elections when the Democrats captured the House for the first time since 1893 and elected many governors. This showing suggested two possibilities: (1) that the insurgents might capture the leadership of the Republican party from the discredited Old Guard; and (2) that, against warring Republicans, the Democrats might have an excellent chance to win the presidency in 1912.

The Republican insurgents were willing to face up to the second possibility when the time came, provided they could bring the first to fruition beforehand. In January 1911 many of them formed the National Progressive Republican League to promote La Follette—the most successful Progressive as governor of Wisconsin and the most militant as United States Senator—as the party's 1912 "logical candidate." Many others, at the same time, looked upon TR as a "natural" and hesitated to join the La Follette boom until certain the Rough Rider would not run. Roosevelt, although pressed by loyal party men to head off La Follette as well as Taft, waited almost a year to make up his mind; and only after La Follette had so worn himself down campaigning for Progressivism within Republican ranks that he collapsed during a major speech on February 2, 1912, did TR publicly announce, "my hat is in the ring." A savage fight followed, and by the time of the Republican convention in Chicago in June, La Follette's support had dwindled to a small group of bitter-enders. Taft's supporters, at the same time, captured the convention and nominated him for a second term on the first ballot, after Roosevelt and his followers, charging that the President had gained his delegates by fraudulent means, stormed out.

In response to questions about his own physical energies, Roosevelt on arriving in Chicago said that he felt "fit as a bull moose," and his supporters now hastily organized a Progressive party convention of their own in that city, hoping to speed him back to the White House. William Allen White explained his own and the crowd's frenzy at this convention by saying, "Roosevelt bit me and I went mad." The delegates nevertheless adopted a sane-enough platform calling for the initiative, referendum, and recall, woman's suffrage, workmen's compensation and social insurance, minimum wages for women, child-labor legislation, and federal trade and tariff commissions to regulate business.

In his *Autobiography,* TR deemed it his "duty," as he put it, "to add this comment" on his abjuration of a third term in 1904 in the light of the events of 1912:

*An ex-President stands precisely in the position of any other private citizen, and has not one particle more power to secure a nomination or election than if he had never held office at all. . . . Therefore the reasoning on which the anti-third-term custom is based has no application whatever to anything except consecutive terms.*

TR felt all the more strongly about this at this juncture, for, as he said early in 1912, "if the people as a whole desire me, not for my sake, but for their own sake, to undertake the job, I would feel honor bound to do so."

Although heartened by the returns of 1910 and the Republican crack-up in 1912, the Democrats had to mend internal divisions of their own to make the most of their opportunity. Bryan, still a power in Democratic ranks, helped matters by announcing that he would not run again. Instead, at the party convention in Baltimore in June, he supported Champ Clark, who had succeeded to the Speakership of the House following the 1910 elections. Though strong in the early balloting, Clark failed to get the two-thirds majority needed for the nomination; and when Bryan, after learning of his gaining conservative eastern support, switched to the Progressive Democratic governor of New Jersey, Woodrow Wilson, the latter won on the forty-sixth ballot.

## IV  Democratic Progressivism

*The 1912 campaign*

Fifty-five years old at the time of his nomination, Wilson had first shown his mettle as an academic reformer while president of Princeton University from 1902 to 1910. His high moral tone made him attractive to Democratic bosses of the state, who in 1910 were seeking a respectable candidate for governor, preferably one they themselves could govern. When they offered Wilson the nomination, he accepted. When he won the gov-

norship, he repudiated the bosses and promoted a variety of reforms that earned him Progressive support.

That Wilson should have been successful in politics is indeed remarkable, for though he had personal and intellectual distinction he lacked the necessary practical qualities. An excellent public speaker, offstage he was ill suited to the give and take of party government. Colonel House, his most intimate confidant, wrote of him in 1915: "his prejudices are many and often unjust. He finds great

Brown Brothers

*Wilson with Andrew Carnegie and others soon after his inauguration as president of Princeton University.*

issue of the trusts. "There is one proposition upon which this campaign turns," Wilson declared in an early speech. "That proposition is this: that monopoly is inevitable, . . . and that is what I deny." As Louis D. Brandeis put it, Wilson was for regulated competition, Roosevelt for regulated monopoly. Wilson held that the business combinations were too powerful to be regulated, "that monopoly can be broken up. If I didn't believe it, I would know that all the roads of free development were shut in this country." A "new freedom" for the individual was more important than a "square deal" from the government.

Probably not many voters followed all the arguments, nor did they need to with two such colorful personalities in the field. Together they altogether overwhelmed Taft, who gained but eight electoral votes. Roosevelt won 88, Wilson 435. Eugene V. Debs, running on the Socialist ticket, won no electoral votes, yet his popular vote of over 900,000 was impressive. Although Wilson's popular vote of 6,293,000 was slightly less than 42 percent of the electorate, the Democratic party captured the House and Senate as well as the presidency; and Wilson, with the additional support of a bloc of Progressive Republicans, took office with excellent prospects for a constructive administration.

difficulty in conferring with men . . . in whom he can find nothing good." Wilson's intense personality projected itself largely in terms of ideals and principles, not in personal loyalties; and some believe that he was often victimized by his own high-sounding words.

The Democrats' great asset in 1912, of course, was the Republican split. Taft, however, soon lagged, and the battle narrowed down to Wilson and TR, and to the central

### The "New Freedom"

Wilson's two terms, running from 1913 to 1921, proved extraordinarily fruitful in reform legislation. Differences on the trust issue may have dominated the electoral contest; but other major subjects demanded even earlier attention. First on the docket was the tariff. In 1913 Wilson called a special session of Congress on this old issue, and with strong support from Senator La Follette and his fellow Republican Progressives, the Democrats that year passed the Underwood Act, which effected the first satisfactory downward revision since the Civil War. To supply the revenue that presumably would be lost through

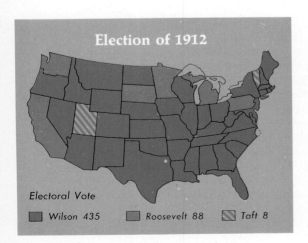

## Election of 1912

*Electoral Vote*

◼ Wilson 435   ◼ Roosevelt 88   ▨ Taft 8

tariff reduction, this act also placed a tax of 1 percent on personal incomes of $4000, and graduated surtaxes of from 1 to 6 percent on higher incomes.

Financial reform, the need for which was recognized by both conservatives and Progressives, came next. A commission set up in 1908 under the chairmanship of Senator Aldrich himself had reported in favor of establishing a great central bank with branches dominated by the leading banking interests. The Democrats denounced this proposal in their 1912 platform, but they agreed with the Aldrich Commission's judgment that the main defect in the banking system was the "unhealthy congestion of loanable funds in great centers," especially in New York City, and especially at times when farmers dispersed over rural areas most needed credit.

As finally passed on December 23, 1913, the Federal Reserve Act renovating the banking system set up twelve regional banking districts, each with a Federal Reserve Bank. The Federal Reserve Banks were owned by the member banks of the Federal Reserve System. All national banks were required to join the system, and state banks also were eligible. Member banks were required to subscribe 6 percent of their capital to the Federal Reserve Bank in their region. On the security of this subscription and commercial and agricultural paper, the Federal Reserve Banks would create a new currency, Federal Reserve notes, issued by the Reserve Banks to member banks and circulated by them to borrowers. The Federal Reserve System was placed under the direction of the Federal Reserve Board, consisting of the Secretary of the Treasury and seven other persons appointed by the President. By 1923, the Federal Reserve System embraced 70 percent of the nation's banking.

Even those who denounced the new setup as one politically "as dangerous as the old United States Bank of Jackson's time" came around to admit its value. The Federal Reserve System created a currency flexible and sound and made it available to all sections of the country through the regional Reserve Banks. It also left banking a private business, under federal supervision.

Further to improve the farmer's access to funds, Congress in May 1916 passed the Federal Farm Loan Act creating a Federal Farm Loan Board of twelve regional Farm Loan banks patterned after the Federal Reserve System. The banks were authorized to lend sums to cooperative farm-loan associations on the security of farm lands, buildings, and improvements, up to 70 percent of the value of these assets. Loans were to be on a long-range basis, interest was not to be more than 6 percent, and profits were to be distributed to the members of the subscribing farm-loan associations. In 1916, another bill was passed for the farmers' financial benefit—the Warehouse Act—which authorized licensed warehouse operators to issue warehouse receipts against farm products deposited with them. Farmers could use these warehouse receipts as currency or as security for personal loans. Legislation for federal support of practical farmer education and rural road improvement also helped the families on the land.

The initial Wilsonian antitrust measure, the Federal Trade Commission Act of September 1914, undertook to prevent rather than punish unfair trade practices. This act created a five-man Federal Trade Commission authorized to investigate alleged violations of antitrust laws. The commission was empowered to issue "cease-and-desist" orders against corporations found guilty of unfair competitive practices. If this recourse failed, the commission could bring accused corporations to court. During Wilson's administration, 379 cease-and-desist orders were issued, and a few dissolutions of trusts were initiated in cooperation with the Department of Justice. Even so, Progressives soon came to feel that the commission was not using its powers vigorously enough, and like the Interstate Commerce Commission earlier, the FTC gradually became a tool of those it purported to regulate.

A second antitrust law, passed in October 1914, was the Clayton Act. This act prohibited a number of business practices: price discrimination that might lessen or destroy competition; tying contracts—that is, contracts that forced purchasers to refrain from buying the product of competitors; the acquisition by corporations of stock in competing firms; and the creation of interlocking directorates in corporations and banks over a specified size as measured by capitalization. Officers of corporations were made personally subject to prosecution if they violated these provisions. Labor unions as such were not to be construed as illegal combinations or conspiracies in restraint of trade, and labor injunctions were forbidden except when necessary to prevent "irreparable injury to property, or to a property right."

But the Clayton Act was passed on the eve of World War I, during which antitrust action was greatly curtailed. During the conservative regimes of the 1920s, a series of Supreme Court decisions nullified its labor provisions.

A few other measures filled out the domestic record of Wilson's first administration, including the Keating-Owen Child Labor Act already described (p. 618). The La Follette-sponsored Seaman's Act of 1915 raised safety requirements on American vessels and, by abolishing the crime of desertion, released American merchant seamen from bondage to labor contracts upon their return to home ports. The Adamson Act of 1916 established the eight-hour day for interstate railway workers. Like the Clayton Act, during World War I and the twenties these measures were largely nullified by administrative negligence and judicial hostility.

## For further reading

The spirit and thought of the early twentieth century may best be captured by reading the contemporary works mentioned in the text. Modern interpretations of Progressive thought include Morton White, *Social Thought in America, The Revolt Against Formalism* (1957 ed.); D. W. Noble, *The Paradox of Progressive Thought* (1958); Charles Forcey, *The Crossroads of Liberalism* (1961); Daniel Aaron, *Men of Good Hope* (1951); Christopher Lasch, *The New Radicalism in America 1889-1963* (1965); Samuel Haber, *Efficiency and Uplift: Scientific Management in the Progressive Era 1890-1920* (1964); H. F. May, *The End of American Innocence: A Study of the First Years of Our Own Time 1912-1917* (1959); Richard Hofstadter, *The Progressive Historians* (1968); August Meier, *Negro Thought in America 1880-1915* (1968); I. A. Newby, *Jim Crow's Defense: Anti-Negro Thought in America 1900-1930* (1965); and works on religion and philosophy cited for Chapter Twenty-two.

R. H. Wiebe, *The Search For Order 1877-1920* (1967), offers a suggestive interpretation of the period somewhat beyond the implication of its title. Wiebe, *Businessmen and Reform* (1962); and Gabriel Kolko, *The Triumph of Conservatism, A Reinterpretation of American History 1900-1916* (1963), and *Railroads and Regulation 1877-1916* (1965), perhaps overemphasize

conservative success, and underemphasize the relationship between the new politics and the new imperialism. Richard Hofstadter, *The Age of Reform* (1955), a target of some of the later scholarship, remains a provocative study. More conventional scholarly surveys include G. E. Mowry, *The Era of Theodore Roosevelt 1900-1912* (1958), and *Theodore Roosevelt and the Progressive Movement* (1947); Ray Ginger, *Age of Excess, American Life from the End of Reconstruction to World War I* (1965); and two short biographies by J. M. Blum: *The Republican Roosevelt* (1954), and *Woodrow Wilson* (1956). The extended introductions in E. E. Morison and others, eds., *The Letters of Theodore Roosevelt* (8 vols., 1951-1954), provide valuable commentary on the invaluable text matter. A. S. Link, *Wilson, The New Freedom* (1956), vol. 2 of Link's extended biography in process, also is indispensable. R. M. Abrams and L. W. Levine, eds., *The Shaping of Twentieth Century America* (1965); Carl Resek, ed., *The Progressives* (1967); Harvey Swados, *Years of Conscience, The Muckrakers* (1962); and Hofstadter, *The Progressive Movement 1900-1915* (1963), are rewarding anthologies.

Many older works, beginning with B. P. Dewitt, *The Progressive Movement* (1915), and Mark Sullivan, *Our Times: The United States 1900-1925* (6 vols.,

1920–1935), retain their value. These include Matthew Josephson, *The President Makers 1896–1919* (1940); John Chamberlain, *Farewell to Reform* (1932); and E. F. Goldman, *Rendezvous with Destiny* (1952).

S. S. McClure, *My Autobiography* (1914), *The Autobiography of Lincoln Steffens* (1931), and Ida M. Tarbell, *All in the Day's Work* (1939), tell much about the leading muckraker publisher and his star reporters. C. C. Regier, *The Era of the Muckrakers* (1932), enlarges the story of their rise and decline. H. S. Wilson, *McClure's Magazine and the Muckrakers* (1970), links muckraking and Progressivism in a new and interesting way. W. E. B. Du Bois, ed., *Atlanta University Publications 1902–1906* (reprinted in 2 vols., 1968), gets at the facts of Negro life that muckrakers did not pursue. Besides La Follette's *Autobiography* (1911), R. S. Maxwell, *La Follette and the Rise of the Progressives in Wisconsin* (1956), and B. C. and Fola La Follette, *Robert M. La Follette* (2 vols., 1953), are illuminating on the "Wisconsin Way." *The Autobiography of William Allen White* (1946) and Claude G. Bowers, *Beveridge and the Progressive Era* (1932), are valuable for other midwestern Progressives. White and others are also accounted for in R. B. Nye, *Midwestern Progressive Politics* (1951). G. E. Mowry, *The California Progressives* (1951), and C. V. Woodward, *Origins of the New South 1877–1913* (1951), are outstanding on their sections. R. M. Abrams, *Conservatism in a Progressive Era: Massachusetts Politics 1900–1912* (1964), casts some oblique but penetrating rays.

S. P. Hays, *Conservation and the Gospel of Efficiency* (1959), and A. T. Mason, *Bureaucracy Convicts Itself* (1941), on the Ballinger-Pinchot controversy, elaborate the conservation story. Illuminating studies of other social and local problems and the Progressive attack upon them include Robert Hunter, *Poverty* (1904); Jane Addams, *Twenty Years at Hull House* (1910); Roy Lubove, *The Progressives and the Slums 1890–1917* (1962); J. P. Felt, *Hostages of Fortune, Child Labor Reform in New York State* (1965); Marc Karson, *American Labor Unions and Politics 1900–1918* (1958);

Irwin Yellowitz, *Labor and the Progressive Movement in New York State 1897–1916* (1965); and R. D. Cross, *The Emergence of Liberal Catholicism in America* (1967). On woman's rights see A. P. Grimes, *The Protestant Ethic and Woman's Suffrage* (1967); and A. S. Kraditor, *The Ideas of the Woman's Suffrage Movement 1890–1920* (1965). Andrew Sinclair, *Era of Excess: A Social History of the Prohibition Movement* (1962), and J. H. Timberlake, *Prohibition and the Progressive Movement 1900–1920* (1963), cover this "reform." O. E. Anderson, Jr., *The Health of a Nation* (1958), is useful on the fight for pure food. Zane L. Miller, *Boss Cox's Cincinnati* (1968), and Walton Bean, *Boss Ruef's San Francisco* (1967), along with Tom L. Johnson, *My Story* (1911), may be profitably added to the books on urban life in this period cited in Chapter Twenty-one. B. D. Karl, *Executive Reorganization and Reform in the New Deal* (1963), is excellent on this earlier period, as its subtitle "The Genesis of Administrative Management 1900–1939" indicates.

The literature on the Progressive Presidents is immense. To the books by Blum, Link, and Morison, cited above, the following may be added: W. H. Harbaugh, *Power and Responsibility: The Life and Times of Theodore Roosevelt* (1961); H. F. Pringle, *Theodore Roosevelt* (1931), and *Life and Times of William Howard Taft* (2 vols., 1939); and J. A. Garraty, *Woodrow Wilson* (1956). The deterioration of the Roosevelt-Taft relationship may be traced in William Manners, *TR and Will* (1969). K. W. Hechler, *Insurgency* (1940), is excellent on the Republican revolt of 1910.

Helpful biographies of others of the era, reformers and conservatives, include A. T. Mason, *Brandeis* (1946); P. C. Jessup, *Elihu Root* (2 vols., 1938); J. A. Garraty, *Right Hand Man, The Life of George W. Perkins* (1960); and N. W. Stephenson, *Nelson W. Aldrich* (1930). F. L. Allen, *The Lords of Creation* (1935), is a spirited account of J. P. Morgan, his friends and enemies. On socialism and the Socialist party, see the contemporary statements of W. E. Walling in *Socialism As It Is* (1912) and *Progressivism and After* (1914); and such scholarly accounts as H. H. Quint, *The Forging of American Socialism* (1953); D. A. Shannon, *The Socialist Party of America* (1955); and Ray Ginger, *The Bending Cross* (1949), a biography of Debs.

633

# WORLD WAR AND WORLD REVOLUTION

On June 28, 1914, Archduke Franz Ferdinand, heir to the throne of the Austro-Hungarian empire, was shot and killed by a revolutionary Slav at Sarajevo in the Austrian province of Bosnia. Austria, aroused by the chronic agitation for self-rule among the captive Slavic people of her empire, claimed that the government of neighboring Serbia, long committed to Slavic nationalism, had known of the impending assassination and had done little to prevent it. To punish her, Austria promptly presented Serbia with a list of demands that involved the surrender of her independence. When Serbia refused to meet one of these demands, Austria, assured of the backing of her German ally, declared war. Russia, the leader of the Slavic world, refused to stand by while Serbia was crushed. Russia's mobilization of her armies on her German and Austrian frontiers signalized to all Europe that a general conflict was to begin.

There was good reason for this European reaction. For a generation and more the European nations had been living in fear of one another, and as their suspicions grew so did their arms. They also began to seek allies. By 1914 Europe was divided roughly into two camps. One was the Triple Alliance, comprising Austria-Hungary, Germany, and Italy— although Italy was soon to break with the two "Central Powers," while Turkey was to join them. The second was the Triple Entente, to become known to Americans as the "Allies," comprising France, Russia, and Great Britain. Each of the nations in these camps also had commitments to nearby smaller nations. The United States, already feeling the strains of a quarter of a century of overseas expansionism and imperialism, had commitments to none.

When Russia refused to check her mobilization on the German frontier, Germany declared war on her on August 1, 1914. In the event of such a war German military leaders had long planned to move first against Russia's ally, France, in the hope of crushing her before Russia could ready her unwieldy forces. Thus on August 3, 1914, Germany declared war on France. When she struck at France through Belgium, Britain on August 4 declared war on Germany. Italy, meanwhile, remained neutral until May 1915, when the Allies in a secret treaty promised her after the war, in exchange for intervention on their side, more territory than she could refuse. Both the Central Powers and the Allies sought American support and flooded the United States with propaganda.

In the war of words between the Allies and the Central Powers, the advantage lay with the Allies, whose language, both literally and philosophically, Americans better understood. The United States, moreover, had a President, in Woodrow Wilson, who seemed, as we have said, peculiarly fond of words, especially high-sounding ones. And when the United States eventually joined the Allies in the European conflict, which then became a world war, Wilson embraced the opportunity to explain the American action in the most elevated language:

> This is the People's War, a war for freedom and justice and self-government amongst all the nations of the world, a war to make the world safe for the peoples who live upon it, ... the German peoples themselves included.

Wilson made a convenient distinction between the "military masters of Germany" and their subjects, and avowed that the United States entered the war against the former "not as a partisan" but as everybody's friend.

Yet it was to be acts rather than words that brought an end to America's abstention from the fighting, and especially aggressive acts by the Central Powers in the war at sea that finally committed the United States to the Allied side. As late as 1916, Wilson campaigned for reelection on the slogan "He kept us out of war" and won. Once the President committed the nation to the Allied cause, however, enthusiasm for "the war to make the world safe for democracy" touched the hearts of the great majority of his countrymen. And once victory was gained, hopes for the attainment of the avowed American purpose in the war ran high. In the same message in which he asked Congress for war on the German government, Wilson welcomed the new Russian government set up by Kerensky after the March Revolution as "a fit partner for a League of Honor"; nor did Lenin's establishment of Bolshevism in the November Revolution shake his faith in Russia as "always in fact democratic at heart."

Wilson's high hopes, nevertheless, were soon dashed by the legacy of Europe's long history of national jealousies and by the American leader's own self-righteousness. Many Americans who took part in the holocaust simply could not equate the realities of trench warfare with the President's idealistic rhetoric. "I was embarrassed," says Lieutenant Henry in Ernest Hemingway's war novel *A Farewell to Arms*, "by the words sacred, glorious, and sacrifice. . . . We had . . . read them, on proclamations, now for a long time, and I had seen nothing sacred, and the things that were glorious had no glory and the sacrifices were like the stockyards in Chicago, if nothing was done with the meat except to bury it. . . . Abstract words such as glory, honor, courage, were obscene."

## I   Toward intervention

### The propaganda campaign

The preoccupation of American leaders with world power since the Spanish-American war could not hide the fact that in many respects the United States remained a provincial nation in 1914. Her small Department of State, as unprofessional as her turn-of-the-century Department of War, was as poorly equipped to understand the transactions of Europe's chancelleries as the latter were to grasp the workings of democracy in the land that had absorbed so many millions of their people. Most Americans were startled by the chain-reaction course of belligerency following the outbreak of the fighting; and when the President, in the early days of the war, appealed to them to be "impartial in thought as well as in act," they felt "the cheering assurance," according to *The Literary Digest*, "that they were in no peril of being drawn in."

It was not long, however, before the loyalties of the more than thirty million Americans of European birth or parentage became engaged with one side or the other, while Wilson personally shared the sympathy of the majority with the Allied cause. Since the turn of the century, moreover, Britain in particular had made a conscientious effort to woo American friendship in view of German competition in Europe and elsewhere, a task made easier by the ties of language and literature that bound the cultivated classes of both countries. Bonds of trade and finance, although strained by prewar competition and wartime jealousies, also united important sectors of the British and American business communities.

For France a somewhat vaguer enthusiasm dated back to the days of Lafayette; and this feeling Americans soon extended to "poor little Belgium," Germany's first victim. The martyrdom of Belgium, at the same time, confirmed many Americans in their belief, fed for decades by the alarming pronouncements of Kaiser Wilhelm about Germany's imperial ambitions, that the German government was ruthless and unprincipled. Mounting evidence early in the war of violence by German and Austrian agents in the United States aimed at crippling industrial production that might assist the Allied cause deepened American revulsion from the "Hun." Americans who had studied in German universities, traveled in the country, and taken Bismarck's advanced social reforms as their models for Progressive programs at home sometimes deplored the barbaric light in which the Central Powers were placed; but their voices were lost in the general hubbub of accusation.

Allied propagandists disseminated such ghastly stories of German rapine, plunder, and cruelty in Belgium, most of them later proved false, that Thomas Mann, in Munich, already a towering figure in German literature, wrote a number of magazine articles in 1915, "an action sprung from rage," as he said, dictated by the "urgent need to come to the intellectual rescue of my reviled nation." The war at sea also favored the public-relations work of the Allies. By 1916 their blockade of Central

Europe brought hunger and malnutrition to women and children, but such slow cruelty was hard to dramatize, while German submarine warfare caused shocking sinkings at sea which struck horror into the hearts of everyone.

### Freedom of the seas

The Allied blockade and the German submarine offensive naturally involved the United States in conflicts with both parties over the rights of neutral carriers. One of the earliest disputes with Britain arose over the definition of contraband—that is, goods which

*An example of British propaganda advantage: This British song of 1912 became immensely popular in the United States when it was found to be the British Tommies' favorite.*

Courtesy Chappell Music Company

in international law may not be supplied by a neutral to one belligerent without risk of lawful seizure by another. The British arbitrarily redefined contraband to embrace *all* articles of importance—including foodstuffs, hitherto not designated—that might give indirect aid to the enemy.

The liberties the British took with the traditional right of visit and search caused additional friction. Under international law a belligerent vessel had the right to stop and search a neutral merchantman for contraband and either release it if none was found or send it to a prize court for legal action if contraband was discovered. The British insisted that the task of searching large modern vessels had grown too complicated for the usual procedure to be observed any longer. Instead, they often conducted neutral vessels to port for a thorough examination, thereby imposing costly delays on American merchantmen. A third source of trouble was Britain's blockading not only enemy ports but neutral ports near enough to Germany to serve as entry points to German markets. Such ports were permitted to land approximately the same volume of goods as before the war and no more.

In November 1914, the British declared the entire North Sea a military area and mined it so thoroughly that no neutral vessel could traverse it without first receiving British directions on how to navigate the mined zones. This again was a radical departure from international practice, but to all complaints Britain replied that she was fighting for her life and would not be bound by maritime laws framed under conditions now obsolete. When in the summer of 1916 the London government drew up a list of eighty-five persons or firms in the United States suspected of giving aid to Germany and forbade British subjects to trade with them, Wilson professed himself "about at the end of my patience with Great Britain and the Allies. This blacklist business is the last straw. . . . Can we any longer endure their intolerable course?"

Yet the United States never really considered going to war against the Allies. "England is fighting our fight," Wilson declared at one point. When members of his Cabinet urged him to embargo exports to Britain in

637

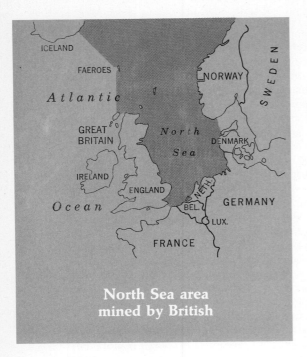

**North Sea area mined by British**

1915, Wilson replied even that early: "Gentlemen, the Allies are standing with their backs to the wall fighting wild beasts." If the Germans should succeed, he once told the British ambassador, "we shall be forced to take such measures of defense here which would be fatal to our form of Government and American ideals." Many thoughtful men agreed, some like Elihu Root in the verbal currency worn threadbare by decades of imperialist propaganda. To an English friend, Root wrote at this time: "The principle of Anglo-Saxon liberty seems to have met the irreconcilable conception of the German State, and the two ideas are battling for control of the world."

Certain nonideological considerations also blunted American complaints. Secretary of State Robert Lansing, who succeeded William Jennings Bryan in that office after the latter's resignation in June 1915 over administration handling of the *Lusitania* sinking (see p. 639), later recalled:

*Short and emphatic notes were dangerous. Everything was submerged in verbosity. It was done with deliberate purpose. It insured continuance of the controversies and left the questions unsettled, which was neces-* *sary in order to leave this country free to act and even to act illegally when it entered the war.*

Profitable trade supplied a second reason for American restraint. True, the Allied blockade so interfered with American trade with the Central Powers that it fell in value from almost $170 million in 1914 to virtually nothing in 1916. But American trade with the Allies in the same period soared from $825 million to about $3.25 billion, a surge that rescued the economy from a recession in 1914 and started a boom that lasted until 1919.

Of even greater significance was the sudden transformation of the United States from a debtor to a creditor nation. The large amounts of American bond issues and corporate securities held especially by British investors were sold out to pay for war materials. To finance further buying, on which Allied success in the war increasingly depended, the British and their friends would be obliged to borrow. The State Department under Bryan discouraged American bankers from making private loans to Allied governments lest the American stake in an Allied victory, despite all the harassment on the seas, become too great to withstand. After Bryan's departure in June 1915, however, the administration altered its position. In August that year, Secretary of the Treasury William G. McAdoo wrote to the President, "To maintain our prosperity, we must finance it."

As time passed, the United States came to have a tremendous economic stake in the Allies' ability to pay back what they borrowed, and in the early thirties a Senate Committee headed by Gerald P. Nye charged that the country finally had entered the war simply to assure the safety of bankers' loans and munitions makers' profits. This charge underlay the neutrality laws of the midthirties, which may have strengthened Hitler's aggressive resolves (see p. 739). It distorts the facts of the situation in World War I, omitting all the other elements of sympathy and policy that impelled Wilson to act as he did.

## Submarine warfare

The more deeply the United States became involved with the Allies, the less constraint she felt in combating the submarine warfare of the Central Powers. A frail craft, the submarine, once it surfaced, could easily be sunk even by the light deck guns of merchant ships. Submarine commanders therefore dared not follow the established practice of halting a suspect vessel, ascertaining its identity, and providing for the safety of passengers and crew before sending it to the bottom. Submarine captains had to hit and run. British practices on the high seas, Wilson said, involved only property damage, which could be adjusted at the end of the war; submarine tactics ignored "the fundamental rights of humanity. . . . The loss of life is irreparable." When the German government, on February 4, 1915, announced its intention of establishing a war area around the British Isles in which all enemy ships would be destroyed without warning, it was clear that neutral vessels would not be safe.

The Germans, on their part, offered to change their submarine tactics if the Allied food blockade were lifted, but there was no hope of altering Allied policy in this respect. Early in 1915, when more and more Allied merchant vessels were being sunk, it became evident that the lives of Americans traveling on belligerent ships were in grave danger. The German government issued warnings about that danger, and Bryan, then Secretary of State, urged the President to forbid Americans to take this risk. Wilson refused, insisting that American travelers were simply exercising a traditional right.

On May 7, 1915, a German submarine sank the unarmed British liner *Lusitania* with the loss of 1198 passengers, 128 of them Americans. Although the ship was carrying rifle cartridges and other contraband, and thus invited attack, the shocking toll of lives dramatized the submarine issue. Some Americans de-

manded an immediate declaration of war, but Wilson demurred. "There is," he said in a public address, "such a thing as a man being too proud to fight." Instead, the administration sent three vigorously worded notes of protest to Germany, one of them, nevertheless, so close to a threat of war that Bryan resigned rather than sign it. Germany later acknowledged responsibility for the loss of American lives and agreed to pay an indemnity. But nothing had been settled when the United States went to war.

After the *Lusitania* tragedy, more sinkings occurred, and American protests elicited German promises that submarine methods would be modified. When in March 1916, however, a submarine torpedoed the unarmed French ship *Sussex,* injuring Americans aboard, Wilson warned Germany that if she did not immediately abandon her monstrous tactics, "the United States can have no choice but to sever diplomatic relations." This threat drew from the Germans the *Sussex* pledge of May 4, 1916, declaring that no more merchant vessels would be sunk without warning, *provided* that the United States held Britain accountable for *her* violations of international law. By ignoring this proviso but accepting the

**German submarine zone, Feb. 15, 1915**

pledge, Wilson succeeded in forcing Germany to place crippling restrictions on her principal maritime weapon.

640

### Election of 1916

Wilson became convinced early in the war that the best way to keep the United States at peace was to bring an end to the fighting. Thus, in January 1915 and again a year later, he sent his personal adviser, Colonel Edward M. House, on peace missions to Europe, but these visits came to nothing. Discouraged by House's failures, Wilson at last yielded to the agitation for preparedness that had been organized by TR, Lodge, and others almost from the moment Belgium had been overrun. Late in January 1916 he took off on a nationwide tour to promote the preparedness idea, and by June Congress had adopted his proposals for enlargement of the army, the navy, and the merchant marine, and for opening officers' training centers at universities and elsewhere. Plans also were made for industrial mobilization.

In taking these steps, Wilson appropriated what might have become a useful Republican issue in the 1916 presidential campaign. Peace-minded Progressives, especially those steadfast in their isolationism where Europe was concerned, were shaken by Wilson's measures; but in fact they were few in number. As early as September 1915, Victor Murdock of Kansas, chairman of the National Committee of the Progressive party, reported that the national party leaders "were in favor of . . . facing forward and throwing themselves into the campaign of 1916 with uncompromising aggression, behind a ticket and platform which will challenge the sense and patriotism of the nation." By January 1916, Murdock's committee unanimously issued a statement denouncing the Wilson administration for failing "to deal adequately with National honor and industrial welfare."

By the time of the Progressive party's national convention in Chicago in June, the party chiefs had taken the lead in urging *compulsory* universal military training. Such a program, said Raymond Robins, the convention chairman, "will do more in one generation to

. . . develop disciplined, vigorous, and efficient citizenship, and to unify the diverse groups of our national life in a vital Americanism than all other forces combined." At this convention, TR was pressed to accept the Progressive nomination once again; but having sought and been denied the regular Republican nomination at that party's Chicago convention, Roosevelt turned the Progressives down. He urged them instead to back the Republican nominee, Supreme Court Justice Charles Evans Hughes, who, he said, stood for the "clean-cut, straight-out Americanism" the Progressives themselves admired. This the Progressives agreed to do. Lodge failed to get the Republicans to accept the Progressives' compulsory military training program; but the Progressives on their part accepted Republicanism once more in full. The Progressive insurgents of six or seven years earlier now forgotten, the party leaders even pressed for a protective tariff that "must be enacted . . . if the industrial invasion from Europe after the war is to be forestalled."

The Democratic party, at its national convention in St. Louis a week after the others, renominated Wilson on the first ballot. Four years earlier Wilson had been elected only because Republican strength had been split between Roosevelt and Taft. This time, with TR vigorously campaigning for Hughes, it was hard to see how Wilson could win. Hughes, however, missed his chance. He so straddled the issue of war and peace that the Democrats soon dubbed him Charles "Evasive" Hughes. Wilson, at the same time, could boast of the *Sussex* pledge which he had wrung from the Germans while keeping the United States out of war. Wilson's domestic reforms also helped him, swaying the votes of farmer, labor, and antiwar groups. In the end, the election hung for the first time on far-western ballots. Wilson carried California by a mere 4000, and with it enough states in the electoral college to give him a majority of 277 to 254. In the popular vote he received 9,129,000 to 8,538,000 for Hughes.

## The decision to fight

A few weeks after his victory Wilson made a new effort to arrange a peace, dispatching notes to all belligerent powers asking them to state acceptable terms. Unfortunately for him, Germany's military fortunes then were at a peak, and a week earlier she had expressed her own willingness to talk peace. The timing of Wilson's note, apparently an echo of the German feelers, deeply offended the Allies, and nothing came of it.

Wilson followed this gesture with another which only deepened Allied suspicions. In a speech before the Senate, January 22, 1917, he announced to the world his own conception of a just and lasting peace and outlined ideas for a League of Nations to maintain it. "It must be a peace without victory," he asserted, adding prophetically,

> Victory would mean peace forced upon the loser, a victor's terms imposed upon the vanquished. It would be accepted in humiliation, . . . and would leave . . . a bitter memory upon which terms of peace would rest . . . only as upon quicksand. Only a peace between equals can last.

Most Americans greeted this speech with enthusiasm, but to the Allies it seemed to be a withdrawal of the informal sympathy they had come to expect from the United States. It also threatened their expansionist and punitive program, at the expense of a defeated Germany, as expressed in secret treaties among themselves, of which Wilson was unaware. Their distress was made especially acute by their deteriorating position in the fighting which, within ten days of Wilson's speech, led the German's boldly to revoke the *Sussex* pledge and strike for complete victory. On January 31, 1917, the Germans announced that their submarines would again sink all vessels on sight, armed or unarmed, within a specified zone around the British Isles and in the Mediterranean. They knew they now risked almost certain war with the United States, but they hoped to knock Britain out of the war by cutting off her food supply before American forces reached the battlefields. They almost won this gamble.

As he had promised, Wilson now broke off diplomatic relations with Germany. He next called upon Congress to authorize the arming of American merchant vessels. When "a little group of wilful men," as Wilson angrily called them, blocked this proposal with a filibuster, presidential aides uncovered an old statute authorizing the Commander-in-Chief to arm vessels without congressional sanction, and on March 12 he issued the appropriate order. Wilson thought he might still avoid war, but two events, one a small incident, the other a world-shaking revolution, killed his and the country's hopes.

In January 1917, British naval intelligence intercepted a message in code from German Foreign Secretary Alfred Zimmermann to the German minister in Mexico, informing him of the German decision to resume unrestricted submarine warfare and instructing him to propose to Mexico that if war came with the United States they fight together. In return, Germany offered to support Mexico in an effort to recover "her lost territory in New Mexico, Texas, and Arizona." In February the British passed this message along to Washington. After holding it for almost a week for fear of its effect on American opinion, Wilson decided to make it public on March 1 to create further support for his armed-ship bill. American sentiment for drastic measures against Germany now rose to fever pitch.

Within two weeks, the March revolution in Russia supplanted the tyrannical czarist regime with a provisional representative government, thereby making it easier to describe the war against the Central Powers as a war of democracies against autocracies. This change in the Allied setup removed one of the last brakes on the United States' joining the Allied cause. At the same time, submarine sinkings of American ships began in the Atlantic, with five going down in March alone.

The President now held many consultations with his Cabinet on the war issue, and when his closest advisers, on March 20, urged him unanimously to commit the nation to the fighting against Germany (Austria-Hungary was already taking secret steps to desert her ally in the Central Powers), the next day he called for a special session of Congress to meet on April 2. In his war message that day he told the legislators, "The present German submarine warfare against commerce is a warfare against mankind." And he added:

*We are now about to accept the gauge of battle with this natural foe to liberty. . . . We are glad . . . to fight thus for the ultimate peace of the world and for the liberation of its people, the German peoples in-* *cluded; for the rights of nations great and small and the privilege of men everywhere to choose their way of life and of obedience. The world must be made safe for democracy.*

On April 4 the Senate voted for war against Germany, 82 to 6. Two days later the House concurred, 373 to 50. Not until December 7, 1917 was war declared against Austria-Hungary.

## II  Embattled at home and overseas

*The Allies' crisis*

The decision of the United States to join the fighting against Germany came when the Allied cause was faring badly almost everywhere. After their courageous stand at Verdun early in 1916, which made "they shall not pass" the heroic slogan of the day, the French had suffered such terrible losses that some of their leaders already were engaging in independent peace talks with the Austrians. In the French army, defeatism had reached the point where ten divisions had mutinied. In the Balkans, at the same time, a carefully prepared Allied offensive had failed. In 1916 alone, the Russian armies lost a million men, and the Russian people were prepared to oppose any government that would not call a halt to the slaughter. After the March revolution in Russia, socialists in the Allied countries, encouraged by the Central Powers, also began a concerted agitation for peace without annexations and indemnities, which further undermined the confidence of the desperate Allied governments.

Worst of all, the new German submarine campaign had proved a great success. In April alone, when Britain had grain enough for only six to eight weeks, 880,000 tons of Allied ship-ping were sunk. At this time Admiral Jellicoe, Britain's naval chief, told the American Admiral William S. Sims, "it is impossible for us to go on, if losses like this continue."

Although many months passed before the United States could put sufficient numbers of men in the field to influence the course of the war on land, the navy could help with the submarine emergency at once. Heretofore, Allied merchant-ship captains had preferred to go it alone at sea, relying upon speed and maneuverability to dodge torpedoes. Obviously this was a poor reliance, and many naval officers had been urging the convoy system in which large fleets of merchant vessels would sail together under cruiser and destroyer escorts. Merchant captains doubted that their ships could hold fixed stations in a convoy. But under Admiral Sims's urging, the convoy system was adopted with impressive results. By November, tonnage lost was down from April's 880,000 to 289,000. Moreover, not one American troop transport was sunk, although two British transports with Americans aboard were lost. Before the war's end, the United States had also launched more than a hundred submarine chasers, had put 500 airplanes to work spotting enemy U-boats, and had taken other effective steps.

## American mobilization

Even before Congress declared war, thousands of American youths had volunteered to serve with the Allies, and many of them saw the full four years of fighting. When the United States entered the war, the combined strength of the regular army and the National Guard was about 375,000 men, from whom were drawn the officers and non-coms of the new army to be created under the Selective Service Act of May 18, 1917. This act required all men between the ages of twenty-one and thirty (it was extended later to eighteen and forty-five) to register for military service. Registrants were placed in five classes, headed by able-bodied unmarried men without dependents. From this group alone the nation drew all the 2,810,000 men actually drafted, although by the end of the war as many as 4,800,000 persons had been enrolled in the army, navy, and marine corps.

Some experts recommended that the administration finance the war on a pay-as-you-go basis, taxing wartime profits and earnings to the utmost; and in fact, about half of the nearly $33 billion spent on the war between April 1917 and June 1920 was raised by taxation. The rest was raised by borrowing, mainly through four Liberty Loan drives in 1917 and 1918. Backed by rallies, parades, and posters spread across the land, volunteers hawked the bonds directly to the public rather than to the banking community, and each issue was oversubscribed.

To mobilize the nation's other resources, Wilson created the Council of National Defense, made up of six Cabinet members and an advisory commission of seven additional civilians. Under the Council's supervision, six huge agencies performed specific wartime tasks. One, the Emergency Fleet Corporation, had been created as early as April 1916 to enlarge the merchant marine. Another, the Food Administration, ably headed by Herbert Hoover, undertook to supply civilians and combatants. The Fuel Administration doled out coal and oil. The Railroad Administration consolidated the nation's railroads and, without removing them from private ownership, operated them as a single system.

In March 1918 the Council of National Defense placed the War Industries Board under the direction of Bernard Baruch and gave him dictatorial powers over American business. Great savings were effected by minute regulations covering everything from the number of trunks traveling salesmen could carry to the number of stops elevators could make, and also by the standardization of products. For example, the number of sizes and styles of plows was reduced from 376 to 76, the number of colors of typewriter ribbons from 150 to 5. The economies effected by such measures taught business much about the advantages of standardization and planning to be applied after the war.

AFL president Samuel Gompers, on becoming one of the civilian advisers of the Council of National Defense, declared that while American workers backed the war, he hoped the government would prevent exploitation and profiteering at their expense. Early in 1918, in return for its pledge not to strike, organized labor was assured of the right of collective bargaining, of the maintenance of the eight-hour day where it existed, and of other privileges. A National War Labor Board was created to mediate labor disputes, and a War Labor Policies Board to deal with labor grievances. Between 1915 and 1917, the number of strikes had tripled and the number of strikers had more than doubled. Strikes fell off thereafter, while the AFL pushed its membership from 1,950,000 in 1915 to 2,800,000 in 1918. The wartime demand for labor, meanwhile, pushed wages up as much as 20 percent in purchasing power in key military industries and approximately 4 percent overall. At the same time, salaried employees suffered from wartime inflation, losing as much as one-third of their prewar purchasing power.

Businessmen and farmers fared best of all. Baruch's War Industries Board, unwilling to delay production by lengthy negotiations,

643

gave up the traditional practice of competitive bidding and made war purchases on the basis of cost-plus contracts. Such contracts guaranteed sellers profits ranging from 2.5 to 15 percent of production costs. By padding costs, some contractors made enough to be able to increase dividend payments and executive salaries substantially and still pile up profits despite high taxes. Large personal fortunes also grew in number. In 1914, only 5000 persons reported annual incomes in the $50,000 to $100,000 tax brackets; in 1918, 13,000 did so. The modern policy of graduated income taxes, placing upon the wealthy a progressively higher share of tax burdens, may be said to have begun during the war and substantially reduced net earnings.

Hoover's Food Administration, meanwhile, set such a high government price on wheat and other staples that farmers stretched their resources to the utmost to acquire more land. From 1916 to 1919 harvested wheat acreage, for example, rose from 53.5 million to 73.7 million acres, the total crop from 635 million to 952 million bushels. Farmers helped to feed the country and its allies and lined their pockets in the process. Farm operators' real income was 29 percent higher in 1918 than in 1915. But soon after the wartime demand ended, the farmers found themselves in deeper financial trouble than ever before.

### High cost of hatred

The success of the Liberty Loan drives could be attributed to some degree to the unwillingness of opponents of the war to incur the brand of "slacker" or "German sympathizer." Strong feeling against fighting in Europe was widespread. "We are going into war at the command of gold," Senator George W. Norris of Nebraska had charged in a popular speech against involvement. Many Americans continued to sympathize with the Central Powers, others had mixed loyalties. Evidence of widespread opposition appeared in the strong showing of the Socialist party in municipal elections in 1917. In some communities socialists won as much as 30 or 40 percent of the vote.

To keep the fires of patriotism burning

brightly, Congress, within two weeks of the declaration of war, established the Committee on Public Information, and Wilson named George Creel, once a prominent muckraker, to head it. Creel conscripted journalists, scholars, and clergymen to convince the country that German depravity was ingrained in the enemy's culture and history, and they seem to have been all too successful. Although the vast majority of German-Americans accepted the necessity of war once the United States joined the Allies, they became the most obvious targets of abuse. Libraries removed German books and sometimes publicly burned them. Schools dropped the German language from the curriculum. A peak in silliness was reached by restaurants that renamed sauerkraut "liberty cabbage" and kennels that rechristened dachshunds "liberty pups." But pacifists, socialists, and left-wing workers like the Wobblies suffered the most repression.

Congress made intolerance official by adopting the Espionage Act of June 1917 and the Sedition Act of May 1918. The Espionage Act prescribed a fine of up to $10,000 and a prison term of twenty years for anyone who interfered with the draft or encouraged disloyalty. The Sedition Act prescribed the same penalties for anyone who obstructed the sale of government bonds, discouraged recruiting, or did "wilfully utter, print, write or publish any disloyal, profane, scurrilous, or abusive language" about the American form of government, the Constitution, the flag, or service uniforms, or "advocate any curtailment of production . . . of anything necessary or essential to the prosecution of the war." Over 1500 persons were imprisoned, including the socialist leader Eugene V. Debs and more than 450 conscientious objectors. Only a few Americans protested that this was a strange way to conduct a war for liberty and democracy.

### The army in action

The first American troops, under General John J. Pershing, arrived in France in

644

June 1917 and were fed into the sagging Allied lines largely to bolster morale. As the American buildup continued, certain contingents began to see independent action, the first such coming near Toul, east of Verdun, in October 1917. When in March 1918 the Germans launched their massive spring offensive, hoping to end the war, about 300,000 American soldiers had reached France and more were arriving every day. By the war's end, of the more than two million men who had been carried to Europe, about 1,400,000 had become actively engaged, all but a few on the Western Front. In April 1918 the Germans enjoyed a numerical superiority on this front of perhaps 320,000. By November, fresh American troops had given the Allies a preponderance of 600,000.

Despite all the mobilization efforts at home, American artillery units were equipped largely with French 75 mm field guns. The American program for airplane production developed so slowly that American aviators were forced to fly foreign-made craft. Ill-prepared to meet the problems of armored-tank production, American industry made negligible contributions in this area. British transports, moreover, carried more American soldiers to Europe than did American vessels.

Of necessity, large numbers of Americans were thrown into battle inadequately trained, but they played a decisive role in the last eight months of the war. The Allies hoped to continue to use American troops largely as replacements, and to brigade them with French or British units. Pershing, however, fought this policy, feeling that the Allies had grown too defensive-minded and that the Americans would be more successful conducting independent offensive operations. Hence the greater part of the American army soon took its place in the lines as a separate force under Pershing's command, subject, after April 1918, to the overall supreme command of Marshal Ferdinand Foch of France.

Pershing's men faced their first major test when assigned to help repulse a menacing

L'Illustration

*Pershing debarking at Boulogne,*
*June 13, 1917. The general wrote later*
*of the "silent wish" that "our Army*
*might have been more nearly ready to fulfill*
*the mission that loomed so large before us."*

German thrust toward Paris. By May 30, 1918, the Germans had reached Château-Thierry on the Marne, only 50 miles from the French capital. The French commander called on Pershing for help, and on May 31 the 2nd and 3rd American Divisions and a brigade of marines went into action in support of French colonial troops. Certain German contingents had actually crossed the Marne. The Americans drove them back and from June 6 to 25 cleared nearby Belleau Wood of enemy forces. In July, when the German General Staff made its last great effort to break through to Paris between Rheims and Soissons, 85,000 Americans helped check the assault.

In its first major offensive assignment, in September 1918, the American army launched an attack on the St. Mihiel salient, a German

United States Signal Corps photo, National Archives

*Doughboy stretcher bearers*
*in the wrecked French town of Vaux, between*
*Chateau Thiérry and Belleau Wood.*

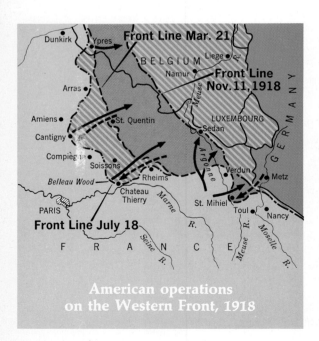

American operations
on the Western Front, 1918

bulge protruding sharply into the Allied lines across the Meuse River southeast of Verdun. Pershing sent American troops against both flanks of the salient and with some French support reduced it in two days. An American army of half a million troops was engaged. At the cost of 7000 casualties, it captured 16,000 German prisoners and over 400 guns, and established a new threat to the fortified center of Metz. By Foch's orders, however, the American army was not sent on toward Metz but was shifted westward and down the Meuse River, through the Argonne Woods toward Sedan, with the object of taking that city and cutting the strategic Sedan-Metz railroad.

The Meuse-Argonne offensive, from late September to early November, became one of the fiercest battles in American military history. Together with the French forces on that front, the Americans captured more than 25,000 prisoners and a great deal of equipment, but at a high cost in casualties. This offensive, part of a coordinated drive against the Central Powers all along the Western Front, in Italy, in Greece, and in Palestine, helped bring Germany and her allies to their knees. At the end of September, Bulgaria surrendered. Turkey followed in October and Austria in November. Finally, on November 11, Germany with her armies everywhere in retreat, her navy on the verge of general mutiny, and her civilian population hungry, exhausted, and dangerously discontented, gave up resistance and signed an armistice.

The war was not over, since terms of peace had yet to be worked out, but fighting on the major fronts had ceased at last. American losses—48,000 killed in battle, 2900 missing in action, 56,000 dead of disease—were light in comparison with those the other great powers had suffered since 1914. Before pulling out of the war early in 1918, Russia counted 1,700,000 battle deaths. Germany lost 1,800,000 men, France 1,385,000, Britain 947,000, and Austria-Hungary 1,200,000. But Americans had had more than a glimpse of the horrors of war and did not soon forget.

## III  Peacemaking in a world in conflict

### The Fourteen Points
### and the Joffe Declarations

While his administration waged its militant propaganda campaign on the home front, Wilson was sending propaganda messages to enemy peoples urging them to give up the struggle. When the United States still was neutral, his appeal for "peace without victory" (see p. 641) had brought hope to a world already war-weary. When the United States went to war, he kept asserting that hostilities were directed not against the German people but against their government. Still unaware of the secret treaties among the Allies for dividing up the spoils of victory, the President asserted that neither punitive damages nor territorial gains were the Allies' real objectives but rather the end of autocratic government and a settlement that would insure permanent peace.

Soon after America's entry into the war, Wilson became privy to these secret treaties. They seemed to him so to sully the avowed civilized aims of the Allies, in contrast to Germany's manifest barbarism, that diplomatically as well as militarily he tried henceforth to conduct his part of the war independently of them. The United States, in fact, never became one of the Allied Powers, but only an "Associated Power" among them.

Following the Bolshevik revolution of November 7, 1917, the new Russian regime invited all belligerents to end the entire war virtually on Wilson's terms—no annexations and no indemnities. No response came from the Allies, a silence the Bolsheviks viewed as casting them upon the mercies of the Germans. Within three weeks, Lenin began negotiations with the Central Powers to close down the Eastern Front, a step the Allies, in turn,

viewed as a stab in the back. Wilson's sympathy with the Bolshevik proposals further alienated him from his partners. When the Bolsheviks next threatened to publish the Allies' secret treaties (to which the deposed Czar had been a party and copies of which had fallen into their hands) and thereby expose Allied hypocrisy to the world, Wilson, after failing again to win Allied agreement on his own peace plans, felt impelled to attempt to diminish the impact of such Bolshevik disclosures with a resounding statement of his own thought. This he did in his message to Congress, January 8, 1918, in which he set forth in his dramatic Fourteen Points all the ideas he had been proposing for foreign as well as domestic consumption at every opportunity during the past two years.

These were the proposals put forward by the President:

*I. Open covenants of peace, openly arrived at.*

*II. Absolute freedom of navigation upon the seas in peace and in war.*

*III. The removal, so far as possible, of all economic barriers among the nations consenting to the peace.*

*IV. Guarantees that national armaments will be reduced to the lowest point consistent with domestic safety.*

*V. An impartial adjustment of colonial claims giving equal weight to the interests of the populations concerned and to the government whose title is to be determined.*

*VI. The evacuation of all Russian territory.*

*VII. The evacuation and restoration of Belgium.*

*VIII. All French territory should be freed, the invaded portions restored, and the wrong done to France in 1871 in the matter of Alsace-Lorraine should be righted.*

*IX. Readjustment of Italian frontiers along clearly recognizable lines of nationality.*

648

*X. The peoples of Austria-Hungary should be accorded opportunity for autonomous development.*

*XI. Rumania, Serbia, and Montenegro should be evacuated, occupied territories restored, Serbia accorded free and secure access to the sea. The Balkan States should be constituted along historically established lines of nationality.*

*XII. The Turkish portions of the Ottoman Empire should be assured a secure sovereignty, the other nationalists under Turkish rule should have autonomous development. The Dardanelles should be open to the commerce of all nations under international guarantees.*

*XIII. An independent Polish state should be erected and should be assured a free and secure access to the sea.*

*XIV. A general association of nations must be formed under specific covenants for the purpose of affording mutual guarantees of political independence and territorial integrity to great and small states alike.*

Lofty though they were, Wilson's ideals found competing ones in Russia. As early as December 22, 1917, indeed, many of his oft-repeated "points," especially those on the self-determination and self-rule of peoples "along historically established lines of nationality" and on freedom of navigation along strategic channels of trade, had been appropriated in the "Joffe Declarations" hopefully asserted to guide the Bolshevik negotiators (whom Adolf Joffe headed) when they sat down for their talks with the Central Powers at Brest-Litovsk, starting January 4, 1918. These declarations, certain to be "taken down and reported by radiotelegraph to all nations," as the Bolshevik delegation said, did them no good in their talks; but as a sort of manifesto to peace-hungry socialists and workers everywhere in Europe, they may have helped make Wilson's points more comprehensive and more urgent.

### Abetting civil war in Russia

The negotiations at Brest-Litovsk dragged out until March 3, 1918—the Bolsheviks using delaying tactics in anticipation of a revolution in Germany to help their cause, the Germans enlarging their demands as the Russians procrastinated. When finally forced to capitulate, the Bolsheviks yielded all of Po-

land, Lithuania, the Ukraine, Russia's Baltic provinces, Finland, and neighboring territories—all told, the home of 30 percent of the Czar's prewar subjects, the source of 90 percent of their coal, 80 percent of their iron. The Germans, on their part, promptly undertook to make good by military occupation those parts of their majestic gains they did not already hold. By May 1918, the British and French had also begun to send troops into Arctic Russia by way of Murmansk on the Barents Sea, and Americans soon followed. If they had in mind a capitalist "crusade" against Bolshevism—their primary goal in the opinion of some historians—their more immediate objective was to occupy the German military machine in the East sufficiently to forestall the transfer of fresh troops to the Western Front in France.

The Allied and American presence in Russia, however, could not fail to encourage dissidents in rebellion against the Bolshevik regime, and by August 1918 the westerners had helped set up an anti-Bolshevik puppet government in northern Archangel. Similarly, anti-Bolshevik contingents in distant Siberia were heartened by the arrival there in August of British, French, American, and Japanese forces, which soon lent them assistance. In this way, the Western powers became involved in the "Great Civil War" of 1918–1920, which raged across the entire Russian Empire.

When the Germans collapsed in the West in November 1918, the Bolsheviks promptly renounced the Treaty of Brest-Litovsk and sought to reclaim surrendered territories. Here too they encountered sharp resistance. Most of the people in these lands detested Bolshevism, a feeling that only strengthened their quest for national self-determination. The French, for whom czarist Russia had offered a vast frontier for investment and development, were most eager among the Western powers to broaden anti-Bolshevik activity. Once the Armistice was signed on November 11, 1918, the British and Americans hung back and also dissuaded the French. Allied and American troops remained in Archangel until near the end of 1919, and Japanese troops still were in Vladivostok late in 1922. But the Bolshevik regime survived.

Years later, Winston Churchill recalled as one of the great mistakes of Allied statesmanship in 1919 "the failure to strangle Bolshevism at its birth and to bring Russia . . . by one means or another into the general democratic system." It remains doubtful, however, that the war-weary West could have been persuaded to make the immense effort needed to attain this goal. The White Russians, moreover, who offered the only alternative to Bolshevik rule, were as far as Lenin's followers from being democrats. Meanwhile, the Allies' inconclusive interference won them nothing but the enduring suspicion of the Bolsheviks, whose survival deepened Western fears that the whole order of capitalism might go down if peace were not soon made in the rest of Europe and reconstruction begun on hopeful terms.

## The Versailles Treaty

His Fourteen Points made Wilson a hero to people everywhere who were eager for a better world; years later his portrait could still be found hanging in peasant shanties in many parts of Europe. Yet as his reputation grew abroad, Wilson confronted mounting opposition at home. Those who believed the United States should never have entered the war could hardly be expected to rally behind him. Many others who had favored the fighting also favored a vengeful, not a Wilsonian, settlement. "Let us dictate peace by the hammering guns," the still popular Teddy Roosevelt demanded, "and not chat about peace to the accompaniment of the clicking of typewriters."

Wilson knew that his role as peacemaker would be sorely weakened if the American people defeated his party at the polls, and in October 1918, facing the off-year elections, he

**649**

*"End of a crusade": U.S. troops returning home after the Armistice.*

United States Army photograph

650

issued a fatal appeal to the voters to express their approval of his leadership by returning a Democratic Congress. His appeal not only failed, it also embittered those many Republicans who had strongly supported the war effort. At the polls, the voters elected Republican majorities to both houses of Congress, and Wilson journeyed to meet his fate at Paris in December 1918 apparently the repudiated head of his country. By then, he had further angered the opposition by failing to appoint a single Republican leader, or a single United States senator even from his own party, to the Peace Commission that accompanied him to the peace talks.

The Paris Peace Conference, a meeting of victors to decide the vanquished's fate, sat at

Versailles Palace from January to June 1919. Representing Britain was her Prime Minister, David Lloyd George, who—unlike Wilson— had called for the severe punishment of Germany in a general election the preceding December and had triumphed. Representing France was Georges Clemenceau, her Premier, a determined promotor simply of French interests and French security. Vittorio. Orlando, the Italian Prime Minister, was in Paris to see that Allied territorial promises to Italy were kept. When it became clear that they would not be, Orlando went home, and the Big Four became the Big Three—Wilson, Lloyd George, and Clemenceau.

Wilson had come to Paris with three cardinal goals: political self-determination for the

*Welcoming sign on the Rue Royale, Paris, December 14, 1918, for the United States President.*

peoples of Europe, and to some extent even for the people of colonial countries, to foster democracy; free trade to foster prosperity; and a League of Nations to insure a lasting peace. He left Paris with his goals only partially attained; unfortunately, his concessions were made largely to secure the League of Nations—which the United States Senate was to strip of power by forbidding the United States to join. Wilson also succeeded in moderating the onerous Allied demands on Germany; but here, too, he was far from attaining his humane goal of "peace without victory." Indeed, the terms of the final treaty, reflecting the Allies' secret treaties among themselves, remained harsh enough almost to insure that the Germans would make every effort to break the peace when they felt strong enough once more to do so.

The Treaty of Versailles, signed by the Germans on June 28, 1919, stripped Germany of her colonies in Africa and the Far East, and of Alsace-Lorraine and the Saar Basin north of Lorraine. France won all rights in the coal-rich Saar for fifteen years, after which its future was to be decided by a plebiscite. On the east, German territory was given to Poland to form the "Polish Corridor" to the Baltic Sea, a provision that split Germany in two and was a bitter pill for her people. The huge indemnity of $5 billion levied on the Germans and the provision for additional "reparations" later on made them look upon the Allies as vultures. Perhaps most distressing to them was the "war guilt" article in the Versailles Treaty, which attempted to justify the indemnity and reparations by forcing Germany to acknowledge responsibility for starting the war. In an effort to avert future aggression by a vengeful people, the treaty deprived Germany of her navy and her merchant marine and limited her to an army of but 100,000 men. Other treaties in conjunction with the Versailles Treaty established such new states as Czechoslovakia and Yugoslavia by virtually dismantling the Austro-Hungarian empire.

For all its harshness, the Versailles Treaty

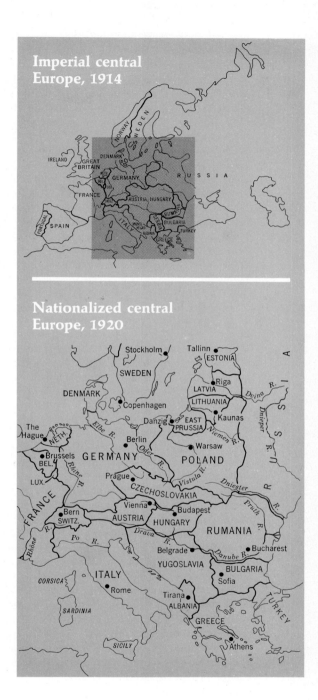

**Imperial central Europe, 1914**

**Nationalized central Europe, 1920**

was no more punitive than the terms Germany would have imposed on the Allies had she been victorious. They had only to recall the Treaty of Brest-Litovsk to be reassured on this point. "It is a very severe settlement with Germany," Wilson said in September 1919, "but there is not anything in it that she did not earn."

The Versailles Treaty, nevertheless, failed to satisfy Clemenceau, who refused to sign until Britain and the United States promised in a separate agreement to come to the aid of France in the event of a future attack upon her. Wilson no doubt suspected that the United States Senate would reject such an "entangling alliance," which it did. His own expectation was that the League of Nations would perform the role given to this alliance, and he strove successfully to get the Allies to include the League Covenant in the treaty. "It is a definite guarantee against the things which have just come near bringing the whole structure of civilization to ruin," Wilson said.

The Covenant set up a permanent Secretariat with headquarters at Geneva, Switzerland, a Council of nine members, and an Assembly. The Council consisted of one representative each from the United States, Britain, France, Italy, and Japan, and four others chosen by the Assembly. The Assembly had a voting representative from every member nation. A Permanent Court of International Justice was set up at The Hague in Holland.

All nations and self-governing dominions were welcomed as members of the League. Members pledged themselves "to respect and preserve as against external aggression the territorial integrity and ... political independence of other members"; to give publicity to treaties and armaments; to recognize the right of each member to bring any threat to peace to the League's attention, and to submit dangerous disputes to arbitration; to refrain from war until three months after the decision of the arbiters; to refrain from war with nations complying with League decisions; and to employ military and economic sanctions against nations resorting to war in violation of League agreements.

The League Council in particular was to make plans to reduce armaments and to miti-

gate the dangers arising from their private manufacture. It was also to set up agencies "to secure and maintain fair and humane conditions of labor," to supervise "traffic in opium and other dangerous drugs" and "in women and children," and "as a sacred trust of civilization" to look after the people of "colonies and territories which as a consequence of the late war" no longer were governed by their former rulers.

Since the Treaty of Versailles covered only the settlement with Germany, other treaties had to be made with her allies. The Treaty of St. Germain with Austria attempted to insure that she would not initiate or consent to union with Germany. The Treaty of Trianon, signed by Hungary in 1920, drastically reduced the borders of the old Magyar kingdom. The Treaty of Neuilly, governing the Bulgarian settlement, trimmed that country's prewar borders. The Treaty of Sèvres with Turkey stripped her of almost all her non-Turkish territory. Turkish nationals prevented its ratification, and in the Treaty of Lausanne, in 1923, Turkey won substantially better terms.

### The League in the Senate

When Wilson returned to the United States from Paris for a few weeks in February 1919, certain senators immediately made clear to him their discontent with the League Covenant. When he formally presented the Versailles Treaty, including the Covenant, to the Senate on July 10, two days after his final return from Paris, he was confronted by the Republican majority elected in 1918 and especially by his sworn foe, Henry Cabot Lodge, now Chairman of the Foreign Relations Committee. Backing Lodge was a strong group of "irreconcilables," including such western Progressives, their eyes always diverted from Europe, as William E. Borah, Hiram Johnson, and Robert M. La Follette. "You cannot yoke a government whose fundamental maxim is liberty," Borah said, "to a government whose first law is force and hope to preserve the former. . . . We may become one of the four dictators of the world, but we shall no longer be master of our own spirit."

Nevertheless, more than the needed two-thirds of the Senate appeared ready to vote for the Versailles Treaty, with some form of League membership, and there is every evidence that the majority of the people would have backed them—despite the opposition of German-Americans because of the harshness of the treaty, of Italian-Americans because of the frustration of their homeland's demands, and of Irish-Americans bitter over Wilson's failure to secure Irish independence.

Through the summer of 1919, as the Senate and the people debated the League, Wilson grew ever more adamant against even minor modifications in the Covenant and more tact-

*The ravaged President,*
*one of the last pictures of Wilson.*

Wide World Photos

less about his all-or-nothing stand. When the irreconcilables, lavishly financed, then opened a tremendous propaganda barrage, the President, although exhausted by work and illness, decided to take his own case to the country on a nationwide speaking tour. While he was gone, Lodge proposed a series of reservations to the Covenant which he knew Wilson would reject and over which the Senate might talk the whole treaty to death.

Lodge's strategy worked. By the time his reservations were introduced in the Senate, Wilson had suffered a physical breakdown forcing him to cancel the rest of his trip. Early in October he suffered a stroke that left him half-paralyzed. His sickbed appeal to "all true friends of the treaty" to spurn the Lodge reservations helped defeat them in the Senate in November. But a resolution to ratify the treaty and hence the League without reservations also failed by 55 to 38, with every Republican but one voting against it. Enough sentiment for the League remained even in the Senate for the treaty to be brought up again in March 1920. This time it won a small majority, 49 to 35, far short of the needed two-thirds, and it and the League issue were dead. The war with Germany thus did not officially end for the United States until July 2, 1921, when Congress passed a joint resolution declaring that hostilities were over and reserving a victor's rights and privileges.

### Election of 1920

Even with the treaty dead in the Senate, Wilson did not give up hope. The election of 1920, he announced, must be "a great and solemn referendum." The people would now vote directly on the issue. But it has rarely been possible in peacetime to make an American presidential election a clear referendum on foreign policy, and 1920 was no exception.

Deprived of their most popular leader by Roosevelt's death early in 1919, the Republicans, at their national convention in Chicago in June, split so badly over the candidacy of TR's friends General Leonard Wood and Governor Frank O. Lowden of Illinois that they yielded at last to the pertinacious pushing of

653

654

the covetous backers of Warren G. Harding of Ohio. This small-town newspaperman, owner and editor of the *Marion Daily Star,* had been elected United States Senator in 1914. As keynoter, he put the 1916 Republican national convention to sleep with two hours of sing-song vaporings. "Nobody could stampede this convention," wrote the *New York Times* correspondent, "and Harding could not stampede any convention." When reminded at the 1920 gathering that Harding still remained virtually unknown outside of Ohio, Senator Frank Brandegee of Connecticut, his Yale refinement rubbed bare by exasperation, shouted: "There ain't any first-raters this year. . . . We got a lot of second-raters and Warren Harding is the best of the second-raters." Perhaps second best was the equally surprising nominee for Vice-President, Calvin Coolidge, a man even more obscure than Harding until, as governor of Massachusetts, he suddenly gained national fame on being credited with having broken the Boston police strike of September 1919 (see p. 666).

To run against Harding, the Democrats, at their convention in San Francisco later in June, named another Ohioan, the popular Governor James M. Cox, who had not been closely identified with Wilson policies. As his running mate they chose Franklin D. Roosevelt, Wilson's Assistant Secretary of the Navy.

Cox, impressed with Wilson's personal gallantry, waged his campaign on the League issue. But the Republicans caught the mood of the public by evading this and all other issues. "Keep Warren at home," advised the dying boss Boies Penrose of Pennsylvania, virtually echoing Boss Platt's admonition about McKinley in the 1896 campaign. "Don't let him make any speeches. If he goes out on a tour somebody's sure to ask him questions, and Warren's just the sort of damned fool that will try to answer them." The Republican platform condemned the League Covenant, but Harding, who had voted against the League in the Senate, now in speeches from his front porch promised to work for "an association of nations." Irreconcilables like William E. Borah and Hiram Johnson supported Harding as an enemy of the League, while thirty-one prominent pro-League Republicans signed an appeal for his election.

Cox was crushed at the polls, 16,152,000 to 9,147,000, receiving only 34 percent of the popular vote. No major-party candidate had ever been defeated so badly. But, as a contemporary observer remarked, Cox was beaten "not by those who dislike him but by those who dislike Wilson and his group." The *New York World* wrote: "The American people wanted a change, and they have voted for a change. They did not know what kind of a change they wanted, and they do not know today what kind of a change they have voted for."

## For further reading

Barbara Tuchman, *The Proud Tower* (1965), is a lively chronicle of Europe on the verge of war. The final three volumes of Mark Sullivan, *Our Times* (6 vols., 1920-1935), are revealing on the United States before and during the fighting. For the diplomatic background see A. J. P. Taylor, *The Struggle for Mastery in Europe 1848-1918* (1954); and S. B. Fay, *Origins of the World War* (2 vols., 1930). Fritz Fischer, *Germany's Aims in the First World War* (1967), is an illuminating if controversial study.

The definitive account of Woodrow Wilson and World War I will be found in the biography in progress by A. S. Link (5 vols., 1947-1965). See also Charles Seymour, ed., *The Intimate Papers of Colonel House* (4 vols., 1926-1928). A. S. Link, *Wilson the Diplomatist* (1957), Harley Notter, *The Origins of the Foreign Pol-*

icy of Woodrow Wilson (1937), and Edward Buehrig, Woodrow Wilson and the Balance of Power (1955), deal illuminatingly with the development of the President's policies. On his policies at maturity, see, in addition, Charles Seymour, American Diplomacy during the World War (1934); E. R. May, The World and American Isolation 1914-1917 (1959); S. W. Livermore, Politics is Adjourned: Woodrow Wilson and the War Congress 1916-1918 (1966); N. G. Levin, Woodrow Wilson and World Politics: America's Response to War and Revolution (1968); and C. P. Parrini, Heir to Empire: United States Economic Diplomacy 1916-1923 (1969).

Walter Millis, Road to War: America 1914-1917 (1935), and C. C. Tansill, America Goes to War (1938), are critiques of Wilson's foreign policy from the isolationist point of view of the thirties. See also Merle Curti, Bryan and World Peace (1931). R. E. Osgood, Ideals and Self-Interest in America's Foreign Relations: The Great Transformation of the Twentieth Century (1953), examines the nation's motivations more broadly.

On wartime propaganda, its truths and untruths, see Arthur Ponsonby, Falsehood in Wartime (1928); Armin Rappaport, The British Press and Wilsonian Neutrality (1950); and George Creel's personal account, How We Advertised America (1920). For wartime restraints on opinion, see Donald Johnson, Challenge to American Freedoms: World War I and the Rise of the American Civil Liberties Union (1963); and H. N. Scheiber, The Wilson Administration and Civil Liberties 1917-1921 (1961).

F. L. Paxson, American Democracy and the World War (3 vols., 1936-1948), is most comprehensive on mobilization and fighting. See also P. W. Slosson, The Great Crusade and After 1914-1928 (1930). On the home front, see G. D. Clarkson, Industrial America in the World War (1923). D. R. Beaver, Newton D. Baker and the American War Effort 1917-1919 (1966), is on the Secretary of War.

Cyril Falls, The Great War (1959), is an outstanding short account. H. R. Rudin, Armistice 1919, is definitive on the end of the fighting. P. Y. Hammond, Organizing for Defense, The American Military Establishment in the Twentieth Century (1961), deals with the maturation of the different services. See also E. E. Mori-

son, Admiral Sims and the Modern American Navy (1942); and J. G. Harboard, The American Army in France 1917-1919 (1936). Laurence Stallings, The Doughboys, The Story of the AEF 1917-1918 (1963), is a spirited account of the American foot soldier. On the air war, see J. J. Hudson, Hostile Skies: A Combat History of the American Air Service in World War I (1968). On the American high command see J. J. Pershing, Final Report (1919), and My Experiences in the World War (2 vols., 1931); and Richard O'Connor, Black Jack Pershing (1961).

J. W. Wheeler-Bennett, Brest-Litovsk: The Forgotten Peace, March 1918 (1938), is excellent. On the Allies and the Russian Revolution, see G. F. Kennan's two volumes on Soviet-American relations: Russia Leaves the War (1956), and The Decision to Intervene (1958); and R. H. Ullman's two volumes on Anglo-Soviet relations: Intervention and the War (1961), and Britain and the Russian Civil War (1968). On the consequences of the Russian Revolution for peacemaking, see J. M. Thompson, Russia, Bolshevism, and the Versailles Peace (1966); and A. J. Mayer, Political Origins of the New Diplomacy 1917-1918 (1959), and Politics and Diplomacy of Peacemaking, Containment and Counterrevolution at Versailles 1918-1919 (1967).

T. A. Bailey, Woodrow Wilson and the Lost Peace (1944), analyzes the President's performance at Versailles; his Woodrow Wilson and the Great Betrayal (1945) discusses American opposition to the League. See also J. P. O'Grady, ed., The Immigrants' Influence on Wilson's Peace Policies (1967); and L. E. Gelfand, The Inquiry: American Preparations for Peace 1917-1919 (1963). John Garraty, Henry Cabot Lodge (1953), makes the case for its subject; see also M. C. McKenna, Borah (1961). J. M. Keynes, The Economic Consequences of the Peace (1919), is a sharp attack on the Big Four, including Wilson. More friendly is Paul Birdsall, Versailles Twenty Years After (1941). See also Robert Lansing, The Peace Negotiations: A Personal Narrative (1921); L. A. R. Yates, The United States and French Security 1917-1921 (1957); and S. P. Tillman, Anglo-American Relations at the Paris Peace Conference of 1919 (1961). On Wilson's heartbreaking last efforts, see Dexter Perkins, "Woodrow Wilson's Tour," in Daniel Aaron, ed., America in Crisis (1952).

On the election of 1920, see Wesley Bagby, The Road to Normalcy (1962); David Burner, The Politics of Provincialism (1967); Frank Freidel, Franklin D. Roosevelt: The Ordeal (1954); and the works on Harding cited in Chapter Twenty-six.

# CRISIS OF PRIVATE CAPITALISM

William Allen White, back in the Republican fold after his Progressive ramble and a delegate to the Chicago assemblage that named Harding for the presidency in June 1920, wrote: "I have never seen a convention—and I have watched most of them since McKinley's first nomination—so completely dominated by sinister predatory economic forces as was this." Shortly thereafter, Hiram Johnson, TR's Progressive party running-mate in 1912 but, like White, returned to the Republican ranks in 1916, declared: "The war has set the people back for a generation. . . . They are docile and they will not recover from being so for many years. The interests which control the Republican party will make the most of their docility."

Actually, the principal predators among the new leaders were not to get in their most selfish licks until postwar repression and "Coolidge prosperity" further softened the people. Harding's administration, at least in domestic affairs, proved little more than one long betrayal of a man wholly unsuited to high office by small-town cronies whose pleasures, such as playing poker and drinking with the President, were not so innocent as they appeared.

Recent attempts to embellish Harding's reputation, while perhaps useful in recalling his neglected industriousness in the White House from time to time, otherwise run counter to the almost universal chagrin or cynicism over his selection, not least among the most hardened party managers of his day. Albert Lasker, a creative genius in the newly glamorous advertising business and publicity director for the 1920 Republican campaign, saw instantly the flabbiness of the candidate entrusted to his care. But having by then made household words of Pepsodent, Puffed Wheat, and Puffed Berries, Lasker undertook, with success, to "humanize Harding," purveying, as he said, the picture of "an old-fashioned, sage, honest-to-the-core Middle Westerner who could be trusted never to rock the boat." Once wafted into the White House by Lasker's puffery, Harding remained a public favorite as long as he held office. Even the ugly disclosures of corruption after his death in 1923 only slowly eroded the popular regard in which he personally was held.

In his inaugural address in March 1921, the new President struck the welcome note when he observed: "We seek no part in directing the destinies of the Old World." What stay-at-home Americans most wanted, he said, was "an end to Government's experiments in business, and ... more efficient business in Government administration," sentiments soon to be echoed more laconically by his successor. Unfortunately for the Republicans, "Coolidge prosperity," even at its crest, proved narrowly based and poorly shared, circumstances that made the eventual economic collapse disastrous beyond precedent. The questioning of business values, deepened by the rival ideologies of fascism and communism that had spread in postwar Europe, also became more general than ever before in the United States. Although forced by the Great Crash of 1929 to take certain limited ameliorative measures, the Republicans stood committed to government hands-off and thereby aggravated the social crisis. In 1932 they were swept out of office as thoroughly as they had swept out the Democrats only twelve years earlier.

## I  This was "normalcy"

### Harding's ordeal

If too much is sometimes made of the return to isolationism in American foreign policy in the twenties (see Chapter Twenty-nine), too little is often made of the persistence of localism and provincialism at home. True, cities grew rapidly, and urbanization, especially of immigrant families and blacks, went on apace. But even this process only deepened the attachment to older values among the older settlers and their offspring:

*The country town [Thorstein Veblen wrote in 1923] ... is the perfect flower of self-help and cupidity standardised on the American plan. ... The country town is one of the great American institutions; perhaps the greatest, in the sense that it has had and continues to have a greater part than any other in shaping the sentiment and giving character to American culture.*

We have only to recall Sinclair Lewis's focus on *Main Street* (1920) and *Babbitt* (1922), and the Lynds' dissection of *Middletown* (1929), for validation of Veblen's view.

When Harding observed that "our supreme task is the resumption of our onward, normal way," that "we must strive for normalcy to reach stability," he had self-help in the business system in mind. "Normalcy's" becoming the trademark of his age and a staple of the language suggests its broader relevance. To assist him in his "supreme task," Harding promised to bring the "best minds" to Washington. He redeemed this promise in part by making such outstanding men as Charles Evans Hughes Secretary of State, Herbert Hoover Secretary of Commerce, and Henry C. Wallace Secretary of Agriculture. But he also brought with him—some no doubt forced themselves upon him—his small-town "Ohio gang," who eventually became as notorious for helping themselves as "normalcy" became apposite for their indiscretions.

At the head of the Ohio gang stood Harry M. Daugherty, a small-time lobbyist for tobacco, meat, and utility interests who first launched the Harding presidential boom. Rewarded with the Attorney-Generalship, he held this position until dismissed by President Coolidge in 1924, when his improprieties were revealed. Daugherty had made a business, while in office, of selling liquor permits, pardons, and paroles to criminals at fancy prices. A year earlier, his henchman Jesse Smith, who conducted a sort of clearinghouse for the Ohio gang's graft, committed suicide and fortunately for Daugherty and others, the gang's worst secrets died with him. Even so, a number of administration insiders soon found their way to jail.

Charles R. Forbes, an adventurer and one-time deserter from the army, had so charmed Harding that he was put in charge of the Veterans Bureau. Here, it was eventually discovered, Forbes swindled the country of no less than $250 million by demanding kickbacks from compliant contractors and suppliers. Forbes also would condemn supplies meant for veterans and sell them at knockdown prices in return for rebates to himself. In 1925 he was sent to Leavenworth Prison. Colonel

Thomas W. Miller, Harding's Alien Property Custodian, in turn, was convicted of conspiracy to defraud the government. For lavish gifts, Miller was found to have distributed to American firms the valuable German chemical and other patents confiscated during the war, charging such firms far less than the patents were worth.

The most spectacular of the Harding scandals was the notorious Teapot Dome affair. Since 1909, when the conservation movement was in full swing, three tracts of oil-rich public land had been set aside under the jurisdiction of the Secretary of the Navy for navy needs. In 1921, with Navy Secretary Edwin Denby's consent, Harding transferred these lands to the custody of his Secretary of the Interior, Albert B. Fall, an intimate of private oil men to whom he was empowered to lease the oil reserves. Within a year, with no competitive bidding, Fall secretly leased Teapot Dome Reserve in Wyoming to Harry F. Sinclair's Mammoth Oil Company and, soon after, leased a second reserve at Elks Hill to a company headed by Edward F. Doheny. Under these leases the private operators were to give the government certain amounts of oil for the privilege of exploiting the fields.

For his favoritism, Fall received about $225,000 in Liberty Bonds and a herd of cattle from Sinclair and a "loan" of $100,000 from Doheny, a surge of wealth that soon attracted the interest of vigilant senators. A committee headed by Senator Thomas J. Walsh of Montana gradually untangled the sordid story, the Supreme Court voided the leases, and public demand for Secretary Denby's resignation mounted. Fall, convicted of accepting a bribe, was fined $100,000 and sentenced to a year in prison, though Doheny and Sinclair, oddly enough, were acquitted of having bribed him. Sinclair, nevertheless, found his own way to jail on conviction for contempt of the Senate for refusing to answer questions and contempt of court for having hired detectives to shadow the jury at his trial.

From the start, Harding was overwhelmed

by all but the ceremonial functions of the presidency. Every decision cost him endless hesitations and torments until at last, exhausted by the tasks of his office, tormented by the realization that he had been betrayed by his friends and that the betrayal would forever blacken his name, he sank under his burdens. In the summer of 1923 he fell ill and on August 2 he died. Still ignorant of the worst of this administration (as the President himself had been to the end), the public went into mourning as deep as that for any leader since Lincoln. Even when the worst came out, the public preferred to forget rather than denounce Harding. Indeed, it was the exposers who were denounced. The *New York Times* called Senator Walsh and his colleagues "assassins of character"; the *Tribune* called them "scandalmongers"; and a prominent patriot charged that "a gigantic international conspiracy" of socialists or communists, he was not sure which, had instigated their probe.

## Uses of the red scare

The almost unshakable tolerance of "normalcy" in the immediate postwar years was matched by unprecedented intolerance of departures from the norm. During the war, Americans had grown accustomed to the suppression of dissent; with the war's end, intolerance that had been directed mainly against those suspected of sympathizing with Germany and the Central Powers embraced a wider variety of persons—foreigners in general, Catholics, Jews, Negroes, radicals, strikers. In large part, the new wave of fear found a scapegoat in the Bolshevik revolution in Russia, after which communist "cells" had been set up in many countries, including the United States—a practice that lent some credence to Soviet threats of worldwide revolution against capitalism. Violence in labor relations right after the war deepened concern, and a bomb scare turned it into panic.

During the war, trade unions had grown enormously in numbers and militancy as work-

ers found them a shield against rising prices. As prices continued to soar, after the Armistice, the unions, largely relieved of wartime no-strike pledges, backed new wage demands with their traditional weapon. In 1919 alone, 3630 strikes involved about 4 million workers, but gains were few. In September 1919, AFL unions struck United States Steel Corporation plants in Pittsburgh, in Gary, Indiana, and elsewhere. Hours, shop conditions, and union recognition itself, as well as wages, were at issue. The corporation, employing its own "security" forces along with state militia and federal troops, broke the strike by January 1920, after eighteen workers had been killed and hundreds beaten.

The steel strike was thoroughly investigated by a Commission of Inquiry of the Interchurch World Movement under the chairmanship of Bishop Francis J. McConnell of the Methodist Episcopal Church. This commission listed as among the leading causes of the defeat of the strike the Steel Corporation's "effective mobilization of public opinion against the strikers through the charges of radicalism, bolshevism, and the closed shop, none of which were justified by the facts." During the strike E. H. Gary, chairman of the corporation, asserted, "There is no good American reason for the strike." The Commission of Inquiry, on its part, concluded that "all the conditions that caused the steel strike continue to exist. . . . In the measure that workingmen become intelligent and Americanized, will they refuse to labor under such conditions."

Allegations of radicalism against the unions were strengthened by some of their demands. When the United Mine Workers struck the bituminous coal pits in November 1919, they were forced a month later to return to work under a federal injunction. In the final settlement the union made a few gains. One of the Mine Workers' unmet demands was nationalization of the coal pits. The railroad unions, in turn, endorsed the widely discussed Plumb Plan, which called for the continuation of wartime government operation of the railroads with labor as well as business participation in management. The principal result of this agitation was simply to speed up the return of the railroads to private control. This was effected by the Esch-Cummins Act of 1920, which also, for the first time, authorized and indeed encouraged the roads to plan combinations to make rail service more efficient.

The avowed adherents of communism and anarchism in the United States after the war came to less than 1 percent of the adult population, mostly intellectuals, not workers. To offset alleged "foreign ideologies" in the unions, employer associations spent large sums promoting the "American Plan," not a program for peaceful industrial relations but simply a set of attitudes, the most important of which was that collective bargaining and the closed shop were "un-American."

Eventually, American Plan associations were organized in every state and nearly every industrial city in the country, where chambers of commerce, local boards of trade, "Constitutional Associations," and other groups all lent a hand. "We have," said one spokesman in 1921, "the school, the pulpit, and the press" through which to "sell" the message. The National Grange, in turn, asserting the right of each individual "to work where his industry is needed at any time and at any wage which is satisfactory to him," mobilized farm support. The temper of the times is evident in the denunciation of women's colleges in 1920 by Wilson's Vice-President, Thomas R. Marshall, following the determination of Radcliffe debaters to uphold the affirmative of the proposition, "Resolved, that the recognition of labor unions by employers is essential to successful collective bargaining."

In 1919 and 1920 a bomb scare intensified the red scare. A time bomb was discovered in the mayor of Seattle's mail; another bomb exploded and blew off the hands of a Georgia senator's house servant. No less than thirty-six bombs addressed to such high-ranking persons as J. P. Morgan, John D. Rockefeller, and Justice Holmes of the Supreme Court were discovered in various post offices.

President Wilson had warned his Attorney-General, "Palmer, do not let this country see red." But A. Mitchell Palmer, who in Josephus Daniels's words "was seeing red behind every bush and every demand for an increase of wages," failed to heed the admonition. "Like a prairie fire," Palmer explained later,

*the blaze of revolution was sweeping over every American institution of law and order. . . . It was eating its way into the homes of the American workman, its sharp tongues of revolutionary heat were licking the altars of the churches, leaping into the belfry of the school bell, crawling into the sacred corners of American homes, seeking to replace marriage vows with libertine laws, burning up the foundations of society.*

To put out the fire, on New Year's Day, 1920, he ordered simultaneous raids on every alleged Bolshevik cell in the country. In about a week, more than 6000 persons were arrested, their property confiscated, their friends who visited them in jail locked up on the grounds of solicitude for revolutionaries. Though supposedly armed to the teeth, the captives yielded the imposing total of three pistols and no explosives. The "Palmer raids" were followed by the eventual deportation of 556 aliens convicted of no crime.

As Wilson anticipated, vigilantism, touched off by the Attorney-General's example, spread across the land, victimizing students, professors, editors, writers, actors, and others sus-

*"I wants to make their flesh creep."*
*Rollin Kirby in the* World, *New York City.*

New York Public Library

pected of harboring subversive ideas or engaging in un-American activities. In January 1920 five duly elected Socialist members of the New York State Assembly were expelled by that body simply because of their party affiliation. In September 1920, just as the red scare had begun to simmer down, a bomb exploded in Wall Street, breaking windows in the House of Morgan, killing thirty-eight persons and injuring hundreds. The perpetrators never were found.

A few months after the Palmer raids, two alien Italian anarchists, Nicola Sacco and Bartolomeo Vanzetti, were arrested for a murder that had been committed in connection with a payroll robbery in South Braintree, Massachusetts. In 1921 the two were brought to trial before Judge Webster Thayer and a jury. On the jury's finding them guilty, the judge sentenced the two defendants to death. At first the trial attracted only slight attention, but as protests against the verdict began to be made throughout the country and the world, more and more Americans questioned its validity. The actual evidence against the men was inconclusive, and the suspicion grew that they had been convicted not because they had committed the crime but because of their political beliefs. Judge Thayer's conduct at the trial only deepened suspicion of the verdict. An investigation committee appointed by Governor Alvan T. Fuller of Massachusetts concluded that the trial judge had been guilty of a "grave breach of official decorum," but nonetheless, it said, justice had been done.

Motions for appealing the verdict delayed the execution of the two men for years, and Vanzetti's dignified demeanor and his and Sacco's quiet persistence in their anarchist beliefs while their lives hung in the balance won additional sympathy for them. When they were electrocuted at last in 1927, amid a new wave of worldwide protest, millions were convinced of their innocence and millions more were convinced that, guilty or innocent, they had not been given a fair trial. Scholarly studies almost half a century after the trial still debate the decision of the court; the world-wide protest against it at the time did much to free the public from the prevailing mood of intolerance.

### "Race suicide" alarms

Xenophobia, or antiforeign feeling, in the wake of the war also brought to a head the anti-immigration sentiment that had been growing in the United States since the 1880s (see p. 500). In 1894, Brahmins and bluebloods had formed the Immigration Restriction League to give strength to their demand for closing the gates. During the Progressive era such xenophobes and labor and business leaders who shared their hostility to newcomers were joined by liberals fearful that immigration was threatening the American way of life in general. The overwhelming surge of "new" immigrants in the decade and a half preceding World War I brought Brahmin alarm to the verge of panic over "race suicide," and paved the way for a complete reversal after the war of the old easygoing terms of admission to the United States.

The Immigration Restriction Act of 1921, reflecting the policy of a "quota system" based on "national origins," assigned each European nation a quota (most Asians were already barred) based on 3 percent of the number of its nationals resident in the United States in 1910. This measure was expected to limit immigration to about 350,000 persons, largely from the United Kingdom and northwestern Europe. The National Origins Act of 1924 cut quotas to 2 percent and made the base year 1890, when the proportion of "Nordics" in the American population had been much higher than in 1910. The National Origins Act also shut the door completely on Japanese immigrants, a step which Japan had warned would have "grave consequences" and which she viewed as a national humiliation. The act of 1924 was to operate only until 1927, after which no more than 150,000 immigrants were to be admitted annually according to quotas based on the ratio of each country's nationals to the whole American population in 1920. In the depression years 1931 to 1939, immigration fell far below even this

Underwood and Underwood

*The Silent Parade, down Fifth Avenue,*
*New York City, July 28, 1917, in which*
*thousands of Negroes marched to the beat*
*of muffled drums protesting the East*
*St. Louis riot. W. E. B. Du Bois*
*shown third from right in second row.*

niggardly allowance, ranging from 12,000 to 63,000 Europeans annually.

Ironically, the desire to restore the "Nordic," Protestant norm in the American population was frustrated to a degree by the failure of these measures to apply to immigrants from Western Hemisphere countries. During the 1920s, almost a million Canadians, many of them French-speaking Catholics, and at least half a million Mexicans, whose enumeration was notoriously careless and whose numbers no doubt were higher, crossed their respective borders to work in the factories of New England and the fields of the South and the Far West.

## Power of the KKK

A larger and much more significant American migration in the twenties was that of southern blacks to northern cities. About 400,000 Negroes served in the armed forces during World War I, half of them overseas in France, where many, indeed, stayed on. When the war ended, many others, having discov-

ered a way of life unimagined in the cotton fields, sought work in urban industry. Here they found many blacks who had come north during the war to take factory jobs in war production. The Negro population of the North soared from 850,000 in 1910 to 1,400,000 in 1920, and to 2,300,000 in 1930. In northern metropolises such as New York, Chicago, Detroit, Cleveland, and Buffalo, the percentage of blacks in the population grew by 100 to 250 percent.

This Negro surge was no more welcome to the white immigrants and other whites than the "new" immigration itself was welcome to the older segments of the population. On July 2, 1917, East St. Louis, Illinois, was the scene of a savage attack on the black community, in which thirty-nine Negroes and nine whites perished. Fear of black competition for white jobs and the employment of black strikebreakers again triggered the race riot, but ignorance and bigotry accounted for its ferocity. Two years later, beginning July 27, 1919, "one of the bloodiest race riots in American history," to quote Allan H. Spear's study of *Black Chicago* (1967), terrorized that metropolis for six days. Before the state militia restored a semblance of seething order, thirty-eight persons had died, 537 had been hurt, and more than a thousand were made homeless. This riot started after a Negro youth, swimming off a Chicago beach, accidentally crossed the unmarked dividing line between white and black sectors of the water and was stoned by white bathers until he drowned. Enraged by police indifference, black bathers attacked the whites and the killing and rapine spread from there.

Racial bloodshed reached such a peak in northern cities in 1919 that that year is still remembered among Negroes as the year of the Red Summer. As blacks increased in number, discrimination became harsher; yet life in the South, as in the "old country" for the white immigrant, remained only something to escape if opportunity offered. Race riots in the North were more than matched in killings by

662

the continuing spread of lynching and rioting in the South. At the same time, even the most menial industrial job offered more hope than sharecropping or farm labor. Northern cities, moreover, offered black children education of a kind; the educated, certain white-collar opportunities; the white-collar man, certain professional careers. Negroes could become teachers, journalists, doctors, lawyers, however few in number.

But, like the "new" immigrant, the northern Negro in particular soon became the target of organized assault, beyond the cruelty of discrimination and segregation. After the red scare, the revival of the Ku Klux Klan provided the most hateful symptom of intolerance. The Klan of Reconstruction days had virtually died out in the 1870s. The new Klan, founded in Georgia in 1915, grew rapidly after 1920, and at its peak in 1924 no fewer than 4,500,000 "white male persons, native-born Gentile citizens," as they said, had joined the hooded group. On its terroristic night rides, the Klan burned fiery crosses to advertise its presence. It flogged or kidnapped blacks and whites alike, acted as a moral censor, especially as an enforcement arm for Prohibition, made and unmade local politicians, and cowed union organizers.

By 1924 Klan leaders decided that their favorite target, the Negro, was "not a menace to Americanism in the sense that the Jew or Roman Catholic is a menace," and thereafter Jews and Catholics bore the brunt of northern Klan violence. The Klan's political influence by then had become so great that the Democratic national convention, after anguished days of debate that deepened the rifts in the party, dared not adopt a resolution condemning the group by name. Nor did the Democrats have a monopoly of the Klan problem. In Indiana, the group's leader, D. C. Stephenson, had built up an organization powerful enough to dominate the Republican party. When Stephenson, in November 1925, was convicted of second-degree murder on the death of a young girl who took poison in their hotel

Underwood and Underwood

*The Klan at its peak*
*in the summer of 1925, marching in full*
*regalia past the White House,*
*on Pennsylvania Avenue, Washington, D.C.*

room after he had abducted and assaulted her, he insisted he had been framed. He took his revenge by giving the newspapers all the sordid details of state officials associated with him. Other exposés disclosed the depths of Klan corruption and soon drove most of its more decorous members away.

### The dry decade

In anticipation of the Prohibition Amendment's becoming law in 1920, Congress in October 1919, over President Wilson's veto, passed the Volstead Act to implement it. This act defined intoxicating liquor as any beverage containing more than one-half of 1 percent of alcohol and forbade any person, except for religious and medical purposes, to "manufacture, sell, barter, transport, import, export, deliver, furnish, or possess" such beverage without a license. The Commissioner of Internal Revenue was to enforce the act.

Making liquor illegal nationwide had two immediate consequences. The old saloon gave way to the covert "speakeasy," where drinking soon took on the glamour of a seemingly harmless conspiracy. At the same time, by

664

putting outside the law a personal habit that millions of Americans would not give up, Prohibition opened up a new field for city gangs. Gangs had existed in American cities before, often exercising great power over local government. National Prohibition made liquor the main source of gang income, raised such income to sybaritic levels, and strengthened gang domination of local police and local politics. Congress, although forced by public pressure to play ball with the "drys," never voted enough money for more than token enforcement of the Volstead Act. The Commissioner of Internal Revenue rarely had as many as 2000 Prohibition agents to police the entire country, whereas the Capone gang alone had a private army in Chicago of at least a thousand well-armed thugs. This and hundreds of other gangs quickly gained control of the undercover liquor business—bootlegging, rumrunning, and speakeasies. At its peak, the Capone gang took in $60 million a year.

Criticism of the "noble experiment," as it was called, mounted as its fruits ripened. Much of the criticism arose within the Democratic party, which appealed more strongly than the Republicans to those urban elements in the population for whom drinking in public was an immemorial social custom. It became an issue in the campaign of 1928, when Alfred E. ("Al") Smith, the Democratic candidate, proposed to do away with national Prohibition and return the problem to the states. Herbert Hoover, his Republican opponent, temporized. After his election, Hoover named a commission headed by the distinguished lawyer George W. Wickersham to study enforcement problems. Its report, published in January 1931, reviewed all the evils of the "experiment" in frank detail; yet a majority of the commission urged its continuance, failure though it was. As one columnist put it:

*Prohibition is an awful flop.*
  *We like it.*
*It can't stop what it's meant to stop.*
  *We like it.*
*It's left a trail of graft and slime,*
*It's filled our land with vice and crime,*
*It don't prohibit worth a dime,*
  *Nevertheless, we're for it.*

After the Democratic victory in the election of 1932, Congress in February 1933 adopted the Twenty-first Amendment repealing the Eighteenth, and by the end of the year it had been ratified. With control of liquor returned to the states only seven chose to continue Prohibition. Mississippi, in 1966, became the last of the seven to go "wet." Some states gave communities a "local option" on the "wet" versus "dry" issue.

### Fundamentalism on trial

The repression of foreigners and "foreign" ideologies and habits soon carried over to the repression of thought and expression. Here, as among the Klansmen and the "drys," Protestant fundamentalists, demanding an absolutely literal reading of the Bible and resisting all modifications of theology in the light of modern science and biblical criticism, led the assault.

The Darwinian theory of evolution became the focus of fundamentalist attacks when a young high school teacher, John T. Scopes, in the country town of Dayton, Tennessee (population 1700), was arrested and tried in 1925 for violating a state law forbidding the teaching of evolution in the public schools. Reporters from all over the country swarmed into Dayton to poke fun at the yokels as well as to cover the court proceedings, which soon supplied their own elements of farce. Religious revivalists and Holy Rollers who also converged on Dayton to preach to curious crowds concerned over the fate of Christianity also drew the reporters' ridicule.

To defend the Bible, William Jennings Bryan, bald and aging, joined the prosecution; Clarence Darrow, perhaps the most brilliant trial lawyer in the country, headed the defense. Bryan began his first speech by denouncing the city slickers come all the way from the Gomorrah of New York to expose the true believers. He soon took up his onslaught on the tree of evolution; and at last, he said, "we have mammals, 3,500, and there is a little circle and man is in the circle. Find him. Find him," he challenged the court. "Talk about putting Daniel in the lion's den. How dared those scientists put man in a little ring like that with lions and tigers and everything that is bad!" One reporter assured Bryan that he was not a mammal because he had no hair and did not suckle his young.

The climax came with Darrow subjecting the "Great Commoner" to pitiless questioning that exposed his ignorance and inconsistencies. After Bryan's wits had been addled by Darrow's barrage, he allowed himself to be lured into one concession that made his followers gasp. "Do you think the earth was made in six days?" asked Darrow. "Not six days of twenty-four hours," answered Bryan. In the end he conceded that the Creation might have lasted for "millions of years." The presiding judge mercifully cut the questioning short. Scopes, found guilty, was fined only the nominal sum of $100, while the country's laughter thereafter took much of the sting from fundamentalist efforts to shore up a shaken system of values by legal compulsion.

## Defense of dissent

Those who cared deeply about American traditions of freedom of expression and personal liberty found the right-wing hysteria, ethnic intolerance, and anti-intellectualism of "normalcy" disheartening. In 1922, when fears of radicalism had waned somewhat, Katherine Fullerton Gerould still could write in *Harper's Magazine:*

*America is no longer a free country in the old sense; and liberty is, increasingly, a mere rhetorical figure. . . . The only way in which [a thinking citizen] . . . can preserve any freedom of expression, is to choose the mob that is most sympathetic to him, and abide under the shadow of that mob.*

Yet the forces of freedom would not be silenced altogether. When the New York legis-

lature expelled its five Socialist members in 1920 simply for their party affiliation, Governor Alfred E. Smith commented:

*Although I am unalterably opposed to the fundamental principles of the Socialist Party, it is inconceivable that a minority party, duly constituted and legally organized, should be deprived of its right to expression, so long as it has honestly, by lawful methods of education and propaganda, succeeded in securing representation, unless the chosen representatives are unfit as individuals. . . .*

*Our faith in American democracy is confirmed not only by its results, but by its methods and organs of free expression. They are the safeguards against revolution. To discard the methods of representative government leads to the misdeeds of the very extremists we denounce . . . and serves to increase the number of the enemies of orderly free government.*

True to these principles, Smith vetoed a proposed loyalty oath for teachers, laws to limit political freedom in New York, and similar measures. When the legislature wished to set up an elaborate apparatus to hunt out and prosecute "criminal anarchy," Smith fought it. "The traditional abhorrence of a free people of all kinds of spies and secret police," he said, "is valid and justified and calls for the disapproval of this measure."

Supreme Court Justice Oliver Wendell Holmes was another who often cautioned against indiscriminate attempts to suppress unpopular ideas. In *Schenck v. U.S.* (1919), Holmes upheld the Socialist Schenck's conviction for conspiracy in distributing a circular aimed to obstruct the wartime draft. In so doing, however, he tried to draw a line between those forms of speech that must be protected and those to be classified as dangerous to the state. "The character of every act depends upon the circumstances in which it is done," he said. "The most stringent protection of free speech would not protect a man in falsely shouting fire in a theatre and causing a panic. . . . The question in every case is whether the words used are used in such circumstances and are of such nature as to create a clear and present danger that they will bring about the substantive evils that Congress has a right to prevent." This "clear and present

665

danger" test for free speech, although it did Schenck himself no good, was cited in many later decisions.

666

Holmes himself soon found occasion to apply his test in an eloquent dissenting opinion in a case superficially similar to Schenck's, *Abrams* v. *U.S.* (1919). Here a majority of the Court had upheld the conviction of a group of Russian immigrants for distributing leaflets opposing American intervention in Russia in 1918. Holmes, with Justice Brandeis concurring, held that the specific statements made by the defendants did not constitute a threat to the government or to the conduct of its war against Germany. The Court had departed, he insisted, from the reasonable line it had drawn in the Schenck case; "Congress certainly cannot forbid all effort to change the mind of the country." Holmes closed his dissent with his most eloquent appeal for "free trade in ideas":

*The best test of truth [he said] is the power of the thought to get itself accepted in the competition of the market. . . . That, at any rate, is the theory of our Constitution. It is an experiment, as all life is an experiment. Every year if not every day we have to wager our salvation upon some prophecy based upon imperfect knowledge. While that experiment is part of our system I think that we should be eternally vigilant against attempts to check the expression of opinions that we loathe and believe to be fraught with death, unless they so imminently threaten immediate interference with the lawful and pressing purposes of the law that an immediate check is required to save the country. . . . Only the emergency that makes it immediately dangerous to leave the correction of evil counsels to time warrants making any exception to the sweeping command, "Congress shall make no law . . . abridging the freedom of speech."*

As the decade wore on, others swelled the chorus of defense of personal liberty "against any encroachments of the Governing part" (to quote eighteenth-century citizens petitioning for bills of rights in state constitutions), and a certain spirited iconoclasm and shedding of taboos gave the twenties their lasting reputation for authentic liveliness of tone (see Chapter Twenty-seven).

## II  Politics of complacency

### Election of 1924

Among the most sensational of the early postwar strikes was that of the Boston police, in 1919, in protest against the refusal of the city's police commissioners to recognize a union organized to raise the policemen's pitifully low wages. Coming at a moment of widespread labor strife and fear of reds and "radicalism," this strike aroused exceptional public hostility. After an appeal from Boston's mayor, Governor Calvin Coolidge called out the state guard to maintain order in the state capital. When AFL President Samuel Gompers protested the firing of some of the leaders of the policemen's union for their organizing activities, Coolidge replied with a resounding statement: "There is no right to strike against the public safety by anybody, anywhere, anytime." Actually, Coolidge's role during the strike had been timid and dilatory, and Boston's difficulties arose in large part from his delay. But this short, no-nonsense avowal established him almost instantly as a national hero and led to his nomination for the vicepresidency in 1920.

When Harding died in August 1923, Coolidge's oath of office as President was administered to him by his father in their simple Vermont farmhouse by the light of an old-fashioned kerosene lamp. This ceremony successfully projected a taciturn Yankee rustic in the Lasker image of his unfortunate predecessor. The new President inherited all the unresolved postwar problems; but the onset of the postwar business revival helped smooth his path. By 1924, "Coolidge prosperity" had become so real that it was a foregone conclusion that the Republican convention in Cleveland would name him for the presidency in his own right.

A boon to the GOP, "Coolidge prosperity" was only one of the hurdles the Democrats faced in 1924. One faction, which backed the candidacy of William G. McAdoo, Wilson's son-in-law and Secretary of the Treasury, found its strength in the rural, Protestant, "dry" segments of the party. A second faction, whose candidate was the "Happy Warrior," New York's Catholic governor, "Al" Smith, drew its support from the city machines and the "wets." After a furious battle in the broiling heat of a New York City summer over the question of denouncing the KKK (the convention refused to denounce the Klan, as we have said), the two factions fell into a sullen deadlock that lasted sixteen days. When it became clear that the party was so badly wrecked that the nomination was worthless, the delegates settled on John W. Davis, an impeccably conservative New York corporation lawyer originally from West Virginia. To con-

ciliate the reform-minded, the convention reached farther west for his running mate, William Jennings Bryan's brother Charles, governor of Nebraska.

Interest was lent to the campaign by the belated third-party candidacy of Robert M. La Follette on a revived Progressive ticket sponsored by the Conference of Progressive Political Action, organized in 1922. One of the novelties of its platform was the demand for a popular referendum for any declaration of war in cases other than invasion of the United States. La Follette drew the concentrated fire of both major candidates who charged him with encouraging the radicalism that had become such a bogey in the public mind. Nevertheless, he polled nearly 5 million votes. Davis received 8,386,000, and Coolidge a thumping 15,725,000, a showing that insured the Republican party a virtually free hand during his administration.

*Republican economic policies*

"No one can contemplate current conditions," said "Silent Cal" in his inaugural address of March 1925, "without finding much that is satisfying and still more that is encouraging." The good times seemed to have justified the Republican measures already taken during Harding's ordeal. These measures had originated mainly with Andrew W. Mellon, the immensely wealthy head of the aluminum trust, owner of oil companies, steel mills, utilities, and banks, a lavish contributor to the party, who became Secretary of the Treasury in 1921—the only Secretary of the Treasury, as one wit put it later, under whom three Presidents had served.

"Anybody knows," Mellon once said, "that any man of energy and initiative can get what he wants out of life. But when that initiative is crippled by . . . a tax system which denies him the right to receive a reasonable share of his earnings, he will no longer exert himself and the country will be deprived of the energy on which its continued greatness depends." Despite the $24 billion national debt created largely by the war, in accord with Mellon's philosophy Congress adopted the Revenue Act of 1921, which repealed the wartime excess-prof-

667

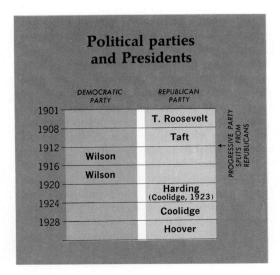

## Political parties and Presidents

| | DEMOCRATIC PARTY | REPUBLICAN PARTY | |
|---|---|---|---|
| 1901 | | T. Roosevelt | |
| 1908 | | Taft | PROGRESSIVE PARTY SPLITS FROM REPUBLICANS |
| 1912 | Wilson | | |
| 1916 | Wilson | | |
| 1920 | | Harding (Coolidge, 1923) | |
| 1924 | | Coolidge | |
| 1928 | | Hoover | |

its tax and reduced the surtax. A revolt of Senate Progressives staved off further cuts for the time being, but after Coolidge's election Congress was not to be stopped. During the debate on the 1925 tax cut (one of many during the next four years), a Nebraska Progressive observed that "Mr. Mellon himself gets a larger personal reduction than the aggregate of practically all the taxpayers in the state of Nebraska."

As taxes went down, tariffs went up. Primed by well-publicized if ill-founded fears, raised as early as 1916, that war-torn Europe would promptly dump its manufactures in the United States once the fighting ended, Congress in 1922 passed the Fordney-McCumber Act, which raised duties to record levels. While checking Allied efforts to reduce war debts by exporting commodities to the United States, this act also caused many nations to adopt retaliatory tariffs against American imports. Nevertheless, protectionism—like xenophobia—was an essential part of "normalcy," one that remained so popular that in 1930, during Hoover's administration, the Hawley-Smoot Tariff raised duties higher still. More than a thousand economists petitioned Hoover to veto this act but to no avail, and foreign retaliatory measures dealt American exports severe new blows.

Apparently pleased to keep American enterprise from competing abroad, the Republican administrations also moved to circumscribe competition at home. To the chairmanship of the Federal Trade Commission, President Coolidge appointed William E. Humphrey, who promised that it would no longer be, as he called it, "a publicity bureau to spread socialistic propaganda." The FTC began to encourage business conferences for the purpose of negotiating industry-wide agreements for corporate—not the public—benefit, a policy furthered by Hoover as Secretary of Commerce under Harding and Coolidge. Hoover's goal, reflecting wartime success with industrial rationalization and standardization, was peacetime industrial cooperation. The more than 200 codes of fair practice he initiated, under which companies shared product and market information, in many respects anticipated the codes of the New Deal's NRA.

The Supreme Court also cleared the air for business cooperation and combination. By introducing the "rule of reason" into its decision dissolving the Standard Oil Company in 1911 (see p. 623), the Court seemed to imply that henceforth its antimonopoly rulings would be even less severe than heretofore. This implication was tested and found accurate in the antitrust suit, approved by President Taft, attacking the United States Steel Corporation (see p. 628). The Steel case lingered on until 1920, when the Court ruled at last that while the billion-dollar enterprise controlled about 40 percent of the steel industry, this was insufficient for it to be considered powerful enough to act in "unreasonable" restraint of trade.

Encouraged by federal agencies and Cabinet-level departments in a favorable judicial atmosphere, businessmen in the 1920s went on a new and unprecedented merger spree. In the field of public utilities alone, 3744 firms were swallowed up, and comparable consolidations occurred in manufacturing, banking, transportation, and wholesale and retail trade.

Organized labor, by contrast, lost ground. The strikes against the great steel, coal, and railroad industries between 1919 and 1922 all failed. Thereafter, employers corralled workers into subservient company unions whose members numbered more than 1.5 million by 1929. Other unions, except those of the old skilled crafts, were kept out of most industries by employers' open-shop policies. AFL membership, at a peak of 4,078,000 in 1920, had fallen under 3 million by 1923 and waned thereafter. Strikes also tapered off in the face of modest annual improvements in real wages during "Coolidge prosperity."

Thirty-four states liberalized workmen's compensation laws in the twenties. At the same time, social legislation fared as badly in the courts as business practices fared well. Two Supreme Court decisions in 1921, *Duplex Printing Press* v. *Deering* and *Truax* v. *Corrigan*, exposed strikers to injunctions thought to be illegal under the Clayton Act of 1914. In 1922, in *Bailey* v. *Drexel Furniture Company*, the Court held that child labor could not constitutionally be regulated by a discriminatory tax levied on products manufactured by children. The next year, in *Adkins v. Children's Hospital,* the Court struck down an act of Congress establishing minimum wages for women and children in the District of Columbia. Only in 1932, after the depression had created a new political mood, did organized labor succeed in pushing through Congress the Norris-LaGuardia Act against labor injunctions, a measure President Hoover reluctantly signed.

### The power issue

During the war, when it became clear that something had to be done to insure a steady supply of nitrates for making explosives, the government built two nitrate plants at Muscle Shoals on the Tennessee River in Alabama and began construction of a power dam, later named Wilson Dam. At the war's end, work on the dam ceased and the House cut off further funds for the entire development. Disturbed by this action, Senator George W. Norris of Nebraska, chairman of the Committee on Agriculture, argued that the Tennessee River projects represented an immense wasted asset and that steps should be taken to complete the dam and bring it and the plants' power into use. Norris had a good case, for the idled plants and the unfinished dam so far had cost $145 million.

Norris's case was weakened by the prevailing political philosophy, which led Congress to dally with the idea of leasing the sites for private development, while the private utilities fought all efforts to keep Muscle Shoals a public project. Finally, in 1928, Norris introduced a bill for government production and sale of power from Wilson Dam and manufacture and sale of fertilizer. Congress, with widespread support from agricultural areas, passed the bill in May 1928, only to have Coolidge veto it. In 1931 Hoover, as President, vetoed a similar measure in a message showing how far Progressive nationalism had receded even in the mind of one so committed to *business* consolidation. "I hesitate," he wrote,

*to contemplate the future of our institutions, of our country, if the preoccupation of its officials is to be no longer the promotion of justice and equal opportunity but is to be devoted to barter in the markets. That is not liberalism, it is degeneration.... Muscle Shoals can only be administered by the people upon the ground, responsible to their own communities, directing them solely for the benefit of their communities, and not for purposes of pursuit of social theories of national politics.*

There the matter stood until the Tennessee Valley Authority was established under the New Deal in 1933.

### Farmers in peacetime

The economic problem most troublesome to the Republicans in the twenties was the distress of staple farmers deeply in debt from wartime overexpansion. Dairy, vegetable, and fruit farmers prospered from expanding city markets in their vicinity. Staple farmers had to sell in world markets, where stronger competition from Canadian, Australian, and Argentine wheat, and Brazilian, Egyptian, and Indian cotton, added to their woes. When women turned from cotton to rayon fabrics, and families altered diets to include more fruits and vegetables at the expense of pork, beef, and flour, the pinch on staple farmers tightened. Republican leaders urged higher tariffs as the sovereign remedy for farmers as for businessmen. But tariffs brought exporters no balm; indeed, besides forcing up prices of farm family purchases they further injured the farmer by focusing foreign tariff retaliation on American agricultural exports. Net farm income, including that of prosperous dairy and truck farmers, fell from $9.5 billion in 1919 to $5.3 billion in 1928.

Farm distress helped create a strong farm bloc in Congress which sponsored the McNary-Haugen bill for federal government support of staple prices. Twice defeated earlier, this bill was passed in 1927 and again in 1928, only to be vetoed both times by the President. "Farmers have never made money," Coolidge averred. "I don't believe we can do much about it." To do something, Congress in June 1929 passed the Agricultural Marketing Act, which President Hoover signed. This act set up a Federal Farm Board to promote cooperatives and endowed it with a revolving fund of $500 million for low-interest loans to

670

assist them in helping staple farmers keep their surpluses off the market when a glut threatened to undermine prices. The Great Crash of October 1929 put this measure to a severe test which it soon failed to meet (see p. 677).

## III   The "golden glow"

### Genuineness of prosperity

Irving Bernstein calls his outstanding history of labor in the twenties *The Lean Years,* and in certain specialized industries and areas, such as textile manufacturing in New England and the southern piedmont and coal mining in Kentucky, suffering among workers became as acute as among small staple farmers. Yet the economy as a whole did well. Between 1921 and 1929, average "real income" for each person in the country rose from $522 to $716; for each person gainfully employed, real income rose from $1308 to $1716. These gains reflected a tremendous increase in the productivity of the individual worker, brought about by improved technology based mainly on the application of electricity to manufacturing and by improved procedures derived in part from theories of scientific management popularized by Frederick Winslow Taylor and his followers. The fact that the stock market seemed to magnify even the real progress of the economy, especially during the later phases of the boom, has caused emphasis to be placed on the speculative side of business in the twenties. Yet the stock-market surge—and the Great Crash— obscure many of the genuine gains of the decade and how they were won.

World War I itself contributed significantly to the boom. For one thing, the liberty bond drives accustomed millions to investing in securities, thereby making it easier for corpora-

tions to finance new or expanded ventures after the war by means of stock and bond issues without knuckling under to the conservative old money trust. Many corporations, moreover, made so much money during the war that they could often pay for expanded or improved facilities without going to the money market at all. Wartime tax policies heightened the effect of wartime financial policies. In particular, the excess-profits tax of the war years had prompted corporations to plow back their heavy earnings into modernized, electrified plant and equipment which paid off in productivity and profits when the war was over. Wartime labor shortages often made such technological advances mandatory for survival.

Many industries that came of age in the twenties also were created by the war or matured by its demands. In 1903 Wilbur and Orville Wright had made the first successful flight in a motor-driven heavier-than-air contraption at Kitty Hawk, North Carolina. But airplane progress languished until the war proved the practicality of the new machines for scouting and eventually for combat. After the war, flyers home from the battlefield worked up a considerable business taking enthusiasts up for five-minute flights. Transcontinental airmail service began in 1920, and in 1923 the first regularly scheduled flights were flown between Chicago and Cheyenne, Wyoming. The Air Commerce Act of 1926 gave substantial mail subsidies to private airlines and helped make commercial flying a big business. After Charles A. Lindbergh, Jr., in May 1927, made his momentous solo flight from New York to Paris, flying became more popular than ever. By 1930, 122 American airlines were carrying almost half a million passengers over 50,000 miles of air routes.

The war gave the American chemical industry an even greater boost than it gave flying. Before 1914 American chemical companies had produced little but the simple heavy acids and alkalis used in basic industrial processes.

During the war, explosives became the principal product of the industry, and many new chemical plants were built to supply Allied needs. Once the war was over, two government measures fostered the growth of a huge chemical industry. The first was the confiscation of German coal-tar patents and their assignment to American chemical corporations. The second, motivated by popular de-

*Wilbur Wright on one of many glider flights at Kitty Hawk, North Carolina, October 10, 1902, made in preparation for brother Orville's first successful takeoff, under power, of a heavier-than-air machine, December 17 the next year.*

Library of Congress

Culver Pictures, Inc.

*"The Hero of the Age,"*
*according to Frederick Lewis Allen in*
Only Yesterday: *"Lucky Lindy" and*
Spirit of St. Louis.

mand for chemical self-sufficiency in the event of another war, was the imposition of forbiddingly high duties on chemical imports. By 1929 certain corporate beneficiaries of these measures, such as Allied Chemicals, Union Carbide, and the old DuPont company, had far outstripped all foreign chemical firms or cartels. The American chemical industry that year produced new plastics, alloys, and "allied products" as well as the older acids and alkalis valued at $3.75 billion.

### An electrochemical revolution

In conjunction with electricity, chemicals revolutionized a number of other in-dustries. Signal advances in the production of electricity itself fostered this development. Between 1920 and 1929, the rise in the efficiency of the power industry was such that a 25 percent increase in coal burned brought a 100 percent increase in kilowatt hours generated. Such progress so cheapened electric power by 1929 that 70 percent of American factory machinery was operated by electricity, compared with but 30 percent fifteen years before. The most striking gains from the combination of electrical and chemical processes were made in the petroleum industry, fortunately for the burgeoning automobile industry. Between 1913 and 1928, electrochemical processes tripled the quantity of gasoline that could be refined from a gallon of crude oil. Electrochemical processes in the steel industry, meanwhile, led to sharp improvement in the quality of the parts of internal-combustion engines, which thus burned with much higher efficiency the gasoline so much more efficiently produced. The combination of electricity and chemistry in metallurgy also brought marked gains in the manufacture of phonographs, refrigerators, radios, washing machines, vacuum cleaners, and other adjuncts of the good life.

Besides revolutionizing industrial technology in the twenties, electricity revolutionized factory organization and procedures. By permitting the transmission of power over tremendous distances, it freed the factory from the river valley and the coal field and gave management much greater opportunity to consider proximity to markets and other "location" factors in deciding on factory sites. By permitting the even flow of power throughout huge plants, electricity added immensely to the flexibility of organization within the factory as well. It made the "straight-line" system of production, the conveyor, and the moving assembly line all more efficient. It also put a premium on the standardization of jobs and commodities, as "rationalization" became the catchword of industrial planners.

## Automobiles come of age

No industry was more firmly rooted in the technological and managerial changes of the postwar years than the automobile industry. For the rubber, glass, and alloys of which body and engine parts were made, the automobile manufacturers depended increasingly on the new chemical and electrical knowledge and the new electrochemical processes. Ultimately, the automobile manufacturers grew into the greatest users of each of the commodities that went into their product, and work on automobile assembly lines became highly mechanized and repetitive.

American experience firmly underpinned the growth of automobile production. From the nation's earliest days, men had been trained by carriage manufacturers in the making of bodies, springs, and wheels. Since the 1850s the building of farm machinery had developed a widespread familiarity with small engines. In the last decades of the nineteenth century, bicycle manufacturers had spurred the development of pneumatic tires. The American environment, in turn, reinforced the impact of American technological experience. The United States was a country of majestic distances and of a growing middle class prosperous enough to purchase thousand-dollar commodities that could traverse the wide-open spaces with satisfying speed. Where railroads had helped concentrate population in metropolises, the automobile tended to disperse it to suburbs and beyond, thereby speeding the decline of great cities.

Many experiments to build a "horseless carriage" run by steam, electricity, alcohol, and other fuels were made before George B. Selden of Rochester, New York, in 1877, produced a workable vehicle with a gasoline engine—which he failed to patent until 1895. By then in the United States and abroad other successful experimenters had entered the field, but not until about 1903 did the auto-mobile become commercially feasible. By 1910 some sixty American companies were producing cars for sale, and General Motors, a combination promoted by William C. Durant to bring chaotic competition in the industry under control, was two years old.

One of the most vulnerable aspects of the General Motors combine was Durant's failure to get Ford into it. By 1908 Henry Ford was already a prominent automobile manufacturer. The next year he introduced the renowned "tin lizzie," Model T, in "any color you choose so long as it's black," list price $950. By 1913 Model Ts were down to $550 and Ford sold 168,000, representing about a third of the nation's entire automobile business that year. In 1914 Ford opened his revolutionary plant at Highland Park, Michigan, equipped with the first electric conveyor belt, which carried the gradually assembled car at a uniform—and rapid—speed past stationary workers, each equipped with the materials and tools to perform his one simple mechanical task. In 1913 it had taken fourteen hours, on the average, to assemble a Model T. In the new plant it could be done in ninety-three minutes. In 1914, Ford built 248,000 cars—45 percent of the total automobile output—at a base price of $490. His profit that year ex-

673

*Chassis on the line
in Ford Highland Park plant, 1924.*

Courtesy of the Ford Archives, Henry Ford Museum, Dearborn, Michigan

ceeded $30 million. By 1925 Ford was turning out a complete car every ten seconds; but by then people were beginning to tire of the tin lizzie, and the drift toward more distinctive models with more comfortable appointments had begun in earnest.

674

In 1920 about 9 million automobiles were registered in the United States. By 1930 registration had risen to nearly 30 million. "We'd rather do without clothes than give up the car," said a "Middletown" housewife in the twenties. "I'll go without food before I'll see us give up the car," said another.

### Small clouds hover

While new production techniques and consumer-goods industries gave a golden glow to "Coolidge prosperity," the older industries contributed their share. Throughout American history the real key to the health of the economy had been the private construction industry, which traditionally engaged more capital and labor than any other, including railroading. In the twenties population and economic growth as well as the wartime construction lag pushed the demand for housing to record levels, while industrial building and railroad rebuilding also soared. The remarkable growth of the power industry and home and factory electrification, in turn, promoted the building of power plants and distrib-

uting facilities. Finally, there was government construction—never, since the days of the canals, a negligible factor in the economy.

In the twenties a large new item began to appear in local, state, and federal budgets: outlays for paved roads. As late as 1921 "chains on all four wheels" and "a shovel with a collapsible handle" were prescribed equipment for touring by automobile. In the next ten years government expenditure for street and highway construction exceeded the capital outlay for most private industries. This was, in effect, a hidden subsidy to the automobile industry and indeed to the entire economy. When private investment slowed down late in the decade and government outlays failed to compensate for it, the crash and depression loomed. Other economic weaknesses of the twenties, such as the maldistribution of wealth and purchasing power and persistent industrial unemployment, recognized after the crash, were obscured by the golden glow. America seemed to have discovered the perpetual-motion prosperity machine, and little sympathy was wasted on those who did not bask in its accomplishments. In the summer of 1929 John J. Raskob, the millionaire chairman of the Democratic National Committee, said:

*If a man saves $15 a week, and invests in good common stocks, and allows the dividends and rights to accumulate, at the end of twenty years he will have at least $80,000 and an income of investments of around $400 a month. He will be rich. And because income can do that, I am firm in my belief that anyone not only can be rich, but ought to be rich.*

### Election of 1928

When "Silent Cal" let slip the announcement that he did not "choose to run" in 1928, Republican leaders took him at his word and turned, appropriately, to his Secretary of Commerce. Born in modest circumstances on an Iowa farm, Herbert Hoover had enjoyed a rewarding career as an engineer and

**Election of 1928**

*Electoral Vote*

Hoover 444          Smith 87

promoter farther west and abroad before winning acclaim for relief work in Europe during the war. After the war, he was also credited with having used American plenty to thwart the advance of communism. These activities had added to his reputation for practicality a reputation for humanitarianism. His attacks on the many unwise aspects of peacemaking, in turn, gave him standing as a statesman.

To oppose Hoover the Democrats this time united behind "Al" Smith who, as governor of New York, had made an outstanding record backing liberal legislation and ideas. But this record proved irrelevant to the nation at large. An Irishman, a Catholic, a New Yorker, and a "wet," Smith stood as the incarnation of everything calculated to arouse rural and small-

town suspicions. Anti-Catholics of the sort who had supported the Klan believed that Smith's election would bring the Pope himself to Washington to take over the government. A whispering campaign that rapidly gained exceptional influence throughout the South spread this idea.

In the light of Hoover's initial advantages, it seems unlikely that any Democrat could have beaten him. His popular *majority* exceeded 6 million votes, and he carried all but eight states, including, for the first time since Reconstruction, five in the Solid South. Many Catholics blamed bigotry alone for Smith's defeat. Other Democrats may have found some balm in his showing. His vote doubled that of Davis in 1924; and in the country's twelve largest cities, strongly Republican in the two preceding presidential elections, his total exceeded Hoover's. The future, moreover, lay with the urban voter.

## IV Politics of depression

### The Great Crash

After taking the oath of office as President on March 4, 1929, Hoover opened his inaugural address with this statement: "If we survey the situation of our Nation at home and abroad, we find many satisfactions." In his closing paragraph he listed some of them:

*Ours is a land rich in resources; stimulating in its glorious beauty; filled with millions of happy homes; blessed with comfort and opportunity. In no nation are the institutions of progress more advanced. In no nation are the fruits of accomplishment more secure.*

Less than eight months later, October 29, 1929, as the *New York Times* said, "stock prices . . . swept downward with gigantic losses in the most disastrous trading day in the stock market's history." In a few hours more than $10 billion of America's "fruits of accomplishment" were washed away. During the next few years, the "glorious beauty" of

the American West, as an observer told Congress, had been caught by "unemployed timber workers and bankrupt farmers" who started forest fires in the state of Washington that raged all summer, "in an endeavor to earn a few honest dollars as fire fighters"; America's bankrupt "happy homes" had closed their doors on thousands of unemployed women who even in winter slept in the public parks; America's shrunken opportunity had drawn "more than 100,000 applications" from such heavily industrialized states as Pennsylvania, Michigan, Massachusetts, and Ohio, according to *Business Week* magazine, for 6000 skilled jobs in Russia that had been announced by the New York office of Amtorg.

The betrayal of the rhetoric of business success by the disastrous course of events disclosed more "pockets" of economic hardship than had been acknowledged, larger ones than had been supposed, and their cancerous tendency to grow. Besides the bottoming out farm receipts and the burdens of industrial underemployment in the twenties, the slowly rising real wages of industrial workers were outdistanced by the salaries, savings, and profits of those higher on the economic ladder. In 1929 the 24,000 richest families had an aggregate income more than three times as large as that of the nearly 6 million poorest families, and 40 percent of all families had incomes under $1500. No wonder consumer purchasing power failed to keep pace with the production potential of the industrial plant and the promotional pyrotechnics of advertising. Those who were getting rich, meanwhile, finding their savings piling up out of all proportion to need and to opportunities for sound investment, turned to speculation in real estate and securities, both indefatigably blown up by pitchmen into a bubble sure to burst.

The economic situation abroad only attenuated the domestic crisis. Dependent upon American credit for imports needed to restore their economies battered in the war and to stabilize their currencies, European nations found their credit limits the more speedily reached by the tariff obstacles to commodity exports. American manufacturers thus found it ever more difficult to sell abroad. American and European economies were so closely linked that the depression soon became worldwide, and Nazism joined fascism among the "parties of order" opposed to socialism, communism, and other radical -*isms*, sometimes called the "parties of movement," also nurtured by hard times.

Hoover himself scorned the ebbing confidence of others. "Prosperity is just around the

**Breadline at Water Street Mission, New York City, 1930.**

Brown Brothers

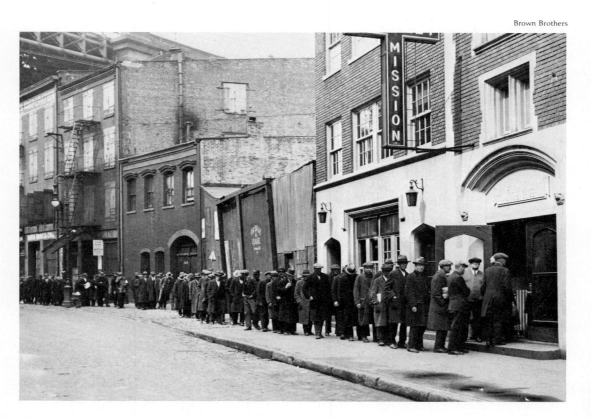

corner," he kept saying, like a prayer. His Democratic rivals, nevertheless, leaving Republicans what use remained of "Coolidge prosperity," promptly branded the new era the "Hoover depression."

### Short reach of government

For all his stress on confidence, Hoover's administration offered some somatic as well as psychological palliatives. In 1930, when the slide of wheat and cotton prices became catastrophic, the Federal Farm Board set up a Stabilization Corporation for each staple to try to reverse the price trend by open-market purchases. It was not long, however, before government warehouses so bulged with such purchases that private dealers, fearful of their being unloaded on the market, sold their own holdings for instant cash. By 1932, when both corporations suspended operations, cotton was 6 cents a pound, down from 16 cents in 1929; wheat 38 cents a bushel, down from $1.00.

To help labor and industry, early in 1930 Congress granted the President $700 million for public works, the start of an unprecedented program that saw Hoover spend almost $3 billion on public construction. The President also tried to get companies to delay discharges and wage cuts, but even the best-willed industrialists could not long keep men at work at a living wage when no markets materialized. By 1932, 12 million people were unemployed, and the wages of the rest had plummeted. In January 1932, in an effort to save insurance companies and philanthropic organizations that had invested so confidently in the securities of great corporations that now faced bankruptcy, Congress created the Reconstruction Finance Corporation, which by the end of the year had loaned $1.5 billion to about 5000 shaky firms.

In the belief that the burden of foreign debts depressed world trade and deterred world recovery, Hoover, in June 1931, proposed a one-year moratorium on debt pay-ments due the United States. A more practical step would have been to cancel such debts outright, which in effect was the outcome, since by 1933, of the fifteen countries involved, none but Finland (which paid in full) made more than token payments.

No previous administration had ever taken such extensive measures to revive the private economy or help the victims of its collapse. Yet they proved wholly inadequate to the crisis, which became especially acute when local and private welfare agencies also crashed under the unprecedented calls upon them. Hoover, the "great humanitarian" of the war years, soon was portrayed as the heartless villain of the depression. The picture of a harsh President became seared in the hearts of millions in the summer of 1932 when, with the November elections approaching, the "Bonus Army" of 12,000 jobless war veterans marched to Washington in hopes of persuading Congress to make a veterans' bonus appropriation. On Hoover's orders, they were driven from the city with tear gas and bayonets.

### Election of 1932

Aware that they had to renominate Hoover in 1932 or accept the allegation of a "Hoover depression," the Republicans, at their early June convention in Chicago, did their duty by the President on the first ballot. When the Democrats met in Chicago later in the month, "Al" Smith was once more strongly in the running for a nomination that was almost certain to lead to the White House. The delegates, however, looked elsewhere. On the fourth ballot they named TR's socialite cousin Franklin D. Roosevelt, Smith's successor as governor of New York, whose victory in the state in 1928 stood out boldly against the Republicans' overwhelming national success that year. In 1930 FDR was reelected governor almost by acclamation.

On receiving the presidential nomination, Roosevelt flew to Chicago to accept the honor in person, something no candidate had done before. "I pledge you, I pledge myself," he told the delegates, "to a new deal for the American people."

In the campaign, Hoover stressed World War I and the unresolved international economic difficulties that followed as the main causes of the crash. Roosevelt did not deny the depression's international character but zeroed in on the flaws it revealed in the American economy. Hoover warned that an excess of governmental zeal would destroy liberty. Roosevelt called for novel methods to meet novel conditions, although his few specific commitments were conventional. Liberals, indeed, were as much disappointed by his campaign as conservatives were frightened. Yet more voters were heartened by his prom-

ises, however vague, than were impressed by Hoover's warnings, however dire. Roosevelt received 22,821,000 votes, Hoover 15,761,000. The victor's electoral college margin, 472 to 59, reflected his success in carrying all but six northeastern states—Maine, New Hampshire, Vermont, Connecticut, Pennsylvania, and Delaware. The Democratic party, moreover, won overwhelming majorities in both houses of Congress.

## For further reading

A. M. Schlesinger, Jr., *The Crisis of the Old Order 1919-1933* (1957), is eminently readable. Shorter general accounts include W. E. Leuchtenburg, *The Perils of Prosperity 1914-1932* (1958); and G. E. Mowry, *The Urban Nation 1920-1960* (1965). R. S. and H. M. Lynd, *Middletown* (1929), and *Middletown in Transition* (1937), provide penetrating analyses of ordinary American life. F. L. Allen, *Only Yesterday* (1931), is an admirable informal history of the twenties. See also Jonathan Daniels, *The Time Between the Wars* (1966). André Siegfried, *America Comes of Age* (1927), is a lively report by a French visitor. G. H. Knoles, *The Jazz Age Revisited* (1955), discusses the experiences of British commentators. For the serious and popular culture of the twenties, see the suggested readings for Chapter Twenty-seven.

Francis Russell, *The Shadow of Blooming Grove, Warren G. Harding in His Times* (1968), is the leading study of the President. See also R. K. Murray, *The Harding Era* (1969). For background on the red scare, see P. G. Filene, ed., *American Views of Soviet Russia 1917-1965* (1968); and L. I. Stakhovsky, *American Opinion About Russia 1917-1920* (1961). R. K. Murray, *Red Scare* (1955), is a scholarly analysis. William Preston, Jr., *Aliens and Dissenters: Federal Suppression of Radicals 1903-1933* (1963), is excellent. Stanley Coben, *A. Mitchell Palmer* (1963), is informative on Wilson's Attorney-General. Francis Russell, *Tragedy in Dedham* (1962), is outstanding on the Sacco-Vanzetti case. See also O. K. Fraenkel, *The Sacco-Vanzetti Case* (1931).

David Brody, *Steelworkers in America, The Nonunion Era* (1960), provides background for the great steel strike described in Brody, *Labor in Crisis, The Steel Strike of 1919* (1965). Contemporary analyses are provided in Commission of Inquiry, Interchurch World Movement, *Report on the Steel Strike of 1919* (1920); and Marshall Olds, *Analysis of the Interchurch World Movement Report on the Steel Strike* (1922). On the "American Plan" and related programs, see vol. IV of J. R. Commons and associates, *History of Labor in the United States* (4 vols., 1918-1935).

On anti-immigrant feeling, John Higham, *Strangers in the Land: Patterns of American Nativism 1860-1925* (1955), is outstanding. R. L. Garis, *Immigration Restriction* (1927), covers the subject in detail. It may be supplemented by R. A. Divine, *American Immigration Policy 1924-1952* (1957). C. S. Johnson, *Shadow of the Plantation* (1966 ed., with R. E. Park's Introduction), provides insight into the backgrounds of black migrants. T. J. Woofter, *Negro Migration* (1920), and E. J. Scott, *Negro Migration During the War* (1920), are useful contemporary accounts. The examples of white response discussed in the text are described in E. M. Rudwick, *Race Riot at East St. Louis July 2,1917* (1964); and A. H. Spear, *Black Chicago, The Making of a Negro Ghetto 1890-1920* (1967). Richard Hofstadter and Michael Wallace, *American Violence: A Documentary History* (1970), reports white as well as black events. Other valuable works on black life in the urban environment include Gilbert Osofsky, *Harlem:*

The Making of a Ghetto, Negro New York 1890-1930 (1966); and St. Clair Drake and H. R. Cayton, Black Metropolis (1945), on Chicago.

D. M. Chalmers, Hooded Americanism, The History of the Ku Klux Klan (1965); A. S. Rice, The Ku Klux Klan in American Politics (1961); and K. T. Jackson, The Ku Klux Klan in the City (1967), tell the story of the hooded group in the twentieth century. On Prohibition, see Andrew Sinclair, Era of Excess, A Social History of the Prohibition Movement (1962). N. F. Furniss, The Fundamentalist Controversy 1918-1931 (1954), is excellent on the battle over evolution theory. W. B. Gatewood, Jr., ed., Controversy in the Twenties: Fundamentalism, Modernism and Evolution (1969), is an illuminating anthology. On the Scopes trial, Ray Ginger, Six Days or Forever? (1958), is amusing as well as scholarly. On dissent and its defense, see Zechariah Chafee, Free Speech in the United States (1941 ed.); and Richard Hofstadter, Anti-Intellectualism in American Life (1963).

D. R. McCoy, Calvin Coolidge, the Quiet President (1967), is a definitive modern biography. W. A. White, A Puritan in Babylon (1938), remains good reading. Alfred E. Smith, Up To Now (1929), may be supplemented by Matthew and Hannah Josephson, Al Smith: Hero of the Cities (1970). David Burner, The Politics of Provincialism, The Democratic Party in Transition 1918-1932 (1968), is excellent. On the party's 1924 convention, see Frank Freidel, Franklin D. Roosevelt, vol. II: "The Ordeal" (1954).

George Soule, Prosperity Decade: From War to Depression 1917-1929 (1947), provides a good introduction to the economy. Herbert Hoover, American Individualism (1922), expresses the business philosophy of the Secretary of Commerce. J. W. Prothro, The Dollar Decade, Business Ideas in the 1920's (1954), offers a different view. On Republican tax and tariff policies, see R. E. Paul, Taxation in the United States (1954); and E. E. Schattschneider, Politics, Pressures and the Tariff (1935). On the power issue, see Fighting Liberal, The Autobiography of George W. Norris (1945); and P. J. Hubbard, Origins of TVA: The Muscle Shoals Controversy 1920-1932 (1961). On the struggles of workers and farmers in the prosperity decade, see Irving Bernstein, The Lean Years, A History of the American Worker 1920-1933 (1960); J. D. Black, Agri-

cultural Reform in the United States (1930); and Theodore Saloutos and J. D. Hicks, Agricultural Discontent in the Middle West 1900-1939 (1951).

"The Golden Glow" is the title of the opening chapter of C. A. and M. R. Beard, America in Midpassage (2 vols., 1939), a work devoted largely to the depression that followed. Siegfried Giedion, Mechanization Takes Command (1948), is unmatched on technology and society.

Two works by A. D. Chandler, Jr., offer the most penetrating accounts of big-business management: Strategy and Structure, Chapters in the History of Industrial Enterprise (1962); and Giant Enterprise, Ford, General Motors, and the Automobile Industry (1964), an excellent anthology. A. P. Sloan, Jr., My Years with General Motors (1964), is best on that company. The three volumes on Ford by Allan Nevins and F. E. Hill fully cover the company and the industry. Among more critical studies of the man see, for example, Keith Sward, The Legend of Henry Ford (1948). On airplanes, F. C. Kelly, The Wright Brothers (1943), and H. L. Smith, Airways: The History of Commercial Aviation in the United States (1942), are illuminating. On Lindbergh, see W. S. Ross, The Last Hero: Charles A. Lindbergh (1967); and K. S. Davis, The Hero: Charles A. Lindbergh and The American Dream (1959). Simon Kuznets, National Income and Its Composition 1919-1938 (1941), is basic. A. A. Berle, Jr., and G. F. Means, The Modern Corporation and Private Property (1932), is a classic study of business concentration. A good example of the excesses of concentration is recounted in Forrest McDonald, Insull (1962). See also, C. D. Thompson, Confessions of the Power Trust (1932). On security speculation W. Z. Ripley, Main Street and Wall Street (1927) is first-rate.

J. K. Galbraith, The Great Crash (1955), is excellent on the 1929 debacle. The onset of the depression is ably reported in Gilbert Seldes, The Years of the Locust (1933). See also Studs Terkel, Hard Times (1970). Herbert Hoover, The Memoirs of Herbert Hoover (3 vols., 1951-1952), contains extensive documentation. More objective is A. U. Romasco, The Poverty of Abundance: Hoover, The Nation, The Depression (1965). How Hoover came to be President is well analyzed in Edmund Moore, A Catholic Runs for President (1956); and R. C. Silva, Rum, Religion and Votes, 1928 Re-examined (1962). How he was unseated is well told in R. V. Peel and T. C. Donnelly, The 1932 Campaign (1935); and Frank Freidel, Franklin D. Roosevelt, vol. III: "The Triumph" (1956).

# THE MODERN TEMPER

Early in 1929, just before the Great Crash, when the well-off could still afford to wonder about their relation to God and the Universe, and not to their fellowmen, Joseph Wood Krutch published *The Modern Temper*. Although its theme was the dissipation of values, the *inevitable* disintegration of the moral structure of society, in a social sense it was an optimistic book. Well-fed, well-clothed, well-housed men, their creature comforts better taken care of than ever before in history and according to the best minds likely to continue so, might "submit," as Krutch says, with the exhilarating "detachment" of the scientist to the tragedy he described. Such submission, indeed, would be but an intellectual coming of age, a willing surrender of "the world of poetry, mythology, and religion," which "represent the world as man would like to have it," and a gallant embracing of the "world of science," the "world as he gradually comes to discover it."

> For the cozy bowl of the sky arched in a protecting curve above him he must exchange the cold immensities of space and, for the spiritual order which he has designed, the chaos of nature.

Krutch himself would set the mature example.

Krutch called *The Modern Temper* "A Study and a Confession." Twenty-five years later he wrote what he permitted others to call a "reply" to *The Modern Temper*. To this book he gave the title *The Measure of Man,* and he described it as "A Study and a Refutation." Krutch insisted here that "the most prevalent educated opinion is still that men are animals and that animals are machines." And yet he now confronted "the stubborn fact of consciousness," accepting, with William James, "the pragmatic ground that whatever we say we believe we never find it possible to act on any assumption other than that there are choices open to us." He also accepted Alfred North Whitehead's dictum that "scientific thinking is, after all, only a *way* of thinking, rather than a description of ultimate reality." And yet the best Krutch would even now begrudge mankind was the possibility of "adjustment" to the "dismal assumptions which make Social Engineering rather than Existentialist resignation the dominant religion of today." Social Engineering itself lay in the hands of "the manipulators of the media of mass communication." They look, said Krutch, to "the creation of a Robot Utopia whose well-adjusted citizens will have comfortably forgotten that their forefathers believed themselves to be Men."

Others in America and elsewhere have usually been more sanguine. In the United States in particular, early in the twentieth century, many intellectuals saw "the masses" not as animals but as the *élan vital* of a society smothered by the genteel tradition. These intellectuals called the "media of mass communication" the "lively arts" and found laughter once again in the movies of Mack Sennett and Charlie Chaplin, in comic strips like "Bringing Up Father" and "Krazy Kat," in dixieland jazz, ragtime, The Follies. They saw these media and the new-fangled radio as liberating, not "conditioning," instrumentalities. In the twenties, moreover, even the most skeptical

and escapist authors in the grand tradition wrote with a disenchantment that itself reflected active moral judgment, not resignation, and as a group they endured more frequent personal crack-ups than any earlier generation of American writers.

The depression of the thirties dragooned many American authors back to social realism, some of them embracing the "Robot Utopia" of the USSR, which seemed to offer a viable alternative to the cruel failures of individualism and capitalism. As late as 1937, when many such authors were abandoning the cruel totalitarianism of Russia under Stalin, the playwright Albert Bein exclaimed: "When I . . . see these people looking, with microscopes, for pimples on the shining face of the Soviet Union, I wonder, am I crazy or what?" The *New Masses* of the thirties became the mouthpiece of the diehard American totalitarians. The original *Masses* of the teens was the mouthpiece of "the lyric years." Krutch's *The Modern Temper,* in its sharp, sophisticated way, serves efficiently to divide the two. The natural determinism and philosophical fatalism it celebrates helped undermine the lyricism and élan of the earlier age, helped underpin the scientism and regimentation of the later one. And yet, as such social crises as the depression at home and the war against Hitler abroad showed, the conventional values of civilization—mercy and justice, liberty and democracy, the humanistic values Krutch and others considered "childish"— were not altogether to be shirked because of the ascribed indifference of the universe to them.

# I  Lyric years

## In quest of the contemporary

The exuberant cultural interlude that ushered in Wilson's presidency in 1912 has been called the "little renaissance." "Little" for being rudely interrupted by America's entry into World War I in 1917, it was "little" also for representing more of an accentuation than an initiation of the artistic war against gentility that had begun after the Civil War and had proceeded thereafter in fits and starts (see Chapter Twenty-two). The new writers who came of age around 1912, like their rebel predecessors, attacked the genteel tradition for its deliberate cloaking of reality, its polite protective evasions. But worse than its artistic doctrine in general was its particular failure, in the words of Van Wyck Brooks (1886-1963), "to grasp the contemporary American mind and its problems."

Brooks's generation and a brilliant group of younger writers and artists proceeded to examine "the contemporary mind" and to arrive at some interesting if not always flattering conclusions about it. Many of these writers and artists came from regions and ethnic backgrounds heretofore skimpily represented in creative circles in America. Some of the most talented lived beyond the precincts of the eastern seaboard. A number had attended no university; nor could they be considered "gentlemen" as the genteel understood that term. Some formed groups with artistic, cultural, or political programs. Others worked as lone wolves to perfect themselves as artists rather than try to save the world. Yet, especially before the war, they also found a solidarity with the joiners in the informal "league of youth"—"freely experimental," as one of their manifestoes said, "skeptical of inherited values, ready to examine old dogmas, and to submit afresh its sanctions to the test of experience."

## The "league of youth"

The cultural program of the young radicals reaffirmed a creed set forth more than a century before: the idea that America must produce a civilization that reflected American democracy and American life. They advocated no break with the European past, but they deplored the everlasting dependence of creative Americans on European models and European approval.

Van Wyck Brooks expressed the new generation's convictions and hopes in a series of challenging books. By 1913 he had come to believe, with the Harvard philosopher and poet George Santayana, that "all nationalities are better at home," that a transplanted culture sickens and dies. He had accepted the injunction of the Irish poet William Butler Yeats that "one can only reach out to the universe with a gloved hand,—that glove is one's nation." What Brooks and his friend in the "league of youth" Randolph Bourne (1886-1918) were groping for was "a socialized world culture" in which America would play a leading part. "How many drafts we have issued in the past upon European thought, unbalanced by any investment of our own!" Brooks wrote. "The younger generation have come to feel this obligation acutely." He concluded: "Certainly no true social revolution will ever be possible in this country till a race of artists, profound and sincere, have brought us face to face with our own experience."

Others no less dedicated joined in this crusade. Even Ezra Pound in *Patria Mia* (written before 1913 but unpublished for many years thereafter) predicted that America was prepar-

ing for an intellectual awakening, a "risorgi-
mento." Foreshadowing a slogan of the 1912
presidential campaign, Pound declared that
the "first duty of a nation is to conserve its
human resources." Like Brooks, who in *America's Coming of Age* (1915) spoke of the gulf
between the "highbrows" living in an abstract
dream world far removed from the realities of
American life and the "lowbrows" dedicated
to practical, vulgar ends and "cynically contemptuous of ideals," Pound repudiated the
"dry rot" of gentility and the "red blood" of
"the school of virility," and believed then that
America had more to say than both.

Across the country, in large cities and in
small towns, such "intellectually emancipated" Americans began to meet in little
freethinking kingdoms where they might escape the "bourgeois pigs" or the "apathetic,
mawkishly-religious middle class." Bohemia
might be a small circle of artists and writers in

*A gay* Masses *cover.*

Chicago or St. Louis or even Davenport, Iowa,
but its mecca by 1914 had become a few West
Side blocks in downtown New York known as
Greenwich Village. The wildest young rebels
from all over America came to the Village to
be free, to flout convention. Young women,
drawn there from the small towns, bobbed
their hair, threw away their corsets, gave stu-
dio parties, debated all the "new" ideas.

One of the gilded priestesses of the new
Bohemia was Mabel Dodge (Luhan)—a wealthy
lady of advanced views who opened her
Fifth Avenue apartment to Village rebels of
every persuasion. At her famous evenings, the
guests discussed everything from penology
and poetry to birth control—anything, in
short, that came under the heading of "opinions." It was generally conceded that when,
in Mabel Dodge's words, "strangely penetrating intuitions rose to consciousness," they
should not be repressed.

Such oversimplified Freudian notions were
now beginning to be bandied about. Although
Sigmund Freud's influence was not to be fully
felt until the twenties, his visit to America in
1909 and the translation before 1915 of certain of his early works—*The Interpretation of
Dreams* and *Three Contributions to a Theory
of Sex,* for example—had brought him to the
attention of the Village intellectuals. "Puritan"
opposition to the alleged immoralities implicit
in Freud helps explain why the radicals elevated him to a symbol of protest.

To Village denizens, *The Masses,* first published in 1912 under the editorship of Max
Eastman, one of the early popularizers of
Freud, expressed the "correct" attitude toward
art, politics, and morals. Though committed to
socialism, *The Masses* reflected a peculiar
anarchism and paganism—what one of its editors (the poet, novelist, and Village historian
Floyd Dell) called the "play spirit." It was
both passionately reformist and refreshingly
gay. "What made us so 'objectionable,' " Max
Eastman later remarked "was not primarily
our attack on capitalism—that question was
still a trifle academic in America. But we
voiced our attack in a manner that outraged
patriotic, religious, and matrimonial, to say
nothing of ethical and aesthetic tastes and
conventions."

683

684

Distinctive features of *The Masses* were drawings and cartoons of the "Ashcan School." Its master, Robert Henri (1865-1929), a Philadelphia painter, encouraged his disciples, William Glackens (1870-1938), John Sloan (1871-1951), George Luks (1867-1933), and George Bellows (1882-1925), to represent life around them faithfully, even though it meant dignifying saloons and Bowery boys, prostitutes and horsecars.

As early as 1908 the photographer Alfred Stieglitz (1864-1946) had begun to exhibit in his Fifth Avenue gallery the newer experimental painting from abroad known generally as postimpressionism and representing the work of Matisse, Braque, Picasso, and others. The new art, in its more extreme forms of cubism and fauvism, defied "realism" as vigorously as the Ashcan School embraced it. After the postimpressionist Armory Show in New York City in 1913—it was also hung in Boston and Chicago, where thousands flocked to see it—the prestige of the Ashcan School declined even among the young rebels. When academic traditionalists, in particular, denounced the new art, some members of the "league of youth" leapt to its defense.

The abstract designs that bewildered or amused the uninitiated at the Armory Show in time were adopted for commercial use in architecture, advertising, and hundreds of mass-produced articles; but the antagonism between what is loosely called "modern art" and academicism continued long after the individualists of 1913 had expressed in paint and plastic forms their private visions.

### The new theater and new poetry

Out of *The Masses'* circle came an exciting experiment in the theater—the Provincetown Players. A group of Greenwich Village writers had been spending their summers at Provincetown, Massachusetts. In 1913, inspired largely by the roving teacher, philosopher, and writer George Cram Cook, the Provincetown group began to produce amateur plays. Three years later, they were running a theater in the Village with the assistance of sympathetic artists and writers who performed as actors.

The Players' greatest gift to the theater was Eugene O'Neill (1888-1953), who among his other occupations had worked as a common seaman. O'Neill's *Bound East For Cardiff,* a one-act play produced in Cook's theater in 1916, recalled the world of tramp steamers, waterfront dives, and seamen's talk the playwright had observed at first hand. The young O'Neill also contributed poetry to *The Masses,* threatening with his verse to torpedo the "Rust-eaten, grimy galleons of commerce." But before 1920 he put radicalism aside for Freudianism and began to write

*Eugene O'Neill in 1922,*
*when* Anna Christie *won the Pulitzer Prize*
*for drama.*

plays in which characters struggled with natural forces, especially those within themselves. *Anna Christie* (1920), *The Emperor Jones* (1921), *The Hairy Ape* (1922), *Desire Under the Elms* (1924), *Strange Interlude* (1927), and *Mourning Becomes Electra* (1931) make up a partial list of plays that won O'Neill the Nobel Prize in 1936.

Excessive psychological baggage and ponderous grappling with "big" themes often marred O'Neill's work. But in his early plays, and in at least two of his last, *The Iceman Cometh* (1946) and *Long Day's Journey Into Night* (1956), O'Neill most clearly displayed his dramatic gifts: an ability to write dialogue at once vernacular and lyrical and an emotional sincerity that distinguished his plays from the sleazy entertainment of the commercial stage.

Two avant-garde magazines performed for the new poetry a role similar to that of Cook's Provincetown theater for the new drama—Harriet Monroe's *Poetry,* founded in 1912, and Margaret Anderson's *Little Review,* which followed in 1914. Both were published in Chicago, the home of a school of poets whose calliope yells startled the eastern seaboard.

One such poet, Carl Sandburg (1878–1967), crowded into his verse much of the turbulent midwestern life he had observed in the prairie towns of Illinois and in the raw metropolis of Chicago,

*Stormy, husky, brawling,*
*City of the Big Shoulders.*

A child of Swedish immigrants, Sandburg quit school at thirteen and worked at odd jobs before becoming a journalist. *Chicago Poems* (1916), his first book of verse, incorporated the American vernacular long absent from American letters. In successive volumes Sandburg wrote of steelworkers, of towns illuminated at night by coke ovens, of Yiddish restaurants, and the mayor of Gary, Indiana, with his "cream cool pants" and white shoes, of honkytonks in Cleveland. He studded his

verse with slang: "neck-tie parties," "galoots," "chippies," "mouthpiece," "crummy." Sandburg is at his best when he captures the world of silos and cornfields, the band concerts in the small towns where girls with their "flowing and circling dresses" and the "boys driving sorrel horses" giggle

> *Amid the cornet*
> *staccato and the tuba oompa, gigglers,*
>   *God knows,*
> *gigglers daffy with life's razzle-dazzle.*

*Chicago Poems* and *Smoke and Steel* best convey Sandburg's urban mood.

Vachel Lindsay (1879–1931) also dealt with midwestern themes. His reputation today rests on a few poems like "The Congo" and "General Booth Enters into Heaven." But just as Whitman's self-image as a brawny, open-shirted vagabond belies the inner man, so Lindsay's medicine-man pose is less typical of him than his tender and elegiac lyrics about Governor Altgeld of Illinois, Abraham Lincoln, and Johnny Appleseed, or his poems of failure and defeat, such as "The Leaden-Eyed":

> *Let not young souls be smothered out before*
> *They do quaint deeds and fully flaunt their pride.*
> *It is the world's one crime its babes grow dull,*
> *Its poor are ox-eyed, limp and leaden-eyed.*

This poet, artist, mystic, and democrat hoped to make his native city, Springfield, Illinois, a center for his Gospel of Beauty, but he exhausted himself lecturing to audiences who wanted him to recite only the verse he liked least. When Lindsay committed suicide in 1931, Sherwood Anderson observed: "We do very well by our poets here, when they are dead."

Edgar Lee Masters (1869–1947), the third outstanding Chicago poet and also Clarence Darrow's law partner, wrote nothing of importance before *Spoon River Anthology,* published in 1915. Few books so completely strip away the romantic aura of small-town life. Most of Spoon River's children—the good and the bad, the talented and untalented, the saints and the hypocrites—die thwarted and broken: Knowlt Hoheimer, killed by a bullet at Missionary Ridge, wishes that he had been jailed for stealing hogs instead of running away to join the Union army; Editor Whedon, who crushed reputations "or bodies, if need be," to sell his papers, lies buried where the town sewage and refuse are dumped; Elliott Hawkins, who looked like Abraham Lincoln and served the railroad interests faithfully, lies comfortably under his tombstone and asks the "world-savers" what they have gained from their labors. Yet a few survive the travail of living and are toughened and purified by it. Fiddler Jones ends his life "with a broken fiddle" but with "a thousand memories" and "not a single regret." And Lucinda Matlock, dead at ninety-six after a strenuous life, affirms:

*What is this I hear of sorrow and weariness,*
*Anger, discontent and drooping hopes?*
*Degenerate sons and daughters,*
*Life is too strong for you—*
*It takes life to love Life.*

Chicago also fostered what Ezra Pound (1885-1971), *Poetry's* European correspondent, called the "technic and aesthetic" poets. Born in Hadley, Idaho, Pound in 1909 became an expatriate whose influence on American and British poetry is difficult to exaggerate. From his transatlantic outpost he admonished young poets in America (and in Britain as well) to revolt against the old clichés, the "obscure reveries," and "the classics in paraphrase." To the vigor of Whitman, whom he honored as a poetic ancestor, Pound wished to add the precision of Henry James and the fine clarity of the painter Whistler—men who, though expatriates like himself, proved the possibility of being artists and at the same time Americans. The "imagists," led by Pound and Amy Lowell, a Boston lady as aggressive and as opinionated as Pound himself, advocated verse of sharp poetic outlines in concentrated images. Pound soon gave up imagism for new explorations. He encouraged promising young poets like T. S. Eliot (1888-1965), an expatriate Missourian whose now much anthologized "The Love Song of J. Alfred

Prufrock" bewildered even the most advanced American critics when it appeared in *Poetry* in 1915. Pound also praised the verse of Robert Frost when that poet was still unread in America.

Frost (1875-1963), born in San Francisco, moved to New England at the age of ten. His most distinctive poetry evokes the bleak beauty of New Hampshire hills, while the taciturn and self-contained Yankees who speak in his monologues seem a part of the landscape. Before going to England in 1911 so that he could write poetry "without further scandal in the family," Frost worked as a bobbin boy in a textile mill, edited a paper, and studied briefly at Dartmouth and Harvard. His first two books of verse, *A Boy's Will* (1913) and *North of Boston* (1914), were published in England, and when he returned to the United States in 1914, a man of forty, he was still unrecognized here. The American publication of *North of Boston* later in 1914, however, established his reputation as one of America's foremost poets.

*STOPPING BY WOODS ON A SNOWY EVENING*

*Whose woods these are I think I know.*
*His house is in the village though;*
*He will not see me stopping here*
*To watch his woods fill up with snow.*

*My little horse must think it queer*
*To stop without a farmhouse near*
*Between the woods and frozen lake*
*The darkest evening of the year.*

*He gives his harness bells a shake*
*To ask if there is some mistake.*
*The only other sound's the sweep*
*Of easy wind and downy flake.*

*The woods are lovely, dark and deep.*
*But I have promises to keep,*
*And miles to go before I sleep,*
*And miles to go before I sleep.*

By choosing to illuminate the prosaic materials of everyday American life, to derive profound insights about man and eternity from a patch of snow, a bird's nest, a stone wall, a birch tree, from pastures and ax-halves, Frost followed in the tradition of Emerson (one of his favorite poets) and Emily Dickinson. In his work, the emblems of New England were exactly named and placed with a countryman's assured knowledge. They also meant more than met the eye. "A poem," Frost said, "begins in delight and ends in wisdom." Such poems as "After Apple-Picking," "Mending Wall," and "Stopping By Woods on a Snowy Evening" begin as pictures from experience and end as thought.

## II  Years of disenchantment

### War and the intellectuals

In 1917 two events shattered the hopes of Brooks, Pound, and Bourne and brought the "joyous season" to a close. On April 6 the United States went to war in Europe; about seven months later the October Revolution brought the Bolsheviks to power in Russia, *The Masses,* symbol of joy and liberation, was banned late in 1917 after its editors had twice been brought to trial for impeding the war effort. *The Seven Arts,* edited by Paul Rosenfeld and Waldo Frank, soon followed it to extinction. "The mental . . . as well as the financial . . . strain was too great," one of the editors wrote to a subscriber. "Everything liberal (and liberating) is being hounded to death . . . from free speech to free verse."

It was now left to Randolph Bourne to make the most anguished pronouncements on the "league of youth." Many of his friends had begun to support the war, but Bourne, crippled, ill, pursued by government agents, and denied an outlet for his writing, refused to change his views. In June 1917, he wrote:

*To those of us who still retain an irreconcilable animus against war, it has been a bitter experience to see the unanimity with which the American intellectuals have thrown their support to the use of war-technique. . . . And the intellectuals are not content with confirming our belligerent gesture. They are now complacently asserting that it was they who effectively willed it, against the hesitation and dim perceptions of the American democratic masses. A war made deliberately by the intellectuals! A calm moral verdict, arrived at after a penetrating study of inexorable facts! Sluggish masses, too remote from the world-conflict to be stirred, too lacking in intellect to perceive their danger! An alert intellectual class, saving the people in spite of themselves. . . . !*

Gertrude Stein called the postwar writers and artists the "lost generation" because in their youth the war had broken the continuity of their lives. Yet the twenties actually saw as much audacious experimentation in expression as did the "lyric years." The writers of the twenties were by no means so universally fatalistic and nihilistic as they have sometimes been pictured; indeed the jazz age had a kind of desperate frivolity about it, and its corrosive social satire, while fulfilling Bourne's prediction that an appalling skepticism would follow in the wake of war, at the same time belied his judgment that no good could come of disenchantment.

### Postwar expatriates

The many American writers and artists who went abroad before the war had gone to look, to compare, to criticize, to learn. America remained their homeland despite their tirades against her limitations, and they believed that she would yet produce a vital culture. The expatriates of the 1920s felt differently. To be sure, they considered themselves, sometimes belligerently, as cultural representatives of their land, but few wished ever again to endure its Puritanism, "snooping smut-hounds" (H. L. Mencken's phrase), evangelical do-gooders, machine standardization. In Paris, their Mecca, the postwar expatriates' historian Malcolm Cowley explained, the artist enjoyed the "tolerance" of his personal "indiscipline," while his profession earned respect. France, said Gertrude Stein, "surrounds you with a civilized atmosphere and then lets you be yourself."

The habits and attitudes of the Paris expatriates are recounted most enduringly in Ernest Hemingway's *The Sun Also Rises* (1926) and F. Scott Fitzgerald's *Tender Is the Night* (1934). They had a private code and a private language, wrote the novelist Kay Boyle, one of the "exiles." "Those who speak it follow no political leader and take no part in any persecution or conquest; nor have they to do with a vocabulary of the rich or the poor or any country or race; it being simply one way of communication between the lost and the lost."

> And that, I believe [wrote Cowley in Exile's Return (1936)], was the final effect on us of the War; that was the honest emotion behind a pretentious phrase like "the lost generation." School and College had uprooted us in spirit; now we were physically uprooted, hundreds of us, millions, plucked from our own soil as if by a clamshell bucket and dumped, scattered among strange people. All our roots were dead now, even the Anglo-Saxon tradition of our literary ancestors, even the habits of slow thrift that characterized our social class. We were . . . infected with the poison of irresponsibility—the poison of travel, too, for we had learned that problems could be left behind merely by moving elsewhere—and the poison of danger, excitement, that made our old life seem intolerable.

A symbol of this intellectual disaffection was the dadaist movement that flourished briefly in Paris during the twenties and flickered momentarily elsewhere. Dada stood for nihilism in philosophy, incomprehensibility in art, absurdity in literature. Every man rode his own hobbyhorse, his own dada, and the ideal dadaist production was to be shocking, unique, purposeless.

The novelist and critic Waldo Frank recognized that such a movement suited tired and battered Europe; it was, he said, "a salutary burst of laughter in a world that felt itself too old." But he reprimanded young expatriates who joined the dadaists, suggesting that America, with its real Ku Klux Klan, William Jennings Bryan, and Hollywood, was zany enough a subject for any poet.

The American humorist Ring Lardner had his own brand of dada, as in this sample dialogue from his sketch "I Gasperi" (The Upholsterers):

*First Stranger:* Where were you born?
*Second Stranger:* Out of wedlock.
*First Stranger:* That's a mighty pretty country around there.
*Second Stranger:* Are you married?
*First Stranger:* I don't know. There's a woman living with me but I can't place her.

## Mencken and Menckenism

H. L. Mencken (1880–1956), "master of revels" of the jazz age, had begun to practice at home before the war what Waldo Frank thought suitable only later. Mencken's career began in 1899 when, as police reporter for the *Baltimore Morning Herald,* he gained his first familiarity with the underworld and the conventional superstructure of American society. His apprenticeship in literary iconoclasm began with books on Bernard Shaw in 1905 and on his idol, Nietzsche, in 1908. His contributions to *Smart Set* before 1917 set the tone for the *American Mercury,* which he founded with George Jean Nathan in 1924. Unlike the Greenwich Village bohemians, Mencken from the outset attacked social idealists and radicals along with philistines. Antidemocratic both before and after the war, his social philosophy grew especially corrosive in

America, for he insisted that the conventional middle classes, the pillars of society, even more than the masses, were boobs, yokels, or peasants, and the United States was their paradise.

During the prewar period Mencken's iconoclasm served a direct purpose. He defended Dreiser against charges of immorality, spoke out for what he ironically called the "mongrel and inferior" Americans of European ancestry, and lampooned American provincialism in general. Few writers had so steeped themselves in American popular culture. As his splendid *The American Language,* first published in 1919, attests, he gained an unmatched command of the vernacular. With it, and the esoteric vocabulary he culled from wide and indiscriminate reading, he developed a unique prose style, a raffish journalese all his own.

The twenties, especially the early twenties, were made for Mencken. Edmund Wilson aptly refers to his relish "for the squalid, semiliterate writing" produced by his contemporaries, not least those now in high places. President Harding's prose he likened to that of a "rhinoceros liberating himself by main strength from a lake of boiling molasses." Mencken's ferocious assault on every sacred conviction of the common man delighted his followers and made him one of the most hated men in the United States. Democracy was a failure, but it provided "the only really amusing form of government ever endured by mankind." Monogamy was against nature; romantic love a lie. Protestantism was "down with a wasting disease." The "American Husbandman" was "a tedious fraud and ignoramus, a cheap rogue and hypocrite. . . . No more grasping, selfish, and dishonest Mammal, indeed, is known to students of Anthropoidea." Another target was the 100 percenter, the American racist, at whom he leveled broadsides such as this:

*The Anglo-Saxon of the great herd is, in many important respects, the least civilized of men and the least capable of true civilization. His political ideas are crude and shallow. He is almost wholly devoid of aesthetic feeling; he does not even make folklore or walk in the woods. The most elementary facts about the visible universe alarm him, and incite him to put them down.*

Mencken reserved his deepest scorn for the "ordinary Class I Babbitt," the flower of the American "booboisie." In one of his annual volumes of *Prejudices,* which he began publishing in 1919, he asked of himself: "If you find so much that is unworthy of reverence in the United States, then why do you live here?" He replied with another question, "Why do men go to zoos?"

Readers eventually grew fatigued with Mencken, but as late as 1927 Walter Lippmann thought him to have been "the most powerful personal influence on this whole generation of educated people." That his influence was in fact good rather than bad, and deliberately so, Mencken himself acknowledged when he dropped his mask of cynicism and revealed himself a moralist:

*The liberation of the human mind [he once wrote] has best been furthered by gay fellows who heaved dead cats into sanctuaries and then went roistering down the highways of the world proving to all men that doubt, after all, was safe—that the god in the sanctuary was a fraud. One horse-laugh is worth ten thousand syllogisms.*

Mencken's *American Mercury,* moreover, was among the first to welcome with hosannas the most lasting "new" writers of the twenties—the O'Neills, Sinclair Lewises, Hemingways, F. Scott Fitzgeralds—and to force conservative critics to accept their work as that of the much sought voice of America.

### The Harlem renaissance

Some of the cultural influences that accounted for the insurgency of the white intelligentsia in the twenties affected their black counterparts as well. And just as Greenwich Village became the Mecca for white iconoclasts from the hinterlands, so Harlem—that part of northern Manhattan formerly occupied by the Dutch, the Irish, and the Jews—in the words of the black artist and scholar James Weldon Johnson (1871-1938), drew "the sightseer, the pleasure seeker, the curious, the adventurous, the enterprising, the ambitious, and the talented of the entire Negro world."

690

Like the young white rebels, Harlem intellectuals and artists, in large part the children of middle-class parents, rejected many of the values and standards of their seniors. Alain Locke (1886-1954), himself a writer and teacher who spoke for the "New Negro," described the emerging generation of artists in the midtwenties as "the 'race radicals' and realists who have broken with the old epoch of philanthropic guidance, sentimental appeal and protest."

The older generation of cultural leaders, Du Bois's "Talented Tenth," had been so fearful of reinforcing white stereotypes about blacks that they did little justice to the artistic resources of Negro folk forms. Staunchly assimilationist, they espoused a gentility similar to that of the white cultural custodians Menc-

*Louis Armstrong.*

ken lampooned. It is no wonder that the more conservative among them frowned upon the poets, novelists, musicians, and entertainers who, with no "by your leave," celebrated black vitality and substituted anger and irony for the old strategy of humility or imitation. Not even Du Bois's qualified opposition to the Harlem "primitivists" deterred black artists from preferring without apology the Negro vernacular, the blues of Bessie Smith, the hot trumpet of Louis Armstrong, the soft-shoe shuffling of Bojangles Bill Robinson. The Harlem artists were encouraged by their white friends who themselves were discovering the freshness and variety of black culture, but the real force behind the renaissance was the Negro's affirmation of his distinctive Americanism. According to James Weldon Johnson, the black artist wanted to show that the Afro-American had much that he could contribute as well as receive, "that his gifts have been not only obvious and material, but also spiritual and aesthetic; that he is a contributor to the nation's common cultural store."

Of the scores of talented men and women who gave Harlem its unusual distinction in the twenties, certain names stand out. One was the Jamaican Claude McKay (1890-1948), a gifted poet and prose writer and an early leader in the Harlem movement. McKay dramatized in his life and work the New Negro's rebellion against bourgeois inhibitions. Cosmopolitan, Marxist, idealist, and realist, his serious treatment of primitivism and his militant protest against exploitative capitalism and racial bigotry linked him with both the white literary experimentalists and the radical publicists of the postwar decade.

Sterling Brown (born in 1901), who was himself a strikingly original and powerful poet, argued that Negro poets like Langston Hughes (1902-1967)—

Black and white,
Gold and Brown—
Chocolate-custard
Pie of town.

Dream within a dream
Our dream deferred.
Good morning, daddy!
Ain't you heard?

and Countee Cullen (1903-1946)—

*...I doubt not God is good, well-meaning, kind...*
*Yet do I marvel at this curious thing:*
*To make a poet black, and bid him sing!*

reflected more of the Harlem spirit than black novelists. But perhaps one of the most brilliant single achievements of the renaissance was Jean Toomer's (1894-1967) novel *Cane,* a series of poetically delineated black portraits that ranged over hitherto unexplored parts of Negro life.

Not all black writers took kindly to the antiassimilationist proclamations of the New Negroes; but Langston Hughes saw their antagonism as expressions of a desire "to pour racial individuality into the mold of American standardization, and to be as little Negro and as much American as possible."

*We younger Negro artists [he asserted] who create now intend to express our individual dark-skinned selves without fear or shame. If white people are pleased we are glad. If they are not, it doesn't matter. We know we are beautiful. And ugly too. The tom-tom cries and the tom-tom laughs. If colored people are pleased we are glad. If they are not, their displeasure doesn't matter either. We build our temples for tomorrow, strong as we know how, and we stand on the top of the mountain, free within ourselves.*

### Bolshevism and alternatives

If World War I shook the faith of so many intellectuals in American society and American values, the October Revolution in Russia suggested to some that redemption might yet be possible and the grounds on which to seek it. Among the hopeful were old bohemians like Max Eastman, Joseph Freeman, Michael Gold, and Floyd Dell, who now repudiated their carefree past. The Russian experience, Dell declared,

*showed us that "freedom" is a bourgeois myth. It would set up in place of "freedom" certain definite*

*and realizable goals, of a not unfamiliar sort, and it would teach us that these are to be achieved by organizing social activities involving all of the customary personal virtues, including such dull matters as honesty, sobriety, responsibility, and even a sense of duty. . . . [It] would offer us the possibility, in the nature at present of a religious hope, of shaping the whole world nearer to the heart's desire.*

Dell and company made few converts in the United States before the Great Crash of 1929 drove many expatriates back from Europe broke and the Great Depression of the thirties convinced them that capitalism was as bankrupt as themselves. Those among the lost generation of the twenties, in Greenwich Village as in Paris, who deigned at least to take a look at the Soviet Union usually came away with the suspicion that as an alternative to American materialism Bolshevism was simply another Babbitt society in the making, or something worse. "We know at least that we have discovered the trick which has been played on us," wrote Joseph Wood Krutch, "and that whatever else we may be we are no longer dupes."

There remained still a third choice—one closely embraced by those as cold as Krutch to religion yet less willing to abdicate to nature's indifference to man. Their opening manifesto was a fat book of close to 600 pages edited by Harold E. Stearns and published in 1922, *Civilization in the United States, An Inquiry by Thirty Americans.* "We wished to speak the truth about American civilization as we saw it," wrote Stearns, "in order to do our share in making a real civilization possible."

The truth as they saw it and spoke it proved more damning than Mencken's diatribes: The theater, according to contributor George Jean Nathan, was "at once the richest theater in the world and the poorest. Financially it reaches to the stars; culturally . . . it reaches to the drains." "The chronic state of our literature," Van Wyck Brooks said now, "is that of a youthful promise which is never redeemed. . . . For half a century the American writer as a type has gone down in defeat." The universities, said Professor Joel Spingarn, seemed to have been created "for the special purpose of ignoring or destroying scholarship." The American husband, Alfred Kuttner found, "becomes everything in his business and nothing in his home. . . . The wife, on her part, either becomes hysterical or falls victim of religious reformatory charlatanism." The corrective lay deeper than Marx's dialectic: "There must be an entirely new deal of the cards in one sense," wrote Stearns; "we must change our hearts."

Two other important books, published at the beginning and the end of the twenties—Thorstein Veblen's *Absentee Ownership* (1923) and Robert S. and Helen M. Lynd's *Middletown* (1929)—seemed to corroborate these conclusions without the charge to do better.

## III   The lively arts

### The bogus bared

Few Americans of any class read Stearns, Veblen, or even the Lynds during the twenties; their bludgeoning of American culture made few dents on their targets. A broader disenchantment with the mainstream of American business culture was implicit in the welcome given even by certain highbrows to the lowbrow, or the "lively," arts. No one took them more seriously, and contemporary fine art more skeptically, than Gilbert Seldes, Harvard '14, who in 1924 identified the new creative fields and gave them standing in his popular book *The Seven Lively Arts*. What were the "seven" Seldes found? Actually, his title was a catch phrase, numerically inexact. TV, except experimentally, lay in the future. Besides the movies and radio, Seldes emphasized popular music and the dance, the musical theater, the newspaper comic strip.

"Bogus is counterfeit," Seldes wrote, "and counterfeit is bad money, . . . and unless it is discovered, bad money will drive out good. . . . The existence of the bogus is not a serious threat against the great arts, for they have an obstinate vitality and in the end—but only in the end—they prevail. It is the lively arts which are continually jeopardized by the bogus, and it is for their sake that I should like to see the bogus go sullenly down to oblivion." To speed it on, Seldes issued this "manifesto" in his book:

*If there were an Academy I should nail upon its doors the following beliefs:*

*That Al Jolson is more interesting to the intelligent mind than John Barrymore and Fanny Brice than Ethel;*

*That Ring Lardner and Mr. Dooley in their best work are more entertaining and more important than James B. Cabell and Joseph Hergesheimer in their best;*

*That the daily comic strip of George Herriman [Krazy Kat] is easily the most amusing and fantastic and satisfactory work of art produced in America today;*

*That Florenz Ziegfeld is a better producer than David Belasco;*

*That one film by Mack Sennett or Charlie Chaplin is worth the entire* oeuvre *of Cecil de Mille;*

*That Alexander's Ragtime Band and I Love a Piano are musically and emotionally sounder pieces of work than Indian Love Lyrics and The Rosary;*

*That the circus can be and often is more artistic than the Metropolitan Opera House in New York;*

*That Irene Castle is worth all the pseudo-classic dancing ever seen on the American stage; and*

*That the civic masque is not perceptibly superior to the Elks' Parade in Atlantic City.*

"All of these comparisons," Seldes wrote later, "were made, obviously, for purposes of shock. In that, they apparently succeeded."

### The movies

As it happened, the liveliest of the lively arts of the twenties, the movies, were also the most highly mechanized, the most highly capitalized, the one closest to big business in production and distribution methods. Like the programs of their later rivals, radio and TV, movies were mass produced for mass audiences and already alarmed many about the mass conditioning of the mass mind. Others, however, saw the mechanized movies, as they saw the other lively arts, as another broad avenue of escape from the horse-and-buggy sentimentalism of the cultural life. In the twenties, among movies themselves, the bogus was already being separated from the genuine.

The movies began as a humble peep show in a penny arcade. The viewer put a nickel in a device called a kinetoscope (invented by Thomas A. Edison about 1896) and saw tiny figures moving against blurred backgrounds. Edison, regarding his invention as little more than a child's toy, quickly lost interest in it, but others took it up and soon succeeded in projecting images on a screen for the benefit of large audiences. By 1905, more than 5000 "nickelodeons," housed in converted stores and warehouses, were showing rudimentary films for 5-cents admission.

Peep shows had prospered by showing short, presumably comic action—such as a man sneezing. The new films, some a thousand feet long, introduced a multitude of frenetic inventions. There were endless variations on the chase: cowboys after rustlers; sheriffs after badmen; city cops after bank robbers. Comedians threw custard pie at one another, slipped on banana peels, fell into manholes. The first movie with a recognizable plot was *The Great Train Robbery* (1903), and its instant success set every producer to turning out thrillers. But there were still no stars, no sex, no culture.

It was David W. Griffith who liberated the movie camera from nickelodeon themes and the limitations of the stage set. In *The Birth of a Nation* (1914), a partisan and intolerant film about the Civil War and Reconstruction, Griffith showed sweeping panoramas of massed armies, fade-outs, close-ups of the principals, and other shots revealing the scope and flexibility of camera and screen. Budgeted at an unheard-of $100,000 and directed with imagination, *The Birth of a Nation* proved a financial and artistic prototype.

By 1917 the movies had become a multimillion-dollar industry, with Hollywood, California, the film capital. Luxurious movie theatres rapidly replaced the nickelodeons, and Americans were spending $175 million a year on admissions. The first stars—Mary Pickford, Roscoe ("Fatty") Arbuckle, Douglas Fairbanks, Marie Dressler—earned fabulous salaries, lived glamorous lives, and attracted incredible newspaper and magazine attention, much of it promoted by movie press agents to keep the stars in the public eye. The stars themselves sometimes cooperated only too well. In 1920, "America's Sweetheart," Mary Pickford, shocked her fans by divorcing the actor Owen Moore and promptly marrying the dashing Douglas Fairbanks. The next year, "Fatty" Arbuckle gave a fabulous party in a San Francisco hotel at which one of the feminine guests died under suspicious circumstances. The press immediately leapt on the tragedy as a "sex crime." Arbuckle himself was implicated, and though he was acquitted after several trials, his career was ruined.

Such incidents only heightened Hollywood's reputation as a Sodom from which unspeakable vice was spread by movies with titles like *Sinners in Silk* and *Women Who Give*. These films promised considerably more than they gave, but moralists worried about their effect on youth and agitated for official censorship. To forestall their critics by regulating their own affairs, film producers in 1922 hired Will H. Hays, former chairman of the Republican National Committee and Harding's Postmaster General, to act as their conscience. Hays devised a production code setting limitations on lovemaking, décolletage, crime, and profanity.

While sex, or at least the promise of sex, was not easily suppressed by the Hays office and its successors, the industry's ambivalent attitude toward it turned producers to other types of pictures, especially grand spectacles

693

694

in the Griffith vein to exploit the mechanical possibilities of the camera. The most successful of Griffith's imitators was Cecil de Mille, but his grandiose religious concoctions—*The Ten Commandments, The Flood, The King of Kings*—only offended those who had high hopes for the movies as a new art form.

Besides sex and spectacles, slapstick comedy quickly became a movie staple featuring such stars as Arbuckle, Harold Lloyd, and Buster Keaton. The greatest comic of all, Charlie Chaplin, gave movies their standing with the intellectuals. Edmund Wilson, in *The New Republic* in September 1925, reviewed Chaplin in *The Gold Rush:*

> The one performer of Hollywood who has succeeded in doing anything distinguished with this primitive machinery of gags is, of course, Charlie Chaplin. . . . Instead of the stereotyped humor of even the best of his competitors, most of whose tricks could be interchanged among them without anyone's knowing the difference, he gives us jokes that, however crude, have an unmistakable quality of personal fancy.

Wilson added that along with such earlier Chaplin hits as *The Kid* and *The Pilgrim,*

> with their gags and their overtones of tragedy, their adventures half-absurd, half-realistic, their mythical hero, now a figure of poetry, now a type out of the comic strips, [The Gold Rush] represents the height of Chaplin's achievement. He could scarcely, in any field, surpass the best moments of these pictures.

Wilson also found exhilaration in another aspect of the movies, the enlightening, not the "conditioning," one. "The film about Evolution which was shown in New York last summer," he wrote in November 1925, "reminded one of the great possibilities of the cinema for scientific exposition. . . . If the picture could only, I thought, be shown in Dayton, Tennessee, the inhabitants of that backward region might be shaken in their literal faith in the account of creation in Genesis."

### Ragtime and jazz

What the film projector did for motion, the phonograph, another Edison inven-

Guy Gillette

*Chaplin.*

tion, did for sound. The effort to record and reproduce the human voice and musical performances went far back into the nineteenth century. Edison became interested in the problem in the 1870s in order to develop a labor-saving device for use in conjunction with the telegraph. The best telegraph operators could send perhaps forty words a minute, a rate less than half as fast as men normally talked. Edison sought a machine that could take down message after message and then transmit each at a hundred or more words a minute. He took out his first patent on such a machine in 1877 and thereafter, with others, worked out the enormous improvement that led to the process of cutting master disks, reproducing masses of identical records from them, and spinning them on turntables where their sound would be animated by a needle and sent forth through a horn. By 1905 the phonograph had become a successful commercial device by which comedians and actors, and leading singers and musicians in opera and on the stage, could be heard in the home or in places of public entertainment. By 1914 more than half a million phonographs were being manufactured each year, and soon the figure verged on a million.

Before radio the phonograph gave the greatest impetus to the spread of popular music, much of it ragtime and jazz, which the devotees of the lively arts in the twenties hastened to differentiate from the pseudo-Viennese sentimentality of composers like Victor Herbert. "Ragtime," Seldes wrote in *The Seven Lively Arts,* "is not, strictly speaking, time at all." While its composers required syncopation at precisely the right moment and employed other technical devices, the main thing was that their music "has torn to rags the sentimentality of the songs which preceded it." The first great name in ragtime was Irving Berlin, who wrote "Alexander's Ragtime Band," "simple and passionate and utterly unsentimental," thought Seldes in 1924. Then came the characteristic accolade:

*What makes the first rag period important was its intense gaiety, its naïveté, its tireless curiosity about itself, its unconscious destruction of the old ballad form and the patter song. The music drove ahead; . . . led to fresh accents. . . . For half a century syncopation had existed in America, anticipating the moment when the national spirit should find in it its perfect expression; for that half century serious musicians had neglected it; they were to study it a decade later when ragtime had revealed it to them.*

The aspirations of the new musicians are revealed most dramatically in the work of George Gershwin, who made the first and perhaps most successful efforts to write serious music in the ragtime idiom. The New York Symphony Society played Gershwin's Piano Concerto in 1926, the same year in

which Paul Whiteman's band presented Gershwin's opera *135th Street* in Carnegie Hall. Gershwin had written it three years before for George White's *Scandals.* Edmund Wilson, reviewing these events, found the Whiteman band "very fastidious and elegant, and stamped with the ideal of perfection."

Jazz presented a different problem to the critics of the lively arts who, for a long time, remained outside the Negro world, or at least the southern world, from which it sprang. Jazz spread northward, especially to Chicago's South Side and New York's Harlem, only with the accelerated wartime and postwar migration of blacks to the great cities above the Mason-Dixon line. The first dixieland "jass" bands (as it was spelled) played in these cities around 1915, the year W. C. Handy wrote his epochal "St. Louis Blues." In 1922 F. Scott Fitzgerald, already a precocious celebrity, published *Tales of the Jazz Age,* and thereafter (though not necessarily through cause and effect) Harlem in particular became the resort of "fast" young New York socialites prowling for exotic thrills. Not until midway in the decade did jazz strike Seldes and his friends:

*The fact that jazz is our current mode of expression, has reference to our time and the way we think and talk, is interesting; but if jazz music weren't itself good the subject would be more suitable for a sociologist than an admirer of the gay arts. . . . If—before we have produced something better—we give up jazz we shall be sacrificing nearly all there is of gaiety and liveliness and rhythmic power in our lives. Jazz, for us, isn't a last feverish excitement, a spasm of energy before death. It is the normal development of our resources, the expected, the wonderful, arrival of America at a point of creative intensity.*

Thereafter, those who could not get to Harlem obtained jazz phonograph records, and the virtuosos of trumpet, trombone, clarinet, piano, and percussion became as well known to enthusiasts as Caruso to opera lovers and Babe Ruth to baseball fans.

### Radio broadcasting

Unlike the movies, whose commercial possibilities were exploited from the first, the early development of radio was haphazard and accidental. In 1920 perhaps 20,000 amateur "hams" listened on homemade sets to wireless messages, sent mainly from ships at sea. That year, as an experiment, the Westinghouse Electric and Manufacturing Company in Pittsburgh began to broadcast musical programs. Amateurs in the area responded enthusiastically, and soon popular demand induced Westinghouse to put the programs on a regular basis and to introduce reports of baseball scores. A Pittsburgh department store began to advertise radio sets, and in 1920 the first commercial broadcasting station, KDKA, was set up in Pittsburgh to broadcast the results of the Harding-Cox election.

KDKA was an enormous success; overnight, radio too became big business. Within four years, 562 stations were sending out music, stock-market and news reports, bedtime stories, church services, and ringside accounts of prizefights. By 1930, more than 12 million American families had radios; by 1940, more than 28 million. By then 765 radio stations covered the country, approximately a fourth of them controlled by newspapers or newspaper chains bent on dominating competitive news outlets. Now that Americans could listen to nominating conventions and campaign speeches in their homes, interest in politics grew. Millions followed the Smith-Hoover campaign in 1928 by radio, and millions more followed the dramatic developments of the New Deal era by listening to Franklin D. Roosevelt's radio "fireside chats."

As a news medium, radio continued to perform a genuine service. Although it gave fewer details than newspapers, it got those details to the public more swiftly and, under supervision of the Federal Communications Commission after 1937, often more fairly.

Once established as a national habit, radio listening became the object of intensive study by two groups—the advertisers, who paid for most of the entertainment, and the critics of popular culture concerned about its quality. As a selling medium, radio seemed unsurpassed. The advertiser could reach into the homes of millions and repeat his message hour after hour. Most people, surveys showed, tended to accept "commercials" as the price of free radio entertainment. Even illiterates were corralled for the advertiser's message, while the siren sound captured the more sophisticated as well.

Radio's first step toward cultural prestige, taken in the midtwenties, was the weekly nationwide broadcast from the Metropolitan Opera House in New York. Symphony concerts soon followed, under such eminent conductors as Stokowski and Toscanini. From time to time, experimental poetry and drama also were broadcast. Yet, it was time more than talent that radio had to sell; every minute had to be put to productive use. The demand for programs put a tremendous strain on the creative community whose work soon became stereotyped. One of the first victims was popular music itself, sadly corrupted by the specialists of Tin Pan Alley in New York who made a business of supplying radio tunes, as one critic said, "about as fast as manufacturers could roll out cars or lipsticks." The climax of stereotyping came with the "soap opera"—according to Seldes, "the great invention of radio, its single notable contribution to the art of fiction."

Seldes soon looked to radio to reverse the tendency toward the bogus already too apparent in de Mille–type movies. "Ignorant and unhappy People," he wrote in an open letter to the movie magnates in 1924, "a voice is heard in the land saying your day is over. The name of the voice is Radio. . . . It is easier to listen than to read. And it is long since you have given us anything significant to see." Seldes advised them to unearth "a mechanical genius to explain the camera and the projector to you" so as to retrieve the quality of "the pictures of 1910, . . . the way to the real right thing." Instead, the movies went the radio one better, bringing in the talking picture, perfected between 1926 and 1929.

### Lively arts on the stage

The fragility of the lively arts is evident in the constant fears of cannibalism among its nervous practitioners. If radio was going to eat up the movies, the talking pictures were promptly looked upon as carnivores preying on the "legitimate theater." "The Legitimate Theater, usually known as Broadway," wrote Lloyd Lewis in the *New Republic* in March 1929, "is in a panic today, with many of its temples dark and many of its priests and vestals rushing about the streets of the walled city, crying out that the movie vandals are at the gates of the citadel at last, . . . armed with new electrical catapults and strange talking devices." For once, the jeremiads had some justification. Talking pictures propelled the movies to their commercial peak even during the depression years of the thirties. Hollywood, moreover, dangled immense pecuniary lures before the eyes of dramatists, novelists, composers, and actors, and even the most serious succumbed. At the same time, vaudeville and musical revues, the liveliest of the theater's attractions, at least to the admirers of the lively arts, declined.

Seldes called vaudeville "the most immediate of the minor arts," and while he recognized its long history in the United States, "nothing I have heard," he writes in *The Seven Lively Arts*,

leads me to believe that there were better days in vaudeville than those which open benignant and wide over Joe Cook and Fanny Brice and the Six Brown Brothers, over the two Briants and Van and Schenck and the four Marxes and the Rath Brothers and the team of Williams and Wolfus; over Duffy and Sweeney and Johnny Dooley and Harry Watson, Jr., as Young Kid Battling Dugan, and Messrs. Moss and Frye, who ask how high is up.

Most of these luminaries mean nothing to today's readers. What critics like Seldes especially admired in vaudeville made the success of its performers fleeting. This was "the refinement of technique":

I am sure that the vaudeville stage makes such demands upon its artists that they are compelled to perfect everything. . . . The materials they use are trivial, yes; but the treatment must be accurate to the hair's breadth; the wine they serve is light, it must fill the goblet to the very brim, and not a drop must spill over.

"It is, of course, obvious," Seldes concludes, "that the responsibility in this case is exactly that of the major arts."

The revue became a staple of the Broadway stage as early as 1907, when Florenz Ziegfeld produced the first of his *Follies*, lavish "girlie"

*The Ziegfeld Follies line.*

shows spiced with the humor of such vintage stars as Will Rogers, Ed Wynn, and W. C. Fields, the trick dancing of Leon Errol, the chanting of Eddie Cantor. Almost annual editions followed, and by 1923 Edmund Wilson was acclaiming the *Follies* as "a permanent institution" on which "comments . . . are always in order." Within five years the *Follies* were challenged by George White's *Scandals* and Earl Carroll's *Vanities,* and within ten years all had passed on.

Wilson's "comments" contained the usual reservations of the admirers of the lively arts:

*In general, Ziegfeld's girls have not only the Anglo-Saxon straightness—straight back, straight brows, and straight noses—but also the peculiar frigidity and purity, the frank high-school girlishness which Americans like. . . . He tries, furthermore, to represent, in the maneuvers of his well-trained choruses, not the movement and abandon of emotion, but what the American male regards as beautiful: the efficiency of mechanical movement. The ballet at the Ziegfeld Follies is becoming more and more like military drill; . . . it is too much like watching setting-up exercises.*

But there was the capitulation as well:

*Yet there is still something wonderful about the Follies. . . . Among these green peacocks and gilded panels . . . there is realized a glittering vision which rises straight out of the soul of New York. The Follies is such fantasy, such harlequinade as the busy well-to-do New Yorker has been able to make of his life. . . . As I say, there is a splendor about the Follies. It has, in its way, both distinction and intensity.*

### Comic strips

In the midtwenties no fewer than 20 million readers followed the fates of their favorites among the characters of the daily newspaper comic strips. During the depression the comics were the one feature which financially pressed publishers would not curtail or cut out. More people, according to polls then popular, bought newspapers for the comics than for any other reason, and their best creators earned $1000 to $1500 weekly.

The comics, like other lively arts, had a long history in America going back at least to 1889.

The first comics might be called one-shots: neither their characters nor their themes were continued from day to day. "The Katzenjammer Kids," which appeared Sundays in the *New York Journal* beginning in 1894, was the first strip with regular characters. Ten years later some dailies began to publish strips two or three times a week. The first six-day strip was H. C. ("Bud") Fisher's "A. Mutt"—later "Mutt and Jeff"—published in the *San Francisco Chronicle* starting in November 1907. The very names of some of these early comics made permanent contributions to the American vernacular: "Let George Do It," the work of George McManus, was one. Others included "Happy Hooligan," "Hairbreadth Harry," and "Bringing Up Father," another McManus creation starting in 1912. The lasting favorite with the critics of the lively arts, George Herriman's "Krazy Kat," first appeared in 1911.

"Of all the lively arts," Seldes writes, "the Comic Strip is the most despised." One reason for this was its early commercialization. Like the songsmiths of Tin Pan Alley, according to the president of the National Association of Newspaper Circulation Managers in 1906, "even the originators and leaders have found themselves pumped well-nigh dry of ideas in the struggle to keep up the constant output." It was not long, moreover, before professional protectors of children's minds such as the International Kindergarten Union and the League for the Improvement of the Children's Comic Supplement assaulted the fun and fantasy of the growing medium.

The admirers of the lively arts in the twenties could not have cared less. The comic strip, they believed, was essentially adult, not child, fare. "With those who hold that a comic strip cannot be a work of art I shall not traffic," Seldes declared. And warming again to his constant theme, he added:

*The qualities of Krazy Kat are irony and fantasy— exactly the same, it would appear, as distinguish The Revolt of the Angels; it is wholly beside the point to indicate a preference for the work of Anatole France, which is in the great line, in the major arts. It happens that in America irony and fantasy are practiced in the major arts by only one or two men, producing high-class trash; and Mr. Herriman, working in a despised*

*medium, without an atom of pretentiousness, is day after day producing something essentially fine. . . . In the second order of the world's art it is superbly first rate—and a delight!*

The comic strip soon proved a rich recourse to those in other arts—in vaudeville, revues, comedies, songs, and ballets—for characters and ideas.

## IV  Intellectuals turn left

### Writers in the Great Depression

Intellectual spokesmen for the lively arts in the twenties had kept their confidence in the masses despite the prevailing disenchantment of the postwar years. Once prosperity vanished, intellectual disenchantment seemed also to disappear and serious writers and others were drawn more closely once again to the common lot. Expatriates returning from Paris in 1930 and 1931 found the United States stirring with new impulses. Personal and aesthetic rebellion became transformed once more into social and political revolt. Writers thought less about criticizing their country, more about trying to save it. Business culture, formerly discredited for Babbittry and complacency, was now discountenanced for failure and futility.

In the election of 1932, a number of writers supported the Communist candidate, William Z. Foster. As Edmund Wilson put it, Foster was too uncomfortably susceptible to the "awful eye of the Third International" for most, but to some he seemed preferable to the major party candidates, who lacked "either moral force or intellectual integrity." Foster polled a mere 102,000 votes, yet this was the largest number ever received by a presidential candidate on the Communist party ticket. Besides Wilson, those who voted for Foster included John Dos Passos, Sherwood Anderson, Malcolm Cowley, and Waldo Frank. The New Deal drew some writers back from the far left, and after the Nazi-Soviet pact of 1939 (see

p. 741), fewer still remained in the communist camp. During the interval, the "left" writers made a considerable literary stir with important fiction, plays, and poems.

Communist party officials in the United States paid little attention to writers and regarded their work as of small importance to the movement, but Communist editors in the early thirties made serious overtures to them. The *New Masses,* founded in 1926, and lesser left-wing periodicals published the often crude work of literary unknowns. Young writers from lower-middle or laboring class families familiar with hobo "jungles," farm foreclosures, industrial strikes, and lynchings were encouraged to set down their experiences. Few "proletarian" works rated highly as literature, but there were powerful exceptions. Robert Cantwell's *Land of Plenty* (1934) gave a taut and exciting account of a strike in a wood veneer factory. Henry Roth's *Call It Sleep* (1935), a story of an immigrant childhood in New York's East Side, successfully evaded the heavy-handed editorializing that disfigured so much proletarian writing.

By far the most widely read depression novel was John Steinbeck's *The Grapes of Wrath* (1939), the chronicle of an Oklahoma farm family tractored off the land. Steinbeck's saga of the Okies' migration to California and the miseries of the fruit and vegetable pickers in the Salinas Valley showed people victimized by inexplicable economic forces yet worthy of pity and compassion. Although it was in no sense a Marxist work, the Left nevertheless hailed *The Grapes of Wrath* as the *Uncle Tom's Cabin* of the depression years.

As Steinbeck wrote of the rural poor, other novelists dealt with the depressed Irish, Poles, Negroes, and Jews of the cities. In his trilogy *Studs Lonigan* (1932–1935), James T. Farrell traced the lives of Chicago Irish who lacked moral focus despite Church ministrations, who smarted over their rejection by respectable Protestant society, and who fought a losing battle with alcoholism—all their problems deepened by the depression. A similar story was told of Chicago Poles in the fiction of Nelson Algren. Clifford Odets's play *Awake and Sing* dramatized the impact of the depression on a lower-middle-class Jewish family in the Bronx. The most despairing yet original depression novel was *Miss Lonelyhearts* (1933), Nathanael West's tragicomic portrayal of an urban wasteland where irremediable wrongs made life a perpetual horror.

The depression also marked the appearance of the first major black novelist, Richard Wright. His collection of short stories, *Uncle Tom's Children* (1938), and *Native Son* (1940) probed the depths of what Gunnar Myrdal was to call "the American dilemma" with a penetration hitherto unmatched in Negro fiction. Wright's childhood in Mississippi and his coming-of-age in Chicago—"huge, roaring, dirty, noisy, raw, stark, brutal"—enabled him to enter into the lives of the "dispossessed and disinherited." Marxism furnished him a philosophical system for ordering his ideas and impressions and for linking the fates of his characters with their racial past.

If Wright did not constitute a literary model for all of his younger friends and protégés, he became a kind of personal hero to them, and his recognition made the later careers of authors like Ralph Ellison and James Baldwin a little easier. His achievement, according to Ellison, was "in defining the human condition as seen from a specific Negro perspective at a given time in a given place."

*The New Deal and cultural nationalism*

When Adolph Hitler came to power in Germany in 1933, those Americans who had found Mussolini's Italian brand of fascism defensible seemed able for a time to live with the new Nazi version. Many intellectuals, on the Right as well as on the Left, however, grew alarmed at Nazi viciousness, especially since they feared for a time that such New Deal experiments as NRA might lead the United States along a similar totalitarian road. Most of them quickly changed their minds; and further totalitarian successes in the Spanish Civil War, which began in 1936 (see p. 739), turned more Americans to a reexamination of their own culture, where they found heretofore unappreciated virtues.

As the New Deal began to cope more effectively with the problems of the dispossessed, moreover, confidence in the recuperative powers of American society rose. Everything American took on a new interest and seemed worthy of reporting, recording, narrating, photographing, and understanding. Photographers from the Farm Security Administration, set up under the Farm Tenancy Act of 1937, went out to the American land to portray the people who worked on it in all their native plainness and dignity. Without a trace of Veblenism, the authors of the WPA guides went back to small-town history to write the first composite survey of the American states. Still other projects recovered American folklore and recorded white and black spirituals, Indian songs, folk tunes, and a mass of unknown music written by forgotten American composers. On post-office walls all over the country, WPA artists painted regional scenes and memorable local episodes. Americans who had never been theater- or concert-goers flocked to Federal Theater performances like that of Sinclair Lewis's play *It Can't Happen Here*, which in four months in 1936 reached an audience of 275,000. A black *Macbeth* played to 120,000 that year and T. S. Eliot's *Murder in the Cathedral* to 40,000. The Federal Theater charged no admission from those unable to pay and only small sums from others.

Among the most notable converts were the most caustic critics of bygone decades, led by a mellowed Van Wyck Brooks himself, whose work in the late thirties and after, culminating in his five-volume series on American writers, *Makers and Finders,* celebrated much that he once had found intolerable. Others followed Brooks. Lewis Mumford located indigenously American elements in native architecture. Archibald MacLeish castigated his fellow intellectuals for toying irresponsibly with their own disillusionment and infecting the young

with cynicism. John Dos Passos, abandoning his revolutionary views, savored the innocence and virtue of the early Republic in *The Ground We Stand On* (1941). And Charles and Mary Beard, whose *Rise of American Civilization* (1927) had provided radicals with historical ammunition for their assault on the ruling class, now in *The Republic* (1943) praised American political practices and warned against Old World wars and intrigues. Even H. L. Mencken settled down to pleasantly reminiscent autobiographical volumes— *Happy Days* (1940), *Newspaper Days* (1940), and *Heathen Days* (1943).

## V Literature: the major phase

*Dreiser, Anderson, Lewis*

The literary generation of the "lyric years" produced work of such power and maturity that they gained for American writing a firmer place in world literature than ever before. The literary generation that followed built well upon this foundation. In neither period, perhaps, did any single writer emerge of greater stature than Melville, Emerson, Hawthorne, Whitman, Mark Twain, or Henry James, but probably more good writing and more important books were produced in these years than in any comparable period in the nation's history. This was especially true of the novels of the postwar years—those of Anderson and Lewis, of Hemingway, Fitzgerald, and Dos Passos, of Wolfe and Faulkner—who shared many of the values and perspectives of the rebels we have examined but were not to be lured by protests, proclamations, and manifestos from the grand tradition.

These writers owed much to those of the recent past—Norris, Crane, and London, for example—and to *their* contemporary Theodore Dreiser, the "Hindenburg of the American novel," as Mencken called him, who continued to brood over the spectacle of man trying to cope with nature. Dreiser's most widely read novel, *An American Tragedy,* was

published as late as 1926, after which he wrote nothing of permanent value.

Dreiser's closest link with the postwar generation was through his friend Sherwood Anderson (1878-1941). For Anderson, the great evil had been the industrial revolution, which destroyed the community and poetry of the village and isolated man from man. "Time and again," Anderson wrote, "I had told the story of the American man crushed and puzzled by the age of the machine." The loneliness of Americans, he thought—the reaching out for human contact and finding none— produced the aberrations of behavior and outlook he described in *Winesburg, Ohio* (1919), in his best novel, *Poor White* (1920), and in stories like "The Egg." The procession of grotesques that moved through his tales—the drunkards, keyhole peepers, bedroom mutterers—had become twisted and deformed because their emotions found no outlet. As Anderson wrote of one of his *Winesburg, Ohio* characters, "The living force within could not find expression." Anderson's frankly confessional tone, his candor about hitherto unmentionable themes, broke the ice for Hemingway, Wolfe, Faulkner, and others.

Sinclair Lewis (1885-1951) was a midwesterner like Anderson, but his picture of village America was neither so tender nor so elegiac.

In fact Anderson resented Lewis's sardonic view of the small town, as presented in his first successful novel, *Main Street* (1920), which sold almost 400,000 copies in its first year. *Main Street's* setting, Gopher Prairie, with its "unsparing, unapologetic, ugliness," suggested to Anderson that Lewis had missed "the minor beauties" and interior history of the Midwest.

Certainly Lewis never probed very deeply into his characters' minds. His greatest single creation, George Folansbee Babbitt, coined a new word for the English language, but Lewis's long list of novels, which reproduce with varying success the business and professional life, the speech and customs, of middle-class America, seldom did more than crack the surface. Even his major characters seem less real than their possessions, and his minor characters often little more than caricatures.

Yet there was a certain appropriateness in Lewis's winning the Nobel Prize for literature in 1930—the first American writer to do so—for despite his superficiality he presented without apology or mitigation the prevailing brashness and vulgarity of his countrymen. Unlike many of his contemporaries, he did not find American life depressing. On the contrary, Americans were to him "one of the most amusing, exasperating, exciting, and completely mysterious peoples in the world." European readers, who saw him as an angry satirist of American materialism, mistook his real intentions. He could lash out at frauds and bigots with Menckenian gusto, but his castigations were directed at those who betrayed the true mission of the bourgeoisie.

Lewis's work deteriorated after the middle twenties, when he ended up parodying himself. But in *Main Street* (1920), *Babbitt* (1922), and *Elmer Gantry* (1927), Lewis was the red Indian "stalking through the land of his enemies," his inventiveness, sense of the ludicrous, and humanitarianism well blended.

### Fitzgerald and Hemingway

The death of F. Scott Fitzgerald in 1940 ended the career of a writer who twenty years before had attracted almost as much attention as the author of *Main Street*. One book, *This Side of Paradise,* published in 1920 when Fitzgerald was twenty-four, made him a celebrity overnight, the laureate of the glittering carnival world he told about next in *Tales of the Jazz Age* (1922) and *The Beautiful and the Damned* (1922).

Even during the "perpetual Maytime" of the twenties, however, Fitzgerald had sniffed the air of catastrophe:

*All of the stories that came into my head had a touch of disaster in them—the lovely young creatures in my novels went to ruin . . . my millionaires were as beautiful and damned as Thomas Hardy's peasants. In life these things hadn't happened yet, but I was pretty sure living wasn't the reckless, careless business these people thought—this generation younger than me.*

In his best novel, *The Great Gatsby* (1925), he managed to suggest simultaneously the glitter of American prosperity and the treacherous foundations on which it rested. Jay Gatsby,

*F. Scott Fitzgerald and Scotty in 1928.*

Culver Pictures, Inc.

the romantic bootlegger who believes every dream can be made real simply by wishing for it intensely enough, is betrayed by his gangster friends and by the privileged rich who "smashed up things and then retreated back into their money or their vast carelessness."

In his last books, *Tender Is the Night* (1934) and the unfinished *The Last Tycoon,* published in 1941 after his death, Fitzgerald wrote skillfully and movingly of the deterioration of that world whose advent he had announced with such bravado. "America's great promise," he asserted to a friend in the thirties, "is that something is going to happen, and after a while you get tired of waiting because nothing happens to people except that they grow old and nothing happens to American art because America is the story of the moon that never rose. . . . The fresh strong river of America! . . . America is so decadent that its brilliant children are damned almost before they are born."

Although Ernest Hemingway (1899–1961) survived Fitzgerald by more than two decades, his best work was also confined to the years before World War II. Soldier, expatriate, reporter, he had perfected his style by 1924, having learned everything he could from his mentors, Sherwood Anderson, Ezra Pound, and Gertrude Stein. His diction was largely monosyllabic, his sentence structure mechanical, yet his writing glittered all the same. A response to the world of wartime rhetoric and high-sounding abstractions, Hemingway's style (as the critic John Peale Bishop put it) "would record an American experience, and neither falsify the world without nor betray the world within."

From the outset, Hemingway wrote of violence and death, of sport and dissipation. *The Sun Also Rises* (1926) told of expatriates desperately amusing themselves in a postwar wasteland: drinking, boxing, watching bullfights, making love, all to no purpose. *A Farewell to Arms* (1929), the most famous of American war novels, was followed by *To Have and Have Not* (1937), a composite of

fishing trips, sex, machine guns, booze, and literary gossip, and *For Whom the Bell Tolls* (1940), based on the Spanish Civil War. Hemingway wrote of bullfighting in *Death in the Afternoon* (1932) and of big-game hunting in *The Green Hills of Africa* (1935).

In all these books and in his short stories (the best illustrations of his splendid talent), Hemingway celebrated his code of honor: to accept death, the great Nada or Nothingness, with dignity and fortitude. His weak characters cannot bear isolation; they break down, cling to each other, or dope themselves with illusions. The strong and the brave live with style to impose some kind of personal order on the confusion that is life. Hemingway lived and died according to this code.

### Dos Passos and Wolfe

John Dos Passos (1896–1970), a child of well-to-do parents, traveled abroad during his childhood, attended Harvard College between 1912 and 1916 (where he wrote rarefied poetry and prose), and drove an ambulance in World War I (where he met Hemingway). After the war, he traveled in Spain and the Near East and published two successful books— *Three Soldiers* (1921) and *Manhattan Transfer* (1925)—as well as sketches and plays. By the thirties he had completed his transformation from an aesthete who lamented the absence of nymphs and ghosts in America to a realist who incorporated the very rhythms of industry in his prose. Between 1927 and the Spanish Civil War, Dos Passos attached himself to the radical movement as an independent. He had thrown himself passionately into the defense of Sacco and Vanzetti and served on writers' committees investigating strikes. Disillusioned with communism in later years, Dos Passos became increasingly conservative.

Dos Passos's great achievement was his trilogy, *42nd Parallel* (1930), *1919* (1932), and *The Big Money* (1936), in which he tried—as he said of another novelist—"to put the acid test to existing institutions, to strip them of their veils." *U. S. A.*, the collective title of the trilogy, covers the years 1900 to 1930 and introduces a large number of characters representing every class and a variety of occupa-

704

tions. The people in *U. S. A.* are moving up and down the social scale, as in some social maelstrom. Punctuating Dos Passos's narrative are sharp snatches from newspaper headlines and popular songs; short acerbic biographies of representative historical figures; and private interior monologues of the author himself. *U. S. A.* is a massive indictment of America. Unlike orthodox Marxist novelists almost compulsively optimistic about the coming of a new society, Dos Passos saw no grounds for optimism. Social salvation appeared to him not only unlikely but undesirable as well.

Thomas Wolfe (1900–1938) drew on personal experience in his novels with even greater intensity than Hemingway or Dos Passos. A North Carolinian who came to New York to seek his literary fortunes, Wolfe told the story of his life in four huge volumes that totaled more than a million words even after extensive cutting by his devoted editor, Maxwell Perkins. As Wolfe wrote to F. Scott Fitzgerald, he belonged with the "putter-inners" rather than with the "taker-outers." In *Look Homeward, Angel* (1929), *Of Time and the River* (1935), *The Web and the Rock* (1939), and *You Can't Go Home Again* (1940), Wolfe "put in" his material with such unremitting force yet lyrical sensitivity that they remain monuments to his genuine talent and revealing evocations of the native scene he knew almost too well.

### Faulkner

William Faulkner (1897–1962) is ranked by many critics as the foremost American literary artist of the twentieth century, He continued to write after 1940, but his major works were published before that date.

A native of Mississippi who served in the Canadian Air Force during World War I, Faulkner first attracted attention with a bitter book about the aftermath of the war called *Soldiers Pay* (1926). *The Sound and the Fury* (1929), *As I Lay Dying* (1930), *Light in August* (1932), and other novels written in rapid succession established him as a major writer. Although the socially conscious critics of the thirties underrated him, as Faulkner went on to *Absalom! Absalom!* (1936), *The Unvanquished* (1939), and *The Hamlet* (1940), his reputation as an epic commentator on the mind and spirit of the South spread in America and Europe. The Nobel Prize in literature, which he received in 1949, was a belated recognition of his genius.

It is now clear that Faulkner's complicated narratives of Indians, Negroes, planters, townspeople, yeoman farmers, and poor whites who people his imaginary Yoknapatawpha County make up a social history of the Deep South. At the same time, the Yoknapatawpha saga is a private vision of ruin and decay, violence and terror, a chapter in man's tragic destiny. Faulkner's characters, whether they be aristocratic families or poor-white clans like the Snopeses, live in a land already doomed by the curse of slavery and the private exploitation of the wilderness. Their salvation, most succinctly and powerfully worked out in Faulkner's magnificent story "The Bear," lies only in reestablishing contact with natural forces (as represented by the bear, Old Ben, and the primeval) and passively enduring them.

## For further reading

Essential works by Krutch, Seldes, and others, cited in the text, are not repeated here. Good introductions to the literary history covered in this chapter will be found in works cited for Chapter Twenty-two. Henry May, *The End of American Innocence* (1959), is a comprehensive analysis of American culture between 1912 and 1917. Christopher Lasch, *The New Radicalism in America 1889-1963* (1965), traces the radical tradition in biographical portraits. The situation of intellectuals in the recent past is considered in Richard Hofstadter, *Anti-Intellectualism in American Life* (1963). The story of the "Little Renaissance" may be found in H. M. Jones, *The Bright Medusa* (1952); Floyd Dell, *Intellectual Vagabondage* (1926); and the early chapters of Joseph Freeman, *An American Testament* (1936). Daniel Aaron, *Writers on the Left* (1961), deals with the impact of radical ideas between 1912 and 1940. See also Malcolm Cowley, ed., *After the Genteel Tradition* (1936). A good history of avant-garde periodicals is F. J. Hoffman, Charles Allen, and C. F. Ulrich, *The Little Magazines* (1946).

The story of literary Bohemia is told in Albert Parry, *Garrets and Pretenders* (1933), and, out of personal experience, in Floyd Dell, *Love and Greenwich Village* (1926). Of relevant autobiographies, the following are among the best: Max Eastman, *Enjoyment of Living* (1948) and *Love and Revolution* (1965); Mabel Dodge Luhan, *Intimate Memories* (3 vols., 1936); and Floyd Dell, *Homecoming* (1933). Van Wyck Brooks, ed., *The History of a Literary Radical & Other Papers by Randolph Bourne* (1956), is indispensable. Also useful are Brooks, *Scenes and Portraits: Memories of Childhood and Youth* (1954) and *Days of the Phoenix: The Nineteen-Twenties I Remember* (1957).

Van Wyck Brooks, *John Sloan, A Painter's Life* (1955), is an excellent description of the Ashcan School. Especially recommended are Meyer Shapiro's brilliant essay, "Rebellion in Art," in Daniel Aaron, ed., *America In Crisis* (1952), and M. W. Brown, *The Story of the Armory Show* (1963). Helen Deutsch and Stella Hanau, *The Provincetown Players: A Story of the Theatre* (1931), is a good account of this experiment. For the story of the insurgent theater in the 1930s, see Harold Clurman, *The Fervent Years* (1957). The best life of O'Neill is Croswell Bowen, *The Curse of the Misbegotten* (1959).

Harry Hansen, *Midwest Portraits* (1923), is a personal reminiscence of the Chicago poets. See also Bernard Duffey's excellent study, *The Chicago Renaissance in American Letters* (1954). S. T. Coffman, *Imagism* (1951), deals with that poetic school. See also D. D. Paige, ed., *Ezra Pound, Letters 1907-1941* (1950).

Lewis Jacobs, *The Rise of the American Film* (1939), is a comprehensive history. Kevin Brownlow, *The Parade's Gone By* (1968), is rich in contemporary accounts and illustrations. Other works of critical interest include Kenneth Macgowen, *Behind the Screen* (1965),

and Andrew Sarris, *The American Cinema* (1968). D. M. White and R. Averson, *Sight, Sound, and Society* (1969), is an outstanding anthology on the impact of film and TV. Charles Siepmann, *Radio, Television, and Society* (1950), is useful. Sigmund Spaeth, *A History of Popular Music in America* (1948), is a general account. See also Winthrop Sargeant, *Jazz* (1946). James Weldon Johnson, *Black Manhattan* (1930), is a good introduction to the Harlem Renaissance. The social background is well presented in Gilbert Osofsky, *Harlem: . . . 1890–1930* (1966), with a valuable bibliography. Arna Bontemps, ed., *American Negro Poetry* (1963), is a rewarding anthology.

F. J. Hoffman, *The Twenties* (1955), is enlightening. For the thirties see Malcolm Cowley, *Exile's Return* (1951), an indispensable report, and his later *Think Back on Us, A Critical Chronicle of the Thirties* (1967). Selections from Mencken's writings are available in paperback editions. William Manchester, *Disturber of the Peace: The Life of H. L. Mencken* (1950), is informative. Particularly recommended as a guide to the twenties are Edmund Wilson's essays collected in *The Shores of Light* (1952) and in *The American Earthquake* (1958), which documents the thirties as well. For the literary history of the thirties see the previously cited Aaron, *Writers on the Left*; J. W. Beach, *American Fiction: 1920-1940* (1951); and Murray Kempton, *Part of Our Time: Some Monuments and Ruins of the Thirties* (1955). Harvey Swados, ed., *The American Writer and the Great Depression* (1966), and Daniel Aaron and Robert Bendiner, eds., *The Strenuous Decade* (1970), are good anthologies.

Irving Howe, *Sherwood Anderson* (1951), H. M. Jones, ed., *Anderson's Letters* (1953), and Anderson's entertaining but untrustworthy books, *A Story Teller's Story* (1924) and *Sherwood Anderson's Notebook* (1926), account for him. Mark Schorer, *Sinclair Lewis: An American Life* (1961), is the definitive biography. See also Vincent Sheean, *Dorothy and Red* (1970). F. Scott Fitzgerald, *The Crack-Up* (1945), is a compilation of letters and notes edited by Edmund Wilson. It should be read in conjunction with Andrew Turnbull, *Scott Fitzgerald* (1962), and Nancy Milford, *Zelda* (1970). C. H. Baker, *Hemingway, The Writer as Artist* (1956), C. A. Fenton, *The Apprenticeship of Ernest Hemingway* (1954), and Philip Young, *Ernest Hemingway* (1954), all provide useful biographical information as well as interpretation. *A Moveable Feast* (1964) is Hemingway's posthumously published memoir of his expatriate years. Thomas Wolfe, *Letters,* Elizabeth Nowell, ed. (1956), is a massive volume of self-revelation. The best introductions to Faulkner are Malcolm Cowley's long essay that prefaces *The Portable Faulkner* (1946) and Cleanth Brooks, *William Faulkner, The Yoknapatawpha County* (1963).

# THE NEW DEAL

By March 4, 1933, when Franklin D. Roosevelt took the oath of office as the thirty-second President of the United States, three and a half years had passed since the Great Crash of October 1929. Better than any array of the morbid statistics, Roosevelt, in his inaugural address, described the decline, the decay, the prostration of those years:

*Values have shrunken to fantastic levels; . . . the means of exchange are frozen in the currents of trade; the withered leaves of industrial enterprise lie on every side; farmers find no markets for their produce; the savings of many years in thousands of families are gone. More important, a host of unemployed citizens face the grim problem of existence, and an equally great number toil with little return. Only a foolish optimist can deny the dark realities of the moment.*

And yet, Roosevelt continued, "our distress comes from no failure of substance. We are stricken by no plague of locusts," but only by the mental and moral collapse of "the rulers of the exchange of mankind's goods," who "have admitted their failure and abdicated."

*The money changers have fled from their high seats in the temple of our civilization. We may now restore that temple to the ancient truths. The measure of the restoration lies in the extent to which we apply social values more noble than mere monetary profit.*

But "changes in ethics alone," obviously were not enough. "This Nation asks for action and action now. Our greatest primary task is to put people to work. . . . It can be accomplished in part by direct recruiting by the Government itself, treating the task as we would treat the emergency of a war." The new President continued:

*Action in this image and to this end is feasible under the form of government which we have inherited from our ancestors. Our Constitution is so simple and practical that it is possible always to meet extraordinary needs by changes in emphasis and arrangement without loss of essential form. . . . But it may be that an unprecedented demand and need for undelayed action may call for temporary departure from that normal balance . . . of executive and legislative authority. I am prepared under my constitutional duty to recommend the measures that a stricken nation in the midst of a stricken world may require. . . . In the event that*

*Congress shall fail to take [appropriate action], . . . I shall ask the Congress for the one remaining instrument to meet the crisis—broad Executive power to wage a war against the emergency, as great as the power that would be given me if we were in fact invaded by a foreign foe.*

Eleanor Roosevelt found the inaugural ceremony "very, very solemn and a little terrifying." It was especially terrifying "because when Franklin got to that part of his speech when he said it might become necessary for him to assume powers ordinarily granted in war time, he received his biggest demonstration."

## I   A bold experiment in government

*The new brooms*

Charming, self-assured, energetic, and fearless, FDR was the New Deal's greatest asset. Whatever may have lain hidden behind the famous Roosevelt smile, it was an extraordinarily effective instrument in private and public relations. The Roosevelt voice also was a fine political tool. "I loved that voice," exclaimed Mary McLeod Bethune, director of the influential Division of Negro Affairs under the New Deal's National Youth Administration; it made her feel, despite disappointments, that she could keep coming back to the man. In his radio "fireside chats," Roosevelt made the people feel that he was discuss-

ing the important national questions with them directly.

Roosevelt, Rexford G. Tugwell writes in his perceptive biography, "often covered a prayerful calculation with a pleasantry," and he chides historians who make too much of FDR's frequent flippant remarks as evidence of irresponsibility. Yet some Roosevelt pleasantries needed no prayer behind them to be effective. Less than two weeks after his inauguration, he remarked calmly after dinner at the White House, "I think this would be a good time for a beer." Three days later Congress repealed the Volstead Act and permitted the sale of beer and wine before the Eighteenth Amendment itself was repealed.

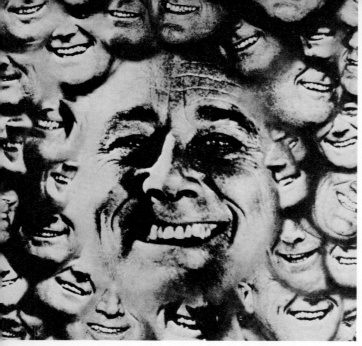

*Vanity Fair,* by permission of Condé Nast

**The Roosevelt victory smile.**

Though hardly a passionate person, Roosevelt was deeply moved by the plight of the destitute. Unlike Cleveland and Hoover, he believed that the underprivileged had a legitimate claim on the sympathies of the federal government. Many people during its early days spoke of the New Deal as an attempt at economic planning, but economic experimentation would be a more accurate description. No one knew of a single panacea, and Roosevelt's policies proved as varied as the men around him. These included veteran politicians such as Postmaster-General James A. Farley of New York, who had a card-index mind in which deserving and undeserving Democrats were sorted out; and Secretary of State Cordell Hull, a national legislator of many years service whose Tennessee background was reflected in his support of the traditional southern quest for lower tariffs and freer world trade. William H. Woodin, a conservative industrialist who enjoyed the confidence of businessmen, became Secretary of the Treasury. When Woodin resigned after giving yeoman service during the urgent bank crisis of 1933, he was succeeded by Henry

Morgenthau, Jr., an old friend of the President's.

The reform element was strongly represented in the Cabinet by the old "Bull Mooser," Harold L. Ickes of Illinois, who became Secretary of the Interior; Henry A. Wallace, the son of Harding's and Coolidge's Secretary of Agriculture, who now filled this post himself; and Frances Perkins, who had worked with Roosevelt in Albany and, as Secretary of Labor, became the first woman Cabinet member. Harry Hopkins, who emerged as perhaps the most influential of all Roosevelt's advisers, although not in the Cabinet until 1939, also had a strong reform bent. Even less formally related to the administration than Hopkins were the members of the "brain trust," notably Raymond Moley, A. A. Berle, Jr., and Tugwell, who in the early days stood perhaps closest to Roosevelt.

Hoover's approach to the problem of recovery had been largely the traditional one of allowing the deflation to run its course. The New Dealers, far less patient, experimented with currency inflation and with heavy government spending to "prime the pump" of business. Some of them hoped also to make the unprecedented crisis an occasion for reforms that far outstripped those of the Progressive movement. They began tentatively here, but when public pressure for change became apparent, led by the politically minded President they moved in a venturesome spirit.

### Rescuing the banks

One of the most dangerous developments of the long depression—the headlong plunge of the nation's banks toward bankruptcy—set the stage for one of the most electrifying New Deal steps. This came within a day or two of Roosevelt's inauguration and gave the public a welcome taste of the energetic new leadership.

By 1933 so many unsound banks had failed that even solvent institutions were menaced by frightened depositors rushing to withdraw their money. To stem the panic, the governors of almost half the states had declared "bank holidays," and by inauguration day, March 4, most of the banks in the country had closed. By proclamation on March 6, Roosevelt suspended all banking operations and gold transactions. Three days later, called into special session, Congress passed the Emergency Banking Act, which ratified the President's actions and established procedures for getting sound banks back in business. Roosevelt then went on the air with his first fireside chat, a brilliant effort in which he reassured the people on the soundness of the banking system that was about to emerge from the reorganization. To speed up the reorganization, the Reconstruction Finance Corporation (see p. 677) was ordered to advance funds where needed, and before the end of March most of the sound banks had reopened and the unsound ones were on the way to being permanently closed. Within another month, more than 12,000 banks, with 90 percent of the country's deposits, were functioning normally.

"In one week," wrote Walter Lippmann of the bank crisis, "the nation, which had lost confidence in everything and everybody, has regained confidence in the government and in itself." Roosevelt's spurning the more radical solution to which he could easily have turned—nationalizing the banks—quieted the suspicions even of many conservatives.

Bank reform followed on the heels of the banking crisis. One of the most salutary reform measures was the Glass-Steagall Act of June 1933, which created the Federal Deposit Insurance Corporation (FDIC) and authorized it to guarantee bank deposits up to $5000 per depositor, thereby making a repetition of the scares of 1932–1933 unlikely. Many banks had got into trouble by speculating in the stock market with depositors' funds through security affiliates. The Glass-Steagall Act forbade national banks to maintain such affiliates and prescribed other reforms to divorce commercial from investment banking. The simple sanity of this law did not prevent the

American Bankers Association from fighting it "to the last ditch," as its president said.

While on the subject of stocks and bonds, Congress in May 1933 passed the Securities Act, requiring greater publicity for the details of stock promotions and closing the mails to sellers failing to provide it. This measure was followed in June 1934 by the Securities Exchange Act creating the Securities and Exchange Commission (SEC), authorized to require the registration of all securities traded on the stock exchanges and to cooperate with the Federal Reserve Board in regulating the purchase of securities on margin. The Public Utility Holding Company Act of 1935 (see p. 719) gave the SEC supervisory powers over the management of holding companies. A number of other measures further enlarged the SEC's power to provide protection for the investor. The Banking Act of 1935, meanwhile, greatly increased federal authority over the banking system by empowering the Federal Reserve Board to regulate interest rates.

### Playing with money

Business recovery proved more elusive than banking reform. The New Deal tried many nostrums to stimulate industrial activity, most of them without success. One of its earliest expedients was to cheapen the dollar and thereby reduce the burden of fixed debts, which had become such a drag on expansion, and at the same time raise domestic prices to encourage output. Cheapening the dollar was also expected to stimulate exports by making the American medium of exchange more easily obtainable by those using foreign currencies. Roosevelt was skeptical of this device, but Congress, in May 1933, pressed by urgent demands from the western wing of the Democratic party for such nostalgic inflationary measures as the printing of greenbacks and the free coinage of silver, authorized the President to issue up to $3 billion in paper money with which to pay federal obligations and even redeem United States bonds. This measure also authorized him to reduce the gold content of the dollar by as much as 50 percent, provide for unlimited coinage of both gold and silver at a ratio that he could set, accept a limited amount of silver in debt payments from foreign governments, and issue silver certificates against bullion received.

In June, by a joint resolution, Congress took the further step of explicitly voiding all clauses in past or future contracts, government or private, requiring payment of obligations in gold, thereby taking the United States off the gold standard in effect since 1900. The constitutionality of this measure was upheld by the Supreme Court in the *Gold Clause cases* of 1935.

Although Congress had surrendered to the greenbackers and the silverites, the President used his new authorization with great caution. Even so, he promptly got into trouble with foreign governments whose representatives had assembled in mid-June at the London Economic Conference for the specific purpose of *stabilizing* world currencies so that importers and exporters might gain a clearer grasp of the profitability of their transactions. These governments counted on a stable dollar as the linchpin of any agreements they might make. But if the United States intended to indulge in manipulation of the value of the dollar with a free hand, the cause of renewed international trade and hence of international recovery was lost. On July 3 Roosevelt sent a radio message to the conference saying the United States would pursue its own course. This message wrecked the conference; but supporters of the New Deal defended the action on the grounds that the participating nations had themselves offered no concessions to compensate for the rigid dollar they wanted.

By October 1933 it had become clear to the administration that, while the powers granted to it by Congress were imprudently broad, Congress's resolution simply taking the dollar off the gold standard was ineffectually narrow. In a new effort to boost commodity prices by monetary manipulation, the Treasury was now ordered to purchase gold at rising dollar rates. Purchases of domestically mined gold began in October, and soon foreign gold was bought as well. But even this expedient was given up by the end of January 1934, when the President, by proclamation, fixed the dollar's gold content at 59.06 cents.

Subsequently, again contrary to its will, the administration was also forced by a ruthless bloc of western senators to launch upon an extraordinary silver-purchase program. It became clear that if the administration did nothing for silver the silver bloc would sabotage its entire legislative program. Under the terms of the Silver Purchase Act of June 19, 1934, the Treasury was obliged to buy the entire output of the domestic silver mines at an artificially high price. The immense subsidy to silver producers entailed by this act cost the government almost $1.5 billion in the next fifteen years. Secretary of the Treasury Henry Morgenthau admitted in 1935: "Our silver program is the only monetary fiscal policy that I cannot explain or justify." The net result of the whole monetary experiment was that, at some cost to the Treasury but with little benefit to the nation, an abnormally large portion of the world's bullion supply found its way to United States vaults.

## The NRA

Currency experiments implied that under favorable monetary conditions the ordinary market mechanisms of the economy might themselves push prices up. But the New Dealers were not alone in their awareness that the market mechanisms themselves needed artificial respiration and probably a permanent iron lung. To help the economy breathe once more, Congress, in June 1933, passed the National Industrial Recovery Act (NIRA). The President hailed it "as the most important and far-reaching legislation ever enacted by the American Congress." Its labor clauses prompted John L. Lewis, president of the United Mine Workers, to declare: "We are convinced that there has been no legal instrument comparable with it since President Lincoln's Emancipation Proclamation." In fact, the act's most far-reaching consequence was to disqualify all such Rube Goldbergs in the future.

The main intent of NIRA was not so much to expand the economy as to ration the nation's business among the surviving corporations consistently with Roosevelt's goal of stabilization "for all time." In this respect it had the support, and in some cases the sponsorship, of such big business men as Bernard Baruch, Gerard Swope, president of General Electric, and leaders of the United States Chamber of Commerce. Under its provisions the antitrust laws were, in effect, suspended, and trade associations and other business groups were permitted to draw up "codes of fair competition" which would include comprehensive price agreements, firm production quotas, and wage scales high enough significantly to improve the condition of the poorest-paid workers. Each type of business was empowered to draw up its own code. The government reserved the right to accept or reject the codes, to set up its own when companies in any industry failed to agree, and to enforce them. Section 7(a) of the NIRA guaranteed labor the right of collective bargaining. A National Recovery Administration (NRA) was formed to administer the codes under the chairmanship of the ebullient and profane General Hugh Johnson, a protégé of Baruch who had worked under him on the War Industries Board during World War I.

In order to make NRA comparable to mobilization for war, administrators organized parades and mass meetings. They adopted a placard with a Blue Eagle as a symbol to be awarded for display to businessmen and even to consumers who cooperated. One of their hoped-for effects was to stir up boycotts of recalcitrant firms, thereby substituting public pressure for legal enforcement. General Johnson blared forth in his characteristically grandiloquent war: "When every American housewife understands that the Blue Eagle on everything she permits to come into her home is a symbol of its restoration to security, may God have mercy on the man or group of men who attempt to trifle with this bird." Asked what would happen to those who did not cooperate, Johnson replied: "They'll get a sock on the nose." In fact, violators of the codes or

objectors like Henry Ford, who met code requirements but refused to sign up, were seldom prosecuted. NRA administrators may have anticipated that, put to the judicial test, the entire scheme would collapse.

No less than 746 NRA codes were adopted by businessmen eager to get started again. But friction soon retarded recovery. The paper work required to supply needed information to the government quickly reached fantastic proportions and was resented. Big corporations resisted all further signs of bureaucratic interference. Small firms, in turn, complained that the codes, drawn up by the larger firms in each industry, discriminated against the little fellows. Workers, who at first rallied to NRA, soon nicknamed it the "National Run Around." Code administrators, they said, characteristically sided with antiunion employers in labor disputes. Employers, on their part, detested the very existence of Section 7(a) and the expansion of organized labor it foretold. Moreover, insofar as the codes succeeded in reviving production by raising prices, they aroused consumer discontent.

NRA had reached a low point in popularity when the Supreme Court, in May 1935, killed it. In the case of *Schechter Poultry Corporation* v. *United States,* the Court unanimously found that the National Industrial Recovery Act was unconstitutional on two counts: first, that it improperly delegated legislative powers to the executive; and second, that the provisions of the poultry code constituted a regulation of intrastate, not interstate, commerce.

NRA had not been entirely in vain. For example, at the time the codes were adopted, some of the most exploited workers in the textile industry had been receiving wages as low as $5 a week. To such workers the cotton textile code, which prescribed minimum wages of $12 to $13 a week, was heaven-sent. As Arthur M. Schlesinger, Jr., has observed, NRA fostered many social reforms: It established the principle of maximum hours and minimum wages on a national basis. It reduced child labor. It made collective bargaining a national policy. Cancellation of the codes brought about in many instances a return to poor working conditions to which the labor movement soon addressed itself directly.

*The future of agriculture*

In the summer of 1932, Milo Reno of the Farmers' Holiday Association said:

> We have issued an ultimatum to the other groups of society. If you continue to confiscate our property and demand that we feed your stomachs and clothe your bodies, we will refuse to function. We don't ask people to make implements, cloth, or houses at the price of degradation, bankruptcy, dissolution, and despair.

In January 1933, before Roosevelt's inauguration, the normally conservative head of the Farm Bureau Federation, Edward A. O'Neal, told a Senate committee: "Unless something is done for the American farmer we will have revolution in the countryside within less than 12 months." Soon farmers began to take matters into their own hands. They forcibly halted eviction sales and mortgage foreclosures, and intimidated and assaulted public officials and agents of banks and insurance companies. Violence became so widespread in Iowa by April 1933 that the governor put several counties under martial law and called out the National Guard. "Americans are slow to understand," commented the *New York World-Telegram*, "that actual revolution already exists in the farm belt. . . . When the local revolt springs from old native stock, conservatives fighting for the right to hold their homesteads, there is the warning of a larger explosion."

The New Dealers were well aware of the need for prompt action, and when they took it they approached the farm problem in the same mood with which they approached the problems of industry. The farm plan was incorporated in the Agricultural Adjustment Act of May 1933, which established the Agricultural Adjustment Administration (AAA).

Abandoning all hope of regaining the lost foreign market for staples (see p. 669), AAA hoped to raise farm prices by cutting back production to domestic needs and rationing the domestic market among producers. In this way it planned to bring farm prices up to "parity" with those of the prosperous prewar years 1909–1914. Further to compensate farmers for cooperating with the government plan, AAA was authorized to pay various sorts of subsidies for acreage withdrawn from production and for certain marketing practices. Funds to finance the program were to come from taxes levied on the processors of farm products, such as millers, cotton ginners, and meat packers. At first, the act provided for crop reductions only in cotton, wheat, corn, hogs, rice, tobacco, and milk; later, other products were included.

To cut production when people were hungry was bound to invite criticism. But farm spokesmen insisted that if the profit system meant anything, the farmers had the same right to do this as businessmen. "Agriculture," said Secretary Wallace, "cannot survive in a capitalistic society as a philanthropic enterprise." To make matters worse, AAA did not begin to function until after the spring planting of 1933. To achieve its desired reduction in marketable staples that year, it was forced to supplement acreage restriction with orders to farmers to "plow under" a large part of their crops. With millions starving in the cities, AAA's action seemed heartless. It also fell short of its goal. Many farmers accepted government checks for reducing acreage and then calmly proceeded to cultivate their remaining acres more intensively. As a result, the net reduction in crops fell far short of what government planners had hoped for.

In 1934 Congress supplemented acreage restriction with production quotas and imposed taxes on violators. The new and old laws helped double and triple farm staple prices and brought about a dramatic rise in the total net income of farm operators from $1.8 billion in 1932 to $5 billion in 1936.

On January 6, 1936, in the Hoosac Mills case *(U.S. v. Butler et al.)*, the Supreme Court, in an even more stunning decision than the NRA ruling, found that AAA crop-control methods unconstitutionally invaded powers reserved to the states. They also found the processing tax not the general revenue measure it pretended to be but an illegal means "to take money from the processor and bestow it upon farmers [simply] to help farmers attain parity prices and purchasing power."

Following the Hoosac Mills decision, Congress passed the Soil Conservation and Domestic Allotment Act which put crop restriction on a sounder constitutional basis, with the avowed object now to increase soil fertility and conserve resources. AAA was authorized to pay farmers for adopting soil-conservation measures and for reducing acreage used for soil-depleting crops. Congressional appropriations instead of the outlawed processing tax

*Ben Shahn poster for the RA, 1937.*

Collection, The Museum of Modern Art, New York; gift of the designer

were to finance the new program. When prices tumbled again in 1937, Congress in February 1938 supplemented the Soil Conservation Act with a second Agricultural Adjustment Act. This law embodied Secretary Wallace's idea of the "ever-normal granary." The price fall in 1937 had come from bumper crops produced in response to the high prices of 1936. This new act aimed to keep such bumper crops off the market by compensating farmers for storing them until years of shortages made it possible to bring them on to the market without fear of undermining it. Large sums were paid to farmers under this measure, but staple growers did not really prosper until wartime demand in the 1940s again pushed crop prices up.

Of course, there were millions of farm families that gained nothing from commercial-farm legislation. As the depression wore on, concern for sharecroppers, farm tenants, and hired farm laborers grew. The New Deal's response in this area was the Resettlement Administration (RA), created in April 1935. Rural poverty was hard to ameliorate, but RA made a noble effort. It withdrew 9 million acres of virtual wasteland from cultivation, moved the families on them to resettlement areas, extended loans to farmers who could not obtain credit elsewhere, and encouraged cooperation among farmers who had always insisted on going it alone.

Late in 1936 Secretary Wallace reported on a trip he had taken through the South:

*I have never seen among the peasantry of Europe poverty so abject as that which exists in this favorable cotton year in the great cotton states from Arkansas to the East Coast. . . . I am tempted to say that one third of the farmers of the United States live under conditions which are so much worse than the peasantry of Europe that the city people of the United States should be thoroughly ashamed.*

In response to the report of a presidential committee on rural poverty, Congress in 1937 passed the Farm Tenancy Act to provide loans to sharecroppers, tenant farmers, and farm laborers for the purchase of land, livestock, supplies, and equipment. By June 1944, 870,000 rural families had been helped.

713

## The TVA

One of the poorest of all American farm areas was the Tennessee Valley; and nowhere was the indictment of American farm poverty more justifiable, for the valley was immensely rich in natural resources. Government projects to harness the mighty Tennessee River itself were begun at Muscle Shoals during World War I but were checked later, as we have seen, by the opposition of private power interests and vetoes of enabling legislation by Coolidge and Hoover. Roosevelt, as governor of New York in this era, by contrast, had fostered the idea of public power and had helped set up a state power authority.

In January 1933, after his election as President, Roosevelt visited Muscle Shoals in the company of experts and soon had a grand plan in view for the whole valley. This plan came to fruition when Congress, on May 18, 1933, created the Tennessee Valley Authority (TVA), and empowered it to buy, build, and operate dams in the valley, generate and sell electric power, plan reforestation and flood control, withdraw marginal lands from cultivation, and in general to further the well-being of the people.

Of all the New Deal experiments in government, TVA, an unprecedented independent public corporation national in scope, probably was the boldest and most original. Its area of responsibility embraced no less than 40,000 square miles in seven states. In this region, partly with the assistance of PWA (see p. 716), TVA built sixteen new dams and took over five others. The first of the new ones, the Norris Dam northwest of Knoxville, Tennessee, and justly named for the Nebraska Senator and tenacious public-power advocate, was completed in 1936. By 1940 four dams were generating electric power in the TVA region, and over 400,000 users, many of them farmers

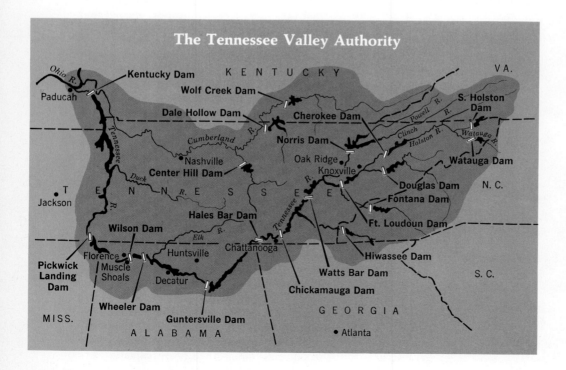

The Tennessee Valley Authority

with no previous access to electricity, were directly or indirectly served. TVA rates generally were low, and its "yardstick" forced private companies in the area also to keep rates down. Land redeemed by TVA from flooding was made productive for the first time. The attention of TVA awakened a new pride in the depressed people of the valley.

Like earlier valley plans, TVA was ceaselessly fought by the power companies. They, in turn, gained the support of many disinterested conservatives who saw in the experiment a threat to the system of private enterprise and rugged individualism. And like other New Deal measures, TVA was taken to court at an early opportunity. Unlike some other measures, it survived. In 1936, in *Ashwander* v. *Tennessee Valley Authority,* the Supreme Court ruled that at no point had the Authority exceeded constitutional powers. TVA became a pillar of strength in World War II.

The plan for a similar development in the Missouri Valley, the projected MVA, was never completed. Other New Deal hydroelectric projects—Grand Coulee and Bonneville Dams on the Columbia River, Hoover Dam on the Colorado, Fort Peck Dam on the upper Missouri—did not include TVA's broad social program nor its concern for conservation rather than careless exploitation of irreplaceable natural phenomena and resources.

### Work for the unemployed

When Roosevelt took office, at least 12 million workers were unemployed; with their families they added up to about 50 million persons, many of them on the verge of starvation. The New Deal's bold experiments in economic legislation only once, in 1937, managed to bring the number of unemployed below 8 million, and in 1940 it was back above that figure, at a level five times as high as in 1929.

Heretofore the government had held hands off the problem of the unemployed. Much as he helped coordinate private relief efforts,

Hoover subscribed to Cleveland's old dictum that it was the people's duty to support the government, not the government's duty to support the people. The writer Martha Gellhorn, touring the country in 1933, reported to Harry Hopkins on the unemployed: "I find them all in the same shape—fear, fear driving them into a state of semicollapse; cracking nerves; and an overpowering terror of the future . . . each family in its own miserable home going to pieces." But Hoover refused to "Prussianize" the poor, as he said, with public assistance.

The New Deal brought a new philosophy to the problem of relief just as it did to the problem of recovery. In 1933 the issue was no longer whether the federal government should act—this question had been settled by the 1932 election. The issue now was whether the government should simply make handouts to the poverty-stricken, which was the cheapest plan, or whether it should provide work relief, which seemed less wasteful and more humane. In accordance with suggestions made by Roosevelt in an address to Congress in March 1933, several lines of action were adopted.

The first New Deal measure providing assistance to the unemployed was an act of March 1933 creating the Civilian Conservation Corps (CCC). This act looked to the youth of the country, not the aged. At one point CCC had on its rolls 500,000 young men, eighteen to twenty-five, recruited from cities, sent to camps built by the War Department, and put to work on reforestation, road and dam construction, the control of mosquitoes and other pests, and similar tasks. Of the $30 a month wages, $22 was sent to the young men's families. By the end of 1941, some 2,750,000 youths had spent some part of their lives in CCC camps.

The first comprehensive New Deal relief measure was the act of May 1933 creating the Federal Emergency Relief Administration (FERA) under Harry Hopkins and providing it with half a billion dollars to be used for direct emergency relief. Although the federal government provided the money, the relief itself was to be administered by the states. At first, cash payments were distributed, but Hopkins believed work relief to be psychologically and economically superior to a dole. He also was concerned with quick results. When approached with a project that needed long and detailed planning, one that he was assured would "work out in the long run," Hopkins snapped, "People don't eat in the long run— they eat every day." In time, almost half of those receiving relief were put to work on jobs that presumably did not compete with private business. Pay began at 30 cents an hour. In all, FERA spent about $4 billion.

The Civil Works Administration, set up in November 1933, run entirely from Washington and given wholly to work relief, supplemented FERA for a short time. Widely criticized by opponents of the New Deal on the ground that it "made work" through leaf raking and similar futile tasks, it in fact performed many useful services, such as repairing roads and improving schools and parks, before being absorbed in the spring of 1934 into the expanding FERA program.

A month after FERA, the National Industrial Recovery Act had created as part of the recovery program the Public Works Administration (PWA) under Secretary of the Interior Ickes. PWA was more a "pump-priming" than a relief agency; its duties included the planning of bridges, dams, hospitals, and similar public projects and contracting for their construction by private companies. But Ickes proved so cautious in approving contracts that PWA took disastrously long in getting started. Eventually, however, the $4.25 billion it spent by 1937 on about 35,000 projects was credited with stimulating the business recovery that seemed then to be on the way. Among PWA's achievements were the Triborough Bridge in New York City, a new sewage system for Chicago, a municipal auditorium for Kansas City, a water supply system for Denver, and two new aircraft carriers, *Yorktown* and *Enterprise.*

Many persons complained that New Deal relief agencies, besides duplicating one another's tasks, made no effort to distinguish between employable persons who needed relief and "unemployables" who could not have found work even in good times. Early in 1935

Roosevelt proposed a reorganization of the entire relief program, with the federal government to aid employables only, the care of others to be left to the states and municipalities. In May, that year, Congress passed the Emergency Relief Act putting these proposals into effect. CCC and PWA were continued. All other federal relief was brought under a new agency, the Works Progress Administration (WPA), directed by Harry Hopkins. When its operations ended in July 1941, WPA had spent no less than $11.3 billion. At its peak, in November 1938, nearly 3.3 million persons were on its payroll, and all told WPA provided work for 8 million individuals. Among its more than 250,000 projects were hospitals, bridges, municipal power plants, post offices, school buildings, slum clearance, and the rehabilitation of army posts and naval stations.

WPA also recognized the claims of the arts, whose practitioners, like other workers, were left stranded by the depression. Its projects in the fine arts, music, and the theater gave employment to painters, writers, actors, singers, instrumentalists, stage hands, and many others (see p. 700). WPA's cultural work was supplemented by a National Youth Administration (NYA), which helped meet the needs of young persons with intellectual interests. Through NYA young people aged sixteen to twenty-five found part-time employment in high schools, colleges, and universities.

No part of the New Deal drew more criticism than its relief program. The cost was truly enormous for the times, and the tax burden had to be shouldered by the depressed private sector of the economy. Many critics charged, usually inaccurately, that relief was inefficiently handled. Others, often justly, accused the administration of using relief for political purposes. No part of the relief program, in turn, drew more criticism than its support of cultural activities. Many Americans had no sympathy with the idea that musicians, writers, and artists had as much claim on the community as did workers in other fields. It was said, also, and often with truth, that persons with radical and unconventional views were being employed on the cultural projects. Few such critics seemed to realize that these projects might restore to such persons a sense of security and personal pride sufficient to mitigate their radicalism, nor that in any case the exercise of freedom of expression was not a valid ground for discrimination in employment. Elsewhere in the world, neglect of intellectuals and artists often turned them toward fascism, national socialism, or communism.

## II  Endorsement and enlargement

### Referendum of 1934

Most of the New Deal's famous "alphabetical agencies"—NRA, TVA, AAA, SEC, CCC, PWA—had their inception in the first stirring "hundred days" of the Roosevelt administration. These were the days of the special session of the 73rd Congress, March 9 to June 16, 1933, probably the most creative congressional session since the first one in 1789. The opposition, which had shunned responsibility for alleviating the social terror of the early depression years, appeared for the moment shamed, shocked, or stunned into silence. Supported by the President's courage and contagious optimism, the unprecedented measures of relief and reform were adopted with near unanimity.

When recovery itself proved elusive, however, the enemies of the New Deal took heart. Such signs of recovery as there were, moreover, brought them many followers who believed, with the emergency thankfully passing, that "normalcy" should again be restored, and the sooner the better. The New Deal fathered enemies on the left as well as on the conservative right, but it was those on the right who, after eighteen months of Roosevelt, did most to make the congressional elections of 1934 an immensely important referendum. Aghast at the abandonment of the gold standard, these enemies resented SEC as a slur on Wall Street's honesty, feared the implications of TVA for the electric-power industry and pri-

vate enterprise in general, deplored the collectivism of NRA and AAA, and denounced the break from the sturdy traditions of individualism and decentralization manifest in federal relief policies. Aggravating every innovation was the thoroughly objectionable President himself, a Judas to his class. The Republican leader Ogden Mills expressed the feelings of the Roosevelt haters when he said: "We have to turn back many centuries to the days of absolute autocrats to find so great a power over millions of men lodged in the hands of a single fallible being."

Walter Lippmann warned those whom he called the "hysterical conservatives" that they had "not a ghost of a chance to win" in 1934. But Roosevelt, taking no risks, made a few astute appeals to the public to support liberal candidates. When the people were told that the New Deal was destroying the Constitution and tearing up the Bill of Rights, Roosevelt suggested that they read the Bill of Rights for themselves and "ask yourself whether you personally have suffered the abatement of a single jot of these great assurances." Again, when they were told that the New Deal was ruining the country, he asked them to judge by their own situations. "Are you," he asked in June, "better off than you were last year? Are your debts less burdensome? Is your bank account more secure? Are your working conditions better?"

These questions were put in full confidence that most people could answer in the affirmative. And at the polls they did. The Republicans' crushing defeats in 1932 were exceeded in 1934. In the Senate, the Democratic margin rose from 25 to 44 seats; in the House the already huge Democratic majority soared over 200. Arthur Krock, the *New York Times* commentator, called this repudiation of the New Deal's critics "the most overwhelming victory in the history of American politics."

### Voices of the demagogues

If the referendum of 1934 buried those who believed that the President was going too far too fast, it must also have reminded him, if he needed reminding, that the spirit of protest was still rising and that those who believed the New Deal moved too little and too slowly would be heard from. In the second half of his first term, Roosevelt became increasingly concerned with the voices on the left, and especially those of a new breed of demagogue who arose to deepen the widespread discontent.

Most formidable among these demagogues was Senator Huey Long, the "Kingfish" of Louisiana. A skilled rabble-rouser with a remarkable command of the popular idiom, Long had built up a national following, especially large in the Mississippi Valley and on the Pacific Coast, on the strength of his vague plan to "share the wealth." In 1935 a Democratic National Committee survey disclosed that Long might win from 3 to 4 million votes on a third-party ticket, thereby gaining the balance of power in American politics, with perhaps disastrous consequences for the Democrats in the 1936 campaign. This alarming possibility was dissipated by Long's assassination in September 1935.

A second popular threat was the elderly California physician Dr. Francis E. Townsend, who, in January 1935, announced the "Townsend Plan" by which the government would give $200 a month to every citizen 60 years old or older, the cost to be paid by a sales tax. Each pensioner would be required to spend his allowance within the month, thereby, according to the plausible doctor, starting such a

wave of consumer buying that business would boom and make it easy for the rest of the country to bear the cost. Responsible economists dismissed the Townsend Plan as a crackpot scheme; one of them, Paul Douglas, estimated that it would require half the national income to be turned over to 8 percent of the population. But Townsend Clubs organized throughout the country attracted desperate old men and women. Their combined membership was said to be about 3 million in 1935, with perhaps as many as 7 million unaffiliated supporters. When frightened politicians began to endorse Townsend's scheme, Roosevelt had to face the fearsome possibility that a large proportion of voters over 60

*"Battle Royal," Daniel Fitzpatrick cartoon, 1935, showing the demagogues Gerald L. K. Smith (left), Father Coughlin, and Huey Long competing for a hearing on the air.*

Fitzpatrick in the *St. Louis Post-Dispatch*

would be forged into a bloc in full cry for an impossible "reform."

More forceful yet more vague than Dr. Townsend was the "radio priest," Father Charles E. Coughlin, who broadcast weekly from Royal Oak, Michigan. Coughlin won an enormous audience for his assaults, in the old Populist idiom, on Wall Street and the international bankers. His spuming "hate" harangues seemed more satisfying to his followers than his conventional demands for a "living annual wage" and "nationalization of banking and currency and of national resources." Originally one of Roosevelt's supporters, Coughlin, in January 1935, began to flay the administration for failing the people.

To those concerned over the rise of Hitler, Mussolini, and other dictators abroad, Long, Coughlin, and company loomed as the "forerunners of American fascism," as the able journalist Raymond Gram Swing called them. Their popularity, coinciding as it did with organized labor's growing discontent with NRA, suggested in the spring of 1935 that Roosevelt's mass appeal, so strong in the early months of the New Deal, might soon dissolve. The President well understood the real grievances underlying the demagogues' broad appeal and privately even spoke of doing something "to steal Long's thunder." The Wealth Tax, the Social Security Act, the National Labor Relations Act, and some others all were responses to this thunder from below. But their natural consequence, by the time of the election of 1936, was to deepen the thunder from above.

### 1935 reforms

Three of the new reform measures were enacted in one month, August 1935. One of the August laws, inspired by the administration's desire to check the growth of gigantic personal fortunes, was the Revenue Act of 1935, sometimes called the Wealth Tax or the "soak the rich" law. Tax rates, which

had already been raised by earlier New Deal measures, were now pushed much higher, reaching 75 percent on individual incomes above $5 million. Holding companies used for the management of private fortunes also were heavily taxed, and corporation levies were lifted to an historic peak. Roy W. Howard, the publisher of a chain of newspapers heretofore sympathetic toward Roosevelt, now wrote the President in an open letter that businessmen believed the Wealth Tax to be simply a punitive measure inspired by revenge against political opponents. Roosevelt replied that the act was intended to "create broader range of opportunity" and to impose needed taxes in accordance with ability to pay. He took the caution to heart, however, and promised that business would now have a "breathing spell."

The second August law was the Public Utility Holding Company Act. As we have said, holding companies were corporations permitted to hold the securities of other corporations. Often, by holding only a tiny fraction of a great corporation's securities, but a fraction still large enough to exercise strong leverage where other holdings were scattered, the holding company could dominate policies to its own advantage. Many other technical and legal devices—such as the designation of only a small part of a corporation's stock as "voting stock," which could then be acquired for a song, along with the full power of the voting privilege—furthered holding companies' domination of basic industries. Domination could be pushed to still broader ranges by the practice of "pyramiding"—a procedure by which holding companies, in a manner similar to that by which they gained control of operating corporations, also gained control of other holding companies and hence of the operating corporations *they* controlled.

Holding companies, and especially those engaged in the practice of pyramiding, had become especially active in the rapidly expanding electric-power industry during the 1920s; and in 1932, thirteen of the largest of them controlled no less than 75 percent of the electric-power market. The most fantastic public power pyramid was that created by Samuel Insull of Chicago. At his peak, Insull was board chairman of 65 corporations out of a total of 111 that made up his empire. When the whole pyramid collapsed in 1932, it was called "the biggest business failure in the history of the world." Insull himself fled the country. Efforts to extradite him to stand trial for fraudulent use of the mails, embezzlement, and other crimes made him as much a front-page story as the New Deal, and his trial in 1934 kept the glare of publicity on the whole industry, its reputation already soured by its ceaseless battle against TVA.

Consumers as well as investors had suffered from public-utility holding companies, and the Act of August 1935 required that those which could not, within five years, demonstrate that they had brought about economies in management must be dissolved. This "death sentence" clause touched off a bitter struggle in Congress, and holding companies spent large sums trying to defeat it. At length, after some compromises, the "death sentence" remained in the measure, which was signed on August 28. Its constitutionality was quickly questioned, but the Supreme Court eventually upheld it. Every effort to impose the "death sentence," however, continued to be stubbornly resisted at immense legal costs, which provided a windfall for lawyers almost wholly engaged in this practice.

The third August enactment was the Social Security Act to secure "the men, women, and children of the Nation against certain hazards and vicissitudes of life." This measure, for the first time, provided federal payments, directly or through the states, for pensions to the aged and the infirm, for unemployment insurance, and for benefits to dependent mothers and children. Federal pensions of up to $15 a month to the poor over sixty-five years of age were expected to be matched by the states. Federal retirement funds, ranging from $10 to $85 a month, were to be paid to workers who retired at sixty-five and who had participated in the plan before their retirement. Agricultural workers, household servants, government employees, and those working for nonprofit religious or charitable organizations were among those excluded. The money for those included was to be raised by a payroll tax levied equally on employers and employees.

Most states promptly set up old-age pension and unemployment insurance systems conforming to the provisions of the act. A worker who lost his job could collect from $5 to $15 a week for a period of about fifteen weeks while he looked for work.

By 1940 about 50 million workers were protected by social security. From time to time since then, new classes of workers have been covered, money payments increased, and the period for receiving unemployment insurance extended. A nonpartisan Social Security Board administers the program.

The Social Security Act passed the House and Senate with far larger majorities than the other reform measures. Its opponents, however, made up in emphasis what they lacked in numbers. Several of them asserted that it would mean the end of free government. "The lash of the dictator will be felt," said one.

Those who participated in the act, as in other New Deal measures, felt otherwise. So much has been made of the bureaucratization of government under the New Deal that its democratizing tendencies, especially among those heretofore deprived of the right or impulse to participate in decisions critical to their well-being, have been lost sight of. The NIRA, for example, asserted that "employees shall have the right to organize and bargain collectively *through representatives of their own choosing,* and shall be free from the interference, restraint, or coercion of employers ... or their agents." The National Labor Relations Act of July 1935 stated this right in even stronger terms. The AAA, in turn, gave thousands of Negro cotton farmers in the South who had never voted before the right to participate equally with others in the referendums by which regional crop controls were voted up or down. Under the Social Security Act, finally, millions of aged and incapacitated workers in the cities and in rural areas found a new interest in state governments made responsible by the act for state contributions to pension and other funds. "Yes ma'am," said a destitute old woman after a week of publicity for "human security" in her state, "we all know about it. . . . Now that we know all the facts the legislators just can't rightly afford not to find the money."

## The labor movement in industry and politics

When the Supreme Court, in May 1935, found the National Industrial Recovery Act unconstitutional, and thereby invalidated Section 7(a) guaranteeing labor the right of collective bargaining, Congress did little about the rest of the defunct act, but it promptly, in July 1935, enacted the National Labor Relations Act to afford labor a more defensible framework for organizing activities. The long-run effects of this measure for the political future of the New Deal, for the Democratic party, and for the country generally were to prove as profound and lasting as its economic consequences.

Even while Section 7(a) had been in operation, militant labor organizers, especially in the mass-employment industries, had gone to the workers with great success with the argument, "The President wants you to join." With this approach, immense gains were made in industries already partially organized, and in new ones, like the automobile and the rubber-tire industries, where there had been no large unions before. Total union membership, which had stood at 2,857,000 in 1933, rose to 3,728,000 by 1935. Collective bargaining under Section 7(a) never worked to the satisfaction of labor leaders largely because of management domination of code machinery, but it had given them a remarkable organizing weapon which was easily made into a political one as well. The National Labor Relations Act of July 1935, or the Wagner Act as it is often called after Senator Robert F. Wagner of New York, was one of its first victories.

The Wagner Act established a National Labor Relations Board (NLRB) of three members, in place of 7(a)'s National Labor Board. It also reenacted in almost the same words the

collective bargaining guarantees of 7(a), but it tightened the restrictions on "unfair labor practices" by employers who tried to coerce workers into joining company unions, to dominate outside unions, and to interfere with a worker's decision to join a union. The act provided that the representative of the majority of the employees in any plant should be the *exclusive* bargaining representative of *all* the employees, and it empowered the NLRB to investigate and certify the proper representatives and to hold supervised elections among employees when there was a dispute over which union should represent whom.

Business organizations led by the powerful National Association of Manufacturers protested that the National Labor Relations Act was one-sided. But labor and government replied that its aim was to rectify the great one-sidedness of corporate power in dealing with unorganized workers. Under the new act no less than 340 company unions were broken up. Membership in free trade unions continued to grow, until in 1941 it had reached 10.5 million. By then the NLRB had handled 33,000 cases affecting more than 7 million workers. More than 90 percent of the cases had been settled amicably, and over 75 percent of the strikes certified to the Board had been settled peaceably.

The marked rise of organized labor, nevertheless, was accompanied by considerable strife, not only between workers and employers but also within labor's ranks. The AFL was badly split. The leaders of the old craft unions that had first come together in the Federation sought to retain their power and standing as the "aristocracy of labor." Loath to bring in the unskilled and semiskilled workers of mass-production industries, they also refused to permit other leaders to organize such workers in new unions. But these leaders did not brook obstruction for long.

The issue came to a head in the national AFL convention of October 1935, when a majority of the delegates stood fast for craft unionism. A month later, John L. Lewis of the United Mine Workers and seven other AFL leaders met separately and organized the Committee for Industrial Organization (CIO), nominally to advise the AFL on how to orga-

722

nize the mass-production industries. Lewis became chairman of the committee. In January 1936 the AFL executive council ordered the CIO to disband. On refusing, they were suspended in August. Expelled in March 1937, they took with them unions representing 1,800,000 workers. A massive organizing campaign followed, contributing heavily to the record 4740 strikes that year. Early in 1938, when the CIO boasted nearly 4 million members, the leaders formed a new, independent organization with the same initials, the Congress of Industrial Organizations.

One of the CIO's novel weapons, outlawed by the Supreme Court in 1939, was the "sit-down" strike. Instead of walking off the job and picketing, workers went to their posts in the plants and stayed there, making it difficult for scabs to replace them. Sit-down strikes against two giant automobile companies, General Motors in January 1937 and Chrysler in April, won the CIO recognition as bargaining agent for their workers. In March 1937 United States Steel Corporation, once the terror of organized labor, also capitulated.

"Little Steel" proved harder to crack. On Memorial Day, 1937, Chicago police killed ten pickets during a strike against the Republic company, Little Steel's leader. Other strikes—

*Police and strikers clash
at Republic Steel's South Chicago plant,
May 30, 1937.*

Wide World Photos

like that against Republic, all lost—brought violence in Youngstown, Massillon, and Cleveland, Ohio. Little Steel did not fall until 1941 when it signed contracts even conforming to the NLRB order to reinstate workers fired during the 1937 struggle.

As labor grew more aggressive and important in politics as well as business, the split in its ranks caused much irritation and many difficulties. A peace movement finally brought about a merger of the AFL and CIO in 1955; but lingering bitterness over the old battles forestalled a genuine reconciliation.

### The Roosevelt coalition, white and black

Toward the end of Theodore Roosevelt's administration in 1908, the *New York Tribune* commented that the lasting value of the Square Deal lay in its "calling public attention to social problems and bringing them into politics." The lasting value of the New Deal lay in its transforming political discussion of social justice into far-reaching legislation and administration. This transformation had been largely accomplished by the end of 1935 and helped Franklin D. Roosevelt forge an extraordinary political coalition with which to push on with the work. "We will win easily next year," he told his Cabinet in November 1935, about the coming presidential election, "but we are going to make it a crusade."

The elements of Roosevelt's coalition were partly traditional and partly new. First among the traditional forces stood the solid Democratic South. Southerners had backed the greater part of the New Deal reforms thus far, though some of them regretted the administration's solicitude for Negroes. Southern industrialists thought relief payments, NRA wage scales, and encouragement of unions were undermining the sweatshop wages paid white factory hands. Cotton, tobacco, and other staples, however, had done well under the New Deal, and the Democratic party in the still largely agrarian South held firm.

Second among the traditional forces were

the Democratic machines in northern cities. Roosevelt did not set himself up as a crusader against machines. He preferred to use, not to destroy, them. True, his relations with Tammany were touchy, for as a governor of New York with presidential aspirations he had found it necessary to avoid too close an identification with such an unsavory body. Tammany men found it hard to forgive this; they also continued to resent FDR's national convention victory over Al Smith in 1932. But Jim Farley opened new lines to New York's Democratic leaders, while Roosevelt attracted additional support from such militant independents as New York City's mayor, Fiorello H. La Guardia, and from the American Labor party, an unaffiliated group that massed the city's labor and left-wing strength behind him. Elsewhere, Roosevelt played ball with city machines and their bosses, happy after a long dry season of Republican Presidents to have a Democrat in the White House. The Hague machine in New Jersey, the Flynn machine in the Bronx, the Kelly-Nash machine in Chicago, the Pendergast machine in Kansas City, Missouri, all could be counted on to deliver the votes.

Roosevelt's success with urban voters was furthered by his strong appeal to new immigrant groups who with other minorities were especially hard hit by the depression and also had begun to play a more active role in politics. Where Al Smith had spoken for the religious and ethnic aspirations of these people and supported their demand for respect within the American political system, Roosevelt responded to their desperate economic need. Anglo-Saxon old-fashioned America, as represented by Hoover, had turned a cold shoulder to "minorities." Roosevelt had helped them.

Among ethnic elements, Negroes had ample grounds to shun the administration. Virtually all NRA codes, for example, discriminated against black workers on employment, wages, and job-improvement opportunities. AAA crop-control payments went largely to farmers with sizable acreage, leaving the black share-

cropper's hand empty, his market curtailed. The CCC, in turn, began as a "lily white" agency; fewer than 3 percent of the first quarter million enrolled were blacks. Complete segregation, moreover, remained the rule here even when black participation was enlarged. Aubrey Williams, a white southerner and Negro champion among New Deal aides, wrote his boss, Harry Hopkins, in 1934 about FERA: "Negroes don't get a fair deal; I don't know how to secure one for them." In the NYA only Mary Bethune's pertinacity won black students some semblance of a fair shake. New Deal agencies and New Deal funds often were administered on a state or local basis. In such instances, local patterns of discrimination ruled.

And yet the Negro voter responded to the New Deal with enthusiasm and formed a strong part of the Roosevelt coalition. The reasons are not hard to find. In the first place, however partial his share, he, like others, did participate in New Deal relief, where there had been little or none under Hoover. Despite almost universal second-class treatment, he, like others, did benefit from New Deal reforms. And, however circumscribed his stake, he, like others, did share in New Deal economic recovery, often through the new labor movement the New Deal fostered.

The New Deal approached relief, reform, and recovery on a national and a general basis. Many of its leaders, Roosevelt often included, feared for their over-all goals if established social patterns were to be attacked. Party solidarity, not to be discounted, also suggested caution on race matters to Democratic chieftains. They did little or nothing, for example, to fight the poll tax that disqualified most blacks of voting age in the South or to check lynching. At the same time, especially in Washington itself, Roosevelt and many of his aides showed the same warmth to Negro leaders as they did to others. In the Cabinet, Ickes and Miss Perkins always proved strong Negro champions who gave black spokesmen a hearing and fought discrimination where they could. The New Deal also employed numerous Negro administrators. The black community itself had not yet developed many leaders of national stature. The concern for

Negro problems shown by certain New Dealers furthered the careers of such leaders and respect for them among their people. Perhaps above all, Eleanor Roosevelt's liberality of spirit and unstinted support of Negro, as of other minority, aspirations rubbed off on the urban black voter and carried him from his traditional allegiance to the party of Lincoln to the FDR bandwagon.

The success of the New Deal's agricultural program also brought into Democratic ranks many normally Republican westerners. Iowa, for example, had gone Republican in every election from 1916 to 1928, often overwhelmingly so. In the anguish of 1932, it had swung to Roosevelt and in 1936 still stood solidly behind him.

Labor's newly organized millions also swung heavily into the Roosevelt camp during 1935 and 1936 and were made welcome. John L. Lewis and other CIO leaders organized Labor's Non-partisan League to mobilize the labor vote in industrial centers. The CIO gave half a million dollars to the 1936 Democratic campaign. Nor did Roosevelt suffer from the split in labor's ranks, for AFL President William Green, after visiting FDR, announced that 90 percent of labor's vote would be his.

The course followed by labor paralleled that of many intellectuals throughout the country. Suspicious at first of the retrogressive features of NRA and AAA, and troubled by the inadequacy and inconsistency of the many New Deal measures, teachers, writers, clergymen, artists, and journalists rallied behind the New Deal after the 1935 reforms. Intellectuals were

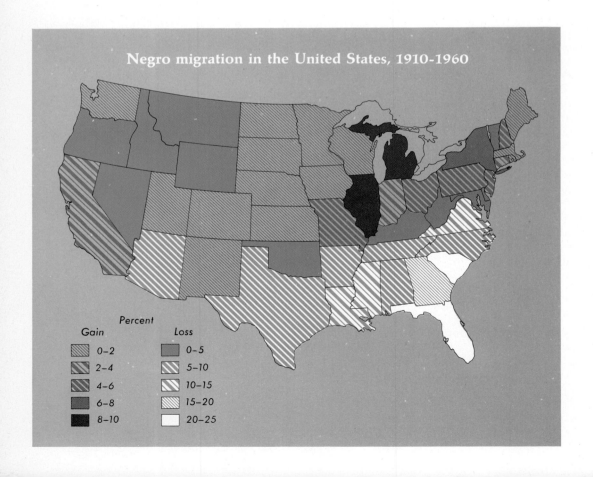

Negro migration in the United States, 1910-1960

Percent

Gain
0–2
2–4
4–6
6–8
8–10

Loss
0–5
5–10
10–15
15–20
20–25

heartened by the administration's receptivity to ideas and experts and by its readiness to assist unemployed artists, scholars, and writers. The shrillness of the conservative business attack on Roosevelt caused many a writer or teacher to give him even more cordial support.

Nor, for that matter, were businessmen altogether absent from the coalition. Roosevelt counted many loyal personal friends among businessmen. Others, notably antitariff merchants and bankers, were traditionally Democrats. Still others represented the socially minded rich long familiar to America. A large number also came from sectors of the economy—consumer-goods manufacturers, for example, and chain and department store owners and other retailers—who benefited directly from gains in mass purchasing power brought about by New Deal reform and relief measures. From them Roosevelt won a gratifying response when the chips were down. Their contributions were feeble compared with the immense outpourings to the Republicans from corporate and personal holders of "the big money," but Roosevelt needed considerably less money than his opponents to win votes.

## Election of 1936

By the time of the 1936 election, the New Deal had made most of the progress it was going to make in fostering business recovery, forwarding labor organization, relieving distress on the farms, and aiding the unemployed. The general economic statistics, moreover, confirmed the success of the program. Farm income, as we have seen (p. 712), had shot up dramatically. Average weekly earnings of workers in manufacturing had risen since 1932 from $17 to almost $22. While some 7 million remained unemployed, this figure had dropped by 4 or 5 million since Roosevelt took office, and the unemployed were receiving enough to keep body and soul together. The rise in national income from $40.2

billion in 1933 to $64.7 billion in 1936 reflected the general advance.

The Republicans, who held their national convention in Cleveland in June, however, did not shrink from a head-on battle. They raked the New Deal from stem to stern. "America is in peril," their platform began. "We invite all Americans, irrespective of party, to join us in defense of American institutions." For President the convention nominated Governor Alfred M. Landon of Kansas, and for Vice-President, Frank Knox, a Chicago publisher.

The Democrats, meeting in Philadelphia, renominated Roosevelt and Vice-President Garner by acclamation. "These economic royalists," Roosevelt told the convention, "complain that we seek to overthrow the institutions of America. What they really complain of is that we seek to overthrow their power." "Presidents do make mistakes," he added, "but the immortal Dante tells us that divine justice weighs the sins of the cold-blooded and the sins of the warm-hearted in different scales."

Coughlinites and other malcontents came together in Cleveland to form a third party, the Union party, and nominated William Lemke, a Republican congressman from North Dakota, as their standard-bearer. The ranks of the demagogues, however, had become sadly depleted after the Social Security Act of 1935 had stolen much of Dr. Townsend's thunder and after the assassination of Huey Long. Coughlin, moreover, had received unmistakable evidence that the Roman Catholic hierarchy found his political behavior embarrassing. Lemke was to poll fewer than a million votes and carry not a single state.

Some disaffected Democrats, including Al Smith, went over to Landon during the campaign, but the Republican's principal support came from the Liberty League, financed by conservative millionaires. Near the end of the campaign, before a wildly enthusiastic crowd in New York City's Madison Square Garden, Roosevelt declared that the New Deal had been struggling with "business and financial monopoly, speculation, reckless banking, class antagonism, sectionalism, war profiteering." He went on: "Never before in all our history have these forces been so united against one candidate as they stand today. They are unanimous in their *hate* for *me—and I welcome their hatred."*

726

In the balloting Roosevelt carried all but two states, Maine and Vermont; his 27.75 million popular votes represented 60 percent of the total cast. In the cities his margins reached record levels. By winning even more overwhelmingly than in 1932, he made the Democratic party the normal majority party of the country.

The fate of the minor parties testified to the inclusiveness of the Roosevelt coalition. Lemke's showing disappointed not only his followers but also those Republicans who had hoped in the early days of the campaign that he would draw enough traditionally conservative farm votes from Roosevelt to swing some states to Landon. The record of the Socialist and Communist candidates, at the same time, showed that the New Deal had completely broken the forces of independent political radicalism. Four years earlier, Norman Thomas, the Socialist party nominee, won 881,000 votes; in 1936, only 187,000. William Z. Foster, the Communist candidate in 1932, won 102,000 votes; Earl Browder, his successor in 1936, but 80,000.

Roosevelt's second inauguration took place, not on the traditional date of March 4, but on January 20, 1937—the date prescribed by the Twentieth Amendment to the Constitution, the "Lame Duck" Amendment, ratified in 1933. By pushing forward the installation of newly elected Presidents and Congresses, this amendment eliminated lame duck sessions formerly held between January and the old inauguration date and often attended by defeated members under a defeated President.

In his second inaugural address, Roosevelt expressed no complacency over his victory or his achievements:

*In this nation [he said] I see tens of millions of its citizens—a substantial part of its whole population— who at this very moment are denied the greater part of what the very lowest standards of today call the necessities of life.*

*I see millions of families trying to live on incomes so meager that the pall of family disaster hangs over them day by day. . . .*

*I see one-third of a nation ill-housed, ill-clad, illnourished.*

Roosevelt promised that the New Deal would continue to do everything in its power to remedy these conditions. At the start of the New Deal, he said. "we did . . . first things first." But:

*Our covenant with ourselves did not stop there. Instinctively we recognized a deeper need—the need to find through government the instrument of our united purpose to solve for the individual the ever-rising problems of a complex civilization. Repeated attempts at their solution without the aid of government had left us baffled and bewildered. . . . We refused to leave the problems of our common welfare to be solved by the winds of chance and the hurricanes of disaster.*

*In this we Americans were discovering no wholly new truth; we were writing a new chapter in our book of self-government.*

As it happened, the growing self-consciousness of the New Deal also helped strengthen the opposition.

## III  Climax of the New Deal

*The court fight*

In some ways Roosevelt's triumph in the 1936 election was too sweeping. American political parties, being loose coalitions, almost always suffer inner splits of some kind; and when the opposition party becomes inordinately weak, internal differences among the victors come quickly to the fore, and feuds are fought out. The climax of the New Deal was reached when Roosevelt, trying to clear the way for further reforms, challenged the power of the Supreme Court, and when, having failed in this enterprise, he tried unsuccessfully to reshape his own party into the more consistently liberal instrument foreshadowed by his inaugural speech. These undertakings were costly enough, but his woes were increased by a sharp business recession in 1937–1938, which raised once more the question of whether his administration really knew where it was going. The overwhelming public endorsement of 1936 was followed by some of Roosevelt's most striking political failures. Even so, he was to make progress with his promised reforms.

The President's attack on the Supreme Court came out of a clear blue sky on February 5, 1937, when, apparently having consulted no one but his Attorney-General, Hom-

er S. Cummings, who drafted the bill for him, Roosevelt proposed to Congress what was promptly called his "court-packing bill." In it he asked that whenever a federal judge failed to retire within six months after reaching the age of 70, an additional federal judge should be appointed. Although the proposal applied to the entire federal judiciary, it was obviously aimed at the Supreme Court, where six of the judges were already over 70 and thus as many as six judges could be added, bringing the full Court to 15.

Although the announcement came as a shock, the need for some such bill seemed clear enough. The people had undeniably approved of the New Deal, but the Supreme Court had emphatically opposed its early legislation. Only in the Gold Clause and TVA cases had it sustained major New Deal measures. In 1935 and 1936 the Court had struck down NRA and AAA. It had rejected a railroad retirement plan and the Bituminous Coal Act, which was intended to reorganize a sick industry. It had invalidated congressional legislation to protect farm mortgages, and it had thrown out a municipal bankruptcy act. To those who sympathized with the New Deal social program, the Court seemed to be creating a no-man's land where neither state nor federal power could be brought to bear on critical problems.

The number of Supreme Court Justices had, in fact, been changed several times in the past, but the present array of nine had become fixed for so long it almost had the sanction of constitutional authority. To attempt to reduce the Court's power by a constitutional amendment, at the same time, would take years, and most likely could not be affected at all. Roosevelt's plan was a short cut, but his assertion that it was intended simply to help the federal courts generally to catch up with their business seemed so disingenuous that, even to a large number of New Dealers, it gave color to the charge that he was indeed seeking those dictatorial powers that his opponents all along had said he wanted.

Even while debate on the bill was in progress, events occurred that further weakened its chances. Most important, within a few weeks of Roosevelt's bombshell, Justice Owen

*C. K. Berryman cartoon, February 10, 1937, on FDR's court-packing plan.*

J. Roberts, influenced perhaps by the clamor over the Court's conservatism and by the results of the 1936 election, began to vote on the liberal side in some cases. "A switch in time saves nine," said a legal wit.

728

The sudden liberalism of Justice Roberts became apparent on March 29, 1937, when the Supreme Court handed down three decisions that bespoke its change of heart. In *West Coast Hotel Co.* v. *Parrish,* by 5-to-4, it sustained a state minimum-wage law, thus overruling the reactionary decision in *Adkins* v. *Children's Hospital* (1923) (see p. 669) and even a very recent decision by the same majority in *Morehead* v. *New York ex. rel. Tipaldo* (1936). On the same day the Court unanimously sustained the revised Farm Mortgage Act of 1935 and the Railway Labor Act as amended in 1934. Even more important for the course of the New Deal were five decisions on April 12 upholding the National Labor Relations Act. Six weeks later, in two 5-to-4 rulings, the Court sustained the social security legislation.

In May, Justice Van Devanter, one of the most conservative men on the bench, struck another blow at the court-reform bill when he announced his intention to retire, thus making it clear that Roosevelt would have at least one appointment of his own. Then in June the Senate Judiciary Committee gave the *coup de grâce* to the bill, reporting against it by the narrow vote of 10 to 8. It "should be so emphatically rejected," said the report, "that its parallel will never again be presented to the free representatives of the free people of America." On July 22 the Senate voted overwhelmingly, 70 to 20, to recommit the bill to the Judiciary Committee, where it died.

And yet Roosevelt had a sort of triumph after all, over and above the recent heartening decisions. In August 1937 he appointed the liberal Hugo L. Black of Alabama to Van Devanter's place on the Court. In the next few years six other aging justices also took the cue and began to retire. To five of the vacancies thus created, Roosevelt appointed liberals and New Dealers, to the sixth the southern Democrat James F. Byrnes. To the Chief Justiceship vacated by Hughes, Roosevelt shifted the learned, liberal Harlan Fiske Stone, a firm advocate of ample federal powers. New Dealers could thus be consoled by the thought that they had lost the battle but won the war, even though the whole procedure opened a lasting rift in the party and cost it voter support.

### Straining toward the welfare state

Many reforms were gained or extended during FDR's second term; but, as in the Court fight, the political costs were high, indicating that the reform potential of the Democratic coalition was becoming exhausted.

Among the reform measures that extended earlier programs were the Farm Tenancy Act of 1937 (see p. 713), strongly opposed by southern conservatives; the second Agricultural Adjustment Act, passed in 1938 (see p. 713); and the Food, Drug, and Cosmetic Act of 1938. The last of these, remedying serious defects in the Pure Food and Drugs Act of 1906, prohibited the misbranding of products and misleading advertising.

Two new reform measures attempted to strike more vigorously at inadequate housing and low wages. As early as 1933 the administration had created the Home Owners Loan Corporation (HOLC) with huge resources to protect impoverished householders from losing their property through mortgage foreclosure. In June 1934 it had set up the Federal Housing Administration (FHA) to lend money mainly to middle-income families for repairing old homes or building new ones. HOLC had also undertaken housing development and had helped more than a million home owners. But positive action in *low-income housing* came only now with the Wagner-Steagall Housing Act of September 1937, creating the United States Housing Authority (USHA) and authorizing it to make long-term, low-interest loans to state or city public-housing agencies to clear slums and build new houses that met federal standards. Occupancy of these houses was to be restricted to those who evidently could not pay rents high enough to induce private builders to construct dwellings for them. By 1941 USHA had torn down more than 78,000 substandard buildings and built new homes for 200,000 families. This accomplishment met only a tiny portion of the need, but private building interests succeeded in checking the program at this point.

The last major New Deal reform measure was the Fair Labor Standards Act of June 1938. The outcome of long-standing liberal agitation, this measure had failed to pass Congress on its first try. Finally, after Roosevelt gave it his open endorsement, it became law over the opposition of southern Democrats. For those covered by this act, which included most industrial workers but conspicuously omitted farm labor on the insistence of rural congressmen, it aimed to secure a minimum wage of 40 cents an hour and a maximum workweek of 40 hours. Even these modest goals were to be reached gradually. Beginning at 44 hours, the workweek was to be lowered to 40 hours in three years. Beginning at 25 cents an hour, the minimum wage was to be raised to 40 cents after eight years. The law also called for time-and-a-half for overtime. Many Americans were shocked to discover that over 750,000 workers were so poorly paid that they received immediate wage increases when the law first went into effect in August 1938. The hours of 1.5 million workers were shortened at the same time.

### Revival of conservative opposition

Even before Congress unwillingly passed the Fair Labor Standards Act, a Democratic member had implored the White House, "For God's sake, don't send us any more controversial legislation! " In May 1938, a newly formed southern Democratic–Republican coalition passed a bill cutting taxes on large corporations, which Roosevelt allowed to become law without his signature. General Hugh Johnson, an old associate turned foe, exulted at this time, "The old Roosevelt magic has lost its kick."

Much of FDR's belated political difficulty could be attributed to the 1937 Roosevelt recession, so-called, when no less than 4 million workers returned to the rolls of the unemployed. The reversal of the steady business revival appears to have been brought about partly because the administration, encouraged by the business advance, had called for a reduction of expenditures by WPA and other New Deal agencies. The high taxes enacted in 1935 and 1936 also seem to have cut private investment, while the accumulation of funds in the Treasury under the social security laws curtailed purchasing power.

The speed with which retrenchment in government expenditures started the downward trend suggested that neither the administration nor private industry could sustain economic growth without large-scale public spending. Early in 1938, the President and Congress put the spending program back into high gear, and the business revival was resumed, but at a slower pace. In the meantime, in April 1938, FDR also lashed out at the "economic royalists" who, he said, were choking American opportunity. "Big Business collectivism in industry," he told Congress, "compels ultimate collectivism in government." He now launched the broadest trust-busting campaign since Taft, while in June, at his urging, Congress created the Temporary National Economic Committee (TNEC) to restudy the whole structure of American private enterprise. TNEC's work, collected in thirty-seven volumes of testimony and forty-three monographs, remains a landmark in government economic investigations.

These drastic administration steps seemed only to strengthen the growing dissatisfaction with the New Deal. On the eve of the congressional elections of 1938, Roosevelt recalled his efforts to "pack" the Supreme Court by attempting to "purge" the Democratic party of conservative southerners and others who themselves were alienated by the growing prestige of labor in New Deal ranks. Again, he succeeded only in adding numbers to the discontented while purging almost no one.

In the elections the Democrats, northern and southern, retained majorities in both houses, but the Republicans made large gains, raising their representation in the House from

89 to 164 and in the Senate from 16 to 23. Even the President now seemed ready to acknowledge that the reform urge in the New Deal was spent. In his annual message to Congress in January 1939, he said: "We have now passed the period of internal conflict in the launching of our program of social reform. Our full energies may now be released to invigorate the processes of recovery in order to preserve our reforms." Recovery was soon to come, but by way of a new war in Europe and not in the application of energy at home.

## An assessment

Although the New Deal commanded the loyalty of the great majority of Americans, as shown by election results, it was hotly contested at every turn and is still questioned.

Anti-New Dealers point out that the New Deal persistently failed to balance the budget, that, on the contrary, from 1933 to 1940 it increased the national debt from $22.5 billion to almost $43 billion, that all in all it was a costly "experiment" with national welfare. The New Deal, they argue, also built up a large bureaucracy: The number of civilian federal employees jumped from 600,000 in 1932 to more than a million in 1940. At the same time, it had failed to restore the confidence of the business community which held the real key to recovery. In 1939, when all the experiments were over, more than 8.7 million workers remained unemployed by private industry, a situation for which the government was somehow held to blame.

Defenders of the New Deal have strong counterarguments. New Deal policies raised the debt, but they also helped raise national income from $40.2 billion in 1933 to $72.8 billion in 1939. Furthermore, pro-New Dealers contend that if unemployment under the New Deal is measured in terms of real human suffering and social waste, it was far less burdensome than in the earlier days. Finally, the New Deal had placed on the statute books a number of measures to make life more comfortable and secure, measures that would benefit not only contemporaries, but also millions yet to be born. After 1936 not even the Republicans quarreled in their party platforms with such reforms as the Social Security Act, minimum wages and hours, improved housing for low-income families, or the insuring of bank deposits. By taking the fateful step of involving the "public sector" in the economic well-being of the nation, the New Deal also laid the foundation for the epochal Maximum Employment Act of 1946 (see p. 777), which institutionalized federal responsibility for full utilization of resources and thereby helped avert a repetition of the 1929 Crash and the Great Depression.

When Roosevelt came into office in 1933, many Americans were flirting with thoughts of violence, doubts of democracy, political panaceas of the extreme right and the extreme left. The New Deal restored their belief that a democratic people could cope with its problems in a democratic way. This demonstration had significance for the Western world. Tyranny ruled in Russia, Germany, Italy, and Japan. But in the most powerful of the Western democracies, the people still moved, erratically but freely, toward the solution of their problems through constitutional means.

## For further reading

The best short introduction to the New Deal is W. E. Leuchtenburg, *Franklin D. Roosevelt and the New Deal* (1963). See also Dixon Wecter, *The Age of* the Great Depression 1929-1941 (1948), and Dexter Perkins, *The New Age of Franklin Roosevelt* (1957). A. M. Schlesinger, Jr., *The Coming of the New Deal*

(1959) and *The Politics of Upheaval* (1960), carry his history of The Age of Roosevelt through the 1936 election. R. G. Tugwell, *The Democratic Roosevelt* (1957), is comprehensive and thoughtful.

Beside's Tugwell's, the best "inside" narratives include Frances Perkins, *The Roosevelt I Knew* (1946); Raymond Moley, *After Seven Years* (1939); Moley's retrospective account with E. A. Rosen, *The First New Deal* (1966); and R. E. Sherwood, *Roosevelt and Hopkins* (1948). Samuel Rosenman, ed., *The Public Papers and Addresses of Franklin D. Roosevelt* (9 vols., 1938–1941), is invaluable. J. M. Blum, *From the Morgenthau Diaries, Years of Crisis 1928-1938* (1959) and *Years of Urgency 1938-1941* (1964), and *The Secret Diary of Harold L. Ickes* (3 vols., 1953–1954), cover the Treasury and the Interior. Eleanor Roosevelt, *This I Remember* (1949), is a valuable personal account. Further insight into New Deal ideas may be gained from Howard Zinn, ed., *New Deal Thought* (1966). B. D. Karl, *Executive Reorganization and Reform in the New Deal* (1963), is outstanding on the revised machinery of government.

Frank Freidel, ed., *The New Deal and the American People* (1964), is an anthology of contemporary material. On the common lot see Robert Bendiner, *Just Around the Corner* (1968); Cabell Phillips, *From the Crash to the Blitz 1929-1939* (1969); and Studs Terkel, *Hard Times* (1970). C. A. and M. R. Beard, *America in Midpassage* (2 vols., 1939), contains much social history.

The best introduction to the spirit of the NRA is Hugh S. Johnson, *The Blue Eagle, From Egg to Earth* (1935). See also Sidney Fine, *The Automobile Under the Blue Eagle* (1963). On the AAA, see J. D. Black, *Parity, Parity, Parity* (1942); R. S. Kirkendall, *Social Scientists and Farm Politics in the Age of Roosevelt* (1966); and C. M. Campbell, *The Farm Bureau and the New Deal* (1962). On other farm problems, see J. L. Shover, *Cornbelt Rebellion: The Farmers' Holiday Association* (1965); D. E. Conrad, *The Forgotten Farmers: The Story of Sharecroppers in the New Deal* (1965); and Sidney Baldwin, *Poverty and Politics, The Rise and Decline of the Farm Security Administration* (1968). On TVA see C. H. Pritchett, *The Tennessee Valley Authority* (1943).

D. S. Howard, *The WPA and Federal Relief Policy* (1943); J. A. Salmond, *The Civilian Conservation Corps 1933-1942* (1967); and J. K. Galbraith and G. G. Johnson, Jr., *Economic Effects of Federal Works Expenditures 1933-1938* (1940), deal with the attack on unemployment. S. F. Charles, *Minister of Relief: Harry Hopkins and the Depression* (1963), supplements Sher-

wood's work, above. E. E. Witte, *The Development of the Social Security Act* (1962), and A. J. Altmeyer, *The Formative Years of Social Security* (1966), cover this basic reform. Labor under the New Deal is dealt with authoritatively in Walter Galenson, *The C.I.O. Challenge to the A.F.L., . . . 1935-1941* (1960); Philip Taft, *The A.F. of L. From the Death of Gompers to the Merger* (1959); and Sidney Fine, *Sitdown: The General Motors Strike of 1936-1937* (1969). H. R. Cayton and G. S. Mitchell, *Black Workers and the New Unions* (1939), and H. S. Northrup, *Organized Labor and the Negro* (1944), are revealing studies.

E. W. Hawley, *The New Deal and the Problem of Monopoly* (1966), covers the ground from NRA days. Thurman Arnold, *The Folklore of Capitalism* (1937), bared some of the pitfalls of trustbusting before he assumed responsibility for it in 1937. David Lynch, *Concentration of Economic Power* (1946), offers a professional summary of TNEC reports and conclusions.

Bernard Sternsher, ed., *The Negro in Depression and War, Prelude to Revolution 1930-1945* (1969), presents ample background on the Negro and the Roosevelt coalition, with an excellent bibliography. E. L. Tatum, *The Changed Political Thought of the Negro 1915-1940* (1951), is informative. J. J. Huthmacher, *Senator Robert F. Wagner and the Rise of Urban Liberalism* (1968), and Charles Garrett, *The LaGuardia Years, Machine and Reform Politics in New York City* (1961), are good on the urban whites in the coalition. G. Q. Flynn, *American Catholics and the Roosevelt Presidency 1932-1936* (1968), is illuminating. G. B. Tindall, *Emergence of the New South 1913-1945* (1968), discusses the sectional Democratic party. See also Frank Freidel, *F.D.R. and the South* (1965).

T. H. Williams, *Huey Long* (1969), definitive on one of Roosevelt's major opponents, is also revealing on his followers. See also C. J. Tull, *Father Coughlin and the New Deal* (1965), and Abraham Holtzman, *The Townsend Movement* (1963). D. R. McCoy, *Angry Voices: Left-of-Center Politics in the New Deal Era* (1958); Irving Howe and Lewis Coser, *The American Communist Party: A Critical History 1919-1957* (1957); and Earl Latham, *The Communist Controversy in Washington: From the New Deal to McCarthy* (1966), discuss the radical left. On the challenge from the right see J. T. Patterson, *Congressional Conservatism and the New Deal . . . 1933-1939* (1967), and George Wolfskill, *The Revolt of the Conservatives: A History of the American Liberty League 1934-1940* (1962).

The Court fight is well described in Joseph Alsop and Turner Catledge, *The 168 Days* (1938). E. S. Corwin, *Court over Constitution* (1938), and R. H. Jackson, *The Struggle for Judicial Supremacy* (1941), state the case against the Court. See also C. H. Pritchett, *The Roosevelt Court: A Study in Judicial Politics and Values 1937-1947* (1948).

# WORLD WAR II AND THE ATOMIC REVOLUTION

The war that began in Europe when Hitler invaded Poland, September 1, 1939, awakened the American people from the dream of continentalism, and isolation from Europe, into which they again had fallen after Wilson's fruitless effort to make the *world* safe for democracy twenty years earlier.

It had not been a peaceful dream. Even those expatriates who found in postwar Europe high cultural standards and a more congenial intellectual atmosphere than at home rubbed most of their countrymen the wrong way. Europe, it was said in the twenties, was a political wasteland inhabited by quarrelsome people always at one another's throats. Europeans had no character; they did not even pay their debts.

Will Rogers, the most popular humorist of the day, gave voice to the American attitude during a trip abroad in 1926. "A bunch of American tourists were hissed and stoned yesterday in France," Rogers gibed, "but not until they had finished buying." On his return home, Rogers remarked: "France and England think just as much of each other as two rival bands of Chicago bootleggers. Gloating over our unpopularity is the only thing they have ever agreed on perfectly." Of Old World governments he had this to say:

*I arrived in Paris late at night. The next day we had Briand Premier for breakfast; Herriot Premier for lunch; Poincaré Premier for dinner; and woke up the next morning and Briand is back in again. This is not a Government; it's an old-fashioned Movie, where they flash on the screen: "Two minutes, please, while we change Premiers."*

During the twenties few Americans condemned Italian fascism, which seemed to have imposed an admired discipline on an unruly people. The rise of Nazism in Germany in the thirties only confirmed the opinion that Europeans should be abandoned to their own devices, not least in dealing with such other European "isms" as socialism and bolshevism, poisonous infections only too easily spread. The Nazi movement in particular, with Adolf Hitler at its head, was to grow sufficiently aggressive in policy to menace American interests and sufficiently inhumane in character to trouble the American soul. Yet the United States long remained cool toward its victims.

The prevailing American attitude toward the Far East differed from that toward Europe. America's "continental destiny," drawing her westward toward the Pacific, soon fixed her gaze beyond that ocean for further trade and future empire. Many Americans who believed that Europe was the land of the past felt, however irrationally, that the Orient was the land of the future. The trouble here was that American aspirations soon encountered the much more imperious ambitions of Japan, which the United States itself had done much to quicken and which had at least the justification of proximity.

In the thirties the United States often tried to interest European nations in collective action to check Japanese expansion. At the same time the United States remained aloof from Europe's systems of collective security. Both policies failed. Weakened by American isolation, European collective security collapsed in the face of Nazi aggression. With the Europeans sorely tried on their own continent, American efforts to involve them in the Orient were doomed.

The distress of America's old Allies after Hitler's Polish adventure had spread into a new general war was the signal for Japan to strike at the United States. What confronted Americans after the catastrophe at Pearl Harbor, December 7, 1941, was no longer the Wilsonian task of making their political institutions prevail throughout the world but simply that of keeping them intact at home. In candid recognition of this predicament, one similarly faced by him in the unprecedented domestic crisis of the depression almost ten years before, Franklin D. Roosevelt called World War II the "War for Survival."

The war against the Axis was won more convincingly than the war on the depression. Yet one may question how well American political institutions, already profoundly altered in meeting the domestic crisis, survived the international one. The massive national mobilization made inescapable by the war tremendously enlarged the role of the military in the American economy, in American education, and in other areas of American life. The war also hastened the collapse of empire among victors and victims alike, leaving power vacuums that sucked in military force. The unleashing of the new demon of atomic energy at the moment of final victory, with the international rivalry for atomic preeminence that followed, gave fresh momentum to militarism that also invited new worldwide responsibilities and irresponsibility—and accelerated change at home.

# I Between-wars diplomacy

## The Washington Conference of 1921-1922

The futility of trying to keep separate the European and Oriental theaters of international friction must have become evident to the United States when Japan persisted in nibbling away at Russian Siberia as well as China even while World War I was in progress. Once that war was over, Japan also grasped formerly German islands in the Pacific. What made her activities the more menacing was her treaty of alliance with Britain which she had renewed for ten years in 1911 and which continued in force.

This combination of two great naval powers was itself enough to compel the United States in 1916 to embark on a vast program of battleship construction which had nothing to do with the German submarine menace. When World War I ended two years later with the German navy dispersed, world naval imbalance became greater than ever, and the United States felt it must become a counterweight to Britain's dominance on the Atlantic as well as to Japan's strength on the Pacific. Rivalry with the British for Middle Eastern petroleum, which the war had made into a vital strategic resource, itself threatened to cause an Anglo-American conflict that American naval leaders felt they must urgently prepare for.

The obvious way to prepare was to build more and more capital ships—that is, battleships and cruisers. But another possibility presented itself: an agreement to check the monstrously costly naval race. In 1920 the United States began to explore the feasibility of a great-power conference to work out such an agreement. These explorations resulted in invitations from President Warren G. Harding in July 1921 to France and Italy as well as Britain and Japan to meet with the United States in Washington, beginning Armistice Day, November 11.

The delegates had hardly settled in their seats on the first business day of the conference when United States Secretary of State Hughes, the presiding officer, electrified them with a blunt proposal for a ten-year suspension in the construction of capital ships. Hughes went farther. He urged that the capital-ship tonnage of the United States and Britain be limited to 500,000 and that of Japan to 300,000. This was in keeping with their then current power ratio of 5-5-3; but it also meant that Britain and Japan would have to jettison no less than sixty-six ships and the United States thirty ships in order to get down to their allotted strength.

Heated bargaining followed the Secretary's proposal, but some time before the conference ended in February 1922, a five-power naval treaty was signed that endorsed the 5-5-3 ratio virtually at Hughes's tonnage figures and permitted France and Italy capital ship tonnages of 175,000. Although smaller ships were not covered by the agreement, the naval race was thus at least partially checked.

Two other important agreements made at the Washington meeting were the so-called Four-Power Pact and Nine-Power Pact. The first replaced the irritating Anglo-Japanese alliance with a new agreement which included the United States and France, and pledged the four signatories to keep the peace in the Pacific region by respecting one another's rights there. The second agreement, in which China, Italy, Belgium, the Netherlands, and Portugal joined the members of the Four-Power Pact, reaffirmed the Open Door principle in China and guaranteed her sovereignty, independence, and territorial integrity.

## Japan in China

The Washington Conference was welcomed in most of the world as a triumph of diplomacy in the quest for enduring peace. When it was followed in 1928 by the Kellogg-Briand Pact renouncing war as an instrument of national policy (which sixty-two nations, including Japan, signed) a fragile world order seemed somewhat strengthened. Japan, however, was simply marking time, while her hunger for a continental empire to cap her extraordinarily rapid industrialization and modernization was suddenly sharpened by the Great Depression. In September 1931, using as an excuse a provocative incident on the Japanese-controlled South Manchurian Railway, Japanese forces stormed into China's Manchuria province.

The United States and the League of Nations promptly reminded Japan of her treaty responsibilities, but to no avail, and by January 1932 the Japanese army had crushed all resistance in Manchuria.

When it had become clear that reminders alone would have no effect on Japan, the question was raised for Western diplomats whether Japan should be subjected to economic sanctions. Secretary of State Henry L. Stimson suggested this possibility to President Hoover, but feeling that sanctions might lead the United States once more into an unwanted war, the President firmly opposed them. His decision, and the reluctance of the League powers to go beyond it, limited Western action to moral pressure which Japan felt free to ignore.

On January 7, 1932, Secretary Stimson stated in a note to Japan and China that the United States could not recognize any treaty or agreement in the Orient that infringed her rights. This policy—refusing to recognize territorial conquest in Asia—became known as the "Stimson Doctrine," though it had earlier been enunciated and applied by Secretary of State Bryan. The Stimson Doctrine, however,

foresaw no use of arms to back it up. Stimson had hoped that the British government would associate itself with his declaration, but the British Foreign Office, instead, issued a statement which, as Stimson later said, could be interpreted by the world, including the Japanese government, only as "a rebuff to the United States." The American people, too absorbed in domestic difficulties to care much about Manchuria, did not "give a hoot in a rain barrel" (as a Philadelphia newspaper said) who controlled North China. And the administration, to its credit, refrained from using the incident to distract the public from depression woes.

The situation deteriorated after January 28, 1932, when Japan, stung by a Chinese boycott outside of Manchuria, invaded Shanghai, wiped out the Chinese force there and killed defenseless civilians. For the first time, militant sentiment against Japan began to appear in the United States, but President Hoover continued to oppose even economic coercion.

Secretary Stimson, fearing that he would only court another humiliating rebuff if he appealed to the signers of the Nine-Power Pact against Japan, decided to issue a message to the world in an informal way by expressing his views in a letter to Senator Borah, chairman of the Senate Committee on Foreign Relations. In this letter, Stimson asserted that the United States would stand on its treaty rights in the Far East, specifically those recognized in the Nine-Power Pact, and invited other nations to do the same. He pointedly warned that the violation of one of the Washington treaties released the parties from the other treaties. This move was greeted with strong approval in the American press, and on March 11, 1932, the League of Nations Assembly adopted a resolution using much the same language. Subsequently, the League's Lytton Commission issued a report condemning Japan's actions and refusing to recognize the validity of the puppet regime that Tokyo had established in Manchuria as the state of Manchukuo. When, as a substitute, the Lytton Commission, in February 1933, proposed an autonomous Manchurian state under face-saving Chinese sovereignty but effective Japanese control, Japan's only response was to withdraw from the League the following month. In December 1934 she also renounced the Washington Conference naval agreement; and when the United States and Britain refused in 1936 to grant her naval parity with themselves, she embarked on a naval expansion program which the other two felt impelled to match.

### Recognition of the Soviet Union

Japan's aggression in China made the Soviet Union fearful that her East Asian rival would soon assault her Maritime Province, ranging along the farthest boundary of Siberia. Despite the World War I western intervention in Russia, such fears made Stalin and his advisers receptive to Roosevelt administration probes in 1933 about the acceptability of offers of recognition by the United States. All other major powers, including Japan, had long since recognized Russia's Bolshevik regime.

The United States, on its part, had good reasons to seek to extend recognition at this time despite a generation of revulsion deepened by the communists' repudiation of World War I czarist debts, confiscation of private property without compensation, preachment of world revolution against capitalism and imperialism, and sponsorship of revolutionary parties in capitalist countries including the United States. Perhaps the principal reason was American fear also of Japanese ambitions on the Asian mainland; but the Great Depression gave added force to the reasons as well. One was the wish for new outlets for American exports in the vast Russian empire (how Russia would pay for such exports was conveniently neglected). A second was the growing interest among American intellectuals and writers in the communist social experiment after the perpetual-motion prosperity machine in the United States failed.

A major center of opposition to recognition was the United States Department of State, where Secretary Hull made little effort to offset the attitudes of highly placed career men despite the President's recognition initiatives. Roosevelt made short shrift of such opposition by ignoring the record—largely unsupported—worked up by the career men of al-

leged Soviet involvement in Cuban revolutionary activity in the early thirties, and by dispatching Hull to the Latin American Montevideo Conference late in 1933 (see p. 738), when final negotiations with Stalin's emissary Maxim Litvinov were in progress. Formal recognition was effected by an exchange of notes in Washington, November 16, 1933, in which Litvinov on his part, after waiving Soviet damage claims against the United States arising from the 1918–1919 intervention, agreed to negotiation of United States claims on czarist debts. Litvinov also agreed to halt Soviet propaganda in the United States and to divorce the Soviet government from subversive organizations heretofore "under its direct or indirect" control.

Recognition gave the United States an official observation post in Moscow. Assistant Secretary of State William C. Bullitt, who had remained closest to Roosevelt in the recognition project, became the first United States ambassador to the USSR. While little was effected in enlarging trade, voice was given to the value of Soviet friendship in relation to German as well as Japanese militarism. Unfortunately, friendship did not long survive the closer contact. Americans in Russia were subjected to personal harassment, while negotiations over debts and debates over continued communist activity in the Western Hemisphere almost led to American withdrawal of recognition within two years. Diplomatic relations, nevertheless, continued.

### "Good neighbors" in Latin America

While fear of war stayed the American hand in the Far East, in Latin America strategic, diplomatic, and economic considerations had led between the end of World War I and 1927 to United States interference in the government of no less than ten Latin American countries. Often United States armed forces became involved—as in Panama in 1921, the Dominican Republic from 1921 to 1924, and Honduras in 1923. Since 1912, more-

736

over, United States marines, on invitation from Nicaragua, had helped keep order in that country. When the marines were withdrawn at last in 1925, Nicaragua again became so turbulent that President Coolidge almost immediately sent them back in force to exercise our "moral responsibility" there. Early in 1927 a special presidential envoy won over rebel and government leaders in Nicaragua to the idea of an election in 1928 under United States supervision. The results were generally satisfactory to both sides. The followers of General Augusto César Sandino, one of the rebel leaders, however, refused to be pacified, retired to the hills, and harassed American marines until 1933, when the last of them were called home.

Intervention in Panama arose largely over strategic concern for the safety of the Panama Canal. Elsewhere, diplomatic responsibility assumed unilaterally under the "Roosevelt Corollary" to the Monroe Doctrine (see p. 603) seemed to justify military involvement. In Mexico, protection of American private economic interests became the main ground for United States policy.

The Mexican Constitution of 1917 had reaffirmed the old Mexican principle, violated during the long Díaz regime (1877-1911), that the government retained the ownership of all Mexican mineral and oil resources. By then, United States businessmen, encouraged by Díaz, had invested heavily in Mexican development, and they feared that application of this principle might be made retroactive and their properties liable to confiscation. When President Plutarco Calles took office in 1924, he announced his desire to make just such a change. The Mexican Congress then provided that petroleum rights acquired before 1917 would be limited to fifty years.

The pressure of American oil interests and the influence of American Catholics who resented Calles's anticlerical policy, together with the conventional interventionist tradition, soon sparked talk of a new war with Mexico. But in 1927 President Coolidge, taking his cue

from a unanimous Senate resolution for peaceful arbitration, sent his former Amherst classmate Dwight L. Morrow, a partner in the House of Morgan, south of the border with the curt instruction: "Keep us out of war." Morrow proved an excellent diplomat, and his friendly feeling for the Mexicans was soon returned. Favored by a decision of the Mexican Supreme Court, he worked out with Calles a compromise by which American investors could retain permanently the oil properties they had held before the Constitution of 1917 went into effect. Later expropriation under the Cárdenas regime in 1938 led to a complex settlement in 1941 under which American oil properties and other claims were bought out by Mexico. American oil companies received about $42 million for their properties, and other American interests another $40 million.

Morrow's success in Mexico heralded a major change in United States diplomacy in Latin America. This became apparent at the Washington Conference on Conciliation and Arbitration in December 1928, when treaties were signed with Latin countries that amounted to a promise to refrain from unilateral action in the future. In 1930 a State Department memorandum expressly repudiated the Roosevelt Corollary, and in the next two years the government showed it meant business by refraining from intervening in El Salvador, Haiti, and elsewhere where the Corollary once would have made intervention a matter of course.

In his first inaugural address in March 1933, FDR said he hoped "to dedicate this nation to the policy of the good neighbor." His good intentions soon were severely tested in Cuba—where, in August 1933, President Gerardo Machado, iron-fisted dictator though he was, could not check civil strife brought on by depression conditions and was ousted by the army, perhaps with a push from Roosevelt's ambassador, Sumner Welles. When further revolutionary activity brought Ramón Grau San Martín to the provisional presidency of Cuba, Roosevelt withheld recognition. San Martín's military backers, led by Sergeant Fulgencio Batista, quickly took the cue and in January 1934 conducted an election which

**738**

carried the United States-backed candidate, Carlos Mendieta, the first of a string of Batista puppets, to the presidency. "I fell because Washington willed it," San Martín declared. Roosevelt did not deny that nonrecognition was intervention, but prided himself, by refraining from landing troops, on the discovery, as he said, of a practical way in which the United States "could apply the doctrine of the Good Neighbor."

A still more practical way was found in May 1934, when the United States, on Ambassador Welles's urging, negotiated with the Mendieta government a treaty abrogating the Platt Amendment (p. 597), thereby releasing Cuba from formal liability to United States interference. At the Montevideo Conference of American States in 1933, Secretary Hull and Latin delegates approved a proposal stating that "no state has the right to intervene in the internal or external affairs of another." At this conference Hull also announced a new plan to reduce tariffs through reciprocal trade agreements, further pleasing the delegates. In the spirit of the Montevideo agreement, United States representatives, in March 1936, signed a treaty with Panama surrendering American rights to interfere in that nation's affairs and raising the annual payments for canal use. Not until Panama agreed in 1939 to permit the United States in emergencies to defend the canal unilaterally, however, did the Senate approve this treaty.

Efforts to overcome the deep suspicion of "Yanqui imperialism" gained ground slowly, but by the time of the attack on Pearl Harbor relations had improved enough for the United States to be assured of cooperation in the Southern Hemisphere.

### Dictatorship in Europe

New friends in Latin America became all the more welcome to the United States as lack of sympathy and understanding with Europe grew. American immigration and protectionist policies in the twenties shut out European peoples and European goods. The acrimonious arguments over Allied war debts, which the United States refused to cancel and

European nations neglected to pay, reflected the breakdown of mutual respect.

As for the League of Nations, perhaps nothing bespoke American sentiment so well as Harding's remark in 1923 that the United States "does not propose to enter now by the side door, or the back door or the cellar door." True, eminent American individuals like John Bassett Moore served on the World Court, the League's judicial agency, and American observers attended sessions of the League, giving their country, as Clemenceau said, representation "by an ear but not by a mouth." By 1930 the United States had actually taken part in forty League conferences, but even to suggest the possibility of overt cooperation with the League, as Secretary Stimson did in 1931 over the Far Eastern crisis, was to risk the wrath of powerful newspapers across the country. The next year, before his nomination for the presidency, even so good a Wilsonian as FDR allowed himself to be pressured by the Hearst press into repudiating the League. "American participation in the League," he said then, "would not serve the highest purpose of the prevention of war and a settlement of international difficulties in accordance with fundamental American ideals." Roosevelt's disruption of the London Economic Conference of 1933 (see p. 710) seemed to indicate that the New Deal itself, except for Hull's success in realizing substantial decreases in world tariffs under the Trade Agreements Act of June 1934, was committed to economic nationalism and political isolation.

Isolationism gained ground in the midthirties from the widespread belief, fostered by the growing disrepute of American business leaders during the depression, that international bankers and munitions makers had conspired to draw the United States into World War I for selfish purposes. The sensational "merchants of death" investigation of 1934, conducted by a Senate committee headed by Gerald P. Nye of North Dakota, gave more or less official sanction to this view that wars were fought for the benefit of a favored few and to the policy of trying to keep out of war simply by making it unprofitable under the law for citizens to trade with belligerents.

The first test of this policy came in mid-1935 when Benito Mussolini, after intensive military preparations, made it clear that nothing short of Italian annexation of the ancient state of Ethiopia, after a border clash with adjoining Italian Somaliland in East Africa, would placate him. By the time the fascist dictator had launched a full-scale attack on Ethiopia in October 1935, Congress (in August) had passed the first of a series of Neutrality Acts authorizing the President, after proclaiming that a state of war existed between foreign nations, to forbid Americans to sell or transport munitions to them. Such basic war materials as oil, steel, and copper were excluded from the ban. Under administration pressure, Congress put a six-month limit on this embargo, and Roosevelt reluctantly signed it on August 31. The arms embargo, he said later, by impeding unprepared victims while leaving unaffected those who had built up massive military machines in advance, "played right into the hands of the aggressor nations [which] were actually encouraged by our laws to make war upon their neighbors."

When the League of Nations branded Italy an aggressor at the outset of the invasion and required member countries to impose economic sanctions on her, only to withdraw the charge and the sanctions after Italy's complete victory in May 1936, another supposed impediment in the dictators' path fell away. Congress, meanwhile, in February 1936, extended the six-month act of August 1935 to May 1, 1937, and added loans and credits to belligerents to the ban.

After his gratifying triumph in Ethiopia, Mussolini embarked on other adventures. In July 1936, when Spanish fascists under General Francisco Franco, with strong church support, rebelled against their country's republican government, he promptly sent 50,000 to 75,000 "volunteers," along with planes and supplies, to aid them. Not to be outdone, Hitler also soon took this course.

Opinion in the United States became deeply divided over the Spanish war. Many Americans sided with the government there, which the United States had long recognized, and some even went over to fight for it. Soviet support of this government, however, lent color to the fascist charge that it was communists they were opposing; it also made it easier for American fascist sympathizers and Catholic supporters of Franco's uprising to win congressional backing for a joint resolution forbidding the export of munitions to either side. Congress adopted such a resolution on January 6, 1937. Naturally this action hurt the government more than the rebels, who were receiving ample foreign assistance. At the expiration of the first Neutrality Act and its extensions on May 1, 1937, Congress adopted a new measure authorizing the President to decide not only when wars between nations existed but also when civil wars like that in Spain endangered world peace, and in such situations an embargo was to begin at once on the export of munitions and on credits for them. A "cash-and-carry" plan, limited to two years, also empowered the President under this act to require belligerents buying *nonmilitary* goods in this country to take them away in their own ships. The act also made it unlawful for Americans (heretofore only warned that they did so at their own risk) to travel on belligerents' vessels.

In March 1939, after an exhausting war, government forces were overwhelmed in Spain and the entire country fell under the rule of General Franco, a dictator heavily obligated to Mussolini and Hitler. By then other totalitarian adventures had soured more and more Americans on isolationism.

## II   Again to the verge of war

### The totalitarian challenge

As might have been expected, the first official abandonment of neutrality was provoked not by the European totalitarians but by the Japanese. After Japanese and Chinese forces clashed at Peiping near the Manchukuoan border in July 1937, large Japanese detachments overran North China. Roosevelt attacked the aggression in his famous "quarantine speech" of October 5, 1937. Ninety percent of the people of the world wanted peace, he said, but their security was threatened by the other 10 percent; peace-loving nations must act together to quarantine aggressors:

There is a solidarity, an interdependence about the modern world, both technically and morally, which makes it impossible for any nation completely to isolate itself from economic and political upheavals in the rest of the world, especially when such upheavals appear to be spreading and not declining. . . . We are determined to keep out of war. . . . We are adopting such measures as will minimize our risk of involvement, but we cannot have complete protection in a world of disorder in which confidence and security have broken down.

As in the recent past, no action was taken against Japan, but in January 1938 Roosevelt called on Congress for a billion dollars to enlarge the navy, a sum Congress voted in May. Within the year, totalitarian experiments in aggression in Europe brought on a crisis there. Hitler, who had come to power in Germany in January 1933 and fifteen months later had renounced the Versailles Treaty terms on German disarmament, had long been campaigning for the return of German territory lost in World War I, where German people still lived.

In March 1936, while Mussolini's adventure in Ethiopia engaged the attention of western Europe, Hitler's forces, unopposed, had actually occupied the Rhineland territory adjacent to France. Now, in September 1938, he was poised to grab the Sudetenland of Czechoslovakia. Again France, along with Britain, remained unprepared to confront a rearmed

*"The sleeping giant begins to feel it"—Hutton cartoon in* Philadelphia Inquirer, *July 18, 1937, on Japan's aggressions in China.*

Germany in battle, and at the disastrous meeting in Munich on September 29 they let Hitler have what he wanted. We secured "peace with honor . . . peace in our time," at Munich, British Prime Minister Neville Chamberlain told his people, but his words carried little conviction.

At Munich, having gained the Sudetenland, Hitler promised to leave the rest of Czechoslovakia alone; but in March 1939 he swallowed up the remainder of the small republic. Not to be outdone, Mussolini three weeks later took Albania. Hitler's word obviously was worthless. Yet the frightened world applauded FDR when, in April 1939, he wrote to Hitler and Mussolini asking them to pledge, for a period of ten years, that they would not attack any one of a list of thirty-one nations. Hitler replied for both with the suggestion that the danger of aggression existed only in Roosevelt's mind. The reality of the danger was brought closer in May 1939, when a stubborn group of Senate isolationists blocked an administration request for revisions of the neutrality laws to permit economic aid to Britain and France in case of war.

Apparently safe from American industrial might on his Western Front, Hitler, in August 1939, shocked the world by making a nonaggression pact with the Russian totalitarians on his Eastern Front. This double protection left him free to attack Poland, which with British and French encouragement had been sturdily resisting demands similar to those made on Czechoslovakia for the return of territory. At the same time, the new pact left Russia free to satisfy her own territorial ambitions. On September 1, 1939, Hitler's legions invaded Poland while his air force rained bombs on Polish cities. Despite the discouraging stand of the United States Senate, Britain and France honored their Polish commitments by declaring war on Germany only two days later. As the law still required, Roosevelt invoked the Neutrality Act against the belligerents, but he did not repeat Woodrow Wilson's appeal for neutrality in thought as well as in deed. "Even

a neutral," said Roosevelt, "cannot be asked to close his mind or his conscience."

Before Munich, public opinion polls showed only a third of the American people in favor of selling arms to Britain and France in the event of war. By mid-September 1939, when Roosevelt called a special session of Congress to revise the neutrality laws, and specifically to repeal the arms embargo so that munitions could be sold to the old Allies, he appeared to have the support of at least two-thirds of the people. In his message to Congress, Roosevelt also asked for authority to prevent American ships from sailing into danger zones so that provocative incidents on the high seas could be avoided; belligerents must carry their own cargoes. All these requests were voted by Congress on November 3, 1939. Lifting the arms embargo pleased the interventionists; restoration of cash-and-carry pleased the still-formidable isolationists.

In addition to its traditional stay-at-home exponents, isolationism attracted a mixed group: pacifists and socialists opposed on principle to war; German- and Irish-Americans who hated France and Britain more than they feared dictatorship; irreconcilable Roosevelt haters, fearful of further aggrandizement of government in case of war; and outright fascist sympathizers. After the Russo-German pact of August 1939, the American Communist party, all out for nonintervention as long as this policy remained in Russian interest, made strange bedfellows for the others.

In September 1940, at the instigation of some big business opponents of the New Deal, the America First Committee was formed to mobilize isolationist opinion, with General Robert E. Wood, Board Chairman of Sears, Roebuck, as national chairman. The Committee drew many eminent spokesmen before its disbandment when Pearl Harbor was attacked. Colonel Charles A. Lindbergh, Jr., expressed their sentiments when he declared: "In the future we may have to deal with a Europe dominated by Germany. . . . An agreement between us could maintain peace and civilization throughout the world as far into the future as we can see."

Interventionists found their voice in the Committee to Defend America by Aiding the

741

Allies, whose chairman was William Allen White. White replied to Lindbergh that many countries that had tried to be neutral, as Lindbergh advised, had been destroyed: "Hitler's whole philosophy, his idea of government, his economic setup, his insatiable ambitions, all make it impossible for a free country and a free people to live beside Hitler's world enslaved."

*Toward intervention*

When Hitler delayed until April 1940 to move on the Western Front, many even in Europe were lulled by the seemingly "phony war." When Hitler did move, however, he did so with such terrifying speed and force that neutral Denmark and Norway and the Low Countries—Belgium, Holland, and Luxembourg—and France herself were all brought to their knees by the *blitzkrieg* within seven weeks. When Belgium fell, Britain had to strain every resource to rescue her own expeditionary force from the Continent. This rescue was effected under the pounding of German planes and guns between May 28 and June 4, when the last of more than 335,000 men had been evacuated safely home from Dunkirk, France, near the Belgian border. On June 10, Mussolini attacked France from the south, while her armies were reeling back from Hitler's in the north. On June 22, completely crushed, France signed an armistice.

The British Empire now stood suddenly alone against German arms and the Berlin-Rome Axis.

*The battle of France is over [Churchill told the House of Commons]. I expect that the Battle of Britain is about to begin. Upon this battle depends the survival of Christian civilization. . . . If we fail, then the whole world, including the United States, . . . will sink into the abyss of a new Dark Age. . . . Let us therefore brace outselves to our duties, and so bear ourselves that, if the British Empire and its Commonwealth last for a thousand years, men will say "This was their finest hour."*

During the summer and fall of 1940, in a tremendous effort to bring Britain to her knees, Hitler sent clouds of planes to bomb

English cities, and tens of thousands of civilians were killed and wounded. But the Royal Air Force fought back with extraordinary courage, and by fall it was clear that Hitler's attempt to bomb Britain into defeat would fail. If Britain was to be subjugated it must be by invasion, and Churchill, at the time of Dunkirk, had promised to resist that "to the end, . . . whatever the cost may be . . . until, in God's good time, the New World, with all its power and might, steps forth to the rescue and liberation of the Old."

Churchill's effort not only to brace his own people but also, as he explained later, to assure America of their resolution, was not lost on the administration. As early as May 1940, Roosevelt requested funds from Congress for "at least 50,000 planes a year." In June, denouncing Mussolini's attack on France, he promised not to recognize infringements of her territory. In August, with the Canadian Prime Minister, Mackenzie King, he agreed to set up a joint board for the defense of the northern half of the Western Hemisphere. Throughout the summer, moreover, aid was being rushed overseas. Military equipment that could not legally be transferred directly from government to government was sold to American private firms, which then resold it to Britain.

On September 3, Roosevelt took his most daring step. By executive agreement, which did not require Senate concurrence, he made the famous deal with Britain, transferring to her fifty overage but still effective destroyers desperately needed to stave off German submarines. In exchange, Britain gave the United States sites for naval bases in Newfoundland and Bermuda and rent-free leases on six additional sites in the Caribbean and South Atlantic. As outraged as many senators by this high-handed trade was Hitler himself, who had every right to consider it an act of war. As Churchill later observed, "it marked the passage of the United States from being neutral to being nonbelligerent." But Hitler did nothing to bestir the United States to join the

Allies, and some of the senators, two weeks later, helped enact the first peacetime draft in American history. By then, too, Congress had appropriated about $16 billion for airplanes, warships, and other defense needs.

The climax of the isolationist-interventionist debate came at about the same time as the presidential election of 1940. The Democrats, at their convention in Chicago in mid-July, boldly broke the two-term tradition and renominated FDR, naming Secretary of Agriculture Wallace as his running mate. The Republicans leaned heavily toward two outspoken isolationist senators, Arthur H. Vandenberg of Michigan and Robert A. Taft of Ohio. Their strength also tinged with isolationism the stand of a third aspirant, the flashy young District Attorney of New York, Thomas E. Dewey. But the drift of the times became abundantly clear when the bright young men in the party rallied so strongly behind a newcomer to politics, Wendell L. Willkie of New York, that they put him across on the sixth ballot at the Philadelphia convention at the end of June. Senator Charles L. McNary of Oregon was named for the vice-presidency.

A magnetic public-utilities executive, Willkie first came into prominence as a leader in the fight of private power interests against the TVA. His charm, apparent then, grew with his own growing liberalism; and by 1940 his stand on the war in Europe was close to Roosevelt's. This similarity probably hurt more than it helped him in the campaign. It left Willkie with a popular position, but deprived him of an issue on which to set himself off from his veteran opponent. Willkie lost by a popular vote of 22,305,000 to 27,244,000 and an electoral vote of 82 to 449, but he restored the Republican party to a position of vigorous opposition without accepting the views of its isolationist wing—an outstanding personal success. His premature death in 1944 was a blow to the GOP.

The election hardly over, Roosevelt renewed the debate over foreign policy in a fireside chat to the people on December 29, 1940.

"There will be no 'bottlenecks' in our determination to aid Great Britain," he said then; "all our present efforts are not enough. We must have more ... of everything. . . . We must be the great arsenal of democracy."

One week later, in his annual message to Congress on January 6, 1941, he went further: "The time is near when ... those nations which are now in actual war with aggressor nations ... will not be able to pay ... in ready cash. We cannot, and will not, tell them they must surrender, merely because of inability to pay for the weapons we know they must have." He then proposed "lend-lease" as the most practical means by which the United States, while remaining at peace herself, could help arm Britain and her allies not only to defeat the totalitarian menace, but in the future to build a better world in which the "four essential human freedoms"—freedom of speech, freedom of worship, freedom from want, and freedom from fear—might animate all nations.

The lend-lease bill—to supply Britain and her allies with arms carried in their own ships and to be returned or replaced when the war ended—was fiercely opposed in Congress as a step toward American involvement in the fighting. Senator Burton K. Wheeler of Montana called it the "New Deal's 'triple A' foreign policy—to plow under every fourth American boy"—a remark that Roosevelt branded "the most untruthful, the most dastardly, unpatriot-

**743**

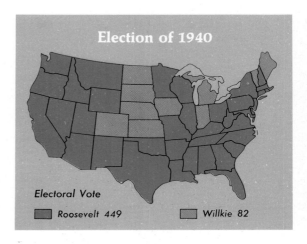

Election of 1940

*Electoral Vote*

Roosevelt 449  Willkie 82

ic thing that has been said in public life in my generation." But public opinion favored lend-lease, and on March 11, 1941, Congress at last having approved it, the President signed the measure. Churchill referred to it as "the most unsordid act in the history of any nation." Lend-lease had a salutary effect on British finances and British morale even before the massive flow of arms began. It also gave a strong impulse to American intervention despite official disclaimers. Indeed, Admiral Harold R. Stark, United States Chief of Naval Operations, promptly wrote his fleet commanders: "The question as to our entry into the war now seems to be *when*, and not *whether*."

### The American commitment

To insure that American lend-lease ended up at its destination and not at the bottom of the sea, Roosevelt, once the measure had become law, immediately took steps to help Britain fight the "wolf-packs" of German submarines that infested the Atlantic, and he soon extended American "defense" lines all the way to Greenland and Iceland. In a more aggressive move still, on March 31, 1941, he ordered the coast guard to seize sixty-five German or German-controlled ships then in American ports. On May 15 a German torpedo sank the American merchantman *Robin Moor* in the South Atlantic. Roosevelt responded by proclaiming an unlimited national emergency, and on June 16 he requested Germany and Italy to close their consulates in the United States. These Axis countries replied by ordering American consulates in their countries closed as well.

Thereafter the United States edged ever closer to war in the Atlantic. In July the President announced that the United States, by agreement with the Icelandic government, was taking over the defense of Iceland, hitherto in the hands of the British, for the duration of the war—and that the United States Navy would keep convoy lines open as far as Iceland. In August he dramatically met with Churchill on a British battleship at sea. Here the two "naval persons," as they liked to call themselves, drew up the eight-point declaration named the Atlantic Charter, in which they professed what amounted to common war aims (see p. 745).

In September, when a German submarine near Iceland fired two torpedoes at the United States destroyer *Greer,* and when two American-owned merchantmen were sunk, Roosevelt in a radio talk declared that United States patrols would henceforth defend the seas against German "piracy" by striking the first blow at any Axis raiders they encountered. In October, when the American destroyer *Kearney* was damaged near Iceland in a battle with German submarines, Roosevelt asserted, "America has been attacked. . . . The shooting has started." At the end of October the destroyer *Reuben James* was sunk off Iceland while engaged in convoy duty, and Congress responded in November by removing the restriction in the Lend-Lease Act prohibiting American vessels from sailing "into a combat area in violation of . . . the Neutrality Act of 1939." Henceforth, American merchant ships were to be allowed to sail well-armed and were to be permitted to carry lend-lease supplies direct to Britain.

Thus, by the fall of 1941 the United States had become an open ally of Britain without formally having declared war. By then Britain had gained still another ally when Hitler, on June 22, 1941, began his invasion of the Soviet Union, so recently his partner in the nonaggression pact.

What led Hitler to take this momentous step at this time remains uncertain, although the geopolitical theories prevalent in Germany in the thirties, and not neglected by American Firsters and others, certainly offer a clue. In 1939, before the Nazi invasion of Poland, Dr. Karl Haushofer, director of the Geopolitik Institut, declared: "If I thought war were coming, I would inscribe over my door: 'Great Britain must not be attacked before the Greater Reich has been established in Mitteleuropa.'" This was also the view of Friedrich Neumann, who died in 1917, but whose book on Greater Germany, as Waverley Root puts it, "was Hitler's breviary." Most likely Hitler hoped quickly to capture the wheat of the Ukraine, the oil of the Caucasus, and the greater part of Russia's industrial resources, all of which Germany had grasped at Brest-Litovsk in 1918 only to be forced within months to relinquish them. Such reconquests might make Britain—having already checked the "1000-year Reich" in the air war—and her friends across the sea recognize at last that they confronted the invincible continental land mass, that phantom of geopolitical empire, with which they had best come to terms. Success in Russia might also inspire Nazi forces with renewed hopes of total victory, so hatefully frustrated in the past.

Whatever his calculations, Hitler obviously underestimated by a wide margin the Soviet's potential for resistance. Others did likewise. In June 1941, for example, immediately after the Nazi attack, Henry L. Stimson, now Roosevelt's Secretary of War, estimated that it would take Hitler from one to three months to conquer the communists. Secretary of the Navy Knox thought it would take "anywhere from six weeks to two months." Yet when winter came, the Nazi armies still were outside Moscow and Leningrad, and Russia was still mustering her strength.

Churchill, an inveterate foe of bolshevism, nevertheless welcomed the Russians as comrades in arms, just as he had welcomed the American "arsenal." "I have only one purpose, the destruction of Hitler," he told his secretary. "If Hitler invaded Hell I would make at least a favorable reference to the Devil in the House of Commons."

In the Atlantic Charter of August 1941, both Roosevelt and Churchill had endorsed generously broad goals in the war against the Axis: no territorial aggrandizement; self-government for all peoples; free access to trade and raw materials; the abandonment of war as an instrument of international relations. The Atlantic Charter goals were disturbingly reminiscent of Wilson's Fourteen Points. Churchill, moreover, accepted the "self-government" principle only with strong, if strategically silent, reservations regarding the British Empire. In February 1942, when Britain's hopes had risen, he publicly chided the United States for interference on behalf of the self-government seekers in India. In November, further exhilarated by events, including his first meeting with Stalin, "the great Revolutionary Chief and profound Russian statesman," in August that year, Churchill made his famous resounding pronouncement: "We mean to hold our own. I have not become the King's First Minister in order to preside over the liquidation of the British Empire."

Russia's qualified endorsement of the goals of the Atlantic Charter when the United States extended lend-lease to her in November 1941 was even more disturbing than Britain's reservations. Russia's endorsement contained the ominous proviso: "Considering that the practical application of" the principles of the Charter "will necessarily adapt itself to the circumstances, needs, and historic peculiarities of particular countries." This was a threat as well as a caution. But the problems of the present had become too urgent to allow much time for worrying about future difficulties.

## III   Engaging the Axis

### Pearl Harbor

When Churchill agreed to the Atlantic Charter's principles for the postwar world, he also stated the Charter's more immediate objectives: "to cause our enemies concern," to "cheer our friends," and to "make Japan ponder." Japan, her appetite whetted by the Indochina possessions of fallen France and the East Indian colonies of occupied Holland, had joined Italy and Germany in the Axis back in September 1940. Now, even if she pondered the Allies' growing strength, her militant war party would not on that account put aside its grandest ambitions.

Early in the afternoon of December 7, 1941, a strong carrier-borne force of Japanese planes swooped down on the American naval base at Pearl Harbor in Hawaii. Although the American naval and military commanders there had been warned by the administration that a Japanese attack was likely, they had failed to prepare for such an eventuality and were caught by surprise. Most American aircraft there were destroyed on the ground, and the unprotected naval vessels suffered frightful damage. In this one assault, 2335 American servicemen and 68 civilians died; 1178 were wounded. The next day a shocked Congress voted to declare war on Japan. When on December 11 her Axis partners, Germany and Italy, declared war on the United States, Congress responded immediately with declarations of war against them.

Since his 1937 "quarantine" speech, Roosevelt had been cautious in dealing with continuing Japanese aggression. As early as December 1937, when Japanese planes sank the American gunboat *Panay* in the Yangtze River, war had seemed possible; but Japan quickly apologized for the attack and paid reparations for the lives lost. From then on, the United States followed an ambiguous line. On the one hand, Roosevelt refused to invoke the Neutrality Act lest it halt the movement of supplies over the tortuous Burma Road to Chinese forces opposing Japan. Yet Americans continued to sell large quantities of scrap metal, steel, copper, oil, lead, and machinery to the Nipponese. It would have been possible, after January 1940, to end this traffic by imposing embargoes on it. But the President hesitated at first to take this step because he thought it would only cause Japan to seek these commodities by further conquest in Asia. In May 1940, as a deterrent to Japan, Roosevelt ordered the transfer of the United States Pacific fleet base from San Diego, California, to Pearl Harbor.

As a further deterrent, after the fall of France in June 1940, Congress in July passed a law requiring Americans henceforth to obtain federal licenses for the export of oil and scrap metal. Under this law, Roosevelt, on July 26, ordered critical aviation gasoline withheld from Japan, a step which drew a strong but futile Japanese protest. The next month Japan forced the helpless Vichy government in France to surrender bases in *northern* Indochina, a move which prompted Roosevelt, on September 25, to extend the embargo to iron and steel scrap and to grant a large new loan to Chiang Kai-shek in China. Two days later Japan joined the German-Italian coalition.

The formation of the Berlin-Rome-Tokyo Axis, ostensibly to promote Hitler's "New Order" in Europe and the prosperity of "Greater East Asia" under Japan, was explicitly intended to warn the United States to keep hands off both. If she attacked any of the signatories, the other two agreed to come to the assistance of the victim. The first major change in the Pacific thereafter followed the Nazi invasion of Russia in June 1941, which removed the last possibility that sizable Soviet forces could be deployed against Japan. That July, Tokyo compelled the Vichy government to yield new French bases, this time in *southern* Indochina. Roosevelt retaliated promptly by freezing all Japanese assets in the United States, an action Japan as promptly reciprocated, thereby all but paralyzing trade between the two countries. On August 17, 1941, Roosevelt warned the Japanese that if they made any further moves to impose military domination on neighboring countries, the United States would take "all steps which it may deem necessary toward safeguarding [its] legitimate right and interest."

The previous December, United States Naval Intelligence cryptographers had broken Japan's secret diplomatic code, "Magic," and Washington was enabled to listen in on messages from Tokyo to its emissaries in the American capital. One thing seemed certain from these messages—Japan had no intention of foregoing the annihilation of Chiang Kai-shek. At the same time, the United States had

746

no intention of sacrificing him to Japan's ambition. Further negotiations between the two countries foundered principally on this issue.

In Japan itself in mid-October 1941 the relatively conciliatory government of Prime Minister Fumimaro Konoye was forced to resign in favor of General Hideki Tojo, who feared for his army's morale if, after years of sacrifice, it must yield its Chinese goal under American pressure. "If a hundred million people merge into one iron solidarity to go forward," Tojo declared, "nothing can stop us." He would have been glad to have China without war with the United States; but on October 23 his Cabinet agreed to speed up military preparations, and by November 3 his government had decided to attack Pearl Harbor if negotiations did not permit Japan to have her way. At the same time, negotiations at Washington were to continue—after November 17 under the direction of Saburo Kurusu, a special envoy dispatched by air.

From the secret code, Washington knew that if satisfactory negotiations were not completed by November 29, "things are automatically going to happen." On November 20 Kurusu and the Japanese ambassador presented Secretary of State Hull with proposals which seemed no less than a demand that the United States approve and abet Japan's conquests in Asia. On November 26 the State Department presented counterproposals offering Tokyo favorable trade relations in exchange for the withdrawal of her forces from China and Indochina and her joining a nonaggression pact with other nations that had interests in the Far East. Japan obviously would not accept such terms. "I have washed my hands of it," said Hull to Secretary of War Stimson that day, "and it is now in the hands of you and Knox, the Army and Navy."

Hull did not realize how right he was. Unknown to the American negotiators, a Japanese carrier force had just set out from its base in the Kurile Islands on its fatal errand. On December 1, dismissing the American demands as "fantastic," Kurusu nevertheless asked that discussions continue, a gesture that can be construed only as a blind for the impending raid. Washington already knew of Japanese troop movements, which Roosevelt thought foreshadowed only an attack in the Southwest Pacific—on Thailand, Malaya, and the Dutch East Indies, which were, in fact, the main Japanese objectives. On December 6 he sent to the Japanese emperor a hasty peace appeal which was followed on December 7 only by the bombs at Pearl Harbor.

As one consequence of the disaster, Roosevelt's most bitter critics later accused him of having provoked Japan to attack in order to bring the United States into the war in Europe and of having deliberately exposed the navy to disaster at Pearl Harbor in order to create a situation that would unite Americans behind his war. That Roosevelt wanted to enter the war by November and that he knew that a firm stand against Japan might bring about drastic action on her part seem beyond doubt. However, had the alternative policy been adopted, and had the United States stood quietly by while Japan conquered an immensely rich empire in China and nearby lands, Roosevelt would have been at least as severely criticized for inaction. The notion that Roosevelt conspired to defeat and destroy a substantial part of the navy he had served and lovingly built up and that his administration and high military authorities were involved in the plot may be left to those who find such notions plausible. No doubt there was slackness both in Washington and at Pearl Harbor, and the naval intelligence coup in deciphering the Japanese code was wasted.

The sequel to Pearl Harbor was immediate and unmitigated disaster. Japan followed up her startling triumph with attacks on the Philippines, Wake Island, Guam, Hong Kong, British Malaya, and Thailand. Thailand surrendered immediately, Guam on December 13, Wake Island on December 20, and Hong Kong on December 25. American troops in the Philippines under General Douglas MacArthur made brave stands on the Bataan Peninsula and on the fortress island of Corregidor, but after MacArthur managed to escape to take command in Australia, Bataan surrendered in April 1942, Corregidor in May.

748

In the Southwest Pacific on December 10, the Japanese paralyzed British striking power by sinking the battle cruiser *Repulse* and the battleship *Prince of Wales*. They then captured Singapore, the center of British authority in Asia, and pushed the defenders out of the Netherlands Indies. By March 1942 they had conquered Burma and closed the Burma Road, reducing aid to China to a trickle.

The only offsetting Allied gains came in Latin America. Here, within a few days of the assault on Pearl Harbor, twelve countries—with Argentina, most heavily populated by families of Italian descent, a conspicuous exception—either declared war on the Axis or broke relations with its members. As early as July 1940, a meeting of hemisphere foreign ministers had adopted the "Havana declaration" to the effect that any non-American at-

tack on an American state "shall be considered as an act of aggression against the states which sign this declaration." This step converted the Monroe Doctrine virtually into a mutual defense agreement. Latin Americans were to suffer humiliations at American hands after the war (see p. 786); but hemispheric harmony—and also prosperity—reached new peaks while the fighting after Pearl Harbor raged.

### Balance of forces

The anti-Axis powers, in the spring of 1942, had little reason to expect they could

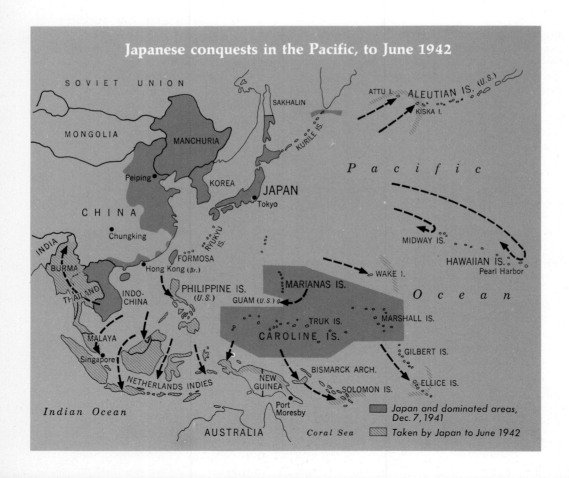

Japanese conquests in the Pacific, to June 1942

win the war quickly, if indeed they could win at all. To be sure, they outnumbered the Axis powers, but the latter could draw on enormous labor resources in Central Europe, the occupied part of Russia, and the Southwest Pacific. Occupied France and friendly Spain could add materially to the German war potential, not least by helping to make the Atlantic and the western Mediterranean hazardous for Allied shipping. Axis forces also occupied North Africa from Tunis to the Egyptian border, and Germany's formidable Afrika Korps, under General Erwin Rommel, seemed on the verge of smashing eastward to Alexandria, closing the Suez Canal, and forcing Turkey to join the dictators. When the eastern Mediterranean became impassable on this account, Allied ships had to take the long route around the Cape of Good Hope to supply British forces in the Middle East. In southern Russia, the Germans were hammering, too, at the Caucasus, and threatening to drive through to Iraq and Iran and complete the conquest of the routes to the East, cutting Britain off entirely from her empire.

At best, a war lasting seven to fifteen years seemed in the offing for the Allies. But such a pessimistic forecast neglected some Allied assets, notably American resources and American industrial capacity. Moreover, Allied planning and administration proved vastly superior to the vaunted centralization of authority by the dictatorships, both in individual countries and in the coordination of joint efforts. Coordination presented a special challenge after January 1, 1942, when at a meeting in Washington, twenty-six nations, the first of the United Nations (see p. 770), pledged full employment of their resources to defeat the Axis.

The United States and Britain in particular, through their combined Chiefs of Staff and the intimate collaboration of Roosevelt and Churchill, worked together with remarkable harmony during most of the war. At an early point in their joint effort, their military planners made an important over-all decision.

They would conduct a holding operation in the Pacific until the United States could mobilize enough aid for Britain and Russia to take the offensive in Europe. After the Axis had been defeated in Europe, Japan's turn would come. Those in the United States who wanted to concentrate all effort immediately on the Oriental challenger hotly criticized this decision.

In the spring of 1942 two important naval victories strengthened Allied hopes that Japan could be held at bay. One was the battle of the Coral Sea, in which a Japanese assault on Port Moresby in New Guinea, an important site in American-Australian communications, was turned back. Coral Sea, said Admiral Ernest J. King, was "the first naval engagement in . . . history in which surface ships did not exchange a single shot." In fact they never saw one another. The entire battle, which set a pattern for most other Pacific engagements, was fought by carrier-based planes beyond their respective ships' horizons. The second Allied victory came in the battle of Midway Island, June 3–6. Japanese capture of Midway would have made Pearl Harbor unusable. To save the island, Admiral Chester Nimitz in Pearl Harbor mobilized the remnants of the American fleet and sent them out, under Admirals Frank Jack Fletcher and Raymond A. Spruance, to meet the much larger Japanese force. After sustaining heavy losses they sent the enemy reeling homeward in her first major naval defeat.

## American mobilization

The attack on Pearl Harbor closed the debate over isolation. Since almost no one now questioned the necessity for war, there was much less intolerance than in World War I. The harsh exception was the expulsion in February and March 1942 of about 110,000 Japanese-Americans from their homes on or adjacent to the West Coast and their incarceration in inland relocation centers. Supreme Court Justice Frank Murphy found in this act "a melancholy resemblance" to the Nazi treatment of the Jews, and the American Civil Liberties Union called it "the worst single wholesale violation of civil rights of American citi-

750

zens in our history." Even such hysterical racial repression, however, did not deter many Nisei units—made up of Americans of Japanese descent—from performing heroically in the United States armed forces. Their work, along with a growing realization of how unfairly Japanese-American families had been treated, led the federal government to pay more than $35 million to the evacuees for property losses.

An American army of 1.6 million men was already in existence at the time of Pearl Harbor, most of them recruited through the first peacetime draft (see p. 743). Eventually, all men between eighteen and forty-five were made subject to military service, and for the first time women were permitted to volunteer in the armed forces. By the war's end, 15 million men and more than 200,000 women had served in the army, navy, marines, and coast guard.

Behind these men and women stood American industry, agriculture, labor, and science. Critics of the President had dismissed as wishful thinking his call for 50,000 planes a year in 1940. In 1942 over 47,000 aircraft were built; for 1944 the figure rose above 96,000. By 1945 no less than 55 million tons of merchant shipping and 71,000 naval vessels had been launched by American yards. Because

*Celebrating the five-thousandth
B-17 bomber at the Boeing Seattle plant
in 1944.*

The Boeing Company

Malayan and East Indian raw rubber supplies had been cut off early in the war, an entirely new synthetic rubber industry had to be established; by 1944, the industry was producing no less than 762,000 tons of synthetic rubber a year.

In other American industries, first lend-lease and then American war production ended the dreary course of the depression. The "hate Roosevelt" attitude of big business did not die with the onset of war mobilization. The steel industry, for example, was slow in responding to appeals to expand capacity before Pearl Harbor. Nor was this attitude absent from the automobile industry's "business as usual" policy, reflected in its reluctance to convert to armaments just when the boom created by the "arsenal of democracy" was reviving the market for cars. Almost complete conversion ultimately was achieved; but private industry's old fear of excess plant capacity forced the government, through the Defense Plant Corporation, to build about 85 percent of the new facilities needed for war production. Most of the government-built plants were run during the war by private corporations under liberal contracts with the armed services, with liberal options for purchase after the war that were speedily taken up.

The dreary course of depression unemployment also ended with wartime mobilization. Negroes, who were called equally with whites to serve in the armed forces, also resumed their migration to the factories that had been checked by the depression. Many Americans sensed the hypocrisy of waging a war against racism abroad while full rights were denied millions at home, and for the first time, in 1941, a federal Fair Employment Practices Committee (FEPC) was created to protect minorities from job discrimination on grounds of race, color, or creed. During the war millions of women joined or replaced men on the assembly lines and kept war plants going day and night. A War Manpower Commission shifted workers into areas where they were most needed and made other arrangements for efficient use of the labor force.

The inducement to work in war plants grew as average weekly earnings rose from $23.86 in 1939 to $46.08 in 1944. After the attack on Pearl Harbor, the AFL and CIO made no-strike pledges. But later, as prices rose and as the most desperate period of the war passed, strikes became quite frequent, but seldom in industries contributing directly to the war effort. Workers were widely criticized for the strikes. But the slogan "There are no strikes in foxholes" was met with the retort "There are no profits either." Corporate profits after taxes rose from $5 billion in 1939 to almost $10 billion in 1944, and many new fortunes were made.

Although the farm population fell during the war (despite draft exemptions for many agricultural workers), farm production soared. In 1945 output per farm worker, responding to favorable weather and scientific aids, almost doubled the level that had been reached during 1910 to 1914, agriculture's golden years. Farm income also doubled. The war showed, too, that a small farm-laboring force, working with improved agricultural techniques, could meet the normal needs of the domestic market, a demonstration that soon influenced farm and financial policies.

To protect farmers from a postwar collapse such as that following the wartime expansion in 1917-1918, the Price Stabilization Act of 1942 contained special agricultural concessions. Some staple prices were to be supported at 90 percent of parity (see p. 712) for two years after the end of hostilities. No price ceilings were to be set on agricultural products until their prices had reached either 110 percent of parity or the level that existed from 1919 to 1929, whichever might be higher. The Stabilization Extension Act of 1944 in effect continued these arrangements. The farmers had driven a hard bargain with the government. Some farm produce prices rose above the ceiling prices paid by consumers, and the government itself was forced to make up the difference. Roosevelt protested, but members of the agricultural bloc in Congress exerted all their influence to make sure that the practice continued.

A concerted effort was made during the war by the Office of Price Administration, under the chairmanship of Leon Henderson, to control inflation elsewhere in the economy. Price ceilings were set on a wide variety of consumer goods, and a few products, such as sugar, coffee, and meat, especially in demand in the armed services, were rationed without causing undue hardship. Prices had already risen about 25 percent when controls were first authorized in January 1942, and they continued to rise slightly. But serious inflation was avoided.

Wartime science in the United States came under the direction of the Office of Scientific Research and Development, headed by Vannevar Bush, president of the Carnegie Institution of Washington and former vice-president of the Massachusetts Institute of Technology, and James Conant, since 1933 president of Harvard. Their work profited greatly from the contributions of refugee scientists from Axis countries and the cooperation of British scientists as well. Among the major developments were those in radar, essentially a British invention. Radar employed a form of microwave detection that made it possible to locate attacking planes at night and to spot submarines trying to make speed by running surfaced in fog or darkness. But the most lethal development was the atomic bomb.

Even before Munich, Nazi scientists, following an old Albert Einstein lead, had become the first in the world to release energy by splitting the uranium atom. Thereafter they worked feverishly to find a way to employ this incredible energy in a deliverable weapon. As early as January 1939 certain American scientists had learned from the eminent Danish physicist Niels Bohr the nature of the German experiments. Later that year Einstein, who had fled Germany when Hitler took power, and two other refugee scientists, Leo Szilard and Eugene Wigner, had managed to convey to FDR the full meaning of the approaching mastery of atomic science by the "master race." Roosevelt promptly established

752

an advisory committee on uranium; but the "crash" program on the production of an atomic bomb was not decided upon until the spring of 1941, when the British, whose atomic research was considerably ahead of that in the United States, agreed to share their knowledge.

From the very first, these great scientists knew they had the alternative of withholding their epochal findings from political leaders whose initial application of atomic energy would be in atomic warfare. At the same time, almost to a man they had suffered under Axis regimes, and their hatred and fear of Hitlerism had grown as strong as the new physical force itself. Either way, civilization, especially as scientists knew it with their free international communication, seemed doomed; perhaps Hitler's end might offer the better chance of resurrection. In any case, it was they who pressed the bomb on governments and not the other way around.

The most fruitful work on the atom thereafter was done at the University of California, the University of Chicago, and Columbia University in New York. This work showed that a practical bomb could be made by employing plutonium as the "fissionable element." Plutonium was a new element produced by splitting the uranium atom in a cyclotron, or atom smasher. On May 1, 1943, the job of producing plutonium in large quantities was given to the sacredly secret Manhattan District Project established under General Leslie R. Groves at Oak Ridge, Tennessee, where the immense water and electric power resources of TVA were available. At approximately the same time, the responsibility for building a practical bomb was placed upon Dr. J. Robert Oppenheimer and the brilliant team of British, American, and European scientists he gathered at Los Alamos, New Mexico. On July 12, 1945, final assembly of the first atomic bomb began. At 5:30 in the morning four days later, at Alamogordo air base in New Mexico, the terrible weapon was detonated.

By mid-1943 American war costs, including those for atom-bomb development, were running at $8 billion a month, as high as the *yearly* budgets of the peacetime New Deal. In 1945, for the first time in history, the federal government spent over $100 billion. The total cost of the war to the United States was about $350 billion—which was ten times the cost of World War I.

After July 1, 1943, employers began to collect income taxes for the government by withholding them from employee payrolls, an innovation that continued to be used after the war and one that assured the government of its revenues and kept the workers abreast of the tax liabilities from month to month. Income and other taxes paid for two-fifths of the war's huge cost. Yet between 1941 and 1945, the national debt rose from about $48 billion to $247 billion.

Politics was not suspended in the war years. In the congressional elections of 1942, the Republicans gained considerable ground by capitalizing on public discontent with military defeats. But by 1944 the military situation had completely changed, and the Republicans had to contend once again with Roosevelt's popularity. Thomas E. Dewey, now risen to governor of New York, became their candidate. The Democrats, with the third-term tradition shattered, nominated Roosevelt with little ado. The convention spotlight, since FDR's health had already become an issue, centered on the choice for Vice-President. After a stormy session, Henry Wallace, unpopular with city bosses and southern conservatives, was dropped in favor of Senator Harry S. Truman of Missouri, who had gained attention as chairman of a Senate committee investigating malpractices under wartime production contracts.

Dewey had no sound issue on which to campaign, since he and his party had accepted most of the administration's program, including the President's commitment to a new international organization. The Republicans put much emphasis on Roosevelt's fatigue, hoping to deepen American fatigue with him. But this tactic boomeranged. Dewey's freshness appeared by comparison to reflect his limited participation in war work, in which the President exhausted himself to save the country. Now "Dr. Win the War" instead of "Dr. New Deal," Roosevelt won by a vote of 25,602,000 to 22,006,000 and by 432 to 99 in the electoral college. The Democrats' choice of a Vice-President proved fateful, indeed, for Roosevelt was to serve less than four months of his fourth term.

## IV  Toward victory

*At war in Europe and Africa*

To win the war, it was vital for the Western powers to gain mastery of the sea and air. For months after the United States entered the war, German U-boats infested the Caribbean Sea and the waters off American Atlantic and Gulf coasts. Sinkings ran extremely high, while the toll of U-boats held relatively low until a new system of convoys was worked out, using a host of light ships on the deep and patrolling coastal waters with bombers and blimps. Still, the cost in tonnage and lives continued at extravagant levels, and it was only the tremendous rate of American merchant-ship production that chiefly offset the submarine offensive.

In the air, supremacy had passed to Britain's RAF during the great clashes over England in 1940. By 1941, when British aircraft production alone surpassed Germany's, the RAF went on the offensive, returning in kind the terrible attacks that Germany had inflicted on British cities. Sustained RAF bombing reached a peak during July 1943, when night raids over Hamburg destroyed more than a third of the port and killed over 60,000 persons. In August 1942 American airmen joined the British in raids over the Continent, supplementing RAF saturation bombings after dark with precision bombing of specific targets by day. Between them, the two air forces dropped more than 2.6 million bombs on enemy sites.

At one point, there was talk among the Allies of trying to bring Germany down by air attack alone, thereby avoiding the immense casualties an invasion of Hitler's "Fortress Europe" on the Continent would almost surely entail. But this strategy had to be abandoned. Air attacks never succeeded in biting deeply enough into Axis production of such essentials as planes, submarines, or synthetic rubber. On the other hand, air assaults in the long run crippled two major targets: transportation and refineries. When the time came for the Allies to invade the Continent, Germany found her defenses gravely hampered by the damage inflicted on railways, roads, and bridges at home and in France, and by shortages of fuel for her planes, tanks, and other vehicles.

Any invasion of the Continent was still some time off in June 1942, when beleaguered Russia's demand for a second front had become importunate. Churchill and Roosevelt, meeting in Washington at this time, learned that General Rommel's army, now sweeping over Egypt (see p. 749), was to be reinforced. With disaster facing the thin line of defenders of the Middle East, this new information settled all argument for the time being over Churchill's eagerness to strike first at Fortress Europe in the presumed "soft under-belly" of the Balkans (chiefly to keep the Russians out) and the Americans' enthusiasm for a limited assault in France in anticipation of an all-out attack in the future. Instead, plans were promptly made for Allied reinforcement of the British troops confronting Rommel, which included the assignment of the imperious General Bernard L. Montgomery to command the key Eighth Army. The over-all North African operation was placed under General Dwight D. Eisenhower, who had just been named Supreme Allied Commander in the Mediterranean theater.

754

Rommel's frightening course across Egypt had halted, spent, at El Alamein, on the Mediterranean, and there, on October 23, 1942, the first great Allied land offensive of the war began. In twelve days Montgomery's army sent Rommel's tanks and his Italian contingents streaming back toward Libya and Tripoli. "Up to Alamein," crowed Churchill, "we survived. After Alamein we conquered." Quickly broadening the conquest was the Allied assault from the west which began on November 8, 1942. On that date, three Allied armies, 185,000 strong, under Eisenhower, two starting from England and one from the United States, began landing at Algiers, Oran, and Casablanca in French North Africa. The landings were as tricky politically as tactically. The politics of Torch, the code name for this offensive, revolved around the touchy relations of the Allies with leaders both of the Vichy collaborators and the devoted underground (often dominated by trained and disciplined communists) in Hitler's Europe.

The Allies hoped in French North Africa to land their troops as expeditiously and safely as possible. But it was difficult to keep Torch secret from the Germans and thereby gain all the advantages of surprise while at the same time informing the French there that friendly forces were approaching. Moreover, most of the French administrators and the French navy in North Africa (largely out of hatred for the British) had remained loyal to Vichy, so the invaders were not necessarily friends.

The landings at Algiers met little resistance; those at Casablanca and Oran encountered heavy fire and heavy fighting from the French fleet, parts of which were sunk. French land forces, in turn, would have nothing to do with General Henri Giraud, a hero of the fall of France who had escaped from prison in Germany and was brought to North Africa by Eisenhower. The troops proved more responsive to Admiral Jean Darlan, chief of all Vichy forces, who was visiting a sick son in Algiers (perhaps a pretext) and became impressed with Eisenhower's strength. Darlan imposed a cease-fire on Vichy-oriented French troops in North Africa on November 11.

Conveniently for the Allies, this political chameleon was assassinated on Christmas Eve,

1942. A tussle for French African leadership followed between Giraud and General Charles de Gaulle, the uncompromising foe of Vichy. Giraud emerged as Darlan's successor as head of the French government in North Africa; but de Gaulle became the chief of the Committee of National Liberation, which the United States recognized in July 1943 as the *de facto* government of all liberated parts of France. While he became a thorn to Churchill and Roosevelt, de Gaulle's work and that of his Free French forces contributed to victory and to the subsequent French revival.

Rommel, now under severe pressure from the west as well as from the east, managed to frustrate both Montgomery and Eisenhower for months. Nevertheless, the momentum of El Alamein in October, strengthened by the Russians' tremendous effort in checking the German assault at Stalingrad in November (see p. 759), gave hope and flair to Allied planning; and when Churchill and Roosevelt met at Casablanca in January 1943, they confidently made plans for victory on all fronts.

At Casablanca the Allied leaders decided to invade Sicily and Italy after the Axis had been cleared out of North Africa, agreed to send sufficient forces to the Pacific to take the offensive there, and promised to ease pressure on the Russians by setting up another front in Europe that would engage enemy armies "as heavily as possible." They also announced that they would accept only the "unconditional surrender" of the Axis. This menacing phrase, Churchill wrote later, raised many issues at the time and would "certainly be long debated." He himself debates its origins and implications at length in Volume IV of his history of *The Second World War.* By this phrase, he writes, quoting his statement of June 30, 1943,

*we mean that [the] will power to resist . . . of the Nazi, Fascist, and Japanese tyrannies . . . must be completely broken, and that they must yield themselves absolutely to our justice and mercy. It also means that we must take all those far-sighted measures which are*

*necessary to prevent the world from being again con-*
*vulsed, wrecked, and blackened by their calculated*
*plots and ferocious aggressions. It does not mean, and*
*it never can mean, that we are to stain our victorious*
*arms by inhumanity or by mere lust of vengeance, or*
*that we do not plan a world in which all branches of*
*the human family may look forward to what the Ameri-*
*can Declaration of Independence finely calls "life, lib-*
*erty, and the pursuit of happiness."*

Of the Germans in particular, Roosevelt added
later that year:

*We wish them to have a normal chance to develop in*
*peace, as useful and respectable members of the Euro-*
*pean family. But we most certainly emphasize the*
*word "respectable," for we intend to rid them once*
*and for all of Nazism and Prussian militarism and the*
*fantastic and disastrous notion that they constitute the*
*"Master Race."*

After the war, when searching helplessly for
strong European allies with whom to rebuild
the balance of power on the Continent, Churchill reopened the controversy over unconditional surrender by asserting that it had made
enemy resistance desperate and prolonged the
slaughter. But that is not what he thought at
Casablanca, where he reached for credit for
the idea. Those, on the other hand, who
thought the threat might shorten the war by
prompting the enemy to sue for an early
peace to avert being "completely broken"
were soon proved wrong, at least where the
Germans and Japanese were concerned.

Following the Casablanca Conference, the
Allies regained full possession of North Africa
when General Von Arnim surrendered Rommel's army of 350,000 men (the "Fox" himself
having evaded capture) in Tunisia on May 13,
1943. The liquidation of Nazi North African
submarine and air bases quickly followed.
Franco Spain, moreover, was deterred from intervening on the Axis side; the southern Mediterranean again became available to the
Allies at normal wartime risk, and pressure on
the Middle East was eased. Two months be-

fore the capitulation of Rommel's army, General Giraud had restored representative government in French North Africa, voided all
legislation enacted there under the Vichy
regime, and, with Algiers as his base, worked
with de Gaulle for the liberation of mainland
France.

The projected attack on Italy began on
July 10, which was as early as sufficient landing craft could be assembled; and by August 17, when Sicily was cleared, 100,000 German prisoners had been taken. Meanwhile,
King Victor Emmanuel and members of the
Fascist Grand Council had deposed Mussolini
and had set up a new government under Marshal Pietro Badoglio, who immediately sued
for peace. On September 8, 1943, the Italian
government signed an unconditional surrender, but Italy herself was still occupied by
strong German forces, which Hitler, on learning of the perfidy of his Axis partner,
promptly strengthened. The Allies' objective
was to wipe out these forces, or at least so to
occupy them that they could not be used
against the Russians. At the same time, the
Western powers had another objective. Control of Italy would permit them to move eastward into the Balkans and forestall the Soviets from overrunning southern Europe when
the final push against Hitler came.

Unfortunately for them, the Italian campaign, in the words of British General Maitland Wilson, deteriorated into a "slow painful
advance through difficult terrain against a determined and resourceful enemy." The Allies
had taken Naples on September 28, 1943.
Rome lay but 100 miles north, but could not
be captured until June 4, 1944, only two days
before the cross-channel invasion of France
was to begin. On April 28, 1945, Italian partisans captured Mussolini, murdered him, and
mutilated his body. But the Nazis in Italy
fought on until May 2, a mere five days before the Reich itself collapsed.

### Conference diplomacy

Following the Casablanca Conference
of January 1943, Roosevelt and Churchill had
met in Washington in May and agreed tentatively on starting the invasion of France by

way of Normandy within twelve months. In August they met again in Quebec to firm up and elaborate the invasion plans. They also confirmed the recognition granted in July by the United States to the French Committee of National Liberation as the government of liberated French territories. In October in Moscow, the Foreign Ministers of the Big Three—Hull for the United States, Eden for Britain, and Molotov for the USSR—drew up the first general understanding among themselves. The Western spokesmen promised the Russians to open the invasion of France in 1944. All three declared their intention to establish as soon as possible a general international organization "for the maintenance of international peace and security." They also proposed to foster a democratic future for Italy. The future of eternally troubled Poland, where Russia's dominance was really unnegotiable, proved a snare now as so often before, but it did not dampen Roosevelt's satisfaction with the Moscow proceedings, which only strengthened his resolve at long last to meet with Stalin personally. This momentous meeting, with Churchill joining the other two, was set for Teheran, the capital of Iran, late in November 1943.

FDR also had an urgent desire to meet with Chiang Kai-shek, whom he invited to join himself and Churchill at Cairo on the way to Teheran. After conferring from November 23 to 27, the three leaders subscribed to the Cairo Declaration in which, to bolster Chiang's willingness to fight Japan to the finish, they themselves promised not to give up the struggle until Japan surrendered unconditionally, at which time coveted territories, including Manchuria and Formosa would be returned to China. They also foresaw a "free and independent Korea." The Cairo Declaration was publicly announced on December 1, after the Russians, at Teheran, endorsed it. At Cairo, Roosevelt and Churchill also agreed that Eisenhower would become the supreme commander of the forces to invade Europe.

The Big Three conference at Teheran ran from November 28 to December 2. Here D-day for the Normandy invasion, under the code name "Overlord," was definitely set for May or June 1944, when it was to synchronize with a Russian offensive against Hitler from the east. Stalin also confirmed the promise made at the Moscow Conference of Foreign Ministers to enter the war against Japan after Germany was defeated. The Grand Alliance agreed to aid Marshal Tito and the Yugoslav "partisans" in ridding their country of Hitler's forces. They also promised to amend the Polish borders, with Russia taking part of the much-divided country on the east and Poland to be compensated on the west at Germany's expense. Germany, in turn, was to be destroyed as a military power.

Although these important decisions were in general harmoniously reached, Churchill left Teheran with deep misgivings. Roosevelt, he felt, gave too much credence to Russian assertions of cooperation in the long future. At the close of the meeting the Big Three announced: "We came here with hope and determination. We leave here, friends in fact, in spirit, and in purpose." Roosevelt's optimism was apparent when he told Congress on his return that he "got along fine with Stalin," and predicted: "We are going to get along with him and the Russian people—very well indeed."

## Hitler's end

Everything abetted Operation Overlord except the weather. Victory in the Battle of Britain had gained the Allies command in the air. Victory in the Battle of the Atlantic and in North Africa had secured command of the seas. The amphibious landings and the establishment of beachheads at Casablanca, Oran, Sicily, and Salerno had yielded invaluable experience. Even the disappointing stalemate in Italy, which engaged needed Allied manpower, also tied down enemy troops and equipment that Hitler needed much more desperately in France. Above all else, victory depended on success in the battle of production, and in the very first weeks following D-day American production met its sternest test.

For four years Hitler had concentrated on making northern France the most impregnable wall of his fortress. For six weeks Allied air attacks pulverized this wall and the communication lines leading to it. Then, on June 4, 1944, a force of nearly 2.9 million men—supported by 2.5 million tons of supplies, 11,000 airplanes, and a vast fleet of ships—stood straining in England for the takeoff. Tension mounted unbearably when a storm over the Channel forced Eisenhower to withhold the signal twenty-four hours. The next night's weather was scarcely better, but Overlord was on. The first troop carriers with 176,000 men anchored off the Normandy beaches at 3 A.M., June 6. Two weeks later, almost half a million Allied soldiers were fighting in Normandy when a mighty hurricane ripped up the shore. The havoc it left was terrifying, and only the prior success of the air arm in sealing off the ravaged zone from enemy reinforcements averted a dreaded German counterattack.

There were other checks in Normandy. The landings there—as against obviously more suitable places—had caught the Nazis by surprise; but so intensive had been their preparation that they were able to mobilize resistance quickly. Then came their V-1s and V-2s, whose rain of terror on London was not stemmed until their very launching sites were captured. The V-1, a pilotless airplane loaded with explosives, had a mechanism that enabled it to hold a predetermined course until on contact with its target it blew up with terrible force. The V-2 was a rocket which descended from the immense height of its arc with such speed that the first warning of its coming was the explosion. The first V-1 struck London on June 12, 1944, six days *after* D-Day; the first V-2, early in August.

"The effect of the new German weapons," Eisenhower wrote in *Crusade in Europe,*

*was very noticeable upon morale. Great Britain had withstood terrific bombing experiences. But when in June the Allies landed successfully on the Normandy coast the citizens unquestionably experienced a great sense of relief. . . . When the new weapons began to come over London in considerable numbers their hopes were dashed.*

757

United States Army photo

*General Dwight D. Eisenhower addressing paratroopers in England just before they took off for first assault on the continent of Europe on D-day. "Full victory—nothing else" was the order of the day.*

General Eisenhower continued:

*It seemed likely that, if the German had succeeded in perfecting and using these new weapons six months earlier than he did, our invasion of Europe would have proved exceedingly difficult, perhaps impossible. I feel sure that if he had succeeded in using these weapons over a six-month period . . . Overlord might have been written off.*

Nevertheless the buildup continued and Overlord progressed. By July 24 more than a million Allied troops had subdued 1500 square miles of Normandy and Brittany. The next day, General George S. Patton, Jr.'s magnificent Third Army swept after the Germans and turned their retreat into a rout. On August 25, assisted by a Free French division under General Leclerc, Patton liberated Paris, where, two days later, de Gaulle installed himself as President of a provisional government. Patton himself kept going, with Omar Bradley's First Army moving more slowly on his left. Farther north, Montgomery, with Canadian and British forces, was hurtling through Belgium, where they liberated the key port of Antwerp on September 4.

The Germans, having lost half a million men and virtually all of France, had decided to take refuge behind their long neglected West Wall in the homeland across the Rhine. Patton hungered to burst after them. At the same time, Montgomery strained for permission to make "one powerful and full-blooded thrust towards Berlin." But the speedy Allied offensives had so stretched supplies of trucks, tires, and fuel that only one of the two could safely be turned loose. In one of his most difficult decisions, Eisenhower leaned toward Montgomery in whose path lay the Nazi access roads

to Antwerp and the bases of the V-weapons. Patton judged this "the most momentous error of the war," and with Bradley's backing acted as though it were not final. Eisenhower, whose overall strategy had favored blunting both Patton's and Montgomery's epic thrusts in order to gain "the whole length of the Rhine before launching a final assault on interior Germany," failed to resolve the conflict over priorities of supply. Montgomery's momentum was dissipated; Patton's progress slowed.

Hitler used the lucky respite to rally his forces. On December 16, 1944, he startled the Allies with his breakout in the thinly defended Ardennes forest in southern Belgium. In ten days his armies advanced 50 miles until checked by the heroic American stand at the crossroads town of Bastogne. By mid-January 1945, in the famous Battle of the Bulge, the Germans had been pushed back to their old line with the satisfaction, such as it was, of having delayed Eisenhower's grand push another month.

In the meantime, the Russians had taken every advantage of Hitler's preoccupation with the second front. The apex of the Nazi inva-

*On a "Red Ball" highway in France, October 1944. Over such designated one-way roads, every vehicle ran at least twenty hours a day straining to keep up supplies for the onrushing armies.*

United States Army photo

sion of the USSR, after devastating the Crimea, had been reached in the summer of 1942 at the level approaches to the industrial city of Stalingrad on the River Volga. The battle for Stalingrad, which had few natural defenses and could only be saved by massed manpower, opened in July. In November Marshal Zhukov grasped the initiative, ordering a sweeping counterattack that encircled the besieging German forces. On January 31, 1943, after one of the "dourest, bloodiest, and most prolonged" battles of the war, the trapped German armies capitulated.

Soviet reclamation of the Crimea began that spring and was completed when the signal for Overlord was given. Elimination of Nazi forces in the Balkans started in the summer of 1944. Only in Greece, where Churchill in October at last got in his Balkan licks by dispatching troops to bend the civil war there to the conservative side, were the communists thwarted in establishing subservient regimes. By February 1945 Finland also had yielded again to Russian arms, Poland had been organized as a communist state, Hungary had fallen, Czechoslovakia had been penetrated, and Vienna's collapse was imminent. At the time of the Yalta Conference, February 4-11, 1945, Soviet armies stood only 50 miles from Berlin. No people besides the Jews had suffered more from Nazi atrocities than the Russians; none of the Western Allies had sacrificed as much as they in the fighting itself. Soviet claims on the sympathy of the free world were immense. Few Americans foresaw what use Stalin would make of it.

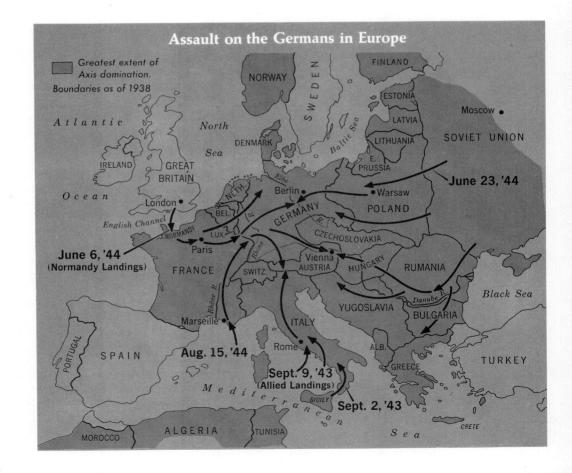

Assault on the Germans in Europe

Greatest extent of Axis domination. Boundaries as of 1938

June 6, '44 (Normandy Landings)

June 23, '44

Aug. 15, '44

Sept. 9, '43 (Allied Landings)

Sept. 2, '43

760

Russia had begun compensating herself long before Yalta. Here she made verbal concessions—to the establishment of the United Nations Organization in April 1945 and to "holding free and unfettered elections as soon as possible" in Poland and elsewhere—in exchange for promises of even larger territorial gains. Most of these were to be at the expense of Japan, with whom Russia was still at peace, so the promises, as well as other Yalta terms, were kept secret (see p. 769). The Soviet was also given, along with reparations in goods, the privilege of the "use of German labor" in her own reconstruction. Tentative decisions also were made at Yalta—and more or less confirmed at the Potsdam Conference in July and August 1945 (see p. 772)—for the multiple administration of Berlin and the partitioning of Germany, for the trial of "war criminals," and the planning of a general peace conference that never was held.

To Churchill the vagueness of the Yalta understandings appeared ominous. By the time of the meeting he had learned—to his fright—of the determination of the United States to withdraw her entire force from Europe within two years of V-E day. To offset the resulting preponderance of Soviet strength on the Continent, he insisted that France be included among the "Great Powers" who would share control of Germany and the emergent world organization. In Roosevelt's eyes, Russian concessions on the prompt establishment of the world organization, and Russian agreement to participate in "liberating China from the Japanese yoke" in "two or three months" after the European war ended, justified everything.

The European war ended soon but not without more tough and costly fighting. On March 7, 1945, the Allies at last plunged across the Rhine over the railroad bridge at Remagen, the only bridge still standing. On April 25, American and Russian troops made contact at the Elbe. On May 1, Hitler committed suicide in Berlin. On May 2, the flaming capital capitulated. On May 7, General Jodl, Chief of Staff of the German army, signed the unconditional surrender at Eisenhower's headquarters.

Two of the Axis partners had succumbed. Within a week half the American air force in Europe was bound for the Pacific and the demobilization of the massive American army had begun. "Meanwhile," Churchill asked in anguish on May 12, "what is to happen about Russia? . . . An iron curtain is drawn down upon their front. We do not know what is going on behind."

Exactly one month earlier, on April 12, 1945, Roosevelt had died suddenly of a cerebral hemorrhage in Warm Springs, Georgia. At Teheran, at the end of 1943, he had presumably suffered a slight stroke, but this became the second best-kept secret of the war. Not since the assassination of Lincoln did the removal of a President so move the American people. Men and women wept openly in the streets. Most appalled of all, perhaps, was FDR's modest successor, Harry S. Truman, who even as Vice-President had been kept in ignorance of the war's best-kept secret, the imminent perfection of atomic bomb production.

## Downfall of Japan

Postwar Russia became President Truman's problem, but embattled Japan required attention first. Back on April 18, 1942, Japan had received a foretaste of the future when sixteen army B-25s led by Colonel James H. Doolittle dropped a load of bombs on Tokyo. The Japanese never learned where these planes came from; nor were they enlightened when FDR jokingly said their base was "Shangri La," which turned out to be aircraft carrier *Hornet* of the Pacific fleet. *Hornet's* own planes had too little range to reach Tokyo, while her deck was too short to receive Doolittle's on return. All the bombers were lost in China, where their crews had to bail out; and the sortie did little damage to the target. Nevertheless it had momentous consequences.

Doolittle's raid is credited with infecting the Japanese with what one of their admirals called "victory disease." To regain face, the Japanese war lords mounted a sudden new offensive even before they had begun to digest the immense fruits of their initial thrust. This offensive was aimed at nailing down a naval and air line of defense from Attu, the westernmost of the Arctic Aleutians, to Port Moresby, the best harbor in New Guinea on the far side of the Equator. Anchor points were to be at Japanese-held Wake and American-held Midway. Inside this line Japan expected to chew up China at her pleasure and perhaps India as well. These plans, as we have seen, were checked by Japanese fleet losses in the Coral Sea in May 1942, and at the disastrous Battle of Midway, June 3–6.

Following their failure at Midway, the Japanese had consoled themselves by grasping Attu and Kiska in the Aleutians. For the moment Alaska seemed on the verge of occupation and Seattle threatened by attack. Men and materials needed elsewhere were rushed to the Territory; the "Alcan Highway" across Canada was begun; and operations were planned which retrieved Attu in May and Kiska in August 1943.

The Japanese were even less successful in a second attack on Port Moresby, this one begun over land in July 1942. To protect this attack, they had begun to clear an air strip on Guadalcanal, one of the nearby (as South Pacific distances go) Solomon Islands. The United States at the same time was eyeing Guadalcanal for the starting point of its own first offensive on Japan's more exposed bastions, especially the island fortress of Rabaul off New Britain.

On August 7, 1942, the first combined American and Australian landings on Guadalcanal were begun against sharp resistance. Two days later a Japanese cruiser force swooped down on the half-unloaded Allied transports in the Solomons' Savo Sea and in "the worst defeat ever suffered by the United States navy" (the words are Admiral S. E. Morison's) sank virtually all the protective fighting ships. The transports ran, and the Japanese force, its mission accomplished, moved off. For six months ill-equipped, half-starved

marines clung to Guadalcanal's air strip at Henderson Field while huge naval actions covering reinforcement attempts by both sides raged in the surrounding waters. The turning point came in mid-November, and in January the Japanese were ordered by Tokyo to evacuate the island, which they did successfully, February 9, 1943.

Before the end of the year the Japanese had also been cleared out of most of New Guinea. In addition, they had been forced to yield enough of Bougainville, the northernmost of the Solomons, for the Allies to maintain air operations there. Bougainville lay only 235 miles from Rabaul—near enough for Allied bombers to neutralize that fortress.

Guadalcanal was the Pacific theater's El Alamein. The Japanese never succeeded in establishing the line behind which they could exploit their "co-prosperity" sphere on the Asian mainland. After Guadalcanal they became fully occupied with defending the Pacific and mainland redoubts they still held as a screen for their home islands. This defense was fanatical. The Japanese navy continued strong and ably led. The Japanese army and air force, much underrated by prewar commentators, was recruited from the impoverished peasantry and treated by the war lords like fatted calves. The soldiers' devotion to their leaders and their cause was beyond reason. Allied leaders like General Douglas MacArthur, chief of Southwest Pacific operations, learned this lesson early and built their strategy upon it. The military Chiefs of Staff in Washington became so impressed with Japanese fortitude that even at the time of the Yalta Conference, when the brilliance of Allied strategy had been well demonstrated, they advised Roosevelt that the Pacific war had at least two years to run with full Russian assistance and considerably longer without.

Allied success in the South Pacific—their establishment in the Solomons, the neutralizing of Rabaul, the clearing of New Guinea—greatly augmented the security of Australia, where MacArthur was preparing for his dramatic return to the Philippines as the last step but one to the taking of Tokyo. The prospect was tempting, but the way bristled with snares. North and east of the Solomons lay

762

the Gilbert Islands; **north** of them, the Marshalls, and farther north **still**, Wake. Together they marked the easternmost advance of Japanese power; and even the barren atolls of each configuration had been armed with air strip, artillery, and adamant men. To the west of this arc, ranging once more from south to north, lay the Palau Islands, the Carolines, Guam, and the Marianas—all, as befit their greater proximity to Japan, even more intensely armed than the outermost line. Farther north and west lay formidable Iwo Jima; and in the shadow of Honshu itself, Okinawa. This defense in depth, extending more than 3000 miles, shielded Tokyo and exposed any invasion from the Philippines to murderous flanking fire.

To roll back this defense island by island, atoll by atoll, fanatic by fanatic, would occupy a generation and still offer scant hope of suc-

cess. MacArthur's command devised the bold alternative of "island hopping," a strategy designed to open quickly a viable path to the heart of Japan while leaving to highly mobile air power the task of neutralizing the uncleared rear. Even so, hundreds of unsung battles were waged by armies as large as those that once decided the fate of nations for atolls where there had probably never been twenty white men assembled together at any one time. The burden of this offensive was placed upon Admiral Chester W. Nimitz and his Central Pacific Fleet. But every assault involved unprecedented coordination of the forces of sea, land, and air. None was easy. Tarawa established the Allied hold on the Gil-

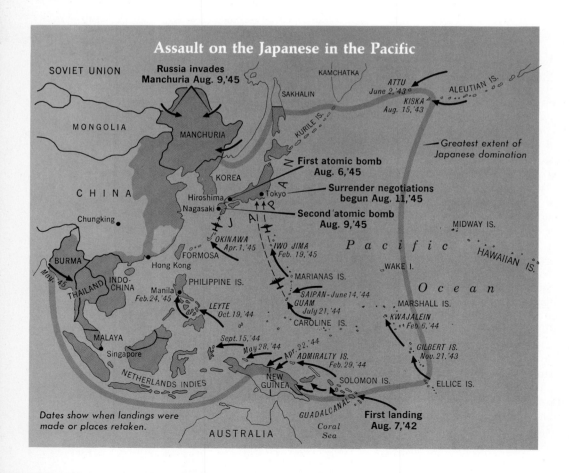

**Assault on the Japanese in the Pacific**

Dates show when landings were made or places retaken.

berts in November 1943; Kwajalein, control of the Marshalls in February 1944. In May, Wake was taken. On June 19-20, in the immense Battle of the Philippine Sea, Admiral Raymond Spruance thwarted a Japanese effort to reinforce the Marianas, and by August 1 Saipan and Tinian there, as well as adjacent Guam, all had succumbed. In September, after some costly hand-to-hand fighting for armed caves, Peleliu in the Palaus was cleaned out.

Three heartening results were earned by this savage surge. First, Truk in the Carolines, Japan's main Central Pacific naval station, was made innocuous without costly frontal assault by the control established over the surrounding island groups. Second, from Saipan and the other Marianas giant superfortresses could reach Tokyo, and the capital and other home island cities henceforth were systematically assaulted with fire bombs that consumed their wooden buildings and decimated the civilian population. Third, the path from New Guinea to the Philippines was opened. On October 19, 1944, a grand armada carrying MacArthur and 250,000 men set out for the Philippine island of Leyte. Four days later virtually the entire Japanese navy converged on Allied transports in Leyte Gulf, and from October 23 to 25 the greatest sea battle in history was fought. At its end the United States emerged in complete command of the Pacific. Manila fell to MacArthur's forces on February 23, 1945, but not until July 5 were the last of the Japanese rooted out.

By then, Iwo Jima and Okinawa had been taken at a sickening cost of 70,000 men. "Kamikaze" attacks by Japanese suicide fliers who plunged their bomb-laden planes into American fighting ships accounted for many of the American casualties at Okinawa. Both campaigns—Iwo had been gained by March 16, 1945, and Okinawa by June 21—wiped out any lingering doubt that the Japanese would resist invaders to the last knife or bullet or breath.

Their power to resist by means of the instruments of modern warfare had by then been

United States Air Force photo

*Mushroom cloud
over Nagasaki, August 9, 1945.*

sorely depleted. The island-hopping campaign had finished all but the remnants of their navy and their air force. American submarines, the silent service, had sunk more than half of their once proud merchant marine which kept them supplied with the oil, rubber, tin, and grain of their mainland conquests. These conquests themselves, moreover, had been under strong attack since the winter of 1943-1944 by British and American forces. The Allies struggled to get Chiang Kaishek to fight harder in China—the British for the protection of India, the Americans for the eviction of Japan—but Chiang was nursing his arms for a future showdown with the communists who were gathering their forces in the Chinese North. Most progress was made against the Japanese in Burma, where Rangoon, the principal port, was retaken in May 1945. But Japan did not yield her other mainland territories until her total collapse at home had been brought about by extraordinary means.

764    On July 26, 1945, three weeks after the reconquest of the Philippines, ten days after the first successful detonation of the A-bomb in New Mexico, Allied leaders assembled at Potsdam sent an ultimatum to the enemy: "The alternative to surrender is prompt and utter destruction." No surrender came. On August 6 the first atomic bomb to be used in warfare was dropped on Hiroshima. Still no word from Japan; but Russia, intent on being in on the imminent kill, declared war on August 8, the very deadline of her "two to three months after V-E day" promise at Yalta, and overran the Japanese forces in Manchuria. On August 9, a second bomb was dropped on Nagasaki. At last, on August 10, Tokyo sued for peace—but made a condition: that Emperor Hirohito be permitted to retain his throne. This condition was accepted by the Allies, and on September 2, 1945, formal surrender ceremonies were conducted in Tokyo Bay on the battleship *Missouri,* with General MacArthur accepting for the victors.

The most terrible war in history had ended in the most terrible display of force. After the bombing of Nagasaki, President Truman said, "We have spent two billion dollars on the greatest scientific gamble in history—and won." A few days later he added, "The atomic bomb is too dangerous to be let loose in a lawless world. That is why Great Britain, Canada, and the United States, who have the secret of its production, do not intend to reveal that secret until means have been found to control the bomb." While Russia had retired behind the "iron curtain," the West had retired, or thought it had retired, behind a scientific curtain of its own, one that was to prove more penetrable.

## For further reading

Alexander DeConde, ed., *Isolation and Security* (1957), Selig Adler, *The Isolationist Impulse* (1957) and *The Uncertain Giant* (1965), and Manfred Jonas, *Isolationism in America 1935-1941* (1966), are illuminating on prewar American attitudes. G. F. Kennan, *American Diplomacy 1900-1950* (1951), and *Memoirs 1925-1950* (1967), offer valuable commentary, rich respectively in hindsight and foresight. D. F. Fleming, *The United States and World Organization 1920-1933* (1938), and *The United States and the World Court* (1945), are useful special studies.

European attitudes may be derived from Hajo Holborn, *The Political Collapse of Europe* (1951); E. H. Carr, *The Twenty Years Crisis 1919-1939* (1942); and G. A. Craig and Felix Gilbert, *The Diplomats 1919-1939* (1953). A. W. Griswold, *The Far Eastern Policy of the United States* (1938), provides relevant background. On Latin-American relations, see J. L. Mecham, *The United States and Inter-American Security 1889-1960* (1961), and Bryce Wood, *The Making of the Good Neighbor Policy* (1961) and *The United*

*States and Latin American Wars 1932-1942* (1966). G. F. Kennan, *Russia and the West Under Lenin and Stalin* (1960), should be supplemented by A. B. Ulam, *Expansion and Coexistence: The History of Soviet Foreign-Policy 1917-67* (1968). The essays in N. A. Graebner, ed., *An Uncertain Tradition: American Secretaries of State in the Twentieth Century* (1961), maintain a high level.

Allan Nevins, *The United States in a Chaotic World 1918-1933* (1950), and *The New Deal and World Affairs . . . 1933-1945* (1951), may be supplemented by L. E. Ellis, *Republican Foreign Policy 1921-1933* (1968); R. H. Ferrell, *American Diplomacy in the Great Depression: Hoover-Stimson Foreign Policy* (1957); and J. E. Wiltz, *From Isolation to War 1931-1941* (1968). The following are authoritative on their subjects: the Washington Conference and its outcome, J. C. Vinson, *The Parchment Peace* (1950), and G. E. Wheeler, *Prelude to Pearl Harbor: the United States Navy and the Far East 1921-1931* (1963); the Stimson Doctrine and beyond, Dorthy Borg, *The United States and the Far Eastern*

Crisis 1933-1938 (1964). On Hitler's rise and the response, K. D. Bracher, *The German Dictatorship* (1971), is outstanding. See also A. A. Offner, *American Appeasement, United States Foreign Policy and Germany 1933-1938* (1969), and Saul Friedlander, *Prelude to Downfall: Hitler and the United States 1939-1941* (1967). C. A. Lindbergh, *The Wartime Journals* (1970), offers rich commentary. See also W. S. Cole, *America First, The Battle Against Intervention 1940-1941* (1953). Gabriel Jackson, *The Spanish Republic and the Civil War 1931-1939* (1965), is excellent.

E. B. Nixon, ed., *Franklin D. Roosevelt and Foreign Affairs* (3 vols., 1969), presents documents from January 1933 to January 1937. In addition to the biographies of FDR cited for Chapter Twenty-eight, see J. M. Burns, *Roosevelt: The Soldier of Freedom 1940-1945* (1970). For the diplomacy of the immediate prewar years see W. L. Langer and S. E. Gleason, *The Challenge to Isolation 1937-1940* (1952), and *Undeclared War 1940-1941* (1953). These may be supplemented by R. A. Divine, *The Illusion of Neutrality* (1962), and *The Reluctant Belligerent* (1965). H. D. Hall, *North American Supply* (1955), is excellent on aid to Britain. R. H. Dawson, *The Decision to Aid Russia 1941* (1959), covers that area. Basil Rauch, *Roosevelt: From Munich to Pearl Harbor* (1950), and Roberta Woblstetter, *Pearl Harbor, Warning and Decision* (1952), defend American policy. Hostile views include C. A. Beard, *American Foreign Policy in the Making 1932-1940* (1946), and *President Roosevelt and the Coming of the War* (1948); C. C. Tansill, *Backdoor to War* (1952); and G. E. Morgenstern, *Pearl Harbor* (1947). Nobutaka Ike, ed., *Japan's Decision for War* (1967), presents official Japanese records. The most comprehensive account of Japan's path to war and of the fighting and its aftermath is John Toland, *The Rising Sun, The Decline and Fall of the Japanese Empire 1936-1945* (1970).

Eliot Janeway, *The Struggle for Survival* (1951), is a good short account of wartime mobilization and its conflicts. An excellent "inside" account is D. M. Nelson, *Arsenal for Democracy* (1944). On the military and the economy R. M. Leighton and R. W. Coakley, *Global Logistics and Strategy 1940-1943* (1955), and *Global Logistics and Strategy 1943-1945* (1968), are invaluable. More general but informative is R. E. Sherwood, *Roosevelt and Hopkins* (1950). Audrie Girdner and Anne Loftis, *The Great Betrayal* (1969), is excellent on the Japanese-American incident. Bernard Sternsher, ed., *The Negro in Depression and War, Prelude to Revolution 1930-1945* (1969), is bibliographically rich. On development of the bomb, see R. G. Hewlett and O. E. Anderson, Jr., *The New World* (1962); N. P. Davis, *Lawrence and Oppenheimer* (1968), and J. I. Lieberman, *The Scorpion and the Tarantula: The Struggle to Control Atomic Weapons 1945-1949* (1970).

A. R. Buchanan, *The United States and World War II* (2 vols., 1964), surveys all phases of American involvement. Winston Churchill, *The Second World War* (6 vols., 1948-1953), is unmatched, but should be checked with Lord Tedder, *With Prejudice* (1966), and Lord Moran, *Churchill* (1966). A. D. Chandler, Jr., ed., *The Papers of Dwight David Eisenhower: The War Years* (5 vols., 1970), is indispensable on the supreme command. See also Eisenhower's *Crusade in Europe* (1948), and S. E. Ambrose, *The Supreme Commander: The War Years of General Dwight Eisenhower* (1970). S. E. Morison, *History of United States Naval Operations in World War II* (15 vols., 1947-1958), is authoritative. Morison, *The Two-Ocean War* (1963), is a short version.

F. W. Deakin, *The Brutal Friendship, Mussolini, Hitler and the Fall of the Italian Fascism* (1962), is excellent on Axis warmaking in the West. Alan Clark, *Barbarossa, The Russian-German Conflict 1941-1945* (1965), and H. E. Salisbury, *The 900 Days, The Siege of Leningrad* (1969), tell much of the Russian story. On the Eastern theater, besides Toland and Morison, see R. J. C. Butow, *Tojo and the Coming of the War* (1961); Louis Morton, *The Fall of the Philippines* (1953), and *Strategy and Command: The First Two Years* (1962); Douglas MacArthur, *Reminiscences* (1964), and Gavin Long, *MacArthur as Military Commander* (1969); William Craig, *The Fall of Japan* (1967); and Herbert Feis, *Japan Subdued, The Atomic Bomb and the End of the War in the Pacific* (1961). Ernie Pyle, *The Story of G. I. Joe* (1945), and Bill Mauldin, *Up Front* (1945), are illuminating on the ordinary soldier.

Herbert Feis, *Churchill, Roosevelt, Stalin* (1957), is outstanding on conference diplomacy. See also his *The China Tangle* (1953), and *Between War and Peace* (1960), and Churchill's *The Second World War* (as cited). Milton Viorst, *Hostile Allies: FDR and Charles de Gaulle* (1965), and Charles de Gaulle, *War Memoirs* (3 vols., 1955-1959), cover relations with France. J. R. Deane, *The Strange Alliance* (1947), and W. H. McNeill, *America, Britain, and Russia* (1953), outstanding early works on wartime Soviet-Western relations, should be read in the light of Gabriel Kolko, *The Politics of War, The World and United States Foreign Policy 1943-1945* (1968); D. F. Fleming, *The Cold War and Its Origins 1917-1960* (2 vols., 1961); and Cold War studies cited for Chapter Thirty.

# A NEW WORLD ORDER

World War II tipped the earth on its axis more violently than any event since the discovery of America almost five hundred years before and probably more violently than any event in recorded history. The harnessing of atomic energy and the maturation of the science of rocketry—making possible both the annihilation of man's planet and the exploration of outer space—no doubt were the most explosive developments of all. Closer to everyday life were the political explosions, especially in the Middle East, Asia, and Africa, that really marked the burning out of long fuses ignited in World War I. Colonial and other economically exploited peoples, made aware by 1918 of the weakness of the imperial powers and their dependence on the products and labor of exotic lands, had been ripening for rebellion a long time before World War II offered them strategic opportunities to strike.

Closer still to life even in the United States were the worldwide technological, social, and medical detonations of the war years. Virtually everywhere, including the United States, unprecedented quantities of nonatomic power were applied to production during the hostilities, and the power surge attained revolutionary velocity once the fighting ended. The new wealth thus produced helped beget a massive population boom. In the more highly developed industrial countries, especially in the Western Hemisphere, where the persistent prewar depression had imposed a degree of birth control, the birth rate soared. In typical underdeveloped countries in both hemispheres, birth rates had always been exceedingly high. Here new medicines and medical hygiene, growing largely out of wartime crash programs in research and application, by improving the health of women and extending their child-bearing years, helped raise the number of births to staggering levels. Advances in infant care and in the control of cholera, yellow fever, and other epidemic diseases, at the same time, kept a revolutionary proportion of the newly born alive, and alive longer.

The "overwhelming and unprecedented" population explosion, to use the words of an outstanding population expert, Kingsley Davis, quickly dissipated any smiling sentimentality about the enrichment children might bring to family life. In countries like India and Egypt, where families struggled over the centuries to extract subsistence from tiny plots of overworked soil, the population explosion simply meant many more mouths to feed from the same poor land. Many wartime and postwar developments made the feeding of the extra mouths possible. As in western and central Europe in the nineteenth century, and to a lesser degree in Russia, so in agrarian countries of our own time brutal reforms in landholding often increased the land's bounty. In combination with improved farm implements and improved husbandry, widespread irrigation projects closely related to the revolutionary spread of power facilities also helped. Yet, as one economist put it after a study of the population burst in Ceylon, "the problem of development was . . . that of keeping the standard of living from falling—not of raising it."

The challenge of poverty in an age of massive gains in productivity was well described by Kingsley Davis when he wrote in 1957:

*If two-thirds of the earth's population was impoverished a century ago and one-third today, there would still be more poor people now than there were then. With many countries multiplying at a rate near 3 percent per year, their economies must somehow move ahead at 4 or 5 percent per year if poverty is to be reduced. This is no easy task when the ratio of people to resources is already excessive and the poverty so great that capital can hardly be accumulated for long-run industrial development.*

The "one world" into which we have all been crowded and jostled since World War II was filled with the youngest population ever known. The persistence of poverty in this world—and the fact that its highest incidence has been in countries where the proportion of clamorous youth is greatest—added ominously to postwar political instability. The extraordinary performance of the American economy in the postwar years in some ways only aggravated worldwide political unrest. American affluence became a goal and a goad to destitute nations, new and old alike. And the elusiveness of the goal, despite lavish American financial and technical infusions, only deepened the prick of the goad. The even more extraordinary gains of the Russian communist economy from a level of poverty below that of Western Europe and the United States even in the depths of the Great Depression were eyed hungrily by youths in many hungry lands and intensified competition between the rival systems for domination of the new world order.

# I  Complex legacy of World War II

*Storm over Yalta*

The conflict between the revolutionary postwar future and the persistence of prewar and wartime thought was nowhere more evident than at the Yalta Conference of February 1945, which came, as Churchill wrote to FDR on the eve of the meeting, "when the Great Allies are so divided and the shadow of war lengthens out before us."

*FDR at Yalta showing the terrible strain of the war years. Beside the jeep at the President's right are Churchill and USSR Foreign Minister V. M. Molotov.*

The Yalta decisions made public at the close of the conference largely concerned the future of the United Nations, and of Germany, Poland, and Yugoslavia, where Stalin's occupying and active armies made Roosevelt-Churchill bargaining with him difficult if not impossible. Those kept secret largely concerned territories and territorial rights to be granted the USSR in East Asia at Japan's expense, including an occupation zone in Korea. Russia won these concessions in return for her promise to intervene against Japan where, as Churchill said, the shadow of war lengthened out as the war in Europe neared a close.

At the time of the Yalta Conference, Manila had not yet been reclaimed, Iwo Jima and

United States Army photo

Okinawa had not yet fallen, the fire bombing of Japanese home-island cities lay still a month or more off. Nor had the atomic bomb been tested; and in any case the skepticism of navy and army chiefs like Admiral King and General MacArthur concerning the ability of air power to terminate a great war had only been deepened by its failure to end the war in Europe. Admiral William D. Leahy, Chief of Staff to FDR and later to Truman, remained skeptical of the A-bomb itself. "It sounds like a professor's dream to me," he told King George VI only a week before its use in Hiroshima. Once it had been dropped, he deplored the adoption by Americans of "an ethical standard common to the barbarians of the Dark Ages." All of these leaders welcomed the prospect of Soviet action in Manchuria to help bring about the unconditional capitulation of the empire of the Rising Sun.

Once the A-bombs had effected Japan's surrender and Yalta's secret provisions stood revealed, Roosevelt, four months in his grave, was assaulted on all counts by many in the United States, the more severely because of Stalin's continued consolidation of his European gains since Yalta and his quick grasp of his Yalta concessions in Asia once Japan fell. Air force General Laurence S. Kuter, stand-in at Yalta for the ill air force chief, General Henry H. ("Hap") Arnold (whom some said might have averted Russia's gains there), declared later that the attacks on FDR stemmed "from misinformation generated by partisan oratory and nourished by shaky memories." One memory that did not waver was Secretary of War Stimson's, who recalled the war weariness of the troops he talked to in Florida in March 1945 on their way from Europe to the Pacific: "These men were weary in a way that no one merely reading reports could readily understand"—a discovery soon to be confirmed by the rioting of the troops remaining in Europe after V-E day demanding their prompt return home (see p. 774). Russia, Stimson felt certain at the time of Yalta, must be brought into the war in Asia; and, for that

matter, when ready, the bomb must be used. Russian forces on the Asian mainland would permit Americans to concentrate on the great object of the Pacific war, the exclusive occupation of Japan; the bomb would hasten that achievement.

Even without the concurrence of Roosevelt and Churchill at Yalta, many believe, Stalin, with more than 1.5 million men in Manchuria, would have seized what he wanted in Asia as he had in Europe—and might have seized even more than he had been granted by agreement. One check upon him may have been the A-bombs themselves. From the outset of the Manhattan District project, Churchill had pressed speed upon its directors and urged FDR to share its results, to enable Britain, as he said in July 1943, "to maintain her future independence in the face of international blackmail that the Russians might eventually be able to employ." Some go so far as to suggest that the main reason for dropping the A-bombs was to overawe the wicked Russians even more than the weakened Japanese. Stimson himself says he gave thought to "this terrible means of maintaining the rule of law in the world" (Churchill's phrase) as an "equalizer" against the "Red Army, which was daily increasing in its relative strength in Europe, as the Americans began their redeployment for the Pacific attack."

Many who assaulted Roosevelt for his territorial concessions at Yalta did so the more severely because they were made not only to hasten the end of the war but, perhaps primarily in Roosevelt's judgement, to win Stalin's full participation in the United Nations once the fighting was over. On returning from Yalta on March 1, 1945, Roosevelt declared that the agreement there "spells the end of the system of unilateral action and exclusive alliances and balances of power and all the other expedients which had been tried for centuries—and have failed. We propose to substitute for all that a universal organization in which all peace-loving nations will finally have a chance to join"—including the USSR.

The old League of Nations had failed at least as badly as traditional balance-of-power arrangements in attempting to keep the world's peace. But this did not deter FDR.

Even he, however, grew disillusioned very quickly. On April 1, 1945, only eleven days before his death, Roosevelt sent Stalin a sharp message decrying "the lack of progress made in carrying out ... the political decisions which we reached at Yalta, particularly those relating to the Polish question," one that so deeply concerned the millions of Polish-American voters. Stalin, on his part, a few weeks before V-E day, had grown suspicious of Western actions which he interpreted as attempts to make a separate peace with Germany, a move forbidden by the United Nations Declaration of 1942. Piqued, Stalin held off until the last moment before sending his delegation to San Francisco, where work on the United Nations Charter began April 25, 1945. Stalin's delay only deepened Western suspicions.

### The UN and the new order

Certain UN instrumentalities had been created even before the Charter was written. As early as November 1943, forty-four nations had set up the United Nations Relief and Rehabilitation Administration (UN-RRA) to assist areas liberated from Germany, Italy, and Japan. The following July the first of two conferences in 1944 to plan the postwar world was held at Bretton Woods, New Hampshire. This conference created an International Monetary Fund to stabilize national currencies and an International Bank for Reconstruction and Development, called the World Bank, to extend loans to nations for rehabilitation. The second conference, beginning in August at Dumbarton Oaks in Washington, D.C., drafted plans for the United Nations Charter. At Yalta the following February, the Big Three agreed to meet at San Francisco in April 1945 to launch the international organization and also ironed out, in a manner of speaking, certain issues that might have wrecked the San Francisco meeting before it even began. Even so, the delegates at San Francisco, representing fifty nations, witnessed a continuous and usually sharp dispute between the Russians and the Western powers that sometimes threatened the conference. By June 26, 1945, however, its work was completed and the Charter signed.

The Charter of the United Nations Organization provided for two major agencies, the General Assembly and the Security Council. In the General Assembly all members had one vote—except the USSR, which at Yalta gained two additional votes for two of its republics with strong independent traditions. The General Assembly was granted the power to discuss all questions falling within the scope of the United Nations Charter and to recommend suitable action to the Security Council. Failing Security Council action, the Assembly, according to a resolution adopted in 1950, could itself recommend action to member nations. The Security Council, which was to remain in continuous session in order to settle international disputes as they arose, was composed of eleven members. The Big Five—the Big Three plus France and Nationalist China—were to have permanent seats; the other seats would rotate for two-year terms among other nations. The decision on voting procedure in the Security Council gave the veto power to any permanent member. This decision virtually insured that the Council would be unable to oppose aggression by the major powers; but it may also have helped save the world from a collision of such powers by allowing them to check the use of force by the UN itself. Whether the UN could oppose aggression even by minor powers remained doubtful.

The Charter provided that when called upon by the Security Council, members were to make armed contingents available to the organization. It was expected that such contingents would be largely supplied by the five great powers on the Council itself. Four of these powers, recognizing differences in their ability to conform to this expectation, promptly agreed that their contributions be "comparable." The USSR, openly scornful of the "great power" status of some of her colleagues on the Council, insisted that contributions be "equal." Equal contributions would have resulted merely in a token army. The issue was resolved by leaving UN forces to later "agreement or agreements," thereby, as the Russians intended, at least temporarily drawing the teeth from the organization.

Four other agencies completed the permanent UN structure: an International Court of Justice; a Secretariat to coordinate the work of the UN; an Economic and Social Council; and a Trusteeship Council to handle colonies taken from Japan and Italy. From time to time additional UN commissions and agencies have been set up for special purposes.

The United States Senate debated the Covenant of the League of Nations for eight months before rejecting it. The Senate debated UN membership for but six days, and approved it by a vote of 89 to 2. The Organization held its first meetings in London in 1946, and then moved to New York City, its permanent home. By 1972 this home housed the delegations of 127 countries, many of them new nations as well as new members; but still absent were such "great powers" as West Germany and Red China.

When the San Francisco conference began few persons in all the world knew of the progress on the A-bomb at Los Alamos, nor were many better informed when the conference ended two months later. Created virtually in ignorance of atomic weapons, the UN was forced to confront atomic warfare as its first major problem, one that more than a quarter of a century later still remained unresolved.

Certain writers believe that the "balance of terror" achieved in the 1950s between the nuclear powers may have done more to avert atomic warfare than the long and fruitless pursuit of the will-o'-the-wisps of control and disarmament; but at first the attempts at control were directed toward checking the atomic arms race that probably began in Germany, the USSR, and Japan even before the Manhattan District Project was far advanced. Scientists in all industrial countries knew of the work on the atom in the thirties, although only those in the United States could mobilize the funds, manpower, and technical equipment required for A-bomb development and manufacture during the war. Once the bomb was dropped, many of the scientists involved wanted frantically to defuse the monster they had created. At the same time, the evidence of its potency spurred others on to develop the bomb in self-defense.

When in June 1946 Bernard M. Baruch, for the United States, submitted to the recently created UN Atomic Energy Commission recommendations for control of atomic weapons, the so-called Cold War had begun (Baruch was to give this rivalry its name one year later; see p. 783), and the atomic arms race became an intrinsic part of it. The Cold War was the second major development of which the architects of the UN were necessarily in ignorance, and it helped frustrate the Organization more and more, beginning with the predictable failure of Baruch's bomb control plan.

Baruch's plan called for the creation of an international agency to which the United States would turn over her atomic secrets provided that this agency be given the power to inspect atomic installations in any country to see that atomic weapons were not being manufactured. As soon as the system of inspection was working, the United States would destroy its stock of atomic weapons and join in the prohibition of their manufacture. But the USSR, still far behind the United States in atomic research and suspicious of international agencies, countered by proposing an international agreement to abandon atomic warfare and prohibit the making of atomic weapons, but with no provision for inspection. This was unacceptable to the United States. In the following decades significant progress was made in employing atomic energy for peaceful as well as wartime purposes, but progress toward regulation of atomic weapons proved slow.

Once the USSR, in September 1949, detonated its own first atomic bomb, Truman's archaic policy of control by means of scientific secrecy crashed as its first victim, while security by the balance of terror loomed as part of civilization under the new world order. A third early postwar development, the often violent dissolution of the overseas empires of

771

Western powers and the aspirations thus promoted among the colored peoples of the world for self-determination and economic advancement, also caught the creators of the UN more or less unawares. These vast areas, sometimes called the "third world," became another stage for superpower rivalry beyond UN control that often menaced the balance-of-terror standoff.

### The conquered nations

The problem of settling the fate of the conquered nations also disclosed the growing tension between the communists and the West. On July 17, 1945, Truman, Churchill, and Stalin met at Potsdam, Germany, to deal with the future of the old Axis members. Following the startling defeat of his party in the British elections on July 26, Churchill two days later gave way to the new Prime Minister, the Labor party leader Clement Atlee. At

Potsdam the new Big Three reaffirmed the four-power occupation of Germany, worked out details of German reparations payments, and tentatively settled the Polish-German frontier. Finally, the Potsdam Conference set up a Council of Foreign Ministers of the United States, Britain, Russia, and China to draw up peace treaties with Italy, Bulgaria, Rumania, Hungary, and Finland. These treaties were signed in February 1947 and, except in Italy and Finland, virtually sanctioned Soviet control over, and United States recognition of, communist regimes.

During 1945 and 1946, the leading Nazis were tried at Nuremberg before an international military court on charges of having started the war and conducting it in ways that violated fundamental human decency. The trial

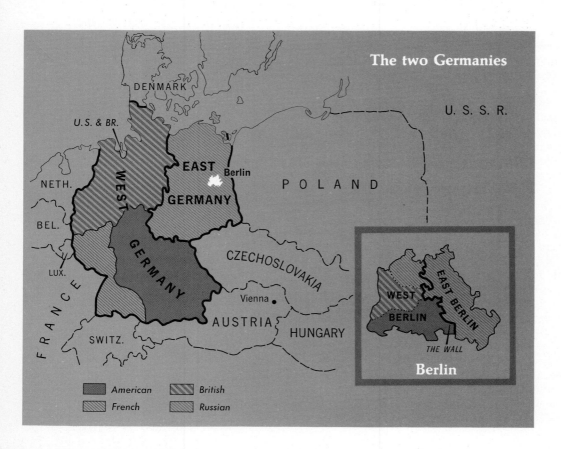

The two Germanies

revealed the full story of Nazi barbarity. Ten leading "war criminals" were executed. In all, over 500,000 Nazis were found guilty in the American zone and received sentences of varying severity. Similar trials in Japan led to the execution of former Premier Tojo and six other war leaders, and lighter sentences for about 4000 other "war criminals." A generation later these trials were to be recalled to the discomfiture of certain of the accusers for their own trespasses on the rules and laws of war when fighting against formerly colonial peoples (see p. 859).

In 1948 the Russians, irked by friction arising from the administration of Germany, ordered a blockade of the city of Berlin, which, though situated deep in their zone, was jointly administered by the USSR and the Western powers. By threatening the Germans in the Western zone of Berlin with starvation, the Soviets hoped to force the Allies to evacuate Berlin altogether. The Allies met the challenge by developing the "air lift," an ingenious technique by which food and supplies were delivered to the city by continuously shuttling cargo planes. In the end, it was the USSR that gave in and lifted the blockade in May 1949.

Frustrated by their failure to reach agreement with the Soviets on Germany, the Western powers met in June 1948 and consented to the creation of an unarmed German Federal Republic, embracing the three Western zones. The new state was launched in September 1949. In October 1949 the Soviets established in the east the German Democratic Republic.

The administration of conquered Japan was left to General Douglas MacArthur. Under American direction, a new constitution went into effect in May 1947, turning the fundamental powers of government over to representatives elected by the people. The Emperor renounced his claim to divinity, and the constitution renounced war as a right of the nation. Many social reforms were carried out, including the dissolution of the great industrial and commercial monopolies and the restoration of large tracts of land to the peasants. In September 1951, following the fall of China to the communists in 1949 (see p. 787) and the outbreak of the Korean War in 1950 (see p. 790), forty-nine nations—the USSR not among them—signed a general peace treaty with Japan restoring her "full sovereignty," including her right to redevelop her armaments industry and her armed services. This treaty was negotiated at the instigation of the United States to rebuild Japan into a power in order to offset communism in Asia as Germany was soon to be strengthened to offset communism in Europe. At this time, mutual security agreements were also made with the Philippines, Australia, and New Zealand.

## II  The Truman administration at home

### Demobilizing military personnel

During World War I, Harry S. Truman, a farm boy from Independence, Missouri, had risen to captain of artillery. He also ran a profitable company canteen with his wartime buddy, "Eddie" Jacobson, and soon after their demobilization in 1919 they opened a haberdashery partnership in Kansas City. When this business died in the postwar depression in 1922, Truman was invited by the Pendergast machine that controlled Kansas City politics to run for county judge, an administrative position. The Pendergasts, under severe pressure for every shade of corruption, needed the politically clean Truman more than he needed them; yet, out of work, he agreed to run, and he won easily. Truman was first elected to the United States Senate in 1934. After his reelection in 1940 he became chairman of a Senate committee to investigate defense contracts, and his zeal in working over wartime big business brought him the prominence that won him the Democratic vice-presidential nomination four years later.

At first overawed by the office he inherited on Roosevelt's death ("Boys, if you ever pray, pray for me now," he told reporters), Truman grew increasingly confident in the White House. Churchill, disconcerted by the loss of his fellow "naval person" and the trend of events, wrote in the last volume of his magisterial history of World War II, "We can see now the deadly hiatus which existed between the fading of President Roosevelt's strength and the growth of President Truman's grip on the vast world problem." Yet Truman, much beholden to FDR's long-time Chief of Staff, General George C. Marshall, only continued Roosevelt's policy of by-passing such civilian agencies as the State and War Departments and dealing directly with the uniformed Joint Chiefs. If it existed at all, Churchill's "hiatus" was short-lived.

Once the war ended in August 1945, the new President was confronted by military men determined to retain the economic power they had gained during the war and to exercise their immense authority through such instrumentalities as universal military training (UMT), of which General Marshall had long been a leading advocate. The goal of UMT now, as after the Spanish-American War and World War I, was not simply to insure military strength in a troubled world. "There is the more reason to fear rule by the military," said the *San Francisco Chronicle* as early as January 1945, "because it is known that in Army and Navy alike there is a group of officers, some of them highly placed, who believe this country needs discipline for discipline's sake alone."

UMT advocates were checked for the short run by the profound war weariness among GIs that Stimson had witnessed in March 1945. With the end of the war in August and delays in demobilization mounting, troop demonstrations, riots, and other mutinous acts seeking release from military life multiplied. These began as early as Christmas Day 1945 in Manila, when 4000 soldiers marched on the local replacement depot to protest cancellation of the sailing of a home-bound troop carrier.

In January 1946, some 20,000 men marched on the general command headquarters in Manila to express their frustrations. By then troop revolts had spread to the European theater. In Frankfort, 4000 soldiers who rushed General McNarney's headquarters demanding that they be sent home were stopped at bayonet point.

Petitions signed by tens of thousands of officers and men, meanwhile, poured in on the President. One of them protested "the vacillation and arbitrary attitude of [the] War Department . . . regarding our welfare, . . . causing deep antagonism in the hearts of GIs overseas." Congress, in turn, was besieged with letters stamped "No Boats, No Votes." At home by September 1945, according to Congresswoman Clare Boothe Luce, soldiers' families had placed the legislature "under constant and terrific pressure." The failure of military authorities to agree upon the appropriate postwar strength of the rival services, and their frequent and obscure manipulation of numbers, lent justification to the soldier revolts. To many GIs, the slowdown in demobilization was only a "subterfuge . . . to force passage of a bill to extend the draft."

Congress and the President bent under all this pressure. By midsummer 1946 the army and air force had been cut from over 8 million to under 2 million men, the navy from nearly 4 million to 980,000. "I termed this," Truman wrote in his *Memoirs,* "the most remarkable demobilization in the history of the world, or 'disintegration,' if you want to call it that." By March 31, 1947, Congress allowed the Selective Service Act of 1940 and its extensions to die.

The armed services, however, did not quit the field. Between January and September 1946, the War Department formed so many Reserve Officer Training Corps (ROTC) units and offered young men of college age such liberal inducements to participate that one writer observed: "Practically, [this policy] would force the nation's colleges to install ROTC units if they wanted male students."

774

Under the Holloway Plan, the navy took a similar course on even more lavish terms. That November, Dr. Francis Brown of the American Council of Education attacked the "insidious" ROTC program: "It is an admission that it is not military skills that are important but the indoctrination of attitudes. . . . No comparable plan," he added, "has been devised to identify, much less subsidize, capable youth for education for leadership in our social, economic, or political life."

This was not exactly true, for under the Servicemen's Readjustment Act of June 1944, commonly known as the "GI Bill of Rights," and later measures, $13.5 billion in federal funds, apportioned according to each man's length of service, was spent between 1945 and 1955 for veterans' education in colleges and vocational schools, including veterans of the Korean War. This act also entitled discharged servicemen to medical treatment at veterans' hospitals, vocational rehabilitation for the crippled, one year's unemployment insurance, and government loans for building homes and establishing businesses.

### Delaying "a permanent war economy"

Although Congress reenacted Selective Service in June 1948 (see p. 779), UMT advocates continued so pertinaciously to press their program that by 1952 the Republican Whip, Congressman Leslie C. Arends of the House Military Affairs Committee, charged that "by hook or by crook, military brass in the Pentagon is determined to . . . realize their dream of a great stockpile of men under their jurisdiction." In the meantime, the "brass" gained other goals. In September 1946, *Business Week* observed: "Partly by design, partly by default, federal support of pure science is today almost completely under military control. Its general direction is being set by military needs; its finances are coming from military funds." The dragooning of science and scientists to military research had reached "such an enormous scale" by 1949 that Van-

nevar Bush himself warned of the existing "danger of the encouragement of . . . grandiose projects, discouragement of individual genius, and hardening of administrative consciences in the universities."

775

Such domination of science in a technological age facilitated domination of the economy itself, the objective of great corporations associated with the military in "hardware" production. Charles E. Wilson, president of General Electric, advocating a permanent war economy in January 1944, urged speed upon the armed forces. In an address at that time to the Army Ordnance Association, Wilson said, "The revulsion against war not too long hence will be an almost insuperable obstacle for us to overcome in establishing a preparedness program and for that reason I am convinced that we must begin now to set the machinery in motion." It "must be a continuing program and not the creature of an emergency. In fact one of its objects will be to eliminate emergencies as far as possible. . . . In the execution of the part allotted to it, industry must not be hampered by political witch-hunts." Later that year, Secretary of the Navy James Forrestal organized the National Security Industrial Association, composed of corporations with sig-

*ROTC classroom at Cornell University, October 1950.*

United States Army photo

nificant military contracts, to insure that "American business will remain close to the services."

One of the principal opponents of this scheme was Donald M. Nelson, executive vice-president of Sears, Roebuck and Company, who became head of the War Production Board in January 1942. In his telltale account of his wartime experiences, *Arsenal of Democracy* (1946), Nelson wrote: "The question of military control will confront us not only in war but in peace. The lesson taught by these recent war years is clear: our whole economic and social system will be in peril if it is controlled by the military men."

While American armed services (especially the navy) and American heavy industry had wooed one another for three quarters of a century before World War II, the global scale of that conflict enlarged the economic ambitions of the military (especially in the army). These were fed by the revolutionary demands on logistics—"the task," as General A. C. Smith, army chief of military history, puts it, "of effecting the orderly assembly, movement, and delivery of great masses of men and matériel throughout the world." General Smith continues:

*Logistical tasks account in large measure for the enormous administrative machinery that the Army developed in the course of the war. Its development, though not a complete surprise, exceeded all anticipations. . . . With this went a 'proliferation of overhead' in the form of complex controls and higher headquarters that ate up officers needed for the training and leading of fighting troops, drew into the service a multitude of specialists, and confused the chain of command. The trend ran counter to the traditional American belief that the overriding mission of the Army is to fight, a conviction so deep that some commanders, like General McNair, fought to keep the Army lean and simple. In World War II they lost this fight.*

The momentum of the army's immense logistical activities naturally carried it into the fiercest conflict with Nelson's civilian War Production Board. "Things [were] said and done," Nelson writes, "in either an inexcusable lust for power or in outright ignorance of how industrial production is accomplished

and what it is necessary for an economy to produce." And he adds:

*The long and bitter controversy with the military over control of America's civilian economy came to its climax in the summer of 1944, with the fight over our reconversion program. To a large extent that battle was lost. To a large extent, the military took control over the economy, and many of the reconversion difficulties which arose later . . . can be traced directly to that fact.*

Truman, from his vantage point in the Senate and the knowledge gained from the work of his investigating committee, sided with the WPB.

Yet just as grass-roots agitation had overcome professional dilatoriness in restoring weary soldiers to civilian liberty, so popular demand for consumer goods among civilians weary of depression privations and wartime sacrifices helped free industry from Pentagon goals. "Rosie the Riveter," Maurice O'Connell of the CIO told the Los Angeles Chamber of Commerce soon after V-J day, "isn't going back to emptying slop jars. . . . Times have changed. People have become accustomed to new conditions, new wage scales, new ways of being treated." Backing up his assertion was the massive $140 billion in savings which "Rosie" and others had come out of the war aching to spend. "The American people," Fred M. Vinson, Director of War Mobilization and Reconversion, declared later in 1945, "are in the pleasant predicament of having to learn to live 50 percent better than they have ever lived before."

Once the fighting ended, the private companies that had operated Defense Plant Corporation facilities (see p. 750) took advantage of their liberal purchase options to buy them up. On this foundation, the business community went on a spree of private expenditure for plant construction that dwarfed any similar movement in the nation's history and provided one of the most explosive features of the postwar boom. Looking toward still further modernization, Congress, in August 1946, created the Atomic Energy Commission, placing it under civilian control after defeating a proposal to give the armed services chiefs a veto on its actions. The commission was to promote private and government research into the peaceful as well as military uses of atomic energy and to develop facilities for its production. Cost and technical problems delayed peaceful applications for almost two decades; and when in the midsixties nuclear electricity-generating plants began to be built by utility companies, the issue of radioactive emissions caused widespread alarm and raised questions of supervision and surveillance still unresolved in the early seventies.

The 1944 Democratic platform, moving beyond the goals of the New Deal itself, pledged to "guarantee full employment" when the war was over. After a long debate on the relative roles of business and government, Congress, in February 1946, passed the landmark Maximum Employment Act to redeem this pledge. This act for the first time committed the federal government fully to utilize the nation's economic resources to insure "maximum employment, production and purchasing power." The act created a Council of Economic Advisers to keep the President informed on economic trends and on proper public measures to soften business downswings and sustain business prosperity.

To stimulate postwar business with an eye to full employment, Congress, in November 1945, cut wartime taxes an estimated $6 billion. In November 1946, despite Truman's veto of such a measure the previous July as too hasty, Congress swept away all wartime price controls under the OPA except those on rents, sugar, and rice. With these further incentives, industrial production soared.

So strong was the pent-up demand, however, that shortages soon intensified the already sharp inflation caused by everyone's catching up at once. Inflation naturally broadened the wave of strikes that swept the country after the removal of wartime restraints and restrictions. Labor, like other seg-

Brookhaven National Laboratory

*Through these holes in the atomic reactor at Brookhaven National Laboratory on Long Island tons of pure uranium metal are introduced. These atoms fission, or split, in a chain reaction, releasing atomic particles used in the production of radioisotopes.*

ments of the economy, had its own catching up to do. One of the most far-reaching strikes was that of the United Mine Workers in April 1946. Although Truman ordered government seizure of the coal pits, the mineworkers eventually made important wage gains. A nationwide railroad strike, followed by fruitless labor-management negotiations, prompted Truman to seize the railroads in May 1946. Only a last-minute settlement halted passage at this time of stern antiunion legislation. Such presidential activity no doubt reflected the lingering spirit of wartime disciplinary habits; yet there was enough of "normalcy" about it as well to avert new fears of a "permanent war economy."

*Resuming party politics*

The postwar inflation and labor conflicts hurt the Democratic party, especially in the cities which had supplied so much Roosevelt strength. The party was also hurt by revelations of successful Soviet atomic espionage, a harbinger of things to come. The most unnerving exposé occurred in Canada, not in the United States, when in February 1946 twenty-three persons, one a member of the Canadian parliament, another an atomic scientist, and the rest in high "positions of trust," were cited as members of a spy ring attached to the Canadian Communist party. Those who for a decade of more had harped on the New Deal's "softness" on communism instantly raised questions about the possible implication of highly placed Americans in this episode and perhaps in others still secret. Strengthened by such spots on the Democratic record, the Republicans, in the elections of 1946, won majorities in both houses of the Eightieth Congress.

Once this Congress convened in January 1947, the Republican leadership resuscitated the House Un-American Activities Committee (HUAC), formed initially as a temporary investigation unit in 1938 largely to advance the personal political fortunes of its chairman, Democrat Martin Dies of Texas. Now with a strong push from the freshman California congressman Richard M. Nixon, victorious after a calculated red-baiting campaign, the committee proceeded to hunt out communists and alleged communists to advance the fortunes of the Republican party generally. Its most resounding coup was the Hiss case, which opened in August 1948, on the eve of the presidential election (see p. 793). To offset the ardor of HUAC, President Truman, in March 1947, ordered a full-scale "loyalty investigation" of all present and prospective federal employees, those under the merit system to be examined by the Civil Service Commission, others by the heads of their departments or agencies. No source of information, however questionable, was to be ignored, and along with all "loyalty" data worked up by government bureaus since 1939, the new dossiers were to become part of a "central master index." Among the "standards for refusal of employment or removal from employment" was "sympathetic association" with any foreign or domestic organization designated by the Attorney-General as "subversive." In compliance with the President's order, Attorney-General Tom C. Clark, in December 1947, issued a list of ninety organizations deemed disloyal to the United States.

Truman realized that the investigation might quickly poison the very freedom it was supposed to protect, and took steps to guard against this. He could not check the proliferation of similar probes in state and local governments and "sensitive" industries, however, where even the few federal safeguards often were omitted. When the federal investigation was completed in April 1951, the records of no less than 3,225,000 civil servants had been scrutinized. Under pressure of the inquiry, 2900 had resigned and a mere 300 had been dismissed. The investigation's broad criteria of what constituted subversion made it possible that none of these individuals was a communist, although no doubt some had been. In any case, so thorough was the screening that when the Republicans took office in 1953 they could not uncover a single communist holdover from the long Democratic regime.

Republican success with the communist issue in 1946 showed that the country could not fall peaceably asleep with sweet dreams of domestic prosperity to be enjoyed once more in isolation. The Soviet menace was real enough, as the Canadian revelations and subsequent events fully demonstrated. The whole question of the confrontation with the USSR around the world occupied the Truman administration from the moment it gained its bearings. (We shall discuss administration foreign policy in detail in the next section.) Before the memorable 1948 presidential campaign, the administration also took steps at home to follow up the reassurance of loyalty probes with reorganization of the military establishment.

One of the most momentous of these steps

came in July 1947 with the passage of the National Security Act unifying the administration of the armed services and enlarging their duties. The issue of unification had been debated ever since the emergence of the air force in World War I, when certain air force leaders had sought to free their service from army control and make it an autonomous arm under an overall General Staff. Secretary of War Newton D. Baker forecast some of the issues that arose after the 1947 legislation when he wrote in his Annual Report of 1919:

*To separate [the ground and air forces] makes them rival services with the whole train of evils which such rivalry creates, evils which in peace time mean contention before Congress for unbalanced appropriations, grievances and fretfulness about relative rank and rapidity of promotion, and in time of war the substitution of combined service prides for a single emotion of pride in one service.*

Secretary of War Dwight F. Davis added in 1926 that a super General Staff under a unified "Department of National Defense" would undertake to do "much more than . . . all the necessary joint planning, . . . more than anyone would want it to do."

The National Security Act of 1947 created a new National Military Establishment, soon to be renamed the Department of Defense, under a new Secretary of Defense on the Cabinet level, to "be appointed from civilian life." The old Department of the Navy was retained intact; the War Department became the Department of the Army; and the autonomous Department of the Air Force, so long sought, was added to them. Each service was to be headed by a Secretary below the Cabinet level, and a uniformed Chief of Staff or of Operations. The uniformed Chiefs of the three services together, along with "the Chief of Staff to the Commander-in-Chief, if there be one," were to make up the Joint Chiefs of Staff, "the principal military advisers to the President." The act also created the National Security Council to be presided over by the

Commander-in-Chief. Under this council, the act set up a Central Intelligence Agency (CIA) to coordinate all government "intelligence activities." Navy Secretary James V. Forrestal became the first Secretary of Defense.

In June 1948, Congress passed a new selective service act to replace the wartime draft which had been permitted to expire the previous March. In July, Truman issued the far-reaching order "that there shall be equality of treatment and opportunity for all persons in the armed services without regard to race, color, religion or national origin," allowing "the time required to effectuate any necessary changes without impairing efficiency or morale."

The urgency of national security measures did not blind the President to the demand for domestic reforms delayed by the Democratic conservatism at the end of the New Deal years and by the total mobilization of wartime. With his own eye on the impending 1948 presidential campaign, he proposed to the Republican dominated Eightieth Congress many new progressive measures aimed especially at rebuilding Democratic urban strength. Among his proposals were comprehensive medicare and civil-rights bills. As anticipated, this program died in the legislature, the civil-rights part of it largely because of southern Democratic opposition. Truman's order for equality of races in the armed services followed his civil-rights failures in Congress.

The Eightieth Congress's most controversial domestic measure, adopted over Truman's veto in June 1947, was the Taft-Hartley Act. This act outlawed the closed shop, forced unions to accept a sixty-day "cooling-off period" before striking, forbade them to contribute to political campaigns, put an end to the checkoff system by which employers helped collect union dues, and required union leaders to file affidavits that they were not communists before their unions could enjoy privileges under the National Labor Relations Board. Labor leaders denounced Taft-Hartley as a "slave-bill," but it did not prevent them from making substantial gains. From 1945 to 1952, union membership rose from 14.6 million to 17 million.

In March 1947 Congress passed the

*A jaunty Harry Truman
out for his summer morning walk
in Independence, Missouri, in August 1946,
accompanied by a member
of his Secret Service staff.*

Twenty-second Amendment to the Constitution, limiting the President to two terms, a backhanded slap at FDR. This amendment was declared ratified in February 1951. As the incumbent, Truman was explicitly exempted from its provisions. In July 1947, Congress also adopted a Presidential Succession Act revising a statute of 1886 which had made the *appointive* Secretary of State the successor to a President serving without a Vice-President. The new measure designated the *elective* Speaker of the House as first in line, with the President *pro tempore* of the Senate next, and the Secretary of State and other Cabinet members only then becoming eligible.

### The Fair Deal

Henry A. Wallace, Truman's Secretary of Commerce until 1946, when he was dropped for opposing the administration's "get tough with Russia" policy, characterized the President's loyalty probe of 1947 as a "witch hunt." In December 1947, Wallace announced that he would run for President on a third-party ticket. Some analysts believed he might win 5 to 8 million votes, enough to sink any Democratic candidate, especially with conservative southerners simmering over their party's liberals' growing concern with Negro equality. Buoyed up by their opponent's differences, the Republicans, at their Philadelphia convention in June, renominated Governor Thomas E. Dewey of New York for President and named Governor Earl Warren of rapidly growing California for Vice-President. They also adopted a platform internationalist on foreign policy and moderate on domestic issues.

For months before the Democrats convened in Philadelphia on July 12, feverish efforts were made to hold the party together. Liberals led by Mayor Hubert H. Humphrey of Minneapolis early in 1948 formed Americans for Democratic Action (ADA) to help keep the Wallaceites in tow. They won the support of many big-city bosses with well-organized black and other ethnic minorities to satisfy. Southerners by and large, certain that a victory for the liberals would alienate millions in their section, fought them. When a broad-based movement to draft the immensely popular General Eisenhower failed, the Truman regulars closed ranks and put him over on July 15. The ADA group, meanwhile, had carried through a liberal platform defending the FDR-Truman tradition, denouncing Taft-Hartley, and promising antilynching and anti-poll-tax laws. As a sop to southerners, the convention named Acting-President of the Senate Alben W. Barkley of Kentucky for Vice-President.

ADA tactics and Barkley's nomination both fell short of their goals. On July 17, the so-called Dixiecrats, meeting in Birmingham, Alabama, formed the States' Rights Democratic party and nominated Governor J. Strom Thurmond of South Carolina for President.

Five days later, the Wallace liberals formed the Progressive party and named their favorite as standard-bearer.

The failure of the unity efforts made Truman's cause seem hopeless. The southerners, however, enhanced his appeal to the strategically important black voters of the North; while Wallace's campaign, quietly manipulated by a small group of communists and their sympathizers, served to dramatize the fact that Truman was no friend of the extreme left. Trusting to Democratic weakness, Dewey never caught the imagination of the voters. Truman, aware of the fight he had to make, stormed up and down the country denouncing "the no good, good-for-nothing Eightieth Congress"—one that, as we have seen, did pass momentous legislation but did little to extend the welfare state. When the ballots were counted, Truman was shown to have pulled off the greatest upset in American political history, winning 24,105,000 popular and 303 electoral votes to Dewey's 21,969,000 and 189. Thurmond carried only four deep-South states, while Wallace carried not a single one. In the Eighty-first Congress, moreover, the Democrats could count a Senate majority of 12 and a House majority of 93.

Convinced that he had received a popular mandate to carry on what he now called his Fair Deal, Truman drew up a program of leg-

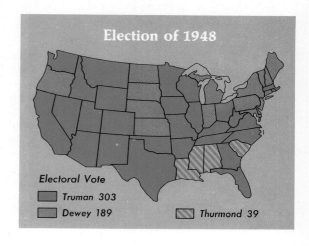

**Election of 1948**

*Electoral Vote*

- Truman 303
- Dewey 189
- Thurmond 39

islation designed to go the New Deal one better. At vital points a newly influential coalition of conservative Democrats and Republicans blocked him, but he made headway despite it. In 1949 he secured an amendment to the New Deal's Fair Labor Standards Act (see p. 729) raising the minimum wage from 40 to 75 cents an hour. A new Social Security Act, in August 1950, added almost 10 million to those eligible for benefits. A National Housing Act, passed in July 1949, provided large sums to cities for aid in slum clearance and for the construction of over 800,000 units for low-income families. Congress, however, defeated the Brannan Plan (an ambitious program for stabilizing farm income), turned down a strong civil-rights program for blacks, and refused to repeal or significantly amend Taft-Hartley.

## III   The Truman administration and foreign affairs

### "Cold War" and "containment" in Europe

While Americans attempted to resume politics as usual once World War II had been won, the Russians undertook to consolidate their most recent territorial gains (see p. 759) and resume their expansive tendencies. Stalin's first new target was oil-rich Iran in the strategic Middle East, but his reach soon

extended to her European neighbor, Turkey, and to Turkey's neighbor, Greece, both keys to the equally strategic Mediterranean.

During the war, Stalin's forces had helped promote a communist separatist movement in Azerbaijan, Iran's northernmost province on the Soviet border. Now, in November 1945, they supported a communist revolt there looking toward the province's autonomy. According to the Big Three agreement at Teheran, Iran's capital, in 1943, all Allied troops were to be removed from Iran by March 2, 1946, but instead of removing his, Stalin only increased them. Iran had already complained to the UN of Soviet interference, and on March 5 Truman backed Security Council efforts to protect Iran by sending a stiff note to Stalin demanding his adherence to the Teheran accord. Stalin took this message to heart and by May 1946 had removed his troops. But he had also forced Iran into an agreement for Soviet participation in Iranian oil production, thereby weakening Britain's long-standing interests there, and for the autonomy of Azerbaijan. With American aid, Iran, in December 1946, regained hegemony over Azerbaijan, but the Soviet threat persisted in the entire Middle Eastern area.

For centuries the Russians had sought access to the Mediterranean by way of the Turkish straits leading out from the Black Sea. In March 1945 and again in August they re-

*Retreat from the Middle East.*
*Members of British Sixth Airborne Division*
*boarding ship for home at Haifa,*
*Palestine, March 1948.*

Wide World Photos

newed their demands for Turkish territory in this region, the second time in terms menacing enough to draw a United States naval task force to the Mediterranean. Still further demands in October elicited stern American and British notes that deterred the Russians for the time being but also impelled them to shift their pressure westward onto Greece. Here, until February 1947, British forces helped the Greek government fight off communist guerrillas strengthened by bands from such adjacent Soviet satellites as Yugoslavia, Bulgaria, and Albania. Britain herself, however, was in dire financial trouble at this time (see p. 783), and on February 24, 1947, she was forced to notify the United States that she no longer could bear the burden of resisting communism in the Mediterranean theater. She planned to withdraw her troops from Greece and to terminate her aid to Turkey.

This step was implicit acknowledgment of the end of British supremacy in the Mediterranean. In March 1946 Britain had acknowledged the independence of Transjordan (renamed Jordan in 1949), and in April 1947 had turned over the future of Palestine to the UN, leading in May 1948 to the creation, with mixed United States reactions, of the independent state of Israel. These steps hastened Britain's decline in the Middle East. France, meanwhile, by August 1946, had completed her promised withdrawal from Syria and Lebanon. If only by default, leadership in the defense of the noncommunist world, with all the obligations it entailed, fell to the United States.

Truman took up the challenge. In March 1947, he went before Congress to make a revolutionary statement known since as the Truman Doctrine:

*I believe that it must be the policy of the United States to support free people who are resisting attempted subjugation by armed minorities or by outside pressure. . . . If we falter in our leadership, we may endanger the peace of the world—and we shall surely endanger the welfare of this nation.*

The President acknowledged that the Greek people were not as free as they might be and that "we have considered how the United Nations might assist in this crisis," but it and "its related organizations are not in a position to extend the kind of help . . . required. . . . We are the only country able to provide that help."

Truman asked Congress for $400 million to assist Greece and Turkey, and "in addition to the funds, . . . to authorize the detail of American civilian and military personnel" to those countries at their request, to oversee the use of American grants and to train Greek and Turkish soldiers. Many Americans were alarmed at the President's expansive policy, but Congress provided what Truman asked. Between 1947 and 1950, the United States spent about $660 million on aid to Greece and Turkey, and their territorial integrity was preserved. In a speech in his native South Carolina in April 1947, Bernard Baruch signified the reawakening of the American people and the nature of their unprecedented commitment when he said: "Let us not be deceived— today we are in the midst of a cold war."

Baruch's catch phrase has since set up another sort of war, that among historians of different persuasions, over who started this rivalry and when it really began. False hopes for the United Nations seemed to obscure the implacable hostility between capitalism and communism evident since the end of czarism in Russia, if not since the Paris Commune of 1870. This hostility has been evident *within* Western nations and within the harshly repressed Eastern nations, as well as in the confrontation of the champions of the rival camps. The wartime alliance of the targets of Nazism in the early 1940s, from the enunciation of the Atlantic Charter in August 1941 onward, represented only an uneasy armistice in this confrontation, and sometimes even less than that, the parties to it often pursuing their independent purposes while the war continued. When the war ended with the victorious Russians grasping lands they felt they needed, and the victorious United States, with

Churchill's urgent blessing, dropping the atomic bomb perhaps to "monitor" the Russian advance, the so-called Cold War intensified. Britain's retreat from her Mediterranean lifeline brought home to the United States the alarming postwar economic predicament of Western Europe and underscored this region's political vulnerability as well. American realization of this position is sometimes viewed as the discovery of an opportunity to reduce the sufferers to permanent economic dependence. But such was scarcely the view of the beneficiaries of American aid at the time of the development of the Marshall Plan, in 1947, by which the United States took the initiative in the Cold War following its effective defensive stand in Greece and Turkey.

Britain, almost entirely dependent upon outside food supplies and on a vigorous world trade for the wherewithal to pay for them, was economically much the worst off in western Europe at this time. The situation in France, however, appeared more ominous because her large Communist party, capitalizing on a century of deprivation among the working classes, thwarted all efforts to revive the economy in order to hasten a general political collapse. In Italy deprivation had an even longer history than in France and communism an even stronger hold. In defeated Germany, hunger was common and chaos ruled. After some early intimations of an aggressive approach to this predicament, projecting nothing less than the reconstruction of the whole European economy as a unit in order to foster conditions favorable to democracy, General George C. Marshall, the first military man, on his appointment in January 1947, to become Secretary of State, announced the new program in his commencement address at Harvard on June 5. As Marshall put it:

*Our policy is directed not against any country or doctrine, but against hunger, poverty, desperation, and chaos. Its purpose should be the revival of a working economy in the world so as to permit the emergence of political and social conditions in which free institutions can exist.*

The USSR and its satellites, although invited to participate in the Marshall Plan, recognized it as a project to revive and preserve Western capitalism and tried everything to subvert it. Western European leaders, on their part, took up the proposal with alacrity and at a meeting in Paris in July drew up a broad program. American isolationists presented additional hurdles, but the communist coup in Czechoslovakia in February 1948, brought on in part by her government's dallying with the idea of participating in the Marshall Plan, made the need for action painfully evident, and isolationist opposition collapsed. In April 1948 Congress passed a bill providing $5.3 billion for the first twelve months of Marshall Plan aid, thus launching the European Recovery Program. Between 1948 and 1952, under the Economic Cooperation Administration, about $12 billion in all in Marshall Plan funds was distributed, more than half the total going to Britain, France, and West Germany. By 1952, economic recovery in these countries was complete, and western Europe was launched on a long business boom. This was topped off by the formation of the European Common Market in 1957 and other economic groupings soon after, as projected by Marshall himself. Moreover, the feared advance of communism on the Continent had been thwarted, and Communist parties in the West languished.

The Marshall Plan was supplemented in 1949 by Truman's Point Four program "for the improvement and growth of undeveloped areas," where resistance to communism might thereby be strengthened. From 1951 to 1954, Congress appropriated nearly $400 million for Point Four, thereby fostering, in conjunction with the economic and social agencies of the UN, the worldwide "revolution of rising expectations."

The animating idea behind the Truman Doctrine, the Marshall Plan, and Point Four was the concept of "containment." Under the signature "X," George F. Kennan, a Foreign Service career man who had spent some time in the USSR during the war, set forth the policy projected by this concept in an article, "The Sources of Soviet Conduct," in *Foreign Affairs* magazine, July 1947.

In brief, the goal of this policy was to "contain" the Soviet Union and its satellite states within their existing boundaries, in the hope that internal divisions and failures would in time so weaken them that they could no longer threaten the security of the Western world. Kennan warned that Soviet leaders had not junked the old communist ideology but also that it should not be assumed that they would commit themselves to some "do-or-die program" to overthrow Western society. Their own belief in the inevitable fall of capitalism through its own divisions and contradictions convinced them that time was on their side. The history of Russia and the teachings of Lenin both argued, he said, that the Soviets would move with caution, retreating when necessary "in the face of superior force." Under such circumstances, Kennan concluded, "the main element of any United States policy toward the Soviet Union must be that of a long-term, patient but firm and vigilant containment of Russian expansive tendencies. . . . The Russians look forward to a duel of infinite duration."

Kennan's counsel dashed all hope for a sudden, spectacular end to the Cold War, which, as we have said, had neither a sudden nor spectacular start. As a more dynamic alternative to containment, the right wing of the Republican party became infatuated with the idea of "liberation"—that is, direct attempts to free captive peoples from the Soviet yoke. "Some voices," Truman wrote later in his *Memoirs,* "were raised in America calling for a break with the Russians" at this time. "These people did not understand that our choice was only between negotiations and war. There was no third way." The possibility of war, even with negotiations, moreover, was not lost sight of, and steps were taken on the home front, as we have seen, to confront it if it came. Further steps were now taken on the diplomatic front as well.

Article 51 of the UN Charter sanctioned "collective self-defense" arrangements until the Security Council could act "to maintain peace and security." In March 1948, under the sanction of this article and of the Marshall

Plan, Britain, France, the Netherlands, Belgium, and Luxembourg signed a treaty of economic cooperation and military alliance. This step prompted the United States Senate in June 1948 to adopt the Vandenberg Resolution to the effect that the United States should seek peace through collective defense arrangements with friendly powers. The Vandenberg Resolution led to the North Atlantic Treaty, signed April 4, 1949, by twelve Western nations. Article 5 of this treaty stated that an armed attack upon any member would be considered an attack upon all and promised that each would go to the assistance of the party attacked by whatever action was thought necessary, "including the use of armed force." After twenty years any member could terminate its affiliation by giving the United States one year notice of intention to do so.

To build up the military strength of the members of the North Atlantic Treaty Organization (NATO), Congress passed the Mutual Defense Assistance Act in September 1949. From October of that year to the end of 1953, the United States supplied almost $6 billion worth of arms and military material to European allies and another $1.7 billion to other

**785**

NATO and Iron Curtain countries, 1949-1952

Original NATO Countries (United States and Canada not shown)

Joined NATO in 1952

Joined NATO in 1955

countries. While the European allies also strained to make their own contributions to NATO, they failed by and large to do so, so that NATO soon came to depend on air power as the principal deterrent to the Soviet Union, and particularly on the American Strategic Air Command (SAC), organized in 1951. SAC in turn imposed on the United States the need for air bases in many parts of the world, not all friendly, and this sometimes awkwardly influenced diplomatic decisions.

*Security of Latin America*

During World War II, all Latin American countries except Argentina and Chile had cooperated readily with the Western Allies to the extent of supplying strategic materials and making bases available. Brazil and Mexico also became active belligerents against the Axis, sending troops overseas. Argentina, aspiring to South American leadership in competition with both Brazil and the United States, grew especially envious of Brazil because of the United States lend-lease aid she received, including arms.

After the strongly pro-Axis military leader Colonel Juan D. Perón became virtual dictator of Argentina in 1944, relations between his country and the United States deteriorated to the extent that the supporters of the Grand Alliance among the Latin American nations began to fear that the war with the Axis would be extended to their hemisphere. To consider and act upon this threat, an inter-American conference, with Argentina excluded and the United States represented, met at the Castle of Chapultepec in Mexico City early in 1945. On March 6 the conference adopted the Act of Chapultepec, an informal agreement declaring that an attack by any state against the territory or "the sovereignty or political independence of an American State shall . . . be considered an act of aggression against" the signers. Argentina, aware of her growing isolation, declared war on the Axis on March 27, 1945, and a few days later accepted the Chapultepec agreement. The United States, in return, over Soviet opposition, helped her win a seat at the San Francisco Conference in April, where she and all other Latin American countries became charter members of the UN.

The end of the war saw the end of the profitable markets for strategic raw materials that Latin American countries enjoyed during the conflict. It also saw the frustration of their hopes for industrialization, to which they had looked forward during the war as a springboard for future economic growth. When neglect by the United States followed hard upon the restoration of peace, suspicion grew that the Good Neighbor policy had been merely a screen for wartime exploitation. A crushing blow came in June 1947, when Latin America found herself excluded from Marshall Plan aid.

The progress of the Cold War soon stirred the Truman administration to seek to mend hemispheric as well as more distant fences. At the Inter-American Conference near Rio de Janeiro in August and September 1947, the United States participated in writing the Rio Pact, sanctioned, like NATO, by the UN charter. This pact made the mutual-defense provisions of the Act of Chapultepec into a permanent treaty and defined the area of its operation. The United States Senate quickly approved this treaty, 72 to 1. A second step was the creation at Bogotá, Colombia, in March 1948, of the Organization of American States (OAS) to supplant the old Pan-American Union. The OAS charter confirmed the Rio Pact and created a permanent executive council with headquarters in Washington to oversee this and other inter-American contacts. Additional charter provisions were aimed mainly at countering communist infiltration. Persistent rejection by the United States of new requests for Marshall Plan-type aid through the OAS soon undid whatever small gains the United States had made at Rio and Bogotá.

*Hot war in China*

"Containment" worked well enough in Europe, but in the Far East an entirely different situation developed with the fall of China to the communist forces there in October 1949. These forces had come into existence long before World War II, and throughout the war the United States and Britain, each for its own purposes, had tried to get them and the Nationalists under Chiang Kai-shek to work together to defeat Japan. But this policy failed dismally. General Joseph W. Stilwell, in charge of coordinating Chinese wartime efforts against Japan, concluded that Chiang's government "is a structure based on fear and favor, in the hands of an ignorant, arbitrary, stubborn man." At the war's end the Chinese communists, encouraged by the Russians, received the surrender of Japanese armies independently, amassed their own arms, and even engaged in skirmishes with the Nationalists.

In an attempt to stave off civil war in China and the extension of communist rule there, United States Ambassador Patrick J. Hurley, in September 1945, arranged a meeting in Chungking, the Nationalist capital, between Chiang and Mao Tse-tung, the communist leader. After a full six weeks of talks, Mao departed for his own capital at Yenan, acknowledging that "there are great difficulties" in the way of reconciliation, "but they can be overcome." Hurley himself doubted this, and on his resignation as ambassador late in November, embittered by his failure, he pointed the finger at career men in the United States Foreign Service who, he said, undermined his efforts to "prevent the collapse of the Nationalist government." Hurley enlarged on this theme on his return to Washington.

As the deterioration of Chiang's regime continued, Truman that December sent General Marshall to the divided country, but without profit. At one point Marshall warned Chiang that the communist forces were too strong for him to defeat militarily, and urged further negotiations. On his final return to Washington in January 1947 to become Secretary of State (he had made a visit home in March and April 1946), Marshall acknowl-

edged his profound discouragement. Sincere efforts to reach a settlement, he said, had been frustrated not merely by the communists but also "by irreconcilable groups within the Kuomintang party interested in the preservation of their own feudal control of China." Marshall did not mention the United States career men.

In July 1947, Truman made still another effort to avert disaster. This time he sent General Albert C. Wedemeyer, who had served as Chiang's chief of staff from late 1945 until the middle of 1946, "to make an appraisal" of the entire situation, "current and projected." Wedemeyer's report of September 19, 1947, made proposals that reflected so harshly on Chiang's ability to control his own territory that Truman and Marshall kept them from the public until the summer of 1949. In the less objectionable parts of his report, Wedemeyer seemed to agree with Marshall's earlier conclusions:

> Today [he wrote] China is being invaded by an idea instead of strong military forces from the outside. . . . The Central Government cannot defeat the Chinese Communists by the employment of force, but can only win the loyal, enthusiastic and realistic support of the masses of the people by improving the political and economic situation immediately.

Despite his criticism of the Nationalist government, Wedemeyer recommended that it be given extensive aid, but the Truman administration decided that Chiang's prospects did not warrant further assistance. In the great civil war that soon developed, the communists swept all the way to Shanghai by May 1949. Preparations for Nationalist withdrawal to the island of Taiwan (Formosa), begun in July 1949, were completed by December. In the meantime, on October 1, scarcely a week after the Russians had exploded their first atomic bomb, the communist "People's Republic of China" was proclaimed. In February 1950, a treaty of alliance and mutual assistance was concluded with the USSR.

In August 1949, the State Department issued a White Paper on the Chinese question revealing, among other items, that from 1945 to 1949 the Nationalists had received $3 billion in American aid, most of it squandered or permitted to fall into communist hands. The White Paper and accompanying documents had so many other provocative things to say that ex-Ambassador Hurley promptly denounced it as a "smooth alibi for the pro-Communists in the State Department who had engineered the overthrow of our ally." A number of senators joined in Hurley's denunciation, and bitterness rose thereafter to the point where Marshall and his advisors were charged with the deliberate betrayal of American interests.

Although she had recognized new communist regimes in Europe, the United States, unlike Britain and other major nations, continued to view Chiang's government in Taiwan as the legitimate government of China and refused to recognize the People's Republic of China or consent to its admission to the UN.

*Conference table at UN Security Council meeting, June 27, 1950. United States Ambassador Warren Austin reads resolution concerning complaint of aggression by North Korea. Note empty USSR seat, second from Austin's right.*

### "Limited war" in Korea

The hot war between Chiang and the communists in China had an almost instant sequel in nearby Korea that soon distressed as many Americans as Chiang's fall. The Cairo Conference of November 1943 had decided that Korea, occupied by Japan during the war, should be made independent, a decision reaffirmed at Potsdam in July 1945. In August, that year, the Russians agreed to accept the surrender of the Japanese in Korea north of the 38th parallel, leaving the United States, on the arrival of its forces in September, to accept the surrender below that line. This military decision probably kept the Russians from overrunning the entire country; but it also created the fateful division of the land which soon hardened. North of the 38th parallel the Soviets characteristically established solid communist control and thereafter resisted all efforts to unify Korea on any grounds short of communist domination. The United States re-

UNATIONS

ferred the question of Korean unity and independence to the UN in September 1947, and although opposed by the USSR, the General Assembly voted to set up a temporary commission to supervise an all-Korean election.

When the Soviets boycotted the UN commission, it held elections in May 1948 for a national assembly in the United States sector alone. The elected national assembly then adopted a constitution, voted Syngman Rhee in as first President, and on August 15 proclaimed the Republic of Korea. The United States and thirty other nations promptly recognized the new nation. That very day the Russians held elections above the 38th parallel leading to the formation of the rival North Korean state, which they and their adherents recognized in turn. By December, leaving the North Koreans heavily armed, the USSR had recalled its troops. The UN, in the meantime,

789

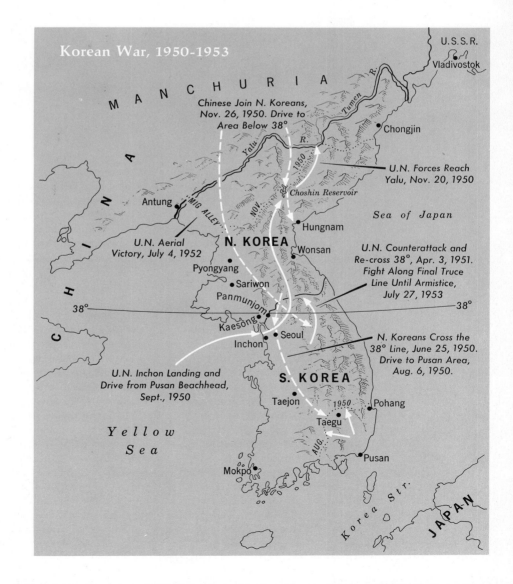

Korean War, 1950-1953

MANCHURIA

Chinese Join N. Koreans, Nov. 26, 1950. Drive to Area Below 38°

U.N. Forces Reach Yalu, Nov. 20, 1950

Chongjin

U.S.S.R.

Vladivostok

Choshin Reservoir

Sea of Japan

Antung

MIG ALLEY

U.N. Aerial Victory, July 4, 1952

N. KOREA

Hungnam

Wonsan

U.N. Counterattack and Re-cross 38°, Apr. 3, 1951. Fight Along Final Truce Line Until Armistice, July 27, 1953

Pyongyang

Sariwon

Panmunjom

Kaesong

Seoul

Inchon

N. Koreans Cross the 38° Line, June 25, 1950. Drive to Pusan Area, Aug. 6, 1950.

38°                                                                 38°

U.N. Inchon Landing and Drive from Pusan Beachhead, Sept., 1950

S. KOREA

Taejon

Pohang

Taegu

Yellow Sea

Pusan

Mokpo

Korea Str.

JAPAN

*Two GIs looking across
the Yalu into Manchuria, November 1950.*

its object being to bring about "the complete independence and unity of Korea," made its temporary commission permanent. At the General Assembly's suggestion, the United States recalled its troops from South Korea in June 1949, leaving much military material and about 500 "advisers" behind.

North and South Korea thus faced one another across an artificial border, each more or less backed by a rival great power committed to unification on its own terms. Border raids soon threatened, in the words of the UN commission, to broaden into a "barbarous civil war." The outbreak of this war may have been hastened by a speech, January 12, 1950, by Secretary of State Acheson outlining United States Asia policy following the establishment of Red China. In this speech, Acheson described the American "defensive perimeter" in the Orient so as to exclude South Korea. In case of attack, he said, "the initial reliance" of nations excluded "must be on the

people attacked to resist it," and then on "the entire civilized world under the Charter of the United Nations." In order to help South Korea resist, Truman, in February 1950, approved an act providing her with $110 million in economic aid. Military aid also was enlarged. Whatever may be said of Acheson's declaration and Truman's aid to South Korea, the North's attack on the South, June 25, 1950, was not, as she claimed, a reprisal for border raids, but, in the words of the UN commission, a "well-planned, concerted, and full-scale invasion."

Truman responded to the emergency with decision and ultimately with restraint. At his urgent request, the UN Security Council met on the afternoon of the invasion and by a vote of 8-0 (the Soviet delegate had boycotted the Council in January over its failure to seat Red China in place of Chiang's government and remained absent until August 1) held North Korea accountable for "a breach of the peace." The Council demanded an immediate end to hostilities and an embargo by all members on aid to North Korea. The next evening, having received a direct appeal from South

*Endless file of South Korean
refugees slogging through January snow,
1951, blocking withdrawal of
South Korean troops.*

Korea for assistance, Truman ordered American naval and air units to help push North Koreans back over the 38th parallel. He also ordered the fleet to keep Chiang Kai-shek from attempting to invade the continent from Formosa and thereby draw Red China into the war. On the following day, June 27, the Security Council urged positive action by UN members against North Korea. Truman then broadened his earlier military instructions and with other nations responded to the Security Council's call. American troops comprised about four-fifths of the UN forces in Korea. The UN troops in turn were more than matched in numbers by the army South Korea eventually put in the field.

The Korean fighting grew as savage as many World War II campaigns, and losses ran high. By the end of August 1950, moreover, the outnumbered UN forces under the command of General MacArthur had been pushed far south and almost into the sea in the area around the port of Pusan. Fortune changed in September when, heavily reinforced, MacArthur opened a counterattack with a brilliant

amphibious landing at the port of Inchon behind the North Korean line. A full-scale offensive in November drove the North Koreans back toward the 38th parallel and destroyed a considerable part of their army. Taking advantage of this moment of superiority, UN forces pushed across the 38th parallel on October 9, 1950, and pressed on toward the Yalu River, North Korea's Chinese boundary. Late that November, Red China threw her own huge armies into the fray and thrust the UN forces back below the 38th parallel, recapturing the South Korean capital of Seoul.

Irked by restraints imposed upon him by the UN's Kennan-like strategy of conducting a limited war for the limited objective of restoring South Korea's frontier, General MacArthur now publicly expressed his dissatisfaction with both the UN and President Truman. Even at the risk of becoming involved in open war with Red China, a development that many sober observers believed might lead to war with the Soviet Union, MarArthur urged an all-out Korean effort. General Omar N. Bradley, Chairman of the Joint Chiefs of Staff, warned that a major war against Red China would be "the wrong war at the wrong place, in the wrong time and with the wrong enemy." MacArthur rejected this decision and finally caused President Truman, on April 11, 1951, for insubordination, to relieve him of his Korean command and of his control of the occupation forces in Japan. MacArthur returned to the United States where he received a hero's welcome, but sympathy for his position quickly faded.

On June 23, 1951, the head of the Soviet delegation in the UN suggested that the Korean conflict might be settled if both parties were willing. This announcement led to armistice negotiations that began on July 10, 1951, and proceeded with exasperating delays for two entire years, during which fighting often broke out.

During the 1952 presidential campaign, General Eisenhower, the Republican candidate, dramatically announced that if elected he would fly to Korea to see about a total cease-fire personally. In December, a month after his victory at the polls, the general fulfilled his promise to fly; but the cease-fire was delayed another seven months. It would have been delayed even longer, in his opinion, had he not threatened once more to extend the war beyond the Korean peninsula, and—despite the deep misgivings of the British and other Europeans—to employ atomic weapons.

The touchy armistice at last was resolved by agreement, on July 27, 1953, to return to the prewar division at the 38th parallel. By then the three-year conflict had cost the United States over $15 billion and more than 140,000 casualties. The United Nations had not won a united Korea, but then neither had the communists. The primary purpose for which their aggression had been met—to show that it would be forcibly withstood—had been accomplished without igniting World War III.

## IV   Onset of McCarthyism

### To the Hiss case

The strains of the Cold War did not deter the American government from taking strong measures to counter communism in Europe, nor did the progress of communism in Asia sap the popular will to confront it there. Yet the inconclusiveness of results in both theaters wore on the nerves of many, causing them to seek scapegoats among their fellow citizens for the elusive finality of victory.

Scapegoats, as in the twenties, were not hard to find, especially by certain descendants of old-time families who had never surrendered their belief in the reality of the "red scare" of the twenties, which they associated with "new immigrant" groups. Their persistent fear of such groups was aggravated by the turmoil of the depression years, when communist and communist "front" organizations enjoyed their American heyday. At the same time, the turmoil of the war years put a great strain on what Fortune magazine in 1942 called the "petrified nationalisms from over there" of the "new immigrant" groups themselves and their offspring, and helped ally them with their elite detractors. The war placed the heaviest burdens on Italian-Americans who, with German-Americans and anti-British Irish-Americans, often felt impelled to be profascist (although the Axis was the enemy) and indiscriminately "anticommunist" (although the Soviets were allies). Once the war ended, the ranks of the red haters were filled out by millions of other "new immigrant" families—those who had roots in countries behind the Iron Curtain where, according to the Republican party platform of 1952, "the negative, futile and immoral policy of 'containment' abandons countless human beings to despotism and godless terrorism."

To all such Americans, and to those who played upon their fears for partisan purposes, Roosevelt's formal recognition of the Soviet Union in 1933 stood out as a telltale act. His wartime aid to Russia beginning in 1941, his "Asia last" military strategy in contrast to Stalin's alleged "Asia first" policy during the fighting, his concessions at Yalta in 1945, and his half-surrender of United States sovereignty to the UN soon after, all apparently confirmed the perfidiousness of his character and that of his associates, thereby making it easy for many to believe Senator Joseph R. McCarthy of Wisconsin in 1950 when he branded "the whole group of twisted-thinking New Dealers" as communists who "have led America near to ruin at home and abroad."

Before Senator McCarthy made this accusation, much additional background for it had been developed by the revived House Un-American Activities Committee (HUAC) following Republican success in the elections of 1946 (see p. 778). The committee's yeastiest adventure in this period was a two-week foray in Hollywood, in October 1947, "to expose those elements that are insidiously trying to . . . poison the minds of your children, distort the history of our country, and discredit Christianity." According to the *New York Herald-Tribune,* itself a Republican paper, the Hollywood investigation soon "dissolved into the ludicrous." Nevertheless, it did frighten movie moguls into an indiscriminate house-cleaning, which soon spread to radio and nascent TV, and into the blacklisting of actors, writers, directors, and others, some of whom remained barred from employment twenty years later.

The Hollywood adventure had been preceded by HUAC's haling before it in Washington, starting in February 1947, of hard-core Communist party functionaries, many of whom preferred citations for contempt to answering the summons. Eugene Dennis, then the General Secretary of the Communist party in the United States, was one of these. At Congressman Nixon's suggestion, HUAC agreed to ask the House to bring contempt charges against Dennis and also to ask the Justice Department to investigate the communist "conspiracy" to violate the Smith Act of 1940, in which he allegedly played a part. The Smith Act made it illegal for a person to advocate "overthrowing . . . any government in the United States by force," or to "affiliate" with groups teaching this doctrine. In July 1948, the Justice Department did procure the indictment of Dennis and ten other high-ranking communist leaders under this act. Their conviction by the federal district court in New York in October 1949 and their heavy fines and jail terms were upheld by the Supreme Court, 6 to 2, in June 1951.

"Certain kinds of speech are so undesirable," Chief Justice Fred M. Vinson said for the Court in the *Dennis case,* "as to warrant criminal prosecution." This view seemed to diminish the value Justice Holmes in 1919 had put on "the free trade in ideas" under the guarantees of the First Amendment (see p. 665). The *Dennis* ruling also encouraged states and municipalities, under local acts and ordinances similar to the Smith Act, to pursue thousands of alleged subversives, sometimes on the basis of mere hearsay or invention offered by frightened or vindictive individuals.

The Hiss case, HUAC's most far-reaching triumph, began on August 3, 1948, on the heels of the Dennis indictment in July. On that day, Whittaker Chambers, admittedly a long-time Soviet agent in the United States who said he quit the Communist party in 1937, was brought before the committee to help corroborate earlier testimony about the communist "apparatus" in Washington. Chambers, an editor of *Time* magazine, told a sensational story, one made no less provocative by his report, later verified, that he had told the same story to the State Department at the time of the Berlin-Moscow nonaggression pact of 1939 with no result. In his story, Chambers named members of the Washington apparatus of the thirties, persons who might still be communists, he said, whose main objective was to infiltrate the uppermost places in the government with party men. Espionage was secondary.

Alger Hiss, in government service in the midthirties and early forties but since 1947 president of the private Carnegie Endowment for International Peace, was one of those Chambers named. On learning of Chambers's accusation, he promptly telegraphed a full denial to the committee and asked for a hearing, which was granted on August 5. This and subsequent hearings, interspersed with re-examinations of Chambers, elicited more and more details of Hiss's activities in the thirties, including alleged espionage. When Hiss persisted in his denials, HUAC Chairman J. Parnell Thomas warned, "Certainly one of you will be tried for perjury." Neither could be prosecuted for other asserted crimes since these had taken place more than seven years before and thus, under the statute of limitations, were beyond legal reach.

On the day of Hiss's first hearing, President Truman had replied to questions about the "spy investigations": "They are simply a red herring. They [the Republicans] are using this as a red herring." The 1948 presidential campaign was then in full swing, and many thought the Democratic victory in this campaign might weaken HUAC and sidetrack the Hiss issue. In December 1948, however, a federal grand jury in New York indicted Hiss for perjury. His trial began in May 1949, and when, at the end of it, the jury disagreed, a second trial opened in November. In January 1950 he was found guilty and sentenced to a $10,000 fine and five years in prison. After appeals to higher courts upheld this verdict, Hiss went to prison in March 1951.

In the earliest denial of Chambers's "complete fabrications," Hiss told HUAC: "I think my record in the Government service speaks for itself." It did, but not in his favor with his listeners. Hiss had been a remarkably fat catch for the committee. A Harvard Law School graduate and secretary to no less a personage than Justice Holmes, he next served as one of the early New Dealers in the AAA. After switching to the State Department, he became involved in planning the United Na-

tions Organization. Hiss was a member, but only a subordinate one, of Roosevelt's Yalta delegation, and finally, before leaving the government in 1946, served as director of the State Department's Office of Special Political Affairs. All in all, he loomed as a likely illustration to the "ethnics" of the penetration of communism even among the country's best people—and to the best people as a traitor to his class as well as his country. The full truth of this episode will not be known until the records of HUAC, the FBI, and the federal grand jury are made available to scholars, if then.

While the Hiss case was in progress, HUAC made other striking accusations and the FBI bestirred itself to uncover additional Soviet agents, so that Truman's "red herring" charge soon came back to haunt him. The news of the first successful Soviet atomic bomb explosion late in September 1949, followed in October by Chaing's fall, and in February 1950 by the mutual-security pact between Red China and the USSR, all deepened the shock of communist gains. Truman's "containment" policy seemed as bankrupt as the Republican Asia Firsters had claimed all along. Their anger grew uncontrollable when, in January 1950, Dean Acheson, having already insisted that he would not turn his back on his friend Alger Hiss, "whatever the outcome," made his "defensive perimeter" speech announcing the United States' newly narrowed Asia policy in the face of the Soviet's dramatically broadened one.

On hearing Acheson's presentation of the new Asia policy, the Asia Firsters led by "Mr. Republican" himself, Senator Robert A. Taft, shattered the bipartisanship in foreign policy so painstakingly constructed by Senator Arthur H. Vandenberg and broadened the assault on the State Department, initiated by Patrick Hurley and others. The State Department, Taft said, echoing the earlier charges, was filled with communists and fellow travelers who had "surrendered to every demand of Russia . . . and promoted at every opportunity the Communist cause in China." Acheson himself "must go." Taft's brutal colleague, Senator McCarthy, as hungry for a partisan issue as Taft, pounced on this theme.

## The Wisconsin Senator
## and his friends

In his "Lincoln-day week-end" speech in West Virginia, February 9, 1950, Senator McCarthy declared that the United States, the strongest nation on earth on V-J day, had been shorn of her strength "because of the traitorous actions of those who have been treated so well by this nation. . . . The bright young men [in the State Department] who are born with silver spoons in their mouths are the ones who have been the worst." None was worse than their chief, Dean Acheson, "this pompous diplomat in striped pants, with a phony British accent," who "could vouch for Hiss absolutely." McCarthy then added: "I have here in my hand," the names of "two hundred and five men that were known to the Secretary of State as being members of the Communist party and who nevertheless are still working and shaping the policy of the State Department."

McCarthy gradually backed away from this figure of 205, keeping in the limelight with new numbers until, in the end, he was unable to substantiate a single name. But nothing was done to check the accuser. On the contrary, Taft gave him the full benefit of his own prestige. "McCarthy should keep talking," he said, "and if one case doesn't work he should proceed with another."

Events soon played into McCarthy's hands. While he was engaging in what became known as "the numbers game," British authorities arrested for atomic espionage Dr. Klaus Fuchs, a German-born nuclear physicist and naturalized British subject who had worked on the American bomb at Los Alamos in 1944. Fuchs admitted the charges and on March 1 was sentenced to fourteen years in prison. He also implicated certain American communists in his activities, which clearly speeded up Russian success with the bomb. Acting on Fuchs's information, the FBI in the summer of 1950 arrested Ethel and Julius Rosenberg and their friend Morton Sobell. For a crime "worse than murder," in the words of the trial judge, the Rosenbergs, in March 1951, were sentenced to death, Sobell to thirty years. After many appeals failed, the Rosenbergs were executed on June 19, 1953.

Such cases helped give credence to McCarthy's charges, which grew in reach and recklessness as the "limited" Korean War eroded American morale. A low point was touched on June 14, 1951, when after General MacArthur's recall from Korea, McCarthy made a bid to retrieve the headlines with a 60,000-word attack in the Senate on MacArthur's rivals, General Marshall and General Eisenhower. Marshall, he said, "with great stubbornness and skill, always and invariably [was] serving the world policy of the Kremlin." Deeply involved with him, "in a conspiracy so immense and an infamy so black as to dwarf any previous such venture in the history of man," was his "firm supporter" and "fast-rising protégé, 'Ike' Eisenhower."

"McCarthyism" by then had passed into the language as an expression for wild charges of disloyalty. More and more Americans, however, came to believe, as the Senator himself told his home following in Wisconsin, that "McCarthyism is Americanism with its sleeves rolled." Money began to pour in on McCarthy, while superpatriot societies like the Daughters of the American Revolution, organizations of professional veterans like the American Legion, and authoritarian "hyphenate" clubs and churches, meanwhile, took up the cudgels. The Supreme Court decision in the *Dennis case* in June 1951 reflected the strength of the McCarthyite spirit.

Congress naturally responded to such grassroots sentiment. On September 23, 1950, over Truman's vigorous veto, it passed the McCarran Internal Security Act, incorporating a drastic new sedition provision making it "unlawful . . . knowingly to . . . conspire . . . to perform any act which would substantially contribute to the establishment within the

796

United States of a totalitarian dictatorship." All "communist-action" and "communist front" organizations were assumed to be such conspiracies and required to register with the Attorney-General. In case of an "Internal Security Emergency," the act authorized the President "to apprehend and . . . detain . . . each person as to whom there is reasonable ground to believe that such person probably will engage in, or . . . conspire with others to engage in, acts of espionage or sabotage." Any alien, moreover, with the slightest "subversive" taint on his record was to be "excluded from admission to the United States." Senator McCarran himself denounced the Internal Security Emergency amendment to his bill as "a concentration-camp measure pure and simple." In his veto message, Truman characterized parts of the Internal Security Act as "the greatest danger to freedom of speech, press, and assembly since the alien and sedition laws of 1798." Far from protecting the nation from dictatorship, he added, the McCarran Act took the United States "a long step toward totalitarianism."

On June 30, 1952, Congress supplemented the Internal Security Act with the McCarran-Walter Immigration Act, passed again after a resounding Truman veto. This act updated but hardly liberalized the widely attacked quota system (see p. 661), which imposed exceptional hardship on displaced persons and refugees from communist countries. More to the point, it required the Attorney-General to screen out "subversives" within the permitted quotas and empowered him to deport such persons even after they had become naturalized American citizens. "Seldom," said Truman, "has a bill exhibited the distrust evidenced here for citizens and aliens alike—at a time when we need unity at home and the confidence of our friends abroad." Yet worse was to come following the frustration of the McCarthyites in the election of 1952.

### Election of 1952

It seemed at first to many shocked Republicans that the press reports, not the voting public, had snatched away a victory already won in the presidential campaign of 1948. Once recovered from their shock, those Republican leaders who had opposed the nomination of the internationalist easterner Thomas E. Dewey and had favored Taft blamed the defeat on bipartisanship in foreign policy and led the attack on it. Following the Truman administration's decision in 1951 to constrain MacArthur and "contain" the Korean War, they accelerated their program to enlist behind their new policy of "liberation" the millions of "ethnics"—some hopefully put their number at nearly 30 million in seventeen key industrial states—distressed by the communist menace at home and abroad. At this time, the Republican National Committee set up an Ethnic Origins Division and under it a Foreign Language Group Activities Section. At the head of this section they placed Arthur Bliss Lane, a former ambassador to Poland who had become one of McCarthy's staunchest backers.

The success of Lane's campaign was evident in the 1952 platform adopted by the party at its national convention in Chicago in July. This platform promised particularly to "repudiate all commitments . . . such as those of Yalta which aid Communist enslavement" and castigated the "containment" policy that "abandoned" so many millions to it. Two years before the convention, John Foster Dulles, the leading Republican adviser to Truman's State Department on bipartisan foreign policy, had written: "If at a time of national peril, two presidential candidates should compete in making novel and unseasoned proposals, designed primarily to win votes, the end of that campaign would leave our foreign relations in a shambles." Now, for practical vote-winning purposes, Dulles became the captive of the "new look" and helped put the appropriate platform planks across.

Yet too many Republicans, rank-and-filers as well as leaders who had backed Dewey, were committed to bipartisanship in principle and to the Truman version of it in practice to yield further to the Asia Firsters. Many of them also loathed McCarthy as deeply as most

Democrats, a feeling they found it ever easier to transfer to his misguided friend Taft, again the Asia Firsters' favorite for the nomination. Their own choice, largely because they believed he alone could stand up to the Wisconsin mudslinger, was Eisenhower, who had turned down the Democrats four years earlier. After tactical successes in unseating southern delegates for Taft, the Eisenhower convention team put "Ike" across on the first ballot. The Taft men took what solace they could from the nomination for Vice-President of Congressman Nixon, the HUAC luminary from California.

The Republicans' snaring of Eisenhower only deepened the pessimism with which the Democrats approached their national convention two weeks later. Many voters believed the McCarthyite charge that their reign had been "twenty years of treason." On the home front, the inflation brought on by the Korean War also depressed the Democrats. The inflation was dramatized by the steel strike in 1952, which Truman failed to arbitrate and which resulted in higher steel prices. Moreover, beginning in 1951, certain petty scandals came to light involving the use of influence by persons close to Truman himself. The fact that it was the Democrats who made most of these revelations did not prevent the administration from being branded by many as corrupt.

After Truman announced in March 1952 that he would not be a candidate, the leading Democratic aspirant became Senator Estes Kefauver of Tennessee, who had gained a national reputation as head of the special Senate Committee that had in fact uncovered so much Democratic graft. When Kefauver failed to win on the first two ballots at the Chicago convention, the delegates drafted Truman's choice, the eloquent but unwilling governor of Illinois, Adlai E. Stevenson. Senator John J. Sparkman of Alabama became his running mate.

Once named, Stevenson conducted a vigorous and unusually eloquent campaign that won him many enduring supporters among intellectuals, often caricatured as "egg heads." He particularly denounced the Republicans' "liberation" promises as a "cynical . . . attempt . . . to play upon the anxieties of foreign nationality groups in this country." Truman himself, foreseeing the actual consequences of the "liberation" line, said, "Nothing could be worse than to incite uprisings that can only end by giving a new crop of victims to the Soviet executioners."

To no one's surprise, Eisenhower's vast appeal, enhanced by his campaign pledge to fly to Korea and end the stalemate there, carried him to a striking triumph. He received 33,824,000 popular votes to Stevenson's 27,314,000. In the electoral college, his margin was 422 to 89, with the Solid South for the first time since 1928 contributing to the Republican total. Yet the Republicans had grounds for misgivings. Even Ike's tremendous popularity brought the party a mere majority of eight in the House and, worse, a standoff in the Senate. The Taft wing should have been especially troubled. Eisenhower, for example, carried Wisconsin by over 350,000 votes; McCarthy won reelection there by less

## Political parties and Presidents

| | DEMOCRATIC PARTY | REPUBLICAN PARTY | STATES' RIGHTS DEMOCRATIC PARTY SPLITS FROM DEMOCRATS |
|---|---|---|---|
| 1932 | F. D. Roosevelt | | |
| 1936 | F. D. Roosevelt | | |
| 1940 | F. D. Roosevelt | | |
| 1944 | F. D. Roosevelt | | |
| 1948 | F. D. Roosevelt (Truman, 1945) | | |
| 1952 | Truman | | |
| 1956 | | Eisenhower | |
| 1960 | | Eisenhower | |
| 1964 | Kennedy (Johnson, 1963) | | |
| 1968 | Johnson | | |
| | | Nixon | |

than 140,000. In numerous Polish-, German-, and Czech-American wards in such key industrial cities as Chicago, Akron, Baltimore, and Cleveland, moreover, the "ethnics," voting as Americans, not "hyphenates," combined with the "egg heads" to give Stevenson majorities of over 60 percent.

The appeal to ethnic blocs, nevertheless, was heightened thereafter. The strong move-

ment of Negroes to the cities in this period added a new element tending to draw all white groups ever more closely together in defense of their own wartime and postwar social gains.

## For further reading

O. T. Barck, Jr., *A History of the United States since 1945* (1965), is a useful survey. E. F. Goldman, *The Crucial Decade—and After, America 1945-1960* (1960), offers an illuminating impressionistic account. Alfred Steinberg, *The Man From Missouri* (1962), H. S. Truman, *Memoirs* (2 vols., 1955), and Cabell Phillips, *The Truman Presidency* (1966), tell Truman's story. Irwin Ross, *The Loneliest Campaign: The Truman Victory of 1948* (1968), is good on Truman on his own. See also B. J. Berstein and A. J. Matusow, eds., *The Truman Administration: A Documentary History* (1966).

Illuminating background for the Yalta Conference and its aftermath is supplied in W. S. Churchill, *Triumph and Tragedy* (1953), vol. VI of his history of World War II; Gabriel Kolko, *The Politics of War, The World and United States Foreign Policy 1943-1945* (1968); Herbert Feis, *Churchill, Roosevelt, Stalin* (1957), and *Between War and Peace: The Potsdam Conference* (1960); and W. L. Neumann, *After Victory: Churchill, Roosevelt, Stalin and the Making of the Peace* (1967). H. L. Stimson and McGeorge Bundy, *On Active Service in Peace and War* (1948), offers first-hand information on the use of the A-bomb on Japan to "monitor" the Russians. See also Herbert Feis, *Japan Subdued* (1961), and the books on the Cold War cited below. J. L. Snell, ed., *The Meaning of Yalta* (1956), offers an able survey. A. B. Ulam, *Expansion and Coexistence, The History of Soviet Foreign Policy 1917-1967* (1968), is outstanding.

Indispensable background for the military and demobilization is supplied in R. W. Coakley and R. M. Leighton, *Global Logistics and Strategy 1940-1943* (1955), and the same, *1943-1945* (1968). D. M. Nelson, *Arsenal of Democracy* (1946), offers first-hand testimony by the head of the War Production Board. See also J. M. Swomley, Jr., *The Military Establishment*

(1964), outstanding among the many books on the Pentagon. For perspective on the National Security Act of 1947 and unification of the armed services, see P. Y. Hammond, *Organizing for Defense: The American Military Establishment in the Twentieth Century* (1961), Walter Millis, ed., *The Forrestal Diaries* (1951), and P. M. Smith, *The Air Force Plans for Peace 1943-1945* (1970), an outstanding case study.

L. M. Goodrich, E. I. Hambro, and A. P. Simons, *Charter of the United Nations* (1969), is standard. A superb modern introduction to the UN is I. L. Claude, Jr., *The Changing United Nations* (1967). Valuable special studies include *The United Nations and Disarmament 1945-1965* (n.d.), issued by the UN; and J. G. Stoessinger, *The United Nations and the Superpowers* (1965). The role of the UN is discussed in J. I. Lieberman, *The Scorpion and the Tarantula* (1970), an informed account of "The Struggle to Control Atomic Weapons 1945-1949," to quote the subtitle.

Hajo Holborn, *American Military Government* (1947), is comprehensive on the occupation of Germany; Walt Sheldon, *The Honorable Conquerors* (1965), affords a good introduction to "The Occupation of Japan 1945-1952." Eugene Davidson, *The Trial of the Germans: Nuremberg 1945-1946* (1966), omits little. Telford Taylor, *Nuremberg and Vietnam, An American Tragedy* (1970), is a thoughtful review of the implications of war-crime trials.

John Spanier, *American Foreign Policy Since World War II* (1968), and W. G. Carleton, *The Revolution in American Foreign Policy* (1967), are scholarly surveys. N. A. Graebner, ed., *Cold War Diplomacy 1945-1960* (1962), includes documents. N. A. Graebner, ed., *An Uncertain Tradition: American Secretaries of State in the Twentieth Century* (1961), offers useful analyses, to be supplemented by R. H. Ferrell, *George C. Marshall* (1966); Dean Acheson, *Present at the Creation*

(1969); G. F. Kennan, *Memoirs 1925–1950* (1967); and W. A. Harriman, *America and Russia in a Changing World* (1971), "A Half Century of Personal Observation." C. S. Maier, "Revisionism and the Interpretation of Cold War Origins," in *Perspectives in American History* (vol. IV, 1970), a series published by Harvard University Press, is an exceptionally able critique of the literature to date, with emphasis on the work of Kolko (above), Gar Alperovitz, *Atomic Diplomacy* (1965), and D. F. Fleming, *The Cold War and its Origins 1917–1960* (2 vols., 1961). Maier also examines the major works of more conventional writers such as Feis and Neumann, already mentioned. From the vast current literature on the Cold War, we may note also M. F. Herz, *Beginnings of the Cold War* (1966); L. J. Halle, *The Cold War as History* (1967); John Lukacs, *A New History of the Cold War* (1966); and G. F. Hudson, *The Hard and Bitter Peace, World Politics Since 1945* (1967). On related issues, see Herbert Feis, *Foreign Aid and Foreign Policy* (1964); Klaus Knorr, ed., *NATO and American Security* (1959); and J. L. Mecham, *The United States and Inter-American Security 1889–1960* (1961).

*China and U.S. Far East Policy 1945–1966* (1967), published by Congressional Quarterly, offers all the details. The State Department's *The China White Paper, August 1949* (2 vols., 1967), and L. P. Van Slyke, ed., *The Chinese Communist Movement, A Report of the United States War Department, July 1945* (1968), are revealing. From the large scholarly literature we may mention A. D. Barnett, *Communist China and Asia: Challenge to American Policy* (1960); and Robert Blum, *The United States and China in World Affairs* (1966). M. B. Ridgway, *The Korean War* (1967); David Rees, *Korea, The Limited War* (1964); and Robert Leckie, *Conflict, The History of the Korean War* (1962), are good. J. W. Spanier, *The Truman-McCarthy Controversy and the Korean War* (1959), is expert.

The Fair Deal is well covered in the general works cited in paragraph one above. Useful special studies are S. K. Bailey, *Congress Makes A Law: The Story Behind the Employment Act of 1946* (1950); H. C. Millis and E. C. Brown, *From the Wagner Act to Taft-Hartley* (1950); A. J. Matusow, *Farm Policies and Politics in the Truman Years* (1967); and R. O. Davies, *Housing Reform During the Truman Administration* (1966). Gunnar Myrdal, *An American Dilemma* (2 vols., 1944), resoundingly reopened the issue of the black man in American society. This subject is updated in Talcott Parsons and K. B. Clark, eds., *The American Negro* (1966). Harold Cruse, *The Crisis of the Negro Intellectual, From its Origins to the Present* (1967), is a seminal study. St. Clair Drake and H. R. Cayton, *Black Metropolis* (1945), and Robert Weaver, *The Negro Ghetto* (1948), are studies of urban Negro life before the Supreme Court decision of 1954.

Preelection voter polling became a powerful political device after World War II. For its use in political analysis, see Samuel Lubell, *The Future of American Politics* (1952) and *Revolt of the Moderates* (1956); and B. R. Berelson and others, *Voting, A Study of Opinion Formation in a Presidential Campaign* (1954). Less restricted methodologically are L. L. Gerson, *The Hyphenate in Recent American Politics and Diplomacy* (1964); and V. O. Key, Jr., *The Responsible Electorate* (1966). On the far right, see Richard Hofstadter, *The Paranoid Style in American Politics and Other Essays* (1965). On the far left, see Earl Latham, *The Communist Controversy in Washington: From the New Deal to McCarthy* (1966); and D. A. Shannon, *The Decline of American Communism: A History of the Communist Party of the United States Since 1945* (1959). R. K. Carr, *The House Un-American Activities Committee 1945–1950* (1952), is a thorough survey. See also Walter Gellhorn, ed., *The States and Subversion* (1952), and Gellhorn, *Security, Loyalty, and Science* (1950); and Alan Barth, *The Loyalty of Free Men* (1951). James Rorty and Moshe Decter examine the evidence in *McCarthy and the Communists* (1954). Richard Rovere, *Senator Joe McCarthy* (1959), places the accuser in context. Alistair Cooke, *A Generation on Trial* (1950), is illuminating on the Hiss case. See also Whittaker Chambers, *Witness* (1952), and Alger Hiss, *In the Court of Public Opinion* (1957). Walter and Miriam Schneir, *Invitation to An Inquest* (1965), attempts to clear the Rosenbergs and their friends.

**799**

# SUPERPOWERS IN THE MISSILE AGE

In *Mandate for Change,* the memoir of his first administration, General Eisenhower wrote of his nomination for President: "The earliest national election that I can recall was that of 1896, in which William McKinley opposed William Jennings Bryan. As a little boy in Abilene [Kansas], I had helped campaign that year by marching in a night-time parade with a flaming torch made of a rag soaked in coal oil. Now, fifty-six years later, my own name was at the head of a Republican ticket." In another four months, "the supreme, the climactic moment" of OVERLORD, as Kenneth S. Davis put it in his early biography of Eisenhower, *Soldier of Democracy* (1945), would be overshadowed by the General's becoming the head of his country.

Like George Washington, the hero of the Revolution; Andrew Jackson, the hero of New Orleans; William Henry Harrison, the hero of Tippecanoe; Zachary Taylor, the hero of Buena Vista; Ulysses S. Grant, the hero of Richmond; and Theodore Roosevelt, the hero of the San Juan hills, in the American way the hero of the Normandy landings had come to his reward.

Eisenhower differed from earlier military Presidents by being elected Commander-in-Chief of the strongest military power on earth. His electoral victory, moreover, came at a moment in the Cold War when his country's way of life seemed menaced by events around the world—in previously unheard of, often unpronounceable, and discouragingly distant places, and at home as well. In 1952 and again in 1956, while virtually discarding his party (the Republicans met an unprecedented third straight setback in the 1958 congressional

800

elections while holding the presidency), the voters appeared to place sublime faith in the smiling general to deal with the communist challenge. Eisenhower suffered a "moderate" heart attack in 1955 and a subsequent digestive disorder that required surgery; yet he remained for most Americans the symbol of military might in the White House capable of charming away the enveloping alien threat.

We know now that the charm failed to work. Although he showed a strong affinity for certain powerful persons, Eisenhower took an ambiguous approach to power itself. Although he made a fetish of strong centralized organization with a clear chain of command, he took a negative view of government, and especially of the central government; and his chain of command became a mere mechanism for inaction, not to say reaction, consistent with his political philosophy.

The general's boyhood home town of Abilene lay almost at the exact geographic center of the United States—"I come from the very heart of America," he told a cheering London crowd in 1945—and no one stressed more than the President his dedication to the "middle way." Yet when millions of Americans and hundreds of millions of others around the world dearly embraced "the revolution of rising expectations," he was "setting in motion," as he writes in *Mandate for Change*, "revolutionary activity" of his own to effect "a reversal of trends . . . which by 1953 were twenty years old," involving the full force of government in the welfare of the people.

During New Deal days, while working on the army budget as a major under General Douglas MacArthur, then Chief of Staff, young Eisenhower had watched the brain-trusters eviscerating private enterprise, as he thought. He discovered then that intellectuals, rare birds in his experience, were distasteful to him. "Those who advocated centralization," he wrote in *Mandate for Change*, "believed they were infallible. They liked power, and they lacked faith in the people." Even though it evidently had the people's blessing, the general believed Truman's Fair Deal even more un-American than FDR's New Deal. The traditional virtues of "individualism" were always on his tongue, yet always reserved for those "of us who are right-thinking." He spoke frequently of "preserving" each man's "equality before the law," as though each man even in the United States enjoyed this fundamental right.

At the very time that David Riesman was making his happy distinction between "other-directed" men afloat in organizational "friendship systems" and the "saving remnant" of "inner-directed" individuals who nursed the divine spark of the creative spirit, the nation chose for its and indeed the Western world's leader "the very model of a modern Major-General" organization man. In *Mandate for Change*, Eisenhower chided "individualistic rather than organizational worker[s]" like writers for their "compulsion . . . to pontificate about organization." They had never organized masses of men for big business or military objectives, he said, yet they "apparently feel themselves experts." But even while he was taking, as he believed, "that straight road down the middle"—backwards, as it turned out—events were polarizing the world and the nation in profound and disconcerting ways that eluded him and his organization but that inner-directed "experts" quickly grasped and John F. Kennedy, his youthful successor in the White House, attempted to turn to political account.

The delicate polarities implicit in such catch phrases as the "Cold War" and the "balance of terror" made up only part of the story. In 1953 Eisenhower put first among the "internal dangers besetting us" the "increasing trend toward unreasonable antagonisms" between business and labor; and he promised his business friends a more favorable political climate. "Our confidence was eroding, too," he said. "Americans have become divided—over questions of loyalty, Communists in government, and corruption of high public officials." A mere array of the arresting titles of contemporary books by "pontifical writers" discloses the superficiality of these observations.

In *The Lonely Crowd* (1950), David Riesman and his colleagues suggested some of the new strains in the American character arising from organization itself. Such strains among heads of families aspiring to traditional success also concerned C. Wright Mills in *White Collar* (1951) and William H. Whyte, Jr., in *The Organization Man* (1956), a study of "the clash between the individualistic beliefs he is supposed to follow and the collective life he actually lives." Paul Goodman, in numerous essays elaborated in *Growing Up Absurd* (1960), probed even deeper into the "Problems of Youth In Organized Society." Lillian Smith, meanwhile, in *Killers of the Dream* (1949), sought to awaken the white South to the surfacing tensions of its black people. Ralph Ellison, in *Invisible Man* (1952), wrote of the "mangled, plucked victim of Authority," not only black, whose sole defense against "loss of self" was the recovery of "his own humanity."

As early as 1937, Harold Lasswell had begun to explore the implications of "the garrison state," requiring "the subordination of every consideration of democracy or welfare to 'military necessity.'" In 1961 Eisenhower made "this conjunction of an immense military establishment and a . . . permanent armaments industry of vast proportions" the sub-

ject of his famous "farewell speech" (see p. 822). But by then what he called "the military-industrial complex" had overrun the traditional instrumentalities of American government despite all the organizational techniques the presidential master of organization had been using to check it for the past eight years. Selfish rivalry among the uniformed services, themselves the admired models of organizational practice, for ever larger slices of the uncontrollable military budget hastened the military ascendancy.

Perhaps more of this story than he intended is disclosed in *The Uncertain Trumpet* (1959) by General Maxwell D. Taylor, Eisenhower's discontented Army Chief of Staff, who became Kennedy's personal adviser on military

*"Ike" and JFK in President's office
a month before Kennedy's inauguration
in January 1961.*

Wide World Photos

nedy, the youngest, approached their high office in ways that magnified the difference in their years even more than in their party affiliation; yet the times imposed a continuity of issues, all overshadowed by the rivalry of the superpowers in the missile age, that both left unresolved.

affairs and after August 1962 served as Chairman of the Joint Chiefs. Eisenhower, the oldest man ever elected President, and Ken-

# I Conservatives in power

## The Eisenhower team

Despite the need for "gargantuan staffs for control and direction" in modern war, it is not true, Eisenhower wrote in *Crusade in Europe,* "that the influence of the individual . . . has become submerged. . . . Personal characteristics are more important than ever before." Yet to rise in the chain of command, the individual needed personal characteristics of a special sort. "The teams and staffs through which the modern commander absorbs information and exercises his authority must be a beautifully interlocked, smooth-working mechanism. Ideally, the whole should be practically a single mind; consequently misfits defeat the purpose of the command organization."

Misfits were few and short-lived on the Eisenhower team. One of the most "delicate problems" confronting the new President was the selection of a "suitable" Secretary of Labor. The quest for a union leader to represent labor's viewpoint in the Cabinet, he said, "was something of an experiment," and the man finally chosen, Martin Durkin of Chicago, head of the AFL Plumbers and Pipe Fitters union, was warned explicitly that in his new post "he would no longer owe personal allegiance to labor, only to the nation." Durkin, Eisenhower observes in *Mandate for Change,* "seemed to have difficulty in making this distinction, which was quite simple to me." He was to be the captive hero's captive labor front. It soon developed that Durkin had difficulties with other distinctions as well, and within a few months he had departed, to be replaced

by a corporation industrial-relations executive, James P. Mitchell.

During the Senate session to confirm Charles E. Wilson, president of General Motors, as Secretary of Defense, Wilson is supposed to have remarked: "What is good for General Motors is good for the country." What he actually said on being questioned closely on the possible conflict of interest between the public good and company profits (GM was a major supplier of defense materiel) was: "I thought what was good for the country was good for General Motors, and vice versa." Unlike Durkin, he moved from the private to the public sector without qualms.

In defending his choice of Wilson, the President commented that "some of our senatorial friends" were "so politically fearful" they carried the conflict-of-interest law beyond the point of reason. The time may come, he warned, when Presidents would "be unable to get anybody to take jobs in Washington except business failures, political hacks, and New Deal lawyers." Perhaps to balance corporate interests he named Harold E. Talbott, a financier with large holdings in the Chrysler Corporation (which he said he would sell on confirmation) as Secretary of the Air Force, a non-Cabinet post under the Secretary of Defense.

Another business luminary in the Cabinet was George M. Humphrey, president of Mark Hanna's old firm, M. A. Hanna and Company, who became Secretary of the Treasury. For Secretary of Agriculture, Eisenhower chose the Taft supporter Ezra Taft Benson, a produce-marketing specialist. One Wall Street lawyer, Herbert Brownell, Jr., became Attorney-General; a second, John Foster Dulles, better known for his diplomatic experience, took his foreordained post as Secretary of State. As Assistant to the President, or chief of the White House staff, the General naturally was tempted to name a military man. "Such an aide," he said, "would have had, of course, the advantage of a thorough knowledge of staff functioning, which regrettably so many persons seem to misunderstand completely—sometimes, I think, deliberately." Fear of "suspicion of excessive military influence," however, deterred him, and eventually the post went to Sherman Adams, the former governor of New Hampshire, who had managed the successful presidential campaign. To assist Adams and Eisenhower himself in running Cabinet meetings efficiently, a Cabinet Secretary was appointed for the first time, with the principal responsibility of preparing and circulating a fixed agenda for each session.

The President in later years expressed satisfaction with his Cabinet associates and with the good spirit in which they worked together. More objective observers attribute the good-fellowship of the Eisenhower team, insofar as it persisted, to the triviality of the agendas often worked up under pressure simply to conform to the system. Cabinet good-fellowship might also be explained by Eisenhower's proclivity, when controversy did arise on basic issues, to fail to press it to a conclusion.

One unresolved hassle between the Department of Defense and the Treasury Department became most acute during the General's tenure because of his total commitment to balancing the budget. Treasury Secretary Humphrey made strenuous efforts to contain the military, but he toppled in the end. "They're beginning to run wild over there again," Humphrey observed of the Pentagon at one juncture in 1956. But he was compelled to add: "I know nothing about the military. Whatever Ike does there is O.K. with me." A White House aide remarked on another occasion, after the Pentagon had mesmerized Secretary Wilson into supporting the requests of the ever more demanding uniformed services, "We just lost control. . . . Charlie's lost it in the programming." *Fortune* magazine said of

this incident: "Wilson has been sandwiched between two layers of military expertise—above him the soldier-President, beneath him the Joint Chiefs of Staff." Despite the President, the latter usually gained their objectives.

At certain crises in foreign relations, the President overruled Secretary of State Dulles; yet in this field even more than in others, his normal policy was to leave decisions to his top administrator. Because of his anxiety to avoid the fate of Dean Acheson at the hands of McCarthyites in Congress, Dulles also became isolated from consultation and advice from below. When Senator McCarthy, at the outset of the Eisenhower regime, succeeded in forcing his own man in as the arbiter of State Department personnel (see p. 807), Dulles even outdid this functionary in demanding "internal inspection" of all Department hands. Beyond that, Hans J. Morgenthau writes in a penetrating essay on Dulles:

> By personally performing many of the major political functions which had traditionally been performed by high-ranking diplomats, Dulles greatly reduced opportunities for the latter to take political initiative of any kind. By divorcing his operations to a considerable degree from those of the Department of State and at the same time taking over the higher political functions of the Foreign Service, Dulles for all practical purposes disarmed the Department of State as a rival in the management of foreign affairs. It must also be kept in mind that the purge of 1953 [see p. 808] and the regime of surveillance accompanying and following it had made it inadvisable for a member of the Department of State of develop a foreign policy of his own.

## Black life and the law

The revolution of rising expectations animated the black community as strongly in the United States as it did colored nations elsewhere in the world. Negro recognition under the New Deal and Negro progress during World War II laid the groundwork for further Negro gains under the Truman administration and in the early years of Eisenhower's first term. In February 1946 a Senate filibuster killed an administration measure for a permanent federal Fair Employment Practices Committee, but before the end of the year five states—New York, New Jersey, Massachusetts, Connecticut, and Washington— had set up their own FEPCs and many more were to follow. In December 1946 Truman named a Committee on Civil Rights, composed of leaders of both races. This committee's report, *To Secure These Rights,* published in 1947 and widely circulated before the presidential election the next year, recommended a broad program for repeal of Jim Crow legislation and advancement of Negro equality. New threats of southern filibusters frustrated administration efforts to implement this program, but Truman took important steps on the executive level, the major one being his order of July 1948 to desegregate the armed forces. Eisenhower continued the implementation of this order on taking office early in 1953. He also promoted the desegregation of public meeting places in the District of Columbia and of public housing there.

Before its momentous decision in May 1954, in *Oliver Brown et al.* v. *Board of Education of Topeka, Kansas,* ordering the end of public-school segregation, the Supreme Court had also taken significant steps toward raising the Negro's status under law.

The nadir of Supreme Court action had come in *Plessy* v. *Ferguson* in 1896, when seven Justices, against one, decided that separate, if equal, facilities provided by a state satisfied the requirement of the Fourteenth Amendment that no state deprive a citizen of the United States of "the equal protection of the laws." The *Plessy* decision upheld the constitutionality of a Louisiana statute requiring blacks and whites to ride in separate railroad cars, but it soon spawned many new Jim Crow laws segregating housing on entire city blocks and also hospitals, parks, schools, and other public facilities. The "equality" of the separate Negro facilities under these laws, moreover, rarely if ever was maintained.

The Supreme Court began eroding the *Plessy* ruling in 1917 when it declared a Louisville Jim Crow housing ordinance unconstitutional. In the 1930s the National Association for the Advancement of Colored People (NAACP) began attacking the inequality of black educational facilities and especially of black teachers' salaries in the courts. A turning point came in the Supreme Court decision in 1938 in *Missouri ex rel Gaines* v. *Canada,* one of a series of cases in higher education through which the idea of the inherent inequality of separate facilities was developed. The University of Missouri Law School, in the absence of a law school for blacks in the state, attempted to meet the "equal" requirement by offering to pay the tuition of Lloyd Gaines, a Negro, in an out-of-state school. The Court, 7 to 2, held that he must be trained in Missouri, in whose courts he would practice, and not in some jurisdiction foreign to them. In the absence of a law school for blacks there, he must be admitted equally with whites to the one at the University of Missouri.

Similar decisions covering medical as well as law schools led the NAACP, and others, to fight not inequality but segregation itself. At the time of the epochal *Brown* ruling in May 1954, cases were pending from South Carolina, Virginia, Delaware, and the District of Columbia, as well as from Kansas, all of which were covered by the decision.

In September 1953 Chief Justice Fred M. Vinson died, and in his place Eisenhower named Governor Earl Warren of California. Some observers believe that Vinson's court would have continued its earlier tendency merely to strengthen the requirement of "equality" in separate facilities, at least until Congress explicitly made segregation illegal. Warren's court, including three southern Justices, decided unanimously to embrace Justice John Marshall Harlan's bold dissent in the *Plessy* case. The doctrine of separate but equal, Harlan had said in 1896, "would stimulate aggressions, more or less brutal and irritating, upon the admitted rights of colored citizens." The "thin disguise of 'equal' accommodations . . . will not mislead anyone, or atone for the wrong this day done." Speaking for his court, Warren undertook to right this wrong:

806

*In approaching ... the effect of segregation itself on public education ... we ... must consider public education in the light of its full development and its present place in American life throughout the Nation. ... Today, education is perhaps the most important function of state and local governments. ... It is the very foundation of good citizenship. Today it is a principal instrument in awakening the child to cultural values, in preparing him for later professional training, and in helping him to adjust normally to his environment. ... In the field of public education the doctrine of "separate but equal" has no place. Separate educational facilities are inherently unequal.*

Much has been made of the sudden and shocking character of the Warren Court's ruling. No doubt it shocked millions, North and South, who had heretofore given little thought to the issue. It probably stunned the President. Yet the particular cases had been before the courts for years before their final resolution, which itself had the concurrence of Justice Department briefs. Great care, moreover, was taken in its implementation, which was placed in the hands of local courts permitted to employ guidelines reflecting local situations, provided only that the courts require "a prompt and reasonable start toward full compliance," which then should proceed "with all deliberate speed."

In border states and in the North, considerable progress was made toward compliance within two years. In the Deep South it became clear that compliance would take time and might involve violence. In September 1957 Little Rock, Arkansas, became the focal point of southern resistance when Governor Orval E. Faubus used the National Guard to prevent nine black children from entering that city's Central High School. President Eisenhower countered by providing the children with federal military protection, and they were subsequently enrolled.

Faubus's overwhelming victory in winning a third term as Arkansas governor in August 1958 was also an endorsement of his segregation stand and a signal to the rest of the South. When the election returns were in, Harry Ashmore, liberal editor of the *Little Rock Gazette,* asserted that the moderate position was now "clearly untenable for any man

in public life anywhere in the region. A period of struggle and turmoil lies ahead."

The handful of black students in Little Rock were subjected to such harassment by extremist white students that the local school board soon asked for a two-and-a-half year suspension of the integration program. The request came to the Supreme Court in September 1958, when attorneys for the school board argued that it could not at present put integration into effect because of "the total opposition of the people and of the State Governor of Arkansas." Over a reasonable length of time, perhaps, the situation would change. Attorneys for the NAACP, led by their chief counsel, Thurgood Marshall, replied: "There can be no equality of justice for our people if the law steps aside, even for a moment, at the command of force and violence." The Supreme Court agreed and on September 12, 1958, unanimously denied the request. Seventeen days later it delivered an unprecedented written opinion on the case in which, to underscore their unanimity, all nine Justices were listed as coauthors. This opinion declared:

*The constitutional rights of respondents [Negro children] are not to be sacrificed or yielded to ... violence and disorder. ... The constitutional rights of children not to be discriminated against in school admissions on grounds of race or color declared by this court can neither be nullified openly and directly by state legislators or state executives or judicial officers, nor nullified by them through any evasive scheme for segregation.*

The outlook, however, remained bleak. During the first integration year, 1955–1956, 450 school districts in the South had been integrated; in the following year, 270; and in the third year, only 60 more had been added. By 1959, of the 2985 biracial southern school districts, only 792 had been integrated, none in the Deep South nor in Virginia, which had taken the lead in adopting the official policy of "massive resistance," authorizing the governor to close any school ordered integrated by the courts. A leading southern lawyer described the situation in these words: "It is like an army advancing. It first overruns the outposts. In the first two hours, it may advance two miles. Then it may hit the hard core of resistance and in the next two days, advance two yards. Now it means advancing from the beachhead, hedgerow by hedgerow, school district by school district, with a bitter fight . . . for each district."

Those in the fight, however, did not flag, least of all blacks themselves. Indeed, while concentrating first on the school issue, they soon broadened their campaign for equality until it encompassed every phase of life, just as repression and segregation did. In 1957 and in 1960, conforming to the blacks' rising militancy, Congress passed the first federal civil-rights acts in almost a century. Broad at the outset, these acts, as adopted, were largely confined to the Negro's right to vote, and they made the procedure for federal intervention in this critical field so tortuous that even the nominal gains were nullified. Nevertheless, these two measures revived dormant federal commitments. "I don't believe you can change the hearts of men with laws or decisions," Eisenhower had said, urging caution in implementing the *Brown* ruling. A few years later, Martin Luther King, Jr., observed, "the law may not change the heart—but it can restrain the heartless." That much and more, sometimes with disheartening consequences, the law was to undertake.

### Climax of McCarthyism

In seeking to improve party unity, Eisenhower often sought Senator Robert A. Taft's advice, and the Senator usually gave his blessing to administration measures. After Taft died in July 1953, the Republican right wing grew increasingly rebellious. They strongly backed an amendment proposed by Senator John W. Bricker of Ohio to limit the treaty-making powers of the President, a mea-

sure only narrowly defeated in the Senate in February 1954. Under right-wing influence, Congress also refused further to revise the Taft-Hartley Act, and rejected administration bills for federal health insurance and aid to schools and highway construction.

One thing Taft failed to do for the new administration was to muzzle Senator McCarthy. The Republican victory in 1952 naturally opened congressional committee chairmanships to party leaders and McCarthy got his. Taft, a dominant Senate figure, averred they had put McCarthy "where he can't do any harm" by giving him the obscure Government Operations Committee; but any committee affording funds and staff would have served McCarthy's purpose, and he soon found occasion to renew his assault on his favorite target, the State Department.

In February 1953, Eisenhower nominated Charles E. Bohlen as ambassador to the USSR. Bohlen was a veteran Foreign Service officer who unfortunately had served as Roosevelt's interpreter at Yalta. No choice could have stung the Senator and his friends more sharply. After vicious condemnations of the nominee, they permitted the Senate to approve him; but their pound of flesh was the appointment of their own man as the State Department's new "security" officer, and henceforth few worked there without McCarthyite consent.

Having cleansed the stables at home, as he thought, McCarthy next turned to operations abroad. His first target here was the Voice of America, the overseas broadcasting unit of the United States Information Agency, where, after the most demoralizing search, he failed to uncover a single Communist party man. On the heels of this venture came another, the victim this time being the State Department's International Information Administration, which disseminated printed materials through libraries in many parts of the world. Many books by eminent American writers, one of them Secretary Dulles's cousin, were ordered withdrawn, and, to the shock of the world, some were publicly burned.

To placate the man his election was supposed to spirit away, the President, on April 27, 1953, issued his own "loyalty order" insti-

808

tuting a probe of government employees to outdo Truman's. The categories for "security risks" were made broader and vaguer than ever, the safeguards fewer and weaker. Not one communist could be found; but in a short time more than half a million civil servants, almost a fifth of the total, resigned in protest. In December 1953, Eisenhower dismayed the whole scientific community by ordering a "blank wall" to be placed between J. Robert Oppenheimer, the great nuclear physicist who had directed the making of the first atomic bomb, and all secret atomic data. Oppenheimer, at this time head of the Institute for Advanced Study at Princeton, also served as chairman of the General Advisory Committee of the Atomic Energy Commission. The administration learned that McCarthy had the physicist in view as another victim for having associated with allegedly communist friends in the thirties, and it wanted to get him first. Oppenheimer soon was cleared of any taint of disloyalty, but in the eyes of AEC he re-

mained a "misfit," unemployable because of "fundamental defects in his character."

The legislature as well as the executive knuckled under to McCarthy's pressure, especially with new security legislation affecting aliens. But the Senator's star began to wane in the summer of 1954 following his attack on the army's "coddling" of communists. After the elections that year returned Democratic majorities to both houses, a move to expel or at least to censure him gained headway. In December 1954, by a vote of 67 to 22, he was "condemned" by the Senate for "conduct unbecoming a member," a mild rebuke in the circumstances. McCarthy died unsung in May 1957, but McCarthyism, a far deeper malady than the red scare of the twenties, continued to alienate creative men from government service.

## II  The "new look" in foreign policy

### Platform promises exposed

The Republicans, as we have seen, took office promising a dynamic alternative to the "negative, futile and immoral policy of 'containment.'" They would "liberate" central Europe from communism's grip, "roll back" Soviet power in eastern Europe, and "unleash" Chiang Kai-shek in Asia. The architect of this ambitious program was to be John Foster Dulles, who soon proved to be more a man of words than acts.

An early test for the "new look" in Europe came suddenly in March 1953 when Stalin died. The struggle to succeed him threw the USSR into such turmoil that Georgi Malenkov, who emerged as the new Premier but was obliged to share power with others, sought to abate external dangers by talking of "peaceful coexistence" with capitalist countries. He also relaxed certain controls

over Russian satellite peoples, a step which, in June 1953, led to an uprising in East Berlin that quickly spread across all East Germany. This revolt, a precursor of others in 1956, had to be suppressed by Soviet troops and only subsided when all hope had gone for "liberation" help from West Germany or elsewhere.

"Roll-back" soon followed "liberation" to the dustbin, with even costlier consequences. To roll back Soviet strength in Europe, NATO would have had to be transformed from a defensive "shield" to an offensive weapon so monstrous that few could take the idea seriously. Even the proposed NATO defensive force of ninety-six divisions had encountered insuperable difficulties when the Republican administration took office. In October 1950, in order to get newly created West Germany to share the cost of Europe's defense while at the same time averting the menace of a new German national army, the French government had suggested the creation of a European Defense Community (EDC) tied to NATO, with nonmember West German units merged into its joint force. This proposal had the backing of the Truman administration as the natural next step following the economic resurgence of Western Europe sparked by Marshall Plan aid, and an EDC treaty for this purpose had been drawn up in May 1952. However, the French people, on their part, viewed any rearming of the Germans with deep misgivings; and this treaty was still being debated in France as late as December 1953.

At this juncture, in order to speed his own policies along, Dulles threatened France with an "agonizing reappraisal" of American troop commitments on the Continent, which might lead to their ultimate withdrawal. The only practical outcome of this threat was the French Assembly's outright rejection of the EDC treaty in August 1954. Following this "shattering blow," as Dulles called it, an alternative British plan was accepted by the United States, France, and others in October. Under this plan, which went into effect in May 1955, West Germany was granted full sovereignty as Japan had been earlier, admitted to NATO with full equality, and permitted to raise an army of twelve divisions to become part of the NATO force. The new German divisions, however, proved discouragingly slow in materializing, while economic and other factors, such as the yearning for the relaxation of tensions

encouraged by the Russians' "peaceful coexistence" line, prompted the older European members gradually to curtail their own contributions. The compulsive economizing of the Eisenhower administration, which in fact had given a touch of credibility to Dulles's "agonizing reappraisal" threat, hastened NATO's decline, while "roll-back" had already died.

For the President, "fiscal morality" required balancing the budget, a goal attainable only by cutting massive military spending. Thus as early as October 1953, conforming to the President's guidelines, the National Security Council had announced a new addition to the "new look" which phrasemaker Dulles soon called "massive retaliation," and which others justified by one more phrase, "more bang for a buck." Under the new "basic decision," dependence on the Army's costly ground forces would everywhere be reduced or eliminated. As a bonus, the United States would no longer be lured into any more hateful little wars like that in Korea. Instead, "security with solvency" would be attained by emphasizing air power, in which the United States still led the world. The administration would simply let the communists in Moscow and Peking know that any new menaces to American security from those quarters would be met by nuclear and thermonuclear assaults on their cities and civilians.

809

*Counterweights in the "balance of terror": parade of Soviet rockets, Red Square, November 1957; and SAC bombers in formation.*

Tass from Sovfoto          United States Air Force photo

Since the United States had already loosed two nuclear bombs in anger and had threatened to employ nuclear weapons in Korea, her NATO allies shuddered at the thought that she might become hardened to the practice. The Russians and the Chinese, at the same time, viewed "massive retaliation" simply as more of Dulles's "vociferous inaction" (the words are those of the *Economist* of London in August 1954). In the belief that only the most extreme military provocation would elicit such a massive retaliatory rejoinder, they felt free to inch ahead once more by intensified political and economic opportunism, leaving "irresponsible and malevolent 'war mongering,'" as they said, to the "Pentagon generals."

Despite "Ike's" great prestige, this "basic decision" also aggravated the chafing of the armed services under civilian considerations and control; and, within the Department of Defense itself, it fanned already dangerously tense interservice rivalry by its massive favoritism toward air power. The reasoning behind it, moreover, was soon proved fallacious by the steeply rising prices of modern air equipment and installations. By the end of 1954, finally, the Russians had not only detonated their own thermonuclear bombs but had developed delivery systems like SAC's as well, thereby confronting the administration, in Churchill's phrase, with a "balance of terror" while giving Dulles grounds for another empty verbal triumph—"brinksmanship," the art of going "to the brink of war without being scared."

### New nationalism in Asia

An early test for the new "new look" in the Far East arose in the first months of 1954. Earlier, the nascent nationalism of colonial peoples in Asia, as in North Africa and the Middle East, had been inflamed by their commitment to World War II by such imperial powers as Britain, Holland, and France, with little or no consultation with native leaders. The wartime difficulties of the imperial powers sorely damaged their prestige and, as it turned out, sapped their power to withstand the postwar nationalist movements.

Britain, the greatest of the imperial powers, was the first to yield to the inevitable in Asia as she had in the Middle East and in the Mediterranean theater. The transition was made easier by her broader preparation for self-government, such as it was, of the native populations of many of her imperial lands. The victory of the Labor party in the British home elections of 1945 also brought into office leaders more responsive to native claims than Churchill and the Conservatives might have been. Thus, one after another in 1947 and 1948, such former British colonies as India (and newly created Pakistan), Ceylon, and Burma were granted independence, all but Burma choosing to remain in the British Commonwealth. A fifth British colony made up of the Malay States and neighboring settlements had gained a more limited degree of self-government by February 1948, but full self-government was postponed by ten years of guerrilla warfare with communists under local Chinese leadership. The Federation of Malaya, set up in 1957 as a member of the Commonwealth, became the Federation of Malaysia in 1963 after the addition of certain adjacent areas.

The Dutch, less well equipped than the British to retain, or rather regain, their prewar Asian empire, proved less ready as well to let it go—to the embarrassment of United States policy in Europe and the Far East. During their wartime occupation of the Dutch East Indies, the Japanese had encouraged an anti-Dutch nationalist movement culminating in the creation of a puppet state, the Indonesian Republic. With Japan's fall, this republic had become virtually independent, and when the Dutch, in an effort to regain their hold there, sent troops to the East Indies, they encountered strong resistance. During the fighting, the Dutch looked to the United States for help in recapturing the imperial sources of so much of their prewar wealth, and the Truman administration, aware of the need of the Dutch in NATO in Europe, felt impelled to give it. On the other hand, the administration was con-

European retreat from colonialism
after World War II

ICELAND

GREAT
BRITAIN

EIRE

PORTUGAL    SPAIN

NORWAY    SWEDEN    FINLAND

DEN.
NETH.
BEL. L.
FRANCE    W. GER.    E. GER.    POLAND
SW.    AUST    CZECH.    HUNG    ROM.
ITALY    YUGO.    BUL.
ALB.
GREECE

U.S.S.R.

MOROCCO
1956
IFNI

TUNISIA
1956

ALGERIA
1962

LIBYA
1951

SPANISH
SAHARA

MAURITANIA
1960
SENEGAL, 1960
GAMBIA
1965
PORT. GUINEA
GUINEA
1958
SIERRA LEONE
1961
LIBERIA
IVORY COAST
1960
MALI
1960

UPPER
VOLTA
1960
GHANA
1957
TOGO
1960
DAHOMEY
1960

NIGER
1960

CHAD
1960

NIGERIA
1960

CAMEROON
1960

EQ.
GUINEA
1968
GABON
1960

REP. OF CONGO
1960

CABINDA
(ANGOLA)

ANGOLA

SOUTH-WEST
AFRICA
(NAMIBIA)
1968

SUDAN
1956

CENTRAL
AFRICAN REP.
1960

CONGO 1960

ETHIOPIA

UGANDA
1962
RWANDA
1962
BURUNDI
1962

TANZANIA
1964

ZAMBIA
1962
RHODESIA
1965
BOTSWANA
1966

MALAWI
1964

MOZAMBIQUE

REP. OF
SOUTH
AFRICA
LESOTHO
1966

SWAZILAND
1968

EGYPT
1951

TURKEY

LEBANON
ISRAEL, 1948
JORDAN
1946
SYRIA
IRAQ

SAUDI
ARABIA

YEMEN

OMAN
&
MUSCAT

S. YEMEN
1967
AFARS & ISSAS
TERR.

SOMALI
REP.
1960

KENYA
1963

IRAN

AFGHANISTAN

W. PAKISTAN
1955

INDIA
1947

TIBET

NEPAL

BHUTAN

E. PAK.
1955

CEYLON
1948

MONGOLIA

CHINA

N. KOREA
1945

S. KOREA
1945

JAPAN

TAIWAN

LAOS
1954

BURMA
1947-8

THAI.

N. VIETNAM
1954

CAM.
1954

S. VIETNAM
1954

MALAYSIA
1957

PHILIPPINE
ISLANDS
1946

INDONESIA 1949

W. IRIAN
1963

NEW
GUINEA

PAPUA

MALAGASY
REPUBLIC
1960

MAURITIUS
1968

Indian Ocean

AUSTRALIA

Atlantic Ocean

Denmark    Spain

France    Portugal

Belgium    Italy

Great Britain    Netherlands

Sudan: Anglo–Egyptian
Namibia: South African Mandate

Papua and New Guinea are territories of Australia
Date indicates Independence

812

strained by its effort to establish an anticolonial posture in the world. In the end American pressure forced the Dutch, in 1949, reluctantly to yield self-government to Indonesia within a hastily formed Dutch-Indonesian Union. When this Union collapsed in 1954, the Republic of Indonesia, under the leadership of Sukarno, a Marxist adventurer hungry for the spoils of power, became entirely independent. As unhappy over American dallying with the Dutch as the Dutch were over what they considered American interference in their internal affairs, Sukarno promptly assumed a "neutralist" position in the Cold War.

In April 1955, Sukarno assembled in Bandung, Java, "the first international conference of colored peoples in the history of mankind." Twenty-nine African as well as Asian nations, most of them newly independent and all together representing at least half the world's population, sent delegates to this conference. Although Sukarno's feigning to employ Western forms of parliamentary democracy had helped him win hundreds of millions of dollars in American aid, at Bandung NATO was denounced as a shield of colonialism, and Chou En-lai, Red China's Premier, took the lead in endorsing third-world "neutrality" against the West.

## The Vietnam test

The French proved even more determined than the Dutch to retain their valuable Southeast Asian possessions centered in Indochina, a mid-nineteenth-century creation including three old troubled kingdoms—Laos, Cambodia, and Vietnam. With Britain and Holland on their way out as Asian powers, the United States wished to help the French, especially after Red China's intervention in Korea seemed to emphasize her aggressive intent.

The situation in Indochina differed in one major way from that in other European imperial domains overrun by Japan. Elsewhere, as in the Dutch East Indies, the Japanese had found it advantageous to employ Western-educated native leaders as their occupation administrators, rather than the more questionably loyal European colonial civil servants who had remained in Asia. They also sought to strengthen the allegiance of these native leaders by catering to their political and cultural nationalism. In Indochina, the Japanese had less need of native leaders because the pro-Vichy French there were Axis-oriented. Thus the nationalist Indochinese, more profoundly hostile to repressive imperialism of the French variety than were most people under British rule, were driven underground. Like the "partisans" in Nazi-occupied countries of Europe during the war, they soon fell under the domination of highly skilled communists led by the Russian-trained Ho Chi Minh, who had begun to work against French rule long before World War II. The principal nationalist group in Indochina was the Vietminh in Vietnam, whose standing by the end of World War II was enhanced by its success in liberating portions of the north from the Japanese. In September 1945, its leaders had proclaimed the Democratic Republic of Vietnam, with Hanoi its capital and Ho Chi Minh its President.

In March 1946, during the struggle for power in postwar France between the Gaullists and others, the new Vietnam administration was recognized as a "free state" within a French Union hastily established like that of the Dutch. In June, Ho was invited to Paris to consult on the future of the new state, a mission from which he returned in September wholly disenchanted with the French attitude toward real independence.

By then local French commanders striving to set up a separatist regime in Cochin China, Vietnam's southernmost region, had clashed repeatedly with Vietminh terrorists seeking to make good Hanoi's claim to overall control. By December other clashes in the north had grown into a general war. The rivalry grew more intense after June 1949, when the French, having successfully set up former native rulers as puppets in Cambodia and Laos, now officially tried the same tactic in Vietnam. Their puppet here was Bao Dai, scion of an old ruling family, who had no popular following and preferred Paris to Saigon.

This challenge led the Vietminh to intensify and extend its military activity. The proclamation of the communist Chinese Republic in October 1949 gave a tremendous boost to Vietminh morale and soon to Vietminh strength as well. Early in 1950 Red China formally recognized the Vietminh regime in Hanoi, making it, in effect, more a captive of communism than before and less able to sustain its avowed nationalist stance. The United States and Britain, especially concerned this time about French support for NATO in Europe, responded by recognizing the Saigon regime of Bao Dai. More than that, the Truman administration began to offset Red Chinese aid to Ho with American aid to Bao.

Chinese military intervention in the Korean War in October 1950 gave the United States almost as much concern about the future of Vietnam as of Korea; and once this war ended, the United States greatly enlarged its assistance to the beleaguered French. By the end of 1953, the Eisenhower administration found itself paying two-thirds of the cost of the French military effort, or about $1 billion per year. But it could not save the French after their main army, early in 1954, allowed itself to be trapped in the untenable fortress of Dienbienphu.

Eisenhower had already stated that the fall of Indochina "would be of a most terrible significance to the United States of America." Southeast Asia, he added, was of "transcendent importance" to American security; a communist victory in Vietnam, with Red China support, might find all noncommunist governments in the Far East soon toppling like a row of dominoes, a phrase to become famous later on. Did he order Dulles, then, to warn Moscow and Peking of "massive retaliation"? Did he order the bombs to rain upon them? He did not. Dulles, with Admiral Arthur W. Radford, Chairman of the Joint Chiefs, on April 3, 1954, met in private with congressional leaders to request authorization for an American air strike on Dienbienphu from navy carriers. The congressmen demurred,

while Eisenhower, on his part, refused to sanction unilateral American military action. On April 10, Dulles flew to London to seek British support but was sternly rebuffed.

On April 16, in a speech before the American Society of Newspaper Editors (an administration trial balloon, "not for attribution"), Vice-President Nixon declared that "if to avoid further Communist expansion in Asia and Indochina we must take the risk now of putting our boys in, I think the Executive has to take the politically unpopular decision and do it." The House at this time had under consideration a rider to an appropriation bill seeking to limit the President's authority to send troops anywhere in the world without congressional consent. Eisenhower's threat to veto the bill helped kill the rider, a proposition probably more popular than the trial balloon, which fell flat.

*Geneva accords*

By the time Dienbienphu, and the French with it, capitulated to Ho Chi Minh on May 7, 1954, the representatives of nine powers—France, Red China, the USSR, Britain, the United States, the two Vietnams, Cambodia, and Laos—had already convened at Geneva to work out some arrangements in the light of the inevitable collapse. Korea was also on the agenda, perhaps simply to justify Secretary Dulles's presence. In any case, at a time when McCarthyism was at its very crest and the State Department most demoralized by it, Dulles, fearful of "Asia First" opinion at home, absented himself from the Geneva discussions on Vietnam, which were certain to end with something less than complete victory over the communists. Under Secretary Walter Bedell Smith sat in for him.

The Geneva settlement, complicated and ambiguous, was meant merely to be temporary. The armistice agreement secured on July 20 provided for a military truce between the Vietminh and the French military command, the latter openly acting for its Saigon puppet regime. The truce set up a "provisional military demarcation line" at the 17th parallel and a narrow "demilitarized zone" on either side of it. North of the line, the Vietminh armies

813

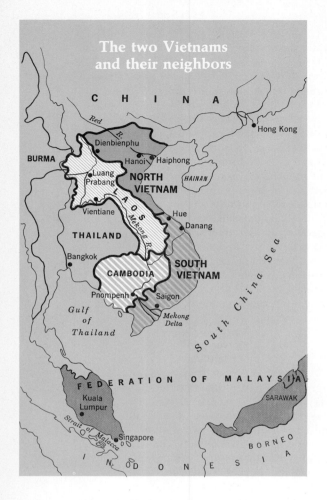

The two Vietnams and their neighbors

"strong man," Prime Minister Ngo Dinh Diem. Fearful of a regimented communist victory in the 1956 elections, Diem found reasons for putting off his approval, not least that, after all, his government had not been a party to the agreement. Meanwhile, the Red Chinese had begun to assist in the further communization of North Vietnam, while the United States gradually increased its aid to Diem's authoritarian regime in the South despite his cruel campaign of suppression and political and religious murders that gave even his American friends pause.

On the day after the Geneva agreements, July 21, 1954, Eisenhower had stated that the Geneva armistice "contains features which we do not like," but "in compliance with . . . the United Nations Charter, the United States will not use force to disturb the settlement." He added: "The renewal of Communist aggression would be viewed by us as a matter of grave concern." That October, he added further, in a letter to Diem, his willingness "to examine" with him "how . . . American aid given directly to your government can assist Vietnam . . . in developing . . . a strong, viable state, capable of resisting attempted subversion or aggression through military means." But such aid must be founded upon "performance on the part of the Government of Vietnam in undertaking needed reforms." Diem's government proved slow in undertaking reforms, but the United States was reluctant to cast him adrift.

The Geneva agreements had promised that civilians as well as soldiers, north or south, would be permitted to move freely to whichever "regrouping zone" they wished. Within two years at least a million persons, mainly Catholics oriented toward the French, had moved south from Ho's region. Among them, no doubt, were infiltrators who soon began to organize Vietcong cadres, their recruiting made easier by the character of Diem's rule. By 1959 terrorist attacks on the Saigon regime were being openly aided by the North, and in September 1960 Ho formally recognized the

were to "regroup"; south of it, the armies of the French.

Like the Korean division at the 38th parallel and the earlier one in Germany, the "provisional" Vietnam settlement soon hardened. One element favoring acceptance of the agreement by the victorious Vietminh was the promise that Vietnam-wide elections to unify the country would be held by July 1956, a promise supported by the United States in its "unilateral declaration" of July 21, with the proviso that elections were "supervised by the United Nations to insure that they are conducted fairly." The "final declaration" at Geneva, signed by no one, also recognized the independence of Cambodia and Laos.

Not until January 1955 did the French turn back the Saigon regime to Bao Dai and his

Vietcong as the National Front for the Liberation of South Vietnam. Most of the supplies from the North came over the Ho Chi Minh trail through northern Laos, a region dominated by the communist group in that country, the Pathet Lao, with Ho's support. Laotian politics consisted of little more than aristocratic family rivalries, and the Eisenhower administration's last efforts to check communism there, as in Vietnam, while now greatly expanded, succeeded largely in alienating the native neutralist opposition by its support of the conservative Boun Oum regime. This policy and its consequences it bequeathed to its own successor administration at home (see p. 831).

### A wall of words

The Geneva accords were widely criticized in the United States and elsewhere as a second Munich, and Dulles, to mend his fences, sought to form a collective organization in Southeast Asia that he hoped would serve as a counterpart to NATO in Europe. This was a retreat to the despised policy of "containment"; but his repeated failures to roll back or even to check communism in Asia left Dulles with little choice. Even in this policy, moreover, he was promptly rebuffed by such significant new South Asia countries as India, Burma, Indonesia, and Ceylon which, resenting American intrusion, also feared that efforts to lock in Red China on the south might simply provoke her to new aggressive acts.

Two mainland countries, Pakistan and Thailand, along with the Philippines, Australia, and New Zealand, proved somewhat more responsive. At Manila in September 1954 they met with the United States, Britain, and France and signed the Manila Pact, creating the Southeast Asia Treaty Organization (SEATO). A special "protocol" gave Laos, Cambodia, and "the free territory under the jurisdiction of the State of Vietnam," all barred by the Geneva accords from making alliances, such protection as the Manila Pact afforded.

Despite repeated attempts by the United States in the Lyndon B. Johnson administration to use her sacred SEATO commitments to justify her immense war machine in Vietnam (see p. 856), these commitments were minimal. The signatory powers merely agreed to meet any "common danger" from "Communist aggression" in accordance with their own "constitutional processes." In case of communist threats short of "armed attack," they would simply "consult" on what should be done. In the meantime, by a provision often overlooked, and perhaps meant to be, they were obliged "to strengthen their free institutions" in order to forestall communist provocation. No SEATO armed force similar to NATO's was contemplated or created. To cover this omission Dulles simply mouthed "massive retaliation" with thermonuclear weapons. "The deterrent power we thus create," he said at the end of the Manila meeting, "can protect many as effectively as it protects one."

The Philippines, for one, remained skeptical; and before leaving Manila, Dulles was obliged to promise more substantial protection in case these islands were attacked. On his way home, Dulles visited Chiang Kai-shek on Taiwan and on December 2 made a SEATO-type pact with him. Both parties agreed, however, to try first to settle peacefully any disputes they became involved in with other countries. By this provision Chiang was only the more securely "leashed," not "unleashed."

Between SEATO countries in the Far East and NATO countries in the West lay the strategic, oil-rich Middle East, where Arab nationalism, already inflamed by the creation of Israel in 1948, was reinforced after 1952 by the overthrow of King Farouk in Egypt. A new Egyptian republic emerged in place of the monarchy, and Colonel Gamal Abdel Nasser emerged as its strong man with ambitions to unite the neighboring Arab lands under Egyptian leadership. An elementary first step was the elimination of remaining vestiges of colonialism, most provokingly evident in Britain's continuing control of a powerful military base at the Suez Canal. Dulles hoped to draw Nasser's growing strength toward the West by

816

pressing the British to yield the base, which they reluctantly did in October 1954.

Dulles by then, for more than a year, had been promoting a Middle East defense organization to close the gap between SEATO and NATO. Greece and Turkey had been admitted to NATO in 1952; and in April 1954 Turkey and Pakistan, a SEATO member, had signed a mutual defense treaty. In February 1955, Turkey and her neighbor Iraq, meeting at Baghdad, Iraq's capital, signed a similar treaty, to which, at Dulles's behest, Britain, Pakistan, and Iran also subscribed in October. These arrangements became known as the Baghdad Pact, under which the Middle East Treaty Organization (METO) was formed, one more in keeping with SEATO's weaknesses than with NATO's relative strengths. METO became CENTO on Iraq's withdrawal from the Baghdad Pact in 1959.

To the confusion of all parties, Dulles kept the United States out of METO, and she stayed out of CENTO as well. Widespread sympathy for Israel, especially among Jews who contributed heavily to the urban vote, constrained the administration from appearing to huddle too closely with Arab powers who had sworn to destroy the Jewish state. A second reason for Dulles's action was the fear that overt American participation in METO, which ran across Russia's southern frontier the way SEATO ran across Red China's, might be the more provocative of Soviet retaliation.

Dulles was not the only one to abstain from METO. Nasser himself, who was particularly to be lured into the organization, also stayed out, to Dulles's great discomfiture. Nasser resented the inclusion of Iraq, an Arab state which preferred American aid to Arab unity. He also wished freedom of action in playing off the USSR and the West against one another to Egypt's national advantage. India, whose anti-NATO, anti-imperialist position had been made clear at the Bandung Conference of April 1955, represented an even more important rift in Dulles's verbal cordon.

Nasser's neutralist policy appeared to pay the desired dividends in September 1955 when he made a deal with the Russians for arms and military training following the expo-sure of Egypt's military weakness by large-scale Israeli raids the previous February in the controversial Gaza strip on the Israeli-Egyptian border. To counter such Russian aid, Dulles, along with Britain and the United Nations itself, soon offered to help Egypt build the Aswan Dam—a project that was to make much more of the Nile's water available for irrigation in the largely desert country. Nasser accepted the American offer in July 1956; but within a week certain of his anti-Western gestures prompted Dulles to withdraw it. On July 26, Egypt responded by announcing the nationalization of the Suez Canal, heretofore run by an Anglo-French company, and her intention of using canal tolls to construct the dam herself.

The rising tensions in the Middle East led Israel to launch an invasion of Egypt in October 1956, with the declared objective of destroying the bases from which raids had been made on her territory. Israel's action was promptly followed by the remarkable Anglo-French invasion of the Suez region on October 31. Even more remarkable was the collaboration of the United States and the Soviet Union in the United Nations General Assembly, where they jointly condemned this resort to arms by NATO nations. The General Assembly then voted to organize a force to supervise a cease-fire; but the UN call for peace went unheeded until November 6, and then it was only the Russian threat to intervene unilaterally with "volunteers" that checked the British and the French. American threats combined with those of the USSR brought the Israeli invasion to a halt a week later. The first detachments of the United Nations Emergency Force began to arrive on November 15 to help keep the peace. But this was only a stopgap measure which solved nothing in the Middle East. The NATO alliance, moreover, was slow to recover from the divisions deepened here.

When the Soviets continued to arm Arab nations, METO members, in turn, called on the United States once more to join the Baghdad Pact. This the administration refused to do lest Soviet intervention be accelerated. Instead, in a message to Congress in January 1957, the President asked for endorsement of the "Eisenhower Doctrine," a unilateral warning to the USSR that the United States would defend the entire Middle East against Soviet attack. Congress foresaw no direct Soviet attack, only increased Soviet subversion. It withheld approval until March of that year when, by a joint resolution, it gave the President, at his discretion, the power to use American forces to help any Middle East nation, at its request, to resist "armed attack from any country controlled by international communism."

## III  Maturation of the Cold War

### Thaw and freeze

Soviet-American cooperation in the UN on the issue of Egypt and Israel early in November 1956 marked the last glimmering evidence of the "thaw" that seemed to soften the Cold War as the policy of "massive retaliation" failed and the idea of "peaceful coexistence" spread. Even Winston Churchill, in June 1954, had urged the West to give this Russian gambit "a real good try." The ambiguities of the thaw quickly became apparent with the signing of the Warsaw Pact in May 1955, which placed all Soviet satellite forces, as a counterweight to NATO, under Moscow's unified command. Just at this time, nevertheless, the USSR agreed to end the four-power occupation of Austria and to recognize her independence despite her obvious Western leanings; and a few months later, on a visit to Moscow, Chancellor Konrad Adenauer secured Soviet recognition of the Bonn government of West Germany.

In June 1955, Premier Nikolai A. Bulganin, Malenkov's successor, and Nikita Khrushchev, the Communist party head, paid a momentous visit to Yugoslavia, where Marshal Tito, in defiance of Stalin in 1948, had set up his own national version of a communist state. Now, Tito and the Russians declared openly that "differences in the concrete forms of socialist development are exclusively the concern of the peoples of the respective countries"—an extraordinary acknowledgment of the first break in the Soviet monolithic structure that would soon have far-reaching consequences in Europe and Asia.

The high point of the thaw came in July 1955, when the Big Four—the United States, the USSR, Britain, and France—met in Geneva for the first "summit conference" since World War II. On the agenda were such touchy old subjects as the unification of Germany, European security, and disarmament, all made the more abrasive by the Warsaw Pact. But since they were abrasive, they were not pressed. In December 1955, such satellites as Albania, Bulgaria, Rumania, and Hungary were admitted to the UN, where they joined Czechoslovakia and Poland, charter members —a peaceful Soviet gain not quite offset by the simultaneous admission of Italy, Spain, and numerous other more independent countries.

Khrushchev lunged so far forward in his quest for full personal power at the Communists' famous Twentieth Party Congress in February 1956 that he almost toppled over. It was this Congress that gave the Soviet's thawed "new look" in foreign policy official confirmation. But the party leader himself stole the show not only with his denunciation of Stalinism, already foreshadowed in his reconciliation with Tito, but of Stalin personally. He was, Khrushchev said, a monster and a brute who "doubtlessly performed great services" for the country (there was other hedging for the benefit of surviving Stalinists, eagerly overlooked by the reformers), but at a cost distressing to contemplate and intolerable any longer to bear.

In this "destalinization" speech, Khrushchev conspicuously stigmatized the dead dictator's "unrealistic appreciation" of Western determination to defend Korea by arms, and he deplored Soviet involvement in the whole "risky" adventure. This passage clearly burned the ears of Chou En-lai in Red China. After *his* adventure in the Korean war, according to David J. Dallin, "the very term, 'great power,' seemed to have enormously excited [China's] new leadership." When Khrushchev so boldly cast off Stalin's gauntlet, Chou forebodingly picked it up; he and Mao Tse-tung now asserting their "legitimacy" in the monolithic Leninist-Stalinist succession. When destalinization, moreover, quickly led Poland and Hungary in particular, among the restive Soviet satellites in Europe, to seek those "different paths to socialism" that Tito had so profitably explored and the Twentieth Congress had sanctioned, the Chinese found the occasion to exercise their leadership. By helping to rescue the floundering Soviet rulers, they hoped to deepen their own stamp on the monolithic system.

Both the Polish and Hungarian "counterrevolutions" had reached their turning points in October 1956, just when the world and the UN were absorbed in the Middle East crisis and the United States, in addition, was approaching the climax of the presidential election. At this juncture, Chou turned up in Moscow. Why Poland, after a tremendous show of Soviet force, was permitted significant relaxations of police terror and political tyranny under the then liberal communist leadership of Wladyslaw Gomulka, while Hungary under the liberal Imre Nagy was belatedly overrun by the Soviet army (with no attempted check by the United States or the UN despite the most desperate pleas for aid), is not exactly clear; but that Chou had a hand in both decisions appears certain. It is likewise certain that Khrushchev's Stalinist enemies in the Kremlin were strengthened by Chou's work and that the party head, to save his skin, began the "qualified rehabilitation" of the dead despot even before the Hungarian dead were counted.

The satellite uprisings, Khrushchev now conceded, were "provoked by enemy agents," not by Stalinist oppression; Nagy himself was in league with "counterrevolutionary fascists" in West Germany and Austria and earned the Stalinist fate that befell him: abduction late in October by Soviet agents in Budapest and the announcement a year and a half later of his execution for treason. In the succeeding months, Gomulka's Poland began to feel the first stings of retribution, which gradually ate away her Titoist gains; while Yugoslavia, for sympathy with the rebellions, was subjected to dire economic warfare. Khrushchev's Stalinist enemies at home also were purged in Stalinist fashion as soon as he won the bitter struggle for his political life in the party's Central Committee. By the time Sputnik I was placed in orbit early in October 1957, Khrushchev had made himself as secure as he would ever be as head of the party, and he had made the party secure once more as head of the state. In March 1958, on supplanting Bulganin, he, like Stalin, became Premier as well as party chief.

## Election of 1956

Often during the 1952 campaign, Eisenhower had promised to "overhaul the entire creaking federal administration," and in March 1953, at his urging, Congress created a Commission on Intergovernmental Relations "to take a hard look at all programs of financial aid that reached down from Washington into the state and the individual community." One outcome of its work was the creation in April of the first new Cabinet department in forty years, the Department of Health, Education, and Welfare, principally, in the President's words, to bring the management of social security and related programs under "more disciplined and efficient" control. In September 1954, on the eve of the congressional elections, at the same time, Eisenhower signed an act adding seven million persons to those eligible for social security benefits, for the first time including farm workers and domestics.

While few other New Deal and Fair Deal programs were enlarged by the "moderate" Republican administration, few were cancelled. One exception was the Democrats' long-term public-housing program, which was given but one more year. Another was their farm program. To slow down the accumulation of farm surpluses in government warehouses under the price-support policy, Secretary of Agriculture Benson first reduced the point at which payments were to begin from Truman's 90 percent of parity to 75 percent, and then secured congressional authorization for a flexible scale ranging from 82.5 to 90 percent. Under Benson's management so many big staple farmers grew rich, so many small farmers, white and black alike, stayed poor, that *Time* magazine, a friend of "modern Republicanism," in August 1957 branded the new program as "The $5 Billion Farm Scandal."

Other significant gaps in economic performance appeared during the first Eisenhower administration. *Business Week,* for example, in July 1955, ran this scare headline: *Lagging Public Construction—A Spreading National Blight.* "In sharp contrast," said the business journal, "to the expansion and modernization of private plant and equipment, which doubled manufacturing capacity at the end of World War II," is the scandalous "condition of our *public* plant and equipment—the roads, schools, water supply, health and sanitation facilities upon which industry, as well as the average family, depends." This was one of the economic consequences of the "peace" following World War II, which absorbed so great a share of federal funds for "security" that, despite the explosive business boom, little seemed to be left to the federal government or local governments for "service."

Public clamor over the decay of "public plant and equipment" was to be postponed for nearly a decade. At the same time, the private business boom, with a strong boost from government spending and government guarantees of home mortgages and other private credit, was genuine enough for the Republicans to campaign in 1956, as in 1928, on the slogan "Peace, Progress, and Prosperity." "By virtually every economic measure," wrote *Time,* "1956 was the greatest year in history." Failures in foreign affairs only seemed to inspire public sympathy for "Ike" while the good times lasted, and his heart attack of 1955 and serious surgery in 1956 brought him closer still to the common lot. Inordinately dependent on the general's personal appeal, Republican leaders thus urged him to run again despite his questionable health, and at the San Francisco convention in August they renominated him by acclamation, along with Vice-President Nixon.

Eisenhower's illnesses and Nixon's controversial reputation at the same time made many Democrats feel that they had a chance to reenter the White House. Despite Truman's opposition, Adlai E. Stevenson easily won renomination at the Democratic convention in Chicago, with Senator Kefauver becoming his running mate. The Democrats made what they could of the threat of a Nixon succession, of economic discontent in the farm belt, and of the failure of the "new look" in foreign affairs. But "Ike's" personal appeal carried him to victory even more decisively than in 1952. With 34,751,000 votes to Stevenson's 25,427,000 he won 58 percent of the ballots. In the electoral college his margin was 457 to 73. At the same time, the Democrats were far from shut out, maintaining their 49-to-47 margin in the Senate and enlarging by two seats their comfortable majority in the House. Not since the time of Zachary Taylor had a President been elected without carrying at least one house of Congress for his party.

### Shock of the Sputnik

In his second inaugural address, January 21, 1957, Eisenhower expressed his continuing hopes for the thaw when he said: "We honor, no less in this divided world than in a less tormented time, the people of Russia. We do not dread, rather do we welcome, their progress in education and industry." A few

819

months later the President and the American people suffered a shock which suggested that they would not, after all, welcome Soviet progress quite so heartily. On August 26, 1957, the Russians reported the first successful tests of an intercontinental ballistic missile (ICBM). Within six weeks, on October 4, they electrified the world by using the missile's rocket engine to launch man's first space satellite, Sputnik I. On November 3, the Soviets sent up Sputnik II, carrying a small dog.

During the course of the next year, the successful launching of four American satellites brought some comfort, which again was dissipated by the Russian success on January 2, 1959, with Lunik I, the first space vehicle to traverse the full distance of about 250,000 miles to the moon. Lunik did not hit the moon but soared into space to become the first artificial planet in orbit around the sun. Two months later, on March 10, the United States successfully put a planet of its own in orbit. The next stage in space exploration involved putting a man in orbit around the earth. This feat, and more spectacular ones, were accomplished in the sixties.

The shock of the Sputniks led Congress in September 1958 to pass the National Defense Education Act. To stimulate scientific education, this act offered loans and scholarships to qualified high-school and college students and grants to educational institutions for laboratories and equipment. At the same time, borrowers and assisted scholars were required to disclaim any communist sympathies and to take an exceptional oath of allegiance to the United States. Certain schools and colleges refused to participate in the program because of this element of thought control, which also alienated many students. Campus unrest was aggravated by the greatly enlarged contributions of government agencies and business corporations to university scientific research which drew more faculty members than ever from the classroom and left students with a sharp sense of neglect.

### Republicanism under stress

During Eisenhower's second administration, the United States suddenly found itself shuffling along with a slowdown in business expansion, a disturbingly high level of unemployment, and serious racial strife. At the same time, the communists made so much of their space triumphs that the President declared in 1958 that they were waging "total cold war." His immediate concern was with the "massive economic offensive that had been mounted by the Communist imperialists against free nations," especially in the oil-rich Middle East. But there was more to it than that. As George Kennan had foretold, they now fed political crises as well, not only in the Middle East but also in Asia and divided Germany.

In July 1958, following an anti-Western revolution in Iraq that led eventually to her withdrawal from the Baghdad Pact, the United States and Britain felt impelled to send troops to Lebanon and Jordan to forestall similar uprisings in these countries with Egyptian and Soviet support. In August that year, Red China resumed the systematic bombing of Quemoy and Matsu, two Nationalist islands just off her coast that she had first bombed in 1954. In October, Khrushchev raised a new storm over the flow of refugees from East to West Berlin and demanded the latter's demilitarization.

Nearer home, meanwhile, Latin America had begun to boil. In April and May 1958, Vice-President Nixon visited a number of Latin American countries in an effort to revive friendliness toward the United States. He was hostilely received, and in Venezuela and Peru he was stoned. When on January 1, 1959, Fidel Castro established his government in Cuba after a five-year struggle to overthrow the hateful Batista regime, many Americans saluted his success. But it was not long before Castro took a hostile line, exploiting the deep antipathy toward the United States in the rest of Latin America, and Khrushchev began using Castro for his own ends.

The Eisenhower administration had come into office after crusading against Democratic corruption. In mid-1958 it was itself besmirched by revelations of scandals so far-reaching that no less a personage than Sherman Adams, the confidential Assistant to the President, was forced, along with other high officials, to resign in September 1958. The depths of the party's trouble on all fronts was disclosed in the 1958 congressional elections, when it suffered a disaster comparable only to those of early New Deal years. In the Senate the Democrats widened their two-vote margin to an overwhelming 64 to 34. In the House their already substantial lead of 235 to 200 was broadened to 283 to 153. The shadow cast by these elections was deepened during the administration's last two years when Dulles's death in May 1959, following Adams's resignation, left the President largely on his own.

On the domestic front, unemployment and inadequate economic growth persisted, along with such unprecedented inflation during hard times that observers began to worry once more about monopoly and "administered" prices. Millions, moreover, were living in poverty. In "distressed areas" in certain states, such as the coal regions of Pennsylvania, West Virginia, and Kentucky and the old industrial regions of New England, "structural unemployment" and hard times had become part of the way of life. In other sections of the country, unemployment grew especially acute among Negroes. Besides encountering almost universal discrimination in the job market, blacks were prevented by the lack of educational opportunities from seeking white-collar work where personnel was most in demand. The continued rapid mechanization of agriculture, meanwhile, and the operation of the price-support program for staples both so favored large farm corporations that overall farm-family income fell off, while those who fled the land for the towns swelled the ranks of the unemployed.

New crises in foreign affairs further damaged the administration. By heating up the Cold War on all fronts, Khrushchev had hoped to convince the President that it would be well to hold the summit meeting he had

vainly sought since his space triumphs and missile gains. When this approach failed, Khrushchev, during Vice-President Nixon's visit to Moscow in July 1959 to open an American exhibit, reversed his tactics. He engaged in such a high-spirited TV debate with the Vice-President that Nixon came to believe that the Premier should get to know more about the United States at first hand. This led to a prompt invitation from the President, "to melt a little of the ice," and on September 15 Khrushchev arrived. After a peaceable address at the UN and a lively cross-country speaking tour, he met with Eisenhower at the President's country retreat with such success that a summit was informally agreed upon to continue "the spirit of Camp David," the site of their talks.

Eisenhower met considerable difficulty in lining up his Western summit colleagues. The imperious Charles de Gaulle, who had become Premier of France in June 1958 and President in December and who wanted reassurances about Germany's future after the Berlin crisis that year, proved especially recalcitrant. But the date May 16, 1960 finally was agreed upon by all parties for a Paris summit conference. On May 5, however, came news of the shooting down of an American U-2 reconnaissance plane over Soviet territory. Before acknowledging the truth of Soviet protests that the plane was on a regular spying mission, the administration trapped itself in a web of denials and half-truths. Khrushchev arrived in Paris for the scheduled meeting, demanding American apologies for "aggression" and punishment of those responsible. Eisenhower declined to apologize, and by taking upon himself full responsibility for the U-2 flights he stilled all punishment talk. The spirit of Camp David instantly dissolved in the Paris confrontation, and the summit conference ended within three hours.

While East-West relations deteriorated once more, relations among the anticommunist powers also worsened. Relations with de Gaulle became so bad that he refused to allow the United States to build NATO missile bases in France or to store nuclear weapons there. The violence that broke out in the Congo when Belgium reluctantly agreed to the formation of the Republic of the Congo in June 1960 further weakened Western unity and raised the curtain on a new region for East-West conflict. Many Japanese, in turn, resented the continuing United States occupation of Okinawa and the militarization of their homeland. When Eisenhower visited the Far East in June 1960, anti-American demonstrations in Tokyo became so militant that he was officially advised to omit Japan from his itinerary since his personal security could not be assured.

### Eisenhower's farewell

Eight years in office proved a great strain on the Republican party, especially since it had failed to balance the budget, reduce the national debt, end the upward wage-price spiral, restore farm income, significantly cut taxes—all goals dear to the heart of the conservative wing. It had also failed to roll back the communists and restore the good old days of continental security for which even Dulles had often expressed a strong nostalgia.

When the time came to choose a candidate at the 1960 convention in Chicago, the conservatives were so fully in command of the party machinery that an internationalist like the Republican governor of New York, Nelson A. Rockefeller, who had won a brilliant victory in 1958 when most other Republicans were going down to crashing defeats, had already

been warned to stand aside. On the first ballot the convention named Richard M. Nixon for President. As a sop to the party liberals it chose Henry Cabot Lodge, United States delegate to the UN, as his running mate.

The Democrats, heartened by the Twenty-second Amendment which kept the still popular "Ike" from seeking a third term, had begun to look to 1960 even before the 1956 campaign. Many hats were in the ring; but after his extraordinary performance in a series of primaries, Senator John F. Kennedy of Massachusetts clearly overshadowed the opposition. At the Los Angeles convention he won on the first ballot. Fearful of the effects of the strong civil-rights stand of the party's northern wing and of Kennedy's Catholicism, the Democrats, in an attempt to hold the South, asked Senator Lyndon B. Johnson of Texas to run for Vice-President.

The campaign was highlighted by the first TV debates between presidential candidates, from which Kennedy seemed to have gained more than his opponent. Nixon suffered from "Ike's" merely lukewarm support and from his own checkered past. Kennedy's winning margin was a mere 113,000 out of a record 68.8 million votes cast. What probably saved him from defeat (when as popular a Protestant might have won an easy victory) was the solid support he received from Catholics and Negroes. At least 70 percent of such voters, according to reliable estimates, endorsed him. The first Catholic President, and at 43 also the youngest ever to be elected, Kennedy soon surrounded himself with young advisers pledged, like himself, to get the country moving again across "new frontiers."

On his part, seeking the "most challenging message I could leave with the people of this country," Eisenhower sharpened the warnings of the recent past in his famous "farewell speech" of January 17, 1961:

*This conjunction of an immense military establishment and a . . . permanent armaments industry of vast proportions . . . is new in the American experience. The*

## Election of 1960

ALASKA
HAWAII

**Electoral Vote**

Kennedy 303        Nixon 219

Byrd 15

total influence—economic, political, even spiritual—is felt in every city, every state house, every office of the federal government. We recognize the imperative need for this development. Yet we must not fail to comprehend its grave implications. . . .

In the councils of government we must guard against the acquisition of unwarranted influence, whether sought or unsought, by the military-industrial complex. The potential for the disastrous rise of misplaced power exists and will persist. We must never let the weight of this combination endanger our liberties or democratic processes. We should take nothing for granted . . . so that security and liberty may prosper together.

In his book *Waging Peace 1956-1961*, furthermore, the President offered his analysis of the "intrinsic dynamics" of this "almost overpowering" danger that had overpowered all his own organizational safeguards:

*Many groups find much value to themselves in constant increases in defense expenditures. The military services, traditionally concerned with 100 percent security, are rarely satisfied with the amounts allocated to them. . . .*

*The makers of the expensive munitions of war, to be sure, like the profits they receive, and the greater the expenditures the more lucrative the profits. Under the spur of profit potential, powerful lobbies spring up to argue for even larger munitions expenditures. And the web of special interest grows.*

*Each community in which a manufacturing plant or a military installation is located profits from the money spent and the jobs created in the area. This fact, of course, constantly presses on the community's political representatives—congressmen, senators, and others— to maintain the facility at maximum strength.*

Nor did the retiring general fail to add another warning: "In holding scientific research and discovery in respect, as we should, we must also be alert to the . . . danger that public policy itself could become the captive of a scientific-technological elite."

## IV   "The New Frontier is here"

### Kennedy without tears

Young as he was when he delivered his first State of the Union message in January 1961, John F. Kennedy had already served fourteen years in Congress, the last eight in the Senate. Judged by the standards of his presidential years, Kennedy's congressional record was in some respects worse than undistinguished. "There is an old saying in Boston," he once recalled, "that 'we get our religion from Rome and our politics at home.'" In the home of his father, Ambassador Joseph P. Kennedy, young Jack in the early forties had found "America Firsters" highly in favor, in the early fifties McCarthyites most welcome. It took time for the home environment, so congenial to his Irish Catholic constituency, to rub off the political aspirant.

In the late forties the young congressman consorted with the most malignant critics of his party's China policy. In 1950, in a talk at Harvard, his alma mater, he declared about the alleged communists in governments who presumably sold Chiang out: "McCarthy may have something." Later that year he helped carry the McCarran Internal Security Act through the House over Truman's veto. The Senate's condemnation of McCarthy in December 1954 found Kennedy, who had been elected to that body in 1952, in a hospital fighting for his life after spinal surgery. His absence absolved him from having to decide whether to vote for condemnation or not; and ever after, although under liberal pressure to do so, he manfully refrained from indicating how his vote might have gone. Perhaps he did not know. In another field, Kennedy's liberal supporters took what solace they could from his outstanding prolabor record, one not altogether disinterested since he represented a district with many wage earners.

824

Liberals had trouble with still other aspects of Kennedy's congressional behavior, including his willingness as late as 1957 to expose civil-rights workers to the mercies of all-white southern juries. When, the next year, Massachusetts sent Kennedy back to the Senate with a majority of 873,000 votes—by far the largest majority ever polled in any Massachusetts campaign—his illiberal record seemed to justify itself. Kennedy's election showing, oddly enough, also justified power-hungry liberals in jumping on the bandwagon. Their course was made easier, as Tom Wicker of the *New York Times* said in *Kennedy Without Tears,* by the Senator's "undue regard for Harvard and a craving for its approval." Few defeated candidates for Harvard's Board of Overseers presumed to try a second time, and few Catholics ever gained consideration. But Kennedy, after his rejection in 1955, "grimly ran again," Wicker writes, "and his election to the Board was a cherished triumph."

In 1956, Kennedy also had made an unsuccessful bid for the Democratic vice-presidential nomination, a setback that similarly strengthened his resolve to seek the presidency, his real goal, in 1960. His dallying with southerners on civil-rights legislation in 1957 has been excused as a quest for party unity on behalf of his candidacy. In his high-powered senatorial campaign of 1958, politics first felt the full force of Kennedy money and clan loyalty translated into an organized assault on the citadels of complacency and prejudice. It was really the proud family that was running Jack, with the goal of stunning recalcitrant party leaders into submission. That objective gained in spectacular fashion in Massachusetts, there remained the rest of the country to conquer. Despite all his congressional years, the young senator still lacked a national reputation. How was he to combat the profound public antipathy to his religion and the selfish resistance of party hacks? His chief asset, perhaps, was his engaging personality.

On January 2, 1960, Kennedy announced his candidacy for the topmost place on the party ticket, challenging any other Democratic aspirant to "submit to the voters his views, record and competence in a series of primary contests." If the nomination "ever goes into a back room," he said, "my name will never emerge." In the first half of 1960, usually in his wife's company, the Senator traveled over 65,000 miles in some twenty-five states and made more than 350 speeches. The results we know. Kennedy "outsmarted all the pros," said Tammany boss Carmine De Sapio. Stuart Symington, the pros' early favorite, acknowledged that Kennedy "had just a little more courage, . . . stamina, wisdom and character than any of the rest of us." No one was more willing than the victor to admit that he also had more money; yet he knew that some even richer men had tried the same course only to fail before the starting gun.

Kennedy's long contact with politics had been shallow enough to leave the glow of youth undimmed, the candor credible, the humor fresh, the modesty unfeigned. His infectious zest for life seemed only to have been heightened by a long history of personal sorrow that continued into the White House—by the violent deaths of young relatives and friends, the mental illness of a sister, his own questionable health and close brushes with eternity. He did not expect to live forever. "If someone is going to kill me," he would say in discussing security precautions with his aides, "they're going to kill me." Such fatalism, for him, only reinforced a native skepticism of absolutes, an eager acceptance of growth and change. Nixon, almost as young as himself, Kennedy said at the outset of the final campaign, "has the courage of our old convictions." But "the New Frontier is here, whether we seek it or not."

During the 1960 campaign, as his aide T. C. Sorensen tells the story, Kennedy learned that the father of the Negro leader Martin Luther King, Jr., had announced his support after having earlier decided to vote against Kennedy on religious grounds. " 'That was a hell of an intolerant statement, wasn't it?' said Kennedy.

'Imagine Martin Luther King having a father like that.' Then a pause, a grin and a final word: 'Well, we all have fathers, don't we.' " Kennedy really was unprepared for the presidency, but perhaps no more than most other successful bidders. By 1960 he had come far from "my father's house" and would come farther still.

### Youth at the helm

"Anybody who would spend $40 billion in a race to the moon for national prestige is nuts," General Eisenhower said after he had retired from the presidency. The new President, although at first as doubtful as his conservative predecessor, soon nurtured other ideas. In May 1961, under the heading "Urgent National Needs," he told Congress: "No single space project in this period will be more impressive to mankind" than that of "landing a man on the moon and returning him safely to earth." The following year, in a speech in Houston, Kennedy said: "The exploration of space will go ahead whether we join in it or not. . . . We mean to be a part of it—we mean to lead it." It was during Kennedy's administration that annual space appropriations soared over $5 billion.

The new administration, nevertheless, was soon brought down to earth by persistent domestic and world problems. The very first of these, an exceedingly critical one since the McCarthyite destruction of government morale and the widespread resignations following the Eisenhower loyalty order, was manning the administration. Kennedy's own youthfulness seemed to give hope and courage to the unprecedentedly youthful population of the entire world, and he soon surrounded himself with youthful advisors. The dynastic heir-apparent, his younger brother Robert, became Attorney-General with perhaps broader powers than any previous holder of that office. Robert S. McNamara, one of the statistical "whiz kids" of the Ford Motor Company, was named Secretary of Defense. His assignment

was, with the aid of computers, to bring Pentagon feuding under civilian control. McGeorge Bundy, Kennedy's Special Assistant for National Security Affairs, "the second smartest man I know," was said to have gone from Dean of Harvard to Dean of the World and probably outranked the official Secretary of State, Dean Rusk. Walter W. Heller, as Chairman of the Council of Economic Advisors, offset with his witty advocacy of Keynesian "new economics" the traditional attitudes of the Secretary of the Treasury, banker C. Douglas Dillon. "Ted" Sorensen, the boyish campaign head, as Special Counsel probably remained closer to the President than anyone but brother "Bobby."

Below these luminaries, the President sought a revivified civil service. Kennedy's victory, essentially one for northern cities, religious and racial minorities, big government, and internationalism, seemed to draw dissident conservatives more firmly together and more decidedly to the right. Both major parties had taken formal notice of the again-burgeoning Klan, the rising John Birch societies, and similar "hate" organizations that flooded Congress and the private mails with blood-curdling reports of the sellout of Americanism even by such respected figures as Eisenhower and Chief Justice Warren. Having overcome these elements in the campaign, Kennedy meant to keep them in their place. "Let it be clear," he stated at the outset, "that this Administration recognizes the value of dissent and daring, that we greet healthy controversy as the hallmark of healthy change. Let the public service be a proud and lively career."

### Domestic projects
### of the thousand days

Other domestic issues—the "clutter" of "unfinished and neglected tasks"—faced by the Kennedy administration had, by the early 1960s, assumed a familiar ring. Kennedy noted them in his first State of the Union message: the "squalor" of our cities; the vast overcrowding of our classrooms; the termination because of financial need of the education of "one-third of our most promising high

Wide World Photos

*"Freedom Riders" were first sent
into Alabama in May 1961 by Congress
of Racial Equality (CORE) to test
segregation laws and practices
in interstate travel. Illustration shows
Greyhound bus that carried first
Freedom Riders, after being set
afire by mob outside Anniston, Alabama.*

school graduates"; persistent recession resulting in the "highest peak in our history" of "insured unemployment"; the continuing decay of long-term "distressed areas"; the drain of American gold abroad, largely for military assistance, and the menace this held for the stability of the dollar; the neglect of growing numbers of indigent old people, of the indigent sick, and of others in need; the waste of natural resources as basic as our threatened water supply.

But all these issues paled before that of Negro equality, which Kennedy in 1961 failed to mention but which by the summer of 1963 rightfully dominated the headlines. The year 1963 marked the hundredth anniversary of the Emancipation Proclamation. Largely because thousands of Negroes had by then risen from their heritage of slavery to become part of the American middle class, the mass of the

black American population found the inspiration, the leadership, and even the economic leverage to seek first-class citizenship for themselves.

In February 1963, Kennedy proposed his first civil-rights legislation to Congress, which liberals branded "thin." A few weeks later mass demonstrations of blacks began in Birmingham, Alabama, and before the summer was over more than 800 cities and towns had seen peaceful protests, often in the face of dogs and fire hoses employed by police. The climax of the campaign came on August 28, when over 200,000 blacks and sympathetic whites marched on Washington "for Jobs and Freedom Now." In June the administration had beefed up its civil-rights proposals, but they languished in committee until 1964.

To the embarrassment of American foreign policy, the headlines of 1963 made known around the world the brutality with which Negro demonstrations often were suppressed. Yet the most remarkable feature of the equality movement was the restraint of whites and blacks alike. Leadership in the Negro nonviolence movement rested with Martin Luther King, Jr., a young minister from Atlanta barely in his thirties, but as the movement spread, as Kennedy feared, white resistance deepened; and when other Negro leaders challenged King's program, the prospect of violence grew.

In the 1950s and 1960s, as southern farming became increasingly mechanized, black sharecroppers and farm laborers displaced from the land flowed to northern cities in record numbers. Here the "upward spiral of mutual fear and corrosive hostility between white and Negro communities"—the words are those of John W. Gardner, who became Secretary of Health, Education, and Welfare in 1965—was matched by the downward spiral of hope and opportunity. Many businesses followed white, and white-collar, workers to safer urban areas and to the suburbs, leaving the urban ghettos ever more isolated and explosive. As the cities succumbed to the poverty and frustration of their new denizens, most of them unprepared for urban and for political life, the likelihood of congressional action to assist them diminished. A sign of the times was Congress's failure to create a Department of Urban Affairs on the Cabinet level, despite Kennedy's urging. The President's efforts to enlarge federal aid to education and to extend federal "medicare" to the aged also failed. But Kennedy's urgent pushing of these measures helped set the stage for their adoption under his successor.

## V Militarism at home and overseas

### Militarism and prosperity

"To get the country moving again" in the economic sphere, the "new economists" of the Kennedy administration explored every avenue for engaging the energies of the entire population and not simply those of the recently favored "private sector." Early in 1962, the President proposed a broad tax cut for consumers as one way to stimulate demand for goods. But this measure, like so many of his proposals, lay becalmed in Congress. One reason for congressional inaction was the marked business upswing in 1962 and 1963, following substantial new expenditures and appropriations for the space program, the related missile program, and other "national security" items. While the strength of the country in foreign affairs indubitably depended upon the strength of the domestic economy, it seemed to be increasingly true that the strength of the domestic economy depended on the volume of production of military hardware and associated material and the scale of military installations and personnel.

One particularly disconcerting aspect of this situation was the rapid acceleration of United States arms sales abroad. "Since 1962, when the current arms sales program began," Jack Raymond, the veteran *New York Times* Pentagon reporter, wrote in 1968, "Pentagon officials have been as aggressive as private arms merchants, with the result that the United States has sold over $11.1 billion worth of arms. In a speech . . . in the spring of 1966, the Pentagon official in charge of the sales program proudly estimated that it had yielded . . . 1.2 million man years of employment for companies throughout the country." Its needless drain on the economies of purchasing countries, especially poor countries in Africa and Latin America, and the internal repression and international insecurity it fostered among them, caused Congress in 1967 to make an effort to curtail this program. "However," Raymond concluded, "the sales of arms abroad continues to be a big—very big—business."

Kennedy as a senator had become by 1959 one of the most active opponents of the growing militarization of the foreign-aid program just when Khrushchev was launching his all-out economic offensive. As President, his efforts to reverse this trend were strengthened by his opposition as well to the military straitjacket of "massive retaliation" that so confined the Eisenhower-Dulles foreign policy of "deterrence." "We intend," he declared in July 1961, "to have a wider choice than humiliation or all-out nuclear action."

By then, Kennedy had already taken certain steps in pursuit of a more "flexible response." One experiment was the establishment of the Peace Corps, "a pool of trained men and women," as the President described it, "sent overseas . . . to help foreign countries meet their most urgent needs for skilled manpower." Created on a pilot basis by executive order in March 1961, the Peace Corps had done so well by September that Congress made it permanent.

In March 1961, Kennedy also outlined his plan for an Alliance for Progress with Latin

American nations, on the model of the Marshall Plan from which, with much resulting bitterness, as we have seen, they had been excluded. In August, at a general conference at Punta del Este in Uruguay, all Latin American countries but Castro's Cuba subscribed to the grandiose scheme envisioning an infusion of $100 billion in new capital in ten years, 80 percent of it to be supplied by the Latin Americans themselves.

The administration also had a "grand design" for Europe despite the lasting NATO strains. One objective of this program was Britain's entry into the European Common Market in order to strengthen the Atlantic Partnership in its confrontation with communism on the Continent begun under the Marshall Plan of 1947 (the enlarged Market was still only on the verge of attainment in mid-1971). A second was increased European participation in aid to poor countries on other continents in competition with the USSR and Red China (a goal only minimally gained). A third was expansion of United States trade with highly industrialized nations, especially Britain and those already in the Common Market. To further the last of these, Congress in October 1962 passed the Trade Expansion Act, enlarging the President's powers to reduce tariffs and otherwise liberalize the terms of international exchange. This was one means to circumvent the Common Market tariff structure, which gave members many advantages over nonmembers. Its effect was small compared to another more or less unforeseen outcome of the success of the Common Market—unprecedented private American investment in Common Market countries, where many United States firms built major plants run by highly trained American personnel.

The "flexible response," nevertheless was quickly shown to require more care and consideration than the administration at first lavished upon it. This demonstration arose from an unfortunate legacy of the outgoing administration's "roll-back" policy that caught the Kennedy team off balance before its own new look materialized. It also precipitated the most extreme provocation of the decade, which helped push military expenditures over the $50 billion mark in 1962 for the first time since the Korean war.

## Castro and Khrushchev

In one of his last acts as President, Eisenhower had broken off diplomatic relations with Cuba in protest against "a long series of harassments, baseless accusations, and vilifications." One of the accusations proved far from baseless. For nine months, as Castro had charged, about 1500 anti-Castro Cuban exiles had been secretly training in Guatemala under United States CIA men for an invasion of their island. Mass internal uprisings were certain to follow, their leaders said, on the heels of their arrival, leading to the overthrow of Castro's regime with their help.

Assured of the success of this misguided adventure by the Joint Chiefs of Staff and other personages he had inherited and by some of his "new frontiersmen" as well, the new President allowed it to proceed. In April 1961, in anticipation of American air support, the trainees with some Americans in the vanguard attempted to land at the Bay of Pigs, 90 miles from Havana. Air support, only wishfully talked of, was not forthcoming, and the assault instantly collapsed amidst recriminations that persisted years later. Over 1200 of the invaders were taken prisoner and held for almost two years.

From this triumph over his manifestly "imperialist" enemies, Castro moved ahead to make Cuba a more sturdy outpost of the Soviet regime, complete with Russian missile installations aimed at United States targets. In October 1962, Soviet strengthening of these installations almost led to "massive retaliation" and the nuclear holocaust that "flexible response" was intended to forestall. On October 22, Kennedy warned Khrushchev that he would not tolerate his "clandestine, reckless and provocative threat to world peace." War was never nearer; but the Soviets, recognizing the gravity of Kennedy's stand, promptly agreed to recall their ships on the high seas carrying more supplies for Cuba and to remove the offending missile bases.

Castro's performance helped kill what small chance for success the Alliance for Progress may have had. By 1963 it had become evident that countries below the border would find it impossible to carry out reforms at home sufficient to develop the broad-based capitalist economy the Alliance projected. Nor would the United States any longer wink at "anti-imperialists" with a popular following who might undertake even more fundamental social changes. This was made clear in Guatemala before the elections scheduled there in November 1963 in which Juan José Arévalo, a former President with a Marxist following and a strong record in agricultural reform, was the leading candidate. As one high-level Kennedy official said of Arévalo early that year: "I don't give a damn whether he is or is not a communist. He talks like a communist, he acts like a communist, and if he's elected he'll be soft on the communists." In March 1963, while CIA men at least turned the other way (some suppose they helped engineer the shift) President Miguel Ydígoras Fuentes was deposed by a military faction which directly installed the minister of defense as President, and the November elections were not held.

A mere two days before Kennedy's warning to Khrushchev over Castro the Chinese communists appeared to have invaded India at many points (although India also appears to have provoked the confrontation), and a general Asian war seemed to be in the offing just when the Cuban missile crisis reached its crest in the West. One month later, although meeting little effective opposition, the Chinese called off the war, but the threat to India persisted. The most striking feature of this conflict was the support the Soviets gave not to their fellow communists but to neutralist India. This policy dramatized the profound split in the communist camp that first became public knowledge in 1956 and now raised new hopes for a détente between the Soviets and the West.

These hopes were strengthened in July 1963, when the three nuclear powers, the United States, Britain, and the USSR, signed a fairly innocuous treaty pledging themselves to end nuclear testing which "causes radioactive debris" outside their own borders. They recognized that this was only a first step, as the preamble to the treaty said, toward "the speediest possible achievement of an agreement on general and complete disarmament under strict international control in accordance with the objectives of the United Nations." The three powers invited all others to sign the treaty. In the West, Germany had misgivings and France, eager for nuclear arms of her own, was openly hostile. In the East, Red China denounced the Soviets and the Western powers alike. In the United States itself, moreover, and no doubt in the USSR as well, armament rather than disarmament had gained the irreversible momentum of which Eisenhower had spoken in his farewell.

### The fatal dynamics of "flexible response"

Following the Bay of Pigs fiasco, according to Arthur M. Schlesinger, Jr., Kennedy declared he would never "be overawed by professional military advice again. . . . The first lesson [of the Bay of Pigs] was never to rely on the experts." Kennedy acted, instead, "to tighten his personal hold on the sprawling mystery of government." And yet, in December 1962, despite his own recent stirring success in Cuba, on reviewing his first two years in office, he acknowledged to the electorate on nationwide TV: "The responsibilities placed upon the United States are greater than I imagined them to be and there are greater limitations upon our ability to bring about a favorable result than I had imagined them to be. . . . It is much easier to make the speeches than it is finally to make the judgments."

Kennedy hoped to identify the country's power with its political ideals, its strength with it social values. At the same time, he said early in 1961, "we must never be lulled into believing that either [Russia or China] has yielded its ambitions for world domination." The tragic irony of his policy of "flexible response," with its "strategic pluralism," was that, while seeking political solutions to "limited" international provocations, he nevertheless felt obliged to build up the tactical power of the armed services, especially the army, the orphan of the Eisenhower administration's emphasis on massive air power alone. More than that, to insure that the absolute "deterrent" itself gained the "credibility" required to make it operative, thereby reducing the likelihood of extreme rather than "limited" provocation, he dared not impede the further rapid and continuous development of the instruments of the old "strategic monism," or "massive retaliation."

Secretary McNamara analyzed the dramatic dynamics of this predicament in a speech in September 1967:

*In 1961, when I became Secretary of Defense, the Soviet Union possessed a very small operational arsenal of intercontinental missiles. However, they did possess the technological and industrial capacity to enlarge the arsenal very substantially over the succeeding several years. Now, we had no evidence that the Soviets did in fact plan to fully use that capability. But as I have pointed out, a strategic planner ... must prepare for the worst plausible case and not be content to hope and prepare for the most probable. ...*

*Thus, in the course of hedging against what was then only a theoretically possible Soviet build-up, we took decisions which have resulted in our current superiority in numbers of warheads and deliverable megatons. But the blunt fact remains that if we had more accurate information about planned Soviet strategic forces, we simply would not have needed to build as large a nuclear arsenal as we have today.*

*Now let me be absolutely clear. I am not saying that our decision in 1961 was unjustified. I am simply saying that it was necessitated by the lack of accurate information.*

*Furthermore, that decision in itself—as justified as it was—in the end, could not possibly have left unaffected the Soviet Union's future nuclear plans.*

"This," McNamara said, "is a significant illustration of the intrinsic dynamics of the nuclear arms race," which, for all Kennedy's philosophical precautions, foiled his quest for "personal hold" on his government just as they foiled Eisenhower's organizational apparatus. Together with the new requirements of "flexible response," moreover, these dynamics gave that "dreadful momentum" to the reach and power of the Department of Defense and its industrial, scientific, and academic auxiliaries which dominated the economy and so deeply troubled Eisenhower personally. It also troubled growing numbers of Americans, especially American youths, who had been so strongly drawn to the Kennedy standard.

Through McNamara's strenuous efforts to bring the military under civilian dominance—"This place is a jungle—a jungle," he exclaimed after his first confrontations in the Pentagon—Kennedy at least was spared full exposure to the expertise of the Joint Chiefs. But to keep them at bay, McNamara himself leaned ever more heavily on his own experts, the so-called academic strategists topped by a "civilian General Staff," as greedy for power as the uniformed services themselves. "They seem to feel, with Mirabeau," complained Admiral Hyman G. Rickover, one of the least hidebound of the military, after long and frustrating experience with them, that "to administer is to govern."

One of McNamara's basic criteria in dealing with the demands of the uniformed services was "cost effectiveness." This statistical system for selecting weapons and strategy seemed to employ the most elaborate "data-processing" hardware—and a phenomenally large and costly civilian technical labor force to run it—to the exclusion of all the judgment and know-how, for what these were worth, of high-ranking field commanders. Charles J. Hitch, an economist who became McNamara's comptroller, acknowledged that "there will always be considerations which bear on the very fundamentals of national defense which are simply not subject to any sort of rigorous, quantitative analysis." Yet even one of the skeptics among Kennedy's top advisers admired "the definition of the 'options' in quantitative terms in order to facilitate choice."

The addition of the strategy of "flexible response" to that of "massive retaliation," by greatly multiplying Kennedy's "options," simply opened entirely new fields for the experts he deplored, drawing the Department of Defense and its auxiliaries ever more deeply into covert, clandestine interference with the American government and its citizens and with foreign governments and their subjects. Many of those involved in such activities were associated with "think tanks" on the model of the RAND ("R"-and-"D," for research and development) Corporation, first set up at the end of World War II by the Air Force as an adjunct of the Douglas Aircraft Company in Santa Monica, California, to project future air-space needs. RAND soon became the envy of the other services, which developed competitive agencies of their own. Many great universities under contract to the Department of Defense or to the Central Intelligence Agency (CIA) also succumbed to the lures of money and power, enlarging the danger, as one university president put it in 1965, of their becoming "institutions always for hire."

## Kennedy and Southeast Asia

Following Sputnik I, one of the vaunted functions of the novel intellectual factories became "thinking about the unthinkable," or shadow combat with the second nuclear power—that is, the USSR. But they also boasted of their "realism," the deadly quality of which eventually took the form of requiring the *doing* of unthinkable things to the "live examples" one such thinker wanted for the strengthening of war-game theory. Only "timidity," another said, held the government's hand off the "nuclear option" in such experiments. By contrast, McNamara himself testified in January 1963 before the House Armed Services Committee: "While it does not necessarily follow that the use of tactical nuclear weapons must inevitably escalate [as in the use of "strategic" nuclear weapons] into global nuclear warfare, it does present a very definite threshold, beyond which we enter a vast unknown."

Despite Kennedy's emphasis on developing *political* "options," the most conspicuous product of "flexible response" became the elaboration and application of the concept of "limited war," the Army's gambit for retrieving predominance from the Air Force by "bringing the battle back to the battlefield." After Korea, writes William W. Kaufmann, a former RAND social scientist and McNamara consultant, in his book *The McNamara Strategy*, "a great deal of debate [among the "academic strategists"] centered upon the desirability and feasibility of another such limited war. . . . Some of its students even maintained [of the Korean conflict] that without it, someone would have had to invent it."

While the academic debate went on—"The outcome of the debate remains inconclusive," Kaufmann wrote in 1964; "the dynamics of escalation are hardly better understood today than they were a decade ago"—the professionals began to act. In October 1961, as Kennedy's special military representative, General Maxwell D. Taylor went to South Vietnam to appraise the situation there under the Diem regime, with the result that the flow of American instructors, pilots, and other military personnel was greatly accelerated. By the end of 1962, after Taylor had become Chairman of the Joint Chiefs in August, the number of Americans in South Vietnam had reached 10,000. In June 1964, the general became President Johnson's ambassador to Saigon. At that time he was succeeded as head of the Joint Chiefs by another army man, General Earle G. Wheeler.

Vietcong activities in Vietnam made it a natural arena for the Army's demonstration of the values of "limited warfare" in a nuclear age; and while Kennedy at first resisted both the "overmilitarization" and "over-Americanization" of the war there, he was impelled by circumstances other than military pressure to countenance the growing military bent of American intervention. Ironically, the strongest impelling force was itself political—the continuing McCarthyite concern with "Asia First" and the China "tragedy," which made it hazardous for any administration, but especially for a Democratic one that had come into office by such a narrow margin, to manifest any tendency to revert to "appeasement" in this region. Kennedy felt the full strength of this position in his last meeting with Eisenhower before the inauguration, when the outgoing Republican warned him that, while he hoped to support the foreign policy of the new administration, any movement toward seating Red China in the UN would force him to return to public life to fight it.

A second Asian legacy of the Eisenhower administration was the struggle to control Laos, a country, according to Kennedy, not "worthy of engaging the attention of great powers," yet, according to Arthur M. Schlesinger, Jr., one on which, "in the first two months of his administration, he probably spent more time . . . than on anything else." In the end Kennedy decided that "we cannot and will not accept any visible humiliation over Laos." By May 1962 the Communist Pathet Lao controlled almost two-thirds of the small country, apparently with little popular opposition, and had forced Eisenhower's favored conservative Boun Oum government to flee to Thailand. To thwart any possible invasion there, Kennedy quickly dispatched protective naval and military contingents. This show of might helped bring about an agreement in July 1962 on a coalition government; but the Pathet Lao kept up its harassment of its partners and, more important, also kept open the path of North Vietnamese aid to the Vietcong in South Vietnam.

The American goal in South Vietnam, even more than in Laos, Kennedy said in July 1963, is the attainment of "a stable government . . . carrying on a struggle to maintain its national independence. We believe strongly in that. . . . For us to withdraw from that effort," he added, genuflecting more deeply than merited to the Eisenhower "domino theory," would "mean a collapse not only of South Vietnam but Southeast Asia. So we are going to stay there." In the succeeding months, American military assistance to the Diem regime soared, and the number of American military personnel edged toward 17,000, even though such stability as Diem's regime retained was promptly sacrificed by his savage assaults on the Buddhists, who made up most of the neutral opposition to the French-oriented

Catholic ruling class. As his attacks on the Buddhists spread, moreover, Diem's militancy against the Vietcong declined.

As early as 1954, although the highest echelons of military experts continued right up to the fall of Dienbienphu to forecast that "the French are going to win" (as, a decade later, they shamelessly forecast the always imminent yet somehow elusive American triumph), Kennedy had said, "I am frankly of the belief that no amount of American military assistance in Indochina can conquer . . . 'an enemy of the people' which has the sympathy and covert support of the people." The emergence of the Vietcong some years later apparently did not alter his conviction that "counterinsurgency" must fail "if its political objectives do not coincide with the aspirations of the people, and their sympathy, cooperation and assistance cannot be gained."

In keeping with these deeper feelings, Kennedy, in September 1963, declared of the South Vietnamese: "In the final analysis, it's their war. They're the ones who have to win it or lose it. We can help them as advisers but they have to win it." To improve the prospects of winning, South Vietnamese General Duong Van Minh, with American encouragement, on November 1, 1963, overthrew the Diem regime and shortly thereafter executed Diem and his brother. The new government (the first of nine in the next five years—such was the political stability the United States was gaining in South Vietnam) was accorded prompt American recognition, but by the time of Kennedy's assassination on November 22, it had won few military laurels.

On October 2, 1963, in the light of his new stand, Kennedy had McNamara and Taylor announce from the White House the administration's intention of withdrawing most United States forces from South Vietnam by the end of 1965. Whether the slain leader could have effected this withdrawal will never be known, but his own violent removal from power presented an opportunity to others less willing to follow where he had pointed. Within three weeks of the assassination, McNamara and CIA chief John A. McCone visited Saigon. On their return, on New Year's Day 1964, they announced that they had "told the [Duong] junta leaders that the United States was prepared to help . . . as long as aid was needed." This only seconded President Johnson's New Year's Eve promise to them of "the fullest measure of support . . . in achieving victory."

Thus was the stage set for clarification in the field of the "academic" debate over the "dynamics of escalation" of "limited wars."

### The onset of political assassination

In Europe, meanwhile, the wall the communists had built early in August 1961 separating East from West Berlin was still the scene of intermittent violence. In Africa, UN troops in the Congo succeeded in bringing about a precarious truce in December 1962. The UN, in financial straits largely because of the failure to receive payment of peace-keeping levies from the USSR and France, gingerly withdrew its forces in June 1964, but not without repeated warning of the still dangerous situation, which again almost immediately deteriorated.

In space, Russian scientists continued to set the pace. The big breakthrough came on April 12, 1961, when Major Yuri Gagarin successfully orbited the earth in a Soviet space capsule. On February 20, 1962, after preliminary flights in space by Commander Alan B. Shepard, Jr. (May 5, 1961) and Captain Virgil I. Grissom (July 21, 1961), Colonel John H. Glenn, Jr., became the first American to orbit the earth. In these years, weather and communication satellites also were successfully launched, while probes toward immensely distant Venus and Mars were conducted by both countries. The tantalizingly nearby (by space standards) moon, however, exerted the greatest pull after Lunik II struck its surface in October 1959 and Lunik III soon after sent back the first pictures of the dark side. Under Kennedy the American commitment to land a man on the moon by the end of the decade had become firm, and in July 1969 it was to be fulfilled (see p. 845).

Such remained the ambiguous state of the world and the nation in the summer of 1963. The previous November, 51 million Americans, the largest ever in a nonpresidential year, went to the polls and broke tradition by fully supporting the administration in power. The Republicans were surprised, as well, by Nixon's defeat in the California race for governor. In Pennsylvania, however, they found in William W. Scranton, and in Michigan in George Romney, two successful gubernatorial candidates who became aspirants for the 1964 presidential sweepstakes. Senator Barry Goldwater of Arizona and the liberal Governor Rockefeller of New York, as well as Nixon himself, however, remained the leaders in the contest to face the Democratic candidate. The assassination of President Kennedy in Dallas, Texas, on Friday, November 22, 1963, obscured for the time being who this candidate might be. The new President, Lyndon B. John-

833

*The assassination of President Kennedy in Dallas, November 22, 1963, showing Mrs. Kennedy climbing to car trunk to seek aid just after her husband was shot.*

United Press International

son of Texas, however, took office with a show of firmness that foretold for 1964 his own likely quest for the candidacy which he had vainly sought in 1960.

834

Kennedy's assassination threw the United States and most of the world into deepest mourning. If there had been any question earlier about the place of the United States as the leader of the free world, the free world's response to his passing answered this question resoundingly. But perhaps Fidel Castro put it best when, on learning the dreadful news, he blurted out in his excitable fashion to the French journalist Jean Daniel: "Everything is changed. The United States occupies such a position in world affairs that the death of its President affects millions of people in every country of the globe. . . . I'll tell you one thing; at least Kennedy was an enemy to whom we had become accustomed."

## For further reading

Many works cited for Chapter Thirty are valuable for this chapter as well. Insight into Eisenhower the man will be gained from K. S. Davis, *Soldier of Democracy* (1945), Eisenhower's war years' *Papers* (5 vols.), cited in Chapter Twenty-nine, his *Crusade in Europe* (1948), and his two volumes on the White House years, *Mandate for Change* (1963) and *Waging Peace* (1965). The following contemporary accounts by insiders or observers are revealing: R. J. Donovan, *The Inside Story* (1956), E. J. Hughes, *The Ordeal of Power* (1963), and Marquis Childs, *Eisenhower: Captive Hero* (1958). E. J. Dale, Jr., *Conservatives in Power: A Study in Frustration* (1960), is an able critique of administration economic policies. Herblock's contemporary cartoons, with text, in *Here and Now* (1955) and *Special for Today* (1958), offer telling comment. Several articles in *Fortune,* an organ of the so-called New Republicanism, also are illuminating, especially on the high hopes in the issues of February and March 1956 and on the growing disenchantment in the issue of July 1957. D. A. Frier, *Conflict of Interest in the Eisenhower Administration* (1971), is a scholarly dissection. The "efficiency" issue is well presented in Charles F. Fenno, Jr., *The President's Cabinet* (1959). See also Sherman Adams, *First-Hand Report* (1961). H. J. Morgenthau, "John Foster Dulles," in N. A. Graebner, ed., *An Uncertain Tradition* (1961), is excellent on the role of the Secretary of State in the administration. On social issues arising from the new economic environment and the Cold War, see the works cited for Chapter Thirty-three, to which we may add J. K. Galbraith, *The Affluent Society* (1958), and Lauren Soth, *Farm Trouble in an Age of Plenty* (1957).

H. M. Christman, *The Public Papers of Chief Justice*

*Earl Warren* (1966), contains the *Brown* decision of 1954 and other illuminating material. J. D. Weaver, *Warren, The Man, The Court, The Era* (1967), is an able biography. Loren Miller, *The Petitioners, The Story of the Supreme Court of the United States and the Negro* (1966), supplies essential background. A. P. Blaustein and C. C. Ferguson, Jr., *Desegregation and the Law, The Meaning and Effect of the School Segregation Cases* (1957), carries the story forward. W. F. Murphy, *Congress and the Court* (1962), deals with the legislative response. Anthony Lewis, *Portrait of a Decade, The Second American Revolution* (1964), is an outstanding "first-hand account of the struggle for Civil Rights from 1954 to 1964." The fate of integration in the same period is covered in Benjamin Muse, *Ten Years of Prelude* (1964). On certain aspects of the southern response see N. V. Bartley, *The Rise of Massive Resistance* (1969), Hodding Carter, *The South Strikes Back* (1959), and Robert Coles, *Children of Crisis, A Study in Courage and Fear* (1967). J. W. Anderson, *Eisenhower, Brownell, and the Congress* (1964), is a scholarly account of "the tangled origins of the Civil Rights bill of 1956–1957." D. M. Berman, *A Bill Becomes a Law: The Civil Rights Act of 1960* (1962), covers that measure. Staughton Lynd, ed., *Nonviolence in America: A Documentary History* (1966), and Richard Hofstadter and Michael Wallace, *American Violence: A Documentary History* (1970), supply useful background for these polarities. Martin Luther King, Jr., *Stride Toward Freedom* (1958) and *Why We Can't Wait* (1964), are parts of the testament of the slain Negro leader. For other works on the Negro revolution, see literature cited for later chapters.

To the works on McCarthyism cited for Chapter

Thirty, we may add J. L. O'Brian, *National Security and Individual Freedom* (1955), on the Eisenhower program; and on the Oppenheimer case, Lewis L. Strauss, *Men and Decisions* (1962), United States Atomic Energy Commission, *In the Matter of J. Robert Oppenheimer, Transcript of Hearing Before the Personnel Security Board* (1954), and P. M. Stern and others, *The Oppenheimer Case, Security on Trial* (1969). N. P. Davis, *Lawrence And Oppenheimer* (1968), offers a good introduction to the problems of scientific genius in a military age.

To the books on Cold War diplomacy and foreign relations cited in Chapter Thirty we may add for the Eisenhower years, besides the general's own books cited above, D. A. Baldwin, *Economic Development and American Foreign Policy 1943-1962* (1966); Arnold Wolfers, ed., *Alliance Policy in the Cold War* (1959); C. L. Sulzberger, *What's Wrong with United States Foreign Policy* (1959); W. A. Williams, *The Tragedy of American Diplomacy* (1959); Edmund Stillman and William Pfaff, *The New Politics: America and the End of the Postwar World* (1961); H. A. Kissinger, *Nuclear Weapons and Foreign Policy* (1957); and Herman Kahn, *On Thermonuclear War* (1960), an early "think-tank" product on the "unthinkable" balance of terror.

Edward Crankshaw, *Khrushchev, A Career* (1966), helps keep *Khrushchev Remembers* (1970), the Premier's controversial memoir, in perspective. M. L. Lasky, ed., *The Hungarian Revolution* (1957), affords moving documentation of one of the fruits of "liberation." On the Russia-China break, see D. S. Zagoria, *The Sino-Soviet Conflict 1956-1961* (1962), and John Gittings, *Survey of the Sino-Soviet Dispute . . . 1963-1967* (1968), which includes documents. On Middle Eastern issues, see J. C. Campbell, *Defense of the Middle East* (1960); Nadav Safran, *The United States and Israel* (1963); Anthony Eden, *Full Circle* (vol. III of *The Memoirs of Anthony Eden*, 3 vols., 1960-1965); Anthony Nutting, *No End of a Lesson, The Story of Suez* (1967); and Herman Finer, *Dulles Over Suez* (1964). For Latin American relations, see D. M. Dozer, *Are We Good Neighbors? Three Decades of Inter-American Relations 1930-1960* (1959). K. H. Silvert, ed., *Expectant Peoples, Nationalism and Development* (1963), supplies a fine introduction to poor nations, mostly new nations, in other parts of the world.

G. Coedès, *The Making of South East Asia* (1966), illuminates the long history of Vietnam and its neighbors. B. B. Fall, *The Two Viet-Nams, A Political and Military Analysis (1964),* and Robert Shaplen, *The Lost Revolution* (1965) and *Time Out of Hand, Revolution*

*and Reaction in Southeast Asia* (1969), reach somewhat less distantly backwards but are informative. Ellen Hammer, *The Struggle for Indochina 1940-1955* (1966), is a scholarly study of "Viet Nam and the French Experience." J. D. Montgomery, *The Politics of Foreign Aid, American Experience in Southeast Asia* (1962), is enlightening on neighboring nations as well as Vietnam. Publication of *The Pentagon Papers* in book form (1971) does not detract from the value of other books cited, both for the United States in Asia and militarism in Washington. On the deepening tragedy of American military involvement see below and works cited in Chapter Thirty-two.

The 1960 campaign is well covered in T. H. White, *The Making of the President* (1960), R. M. Nixon, *Six Crises* (1962), T. C. Sorensen, *Kennedy* (1965), and L. H. Fuchs, *John F. Kennedy and American Catholicism* (1967). R. J. Whalen, *The Founding Father, The Story of Joseph P. Kennedy* (1964), is a revealing introduction to "the family he raised to power." See also Tom Wicker, *Kennedy Without Tears, The Man Beneath the Myth* (1964) and *JFK and LBJ: The Influence of Personality Upon Politics* (1968). Especially valuable for the curtailed administration are Sorensen (above), and A. M. Schlesinger, Jr., *A Thousand Days, John F. Kennedy in the White House* (1965). Patrick Anderson, *The President's Men* (1968), is helpful on advisers. J. K. Galbraith, *Ambassador's Journal* (1968), by the President's friend and ambassador to India, shows the advantages of distance from the day-to-day White House hubbub. J. W. Gardner, ed., *To Turn the Tide* (1962), and A. Nevins, ed., *The Burden and the Glory* (1964), present short selections from Kennedy's statements, published in full in *Public Papers of the President of the United States, John F. Kennedy* (4 vols., 1962-1964). Some insight into Kennedy's failures with Congress are provided in J. M. Burns, *The Deadlock of Democracy: Four-Party Politics in America* (1963). His relations with the people through the press are discussed in H. W. Chase and A. H. Kerman, eds., *Kennedy and the Press: The News Conferences* (1965).

Kennedy's approach to the national economy is well presented in W. W. Heller, *New Dimensions of Political Economy* (1966), by his chairman of the Council of Economic Advisors. Independent views of economic organization and trends are presented in such works as Richard Caves, *American Industry: Structure, Conduct, Performance* (1964); and Eli Ginzberg and others, *The Pluralistic Economy* (1965). B. J. Wattenberg and R. M. Scannon, *This U.S.A., An Unexpected Family Portrait . . . Drawn from the Census* (1965), affords an exceptional survey of American society with many tables based on the 1960 census. The question of poverty in the affluent society was newly opened by Michael Harrington, *The Other America, Poverty in the United States* (1962), and further developed in Harrington's later works. Herman Miller, *Rich Man, Poor Man* (1964), offers valuable commentary on Harrington's thesis. See also Gunnar Myrdal, *Challenge to Affluence* (1963), and R. L. Heilbroner, *The Limits of American Capitalism* (1966). Oscar Lewis, *La Vida, A Puerto Rican Family in the Culture of Poverty—San Juan and New York* (1966), provides a good introduction to this anthropologist's work. "Cities," the subject of the entire September 1965 issue of *Scientific American*, offers a broad introduction to urban life in the sixties. See also Blake McKelvey, *The Emergence of Metropolitan America 1915-1966* (1968), with up-to-date bibliographical notes. Kennedy and Negro civil rights is discussed in some depth in Sorensen and Schlesinger (above) and in the works on education and the desegregation decision. Powerful black statements of the early sixties include James Baldwin, *Nobody Knows My Name* (1961) and *The Fire Next Time* (1963), and *The Autobiography of Malcolm X* (1964). See also J. H. Clarke, ed., *Malcolm X, The Man and His Times* (1969).

Roger Hilsman and R. C. Good, eds., *Foreign Policy in the Sixties* (1965), is a valuable anthology on worldwide relationships during the Kennedy years; Hilsman, *To Move a Nation* (1967), is a first-hand report on "The Politics of Foreign Policy in the Administration of John F. Kennedy." R. J. Walton, *The Remnants of Power, The Tragic Last Years of Adlai Stevenson* (1968), is outstanding on Kennedy and the UN. Tad Szulc and K. E. Meyer, *The Cuban Invasion, The Chronicle of a Disaster* (1962), offers interesting reporting on the Bay of Pigs. Elie Abel, *The Missile Crisis* (1966), does the same for Khrushchev's Cuban adventure. See also R. F. Kennedy, *Thirteen Days, A Memoir of the Cuban Missile Crisis* (1969). Lincoln Gordon, *A New Deal for Latin America: The Alliance for Progress* (1963), reflects the early high hopes. W. D. Rogers, *The Twilight Struggle, The Alliance for Progress and the Politics of Development in Latin America* (1967), recounts the intransigence of the difficulties. The ultimate failure is analyzed in Jerome Levinson and Juan de Onís, *The Alliance That Lost Its Way* (1970).

Urs Schwarz, *American Strategy: A New Perspective, The Growth of Politico-Military Thinking in the United States* (1966), provides a good short introduction to the military side of the military-industrial complex and its relation to modern warmaking. Maxwell D. Taylor, *The Uncertain Trumpet* (1959) and *Responsibility and Response* (1967), reveal some implications of such thinking for a leading general and diplomat. W. W. Kaufmann, *The McNamara Strategy* (1964), and R. S. McNamara, *The Essence of Security, Reflections in Office* (1968), are illuminating on the applications of such thinking. Philip Green, *Deadly Logic, The Theory of Nuclear Deterrence* (1966), affords a penetrating critique of "think-tank" thinking that goes well beyond simple deterrence itself. An example of such broader thinking is T. C. Schelling, *Arms and Influence* (1966). The place of science in this intellectual environment is examined in such books as Robert Gilpin, *American Scientists and Nuclear Weapons Policy* (1962), and H. L. Nieburg, *In The Name of Science* (1966). For works on the onset and extent of escalation of American involvement in the "limited war" in Vietnam see readings suggested for Chapter Thirty-two.

On Kennedy's assassination, see *A Concise Compendium of the Warren Commission Report* (1964); E. J. Epstein, *Inquest, The Warren Commission and the Establishment of Truth* (1966); and William Manchester, *Death of a President* (1967).

# Violent peace

Ever since that September day [1945] . . . not a single war has been declared . . . .
Yet violence and warlike episodes have not diminished in these
two decades . . . [nor] the bitter contest for supremacy between the power nations, the struggle
for independence in the colonies, the clashes over territory,
and the civil wars and insurrections against established governments.
(Carl and Shelly Mydans, The Violent Peace, 1968)

Willingness to incur the wrath and punishment of government
can represent the highest loyalty and respect for a democratic society.
(Mrs. Patricia Roberts Harris, member National Commission
on the Causes and Prevention of Violence, 1969)

The complaints of our young and disadvantaged are not directed
to the workings of small-scale enterprise . . . but . . . to the several hundred firms that . . .
exercise a significant amount of power . . . over vast numbers of . . . human beings.
(Morton Mintz and Jerry S. Cohen, America, Inc., 1971)

Future shock is the dizzying
disorientation brought on by the premature arrival of the future.
(Alvin Toffler, Future Shock, 1970)

Scientists' Timetable According to CBS
  1975—Biological agents to destroy an enemy's will to resist.
  1982—Artificial plastic and electronic organs for humans.
  1989—Primitive forms of life created in the laboratory.
  2007—Biochemicals to aid the growth of new organs and limbs.
(The Futurist, February 1967)

The future is, of course, always "guerrilla country" in which the unsuspected
and apparently insignificant derail the massive and seemingly invincible trends of today.
(Peter F. Drucker, The Age of Discontinuity, 1969)

FREEDOM MARCHERS AT WASHINGTON MONUMENT, 1963. (Robert W. Kelley photo,
LIFE Magazine, © Time Inc.)

1

2

1. TOKYO POLICE BATTLE RIOTERS, 1960. (Wide World Photos)   2. CAPTIVES OF REBEL SOLDIERS, Santo Domingo, 1965. (Wide World Photos)   3. MASKED BRITISH TROOPS CLASH WITH IRISH CATHOLICS in Londonderry, 1969. (Wide World Photos)   4. FRENCH SOLDIERS GUARDING ARRESTED MOSLEMS, Algeria, 1961. (Wide World Photos)   5. RED CROSS NURSES WITH SICK AND STARVING IBO CHILDREN, Nigeria, 1968. (Wide World Photos)   6. CIVILIANS ROUNDED UP DURING AMERICAL UNIT SWEEP of Vietnam village. (P. Jones-Griffiths photo, Magnum)

3

*There have been so many opportunities for war reportage
in the past two decades that some reporters and photographers
have virtually traveled the world from war to war ...
(Carl and Shelly Mydans, The Violent Peace, 1968)*

4

5

6

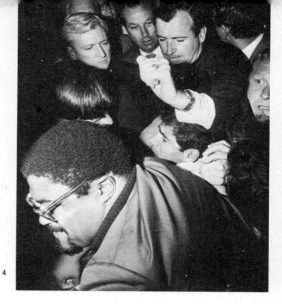

1

2

3

4

*The postures and expressions*
*of warfare have carried over into*
*our peacetime activities.*
*(Millard Daniels,* Redding Seminars, *1971)*

1. WALLACE CAMPAIGNERS, 1968. (Kubota photo, Magnum) 2.
HELL'S ANGELS and gear, 1967. (Wayne Miller photo, Magnum)
3. LAW ENFORCEMENT ON BERKELEY CAMPUS, California, 1969. (Lou de
la Torre photo) 4. SIRHAN SIRHAN SURROUNDED just after shooting
Robert Kennedy, 1968. (United Press International) 5. THE
FOOTBALL FRONT, Shea Stadium, New York City, 1969. (Ernest
Baxter photo, Black Star)

5

1. PILING JUNK. (Bruce Davidson photo, Magnum)
2. SHOOTING JUNK. (Steve Shapiro photo, Black Star)
3. THE OLDER GENERATION RESTING. (Franklynn Peterson photo, Black Star) 4. NASA ROBOT, 6 feet, 2 inches, 230 pounds, for determining stresses in astronauts' space suits. (United Press International) 5. GENERAL ELECTRIC'S "HARDIMAN," when attached to worker, enables him to lift 1500-pound load. (United Press International)

*Is a society a success if it creates conditions that impair its finest minds and make a wasteland of its finest landscapes?*
*(Stewart L. Udall, The Quiet Crisis, 1963)*

*. . . It is easy to be young. (Everybody is,*
*at first.) It is not easy*
*to be old. It takes time.*
*(May Swenson, "How to be Old," in To Mix with Time, 1963)*

*In [the] field of robotology . . . technicians have created . . .*
*computer-controlled humanoids capable of . . .*
*grimacing, smiling, glowering, . . . [doing] "everything but bleed."*
*(Alvin Toffler, Future Shock, 1970)*

1. WOMEN'S LIB, 1970. (Burt Glinn photo, Magnum) 2. RALPH NADER at Syracuse University, 1970. (Ron Sherman photo, Nancy Palmer Agency) 3. YOUNG MAN AT MIKES, FIRST EIGHTEEN-YEAR-OLD TO REGISTER for voting in New York City, 1971. (United Press International) 4. GIRL OFFERING NATIONAL GUARDSMAN A FLOWER during peace march, Washington, D.C., 1967. (Marc Riboud photo, Magnum)

*These chicks are our natural enemy....*
*It is time to do battle with them.*
*(Memo of Hugh Hefner, editor of Playboy, 1971)*

*They say on campus that getting a job*
*with Nader is "tougher than getting into Yale Law School."*
*(From Fortune, p. 147, May 1971)*

*The crisis on American campuses has no parallel*
*in the history of the nation.... This crisis has two components:*
*A crisis of violence and a crisis of understanding.*
*(Report of the President's Commission on Campus Unrest, 1970)*

# BOUND TO PLANET EARTH

In August 1966, just as Lunar Orbiter I cruised around the moon only 28 miles from its surface and took some 200 pictures—the first successful American enterprise of its kind—Walter Sullivan, science editor of the *Times,* raised this question in the *New York Times Magazine:* "What Earthly Use Is the Moon?"

After some very earthly answers in terms of the possible makeup of moon rocks and other surface materials, Sullivan speculated about the ultimate use to earthlings of the moon's low gravity and lack of air:

*As our knowledge of chemistry, metallurgy, and solid-state electronic devices becomes more advanced it is likely that many industrial processes will emerge that must be carried out in a deep vacuum. On the moon [where the natural] vacuum is more nearly complete than any achievable in ordinary laboratories, . . . that would mean out-of-doors and some have proposed that the moon may therefore become the home of specialized industries.*

Stretching his earthly imagination somewhat farther, Sullivan continued: "A lunar colony could be largely self-sustaining," for "studies of meteorites and observations of stellar spectra (which indicate the chemical composition of the stars) show that essentially the same elements, with the same properties, abound everywhere." Thus on the moon as on earth we may expect to find even those elements "required to generate nuclear energy," and others "that combine to form organic molecules . . ." from which, "with improved knowledge of chemical synthesis," could be made "proteins, carbohydrates and fats in special food factories."

All this may lie in the far distance, may even be visionary, Sullivan conceded: "The moon's chief immediate resource is knowledge. Written upon the face of the moon is much of the history of the solar system—a record steadily erased from the surface of the earth. . . . For a true understanding of the past—and some glimpse of the future—we must look to the moon."

By mid-1966, when employment for National Aeronautics and Space Administration (NASA) programs reached its peak for the sixties, and projects reaching as far ahead as an Apollo 20 mission had been largely paid for, the United States alone was looking to the moon to the tune of over $5 billion annually. This sum was exceeded in the federal budget, aside from such fixed commitments as interest payments and disbursements for social security, only by that for "National Defense," to which, indeed, it might justifiably have been added.

Nothing could be more rational, more intellectually orderly, than celestial exploration looking to moon landings and the light they may throw on the universe, past and future. Yet the terrestrial creature engaged in it remained simultaneously as irrational as he was rational, spontaneously as instinctive as he was intellectual, a being as likely as not, under any momentary provocation, to forgo his future, to forget his past. Would moon landings and moon settlements, then, transform this natural earth satellite into a *rational* extension of its planet, its vacuum filled with mankind intellectually modified for survival there—and here? Or would the earth itself revert to the condition of the moon?

Some scientists in the midsixties professed an extraordinary optimism about man and his chances. In an age of cascading scientific, man-made change, they said, man himself must also change, even, according to the biophysicist John R. Platt, in "emotional reactions and social behavior." The eminent behavioral physiologist Konrad Lorenz observed in 1966 in his book *On Aggression*:

*We know that, in the evolution of vertebrates, the bond of personal love and friendship was the epoch-making invention created by the great constructors when it became necessary for two or more individuals of an aggressive species to live peacefully together and to work for a common end.*

Lorenz then confidently conjectured that space might inspire a similar invention for societies of the aggressive species: "I believe," he wrote, "that the tremendous and otherwise not quite explicable public interest in space flight arises from the subconscious realization that it helps to preserve peace." Lorenz added:

*I agree with Dr. [J.] Marmor's assertion that modern war has become an institution, and I share his optimism in believing that, being an institution, war can be abolished.*

Others perhaps too close to war, too removed from science and space, found it harder, in the sixties, to yield to what William James before both world wars called "the will to believe." They found it hardest to build hopes on what James also called war's "moral equivalents," celestial or terrestrial. U Thant, Secretary-General of the United Nations, was one of the least sanguine. In the introduction to his annual report for 1965–1966, he wrote:

844

*Generally speaking and as reflected by positions taken in the United Nations, the powerful nations have not during this period shown themselves able to rise above the suspicions, fears and mistrust that spring from their different ideologies and from their different conceptions of the best interests of the rest of the world; nor the rich nations above their concern for the continuation of their own prosperity; nor the poor nations above the dead weight of their chronic poverty and their anachronistic social structures.*

Some believed U Thant's pessimism as excessive as the scientists' optimism. Yet by the midsixties "economic development" had encountered discouraging setbacks—in the assisting countries largely because of its subordination to primarily military objectives; in the assisted countries largely because of the disheartening corruption characteristic of "anachronistic social structures." By 1966, in fact, a "development weariness" seemed to have set in which forced the congenital optimists of that decade to scan the seventies for new hope. Early in 1968 the UN Economic Commission for Latin America deplored the "weak development performance there," and declared that "scant progress was made in the living conditions of the population." At the same time the UN Conference on Trade and Development in Asia collapsed after eight weeks of futile negotiations. "The results were denounced . . . as meaningless" by the representatives of the rich and poor nations alike, according to press reports.

Within the "developed countries" themselves, moreover, the "democracy of the automobile" and of consumer credit in Europe, the democracy of desegregation and of higher education in America—each encountered "backlash" resistance. Many Europeans feared the growing mechanization of their society—or "Americanization," as they often called it; many Americans feared the growing "socialization" of theirs. The unprecedented list of individual leaders murdered in the United States, beginning with the assassination of President Kennedy, also gave optimists pause, while the social violence, hatred, and absence

of commitment all gave pessimists support. "Our cities have become armed camps," said one federal report in 1969. Segregation in the nation's public schools is at a twentieth-century peak, said another. Welfare lists have grown stratospheric, said a third. The conscienceless pollution of air and water soon will make the land uninhabitable, added a fourth. The $35 billion spent on space exploration represented warped priorities, said a fifth.

Finally, war seemed hardly on the verge of being abolished; indeed, after the fateful American "escalation" of the war in Vietnam in February 1965, war with new weapons and new tactics seemed to have grown uglier and more insupportable than ever.

Nor could this dark prospect on earth be attributed to any lack of space competition and space progress. Fatal mishaps in the space programs of the United States and the Soviet Union in 1967 appeared to have dampened the ardor of both contestants for moon research and moon landings. A year later, nevertheless, two unmanned Soviet spacecraft, Zond 5 in September and Zond 6 in November, were for the first time brought successfully back to earth after orbiting the moon. Then, early in the morning of December 24, 1968, "in the most far reaching voyage of the space age—or any previous age," as the *New York Times* put it, the American spaceship Apollo 8, commanded by Colonel Frank Borman of the air force, a veteran astronaut, went into orbit around the moon. This flawless flight took it within 70 miles of the desolate celestial sphere, from whose orbit the astronauts then broke free to return to earth.

Apollo 9, in March 1969, commanded by air force Colonel James A. McDivitt, and Apollo 10, that May, commanded by air force Colonel Thomas Stafford, first tested in space the lunar module (LM) which was to land on the moon and then return to dock with the orbiting command ship.

Even while Apollo 10 was aloft, Apollo 11, commanded by a civilian, Neil A. Armstrong, accompanied by Colonel Edwin E. Aldrin, Jr., and Lieutenant Colonel Michael Collins, both of the air force, was being readied at Cape Kennedy for the epochal moon-landing adventure. Blastoff came at 9:32 A.M., Eastern daylight time, Wednesday, July 16, 1969, after President Richard M. Nixon had declared the Monday following Sunday's scheduled landing a national holiday to mark the "moment of transcendent drama." The drama was played on schedule, when Armstrong's LM, with Aldrin along (while the younger Collins navigated the command ship), came down on a level rock-strewn plain on the arid Sea of Tranquility at 17 minutes, 40 seconds past 4 P.M., Eastern daylight time, Sunday, July 20. "The Eagle has landed," said their message home to the NASA center at Houston, Texas. About six and a half hours later, 56 minutes and 20 seconds past 10 P.M., Eagle's head passenger, Neil Armstrong, at last set foot on the moon's "very, very fine grained surface." "That's one small step for man, one giant leap for mankind," Armstrong declared.

Aldrin soon followed the commander to the surface for their moon walk and rock-sample collecting. Monday, July 21, 1:55 P.M., 21 hours and 37 minutes after landing, Eagle blasted off the moon. At 5:35 P.M., some 69 miles from that sphere, she rejoined Collins's spaceship for the voyage home. Splashdown, only 11 miles from aircraft carrier *Hornet,* the recovery ship in the Pacific, came at 12:50 P.M., Thursday, July 24. For two years thereafter Lorenz's "tremendous and otherwise not quite explicable public interest in space flight" seemed to diminish. Even the first spectacular moon landing, in fact, fathered misgivings on earth. Babette Deutsch caught some of man's ambivalence toward this feat in her poem "To The Moon, 1969":

> You are not looked for through the smog,
>   you turn blindly
> Behind that half palpable poison—you
>   who no longer
> Own a dark side, yet whose radiance falters,
>   as if it were fading. . . .

> Once, it was said, the cry: "Pan is dead!
>   Great Pan is dead!"
>   shivered, howled through the forests:
>   the gentle
> Christ had killed him.
> There is no lament for you—who are silent
>   as the dead always are.
> You have left the mythologies,
>   the old ones, our own.
> But, for a few, what has happened
>   is the death of a divine Person,
>   is a betrayal, is a piece of
> The cruelty that the Universe feeds,
>       while displaying its glories.

The spectacular success of the Apollo 15 mission, July 26 to August 7, 1971, nevertheless may have restored and enlarged the excitement of the space program. Commanded by Colonel David R. Scott of the air force, Apollo 15 carried not only a more sophisticated LM but Rover I as well, a four-wheeled

845

*Apollo 15's Lieutenant-Colonel Irwin
and Rover I on moon,
with Mount Hadley in background.*

NASA

vehicle for travel on the moon. After one day's 7-hour and 13-minute excursion, Scott and his companion, air force Lieutenant-Colonel James B. Irwin, made such remarkable finds that Gerald D. Griffin, the flight director at NASA headquarters in Houston, exclaimed: "We have witnessed the greatest day of scientific exploration that we've ever seen in the

space program." Additional exploration added so much to the astronauts' discoveries that the full scientific impact of the mission would not be known for some time.

## I  "The Great Society"

*LBJ's succession year*

Few Presidents in American history had had such long careers in down-to-earth politics and self-help before entering the White House as Lyndon B. Johnson and Richard M. Nixon, the inheritors of space-age triumphs. "By political background, by temperament, by personal preference," writes Philip Geyelin in his perceptive book *Lyndon B. Johnson and the World* (1966), LBJ "was the riverboat man. He was brawny and rough and skilled beyond measure in the full use of tricky tides and currents, in his knowledge of the hidden shoals. He was a swashbuckling master of the political midstream—but only in the crowded, well-traveled familiar inland waterways of domestic politics. . . . He was king of the river and a stranger to the open sea."

Although he had difficulties with the bereaved Kennedy family on the day of the assassination, Johnson swiftly made the transition from Vice-President to President. In this he was aided by the loyalty of top Kennedy men, all of whom stayed on. Little time elapsed before LBJ began working his old magic with Congress, speeding the progress of strong Kennedy bills for the prosperity tax cut and civil rights.

At his last news conference, Kennedy said of the coming session of the Eighty-eighth Congress: "I am looking forward to the record of this Congress, but . . . this is going to be an 18-month delivery." It was only a few months after that, on February 26, 1964, that President

Johnson signed the tax bill providing cuts of $11.5 billion, and significantly reducing the withholding rate from 18 to 14 percent. Only a few months later, on July 2, he signed the Civil Rights Act. James Farmer, the militant black leader of the Congress of Racial Equality (CORE), said this measure was an "act of goodwill and reconciliation" between blacks and the white community, following the cruel summer of 1963. But Farmer warned that "there will be no breathing spell on demonstrations. . . . We will continue to use our body and spirit to secure . . . the reality of equality."

The most sweeping civil rights act in American history, the new law enlarged *federal* power to protect voting rights, to provide open access for all races to public facilities, to sue to speed up lagging school desegregation, and to insure equal job opportunities in businesses and unions.

In promoting the Civil Rights Act in his first State of the Union message in January 1964, Johnson said: "Unfortunately, many Americans live on the outskirts of hope, some because of their poverty and some because of their color, and all too many because of both." To raise the hopes of such people, he proposed a new measure of his own, an "unconditional" declaration of "war on poverty in America." This war Congress also endorsed, in August 1964, when it appropriated almost $950 million for ten separate antipoverty programs to be supervised by the Office of Economic Opportunity set up by the bill as part of the Executive Office of the President. Key features included a Job Corps to train underprivileged youths for the labor market; a work-training program to employ them; an adult education program; a program to make or guarantee loans to establish or strengthen small businesses; and a "domestic peace corps" (officially, Volunteers in Service to America, VISTA) to enlist the privileged on behalf of the poor.

The rapid tempo of far-reaching change under the new administration was kept up by the Warren Court. In June 1964, in a 6 to 3 decision in *Reynolds* v. *Sims,* the Chief Justice, speaking for the majority, declared that both houses of state legislatures "must be apportioned on a population basis" in order that citizens gain the constitutional guarantee of "equal protection of the law." This decision appeared to be a blow to rural areas which dominated state senates. At the same time it gave cities and the fast-growing suburbs the potential of unchecked legislative power. By 1968 most states had reapportioned their legislatures more or less in conformity with the Court's 1964 ruling and subsequent decisions and congressional action.

On October 16, 1964, Nikita Khrushchev suddenly was ousted from power in the USSR, to be succeeded as premier by Alexei Kosygin and as party secretary by Leonid Brezhnev. That Khrushchev was not disgraced or executed showed that the Russians had made some little progress of their own in achieving peaceful successions.

Yet the USSR remained for some time thereafter ridden by uncertainty, especially over relations with Red China. The conflicts in the communist camp may have increased the likelihood that one or the other of the great dictatorships would embark on new foreign military adventures. But their domestic problems and their strained relations may also have held them back. In any case, the communists' dilemmas underlay in part President Johnson's willingness to risk escalating the Vietnam War after his landslide victory in November.

## The Johnson landslide

Kennedy's assassination while on a party fence-mending mission in Dallas rocked the Republican party as much as it did the Democrats, the country, and the world. The election campaign of 1964 had in fact already begun, with the assumption by both parties that Kennedy would be the Democratic candidate. His removal left the Republicans without a clear target. It did not faze Barry Goldwater and his backers, however. As early as June 1963, Goldwater spoke confidently of winning the Republican nomination. "You see," he said then, "I have one advantage. I've done my political homework. I've spent the last 5½ years traipsing around the country helping precinct chairmen elect candidates and raise money." Goldwater's determination to end Republican "me-tooism" did not frighten the many party veterans who secretly shared his views. "I will offer a choice, not an echo," he said in announcing his candidacy in January 1964. "This will not be an engagement of personalities. It will be an engagement of principles." Goldwater soon lost a series of primaries, but he won the big one in California early in June, gaining that state's 86 delegates by defeating Rockefeller. In states where conventions rather than primaries ruled, his "homework" paid off handsomely.

Immediately following Rockefeller's California defeat, a frantic stop-Goldwater movement was launched, with Pennsylvania's liberal Republican Governor Scranton the chief hope. Even after being warned by Eisenhower of the dangers of an anti-Goldwater "cabal," Scranton persisted in seeking the nomination. But at the national convention in San Francisco in July Goldwater won on the first ballot. "Extremism in the defense of liberty is no vice," he said in his acceptance speech; "moderation in the pursuit of justice is no virtue"—observations that brought "amazement and shock" to the liberals.

In June 1964, segregationist Governor George C. Wallace of Alabama entered the presidential race by running in a number of Democratic primaries. He did well enough to frighten many already worried by Goldwater;

847

but the latter's nomination deprived Wallace of the conservative support he sought. When the Democrats met at their convention in Atlantic City in August, Johnson's nomination was a foregone conclusion, and after a spirited contest for LBJ's nod, Senator Hubert H. Humphrey of Minnesota won the ticket's second place.

The campaign itself gradually deteriorated into a conflict of personalities rather than of principles, despite Goldwater's boast. When it was over, the Fair Campaign Practices Committee declared: "Rarely have the reputations of two opponents for the Presidency been pried by so many into the stereotypes of maniac and thief." In the balloting, Goldwater scored only in Alabama, Georgia, Louisiana, Mississippi, and South Carolina—George Wallace country—and in his home state of Arizona. His popular vote was 27,176,873, his electoral vote 52. Johnson's popular vote of 43,128,918 gave him 61 percent of the total, surpassing even FDR's record showing in 1936. His electoral vote was 486. The Republican party seemed finished; yet it was to have a significant revival in 1966, and in 1968 completed its comeback by regaining the presidency. The election of Richard M. Nixon that year reflected a remarkable personal comeback as well.

### "Great Society" legislation

During the 1964 campaign, columnist James Reston wrote of LBJ: "On the platform, . . . when he is at his shouting best, arms waving like a helicopter, he not only commands but almost stuns his audience." Johnson's platform fury was carried into closed-room confrontations as well. When he was Majority Leader of the Senate, a witness recalled his "monumental chewing-out" of his long-time loyal aide George Reedy: "He was using language that I had never heard one human being use to another." A Washington correspondent reported of a second Johnson aide that "over the years Johnson systematically broke him down, destroyed him, left him a shell of what he had been." Patrick Anderson, a Texan who worked in the administration, wrote later of "the most conspicu-

ous fact about Johnson's staff: its ceaseless turnover."

At the same time, it must be noted that few Presidents kept on, and kept on for so long, so many of a predecessor's Cabinet members, notably Rusk, Dillon, and McNamara in State, Treasury, and Defense. Major holdovers, perhaps their equal in influence and power if just below them in rank, included such congenial war hawks as McGeorge Bundy and Walt W. Rostow.

In November 1961, after nearly a year in office, Kennedy had written: "There has been a growing recognition that we must fit our power to our responsibilities." Only a year later, as we have seen, he acknowledged that it might perhaps be the other way around, that we must fit our responsibilities to our power. As President, Johnson's experience seemed to run in the opposite direction. In his first State of the Union message as an elected Chief Executive, in January 1965, he said, "We will not, and should not, assume it is the task of Americans alone to settle all the conflicts of a torn and troubled world." Yet, a year later, on the same occasion, he said, "This nation is mighty enough—its society is healthy enough—its people are strong enough—to pursue our goals in the rest of the world while still building a great society here at home."

The "Great Society" became the central theme of LBJ's first message to the Eighty-ninth Congress that convened in January 1965. When that Congress terminated its business in the fall of 1966, it had made one of the most constructive records in history—too constructive, indeed, for many Americans who, in the by-elections of November 1966, shocked the Democrats by undermining their domination of House and Senate and the governorships of the states. One of the most extraordinary Republican victories was that of the movie actor Ronald Reagan, a conservative political neophyte, over the veteran liberal Democrat Edmund G. ("Pat") Brown, for the governorship of California, the new number-one state in the Union. Reagan's campaign was based mainly on the administration's excessive "interventionism," with interventionism on behalf of the Negro an important "backlash" factor but not necessarily the predominant one.

The first of the striking new measures of the Eighty-ninth Congress, adopted in April 1965, was the Elementary and Secondary Education Act, which provided $1.3 billion in federal aid to all pupils in school districts. By earmarking these funds for pupils instead of for schools directly, Congress was able to include those who attended parochial as well as public institutions, thereby circumventing for the time being constitutional issues on the separation of church and state (the Supreme Court disallowed this distinction in 1971) and quieting the powerful parochial-school lobby, which had helped defeat Kennedy's education bill. Later in 1965 Congress also appropriated $2.3 billion for federal loans to college students and other aid to higher education.

The United States Office of Education, meanwhile, as a condition for federal aid under this act, for the first time demanded proof rather than paper promises that, beginning with the school term of 1966-1967, desegregation of classrooms both for students and for teachers had been undertaken in good faith. Southern governors rebelled against the new "guidelines" for federal aid, declaring that no less than 200 school districts would reject the federal standards. But the Office of Education, strengthened by a United States Circuit Court decision in December 1966 requiring rapid desegregation under the guidelines, stuck to its guns and soon registered significant increases in the number of blacks going to school with whites in the South.

The Office of Economic Opportunity, in turn, in the summer of 1965, began both the Head Start and Upward Bound programs, manned mainly by young volunteers. Head Start was designed to help pre-school-age youngsters from deprived families to enter kindergarten or first grade. Upward Bound was to prepare talented, poverty-stricken youths for college by overcoming psychological and social disabilities.

A second far-reaching measure of the Eighty-ninth Congress was the Voting Rights Act, signed by the President on August 6, 1965. The failure of certain southern states to enforce the voting provisions of the Civil Rights Act of 1964 had brought the resumption of Negro demonstrations that James Farmer promised. These took place first in Alabama, particularly in the town of Selma, where on February 1, 1965 Martin Luther King, Jr., and 770 other Negroes were arrested. Early in March, Alabama state troopers and auxiliaries, using tear gas and whips, frustrated an attempted civil-rights march from Selma to Montgomery, the state capital. After President Johnson, on March 20, federalized the Alabama National Guard and ordered it to protect the marchers (Governor Wallace having earlier refused to do so), the procession of some 25,000 blacks and sympathetic whites from all over the country began. The night the march ended, one white woman participant was killed by Klan gunfire and soon after a Boston minister was slain. Their deaths enlarged the decade's toll of political activists.

Congress responded to the evident need with the Voting Rights Act. This measure suspended all literacy tests and other devices still used in certain southern states and in districts in a few others from Alaska to Maine to keep voting lily white. It also empowered "federal examiners" in effect to register all who qualified simply under age, residence, and objective educational requirements. By November over half a million Negro voters had been added to the rolls in five deep southern states, and their number soared after March 7, 1966, when the Supreme Court in *South Carolina* v. *Katzenbach* unanimously upheld the major provisions of the legislation.

Although the Twenty-fourth Amendment to the Constitution, ratified January 1964, abolished the poll tax in federal elections, certain states failed to enforce the ban or quickly adopted substitute voter taxes. Some also retained the poll tax for state elections. In April 1965, the Supreme Court unanimously upheld the absolute ban imposed by the amendment,

850

and declared as well that "no equivalent or milder substitute may be imposed." The Voting Rights Act of 1965, in turn, directed the Attorney-General to start suits against the surviving poll taxes in *state* elections, and Nicholas deB. Katzenbach, Robert Kennedy's successor as Attorney-General, initiated such suits the day after the act was signed. The last of the poll taxes was killed by a 6 to 3 vote of the Warren Court, March 17, 1966. By then a new drive to register the full 2 million eligible blacks in eleven southern states was underway, while many black candidates for office soon appeared on the ballots.

A third far-reaching congressional achievement was the adoption of the "medicare" amendments to the Social Security Act, which the President approved on July 30, 1965. These amendments, a victory for the aged over the relentless lobbying of the American Medical Association, provided hospital insurance and certain posthospital care for virtually all Americans on reaching the age of 65, although in anticipation of the expanded coverage of the Social Security Act itself, the new laws stipulated that after 1968 only those under social security would receive the hospital insurance. This insurance was to be paid for out of compulsory increases in social security taxes. A second part of the new program provided a voluntary system of medical insurance covering doctor bills, diagnosis procedures, and other medical services and supplies. This insurance was to be available to all over 65 who agreed to pay $3 per month for it.

Other notable domestic legislation of the Eighty-ninth Congress included a new immigration act terminating the discriminatory national-origins quota system (see p. 661); special assistance legislation for the redevelopment of the eleven depressed states in "Appalachia"; acts to promote the beautification of highways, the purification of smog-laden air, and the restoration of polluted waterways; a constitutional amendment covering the presidency during the incumbent's disability (see Amendments in the Appendix); and acts creating two new departments on the Cabinet level: Housing and Urban Affairs (September 1965) and Transportation (October 1966).

In addition, massive new appropriations were made for older "Great Society" programs, including the war on poverty and the regeneration of cities. Both goals were sought by the controversial Model Cities Act, passed in October 1966. The main purpose of this measure was to promote improvement of the entire urban environment by setting up "Model Cities" demonstrations in certain older metropolises and model new cities in selected areas.

## Downward from Watts

When the Eighty-ninth Congress adjourned in October 1966, the American economy had enjoyed six solid years of extraordinary economic expansion, pushing the annual gross national product almost to $740 billion, employment almost to 73 million persons. Thus, the brilliant legislative record was underpinned by a record-smashing prosperity. Yet deep social dissatisfaction seemed to darken the hue of good times and good prospects. Young persons and black persons still found it hard to get jobs or to take satisfaction in other aspects of American domestic success. Life on family farms, moreover, remained dreary, while city dwellers were exposed to unprecedented violence and fears.

Two situations in particular intensely aggravated the general malaise made evident in the 1966 elections. One was the sharp deterioration in race relations; the second, the sharp escalation of the Vietnam War. "We have become so overwhelmed in our troubles—terribly real troubles like race and Vietnam," Edwin L. Dale, Jr., the *New York Times* Washington economics reporter, wrote in November 1967, "that the blessing of prosperity has slipped from our vision. In some circles, it is almost a word of opprobrium."

An early sign of the "Great Society's" failure to deal with the question of blacks among whites appeared with the spread of large-scale Negro demonstrations to northern metropolises, starting with the murderous riots in the Watts ghetto of Los Angeles in mid-August 1965. Thirty-five persons died, and property damage soared over $100 million.

Watts was a stunning blow to the "Great Society" idea. "The burning, looting and violence of Watts," Darwin W. Bolden of the Interracial Council for Business Opportunity wrote in January 1970, "drove a wedge through the heart of the nation, dividing black from white and opening a wound for which we still seek sutures." Later in 1965 and in 1966, similar rioting occurred in the Harlem district of New York and in Chicago, San Francisco, and other cities. These events further exposed the deprivation and desperation of the black slums and slum dwellers as well as the savage determination of urban whites in defending their own recent social advances.

In the summer of 1967 racial rioting struck no fewer than sixty-seven cities across the nation. In Newark, New Jersey, where black unemployment rates ran spectacularly high and ghetto housing shortages were among the most acute in the country, the riots of July 12–17 took twenty-five lives. Rioting a week later in Detroit, Michigan, took forty-three lives; and the more than 4000 fires set there pushed the toll of property losses above even that of Watts. The violence in Detroit defeated all pacification efforts until for the first time in twenty-four years—in fact, since the 1943 Detroit race riots—federal troops were called for by a governor to restore civil order. Army tanks on Detroit streets adorned newspapers around the world that summer, *Pravda* in Moscow running pictures of the event on page one.

Negro efforts at self-help in enforcing the "Great Society's" Voting Rights Act of August 1965, in turn, spawned new violent confrontations in the South. The most far-reaching of these took place in Mississippi during the "Meredith March" of June 1966.

James Meredith, a black student whose admission to the University of Mississippi in 1962 had led to such fighting and harassment that he soon withdrew, returned to the state

on June 5, 1966 for a 220-mile "pilgrimage" from the Tennessee border to the capital at Jackson. His object was to demonstrate to the 450,000 unregistered Mississippi adult blacks that they need no longer fear murder for attempting to sign up and cast their ballots. Only a day later, June 6, Meredith was struck three times by a shotgun blast while on the pilgrimage route. Police promptly seized his white assailant and charged him with assault with intent to kill.

Meredith's wounds, while superficial, were sufficiently serious to remove him from the march, and on June 7 three topmost black leaders announced that the pilgrimage would be resumed promptly, and on a more ambitious basis. These were the Reverend Martin Luther King, Jr., of the Southern Christian Leadership Conference; Floyd McKissick, of the Congress of Racial Equality (CORE); and Stokely Carmichael, of the Student Non-Violent Coordinating Committee (SNCC), an interracial group. The marchers, now about 1000 strong, altered the initial route in order to visit more Mississippi towns, and within two weeks they succeeded in registering about 4000 black voters in that state. On June 21, a white mob attacked the marchers at Philadelphia, Mississippi, but they persisted until they reached Jackson at last, on June 26, when they held a rally attended by about 15,000 persons.

The violence along the march route aggravated the growing differences among the three black leaders, especially on two basic issues: (1) nonviolence in the Negro campaign for first-class citizenship, to which Dr. King, the most eminent of the three, was dedicated, but from which the others dissented; and (2) "black power," with the abandonment of integration as the primary goal of American Negroes—again an issue that divided Dr. King from the others and soon fostered further fragmentation among the various dissident black groups.

The chant "black power" probably first was heard in the 1960s during the Watts rioting of 1965; but only after the Meredith march the next year did the idea attract a national following. The black poor who felt neglected by the intellectual black leadership of the recent past made up the "black power" rank and

Eve Arnold photo, Magnum

*Malcolm X addressing black Muslims, 1961.*

file; the numerous aspirants for power on the poor's behalf, and their own, gave it what leadership they could. The autobiography of Malcolm X, published in a widely distributed paperback edition in 1966, helped spread the "black power" idea.

Malcolm X came naturally to his "black nationalism" program. His father, the Reverend Earl Little, a Baptist minister in Omaha, Nebraska, was a devout follower of Marcus Aurelius Garvey, whose campaign, "raising the banner of black-race purity," as Malcolm himself put it, "and exhorting the Negro masses to return to their ancestral African homestead," engaged the allegiance of many blacks at the time of World War I and into the twenties. The violence and humiliation that Reverend Little's family suffered from "the good Christian white people" in the urban North deepened his son's alienation. In the religion of Islam, Malcolm later found a path from the total ghetto and gutter experience he recounts so fully. "Yes, I'm an extremist," he said near the end. "The black race here in North America is in extremely bad condition. You show me a black man who isn't an extremist and I'll show you one who needs psychiatric attention."

Strife within the black nationalist movement appears to have brought about Malcolm's death, February 21, 1965, while he was on stage to speak at the Audubon Ballroom in upper Manhattan. "It looked like a firing squad," said a member of the audience about the three men who stood up, took aim, and pulled the triggers. The whole black nationalist movement at this time probably numbered no more than 40,000 followers. But "black power" had its martyr, one of the most articulate writers and speakers of the age.

The urban riots in the North from 1965 to 1967 appeared to draw ghetto blacks more closely to one another, a tendency deepened by the necessity to reconstruct their devastated communities largely with their own resources and leadership. Even Negroes depressed by the call for "black power" began to put autonomous black action above integration, especially since the rioting and its "black power" sequel had clearly alienated many liberal white supporters of the Negro cause.

Among those alienated were some northern Republican legislators who, in collaboration with their southern colleagues in the Senate, permitted the administration bill for open housing to die with the close of the Eighty-ninth Congress. The crucial Senate vote had come on September 14, 1966; and with the death of the bill at that time, Senator James O. Eastland of Mississippi issued a press release: "The civil rights advocates who hope to force an interracial society have been completely routed. The old-time coalition of Southern Democrats and Republicans were united and effective." Eastland, referring to earlier civil-rights acts, now looked forward to starting "the fight to repeal those vicious measures." He gained further encouragement from the November elections, when over forty northern Democratic representatives who had voted for open housing lost their seats.

Congressional advocates of open housing, however, refused to be deterred by the events of 1966 and two years later actually pushed through a measure that prohibited discrimination, by 1970, in the sale or rental of about 80 percent of the nation's housing. Senator Walter F. Mondale, Democrat of Minnesota, who had agreed to sponsor the bill, indicated the expiration of the "Great Society" idea when he characterized his success as "a miracle."

Two events helped bring this miracle about. One was the inclusion in the 1968 act of an antiriot section. This provided severe penalties for persons, such as civil-rights workers, who crossed state lines or used interstate facilities like the mail or telephones "with intent" to take part in or induce others (as few as three) to take part in actions (including speech-making) involving at least the threat of violence, the danger of property damage, or personal injury. This section gratified men like Congressman William Colmer of Mississippi. "Here we are," he said, "with one Stokely Carmichael and one Rap Brown, who among others we find traveling from state to state and from city to city, and in their wake comes conflagration, blood-spilling, wholesale pilfering and the loss of life and property."

The second event promoting passage of the open-housing legislation was the assassination of Dr. Martin Luther King, Jr., in Memphis, Tennessee, April 4, 1968. The tensions and riots stemming from that evil act seemed to impel certain opponents of the measure to reconsider. Final congressional action came on April 10, and the next day President Johnson signed the bill.

The *New Yorker* magazine observed on Martin Luther King's assassination: Dr. King "was the most important example of a new kind of political leader in America—one who cannot exercise leadership without first coming to terms with the probability of his own

Wide World Photos

*Dr. Martin Luther King, Jr.,*
*demanding "stop the bombing" in Vietnam*
*at UN Plaza, New York, April 1967.*

violent death." "A gunman needs a climate of hate," the *New York Times Magazine* said at the same time. A contributor to *Esquire* epitomized the divided and decayed spirit of the country when he wrote two months later: "It may be that Looting, Rioting and Burning . . . are really nothing more than radical forms of urban renewal, a response not only to the frustrations of the ghetto but to the collapse of all ordinary modes of change. As if a body despairing of the indifference of doctors, sought to rip a cancer out of itself." Meanwhile, *Life* commented, "The President [now] seems readier to deal with the violence than with the Negro indignation from which it springs"—a conclusion justified by the preparations of Defense Department weapons scientists and "riot-control" experts to beef up local police for the summer ahead, "as if they expected to take on the Vietcong," added *Look* in May that year.

## II  LBJ and the world

*Regions of negation and neglect*

The trouble with foreigners, Lyndon Johnson once said, "is that they're not like folks you were reared with." One trouble

with Lyndon Johnson's foreign policy was his urge to make the world more congenial to Americans by making all people similar to ourselves.

In August 1965, after signing a bill for a

year's extension of the Peace Corps, LBJ read from Scripture to a group of volunteers invited to his office: "They therefore that were scattered abroad went about preaching the word, . . . and many that were palsied, and that were lame, were healed." The President read on: "And besides this, giving . . . to your faith virtue; and to your virtue knowledge; and to your knowledge temperance; and to your temperance patience; and to your patience godliness; and to godliness brotherly kindness; and to brotherly kindness love"— that, he said, "is what the Peace Corps is to me. That is what my religion is—that is what the Great Society is, . . . and that is the foreign policy of the United States."

LBJ was so taken by Barbara Ward's book *The Rich Nations and the Poor Nations* (1962) that he pressed it upon his staff as required reading. He was particularly struck by her emphasis on "the ancient enemies of mankind: . . . the servitude of poverty; the servitude of ignorance; the servitude of ill-health." In Vietnam, the Mekong River appeared to him only as a grander Pedernales in his native Texas county; and he saw its development with Texas know-how and technology as the best insurance for the continued Americanization of this ancient Asian land, which the Vietnam War was said to be all about.

Yet Americanization by godliness and knowledge, in Asia and elsewhere, did not have a free field; and nothing, not even profound if fragile Orientalism, thought LBJ, could be more foreign to it than the worldwide communist conspiracy. Early in the Johnson administration Walter Lippmann pointed out that the commitment of the United States by earlier administrations "to a global ideological struggle against revolutionary Communism" lay "at the root of our difficulty in appraising . . . the importance of our engagement in Vietnam." Lippmann went on to suggest that "the test of statesmanship" now was to find "a stopping point between globalism and isolationism." Vietnam, he believed, was hardly such a point. But LBJ thought differently. "If we don't stop the Reds in South Vietnam," he instructed a demurring Senator, "tomorrow they will be in Hawaii, and next week

they will be in San Francisco." And if that were so, if we did not stop them nearer home as well, the menace would only be magnified.

Nearer home lay Latin America, where Barbara Ward's three "servitudes" seemed only to worsen each year and the charge of "communist" against every ameliorative effort had become routine, especially for United States consumption. The first major test of LBJ's Latin American policy came in the Dominican Republic in April 1965. Four years earlier the brutal reign of Rafael Trujillo had ended after three decades when he was shot down on a lonely country road by one of his henchmen. The dispatch of American warships and 1200 marines at this time forestalled a coup by the slain dictator's relatives; and the next year, in the first free election since Trujillo's takeover, the often-exiled poet Juan Bosch won the presidency. The Kennedy administration made much of this democratic event; but Bosch soon showed his inexperience of power, and when in September 1963 he sought to oust certain army commanders friendly to American military advisers, he was overthrown without United States opposition. Kennedy, however, wanted a civil regime and one was quickly instituted under Donald Reid Cabral.

On April 24, 1965, army officers friendly to Bosch unseated the Reid regime, but they were promptly confronted by traditionalist military forces with American connections, and a civil war began. The next day, to leading questions from Washington about "Castroite extremists" in the pro-Bosch group, the American embassy in Santo Domingo, the Dominican Republic capital, obliged with appropriate answers. On April 28, LBJ disclosed the landing of 400 marines in Santo Domingo to protect American lives; but a high-ranking navy officer said they were also "to see that no Communist government is established." In the meantime, the dispatch of American forces was speeded up until by May 5, when a truce was worked out, they exceeded 20,000 men, a number many thought incredible.

Among the skeptical was Adlai Stevenson, United States Ambassador to the UN, upon whose shoulders fell the responsibility of explaining this invasion, contrary to all the tenets of the Organization of American States, and explaining administration contradictions as well. On his part, LBJ on May 2 went on nationwide TV to share his Castroite panic with the public:

> What began as a popular democratic revolution [he said] . . . moved into the hands of a band of Communist conspirators. . . . The American nation cannot, must not, will not, permit the establishment of another Communist government in the Western Hemisphere.

The administration soon backed away from these assertions and worked out a compromise settlement including Bosch men in a new government. But these steps only deepened the consternation of many in Congress, among the American people, and throughout Latin America over having been misled earlier by hasty if not calculated White House pronouncements. The whole episode enlarged the "credibility gap" already evident in White House reporting on the Vietnam War.

In Vietnam so little love seemed to accompany the avowed Americanization of economic development, so little virtue to soften the Americanization of politics, so little godliness to temper the Americanization of war technology, that the best friends of the United States in Europe—themselves already alienated by persistent policies of Americanization of their continent—soon recoiled from the Atlantic Partnership. Scandinavians also became ever more outspoken in their revulsion, and even dependent Italy and West Germany gave the adventure only what lip service seemed to be politic. Solid support for the United States came only from the three most authoritarian European states outside the Soviet orbit: Portugal, Spain, and Greece.

In the Middle East, meanwhile, after U Thant, in May 1967, complied with Nasser's demand that UN troops be withdrawn after keeping Egypt and Israel apart for ten years, the Egyptian leader immediately called for a "Holy War" of Arabs against the Jewish state. Israel, however, beat him to the punch with an overpowering assault in the Six-Day War, June 5 to 10. In this war 15,000 Arab officers and men died, 80 percent of the Arab military equipment was destroyed, and strategic Arab territory was taken. The Six-Day War humiliated the USSR as well, for it was Russian aid in arms and training that had encouraged Nasser's militancy. In Washington the conviction was "almost universal," to quote one reporter, "that the Soviet Union had been dealt an almost irreparable setback."

Yet the profound unrest in the Middle East following Israel's triumph only fostered a bigger arms buildup than ever, one which the USSR itself promoted. While the United States became preoccupied with Vietnam and with rebellion at home against the deadly futility of the war there, the Russians not only regained their standing in the Middle East but enlarged their influence in the entire Mediterranean region as well. Among their own satellites, moreover, where the United States had pressed Westernization to loosen Moscow's grip, the Russians soon felt free to crush all libertarian leanings. The worst sufferer was Czechoslovakia in August 1968. There, with a show of force even greater than that used in Hungary twelve years before, the Alexander Dubcek regime was broken and every libertarian light extinguished.

Two years earlier, both Moscow and Peking had made trade treaties with Japan, where anti-Americanism had hardly declined since 1960 when President Eisenhower was forced to omit Tokyo from his Far Eastern itinerary for security reasons. Red China's success in perfecting nuclear weapons in the midsixties helped remind the Japanese of the value of their security treaty with the United States, first signed in 1951. But the accelerating antagonism toward Japanese imports in the United States, at the same time, also reminded them of the value of their traditional markets in China, disregarding American concern over Chinese intentions in Vietnam.

*Upward from Tonkin Gulf*

856

Few wars in history have been marked by such an array of inaccurate, inconsistent, contradictory official pronouncements as to its purpose and progress as the American war in Vietnam; and nothing contributed more to public discontent over the war than the mistrust created by the policy of obfuscation and the policy of secrecy. Even such an august body as the Senate Foreign Relations Committee had to scratch for elementary information, and despite the pertinacity of its long-term chairman, Democrat J. William Fulbright of Arkansas, the White House, the Defense Department, and other executive agencies routinely denied it documentary materials.

Publication of excerpts and analysis of the secret "Pentagon Papers" by the *New York Times,* beginning June 13, 1971, and subsequently by the *Washington Post* and nearly a score of other newspapers across the country, showed how much the administrations involved in the Vietnam War had to hide. "A feeling is widely and strongly held," John T. McNaughton, Assistant Secretary of Defense, wrote to his chief, McNamara, in May 1967, "that 'the Establishment' is out of its mind. . . . Related to this feeling is the increased polarization that is taking place in the United States with seeds of the worst split in our people in more than a century." A month later, McNamara authorized the "objective and encyclopedic" study that McNaughton had recommended, that the *Times* began to make public in mid-1971, and that the Nixon administration tried to recall and sequester until checked by a Supreme Court decision in favor of the *Times* and *Post,* June 30, 1971.

No incidents in the war were more clouded by contradictory pronouncements and the classification of essential documents than the naval events in Tonkin Gulf, off North Vietnam, on August 2 and 4, 1964. Compounding the confusion was the fact that the United States at this time was in the midst of the presidential campaign between the avowed Arizona "hawk," Senator Goldwater, and a Democratic seeker after "consensus" who

dared not allow allegations of his being "soft on communism" in Asia or elsewhere to mar his image. When early in July 1964, in response to saber rattling by a new Saigon regime, UN Secretary-General U Thant declared that "the only sensible alternative is the political and diplomatic method of negotiations" and proposed a reconvening of the Geneva Conference for this purpose, the new administration's response was "brusque and uncompromising," according to one analyst. The President himself stated, "we do not believe in conferences to ratify terror," and the next day he announced a 30 percent increase in the American "military mission" to Vietnam from 16,000 to 21,000 persons.

Neither side in the Tonkin Bay controversy three weeks later denied that on August 2, North Vietnamese PT boats attacked the U.S. destroyer *Maddox* in Tonkin Gulf, and were driven off with the help of carrier-based fighter planes, *Maddox* suffering neither damage nor casualties. The United States asserted that the attack was "unprovoked" while *Maddox* sailed "on routine patrol in international waters," a phrase McNamara was to repeat practically by rote in response to later Senate queries. But Hanoi on July 30 and 31 had already filed a formal protest with the International Control Commission set up under the Geneva agreements, declaring that Saigon vessels had raided North Vietnamese fishing boats and that, under cover of protection by an American destroyer, had bombarded two North Vietnamese islands. The attack on *Maddox,* Hanoi held, was aimed to stop such activities.

It is clear now (from Joseph C. Goulden's excellent book *Truth is the First Casualty: The Gulf of Tonkin Affair—Illusion and Reality,* published in 1969, as well as from the Pentagon Papers) that North Vietnamese islands had been bombarded. It is also clear that the bombardment was part and parcel of deliberate United States policy to exert "new and significant pressures on North Vietnam," adopted in February and March 1964, to elicit overt action on her part in order to gain congressional authorization of whatever further "is necessary with respect to Vietnam."

This policy was stiffened after the attack on *Maddox,* when the President directed the navy to assign a second destroyer to join *Maddox's* patrol and to order both vessels, together with the necessary air power, to repel any further assaults, "with the object not only of driving off the force but of destroying it." Two days later, on August 4, the Defense Department announced that North Vietnam had attacked both *Maddox* and its companion, the destroyer *C. Turner Joy,* 65 miles offshore in the Gulf, and that the attackers had been driven off with the loss of at least two boats while the American vessels went unscathed. North Vietnam denied that any such attack had taken place.

That very night, allowing no time for detailed investigation, the President went on TV:

*Repeated acts of violence against the armed forces of the United States must be met not only with alert defense but with positive reply. That reply is being given, as I speak to you tonight. Air action is now in execution against gunboats and certain facilities in North Vietnam . . . used in these hostile operations.*

Johnson was wholly aware, of course, that this initial attack on Ho's country was more than a mere escalation of a war officially described as one for the defense of Saigon governments against guerrilla groups as yet made up mainly of South Vietnamese. In accordance with the "pressure" policy, just prior to his telecast the President informed legislative leaders that he would the next day send Congress a retroactive joint resolution to be adopted "before dark" and without amendment. This resolution the administration promptly and thereafter persistently interpreted as a "functional equivalent" of a formal declaration of war in Southeast Asia.

Restating the United States version of the events of August 2 and 4, the fateful Tonkin Gulf Resolution of August 7, 1964, declared:

*The Congress approves and supports the determination of the President, as Commander in Chief, to take all necessary measures to repel any armed attack against the forces of the United States and to prevent further aggression.*

857

The resolution was to remain operative until "the President shall determine that the peace and security of the area is reasonably assured, . . . except that it may be terminated earlier by concurrent resolution of Congress."

Rushed into session in a crisis mood, the House adopted the wanted resolution without a dissenting vote. The Senate, after two days of debate wrung from the leadership by Wayne Morse of Oregon by threats of a filibuster (hence the August 7 date of the measure), counted but two opposed—Morse and Ernest Gruening of Alaska. Both, to their credit, saw through the smokescreens of at least two administrations. Gruening even then called the administration resolution "a predated declaration of war." Morse said during the two-day debate: "I shall . . . state categorically that high officials of the government have admitted on the record that they were aware of plans for the bombardment." To Senator Lausche's objection, "There is no testimony to that effect whatsoever. That is an inference made by the Senator from Oregon," Morse replied: "Get permission of the State Department or the Pentagon to publicly release the whole transcript without a single word deleted, and let the country know what they said."

As late as May 1966, Senator Fulbright told Eric Sevareid in an interview that "this Gulf of Tonkin incident . . . was a very vague one. We were briefed on it, but we have no way of knowing even to this day, what actually happened." In February 1968, again, Fulbright's committee conducted an examination of Secretary McNamara on the Tonkin Gulf incident, seeking light, as he said, simply on "the decision-making process of our Government in time of crisis." At the end of this examination, McNamara was reported as having described his "grilling" as "pure hell," a phrase seemingly justified by the straits of evasion, convenient lapses of his famous memory, concoctions of technicalities, and above all of

858

simple concealment under cover of "classification," to which he was forced to resort. On closing the hearings, Fulbright said he found it "awfully hard to believe . . . [that the Secretary's secrecy was] of any significance to current security. It is just incredible."

The bombing of North Vietnam in August 1964 appears to have been as much a political as a military adventure. Regular missions of this sort did not begin until February 1965, when, with the election won and the new administration seated, McGeorge Bundy, now one of Johnson's hard-line advisers, returned from a visit to Saigon full of the need to buck up the South Vietnamese. Even then, the persistent fear of "bringing the Chinese down on us," as another adviser put it, contributed to giving the President pause. "He's filibustering," one observer remarked, "so that he won't have to make up his mind one way or another." Even after February 1965, Tom Wicker writes in *JFK and LBJ*, the bombing missions went on "hesitantly and reluctantly"

for six weeks, "as if those who loosed the beast tried at first to restrain it, only to find its innate power greater than theirs, and at last uncontrollable."

American ground troops engaged the Viet Cong in direct fighting for the first time in June 1965. By the end of the year American forces in Vietnam had soared above 200,000. The South Vietnamese also promised to step up their efforts in June 1965 after Vice Marshal Nguyen Cao Ky took over as Premier of the eighth South Vietnam government since the end of Diem. In November 1965, some 30,000 persons participated in a "March on Washington for Peace in Vietnam," evidence of the growing unpopularity of the war. And yet the continuing "escalation" of military appropriations by congressmen needing to confront constituent opinion seemed to indicate that most Americans continued to share the President's "dogged optimism," as one reporter put it, about getting North Vietnam to the peace table by "shooting his way there." Air force "think-tank" planners even considered the advisability of removing the inhibiting uncertainty of Chinese involvement by "a nuclear strike on Chinese atomic-weapons

*(Left) American infantry sortie in South Vietnam. Photo by* LIFE *photographer Larry Burrows, killed in war area, 1971.*
*(Right) The "body count": Viet Cong dead after attack on South Vietnam outpost, November 1967.*

LIFE Magazine © Time Inc.                    Wide World Photos

plants," thereby "denuclearizing the Chinese," in Philip Geyelin's words, "even before they had really gotten started." But there appeared little appetite for a new Tonkin Gulf–type incident to trigger such "further engagement."

During the President's extraordinary Asian tour in October 1966, culminating in the "summit conference" in Manila among Asian supporters of his policy, Johnson proposed to extend the "Great Society" not only to all Southeast Asia but to all other underdeveloped regions. By then, there was no let up in "peace feelers" by the UN, the Pope, the Italians, and many other parties, and no let up in bombing North Vietnam, presumably to improve Hanoi's receptivity to peace moves and Ho Chi Minh's willingness to communicate them to the Viet Cong.

By the end of 1966, American forces in Vietnam had reached 380,000. American "hardware" commitments, officially and no doubt properly secret, by then probably exceeded those of any other war in history. "What kind of a war are we fighting anyway?" asked an American soldier in his Vietnam diary in 1967. "They say we've got more fire-power out here than they had in both World War I and II. Yet these damn kids in black pajamas continue to hold out. I can't understand it. Each one of them must have 40 lives." Widespread chemical warfare and the employment of other new weaponry, also largely concealed from Americans at home, contributed heavily to the devastation of South Vietnam while contributing little to "pacification" of the Viet Cong.

In a struggle that had devolved into a war of "body counts," pacification had come largely to mean extermination, with Vietnamese civilians, North and South, almost routinely included in the slaughter to help provide a better showing. The counts themselves, moreover, soon grew as suspect as all other aspects of this tragedy, while the means employed added anxiety over war crimes to the other sources of revulsion. In May 1967, Secretary McNamara himself recoiled.

*The picture of the world's greatest superpower killing or seriously injuring 1,000 noncombatants a week [he wrote then], while trying to pound a tiny backward nation into submission on an issue whose merits are hotly disputed, is not a pretty one.*

By the end of 1967 United States troop strength in Vietnam approached 475,000 men, about 1500 more than the peak of the Korean War, and casualties rose proportionately. By then the military futility of bombing North Vietnam and its immense political cost both at home and abroad were being acknowledged by all but the most impenitent administration spokesmen. McNamara admitted it *publicly* in August 1967, three months before his announced departure from the Cabinet—an event characteristically unexplained by the President but presumably following upon the Secretary's altered opinion.

Hanoi's "Tet" (New Year's) offensive against Saigon and other South Vietnam cities in February 1968 seemed next to testify to two suggestive conclusions: (1) that Ho, despite the bombing, could launch massive assaults that caught both hardened United States field commanders and veteran administration travelers wholly by surprise; and (2) that the USSR, in any case, would not leave North Vietnam to confront high American military technology simply with captured or stolen American weapons. Hanoi used Soviet jet planes and tanks in the Tet offensive for the first time in the ever escalating conflict.

Worldwide pressure for peace had grown very heavy by this time. In the United States, the strength of the peace movement became evident in the showing of one of its leading congressional advocates, Senator Eugene J. McCarthy of Minnesota, in the Democratic presidential primary in New Hampshire, March 12, 1968. Although given little chance against LBJ, McCarthy shocked the administration by gaining 42 percent of the votes to the President's 49 percent. It took little time for the lesson of this event to penetrate the White House. On March 31, Johnson said on nationwide TV: "We are prepared to move immediately toward peace through negotiations. So tonight, in the hope that this action will lead to early talks, I am taking the first

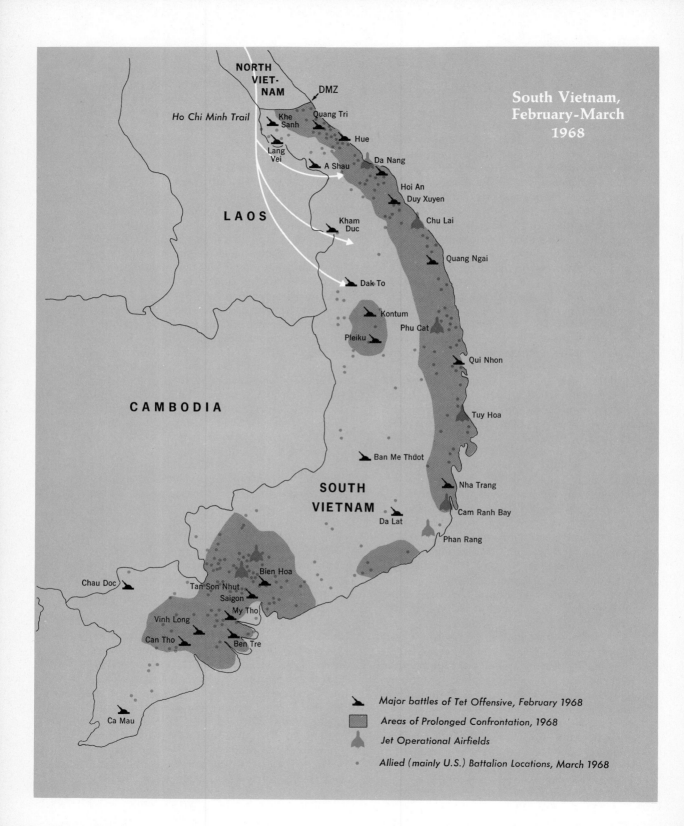

South Vietnam,
February-March
1968

NORTH VIET-NAM

DMZ

Ho Chi Minh Trail

Khe Sanh
Quang Tri
Hue
Lang Vei
A Shau
Da Nang
Hoi An
Duy Xuyen
Chu Lai

LAOS

Kham Duc

Quang Ngai

Dak To

Kontum
Phu Cat

Pleiku

Qui Nhon

CAMBODIA

Tuy Hoa

Ban Me Thuot

SOUTH VIETNAM

Nha Trang

Da Lat
Cam Ranh Bay

Phan Rang

Chau Doc

Bien Hoa

Tan Son Nhut
Saigon
My Tho

Vinh Long

Can Tho
Ben Tre

Ca Mau

Major battles of Tet Offensive, February 1968

Areas of Prolonged Confrontation, 1968

Jet Operational Airfields

Allied (mainly U.S.) Battalion Locations, March 1968

step to deescalate the conflict." This step was his order to halt all air and naval bombardment of North Vietnam, except in the area just north of the demilitarized zone where the enemy arms buildup was most active. The North Vietnamese response came quickly. On April 3, Ho Chi Minh's government "declared its readiness" to confer on peace with a United States representative, and just one month later preliminary talks began in Paris.

The war, nevertheless, diminished little in ferocity. On June 4 the United States command in Vietnam announced that American battle deaths in the first six months of 1968 exceeded those of all 1967. By June 23, reckoning from December 22, 1961, the date of the first death of an American serviceman in Vietnam, the war there had become the longest in American history, surpassing by a day the six years and six months usually ascribed to the fighting in the American Revolution. The direct cost of the war also had soared to an acknowledged $25 billion a year, with unacknowledged costs for weapons development and other programs associated with the conflict also rising dramatically. At the same time, little progress was reported from Paris until November 1, a few days before the United States presidential elections. Then, following favorable information from the French capital, Johnson announced: "I have now ordered that all air, naval and artillery bombardment of North Vietnam cease." The President looked forward to the scheduled meeting of the Paris conferees on November 6, the day after the elections, for the sweet fruits of his decree; but conflicts over the Paris roles of South Vietnam and its official enemy, the Viet Cong, dissipated his hopes.

For McNamara's benefit, in the Pentagon Papers Assistant Secretary John T. McNaughton "capsulized" American aims in Vietnam:

*70 pct.—To avoid a humiliating U.S. defeat (to our reputation as a guarantor).*

*20 pct.—To keep SVN [South Vietnam] (and then adjacent territory) from Chinese hands.*

*10 pct.—To permit the people of SVN to enjoy a better, freer way of life.*

*Also—To emerge from crisis without unacceptable taint from methods used.*

*NOT—To "help a friend," although it would be hard to stay in if asked out.*

The Pentagon Papers are massive—2.5 million words, with 4000 pages of official documents and 3000 pages of analysis, all the work of thirty to forty researchers and authors, covering American involvement in Southeast Asia from World War II to the opening of the Paris peace talks in May 1968. Yet they provide, as the *Times* says, "far from a complete history. . . . There are gaps in the Pentagon study—the researchers lacked access to Presidential files," for example, while the *Times* and other newspapers did not obtain "the chapter on diplomatic initiatives, some of which are continuing." Only fragments of the whole, again, could be published in newspaper or book form. Their revelations, moreover, may in fact be little different in character from those obtainable in the archives of many other wars in many other countries; and for all their bulk, they are likely to provide the foundation only for far larger quantities of elucidation, extenuation, and rebuttal in the coming years.

But all that lay ahead in mid-1971. At the time of their publication the Pentagon Papers caused a sensation largely because of the unprecedented concealment and distortion by the executive department of information which a free society must have to preserve its liberties, especially under the stress of a distant and disconcerting war. Not only the public but Congress—the legislative branch of a constitutional government of checks and balances—was deliberately misled or calculatingly kept ignorant, largely for self-serving rather than security reasons. The Vietnam conflict coined a new phrase in American politics—the "credibility gap"—long before publication even of a small part of the Pentagon Papers appeared to verify the credibility of the phrase. Nor was the Nixon administration's response of instant suppression of the disclosures reassuring on the prospects of the people's right to know.

## III  The "silent majority" on trial

### Nixon's comeback

One of the major casualties of the war in 1968 was LBJ's political career. In his dramatic deescalation speech of March 31 he had added the even more dramatic announcement of his decision not to seek reelection later that year, a gesture made deliberately to remove the most conspicuous abrasive from society's lesions. Even Herbert Hoover at the bottom of the Great Depression in 1932 had resisted such a step. One needed perhaps to go back to Jefferson "panting for retirement" toward the end of his second term in 1808 to find even a near precedent. Jefferson in 1804 had gained the presidency with an approach to unanimity that matched Johnson's record victory in 1964, and the success of his domestic policies rivaled that of the Texan's in the Eighty-ninth Congress in 1965–1966. Jefferson forfeited the confidence of the country by holding to a peaceful course in foreign affairs against the shrill demands of the war hawks of his day. Johnson failed by obdurately enlarging an increasingly suspect war while the cry for peace enveloped the land.

The presidential elections of 1968 may themselves be said to have begun with the decision to bomb North Vietnam in February 1965. The ranks of the doves swelled thereafter, not only among McCarthy's colleagues in the Senate but among the youth of the nation as well. McCarthy's performance in the New Hampshire primary in March 1968 showed that he had grown strong enough to split the party. When, a few days later, Senator Robert F. Kennedy of New York decided to enter the campaign, it seemed that the opposition to the administration would also be split. Johnson's

*(Left) LBJ aboard Air Force One with hard-line advisers, Rostow, Rusk and General Taylor, and others.*
*(Right) LBJ showing his Vietnam scar, in cartoon by David Levine, 1966.*

(Left) Y. R. Okamoto photo, Lyndon Baines Johnson Library; (Right) With permission of *The New York Review of Books,* © 1966, NYREV, Inc.

withdrawal two weeks later deepened the conflict between his would-be Democratic successors.

Domestic issues were brought violently to the foreground by the assassination of Martin Luther King, Jr., on April 4 and by the new rioting that followed in Washington, D.C., and other cities. The Kennedy mantle and mystique drew millions of American young people, black and white alike, to the Kennedy camp. When Robert Kennedy himself was felled by an assassin on June 5, the very night of his victory in the California Democratic primary, a gaping vacuum appeared in American life which Senator McCarthy tried vainly to fill. Hubert H. Humphrey, Johnson's Vice-President, who did not enter any primaries, had joined the Democratic contest late in April and his quest for delegates did not end until the very moment of the first ballot at the Democratic convention in Chicago, August 26-29.

This convention set many precedents in American political history, most of them involving violence. On orders of Mayor Richard J. Daley of Chicago, an administration Democrat, the International Amphitheater, where official sessions of the convention met, was ringed with barbed-wire fencing broken only by check points for entering delegates, reporters, and guests. An area of several blocks around the Amphitheater and around major downtown hotels, meanwhile, swarmed with police, federal agents, and finally with National Guardsmen called in to keep antiwar demonstrators away. According to the Walker Report of November 1968 to the National Commission on the Causes and Prevention of Violence, these "security" forces, their own ubiquitousness an incitement to the trouble they were primed to anticipate, endured manifest provocation. But "the nature of the response was unrestrained and indiscriminate police violence, particularly at night," itself provoked in part by Mayor Daley's rebukes to the police for their restraint in handling earlier demonstrations.

The convention week violence, the report continues,

*was made all the more shocking by the fact that it was often inflicted upon persons who had broken no law, disobeyed no order, made no threat. These included peaceful demonstrators, onlookers, and large numbers of residents who were simply passing through, or happened to live in, the areas where confrontations were occurring.*

*Newsmen and photographers were singled out for assault, and their equipment deliberately damaged. Fundamental police training was ignored; and officers, when on the scene, were often unable to control their men.*

Violence in the vicinity of the convention reached its peak on Wednesday evening, August 28, after the delegates that afternoon had rejected an antiwar platform plank. This plank called for immediate cessation of all bombing of North Vietnam (which the President, as we have said, did order the following November on the eve of the elections) and other steps leading to a prompt end of the fighting. Among those arrested that evening were the "Chicago 8," who were indicted by a federal grand jury in March 1969 for conspiracy—based heavily on wiretap evidence surreptitiously collected earlier by United States agents without a court order—as well as for direct violations of the antiriot act of 1968 during the convention week. Among the "8" was Black Panther leader Bobby Seale, whose courtroom conduct during the trial that began in September 1969 led Judge Julius J. Hoffman to cite him for contempt and to sentence him to four years in jail forthwith. Seale's removal reduced the "8" to the "Chicago 7."

"In choosing the eight of us," one of the defendants declared on the eve of the September trial, "the government has lumped together all the strands of dissent in the '60s. We respond by saying the movement of the past decade is on trial here." Eight policemen—no more, no less—also were indicted, but they were acquitted before the trial of the other "8" began.

While violence was occuring in the convention area that Wednesday evening, hundreds of "Daley's people" planted inside the Am-

863

phitheater without credentials began physically to eject delegates who refused, on demand, to show their own credentials. The McCarthy forces and other liberals, charging "atrocities," tried without success to get the convention postponed two weeks. Amidst pandemonium inside and outside the convention hall—all visible to millions on TV— Humphrey, a few minutes before midnight, gained the nomination on the first ballot. The next day he announced—and the convention confirmed—his choice for Vice-President, Senator Edmund S. Muskie of Maine.

Three weeks before the Democratic convention the Republicans had held their's at Miami Beach, where they nominated Nixon on the first ballot. A platform warning that "lawlessness is crumbling the foundations of American society" launched their "law and order campaign." In his acceptance speech, Nixon welcomed as the core of his constituency the "silent majority" of "forgotten Americans"—"the non-shouters, the non-demonstrators, that are not racist or sick, that are not guilty of the crime that plagues the land." This speech was well received. Liberal Republicans, however, were so aroused by his selection of Governor Spiro T. Agnew of Maryland, a convert to stern repression of blacks and other dissidents, as his running mate that they tried to nominate a liberal vice-presidential candidate from the floor, a move that fell flat. The choice of Agnew, a southern candidate nominated in a southern convention city, could only strengthen the Republicans' "southern strategy," already manifest in Nixon's promise to southern delegations the day before the convention balloting. If elected, he said, his administration would not "ram anything down your throats." He disliked federal intervention in local school board affairs; he opposed school busing; and he would appoint "strict constitutionalists" to the Supreme Court.

Nixon's stand may have taken some of the wind from the sails of a third candidate for President, George C. Wallace, the Alabama segregationist, who was thought by many to be strong enough to deprive both regular party candidates of the electoral majority needed to win. Were Wallace able to accomplish this, the election would be thrown into the House of Representatives, where Humphrey's only hopes seemed to lie.

Despite the almost decade-long violence that had preceded it, the 1968 presidential campaign passed without bloodshed. Humphrey, with exceptional support from the old Democratic coalition of urban liberals, organized labor, and minority groups, made a remarkably strong finish in the big industrial states, virtually equaling the popular vote Nixon gained elsewhere. Nixon carried by small majorities the critical states of Ohio, Illinois, New Jersey, and California; but Humphrey won in Michigan and Texas as well as New York and Pennsylvania. Wallace's poor southern showing outside the few deep South states he was certain to carry also helped Nixon gain a clear electoral majority with 301 votes to 191 for Humphrey and 46 for Wallace. Like Eisenhower in 1956, nevertheless, he failed to carry enough legislative candidates with him to diminish significantly the Democratic majorities in House and Senate.

While winning the electoral majority, moreover, Nixon failed to gain a popular majority. His margin over Humphrey, a mere 510,000 out of 73.2 million votes cast, gave

**Election of 1968**

ALASKA
HAWAII

*Electoral Vote*

Nixon 301
Humphrey 191
Wallace 46

him only 43.4 percent of the popular vote, the lowest by a successful candidate since Wilson in 1912. Humphrey gained 42.7 percent of the popular vote; Wallace 13.5 percent.

Many believed that relatively few blacks would vote in the 1968 elections, their abstention having been urged by "black power" forces and other disaffected Negro groups. And it is true that fewer blacks did vote in 1968 than in 1964. The difference between the two election years, however, appears to have been much smaller than anticipated. More remarkable still, since he was saddled with so many of the failures of the Johnson administration at home as well as abroad, was Humphrey's command of those Negroes who balloted. His margin in some precincts soared well over 90 percent. Nixon's analysts acknowledged that overall their candidate received no more than 10 percent of the Negro vote, a showing that suggests that Nixon's victory may well be viewed as a Negro defeat. As James Reston wrote two days after the balloting: "Mr. Nixon's greatest problem is likely to be with the people who didn't vote for him: the very poor, the Negroes, the vast numbers of organized workers, and the rebellious and articulate young intellectuals." There were also those, Reston added, concerned with "the control of military arms."

### "Halfway—Where?"

In his inaugural address, January 20, 1969, Richard M. Nixon let it be known that the deepening mood of desperation in the United States had touched even the coldest of calculating minds. Summing up the experience of the Democratic sixties, the new President said, "We have endured a long night of the American spirit"; and he described a nation "reaching with magnificent precision for the moon, but falling into raucus discord on earth." Not above aping John F. Kennedy in some of *his* more inspiring inaugural phrases (as Garry Wills perspicaciously points out in

*Nixon Agonistes,* 1970) Nixon on his own urged Americans to "stop shouting at one another," to "lower our voices," in order to smooth the path for our "coming together" once more.

Millions of older Americans raised on the antagonisms of the 1940s and 1950s and recalling Nixon's role in them may have doubted that the new President was the right man to heal the fractured nation. Millions of younger people, distressed by the adventures and misadventures of the 1960s, no doubt shared the skepticism of their elders, and beyond that, had learned to distrust anyone wielding the greatly enhanced authority of the President's office. It was clear, at the same time, that the new President embodied the sentiments of tens of millions of his countrymen, many of them dismayed by the melancholy harvest of the liberal tradition to which they once subscribed. Perhaps more of them had always been conservative, or at any rate conventional, in politics as well as in religion and morality and had awaited a spokesman to articulate their grievances and hopes.

The irony is that more than halfway in his administration—after having suffered sharp reversals in the 1970 elections despite campaign activity by himself and Agnew matched by few administration leaders in the past—Nixon continued to sing the same sad tune. "Sometimes when I see those columns [of Washington's pseudo-classic public structures]," he said a few days after the Fourth of July 1971, "I think of what happened to Greece and Rome, and you see what is left of great civilizations of the past—only the pillars. . . . As they lost their will to live, to improve, they became subject to the decadence that destroys the civilization." "The United States," he concluded without qualification, "is now reaching that period."

As so often in the past, Nixon put less of the blame for America's plight on the lawless acts of authoritarians in power who undermined the people's faith, and more of it on the media and the schools—"editors, television, radio commentators, teachers"—for not "reassuring" the people by reporting or repeating government handouts. Nevertheless, jour-

865

nalists and commentators were not lacking who took up his theme. On July 16, 1971, C. L. Sulzberger, writing from Rome itself on Nixon's "pessimistic musing," declared: "This has become America's primordial problem. As the President said, 'the critical question is whether the United States will be a healthy nation in terms of its moral strength.' When that same question was posed in ancient Rome, the answer was a flat no." Three days later, the syndicated columnist Stewart Alsop observed:

> Past history suggests that mass defiance invites, sooner or later, an authoritarian and repressive response. Today in this country there is less repression of dissent than in any other nation. . . . Moreover, no man on horseback is even dimly visible. . . . The danger is not immediate. But the disintegration of the authority of the "established government" could produce an authoritarian regime, if it were combined with a severe economic depression. That combination could happen here.

As early as 1957, Amaury de Riencourt wrote in his book *The Coming Caesars:* "It is in Washington and not in London, Paris, or Berlin that the Caesars of the future will arise. . . . Caesarism is not dictatorship, not the result of one man's overriding ambition, not a brutal seizure of power through revolution. It is not based on a specific doctrine or philosophy. It is essentially pragmatic and untheoretical. It is a slow . . . unconscious development that ends in a voluntary surrender of a free people escaping from freedom to one autocratic master." Riencourt then had in mind President Eisenhower, to whom, two years before, Congress had eagerly passed on the "terrifying responsibility" of protecting Taiwan from the Red Chinese. But "Ike" was an old-fashioned hero simply fronting for congenial conservatives. Perhaps Nixon's "musing" on Rome's fate was that of a veteran nonhero committed to performing pragmatic services for constituents he was unwilling to constrain.

Nixon delayed his first State of the Union message until January 22, 1970, and then dealt chiefly with such issues as law and order, already threadbare from the 1968 campaign. Many who voted for him then had grown weary of the strenuous and militant Democratic Presidents of the recent past and their sponsorship of overweening federal intervention in state and community affairs. A certain quietness in Washington promised a welcome relaxation, gratifying not only to the "silent majority" but to others as well. At the same time, Nixon's efforts to satisfy his southern constituency by fulfilling his promise of "strict-constructionist" Supreme Court nominations blew up a great storm.

The President's selection of Warren E. Burger of Minnesota to replace Earl Warren as Chief Justice was confirmed by the Senate with little ado in June 1969. For the remaining vacancy, in August that year, Nixon named Clement F. Haynesworth, Jr., of South Carolina, whom the Senate turned down in November, largely for past carelessness in conflict-of-interest cases. Shocked by this setback, the President vowed to place a southerner on the Court, and in January 1970 chose G. Harrold Carswell of Florida for the honor. Carswell proved more vulnerable to attack on his racial record as well as his professional competence than the President perhaps had realized; but when he too was rejected in April as unfit, Nixon assaulted the Senate as unremittingly hostile to the South and more than that as a usurper of Executive prerogatives. "What is centrally at issue in this nomination," he said, "is the constitutional responsibility of the President to appoint members of the Court." Nothing was added on the constitutional powers of the Senate to advise and consent. The Court vacancy was finally filled by Harry A. Blackmun of Minnesota, whom the Senate unanimously confirmed in May.

One feature of Nixon's second State of the Union message, January 1971, was his proposal for a massive overhauling of the Executive bureaucracy, so vastly enlarged by LBJ's three wars—on poverty, on racism, and on North Vietnam. Like other Nixon steps, this would have considerably enlarged the authority of the White House; but Congress again proved slow to act.

A second feature was the President's proposal for "revenue sharing" between federal and state governments, which became the avowed keystone of his domestic program. Deceptively neutral sounding and statesmanlike in bringing a fresh approach to reduction of state burdens in welfare and domestic security costs, this proposal was another "southern-strategy" weapon. In his essay on the Nixon administration "Halfway—Where?" in *The Center Magazine,* March/April 1971, the magazine's executive editor, Donald McDonald, wrote of this aspect of the State of the Union message:

*Mr. Nixon's State of the Union appeal for a "peaceful revolution in which power [is] turned back to the people" may spell regression unless his Administration is prepared to enforce what it has, on the whole, failed to enforce in its first two years: equitable distribution of power among all the people and the just use of that power for the benefit of all the people, rich and poor, white and black. The President said that the people must have "a bigger voice in deciding for themselves those questions that so greatly affect their lives." But*

*"Southern strategists" at bay.*
*Nixon and Mitchell after Carswell fiasco.*

*for millions of people, the only voice they have had has been that of the federal government. If that voice, already enfeebled, muted, and ambivalent, is now going to be withdrawn; if Mr. Nixon, in effect, proposes to wash his hands of federal responsibility in the necessary but unpleasant and politically unpopular task of insuring universal justice in the society, then the prospect for an amplification of the people's voice is not promising.*

By then the President had vetoed as inflationary congressional appropriations for the Department of Health, Education, and Welfare, leading to major cuts in civil-rights programs that only heightened the discontent that had come to permeate HEW workers. In October 1970, the United States Commission on Civil Rights reported, in turn, that "a major breakdown" in enforcement of civil-rights legislation had occurred not only in HEW but in the Justice Department as well. Moreover, while inflation soared, the economy by mid-1970 had fallen into a recession, or depression, of the sort columnist Alsop feared. The administration frequently scouted the economic reports of its own professional agencies such as the Bureau of Labor Statistics and the Federal Reserve Board and sought politically sensitive adjustments in their data. In the meantime unemployment, especially among the underprivileged and the young, added significantly to welfare rolls and welfare costs and to the cost of other relief efforts. Unemployment also became widespread in war industries, which were especially hard hit by the President's "winding-down" of the American involvement in the Vietnam War.

In his "game plan" for reversing the inflationary surge the President persistently put off as "unworkable" Democratic proposals for concrete wage and price controls, which also had the backing of certain administration experts. But as the maneuvering for the 1972 elections intensified, he yielded at last in mid-August 1971 to the strength of the "economic issue" in the country. At that time, in a world-shaking TV speech, he ordered a ninety-day wage-price freeze. He also asked Congress to repeal the 7 percent excise tax on automobile sales; to grant business an investment tax credit of 10 percent for one year and of 5 percent thereafter; and to advance to January 1, 1972, the $50 additional personal income-tax exemption not due to take effect until a year later.

868

Beyond all that, in an effort to recoup American markets abroad, the President declared virtual economic warfare on other industrial nations. His strategy here included taking the dollar off the gold standard, with the hope that such implicit devaluation would cut the cost of American exports in terms of foreign currencies; and imposing a virtual across-the-board 10 percent surcharge on imports. The President also took this occasion to get out from under his revenue-sharing and other welfare-reform measures which had encountered hard going in Congress.

The business community seemed to give the President's new game plan a resounding vote of confidence when, the day following its announcement, purchases on the New York Stock Exchange reached a record 31.7 million shares and the Dow Jones averages of stock values soared a record 32.9 points. Labor leaders, however, miffed by the omission of a profit freeze, immediately voiced militant opposition to the wage freeze, which even countermanded wage increases stipulated for the future in existing contracts. For the tens of millions of victims of structural unemployment—joblessness among black youths, for example, had soared over 40 percent in the summer of 1971—there was little balm or hope in the new economic policy. Structural unemployment, once limited to pockets of declining industries such as coal mining in Appalachia and textile manufacture in New England, had by now spread to most central cities; and its predominantly racial character had made it a profound social as well as economic issue to which the President's new economic steps were as irrelevant as his moribund welfare-reform program. The response of industrial nations abroad, moreover, surly at first, had yet to take either retaliatory or accommodating form.

### The President at war

During the 1968 campaign, Nixon said of the presidency:

*I have always thought this country could run itself domestically without a President. All you want is a competent Cabinet to run the country at home. You need a President for foreign policy; no Secretary of State is really important. The President makes foreign policy.*

More than any Cabinet member, the Counsel to the President, John D. Ehrlichman, became in effect Nixon's "domestic president." In foreign affairs, Henry A. Kissinger and his 110-man White House staff overshadowed not only the 11,000-man State Department but the Department of Defense and the National Security Council as well.

In foreign policy the President took many "initiatives," capped by Kissinger's successful mission to Peking in July 1971, where he obtained an invitation from Chou En-lai for the President to visit Red China before May 1972. Few peaceful events in foreign policy elicited such excitement, especially as the President promptly called his proposed visit a "peace mission." Characteristically, however, he soon veered away from discussing the relation of this visit to the Vietnam War, which remained the most provocative issue not only in foreign policy but in many respects in domestic policy as well.

In February 1969, American troop strength in Vietnam reached a peak of 542,500 men. That June, after nominal peace proposals by both sides, the President announced his program for "Vietnamization" of the war, signifying his intention to bring home by the end of August 25,000 American combat troops, who would be replaced by South Vietnam contingents. Many doubted the ability of the South Vietnamese to function without large-scale American assistance; and some even denounced as immoral the "hiring of Asians to fight Asians" for American objectives.

By October 1969 further troop withdrawals had been announced, but neither the pace of withdrawal nor the progress of the war satisfied many Americans. In the largest public protest since the war began, hundreds of thousands across the country, most of them students and young people, observed a war "moratorium." Administration supporters also were in evidence in larger numbers than before. On Law Day, May 1, 1969, Attorney-General John N. Mitchell, who directed Nixon's 1968 "law and order" campaign, warned that "the time has come for an end to patience" in dealing with student war dissenters. They were "nothing but tyrants," he said. Mitchell's Deputy Attorney-General called them "ideological criminals." The moratorium itself, marred only by small and isolated disturbances, elicited from Vice-President Agnew the view that it had been led by "an effete corps of impudent snobs who characterize themselves as intellectuals." Far more provocative was his observation a few days later that the country should "separate" dissenting students from society "with no more regret than we should feel over discarding rotten apples from a barrel."

On April 20, 1970, Nixon announced that Vietnamization was proceeding so successfully that all American troops in Vietnam "can and will be withdrawn." Within ten days, however-

er, occurred the invasion of Cambodia by American forces to clear out "enemy sanctuaries." The administration denied that this was another undeclared war on an independent nation: it was an "incursion"; and by June 29, it was said, all American forces had been withdrawn, their objective presumably gained. In November, the full-scale bombing of North Vietnam was resumed; but these attacks were called "protective retaliation strikes." By mid-1971, the number of such strikes had reached forty-seven. In February 1971, Laos was invaded in turn, another "incursion," this one by South Vietnam forces with heavy American bombing support and with results as indefinite as those in Cambodia. Each in turn aroused the war weary at home.

One of the liabilities of Nixon's view of the relationship between the presidency and foreign affairs was the encouragement it gave to Executive secrecy and manipulation, already too evident here as well as in the vast Executive bureaucracy responsible for the implementation of domestic programs voted by Congress and upheld by the Supreme Court.

**869**

*Antiwar protesters in Washington, D.C., corralled behind hurricane fencing, May Day 1971.*

Charles Harbutt photo, Magnum

Startling Executive coups in both areas gave a strong scent of realism to the animadversions of the President himself and his friendly spokesmen on the subject of the Roman Republic's decline and fall.

Nor did the disarray in the Democratic party on the national level appear to help matters. No leader of national stature emerged after LBJ's withdrawal and the assassination of Robert Kennedy. The aspirations of Edward M. Kennedy, the last and youngest of the Kennedy brothers and Senator from Massachusetts, were short-circuited by the death of Mary Jo Kopechne, a young woman formerly on Robert Kennedy's staff, in a car driven by the Senator that plunged off a bridge in July 1969.

The youth vote which the Kennedy clan seemed especially to attract was certain to be vastly enlarged by the ratification in June 1971 of the Twenty-sixth Amendment to the Constitution providing the franchise in national elections for eighteen-year-old citizens. Although political memories are notoriously short-lived, Nixon's and Agnew's assaults on college youth during the 1970 congressional campaign—an attempt to submerge the rising "economic issue" under the old "social issue" of dissent—could hardly be expected to improve the President's chances with young voters. Yet his Roman holiday with a new economic policy and a new China policy left the Democrats a narrower field for maneuver in 1972.

## For further reading

Many books cited for chapters Thirty and Thirty-one on American militarism, the Vietnam War, and blacks in white society are also recommended for this chapter. An interesting introduction to the space drama is available in Walter Sullivan, ed., *America's Race for the Moon* (1962). See also *The Next Ten Years in Space 1959-1969* (1959), a staff report to the House Committee on Science and Astronautics. *Report of Apollo 204 Review Board* (1967), set up to investigate the accident of January 27, 1967, taking the lives of three astronauts on the "Launch Complex," discloses many of the details of space flight preparation as well as what went wrong. The subsequent space triumphs are best reported, so far, in the contemporary journalistic accounts. Norman Mailer, *Of a Fire on the Moon* (1970), is a successful attempt to get at the blood-and-guts side of the astronauts and their machines, so often buried under "computerese."

Alfred Steinberg, *Sam Johnson's Boy* (1968), is a comprehensive if critical biography. Interesting inside information is provided in Sam Houston Johnson, *My Brother Lyndon* (1970). Other outstanding accounts include Tom Wicker, *JFK and LBJ, The Influence of Personality upon Politics* (1968), Robert Novak and Rowland Evans, *Lyndon B. Johnson: The Exercise of Power* (1966), and Philip Geyelin, *Lyndon B. Johnson and the World* (1966). Neil Sheehan and others, *The Pentagon Papers* (1971), tells much of LBJ, his advisers, and their adventure in Vietnam. To the numerous books on Richard M. Nixon cited in earlier chapters, we may add here Garry Wills, *Nixon Agonistes: The Crisis of the Self-Made Man* (1970), Jules Witcover, *The Resurrection of Richard Nixon* (1970), and Gladwin Hill, *Dancing Bear, An Inside Look at California Politics* (1968).

Harold Faber, ed., *The Road to the White House: The Story of the 1964 Election by the Staff of the New York Times* (1965), is outstanding. See also T. H. White, *The Making of the President* (1965); S. C. Shadegg, *How to Win an Election* (1964); and R. J. Huckshorn, *Republican Politics: The 1964 Campaign and Its Aftermath for the Party* (1968). On the 1968 election see Mike Ryko, *Boss, Richard J. Daley of Chicago* (1971); Norman Mailer, *Miami and the Siege of Chicago, An Informal History of the Republican and Democratic Conventions of 1968* (1968); *Rights in Conflict* (1968), the Walker Report on the violence at the Democratic convention; Joe McGinniss, *The Selling of the President 1968* (1969); K. P. Phillips, *The Emerging Republican Majority* (1969); and Jeremy Larner, *Nobody Knows, Reflections on the McCarthy Campaign of 1968* (1970). T. R. Gurr, *Why Men Rebel* (1970), provides an able introduction to the "law and order" issue. See also Paul Chevigny, *Police Power* (1969), by the director of the Police Practices Project of the Civil Liberties Union.

The brief ascendancy of "Great Society" thinking,

its limitations and decline, is well presented in M. E. Gettleman and David Mermelstein, *The Great Society Reader* (1967). A. L. Schorr, *Explorations in Social Policy* (1968), is a brilliant analysis of the limitations of conventional political approaches to poverty and related problems. Johnson's "war on poverty" is also dissected in J. C. Donovan, *The Politics of Poverty* (1967). See also Robert M. O'Neil, *The Price of Dependency: Civil Liberties in the Welfare State* (1970). Gary Orfield, *The Reconstruction of Southern Education: The Schools and the 1964 Civil Rights Act* (1969), is a scholarly account of the "guidelines" for desegregation. L. E. Panetta and Peter Gall, *Bring Us Together* (1971), is an opening gun, to quote the subtitle, on "The Nixon Team and the Civil Rights Retreat." Richard Harris, *Justice* (1970) and *Decision* (1971), are revealing if not dispassionate on Attorney-General John N. Mitchell and on the Carswell Supreme Court nomination, respectively. On another domestic issue of growing importance, A. R. Miller, *The Assault on Privacy: Computers, Data Banks, and Dossiers* (1971), updates Senator Edward V. Long, *The Intruders* (1966), and A. F. Westin, *Privacy and Freedom* (1967).

To the works on civil-rights legislation and judicial decisions, and civil-rights literature and demonstrations cited in previous chapters we may add here the following on ghetto violence in the late sixties: *Report of The National Advisory Commission on Civil Disorders* (1968); H. G. Graham and T. R. Gurr, eds., *Violence in America, Historical and Comparative Perspectives* (1969); Jerry Cohen and W. S. Murphy, *Burn, Baby, Burn, The Watts Riot* (1966); Hubert G. Locke, *The Detroit Riot of 1967* (1969); and M. R. Berube and Marilyn Gittell, *Confrontation at Ocean Hill–Brownsville* (1969). On other aspects of the Negro in American society in this period, see D. M. Heer, ed., *Social Statistics and the City* (1968), on underenumerating urban blacks; Bureau of Labor Statistics, *Social and Economic Conditions of Negroes in the United States* (1967); and U.S. Department of Health, Education, and Welfare, *Equality of Educational Opportunity* (1966). J. W. Prothro, *Negroes and the New Southern Politics* (1966), offers useful background for the Republicans' "southern strategy." Other illuminating studies include Paul M. Gaston, *The New South Creed, A Study in Southern Mythmaking* (1970), and Robert Sherrill, *Gothic Politics in the Deep South* (1968). To the works on the Warren Court and its enemies already cited, we may add A. M. Bickel, *The Supreme Court and the Idea of Progress* (1970), especially good on the desegregation issue; and Fred B. Graham, *The Self-Inflicted*

*Wound* (1970), on "the Warren Court's revolutionary rulings on criminal law."

J. L. Clayton, ed., *The Economic Impact of the Cold War* (1970), provides an excellent introduction to the relationship between militarism and economic life. *The National Impact of Defense Spending* (1965), the Report of the President's Committee on the Impact of Defense and Disarmament, is an illuminating official document. R. E. Lapp, *The Weapons Culture* (1968), George Thayer, *The War Business, The International Trade in Armaments* (1969), R. J. Barnet, *The Economy of Death* (1969), Nigel Calder, ed., *Unless Peace Comes, A Scientific Forecast of New Weapons* (1968), and Eugene Rabinowitch and Ruth Adams, *Debate the Antiballistic Missile* (1967), are examples of recent literature. H. A. Marmion, *Selective Service* (1968), and G. E. Reedy, *Who Will Do Our Fighting for Us* (1969), discuss the draft and the volunteer army proposals.

Philip Geyelin on LBJ, cited above, provides an excellent introduction to the President and the world. On relations with Europe see the suggestive G. W. Ball, *The Discipline of Power* (1968), and John Newhouse, *De Gaulle and the Anglo-Saxons* (1970). See also Altiero Spinelli, *The Eurocrats: Conflict and Crisis in the European Community* (1969 edition). On the sharpening of the decline of the United Nations in American thinking, see R. J. Walton, *The Remnants of Power: The Tragic Last Years of Adlai Stevenson* (1968). On the 1965 intervention in the Dominican Republic, see J. B. Martin, *Overtaken by Events* (1966), Theodore Draper, *The Dominican Revolt* (1968); and on its consequences for hemispheric policy, Jerome Levinson and Juan de Onís, *The Alliance That Lost Its Way* (1970). On Israel's Six-Day War and related Middle East issues see Amos Elon, *The Israelis: Founders and Sons* (1971).

On the violence in Vietnam, *The Pentagon Papers* (1971), is of course invaluable. But other works, besides those already cited in previous chapters, remain useful—for example: J. C. Goulden, *Truth Is the First Casualty: The Gulf of Tonkin Affair—Illusion and Reality* (1969); R. L. Sansom, *The Economics of Insurgency in the Mekong Delta of Vietnam* (1970); Franz Schurman, P. D. Scott, and Reginald Zelnik, *The Politics of Escalation in Vietnam* (1966); David Kraslow and S. H. Loory, *The Secret Search for Peace in Vietnam* (1968); Frank Harvey, *Air War—Vietnam* (1968); W. R. Corson, *The Betrayal* (1968); Townsend Hoopes, *The Limits of Intervention* (1969); and Telford Taylor, *Nuremburg and Vietnam* (1970). R. J. Barnet, *Intervention and Revolution* (1968), is a study of "The United States in the Third World" in Vietnam and other areas of "insurgency." Carl and Shelley Mydans, *The Violent Peace* (1968), offers a telling firsthand "Report on Wars in the Postwar World," splendidly illustrated.

871

# FRENZY AND CONCERN

The American experience in the sixties has been compared to weird pieces of science fiction or comic-book fantasy replete with episodes beyond the most bizarre imaginings. The scenario features cities burned out by their own people, street warfare with knives, masked soldiers in fogs of tear gas, massed music-sick youth stoned with drugs and sprawling over the countryside, campus violence, cult murders, projects to kidnap high officials, stolen FBI files, terrorist bomb factories, and courtroom shoot-outs.

What an English critic found in American fiction of the past twenty years—"hidden persuaders, hidden dimensions, plots, secret organizations, evil systems, all kinds of conspiracies against spontaneity of consciousness, even cosmic take-overs"—all seemed more credible than the actualities which in fact left fiction behind, while poetry was enjoying a renaissance:

*He didn't die in the whirlpool by the mill . . .*
*And when he came out, he was changed forever,*
*that soft heart of his had hardened*
*and he really was a monster now. . . .*
*His idea—if his career now had an idea—*
*was to kill them all,*
*keep them in terror anyway,*
*let them feel hunted.*
*Then perhaps they would look at others*
*with a little pity and love.*
*Only a suffering people have any virtue.*
(From "The Return of Frankenstein"
by Edward Field, 1967)

The crises of the decade came to a head in a run of "confrontations" (worked-up social encounters) and court trials made to order for the mass media. For this was a time when government officials, politicians, professors, and priests competed with athletes, hippies, hairy writers, and revolutionaries for machine-made national images.

Late in the decade the Black Panthers, organized in the Oakland, California, ghetto by Bobby Seale and Huey P. Newton in 1966, showed how frightening an attuned few could become.

*Well then, believe it, my friend*
*That this silence will end*
*We'll just have to get guns*
*And be men. . . .*

So went the Black Panther ballad. A knowing journalist wrote of the Panthers early in 1970:

*They are Media Age revolutionaries, gifted with words, good at sloganeering, irresistibly photogenic, scary on television, masterful at poster art. . . . They put "pig," for policemen, into the radical vocabulary. They made berets and black leather de rigueur for splinter groups of Latin, Indian, Chinese and even Appalachian white dissidents. Ghetto kids walk with the Panther walk and talk the Panther talk. White student radicals are entranced by Panther machismo.*

All this by a violent group that never numbered as many as a thousand at one time and whose leadership and ranks were quickly depleted by shoot-outs and arrests.

In his much discussed *The Greening of America*, Charles A. Reich, a Yale law professor, forecast in 1970 that the "corporate state" would soon destroy itself, and then the emerg-

ing "youth-culture" would eventually insure the end of established attitudes toward business, politics, leisure, and the daily conduct of life. The new "consciousness of the kids," reflected in current styles of dress, automobiles, study, and social behavior, helped make him both a prophet of doom and a prophet of Utopia, not unlike the Transcendentalist radicals almost a century and a half before. Nor did the "state" in the early 1970s give any more evidence of concern, beyond speechmaking and "security" mobilization, than the state in the 1840s.

*—corporal jesus*
*commander grinly*
  *said—see that hill*
*the one with three sad trees*
    *take it . . .*
      *Check*
  *It is finished.*
      *except for that hill*
*where the singing*
    *will not stop . . .*
  *We gunned and gunned—*
  *We bombed and bombed*
    *till the sad trees*
*bent into belcanto, till bullets turned and*
*blossomed back to us, till pits healed them-*
*selves and propellers whispered a treason of*
*love and rest.*
  *This is to inform the*
*commander (who grims an ending grin)*
      *We have*
*gone over to the flowers, . . .*
  *we are finished with thunder . . .*
(From "Communique: I"
by John William Corrington, 1964)

At the same time, the divorce of the people from the state seemed to grow apace, and the concern for peace in place of needless war, for humane applications of technological prowess, for ecological protection of the earth's bounty and beauty, for peacefulness of mind in place of drugs, seemed to have gained a larger follow-ing among all age groups, if only because of the mounting and powerful evidence of danger.

## I  The 1970 census

Pessimistically or superficially inspected, the 1970 census supported dark apprehensions. By April, that year, the United States population had reached 203,184,772, not including the 1.5 million living abroad as soldiers and government employees—and the even more numerous homeless, transient, poor, and illiterate in the fifty states not caught by the mailed census forms or the individual census takers. As never before, Americans had become aware of the danger of overpopulation, and it took no special expertise to recognize its bearing on pollution, poor relief, housing, public education, health, and crime. In fact a good many radical social programs, such as campaigns to legalize abortion, popularize the "pill," and remove legal disabilities from consenting adult homosexuals, were in part spurred on and condoned by the prospect of runaway population growth.

In one respect the alarm over numbers was misplaced. The new count, in fact, reflected an overall growth rate 5 percent less for the sixties than for the fifties. Some aspects of the altered physical distribution of the population perhaps should also have tempered concern. All the publicized evils linked with overpopulation, for example, were also linked with great cities. Yet census figures for twenty-five of the largest cities, including Chicago and Philadelphia, actually declined, while for the first time, thanks to the influx of whites from the beleaguered metropolises, the nation's overall suburban population (76.3 million) exceeded that of the cities (63.9 million). But the census figures also indicated the beginnings of a black movement to the suburbs.

The metropolises, at the same time, were sustained by the continuing influx of blacks (and in some areas by other minorities, such as Puerto Ricans in the Northeast and Mexican-Americans in the Southwest). By 1970, fully a third of the nation's 22 million blacks were concentrated in but fifteen cities, with Washington, D.C., Atlanta, Newark, and Gary, Indiana, reporting actual majorities. By almost every social test—family income, employment, housing, health, military status—blacks continued to fare far less well than whites in all sections of the country.

Blacks also made some very marked gains in some areas. A 1970 survey of Negro success reported that there were nearly 1500 black officials in the United States, including 48 mayors, 168 state legislators, and 99 law-enforcement administrators. Other surveys registered growing numbers of successful black business and professional men and women. Yet black militants and others scoffed at such showings and would have scoffed at numbers ten times as large.

With rare exceptions—principally writers, artists, athletes, and entertainers—Negroes who rose in white society in the 1960s as in the late nineteenth century formed a middle-class elite whom the militants accused of deserting the black masses for white friendships and favors. Outside the black community, moreover, Negro successes were used once more to support the attribution of widespread lack of progress to personal rather than social failings. Indeed, as Harold S. Sims, the new Director of the National Urban League, said in July 1971: In view of "the frustrating conditions that the nation has suffered, there is the danger that [the majority] will continue to blame the victims, . . . like in Nazi Germany," rather than work toward solutions of the real problems. To Sims at this time the "greatest danger" facing blacks was "massive repression." Legislators, he pointed out, "were seeking to solve economic problems by punishing welfare mothers." The money sought for

"so-called domestic security," he added, was "a frightening kind of thing."

The 1970 census suggested that sheer numbers might also have added to the frenzy and concern over certain social ills. Certainly the housing and education crises, to name only two, were aggravated by the 44.4 percent jump in the 15- to 19-year-old age group between 1960 and 1970. It seems likely, too, that the rapid acceleration in juvenile crime rates during the same period had more to do with demographic changes than with parental permissiveness.

## II Collision of law and order

*To assassinate the Chase Manhattan Bank*
*Is not as easy as you'd think.*
*I walked in, see, and yelled "Kings-X!"*
*and saw what looked like great machines*
*come rumbling to a halt, and I thought,*
*fine—I'm halfway home. Then God rose from*
*the Office of President,*
*a little miffed, I think, and said,*
*"What's on your mind?"*
*"I came up from the Coast," I said,*
*"to blow this pad to—if you will*
*excuse my pun—to Kingdom Come."*
*"You can't do that, my Son," he said,*
*. . ."Put down your bomb,*
*let's have a talk," he said, and smiled.*
*I laid the bomb aside and followed him*
*into his office, and sat down.*
(From "The Plot to Assassinate the Chase Manhattan Bank" by Carl Larsen, 1961)

In his first State of the Union message on January 22, 1970, President Nixon declared:

*As we move into the decade of the seventies we have the greatest opportunity for progress at home of any people in world history. . . .*

*The critical question is not whether we will grow but how we will use that growth. The decade of the sixties was also a period of great growth economically. But in the same 10-year period we witnessed the great-*

*est growth of crime, the greatest increase in inflation, the greatest social unrest in America in 100 years. Never has a nation seemed to have more and enjoyed it less.*

At this time a number of trials and hearings were in progress or impending to which the government was a party. Each grew directly or indirectly from the Vietnam War and blurred distinctions between legality and immorality. Each, furthermore, had grotesque features which became the hallmark of the sixties.

Perhaps the most celebrated of these trials was that of the "Chicago 7," arising out of the violence that marred the 1968 Democratic National Convention. This trial began in September 1969 and ended in February 1970. Some lawyers compared it to the Roman Circus Maximus, as much for the antics of government prosecutors and Judge Hoffman as for those of the uninhibited defendants. In his final summation to the jury, United States Attorney Thomas A. Foran said of the "7": "They're sophisticated, they're smart, they're well-educated, and they're as evil as they can be." Their deepest evil, Foran said, lay in this:

*American young people are disillusioned these days. The kids do feel the lights have gone out in Camelot; the parade is over; the banners are furled. But these men take advantage of that, use it for their own purposes, for their own intents.*

876

Foran especially flayed the defendants for comparing themselves with Jesus, Martin Luther King, Jr., Mahatma Gandhi, and Robert F. Kennedy. "Can you imagine any of those figures supporting liars and obscene haters like these men?" Foran asked. William M. Kunstler, the principal defense attorney for the "7," told the jury, in turn, that by their verdict they could substantiate "the right of men to speak boldly unafraid, to be masters of their souls, to live free and die free. It is your responsibility," he said. "Perhaps if you do what is right, Allen Ginsberg [who testified for the defense] will never have to say again, as he did in his poem, 'Howl,'—'I saw the best minds of my generation destroyed by madness.'"

After five days of fatiguing deliberation, the jury of ten women and two men in this trial, most of them ordinary members of the "silent majority," acquitted all seven defendants of the government's conspiracy charges, based on evidence lawlessly obtained by wiretapping. As a result of a compromise within the jury—because "we had to give the government something after they had spent all this money on the trial," the jury foreman explained later—five of the seven were convicted on the antiriot provisions of the 1968 Open-Housing Act for crossing state lines with riotous intent. While the jury deliberated, the judge had cited all seven and their lawyers for contempt for actions during the trial and had sentenced them to jail terms ranging over two years, denying them bail at the same time. But a few days after the jury verdict, a United States Court of Appeals granted all defendants their release on bail pending hearings of their appeals.

The trial in 1968 of the "Boston 5"—Dr. Benjamin Spock, famous author of *The Pocket Book of Baby and Child Care,* and four others including the Reverend William Sloane Coffin, Jr., chaplain of Yale University—on charges of conspiracy to aid and counsel evasion of the draft lacked much of the circus character of the Chicago trial. Yet largely because of the attitude of the 85-year-old judge, who seemed to hear only the argument for the prosecution, this trial was deemed a national disgrace by many lawyers. This opinion

was strengthened by the action of the Court of Appeals in reversing the conviction of four of the five found guilty in Boston's Federal District Court.

The government case grew out of the defendants' denunciation of a letter of General Lewis B. Hershey, head of Selective Service, in October 1967, ordering that "misguided registrants" who participated in antiwar demonstrations or related activities be made subject to immediate induction. Kingman Brewster, Yale's president and a former Professor of Law at Harvard, denounced this letter as an "absolutely outrageous usurpation of power." But just as bad were the *conspiracy* charges worked up by the Department of Justice against persons who in some instances had to be introduced to each other at the trial. Certain lawyers have observed that conspiracy charges cast a wide net; and in this case, that they were brought, on very flimsy grounds, not so much because the government expected convictions, or cared about reversals of convictions by higher courts, but principally to intimidate other war protesters.

Others who like Spock and his "co-conspirators" believed in the urgency of direct action against the war were the Catholic priests Daniel and Philip Berrigan. Convicted in June 1969 of burning draft records and related charges (along with seven other priests, known collectively as the "Catonsville 9"—after the town in Maryland, scene of their activities), the Berrigans became fugitives but eventually were taken and imprisoned.

A trial of far greater magnitude and one posing even knottier moral problems ended in April 1971 when a military court sentenced First Lieutenant William Calley to life imprisonment for murdering twenty-two Vietnamese civilians at My Lai village in 1968. Calley's conviction at the close of the longest court-martial in United States history touched off an explosion of protest throughout the country. A Gallup Poll disclosed that 71 percent believed that others shared responsibility for the massacre and 69 percent thought Calley had been made a scapegoat. When President Nixon ordered Calley released from the Fort Benning stockade pending appeal, 83 percent of those polled approved.

Apart from its political reverberations and its disastrous impact on army morale, this trial brought home to the American people—as no previous event had done—the question of national complicity in the Vietnam holocaust. As more evidence came to light about other mas-sacres, of saturation bombing, forced evacuation of villages in "free-fire" zones, and the like, the line between legitimate and illegitimate warfare virtually disappeared. Who were the criminals—soldiers carrying out orders or the men who gave them? "You did not strip him of his honor," Captain Aubrey Daniel III, the prosecutor, told the military panel. "What he did stripped him of his honor. . . . It is not honor—and never can be considered an honor—to kill men, women, and children." Yet the court-martial implicated many more than Calley, and more questions were raised than resolved.

## III The "forerunners"

"No other society in history," wrote *Fortune* in its intensive survey of the younger generation of 1968, "has ever had to deal with *mass* educated youth." Not all the college men surveyed belonged to *Fortune*'s "forerunners" of a new ethos. Indeed, 60 percent stood on "the 'practical' side of the line," committed to careers in big business or big government, or in adjunct professions, more or less as they found them. These composed the nonmilitant majority during the tumultuous student riots of 1968, more interested—as *Fortune* put it—"in learning to build new cities than in learning old theologies" and in preparing themselves for the emoluments of power and the amenities of affluence. But even they appeared much less likely to be absorbed into conventional society than were their conspicuous predecessors in the Jazz Age and the campus radicals of the Great Depression.

In contrast to the practical "responsibility seekers," the "forerunners" sought to avoid ensnarement in the "paper trap" of white-collar life. To "change things" did not necessarily mean that they, any more than the "practical," wanted to wreck their universities or their society. Disenchanted they clearly were, but largely with the sterile values of practicality.

America's sudden awakening to the contami-nation of the environment after at least a quarter century of warning by prophets like Rachel Carson seemed to provide many "forerunners" with a congenial outlet for constructive social action. The pollution crisis evoked the familiar prophecies of cosmic disaster often heard during the sixties, and "ecology" became a battle cry for the reformers. Business spokesmen soon complained that their adversaries tended to oversimplify the complex and expensive task of dealing with the pollution crisis. Yet at the end of the decade, largely because of "forerunner" leadership, enough significant legislation had been passed to give promise of better things to come.

Most of the progress in this field resulted from the work of Ralph Nader, a young lawyer who attracted congenial lawyers, doctors, and engineers, all willing to work for little or nothing. These young people became known as "Nader's raiders," and they attracted especially strong support on the nation's campuses by their convincing demonstrations of effective action against formidable corporate and political obstructionists. If all students contributed the $250 each of them spent annually on cokes, tobacco, and alcohol to some national student lobby, Nader once said, they could become the most powerful political force in Washington.

## IV  The coming American Revolution?

Henry Adams in 1891 closed his classic nine-volume history of Jefferson's and Madison's administrations with this passage on the young republicans in 1815:

*They were intelligent, but what paths would their intelligence select? They were quick, but what solution of insoluble problems would quickness hurry? They were scientific, and what control would their science exercise over their destiny? They were mild, but what corruptions would their relaxations bring? They were peaceful, but by what machinery were their corruptions to be purged? What interests were to vivify a society so vast and uniform? What ideals were to ennoble it? What object, besides physical content, must a democratic continent aspire to attain? For the treatment of such questions, history required another century of experience.*

Henry Adams was a pessimist; the very way he framed his questions suggested the unlikelihood of satisfactory answers, century after century. His generation, at the same time, counted many more optimists than our own, and they set the United States upon a course that became at once a model and a menace to older societies around the world. The model is somewhat tarnished now, the menace enlarged. Pessimism has become more general, and with good reason. To many, the degeneration of the democratic model has become irreversible, the menace of technological blind strength one of the principal sources of discontent. And yet the people remain their own best resource, and unprecedented dangers may have strengthened their resolve.

After eight years of terrible stress, Americans were still able to make a realistic appraisal of the Vietnam War, criticize official governmental blunders, and generally agree that the whole thing was a mistake. In a national poll in June 1970, only 36 percent said they believed the United States to be right in Vietnam. The Calley conviction, however one looked at it, was a concession of error if not sin. No other American military trial had been so minutely reported nor so freely criticized in the media.

The outcome of the rash of government conspiracy trials, in turn, showed the strength and value of the jury system, while the Supreme Court decision on the Pentagon Papers, whatever may be said of the administration's suit, could hardly have been duplicated in other countries. When the House of Representatives in July 1971 denied demands for a contempt citation against the Columbia Broadcasting System for refusing to yield unused portions of its informative nationwide telecast "The Selling of the Pentagon," it too showed a responsiveness to the voters and an independence of the Executive already strongly evident for many years among the Vietnam doves of the Upper House.

Television, indeed, often feared as an instrument of centralized government information control, may have become one of the major instrumentalities of popular education and expression. More effectively than any other medium, television brought all of life into focused image, turning individuals and groups into media performers: combat teams and tormented villagers in Vietnam; starving children in Biafra; moon-bound astronauts; Mexican-American striking grape pickers; the welfare poor in New York City hotels; courtroom characters; celebrities from the world of sport and entertainment—all competed for "prime time" on the "boob tube." The vast unseen audience wanted as much to be informed and edified as thrilled and amused.

The very ease with which any opinion from

the most shocking and heterodox to the most reactionary could receive a hearing in some branch of the communication media might have indicated to radicals left and right that the "establishment" was not exactly tottering. The threats and warnings and the strategies for upheaval or repression produced no per-

manent "armies of the night" nor guerrillas in the hills. Mounting episodes of violence in the sixties and early seventies caused blacks and whites alike to express the conviction that America could only be cleansed by killing. Yet sporadic riots and bombings, murders of and by police, did not constitute a revolution; and as the 1972 elections approached, under widespread popular pressure the issue of peace at home and abroad seemed to have regained national attention.

## For further reading

Many books cited for Chapter Thirty-two are useful for this chapter as well. Good introductions to the media include G. A. Steiner, *The People Look at Television* (1963), Andrew Sarris, *The American Cinema* (1968), and D. M. White and R. Averson, eds., *Sight, Sound and Society* (1969). Jonathan Bombach, *The Landscape of Nightmare* (1965), and Robert Scholes, *The Fabulators* (1967), cover recent fiction. Recent poetry is discussed in Richard Howard, *Alone with America* (1969). See also Bruce Cook, *The Beat Generation* (1971).

C. A. Reich, *The Greening of America* (1970), became one of the most popular accounts of the changing values of young people. See also Alvin Toffler, *Future Shock* (1970). Other illuminating studies of this subject include Keith Kenniston, *The Uncommitted: Alienated Youth in American Society* (1965); Paul Goodman's writings, beginning with *Growing up Absurd* (1960); and Erik Erikson's books, beginning with *Childhood and Society* (1950). The populist philosopher Eric Hoffer is well represented in his *The Temper of Our Time* (1967). R. P. Warren, *Who Speaks for the Negro?* (1966), has lasting value for its tape-recorded interviews and reflections of the author on the situation in the South. K. B. Clark, *Dark Ghetto* (1965), and Oscar Lewis, *La Vida: A Puerto Rican Family in the Culture of Poverty—San Juan and New York* (1966), are of lasting value on ghetto life.

Christopher Jencks and David Riesman, *The Academic Revolution* (1968), is comprehensive on the changing college scene. See also Sidney Hook, *Academic Freedom and Academic Anarchy* (1970), and G. R. and J. H. Weaver, eds., *The University and Revolution* (1969). Robert Bendiner, *The Politics of Schools* (1969), affords nationwide coverage on public education. J. J. Hadden, *The Gathering Storm in the Churches* (1970), and D. R. Cutler, ed., *The Religious Situation* (1969), appraise the religious schisms.

Informative on the issue of law and order are such official publications as *To Establish Justice, To Insure Domestic Tranquility* (1969), "Final Report of the National Commission on the Causes and Prevention of Violence"; and *Campus Unrest* (1970), "The Report of the President's Commission." Jessica Mitford, *The Trial of Dr. Spock* (1969), and Robert Sherrill, *Military Justice is to Justice as Military Music is to Music* (1970), are examples of useful popular studies of courtroom practice.

P. R. and A. H. Ehrlich, *Population, Resources, Environment* (1970), is outstanding on worldwide "Issues in Human Ecology," with a valuable bibliography. See also Paul Shepard and Daniel McKinley, eds., *The Subversive Science, Essays Toward an Ecology of Man* (1969). V. C. Ferkiss, *Technological Man* (1969), is a well-informed analysis, as is E. E. Morison, *Men, Machines and Modern Times* (1968). Morton Mintz and J. S. Cohen, *America, Inc., Who Owns and Operates the United States* (1971), is an outstanding example of the work of Ralph Nader's "raiders." See also P. F. Drucker, *The Age of Discontinuity* (1969). Stuart Chase, *The Most Probable World* (1968), is an informed projection of the twenty-first century.

# APPENDIX

THE DECLARATION OF INDEPENDENCE

When in the course of human events it becomes necessary for one people to dissolve the political bands which have connected them with another and to assume, among the powers of the earth, the separate and equal station to which the laws of nature and of nature's God entitle them, a decent respect to the opinions of mankind requires that they should declare the causes which impel them to the separation.

We hold these truths to be self-evident, that all men are created equal; that they are endowed by their Creator with certain unalienable rights; that among these are life, liberty, and the pursuit of happiness. That, to secure these rights, governments are instituted among men, deriving their just powers from the consent of the governed; that, whenever any form of government becomes destructive of these ends, it is the right of the people to alter or to abolish it, and to institute a new government, laying its foundation on such principles, and organizing its powers in such form, as to them shall seem most likely to effect their safety and happiness. Prudence, indeed, will dictate that governments long established should not be changed for light and transient causes; and, accordingly, all experience hath shown that mankind are more disposed to suffer, while evils are sufferable, than to right themselves by abolishing the forms to which they are accustomed. But when a long train of abuses and usurpations, pursuing invariably the same object, evinces a design to reduce them under absolute despotism, it is their right, it is their duty, to throw off such government and to provide new guards for their future security. Such has been the patient sufferance of these colonies, and such is now the necessity which constrains them to alter their former systems of government. The history of the present King of Great Britain is a history of repeated injuries and usurpations, all having, in direct object, the establishment of an absolute tyranny over these States. To prove this, let facts be submitted to a candid world:

He has refused his assent to laws the most wholesome and necessary for the public good.

He has forbidden his governors to pass laws of immediate and pressing importance, unless suspended in their operation till his assent should be obtained; and, when so suspended, he has utterly neglected to attend to them.

He has refused to pass other laws for the accommodation of large districts of people, unless those people would relinquish the right of representation in the legislature; a right inestimable to them and formidable to tyrants only.

He has called together legislative bodies at places unusual, uncomfortable, and distant from the depository of their public records, for the sole purpose of fatiguing them into compliance with his measures.

He has dissolved representative houses, repeatedly for opposing, with manly firmness, his invasions on the rights of the people.

He has refused, for a long time after such dissolutions, to cause others to be elected; whereby the legislative powers, incapable of annihilation, have returned to the people at large for their exercise; the state remaining, in the meantime, exposed to all the danger of invasion from without and convulsions within.

He has endeavored to prevent the population of these States; for that purpose, obstructing the laws for naturalization of foreigners, refusing to pass others to encourage their migration hither, and raising the conditions of new appropriations of lands.

He has obstructed the administration of justice by refusing his assent to laws for establishing judiciary powers.

He has made judges dependent on his will alone for the tenure of their offices and the amount and payment of their salaries.

He has erected a multitude of new offices and sent hither swarms of officers to harass our people and eat out their substance.

He has kept among us, in time of peace, standing armies, without the consent of our legislatures.

He has affected to render the military independent of, and superior to, the civil power.

He has combined with others to subject us to a jurisdiction foreign to our Constitution and unacknowledged by our laws, giving his assent to their acts of pretended legislation—

For quartering large bodies of armed troops among us;

For protecting them by a mock trial from punishment for any murders which they should commit on the inhabitants of these States;

For cutting off our trade with all parts of the world;

For imposing taxes on us without our consent;

For depriving us, in many cases, of the benefit of trial by jury;

For transporting us beyond seas to be tried for pretended offences;

For abolishing the free system of English laws in a neighboring province, establishing therein an arbitrary government, and enlarging its boundaries, so as to render it at once an example and fit instrument for introducing the same absolute rule into these colonies;

For taking away our charters, abolishing our most valuable laws, and altering, fundamentally, the powers of our governments;

For suspending our own legislatures and declaring themselves invested with power to legislate for us in all cases whatsoever.

He has abdicated government here by declaring us out of his protection and waging war against us.

He has plundered our seas, ravaged our coasts, burnt our towns, and destroyed the lives of our people.

He is, at this time, transporting large armies of foreign mercenaries to complete the works of death, desolation, and tyranny already begun with circumstances of cruelty and perfidy scarcely paralleled in the most barbarous ages, and totally unworthy the head of a civilized nation.

He has constrained our fellow citizens, taken captive on the high seas, to bear arms against their country, to become the executioners of their friends and brethren, or to fall themselves by their hands.

He has excited domestic insurrections amongst us and has endeavored to bring on the inhabitants of our frontiers, the merciless Indian savages, whose known rule of warfare is an undistinguished destruction of all ages, sexes, and conditions.

In every stage of these oppressions, we have petitioned for redress in the most humble terms; our repeated petitions have been answered only by repeated injury. A prince whose character is thus marked by every act which may define a tyrant is unfit to be the ruler of a free people.

Nor have we been wanting in attention to our British brethren. We have warned them, from time to time, of attempts made by their legislature to extend an unwarrantable jurisdiction over us. We have reminded them of the circumstances of our emigration and settlement here. We have appealed to their native justice and magnanimity, and we have conjured them, by the ties of our common kindred, to disavow these usurpations, which would inevitably interrupt our connections and correspondence. They, too, have been deaf to the voice of justice and consanguinity. We must, therefore, acquiesce in the necessity which denounces our separation, and hold them, as we hold the rest of mankind, enemies in war, in peace, friends.

We, therefore, the representatives of the United States of America, in general Congress assembled, appealing to the Supreme Judge of the world for the rectitude of our intentions, do, in the name and by the authority of the good people of these colonies, solemnly publish and declare, that these united colonies are, and of right ought to be, free and independent states: that they are absolved from all allegiance to the British Crown, and that all political connection between them and the state of Great Britain is, and ought to be, totally dissolved; and that, as free and independent states, they have full power to levy war, conclude peace, contract alliances, establish commerce, and to do all other acts and things which independent states may of right do. And, for the support of this declaration, with a firm reliance on the protection of Divine Providence, we mutually pledge to each other our lives, our fortunes, and our sacred honor.

## THE CONSTITUTION OF THE UNITED STATES OF AMERICA

We the people of the United States, in order to form a more perfect union, establish justice, insure domestic tranquillity, provide for the common defense, promote the general welfare, and secure the blessings of liberty to ourselves and our posterity, do ordain and establish this Constitution for the United States of America.

*Article I*

SECTION 1. All legislative powers herein granted shall be vested in a Congress of the United States, which shall consist of a Senate and House of Representatives.

SECTION 2.  1. The House of Representatives shall be composed of members chosen every second year by the people of the several States, and the electors in each State shall have the qualifications requisite for electors of the most numerous branch of the State legislature.

2. No person shall be a representative who shall not have attained to the age of twenty-five years, and been seven years a citizen of the United States, and who shall not, when elected, be an inhabitant of that State in which he shall be chosen.

3. Representatives and direct taxes[1] shall be apportioned among the several States which may be included within this Union, according to their respective numbers, which shall be determined by adding to the whole number of free persons, including those bound to service for a term of years, and excluding Indians not taxed, three fifths of all other persons.[2] The actual enumeration shall be made within three years after the first meeting of the Congress of the United States, and within every subsequent term of ten years, in such manner as they shall by law direct. The number of representatives shall not exceed one for every thirty thousand, but each State shall have at least one representative; and until such enumeration shall be made, the State of New Hampshire shall be entitled to choose three, Massachusetts eight, Rhode Island and Providence Plantations one, Connecticut five, New York six, New Jersey four, Pennsylvania eight, Delaware one, Maryland six, Virginia ten, North Carolina five, South Carolina five, and Georgia three.

4. When vacancies happen in the representation from any State, the executive authority thereof shall issue writs of election to fill such vacancies.

5. The House of Representatives shall choose their speaker and other officers; and shall have the sole power of impeachment.

SECTION 3.  1. The Senate of the United States shall be composed of two senators from each State, chosen by the legislature thereof,[3] for six years; and each senator shall have one vote.

2. Immediately after they shall be assembled in consequence of the first election, they shall be divided as equally as may be into three classes. The seats of the senators of the first class shall be vacated at the expiration of the second year, of the second class at the expiration of the fourth year, and of the third class at the expiration of the sixth year, so that one third may be chosen every second year; and if vacancies happen by resignation, or otherwise, during the recess of the legislature of any State, the executive thereof may make temporary appointments until the next meeting of the legislature, which shall then fill such vacancies.[4]

3. No person shall be a senator who shall not have attained to the age of thirty years, and been nine years a citizen of the United States, and who shall not, when elected, be an inhabitant of that State for which he shall be chosen.

4. The Vice President of the United States shall be President of the Senate, but shall have no vote, unless they be equally divided.

1 See the Sixteenth Amendment.
2 See the Fourteenth Amendment.
3 See the Seventeenth Amendment.
4 See the Seventeenth Amendment.

5. The Senate shall choose their other officers, and also a president pro tempore, in the absence of the Vice President, or when he shall exercise the office of the President of the United States.

6. The Senate shall have the sole power to try all impeachments. When sitting for that purpose, they shall be on oath or affirmation. When the President of the United States is tried, the chief justice shall preside: and no person shall be convicted without the concurrence of two thirds of the members present.

7. Judgment in cases of impeachment shall not extend further than to removal from office, and disqualifications to hold and enjoy any office of honor, trust or profit under the United States: but the party convicted shall nevertheless be liable and subject to indictment, trial, judgment and punishment, according to law.

SECTION 4.  1. The times, places, and manner of holding elections for senators and representatives, shall be prescribed in each State by the legislature thereof; but the Congress may·at any time by law make or alter such regulations, except as to the places of choosing senators.

2. The Congress shall assemble at least once in every year, and such meeting shall be on the first Monday in December, unless they shall by law appoint a different day.

SECTION 5.  1. Each House shall be the judge of the elections, returns and qualifications of its own members, and a majority of each shall constitute a quorum to do business; but a smaller number may adjourn from day to day, and may be authorized to compel the attendance of absent members, in such manner, and under such penalties as each House may provide.

2. Each House may determine the rules of its proceedings, punish its members for disorderly behavior, and, with the concurrence of two thirds, expel a member.

3. Each House shall keep a journal of its proceedings, and from time to time publish the same, excepting such parts as may in their judgment require secrecy; and the yeas and nays of the members of either House on any question shall, at the desire of one fifth of those present, be entered on the journal.

4. Neither House, during the session of Congress, shall, without the consent of the other, adjourn for more than three days, nor to any other place than that in which the two Houses shall be sitting.

SECTION 6.  1. The senators and representatives shall receive a compensation for their services, to be ascertained by law, and paid out of the Treasury of the United States. They shall in all cases, except treason, felony, and breach of the peace, be privileged from arrest during their attendance at the session of their respective Houses, and in going to and returning from the same; and for any speech or debate in either House, they shall not be questioned in any other place.

2. No senator or representative shall, during the time for which he was elected, be appointed to any civil office under the authority of the United States, which shall have been created, or the emoluments whereof shall have been increased, during such time; and no person holding any office under the United States shall be a member of either House during his continuance in office.

SECTION 7. 1. All bills for raising revenue shall originate in the House of Representatives; but the Senate may propose or concur with amendments as on other bills.

2. Every bill which shall have passed the House of Representatives and the Senate, shall, before it become a law, be presented to the President of the United States; If he approves he shall sign it, but if not he shall return it, with his objections, to that House in which it shall have originated, who shall enter the objections at large on their journal, and proceed to reconsider it. If after such reconsideration two thirds of that House shall agree to pass the bill, it shall be sent, together with the objections, to the other House, by which it shall likewise be reconsidered, and if approved by two thirds of that House, it shall become a law. But in all such cases the votes of both Houses shall be determined by yeas and nays, and the names of the persons voting for and against the bill shall be entered on the journal of each House respectively. If any bill shall not be returned by the President within ten days (Sundays excepted) after it shall have been presented to him, the same shall be a law, in like manner as if he had signed it, unless the Congress by their adjournment prevent its return, in which case it shall not be a law.

3. Every order, resolution, or vote to which the concurrence of the Senate and the House of Representatives may be necessary (except on a question of adjournment) shall be presented to the President of the United States; and before the same shall take effect, shall be approved by him, or being disapproved by him, shall be repassed by two thirds of the Senate and House of Representatives, according to the rules and limitations prescribed in the case of a bill.

SECTION 8. The Congress shall have the power

1. To lay and collect taxes, duties, imposts, and excises, to pay the debts and provide for the common defense and general welfare of the United States; but all duties, imposts, and excises shall be uniform throughout the United States;

2. To borrow money on the credit of the United States;

3. To regulate commerce with foreign nations, and among the several States, and with the Indian tribes;

4. To establish an uniform rule of naturalization, and uniform laws on the subject of bankruptcies throughout the United States;

5. To coin money, regulate the value thereof, and of foreign coin, and fix the standard of weights and measures;

6. To provide for the punishment of counterfeiting the securities and current coin of the United States;

7. To establish post offices and post roads;

8. To promote the progress of science and useful arts, by securing for limited times to authors and inventors the exclusive right to their respective writings and discoveries;

9. To constitute tribunals inferior to the Supreme Court;

10. To define and punish piracies and felonies committed on the high seas, and offenses against the law of nations;

11. To declare war, grant letters of marque and reprisal, and make rules concerning captures on land and water;

12. To raise and support armies, but no appropriation of money to that use shall be for a longer term than two years;

13. To provide and maintain a navy;

14. To make rules for the government and regulation of the land and naval forces;

15. To provide for calling forth the militia to execute the laws of the Union, suppress insurrections and repel invasions;

16. To provide for organizing, arming, and disciplining the militia, and for governing such part of them as may be employed in the service of the United States, reserving to the States respectively, the appointment of the officers, and the authority of training the militia according to the discipline prescribed by Congress;

17. To exercise exclusive legislation in all cases whatsoever, over such district (not exceeding ten miles square) as may, by cession of particular States, and the acceptance of Congress, become the seat of the government of the United States, and to exercise like authority over all places purchased by the consent of the legislature of the State in which the same shall be, for the erection of forts, magazines, arsenals, dockyards, and other needful buildings; and

18. To make all laws which shall be necessary and proper for carrying into execution the foregoing powers, and all other powers vested by this Constitution in the government of the United States, or any department or officer thereof.

SECTION 9. 1. The migration or importation of such persons as any of the States now existing shall think proper to admit, shall not be prohibited by the Congress prior to the year one thousand eight hundred and eight, but a tax or duty may be imposed on such importation, not exceeding ten dollars for each person.

2. The privilege of the writ of habeas corpus shall not be suspended, unless when in cases of rebellion or invasion the public safety may require it.

3. No bill of attainder or ex post facto law shall be passed.

4. No capitation, or other direct, tax shall be laid, unless in proportion to the census or enumeration hereinbefore directed to be taken.[5]

5. No tax or duty shall be laid on articles exported from any State.

6. No preference shall be given by any regulation of commerce or revenue to the ports of one State over those of another: nor shall vessels bound to, or from, one State be obliged to enter, clear, or pay duties in another.

7. No money shall be drawn from the treasury, but in consequence of appropriations made by law; and a regular statement and account of the receipts and expenditures of all public money shall be published from time to time.

8. No title of nobility shall be granted by the United States: and no person holding any office of

[5] See the Sixteenth Amendment.

profit or trust under them, shall, without the consent of the Congress, accept of any present, emolument, office, or title, of any kind whatever, from any king, prince, or foreign State.

section 10. 1. No State shall enter into any treaty, alliance, or confederation; grant letters of marque and reprisal; coin money; emit bills of credit; make any thing but gold and silver coin a tender in payment of debts; pass any bill of attainder, ex post facto law, or law impairing the obligation of contracts, or grant any title of nobility.

2. No State shall, without the consent of the Congress, lay any imposts or duties on imports or exports, except what may be absolutely necessary for executing its inspection laws: and the net produce of all duties and imposts laid by any State on imports or exports, shall be for the use of the treasury of the United States; and all such laws shall be subject to the revision and control of the Congress.

3. No State shall, without the consent of the Congress, lay any duty of tonnage, keep troops, or ships of war in time of peace, enter into any agreement or compact with another State, or with a foreign power, or engage in war, unless actually invaded, or in such imminent danger as will not admit of delay.

*Article II*

section 1. 1. The executive power shall be vested in a President of the United States of America. He shall hold his office during the term of four years, and, together with the Vice President, chosen for the same term, be elected, as follows:

2. Each State shall appoint, in such manner as the legislature thereof may direct, a number of electors, equal to the whole number of senators and representatives to which the State may be entitled in the Congress: but no senator or representative, or person holding an office of trust or profit under the United States, shall be appointed an elector.

The electors shall meet in their respective States, and vote by ballot for two persons, of whom one at least shall not be an inhabitant of the same State with themselves. And they shall make a list of all the persons voted for, and of the number of votes for each; which list they shall sign and certify, and transmit sealed to the seat of the government of the United States, directed to the president of the Senate. The president of the Senate shall, in the presence of the Senate and House of Representatives, open all the certificates, and the votes shall then be counted. The person having the greatest number of votes shall be the President, if such number be a majority of the whole number of electors appointed; and if there be more than one who have such majority, and have an equal number of votes, then the House of Representatives shall immediately choose by ballot one of them for President; and if no person have a majority, then from the five highest on the list the said House shall in like manner choose the President. But in choosing the President, the votes shall be taken by States, the representation from each State having one vote; a quorum for this purpose shall consist of a member or members from two thirds of the States, and a majority of all the States shall be necessary to a choice. In every case, after the choice of the President, the person having the greatest number of votes of the electors shall be the Vice President. But if there should remain two or more who have equal votes, the Senate shall choose from them by ballot the Vice President.[6]

3. The Congress may determine the time of choosing the electors, and the day on which they shall give their votes; which day shall be the same throughout the United States.

4. No person except a natural born citizen, or a citizen of the United States, at the time of the adoption of this Constitution, shall be eligible to the office of President; neither shall any person be eligible to that office who shall not have attained to the age of thirty-five years, and been fourteen years a resident within the United States.

5. In case of the removal of the President from office, or of his death, resignation, or inability to discharge the powers and duties of the said office, the same shall devolve on the Vice President, and the Congress may by law provide for the case of removal, death, resignation or inability, both of the President and Vice President, declaring what officer shall then act as President, and such officer shall act accordingly, until the disability be removed, or a President shall be elected.

6. The President shall, at stated times, receive for his services a compensation, which shall neither be increased nor diminished during the period for which he shall have been elected, and he shall not receive within that period any other emolument from the United States, or any of them.

7. Before he enter on the execution of his office, he shall take the following oath or affirmation:—"I do solemnly swear (or affirm) that I will faithfully execute the office of President of the United States, and will to the best of my ability, preserve, protect and defend the Constitution of the United States."

section 2. 1. The President shall be commander in chief of the army and navy of the United States, and of the militia of the several States, when called into the actual service of the United States; he may require the opinion, in writing, of the principal officer in each of the executive departments, upon any subject relating to the duties of their respective offices, and he shall have power to grant reprieves and pardons for offenses against the United States, except in cases of impeachment.

2. He shall have power, by and with the advice and consent of the Senate, to make treaties, provided two thirds of the senators present concur; and he shall nominate, and by and with the advice and consent of the Senate, shall appoint ambassadors, other public ministers and consuls, judges of the Supreme Court, and all other officers of the United States, whose appointments are not herein otherwise provided for, and which shall be established by law: but the Congress may by law vest the appointment of such inferior officers, as they think proper, in the President alone, in the courts of law, or in the heads of departments.

6 Superseded by the Twelfth Amendment.

3. The President shall have power to fill up all vacancies that may happen during the recess of the Senate, by granting commissions which shall expire at the end of their next session.

SECTION 3. He shall from time to time give to the Congress information of the state of the Union, and recommend to their consideration such measures as he shall judge necessary and expedient; he may, on extraordinary occasions, convene both Houses, or either of them, and in case of disagreement between them with respect to the time of adjournment, he may adjourn them to such time as he shall think proper; he shall receive ambassadors and other public ministers; he shall take care that the laws be faithfully executed, and shall commission all the officers of the United States.

SECTION 4. The President, Vice President, and all civil officers of the United States, shall be removed from office on impeachment for, and conviction of, treason, bribery, or other high crimes and misdemeanors.

## Article III

SECTION 1. The judicial power of the United States shall be vested in one Supreme Court, and in such inferior courts as the Congress may from time to time ordain and establish. The judges, both of the Supreme and inferior courts, shall hold their offices during good behavior, and shall, at stated times, receive for their services, a compensation, which shall not be diminished during their continuance in office.

SECTION 2. 1. The judicial power shall extend to all cases, in law and equity, arising under this Constitution, the laws of the United States, and treaties made, or which shall be made, under their authority;—to all cases affecting ambassadors, other public ministers and consuls;—to all cases of admiralty and maritime jurisdiction;—to controversies to which the United States shall be a party;[7]—to controversies between two or more States;—between a State and citizens of another State;—between citizens of different States;—between citizens of the same State claiming lands under grants of different States, and between a State, or the citizens thereof, and foreign States, citizens or subjects.

2. In all cases affecting ambassadors, other public ministers and consuls, and those in which a State shall be party, the Supreme Court shall have original jurisdiction. In all the other cases before mentioned, the Supreme Court shall have appellate jurisdiction, both as to law and fact, with such exceptions, and under such regulations as the Congress shall make.

3. The trial of all crimes, except in cases of impeachment, shall be by jury; and such trial shall be held in the State where the said crimes shall have been committed; but when not committed within any State, the trial shall be at such place or places as the Congress may by law have directed.

SECTION 3. 1. Treason against the United States shall consist only in levying war against them, or in adhering to their enemies, giving them aid and comfort. No person shall be convicted of treason unless on the testimony of two witnesses to the same overt act, or on confession in open court.

2. The Congress shall have power to declare the punishment of treason, but no attainder of treason shall work corruption of blood, or forfeiture except during the life of the person attainted.

## Article IV

SECTION 1. Full faith and credit shall be given in each State to the public acts, records, and judicial proceedings of every other State. And the Congress may by general laws prescribe the manner in which such acts, records and proceedings shall be proved, and the effect thereof.

SECTION 2. 1. The citizens of each State shall be entitled to all privileges and immunities of citizens in the several States.[8]

2. A person charged in any State with treason, felony, or other crime, who shall flee from justice, and be found in another State, shall on demand of the executive authority of the State from which he fled, be delivered up to be removed to the State having jurisdiction of the crime.

3. No person held to service or labor in one State under the laws thereof, escaping into another, shall, in consequence of any law or regulation therein, be discharged from such service or labor, but shall be delivered up on claim of the party to whom such service or labor may be due.[9]

SECTION 3. 1. New States may be admitted by the Congress into this Union; but no new State shall be formed or erected within the jurisdiction of any other State; nor any State be formed by the junction of two or more States, or parts of States, without the consent of the legislatures of the States concerned as well as of the Congress.

2. The Congress shall have power to dispose of and make all needful rules and regulations respecting the territory or other property belonging to the United States; and nothing in this Constitution shall be so construed as to prejudice any claims of the United States, or of any particular State.

SECTION 4. The United States shall guarantee to every State in this Union a republican form of government, and shall protect each of them against invasion; and on application of the legislature, or of the executive (when the legislature cannot be convened) against domestic violence.

## Article V

The Congress, whenever two thirds of both Houses shall deem it necessary, shall propose amendments to this Constitution, or, on the application of the legislatures of two thirds of the several States, shall call a convention for proposing amendments, which in either case, shall be valid to all intents and purposes, as part of this Constitution, when ratified by the legislatures of three fourths of the several States, or by conven-

7 See the Eleventh Amendment.

8 See the Fourteenth Amendment, Sec. 1.
9 See the Thirteenth Amendment.

tions in three fourths thereof, as the one or the other mode of ratification may be proposed by the Congress; Provided that no amendment which may be made prior to the year one thousand eight hundred and eight shall in any manner affect the first and fourth clauses in the ninth section of the first article; and that no State, without its consent, shall be deprived of its equal suffrage in the Senate.

### Article VI

1. All debts contracted and engagements entered into, before the adoption of this Constitution, shall be as valid against the United States under this Constitution, as under the Confederation.[10]
2. This Constitution, and the laws of the United States which shall be made in pursuance thereof; and all treaties made, or which shall be made, under the authority of the United States, shall be the supreme law of the land; and the judges in every State shall be bound thereby, any thing in the Constitution or laws of any State to the contrary notwithstanding.
3. The senators and representatives before mentioned, and the members of the several State legislatures, and all executive and judicial officers, both of the United States and of the several States, shall be bound by oath or affirmation to support this Constitution; but no religious test shall ever be required as a qualification to any office or public trust under the United States.

### Article VII

The ratification of the conventions of nine States shall be sufficient for the establishment of this Constitution between the States so ratifying the same.

Done in Convention by the unanimous consent of the States present the seventeenth day of September in the year of our Lord one thousand seven hundred and eighty-seven, and of the independence of the United States of America the twelfth. In witness whereof we have hereunto subscribed our names.

[Names omitted]

\*   \*   \*

*Articles in addition to, and amendment of, the Constitution of the United States of America, proposed by Congress, and ratified by the legislatures of the several States, pursuant to the fifth article of the original Constitution.*

### Amendment I [First ten amendments ratified December 15, 1791]

Congress shall make no law respecting an establishment of religion, or prohibiting the free exercise thereof; or abridging the freedom of speech, or of the press; or the right of the people peaceably to assemble, and to petition the government for a redress of grievances.

[10] See the Fourteenth Amendment, Sec. 4.

### Amendment II

A well regulated militia, being necessary to the security of a free State, the right of the people to keep and bear arms, shall not be infringed.

### Amendment III

No soldier shall, in time of peace be quartered in any house, without the consent of the owner, nor in time of war, but in a manner to be prescribed by law.

### Amendment IV

The right of the people to secure in their persons, houses, papers, and effects, against unreasonable searches and seizures, shall not be violated, and no warrants shall issue, but upon probable cause, supported by oath or affirmation, and particularly describing the place to be searched, and the persons or things to be seized.

### Amendment V

No person shall be held to answer for a capital, or otherwise infamous crime, unless on a presentment or indictment of a grand jury, except in cases arising in the land or naval forces, or in the militia, when in actual service in time of war or public danger; nor shall any person be subject for the same offense to be twice put in jeopardy of life or limb; nor shall be compelled in any criminal case to be a witness against himself, nor be deprived of life, liberty, or property, without due process of law; nor shall private property be taken for public use, without just compensation.

### Amendment VI

In all criminal prosecutions, the accused shall enjoy the right to a speedy and public trial, by an impartial jury of the State and district wherein the crime shall have been committed, which district shall have been previously ascertained by law, and to be informed of the nature and cause of the accusation; to be confronted with the witnesses against him; to have compulsory process for obtaining witnesses in his favor, and to have the assistance of counsel for his defense.

### Amendment VII

In suits at common law, where the value in controversy shall exceed twenty dollars, the right of trial by jury shall be preserved, and no fact tried by a jury shall be otherwise reëxamined in any court of the United States, than according to the rules of the common law.

### Amendment VIII

Excessive bail shall not be required, nor excessive fines imposed, nor cruel and unusual punishments inflicted.

## Amendment IX

The enumeration in the Constitution of certain rights shall not be construed to deny or disparage others retained by the people.

## Amendment X

The powers not delegated to the United States by the Constitution, nor prohibited by it to the States, are reserved to the States respectively, or to the people.

## Amendment XI [January 8, 1798]

The judicial power of the United States shall not be construed to extend to any suit in law or equity, commenced or prosecuted against one of the United States by citizens of another State, or by citizens or subjects of any foreign State.

## Amendment XII [September 25, 1804]

The electors shall meet in their respective States, and vote by ballot for President and Vice President, one of whom, at least, shall not be an inhabitant of the same State with themselves; they shall name in their ballots the person voted for as President, and in distinct ballots, the person voted for as Vice President, and they shall make distinct lists of all persons voted for as President and of all persons voted for as Vice President, and of the number of votes for each, which lists they shall sign and certify, and transmit sealed to the seat of the government of the United States, directed to the President of the Senate;—The President of the Senate shall, in the presence of the Senate and House of Representatives, open all the certificates and the votes shall then be counted;—The person having the greatest number of votes for President, shall be the President, if such number be a majority of the whole number of electors appointed; and if no person have such majority, then from the persons having the highest numbers not exceeding three on the list of those voted for as President, the House of Representatives shall choose immediately, by ballot, the President. But in choosing the President, the votes shall be taken by States, the representation from each State having one vote; a quorum for this purpose shall consist of a member or members from two thirds of the States, and a majority of all the States shall be necessary to a choice. And if the House of Representatives shall not choose a President whenever the right of choice shall devolve upon them, before the fourth day of March next following, then the Vice President shall act as President, as in the case of the death or other constitutional disability of the President. The person having the greatest number of votes as Vice President shall be the Vice President, if such number be a majority of the whole number of electors appointed, and if no person have a majority, then from the two highest numbers on the list, the Senate shall choose the Vice President; a quorum for the purpose shall consist of two thirds of the whole number of Senators, and a majority of the whole number shall be necessary to a choice. But no person constitutionally ineligible to the office of President shall be eligible to that of Vice President of the United States.

## Amendment XIII [December 18, 1865]

SECTION 1. Neither slavery nor involuntary servitude, except as a punishment for crime whereof the party shall have been duly convicted, shall exist within the United States, or any place subject to their jurisdiction.

SECTION 2. Congress shall have power to enforce this article by appropriate legislation.

## Amendment XIV [July 28, 1868]

SECTION 1. All persons born or naturalized in the United States, and subject to the jurisdiction thereof, are citizens of the United States and of the State wherein they reside. No State shall make or enforce any law which shall abridge the privileges or immunities of citizens of the United States; nor shall any State deprive any person of life, liberty, or property, without due process of law; nor deny to any person within its jurisdiction the equal protection of the laws.

SECTION 2. Representatives shall be apportioned among the several States according to their respective numbers, counting the whole number of persons in each State, excluding Indians not taxed. But when the right to vote at any election for the choice of electors for President and Vice President of the United States, representatives in Congress, the executive and judicial officers of a State, or the members of the legislature thereof, is denied to any of the male inhabitants of such State, being twenty-one years of age, and citizens of the United States, or in any way abridged, except for participating in rebellion, or other crime, the basis of representation therein shall be reduced in the proportion which the number of such male citizens shall bear to the whole number of male citizens twenty-one years of age in such State.

SECTION 3. No person shall be a senator or representative in Congress, or elector of President and Vice President, or hold any office, civil or military, under the United States, or under any State, who having previously taken an oath, as a member of Congress, or as an officer of the United States, or as a member of any State legislature, or as an executive or judicial officer of any State, to support the Constitution of the United States, shall have engaged in insurrection or rebellion against the same, or given aid or comfort to the enemies thereof. But Congress may by a vote of two thirds of each House, remove such disability.

SECTION 4. The validity of the public debt of the United States, authorized by law, including debts incurred for payment of pensions and bounties for services in suppressing insurrection or rebellion, shall not be questioned. But neither the United States nor any State shall assume or pay any debt or obligation incurred in aid of insurrection or rebellion against the United States, or any claim for the loss or emancipation of any slave; but all such debts, obligations, and claims shall be held illegal and void.

SECTION 5. The Congress shall have power to enforce, by appropriate legislation, the provisions of this article.

## Amendment XV [March 30, 1870]

SECTION 1. The right of citizens of the United States to vote shall not be denied or abridged by the United States or by any State on account of race, color, or previous condition of servitude.

SECTION 2. The Congress shall have power to enforce this article by appropriate legislation.

## Amendment XVI [February 25, 1913]

The Congress shall have power to lay and collect taxes on incomes, from whatever source derived, without apportionment among the several States, and without regard to any census or enumeration.

## Amendment XVII [May 31, 1913]

The Senate of the United States shall be composed of two senators from each State, elected by the people thereof, for six years; and each senator shall have one vote. The electors in each State shall have the qualifications requisite for electors of the most numerous branch of the State legislature.

When vacancies happen in the representation of any State in the Senate, the executive authority of such State shall issue writs of election to fill such vacancies: *Provided,* That the legislature of any State may empower the executive thereof to make temporary appointments until the people fill the vacancies by election as the legislature may direct.

This amendment shall not be so construed as to affect the election or term of any senator chosen before it becomes valid as part of the Constitution.

## Amendment XVIII[11] [January 29, 1919]

After one year from the ratification of this article, the manufacture, sale, or transportation of intoxicating liquors within, the importation thereof into, or the exportation thereof from the United States and all territory subject to the jurisdiction thereof for beverage purposes is thereby prohibited.

The Congress and the several States shall have concurrent power to enforce this article by appropriate legislation.

This article shall be inoperative unless it shall have been ratified as an amendment to the Constitution by the legislatures of the several States, as provided in the Constitution, within seven years from the date of the submission hereof to the States by Congress.

## Amendment XIX [August 26, 1920]

The right of citizens of the United States to vote shall not be denied or abridged by the United States or by any State on account of sex.

Congress shall have the power to enforce this article by appropriate legislation.

[11] Repealed by the Twenty-first Amendment.

## Amendment XX [January 23, 1933]

SECTION 1. The terms of the President and Vice President shall end at noon on the 20th day of January, and the terms of Senators and Representatives at noon on the 3d day of January, of the years in which such terms would have ended if this article had not been ratified; and the terms of their successors shall then begin.

SECTION 2. The Congress shall assemble at least once in every year, and such meeting shall begin at noon on the 3d day of January, unless they shall by law appoint a different day.

SECTION 3. If, at the time fixed for the beginning of the term of President, the President-elect shall have died, the Vice President-elect shall become President. If a President shall not have been chosen before the time fixed for the beginning of his term, or if the President-elect shall have failed to qualify, then the Vice President-elect shall act as President until a President shall have qualified; and the Congress may by law provide for the case wherein neither a President-elect nor a Vice President-elect shall have qualified, declaring who shall then act as President, or the manner in which one who is to act shall be selected, and such person shall act accordingly until a President or Vice President shall have qualified.

SECTION 4. The Congress may by law provide for the case of the death of any of the persons from whom the House of Representatives may choose a President whenever the right of choice shall have devolved upon them, and for the case of the death of any of the persons from whom the Senate may choose a Vice President whenever the right of choice shall have devolved upon them.

SECTION 5. Sections 1 and 2 shall take effect on the 15th day of October following the ratification of this article.

SECTION 6. This article shall be inoperative unless it shall have been ratified as an amendment to the Constitution by the legislatures of three-fourths of the several States within seven years from the date of its submission.

## Amendment XXI [December 5, 1933]

SECTION 1. The Eighteenth Article of amendment to the Constitution of the United States is hereby repealed.

SECTION 2. The transportation or importation into any State, Territory, or possession of the United States for delivery or use therein of intoxicating liquors in violation of the laws thereof, is hereby prohibited.

SECTION 3. This article shall be inoperative unless it shall have been ratified as an amendment to the Constitution by conventions in the several States, as provided in the Constitution, within seven years from the date of the submission thereof to the States by the Congress.

## Amendment XXII [March 1, 1951]

No person shall be elected to the office of the President more than twice, and no person who has held the office of President, or acted as President, for more than two years of a term to which some other person was elected President shall be elected to the office of the President more than once.

But this article shall not apply to any person holding the office of President when this article was proposed by the Congress, and shall not prevent any person who may be holding the office of President, or acting as President, during the term within which this article becomes operative from holding the office of President or acting as President during the remainder of such term.

This article shall be inoperative unless it shall have been ratified as an amendment to the Constitution by the legislatures of three-fourths of the several States within seven years from the date of its submission to the States by the Congress.

## Amendment XXIII [March 29, 1961]

SECTION 1. The District constituting the seat of Government of the United States shall appoint in such manner as the Congress may direct:

A number of electors of President and Vice President equal to the whole number of Senators and Representatives in Congress to which the District would be entitled if it were a State, but in no event more than the least populous State; they shall be in addition to those appointed by the States, but they shall be considered, for the purposes of the election of President and Vice President, to be electors appointed by a State; and they shall meet in the District and perform such duties as provided by the twelfth article of amendment.

SECTION 2. The Congress shall have power to enforce this article by appropriate legislation.

## Amendment XXIV [January 23, 1964]

SECTION 1. The right of citizens of the United States to vote in any primary or other election for President or Vice President, for electors for President or Vice President, or for Senator or Representative in Congress, shall not be denied or abridged by the United States or any State by reason of failure to pay any poll tax or other tax.

SECTION 2. The Congress shall have power to enforce this article by appropriate legislation.

## Amendment XXV [February 10, 1967]

SECTION 1. In case of the removal of the President from office or of his death or resignation, the Vice President shall become President.

SECTION 2. Whenever there is a vacancy in the office of the Vice President, the President shall nominate a Vice President who shall take office upon confirmation by a majority vote of both Houses of Congress.

SECTION 3. Whenever the President transmits to the President pro tempore of the Senate and the Speaker of the House of Representatives his written declaration that he is unable to discharge the powers and duties of his office, and until he transmits to them a written declaration to the contrary, such powers and duties shall be discharged by the Vice President as Acting President.

SECTION 4. Whenever the Vice President and a majority of either the principal officers of the executive departments or of such other body as Congress may by law provide, transmit to the President pro tempore of the Senate and the Speaker of the House of Representatives their written declaration that the President is unable to discharge the powers and duties of his office, the Vice President shall immediately assume the powers and duties of the office as Acting President.

Thereafter, when the President transmits to the President pro tempore of the Senate and the Speaker of the House of Representatives his written declaration that no inability exists, he shall resume the powers and duties of his office unless the Vice President and a majority of either the principal officers of the executive departments or of such other body as Congress may by law provide, transmit within four days to the President pro tempore of the Senate and the Speaker of the House of Representatives their written declaration that the President is unable to discharge the powers and duties of his office. Thereupon Congress shall decide the issue, assembling within forty-eight hours for that purpose if not in session. If the Congress, within twenty-one days after receipt of the latter written declaration, or, if Congress is not in session, within twenty-one days after Congress is required to assemble, determines by two-thirds vote of both Houses that the President is unable to discharge the powers and duties of his office, the Vice President shall continue to discharge the same as Acting President; otherwise, the President shall resume the powers and duties of his office.

## Amendment XXVI [June 30, 1971]

SECTION 1. The right of citizens of the United States who are eighteen years of age or older to vote shall not be denied or abridged by the United States or by any State on account of age.

SECTION 2. The Congress shall have power to enforce this article by appropriate legislation.

| President | | Vice-President | | Secretary of State | | Secretary of Treasury | |
|---|---|---|---|---|---|---|---|
| 1. George Washington | 1789 | John Adams | 1789 | T. Jefferson<br>E. Randolph<br>T. Pickering | 1789<br>1794<br>1795 | Alex. Hamilton<br>Oliver Wolcott | 1789<br>1795 |
| 2. John Adams<br>Federalist | 1797 | Thomas Jefferson<br>Democratic-<br>Republican | 1797 | T. Pickering<br>John Marshall | 1797<br>1800 | Oliver Wolcott<br>Samuel Dexter | 1797<br>1801 |
| 3. Thomas Jefferson<br>Democratic-<br>Republican | 1801 | Aaron Burr<br>Democratic-<br>Republican<br>George Clinton<br>Democratic<br>Republican | 1801<br><br><br>1805 | James Madison | 1801 | Samuel Dexter<br>Albert Gallatin | 1801<br>1801 |
| 4. James Madison<br>Democratic-<br>Republican | 1809 | George Clinton<br>Independent-<br>Republican<br>Elbridge Gerry<br>Democratic-<br>Republican | 1809<br><br><br>1813 | Robert Smith<br>James Monroe | 1809<br>1811 | Albert Gallatin<br>H. W. Campbell<br>A. J. Dallas<br>W. H. Crawford | 1809<br>1814<br>1814<br>1816 |
| 5. James Monroe<br>Democratic-<br>Republican | 1817 | D. D. Thompkins<br>Democratic-<br>Republican | 1817 | J. Q. Adams | 1817 | W. H. Crawford | 1817 |
| 6. John Q. Adams | 1825 | John C. Calhoun | 1825 | Henry Clay | 1825 | Richard Rush | 1825 |
| 7. Andrew Jackson<br>Democrat | 1829 | John C. Calhoun<br>Democrat<br>Martin Van Buren<br>Democrat | 1829<br><br>1833 | M. Van Buren<br>E. Livingston<br>Louis McLane<br>John Forsyth | 1829<br>1831<br>1833<br>1834 | Sam D. Ingham<br>Louis McLane<br>W. J. Duane<br>Roger B. Taney<br>Levi Woodbury | 1820<br>1831<br>1833<br>1833<br>1834 |
| 8. Martin Van Buren<br>Democrat | 1837 | Richard M. Johnson<br>Democrat | 1837 | John Forsyth | 1837 | Levi Woodbury | 1837 |
| 9. William H. Harrison<br>Whig | 1841 | John Tyler<br>Whig | 1841 | Daniel Webster | 1841 | Thos. Ewing | 1841 |
| 10. John Tyler<br>Whig and<br>Democrat | 1841 | | | Daniel Webster<br>Hugh S. Legare<br>Abel P. Upshur<br>John C. Calhoun | 1841<br>1843<br>1843<br>1844 | Thos. Ewing<br>Walter Forward<br>John C. Spencer<br>Geo. M. Bibb | 1841<br>1841<br>1843<br>1844 |
| 11. James K. Polk<br>Democrat | 1845 | George M. Dallas<br>Democrat | 1845 | James Buchanan | 1845 | Robt. J. Walker | 1845 |
| 12. Zachary Taylor<br>Whig | 1849 | Millard Fillmore<br>Whig | 1849 | John M. Clayton | 1849 | Wm. M. Meredith | 1849 |
| 13. Millard Fillmore<br>Whig | 1850 | | | Daniel Webster<br>Edward Everett | 1850<br>1852 | Thomas Corwin | 1850 |
| 14. Franklin Pierce<br>Democrat | 1853 | William R. D. King<br>Democrat | 1853 | W. L. Marcy | 1853 | James Guthrie | 1853 |
| 15. James Buchanan<br>Democrat | 1857 | John C. Breckinridge<br>Democrat | 1857 | Lewis Cass<br>J. S. Black | 1857<br>1860 | Howell Cobb<br>Philip F. Thomas<br>John A. Dix | 1857<br>1860<br>1861 |
| 16. Abraham Lincoln<br>Republican | 1861 | Hannibal Hamlin<br>Republican<br>Andrew Johnson<br>Unionist | 1861<br><br>1865 | W. H. Seward | 1861 | Salmon P. Chase<br>W. P. Fessenden<br>Hugh McCulloch | 1861<br>1864<br>1865 |
| 17. Andrew Johnson<br>Unionist | 1865 | | | W. H. Seward | 1865 | Hugh McCulloch | 1865 |
| 18. Ulysses S. Grant<br>Republican | 1869 | Schuyler Colfax<br>Republican<br>Henry Wilson<br>Republican | 1869<br><br>1873 | E. B. Washburne<br>Hamilton Fish | 1869<br>1869 | Geo. S. Boutwell<br>W. A. Richardson<br>Benj. H. Bristow<br>Lot M. Morrill | 1869<br>1873<br>1874<br>1876 |
| 19. Rutherford B. Hayes<br>Republican | 1877 | William A. Wheeler<br>Republican | 1877 | W. M. Evarts | 1877 | John Sherman | 1877 |

*No distinct party designations.

| Secretary of War | | Attorney-General | | Postmaster-General † | | Secretary of Navy | | Secretary of Interior | |
|---|---|---|---|---|---|---|---|---|---|
| Henry Knox | 1789 | E. Randolph | 1789 | Samuel Osgood | 1789 | Established April 30, 1798. | | Established March 3, 1849. | |
| T. Pickering | 1795 | Wm. Bradford | 1794 | Tim. Pickering | 1791 | | | | |
| Jas. McHenry | 1796 | Charles Lee | 1795 | Jos. Habersham | 1795 | | | | |
| Jas. McHenry | 1797 | Charles Lee | 1797 | Jos. Habersham | 1797 | Benj. Stoddert | 1798 | | |
| John Marshall | 1800 | Theo. Parsons | 1801 | | | | | | |
| Sam'l Dexter | 1800 | | | | | | | | |
| R. Griswold | 1801 | | | | | | | | |
| H. Dearborn | 1801 | Levi Lincoln | 1801 | Jos. Habersham | 1801 | Benj. Stoddert | 1801 | | |
| | | Robert Smith | 1805 | Gideon Granger | 1801 | Robert Smith | 1801 | | |
| | | J. Breckinridge | 1805 | | | J. Crowninshield | 1805 | | |
| | | C. A. Rodney | 1807 | | | | | | |
| Wm. Eustis | 1809 | C. A. Rodney | 1809 | Gideon Granger | 1809 | Paul Hamilton | 1809 | | |
| J. Armstrong | 1813 | Wm. Pinkney | 1811 | R. J. Meigs, Jr. | 1814 | William Jones | 1813 | | |
| James Monroe | 1814 | Richard Rush | 1814 | | | B. W. Crownin-shield | 1814 | | |
| W. H. Crawford | 1815 | | | | | | | | |
| Isaac Shelby | 1817 | Richard Rush | 1817 | R. J. Meigs, Jr. | 1817 | B. W. Crownin-shield | 1817 | | |
| Geo. Graham | 1817 | William Wirt | 1817 | John McLean | 1823 | Smith Thompson | 1818 | | |
| J. C. Calhoun | 1817 | | | | | S. L. Southard | 1823 | | |
| Jas. Barbour | 1825 | William Wirt | 1825 | John McLean | 1825 | S. L. Southard | 1825 | | |
| Peter B. Porter | 1828 | | | | | | | | |
| John H. Eaton | 1829 | John M. Berrien | 1829 | Wm. T. Barry | 1829 | John Branch | 1829 | | |
| Lewis Cass | 1831 | Roger B. Taney | 1831 | Amos Kendall | 1835 | Levi Woodbury | 1831 | | |
| B. F. Butler | 1837 | B. F. Butler | 1833 | | | Mahlon Dickerson | 1834 | | |
| Joel R. Poinsett | 1837 | B. F. Butler | 1837 | Amos Kendall | 1837 | Mahlon Dickerson | 1837 | | |
| | | Felix Grundy | 1838 | John M. Niles | 1840 | Jas. K. Paulding | 1838 | | |
| | | H. D. Gilpin | 1840 | | | | | | |
| John Bell | 1841 | J. J. Crittenden | 1841 | Francis Granger | 1841 | George E. Badger | 1841 | | |
| John Bell | 1841 | J. J. Crittenden | 1841 | Francis Granger | 1841 | George E. Badger | 1841 | | |
| John McLean | 1841 | Hugh S. Legare | 1841 | C. A. Wickliffe | 1841 | Abel P. Upshur | 1841 | | |
| J. C. Spencer | 1841 | John Nelson | 1843 | | | David Henshaw | 1843 | | |
| Jas. M. Porter | 1843 | | | | | Thos. W. Gilmer | 1844 | | |
| Wm. Wilkins | 1844 | | | | | John Y. Mason | 1844 | | |
| Wm. L. Marcy | 1845 | John Y. Mason | 1845 | Cave Johnson | 1845 | George Bancroft | 1845 | | |
| | | Nathan Clifford | 1846 | | | John Y. Mason | 1846 | | |
| | | Isaac Toucey | 1848 | | | | | | |
| G. W. Crawford | 1849 | Reverdy Johnson | 1849 | Jacob Collamer | 1849 | Wm. B. Preston | 1849 | Thomas Ewing | 1849 |
| C. M. Conrad | 1850 | J. J. Crittenden | 1850 | Nathan K. Hall | 1850 | Wm. A. Graham | 1850 | A. H. Stuart | 1850 |
| | | | | Sam D. Hubbard | 1852 | John P. Kennedy | 1852 | | |
| Jefferson Davis | 1853 | Caleb Cushing | 1853 | James Campbell | 1853 | James C. Dobbin | 1853 | Robert McClelland | 1853 |
| John B. Floyd | 1857 | J. S. Black | 1857 | Aaron V. Brown | 1857 | Isaac Toucey | 1857 | Jacob Thompson | 1857 |
| Joseph Holt | 1861 | Edw. M. Stanton | 1860 | Joseph Holt | 1859 | | | | |
| S. Cameron | 1861 | Edward Bates | 1861 | Horatio King | 1861 | Gideon Wells | 1861 | Caleb B. Smith | 1861 |
| E. M. Stanton | 1862 | Titian J. Coffey | 1863 | M'tgomery Blair | 1861 | | | John P. Usher | 1863 |
| | | James Speed | 1864 | Wm. Dennison | 1864 | | | | |
| E. M. Stanton | 1865 | James Speed | 1865 | Wm. Dennison | 1865 | Gideon Wells | 1865 | John P. Usher | 1865 |
| U. S. Grant | 1867 | Henry Stanbery | 1866 | A. W. Randall | 1866 | | | James Harlan | 1865 |
| L. Thomas | 1868 | Wm. M. Evarts | 1868 | | | | | O. H. Browning | 1866 |
| J. M. Schofield | 1868 | | | | | | | | |
| J. A. Rawlins | 1869 | E. R. Hoar | 1869 | J. A. J. Creswell | 1869 | Adolph E. Borie | 1869 | Jacob D. Cox | 1869 |
| W. T. Sherman | 1869 | A. T. Ackerman | 1870 | Jas. W. Marshall | 1874 | Geo. M. Robeson | 1869 | C. Delano | 1870 |
| W. W. Belknap | 1869 | Geo. H. Williams | 1871 | Marshall Jewell | 1874 | | | Zach. Chandler | 1875 |
| Alphonso Taft | 1876 | Edw. Pierrepont | 1875 | James N. Tyner | 1876 | | | | |
| J. D. Cameron | 1876 | Alphonso Taft | 1876 | | | | | | |
| G. W. McCrary | 1877 | Chas. Devens | 1877 | David M. Key | 1877 | R. W. Thompson | 1877 | Carl Schurz | 1877 |
| Alex. Ramsey | 1879 | | | Horace Maynard | 1880 | Nathan Goff, Jr. | 1881 | | |

†Not in Cabinet until 1829.

| President | | Vice-President | | Secretary of State | | Secretary of Treasury | | Secretary of War* | |
|---|---|---|---|---|---|---|---|---|---|
| 20. J. A. Garfield<br>Republican | 1881 | C. A. Arthur<br>Republican | 1881 | James G. Blaine | 1881 | Wm. Windom | 1881 | R. T. Lincoln | 1881 |
| 21. Chester A.<br>Arthur<br>Republican | 1881 | | | F. T. Freling-<br>huysen | 1881 | Chas. J. Folger<br>W. Q. Gresham<br>Hugh McCulloch | 1881<br>1884<br>1884 | R. T. Lincoln | 1881 |
| 22. G. Cleveland<br>Democrat | 1885 | T. A. Hendricks<br>Democrat | 1885 | Thos. F. Bayard | 1885 | Daniel Manning<br>Chas. S. Fairchild | 1885<br>1887 | W. C. Endicott | 1885 |
| 23. Benj. Harrison<br>Republican | 1889 | Levi P. Morton<br>Republican | 1889 | James G. Blaine<br>John W. Foster | 1889<br>1892 | Wm. Windom<br>Charles Foster | 1889<br>1891 | R. Proctor<br>S. B. Elkins | 1889<br>1891 |
| 24. G. Cleveland<br>Democrat | 1893 | A. E. Stevenson<br>Democrat | 1893 | W. Q. Gresham<br>Richard Olney | 1893<br>1895 | John G. Carlisle | 1893 | D. A. Lamont | 1893 |
| 25. William Mc-<br>Kinley<br>Republican | 1897 | Garret A. Hobart<br>Republican<br>Theo. Roosevelt<br>Republican | 1897<br><br>1901 | John Sherman<br>Wm. R. Day<br>John Hay | 1897<br>1897<br>1898 | Lyman J. Gage | 1897 | R. A. Alger<br>Elihu Root | 1897<br>1899 |
| 26. Theodore Roose-<br>velt<br>Republican | 1901 | Chas. W. Fair-<br>banks<br>Republican | 1905 | John Hay<br>Elihu Root<br>Robert Bacon | 1901<br>1905<br>1909 | Lyman J. Gage<br>Leslie M. Shaw<br>G. B. Cortelyou | 1901<br>1902<br>1907 | Elihu Root<br>Wm. H. Taft<br>Luke E. Wright | 1901<br>1904<br>1908 |
| 27. W. H. Taft<br>Republican | 1909 | J. S. Sherman<br>Republican | 1909 | P. C. Knox | 1909 | F. MacVeagh | 1909 | J. M. Dickinson<br>H. L. Stimson | 1909<br>1911 |
| 28. Woodrow Wil-<br>son<br>Democrat | 1913 | Thomas R.<br>Marshall<br>Democrat | 1913 | Wm. J. Bryan<br>Robert Lansing<br>Bainbridge Colby | 1913<br>1915<br>1920 | W. G. McAdoo<br>Carter Glass<br>D. F. Houston | 1913<br>1918<br>1920 | L. M. Garrison<br>N. D. Baker | 1913<br>1916 |
| 29. Warren G.<br>Harding<br>Republican | 1921 | Calvin Coolidge<br>Republican | 1921 | Chas. E. Hughes | 1921 | Andrew W. Mellon | 1921 | John W. Weeks | 1921 |
| 30. Calvin Cool-<br>idge<br>Republican | 1923 | Charles G.<br>Dawes<br>Republican | 1925 | Chas. E. Hughes<br>Frank B. Kellogg | 1923<br>1925 | Andrew W. Mellon | 1923 | John W. Weeks<br>Dwight F. Davis | 1923<br>1925 |
| 31. Herb. Hoover<br>Republican | 1929 | Charles Curtis<br>Republican | 1929 | Henry L.<br>Stimson | 1929 | Andrew W. Mellon<br>Ogden L. Mills | 1929<br>1932 | James W. Good<br>Pat. J. Hurley | 1929<br>1929 |
| 32. Franklin D.<br>Roosevelt<br>Democrat | 1933 | J. Nance Garner<br>Democrat<br>H. A. Wallace<br>Democrat<br>H. S. Truman<br>Democrat | 1933<br><br>1941<br><br>1945 | Cordell Hull<br>E. R. Stettinius,<br>Jr. | 1933<br><br>1944 | Wm. H. Woodin<br>Henry Morgenthau,<br>Jr. | 1933<br><br>1934 | Geo. H. Dern<br>H. A. Woodring<br>H. L. Stimson | 1933<br>1936<br>1940 |
| 33. Harry S.<br>Truman<br>Democrat | 1945 | Alben W.<br>Barkley<br>Democrat | 1949 | James F. Byrnes<br>Geo. C. Marshall<br>Dean G. Acheson | 1945<br>1947<br>1949 | Fred M. Vinson<br>John W. Snyder | 1945<br>1946 | R. H. Patterson<br>K. C. Royall | 1945<br>1947 |
| 34. Dwight D.<br>Eisenhower<br>Republican | 1953 | Richard M.<br>Nixon<br>Republican | 1953 | J. Foster Dulles<br>Christian A.<br>Herter | 1953<br><br>1959 | George C.<br>Humphrey<br>Robert B. Anderson | 1953<br><br>1957 | *Sec'y of Defense*<br>Est. July 26, 1947<br>J. V. Forrestal<br>L. A. Johnson<br>G. C. Marshall<br>R. A. Lovett<br>C. E. Wilson | <br><br>1947<br>1949<br>1950<br>1951<br>1953 |
| 35. John F.<br>Kennedy<br>Democrat | 1961 | Lyndon B.<br>Johnson<br>Democrat | 1961 | Dean Rusk | 1961 | C. Douglas Dillon | 1961 | N. H. McElroy<br>T. S. Gates, Jr.<br>R. S. McNamara | 1957<br>1959<br>1961 |
| 36. Lyndon B.<br>Johnson<br>Democrat | 1963 | Hubert H.<br>Humphrey<br>Democrat | 1963 | Dean Rusk | 1963 | G. Douglas Dillon<br>Henry H. Fowler<br>Joseph W. Barr | 1963<br>1965<br>1968 | C. M. Clifford<br>M. R. Laird | 1968<br>1969 |
| 37. Richard M.<br>Nixon<br>Republican | 1969 | Spiro T.<br>Agnew<br>Republican | 1969 | William P.<br>Rogers | 1969 | David M. Kennedy<br>John B. Connally | 1969<br>1971 | | |

*Lost cabinet status in 1947.

| Attorney-General | Postmaster-General | Secretary of Navy† | Secretary of Interior | Secretary of Agriculture‡ | Other members |
|---|---|---|---|---|---|
| W. MacVeagh 1881 | T. L. James 1881 | W. H. Hunt 1881 | S. J. Kirk-<br>wood 1881 | | *Sec'y of Commerce<br>and Labor*<br>Est. Feb. 14, 1903<br>G. B. Cortelyou 1903<br>V. H. Metcalf 1904 |
| B. H. Brewster 1881 | T. O. Howe 1881<br>W. Q. Gresham 1883<br>Frank Hatton 1884 | W. E. Chandler 1881 | Henry M.<br>Teller 1881 | | O. S. Straus 1907<br>Chas. Nagel 1909<br>(Dept. divided,<br>1913) |
| A. H. Garland 1885 | Wm. F. Vilas 1885<br>D. M. Dickinson 1888 | W. C. Whitney 1885 | L. Q. C. Lamar 1885<br>Wm. F. Vilas 1888 | N. J. Colman 1889 | |
| W. H. H. Miller 1889 | J. Wanamaker 1889 | Benj. F. Tracy 1889 | John W.<br>Noble 1889 | J. M. Rusk 1889 | |
| R. Olney 1893<br>J. Harmon 1895 | W. S. Bissell 1893<br>W. L. Wilson 1895 | Hilary A. Herbert 1893 | Hoke Smith 1893<br>D. R. Francis 1896 | J. S. Morton 1893 | *Sec'y of Commerce*<br>Est. March 4, 1913<br>W. C. Redfield 1913<br>J. W. Alexander 1919<br>H. C. Hoover 1921<br>H. C. Hoover 1925<br>W. F. Whiting 1928 |
| J. McKenna 1897<br>J. W. Griggs 1897<br>P. C. Knox 1901 | James A. Gary 1897<br>Chas. E. Smith 1898 | John D. Long 1897 | C. N. Bliss 1897<br>E. A. Hitch-<br>cock 1899 | James Wilson 1897 | R. P. Lamont 1929 |
| P. C. Knox 1901<br>W. H. Moody 1904<br>C. J. Bonaparte 1907 | Chas. E. Smith 1901<br>Henry C. Payne 1902<br>Robt. J. Wynne 1904<br>G. B. Cortelyou 1905<br>G. von L. Meyer 1907 | John D. Long 1901<br>Wm. H. Moody 1902<br>Paul Morton 1904<br>C. J. Bonaparte 1905<br>V. H. Metcalf 1907<br>T. H. Newberry 1908 | E. A. Hitch-<br>cock 1901<br>J. R. Garfield 1907 | James Wilson 1901 | R. D. Chapin 1932<br>D. C. Roper 1933<br>H. L. Hopkins 1939<br>Jesse Jones 1940<br>H. A. Wallace 1945 |
| G. W. Wicker-<br>sham 1909 | F. H. Hitchcock 1909 | G. von L. Meyer 1909 | R. A. Ballinger 1909<br>W. L. Fisher 1911 | James Wilson 1909 | W. A. Harriman 1946<br>C. W. Sawyer 1948<br>S. Weeks 1953<br>L. L. Strauss 1958<br>F. H. Mueller 1959<br>L. H. Hodges 1961 |
| J. C. McReynolds 1913<br>Thos. W. Gregory 1914<br>A. M. Palmer 1919 | A. S. Burleson 1913 | Josephus Daniels 1913 | F. K. Lane 1913<br>J. B. Payne 1920 | D. F. Houston 1913<br>E. T. Mere-<br>dith 1920 | L. H. Hodges 1963<br>John T. Conner 1965<br>A. B. Trowbridge 1967<br>C. R. Smith 1968<br>M. H. Stans 1969 |
| H. M. Daugherty 1921 | Will H. Hays 1921<br>Hubert Work 1922<br>Harry S. New 1923 | Edwin Denby 1921 | Albert B. Fall 1921<br>Hubert Work 1923 | H. C. Wallace 1921 | |
| H. M. Daugherty 1923<br>Harlan F. Stone 1924<br>John G. Sargent 1925 | Harry S. New 1923 | Edwin Denby 1923<br>Curtis W. Wilbur 1924 | Hubert Work 1923<br>Roy O. West 1928 | H. M. Gore 1924<br>W. M. Jardine 1925 | |
| Wm. D. Mitchell 1929 | Walter F. Brown 1929 | Chas. F. Adams 1929 | Ray L. Wilbur 1929 | Arthur M.<br>Hyde 1929 | *Sec'y of Labor*<br>Est. March 4, 1913<br>W. B. Wilson 1913<br>J. J. Davis 1921<br>W. N. Doak 1930<br>Frances Perkins 1933<br>L. B. Schwellen-<br>bach 1945 |
| H. S. Cummings 1933<br>Frank Murphy 1939<br>Robt. H. Jackson 1940<br>Francis Biddle 1941 | James A. Farley 1933<br>Frank C. Walker 1940 | Claude A.<br>Swanson 1933<br>Chas. Edison 1940<br>Frank Knox 1940<br>James V.<br>Forrestal 1944 | Harold L.<br>Ickes 1933 | H. A. Wallace 1933<br>C. R. Wickard 1940 | M. J. Tobin 1948<br>M. P. Durkin 1953<br>J. P. Mitchell 1953<br>A. J. Goldberg 1961 |
| Tom C. Clark 1945<br>J. H. McGrath 1949<br>J. P. McGranery 1952 | R. E. Hannegan 1945<br>J. L. Donaldson 1947 | James V.<br>Forrestal 1945 | H. L. Ickes 1945<br>Julius A. Krug 1946<br>O. L. Chapman 1951 | C. P. Ander-<br>son 1945<br>C. F. Brannan 1948 | W. W. Wirtz 1962<br>G. P. Schultz 1969<br>J. D. Hodgson 1970 |
| Herbert Brown-<br>ell, Jr. 1953<br>W. P. Rogers 1957 | Arthur E.<br>Summerfield 1953 | *Sec'y of Health<br>Educ. & Welfare*<br>Est. April 1, 1953<br>O. C. Hobby 1953<br>M. B. Folsom 1955<br>A. S. Flemming 1958 | Douglas<br>McKay 1953<br>Fred Seaton 1956 | Ezra T.<br>Benson 1953 | *Sec'y of Housing<br>and Urban<br>Development*<br>Est. Sept. 9, 1965<br>R. C. Weaver 1966<br>G. W. Romney 1969 |
| Robt. F. Kennedy 1961 | J. Edward Day 1961<br>John A. Gronouski 1963 | Abraham A.<br>Ribicoff 1961<br>A. Celebrezze 1962 | Stewart L.<br>Udall 1961 | Orville L.<br>Freeman 1961 | *Sec'y of<br>Transportation*<br>Est. Oct. 15, 1966<br>Alan S. Boyd 1967<br>John A. Volpe 1969 |
| Robt. F. Kennedy 1963<br>Nicholas deB.<br>Katzenbach 1965<br>Ramsey Clark 1967 | John A. Gronouski 1963<br>Lawrence F.<br>O'Brien 1965<br>Marvin Watson 1968 | A. Celebrezze 1963<br>John W. Gardner 1965<br>Wilbur J. Cohen 1968 | Stewart L.<br>Udall 1963 | Orville L.<br>Freeman 1963 | |
| John N. Mitchell 1969 | Winton M.<br>Blount 1969 | Robert H. Finch 1969<br>Elliot L.<br>Richardson 1970 | Walter J. Hickel 1969<br>Rogers C. B.<br>Morton 1971 | Clifford M.<br>Hardin 1969<br>E. L. Butz 1971 | |

†Lost cabinet status in 1947.    ‡Cabinet status since 1889.

| Year | Number of states | Candidates | Party | Popular vote* | Electoral vote † | Percentage of popular vote |
|------|------------------|------------|-------|---------------|------------------|----------------------------|
| 1789 | 11 | GEORGE WASHINGTON | No party designations | | 69 | |
|      |    | *John Adams* | | | 34 | |
|      |    | *Other Candidates* | | | 35 | |
| 1792 | 15 | GEORGE WASHINGTON | No party designations | | 132 | |
|      |    | *John Adams* | | | 77 | |
|      |    | *George Clinton* | | | 50 | |
|      |    | *Other Candidates* | | | 5 | |
| 1796 | 16 | JOHN ADAMS | Federalist | | 71 | |
|      |    | *Thomas Jefferson* | Democratic-Republican | | 68 | |
|      |    | *Thomas Pinckney* | Federalist | | 59 | |
|      |    | *Aaron Burr* | Democratic-Republican | | 30 | |
|      |    | *Other Candidates* | | | 48 | |
| 1800 | 16 | THOMAS JEFFERSON | Democratic-Republican | | 73 | |
|      |    | *Aaron Burr* | Democratic-Republican | | 73 | |
|      |    | *John Adams* | Federalist | | 65 | |
|      |    | *Charles C. Pinckney* | Federalist | | 64 | |
|      |    | *John Jay* | Federalist | | 1 | |
| 1804 | 17 | THOMAS JEFFERSON | Democratic-Republican | | 162 | |
|      |    | *Charles C. Pinckney* | Federalist | | 14 | |
| 1808 | 17 | JAMES MADISON | Democratic-Republican | | 122 | |
|      |    | *Charles C. Pinckney* | Federalist | | 47 | |
|      |    | *George Clinton* | Democratic-Republican | | 6 | |
| 1812 | 18 | JAMES MADISON | Democratic-Republican | | 128 | |
|      |    | *DeWitt Clinton* | Federalist | | 89 | |
| 1816 | 19 | JAMES MONROE | Democratic-Republican | | 183 | |
|      |    | *Rufus King* | Federalist | | 34 | |
| 1820 | 24 | JAMES MONROE | Democratic-Republican | | 231 | |
|      |    | *John Quincy Adams* | Independent Republican | | 1 | |
| 1824 | 24 | JOHN QUINCY ADAMS | | 108,740 | 84 | 30.5 |
|      |    | *Andrew Jackson* | | 153,544 | 99 | 43.1 |
|      |    | *William H. Crawford* | | 46,618 | 41 | 13.1 |
|      |    | *Henry Clay* | | 47,136 | 37 | 13.2 |
| 1828 | 24 | ANDREW JACKSON | Democrat | 647,286 | 178 | 56.0 |
|      |    | *John Quincy Adams* | National Republican | 508,064 | 83 | 44.0 |
| 1832 | 24 | ANDREW JACKSON | Democrat | 687,502 | 219 | 55.0 |
|      |    | *Henry Clay* | National Republican | 530,189 | 49 | 42.4 |
|      |    | *William Wirt* | Anti-Masonic | } 33,108 | 7 | } 2.6 |
|      |    | *John Floyd* | National Republican | | 11 | |
| 1836 | 26 | MARTIN VAN BUREN | Democrat | 765,483 | 170 | 50.9 |
|      |    | *William H. Harrison* | Whig | | 73 | |
|      |    | *Hugh L. White* | Whig | } 739,795 | 26 | } 49.1 |
|      |    | *Daniel Webster* | Whig | | 14 | |
|      |    | *W. P. Mangum* | Whig | | 11 | |
| 1840 | 26 | WILLIAM H. HARRISON | Whig | 1,274,624 | 234 | 53.1 |
|      |    | *Martin Van Buren* | Democrat | 1,127,781 | 60 | 46.9 |

*Percentage of popular vote given for any election year may not total 100 percent because candidates receiving less than 1 percent of the popular vote have been omitted.

†Prior to the passage of the Twelfth Amendment in 1804, the electoral college voted for two presidential candidates; the runner-up became Vice-President. Data from *Historical Statistics of the United States, Colonial Times to 1957* (1961), pp. 682–683, and *The World Almanac.*

| Year | Number of states | Candidates | Party | Popular vote | Electoral vote | Percentage of popular vote |
|------|------|------------|-------|--------------|----------------|----------------------------|
| 1844 | 26 | JAMES K. POLK | Democrat | 1,338,464 | 170 | 49.6 |
|      |    | Henry Clay | Whig | 1,300,097 | 105 | 48.1 |
|      |    | James G. Birney | Liberty | 62,300 | | 2.3 |
| 1848 | 30 | ZACHARY TAYLOR | Whig | 1,360,967 | 163 | 47.4 |
|      |    | Lewis Cass | Democrat | 1,222,342 | 127 | 42.5 |
|      |    | Martin Van Buren | Free Soil | 291,263 | | 10.1 |
| 1852 | 31 | FRANKLIN PIERCE | Democrat | 1,601,117 | 254 | 50.9 |
|      |    | Winfield Scott | Whig | 1,385,453 | 42 | 44.1 |
|      |    | John P. Hale | Free Soil | 155,825 | | 5.0 |
| 1856 | 31 | JAMES BUCHANAN | Democrat | 1,832,955 | 174 | 45.3 |
|      |    | John C. Frémont | Republican | 1,339,932 | 114 | 33.1 |
|      |    | Millard Fillmore | American | 871,731 | 8 | 21.6 |
| 1860 | 33 | ABRAHAM LINCOLN | Republican | 1,865,593 | 180 | 39.8 |
|      |    | Stephen A. Douglas | Democrat | 1,382,713 | 12 | 29.5 |
|      |    | John C. Breckinridge | Democrat | 848,356 | 72 | 18.1 |
|      |    | John Bell | Constitutional Union | 592,906 | 39 | 12.6 |
| 1864 | 36 | ABRAHAM LINCOLN | Republican | 2,206,938 | 212 | 55.0 |
|      |    | George B. McClellan | Democrat | 1,803,787 | 21 | 45.0 |
| 1868 | 37 | ULYSSES S. GRANT | Republican | 3,013,421 | 214 | 52.7 |
|      |    | Horatio Seymour | Democrat | 2,706,829 | 80 | 47.3 |
| 1872 | 37 | ULYSSES S. GRANT | Republican | 3,596,745 | 286 | 55.6 |
|      |    | Horace Greeley | Democrat | 2,843,446 | * | 43.9 |
| 1876 | 38 | RUTHERFORD B. HAYES | Republican | 4,036,572 | 185 | 48.0 |
|      |    | Samuel J. Tilden | Democrat | 4,284,020 | 184 | 51.0 |
| 1880 | 38 | JAMES A. GARFIELD | Republican | 4,453,295 | 214 | 48.5 |
|      |    | Winfield S. Hancock | Democrat | 4,414,082 | 155 | 48.1 |
|      |    | James B. Weaver | Greenback-Labor | 308,578 | | 3.4 |
| 1884 | 38 | GROVER CLEVELAND | Democrat | 4,879,507 | 219 | 48.5 |
|      |    | James G. Blaine | Republican | 4,850,293 | 182 | 48.2 |
|      |    | Benjamin F. Butler | Greenback-Labor | 175,370 | | 1.8 |
|      |    | John P. St. John | Prohibition | 150,369 | | 1.5 |
| 1888 | 38 | BENJAMIN HARRISON | Republican | 5,447,129 | 233 | 47.9 |
|      |    | Grover Cleveland | Democrat | 5,537,857 | 168 | 48.6 |
|      |    | Clinton B. Fisk | Prohibition | 249,506 | | 2.2 |
|      |    | Anson J. Streeter | Union Labor | 146,935 | | 1.3 |
| 1892 | 44 | GROVER CLEVELAND | Democrat | 5,555,426 | 277 | 46.1 |
|      |    | Benjamin Harrison | Republican | 5,182,690 | 145 | 43.0 |
|      |    | James B. Weaver | People's | 1,029,846 | 22 | 8.5 |
|      |    | John Bidwell | Prohibition | 264,133 | | 2.2 |
| 1896 | 45 | WILLIAM MCKINLEY | Republican | 7,102,246 | 271 | 51.1 |
|      |    | William J. Bryan | Democrat | 6,492,559 | 176 | 47.7 |
| 1900 | 45 | WILLIAM MCKINLEY | Republican | 7,218,491 | 292 | 51.7 |
|      |    | William J. Bryan | Democrat; Populist | 6,356,734 | 155 | 45.5 |
|      |    | John C. Woolley | Prohibition | 208,914 | | 1.5 |
| 1904 | 45 | THEODORE ROOSEVELT | Republican | 7,628,461 | 336 | 57.4 |
|      |    | Alton B. Parker | Democrat | 5,084,223 | 140 | 37.6 |
|      |    | Eugene V. Debs | Socialist | 402,283 | | 3.0 |
|      |    | Silas C. Swallow | Prohibition | 258,536 | | 1.9 |

*Because of the death of Greeley, Democratic electors scattered their votes.

| Year | Number of states | Candidates | Party | Popular vote | Electoral vote | Percentage of popular vote |
|------|------|------------|-------|--------------|----------------|-----------------------------|
| 1908 | 46 | WILLIAM H. TAFT | Republican | 7,675,320 | 321 | 51.6 |
| | | William J. Bryan | Democrat | 6,412,294 | 162 | 43.1 |
| | | Eugene V. Debs | Socialist | 420,793 | | 2.8 |
| | | Eugene W. Chafin | Prohibition | 253,840 | | 1.7 |
| 1912 | 48 | WOODROW WILSON | Democrat | 6,296,547 | 435 | 41.9 |
| | | Theodore Roosevelt | Progressive | 4,118,571 | 88 | 27.4 |
| | | William H. Taft | Republican | 3,486,720 | 8 | 23.2 |
| | | Eugene V. Debs | Socialist | 900,672 | | 6.0 |
| | | Eugene W. Chafin | Prohibition | 206,275 | | 1.4 |
| 1916 | 48 | WOODROW WILSON | Democrat | 9,127,695 | 277 | 49.4 |
| | | Charles E. Hughes | Republican | 8,533,507 | 254 | 46.2 |
| | | A. L. Benson | Socialist | 585,113 | | 3.2 |
| | | J. Frank Hanly | Prohibition | 220,506 | | 1.2 |
| 1920 | 48 | WARREN G. HARDING | Republican | 16,143,407 | 404 | 60.4 |
| | | James M. Cox | Democrat | 9,130,328 | 127 | 34.2 |
| | | Eugene V. Debs | Socialist | 919,799 | | 3.4 |
| | | P. P. Christensen | Farmer-Labor | 265,411 | | 1.0 |
| 1924 | 48 | CALVIN COOLIDGE | Republican | 15,718,211 | 382 | 54.0 |
| | | John W. Davis | Democrat | 8,385,283 | 136 | 28.8 |
| | | Robert M. La Follette | Progressive | 4,831,289 | 13 | 16.6 |
| 1928 | 48 | HERBERT C. HOOVER | Republican | 21,391,993 | 444 | 58.2 |
| | | Alfred E. Smith | Democrat | 15,016,169 | 87 | 40.9 |
| 1932 | 48 | FRANKLIN D. ROOSEVELT | Democrat | 22,809,638 | 472 | 57.4 |
| | | Herbert C. Hoover | Republican | 15,758,901 | 59 | 39.7 |
| | | Norman Thomas | Socialist | 881,951 | | 2.2 |
| 1936 | 48 | FRANKLIN D. ROOSEVELT | Democrat | 27,752,869 | 523 | 60.8 |
| | | Alfred M. Landon | Republican | 16,674,665 | 8 | 36.5 |
| | | William Lemke | Union | 882,479 | | 1.9 |
| 1940 | 48 | FRANKLIN D. ROOSEVELT | Democrat | 27,307,819 | 449 | 54.8 |
| | | Wendell L. Willkie | Republican | 22,321,018 | 82 | 44.8 |
| 1944 | 48 | FRANKLIN D. ROOSEVELT | Democrat | 25,606,585 | 432 | 53.5 |
| | | Thomas E. Dewey | Republican | 22,014,745 | 99 | 46.0 |
| 1948 | 48 | HARRY S. TRUMAN | Democrat | 24,105,812 | 303 | 49.5 |
| | | Thomas E. Dewey | Republican | 21,970,065 | 189 | 45.1 |
| | | J. Strom Thurmond | States' Rights | 1,169,063 | 39 | 2.4 |
| | | Henry A. Wallace | Progressive | 1,157,172 | | 2.4 |
| 1952 | 48 | DWIGHT D. EISENHOWER | Republican | 33,936,234 | 442 | 55.1 |
| | | Adlai E. Stevenson | Democrat | 27,314,992 | 89 | 44.4 |
| 1956 | 48 | DWIGHT D. EISENHOWER | Republican | 35,590,472 | 457† | 57.6 |
| | | Adlai E. Stevenson | Democrat | 26,022,752 | 73 | 42.1 |
| 1960 | 50 | JOHN F. KENNEDY | Democrat | 34,227,096 | 303‡ | 49.9 |
| | | Richard M. Nixon | Republican | 34,108,546 | 219 | 49.6 |
| 1964 | 50 | LYNDON B. JOHNSON | Democrat | 42,676,220 | 486 | 61.3 |
| | | Barry M. Goldwater | Republican | 26,860,314 | 52 | 38.5 |
| 1968 | 50 | RICHARD M. NIXON | Republican | 31,785,480 | 301 | 43.4 |
| | | Hubert H. Humphrey | Democrat | 31,275,165 | 191 | 42.7 |
| | | George C. Wallace | American Independent | 9,906,473 | 46 | 13.5 |

†Walter B. Jones received 1 electoral vote.     ‡Harry F. Byrd received 15 electoral votes.

| Name (Chief Justices in Italics) | Service (Term) | (Years) | Name (Chief Justices in Italics) | Service (Term) | (Years) |
|---|---|---|---|---|---|
| *John Jay* (N.Y.) | 1789–1795 | 6 | David J. Brewer (Kans.) | 1889–1910 | 21 |
| John Rutledge (S.C.) | 1789–1791 | 2 | Henry B. Brown (Mich.) | 1890–1906 | 16 |
| William Cushing (Mass.) | 1789–1810 | 21 | George Shiras, Jr. (Pa.) | 1892–1903 | 11 |
| James Wilson (Pa.) | 1789–1798 | 9 | Howell E. Jackson (Tenn.) | 1893–1895 | 2 |
| John Blair (Va.) | 1789–1796 | 7 | Edward D. White (La.) | 1894–1910 | 16 |
| James Iredell (N.C.) | 1790–1799 | 9 | Rufus W. Peckham (N.Y.) | 1895–1909 | 14 |
| Thomas Johnson (Md.) | 1792–1793 | ½ | Joseph McKenna (Calif.) | 1898–1925 | 27 |
| William Paterson (N.J.) | 1793–1806 | 13 | Oliver W. Holmes (Mass.) | 1902–1932 | 30 |
| *John Rutledge* (S.C.)* | 1795–1795 | | William R. Day (Ohio) | 1903–1922 | 19 |
| Samuel Chase (Md.) | 1796–1811 | 15 | William H. Moody (Mass.) | 1906–1910 | 4 |
| *Oliver Ellsworth* (Conn.) | 1796–1800 | 4 | Horace H. Lurton (Tenn.) | 1910–1914 | 4 |
| Bushrod Washington (Va.) | 1798–1829 | 31 | *Edward D. White* (La.) | 1910–1921 | 11 |
| Alfred Moore (N.C.) | 1800–1804 | 4 | Charles E. Hughes (N.Y.) | 1910–1916 | 6 |
| *John Marshall* (Va.) | 1801–1835 | 34 | Willis Van Devanter (Wyo.) | 1911–1937 | 26 |
| William Johnson (S.C.) | 1804–1834 | 30 | Joseph R. Lamar (Ga.) | 1911–1916 | 5 |
| Brock. Livingston (N.Y.) | 1806–1823 | 17 | Mahlon Pitney (N.J.) | 1912–1922 | 10 |
| Thomas Todd (Ky.) | 1807–1826 | 19 | James C. McReynolds (Tenn.) | 1914–1941 | 27 |
| Joseph Story (Mass.) | 1811–1845 | 34 | Louis D. Brandeis (Mass.) | 1916–1939 | 23 |
| Gabriel Duval (Md.) | 1811–1835 | 24 | John H. Clarke (Ohio) | 1916–1922 | 6 |
| Smith Thompson (N.Y.) | 1823–1843 | 20 | *William H. Taft* (Conn.) | 1921–1930 | 9 |
| Robert Trimble (Ky.) | 1826–1828 | 2 | George Sutherland (Utah) | 1922–1938 | 16 |
| John McLean (Ohio) | 1829–1861 | 32 | Pierce Butler (Minn.) | 1923–1939 | 16 |
| Henry Baldwin (Pa.) | 1830–1844 | 14 | Edward T. Sanford (Tenn.) | 1923–1930 | 7 |
| James M. Wayne (Ga.) | 1835–1867 | 32 | Harlan F. Stone (N.Y.) | 1925–1941 | 16 |
| *Roger B. Taney* (Md.) | 1836–1864 | 28 | *Charles E. Hughes* (N.Y.) | 1930–1941 | 11 |
| Philip P. Barbour (Va.) | 1836–1841 | 5 | Owen J. Roberts (Pa.) | 1930–1945 | 15 |
| John Catron (Tenn.) | 1837–1865 | 28 | Benjamin N. Cardozo (N.Y.) | 1932–1938 | 6 |
| John McKinley (Ala.) | 1837–1852 | 15 | Hugo L. Black (Ala.) | 1937–1971 | 34 |
| Peter V. Daniel (Va.) | 1841–1860 | 19 | Stanley F. Reed (Ky.) | 1938–1957 | 19 |
| Samuel Nelson (N.Y.) | 1845–1872 | 27 | Felix Frankfurter (Mass.) | 1939–1962 | 23 |
| Levi Woodbury (N.H.) | 1845–1851 | 6 | William O. Douglas (Conn.) | 1939– | |
| Robert C. Grier (Pa.) | 1846–1870 | 24 | Frank Murphy (Mich.) | 1940–1949 | 9 |
| Benjamin R. Curtis (Mass.) | 1851–1857 | 6 | *Harlan F. Stone* (N.Y.) | 1941–1946 | 5 |
| John A. Campbell (Ala.) | 1853–1861 | 8 | James F. Byrnes (S.C.) | 1941–1942 | 1 |
| Nathan Clifford (Maine) | 1858–1881 | 23 | Robert H. Jackson (N.Y.) | 1941–1954 | 13 |
| Noah H. Swayne (Ohio) | 1862–1881 | 19 | Wiley B. Rutledge (Iowa) | 1943–1949 | 6 |
| Samuel F. Miller (Iowa) | 1862–1890 | 28 | Harold H. Burton (Ohio) | 1945–1958 | 13 |
| David Davis (Ill.) | 1862–1877 | 15 | *Fred M. Vinson* (Ky.) | 1946–1953 | 7 |
| Stephen J. Field (Calif.) | 1863–1897 | 34 | Tom C. Clark (Tex.) | 1949–1967 | 18 |
| *Salmon P. Chase* (Ohio) | 1864–1873 | 9 | Sherman Minton (Ind.) | 1949–1956 | 7 |
| William Strong (Pa.) | 1870–1880 | 10 | *Earl Warren* (Calif.) | 1953–1969 | 16 |
| Joseph P. Bradley (N.J.) | 1870–1892 | 22 | John M. Harlan (N.Y.) | 1955–1971 | 16 |
| Ward Hunt (N.Y.) | 1872–1882 | 10 | William J. Brennan (N.J.) | 1956– | |
| *Morrison R. Waite* (Ohio) | 1874–1888 | 14 | Charles E. Whittaker (Mo.) | 1957–1962 | 5 |
| John M. Harlan (Ky.) | 1877–1911 | 34 | Potter Stewart (Ohio) | 1958– | |
| William B. Woods (Ga.) | 1880–1887 | 7 | Byron R. White (Colo.) | 1962– | |
| Stanley Matthews (Ohio) | 1881–1889 | 8 | Arthur J. Goldberg (Ill.) | 1962–1965 | 3 |
| Horace Gray (Mass.) | 1881–1902 | 21 | Abe Fortas (Tenn.) | 1965–1969 | 4 |
| Samuel Blatchford (N.Y.) | 1882–1893 | 11 | Thurgood Marshall (Md.) | 1967– | |
| Lucius Q. Lamar (Miss.) | 1888–1893 | 5 | *Warren E. Burger* (Minn.) | 1969– | |
| *Melville W. Fuller* (Ill.) | 1888–1910 | 22 | Harry A. Blackmun (Minn.) | 1970– | |

*Appointed and served one term, but not confirmed by the Senate.

| | | | | |
|---|---|---|---|---|
| 1. | *Delaware* | Dec. 1, 1787 | 26. *Michigan* | Jan. 26, 1837 |
| 2. | *Pennsylvania* | Dec. 12, 1787 | 27. *Florida* | Mar. 3, 1845 |
| 3. | *New Jersey* | Dec. 18, 1787 | 28. *Texas* | Dec. 29, 1845 |
| 4. | *Georgia* | Jan. 2, 1788 | 29. *Iowa* | Dec. 28, 1846 |
| 5. | *Connecticut* | Jan. 9, 1788 | 30. *Wisconsin* | May 29, 1848 |
| 6. | *Massachusetts* | Feb. 6, 1788 | 31. *California* | Sept. 9, 1850 |
| 7. | *Maryland* | Apr. 28, 1788 | 32. *Minnesota* | May 11, 1858 |
| 8. | *South Carolina* | May 23, 1788 | 33. *Oregon* | Feb. 14, 1859 |
| 9. | *New Hampshire* | June 21, 1788 | 34. *Kansas* | Jan. 29, 1861 |
| 10. | *Virginia* | June 25, 1788 | 35. *West Virginia* | June 19, 1863 |
| 11. | *New York* | July 26, 1788 | 36. *Nevada* | Oct. 31, 1864 |
| 12. | *North Carolina* | Nov. 21, 1789 | 37. *Nebraska* | Mar. 1, 1867 |
| 13. | *Rhode Island* | May 29, 1790 | 38. *Colorado* | July 1, 1876 |
| 14. | *Vermont* | Mar. 4, 1791 | 39. *North Dakota* | Nov. 2, 1889 |
| 15. | *Kentucky* | June 1, 1792 | 40. *South Dakota* | Nov. 2, 1889 |
| 16. | *Tennessee* | June 1, 1796 | 41. *Montana* | Nov. 8, 1889 |
| 17. | *Ohio* | Mar. 1, 1803 | 42. *Washington* | Nov. 11, 1889 |
| 18. | *Louisiana* | Apr. 30, 1812 | 43. *Idaho* | July 3, 1890 |
| 19. | *Indiana* | Dec. 11, 1816 | 44. *Wyoming* | July 10, 1890 |
| 20. | *Mississippi* | Dec. 10, 1817 | 45. *Utah* | Jan. 4, 1896 |
| 21. | *Illinois* | Dec. 3, 1818 | 46. *Oklahoma* | Nov. 16, 1907 |
| 22. | *Alabama* | Dec. 14, 1819 | 47. *New Mexico* | Jan. 6, 1912 |
| 23. | *Maine* | Mar. 15, 1820 | 48. *Arizona* | Feb. 14, 1912 |
| 24. | *Missouri* | Aug. 10, 1821 | 49. *Alaska* | Jan. 3, 1959 |
| 25. | *Arkansas* | June 15, 1836 | 50. *Hawaii* | Aug. 21, 1959 |

ACKNOWLEDGMENTS

The selection from "Chicago," on page 685, is from *Chicago Poems* by Carl Sandburg. Copyright 1916 by Holt, Rinehart and Winston, Inc. Copyright 1944 by Carl Sandburg. The selection from "Band Concert," on page 685, is from *Cornhuskers* by Carl Sandburg. Copyright 1918 by Holt, Rinehart and Winston, Inc. Copyright 1946 by Carl Sandburg. Both reprinted by permission of Holt, Rinehart and Winston, Inc.

The selection from "The Leaden-Eyed," on page 685, is reprinted with permission of The Macmillan Company from *Collected Poems* by Vachel Lindsay. Copyright 1914 by The Macmillan Company, renewed 1942 by Elizabeth C. Lindsay.

The selection from "Lucinda Matlock," on page 686, is from *Spoon River Anthology with Additional Poems* by Edgar Lee Masters. Copyright 1963 by The Macmillan Company. Reprinted by permission of Mrs. Ellen Masters.

"Stopping by Woods on a Snowy Evening," on page 686, is from *The Poetry of Robert Frost,* edited by Edward Connery Lathem. Copyright 1923 by Holt, Rinehart and Winston, Inc. Copyright 1951 by Robert Frost. Reprinted by permission of Holt, Rinehart and Winston, Inc.

The selection from "Good Morning," on page 690, is from *Montage of a Dream Deferred* by Langston Hughes, published 1951 by Holt, Rinehart and Winston, Inc. Copyright 1951 by Langston Hughes. Reprinted by permission of Harold Ober Associates Incorporated.

The abridgment of "Yet Do I Marvel," on page 691, is from *On These I Stand* by Countee Cullen. Copyright 1925 by Harper & Row, Publishers, Inc.; renewed 1953 by Ida M. Cullen. Reprinted by permission of Harper & Row, Publishers, Inc.

The selection from "How to be Old," on page 840, is reprinted by permission of Charles Scribner's Sons from *To Mix with Time* by May Swenson. Copyright 1963 by May Swenson.

The selection from "To the Moon, 1969," by Babette Deutsch, on page 845, was first published in *The New York Times,* July 21, 1969. Copyright 1969 by The New York Times Company. Reprinted by permission.

The selection from "The Return of Frankenstein," on page 872, is from *Variety Photoplays* by Edward Field. Reprinted by permission of Grove Press, Inc. Copyright 1967 by Edward Field.

The selections from "Communique: I," by John William Corrington, on page 873, and "The Plot to Assassinate the Chase Manhattan Bank," by Carl Larsen, on page 875, are from *Poets of Today: A New American Anthology,* edited by Walter Lowenfels, International Publishers Co., Inc. Copyright 1964. Reprinted by permission of the poets.

# INDEX

1

Lunar Orbiter I, 842
Lunik I, II and III, 820, 833
*Lusitania* (ship): sinking of, 638, 639
Luther, Martin, 18
Lutheranism, 18, 19, 58-59
Luks, George, 684
Luxembourg, 742, 784-785
Lyceums: growth of (1835-1860), 284
Lynching, 269, 663
Lynd, Helen M., 658, 692
Lynd, Robert S., 658, 692
Lyon, Matthew, 180

McAdam, John L., 273
McAdoo, William G., 638, 667
MacArthur, Gen. Douglas, 801; in World War II, 747, 761-764, 769; as administrator of Japan, 773; in Korean War, 791-792; recalled, 792, 795, 796
*McCall's* (magazine), 547
McCarran Internal Security Act (1950), 795-796, 823
McCarran-Walter Immigration Act (1952), 796
McCarthy, Eugene J.: 1968 elections and, 859, 862-864
McCarthy, Joseph R., 793-797, 807-808
McCarthyism, 804, 823; onset of, 792-798; climax of, 807-808
McClellan, Gen. George: in Civil War, 395, 400-404; 1864 elections and, 412
McClure, S. S., 614
*McClure's* (magazine), 614
McCone, John A., 833
McConnell, Bishop Francis J., 659
McCormick, Cyrus Hall, 344-345
McCormick Harvester Company, 497, 628
McCormick reaper-mower, 344
McCosh, James, 562
McCoy, Joseph G., 463-464
*McCulloch* v. *Maryland* (1819), 210, 259
McDivitt, Col. James A., 844
McDonald, Donald, 867
McDowell, Gen. Irwin, 397, 398
Machado, Gerardo, 737
Machine politics: in New Deal, 722-723
Machines: industrial accidents and, 493
McKay, Claude, 690
McKay, Donald, 348
Mackay, John W., 460, 487
McKim, Meade and White, 541, 549
McKinley, William, 516, 622; 1896 election of, 523-525, 654; 1900 election of, 526, 597; annexation of Hawaii and, 584-585; Spanish-American War and, 590-593, 595-596; assassination of, 596
McKinley Tariff (1890), 526
McKinley Tariff (1893), 517, 518
McKissick, Floyd, 851
Maclay, William, 165, 184
McLean, John, 248, 262
McLeod, Alexander, 293
McNamara, Robert S., 825, 830-831, 848; Vietnam War and, 856-857, 859, 861
McNarney, Gen. Joseph T., 774
McNary, Charles L., 743
McNary-Haugen bill (1927 and 1928), 669-670
McNaughton, John T., 856, 861
McParlan, James, 494

Macune, C. W., 521
MacVeagh, Wayne, 502
*Maddox* (ship), 856, 857
Madero, Francisco, 603
Madison, James, 163, 194-208, 878; on power of state legislatures, 139; at Constitutional Convention (1787), 149, 150, 153, 156; ratification of Constitution and, 157; as House leader, 161-162; Hamilton opposed by, 166-167; formation of Republican party and, 171, 173; in J. Adams's Cabinet, 179, 187; Sedition Act and, 180-181; continental destiny and, 185; in Jefferson's Cabinet, 186; first administration of, 194-198; second administration of, 199-205; Monroe Doctrine and, 206; 1816 elections and, 207-208
Magellan, Ferdinand, 15
"Magic" (Japanese code), 746
Mahan, Adm. Alfred T., 555; Blaine and, 585-587; Spanish-American War and, 590; influence of, 598, 599
Mail subsidies to airlines, 670-671
Maine, 32, 34, 43, 144, 212, 242, 543
*Maine* (ship), 586, 591
Malaya (British), 747
Malaysia, Federation of, 810
Malcolm X, 852
Malenkov, Georgi, 808, 817
Malthus, T. R., 559
Mangum, Willie P., 262
Manhattan District Project: atomic bomb and, 752, 769, 771
Manifest Destiny: as slogan for expansionism, 290-313
Manila (Philippines), 763, 768, 774; occupied, 595
Manila Bay, Battle of (1896), 593-594
Manila Conference (1966), 859
Manila Pact (1954), 815
Mann, Horace, 282-283, 333
Mann, Thomas, 636
Mann-Elkins Act (1910), 627
Manufacturing: development of, 21; Dutch, 22; effect of embargo of 1807 on, 195; War of 1812 and, 208; beginnings of, 228-229; southern-produced goods (1860), 330; growth of (by 1860), 355
Manumission, 137
Mao Tse-tung, 787, 818
Marbury, William, 187
*Marbury* v. *Madison* (1803), 187, 209
March on Washington for Peace in Vietnam (1965), 858
March Revolution (Russian; 1917), 635, 641, 642
Marcy, William L., 365
Mariana Islands, 762, 763
Marie Antoinette (Queen of France), 540
Marion, Francis, 131
*Marion Daily Star* (newspaper), 654
Maritime explorations: Spanish, 2-4, 11-13, 14-16; Asian, 4-5; Norwegian, 8-9; Greek and Alexandrian contributions to, 9-11; Portuguese, 12-14; French, 21-22; Dutch, 22-24; English, 24-25
Maritime trade: New England, 44-45; navigation acts and, 50-52; growth of colonial, 70-72; decline of post-Revolutionary War, 144; Barbary War and,

188; freedom of seas (early 1800s), 192-193; early 19th century, 227-228; Caribbean, 256
Marquette, Father Jacques, 76
Marryat, S. F., 292
Marshall, Gen. George C., 774, 783, 787-788, 795
Marshall, John: decisions rendered by, 154, 155, 180, 182, 187, 189, 209-210, 222, 251-252, 259; Burr tried by, 192; nationalism of, 209-212
Marshall, Thomas R., 660
Marshall, Thurgood, 806
Marshall Plan (1947), 783-784, 786, 828
Martin, Bradley, 540
Martinique, 80, 81
Marx, Karl, 692
Marxism, 608-609
Mary (Stuart; Queen of Scots), 20, 31
Mary I (Queen of England; "Bloody Mary"), 20, 30
Mary II (Queen of England), 52
Maryland: as refuge for Catholics, 37; colony, 37-39, 59, 65; free Negroes in (1790), 137; representative government in, 138; Articles of Confederation and, 140, 141; ratifies Constitution, 157; franchise in, 242; tobacco growing in, 327; railroads in, 351; secession and, 380, 384; in Civil War, 394
Mason, George, 155, 157
Mason, James Murray, 405
Mason, John Y., 365
Mason, Lowell, 281
Mason-Dixon Line, 396
Masonry, 257
Massachusetts (*see also* Massachusetts Bay Colony): constitution of, 135-136, 139; absence of slavery in (1790), 136; representative government in, 137; excess taxation of farmers in, 147; ratifies constitution, 157; in War of 1812, 199, 202; population of (1820), 208; canal building by, 225; franchise in, 242; railroads in, 351
Massachusetts Bay Colony: beginnings, 40-45; charter annulled, 51, 52; Puritan revolt in, 52-53; development of, 70-71; franchise in, 73; land banks prohibited in, 74-75; education as public responsibility in, 99
*Masses, The* (magazine), 683-684, 687
Massive retaliation doctrine, 809-810, 813, 817, 827, 830-831
Mass-production methods, 490
Masters, Edgar Lee, 685-686
Materialism, 472-474
Mather, Cotton, 41, 52, 71, 72, 83, 85-87; Salem witchcraft hysteria and, 89-90; ideas of, 94-95; scientific speculations of, 97; on Wampanoag Indians, 454
Mather, Increase, 52, 86, 89-90
Mather, Richard, 86, 94
Matisse, Henri, 684
Maximilian (Archduke of Austria and briefly Emperor of Mexico, 1863-1867), 405, 580
Maximilian I (Holy Roman Emperor), 19
Maximum Employment Act (1946), 777
Maya Indians, 6-7, 17
*Mayflower* (ship), 39, 454
Mayflower Compact (1620), 39-40
Mayhew, Jonathan, 102

White supremacy, 435, 440-448
White trash, 320
Whitlock, Brand, 615
Whitman, Marcus, 299
Whitman, Walt, 272, 276, 386, 420, 701; biography of, 277; slavery condemned by, 287; fall of Fort Sumter and, 381; on late 19th-century literature, 571, 572; Lindsay compared with, 685; Pound and, 686
Whitney, Eli, 195, 220
Whittier, John Greenleaf, 92, 287
Whittlesey, Derwent, 4
Whyte, William H., Jr., 802
Wicker, Tom, 824, 858
Wickersham, George W., 664
Wigfall, Louis T., 376
Wigner, Eugene, 751
Wilderness, Battle of (1864), 411
Wild West, 450-451, 462, 463
Wiley, Harvey W., 625
Wilhelm II (Emperor of Germany), 586, 636
Wilkinson, Gen. James, 192
Willard, Emma, 283, 619
Willard, Frances E., 543
William III (King of England), 52, 53, 77
William and Mary College, 65, 100
Williams, Aubrey, 723
Williams, Roger, 42-43, 287
*Williams* v. *Mississippi* (1898), 448
Willkie, Wendell L., 743
Wills, Gary, 865
Wilmot, David, 307
Wilmot Proviso (1846), 307, 309, 310, 371
Wilson, Charles Edward (president, General Electric Co.), 775
Wilson, Charles Erwin (president, General Motors Corp.): as Secretary of Defense, 803, 804
Wilson, Edmund, 689, 694, 698, 699
Wilson, Gen. Maitland, 755
Wilson, James, 115, 149, 151-152
Wilson, Woodrow, 565, 635-654, 682, 732, 741; Latin American policy of, 602-604; New Freedom of, 612-613, 630-632; woman's suffrage and, 620; 1912 election of, 629-630; World War I and, 635-644; 1916 election of, 640; Fourteen Points of, 647-648, 745; Versailles Treaty and, 649-653; 1920 elections and, 653, 654; red scare and, 660; Prohibition and, 663
Wilson Dam, 669
Wilson-Gorman Tariff (1894), 589
Winder, Gen. William H., 200

Winthrop, John, 40-42, 83, 97, 100
Wiretapping, 876
Wirt, William, 257-258
Wisconsin: settled, 295; statehood granted, 339; immigrants to, 340; resources of, 343, 469; railroads of, 352; population of, 467; Progressivism in, 617
Wisconsin Way, 613-614
Wise, Henry A., 376
Wise, John, 93, 102
Wolcott, Oliver, 170, 177
Wolfe, James, 80
Wolfe, Thomas, 701, 704
*Woman's Home Companion* (magazine), 547
Women: as mill workers, 228-230, 232; franchise for, 429, 620; education of, 568; in Progressive movement, 609-610; in labor force, 618; in armed forces, 750; liberation of, 841
Women's Christian Temperance Union (WCTU), 543, 620
Women's liberation movement, 841
Wood, Gen. Leonard, 595, 596, 653
Wood, Gen. Robert E., 741
Woodford, Gen. Stewart L., 590-593
Woodin, William H., 708
Woodward, C. Vann, 570, 607
Wool, Capt. John, 198
Wool Act (1699; British), 54
Woolman, John, 92
Worcester, Samuel, 252
*Worcester* v. *Georgia* (1832), 247, 251-252
Work, Henry C., 281
Work day: ten-hour, 565, 618
Workers: cotton mill, 228-230; communitarianism among, 285-287; southern industrial (1850-1860), 330; numbers of (1857), 359; blacklisting, 494; Protestants and, 543-544; World War I and, 643, 644; protecting, 668, 729, 818-819; suffering (1920s), 670; in New Deal coalition, 724; World War II and jobs for, 750-751 (*see also* Farm laborers; Unemployment)
Working conditions: in textile mills, 231-233; plantation, 323, 326; post-Civil War, 492-500; Chinese labor, 507-508; church view of changes in, 543-544
Workingmen's party, 495
Workmen's compensation laws, 668
Works Progress Administration (WPA), 700, 716, 729

Work week, 493, 711, 729
World's Columbian Exposition (Chicago; 1893), 488, 548-549
World's Fair (London; 1851), 356
World War I, 634-655; American volunteers in, 555; U.S. intervention in, 635-646; mobilization for, 643-644; peace derived from, 647-654; Negroes serving in, 662
World War II, 732-765; prosperity and, 670; industry in, 670-672, 749-751; czarist debt, 736; merchants of death and, 738-739; begins, 740-742; intervening in, 742-745; Axis engaged, 745-753; U.S. war costs, 752; unconditional surrender terms in, 754-755; new world order and, 766-773
Wounded Knee, "battle" of (1890), 457
Wright, Chauncey, 563
Wright, Frances, 286
Wright, Orville, 670
Wright, Richard, 700
Wright, Wilbur, 670, 671
Writers: mid-19th century, 272-278; southern, 334-336; late 19th century, 571-576; depression and, 681-684; disenchantment of, 687-692; in relief programs, 716-717
Writs of assistance, 106-107
Wyeth, Nathaniel J., 299
Wynn, Ed, 698
Wyoming, 458, 461

XYZ affair (1798), **178**, 181

Yalta Conference (1945), **759**, 760, 764, 794, 807; conflict over, 768-770
Yeager, Joseph, 236
Yeats, William Butler, 682
Yellow journalism, 546-547
York, Duke of (later James II of England), 47-49, 51-53
*Yorktown* (ship), 716
Youmans, Edward Livingston, 558
Young, Brigham, 303
Youth culture, 873
Yugoslavia, 782; established, 651; Yalta Conference and, 768; differences in socialist development and, 817

Zenger, John Peter, 100
Zhukov, Marshal Georgi, 759
Ziegfeld, Florenz, 692, 697
*Ziegfeld Follies*, 697-698
Zimmermann, Alfred, 641
Zola, Emile, 574
Zond 5 and 6, 844
Zuñi Indians, 453